Encyclopedia of
ETHICS

Board of Consulting Editors

Encyclopedia of
ETHICS

Second Edition

Lawrence C. Becker and Charlotte B. Becker

Editors

Volume III
P–W
Indexes

Routledge
New York and London

To G.S.K.

Published in 2001 by
Routledge
29 West 35th Street
New York, NY 10001

Published in Great Britain by
Routledge
11 New Fetter Lane
London EC4P 4EE

Routledge is an imprint of Taylor & Francis Books, Inc.

Printed in the United States of America on acid-free paper.

First edition published by Garland Publishing, New York, 1992.

Portions of Derk Pereboom's "free will" were drawn from his introduction to *Free Will*,
    edited by Derk Pereboom, Indianapolis: Hackett, ©1997, all rights reserved.
"deceit" © 2001 by Sissela Bok
"etiquette" © 2001 by Judith Martin and Gunther Stent
"moral terms," "prescriptivism," "slavery," "universalizability," and "weakness of will"
    © 2001 by R. M. Hare

10 9 8 7 6 5 4 3 2 1

Library of Congress Cataloging-in-Publication Data

Encyclopedia of ethics / Lawrence C. Becker and Charlotte B. Becker, editors.— 2nd ed.
    p. cm.
    Includes bibliographical references and index.
    ISBN 0-415-93672-1 (set : alk. paper) — ISBN 0-415-93673-X (vol. 1 : alk. paper) —
ISBN 0-415-93674-8 (vol. 2 : alk. paper) — ISBN 0-415-93675-6 (vol. 3 : alk. paper)
    1. Ethics—Encyclopedias. I. Becker, Lawrence C. II. Becker, Charlotte B., 1944–

BJ63 .E45 2001
170′.3—dc21
                                                    2001019657

P

pacifism

The word "pacifism" was introduced about 1902 as a synonym for "anti-warism." It still carries with it the vagueness and variability suggested by this origin. At times there is no doctrine at all associated with being a pacifist; when there is, it need not be the same doctrine in all cases. The main idea is privative: opposition to war. Often, however, the opposition is to more than actual war: to "warism" (Cady), to pugnacity (Shaw [1856–1950], preface to *Heartbreak House,* 1919), to nationalism or statism, to "zero-sum" thinking (Boulding, Rapoport), to violence (Muste), or to any use of force (GANDHI [1869–1948]; the twelfth-century Cathari of southwestern France). Its expression is so varied that useful discussions of pacifism (Brock, Cady, Teichman) all begin with a description of its different varieties. These variations broaden the concept of pacifism historically as well as conceptually, for there is eloquent opposition to war and to pugnacity in AUGUSTINE (354–430), and WEIL (1909–1943) has inferred it in Homer.

Besides being identified through opposition to war or to warism, pacifism is sometimes identified by reference to well-known pacifists such as Norman Angell (1872–1967), A. J. Muste, Jane Addams (1860–1935), Grace Paley, Virginia Woolf (1882–1941), and Dorothy Day (1897–1980). Tolstoy (1828–1910), Gandhi, and Martin Luther KING, Jr. (1928–1968) are frequently mentioned as propo-

nents of a pacifism which merges with active nonviolence. Although this definition by paradigm cases is undoubtedly useful, it, too, leaves one with a wide range of variations.

Practical Pacifism

Practical pacifism is the refusal of war service and the active opposition to war preparations. It may be general, applying to all wars, in which case the pacifism is said to be "absolute"; it may apply to a particular war, such as World War I or the Vietnam War; or it may be against a particular type of war, as it is with "nuclear pacifists." In none of these cases need there be a doctrine associated with the refusal. Where there are doctrines that underlie the refusal, they may be religious and hence relatively insulated from rational scrutiny, as is the historic "peace testimony" of the Quakers and Anabaptists.

Personal Pacifism

Personal pacifism takes the form of conscientious objection to military service. Fundamentally a witness against war, it is generally also a witness for something else: for reverence for life (SCHWEITZER [1875–1965]); for a community or a way of life based on religious principles (Gandhi; the Cathari); for anarchism (Tolstoy); for replacement of hierarchical domination by cooperative and integrative social processes (Boulding, Rapoport); for universal

LOVE (Gandhi, Muste); and so on. Even when no reasons are given, refusing to fight makes as much sense as agreeing to fight. Although fighting is a natural behavior pattern, avoiding fights is also a natural behavior pattern: each stands as much—or as little—in need of justification as the other.

Pacifist Movements

In the twentieth century, pacifist movements center around getting people to make a personal commitment to refuse military service and to campaign against military expenditures. These movements impinge on politics, of course, but can be considered apolitical in the sense that they are nonpartisan. In Britain, the Peace Pledge Union was a major force during the 1930s, but the pledges often did not hold firm when war came. Pacifist movements seem to flourish better when there is threat of war than during actual war, unless, as with the Vietnam War, the war is remote and unpopular.

Pacifist Theory

There is no firmly established pacifist theory. Rather than an independent doctrine with its own theory, pacifism is generally an offshoot of other doctrines. Precise definitions and clear theories of the principles of pacifism are more apt to be offered by opponents, who then reject them, than by proponents. In recent decades, pacifists (Richardson, Galtung, Rapoport, K. and E. Boulding) have instituted an international peace research movement and introduced peace studies in university curricula—developments which clearly imply a search for ideas rather than a commitment to existing theory.

Objections to Pacifism

The popular charge that pacifists lack COURAGE cannot be taken seriously; it usually forms part of war propaganda and is obviously false in very many cases. There are, however, more respectable objections. Traditionally the principal criticism comes from the just war doctrine. Other criticisms are charges of inconsistency, of impracticality, and of disloyalty or subversion.

Just war theory specifies conditions under which wars are just. Since such conditions are seldom realized, just war thinkers often oppose wars. Their opposition differs from that of other pacifists in that (a) they oppose particular wars but not war as such; and (b) their opposition is based on principles of justice rather than of pacifism. RUSSELL (1872–1970) and Jägerstätter (1907–1943) are excellent examples of just war pacifists.

This doctrine may lead to a criticism of absolute pacifism in the name of justice. What is interesting philosophically is whether such a pacifist is bound to say, in the case of a putatively just war, that a just war theorist is wrong. I think not, on the ground that one can have a right, or be justified, in cases where exercising that right would be foolish. Pacifists can allow that their country has a right to fight and still rationally refuse to participate on the ground that fighting is foolish or that it violates other principles. A different pacifist reply is that the hypothetical conditions for just war never actually obtain. It is certainly true that if the just war theory collapsed—that is, if it were shown that there are no conditions for just war—the case for pacifism would be immeasurably improved. But the converse does not hold: a viable just war theory does not present a formidable obstacle to practical pacifism.

Inconsistency is a charge brought against pacifists on the ground that they accept the benefits of wars they do not serve in. There is something disquieting about the assumption in this argument that one is responsible for what one cannot possibly help: it is after all other people who choose to use force to keep the public peace. Still, the objection does have merit when brought against pacifists who object to all use of force in human affairs. It is not, however, an objection against pacifism generally, for, as Cady and Teichman argue, there is nothing contradictory in approving parental discipline and police work while disapproving of war.

A related charge of incoherence arises from considering pacifism to be a speculative or substantive philosophical theory with universal truth-claims and universal precepts. Truth-claims about the power of non-violence to win over aggressors or about peace having ultimate value turn out to be difficult to sustain; and pacifist precepts, such as that it is always impermissible to fight in a war or to resist violence with force, seem neither able to stand on their own nor to fit comfortably with any obvious system of precepts and values. Jan Narveson has been vigorous in presenting such criticism and at blocking escape routes sought by philosophical pacifists, as he does in his response to Carlo Filice.

Impracticality is the charge against idealists of all sorts, as well as against pacifists specifically, that has led to the exclusion of morals from *Realpolitik*. It is true that pacifist ideas will not help to win at chess or football; but the enormous social and commercial benefits from cooperative and integrative rather than combative solutions to conflict make it doubtful whether such zero-sum games are a useful model for much of human life.

Subversion or disloyalty are charges brought against pacifists in the context of wars and militaristic nationalism. In this context they are valid. While there is nothing unfriendly or hostile in pacifism, nor disloyal to communities or societies as such, the refusal to fight in wars certainly does amount to disloyalty toward certain political regimes, and can subvert certain political policies.

See also: AMNESTY AND PARDON; AUGUSTINE; AUTHORITY; CHRISTIAN ETHICS; CIVIL DISOBEDIENCE; CIVILITY; COOPERATION, CONFLICT, AND COORDINATION; COURAGE; FEMINIST ETHICS; GANDHI; INTERNATIONAL JUSTICE: CONFLICT; KING; LOYALTY; MILITARY ETHICS; NUCLEAR ETHICS; OBEDIENCE TO LAW; REVOLUTION; RUSSELL; SCHWEITZER; TERRORISM; THOREAU; VIOLENCE AND NON-VIOLENCE; WAR AND PEACE; WEIL.

Bibliography

Brock, Peter. *Pacifism in the United States: From the Colonial Era to the First World War.* Princeton: Princeton University Press, 1968. A scholarly study with extensive bibliography.

———. *Twentieth Century Pacifism.* New York: Van Nostrand Reinhold, 1970.

Cady, Duane. *From Warism to Pacifism: A Moral Continuum.* Philadelphia: Temple University Press, 1989. Fine characterization of the varieties of pacifism.

Defrasne, Jean. *Le pacifisme.* Paris: Presses Universitaires de France, 1983.

Eagleton, Clyde. *Analysis of the Problem of War.* New York: Garland, 1972 [1937]. Includes new introduction by Kenneth Boulding.

Filice, Carlo. "Pacifism: A Philosophical Exploration." *Journal of Philosophical Research* 17 (1992): 119–53.

Gallie, W. B. *Philosophers of Peace and War: Kant, Clausewitz, Marx, Engels and Tolstoy.* Cambridge: Cambridge University Press, 1978.

Gioseffi, Daniela, ed. *Women on War: Essential Voices for the Nuclear Age.* New York: Simon and Schuster, 1988.

Gregg, Richard B. *The Power of Nonviolence.* Rev. ed. Nyack, N.Y.: Fellowship Publications, 1959. Classic exposition of Gandhian pacifism.

Lewis, John. *The Case Against Pacifism.* New York: Garland, 1973 [1940]. Includes new introduction by Carl Marzani.

Muste, A. J. *The Essays of A. J. Muste.* Edited by Nat Hentoff. New York: Bobbs-Merrill, 1967. Includes a long autobiographical essay.

Narveson, Jan. "Filice's Defense of Pacifism." *Journal of Philosophical Research* 17 (1992): 483–91.

———. "Pacifism: A Philosophical Analysis." *Ethics* 75 (1965): 259–71.

Roquebert, Michel. *L'épopée Cathare: 1198–1212, L'invasion.* Toulouse: Edouard Privat, 1970.

Russell, Bertrand. *Which Way to Peace?* London: Michael Joseph, 1936.

Teichman, Jenny. *Pacifism and the Just War: A Study in Applied Philosophy.* Oxford: Basil Blackwell, 1986.

Weil, Simone. *The Simone Weil Reader.* Edited by George A. Panichas. New York: David McKay, 1977. See "The Iliad, Poem of Might," pp. 153–83.

Woolf, Virginia. *Three Guineas.* New York: Harcourt Brace Jovanovich, 1966 [1938].

Zahn, Gordon. *In Solitary Witness: The Life and Death of Franz Jägerstätter.* New York: Holt, Reinhart and Winston, 1964. The remarkable story of a peasant's persistent refusal to fight in Hitler's war.

Newton Garver

pain and suffering

Knowledge concerning the nature, causes, and extent of human and animal pain and suffering is of the greatest importance in consequentialist ethics, and most of the major deontological ethics as well. Yet there is a poverty of writings concerning pain and suffering both in ethics and philosophical psychology. Notwithstanding UTILITARIANISM's long dominance, little has developed from BENTHAM's (1748–1832) very preliminary analyses of the concepts and accounts of the kinds, causes, and estimations of pain and suffering. Instead, utilitarians such as JOHN STUART MILL (1806–1873) concentrated on PLEASURE and HAPPINESS, including the so-called higher pleasures. In philosophical psychology, pain and suffering have most commonly, wrongly, been assumed to be the opposites of pleasure and happiness, despite significant differences relevant to the morally appropriate treatment of persons, infants, fetuses, and animals.

Pain as in toothaches, pinches, burns, wounds,

etc., has been characterized as a sensation, an episode, an emotion, a perception of a state of one's body. The most plausible account is that such pain is a sensation. The pain referred to as suffering—fear, grief, anxiety, despair—is to be explained as an emotion. Pain the sensation is typically but not always associated with damage or the likelihood of damage to the organism; it has felt location, although infants may need to learn to locate pain. By contrast, most pleasures are unlocated emotions. Only some few pleasures, such as of touch and taste, have been claimed by some to be sensations located in the body. Pain has a felt quality, a felt intensity. It operates through the nervous system, although such pains as *tic douloureux,* causalgia, and pain in phantom limbs, which may persist after nerves are severed, make necessary the development of complex accounts of the processes in the nervous system. Science has yet to unravel the problem of explaining such phenomena.

The pain (emotion) of suffering is not located in the body; its intensity and quality differ from those of pain the sensation. Suffering as with grief, ENVY, and anxiety, does not relate to the nervous system as does the sensation pain.

The sensation-emotion dichotomy raises problems. If emotions involve beliefs and objects of belief, what of floating, objectless, beliefless anxiety, depression, guilt, remorse? What of those suffering experiences—itches, tickles, nausea, hangovers, cravings—which are more akin to nonemotion feelings? More importantly, as C. S. Lewis (1898–1963) and others have noted, the dichotomy leads to paradoxical conclusions. The common-sense view is that pain must involve unpleasantness, unwantedness, dislike. Yet pain can be separated from the response to it, just as other sensations can be separated from our reactions to them. The literature is rich in citing pain that is neither disliked nor unpleasant: minor pain, certain pain experiences of those who have undergone leukotomies, some pain recalled after light hypnosis, certain experiences of natural childbirth, pain that is not attended to, is unnoticed, or even 'unfelt.' The wounded Anzio soldiers cited by Beecher seemed either not to feel pain or to feel it and not to be distressed by it. There are also those who, under hypnosis, immerse a limb in icy water and exhibit no discomfort, but if so instructed under hypnosis, may report in writing or verbally that they are experiencing pain. By contrast, the masochist appears to experience pain as painful but enjoys it.

Whether suffering must be unpleasant, or disliked, is less often discussed. If to be disliked is for suffering to be something that we wish to be rid of, the unpleasantness or dislike of suffering need not be an essential feature of it. The masochist relishes both the pain and the suffering it brings; his enjoyment of his humiliation, whilst parasitic on first-order distress, is real. Normal persons also reject relief from the suffering attached to grief, remorse, or guilt. There are then problems in explaining and characterizing the unpleasantness of suffering when it occurs. Lewis and others cannot be followed in claiming that suffering is simply what we dislike. Yet, whether and when pain the sensation and suffering the emotion are distressing are central to moral issues in the treatment of humans and animals. Further, if the "awfulness" of pain and suffering consisted only in their being disliked, many ethical issues, including the problem of EVIL, would need drastic reassessment.

The vast amount of recent scientific research concerning pain and suffering phenomena has created problems for both scientific and philosophical theory. All traditional and modern scientific accounts of pain and suffering, including the gate-control theory, are exposed to difficulties that are in part due to the range and complexity of factors claimed to affect these experiences, and in part to the problems of interpretation of the reported phenomena. The scientific data fit ill with the claims of philosophical behaviorism and the current confidence in functionalism.

The pains most stressed by Bentham, Lewis, and many others are those of suffering that presuppose a whole range of rational, mental capacities, such as understanding, memory, imagination, foresight, sympathetic identification, consciousness, and self-consciousness, not all of which relate to the sensation pain. They bear more directly on the subject's capacity to control or affect its pain and suffering. To understand the meaning of pain or suffering may decrease or increase it.

Despite great endeavors of scientists in many areas, the achievements in assessing pain and suffering remain extremely disappointing. Philosophers have contributed even less here.

The traditionally orthodox view that honest reports about a speaker's pain are incorrigibly true has not escaped persistent questioning. PLATO (c. 430–347 B.C.E.) believed we could mistake unreal pleasures/pains for real pleasures/pains. J. S. Mill held that SOCRATES (c. 470–399 B.C.E.) could believe himself to be dissatisfied yet to be enjoying great pleasure. Today some argue that those who have undergone leukotomies and experience cancer pain without distress lack the concept of pain—even though they find noncancer pains distressing. Similarly with the masochist. Thus it is urged we must choose between the incorrigibility of pain statements or the awfulness of pain.

Theologians and scientists alike stress the value of pain and its related suffering as a warning system, albeit a very imperfect one. Persons congenitally incapable of pain are subject to grave injuries. Clearly the traditional approach of treating pain and suffering as adjuncts to pleasure and happiness is unsatisfactory. ARISTOTLE (384–322 B.C.E.), with his emphasis on pleasure and happiness, must share responsibility for this.

See also: ANIMALS, TREATMENT OF; ARISTOTLE; BENTHAM; CONSEQUENTIALISM; CRUELTY; DEONTOLOGY; EMOTION; ENVY; EUTHANASIA; EVIL; EXISTENTIAL ETHICS; GUILT AND SHAME; HAPPINESS; HARM AND OFFENSE; KIERKEGAARD; KILLING/LETTING DIE; MEDICAL ETHICS; MERCY; PLEASURE; PSYCHOLOGY; RESENTMENT; SARTRE; STOICISM; SUICIDE; TORTURE; TRAGEDY; UTILITARIANISM.

Bibliography

Beecher, Henry K. "Pain in Men Wounded in Battle." *Annals of Surgery* 123 (1946): 96–105. A report on the much cited pain phenomenon.

Bentham, Jeremy. *An Introduction to the Principles of Morals and Legislation.* Reprinted, Oxford: Clarendon, 1907 [1780]. Classical statement of hedonistic utilitarianism and of the pleasure-pain calculus.

Dennett, Daniel C. *Brainstorms: Philosophical Essays on Mind and Psychology.* Montgomery, VT: Bradford Books, and Hassocks, Sussex: Harvester, 1979. Chapter 11 is a tentative exploration of tensions in the philosophical concept of pain.

Edwards, R. *Pleasures and Pains.* Ithaca: Cornell University Press, 1979. Sensitive discussion of the thesis of higher and lower pleasures and pains.

Hospers, John. *Human Conduct.* San Diego, Calif.: Harcourt, Brace and World, 1961. Chapter 3 contains a useful, brief discussion of pain and pleasure.

Kenny, Anthony. *Action, Emotion and the Will.* London: Routledge and Kegan Paul, 1963. Competent discussion of issues relevant to pain and suffering, but insensitive to subtleties of interpretation of pain phenomena and masochism.

Lewis, C. S. *The Problem of Pain.* London: Godfrey Bles, 1940. Discussion of theological problem. Contains an interesting definition of pain on p. 78.

McCloskey, Mary A. "Pleasure." *Mind* 80 (1971): 542–51. Examines differences between pleasure and pain, and statements concerning them.

Melzack, Ronald, ed. *Pain Measurement and Assessment.* New York: Raven Press, 1983. Contains informative articles about pain phenomena.

Melzack, Ronald, and Patrick D. Wall. *The Challenge of Pain.* Harmondsworth, England: Penguin, 1982. Survey work which places and explains the gate-control theory.

Mill, John Stuart. "Utilitarianism." *Fraser's Magazine,* October–December 1861. Also in vol. 10 of *Collected Works of John Stuart Mill,* Toronto: University of Toronto Press, 1969. Contains celebrated discussion of higher and lower pleasures and pains.

Penelhum, Terence. "The Logic of Pleasure." *Philosophy and Phenomenological Research* 17 (1956–7): 488–503. Discusses case for localized pleasures.

Pitcher, George. "Pain Perception." *Philosophical Review* 79 (1970): 368–93. Examines the coherence of our concept of pain.

Plato. *Republic.* Book IX.

Ryle, Gilbert. *The Concept of Mind.* London: Hutchinson, 1950. Brief discussions directed at pain and suffering.

Teichman, Jenny. *Philosophy and the Mind.* Oxford: Blackwell, 1988. Pithy, perceptive discussions of materialist theories and other problems with pain.

Trigg, Roger. *Pain and Emotion.* Oxford: Clarendon Press, 1970. Excellent sustained investigation of the concepts of pain and suffering.

Weisenberg, Matisyohu, ed. *Pain: Clinical and Experimental Perspectives.* St. Louis: C. V. Mosby, 1975. One of many good collections which report on and examine pain and suffering phenomena.

Henry John McCloskey

Paine, Thomas [Tom] (1737–1809)

English-born political radical and polemicist. Paine passed an obscure life of failure during his first thirty-seven years. His writing career began after he immigrated to America in 1774. His ethical theory and political thought emerged as a response to the events in America and France in the last three decades of the eighteenth century.

With the publication of *Common Sense* (1776),

his most well-known work, Paine became the first public advocate to defend the American colonies' separation from Britain. During the REVOLUTION, he inspired the colonies to support the American cause with a series of essays known collectively as *The American Crisis* (1777–1783). He later supported the revolution in France and was one of the first writers to respond to Edmund BURKE's (1729–1797) attack in *Reflections on the French Revolution* (1790). In *Rights of Man* (1791, 1792), Paine most clearly articulated his ethical views, especially the moral imperative of one person to come to the aid of another. Prior to his imprisonment in France under the Reign of Terror in 1793–1794, Paine wrote the first volume of *The Age of Reason* which, along with a subsequent one, contributed to his reputation as an atheist. His last major work, *Agrarian Justice* (1796), placed him in the forefront of radical social thought with its emphasis on a large inheritance tax on land to ameliorate the condition of the poor.

Throughout his career, Paine attacked tyranny in every form. He consistently argued that every person's duty was to promote the creation of a social and political environment in which all people would flourish intellectually and economically. Initially influenced by the ideas of John LOCKE (1632–1704), Paine believed in the natural sociability of people who could work together to form the best government. In *Common Sense,* he suggests that the new American landscape offered its virtuous people "every opportunity . . . to form the noblest, purest constitution on the face of the earth. We have it in our power to begin the world over again." For Paine, the moral imperative of a virtuous America separating from corrupt Britain was self-evident. Once the Americans create a strong, democratic constitution, their natural sociability will drive them to live in peace and harmony with each other. The death of tyranny is a sufficient cause for people's true nature to surface.

By the French revolutionary years, Paine's focus dramatically changed. In *Rights of Man,* he sees that even in America social differentiation and indifference led to the growth of a class of poor people. He argues that only through governmental intervention will the poor become fully productive members of society. Although he never proposed absolute EQUALITY among all citizens, he did propose a detailed social welfare program designed to aid young married couples, the aged, and the poor through direct monetary grants from the government. The state was to fund the program through direct taxes and a graduated income tax. His plan also included a system of public education. Paine's social welfare program is a direct consequence of the principle that the purpose of a revolution is "a change in the moral condition of government." This change is accompanied by the people's realization of how they may help their fellows, particularly the poor. The old tyrannies of Europe taxed the class least able to pay so that kings and lords could live in luxury. In contrast, Paine argues that now many people, not only the highborn and wealthy, will benefit. "I speak an open and disinterested language," he proclaims, "dictated by no passion but that of humanity."

Paine continued this theme in *Agrarian Justice,* in which he supports direct public assistance payments to all people through a national program funded by a heavy inheritance tax on land. All people at age twenty-one were to receive fifteen pounds sterling. After they were fifty years old, they would be paid an additional ten pounds annually for the rest of their lives. This scheme was designed to compensate people for the loss of their "natural inheritance," the earth which God had created for the use and enjoyment of all, but which had become encumbered by private ownership. Because everyone received a portion of the fund, there would be neither absolute equality nor social friction. At the same time, the lot of the poor would substantially improve.

Paine never developed his social, political, or ethical theory into a cohesive philosophy. His major works are, however, an important part of late-eighteenth-century thought and served as the foundation for later British and American social and political radicalism in the nineteenth and twentieth centuries.

See also: BURKE; ELITE, CONCEPT OF; EQUALITY; LIBERTY; LOCKE; NATURE AND ETHICS; PROPERTY; REVOLUTION; RIGHTS; SOCIAL AND POLITICAL PHILOSOPHY; WELFARE RIGHTS AND SOCIAL POLICY.

Bibliography

Works by Paine

Common Sense. Edited by Isaac Kramnick. Harmondsworth, England: Penguin, 1976 [1776]. For passage noted, see p. 120.

Rights of Man. Introduction by Eric Foner. Harmondsworth, England: Penguin, 1984 [1791, 1792]. For passages noted in this article, see part 2, pp. 212, 228.

The Complete Writings of Thomas Paine. Edited by Philip S. Foner. 2 vols. New York: Citadel Press, 1945.

The Writings of Thomas Paine. Edited by Eric Foner. New York: Library of America, 1995.

The Thomas Paine Reader. Edited by Michael Foot, and Isaac Kramnick. Harmondsworth, England: Penguin, 1987.

Works about Paine

Blakemore, Steven. *Crisis in Representation: Thomas Paine, Mary Wollstonecraft, Helen Maria Williams, and the Rewriting of the French Revolution.* Madison, Wis.: Fairleigh Dickinson University Press, 1997.

Claeys, Gregory. *The Political Thought of Thomas Paine.* Winchester, Mass.: Unwin Hyman, 1989.

Davidson, Edward H., and William J. Scheick. *Paine, Scripture, and Authority: The Age of Reason as Religious and Political Idea.* Bethlehem, Pa.: Lehigh University Press, 1994.

Foner, Eric. *Tom Paine and Revolutionary America.* London: Oxford University Press, 1976.

Fruchtman, Jack, Jr. *Thomas Paine and the Religion of Nature.* Baltimore: Johns Hopkins University Press, 1993.

———. *Thomas Paine: Apostle of Freedom.* New York: Four Walls Eight Windows, 1994.

Keane, John. *Tom Paine: A Political Life.* Boston: Little, Brown, 1995.

Jack Fruchtman, Jr.

Paley [variant: Payley], William (1743–1805)

English moral philosopher and theologian. In his only ethical work, *Principles of Moral and Political Philosophy* (1785), Paley elaborated and defended a theological version of UTILITARIANISM whereby God both justifies and supplies the motivating power for the utility principle. Although Paley was not the only proponent of religious utilitarianism, his *Principles* was a huge success. Based on lectures he gave while teaching at Cambridge, the book went through numerous reprintings and was used as a textbook in both Great Britain and the United States well into the 1830s. The success of his book is said to have spurred BENTHAM (1748–1832) to finally publish his *Introduction to the Principles of Morals and Legislation* (1789). Paley wrote three other books, all theological or apologetical. In his *Horae Paulinae* (1790) he argues for the authenticity of the scriptural history of St. Paul. Paley defends the genuineness of Christian miracles in his *A View of the Evidences of Christianity* (1794). His third, *Natural Theology* (1802), the best known of his works today, provides a detailed restatement of the argument from design.

It is no accident that the *Principles* reads more like a rule book detailing our duties than a philosophical work. The aim of moral philosophy, as Paley saw it, is simply to "teach men their duty, and the reasons of it." For Paley the former is the more important: we need help in discerning our duties because the typical sources of guidance—the law of HONOR, positive law, and scripture—are incorrect or incomplete or, because, as is the case with scripture, we may misapply general rules in particular cases.

Paley's *Principles* is important because it is one of a number of works in Great Britain in the early- and mid-nineteenth century which marked the transition to utilitarianism from sentimentalist—HUTCHESON (1694–1746), HUME (1711–1776), Adam SMITH (1723–1790)—and intuitionist—CLARKE (1675–1729), PRICE (1723–1791)—theories. As was the case with later utilitarians such as Bentham and JOHN STUART MILL (1806–1873), Paley collapsed these competing theories into one view. According to Paley, both sentimentalists and intuitionists claim that we require a special moral faculty in order to discern our duties: either a special moral sense, an instinct, or our natural CONSCIENCE enables us to immediately intuit right and wrong and is the source of innate moral maxims. Paley opposed this view on a variety of grounds. He doubted that there are any innate moral maxims because moral maxims need to be flexible. There are no moral maxims "absolutely and universally true; in other words, which do not *bend* to the circumstances." The dictates of the alleged moral sense are, he maintained, really the result of education, custom, general practice, or prejudice and so are not to be relied upon in MORAL REASONING. They support the *status quo* without correcting or reforming it. Finally, if there were such a thing as a moral conscience, it would lack authority or motivating POWER. It may turn out that the pleasures of sin may exceed the pains of violating the dictates of conscience and in such a case moral instinct "has nothing to offer."

The key elements of Paley's theory are summed up in his three part definition of virtue: "The doing of good to mankind, in obedience to the will of God, and for the sake of everlasting happiness." Paley advocates a version of the divine command theory: What makes actions morally right is the will of God. Although Paley was aware of the standard objection to divine command theory—if God's will makes actions right then the statement that what God wills is right is an insignificant tautology—his response is inadequate.

Paley confidently asserted that there are two ways of knowing what God wills and so what our duties are: his will as revealed in scripture and his INTENTION or purpose as discovered in nature. Both lead to the same conclusions. Relying on the argument from design, Paley claimed it is evident that God created us for the purpose of making us happy. The test then of the rightness or wrongness of an action is its tendency to promote or diminish the general HAPPINESS. According to Paley, the ingredients of happiness include, among other things, cultivating and exercising our social affections and our talents and faculties.

Paley sharply separated the question of what makes actions right from the question of what motivates us to do what is right. The answer to the first is just that God wills it. That answer, however, does not provide us with a motive for doing what is right. We may still legitimately ask, "What motive do I have for doing what God wills?" Paley asks the latter question in this way: "Why am I obliged to do what is right?" By "obliged" he means being "urged by a violent motive resulting from the command of another." The violent motive is hope of reward and fear of PUNISHMENT in an afterlife; the commander is God. Thus we are moved to do the right thing by a self-interested motive.

Paley anticipated a number of problems utilitarians discuss to this day. For example, he worried that in particular cases an action (robbing a miser or killing a tyrant) may be useful although common sense would say it is not right. Paley replied that we need to take into account the precedent that would be established. If killing a tyrant is allowable because he is not useful, then it is permissible to kill any useless person. This would result in a state of affairs that would "fill the world with misery and confusion." Paley moved to rule-utilitarianism for a solution. If such actions are wrong because of the ex-

amples they set, what about actions done in secret? Paley appealed to the claim that God knows what we are doing. He also argued that a system of rewards and punishments is efficacious only if based on general rules. Without rules, the same act might be rewarded in one case and punished in another, with the result that no one would know how to act.

Most of the *Principles* consists in a detailed discussion of our duties to God, to others, and to ourselves, although Paley does not always show that these duties may be derived from the utility principle. The final part contains the outlines of a political theory.

See also: BENTHAM; CONSCIENCE; HAPPINESS; HUME; HUTCHESON; JOHN STUART MILL; MORAL EDUCATION; MORAL REASONING; MORAL RULES; MORAL SENSE THEORISTS; MOTIVES; REID; THEOLOGICAL ETHICS; UTILITARIANISM.

Bibliography

Works by Paley

The Principles of Moral and Political Philosophy. London, 1785. 12th ed. pub. 1799.

A View of the Evidences of Christianity. 2 vols. London, 1794.

Natural Theology; Or, Evidences of the Existence and Attributes of the Deity, Collected from the Appearances of Nature. London, 1802.

There is no modern edition of Paley's works; currently available selections from the *Principles* may be found in the following:

Raphael, D. D., ed. *British Moralists: 1650–1800.* Indianapolis: Hackett, 1991 [1969].

Schneewind, Jerome B., ed. *Moral Philosophy from Montaigne to Kant.* Cambridge: Cambridge University Press, 1990.

Works about Paley

Albee, Ernest. *A History of English Utilitarianism.* New York: Collier, 1962 [1902].

Barker, Ernest. *Traditions of Civility.* Cambridge: Cambridge University Press, 1948.

Clark, M. L. *Paley.* Toronto: University of Toronto Press, 1974.

LeMahieu, D. L. *The Mind of William Paley.* Lincoln: University of Nebraska Press, 1976.

Schneewind, Jerome B. *Sidgwick's Ethics and Victorian Moral Philosophy.* Oxford: Clarendon Press, 1977.

———. *The Invention of Autonomy: A History of Modern*

Moral Philosophy. Cambridge: Cambridge University Press, 1998.

Charlotte Brown

pardon

See amnesty and pardon.

partiality

To favor one person or group more than another is to show partiality. Some philosophers define 'partiality' more specifically as favoring "one's own": one's own projects, or those who stand in special relationships to oneself, such as family members, friends, or social groups. 'Partialists' maintain that the favored treatment of those to whom one is specially related is essential to such relationships. However, the two dominant theoretical traditions of modern moral philosophy, utilitarian CONSEQUENTIALISM and Kantian DEONTOLOGY, each define the MORAL POINT OF VIEW as requiring impartial concern for all persons and an equal consideration of the INTERESTS of all. Partialist critics argue that this requirement of IMPARTIALITY has led moral theories to neglect or deny the value of special relationships—relationships which are necessary to personal identity, INTEGRITY, and fulfillment in life.

The Partialist Challenge

Generally, partialists argue that the impartial standpoint calls for various attitudes and concepts which alienate persons from their loved ones and are inimical to PERSONAL RELATIONSHIPS. These attitudes and concepts include detachment from personal concerns and loyalties, disinterest, dispassion, an overemphasis on justice and RIGHTS, a sense of duty as the main moral motivation (in KANTIAN ETHICS), and a regard for other persons which focuses on their generalized moral EQUALITY while abstracting from their particularity and uniqueness. Personal relationships, by contrast, call for personal concern, LOYALTY, interest, PASSION, an emphasis on CARE and responsiveness, and attentiveness to the uniqueness of others and to their particular needs, interests, and so on.

UNIVERSALIZABILITY is a hallmark of the impartial standpoint: if a moral choice is genuinely impar-

tial, then it must also be the morally appropriate choice for anyone to make who faces the same circumstances. However universalizability, argue the partialists (*e.g.,* Blum, Oldenquist), is also ill-suited to personal relationships. The ways in which we benefit those we care about and our particular responsibilities toward them should reflect and express the specific natures of each special relationship, and cannot sensibly be universalized. Partialities toward persons or groups are nonuniversalizable also because they involve ineliminable egocentric references, such as "my" child, "my" country—references which are essential to identifying the objects of those loyalties.

Partialists (*e.g.,* MACINTYRE) defend favoritism to social groups on the additional grounds that morality is always at least partly tied to social contexts and traditions, and that individuals are identified through their social roles and their memberships in social groups. Social traditions thereby define many of the nonuniversalizable particulars of individual moral lives. Furthermore, group loyalty is essential to moral community by constituting a common, noninstrumental good which binds all community members together.

Many feminist critics (*e.g.,* S. Benhabib in Kittay and Meyers) emphasize, further, that the impartiality/partiality dichotomy has been traditionally aligned with both the public/private and the male/female dichotomies. Impartial reason has been revered as the perspective of (traditionally male) participants in the esteemed public realm of civic community, where citizens meet as equals to decide matters of justice and rights. By contrast, partiality and EMOTION have been unjustifiably devalued—along with women and their socially ascribed caretaking roles in the private realm of family and personal life. The twin philosophical insistence on moral impartiality and neglect of special relationships thus contributes to the unwarranted devaluation of women's moral capacities.

Partialist Solutions

Partialists have variously used two different strategies when accommodating the partiality of special relationships to impartialist moral traditions.

One strategy (*e.g.,* Blum, Nagel, Scheffler, and WILLIAMS) has been to argue that the domain of morality comprises partial as well as impartial considerations. Moral demands of justice, rights, and other impartial duties may often be overridden by partial moral considerations. Impartiality is typically required only of persons who either interact as equals in the impersonal realm of social justice, or act in an official capacity, as defined by a public institution, with equal responsibilities to all the members of some identifiable group. Apart from such institutional requirements, partial care for particular others is not only morally permissible but also has intrinsic and nonderivative moral value.

A second strategy (*e.g.,* Oldenquist) has been to challenge altogether the requirement of moral impartiality. On this view, impartial reasoning is impossible; self-love and concern for loved ones are ineradicable aspects of human nature. Furthermore, equal concern for the whole of humanity is too weak in most people to generate effective moral motivation or to outweigh narrower loyalties. At any rate, an equal concern for all human beings would itself be a form of partiality, differing only in being partiality for a larger group. For some critics (*e.g.,* Friedman, McIntyre), human beings cannot attain an impartial point of view because they cannot abstract entirely from their particular ends, desires, history, community, and embodiment. No actual human point of view is possible which is not intrinsically particularized in those ways.

For many such critics, VIRTUE ETHICS offers a more adequate account of the value of interpersonal partiality than do either Kantian ethics or utilitarianism.

In response, impartialist moral philosophers have agreed that partial concern for loved ones has great moral value. Defenders of impartialist moral theories, however, have attempted to construe these values as either derivable from, or at least constrained by, traditional impartialist moral principles.

Deontological Responses

Deontological impartialists tend to distinguish theoretically between levels of MORAL REASONING and to argue that only the universal level requires impartiality. One such version (*e.g.,* T. E. Hill, Jr., in Kittay and Meyers) construes impartiality as a standpoint for deciding fundamental moral principles and values, but not for making the specific moral choices of daily life. When deciding the most general moral principles, one is not to give any special standing to one's own interests or to those of people identified solely by their relationships to oneself. The specific moral choices of daily life, however, may be made with full particularized responsiveness toward loved ones, so long as those choices are consonant with the relevant impartial moral principles.

Another version (*e.g.,* Baron, Herman) differentiates levels of motivation: a sense of duty, the only moral motivation recognized by Kantian deontology, is a "secondary" motive, a long-term, overarching commitment to doing what one ought to do, and to finding out what one ought to do. A sense of duty functions as a limiting condition on what may be done from other, "primary" MOTIVES. In that role, a sense of duty is compatible with all the sentiments of LOVE, SYMPATHY, and so on which are essential to close personal relationships and which operate as primary motives to favor loved ones.

On a third version (*e.g.,* GEWIRTH), moral principles calling for the impartial treatment of all persons may apply directly to individual actions, or they may apply directly to social institutions and practices, and, through them, only indirectly to individual actions. A social institution can impartially further the highest moral ends (on this account, freedom and well-being) by establishing forms of role differentiation which themselves authorize partial behavior by those participant individuals.

Utilitarian (and other Consequentialist) Responses

Analogous to the deontologists's distinction between moral levels, many consequentialists (*e.g.,* Brink) distinguish general criteria of rightness from decision procedures for making right choices on particular occasions. The overriding criterion of rightness is the equal consideration of all interests. However, such a requirement is not itself a decision procedure for all specific occasions of moral deliberation. Partiality is permissible, possibly even required, at the level of individual moral deliberation.

Some consequentialists (*e.g.,* Railton) also defend a pluralism of ultimate values. This enables them to recognize the intrinsic value of those personal projects and commitments, including special relationships and their partiality, which are essential to self-identity and integrity.

Another consequentialist response (*e.g.,* Singer) calls for working moral codes which take into account the nature of human inclination. People are capable of strong affection toward only a few human beings and have the knowledge and ability to benefit only a few additional others. Also people do not or cannot always make good consequentialist calculations, for example, in emergency situations, and, in general, because of the problems of interpersonal comparison and long-range projection. People should, thus, cultivate dispositions and rules for decision making which are tailored to typical cases, and which will approximate the greatest value for the greatest number overall, even if, on occasion, there will be outcomes which depart from such a result. There is good reason to think that such rules and dispositions will permit partiality to friends and relatives.

Finally, some consequentialists (*e.g.,* Goodin) endorse the partiality of special relationships in light of two considerations. One is the empirical observation that moral conventions assign special duties of care for particular sorts of persons, such as young children and aged parents, to specific sorts of other persons. The second consideration is the alleged impartial moral duty of all persons to protect the vulnerable. Those for whom one has been assigned special caring responsibilities thereby become particularly vulnerable to one's actions and, accordingly, deserve one's partiality in caretaking.

Besides accounting for partiality in impartialist terms, many deontologists and consequentialists also warn that some forms of partiality are morally problematic, for example, sexism, racism, and nepotism. On this view, impartial moral principles remain the best basis for differentiating permissible from prohibited forms of partiality. At the same time, some philosophers (*e.g.,* Nagel) remain dissatisfied with all attempts thus far to reconcile the claims of impartial morality with the partial concerns of the personal point of view.

See also: ALIENATION; CARE; CHILDREN AND ETHICAL THEORY; CONSEQUENTIALISM; DELIBERATION AND CHOICE; DEONTOLOGY; DISCRIMINATION; DUTY AND OBLIGATION; EGOISM; EQUALITY; ETIQUETTE; FAMILY; FEMINIST ETHICS; FRIENDSHIP; GROUPS, MORAL STATUS OF; IDEAL OBSERVER; IMPARTIALITY; INSTITUTIONS; INTERESTS; INTEGRITY; KANTIAN ETHICS; LOVE; LOYALTY; MORAL COMMUNITY, BOUNDARIES OF; MORAL PLURALISM; MORAL REASONING; NEEDS; PASSION; PERSONAL RELATIONSHIPS; PUBLIC AND PRIVATE MORALITY; RECIPROCITY; RESPONSIBILITY; RACISM AND RELATED ISSUES; UNIVERSALIZABILITY; UTILITARIANISM; VIRTUE ETHICS.

Bibliography

Baron, Marcia. "The Alleged Moral Repugnance of Acting from Duty." *Journal of Philosophy* 81, no. 4 (1984): 197–219. Kantian response.

Becker, Lawrence C. [ed.]. "Symposium on Impartiality and Ethical Theory." *Ethics* 101, no. 4 (1991): 698–864. Broad spectrum of views.

Blum, Lawrence A. *Friendship, Altruism, and Morality.* London: Routledge and Kegan Paul, 1980. Partialism.

Brink, David O. "Utilitarian Morality and the Personal Point of View." *Journal of Philosophy* 83, no. 8 (1986): 417–38. Utilitarian response.

Cottingham, John. "Ethics and Impartiality." *Philosophical Studies* 43 (1983): 83–99. Partialism.

Friedman, Marilyn. *What Are Friends For? Feminist Perspectives on Personal Relationships and Moral Theory.* Ithaca: Cornell University Press, 1993. Criticisms of both impartiality and partiality.

Gewirth, Alan. "Ethical Universalism and Particularism." *Journal of Philosophy* 85, no. 6 (1988): 283–302. Deontological response.

Goodin, Robert. *Protecting the Vulnerable: A Reanalysis of Our Social Responsibilities.* Chicago: University of Chicago Press, 1985. Consequentialist response; extensive bibliographical references.

Herman, Barbara. *The Practice of Moral Judgment.* Cambridge, MA: Harvard University Press, 1993. Kantian response.

Kittay, Eva F., and Diana T. Meyers, eds. *Women and Moral Theory.* Totowa, N.J.: Rowman and Littlefield, 1987. Feminist Partialism and some impartialist responses.

MacIntyre, Alasdair. *After Virtue.* 2nd ed. Notre Dame, Ind.: University of Notre Dame Press, 1984 [1981]. Sweeping anti-impartialism.

Nagel, Thomas. *Equality* and *Partiality.* New York: Oxford University Press, 1991. Part impartialist, part partialist.

Oldenquist, Andrew. "Loyalties." *Journal of Philosophy* 79, no. 4 (1982): 173–93. Partialism.

Railton, Peter. "Alienation, Consequentialism, and the Demands of Morality." *Philosophy* and *Public Affairs* 13, no. 2 (1984): 134–71. Consequentialist response.

Scheffler, Samuel. *The Rejection of Consequentialism.* Oxford: Clarendon, 1982. Partialism.

Singer, Peter. *The Expanding Circle: Ethics and Sociobiology.* New York: Farrar, Straus and Giroux, 1981. Utilitarian response.

Stocker, Michael. "The Schizophrenia of Modern Ethical Theories." *Journal of Philosophy* 73, no. 14 (1976): 453–66. Partialism.

Williams, Bernard. *Moral Luck.* Cambridge: Cambridge University Press, 1981. Partialism.

Marilyn Friedman

Pascal, Blaise (1623–1662)

French philosopher and mathematician. In his writings and life, Pascal exhibited the conflict in his own soul between a yearning for uncomplicated Christian faith and the skeptical doubts of an intellect of genius. He could not suspend judgment like Michel de MONTAIGNE (1533–1592), nor could he champion reason like René DESCARTES (1596–1650), whose *sang-froid* Pascal dubbed *inutile et incertain*. In subordinating reason to religious AUTHORITY or faith, Pascal concluded that "the heart" rather than reason has moral priority. This in effect denied the viability of any human morality based on natural reason. Pascal saw himself and man suspended between the infinitely small and the infinitely great, and thus threw himself on the mercy of God in the hope that his sinful human PRIDE would be crushed by divine grace.

To his own agony, Pascal had difficulty overcoming reason. He thus proposed that skeptics take what became known as the Pascalian Wager: If you believe in God, and God exists, then you will have eternal bliss; if you believe and God does not exist, you lose nothing. Any gambler would choose belief. But following the Jansenists (Cornelius Jansen, 1585–1638), Pascal also said that God's grace is required for belief and salvation. Reason and yearning—as he discovered—are of no help; to have faith, the incomprehensible grace of God is required. Thus his game-theory advice is both ironic and tragic. In 1654, he had a profound religious experience. Thereafter he believed that the certitude of the Christian religion had been revealed to him, and that reason had nothing to do with it.

Pascal utilized his great wit and reason in his *Lettres provinciale* (1656–1657), in which he attacked the CASUISTRY of the Jesuits and defended the Jansenists. He purported to show just how corrupt the use of reason can be. But the Jesuits were in favor in the court of Louis XIV (1638–1715), and Pascal's attack was taken to threaten both the Church and the state. The *Lettres* were condemned and the Jansenists were persecuted. Nevertheless, Pascal continued his attacks in his *Pensées sur religion* which were published only after his death. The *Pensées* contain no systematic ethical position, but their epigrammatic eloquence and sardonic wit have assured both Pascal's place as a religious thinker and his literary fame.

Pascal's foundation in faith as a gift of the grace of God led him to stress the Christian VIRTUES of HUMILITY, asceticism, and worldly ignorance, and to favor the doctrine of predestination, thus putting him in diametric opposition to Descartes who believed that we can reach truth and salvation by use of reason and FREE WILL alone.

Pascal said that skepticism is the best route to fideism because skepticism shows how miserable we are without the certitude that can be provided only by the grace of God. In ethical terms, we can know what is good and right only if we have basic moral principles that are certain. But no principles—in mathematics, science, RELIGION, or ethics—can be established by reason alone. Thus Pascal says that even the great advances in mathematics and science of his time (to which he made major contributions) are trivial and futile in the face of revealed knowledge of God. Pascal's claim that such religious knowledge is beyond reason and requires a leap of faith makes him a predecessor of existentialist theology and a critic of the (human) ethical stance.

Thus Pascal is superficially an intuitionist and profoundly an irrationalist in ethics: "We know truth not by reason but more so by the heart. It is in this latter way that we know first principles, and it is in vain that reason, which plays no part in this, tries to combat them" (*Pensées*). Pascal thus moves from rationalism to MYSTICISM. Like Descartes, Pascal believed that God's assurance is necessary for us to be absolutely certain about first principles; but unlike Descartes, he believed that we require certainty for practical actions in life. The general lack of faith and of moral certainties among the general run of humankind led him to a profound pessimism.

In sum, despite his appeal to the heart, Pascal's ethics is that of an ascetic Christianity that denies any human comfort other than hope for grace. The Jesuits showed how reason can lead to sin, and all their casuistic arguments were to be cast aside as deception. Similarly, the pride of the new scientists, particularly of the Cartesians, in the progress of the new science is a snare and a delusion. By reducing man's dependence for knowledge to revelation, by posing salvation as the only serious concern of mankind, and by stressing grace over good works as the only (possibly predestined) way to salvation, Pascal trivializes all merely human concerns such as science and mundane morality.

See also: CASUISTRY; CHRISTIAN ETHICS; DESCARTES; EXISTENTIAL ETHICS; FREEDOM AND DETERMINISM; HUMILITY; INTUITIONISM; MORAL REASONING; MYSTICISM; PRIDE; RATIONALITY VS. REASONABLENESS; RELIGION; SKEPTICISM IN ETHICS; THEOLOGICAL ETHICS; VIRTUES.

Bibliography

Works by Pascal

Oeuvres complètes. Edited by Jouis Lafuma. Paris: Éditions du Seuil, 1963.

Pensées. Translated by Martin Tunell. New York: Harper, 1962 [1669].

Works about Pascal

Armour, Leslie. *"Infini rien": Pascal's Wager and the Human Paradox.* Carbondale: Southern Illinois University Press, 1993.

Baird, A. S. W. *Studies in Pascal's Ethics.* The Hague: Nijhoff, 1975.

Brunschvicg, Léon. *Descartes et Pascal: lecteurs de Montaigne.* New York: Brentano's, 1944.

Carraud, Vincent. *Pascal et la philosophie.* Paris: Presses Universitaires de France, 1992.

Goldman, Lucian. *The Hidden God: A Study of the Tragic Vision in the Pensées of Pascal and the Tragedies of Racine.* New York: Humanities Press, 1964.

Mesnard, Jean. *Pascal: His Life and Works.* New York: Philosophical Library, 1952.

Richard A. Watson

passion

Do our passions, as the Stoics thought, distract us from our true vocation, the following of reason? Is "apathy" (ἀπάθεια), absence of all passions (πάθη), a proper goal for us? Are our passions not really *ours,* but forces that interfere with the expression of our true (better) nature, or do they help constitute our better nature? Are we passive when they are active, active only when reason is in control?

Passions are usually contrasted with actions and seen as being under less direct control of the will. But when they are seen to include desires and MOTIVES, they are activating forces. Even when they show in reaction rather than intentional action, they actively affect the moral scene. They are often also contrasted with reason. One significant fact about them is that there are many of them, different ones dominating in different persons, whereas we supposedly all share the same one reason, one of whose voices is taken to be the voice of duty. Passions have been of interest to moral philosophers either as psychological forces that morality is to counter and control, or as forces that morality itself depends upon and appeals to, or as a mixture of these. Whether to know our moral enemies, or to know our moral allies, or to know which particular passions are likely to be enemies of morality, which ones sources or allies of morality, moralists may want to understand the variety and various workings of human passions.

PLATO (c. 430–347 B.C.E.), like many later moral philosophers, thought that all passions should be controlled by reason. He selected our capacity for ANGER, self-assertion, and SELF-DEFENSE (θυμός) as reason's needed ally among the passions. Later philosophers, such as SPINOZA (1632–1677) and HUME (1711–1776), followed Plato in taking a form of self-assertive PRIDE as one source of moral motivation.

ARISTOTLE'S (384–322 B.C.E.) long list of moral VIRTUES is a list of social human beings' desires and passions when these take their most appropriate forms. He clearly based his ethics on a careful study of the MORAL PSYCHOLOGY of human passions. For him there is a virtuous form of every normal human passion, including pride, anger, and desire for PLEASURE. But he agreed with Plato that reason is to make the decision as to which version of each of these psychological forces is the humanly appropriate one. The intellectual virtues of WISDOM and PRUDENCE take priority over the other virtues, in that they are needed for the recognition of them. For the cultivation of any virtue, however, Aristotle held that friendly parental training in good habits is a first essential, so that intellectual and more passionate virtues are interdependent.

The Christian tradition, especially its Augustinian strand, takes our capacity not just for friendship but for passionate LOVE, to be an ally with reason in motivating us to embrace our true good. DESCARTES (1596–1650), in *The Passions of the Soul* (1649), agreed in giving this high honor to love, which, when guided by reason, "can never be too great" (Article 139). It unites the soul with a whole of which it sees itself to be a lesser part, and in so doing it perfects the soul, and gives it the "sweetest of all joys," that of self-satisfaction (Article 190). "It represents to us what we love as a good which belongs to us" ("*qui nous appartient,*" Article 139). Joy is the soul's awareness that it possesses its own true good. "For the soul receives no other yield [fruit] from all the good things that it possesses, except this joy" (Article 91). Descartes' rationalist epistemology is completed by an ethics of love and joy. Reason guides, but, for the reasoning not to have been fruitless, what it guides one to has to be willingly embraced, claimed as one's own, and enjoyed. The highest object of love is God-or-universe, but lesser loves point us in the right direction. "*Generosité*" to all fellow persons is the expected effect of the highest love, and of consequent satisfaction with oneself as perfected by it. Persons with this first virtue "do not hold anything more important than to do good to other men and to disdain their individual interests, they . . . are always perfectly courteous, affable and obliging to everyone" (Article 156).

HOBBES (1588–1679), like Descartes, Spinoza, and Hume, made an analytical list of human passions as a preliminary to his moral endorsements. More than Descartes or Hume, he tried to give a mechanist analysis of them, reducing them all to versions of "endeavour" or "vital motion," *i.e.,* the "small beginnings" of animal or voluntary motion. Endeavour is "for divers considerations diversified" into the full spectrum of human passions. The diverse considerations include whether the motion is to or from some external thing, what sort of thing it is, the perceived likelihood of the success of the endeavour, and its place in different sequences and mixtures of endeavours. As Descartes, Spinoza, and Hume found a positive moral role for the Christian sin of pride, so Hobbes did for that pagan vice, fear of DEATH. Fear of death, and hope for the POWER and assurance of more commodious living incline Hobbist natural persons to follow the theorems of reason, and replace fighting over scarce goods with peace. The insatiable desire for eminent power to satisfy our desires, the desire for the acknowledgment of our superior power, an immoderate appetite for "glory," and joy in our sense of power, all put obstacles in the way of peace, and even in the way of recognizing right reason. Vain persons all want their own fallible disagreeing reason ("Professors themselves may often err, and cast up false"—*Leviathan,* chapter V) to be treated as right reason, and so add to the quarrels they presume to arbitrate.

(Hobbes was not himself a professor, and seems confident enough that he himself has not cast up false.) Hobbes takes morality to be the enlightened self-interest of persons who have the passions, intelligence, and reason he has analyzed, persons who face scarcity and live "in multitudes," and so are forced to relate somehow to one another. The RATIONAL CHOICE is cooperation. The danger is self-defeating defensive aggression, a rash of would-be preemptive strikes.

In Book Two of *A Treatise of Human Nature* (1737) and in subsequent writings about human passions, Hume followed SHAFTESBURY (1671–1713) and French moralists, such as MONTAIGNE (1533–1592) and La Bruyère (1645–1696), as much as Hobbes. He gave an associationist but not a mechanist account of the "objects" of human passions, and of the way one passion is followed by others. He saw that SYMPATHY communicates passions from person to person, but "comparison" can prevent this sharing of goods and ills. One person's good cannot but conflict with that of her fellows, if she has to see herself as better off than they are in order to be content. For Hume, conflict, either between the various passions of one person, or between the strong passions of different persons, makes the conflicting passions "violent." It is the job of an enlightened morality to reconcile and calm our passions, but not to frustrate them. Indeed, moral judgment itself is the verdict of a special meta-passion, joy or sorrow in a human passion, habit, or in an action expressing passions or habits. We call this special reflective moral sentiment "approbation" and "disapprobation." Morality on Hume's view is thus a matter of human passions controlling themselves. But reason automatically serves the passions, and is an indispensable servant in their self-regulation.

KANT (1724–1804) found a positive moral role for a few human passions: reverence for the moral law, and for the rational wills that are its legislators; GUILT AND SHAME at one's failures to be adequately guided by respect for this law and its legislators; loathing of indulgence of our "animal inclinations"; good cheer in performance of our moral duties. But he saw that most human passions express only our empirically determined phenomenal nature, not our rational free noumenal nature, and so have no moral worth. They play the role of the governed, not the governor, in the moral life of a Kantian virtuous person of good will.

NIETZSCHE (1844–1900) said very acute things about the different passions to which different versions of morality give expression. He distinguished between moralities animated by reactive passions like pity, guilt, and RESENTMENT, and those that express freer and more active passions, such as pride and GENEROSITY. Moralities of the latter sort, he believed, will tend to speak of good and bad, rather than of good and EVIL. Most previous moral philosophies, including the Christian, the utilitarian, and the Kantian, come in for his merciless diagnosis: "*Schlechte Luft! Schlechte Luft!*" ("Foul air! Foul air!") He evaluated moralities by evaluating the passions to which they give covert or open satisfaction.

Contemporary discussions about the place of reason and passion in morality often follow Plato, Hobbes, and Kant, rather than Descartes, Hume, or Nietzsche, tending to see the passions as on the whole an unruly lot that needs to be governed by reason and its few picked passion cohorts. A sound morality is then seen to get its authority from reason, which harmonizes the passions, weeds out troublemakers among them, and works out the means to satisfying the rest. When construed as merely instrumental, what it is seen to serve is informed "preference" or "self-interest," a kind of anonymous outcome of each person's cleaned up passions, particularly her desires, given her information about the conditions and chances of their satisfaction. The detailed study of different human passions, and the particular workings of each of them, then gets left to psychologists like Freud (1856–1939) ethologists like DARWIN (1809–1882), and moral psychologists like Nietzsche. But moral philosophers who agree with Aristotle, Descartes, and Hume that annotated lists of virtues may be a more helpful codification of morality than sets of "laws" or rules, will want to learn about the special features of different passions, to reflect on their various relations to various versions of reason, and to evaluate their individual and collective capacity for self-regulation and self-acceptance.

See also: ANGER; ARISTOTLE; DESCARTES; DESIRE; EMOTION; HOBBES; HUME; KANT; NIETZSCHE; PLATO; REASONS FOR ACTION; SELF-CONTROL; STOICISM; VIRTUE ETHICS; VIRTUES.

Bibliography

Aristotle. *The Basic Works of Aristotle.* Edited by R. McKeon. New York: Random House, 1971. See *Rhetoric, De anima, Poetics,* and *Nicomachean Ethics.*

Cicero, Marcus Tullius. *De finibus bonorum et malorum.* Translated by H. Rackham. London: Heinemann, 1931.

———. *Tusculanae disputationes.* Translated by J. E. King. Cambridge, MA: Harvard University Press, 1971.

Darwin, Charles. *The Expression of the Emotions in Man and Animal.* New York: D. Appleton, 1873.

De Sousa, Ronald. *The Rationality of Emotion.* Cambridge, MA: MIT Press, 1987.

Descartes, Renè. *The Passions of the Soul.* Translated by Stephen H. Voss. Indianapolis/Cambridge: Hackett, 1989 [1649].

Freud, Sigmund. *Civilisation and Its Discontents.* Translated by J. Strachey. New York: W. W. Norton, 1961 [1930].

Gordon, Robert. *The Structure of Emotions.* Cambridge: Cambridge University Press, 1987.

Greenspan, Patricia. *Emotions and Reasons.* New York: Routledge, 1988.

Hobbes, Thomas. *Leviathan.* London: J. M. Dent, 1914 [1651].

Hume, David. *A Treatise of Human Nature.* Edited by L. A. Selby-Bigge. Oxford: Clarendon Press, 1958 [1737]. Especially book 2.

———. *Essays, Moral, Political, and Literary.* Edited by Eugene Miller. Indianapolis: Liberty Classics, 1985 [1741–1742]. See "Of the Delicacy of Taste and Passion"; "Of the Standard of Taste"; and "Of Tragedy."

Izard, Carroll. *Human Emotions.* New York: Plenum, 1977.

Kant, Immanuel. *Lectures on Ethics.* Edited by L. W. Beck. New York: Harper and Row, 1963 [1780].

———. *Metaphysics of Morals.* Indianapolis: Bobbs-Merrill, 1964 [1797].

———. *Anthropology from a Pragmatic Standpoint.* Translated by M. J. Gregor. The Hague: Martinus Nijhoff, 1974 [1798].

Nietzsche, Friedrich. *The Genealogy of Morals.* Edited by W. Kaufmann. New York: Vintage, 1967 [1887].

Plato. See the following titles and translations: *Phaedrus* (R. Hackforth); *Symposium* (B. Jowett); *Republic* (G. M. A. Grube); *Philebus* (J. C. B. Gosling).

Solomon, Robert. *The Passions.* Garden City, N.Y.: Anchor Press, 1976.

Spinoza, Baruch. *Ethics and Selected Letters.* Translated by S. Shirley. Edited by S. Feldman. Indianapolis: Hackett, 1982 [1677].

Taylor, Gabriele. *Pride, Shame, and Guilt: Emotions of Self-Assessment.* Oxford: Clarendon Press, 1985.

Annette C. Baier

paternalism

The normative issue raised by paternalism is when, if ever, one person is entitled to interfere with another for that other person's good. Philosophically, discussion of the issue has as its focus paternalistic interventions by the state seeking to promote the welfare of its citizens—legal paternalism. Such discussion takes as its starting point the strong anti-paternalistic views of JOHN STUART MILL (1806–1873). In his *On Liberty* (1859), he denies the state the right to make someone do or forbear from doing something "because it will be better for him to do so, because it will make him happier, because in the opinion of others, to do so would be wise." Contemporary philosophical argument attempts to sustain this conclusion or to argue for various exceptions to such a strong anti-paternalism.

This article is divided into two parts. The first is a discussion of the conceptual problems associated with the effort to define the concept of paternalism. The second is a discussion of various ethical theories that are used to clarify the normative questions.

Conceptual Issues

Any analysis of the term "paternalism," like that of other philosophical terms, is relative to some set of problems. If one were interested in comparing the organizational behavior of large corporations with respect to their employees' welfare, one might adopt a different definition of paternalism than if one were concerned with limits on the state's right to exercise COERCION. It is useful, therefore, to give examples of the kinds of laws and actions which have been central to most writing on the topic.

1. Laws requiring motorcyclists to wear helmets.
2. Laws forbidding swimming while lifeguards are not on duty.
3. Laws requiring individuals to save for their retirement (in the United States, Social Security).
4. Court orders allowing physicians to transfuse Jehovah's Witnesses against their wishes.
5. Required waiting periods for marriage and divorce.
6. Deception of patients by medical personnel to avoid upsetting the patient.
7. Civil commitment of persons judged dangerous to themselves.
8. Requiring students to take certain courses.
9. A wife hiding sleeping pills so that her depressed husband cannot attempt suicide.
10. Infanticide of severely defective newborns.

In all these cases we have some kind of interference with a person; its purported justification would be in terms of reasons referring to the promotion of the person's good or the prevention of harm to the person. One can make these elements more precise by adopting the following definition.

P acts paternalistically towards Q if and only if
(a) P acts with the intent of averting some harm or promoting some benefit for Q.
(b) P acts contrary to the current preferences, desires or dispositions of Q.
(c) P's act is a limitation on Q's autonomy.

This definition has the following features. It is evaluatively neutral in that it does not beg any questions with respect to the legitimacy or illegitimacy of paternalistic actions. It makes clear that while the action has a benevolent intent there are normative questions raised by clauses (b) and (c). Clause (c) in particular raises the most obvious ethical issues and is most difficult to formulate accurately. The problem is that not everything that is done contrary to the wishes of others, and intended for their good, is best viewed as paternalism. Some authors have added as an additional ingredient that the action must be an interference with LIBERTY. But lying to people, or even injuring them, is not clearly an interference with liberty. Others have pointed out that one can act paternalistically by telling people the truth (as when a doctor insists that a patient know the exact nature of her illness, contrary to her wishes). Only some broad notion of limitation of autonomy seems capable of encompassing the many ways in which we can act paternalistically, while not allowing all benevolently intended actions contrary to someone's wishes to fall under the definition.

Normative Issues

This definition makes clear the elements which both raise questions of justification and provide possible justifying considerations. The reasons which support paternalism are those which support any altruistic action—the welfare of another person. The reasons against paternalism are those which militate against any interference with the autonomy of individuals—respect for their desire to lead their own life. It should be noted that I am assuming throughout that we are dealing with competent adults. Few deny that young children, the profoundly retarded, the severely depressed, the psychotic, may be subjected to various forms of paternalism.

The simplest theory which could be advanced to support some paternalistic acts is a maximizing CONSEQUENTIALISM. Given some conception of the good, according to which it is possible to produce good for an agent while acting against her current preferences, paternalism is justified whenever more good than bad is produced by the intervention. The best known consequentialist theory, UTILITARIANISM, defines the good as some form of preference satisfaction. But one could have a different value theory, one which, say, regarded liberty as intrinsically valuable. One could then argue that certain forms of paternalism are justified because they maximize the person's liberty. So one could argue against addictive drugs that people ought not to be free to use them because their freedom is reduced. Mill uses some form of this argument when he urges that a person should not be allowed to sell herself into SLAVERY.

Criticism of any consequentialist justification of paternalism can take two forms. On the empirical level one could argue that the facts are such that it is very unlikely that paternalistic POWER, as exercised by the state or by, say, physicians, will lead to better consequences than the denial of such power. Support of such an argument will involve claims about persons being the best judges of their own INTERESTS, the difficulty of drawing the line between some interventions and others, the importance to individuals of being allowed to make their own decisions, and so forth. While such arguments are often cogent, it seems unlikely they can lead to any stronger conclusion than a general presumption against paternalism, a burden of proof on those who wish to interfere. It is plausible, however, that the burden of proof can be met in some cases. For example, it appears that the harm produced by a legal requirement that hunters wear brightly colored jackets is less than the good produced by saving hunters from accidental shootings.

The second, and more important, criticism of a consequentialist theory is that such a theory is mistaken in its single-minded focus on the total good produced for someone. To regard another person as a moral equal is to give considerable weight to her view of the world. Most of us do not simply want to have our desires satisfied, but to be active in determining the nature of those desires, to determine for ourselves a conception of the good, to have a sphere of self-determination in which we are allowed to make our own mistakes. For someone else to impose upon us his conception (even if in some sense "better") of our good is to deny us the respect due to equal moral agents. To use a different mode of analysis, just as RIGHTS put limits on what we can do to people in pursuit of the good of others, so rights of autonomy put limits on what may be done to people in pursuit of their good.

For these reasons those who defend a limited paternalism rely on arguments concerning when autonomy may be limited. The central idea is that of hypothetical CONSENT. Consider a person who is found unconscious in the wreckage of an automobile accident. He requires an immediate operation to save his life. Since we believe the person *would* consent to such an operation, were he conscious, competent, and informed of the relevant facts, we proceed with the operation in the absence of actual consent. And, as is shown by J. S. Mill's famous example—a man walking across a bridge which, unknown to him, is about to collapse—we are entitled to intervene paternalistically even if the person actively resists our efforts.

Generalizing from such examples, hypothetical consent theorists claim that we are justified in paternalism if the person would have consented to our action if she were fully rational and informed of the facts. Such theorists assume that in any case in which we are entitled to act paternalistically there is some specific cognitive or emotional defect which is present, and which prevents the person from making a prudent decision. They assume that the agent is not acting in a fully voluntary fashion and that only in such cases, or in cases when it is necessary to establish whether the person is acting voluntarily, is paternalism justified. Feinberg calls this thesis "soft paternalism." It is distinct from "hard" paternalism which maintains that it is sometimes legitimate to interfere with competent adults to protect them from harm even if they are acting completely voluntarily.

Consider, as a case in which the two views differ, a law allowing people to sell themselves into slavery. A soft paternalist will be very suspicious of such CONTRACTS, believing that our experience establishes a general presumption that persons would not voluntarily enter into such contracts. The soft paternalist will want to make such contracts have a period in which the potential slave can change his mind, but if convinced of the voluntary character of the contract, must allow them as valid. A hard paternalist, on the other hand, argues that the condition of being a slave is so harmful and morally degrading that people should not be allowed to enter that condition no matter how voluntary their agreement is.

Deciding between these two positions, or between them and an absolute ban on paternalism, is not just a matter of how we react to particular examples. It is a matter of assessing competing principles in terms of their consistency, their coherence with other parts of our moral and political theory, their grounding in attractive conceptions of the type of persons we want to be, the conceptual and normative difficulties of alternative principles, and the quality of the arguments we can muster in defense of the favored principles.

See also: AGENCY AND DISABILITY; ALTRUISM; AUTONOMY OF MORAL AGENTS; BENEVOLENCE; CHARITY; CHILDREN AND ETHICAL THEORY; COERCION; CONSENT; CONSEQUENTIALISM; CONTRACTS; DECEIT; DELIBERATION AND CHOICE; FREE WILL; FREEDOM AND DETERMINISM; INSTITUTIONS; INTERESTS; KANT; LIBERTY; LIBERTY, ECONOMIC; JOHN STUART MILL; NEEDS; OPPRESSION; POWER; PRIVACY; RIGHT HOLDERS; RIGHTS; SECRECY AND CONFIDENTIALITY; SLAVERY; UTILITARIANISM; VOLUNTARY ACTS; WELFARE RIGHTS AND SOCIAL POLICY.

Bibliography

Arneson, Richard. "Mill versus Paternalism." *Ethics* 90 (1980): 470–89.

Dworkin, Gerald. "Paternalism." In *Morality and the Law,* edited by R. Wasserstrom. Belmont, Calif.: Wadsworth, 1971.

Feinberg, Joel. "Legal Paternalism." *Canadian Journal of Philosophy* 1 (1971).

———. *Harm to Self.* New York: Oxford University Press, 1986.

Gert, Bernard, and Charles Culver. "Paternalistic Behavior." *Philosophy and Public Affairs* 6 (1976): 45–57.

Kleinig, John. *Paternalism.* Totowa, N.J.: Rowman and Allenheld, 1983.

Mill, John Stuart. *On Liberty.* Indianapolis: Bobbs-Merrill, 1956 [1859].

Sartorius, Rolf, ed. *Paternalism.* Minneapolis: University of Minnesota Press, 1982.

VanDeVeer, Donald. *Paternalistic Intervention.* Princeton: Princeton University Press, 1986.

Gerald Dworkin

Paul, the Apostle, Saint (C.E. 5–67?)

Christian saint; an apostle and author of several epistles in the New Testament. Born to Jewish parents in the Hellenistic city of Tarsus in Cilicia, Paul grew comfortable with the Greek language and familiar with the terminology and style of popular philosophy, but he grew committed to the ancestral heritage and faithful to the God of Abraham. He became a strict Pharisee (Phil. 3:5) and was evidently trained as a rabbi. (According to Acts 22:3 Paul studied in Jerusalem with the famous Gamaliel [died c. C.E. 50], but the reliability of the biographical data in Acts is disputed by many scholars.) Paul's zeal for the law of Moses led him to become "a persecutor of the church"; he evidently saw among some of the followers of JESUS a dangerous threat to the legal traditions of the Jews. In the early thirties in a vision of the risen Christ he was called to cease the persecution and to begin proclamation of the gospel of Jesus Christ among the Gentiles. In obedience to this call Paul became an itinerant missionary, establishing and nurturing churches throughout the northeastern Mediterranean. On a trip to Jerusalem to deliver a collection for the poor in Judea, a collection which was for Paul not only a gesture of CHARITY but also a symbol of the unity of Jew and Gentile in the church, Paul was arrested. Imprisoned first at Caesarea and then at Rome, he was probably executed in Rome during the reign of Nero (C.E. 37–68, r. 54–68).

Letters

Paul's literary legacy is in the form of letters to the churches. There is almost unanimous agreement that Romans, I and II Corinthians, Galatians, Philippians, I Thessalonians, and Philemon were written by Paul; there is considerable agreement that I and

II Timothy and Titus were written by a member of the Pauline "school"; but there remains considerable disagreement about the authorship of Colossians, Ephesians, and II Thessalonians. Set in the service of Paul's mission as an apostle, the moral exhortations in the letters present no "timeless truths" in the style of either a philosopher or a code-maker; they are rather the timely and pastoral proclamation of the gospel to particular churches facing concrete problems.

The Gospel and Morality

Paul's proclamation of the gospel, of "the power of God for salvation" (Rom. 1:16), sometimes took shape in the indicative mood and sometimes in the imperative mood. Both moods are appropriate—indeed, necessary—for Paul. In the crucified and risen Christ, God has acted to end the reign of sin and death and to begin the coming age of God's unchallenged and cosmic sovereignty. The indicative mood describes the power of God to provide the eschatological salvation of which Christians have already the "first-fruits" (Rom. 8:23) and the "guarantee" (II Cor. 5:5) in the Spirit. The imperative mood acknowledges that Christians are still threatened by the powers of sin and death and responsible for holding fast to the life given them in Christ. So, "if we live by the Spirit, let us also walk by the Spirit" (Gal. 5:25).

Reflection about conduct and CHARACTER was to be radically qualified by the gospel. Paul admonished the Roman churches to a new discernment, not conformed to this age but transformed by the renewal of their minds by the power of God (Rom. 12:2). There is no Pauline recipe for this new discernment, no wooden scheme or fixed checklist, but some features of it are clear.

1. Christians' self-understanding as moral agents was to be determined by their incorporation into Christ (Gal. 2:20; Rom. 6:1–11).
2. Their perspective on moral situations was to be eschatological, attentive both to the ways the power of God was already effective in the world and to the continuing assertiveness of the doomed powers of sin and death. (The Galatians, tempted to submit again to the yoke of the law, needed to be reminded that Christ had already established a new creation, while the Corinthians needed to be reminded that they were not yet, despite their pretensions, fully in the coming age.)
3. Freedom (Gal. 5:1; II Cor. 3:17) and LOVE (I Cor. 13; Phil. 1:9) were fundamental values for the community; they provided tokens of the age to come.
4. The new discernment was not simply a spontaneous intuition granted by the Spirit; nor were guidelines and judgments created *ex nihilo*. The existing moral traditions of Judaism, Hellenism, and the Church were utilized by Paul and his communities as they had been selected, assimilated, and qualified by the gospel.

The existing moral traditions were good and useful but never normative for Paul in the same way God's action in Jesus Christ was. The law of Moses was "good" (Rom. 7:16), but as secondary to the promise and provisional to the fulfillment of promise, it could not be allowed either the first or last word in Christian congregations. The moral traditions of the Greek philosophical schools could provide elements of style (*e.g.,* the diatribe) and moral concepts (*e.g.,* CONSCIENCE or *suneidesis;* contentment or *autarkeia*), but both style and concepts are in the service of Paul's mission as an apostle. (In Rom. 1:14–15, with its reference to a law "written on their [*i.e.,* Gentiles's] hearts," Paul does not so much affirm a philosophical doctrine of "natural law" as utilize Hellenistic Jewish traditions polemically against Jewish Christians in Rome who would condemn Gentiles and repudiate Paul's mission to Gentiles.) The churches' tradition of Jesus' sayings was accepted as morally authoritative, but not as "the basis for a kind of Christian Halakah" (Davies, 144). Existing traditions were used but always also qualified by the moral identity, perspective, and fundamental values formed by the gospel. By means of such discernment the gospel was brought to bear on the many and varied concrete problems faced by the Pauline churches. There were questions, for example, about the relationship of Jews and Gentiles in the churches. Paul requires neither Jewish Christians to act like Gentiles nor Gentile Christians to observe the Jewish laws, but he does require them both to "welcome one another" (Rom. 15:7), not to con-

Paul, the Apostle

demn and repudiate each other. Indeed, the unity and equality of Jew and Gentile in the Church are closely related for Paul to "the truth of the gospel" (Gal. 2:4, 14) and to the "obedience of faith" (Rom. 1:5; 16:26).

There were questions, too, about other relationships in the church, relationships between the free and the slaves and between male and female. Paul does not lead a slave revolt or proclaim a woman's year, but neither does he simply condone existing social roles and existing relationships. Paul cannot simply create *ex nihilo* new social traditions and role assignments; instead he qualifies existing traditions in the light of a new identity in Christ in whom "there is neither Jew nor Greek, there is neither slave nor free, there is neither male nor female, for you are all one in Christ Jesus" (Gal. 3:28; cf. Longenecker). This new identity in Christ yielded its first fruits when slaves like Onesimus were received "no longer as a slave but . . . as a beloved brother . . . both in the flesh and in the Lord" (Philem. 16), and when a woman like Prisca was a "fellow-worker" (Rom. 16:3–5) and Euodia and Syntyche "labored side by side" with Paul (Phil. 4:2). Some passages in Paul (*e.g.,* I Cor. 11:3–16 and 14:33–35) are difficult to reconcile with each other and more difficult still to reconcile with Paul's practice or with his eschatological perception of a new order in which there is no male and female. But this much is clear: Paul's discernment enables the criticism and qualification of existing traditions and rejects any attempt to construe freedom in Christ merely as independence rather than as interdependence, *i.e.,* as mutual service (*e.g.,* I Cor. 11:11, 12).

Other concrete problems include the question of the relationship of rich and poor in the churches—whether at the table of the sacrament (I Cor. 11:22) or in the collection for the poor in Judea (*e.g.,* II Cor. 8:8–14); the question of the appropriate attitude toward sexual intercourse when the claim of some enthusiasts that they are already altogether "spiritual" leads to either ascetic or libertine inferences (*e.g.,* I Cor. 6:12–21, 7:1–40); the question of political RESPONSIBILITY, which Paul handles according to Hellenistic Jewish traditions but sets in the context of the love of the neighbor (Rom 13:1–7); the question of eating meat routinely sacrificed to idols (I Cor. 8).

In none of these is Paul providing a timeless moral code in the style of either rabbi or philosopher. Rather he continually and pastorally brings the gospel to bear upon particular problems faced by specific congregations and upon the moral traditions and resources they have for dealing with those problems. He nurtures the communities he addresses as communities of moral discourse and discernment, as "full of goodness, filled with knowledge, and able to instruct one another" (Rom. 15:14).

See also: CHRISTIAN ETHICS; JESUS OF NAZARETH.

Bibliography

Davies, W. D. *Paul and Rabbinic Judaism.* 4th ed. Philadelphia: Fortress Press, 1980 [1948]. Classic study highlighting Paul's Pharisaic background.

Furnish, Victor Paul. *Theology and Ethics in Paul.* Nashville: Abingdon Press, 1968. An excellent account of the theological character of Paul's ethic. Appendix surveys interpretations of Paul's ethic. Extensive bibliography.

———. *The Moral Teaching of Paul.* 2d ed. Nashville: Abingdon Press, 1985 [1979]. Account of Paul's teaching on some concrete moral questions.

Hays, Richard B. *The Moral Vision of the New Testament: Community, Cross, New Creation: A Contemporary Introduction to New Testament Ethics.* New York: Harper Collins, 1996.

Longenecker, Richard. *New Testament Social Ethics for Today.* Grand Rapids, Mich.: Eerdmans, 1984. An account of Paul's application of Galatians 3:28 in his preaching and practice.

Meeks, Wayne, ed. *The Writings of Paul.* New York: W. W. Norton, 1972. Convenient combination of primary texts with critical notes and selected essays.

Rosner, Brian S., ed. *Understanding Paul's Ethics: Twentieth-Century Approaches.* Grand Rapids, Mich.: Eerdmans, 1995. A collection of diverse and important essays on Paul's ethics.

Stendahl, Krister. *Paul Among Jews and Gentiles.* Philadelphia: Fortress Press, 1976. Provocative study which argues "justification by faith" is, for Paul, not the answer to a troubled conscience but the solution to the social question of relations between Jews and Gentiles.

Verhey, Allen. *The Great Reversal: Ethics and the New Testament.* Grand Rapids: Eerdmans, 1984. See pp. 102–29. A fuller account of Pauline discernment and its application to concrete problems.

Allen D. Verhey

peace

See war and peace.

Peirce, C[harles] S[anders] (1839–1914)

American philosopher, mathematician, and physicist. Born in Cambridge, Massachusetts, in 1839, Peirce was graduated from Harvard in 1859, and four years later earned a degree in chemistry, *summa cum laude,* from the Lawrence Scientific School. For the next fifteen years he wrote philosophy while working as an astronomer and a physicist. The recognition he gained from these writings led to his appointment to the faculty of Johns Hopkins University. After retiring in 1887, he lived in Milford, Pennsylvania, where he died in 1914.

Peirce was a systematic thinker whose writings cover virtually all areas of philosophy. He is considered the founder of PRAGMATISM, and made important contributions to logic, semiotics, philosophy of science, philosophy of mathematics, epistemology, metaphysics, cosmology, PHENOMENOLOGY, RELIGION, AESTHETICS, and ethics. His ethics cannot be severed from his logic and aesthetics or from his central doctrine of the threefold division of categories.

Although Peirce for many years considered ethics a practical discipline of no philosophic importance, he gradually came to recognize it as an important normative science upon which logic depends. His tripartite categorial distinctions of Firstness, Secondness, and Thirdness, originally based on logic, became founded in phenomenology. Logic, ethics, and aesthetics became the three normative sciences. According to Peirce's triadic architectonic, these normative sciences, along with phenomenology and metaphysics, constitute the three branches of philosophy. Within the division of the normative sciences, logic deals with thought or Thirdness, ethics with ACTION or Secondness, and aesthetics with the qualitative or Firstness.

Peirce characterizes the normative sciences of logic, ethics, and aesthetics as the sciences of ends. They are the sciences which distinguish, respectively, good and bad in the representations of truth, in the efforts of the will, and in objects regarded simply in their presentation. Logic is the first normative science accepted by Peirce, then ethics, then aesthetics. However, the logical order of dependence is precisely the reverse. Logic deals with thinking, which is a type of deliberate activity. It involves the ongoing correction of our methods of reasoning, and its end is truth. But the question remains concerning what truth is, what reasoning ought to aim toward. Ethics defines that end. The general issue of ethics for Peirce is the deliberate acceptance of goals. It concerns the regulation of conduct in accordance with ends. Ethics in turn depends upon the determination of the ultimate end, the *summum bonum,* which is not a means to anything further, which needs nothing further for its own justification, but which is good in and of itself. This lies in the domain of aesthetics. Thus, ethics is ultimately dependent upon aesthetics, just as logic is ultimately dependent upon ethics.

Peirce was opposed to almost all the positions of his day in the area of ethics. In particular he attacked the two views to which his own stance was held susceptible: psychologism and HEDONISM. The problem of psychologism came from the direction of his logic. Peirce argued, however, that logic, like ethics and aesthetics, involves normative judgments which criticize in order to correct, and thus exert a control over what is being criticized. The various sciences presuppose the use of logic, and thus validity of their respective inquiries will depend upon good reasoning. The science of PSYCHOLOGY, in none of its variations, determines good reasoning, but rather presupposes it.

The problem of hedonism resulted from the direction of his aesthetics. The claim was that the ultimate dependence of ethics upon aesthetics makes the ethics a hedonism. Peirce held, however, that to base morality on aesthetic judgment is not to embrace hedonism but to oppose it. While aesthetic experience involves a quality of feeling, it involves a reasonable feeling, a consciousness belonging to the category of Thirdness or representation. Aesthetics concerns the Thirdness of Firstness or quality of feeling, just as ethics concerns the Thirdness of action or Secondness. For Peirce, something is pleasurable because it is approvable or reasonable rather than the reverse. Ultimately, then, the *summum bonum* is itself reasonable, deliberative conduct.

Peirce's thinking was systematic in nature, and it is nearly impossible to isolate any one aspect of his philosophy from the rest. His understanding of ethics and the normative sciences in general ties in ultimately to key features of his wide-ranging cosmic vision.

See also: AESTHETICS; LOGIC AND ETHICS; METAPHYSICS AND EPISTEMOLOGY; PHENOMENOLOGY; PRAGMATISM.

Peirce, C. S.

Bibliography

Works by Peirce

Collected Papers. 8 vols. Cambridge: Belknap Press; Harvard University Press, 1931–1958. Vols. 1–6 edited by Charles Hartshorne and Paul Weiss; vols. 7–8 edited by Arthur Burks. The standard published collection of Peirce's writings. Citations are usually made thus: volume number.paragraph number

Writings of Charles S. Peirce: A Chronological Edition. 20 vols. projected. Bloomington: Indiana University Press, 1982–. Various editors. Intended as the definitive collection of Peirce's works. Even this edition, however, will not be exhaustive, as it has been estimated that a complete set of his published and unpublished works would require 104 volumes.

Charles Sanders Peirce: Contributions to the Nation. 4 vols. Lubbock: Texas Tech Press, 1975–1979. Compiled and annotated by Kenneth Ketner and James Cook. The first three volumes are a chronological presentation of Peirce's contributions from 1869–1908. The fourth volume is a detailed index.

Charles S. Peirce's Letters to Lady Welby. Edited by Irwin Lieb. New Haven: Whitlock's, 1953.

Works about Peirce

Ketner, Kenneth, ed. *A Comprehensive Bibliography of the Published Works of Charles Sanders Peirce with a Bibliography of Secondary Studies.* 2d rev. ed. Bowling Green, Ohio: Philosophy Documentation Center, 1986. Contains a virtually exhaustive and recent listing of secondary sources.

Robin, Richard, ed. *Annotated Catalogue of the Papers of Charles S. Peirce.* Amherst: University of Massachusetts Press, 1967. A catalogue of the Peirce manuscripts in the Houghton Library at Harvard.

———. "The Peirce Papers: A Supplementary Catalogue." *Transactions of the Charles S. Peirce Society* 7 (1971): 37–57. Additional Houghton listing.

Sandra B. Rosenthal

perception

See moral perception.

perfectionism

In everyday English the term "perfectionism" connotes an insistence on the highest standards of evaluation. It has both a favourable use, where it implies a laudable dedication to EXCELLENCE, and a pejorative use, where it connotes neurotic fussiness. The philosophical use of "perfectionism" is quite different from this. It refers to one of the leading moral and political theories of the Western tradition, wholly or in part that of PLATO (c.430–347 B.C.E.), ARISTOTLE (384–322 B.C.E.), THOMAS AQUINAS (1225?–1274), G. W. LEIBNIZ (1646–1716), G. W. F. HEGEL (1770–1831), Karl MARX (1818–1883), Friedrich NIETZSCHE (1844–1900), T. H. GREEN (1836–1882), F. H. BRADLEY (1846–1924), and G. E. MOORE (1873–1958). Despite its historical importance, perfectionism in this sense was virtually ignored by English-speaking philosophers during the middle part of the twentieth century. More recently, interest in it has revived.

Broad vs. Narrow Perfectionism

Perfectionism is a teleological or consequentialist moral theory. It first identifies some state or states of human beings as intrinsically good, and then characterizes the right act in any circumstance as that which results in the most such good possible. In egoistic versions of perfectionism the good an agent is to maximize is only her own; in agent-neutral versions it is that of all humans. But in all versions the rightness of an act depends on the quantity of good that will result if it is performed.

The basic structure of perfectionism, then, is similar to that of other teleological theories such as UTILITARIANISM. But whereas utilitarians identify the good with HAPPINESS, understood variously as PLEASURE or the fulfilment of desires, perfectionists value states other than happiness. They hold that, for example, knowledge, the achievement of difficult goals, virtue, FRIENDSHIP, and aesthetic appreciation are good apart from any pleasure or satisfaction they may bring. The presence of these states in a life makes that life better regardless of how much they are wanted or enjoyed, and their absence impoverishes it even if it is not a source of regret. Whereas utilitarianism has a subjective theory of the good, perfectionism has an objective theory, one on which certain states of humans are good independently of any attitudes humans have to them.

The goods recognized by perfectionism are often referred to in distinctive language, for example, as "perfections" or "excellences." This has suggested to some that perfectionism uses different moral concepts than just those of goodness and rightness, for example, specifically "aretaic" concepts. But it is not clear how much turns on this issue. If the life called "excellent" is both a desirable life and one people should try to lead, how is it different from a life called "good"? It is true that some perfectionist goods such as achievement and virtue can be not only produced by acts as an external consequence but also embodied in them, so a person can have reason to perform these acts because of what they themselves involve. If a theory used only goods that can be embodied in acts when evaluating them, it would at least look very different from, say, utilitarianism. But it would still derive its claims about rightness from claims about the good. And in any case, most plausible versions of perfectionism also count as relevant to evaluating acts goods that the acts will allow or encourage in the future.

This initial characterization of perfectionism is very general, and allows disagreement about what states of humans are in fact good. (Compare the ideals of human life of Plato and Marx, or of Nietzsche and Moore.) Nonetheless, many perfectionists agree in their deepest account of the good. They hold that what is good, at bottom, is the development of properties fundamental to human nature. These properties make humans human, and the ideal human life involves their full development. If these perfectionists disagree about particular intrinsic values, it is because they disagree about human nature. Their shared foundational idea defines perfectionism in a narrower sense: a teleological theory with an objective theory of the human good grounded in some theory of human nature. In a broader sense, perfectionism (also called "ideal utilitarianism") is a teleological theory with an objective theory of the good.

In its history, the narrower version of perfectionism has often been accompanied by doctrines that are not strictly speaking moral. Perfectionists have held the metaphysical view that developing human nature is our "function" or natural purpose as humans; the psychological view that it is what each human most centrally wants; and the metaethical view that from claims about what human nature is there follow directly conclusions about how humans ought to live. These views are accretions to perfectionism considered as a moral theory, and in a moral discussion should be set aside. We should understand narrow perfectionism as formulating an ideal of life that humans ought to pursue apart from any claims about functions, desires, or entailments. To make its ideal determinate, this perfectionism must do two things. It must explain what kinds of properties it takes human nature to consist in (those distinctive of humans? or essential to humans? or distinctive of and essential to humans?). And it must show, empirically, what properties fall under human nature as so defined. This will tie its foundational idea to a list of objective goods like those in any broad perfectionism.

Theoretical and Practical Perfections

An important difference among perfectionist theories, whether broad or narrow, concerns their specific accounts of the human good. Some perfectionists find the highest good in the development of our theoretical faculty, through which we form beliefs about the world (Plato, Aristotle, Aquinas). Others find it in our practical faculty, through which we act (Marx, Nietzsche), while a third group values both faculties equally (Bradley). What follows is a sample account of theoretical and practical perfections, drawn from several historical figures' but not identical to any one's. In a narrow perfectionism the account might be tied to the view that one part of human nature is rationality, both theoretical and practical.

On the most common view, theoretical perfection consists in knowledge or understanding, of the world and of oneself. If knowledge is, roughly, justified true belief, then a person's achievement of this good depends in part on how many such beliefs she has. If she acquires a new justified true belief, this increases value in her life; if she loses one, her theoretical good diminishes. But number of truths known cannot be the only criterion here, for plainly some beliefs are more worth having than others. Here a popular test of value is structural. The best knowledge comes in organized structures, with the beliefs at the top of the structure uniting and explaining those below; and the best items of knowledge are those most explanatory ones that crown these structures.

The practical parallel to knowledge is the successful achievement of a goal, given a justified belief that this would happen. Once again, a person's value is partly a matter of number, this time of the number of his nonlucky achievements. But there are also considerations of quality, which can again be based on structure. Like beliefs, goals can be organized in hierarchical structures, with those at the bottom pursued as means to those above. The best goals are those atop such structures, those achieved by or through the achievement of many others adopted in part as means to them. These goals, and the specifically practical perfection their achievement embodies, appear in a unified life, where a person fits different pursuits into a single life-plan; in complex and difficult activities, such as chess and artistic creation; in political activity; and in the nuanced emotional interactions of friendship.

These theoretical and practical values are not endorsed by all perfectionists, but some of their general characteristics are widely accepted. For most perfectionists the good is essentially active, involves complex psychological states, requires a connection to outside reality, and is achieved essentially in complete lives. These general characteristics explain perfectionists' uniform reaction to a fantasy like Huxley's *Brave New World* (1932). Whereas utilitarians must regard Huxley's (1894–1963) construction as a utopia, perfectionists find it abhorrent. People there are passive, have only simple psychological states, neither understand nor have significant effects on their world, and lack the unity through time that makes for a life in the proper sense.

Virtue as a Perfection

In both its broad and narrow versions, perfectionism gives a central place to self-regarding duties. It holds that humans ought morally to seek knowledge, achievement, and other goods in their own lives, or to develop their talents for these goods. To be intuitively acceptable, however, perfectionism must also capture other-regarding duties, such as the duty not to harm others.

Some perfectionists attempt this within the account of each person's good. They characterize the good so that achieving it in one's own life requires exhibiting other-regarding virtues such as honesty, justice, and BENEVOLENCE. Then other-regarding duties are included within a theory that is formally egoistic, with the only ultimate duty being to seek one's own perfection.

This approach, however, is problematic. If the VIRTUES are simply added to a list of perfectionist goods, with no deeper explanation of why they belong there, it is not clear that the resulting theory differs interestingly from one in which they, or the duties associated with them, are treated as foundational. And it

seems difficult to ground the virtues in a theory of human nature. Aristotle, Aquinas, and other perfectionists hold that it is part of human nature to be practically rational, and that exercising practical rationality involves exhibiting other-regarding virtues. But if there is a sense of "rationality" in which rationality is plausibly part of human nature, *e.g.,* is plausibly essential to human nature, it does not seem specially tied to virtuous action. Rationality in this sense, many would say, can be shown as much in sophisticated malevolence as in kindness.

The alternative is to make perfectionism formally agent-neutral, so each person's ultimate goal is the achievement of perfectionist goods not just by himself but by everyone. Then his duty to seek knowledge, achievement, and other goods in his own life is constrained by a parallel duty to preserve and promote them in others. This agent-neutral approach, which is arguably present in most classical perfectionists, captures other-regarding duties, as desired, though without claiming that virtue is intrinsically good. But a perfectionism that adopts the approach can go on to claim this. It can say that states such as knowledge and achievement are intrinsically good and add, recursively, that it is good to love (desire, pursue) whatever is good. Then moral virtue, or loving (desiring, pursuing) knowledge and achievement in oneself and others, itself has intrinsic worth. This account of virtue may not be admissible in the narrow perfectionism that grounds the good in human nature, but it appears in the broadly perfectionist theories of Moore, Hastings Rashdall (1858–1924), and W. D. Ross (1877–1971).

Perfectionism and Politics

When it is applied to political questions, perfectionism uses the same teleological standard as for evaluating acts by individuals: the best government, legislator, or law is that which results in the most perfectionist good. As Aristotle says, the state exists "for the sake of a good life" and is to be judged for how well it promotes that life. But this perfectionist approach to politics is controversial. Critics worry that perfectionism is hostile to the values of LIBERTY—it wants to force people into the activities it deems excellent—and EQUALITY—it wants resources concentrated on those few with the most talent for such activities. Perfectionism has certainly been formulated in ways that substantiate these worries (Plato, Aristotle, Nietzsche), but in other versions it embraces liberty and equality (Marx, Green). Which line it takes depends on its formal structure and, especially, its substantive values.

Perfectionism can value liberty most easily by making autonomy, or any choice from a wide range of options, itself intrinsically good. Then any government restriction of people's choice carries some perfectionist cost. The classical liberal theories of Wilhelm von Humboldt (1767–1835) and JOHN STUART MILL (1806–1873) start from this perfectionist valuing of autonomy. Perfectionism can also argue that if the good involves people's acting, and doing so from complex psychological states, there are limits on how successfully that good can be promoted by coercive state action. On the contrary, such action is more likely to hinder people's perfection. These arguments do not support an absolute guarantee of individual liberty, but they can make a perfectionism whose values allow them in practice generally liberal.

Some perfectionist theories are anti-egalitarian about distribution because of their formal structure. For example, Nietzsche equates the overall excellence in a society with the excellence of its few best members and wants social policy to aim at that. (Some writers use "perfectionist" to refer to this structural view; a better name is "maximax.") Nietzsche's view has elitist assumptions given almost any assumptions about the world. Other perfectionists think distribution should be in accordance with desert, so those who have achieved more excellence should on that basis receive more. But perfectionism can equally well have the same summative structure as utilitarianism, so its ultimate moral goal is the greatest total excellence of all in society, with equal gains for all people having equal moral weight. Then the theory's distributive implications depend very much on certain empirical issues.

Given a summative structure, perfectionism will favour elitist distributions if (a) people's talents for perfectionist goods are very unequal; (b) the most or only valuable activities are very expensive; and (c) perfection is competitive, in that one person's achieving it makes others' doing so less likely. Conversely, perfectionism will favour distributive equality if (a) people's abilities are close to equal; (b) there are many inexpensive perfections; and (c) perfection is cooperative, in that one person's achieving it encourages and is encouraged by oth-

ers'. Which of, and how far, these various claims are true depends in large part on what in particular a perfectionist theory takes to be good. Plato and Aristotle endorse values that tend to validate the first trio of assumptions, while Marx's and Green's values support the second trio. Here as elsewhere much that is crucial in perfectionism depends on its specific claims about intrinsic human goods.

This political application of perfectionism is the core of the view recently discussed under the name "COMMUNITARIANISM." Communitarians start with the perfectionist claim, which is rejected by contemporary "neutralist" LIBERALISM, that the state may and should act to promote objectively good lives. They then supplement this claim with either or both of the following: (a) a or even the, central part of each person's good is communal, and especially political, activity with other members of a society; (b) what is good in a society is determined by its own values, traditions, and so on. These latter claims are independent of the first one, and many perfectionists reject them. They hold that purely individual states such as knowledge and achievement are the chief goods, and are so in all societies everywhere. Nonetheless, the communitarianisms that accept the claims are built on a simpler perfectionist core.

Conclusion

Perfectionism differs from other moral theories in the central place it gives questions about how best to live one's own life. It holds that there are intrinsically better and worse activities, and that people ought to pursue those that are better. Many contemporary approaches to ethics deemphasize these questions, confining serious or even all moral evaluation to acts that affect other people. For those who find this contemporary approach impoverished, perfectionism's prominent concern with self-regarding duties will be an attractive feature. Where perfectionism is more problematic is in its application to larger questions of social policy, for here it has been, and can be, hostile to important political values. The important question here is whether the version of perfectionism that is independently most attractive endorses the political values of liberty and equality (assuming it should) and, if it does, whether this is for the right explanatory reasons.

perfectionism

See also: AUTONOMY OF MORAL AGENTS; COMMUNITARIANISM; COMPETITION; CONSEQUENTIALISM; COOPERATION, CONFLICT, AND COORDINATION; DUTY AND OBLIGATION; EGOISM; EQUALITY; EXCELLENCE; GOOD, THEORIES OF THE; IDEALIST ETHICS; JUSTICE, DISTRIBUTIVE; LIBERALISM; LIBERTY; MARXISM; MERIT AND DESERT; METAETHICS; METAPHYSICS AND EPISTEMOLOGY; MORAL PSYCHOLOGY; MORAL PURITY; MORAL SAINTS; SOCIAL AND POLITICAL PHILOSOPHY; SUBJECTIVISM; TELEOLOGICAL ETHICS; UTILITARIANISM; VALUE, THEORY OF; VIRTUES.

Bibliography

Aristotle. *Nicomachean Ethics.* Highly influential version of narrow perfectionism.

Attfield, Robin. *A Theory of Value and Obligation.* London: Croom Helm, 1987. Narrow perfectionism extended from humans to all living organisms.

Bradley, F. H. *Ethical Studies.* 2d ed. Oxford: Clarendon Press, 1927 [1876]. Idealist perfectionism.

Green, Thomas Hill. *Prolegomena to Ethics.* Oxford: Clarendon Press, 1883.

———. *Lectures on the Principles of Political Obligation.* London: Longmans, 1891. In vol. 2 of his *Works,* edited by R. L. Nettleship. Moderately liberal-egalitarian perfectionism.

Humboldt, Wilhelm von. *The Limits of State Action.* Translated by J. W. Burrow. Cambridge: Cambridge University Press, 1969 [1854]. Perfectionism as a basis for liberalism.

Hurka, Thomas. *Perfectionism.* New York: Oxford University Press, 1993. Survey of narrow and broad perfectionism.

Marx, Karl. *Economic and Philosophical Manuscripts.* New York: International Publishers, 1975. In Marx and Engels, *Collected Works,* vol. 3. Human perfection as productive, cooperative activity.

Moore, G. E. *Principia Ethica.* Cambridge: Cambridge University Press, 1903. Chapter 6 proposes objective theory of value with doctrine of "organic unities."

Nietzsche, Friedrich. *Beyond Good and Evil.* Translated by W. Kaufmann. New York: Vintage, 1966 [1886].

———. *The Will to Power.* Translated by W. Kaufmann and R. J. Hollingdale. New York: Vintage, 1968 [1901; 1906]. Brazenly anti-egalitarian perfectionism.

Nozick, Robert. *Philosophical Explanations.* Cambridge, MA: Harvard University Press, 1981. Chapter 5 finds intrinsic value in organic unity.

Nussbaum, Martha. "Nature, Function, and Capability: Aristotle on Political Distribution." *Oxford Studies in Ancient Philosophy,* Supplementary Volume 1 (1988): 145–84.

———. "Aristotelian Social Democracy." In *Liberalism and the Good,* edited by R. B. Douglas, G. M. Mara, and H. S. Richardson. New York: Routledge, 1990. Liberal-egalitarian perfectionism.

Rashdall, Hastings. *The Theory of Good and Evil.* Oxford: Oxford University Press, 1907. See Book 1, chapters 7, 8 on "ideal utilitarianism."

Rawls, John. *A Theory of Justice.* Cambridge, MA: Harvard University Press, 1971. Section 50 contains influential liberal critique of perfectionism.

Raz, Joseph. *The Morality of Freedom.* Oxford: Clarendon Press, 1986. Perfectionism in political philosophy, with autonomy as central value.

Ross, W. D. *The Right and the Good.* Oxford: Clarendon Press, 1930. Chapters 5–7 expound a largely perfectionist account of the good.

Sher, George. *Beyond Neutrality: Perfectionism and Politics.* Cambridge: Cambridge University Press, 1997. Careful examination of anti-perfectionist arguments.

Thomas Aquinas. *Summa Theologiae.* 1266–73. Books I–II, II–II. Aristotle's perfectionism accommodated to Christian theology.

Thomas Hurka

Perry, R[alph] B[arton] (1876–1957)

Born in Vermont, educated at Princeton and Harvard, Perry taught philosophy at Harvard for more than forty years. His *General Theory of Value* (1926) played a foundational role in general value theory in America for half a century. He sought the generic meaning for value in terms of the biological-evolutionary efforts of humans to survive, expand, cooperate, and flourish. Starting from a realistic epistemology (he was one of the co-authors of *The New Realism,* 1912), he approached purposive ACTION through experience and observable behavior; however, he used *interest* rather than purpose or PLEASURE to designate the attitude involved in value, construing it as selective behavior, a motor-affective for-or-against that shapes action. Value was defined as any object of any interest. Since every interest thus had some initial value, a moral critique could be carried out only in terms of its effects on one's own or others' INTERESTS; a liberal equalitarian INDIVIDUALISM thus lies at the base of his idea of value.

The processes that give structure to ethics and value theory consist of efforts to expand and carry through interests, to reconcile and organize them into progressive effective systems. In his early *The Moral Economy* (1909), Perry compares interests to enterprises in an economy, with ethics as the regulations of the system that allows harmonious economic growth. The later value theory studies in detail biological and psychological aspects of organization, modes of interest that run through human experience in feelings and varieties of relations, and ways of social integration. Perry's approach to ordering in evaluation, less stringent than BENTHAM's (1748–1832) hope of cardinal measurement, uses more general standards of intensity, preference, and inclusiveness. His later *Realms of Value* (1954), after reckoning with problems of analysis and definition that had engaged philosophical energies in the intervening quarter of a century, explores the provinces of value—social, institutional, and cultural structures, including the enterprises of science, art, and education, in which values are found.

Perry's extensive work in social philosophy—carried out through books, articles, lectures, letters to newspapers—was geared to public crises. During World War I, in addition to military work in education and special training, he wrote on the conflict of ideals. In World War II, in the prevailing atmosphere of ideological controversy, he urged competing groups to reserve their metaphysical disagreements for their adherents and take as a basis for common struggle an emphasis on common human welfare.

Perry's many writings also included studies of philosophical trends; he won a Pulitzer prize for his biography of William JAMES (1842–1910). His major historical contribution may be seen as consolidating the naturalistic turn in value theory, opening it to fuller scientific inquiry.

See also: BIOLOGICAL THEORY; EVOLUTION; GOOD, THEORIES OF THE; METAPHYSICS AND EPISTEMOLOGY; MORAL REALISM; NATURALISM; VALUE, THEORY OF.

Bibliography

The Moral Economy. New York: Scribner, 1909. Charts a broadening direction in moral theory.

General Theory of Value: Its Meaning and Basic Principles Construed in Terms of Interest. New York: Longmans, Green, 1926. His major contribution to the development of the field.

Realms of Value: A Critique of Human Civilization. Cambridge: Harvard University Press, 1954. The mature reformulation, rounding out the theory.

Present Conflict of Ideals. New York: Longmans, Green, 1918. A study of the philosophical background of World War I.

Our Side Is Right. Cambridge: Harvard University Press, 1942.

The Citizen Decides: A Guide to Responsible Thinking in Time of Crisis. Bloomington: Indiana University Press, 1951.

Puritanism and Democracy. New York: Vanguard Press, 1944.

Philosophy of the Recent Past: An Outline of European and American Philosophy since 1860. New York: Scribner, 1926.

The Thought and Character of William James. 2 vols. Boston: Little, Brown, 1935. Subtitle: As revealed in unpublished correspondence and notes, together with his published writings.

Abraham Edel

person, concept of

For as long as human beings have engaged in ethical thought, persons have occupied its central position. Virtually every issue in ethics rests on postulates about the normative status of persons. They are the paradigmatic, if not the only, bearers of RIGHTS and duties, and interactions with persons are radically unlike those with other beings. One eats animals but sleeps with persons; any inversion of this procedure is apt to occasion considerable attention. The presumption that ethics is for and about persons has, historically, been so ubiquitous and unquestioned that explicit reflection on the concept of a person has been infrequent. Most often, the importance of personhood is taken for granted rather than overtly stated.

Persons as Human Beings

In common usage, persons are human beings and human beings persons. "How many persons are there in the room?" is answered by counting the number of human individuals. So understood, personhood is constituted by membership in the biological species *homo sapiens*. Still, it is a mistake to conclude that ascriptions of personhood function in a purely descriptive manner. Declarations of the form, "She is, after all, a person," are usually meant to emphasize the individual's normative standing, implying that treatment of her as a mere thing is inappropriate. It should be noted that reference to an individual as a 'human being' also typically conveys much the same normative significance, as do even more emphatically such cognates as 'humane' and 'inhuman.'

Aristotelian Conception of Persons

ARISTOTLE (384–322 B.C.E.) classifies human beings as rational animals and also describes them as being by nature political animals. Like other animals, human beings move from place to place and perceive via their senses, but alone among animals they possess a rational soul (*psyche*). It is only a slight overstatement to say that development of the implications of rationality and sociality pervades all of Aristotle's writings on human subjects. In particular, the *Nicomachean Ethics* defines the good for humans as HAPPINESS (*EUDAIMONIA*), which in turn is characterized as activity guided by reason. Aristotle classifies as a "natural slave" an individual in whom this rational capacity is absent. Although ostensibly human, natural slaves are persons only in a secondary sense and so may properly be used as instruments for the projects of others. Human beings achieve their flourishing only in association with others, and most completely in the *polis*. Thus, ethics is continuous with politics. They differ with respect to their context of application but aim at the same end: the good life for humankind.

Biblical Conception of Persons

The book of Genesis describes human beings as being made in the image (*tselem*) of God. In its original sense, this may have simply meant that human beings bear a physical resemblance to God. By the time the Hebrew scriptures take on the form in which they have been preserved, however, it is a matter of settled religious doctrine that God possesses no physical likeness. Therefore, our resemblance to God must be understood other than anatomically. Within the biblical tradition it is possession of reason, construed especially as the knowledge of good and EVIL, that is typically taken to be the crucial nexus of similarity between the human and the divine.

Humans are characterized as occupying a unique in-between status: made from the dust to which we return, but little lower than the angels; merely creatures, but ones that enjoy stewardship over the rest of creation. The Hebraic understanding of the nature of persons is, prior to contact with Hellenism in the fourth century B.C.E., thoroughly monistic. That is, no substantial separation between soul and body is admitted: Genesis describes a human as *being* a living soul rather than *having* a soul; the death of the body is, accordingly, death of the human being.

Fusion of Greek and Biblical Conceptions

Because both Greek and Hebraic thought conceive of human beings as essentially rational, and because both accord to human beings a sort of midway status between the animal realm and higher-order intelligences, subsequent Christian philosophy finds it relatively easy to accommodate the insights of these two traditions. Some thinkers follow PLATO (c. 430–347 B.C.E.) rather than Aristotle in finding a substantial distinction between the soul and body, but this remains a minority position. Authoritative Christian and Jewish doctrines, consistent with their basic monism, insist on describing afterlife as featuring *resurrection* (of the revitalized body) rather than *immortality* (of the soul). The manner in which human beings survive the interregnum between DEATH and resurrection is, for this view, a difficulty, but it is one that philosophers and theologians attempt to resolve within a basically monistic conception of humankind. In medieval cosmological speculation, human beings are often characterized as the linchpin of the chain of being, tying together in their nature the realms of purely material beings and purely spiritual intelligences. They are thereby afforded a metaphysical dignity that reinforces that which ethical and theological doctrine ascribes to persons.

Modern Conceptions of the Person

The most influential dualistic theory of persons after Plato is provided by René DESCARTES (1596–1650) in *Meditations* (1641). For Descartes, a person is a combination of two interacting substances, mind and body. Descartes has, however, relatively little to say about the ethical implications of this conception.

Locke on personal identity. Of more importance to ethics is the work of John LOCKE (1632–1704). Locke acknowledges that we often use "man" and "person" interchangeably, but he nonetheless insists that these properly stand for distinct ideas. While our idea of a man is of a corporeal being, the idea of a person has to do with a connected flow of consciousness and thus refers to something incorporeal. Locke launches the modern examination of the criteria of personal identity over time, arguing in the twenty-seventh chapter of *Essay Concerning Human Understanding* (1690) that memory is the essential glue that links discrete episodes of consciousness such that they constitute items of awareness of the self-same person. A vast and ongoing literature has ensued. For purposes of ethical inquiry, as opposed to metaphysics, of yet greater consequence is Locke's remark that "person" is a "forensic" term. We hold people accountable for deeds only insofar as we assume that the individual who is subjected to praise or blame is the same person as the individual who performed the deed in question. Normally, to be the same person is simply to be the same man, but divergence between the two is possible. In the *Essay*, Locke presents puzzle cases in which the same man proves not to be the same person; these are cases in which the individual on the later occasion is not conscious of the deeds of the one who formerly acted. Such examples have been multiplied many fold by contemporary analysts of personal identity.

Kant. Locke's discussion raises many questions. Perhaps the most important for ethics is: What, specifically, is it that renders "person" a forensic term? That is, what feature of those beings we identify as persons accounts for their possession of a unique moral status that renders them the subject of rights and duties, leaves them liable for praise or blame, affords them DIGNITY and worth? In the writings of Immanuel KANT (1724–1804), consideration of this question takes a decisive turn, indeed assumes the form in which most subsequent discussions of personhood have been couched.

In one respect, Kant's theory is not at all novel. Like Aristotle and the biblical tradition, he ascribes a midway status to persons. Human beings are a part of the natural order, but they also can be moved to act on the basis of reason. How that can be so is, however, not easy to see. Kant believed that he had firmly established in the *Critique of Pure Reason* (1781) that, within the natural order, it is necessarily the case that every event is the causal product of antecedent conditions. Therefore, human actions are causally determined. How those actions can then have any specifically moral value thus becomes problematic. If an action is *merely* the product of

antecedent conditions, it is of no more inherent moral significance than brute happenings within nature. On the other hand, actions *entirely unconstrained* by causality cannot be ascribed to beings such as ourselves who live within the phenomenal realm.

Kant's attempted resolution of this conundrum is intricate and complex. He argues in the *Foundations of the Metaphysics of Morals* (1785) that the only thing that can be called unqualifiedly good is the *good will, i.e.,* action motivated from a sense of duty. One who is moved to act by the spur of some desire is characterized as acting *heteronomously*. Heteronomous activity possesses no moral value. Only activity directed by a reason independent of DESIRE is *autonomous* and thus a candidate for moral considerability. Autonomy, however, presupposes a freedom that transcends causal determination, and such freedom can neither be empirically ascertained nor demonstrated *a priori*. A postulated freedom of the will is, however, consistent with a causally regular natural order because persons as they are in themselves—as *noumenal* beings—can be thought to be self-determiners. Indeed, PRACTICAL REASON requires of us that we make such a postulation. Thus, via a two-tier conception of the self as both phenomenal and noumenal, we can obtain an understanding of persons as being a part of a natural order that they also transcend insofar as they are rational. Thus Kant's theory of moral personhood is not restricted to human beings but includes whatever forms of rational agency there may be.

Consequences of Kantianism

Few philosophers have followed Kant in his delicate attempt to balance phenomenal and noumenal aspects of a self. To a remarkable extent, though, it is Kant who has set the terms of subsequent discussion of the nature of persons. Many philosophers have followed him in distinguishing between (mere) things, possessing only derivative or instrumental value, and persons, whose value is absolute. Persons, unlike things, merit respect. While one may use a thing to satisfy one's various purposes, persons are, says Kant in a much-quoted phrase, "ends-in-themselves" that may not be used merely as a means. The obligations we have are all obligations to persons; whatever rights there may be are the rights of persons. Therefore, it becomes a matter of some philosophical urgency, especially for those who are inclined to borrow liberally from the Kantian ethic while leaving behind his metaphysics, to specify with clarity just what it is about individuals that constitute their being persons. Both Benn and Downie and Telfer pursue a Kantian program of deriving an ethical theory from reflections on the nature of persons.

We can identify both a broad and a narrow impetus for explicating the term 'person.' Because all of ethics is bound up with questions of rights and duties, VIRTUES and vices, any ethical inquiry will have to address itself to the nature of those beings who are the subjects of these MORAL TERMS. More narrowly, several important ethical debates seem to hinge on a proper demarcation of persons from nonpersons. For example, the permissibility of ABORTION is often held to depend on whether fetuses are persons. Similarly, what we may do with or for irreversibly comatose human beings living a vegetative existence depends on whether individuals who formerly were persons retain that status.

Definitions of 'Person'

Definitions of 'person' typically display one of the three following forms:

1. Persons are all and only human beings.
2. Persons are all and only those beings who possess moral standing (or who possess the highest moral standing).
3. Persons are all and only those beings who display attribute F (where F signifies some suitably elevated cognitive ability).

As noted earlier, definitions of the first type correspond most closely with common usage. Nonetheless, few philosophers who take personhood to be a morally portentous concept advance such a definition. Rather, they criticize it for being both question-begging and overly restrictive. It is held to be question-begging because, for example, even if fetuses (or zygotes) are biologically human, it remains an open question whether human organisms of *this sort* possess a right not to be killed. Nothing in the biologists' books would seem to supply a definitive answer. The definition is too restrictive because it arbitrarily assumes that no beings could deserve the protections commonly afforded human beings without themselves being human. Even if, in our imme-

diate environment, it is only biologically human individuals that possess elevated moral standing, that is no more than a contingent truth. Were we to encounter a race of extraterrestrial beings who possess cognitive and affective capacities equal to or in advance of our own, it is evident that they too would count as morally considerable. Biology may be destiny, but it is not adequate morals.

Definitions of the second type are neither question-begging nor arbitrarily anthropocentric. They cannot, however, be directly applied to the task of ethical appraisal. Unless we antecedently know *which* beings possess (the highest) moral standing, we will not know which are the persons. For example, in "Abortion and Infanticide," Michael Tooley characterizes persons as those beings who possess a "serious right to life." Does this mean that abortion is permissible? No answer is forthcoming without an independent means for determining who possesses a serious right to life.

Definitions of the third type purport to supply a criterion in terms of which just that determination can be made. One difficulty that besets such definitions is that the nature of the crucial attribute F is liable to be at least as controversial as are the normative issues that the definition is meant to resolve. Many utilitarians, going back to Jeremy BENTHAM (1748–1832), contend that it is the ability to experience PLEASURE and pain which renders a being worthy of moral consideration. Harry Frankfurt maintains in "Freedom of the Will and the Concept of a Person" that persons are those individuals who display second-order volitions. That is, a person is a being who not only has desires but also desires *of* his desires that they be of such-and-such a nature. Kant, as previously noted, holds that persons are those beings who can act on the basis of moral laws legislated by reason. There seems to be no obvious way to decide among these markedly different views. Rather, each invokes a concept of the person that is inextricably tied to a broad philosophical program. Absent a judgment concerning the general success of the philosophical enterprise of which it is a part, we are entitled to little confidence concerning the adequacy of its particular conception of the person.

A related difficulty attaches to all familiar definitions of the third type: whatever the crucial attribute F is taken to be, counterintuitive implications follow. If it is only the capacity to experience pleasure and pain that is morally salient, then there can be no distinction in principle between using animals as means for our purposes and similarly using human beings. Few will find it acceptable, though, morally to amalgamate keeping domestic animals and enslaving human beings. If possession of second-order volitions is definitive of persons, then fetuses clearly are not persons. Neither, however, are very young children nor, plausibly, many adult human beings. Michael Tooley maintains that only conscious beings who are capable of desiring to go on living possess a serious right to life. Fetuses are thereby excluded from the class of RIGHT HOLDERS, but so too are neonates. Unlike most similarly situated theorists, Tooley enthusiastically embraces the consequences of this theory: both abortion and INFANTICIDE are morally licit, but killing an adult cat may be in violation of its rights.

Common morality recognizes sharp distinctions between, on the one hand, how one may behave with regard to animals and, on the other hand, what is permissible in one's dealing with other human beings. This understanding is encapsulated in the expression 'HUMAN RIGHTS.' And while the moral permissibility of abortion is, of course, hotly disputed, few take abortion to be morally indistinguishable from infanticide. Definitions of the third type are, therefore, distinctly *revisionary;* rather than clarifying and systematizing our familiar moral ascriptions, such definitions would alter them dramatically. Several philosophers have objected that such revisionary programs are insufficiently well-grounded. Common morality is not sacrosanct, it may be in need of substantial house cleaning; yet is the warrant of Bentham's or Frankfurt's or Tooley's theory of the person so clear and evident as to justify superseding judgments such as "Young children should not be killed"? It should be noted that so-called conservatives on the issue of abortion also present themselves as revisionaries insofar as their understanding of the criterion for being a person similarly entails the moral indistinguishability of abortion and infanticide.

Mixed Approaches

A consequence of maintaining that persons and only persons are morally considerable beings is to establish a threshold that generates marked moral discontinuity. To fall on one side of it is to be an agent qualified for the full panoply of rights and duties that characterize persons; to fall on the other side is to be, strictly speaking, a thing. Because thresholds typically yield revisionary moral judgments, some philosophers attempt to smooth the discontinuity. One common way in which this is attempted is to distinguish between *actual* persons and *potential* persons. The former are full moral agents; the latter merit a status intermediate between actual persons and things. This status may itself vary as a direct function of the closeness of the being in question to actual personhood.

One problem with this approach is that it may be difficult to identify which beings qualify as potential persons. If neonates are clear cases, what of advanced fetuses, embryos, a zygote? Will any disjoint pair of sperm and ovum constitute a potential person? If so, the moral universe has experienced a population boom! And if potentiality is a matter of more and less, how are we to devise a morality that embodies infinite gradations of approximations to the status of full personhood?

A further difficulty is that no inferences concerning the moral perquisites of potential persons straightforwardly follow from propositions about the status of actual persons. Consider the following analogy: the individual who is actually the president of the United States possesses constitutionally (and otherwise) defined rights and duties. He or she has, for example, the right to veto congressional legislation and is also entitled to Secret Service protection. Let us suppose that a candidate for the presidency is a potential president. This individual enjoys no right to veto legislation but does have a right to Secret Service protection. It is not, however, the logic of rights that generates these results. Reasoning analogously, from the proposition that actual persons enjoy a right not to be killed, nothing follows concerning whether potential persons possess a similar right not to be killed. We might need an entire additional and independent morality to spell out the claims of potential persons.

A somewhat different approach is taken by Engelhardt. He distinguishes between "strict" persons and "social" persons, *e.g.,* infants, who are treated for the most part as persons although they do not meet the qualifications for strict personhood. Although Engelhardt thereby avoids revisionism, his view is open to the criticism that ascriptions of personhood which are not strict are thereby "loose"— and thus unable properly to bear the moral weight that is placed on them. An alternative strategy is to reject the implicit premise that all persons (in the "strict" sense) must be persons for the same reason. Lomasky argues that functional adult human beings qualify as persons in virtue of their intellectual attainments but that, through a sort of "piggy-back" mechanism, children and nonfunctional adults also are rights-holders. His suggestion may be criticized, though, as an *ad hoc* ploy to preserve the intuitions of common morality which sacrifices foundational rigor.

Personal Identity and Moral Principles

Issues such as abortion and the disposition of permanently vegetative individuals are often framed in terms of whether the party in question is, *at that time,* a person. There are, in addition, a number of ethical issues that can be taken to hinge on whether an individual who unquestionably is a person is the *same* person as one who previously acted. Suppose, for example, that an elderly man some sixty years earlier had perpetrated an atrocity. In the interim, his CHARACTER has been transformed and he views with abhorrence the actions of his earlier self. To what extent is he properly held responsible for those deeds? According to Locke, he is morally accountable if and only if he remembers committing the atrocity. Nearly all contemporary philosophers believe that Locke's memory criterion for personal identity is deficient. Those who follow Locke in taking "person" to be primarily a forensic term typically argue that memory is only one of several psychological attributes that constitute the basis for identity over time. They might maintain that, if the transformation in character has been sufficiently thoroughgoing, the elderly man is not the same person as the youth who committed the atrocity.

Parfit. Derek Parfit has been a leading contributor to contemporary discussions of personal identity. His metaphysical treatments have been conjoined with provocative inquiry into the implications for morality of different theories of personal identity. Parfit acknowledges that identity is, logically, an "all or nothing" relation, *i.e.,* one that either obtains or fails to obtain. However, the psychological continuity of person-stages admits of more and less. In a series of papers, and then in *Reasons and Persons,* he contends that self-identity matters less than do continuity and connectedness among person-stages. His account bears directly on punishment theory and the importance of personal survival but also, though less straightforwardly, on questions concerning distributive justice. For example, a comparative accounting of the benefits and burdens that accrue to various individuals over the course of their lives may be of little salience for assessments of distributive justice if the fact of personal identity over time is not a "deep" further fact beyond continuity and connectedness. Although the implications of his metaphysical account are not entirely clear-cut, they may be seen as favoring UTILITARIANISM over theories for which the "separateness of persons" looms large. Reaction to Parfit's views will figure importantly in forthcoming work in ethical and political philosophy.

See also: ABORTION; ANIMALS, TREATMENT OF; ARISTOTLE; AUTONOMY OF MORAL AGENTS; CHRISTIAN ETHICS; DESCARTES; DESIRE; DIGNITY; EUTHANASIA; EVIL; FREE WILL; FREEDOM AND DETERMINISM; HUMAN RIGHTS; HUMANISM; INFANTICIDE; JEWISH ETHICS; JUSTICE, DISTRIBUTIVE; KANT; KANTIAN ETHICS; KILLING/LETTING DIE; LIFE, MEANING OF; LIFE, RIGHT TO; LOCKE; MEDICAL ETHICS; PRACTICAL REASON; PUNISHMENT; RATIONAL CHOICE; RESPONSIBILITY; RIGHT HOLDERS; RIGHTS; SELF AND SOCIAL SELF; SLAVERY; SUICIDE; THEOLOGICAL ETHICS.

Bibliography

Aristotle. *Nicomachean Ethics.* Politics.

Benn, Stanley I. *A Theory of Freedom.* Cambridge: Cambridge University Press, 1988. Benn's theory is based on an account of moral personhood.

Downie, R. S., and Elizabeth Telfer. *Respect for Persons.* London: George Allen and Unwin, 1969. Analysis of the idea of the supreme worth of the individual person.

Engelhardt, H. Tristram. "Medicine and the Concept of Person." In *What is a Person?*, edited by Michael F. Goodman, 169–84. Clifton, N.J.: Humana Press, 1988.

Frankfurt, Harry G. "Freedom of the Will and the Concept of a Person." *Journal of Philosophy* 68 (1971): 5–20.

Goodman, Michael F., ed. *What is a Person?* Clifton, N.J.: Humana Press, 1988. Sixteen essays on personhood, including those by Engelhardt, Frankfurt, and Tooley; extensive bibliography.

Kant, Immanuel. *Foundations of the Metaphysics of Morals.* 1785.

Locke, John. *Essay Concerning Human Understanding.* 1690. Especially chapter 27.

Lomasky, Loren. *Persons, Rights, and the Moral Community.* Oxford: Oxford University Press, 1987.

Parfit, Derek. *Reasons and Persons.* Oxford: Oxford University Press, 1984.

Perry, John. *Personal Identity.* Berkeley: University of California Press, 1975.

Rorty, Amélie. *The Identities of Persons.* Berkeley: University of California Press, 1976.

Tooley, Michael. "Abortion and Infanticide." *Philosophy and Public Affairs* 2 (1972): 37–65.

Loren E. Lomasky

personal relationships

Personal relationships are fairly long-standing relationships between individual persons who know each other to a substantial degree and who normally have some degree of emotional attachment to one another. Personal relationships have become a major topic within moral philosophy since the 1970s, after playing a relatively minor role in the subject since ARISTOTLE (384–322 B.C.E.) gave FRIENDSHIP a central place in his ethical theory. While some of the great moral philosophers (*e.g.,* Immanuel KANT [1724–1804]) discussed friendship or family relationships, few of them either integrated their discussion adequately into their theoretical framework, or saw personal relations as a central element in a good or moral life. David HUME (1711–1776) is an exception to this in that his ethic centered on VIRTUES concerned with social intercourse, one important element of which was personal relationships. And G. E. MOORE (1873–1958) asserted in *Principia Ethica* (1903) that personal affection was one of only two intrinsically good things.

Recognizing the importance of personal relationships to human life poses some questions for ethical theory. Can the significance of personal relationships be accounted for within traditional moral theories such as Kantianism, UTILITARIANISM, or contractualism? Do personal relationships have a distinctly moral dimension, or are they to be understood solely as a nonmoral good?

Personal relationships can be wholly involuntary, as in the relationship between child and parent. They can be wholly voluntary in the sense that it is entirely up to the individual whether to enter into them or not; marriage and friendship are examples. And there may be cases in between, such as the relation of parent to child; the parent may choose to have a child, but does not choose to have the particular child he or she does end up having. But the voluntariness of entering into these relationships is not paralleled by a comparable voluntariness in exiting from them. Relationships with friends and spouses can be terminated or exited from, but there are generally thought to be greater moral constraints on doing so than on entering into them. And that constraint is generally stronger in the case of marriage than friendship, and in the former case takes legal form as well.

For these reasons, at least some, and perhaps in some degree all, personal relationships are not contractual in nature. They are not formed through explicit contract, nor are the moral expectations and constraints which they involve a product (solely) of implicit or explicit agreements among the parties to the relationship. As HEGEL (1770–1831) said, even the idea of a "marriage contract" is an agreement to transcend the standpoint of contract.

The notion of personal relationship is ambiguous. On the one hand it can be used to refer to a category of relationships of which familial and friendship relations are taken to be the paradigm, contrasting with categories of impersonal or nonpersonal relations, such as professional relationships, fellow citizens, or complete strangers. On the other hand we sometimes say that a given instance of one of the personal types of relationship is not really a personal relationship—either because emotional attachment is lacking, or because one party to the relationship regards or treats the other in an impersonal way. An example of the latter would be liking someone as a friend yet caring for her not in her individuality but rather as a substitutable exemplification of the category "friend."

On the other side, some particular relationships outside of friendship and family—*e.g.,* between teacher and student, doctor and patient—might seem to take on a sufficient degree of emotion, personal interest, individuality, and mutual knowledge to be "personal relationships" in this second sense. Perhaps they will in that case have become a kind of *friendship,* thus preserving the idea that it is at least a necessary (if not sufficient) condition for a relationship to be a personal one that it be a friendship or familial relationship.

Several streams of thought, all of which involve criticism of dominant traditional approaches to ethics (such as utilitarianism, Kantianism, and contractualism) have contributed to the renewed interest in personal relationships within ethics in the last quarter of the twentieth century: (a) a focus on the "personal point of view"; (b) attention to the moral character of special relationships; and (c) feminism.

The Personal Point of View

The personal point of view criticizes utilitarianism's (and, in some versions, Kantianism's) demand that the agent adopt a purely impartial and impersonal standpoint as decisive in ACTION, for according insufficient recognition to the individual agent's own projects and commitments which give meaning to her life. Personal relationships come into this picture as one of the personal commitments which are normally most deeply treasured by human beings.

Utilitarianism has been the major target of this critique. If the ultimate goal of my actions is the welfare of all, then I must treat my own good—and that of persons close to me—as having no more claim on me than anyone else's good. I will, then, often have to sacrifice my own good and those of my friends and family for the greater good of others who have no connection to me.

Henry SIDGWICK (1838–1900), in his defense of utilitarianism, replied to this argument that since I know my own good and the good of those close to me much better than I know the good of strangers—and thus have a higher probability of succeeding in promoting it—in fact utilitarianism will not often require me to sacrifice my own and my loved ones' good for the sake of the greater good of others. Moreover, Sidgwick claimed, following JOHN STUART MILL (1806–1873), that most people are infrequently in a position to confer benefit on more than their close circle of friends and family, so that the conflict seldom arises in the first place. Modern communications, international relief agencies, and the like have made the latter view obsolete; it is now in fact relatively easy to benefit anonymous, needy others. Contemporary utilitarians have not followed Sidgwick in the former argument either, in part because it makes the value of friendship purely instrumental to other aspects of a person's welfare.

Sidgwick makes use of another argument which acknowledges the specific, noninstrumental value of friendship as a type of human good in its own right. He says that if people consider friendship to be an important component of their individual good, then, even if friendship itself involves a nonutilitarian preference of the friend over others, the utilitarian principle will prescribe its promotion. So, while acting from friendship might not maximize overall welfare defined independently of the intrinsic good of friendship (or of personal relations more generally), it would do so if the good of friendship is acknowledged.

This argument—echoed in many contemporary accounts—is unsatisfactory. For to act from friendship is to act for the sake of one's particular friend. One does not act "from friendship" if one acts with the goal of promoting overall good, even if, because the good of friendship is one component (and the salient one in the act in question) of that overall good, that act would be the same as that prompted by genuine friendship. On the proposed account the friend's good is still portrayed as instrumental to overall good or welfare, even if it is a component of that good.

Some utilitarians acknowledge the force of this objection and agree that personal relations are a great personal good which should not be continually at risk from the demands of an impersonal point of view. But they reply to the objection in the following manner: Utilitarianism should not be seen as prescribing a motive or type of PRACTICAL REASONING in all or most situations. Rather utilitarianism should be seen as defining a standpoint for assessment of MOTIVES, traits of character, or dispositions. So utilitarianism does not tell agents to have regard for the overall good in their every action (specifically their actions of friendship). On the contrary, if overall good turns out empirically to be fostered by agents acting spontaneously on behalf of friends while paying no regard (in most situations) to overall welfare, then utilitarianism prescribes such dispositions.

This view greatly mutes the conflict between personal relations and impersonal morality, though it still ultimately justifies action on behalf of friends by its role (via utility-promoting dispositions) in promoting overall good. But proponents of the value of personal relationships may still feel that there is in any case something entirely misguided about attempting to encompass personal relations within an impersonal framework. For the value of personal relations is not just their *general* value as components of human good. Rather, each *particular* friendship (or other personal relationship) has its own unique value; each relationship is (at least partly) incommensurable with any other. The value of friendship involves the irreplaceable and noncomparable value of each particular friendship.

The "personal point of view" critique of utilitarianism—and of impersonal moralities more generally—does not take on personal relations as a distinctly moral or ethical phenomenon. It is concerned only with exhibiting their role in human good or flourishing, and with their legitimacy from the point of view of practical reason more generally.

Special Moral Relationships

A second source of interest in personal relations, as a distinctly moral phenomenon, comes from recognizing that there are many kinds of *special moral relationships* (of which personal relations are only a subset). The paradigm, and in an ultimate sense only, moral relationship in impartialist ethical thinking is of persons regarded simply as persons, human beings, rational beings, or the like. This perspective is insufficient in that we are subject to certain NORMS, responsibilities, and perhaps duties to specific other persons in virtue of the type of specific relationship in which we stand to them—professional to client, friend to friend, parent to child.

This point of view can be associated historically with INTUITIONISM of the type advocated by W. D. ROSS (1877–1971) and discussed by Sidgwick. The intuitionist perspective involves a multiplicity of distinct and irreducible principles, not all applicable to all persons simply as persons.

While accepting that there can be norms and obligations in, for example, professional relationships, some nevertheless object to seeing personal relations in this way. For, they say, action on behalf of friends or family must stem from personal affection or caring. If it stems from duty or obligation something is wrong; this is not what our friends, spouses, and children need or want from us. Thus morality is an intrusion into personal relationships.

Yet we do speak of duties at least of parents toward their children (to nurture, support, take care of). Such usage seems perhaps less natural in the case of friendship (though some philosophers have, without seeming troubled in doing so, referred to duties of friendship as well), and this may be related to the existence of legal obligations toward spouse and children but not toward friends. Sidgwick suggests that we do have duties to have affection for our friends and family (insofar as doing so is, at least

to some extent, within our control), but that in the absence of such affections we also regard parents as under a duty to provide certain goods to their children. The latter view should be treated with some caution, however, as many goods within personal relations (a child's SELF-ESTEEM or a friend's self-confidence, for example) cannot be brought about by the parent or friend unless doing so is motivated by certain emotions or emotional attitudes (of LOVE or CARE or valuing) rather than by duty. (Perhaps it could be argued that there are duties of personal relationship, but that discharging those duties requires motives other than duty itself.)

Alternatively, one could attempt to preserve some notion of personal relations as an arena of moral assessment, but not of obligation or duty, by framing such assessment in terms of virtues. Certain virtues are in some way implicit in these relationships—commitment, care, LOYALTY, honesty, TRUST, and the like. Someone can be criticized for lacking those virtues, and that lack is often in part a lack of a certain kind of emotion toward the other person. This perspective expresses our understanding that one's way of conducting personal relationships reflects on one's CHARACTER, yet avoids problems associated with applying "duty" in the area of personal relations.

Moreover, even if there are duties in personal relationships, there must certainly be a wide area of conduct not covered by such duties. A friend whose actions were only those required by duties of friendship (even if that was not her motive for engaging in them) would be too minimal a friend. That wider area can be captured by the notion of virtue. Yet the virtue perspective should not be taken so far in the other direction as to deny that certain kinds of conduct within personal relations are positively wrong. For example, to betray a friend is to *wrong* the friend—to act wrongly—and not merely to lack a virtue or to exhibit a vice.

Thus there seem to be grounds for saying that moral norms operate within personal relationships, though these norms sometimes involve emotion and feeling in ways that norms do not do in other relationships. In addition, an ethic for personal relationships will have to be decidedly more particularistic than so far indicated, and more particularistic than the way obligations are portrayed on standard accounts. For if there are duties to friends, these are not just general duties but ones very specific to the particular relationship in question. Just as each personal relationship has its own irreplaceable value, so each has its own unique history, character, and set of implicit and explicit understandings about what is to be expected of the parties to it. What I ought to do for my friend (or child or spouse) is, often, not what I ought to do for any friend in comparable circumstances, but rather depends on these particularities of the relationship.

Feminism

A third source of interest in personal relationships has come from the impact of *feminism* on moral theory. An important strand of feminism has criticized moral philosophy for neglecting the domain to which women have been relegated for most of human history, namely the world of domestic activities, of family and personal relationships. Taking this domain seriously requires going beyond the impersonal ethics of utilitarianism, Kantianism, and contractualism. For these theories do not capture the emotion-groundedness of conduct in this area, the often indefinite nature of the responsibilities involved, and the focus on intimacy and deep personal knowledge of another person.

Feminists have claimed that moral philosophy has tended to model morality on the impersonal relationships suitable to the state, the market, professional life, and the bureaucracy—*i.e.,* on the traditional domain of men. This accounts for the domination of moral philosophy by impartialism, by impersonal rules and principles, or by a contract model of relationships. In this way a male bias has been built into the heart of traditional moral theory itself. To give adequate attention to the traditional domain of women, then, would require not only turning traditional theory toward that domain, but also revising the theory itself.

G. W. F. Hegel is the one historically significant philosopher who has given the domain of domestic life an important role to play in his overall ethical system and theory, and he articulates the public/private dichotomy which is the basis for feminist criticism. Nevertheless Hegel devalues women and the private world of family in comparison with the world of "civil society" and the state, precisely *because* he sees the latter realm as regulated by universal rules and principles while the former is governed, he says, by mere feeling and particularity.

Such devaluing of the world of particular personal relationships is part of the target of the feminist critique and of its charge of male bias.

The latter feminist criticism does not assume that the private domain of family, friends, and personal relations more generally is in fact the 'natural' or proper domain of women. Confining women to the private sphere is itself a target of feminist criticism. The claim is rather that the personal domain is an ethically significant domain for everyone.

So one effect of this feminist criticism has been to turn attention toward the domain of personal relations as a moral domain. In this way feminism's effect has supported the turn toward "special relationships" and their moral obligations and responsibilities. In addition, one stream within feminism has focused on the particular moral sensibility and virtues needed to act well within the domain of personal relationships—for example, care, attentiveness to context, and particulars of situations, understanding of persons in their particularity, sensitivity to people's feelings, and the like.

See also: CARE; CHARACTER; CHILDREN AND ETHICAL THEORY; COMMON GOOD; DUTY AND OBLIGATION; EMOTIONS; *EUDAIMONIA,* -ISM; FAMILY; FEMINIST ETHICS; FRIENDSHIP; IMPARTIALITY; LOYALTY; PUBLIC AND PRIVATE MORALITY; RECIPROCITY; SITUATION ETHICS; SYMPATHY; TRUST; UTILITARIANISM; VIRTUE ETHICS.

Bibliography

Badhwar, Neera Kapur, ed. *Friendship: A Philosophical Reader.* Ithaca: Cornell University Press, 1993. Collection of many of the most influential contemporary essays on friendship.

Becker, Lawrence C. *Reciprocity.* Chicago: University of Chicago Press, 1990 [1986]. Chapters 6 and 7 argue that the norm of reciprocity—returning good for good received—applies in the domain of personal relationships.

Blum, Lawrence A. *Friendship, Altruism, and Morality.* London: Routledge and Kegan Paul, 1980.

Buber, Martin. *I and Thou.* New York: Scribner's, 1958 [1922]. A classic statement of the distinctive character of personal encounters.

Friedman, Marilyn. *What Are Friends For: Feminist Perspectives on Personal Relationships and Moral Theory.* Ithaca: Cornell University Press, 1993. Collected essays providing complex feminist perspective on friendship and other personal relationships.

Gilbert, Paul. *Human Relationships.* Oxford: Blackwell,

1991. Discussion of issues in personal relationships, and critique of Freudian, sociobiological, and power perspectives on them.

Goodin, Robert E. *Protecting the Vulnerable: A Reanalysis of Our Social Responsibilities.* Chicago: University of Chicago Press, 1985. Chapters 3 and 4 argue that obligations of personal relationships can be accounted for as obligations to protect those vulnerable to us.

Graham, George, and Hugh LaFollette, eds. *Person to Person.* Philadelphia: Temple University Press, 1989. Articles on morality and personal relationships.

LaFollette, Hugh. *Personal Relationships: Love, Identity, and Morality.* Oxford: Blackwell, 1996. Theory of the nature and value of friendship, love, and kinship relations.

Noddings, Nel. *Caring: A Feminine Approach to Ethics and Moral Education.* Berkeley: University of California Press, 1984. Fullest philosophical statement of nature of caring within personal relationships.

Railton, Peter. "Alienation, Consequentialism, and the Demands of Morality." *Philosophy and Public Affairs* 13 (1984): 134–71. Attempt to express value of personal relationships within consequentialist framework.

Ruddick, Sara. "Maternal Thinking." In *Mothering: Essays in Feminist Theory,* edited by Joyce Treblicot. Totowa, N.J.: Rowman and Allanheld, 1983. Attempt to articulate the virtues and sensibilities of mothering as a moral activity capable of illuminating personal relationship more generally.

Sidgwick, Henry. *Methods of Ethics.* 7th ed. Chicago: University of Chicago Press, 1962 [1874]. Book III, chapter 11, section 4; book IV, chapter 3, section 3, and elsewhere discuss duties in personal relationships and the ability of utilitarianism to encompass them.

Stocker, Michael. "The Schizophrenia of Modern Ethical Theories." *Journal of Philosophy* 73 (1976): 453–66. Germinal statement of critique of traditional moral theories for not accommodating motives in personal relationships.

Lawrence Blum

persuasive definition

The concept of a persuasive definition was introduced by Charles L. STEVENSON (1908–1979) in the 1930s, and is developed in his well-known book, *Ethics and Language* (1944). Stevenson's theory is based on the idea that words have an emotional, as well as a descriptive meaning. When a definition of a word that has familiar conventional meaning is put forward in an ethical discussion, the definition may be partly stipulative. So it may not represent the conventional meaning. When used in arguments, such definitions typically change the conventional meaning by making it more precise, in a direction that suits the INTERESTS or the purposes of the arguer. However, Stevenson observed that the emotional meaning of the word, in such cases, tends to have a certain inertia, retaining the same positive or negative connotations it always had. The effect of the use of a persuasive definition of this kind creates a deception. The audience is subtly influenced to accept the arguer's viewpoint because they see the viewpoint described in language that casts a positive light on it. Or in a negative instance, the audience could be influenced against a viewpoint because of the negative language used to describe it.

Because of an awareness of this deceptively persuasive aspect, logic textbooks have been inclined to be suspicious about persuasive definitions, even classifying them as fallacious in some instances. One textbook, Patrick Hurley's *A Concise Introduction to Logic* (1994), for example, writes, "a persuasive definition masquerades as an honest assignment of meaning to a term while condemning or blessing with approval the subject matter of the (term being defined)." To illustrate, Hurley gives the following pair of opposed persuasive definitions of the term "abortion":

"Abortion" means the ruthless murdering of innocent human beings.

"Abortion" means a safe and established surgical procedure whereby a woman is relieved of an unwanted burden.

One can easily see from this example how common persuasive definitions are in ethical argumentation, how they can be used to influence the attitudes of an audience, and how tricky and deceptive they can be. One can also see how ethical disputes, and legal disputes as well, can turn into protracted and obstructive quarreling about the meanings of words. According to Richard Robinson, a persuasive definition is "at best a mistake and at worst a lie," because the only people who are influenced by it are those who mistakenly take it to be an objective description of the true nature of things. Tentatively adopting this view, Robinson suggested that the practical conclusion following from it is that we should not use persuasive definitions at all. However, one wonders whether ethical argumentation, or even philosophical argumentation generally, would be possible, as we know it, without the liberal use of persuasive definitions.

According to Stevenson, persuasive definitions can often be recognised by being prefaced by the word "real" or the word "true." For example, it might be said that CHARITY, in the true sense of the word, means the giving of understanding, and not just money. Such persuasive definitions are frequently found in proverbs and folk sayings. They are also frequently found in intellectual treatises, in philosophy, literary criticism, the social sciences, and other academic fields. Philosophical arguments, in particular, are often about the true or essential nature of things, and the use of persuasive definitions is an important part of the argumentation, not only in ethics. Sören Halldén cited many cases of intellectual writings that give persuasive definitions of concepts like LOVE, humor, poetry, culture, life, and DEMOCRACY.

One case cited by Halldén is the definition of "pornography" put forward by D. H. Lawrence (1885–1973) in his essay, "Pornography and Obscenity." Lawrence first considered a definition according to which PORNOGRAPHY is intended to be sexually stimulating—a definition that does not seem to imply that pornography is degrading or unpleasant. Lawrence, however, argued that those who advocate this definition to argue that books or pictures that have sex appeal are bad books or pictures, are hypocrites. As an alternative, he proposed his own definition: "pornography" is the attempt to insult sex, to do dirt on it." But as Halldén commented, this definition is "paradoxical" in the sense that it departs considerably from the conventional meaning of the word. What Lawrence is doing is retaining the negative connotations of the word "pornogrphy," but redirecting them so they appear to go against anyone who thinks that sexual impulses should be restrained or repressed. This is an example of how the emotive connotations of a word are retained, but redirected against argumentation the redefiner is opposing.

Stevenson's observations about how common persuasive definitions are in ethical argumentation turn out to be very important to understanding the nature of ethical disputes like the ABORTION issue. Participants not only use persuasive definitions on both sides, but they also try to adopt language that is tilted towards supporting their own point of view (and goes against the opposed point of view). These habits are comparable to argumentation in wars and territorial disputes, where our side is routinely described as "freedom-fighters" and the opposition is described as "terrorists." In the case of the abortion dispute, participants even try to define the issue in a way that favors their own side—one side calls itself "pro-choice" and the other side calls itself "pro-life." Both labels sound positive, but the verbal issue (the conflict of opinions) is no longer evident.

There is controversy over whether the use of persuasive definitions, and emotionally loaded language generally, is legitimate in ethical argumentation. Stevenson saw persuasion of this emotive kind as nonrational, whereas the reality of the situation is that the use of persuasively slanted language is normal in ethical argumentation, and it seems inescapable, given the colorations of words and phrases in everyday natural language. Given this reality, some would defend the use of persuasive definitions by pointing out that commonly used words already have built-in emotional connotations that reflect traditional values, which should not be impervious to criticisms. For example, feminists might defend the redefinition of "pornography" as "violence against women," even though it does not accord with the traditional meaning of that term, on the grounds that the old meaning of the term reflected patriarchal values that are no longer appropriate (they claim) for the modern era.

The tradition of CASUISTRY might see the legitimacy of the use of persuasive definitions in ethics in quite a different way from the way Stevenson did. From the casuistic point of view, there are always two sides to ethical disputes, because such disputes characteristically arise out of cases in personal deliberation when a choice has to be made between two principles or values that conflict with each other in a given case (see Jonsen and Toulmin). So the casuist might see the use of persuasive definitions by a participant in an ethical dispute as a reasonable means of attempting to argue for her point of view, as long as the other side was free to challenge such definitions, or to propose different ones.

From such a perspective then, use of a persuasive definition in ethical argumentation could be viewed as not wholly illegitimate or fallacious, as long as it is clear that such a definition represents a particular viewpoint or interest, and is subject to challenge and critical questioning by someone who is not committed to that viewpoint, or who has a different interest.

The real problem with persuasive definitions is

their deceptive nature, as noted by Robinson above. As Stevenson pointed out, they tend to take advantage of the inertia effect of the persistence of conventional meanings and connotations of words. If a word already in use is redefined, the redefiner may take advantage of the audience's disposition to continue to accept the positive or negative connotations of the word in the old way. This deceptive practice involves a kind of ambiguity that is at odds with any attempt to rationally persuade people to change their commitment to a view, based on logical reasoning of a kind that provides good evidence to support a view.

On the other hand, it is hard to imagine ethical argumentation, of the kind we are familiar with in philosophy, without persuasive definitions being allowed. So Stevenson's theory, that ethical language is persuasive as well as descriptive, raises fundamental questions about ethical argumentation that have not been answered to this day. As Robinson so incisively puts it, "the whole question of what methods of moral persuasion are moral must be re-examined from the beginning." Postmodern skepticism about the biases inherent in all ethical argumentation in natural language has only underscored the importance of this fundamental question.

See also: ABORTION; ACADEMIC ETHICS; ANALYTIC PHILOSOPHY AND ETHICS; CASUISTRY; CONVENTIONS; CRITICAL THEORY; DECEIT; EMOTIVISM; INTERESTS; LOGIC AND ETHICS; MORAL POINT OF VIEW; MORAL REALISM; MORAL REASONING; MORAL TERMS; PARTIALITY; POSTMODERNISM; RATIONALITY VS. REASONABLENESS; SKEPTICISM IN ETHICS; SLIPPERY SLOPE ARGUMENTS; STEVENSON.

Bibliography

Halldén, Sören. *True Love, True Humour and True Religion: A Semantic Study.* Lund, Sweden: Gleerup, 1960. D. H. Lawrence discussion, pp. 75–76.

Hurley, Patrick J. *A Concise Introduction to Logic.* 5th ed. Belmont, N.Y.: Wadsworth, 1994. Cited, p. 92.

Jonsen, Albert R., and Stephen Toulmin. *The Abuse of Casuistry: A History of Moral Reasoning.* Berkeley: University of California Press, 1988.

Robinson, Richard. *Definition.* Oxford: Clarendon Press, 1950. Cited, pp. 169–70.

Stevenson, Charles L. *Ethics and Language.* New Haven: Yale University Press, 1944. Cited, pp. 212, 140.

Walton, Douglas. *One-Sided Arguments: A Dialectical Analysis of Bias.* Albany: State University of New York Press, 1999.

Douglas N. Walton

phenomenology

Many phenomenologists have made substantial contributions to the field of ethics. Yet the concrete ethical theories which phenomenologists have actually proposed are in content often quite different from each other. This is obvious if one compares the views proposed by HUSSERL (1859–1938) with those developed by SARTRE (1905–1980), RICOEUR, Polin, and others. Many phenomenologists have also written on ethical issues from an axiological point of view. But what all phenomenologists have in common is the use of phenomenological methods which are generally either descriptive and eidetic in nature, or transcendental in character. This essay will be limited to a brief description of basic similarities and differences of method and content in the different phenomenological investigations concerning ethical issues.

The history of ethical theories developed by phenomenologists to a great extent parallels the history of value theories in ethics in the twentieth century. Among phenomenologists who have written on ethics from an axiological point of view are Husserl, SCHELER (1874–1928), Nicolai HARTMANN (1882–1950), von Hildebrand, Reiner, and Polin.

The first phenomenologist to publish an ethics from an axiological point of view was Max Scheler, who at that time was deeply influenced in his ideas by Eucken (1846–1926), NIETZSCHE (1844–1900), St. AUGUSTINE (354–430), and Bergson (1859–1941). Yet Husserl, the founder of the phenomenological movement, had already regularly given seminars and courses on ethics between 1889 and 1924. These lectures remained unpublished until 1988.

If we compare Husserl's ethics with that of other phenomenologists, we see immediately that almost all of them are quite different in method or content from the one developed by Husserl. Scheler did indeed develop ethics as a theory of values, as BRENTANO (1838–1917) and Husserl had done before him, and he also made use of the phenomenological method developed by Husserl. Yet for Scheler, phenomenology does not contain a transcendental dimension; phenomenology is a careful description of immediate, intuitive, lived-through experiences with the intention of penetrating to what is given in such experiences. The phenomenologist should be concerned mainly with the possible, not the actual— with the essences of values and not so much with their concrete appearances. Finally, the phenomenologist must try to establish the essential and *a priori* relationships between these essences.

Scheler, like Husserl, took his point of departure from Brentano. Like Brentano and Husserl, Scheler also distinguished purely formal values from material values. But contrary to Husserl, Scheler distinguished five basic types of material values which can be ordered hierarchically with the help of *a priori* criteria. For Husserl, values are ideal entities. For Scheler, although values are given only in our experiences, they are *a priori* in the sense that they do not depend for their being on such experiences. Yet the precise character of this *a priori* status of values was never carefully determined by Scheler. Finally, Scheler derived the moral *ought* from the *a priori* character of values; once this *ought* has been discovered there is room in ethics for concrete NORMS and imperatives. In this latter point, Scheler again approaches Husserl's position.

Nicolai Hartmann also developed his ethics in the form of a theory of values using the phenomenological method. Yet Hartmann was critical of the conception of phenomenology proposed by Husserl and his close followers. For him phenomenology is only the first phase of the philosophical method taken as a whole. Phenomenology is for him no more than a description of what is immediately given, and should be followed by an aporetics in which difficulties, problems, and contradictions in what is immediately given are brought to light. In a third phase, an analytic method gives us access to the categories in terms of which each concrete datum is to be understood. Finally, a dialectical and a synthetic phase are added to place the examined concrete data in their wider perspectives, and to provide a final unification of the categories throughout the various strata of our world. As far as the values themselves are concerned, Hartmann to a large extent incorporated Scheler's material values into his own theory of values. But his primary concern in his *Ethics* appears to have been to present the values themselves in a systematic fashion. In addition to this, he also paid attention to the manner in which we discover values.

He wanted to explain particularly that, although our valuations may change over time and from place to place, the values themselves are independent of these valuations. Human beings discover values; they do not create or constitute them. If one compares the Greek world to the Christian, the modern, and the contemporary worlds, one will see that it is not the values that change, but our value consciousness in which the unchanging values reveal and manifest themselves. Because consciousness is very limited, usually when we discover new values, we forget other older values.

For Sartre, too, phenomenology is limited to what Husserl called eidetic, mundane phenomenology; thus Sartre rejects the transcendental reduction and eliminates Husserl's transcendental ego. Eidetic description in philosophy and ethics leads to immediately given data which then must be interpreted metaphysically. Sartre did not develop a theory of value, but instead based his ethical view on his metaphysics of the human condition in which the notion of "absolute" freedom plays the vital role. Only in his early philosophy did Sartre use the phenomenological method and defend his well-known existentialist ethics of AUTHENTICITY for which *Being and Nothingness* had laid the foundation. In this first phase, the critique of "bad faith" plays a vital role; BAD FAITH conceals an unwillingness to live with the anguish of freedom, choice, and RESPONSIBILITY and is thus to be overcome. In the second phase, Sartre developed an ethics of disalienation whose aim it was to change the social and economic structures of choice which leave the oppressed and poor no choice but submission or death. This conception of ethics was developed during the time in which Sartre was closely associated with the French Communist Party. In his final phase, Sartre developed an ethics of freedom which advocates the virtues of fraternity and mutuality and rejects capitalism on the ground that it is atomistic, deterministic, and antihumanistic; at the same time, it defends socialism's dialectical spirit on the grounds that it is holistic, humanistic, and it promotes freedom. In his final conception of HUMANISM, Sartre ascribes to the members of any institution or society the moral responsibility for social structure and laws.

Dietrich von Hildebrand was methodically deeply influenced by Reinach (1883–1916). He identified the phenomenological method with a metaphysical analysis of essences. Hildebrand's theory of values was at first influenced by Scheler and Husserl. Hildebrand makes a distinction between adequate and inadequate value responses. His conception of value blindness, a phenomenon that can occur in different degrees, is of great importance for modern value theory.

Herbert Spiegelberg, who was influenced by Husserl and Pfänder, developed a practical philosophy upon phenomenological foundations which tried to combine insights of the phenomenology of values (of the kind developed by Scheler and Husserl) with a deepened conception of human existence.

Hans Reiner has made use of a phenomenological, descriptive method which he applied mainly to phenomena such as freedom, will, duty, inclination, DESIRE, HONOR, etc., but above all to the notions of the morally good and EVIL. Reiner developed an ethical theory that is built mainly on the notions of feeling and value. He distinguished absolute values from relative ones that are conditioned by needs; he also made a distinction between subjectively and objectively significant values. Given this distinction, it is possible to explain how the morally good and evil can be defined unambiguously. In Reiner's view, the morally good consists in nothing but the fact that we comply with the demands or the invitations to maintain or materialize a value any time the realization of an objectively significant value is put into our hands in a concrete situation so that we have to act or refrain from action in regard to that value. Inversely, evil consists in the fact that we do not respond to such a demand or invitation to maintain or materialize an objectively valid value. These ideas are developed in detail in his work, *Pflicht und Neigung (Duty and Inclination)*, which appeared in 1951.

Raymond Polin is convinced that philosophy faces grave problems the moment it conceives of man in terms of freedom and nevertheless attempts to develop an ethics as a practical theory of man. Polin rejects the idea that one can attribute to man an invariable structure which determines his essence. The essence of man consists in his freedom, but this freedom is not "absolute"; it is intimately interwoven with what is given. Yet man is free, he has the ability to become on the basis of what he already is, and he has the POWER to create. From this it follows that to determine the meaning of the human condition is to assign a specific end to his function as a human being, and thus to treat him as a

value around which the world of men should be ordered in his regard. Thus the essence of man must be understood in terms of freedom, meaning, and value. The reason for this is that all man's characteristics are merely means to the creation of meaning and value. Among these means, freedom is "the means of all means." Freedom can establish meaning only in relation to a given situation and in relation to an order that is to be established. This order, however, is not something unquestionable and definitive. Polin thinks that he can deny the existence of such an order and still justify the obligatory character of our moral standards and imperatives. For Polin there is a universally valid moral imperative which does not presuppose an absolute order nor deny man's freedom, namely, "Act in such a way that there can be an intelligible theory of your actions."

Finally, Ricoeur, one of the most influential French philosophers today, has always given ethics an important place in his thinking. In his early work he was concerned mainly with the development of a philosophy of the will. In *The Voluntary and Involuntary*, Ricoeur uses the phenomenological method without appealing to its transcendental dimension. He tries to describe accurately certain invariable and essential structures of man's practical and affective life. In other volumes of his *Philosophy of the Will*, Ricoeur uses Nabert's reflective method as well as hermeneutic methods.

In his later work Ricoeur has given us an indication of how he now would go about writing a philosophical ethics. In his view it is not correct to begin with a world of invariable and eternal paradigms that can function as the definitive standard for man's behavior. It is equally wrong to begin with the eternal and the natural law, or with obligation, duty, value, norm, or imperative. The starting point for a genuine ethics must be a reflection on man's freedom, for freedom is the source of ethics. Typical for man's freedom is that it constantly posits itself, but never fully possesses itself. Only after explaining the notion of finite freedom that constantly encounters a world that is already given will it be possible to turn to reflections on duty, norms, imperatives, values, and laws.

See also: AUTHENTICITY; BRENTANO; HARTMANN; HUMANISM; HUSSERL; METAPHYSICS AND EPISTEMOLOGY; RICOEUR; SARTRE; SCHELER; VALUE, THEORY OF.

Bibliography

Hartmann, Nicolai. *Ethics.* 3 vols. New York: Macmillan, 1932.

Hildebrand, Dietrich von. *Fundamental Moral Attitudes.* Translated by Alice M. Jourdain. New York: Longmans and Green, 1950.

Reiner, Hans. *Das Prinzip von Gut und Böse.* Freiburg: Alber, 1960.

———. *Die philosophische Ethik.* Heidelberg: Quelle und Meyer, 1964.

———. *Gut und Böse.* Freiburg: Bielefelds, 1965. For an English translation of pp. 7–41, see *Contemporary European Ethics,* edited by Joseph J. Kockelmans, Garden City: Doubleday, 1972.

Ricoeur, Paul. *Fallible Man.* Translated by Charles Kelbly. Chicago: Regnery, 1965.

———. *The Voluntary and Involuntary.* Translated by Erazim V. Kohak. Evanston, Ill.: Northwestern University Press, 1966.

———. "The Problem of the Foundation of Moral Philosophy." *Philosophy Today* 22 (1978): 175–92.

Sartre, Jean-Paul. *Cahiers pour une morale.* Paris: Gallimard, 1983 [published posthumously; written 1946–1947].

———. *Being and Nothingness.* Translated by Hazel E. Barnes. New York: Philosophical Library, 1956. Tr. of *L'Être et le néant* [1943].

Spiegelberg, Herbert. *Gesetz und Sittengesetz: Strukturanalytische und historische Vorstudien zu einer gesetzfreien Ethik.* Zurich: Niehans, 1935.

———. "Indubitables in Ethics: A Cartesian Meditation." *Ethics* 58 (1947): 35–50.

———. *The Phenomenological Movement.* 2 vols. The Hague: Nijhoff, 1960.

Joseph J. Kockelmans

philosophical anthropology

Philosophical anthropology is the philosophical examination of what it is that human beings are, and what they could reasonably be expected to know or act upon. (This is distinct from the empirical study of what human beings actually do or say.) Because we thereby investigate what we, being human, could be expected to know or act upon, the study cannot avoid a certain circularity, and always has further implications for the study of things other than us. Are we the sort of creature that could discover general truths about the universe?

The characteristics which have usually been identified as essentially human are a capacity to speak a human language, to make choices about one's future, to organize communal actions in accordance with some freshly negotiated plan, and to recognize oneself as one creature among many, having a history, a CHARACTER, a hope of change. The term *homo sapiens* names a species uniquely and universally endowed with language, self-consciousness, and a capacity for life under the law in a community of the like-minded. ARISTOTLE's (384–322 B.C.E.) dicta that humans are political animals, animals with language, animals capable of recognizing and acting upon general principles, all amount to the same thing: a picture of the human essence that identifies human beings as something unlike all other animals. Some have added that the capacity to make tools to alter the environment, and to organize the labor of so doing, makes a crucial difference. These variations often seem to rest upon prior judgements of value: What is it that we think most important of those things we do? Pure thinking, moral action, productive labour, play?

Though Aristotle did identify the human essence in these terms, he did not adopt the full-scale "essentialism" which modern biologists now associate with his name. Modern biologists point out that the classes identified in folk-biology have often turned out to have no single character in common, nor even to have a common ancestor they do not share with creatures from another class. "Fishes" does not name a well-defined biological kind, any more than "weeds" does (the things we call fishes are not members of any single biological group, or *taxon*). But even recognized biological *taxa* do not have so-called "essences." There is no character that a thing has to have if it is to count as a member of a particular biological *taxon*—except the historical character of being a member, by descent, of a named set of populations. A species, in modern terms, is not a set of creatures with a shared and essential nature, but a set of interbreeding populations. It seems to follow that if we consider human beings as a biological class we cannot expect that all such creatures share a nature. Maybe all humans now known to us can talk, or live under negotiated agreements with their fellows, just as all reptiles have three-chambered hearts—but there is nothing to say they must. There is no single nature that species members certainly display. "Humans" might even turn out to be a merely nominal class, like weeds or fishes, identified as such only because a given community chooses to do so. If "humans" does identify a real species (as seems likely), that species is simply a collection of creatures united by genealogical relationships, not phenomenal or genetic resemblances.

One reply to this "objectivist" approach is that we are ourselves the things we seek to find. We don't *find* humans as we might find fishes or monkeys: we are humans (that is, "human" names what we self-consciously are), and we have an *a priori* grasp of our own essence before we locate any others like ourselves. We may find out more things about human beings, whether they are universally true of the class by accident (*e.g.,* all human beings live on the earth) or by necessary but unexpected implication (*e.g.,* all human beings can laugh). But we do not find out what the essence of a human being might be: *that* is evident in the first moment of locating something as human, even if we need to think before we can express it. The tradition now associated with DESCARTES (1596–1650), and continued into the twentieth century chiefly by phenomenological philosophers such as HUSSERL (1859–1938) or HEIDEGGER (1889–1976), prefers to discover what it is to be human by asking what it is to be Me, what can be said of my being as a subject rather than as an object. On this account my self-consciousness, my taking the world as my world and my making a personal history from the shreds of memory and fear for the future, are of my essence. Everything else could be thought away—though later philosophers have been less ready than Descartes to think that I could think away the social and physical nexus in which I find myself. On this view I am essentially, as Aristotle said, a being that does not simply engage in private thoughts but, crucially, communicates and acts, and all other creatures with whom I identify in the act of recognizing myself are essentially the same. Being "human," on this account, is not being a member of a particular biological *taxon* (though it may be that only members of that *taxon* prove to be "human"), but being like us, existing in our own act of defining ourselves.

This last claim, that human beings are creatures who define themselves, is sometimes expressed, as SARTRE (1905–1980) did, by saying that "human beings have no nature." The point here is not the modern biological one that species-membership does not depend on any shared, essential nature, but rather the Aristotelian doctrine that to be human in the sense in which I am self-consciously "human" is to be required to make choices, to be aware of one-self as an entity that has a history, not just a past, and both hopes and fears, not just a future. MARX (1818–1883) would add that the individualist emphasis in this is a product of particular historical and economic circumstances. Aristotle, like Heidegger, also insisted that to be human was to have the option of recognizing and serving Being: that is, our self-conscious humanity rests not on our capacity to do as we please, but on our discovery of a world greater than ourselves. We are not limited—as we suppose that other creatures are—to the world of present phenomena, how things naturally are for us: in dealing with the world, we know that it transcends our knowledge and our present purposes. To be human is to be aware of boundless mystery.

See also: BIOLOGICAL THEORY; DELIBERATION AND CHOICE; EVOLUTION; EXISTENTIAL ETHICS; INDIVIDUALISM; PHENOMENOLOGY; PSYCHOLOGY; RACISM, CONCEPTS OF; SELF-KNOWLEDGE; TRANSCENDENTALISM.

Bibliography

Aristotle. *Nicomachean Ethics.* See Book I for material on human "function" (*i.e.,* what human beings find they have to do: make choices).

———. *Politics.* In Book I, material on naturalness of family and civic bonds.

Baker, John Randal. *Race.* Oxford: Clarendon Press, 1974. A work justly accused of racist stereotyping, but includes a useful discussion of Kantian anthropology.

Banton, Michael. *Racial Theories.* Cambridge: Cambridge University Press, 1987. A critical account of the concepts of race and racial relations.

Cassirer, Ernst. *An Essay on Man.* New Haven, Conn.: Yale University Press, 1944. A neo-Kantian approach to the question.

Grene, Marjorie Glicksman. *Approaches to a Philosophical Biology.* New York; London: Basic Books, 1968. Philosophical biology in the Continental tradition: Buytendjik, Goldstein, and others.

Heidegger, Martin. *Being and Time.* Translated by J. Macquarrie, and E. Robinson. Oxford: Blackwell, 1962 [1927]. Translation of *Sein und Zeit;* analysis of Dasein.

Ingold, Tim, ed. *What is an Animal?* Rev. ed. London: Routledge, 1994 (1988). Philosophers and anthropologists on ways that people define themselves against the nonhuman.

Mayr, Ernst. *Toward a New Philosophy of Biology: Observations of an Evolutionist.* Cambridge, Mass.: Harvard University Press, 1988.

Olafson, Frederick A. *What is a Human Being?: A Heideg-

gerian View. Cambridge: Cambridge University Press, 1995. A clear account of the difference between third-person and first-person approaches to the problem.

Trigg, Roger. *Ideas of Human Nature.* Oxford: Blackwell, 1988. Straightforward introduction to different views of what human beings are essentially like.

S. R. L. Clark

philosophy of law

See legal philosophy.

philosophy of religion

The relation of philosophy of RELIGION to ethics is most controversial in monotheistic religions like Judaism, Christianity, and ISLAM. Philosophical opinion has ranged from the belief that the existence of God destroys the foundations of morality to the belief that God's existence legitimizes the foundations of morality.

As an example of the first sort of opinion, some philosophers have argued that the existence of an omniscient deity would make ethics pointless, since God's foreknowledge, they thought, would preclude human freedom and RESPONSIBILITY. For if God is omniscient, then he knows in advance every action that any agent will do. God's knowing every action in advance (in contrast, say, to his merely guessing about them) entails that the actions must be done just as they are foreseen by him. If all actions must be done as they are foreseen by God, then no agent ever has the power to do otherwise. Since freedom presupposes the power to do otherwise, no agent can be free if God is omniscient. This kind of argument has received considerable philosophical scrutiny. Although some have concluded that we must either deny God's foreknowledge of human actions or deny human freedom, many have challenged one or more of the other presuppositions of the argument. For example, it has been claimed that God's knowing an action in advance does not entail that it *must* happen, but only that it *will* happen, and that is compatible with its being done freely.

The so-called moral arguments for God's existence provide an example of the opposite extreme regarding God's relation to ethics. The arguments form a family whose common feature is the claim that the very objectivity of ethics presupposes either that God exists or that it is reasonable to believe that he exists. The arguments typically appeal to the alleged existence of a supreme moral principle or principles or the alleged convergence of moral principles in different societies. Cruder versions of the argument have as their major premise the claim that if there were no God, then nothing would be right or wrong. Slightly more sophisticated versions identify moral principles with commands or imperatives and argue that the existence of a supreme moral command or imperative implies the existence of a supreme commander. One of the most sophisticated versions was put forward by Immanuel KANT (1724–1804). Kant criticized the traditional proofs in natural theology of God's existence, but he thought nevertheless that the existence of a providential God was a postulate of pure PRACTICAL REASON. We know that we ought to promote the highest good attainable. We also know that HAPPINESS ought to be proportionate to worthiness. Experience tells us that the perfect distribution of happiness proportionate to worthiness lies beyond our power of promoting the good and is not guaranteed by the workings of the natural world. Thus, Kant claimed, if we believe in the compatibility of the two normative claims, we are drawn to believe in the existence of a providential God.

Putting aside the issue of whether God exists, participants to the discussion about the connection between ethics and religion could agree that *if* there were a God, he would be the supreme moral commander, moral agent, and moral judge. Significant disagreement would begin to emerge if it were asked how he is supposed to fulfill each of these roles.

God as Supreme Commander

God's commands (prohibitions) have often been claimed to underwrite the objective rightness (wrongness) of what is commanded (prohibited), and thus to provide a moral code that is binding on all people at all times. But the dispositive nature of God's commands does not in itself imply invariance. It would be consistent for one to hold both that Abraham's killing Isaac would have been right because God had commanded it, and that killing is always wrong because God's sixth commandment to Moses forbids it: one need only add that the enunciation of the Ten Commandments postdates the command to Abraham. Ethicists have pointed out that apparently contradictory practices in different societies might each be the justified result of applying the same general, nonrelativistic moral principle to differing circumstances. It seems possible, then, for a theist to say that God's commands are the objective criterion of rightness and wrongness and yet that his commands may change with place and time.

Voluntarism and Rationalism

To say only this, however, is to leave unresolved the question of *how* God's commands are the criterion of rightness and wrongness. Is something right because God commands it or does God command what is right because it is right? (Variations of this question go back at least as far as PLATO's [c. 430–347 B.C.E.] *Euthyphro.* An analogous question can be asked concerning wrongness.) *Theological voluntarism* is the position that God's will is the source of rightness and wrongness, and his commands, as expressions of his will, determine legislatively what is right and wrong. *Theological rationalism* is the position that what is right is right independently of God's commands. (Plato, LEIBNIZ [1646–1716], and Kant espoused different versions of theological rationalism.) According to the theological rationalist, killing is wrong, for instance, no matter what God's attitudes might have been about it. Being omniscient, God knows that killing is wrong, and being perfectly good, God is concerned to let us know that killing is wrong. God's revealing the Ten Commandments to Moses, then, is a case of his transmitting important items of moral truth.

Theological voluntarists object to the rationalists' conception of God's activity, pointing out that it reduces God's role in ethics to that of moral educator, a role that seems to be merely instrumental and theoretically dispensable. According to voluntarists, God's commands are constitutive of rightness and wrongness. Some voluntarists, such as William PALEY (1743–1805) and Robert Merrihew Adams, have taken the notion of constitution to be metaethical: "I am obligated to do *x*" *means* "God commands me to do *x*" or "*x* is wrong" *means* "*x* is contrary to God's commands." Other voluntarists, such as John DUNS SCOTUS (1266–1308) and WILLIAM OF OCKHAM (c. 1285–c. 1349), seem to have taken the notion of constitution to be causal. According to them, God's prohibition of killing provides the full causal explanation of why killing is wrong. Had he

not prohibited killing, it would not be wrong, and if he were now to revoke or waive the prohibition, killing would not now be wrong.

A standard objection to VOLUNTARISM is to say that according to it, nothing is intrinsically or essentially right or wrong. TORTURE is in fact wrong, but it would have been right had God willed it so. Acting with compassion is right, but it might have been wrong. These consequences strike many as unacceptable. There are at least three different strategies that might be deployed in response. One is to insist on God's sovereignty and accept the consequences. Ockham thought that the rightness or wrongness of any type of action is always separable by God from the action itself, so that God could have commanded us to hate him and the action of hating him would thereby have been obligatory. A second strategy is to claim that some moral principles are in some sense necessary and thus beyond the control of God even if he is omnipotent. Voluntarists have resisted this strategy from two directions. Some, like René DESCARTES (1596–1650), have claimed that God establishes even the necessary truths. Others have rejected the claim on grounds that it simply is rationalism reintroduced and demotes God's legislative role to that of commanding or prohibiting such types of action, as the eating of shellfish, which appear to be of secondary importance. A third strategy is to claim that there are constraints on what God might have commanded, but that the constraints arise from God's nature. God's commanding torture, for example, is impossible because it is inconsistent with his perfect goodness. A difficulty for this third strategy is to give an account of God's goodness compatible with voluntarism that does not amount to saying that God approves of himself: if this is what his goodness consists of, then his goodness seems compatible once again with his commanding just anything.

The debate between rationalism and voluntarism has ramifications for theistic MORAL PSYCHOLOGY. Opponents of rationalism allege that according to that theory, although we might be thankful to God for serving as moral tutor, being thankful falls short of being worshipful, and rationalism can give no plausible account of that dimension of the religious life. Opponents of voluntarism claim that on that theory, the only reason we can have for obeying the commands of a willful, omnipotent God are obvious prudential reasons, and if we think that morality does not reduce to self-interest, we should reject voluntarism. It is not clear that these observations are correct; they deserve further exploration.

God as Moral Agent

Creation. The debate between voluntarists and rationalists can be extended to the case of God's creating the world. Is the world good because God created it, or did God create the world because it is good? Theists have tended to focus their attention on a related issue. How can it be that God is a self-sufficient, free, perfectly good creator? If he is self-sufficient he has no need to create. If he is perfectly free he can create any world he wants to create. But if he is essentially good, then his goodness prevents him from creating evil worlds and thus seems to constrain his freedom. In the *Timaeus,* Plato argued that the Demiurge, being good, has no taint of jealousy and so created a world that is as close to the Demiurge's perfection as a world can be. In the *Enneads,* PLOTINUS (205–270) viewed the world as an indirect emanation from an original One, also characterized as Good. This view was rejected by Christian orthodoxy because the One does not bring about the world directly and the process of emanation involves no free choice on the part of the One. Pseudo-Dionysius the Areopagite (perhaps fifth century C.E.) suggested, in *On the Divine Names,* that it is the very nature of God's goodness to communicate itself to other things. Saint THOMAS AQUINAS (1225?–1274) attempted to adapt the doctrine of the essential diffusiveness of goodness to a view that maintained that God nevertheless freely chooses to create. Leibniz claimed that of all the infinitely many possible worlds God might have created, he chose to create the best. Although free, God's choice was "morally necessitated" in the sense that his knowingly choosing to create a lesser world was rationally impossible. Leibniz's critics challenged the claim that God could be genuinely free under the condition of moral necessity. Other philosophers, such as Aquinas and Adams, have argued that God's being perfectly good does not entail that he create the best world possible.

Evil. It is hard to see how the world can be the creation of an omniscient, omnipotent, perfectly good being and yet contain so much suffering. Attempts to deal with the so-called Problem of Evil often ascribe the existence of suffering to the misuse of freedom on the part of creatures. One version uses the account of the Fall given in the Book of Genesis to maintain that EVIL is the result of a catastrophic free choice made by humanity's progenitors. Another version maintains that freedom is a necessary condition for MORAL DEVELOPMENT, but that freedom carries with it the liability of choosing wrongly. Both versions rely on the assumption that it is logically impossible for there to be creatures who are genuinely free and who never make wrong choices. This assumption has provoked spirited controversy.

Personhood. Theists have typically claimed that although God is a being who takes various personal attitudes toward and enters into various personal relations with his creatures, he may not be a moral agent in many of the ways in which humans are. For example, Aquinas and others have argued for God's *impeccability,* the doctrine that, unlike humans, God not only will not but *cannot* commit a sin. Aquinas considers this doctrine to be compatible with—indeed, entailed by—the thesis that God is omnipotent. Philosophers have observed that some of the VIRTUES distinctive of humans cannot apply to God. God is thought to be wise, charitable, and just, but there is no literal sense in which he can be temperate (having no bodily appetites to control), courageous (knowing that nothing can prevail against him), or faithful or hopeful (being omniscient).

Voluntarists have argued that God can have no moral obligations or duties, on grounds that he is not subject to moral principles that he himself did not institute. Thus if he did have obligations or duties, they could only be owed to himself, and the notion of an obligation or duty to oneself is fatuous. Independently of voluntarism, some philosophers have argued that God's having duties is incompatible with his maximal freedom and essential goodness. Suppose that God promises something and thereby places himself under an obligation to fulfill the promise. If he is essentially good, he cannot fail to fulfill his obligation (without ceasing to be God). But if he cannot fail to fulfill his obligation, then he is not maximally free. One way out of this impasse is to deny that God's promising, or any activity of his, creates an obligation on his part. His carrying out the promise would then be guaranteed, not by his being aware of a duty, but merely by his being perfectly good. On this sort of view, God's actions are supererogatory rather than obligatory.

God as Moral Judge

Fundamental to much theistic thought is the doctrine that God is the ultimate judge of the lives we live and the assigner of appropriate rewards and punishments. The doctrine is usually accompanied by some sort of belief about personal survival in an afterlife, which may or may not involve immortality, resurrection, reincarnation, or the assignment to special regions of reward or punishment. Theists generally have supposed that if God judges one's life in an afterlife, the afterlife must entail the continuity of one's individual self as distinct from other persons. Doctrines according to which at death individual consciousness is obliterated and absorbed into a universal consciousness are not typical to the major theistic religions. The design of human INSTITUTIONS of reward and PUNISHMENT reflects the fact that human judges operate under the liabilities of ignorance and fallibility. Thus human judges consider the agent's overt performance primarily and the state of the agent's mind secondarily. Since ignorance and fallibility are supposed not to characterize God, some theists have argued that God's role as judge is significantly different from the role played by human judges. *Intentionalism* is any doctrine that claims that moral rightness and wrongness attach primarily to an agent's INTENTIONS and only secondarily to the actions that ensue from those intentions. *Theistic intentionalism* adds the claim that an intention is right if and only if it conforms to God's will. (The Stoics and Kant were thus intentionalists but not theistic intentionalists.) Building on a tradition that went back at least to Saint AUGUSTINE (354–430), Peter ABELARD (1079–1142) expounded an extreme version of theistic intentionalism. According to Abelard, rightness and wrongness apply exclusively to intentions; actions and consequences are irrelevant to judgments of rightness or wrongness. Moreover, the moral wrongness of a sinful intention consists entirely of its expressing contempt of God. Human judges properly punish overt behavior even though the real wrongdoing is interior and ultimately punishable by God: this is no more unjust than a case in which following impeccable judicial procedure causes a judge to impose a sanction on a person whom the judge knows to be innocent. Abelard's intentionalism has not won many converts, but it does raise in a provocative way the question of how a theist might justify human systems of reward and punishment.

See also: ABELARD; AUGUSTINE; CHRISTIAN ETHICS; DESCARTES; DUNS SCOTUS; EVIL; FREE WILL; FREEDOM AND DETERMINISM; GOOD, THEORIES OF THE; INTENTIONS; ISLAMIC ETHICS; JEWISH ETHICS; PALEY; PLATO; PLOTINUS; RELIGION; RIGHT, CONCEPTS OF; THEISM; THEOLOGICAL ETHICS; THOMAS AQUINAS; VOLUNTARISM; WILLIAM OF OCKHAM.

Bibliography

Abelard, Peter. *Ethics.* Defends extreme theistic intentionalism.

Adams, Robert Merrihew. *The Virtue of Faith.* New York: Oxford University Press, 1987. Contains essays on God's creating the best possible world, voluntarism, and moral arguments for God's existence.

———. *Finite and Infinite Goods.* New York: Oxford University Press, 1999. Extends Adams's thinking about the foundations and implications of a theistic ethical theory.

Descartes, René. *Reply to the Sixth Set of Objections to the Meditations.* 1642? Defends voluntarism with respect to moral principles and necessary truths.

Helm, Paul, ed. *Divine Commands and Morality.* New York: Oxford University Press, 1981. Contains several contemporary discussions of voluntarism and rationalism.

Idziak, Janine Marie, ed. *Divine Command Morality: Historical and Contemporary Readings.* New York: Edwin Mellen, 1979. Comprehensive selections include relevant material from Plato's *Euthyphro,* Duns Scotus, William of Ockham, and Paley.

Kant, Immanuel. *Religion Within the Limits of Reason Alone.* 1793. Preface to the 1st ed. contains Kant's last statement of a moral argument for God's existence.

Leibniz, Gottfried Wilhelm. *Theodicy.* 1710. Defends rationalism and the claim that this is the best of all possible worlds.

Morris, Thomas V. *Anselmian Explorations.* Notre Dame, Ind.: University of Notre Dame Press, 1987. Contains essays on whether God has duties and on the nature of God's goodness.

Plantinga, Alvin. "On Ockham's Way Out." *Faith and Philosophy* 3 (1986): 235–69. Discussion of God's foreknowledge and human freedom.

Quinn, Philip L. *Divine Commands and Moral Requirements.* Oxford: Clarendon Press, 1978. A detailed exploration of divine command voluntarism.

Thomas Aquinas. *Summa contra Gentiles.* 1259–1264. On God's goodness and creation.

———. *Summa Theologiae.* 1266–1273. On God's impeccability and whether God could create a better world.

William E. Mann

phronesis

In the *Republic,* PLATO (c. 430–347 B.C.E.) calls the state of possessing the highest form of knowledge *phronesis.* According to Plato, to have *phronesis* is to have the intellectual virtue of the philosopher. It is to have the virtue of the person who has come to grasp the nature of the unchanging Forms. This philosopher's knowledge is both scientific and theoretical, since it constitutes a grasp of the unchanging realities through which all other things become known. Thus, Plato not only calls this knowledge *phronesis,* but he also calls it *sophia* (WISDOM). This knowledge is of use to the philosopher in practical contexts. For example, the philosopher is able to propose just laws for others, owing to his grasp of the Form of Justice. But, for Plato, *phronesis* is not limited to the grasp of the objects of moral knowledge. Rather, since he does not propose a substantive division among types of knowledge, *phronesis* is, for him, the finished state of unqualified intellectual virtue.

ARISTOTLE (384–322 B.C.E.) follows his teacher by using *phronesis* to name an intellectual virtue. However, since Aristotle thinks that there are different types of knowledge, he also thinks that there are different types of intellectual virtue. For him, there are three types of knowledge: theoretical knowledge (knowledge of true and explanatory axiomatic systems), productive knowledge (knowledge connected with bringing things, or states of affairs, into existence), and practical knowledge (knowledge dealing with matters of conduct). For each type of knowledge there is a particular intellectual EXCELLENCE. *Sophia* is the intellectual virtue linked with theoretical knowledge; *techne* (craft) is the state of reasoning truly with respect to production; and *phronesis* is the intellectual virtue specifically linked with moral knowledge. Thus, for Aristotle, *phronesis* is not an unqualified intellectual virtue. *Phronesis* is one among the intellectual virtues and it is the only intellectual virtue that has direct bearing on matters of human conduct.

Aristotle thinks that obedience of PASSION to reason is one of the central elements within moral virtue and, so, he thinks that it is one of the central elements within human HAPPINESS. Aristotle is concerned with obedience to right reason (*orthos logos*) and, for him, right reason in respect to matters of conduct is *phronesis.* Consequently, *phronesis* plays a central role in Aristotle's account of moral virtue. He defines moral virtue as "a state . . . concerned with choice, lying in a mean, *i.e.,* the mean relative to us, this being determined by a rational principle, and by that principle by which the man of practical wisdom [the *phronimos:* the man with *phronesis*] would determine it." (*Nicomachean Ethics* [EN] 1106b36–1107a2) This definition may at first seem perplexing, but Aristotle takes pains to explain the important concepts involved. Thus, scholars are typically in agreement when it comes to what he means by, say, "the mean relative to us" in this definition. However, this is not the case when it comes to what he means by "*phronesis*" (or "*phronimos*"). The issue of how to properly demarcate the nature of *phronesis* is a point of some contention and, thus, the issue of how to thoroughly explicate Aristotle's conception of moral virtue is a point of some contention.

Disagreement over *phronesis* is often due to difficulties involved in harmonizing and elucidating certain of Aristotle's claims regarding the distinctive features of *phronesis* and others regarding the general characteristics of matters concerned with conduct. Among these claims the more important are as follows: (1) we possess moral virtue just in case we possess *phronesis* (EN 1144b30–33); (2) *phronesis* is excellence in deliberation about what is advantageous as a means to the good life in general (EN 1140a25–28); (3) *phronesis* is a true grasp of the end (EN 1142b33); (4) moral virtue ensures the rightness of the end, while *phronesis* ensures the rightness of the means toward the end (EN 1144a7–9); and (5) matters concerned with conduct and questions of what is good for us have no fixity (EN 1104a4–11). Among these, (2) and (4) might be taken to suggest that *phronesis* is simply ratiocinative excellence in working out the means toward a given end. On this view, *phronesis* is a type of cleverness which, when combined with an appropriate grasp of the end, brings us to complete moral virtue. However, this view cannot be correct. For it cannot be reconciled with (1). According to (1), a person can have neither *phronesis* without moral virtue nor moral virtue without *phronesis.* (The latter point is also suggested by Aristotle's original definition of moral virtue.) *Phronesis,* then, cannot be found in isolation from moral virtue. Cleverness, however, can be found in isolation, for the vicious person is also a clever person. Thus, *phronesis* cannot simply be a kind of cleverness. Together, (1), (2), and (4) suggest that *phronesis* has two components. It is excellence in deliberation, but it is also something else.

In (3) we find a candidate second component of *phronesis.* Aristotle's claim suggests that *phronesis* is, in addition to deliberative excellence, a true grasp of the end. This view at first seems difficult to reconcile with (4), since in (4) moral virtue, in contrast to *phronesis,* is said to concern the end. However, there is only a seeming opposition between (3) and (4). Aristotle explains two notions of moral virtue: natural moral virtue and full moral virtue. Natural moral virtue is a condition (possessed from childhood) in which the passions are naturally inclined toward states like COURAGE or TEMPERANCE, but are also lacking the guidance of reason. When the passions come under the guidance of right reason (*i.e., phronesis*), natural moral virtue becomes full moral virtue. Thus, in full moral virtue the passions concern the end, but they do so under the guidance of *phronesis.* In (4), Aristotle emphasizes the role of the passions in full moral virtue and contrasts this with the role of deliberative excellence, but this is consistent with his also thinking that the passions concern the end under the guidance of *phronesis. Phronesis,* then, is both excellence in deliberation and a true grasp of the end. Further, this grasp of the end is provided by reason, for otherwise the passions would be neither guided by reason nor obedient to reason.

One view about the second rational component of *phronesis* is that it is a grasp of the end which is determined through deliberation. This view at first seems to clash with Aristotle's claim that deliberation is never about ends, but always about means, *i.e.,* always about what is toward the end (*ta pros to telos*). (EN 1112b13–15) However, it is argued that the end, our conception of human happiness, is constituted by a number of parts and that each of these parts is in a limited sense a means toward the end. For, while constituent parts of an end are not external causal conditions for that end, the realization of some one constituent part is itself a partial realization of the end. Thus, it is thought that we can determine the end by deliberating about the value of some one part of the (candidate) end in light of some other part(s) of the (candidate) end and, so, the end can be determined through deliberation. However, this view fails to provide a complete account of the

rational determination of the end. It requires that, during any episode of deliberation about the end, some part of the end be taken as fixed in respect to some other part(s) of the end. So, it requires that some specification of the end be in place prior to any given deliberation about the end. This view fails to provide a complete account of how reason can determine the end. At best it provides an account of how a preexisting grasp of the end might be further refined.

Another view about the second rational component of *phronesis* is that it is an intuitive grasp of the end. According to this view, the *phronimos* need not have a discursive justification for his conception of the end, but only a special sort of mental vision of the end. This view seems to fit with Aristotle's use of perceptual language in describing *phronesis.* Aristotle does claim that *phronesis* is an "eye" of the soul. (EN 1144a30) However, this view is largely dependent upon a suspect interpretation of Aristotle's account of how we acquire knowledge of scientific principles. Recent scholarship on his *Posterior Analytics* suggests that, for Aristotle, our grasp of scientific principles is discursively justified. This, in turn, suggests that, for Aristotle, *phronesis* does not involve an intuitive grasp of the end. If the second component of *phronesis* is a rational grasp of the end, it must involve discursive justification.

Aristotle describes *phronesis* as involving a grasp of generalities (*kathalou*). (EN 1141b15) This has been taken to suggest that the *phronimos* has an understanding of true and explanatory universals. But, it has also been taken to suggest that he has an understanding of imprecise generalities. On the first view, the "grand end" view, the *phronimos* looks to a set of universal rules, as ends, in his deliberations. On the second view, the "empiric" view, he employs a set of rules of thumb. The "grand end" view is difficult to reconcile with Aristotle's division among types of knowledge. It suggests that ethics is in some way a science and, so, jeopardizes Aristotle's own distinction between *sophia* and *phronesis.* This view is also difficult to reconcile with (5). The "grand end" view suggests a level of fixity and precision in ethics that far exceeds Aristotle's explicit expectations. The "empiric" view is in harmony both with Aristotle's division among types of knowledge and with his claim that questions of what is good for us have no fixity. Further, this view makes sense of Aristotle's claim that *phronesis* requires experience, since generalities and rules of thumb are typically the product of our lived experiences.

Phronesis is, for Aristotle, the intellectual virtue which has direct bearing on matters of human conduct. It requires both excellence in deliberation and a rational grasp of the end. Further (according to the most plausible interpretation), this grasp of the end is an understanding of imprecise generalities and rules of thumb.

See also: ARISTOTLE; DELIBERATION AND CHOICE; EMOTION; *EUDAIMONIA*, -ISM; EXCELLENCE; MORAL PERCEPTION; MORAL REASONING; PASSION; PLATO; PRACTICAL REASON[ING]; PRACTICAL WISDOM; RATIONAL CHOICE; RATIONALITY VS. REASONABLENESS; THEORY AND PRACTICE; VIRTUE ETHICS; VIRTUES; WISDOM.

Bibliography

Aristotle. *Nicomachean Ethics.* Translated by W. D. Ross; revised by J. O. Urmson. In *The Complete Works of Aristotle,* edited by Jonathan Barnes, vol. 2. Princeton: Princeton University Press, 1985.

———. *Nicomachean Ethics: Book Six, With Essays, Notes, and Translation by L. H. G. Greenwood.* Cambridge: Cambridge University Press, 1909; reprinted, New York: Arno Press, 1973. Greenwood introduces the notion that means may be constituents of the end.

Bolton, Robert. "Phronesis: Aristotle's Conception of Moral Virtue." Unpublished. Bolton presents a decisive argument in support of the "empiric" view.

Broadie, Sarah. *Ethics with Aristotle.* New York: Oxford University Press, 1991. In this excellent work, which deals with many of the major themes in the EN, Broadie is critical of the "grand end" view.

Cooper, John. *Reason and Human Good in Aristotle.* Cambridge: Harvard University Press, 1975. The first chapter of this book deals with deliberation and its role in *phronesis.*

Devereux, Daniel T. "Particular and Universal in Aristotle's Conception of Practical Knowledge." *Review of Metaphysics* 39 (1986): 483–504. Devereux offers a critical discussion of part of Cooper's treatment of deliberation together with a defense of the "empiric" view.

Kraut, Richard. "In Defense of the Grand End." *Ethics* 103 (1993): 361–74. A critical treatment of Broadie's discussion of the "grand end" view.

Lennox, James G. "Aristotle on the Biological Roots of Virtue: The Natural History of Natural Virtue." In *Biology and the Foundations of Ethics,* edited by Jane Maienschein and Michael Ruse, pp. 10–31. Cambridge: Cambridge University Press, 1999. A discussion of integration of emotion and reason in *phronesis.*

Wiggins, David. "Deliberation and Practical Reason." In *Essays on Aristotle's Ethics,* edited by Amélie Rorty, 221–40. Berkeley: University of California Press, 1980. Wiggins defends the notion that means may be constituents of the end.

Woods, Michael. "Intuition and Perception in Aristotle's Ethics." *Oxford Studies in Ancient Philosophy* 4 (1986): 145–66. A discussion of the use of perceptual language in Aristotle's treatment of *phronesis.*

John E. Sisko

plagiarism

Plagiarism is defined as appropriating someone else's words or ideas without acknowledgment. To understand plagiarism we must consider two questions: (1) How is plagiarism like or unlike theft? (2) Why is plagiarism considered wrong; why *should* we acknowledge the originator of an idea?

Is Plagiarism Like Theft?

First, plagiarism can easily be distinguished from piracy. Piracy is the sale of attributed but unauthorized copies of a work, an act depriving the author of profit but not credit. Depriving authors of profit that is rightfully theirs is theft, but here we focus on credit rather than profit. Depriving authors of credit might also be a form of theft. We often think that ideas and their expression belong to the author as if they were private PROPERTY, the author's intellectual property. On this view, plagiarists steal the work of others, taking for themselves the credit of ownership and thereby depriving the original authors of this benefit. If intellectual property is like physical property, the analogy helps explain subtler forms of plagiarism. For example, most people know that taking the exact wording of another person without attribution is plagiarism, but believe that paraphrasing the original without attribution is acceptable. Yet taking someone else's idea and changing the wording could be compared to stealing a car and changing its color.

However, literary works that are stolen differ in important ways from physical objects that are the targets of ordinary theft. Ideas are less tangible and identifiable than physical objects. Objects that are stolen remain stolen even if they are taken apart and recombined. Not so with ideas. Building new ideas from old ideas, using existing components and combining them in new ways might be creativity, not plagiarism. It is often difficult to determine what counts as a new idea and what requires acknowledgment as a variation on an old idea. CONVENTIONS for giving credit vary from field to field. For example, much has been written about ill-fated love or problems with parent-child relations without giving credit to Shakespeare or Aeschylus. In literature the *form* of the expression is more important than the basic plot idea. In fact some critics claim that there are only a small number of basic plots in all of literature. To count as plagiarism in literature a description must steal the form of the original, not just the structure. However, in the sciences, reporting the research results of another without attribution is plagiarism, even if the words and style of the report are very different. In order to know what should be credited to others, one has to know the practices of that field. And even then it may not be clear. In areas such as computer programming and music composition, what counts as plagiarism is still being argued in the courts.

Unlike physical objects that belong to someone else, we are expected to pick up the ideas of others and take them with us. We remember ideas without remembering where they came from because recalling the source of an idea is often more difficult than recalling the idea itself. Therefore it is possible to commit plagiarism without realizing that one is doing so. Learning to avoid plagiarism requires careful training in a system of conventions particular to a field, unlike learning to avoid theft. This may explain why several great thinkers of the past have recently been accused of plagiarism. Under today's conventions of attribution, what they did constitutes plagiarism. But the conventions of today are not the same as in the past when writers usually cited another person's work only to invoke AUTHORITY.

Plagiarism differs from theft in a more profound way. Taking an object that has been abandoned or given away is not considered stealing. But copying the ideas of an anonymous author, or claiming credit for an idea given to you by a friend who does not wish to claim authorship, is considered plagiarism.

If words and ideas were merely property, and plagiarism merely a form of theft, then there would be nothing wrong with buying the rights to authorship from another, as in the case of commercial term-paper services. The original authors sell their claim to authorship for money. The plagiarist who uses these services is not *stealing* the credit from another person because the original author does not want the credit. But credit for authorship is not something that can be sold or given away. Credit for authorship is so undetachable that even the reverse of stealing, falsely attributing one's own work to another, is wrong; it constitutes FORGERY.

In the realm of ideas and their expression, one is evaluated not for owning the rights to a work but for having been its originator. Ideas and forms of expression are, in this sense, closer to moral actions than to property. The credit due the originator cannot be transferred to someone else, even if both parties agree to the transfer. As with a moral action, RESPONSIBILITY, whether creditworthy or blameworthy, inheres in the agent.

Why Attribute at All?

There are commonly accepted violations of the rule that works must be attributed to their true authors. Books "by" celebrities are routinely ghostwritten. Highly successful authors use pseudonyms. Books written by committees are published under a famous author's name. Politicians give speeches without crediting their speechwriters. Congressional bills bear the names of legislators who introduce them, not the assistants who write them. Researchers routinely use the assistance of librarians without acknowledgment. People tell jokes without crediting the originators.

Perhaps these failures to give credit are wrong. Some argue that credit should always be given to the originator; that proper attribution is essential to evaluate the contributions of individuals and to reward creativity. Certainly when evaluation is focal, it is wrong to take credit for the work of others. And certainly it is important to identify and reward people who do original work in order to encourage progress.

On the other hand, it is possible that emphasis on evaluation and credit discourages collaboration and fosters destructive COMPETITION and CHEATING. When the result is more important than the process, collaboration and teamwork might be encouraged even at the cost of sacrificing accurate attribution of credit. Under these conditions the reprehensibility of plagiarism might diminish.

See also: ACADEMIC ETHICS; CHEATING; COMPETITION; COMPUTERS; DECEIT; EXPLOITATION; FORGERY; LIBRARY AND INFORMATION PROFESSIONS; LITERATURE AND ETHICS; MERIT AND DESERT; PROPERTY; RIGHT HOLDERS; RIGHTS.

Bibliography

ACI Writing Assistance Center [Daniel K. Berman]. *ACI Net Guide to Termpapers.* http://members.aol.com/aciplus/netguide.htm. (Address valid July, 1999.) An Internet collection of sources for college papers. It comes with the warning "Anything that a student can pull off the Net can be just as easily located by the student's instructors." Another source for student papers (http://www.schoolsucks.com) carries the warning: No Document May Be Reprinted Without Proper Attribution To Our Company As the Original Source.

Broad, W., and N. Wade. *Betrayers of the Truth.* New York: Simon and Schuster, 1983. About research fraud, including plagiarism, by famous scientists.

Brogan, K., and J. Brogan. "Yet Another Ethical Problem in Technical Writing." ERIC Document No. 229782, October, 1988. Plagiarism in technical writing is increasing.

Canuteson, J. "We Can Help Eliminate Plagiarism by Teaching Students What It Is." *Chronicle of Higher Education*, March 16, 1983: 30.

Duguid, Brian, producer. "The Acceptable Face of Plagiarism." *EST,* issue four (Summer 1992). http://www.hyperreal.org/intersection/zines/est/articles/plagiari.html. (Address valid October, 1999.) Interview with John Oswald; discussion of a defense of plagiarism in music.

Goodstein, David. "Conduct and Misconduct in Science." In *The Flight from Science and Reason,* edited by Paul R. Gross, Norman Levitt, and Martin W. Lewis, 31–38. Annals of the New York Academy of Sciences, 1996. Discussion about what kinds of misconduct, including plagiarism, harm the goals of science.

Kelman, H., and C. Hovland. "Reinstatement of the Communicator in Delayed Measurement of Opinion Change." *Journal of Abnormal and Social Psychology.* 48 (1953): 327–35. People remember the idea but not the source.

LaFollette, Marcel C. *Stealing into Print: Fraud, Plagiarism, and Misconduct in Scientific Publishing.* Berkeley: University of California Press, 1992.

Moulton, Janice, and George Robinson. "Cheating for Truth and Glory: The Problem of Research Fraud." *Twenty Questions: An Introduction to Philosophy,* edited by L. Bowie, M. Michaels, and R. Solomon, 108–16. New York: Harcourt, Brace, Jovanovich, 1988. The methodology of a science changes and with it the idea of what is improper practice.

Robinson, George, and Janice Moulton. *Ethical Problems in Higher Education.* New York: Prentice Hall, 1985. Chapter 4 discusses plagiarism and other research frauds.

Shaw, P. "Plagiary." *American Scholar* Summer, 1982: 325–37. Society should enforce sanctions against plagiarism.

Shea, J. "When Borrowing Becomes Burglary." *Currents* 13:1 (January 1987): 38–42. It is sometimes difficult to distinguish inspiration from theft.

Simon, J. F. "Software Owner Wins 'Look and Feel' Victory." *The Boston Globe,* March 14, 1989: 43; 50. Regardless of the code used, it is plagiarism to produce software that looks and feels the same to the customer.

Skom, E. "Plagiarism: Quite a Rather Bad Little Crime." *American Association of Higher Education Bulletin*, October 1986: 3–7. Plagiarism is not understood by many; teachers often do not acknowledge their own sources.

Stillinger, Jack. *Multiple Authorship and the Myth of Solitary Genius.* New York: Oxford University Press, 1991.

For a list of web sites on this topic, search for "plagiarism" using http://www.google.com or another comparable search engine.

Janice Moulton
George Robinson

Plato (c. 430–347 B.C.E.)

Plato was born (variant birth date, 428 B.C.E.) during the early years of the Peloponnesian War (431–404) and was a young adult by the final years of the war, followed by the oligarchic regime of the Thirty (404–403) and the trial and death of Socrates in 399. He founded a philosophical school, the Academy, in Athens, and remained as its head until his death. Much of the evidence on Plato's life is uncertain; the ostensibly autobiographical *Seventh Letter* is probably spurious.

Plato and Socrates

This article is concerned with Plato's middle and late dialogues. In most of these 'Socrates' remains the protagonist, but they are usually thought to expound Plato's own views (or criticisms of them), as opposed to those of the historical SOCRATES (c. 470–399 B.C.E.). Probably Plato retains the character 'Socrates' because he thinks the dialogues defend the central convictions of the historical Socrates; but he believes that a proper defense of these convictions requires considerable revision of them. (In the rest of this article I will use 'Socrates' for the Socrates of the early dialogues, not for the protagonist in the middle and late dialogues.) Moreover, the middle and late dialogues have a much wider philosophical range than we find in the earlier—largely ethical—dialogues. Plato introduces his belief that we are immortal, immaterial souls, that knowledge is the result of recollection of pre-natal knowledge, that the primary objects of knowledge are separated Forms, and that reason must be preferred over the senses as a source of knowledge. These doctrines are often relevant to ethical questions; and Plato's discussions of ethics are often connected to questions in political theory, AESTHETICS, cosmology, metaphysics, epistemology, and theology. This article will not cover all of Plato's views on ethics. Instead it will describe his attitude to Socrates' ethical outlook, and his attempted solutions to Socratic problems. The main focus will be on the *Republic,* with some references to other dialogues.

The main issues on which Plato rejects or revises the Socratic position are these:

1. Socrates believes that virtue is sufficient for HAPPINESS, and that therefore the virtuous person can suffer no genuine harm. Plato believes only a comparative thesis—that the virtuous person is in all circumstances happier than anyone else.
2. Plato explicitly claims, as Socrates does not, that virtue is an intrinsic and noninstrumental good, to be chosen for its own sake, and not simply as an instrumental means to happiness.
3. Plato rejects the Socratic denial of incontinence. He therefore believes that virtue consists of more than knowledge. Since different nonrational desires correspond to different VIRTUES, he rejects the Socratic doctrine of the unity of virtue.
4. Since Plato rejects the Socratic conceptions of virtue and happiness, the defense of justice offered in the *Republic* differs on some central points from the one offered in the *Gorgias.* In particular, Plato develops a theory of LOVE that is intended to explain why a rational concern for one's own good requires concern for the good of others.
5. In *Republic* ix and the *Philebus,* Plato considerably develops and elaborates the re-

flections on PLEASURE and goodness found in the *Protagoras* and the *Gorgias.* He rejects both HEDONISM and the more extreme forms of anti-hedonism.
6. In the *Phaedo,* Plato suggests that the proper focus of ethical concern is the immortal soul, as opposed to the body with its nonrational desires and physical NEEDS.

Virtue and Happiness

In *Republic* i, Plato puts forward a Socratic argument to show that justice is preferable to injustice because justice is sufficient for happiness (352d–354c). In *Republic* ii–ix, however, he argues only for the comparative thesis. He modifies the Socratic position on two related points:

1. He now sets out to prove that justice is a good to be chosen in itself, and for its own sake, apart from its consequences (367b–d). Plato rejects any defense of justice that appeals solely to its good consequences, and condemns the outlook of people who do just actions purely for their consequences as a mere 'facade' of virtue (*Republic* 365c, *Phaedo* 69b), not genuine virtue at all. This claim has no explicit parallel in the Socratic dialogues. In accepting it for justice, Plato commits himself to a general claim about virtue that both disallows some defenses of it and suggests the possibility of other defenses.
2. Since he focuses only on justice taken by itself, apart from its consequences, he defends only the comparative thesis. (At 611e–614a, he reintroduces the consequences that were excluded in Books ii–ix.) He claims that justice, taken by itself and irrespective of its consequences, makes the just person better off than everyone else in all circumstances.

In defending the comparative thesis rather than the Socratic thesis, Plato concedes that there may be aspects of happiness that the just person lacks. Only a later dialogue, the *Philebus,* gives a clear reason for this concession. There Plato argues that the good (*i.e.,* happiness) cannot be identified either with pleasure alone or with intelligence alone, because each of these lacks an essential feature of the good. The good, he insists, must be 'complete' and 'sufficient,' and must need nothing added to it (*Philebus* 20d–21a; cf. *Republic* 505de). Neither pleasure alone nor intelligence alone meets this condition; for it is rational to prefer the mixed life of pleasure plus intelligence over the unmixed life consisting of one of these goods without the other. If this principle is applied to *Republic* ii, it explains Plato's preference for the comparative thesis over the Socratic thesis. For if it is rational to prefer justice plus its usual good consequences over justice without the consequences, then justice without the good consequences is incomplete.

Though Plato does not endorse the Socratic view that virtue is sufficient for happiness, he still accepts EUDAIMONISM. For he assumes that a rational justification of a virtue must show that it promotes the agent's happiness. He does not consider the possibility that we might be justified in benefitting others for reasons that do not refer to our own benefit. If, then, Plato is to prove that justice promotes our happiness by being a noninstrumental good, he needs to show that justice is a component of, not a mere instrumental means to, happiness.

Reason and Desire

In the *Protagoras* Socrates argues that no one who knows or believes that *x* is better than *y* will choose *y;* that is why all ostensible cases of incontinent choice of *y* simply display the mistaken belief that *y* is better than *x*. Plato rejects this connection between evaluative belief and choice. He argues that Socrates cannot account for the persistence of desires (*e.g.,* to drink) even in the face of the belief that it is better not to satisfy them (*e.g.,* the belief that it would be unhealthy or dangerous to take this drink; *Republic* 438a–439d). In these cases Plato argues that the strength of a desire does not correspond to our evaluation of what is desired. Hence we must admit that nonrational desires, not wholly responsive to beliefs about the good, move us to action.

The different relations of desires to beliefs about the good are the basis of Plato's division of the soul into three 'parts' or 'kinds' (435b–441e). This division seems to be primarily a division among desires, supported by examples of different kinds of psychic conflict. Plato recognizes (a) the rational part, whose rational desires are formed by deliberation about the good of the whole soul (441c, 442b); (b) the appetitive part, whose desires (*e.g.,* hunger, thirst, sexual desire) do not depend on considerations about what is good or bad (439d); (c) the 'spirited' or 'emotional' part, whose desires and emotions (*e.g.,* ANGER, PRIDE, shame, love of HONOR) depend on some beliefs about what is good or bad, but not on deliberation about what is best overall for the whole soul (439e–441c).

In recognizing these three types of desires, Plato rejects the Socratic denial of incontinence. Once we recognize that not all desires are rational desires, we need not find it so difficult to believe that we can act against our belief about what is best overall.

Noncognitive Aspects of Virtue

Once he recognizes nonrational desires, Plato must fit them into his account of virtue, and must reject the Socratic view that a virtue is a purely cognitive state. He describes the four 'cardinal' virtues (WISDOM, bravery, TEMPERANCE, and justice; 427e) from two points of view:

1. They are virtues of a state (*polis*), and so they are fully realized in the ideal state sketched in the *Republic*. Plato identifies them with the right functions and structure of the three classes in the ideal state.
2. They are virtues in an individual person, and Plato identifies them with the right functions and structure of the three parts in an individual soul.

His actual argument relies on the assumption that the three parts of the soul are sufficiently analogous to the three parts of the state. But both the division of the soul and the account of the virtues are intelligible and defensible apart from this political analogy.

The four virtues together constitute the best order of the tripartite soul, and each virtue secures a particular aspect of that order. Bravery involves endurance, the good condition of the spirited part that prevents us from being swayed by unreasonable fears (429a–430c). Temperance involves orderliness in the appetitive part, so that we have restrained and orderly appetites (430d–432a). Wisdom requires the appropriate knowledge in the rational part, supported by properly trained desires in the other two parts (428a–429a). Justice requires each part to do its own work (441d–442b).

In treating endurance as an element of bravery, and orderliness as an element of temperance, Plato restores to these virtues the noncognitive components eliminated in the Socratic treatment. (See *Laches* 192b–e, 194cd, *Charmides* 159b, where the noncognitive components are mentioned, but then drop out of the argument. But *cf. Gorgias* 507ab.) This non-Socratic conception of the virtues influences Plato's view of moral training. Elementary MORAL EDUCATION of the sort described in *Republic* ii–iii is intended to fix the right noncognitive responses in people so that they do not suffer the sort of conflict that Plato, unlike Socrates, takes to be psychologically possible and dangerous. Pleasures and pains are to be formed so that we go in the direction that reason will approve when it comes along; and hence when we acquire correct rational judgment we will welcome and accept what it says (401e–402a).

Knowledge, Belief, and Virtue

Plato follows Socrates in insisting that knowledge is necessary for virtue. The Socratic dialogues recognize a distinction between knowledge and true belief (*Gorgias* 445de, 465a, 508e–509a), and Socrates identifies virtue with knowledge rather than simply with true belief; but he does not explain why virtue should require more than true belief. In the *Meno,* however, Plato draws a more explicit distinction between knowledge and true belief (*Meno* 97e–98a), focusing on two aspects of knowledge:

1. Unlike true belief, it is stable and does not easily wander away.
2. It is secured by 'reasoning about the explanation.'

In *Republic* iv, Plato suggests that some people—and especially the nonruling classes in the ideal state—can satisfy the first aspect to some degree without satisfying the second. This is because their moral education gives them stable correct belief, not disturbed by wayward nonrational desires.

Still, the second aspect is important if we are to choose virtue for itself, as Plato demands. If well-educated people without knowledge believe that an action is just, their emotional part responds without

any further inducement. To choose justice for itself, however, we must choose it under the description that makes it what it is—for the property that makes it justice. Without knowledge of what it is, we cannot choose just actions because they have their essential property as just actions. Tenacious right belief without knowledge does not imply the choice of justice for itself.

Plato, then, has good reason for claiming (442c) that virtue requires knowledge—not just true belief—in the rational part of the soul.

The Reciprocity of the Virtues

Since Plato connects the different virtues with different features of the rational and nonrational parts in a well-ordered soul, he has lost one of Socrates' reasons for accepting the unity of the virtues. Socrates believes that each virtue is identical to the very same knowledge of good and EVIL, and hence that all the virtues are really just one virtue. Plato, by contrast, identifies bravery with a particular relation between the spirited and the rational parts, but identifies temperance with a relation between the rational and the appetitive parts. The virtues are distinct conditions, and a correct account of what bravery is would not say what temperance is. Distinct kinds of training are needed for each virtue, and distinct actions are expected from the agent who has each. (The distinctions are emphasized still more strongly at *Statesman* 306a–308b.)

Still, Plato seems to agree with Socrates in accepting the reciprocity of the virtues, believing that you have any one of the virtues if and only if you have them all (cf. *Protagoras* 329e). His reasons emerge from his account of the fourth cardinal virtue, psychic justice ('p-justice').

P-justice, unlike the other virtues, is not concerned primarily with some particular relation between the rational part and a nonrational part. It is the right relation between all the parts, in which each does its own work under the guidance of the wisdom in the rational part (441d–442b). P-justice includes more than mere continence (control by the rational part), and more than mere agreement (acceptance of the rational part's control by the nonrational parts). It requires the rational part to deliberate about the good of the whole soul and each part, and the other parts to agree in accepting the results of this deliberation.

This description of p-justice requires the reciprocity of the virtues. Perhaps we could manage brave or temperate actions without p-justice (if, for example, we did these actions out of fear of PUNISHMENT). But we could not want to do brave or temperate actions for the right reason unless the parts of our soul were properly ordered; and for this proper order we need p-justice. Conversely, if we have p-justice and the proper order in the parts of our soul, nothing more is needed for the other virtues. Plato's conception of p-justice marks the distinction that ARISTOTLE (384–322 B.C.E.) marks in distinguishing virtuous action from the virtuous state of CHARACTER.

The Defense of Justice

The cardinal virtues are different aspects of a well-ordered soul. The true judgments in the rational part make us wise, and the subordination of nonrational to rational desires makes us temperate and brave. The right relation of the parts doing their proper work constitutes p-justice. These virtues, then, clearly belong to the rationally prudent person.

Plato believes that with this conception of p-justice he can prove that justice is always preferable to injustice. He argues that without p-justice we are not reliably guided by rational desires; we cannot act on deliberation about our overall interest, but must simply be victims of our nonrational desires. If we value rational PRUDENCE, then, in his view, we must agree that we are better off with p-justice than we would be without it (443c–445b). P-justice expresses our nature as rational agents; and if we believe that happiness requires the fulfillment of our nature (cf. 352d–353e with 443c–444b), then we must agree that p-justice is necessary for our happiness.

But is this defense of p-justice really a defense of justice—the virtue that was challenged in *Republic* i–ii? When the interlocutors in Books i–ii doubted whether justice is good for the just person, they relied on an intuitive and plausible conception of justice and just action, assuming that the just person obeys laws, avoids CHEATING, and does not seek unfair advantages (343de, 349bc, 358e–359b, 362bc); in short, they assumed that justice is an other-directed virtue, and supposed for that reason that justice benefits others and is harmful to just people themselves (343c, 367c). This conception of justice—fairly close to our conception of morality—is a plausible conception of the ordinary sort of justice ('o-justice'); and the question whether o-justice benefits the o-just person seems to be a clear and legitimate question. But does Plato answer this question? He argues that p-justice benefits the p-just person; but could we not have p-justice without o-justice? It seems conceivable that rationally prudent people might decide sometimes in their own interest to disregard the INTERESTS of others.

Some of the moral implications of Plato's own METAPHYSICS AND EPISTEMOLOGY actually seem to aggravate this difficulty. For he believes that the philosophers who come to know about the Forms—the basic objects of knowledge—will find the contemplation of them so completely absorbing and satisfying that they will want to devote themselves entirely to it (519c). Since the philosophers are dominated by the rational part of the soul, they seem to have p-justice; but since their contemplative outlook seems to encourage them to shirk obligations to other people, why should they not be o-unjust?

Plato answers this challenge briefly. He offers some 'commonplace' indications of the o-justice of the p-just person, suggesting that obviously such a person will avoid some of the most flagrantly o-unjust actions (442d–443b); p-just people refrain from these o-unjust actions because of the p-justice in their soul. Many o-unjust actions are the product of immoderate and uncontrolled EMOTION or appetite; and since p-just people have moderate and controlled emotions and appetites, they will see no reason to commit these o-unjust actions.

This defense, however, hardly shows that p-just people will systematically avoid o-unjust actions, still less that they will avoid them out of respect for other people's good, or that their being p-just will really benefit others. To defend p-justice on these points, Plato needs to explain why rational prudence requires o-just actions.

A Further Defense of Justice

Plato devotes some of *Republic* viii–ix to a fuller description of different types of p-injustice (445c–449a); and in describing this more fully he explains by contrast what is necessary for p-justice, and helps to show why it is at any rate not obviously compatible with o-injustice. (See *e.g.,* 550ab, 553a–c, 558c–561d, 571a–578c.) He describes several 'deviant' people, with souls parallel in structure to the different constitutions (timocratic, oligarchic, etc.) that deviate from the ideal state. These deviant people might appear to have p-justice, insofar as they pursue their rational plans and act on their rational desires. If this is all it takes to be p-just, then Plato cannot reasonably claim that p-justice requires concern for the good of others.

The deviant people, however, are meant to show that p-justice requires more than the steady pursuit of our rational plans. It requires us to form our plans not simply by accepting the desires of the nonrational parts of the soul and planning for their satisfaction, but by deliberation about what is good for the whole soul and for each part. Such deliberation requires more than mere acceptance of the desires of the nonrational parts. The deviant people all plan, to different degrees, to fulfil their overall aims; but their aims are determined by one or more of their nonrational desires, and so they are prone to o-injustice as a means to satisfaction of these desires. (This is most spectacularly true of the tyrannical person.) P-just people, by contrast, do not simply accept their nonrational desires as ultimate ends; they also deliberate rationally about their ultimate ends, and act on the results of this deliberation. But what is required for correct deliberation about ultimate ends? Plato does not answer this question fully in *Republic* viii–ix. But his theory of love (*erôs*), developed in the *Symposium* and the *Phaedrus,* suggests answers. (*Republic* 490ab shows that the theory of love is relevant.)

The Theory of Love

Plato argues that if we have rational concern for ourselves, and understand the nature of this concern, we will see that we also have reason to be concerned for other people. His argument rests on an analysis of self-concern as a desire for 'propagation' (or 'reproduction', *Symposium* 206b–207c). 'Propagation' normally implies bringing a new person into existence; but Plato argues that the difference between our ordinary concern for our own future and a desire to produce another person is less sharp than it might appear. Given the extent of change in a single person through a lifetime, concern for ourselves is really concern for 'intra-personal propagation'—the production of future selves appropriately related to our present selves. For we change in body and soul; our characters, personalities, memories, aims and so on all change, and we keep ourselves in existence in so far as the 'old' self successfully plans for a 'new' self with the right kind of connection between the old traits, memories etc.—especially the ones that we value—and the new (207c–208b).

If, however, rational self-concern essentially involves this concern for intra-personal propagation, it turns out to justify more than concern for myself. For the valuable aspect of self-concern is propagation of my valuable traits; and I can fulfil this valuable aspect of self-concern by propagating these same traits in another person. Hence the value of intra-personal propagation gives us a reason to be concerned about other people as well as ourselves (208c–212a; *Phaedrus* 250e–253c).

Plato's account of love has three important results:

1. It explains love between particular people as a case of interpersonal propagation (*Symposium* 209a–e, *Phaedrus* 253c–256d). A is attracted to B because B already seems beautiful and fine (*kalos*)—a suitable person for receiving the sort of character and personality in which A seeks to propagate himself. The proper process of education causes A to change his mind about the sorts of features that he wants to propagate himself; as he examines different sorts of examples of beauty (*i.e.,* of what is fine and admirable), he eventually comes to see the Form of beauty itself, and so comes to understand the features that all these genuinely admirable things have in common (210a–211c).

2. This account of love between persons indicates one role of Plato's theory of Forms in his moral theory. Philosophers become aware of the Forms of justice and beauty, and ultimately of the Form of the good (*Republic* 504e–506b), which explains the goodness of the other Forms and of all other good things. Their awareness of the Forms produces the desire to reproduce them in their own lives and in other people's (500a–c). This is the motive underlying the philosopher rulers' desire to rule in the ideal state. Despite the disagreeable

aspects of ruling (519b–521b, 540a–c), and their absorption in the contemplation of the Forms, they will see that ruling is necessary and—everything considered—desirable, because they want to propagate their conception of the Forms in other people.

3. Plato's conception of love shows why we have reason to be concerned about other people who reproduce the features we value in ourselves. P-just people, therefore, will be concerned about the interests of the other people whom they regard as suitable people to reproduce their own p-justice. Our concern for our future selves is noninstrumental (we are not concerned about the reproduction of these valuable traits simply for the sake of some other future person to whose interests the interests of our future selves are purely instrumental); hence our concern for the other person who reproduces these valuable traits is also noninstrumental. Moreover, since p-justice is more beneficial than anything else for a p-just person, if A wants to reproduce A's p-justice in B, then A will be doing the best that can be done for B's interest. Since p-just people have this noninstrumental concern for others, they can reasonably claim to be o-just. Hence Plato can claim that his defense of p-justice is also a defense of o-justice.

Pleasure and Happiness

In saying that just people are happier than anyone else, Plato also claims that they have the most pleasure. He does not, however, return to the hedonism of the *Protagoras*. He argues that the quantity of pleasure in A's life depends on the value of the states and activities that A enjoys, and that the enjoyment is not what by itself makes them valuable. The rational part of the soul has its own characteristic pleasures (580de), and Plato argues that these are superior to the pleasures of the other two parts because they are 'true' as opposed to 'false' pleasures; other pleasures are infected by the nature of their objects, or by false beliefs about them, in ways that disqualify such pleasures from being the main constituents of happiness (583c–586c).

This analysis of pleasure is developed more fully in the *Philebus*. The main points in the obscure and complex discussion of pleasures are these:

1. Plato argues from the completeness of the good against a life consisting of pleasure without intelligence. He argues that such a life would be the life of some primitive animal, not of a human being (21c). He assumes that our life is not worthwhile for us as rational agents, unless it includes, as an aspect of its intrinsic value, the sorts of rational activity that are involved in our conception of ourselves as rational agents lasting from one time to another and making plans for our future.

2. Intelligence is needed to select the valuable pleasures and to avoid the others (12c–13d, 28c–31a). Plato believes that differences in the object and cause of our pleasure affect the value of the pleasure itself. Those who take pleasure in the wrong things make themselves worse off precisely insofar as they enjoy such things, not because of some further effects. Judgments of value enter, not simply into considering the consequences of the pleasures, but in the estimate of the value of the pleasures themselves.

3. Plato criticizes several types of pleasures for their falsity, claiming that they depend on beliefs whose falsity reduces the value of the pleasures (32b–50e). In some cases I take pleasure in *x* by anticipation, when in fact *x* will not happen (32b–40e). In other cases my error is more complex; if, for instance, I think there is nothing more to pleasure than relief from pain, then I will think I have achieved pleasure when I have really achieved something different (42c–44a). The long discussion of false pleasures suggests that a life devoted to pleasure, without the evaluative guidance of intelligence, must include elements that clearly have no place in the best life; hence the mere maximization of pleasure cannot be a reasonable policy for the best life.

Though the details are complicated, the main argument of the *Philebus* supports claims that Plato more or less takes for granted in the *Republic*. It tries to explain why general and plausible criteria for the best life—completeness and rational activity—favor some lives over others, and especially why these conditions rule out a life devoted simply to the satisfaction of whatever desires we may happen to have. In moving the argument to these more abstract questions about the structure and composition of the good, the *Philebus* anticipates Aristotle.

Soul and Body

Socrates advises people to take care of their souls, rather than their bodies or their possessions (*Apology* 29de, *Crito* 47e). He says this to express the importance of virtuous character, as opposed to the external circumstances that may befall us. Plato reinterprets this contrast between concern for oneself and concern for externals in the light of his dualist conception of body and soul. He argues that persons are to be identified with their reason and capacity for thought, and that since the rational intellect is immortal, each person is immortal. The soul is immaterial, imperceptible, and immortal, while the body is material, perceptible, and mortal. The soul can know the Forms without the senses, and like the Forms, is imperceptible and indestructible. Plato suggests that we are aware of ourselves as rational intellects in contrast to nonrational impulses and appetites; he uses examples of psychic conflict to suggest that we identify ourselves with the rational intellect (*Phaedo* 94c–e; cf. *Republic* 441bc).

Plato believes that if we accept this dualist conception of ourselves, we will draw two sorts of ethical conclusions:

1. In cultivating the virtues, we prepare ourselves for the state we will finally reach when we are free of the body. Some people do brave or temperate or just actions only when they see some further material advantage coming from them; these people have a mere 'facade' of virtue. Philosophers, however, are unreservedly committed to the virtues, because they do not care about any worldly loss that the virtues may involve (*Phaedo* 67e–69e; cf. Plotinus, *Enneads* i 2.2–4).

2. Philosophers are less concerned with what happens in the physical world, because they concentrate on contemplation of the Forms (*Theaetetus* 173c–177a; cf. Plotinus, *En-*

neads i 2.5–7). We might think that this second ethical conclusion casts doubt on the first. If philosophers are completely detached, as far as possible, from earthly concerns, why should they have any positive reason to share the virtuous person's concerns?

This question might also raise doubts about Plato's claim that we identify ourselves with our purely rational souls. His conclusion about immortality implies that we are identical to our rational capacities, to the exclusion of all the others. But we might well reject this conception of ourselves. Though we might identify ourselves with the reason that organizes nonrational impulses, we would not thereby identify ourselves with pure intellect without any impulses to organize.

Plato seems to see some of these difficulties. In *Republic* x (611b–612a) he tries to reconcile the tripartite psychology of *Republic* iv with his belief in immortality, by suggesting that the soul has nonrational parts during its life in the body, but sheds them at death. In the *Phaedrus,* however, he attributes nonrational desires to souls even out of the body (*Phaedrus* 246ab). This apparent change in Plato's views about the composition of the immortal soul may suggest that he wants to counter any attempt to argue from dualism to the rejection of moral concerns.

See also: AESTHETICS; ARISTOTLE; CONSEQUENTIALISM; COURAGE; DELIBERATION AND CHOICE; DESIRE; EOGISM; *EUDAIMONIA,* -ISM; GOOD, THEORIES OF THE; HAPPINESS; HEDONISM; LOVE; METAPHYSICS AND EPISTEMOLOGY; MORAL EDUCATION; PLEASURE; PRUDENCE; RATIONAL CHOICE; SELF-CONTROL; SOCIAL AND POLITICAL PHILOSOPHY; SOCRATES; TEMPERANCE; THEOLOGICAL ETHICS; VIRTUE ETHICS; VIRTUES; WEAKNESS OF WILL; WISDOM.

Bibliography

Primary Sources

Complete Works. Edited by J. M. Cooper and D. S. Hutchison. Indianapolis: Hackett, 1997. Translations of all of Plato's dialogues.

Republic. Translated by P. Shorey. London: Heinemann, 1935.

Philebus. Translated by J. C. B. Gosling. Oxford: Clarendon Press, 1975.

Plato

Phaedrus. Translated by R. Hackforth. Cambridge: Cambridge University Press, 1952.

Phaedo. Translated by D. Gallop. Oxford: Clarendon Press, 1975.

Secondary Sources

Annas, Julia. *An Introduction to Plato's* Republic. Oxford: Clarendon Press, 1981.

Cooper, John M. *Reason and Emotion.* Princeton: Princeton University Press, 1998.

Fine, G., ed. *Plato.* Vol. 2. Oxford: Oxford University Press, 1999.

Gosling, J. C. B. *Plato.* London: Routledge and Kegan Paul, 1973.

Gosling, J. C. B., and C. C. W. Taylor. *The Greeks on Pleasure.* Oxford: Clarendon Press, 1982. See chapters 5–10.

Irwin, T. H. *Plato's Ethics.* Oxford: Oxford University Press, 1995.

Kirwan, C. A. "Glaucon's Challenge." *Phronesis* 10 (1965): 162–73. Justice and its consequences.

Kraut, Richard. "Reason and Justice in Plato's *Republic.*" In *Exegesis and Argument,* edited by E. N. Lee, *et al.* 207–24. Assen, Netherlands: Van Gorcom, 1973.

———. "Egoism, Love, and Political Office in Plato." *Philosophical Review* 82 (1973): 330–44.

———, ed. *Cambridge Companion to Plato.* Cambridge: Cambridge University Press, 1992.

Vlastos, Gregory, ed. *Plato II.* Garden City, N.Y.: Doubleday, 1971. Essays; bibliography. See chapter 4, "Is Plato's *Republic* Utilitarian?", by J. D. Mabbot; chapter 6, "Thought and Desire in Plato," by T. Penner; chapter 15, "Plato's Views on the Nature of the Soul" by W. K. C. Guthrie.

———. *Platonic Studies.* 2d ed. Princeton: Princeton University Press, 1981. See especially chapter 5, "Justice and Happiness in the *Republic*" and chapter 1, "The Individual as an Object of Love in Plato."

White, N. P. *A Companion to Plato's* Republic. Indianapolis: Hackett, 1979.

———. "The Rulers' Choice." *Archiv für Geschichte der Philosophie* 68 (1986): 22–46.

T. H. Irwin

pleasure

Moral philosophers have taken an interest in pleasure because it seems to pose a threat to virtue. Crudely, philosophers divide into those who think pleasure should be avoided, those who think it an acceptable, even valuable, adjunct of a good life, and those who think it is the goal whose achievement constitutes the good life (HEDONISM). The first think it a threat to virtue because they think its pursuit selfish and its indulgence morally weakening. The second tend to distinguish kinds of pleasure, and look on pleasure as a reward of reputable activities, and perhaps permissible on occasion as an objective, but to make it one's main objective is a form of EGOISM, which is bad. The third often try to turn the moral tables by claiming that all morality depends on or consists of the pursuit of pleasure. The main object of interest has been the question of the acceptability of hedonism.

Two Main Types of Hedonism

Hedonists fall into two main types, although individuals may try uncomfortably to belong to both. First, there are those who hold that the only possible object of human DESIRE is pleasure. They are called psychological hedonists because they hold that it is a fact of human PSYCHOLOGY that humans can only value pleasure. Secondly, there are evaluative hedonists, who hold that whatever people actually pursue, pleasure is the only thing worth pursuing.

Forms of Psychological Hedonism

There are five main types, at least in theory:

1. *Immediate hedonism.* The view that humans desire/pursue just and only the immediately available perceived pleasure. If there are two such, they desire the pleasanter.
2. *Maximal hedonism.* The view that humans desire/pursue just and only the course which they consider will, of perceived available choices, produce maximum pleasure overall in their lives.
3. *Reflective hedonism.* The view that, although they may not in all their pursuits aim at pleasure, once individuals stand back and reflect on what makes a course worthwhile, the standard they are psychologically bound to use is that of maximal pleasure.

(Note: types 1–3 are to be taken as forms of egoism.)

4. *Nonegoistic hedonism* is a theoretically possible version of any of 1–3, broadened

to make the necessary object of human desire or evaluation the pleasure of any human or sentient being. It is now possible to ring various changes on 1–4.

5. *Conceptual hedonism* bases the thesis not on observation of human practice, but on the claim that the concept of desire requires pleasure for its object. In theory, according to the tie argued from, conceptual analogues of 1–4 are possible.

Forms of Evaluative Hedonism

Corresponding to 1–4 above are possible versions of evaluative hedonism. They have usually corresponded to forms 1–3, often combining the analogues of 2 and 3. Classical UTILITARIANISM (sometimes called ethical hedonism) can be construed as a nonegoistic version of one or both of these.

Compatibility of Types of Hedonism

The usual assumption of evaluative hedonism is that it is worth recommending pleasure because people do not always either desire/pursue it or use it as the basis of their evaluations. It should therefore presuppose the falsity of psychological hedonism. Since psychological hedonism purports to show how we inevitably behave, its truth should show the futility of recommendations, and so of the rhetoric of evaluative hedonism.

Relation of Hedonism to Morality

Psychological hedonism. Since this commits one to saying that all decisions or views on value have pleasure as their object, that must include moral decisions and views. These last have commonly been felt to pose a problem for all forms of psychological hedonism, since many moral decisions and views seem not to be geared to pleasure at all, whether of the agent or of others. Any apparently altruistic motive poses a challenge to any egoistic version. In addition the apparent determinism of these views seems incompatible with the attribution of RESPONSIBILITY.

Evaluative hedonism. Egoistic versions seem subversive of traditional moral views insofar as these last are nonegoistic. A hedonism which recommends pursuit of the pleasure immediately to hand further subverts morality insofar as that requires consideration of longer term consequences. Hedonists such

as the CYRENAICS, who concentrated on bodily pleasures, are seen as hostile to higher moral and spiritual values. Most hedonists adopt a form of CONSEQUENTIALISM, and so attract the moral objections to that. Nevertheless, maximal evaluative hedonism has sometimes (*e.g.,* PLATO's [c. 430–347 B.C.E.] *Protagoras*) been used to defend traditional NORMS, the argument being that the security of our overall pleasure in life requires the acquisition of virtue by ourselves, and the upholding of moral standards generally. *Nonegoistic versions,* of which classical utilitarianism is the main example, sometimes claim to give a more rational alternative to traditional morality; but sometimes they purport to supply the rationale of traditional morality by bringing cohesion to an apparently disparate set of norms.

Arguments for Hedonism

Psychological versions. The evidence should be observations of actual human practices. These have to be able to cope with apparent counterexamples where agents pursue what are realized to be unpleasant goals, or the good of others, or where they are restrained by considerations which do not seem justifiable on pleasure grounds. The danger is to slip into insisting that the agent must really have pleasure in view, whatever the apparent evidence, perhaps surreptitiously inserting the suggestion that any other pursuit would be irrational. Thus one can slip into conceptual hedonism, the arguments for which rely on analysis of the concepts of desire and pleasure.

Evaluative versions. These will depend on views about moral reasoning. It is sometimes difficult to tell whether a given argument is one for psychological reflective hedonism or evaluative: an appeal to the obvious fact that we value only pleasure can look like an appeal to the obvious fact that it alone is valuable, a form of INTUITIONISM. There is dispute as to whether JOHN STUART MILL's (1806–1873) proof in *Utilitarianism* (1861) illicitly crosses the fact/value boundary.

Calculation of Pleasure

A problem for all hedonists other than immediate ones is how pleasure is to be measured. A mixture of intensity, duration, probability, distance, fecundity, and purity is offered by BENTHAM (1748–1832).

Apart from questions of how to balance the criteria, there is a problem about the COMMENSURABILITY of pleasures: whether one can sensibly compare the degrees of pleasure of push-pin (a children's game) and poetry. Mill distinguished between higher and lower pleasures in part to avoid this problem. Higher pleasures are intrinsically more valuable. As they are the pleasures of a civilized life, that life can be taken as more valuable without intricate measurement. "More valuable" here must mean "pleasanter", and Mill's ground for that claim was that those who had experienced both gave their judgment in favor of the higher.

The Range of Pleasures

Hedonistic views take on a different appearance according to the range of pleasures allowed. Thus EPICURUS (341–270 B.C.E.) seems to have allowed only bodily pleasures and anticipations and memories of these. The resultant view is very different from one which makes Mill's higher pleasures the main objective.

The Nature of Pleasure

The difference made to hedonism. Many hedonistic arguments take it for granted that we all know what pleasure is. Yet different views on the nature of pleasure make all the difference to the nature, or even possibility, of hedonism. Pleasure has been thought to be the satisfaction of natural NEEDS or the fulfillment of desire (Plato), the activation of our natural capacities on their proper objects (ARISTOTLE [384–322 B.C.E.]), the (false) belief that we possess some good (Chrysippus [280–207 B.C.E.]), a sensation (perhaps HUME [1711–1776]), and a tone common to very varied experiences (Sprigge). Hedonism will take on a different form according to the view of pleasure, and on some will seem bizarre. If it is of the nature of pleasure to be the (an) object of desire, hedonism will receive some support; if pleasure is a false belief that one possesses a good, it will seem a strange object of pursuit.

The nature of the question. Early answers to the question "What is pleasure?" give supposed necessary and sufficient conditions for the occurrence of either pleasure generally or "real" pleasure. As the examples in the previous paragraph indicate, the answers do not show a concern with analyzing the meaning of "pleasure." Twentieth-century Anglo-Saxon philosophers tend to offer accounts of what "is pleased that," "enjoys," and similar expressions mean. Someone using these predicates of a subject is saying of them that they are experiencing a particular feeling (Zink), or that they are doing or experiencing something they want for its own sake (Taylor). These also yield very different accounts of hedonism.

The concept of pleasure. Modern views often claim to give an analysis of the concept of pleasure. This necessitates an examination of different expressions in the "pleasure" family. Philosophers have not always pursued this with an interest in ethics, but the results have their consequences for hedonism. Some not only distinguish between "is pleased that" and "enjoys," but also between the sorts of explanation offered by, for example, "because A is pleased that," "because A enjoys," "because A wants the pleasure of," and "because A gets pleasure at the thought of." It has been claimed that some forms of hedonism receive extra plausibility because they pass without notice from one to another of these different explanations. Any form of hedonism obviously requires clarity about the concepts of pleasure, enjoyment, desire. If these are the concepts of everyday language, then careful attention to the nuances of everyday expression will be needed. If they are the specialist concepts of some psychological theory, then it will be important not only to delineate these concepts clearly, but also to clarify the relationships between them and the everyday ones, in order to avoid confusions and fallacies.

Arguments for conceptual analyses. Arguments on the conceptual issues take two forms. If they are about the familiar concepts, they produce examples (*e.g.,* a man enjoying a game of golf), and ask what is being said or denied of a person when he is being said or denied to be enjoying it. If they are arguments *for* a certain concept, they will tend to ignore nuances of ordinary usage in favor of considerations which show that the concept as stipulated, while varying somewhat from the day-to-day one, enables us to describe or explain more clearly what the day-to-day concepts describe or explain.

History

Argument about the nature of pleasure and the viability of hedonism was a common theme of classical Greek and Roman philosophers. Plato and Aristotle both gave considerable importance to pleasure (of the proper sort), and EPICUREANISM was one of the major influential philosophical schools. Other philosophers (*e.g.,* the CYNICS), thinking of pleasure mainly in bodily terms, rejected it as incompatible with the good life. The Stoics also held views antipathetic to pleasure. In the Middle Ages interest was muted, reviving with the revival of Aristotelianism, but largely through Aristotelian eyes. In British philosophy from HOBBES (1588–1679) to SIDGWICK (1838–1900), the topic regained major importance, with many philosophers at least flirting with hedonism. In mainland Europe, Helvetius (1715–1771) was a notable proponent. The bibliography suggests some of the interest in the present century.

See also: ARISTOTLE; BENTHAM; BRANDT; CONSEQUENTIALISM; CYNICS; CYRENAICS; DESIRE; EGOISM; EPICUREANISM; EPICURUS; *EUDAIMONIA, -ISM;* EXCELLENCE; GOOD, THEORIES OF THE; HEDONISM; INTERESTS; JOHN STUART MILL; MORAL POINT OF VIEW; MORAL PSYCHOLOGY; NEEDS; PLATO; PSYCHOLOGY; PURITANISM; STOICISM; UTILITARIANISM; VIRTUE ETHICS.

Bibliography

Epicurus. *The Extant Remains.* Edited by C. Bailey. New York, 1970.

Gosling, J. C. B. *Pleasure and Desire.* Oxford: Clarendon Press, 1969.

Gosling, J. C. B., and C. C. W. Taylor. *The Greeks on Pleasure.* Oxford: Clarendon Press, 1982.

Hobbes, Thomas. "Philosophical Rudiments Concerning Government and Society." In *Value and Obligation,* edited by R. B. Brandt. New York: Harcourt, 1961 [1839].

Mill, John Stuart. *Utilitarianism.* Edited by Mary Warnock. Collins, 1962 [1861].

Moore, G. E. *Ethics.* Oxford: Oxford University Press, 1966 [1912].

Perry, David L. *The Concept of Pleasure.* The Hague: Mouton, 1967.

Plamenatz, John. *The English Utilitarians.* Oxford: Blackwell, 1958.

Plato. *Protagoras.* Translated by C. C. W. Taylor. Oxford: Clarendon Press, 1976.

Sprigge, T. *The Rational Foundations of Ethics.* London: Routledge and Kegan Paul, 1987.

Taylor, C. C. W. "Pleasure." *Analysis, supple.* 1963.

Zink, S. *Concepts of Ethics.* New York: St. Martin's, 1962.

Justin Gosling

Plotinus (205–270)

Plotinus was probably born in Lycopolis in Egypt. His nationality is not known for certain: while his name is Roman, he wrote in Greek, which presumably was his native language. The main source for Plotinus's life is the *Life of Plotinus* by his student Porphyry (c. 234–c. 305). For eleven years, from about the age of twenty-seven, Plotinus studied philosophy in Alexandria under the Platonist Ammonius Saccas (c. 175–242). He then made an unsuccessful attempt to travel to Persia and India in order to acquaint himself with the philosophy of these regions. He settled in Rome at the age of forty, where he established a school and stayed almost to the end of his life. His writings are treatises of varying length whose subject matter relates to topics under discussion in his school. Porphyry arranged them into six sets of nine treatises. These sets are called the *Enneads.*

Doctrinal Overview

The main characteristic of Plotinus's views, and that in virtue of which he is considered the founder of Neoplatonism, is the distinction between three principal levels of reality, the so-called *hypostaseis:* the One or the Good; Intellect, containing the archetypal forms of things; and Soul. These three constitute the intelligible realm, which is sharply distinguished from the sensible realm, the latter being an inferior reflection of the former in pure matter. Thus, Plotinus maintains a hierarchical world-picture according to which the One is the source of everything else. His main concern is to account for the structure of this hierarchy in detail and the place of human beings within it. As indicated by Plotinus's designation of "the Good" as the highest principle, there is a clear normative aspect to his metaphysics as a whole and, relatedly, to his philosophy of man. Plotinus's attitude towards the sensible world and to human life within it is somewhat ambivalent. While constantly emphasizing its low worth as compared with the higher realm, he does not consider it totally evil or worthless. Plotinus is primarily a metaphysician and is not much interested in the ethics of interpersonal relations. However, he directly addresses several topics that traditionally have been classified as ethical, such as the VIRTUES, freedom of the will, and HAPPINESS.

The Doctrine of Evil

In the treatise I.8, "On what are and whence come evils," Plotinus discusses at length questions concerning EVIL, a topic also brought up in many other treatises. The intelligible world is perfect and totally self-sufficient; and while the sensible world is not, it is a reflection of the former. It is therefore puzzling how evil can arise. Plotinus argues that evil as such does not exist and he identifies it with matter, understood as total formlessness. This is absolute evil. Other things, such as bodies, are evil in a relative way insofar as they have a share in matter. The existence of absolute evil is required by the fact that the Good exists. Plotinus responds to ARISTOTLE's (384–322 B.C.E.) objections against PLATO's (c. 430–347 B.C.E.) claim that evils must exist because the Good must have its contrary. These objections are founded on the claim that there is no contrary of substance; as the Good is a substance (or, in Plotinus's view, something beyond substance), the Good will have no contrary. Plotinus answers that matter is to be understood as the contrary of the Good in the sense that it is that which is furthest removed from it and which thus is characterized by all the opposite features. Despite this doctrine of matter as absolute evil, Plotinus does not maintain a radical dualism of two ultimate and opposite principles, for matter too is derived from the One. The doctrine of matter as the origin of evil also holds for human evils, such as vice and so-called "weakness of the soul," and for external evils such as illness or poverty. In both cases the deficiency of matter is the cause of evil.

Philosophy of Man

A human being is composed of soul and an organic body. The soul is further divided into a lower soul, which is responsible for the organic functions of the body, and a higher soul, in virtue of which we think and in virtue of which we are individuals rather than merely parts of the sensible world. The individual higher soul has a counterpart at the level of Intellect on which it depends and to which it may return. This return is described by Plotinus as a return to the real man and to one's true self. It is even possible for the soul to ascend to the One and achieve a temporary union with it. Thus, a human being contains, in a way, all the different levels of reality. The main obstacle to the higher life is the body and its NEEDS. The individual soul may become preoccupied with the body and the sensible realm, but it will be purified through philosophy. Our lives become more valuable the better we manage to live at the higher levels. Plotinus stands firmly in the classical Greek philosophical tradition in holding that philosophical training and contemplation, rather than theurgy or asceticism, are the means by which we can ascend to the intelligible realm.

The Virtues

Plotinus's treatise, I.2., is devoted to the virtues. His main objective, as so often, is to reconcile apparent discrepancies in Plato's teaching. In this case it is the doctrine of the four cardinal virtues in the *Republic;* the doctrine of the *Pheado,* according to which virtue is the soul's purification; and the doctrine suggested in *Theaetetus* 176 A–B that the virtues assimilate us to the divine. Plotinus distinguishes between political virtues, purgative virtues, and the archetypes of the virtues on the level of Intellect. These form a hierarchy of virtues. The function of the political virtues (the lowest grade) is to give order to the desires. The question arises whether the political virtues can be said to assimilate us to God (which for Plotinus is Intellect), for the divine does not have any desires that must be ordered and hence cannot possess the political virtues. Plotinus's answer to this is that although God does not possess the political virtues, there is something in God answering to them and from which they are derived. Further, the similarity that holds between a reflection and the original is not reciprocal. Thus, the political virtues may be, as it were, reflections of something belonging to the divine without the divine possessing the political virtues. However, it is not the political virtues that make the sage godlike, but rather the superior purgative virtues, which are the principles of the former and closer to the archetypes. Their object is to make us independent of the body and the sensible realm.

Happiness

The first *Ennead* contains two treatises dealing with happiness or well-being (*eudaimonia*): I.4, "On happiness" and I.5, "On whether happiness increases with time." In the former treatise, Plotinus rests his own position on Platonic and Aristotelian doctrines, while criticizing the Epicureans and the Stoics. He rejects the view that happiness consists at all in PLEASURE, a sensation of a particular sort. One can be happy without being aware of it. He also rejects the Stoic account of happiness as rational life. His own position is that happiness applies to life itself, not to a certain sort of life. There is a supremely perfect and self-sufficient life, that of the hypostasis Intellect, upon which every other sort of life depends. Happiness pertains primarily to this perfect life, which does not depend on any external good. But as all other kinds of life are reflections of this one, all living beings are capable of at least a reflection of happiness according to the kind of life they have. Man is capable of attaining the perfect kind of life. Plotinus holds, with the Stoics, that none of the so-called "external evils" can deprive a happy man of his happiness and that none of the so-called "goods" pertaining to the sensible world are necessary for human happiness.

In the second treatise on happiness, I.5, Plotinus discusses various questions concerning the relation between happiness and time, in particular whether the length of a person's life is relevant to his happiness. His answer is that it is not, because happiness, consisting in a good life, must be the life of real being, *i.e.,* that of Intellect. This life is not dispersed in time but is in eternity, which means here "outside time," not "lasting forever."

Freedom

Plotinus makes several remarks on human freedom or autonomy, in particular in III.1, "On Destiny"; III. 2–3, "On Providence" I and II; and in VI.8.1, "On the voluntary and on the will of the One." It is not clear that he is entirely consistent on this topic. He defines a voluntary act as one which is not forced and is carried out with full knowledge of everything relevant (VI.8.1). It appears that he had doubts that human beings, as agents in the sensible world, can be fully free in this sense, and hence they enjoy at best a limited autonomy. Nevertheless, in so far as the human soul is the agent of human actions, the person is responsible for them. Full autonomy belongs only to the soul that is entirely free from the body and lives on the level of Intellect. Thus, autonomy is possible, but it is questionable whether we are free to seek it and attain it.

See also: AUTONOMY OF MORAL AGENTS; DESIRE; EPICUREANISM; EVIL; *EUDAIMONIA, -ISM;* FREE WILL; FREEDOM AND DETERMINISM; GOOD, THEORIES OF THE; HAPPINESS; METAPHYSICS AND EPISTEMOLOGY; NEEDS; PLATO; PLEASURE; RATIONALITY VS. REASONABLENESS; STOICISM; VIRTUES; VOLUNTARY ACTS; WEAKNESS OF WILL.

Bibliography

Works by Plotinus

Plotini opera. 3 vols. Oxford Classical Texts. Oxford: Oxford University Press, 1964–1982. Scholarly edition.

Plotinus. 7 vols. Loeb Classical Library. Cambridge, MA: Harvard University Press, 1967–1988. Best translation in English.

Works about Plotinus

Armstrong, A. H. "Plotinus." In *The Cambridge History of Later Greek and Early Medieval Philosophy.* Edited by A. H. Armstrong. Cambridge: Cambridge University Press, 1970. Pp. 195–268. Chapters 14 and 16.

Dillon, J. "Plotinus, Philo and Origen on the Grades of Virtue." In *Platonismus und Christentum: Festschrift für Heinrich Dörrie.* Edited by Horst-Dieter Blume and Friedhelm Mann. Münster Westfalen: Aschendorff, 1983.

Haase, Wolfgang, ed. *Aufstieg und Niedergang der römischen Welt (ANRW).* 1951–86. II, 36, 1; bibliographies of fairly recent scholarship by H. Blumenthal, K. Corrigan, and P. O'Cleirigh. Berlin and New York: Walter de Gruyter: 1951–1986.

Henry, P. "Le problem de la liberté chez Plotin." *Revue néoscholastique de philosophie* 33 (1931).

O'Brien, D. "Plotinus on Evil: A Study of Matter and the Soul in Plotinus' Conception of Human Evil." *Downside Review* 87 (1969). Also in *Le Néoplatonisme,* Paris, 1971.

———. "Le Volontaire et la nécessité: Réflexions sur la descente de l'âme dans la philosophie de Plotin," *Rev. Philos. de la France et de l'étrangère* 167 (1977).

Rist, John M. "Plotinus on Matter and Evil." *Phronesis* 6 (1961).

———. *Plotinus: The Road to Reality.* Cambridge: Cambridge University Press, 1967.

Trouillard, Jean. *La purification plotinienne.* Paris: Presses Universitaires de France, 1955.

Volkmann-Schluck, K.-H. "Plotins Lehre vom Wesen und von der Herkunft des Schlecten (*Enn.* I.8)." *Philos. Jahrb.* 75 (1967).

Eyjólfur Kjalar Emilsson

pluralism

See moral pluralism.

police ethics

Lawbreakers (and sometimes the innocent) are apprehended, tried, and incarcerated. The corresponding social INSTITUTIONS—police, courts, and corrections—constitute the domain of criminal justice. The ethical analysis of those institutions and of the behavior of actors within the criminal justice system forms the subject matter of criminal justice ethics.

Police ethics is that branch of criminal justice ethics that treats the moral issues arising from keeping the domestic peace and, when unsuccessful, fighting individual and group crime. It is not a separate brand of ethics, but rather consists of applying philosophical theories to the concrete problems of policing. As such, it is a young field, with a lifespan measured in decades rather than centuries. Its current nature and concerns are due, on the philosophical side, to the general resurgence of normative inquiry and applied ethics together with, on the police side, a shift toward more sophisticated models of policing.

Policing as an Institution

Although most societies have had internal mechanisms for maintaining domestic order, the institution of policing as we know it today is of relatively recent origin. In England, for example, guidelines for sheriffs and constables were established as early as Magna Carta (1215), but the development of modern police administration began only in 1829 with the founding of the London Metropolitan Police. Such chronology has a bearing on philosophical speculation about the police: in earlier periods attention was directed, often in theoretical and fairly sketchy terms, to the place of law enforcement within the legal or governmental structure; contemporary applied philosophy, by contrast, is preoccupied with the details of actual police work and organizations, examining specific police functions with an eye to recommending improved policies and procedures.

Yet the two inquiries are not unrelated. The theoretical question about the justification of policing leads naturally to questions about the police role and the status of policing; these then lead to further questions about the morality of specific police activities and actions.

The standard justification of policing stems from SOCIAL CONTRACT theory of a Lockean sort. The exchange of some freedom in a state of nature for greater security in an organized society is a desirable and reasonable improvement. In the ensuing tripartite division of government, the executive has AUTHORITY for enforcing the law, and a police force is its principal domestic instrument for so doing.

The notion of "force" is paramount, but force can be exercised with varying degrees of subtlety. Thus, the conception of the police role can range from crime fighting at its most brutal to communitarian social service, with all shades of dispute resolution in between. Which model is chosen will determine whether the police are viewed as an occupying army with criminals as their enemies, or as partners in maintaining an orderly and truly civil society. At a more mundane level of police role, there is the related question of how the police are to be distinguished from other executive functionaries such as safety inspectors, traffic wardens, and the like.

The status of police themselves is an increasingly important issue: Is policing a profession, on a par with doctoring or lawyering, or do the police, as John Kleinig argues, exhibit a lesser degree of expertise, discretion, self-regulation, and other qualifying attributes? Indeed, is professionalism a desirable goal at all, or can responsible experts degenerate too easily into cadres of paternalistic elites? Much attention has been paid recently to articulating codes of police ethics, which are valued for providing guidance to individual officers, organizational standards, reassurance to the public, and heuristic devices. But even such superficially laudable efforts may be suspect insofar as they presuppose that ethical dilemmas can be easily settled and codified, that RESPONSIBILITY can be defined in terms of simple obedience rather than rational reflection, that police constitute a club with their own unique set of rules, and that paper policies will translate into informed practice.

Finally, there are institutional questions of management that have, despite their specific twists in the context of policing, analogies to traditional issues in BUSINESS ETHICS: accountability and external controls, LOYALTY and whistleblowing, privatization, DISCRIMINATION and affirmative action, unionization and strikes, "white-collar" *vs.* "blue-collar" divisions, the allotment of scarce resources, and the like. To these can be added consideration of the place of education in the formation of police, and specifically the manner in which ethical issues are treated in any such training.

Police as Actors

Police, in fulfilling their duty to maintain public order and protect persons and PROPERTY from unlawful acts, are an obvious target of moral scrutiny. Within each major area of police work—preserving the peace, detecting crime, and arresting and processing violators—moral philosophers have found ample scope for analysis. While there is no short and simple list of questions that may be raised, several recurrent topics have formed the basis of many philosophical and social science discussions.

Corruption. Most, if not all, police departments have witnessed the truth of Lord Acton's dictum about POWER. CORRUPTION—the presumption, solicitation, or acceptance of extraneous gain for the doing or not doing of one's official duties—has been a lasting and deep problem in the enforcement of law. It is intimately involved with the exercise of discretion, and it can sap the authority of police both individually and collectively. Paradoxically, however, this moral shortcoming so troubling to the popular mind is also the least complex philosophically. Whether in the broader sense of ordinary criminality (committing burglaries, trafficking in controlled substances) or in the narrower sense of exchanging favors for benefits (accepting bribes, performing shakedowns), corruption is the antithesis of what the police must represent in a civilized community. Police have a special obligation to uphold the law in a way that other public employees, such as sanitation workers, do not. Major instances of police corruption may thus serve as data for the social scientist inquiring after causes and effects, or they may provide convenient symbols for MORAL EDUCATION, but they offer little room for ethical analysis. Most of the literature on police corruption has consequently been criminological or journalistic rather than philosophical in nature.

At the other extreme of the paradox, harder ethical issues are posed by more common but more minor temptations (such as accepting a free cup of coffee from a local merchant). In some cases there may not even be a suspect motivation: a police officer may perform a duty despite the knowledge, rather than with the aim, that a gratuity will follow. Some writers, like Lawrence Sherman, have discerned a slippery slope leading gradually from petty rewards to serious venality, with regularized expectations generating obligations or worse. Insofar as the connection between the two ends of the slope is logical, it is open to philosophical analysis; insofar as it is empirical, or psychological, it becomes more a matter of police administration. Those writers, like Michael Feldberg, who countenance the acceptance of small gratuities appeal to "longstanding and universally tolerated practice" and fee-for-service models of police protection to argue that the democratic ethos can encompass trivial hospitable reciprocities. The emphasis is on the motive of the giver as much as that of the taker, and the slope need not be all that slippery.

Further philosophical investigation is needed to relate discussions of corruption to theories of human nature, to examine the effects of CHARACTER and social institutions on each other (the "rotten apple" problem), and to fit specific types of corruption (kickbacks, payoffs, fixes, etc.) into a hierarchy of corruption (reward, gratuity, gift, bribe, etc.).

Deception. The tangled web of deception presents the most dramatic contrast between deontological and utilitarian justifications in policing. Deception can take many forms, including lies, falsehoods, half-truths, prevarications, misrepresentations, distortions, omissions, and fabrications. Within the context of policing, deception may range from routine undercover operations (even an unmarked car is "undercover") to elaborate entrapments. Following Jerome Skolnick, the broad activities of investigation, interrogation, and testifying can be distinguished; "blue lies" can occur, with increasing gravity, in each stage. The common theme is whether laudable ends can justify dubious means. Lawbreakers thrive on deception; is it ethically permissible for police to use similar tools to defeat them? Should police be allowed to use decoys, wear disguises, purchase vice through fronts, trick suspects into confessing, manufacture evidence, or lie to other police and to a court ("testilying") in the name of better law enforcement, or does the very question defeat itself?

Unlike the case of corruption, much of the present literature is directed towards more flagrant deceptions like entrapment, raising fundamental issues of RIGHTS, honesty, TRUST, and proof. The risk is obvious, that of turning police from crime stoppers into crime makers. Can enticement to crime ever be justified morally? If so, what limits and controls should regulate the practice? Should the proper test of entrapment be objective (focusing on police conduct) or subjective (evaluating the offenders' predispositions)? Should targeting be random or selective, by group or by individual? Other promising approaches seek to develop a taxonomy of deceptions and to assess the moral effect on society of official deception, which creates a model of distrust in personal and professional relationships.

Force. Although it can be facilitative as well, most law is coercive, and the legitimate dispensing of force is a central police function. Indeed, to judge from the depiction of police in television programs and the cinema, even excesses of force are considered by some to be normal and admirable, as witness the fighting of force with unauthorized force that Carl Klockars calls the "Dirty Harry" problem, after a film character of that name. However, such high-profile cases of brutality as those against Rodney King (1991) and Abner Louima (1997) have provided notorious examples of what many fear is a far too frequent, and wholly indefensible, police response. Taken together with instances of the literal overkill of citizens who are sometimes unarmed, such practices can easily erode a community's confidence in its police.

While it can be argued that any use of force against a person requires justification, police force has its own dramatic dimension. The police have a large arsenal of weapons and techniques at their disposal for administering force—guns and other firearms, gas and liquid sprays, hitting weapons (clubs, sticks, batons), restraining devices (handcuffs, ropes, nets), physical holding, animals—and moral issues can arise about the use of each of them.

Generally speaking, the greater the use of force the more serious is the resulting ethical problem. Force that simply maintains order or provides for SELF-DEFENSE is less troublesome philosophically than force used intentionally to inflict harm. In the case of extreme or deadly force, philosophers have used Rawlsian contractual models, concepts of PROPORTIONALITY, and analogies to CAPITAL PUNISHMENT to analyze the grounds under which police should be permitted such power. Particularly at a time when most civilized societies have renounced

the death penalty, while also redefining (often expansively) what is to count as a felony, it is good policy to rethink the common law tradition that permits lethal retaliation against "fleeing felons."

In determining standards for forcible police reaction to crimes, philosophers can bring their notions of deterrence and retributive justice to bear on the normative debate. And the audience for change may be receptive: while philosophers and social scientists have noted disturbing statistical anomalies that still exist in police enforcement (concerning disproportions in the receipt of force by race or class and in administering force from department to department), it is to be hoped that modern policing in Europe and America will increasingly distance itself from its stereotype. Police coercion is controlled and humanized when departments move from a military to a social-service model, which not coincidentally corresponds to the principal needs for police response in a stable community.

Privacy. General questions of PRIVACY—what is it, why is it valuable, and is there a right to it?—are explored elsewhere. Specific questions typically relate to police powers to invade the individual's sanctum, be it home, car, telephone, or very person. Most attention has been directed to the legal interpretation and moral criticism of actual statutes and landmark cases, with two main focuses: identifying lawbreakers and developing cases against those arrested. What should be the limits of stop and frisk, search and seizure, and electronic surveillance? What safeguards will balance the need to know and the "right to remain silent," guaranteeing that any confessions will be freely given and accurate? To what extent should modern investigative techniques, such as lie detectors, fingerprinting, and DNA and other bodily analyses, compromise personal INTEGRITY? And, in an age of computerized data banks that provide instant access to life's secrets, what sorts of information about individuals should law enforcement agencies develop and maintain, and how, if at all, may this information be shared?

But privacy works in the other direction as well. What rights to privacy should police officers have for themselves? In order to garner respect and be effective at their jobs, must they be exemplary role models for the community? If so, the door will be open for limiting free speech, political association, consensual sexual activity, and freedom of residence. Frederick Elliston has argued, on grounds of FAIR-

NESS and Aristotelian equal treatment, that police should no more be required than other workers to sacrifice key parts of their private lives, but critics like John Kleinig emphasize occupational differences, particularly concerning discretion, that justify some differential treatment.

Discretion. In its central aspect, police discretion mirrors judicial discretion: given a fixed but imperfectly dispositive set of rules, to what extent may the applier of the rules substitute flexible judgment in approaching individual cases? Or, in Ronald DWORKIN's strong sense of discretion, should the official be free to choose without being subject to independent standards set by some authority? In practice, however, police discretion often means not arresting someone, and it differs from judicial discretion in not generally being recorded.

Some discretion is inevitable because strict enforcement is impossible in the face of numerous violations and limited resources. Even if more resources were available, however, discretion would still have a point, because law is more than a simple system of articulated rules. Of course, the greater the crime the lesser should be the permissible scope of individual prerogative in enforcement; but, provided its use is not arbitrary, capricious, or discriminatory, discretion can be a tool under a community policing model for taking context more fully into account and avoiding overly legalistic outcomes. Police thus become improvising problem solvers who must give all citizens their due as individuals while insuring fair and equitable treatment with no invidious distinctions.

Philosophers have sought to differentiate the types of discretion (Michael Davis distinguishes among discretion as judgment, mere decision, discernment, LIBERTY, and license) and to determine its proper limits. Both efforts raise fundamental questions of completeness and consistency, of authority versus autonomy, and of legality and public morality.

Race. Although the subject of race fits in part under the ethical issues already discussed, particularly those of force and discretion, it also demands discussion in its own right. Moral issues can arise in any setting in which a discrete minority is subjected to discrimination based on race or ethnicity, and hence the problems that relate to the police are part of a larger whole. However, although discrimination in general is often forbidden by legislation, such as the Civil Rights Act of 1964 (United States) and the Race Relations Act of 1976 (United Kingdom), the realities of police practices present some notable MORAL DILEMMAS of their own. It is no secret, especially in the United States and the United Kingdom, that citizens of different racial or ethnic groups systematically receive different treatment from police. Blacks, in particular, are proportionally more likely to be stopped, searched, and arrested, with the result that prison populations are racially skewed.

This overrepresentation of blacks among prison inmates has led to controversy as to its causes. Ultimately, this is an empirical rather than a moral question, a reincarnation along racial lines of the old nature *vs.* nurture debate, although the word "nurture" is a gross misnomer in this context. Given the difficulties even of defining "race" and the genetic evidence that shows greater disparity within a race than across races, historical and cultural explanations of this discrepancy have greater appeal. Certainly the record of racial discrimination in the United States, for example, has been long and severe, leading to a vicious circle from racial prejudice to disparate treatment, to economic disadvantage, to incentives to crime, to the commission of crimes, and ultimately to reinforced stereotypes about inherent criminality that can lead to police overreactions. Magnifying this process is the tendency to define, enforce, and penalize street crimes more aggressively and harshly than crimes the well-off are more likely to commit.

A vivid police example of stereotyping is the practice known as racial profiling, whereby blacks, because they are considered more likely to be lawbreakers than whites, are singled out for harassing police stops. Playing on the acronym DWI (driving while intoxicated), some writers have identified DWB (driving while black) in order to call attention to this tendency. Indeed, abuse of discretion based on racial prejudice has been given more scope by the Supreme Court in *Whren v. United States* (1996). There the Court articulated a broad standard of reasonable stopping based on "probable cause to believe that a traffic violation has occurred." Since such infractions can be minor and numerous, much room is given for police judgment and misjudgment. Polls have shown that white and black Americans alike agree that racial profiling is widespread and that it is wrong.

Confrontations between police and whole communities have presented even more dramatic problems. More than two hundred urban disorders in the United States between 1965 and 1968 led to the Kerner Report (1968). In England, the disorders in Brixton (1981) and other cities led to the Scarman Report (1981). Both Kerner and Scarman found police misconduct to be among the main causes of civil unrest. Attempts to overcome the gap in perspective between police and those whom they are supposed to protect have led to a literature, mostly in the social sciences, that stresses a holistic notion of community policing. Such an approach advocates a partnership between police and law-abiding citizens to gather information, to identify potential risks (not simply with a focus on crime, but also on fear of crime, neighborhood decay, drugs, etc.), and to involve the community in their solution. Of course, in a society with imbedded residential segregation and an underrepresentation of minority citizens on the police force, community policing faces its own underlying problems. Returning to the theme that began this section, the burden of attaining an orderly and just society requires a more thoroughgoing response than mere improvements in policing. Unfortunately, moving from discriminatory treatment by race or ethnicity to greater equality remains an obstinate challenge at the general political, economic, and social levels.

Conclusion

Criminal justice is already more specific than justice itself, and the study of criminal justice ethics, of which police ethics is one branch, is more specific still. While general, theoretical questions about law and its enforcement have long been subjected to ethical analysis, only recently have philosophers focused their attention on moral concerns that are prompted by the practical, institutional realities of police work. Much remains to be done in every area: contemporary police ethics is a workshop whose product is still in the making.

See also: AUTHORITY; BRIBERY; CIVIL DISOBEDIENCE; COERCION; CORRUPTION; DECEIT; DETERRENCE, THREATS, AND RETALIATION; DISCRIMINATION; JUSTICE, RECTIFICATORY; OBEDIENCE TO LAW; PATERNALISM; POWER; PRIVACY; PROPORTIONALITY; PUBLIC AND PRIVATE MORALITY; RACISM AND RELATED ISSUES; RESPONSIBILITY; SECRECY AND CONFIDENTIALITY; SELF-DEFENSE; SOCIAL CONTRACT; TORTURE.

Bibliography

Bailey, William G., ed. *The Encyclopedia of Police Science.* 2d ed. New York: Garland Publishing, 1995. See especially Michael Davis (pp. 83–94) on codes of ethics; Michael Feldberg (pp. 206–11) on discretion; and Carl Klockars (pp. 549–53) on police ethics.

Barker, Thomas, and Julian B. Roebuck. *An Empirical Typology of Police Corruption.* Springfield, Ill.: Thomas, 1974.

Chadwick, Ruth, ed. *Encyclopedia of Applied Ethics.* San Diego, Calif.: Academic Press, 1998. See especially Neil Walker on police accountability (vol. 3, pp. 541–52); Trevor Jones on police and race relations (vol. 3, pp. 553–64); and Gary T. Marx on the ethics of undercover investigations (vol. 4, pp. 427–37).

Close, Daryl, and Nicholas Meier, eds. *Morality in Criminal Justice: An Introduction to Ethics.* Belmont, Calif.: Wadsworth, 1995. A useful compendium of classic philosophical readings, contemporary articles, decisions, and codes, with practical problems for discussion.

Cohen, Howard S., and Michael Feldberg. *Power and Restraint: The Moral Dimension of Police Work.* New York: Praeger, 1991. Applies a social contract perspective on policing to several concrete examples.

Criminal Justice Ethics. 1982– . Semi-annual journal, the only source of its kind. See especially Jerome Skolnick (1/2: 40–54) and Skolnick and Richard A. Leo (11/1: 3–12) on deception; Howard Cohen (5/2: 23–31 and 6/2: 52–60) on authority; Richard R. E. Kania (7/2: 37–49) on gratuities; R. E. Ewin (9/2: 3–15) on loyalty; Michael Davis (10/1: 14–28) on codes of ethics; and Gary T. Marx (11/1: 13–24) on undercover operations.

Davis, Kenneth Culp. *Discretionary Justice: A Preliminary Inquiry.* Baton Rouge: Louisiana State University Press, 1969. Classic analysis of structural constraints on discretion.

Delattre, Edwin J. *Character and Cops: Ethics in Policing.* 3d ed. Washington, D.C.: The AEI Press, 1996. A polemical argument for the development of police character.

Dworkin, Ronald. *Taking Rights Seriously.* Cambridge: Harvard University Press, 1977. See pp. 31–39. Dworkin writes of discretion as "the hole in the doughnut . . . left open by a surrounding belt of restriction."

Elliston, Frederick A., and Michael Feldberg, eds. *Moral Issues in Police Work.* Totowa, N.J.: Rowman & Allanheld, 1985. See especially Lawrence Sherman (pp. 253–65) and Michael Feldberg (pp. 267–76) on police corruption; Jerome Skolnick (pp. 75–98) on deception; Jeffrey Reiman (pp. 237–49) on deadly force; Elliston (pp. 277–88) on police rights to privacy; and Carl Klockars (pp. 55–71) on the "Dirty Harry" problem.

Heffernan, William C., and Timothy Stroup, eds. *Police Ethics: Hard Choices in Law Enforcement.* New York:

John Jay Press, 1985. Sections on discretion, undercover operations, deadly force, etc.

Kerner, Otto. *Report of the National Advisory Commission on Civil Disorders.* Introduction by Tom Wicker. New York: Dutton, 1968. Originally published, Washington, D.C.: GPO, 1968.

Kleinig, John. *The Ethics of Policing.* Cambridge: Cambridge University Press, 1996. The most comprehensive and astute treatment of issues in police ethics.

———, ed. *Handled with Discretion: Ethical Issues in Police Decision Making.* Lanham, Md.: Rowman and Littlefield, 1996. See Michael Davis (pp. 13–35) on types of discretion.

Pollock, Joycelyn M. *Ethics in Crime and Justice: Dilemmas and Decisions.* Belmont, Calif.: Wadsworth, 1994. Section 6 (pp. 91–135) on "Ethics and Law Enforcement."

Scarman, Leslie George. *The Brixton Disorders, 10–12 April 1981: Report of an Inquiry.* Harmondsworth, Middlesex: Penguin Books, 1982. The Scarman Report. Remainder of title: *Presented to Parliament by the Secretary of State for the Home Department by Command of Her Majesty, November 1981.* Originally published, London: HMSO, 1981.

Whren et al. v. United States, 517 U.S. 806 (1996).

Timothy Stroup

political correctness

History and Definition

The term "politically correct" appears to have originally been used in leftist circles either approvingly to refer to someone who correctly adheres to the party line, or more often ironically and disapprovingly to someone whose adherence to the Communist Party line was excessive, tiresome, and beyond good sense. Confessions of being politically incorrect might also be used self-deprecatingly to refer to one's own backsliding.

In the mid- to late-1980s, neoconservative scholars, many of whom were members of the National Association of Scholars, began to use "political correctness" as a term of disparagement for a variety of curriculum transformation projects. Women's studies programs, ethnic studies programs, and curriculum revisions designed to make college courses, especially in literature and history, more multicultural were charged with being part of a new wave of political correctness on college and university campuses. In 1989, Stanford University made a much publicized revision in its core Western Civilization courses to de-emphasize the West and to include women and racial minorities. Major universities like Stanford, the University of Michigan, and the University of Wisconsin instituted speech codes aimed at controlling hate speech. The political correctness debates (also referred to as the culture wars) subsequently took off in 1990 and 1991 in a series of articles in *Newsweek, U.S. News and World Report,* the *New York Times, Time,* the *Village Voice,* and *Atlantic Monthly* about the new political correctness on campuses. In May 1991, President George Bush delivered his commencement address at the University of Michigan on the dangers of political correctness. Since then, "politically correct" has come to be used to characterize curriculum revisions, campus speech codes, harassment policies, affirmative action in college admissions and hiring, the use of new descriptors for minorities (*e.g.,* African American, Native American, learning disabled), new NORMS for interacting with women and racial or cultural minorities (*e.g.,* avoiding genteel "ladies first" policies), and generally, to any change in language, policy, social behavior, and cultural representation that is aimed at avoiding or correcting a narrowly Eurocentric world view and the long-standing subordination of some social groups. Originating in debates over the content of higher education, the terms "politically correct" or "PC" are now routinely used outside of the academy.

The current political correctness debates were preceded by a set of social (or identity politics) movements, legislative initiatives, and theoretical developments that motivated members of the academy to become mindful of the politics of education. The Civil Rights movement of the 1960s that was followed by the women's rights movement, gay and lesbian liberation movement, animal liberation movement, and public attention to the culturally disesteemed status of Native Americans, various ethnic minorities, and the physically and mentally disabled all had substantial cultural and legal impacts that in turn affected the academy. Cumulatively, these movements have underscored the significance of the feminist slogan "the personal is political." That is, areas of social life that were conventionally taken to be apolitical, such as everyday language, the canon of literary classics, jokes, advertising, norms of politeness, hiring decisions, and sports funding, came increasingly to be seen as potential sites for enacting racism, sexism, and Eurocentrism. Attention to the politics of traditional university curricula was a natural outgrowth of this expanded sense of the political. These social movements also issued in a set of legal initiatives that significantly affected educational policy, most notably, the desegregation of education mandated in *Brown v. Board of Education of Topeka* (1954), Title IV of the Civil Rights Act (1964) that prohibited DISCRIMINATION against members of "suspect categories," and Title IX of the Educational Amendments (1972) that prohibited sex discrimination in education. Finally, the rise of POST-MODERNISM and deconstructionism, particularly in literature departments, provided the theoretical apparatus for analyzing the politics of claims to truth and objectivity and for investigating the role that scholarship plays in the social construction of reality. Critics of foundationalist epistemology argued that knowledge is perspectival and historically and culturally situated. More importantly, it was argued that the sciences, social sciences, and humanities have historically excluded the perspectives of nonwestern, nonwhite and nonmale people, have used biased standards for what counts as good scholarship, and have produced theories and "factual" narratives distorted by the cultural ideologies that sustain dominance systems. If truth claims themselves can serve a political function, the academy could not claim to be politically neutral simply because it was devoted to the pursuit of truth.

"Politically correct" now carries a complex set of meanings. To describe an academic program, a bit of social behavior, or a new descriptor (*e.g.,* "chair" rather than "chairman") as politically *correct* is to imply that while it correctly conforms to a liberal academic party line, it is incorrect by some other more important or more substantive measure; it is educationally unsound, unjust, an illegitimate interference with free speech, or simply unnecessary or silly. "Politically correct" also implies the presence of a sufficient power base to enforce compliance with whatever is politically correct, either through formal penalties or informal disapproval and shunning. That is, it implies the presence of political correc*tors* and the threat of being correc*ted*. As a result, political correctness is implicitly linked with authoritarianism, COERCION, CENSORSHIP, and the bad taste to correct others' manners.

To describe an academic program, a bit of social behavior, or a new descriptor as *politically* correct is to imply that political goals have wrongly been given precedence over other goals. For instance, women's studies and African American studies programs have been described as prioritizing political aims at the expense of educational ones. The term "politically correct," partly in virtue of its historical association with the Communist Party, also implies that democratic liberties are being interfered with, most notably free speech and academic freedom. Indeed, political correctness has been equated with "thought police" and a "new McCarthyism."

Because the term "politically correct" implies dogmatic, illiberal toeing of a party line and because "politically incorrect" implies a refusal to give politics priority, both terms exclude what defenders of curriculum transformation projects, speech codes, antiharassment policies, new social norms, and new descriptors for women and minorities in fact advocate—political thoughtfulness.

Moral Language and Cultural Criticism

Becoming thoughtful about the social construction of culturally disesteemed gender, racial, ethnic, economic, national, sexual, religious, age, and ability identities and the ways in which prejudice and second-class citizenship are socially institutionalized is necessarily a political matter. It is thoughtfulness about the way that POWER—economic, epistemic, cultural, and legal—is sustained for some and denied to others. It is thoughtfulness about what it would take to realize two of our most basic political values: EQUALITY and democratic decision making. From the late 1880s through the 1970s, political thoughtfulness about inequality was heavily devoted to critiquing the *formal* differential treatment of racial minorities and women in law and policy. In academia, that originally meant opening college and university doors to blacks, women, and Jews; and later, enforcing antidiscrimination policies. Although formal RIGHTS are critical to securing equality for disadvantaged social groups, extralegal cultural factors affect individuals' ability to exercise those rights and have them respected. Extralegal cultural factors also determine whether or not equal rights translate into equally dignified treatment generally, freedom from bias-motivated violence, equal engagement in the production of knowledge and culture, and equal representation in democratic decision making processes. But if inequality is culturally, and not just legally, institutionalized, political thoughtfulness will involve cultural criticism.

In the 1980s and 1990s, cultural critics within the academy developed a sizable, new, moral language adequate to the task of cultural criticism. Some new terms—that PC critics trivialize as mere "isms"—name morally worrisome systems of domination: for example, racism, sexism, classism, heterosexism, and colonialism. Other new terms were meant to replace the older moral language of discrimination and prejudice and to more accurately describe the nature, mechanisms, and effects of institutionalized inequality: OPPRESSION, domination, cultural imperialism, elitism, hate crimes, marginalization, exclusion, silencing, essentializing, treating as the Other. Supplementing the older moral language of rights and liberties, an additional set of MORAL TERMS captured what full scale sociocultural equality would mean or require: sensitivity, diversity, inclusivity, celebrating difference, empowerment, and attention to a plurality of voices.

The terms "politically correct" and "politically incorrect" belong in this new moral, linguistic landscape. Any policy, norm, educational program, or linguistic change whose rationale is statable using this new moral terminology can also be disparaged as mere political correctness. Because "political correctness" refers to educational, linguistic, and behavioral reforms based on an antidomination rationale, being opposed to political correctness generally is not clearly distinct from being opposed to critiques of and interventions in dominance systems. Were it not for the fact that "political correctness" carries negative implications (for example, of being against academic freedom), it would be more obvious that care needs to be taken in expressing opposition to political correctness to explain how that opposition does not entail being pro racism, sexism, classism, and so on.

Although the term "political correctness" has unfortunately been used to dismiss politically thoughtful educational reforms without suggesting alternative means for remedying structural inequalities or for ensuring that scholarship does not perpetuate cultural ideologies, a term like "political correctness" is a useful, perhaps essential, part of our moral vocabulary. As JOHN STUART MILL (1806–1873) noted over a century ago, any belief no matter how admirable may be held merely as a dead dogma. In addition, it is tempting when faced with political problems as complex and intransigent as racism to focus on quick, easy fixes like a mere change in vocabulary. And even the best political movements attract moral snobs who prize the signs of moral superiority and the AUTHORITY to correct. Carefully used to refer only to a kind of intellectual and moral vice, rather than to dismiss an antidominance viewpoint, "political correctness" could, like "snobbery" and "dogmatism," function as a term of appropriate moral critique.

Liberal Tensions

The PC debates within academia, like larger social debates about affirmative action, sexual harassment policies, the regulation of PORNOGRAPHY, the meaning of equal opportunity, and welfare and bilingual policies, are fueled by long-standing tensions and unclarities within liberal political theorizing. Equality and LIBERTY are both central liberal values. The meaning of both terms is contested. Attempting to improve the campus climate for members of subordinate groups in the name of liberty may conflict with attempts to maximize liberty from legal and quasi-legal restrictions on individual behavior and self-expression. Attempting to promote equal representation of minorities and women on faculties and in curricula may conflict with the equal consideration of all meritorious candidates and equal distribution of resources to all academic programs. It may also be the case that under conditions of institutionalized oppression, tradeoffs between equality and liberty will be unavoidable, and thus so too will be disputes over which value should be given priority in any individual case.

Liberalism's long-standing invocation of the harm principle to justify restrictions on liberty, including free speech, has provoked equally long-standing controversies about what constitutes harm. Must hate speech satisfy the "fighting words" doctrine articulated in *Chaplinsky v. New Hampshire* (1942), or qualify as harassment by being addressed to an individual or a captive audience, like students in a classroom, to be considered harmful? Or do hateful, demeaning, and trivializing images and language in graffiti, newspaper ads, and editorials constitute a harm, even though not directed at a particular individual, because of their chilling effect on campus climate, undermining of esteem, and contribution to institutionalized domination?

The distinction between the right and the good, between what is a matter for political decision-making and what is a matter of individual choice, is central to LIBERALISM. How that line is to be drawn in practice, however, is often a matter of dispute. Domestic violence has, for instance, shifted from being a private familial issue to a concern of the law. Much of the PC debate has been about where to draw the line between freedom of expression and academic freedom on the one hand and what colleges and universities are obligated to provide as a matter of educational responsibility and minority student entitlement on the other.

Finally, what it means to have a liberal education is contestable. Traditionally, a liberal education has meant being broadly educated within the standard disciplines and the classics of Western civilization. Contemporary curricular reform, however, is driven by a different vision of liberal education as education for participation in a multicultural, multiracial, egalitarian nation in a multinational world. It is also driven by a different interpretation of how educational institutions have functioned in the past, namely, not merely as preservers of great works and the custodians of truth, but also as producers of ideology and preservers of an inegalitarian status quo.

See also: ACADEMIC ETHICS; ACADEMIC FREEDOM; AGENCY AND DISABILITY; ANIMALS, TREATMENT OF; AUTHORITY; CENSORSHIP; CIVIL RIGHTS AND CIVIC DUTIES; COERCION; CONSERVATISM; CULTURAL STUDIES; DEMOCRACY; DIGNITY; DISCRIMINATION; EQUALITY; ETIQUETTE; FEMINIST ETHICS; GAY ETHICS; LESBIAN ETHICS; LIBERALISM; MORAL EDUCATION; MULTICULTURALISM; PATERNALISM; PORNOGRAPHY; PUBLIC AND PRIVATE MORALITY; PUBLIC POLICY; RACISM AND RELATED ISSUES; SELF-RESPECT; SEXUAL ABUSE AND HARASSMENT; TOLERATION.

Bibliography

Berman, Paul, ed. *Debating P.C.: The Controversy Over Political Correctness on College Campuses.* New York: Dell Publishing, 1992. An anthology of key essays by major players in the political correctness debate during the late 1980s and early 1990s.

Bloom, Allan. *The Closing of the American Mind.* New York: Simon & Schuster, 1987. In Bloom's words, "on how higher education has failed democracy and impoverished the souls of today's students."

D'Souza, Dinesh. *Illiberal Education: The Politics of Race and Sex On Campus.* New York: Free Press, 1991. Perhaps the most often cited work opposing political correctness.

Fish, Stanley. *There's No Such Thing as Free Speech, and It's a Good Thing Too.* Oxford: Oxford University Press, 1993.

Friedman, Marilyn and Jan Narveson. *Political Correctness: For and Against.* Lanham, Md.: Rowman and Littlefield, 1995. In-depth philosophical evaluations of the arguments on both sides of the debate.

Frye, Marilyn. "Getting It Right." In her *Willful Virgin: Essays in Feminism, 1976–1992.* Freedom, Calif.: Crossing Press, 1992. A defense of the moral ideal of supporting genuinely correct political positions and feminist critiques of affirmative action and multiculturalism.

Kimball, Roger. *Tenured Radicals: How Politics Corrupted Our Higher Education.* New York: Harper and Row, 1990.

National Council for Research on Women. *To Reclaim a Legacy of Diversity: Analyzing the "Political Correctness" Debates in Higher Education.* [Written by Debra L. Schultz.] New York: The Council, 1993. An excellent source book for factual, statistical, and bibliographical information relevant to the PC debates.

Cheshire Calhoun

political philosophy

See social and political philosophy.

political systems, evaluation of

Every organized political entity has some way of allocating the RIGHTS to make legally binding decisions. The range runs from an absolute monarchy to the complex division of powers laid out in the U.S. Constitution. Systematic speculation about the best form of polity constitutes a large part of the subject matter of political philosophy. Most political philosophers have recommended some particular form of political organization, if not for all times and places then at any rate for their own society and others sufficiently like it. We shall be concerned here with the recurrent forms of argument that are put forward in order to advance the claims of certain political institutions over those of others. The object will be to construct an exhaustive classification of types of justification. This is represented as a tree diagram:

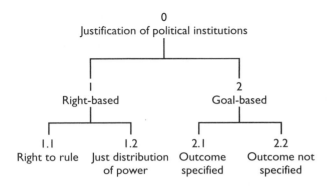

0
Justification of political institutions

1
Right-based

2
Goal-based

1.1
Right to rule

1.2
Just distribution of power

2.1
Outcome specified

2.2
Outcome not specified

A Typology of Justifications

As will be seen in the figure, the most basic distinction drawn is that between right-based and goal-based justifications (see Dworkin). The same distinction could be marked by dividing justifications into procedural and nonprocedural (see Beitz).

1. *Right-based justifications.* Right-based justifications are distinctive in that they do not appeal to any alleged advantages that one decision-making system has over its rivals. The consequences of the system are immaterial to its evaluation: *fiat justitia, ruat coelum*—let justice be done, though the heavens fall. In line with an idea that has now become common in moral philosophy, let us divide right-based justifications into two kinds: those that appeal to an *entitlement* theory and those that appeal to a theory of *distributive justice.*

We must be careful here to specify accurately the subject matter of the two theories in the present context. Someone might have an entitlement theory of PROPERTY and other personal rights, or a theory of distributive justice concerned with the proper distribution of money and social position, and then ask what set of political institutions provides the best guarantee of bringing about and sustaining the rights or the distribution advocated. These are, for the present purpose, examples of goal-based approaches, for they assess political institutions in accordance with their tendency to achieve an independently specified goal: it is irrelevant that the goal is itself right-based.

The subject matter of a right-based justification must be, then, rulership or political POWER. An entitlement theory in relation to political institutions will be one that says that, in virtue of some feature, a certain person or set of persons has a just title to rule. A theory of distributive justice in relation to political institutions treats political power as a good

or resource and then asks what a just distribution of that good or resource would be. It may be seen that, in these pure forms, both of these approaches are genuinely right-based in that they do not ground the case for their preferred form of decision making on its conduciveness to some end.

For better or worse, an entitlement theory of property does not make rights to property rest upon any claim to the effect that the holder of a piece of property will make better use of it than would others, or more generally that a certain allocation of property holdings will bring about a good state of affairs. And a (right-based) theory of distributive justice in relation to economic and social advantages makes the justice of a distribution an ultimate value rather than appealing to the conduciveness of that distribution to anything else, such as harmony or HAPPINESS. A right-based approach to the justification of political institutions is similar in this respect.

1.1 *The claim of a right to rule* has been, in the whole of human history, by far the most common of all justifications for a system of political decision making. An example is the theory lampooned by LOCKE (1632–1704) in the *First Treatise of Government* (1689), according to which monarchs have a hereditary right to rule derived from their being in the eldest line of descent from Adam. This conception of a right to rule takes a democratic form when it is asserted that "the people" in any given country have such a right: this is the doctrine of "popular sovereignty." Problems arise in implementing this principle since it is impractical for everyone to rule (in any sense recognizably similar to that in which an absolute monarch may be said to rule) and in any case "the people" frequently speaks with a divided voice. In sophisticated treatments, therefore, the doctrine of popular sovereignty forms a foundation for a goal-based criterion of type 2.2, where political institutions are assessed according to their tendency to give effect to "the will of the people" (see Nelson).

Sometimes an entitlement to rule is derived by saying that the people who should exercise political power are those who are best qualified to make good use of it. It should be observed, however, that this ceases to be an ultimate justification as soon as it is suggested that these people are best qualified to bring about some specified state of affairs, such as economic development or a communist society. For then the criterion is in the last analysis one of type 2.1: we start with a goal to be achieved by PUBLIC

POLICY and then recommend INSTITUTIONS as a means to its achievement. Only if some people are claimed to be competent without indicating any criterion of political achievement on the basis of which their competence is to be judged can a right to rule derived from competence be a freestanding justification. But in that case the claim of competence adds very little to the straightforward claim of a right to rule. It is interesting to ask (and no answer will be attempted here) exactly how the theory put forward by PLATO (c. 430–347 B.C.E.) in the *Republic* is to be categorized. Is the competence of the rulers metaphysically guaranteed, as it were? Or is there a basis upon which rulers selected in accordance with Plato's prescriptions could ever be said to have failed?

1.2 *The appeal to a just distribution of power* is the alternative way of providing a right-based justification for political institutions. Political power is here regarded as a good whose distribution is subject to criteria of justice. The democratic version of this holds that, ideally, political power should be distributed equally (see Beitz). However, once we try to give some substance to the idea of equal power, we are liable to find that (as with the idea of "popular sovereignty") it has to be cashed out in terms of a type 2.2 criterion for a desirable relationship between preferences and outcomes. That is to say, we start by asking how outcomes would have to be related to preferences if everyone were to have an equal influence over the outcome, and then work back from that to a set of political institutions that comes closest to achieving the desired relationship.

Nevertheless, it may be observed that the simple idea of equal power finds expression in a strong sentiment in favor of each person having one and only one vote. The rejection of "fancy franchises"—giving extra votes to certain people in virtue of educational qualifications or ownership of property, for example—is an axiom of political morality in all societies with any pretensions to DEMOCRACY. Thus, votes are thought of as resources to be shared on an equal basis among citizens, regardless of the impact that this has on the relation between preferences and outcomes (see Pennock). In effect, the construction of institutions to bring about an ideal relation between preferences and outcomes has to accept at the outset the constraint that each person is to have one vote.

In societies where civil rights are equal—in the sense that all citizens are considered equal before the law—equal political rights are a natural concomitant. By the same token, in societies where the idea of equal citizenship is less well established, we may expect to find that those who are superior in other respects will claim superiority in the allocation of political power as well. ARISTOTLE (384–322 B.C.E.), in the *Politics,* analyzed constitutional conflict within the Greek city states in precisely these terms.

> Democracy, for example, arises out of the notion that those who are equal in any respect are equal in all respects: because men are equally free, they claim to be absolutely equal. Oligarchy is based on the notion that those who are unequal in one respect are in all respects unequal; being unequal, that is, in property, they suppose themselves to be unequal absolutely. . . . There is also a superiority which is claimed by men of rank; for they are thought noble because they spring from wealthy and excellent ancestors.

2. *Goal-based justifications.* We now turn to assessments of political institutions that judge them by the outcomes that they tend to produce. We have already met one kind of outcome-orientated justification in the discussion of types 1.1 and 1.2. For we saw there that the idea of popular sovereignty and that of equal power both require, in any sophisticated treatment, to be translated into a specification of the desirable relation between preferences and outcomes. There is, however, a much less esoteric way of justifying political institutions by reference to outcomes, and that is to stipulate certain substantive criteria of good outcomes and then suggest that political institutions are to be assessed in accordance with their tendency to bring about such outcomes. We have in fact already come across this in connection with type 1.1, since it was pointed out in the discussion there that claims of a right to rule grounded on professions of superior competence are liable to reduce to arguments that some desirable state of affairs is most likely to be achieved if power is placed in the hands of a certain set of people.

In this second case the outcome to be aimed at is given specific content. This forms a contrast with the first case, where the outcome to be aimed at is defined only in relation to preferences: until we know the preferences we have no way of saying what is a desirable outcome. Let us look at these in turn, taking up first the case where the outcome is specified and then the case where it is not.

2.1 *Specified outcomes* may be relatively concrete: I earlier alluded to the achievement of a high rate of economic growth or the creation of a communist society as examples. Alternatively, the outcome may be expressed quite abstractly, by saying for example that political institutions should be conducive to justice or to the greatest happiness of the greatest number. The essence of the view in question is simply that political institutions are to be judged instrumentally, according to their predictable tendencies to bring about good or bad outcomes. It follows from this that a certain system of decision making may well be recommended for use under some conditions and not others, since the value of the outcomes it produces may be expected to vary depending on circumstances.

It seems safe to suggest that justification by outcome is by far the most common kind of justification for political institutions provided by political philosophers in the last three centuries. ROUSSEAU (1712–1778) offers a good (though difficult) illustration in his *Social Contract* (1762). Rousseau's starting point is the General Will, a desire for the COMMON GOOD of the citizens of a state. This can, he maintains, be expressed only by the body of citizens meeting in an assembly. But the decisions of an assembly may or may not embody the General Will. The General Will "always tends towards the public utility," but the people may not put the General Will first when voting.

Rousseau argues that, under conditions of approximate equality and complex interdependence of INTERESTS, citizens will put the public good first in their deliberations and votes of the assembly will then realize the General Will. But "when the social bond begins to slacken," votes in the assembly will tend to reflect private interests rather than the public interest. The state then ceases to be legitimate, because the General Will no longer corresponds to a majority vote.

It should be acknowledged that Rousseau makes a bow in the direction of a "popular sovereignty" view of type 1.1 when he says: "The people that is subject to the laws ought to be their author. Only those who are forming an association have the right to regulate the conditions of the society." But this has to be read in conjunction with the claim that direct voting on laws is a necessary (though not sufficient) condition for the expression of the General Will. Thus, the best overall interpretation of Rousseau would seem to make him a theorist of the General Will (with popular sovereignty as an essential prerequisite) rather than a theorist of popular sovereignty.

The classical utilitarians, BENTHAM (1748–1832) and JAMES MILL (1773–1836), offer a more straightforward illustration of an instrumental approach to political institutions.

> Bentham's initial expectation had been that the reign of utility would be inaugurated by an enlightened aristocracy. . . . Bentham became a democrat only when he was convinced that democracy was (at least in [Britain]) the sole form of government in which rulers would be obliged to respect social utility (and thus embark upon his programme of legal reform). Where Utilitarians believed they could control government without representative institutions, they were unsympathetic to them. [James] Mill . . . resolutely opposed in 1831 the idea of the establishment of any sort of representative legislature [in India]. He recommended, rather, a legislative council consisting of a lawyer, a native expert in Indian affairs, the [East India] Company's bureaucrats and 'a person thoroughly versed in the philosophy of man and government', in other words a utilitarian. (Lively and Rees)

The logic of UTILITARIANISM is thus to start by postulating a desirable end—the maximization of utility—and then to ask what political institutions show the best prospect of bringing that about. An enlightened utilitarian autocracy is best; but, failing that, democratic institutions stand a better chance than others. This case for democracy is, however, entirely contingent, resting upon the belief that a majority of voters will support policies that are in accordance with the utilitarian criterion.

In any system of political decision making, policies will reflect the policy preferences of some person or people, whether a utilitarian autocrat, a Rousseauan assembly, or a modern mass electorate voting in parliamentary elections. A consistent adherent of type 2.1 justifications will therefore seek to put power in the hands of those with preferences or policies conducive to the outcome stipulated as desirable. Anyone with a type 2.1 theory must therefore have a theory of the formation of policy preferences, except in the very unusual case represented by James Mill's proposal for India, where the person to be given power is actually picked out by reference to his policy preferences.

We have seen how Rousseau paid careful attention to the conditions under which the decisions of an assembly of citizens could be expected to embody the General Will. James Mill, in his defense of democracy as a second best to an enlightened utilitarian despotism, also put forward a theory of preference formation. The lower orders would, he suggested, take their policy preferences from their social betters, so there was no danger of there being a majority in favor of rash programmes of redistribution. But perhaps the best understanding of the logic of type 2.1 justification was displayed by his son, JOHN STUART MILL (1806–1873), who argued that any set of political institutions is to be judged by asking two questions: "How far it promotes the good management of the affairs of society by means of the existing faculties, moral, intellectual, and active, of its various members, and what is its effect in improving or deteriorating those faculties" (John Stuart Mill; see also Pateman). Representative government, according to Mill, is the best form of government on both criteria; but it is particularly significant for its effects in the second department, and this is, he claims, the more important. "The first element of good government . . . being the virtue and intelligence of the human beings composing the community, the most important point of excellence which any form of government can possess is to promote the intelligence and virtue of the people themselves." And Mill's criterion for political virtue is identical with Rousseau's: "Whenever the general disposition of the people is such, that each individual regards only those of his interests which are selfish, and does not dwell on, or concern himself with, his share of the general interest, in such a state of things good government is impossible."

2.2 Nonspecified outcomes have to be contrasted with specified outcomes rather carefully to get the intended distinction right. In both cases it is supposed that there is a "right answer"—an ideal set of outcomes—and that political institutions are to be assessed in terms of their tendency to produce that answer. Where they differ is that in the first category the "right answer" can be defined independently of anyone's policy preferences, whereas in the second the "right answer" is to be arrived at by aggregating policy preferences, in some way or other. Thus, as we have seen, those who put forward aggregate utility or social justice (or some more concrete outcome) as the criterion by which political institutions are to be judged will value institutions according to their tendency to give power to those who have policy preferences for the specified outcome or to stimulate policy preferences for the specified outcome among those who have power (or both). By contrast, those who take the second position believe that there is no way of specifying a "right answer" without knowing what people's policy preferences are—or at any rate that even if this can be done it is irrelevant to the advocacy of a set of institutions for political decision making. As Michael Dummett puts it: "There are two problems: what the outcome ought to be, given what the voters want; and how to devise a voting procedure that will produce that outcome."

It is worth emphasizing here that the relevant preferences in the second case are preferences *for policies,* not preferences in general. A utilitarian, falling under 2.1, might construe the utility that is to be maximized in terms of the satisfaction of desires, but this would still open up a logical gap between an outcome meeting that criterion and the policy produced by aggregating the policy-preferences of citizens in accordance with some rule. For the preferences relevant to preference-utilitarianism are for states of affairs, whereas the preferences relevant to 2.2 are for policies. And the policies preferred by (say) a majority of citizens may or may not accord with the utilitarian criterion for judging states of affairs, whether construed according to the criterion of HEDONISM or in terms of satisfying wants.

The larger point that follows from this is that when we say that both 2.1 and 2.2 evaluate political institutions in terms of outcomes, the word "outcome" has to be given a different meaning in the two cases. In the case of 2.1 we ask what policies (including laws and so on) a certain set of decision-making institutions is likely to give rise to, then evaluate these policies by their conduciveness to economic growth, communism, justice, maximization of utility, and so on. These are the "outcomes" in terms of which political institutions are ultimately to be assessed. In the case of 2.2, however, the relevant "outcomes" of a set of decision making institutions are the decisions themselves—the laws and policies that they enact or, by inaction, keep in place. We do not look at the consequences of these decisions, but simply at the way in which the laws and policies themselves correspond or fail to correspond to the policy preferences of some set of people (*e.g.*, the citizens of a country) aggregated according to some rule.

The distinction between 2.1 and 2.2 is worth laboring because the whole of modern welfare economics is premised upon ignoring it. Until the 1920s, economic orthodoxy was utilitarian, and it was supposed that economic welfare was to be construed in utilitarian terms. Welfare economics was thus conceived of as the branch of economics that assessed economic policies and institutions according to their tendency to promote welfare. (See Pigou for the definitive work.) During the interwar period, doubts set in about the interpersonal comparison of utilities, and welfare economics was reformulated in terms that avoided them. But the resultant "social welfare function" was still conceived of as telling something about the welfare generated by a set of economic arrangements.

All this was changed by the publication of Kenneth Arrow's *Social Choice and Individual Values* in 1951. Arrow took the problem of constructing a social welfare function to be that of aggregating preferences for states of affairs. "Welfare" was thus to be constructed not out of things like consumption bundles, but out of preferences for overall states of the world. The burgeoning literature of "social choice" is in effect a technical study of ways of aggregating policy preferences into policy outcomes. It thus has nothing to do with social welfare on any uncontorted understanding of the term, but everything to do with the evaluation of political institutions (see Barry and Hardin).

Unfortunately, very little attention is given in this whole literature to the ethical foundations. Why should we drop the earlier idea that policies are to be evaluated by their tendency to promote human welfare, and take up instead the idea that they are to be evaluated by their correspondence with policy preferences? The answer would seem to lie in the skepticism about "value judgments" endemic among economists, which leads to treating the judgment that some policy is a good one as a "preference" for that policy, to be aggregated with other such "pref-erences" (see Barry). It is, in fact, hard to see how the notion that institutions are to be judged by their properties of aggregating policy preferences can be defended except by grounding it in considerations of type 1.1 or 1.2, that is to say either popular sovereignty or political equality.

Conclusion: The Current Debate

Within contemporary Anglo-American political philosophy it may be said that democracy is unchallenged—at least in the sense that there is no serious school of thought that opposes the institution of universal suffrage. In that sense, it may be said that the range of dispute is somewhat restricted. Yet at the same time the range of rationales offered is as wide as it could be: If we examine the four positions at the bottom of the tree diagram, we shall find that each of them has contemporary adherents. We can without difficulty identify believers in popular sovereignty (1.1), equal power (1.2), social justice (2.1), and "fair" preference-aggregation (2.2).

Unquestionably, however, the sharpest dispute lies between those who believe in a substantive "right answer" (usually formulated in terms of justice) and those who reject this and hold that political philosophers have no business second-guessing the outcomes of an appropriately democratic set of political institutions. Proponents of the first position (who include RAWLS, Nelson and Beitz) wish to see fundamental aspects of justice entrenched constitutionally, so as to put them beyond the reach of electoral majorities, and then judge the institutions that are to settle what is left open according to their expected tendency to come up with just outcomes. Echoing Rousseau, these writers pay a good deal of attention to the social conditions under which voters are most likely to support policies required by social justice.

Against them are ranged authors such as Barber and WALZER, who regard the efforts of political philosophers to lay down principles of justice as presumptuous. They are, it is suggested, contemporary Platonists who cast the U.S. Supreme Court in the role of Philosopher King (with themselves as expert advisors). According to these writers, politics should be an activity of creation, and what is created cannot be criticized by the use of external criteria. It is interesting to observe that these writers are also strongly reminiscent of Rousseau in the importance they attach to the creation of a political community of equal citizens, but they depart from him in denying that there is a "right answer" corresponding to Rousseau's General Will.

However, those who hold the first position would surely wish to allow that some things should be done simply because a majority wants them done, while those who hold the second position would certainly draw back from endorsing, say, GENOCIDE or SLAVERY, even if these outcomes had impeccably democratic credentials. It would appear therefore that any complete theory will have to bring together a number of the types of justification analyzed here.

See also: CIVIC GOOD AND VIRTUE; CIVIL RIGHTS AND CIVIC DUTIES; COMMON GOOD; COMMUNITARIANISM; COOPERATION, CONFLICT, AND COORDINATION; DEMOCRACY; ECONOMIC SYSTEMS; ENTITLEMENTS; EQUALITY; INDIVIDUALISM; INSTITUTIONS; INTERNATIONAL JUSTICE ENTRIES; JUSTICE, DISTRIBUTIVE; LIBERALISM; MARXISM; POWER; PUBLIC GOODS; PUBLIC POLICY; RATIONAL CHOICE; RIGHTS; SOCIAL AND POLITICAL PHILOSOPHY; WELFARE RIGHTS AND SOCIAL POLICY.

Bibliography

Aristotle. "Politics." In vol. 2 of *The Complete Works of Aristotle,* edited by Jonathan Barnes, pp. 1986–2129. Princeton: Princeton University Press, 1984. For discussion of conceptions of citizenship, see 1301 a28–b5.

Arrow, Kenneth J. *Social Choice and Individual Values.* 2d ed. New Haven: Yale University Press, 1963 [1951].

Barber, Benjamin R. *Strong Democracy.* Berkeley: University of California Press, 1984.

Barry, Brian. "Lady Chatterley's Lover and Doctor Fischer's Bomb Party." In *Foundations of Social Choice Theory,* edited by Jon Elster, and Aanund Hylland, 11–43. Cambridge: Cambridge University Press, 1986. Reprinted in Barry's *Democracy, Power, and Justice: Essays in Political Theory.* Oxford: Clarendon Press, 1989, 360–91; and Barry's *Liberty and Justice: Essays in Political Theory 2.* Oxford: Clarendon Press, 1991, 78–109.

Barry, Brian, and Russell Hardin. *Rational Man and Irrational Society? An Introduction and Sourcebook.* Beverly Hills, Calif.: Sage, 1982. For discussion of social choice theory, see part 2.

Beitz, Charles R. *Political Equality: An Essay in Democratic Theory.* Princeton: Princeton University Press, 1989. For procedural *vs.* nonprocedural justifications, see p. 20. For equal distribution of power, pp. 4–5.

Dummett, Michael. *Voting Procedures.* Oxford: Clarendon Press, 1984. Voters' preferences and voting procedures, see p. 10.

Dworkin, Ronald. "The Original Position." In *Reading Rawls,* edited by Norman Daniels, pp. 16–53. Oxford: Basil Blackwell, 1975. For right-based *vs.* goal-based justifications, p. 38.

Lively, Jack, and John Rees. "Introduction" to *Utilitarian Logic and Politics: James Mill's "Essay on Government," Macaulay's Critique, and the Ensuing Debate,* edited by Jack Lively and John Rees, pp. 3–52. Oxford: Oxford University Press, 1978. Bentham and Mill on democracy *vs.* utilitarianism, pp. 48–49.

Locke, John. *Two Treatises of Government.* Edited by Peter Laslett. New York: Mentor, 1965 [1689].

Mill, John Stuart. "Considerations on Representative Government." In vol. 2 of his *Essays on Politics and Society,* edited by J. M. Robson, pp. 371–577. Toronto: University of Toronto Press, 1977 [1861]. Pp. 39, 390, 404: government to promote the intelligence and virtue of the people.

Nelson, William. *On Justifying Democracy.* London: Routledge and Kegan Paul, 1980. Goal-based justification and the will of the people, pp. 54–55.

Pateman, Carole. *Participation and Democratic Theory.* Cambridge: Cambridge University Press, 1970. See especially chapter 2.

Pennock, J. Roland. *Democratic Political Theory.* Princeton: Princeton University Press, 1979. Pp. 153–54: one person one vote.

Pigou, A. C. *The Economics of Welfare.* 4th ed. London: Macmillan, 1948 [1920].

Plato. *The Republic.*

Rawls, John. *A Theory of Justice.* Cambridge, Mass.: Harvard University Press, 1971.

Rousseau, Jean-Jacques. *On the Social Contract, with Geneva Manuscript and Political Economy.* Edited by Roger D. Masters. New York: St. Martin's, 1978 [1762]. On the General Will, *Social Contract,* Book II, chapter 1, p. 59, chapter 3, p. 61; Book IV, chapter 1, p. 108. On "popular sovereignty," Book II, chapter 7, p. 67.

Walzer, Michael. "Philosophy and Democracy." *Political Theory* 9 (1981): 379–99.

Brian Barry

pornography

The ethical and political disputes over what to do about pornography are naturally much affected by what range of materials we are referring to when we speak of it. Etymologically, "pornography" meant writing about, or depictions of, female prostitutes. Today the core meaning of the term has been extended far beyond the original sense. It can be used to refer to sexually explicit depictions (including writing) of both men and women, prostitutes and nonprostitutes, and it is also common to speak of "child pornography." Not every sexually explicit picture or text warrants the label, however. Clinical descriptions of human sexuality in medical textbooks are usually exempted, as are essays such as this, no matter how explicit they become. Yet it has proved difficult to get general agreement on a definition of "pornography" as it is currently used.

For example, some define "pornography" evaluatively as involving the endorsement of, or approving portrayal of, women (or men, or children) being subordinated and wrongfully treated in a sexual manner. Defenders of the evaluative definition call attention to brutal cases. They ask us to consider, for instance, a noncondemnatory film of a woman with her nipples being cut off with a chain saw, or a jackhammer being shoved up her vagina. These viscerally jolting images quickly serve to remind us that among the materials referred to as pornographic are those which, although they may induce sexual excitement in some, are misleadingly described as "merely erotic" and which, far from upsetting only the prudish, are found objectionable even by those who "adore sex."

But there are difficulties with adopting such an evaluative definition. It would require settling moral issues in order to apply the term. And because such an evaluative definition is more restrictive than common usage, its use invites confusion. For example, it would accord with common usage to refer to films of happily married couples voluntarily engaging in explicit sexual activity (beyond foreplay) as "pornography." Arguably, the woman (or man) may not be wronged or exploited in such a case. So, the evaluative definition seems much at odds with common usage.

If we aim to reconstruct the meaning of "pornography" in current English, it is preferable to abandon overly restrictive, evaluative definitions. Ideally, we need a reasonably precise definition that accords with prevailing usage, is neither too broad nor too narrow, and is morally neutral. A neutral definition will allow all disputants over the morality of producing such materials, disseminating them, or censoring them, to agree on which materials are the subject of dispute. The failure to separate sharply the tasks of *identifying* which practices are at issue and

the *moral evaluation* of those practices leads to unnecessary confusion.

A more adequate definition is the following. Pornography is the sexually explicit depiction of persons, in words or images, created with the primary, proximate aim, and reasonable hope, of eliciting significant sexual arousal on the part of the consumer of such materials. Several points deserve comment. The dominant goal of most producers of pornography is to make money, but that fact is compatible with our definition. The definitional feature that the one proximate aim is to elicit sexual arousal will distinguish pornography from, say, nude photographs in a medical text, a case in which, presumably, no aim to arouse is present. A similar point may be made for other photography, painting, or sculpture in which aesthetic goals supplant such an aim. Assuming no primary, proximate intention by Michelangelo to cause sexual arousal, his statue of David is not pornographic, even if its effect on some is to evoke such arousal. Further, the "reasonable hope" clause in our definition implies that lovely, vivid photographs of juicy red strawberries normally, or always, fail to qualify as pornography. Similarly, the earnest would-be pornographer (for the general market) who thinks that his photograph of anorexic women in overcoats will be arousing will fail thereby to produce pornography. In both cases it is unreasonable to expect to evoke sexual arousal in a randomly chosen adult, and in neither case is there what would ordinarily be called a sexually explicit depiction.

Consider films of other (naked) primates engaged in orgasmic sexual activities, or photographs of newly dead, naked humans. These are not instances of pornography on the proposed definition (not being depictions of persons). It may be unimportant how we decide whether or not such cases are instances of pornography, or whether to amend our definition slightly. These cases are at least marginally pornographic, or are quasi-pornographic, or "near pornography." If we wish to discuss them we can (as we have here).

Our broad characterization of pornography sweeps into its conceptual net a wide variety of materials. It will be useful for certain purposes, then, to identify relevant subcategories, *e.g.,* child versus adult pornography, or violent and non-violent.

Several worries remain. There is the familiar problem of vagueness, *i.e.,* the definition is not sufficiently precise to preclude the possibility of a variety of borderline cases. Since "rape" is often defined (partly) as involving the use of *duress,* "rape" is vague; no one infers from this that "although rape cannot be defined, I know it when I see it." Those who insist that anti-pornography laws in the United States are too vague to be constitutional run the risk of invoking unreasonable standards of precision.

An element of vagueness in our definition is due largely to the fact that we lack precise criteria (though it may be reasonable to stipulate some) for "sexually explicit depiction" and "significant sexual arousal." What is "sexually explicit" is not plausibly interpreted as merely what clearly reveals gender membership. What else is needed cannot be pursued here. Certain images, by provoking the imagination or by a certain identification with the role of one depicted, normally arouse significant sexual DESIRE in those consuming (reading or looking at) the pornography. The insistence and persistence of this desire, its physiological effects, its taking over of one's awareness, are familiar indices of the extent of sexual arousal. Important in deciding whether material is likely to evoke significant sexual arousal is its probable effect on an average person in a certain population, *e.g.,* females of normal (understood statistically) mind and body between fifteen and sixty years of age. The reactions of particular individuals are inconclusive.

It may be objected that our definition fails to distinguish between the pornographic and the erotic, or fails to bring out what is so bad about pornography as opposed to the erotic. Consider the first point. The term "pornographic" is often used pejoratively and the term "erotic" less so or not at all. It is sufficient to note that the pejorative connotation of "pornography" is defeasible; it is not contradictory to say that one likes or approves of (some) pornography. Mainly, it is important to be clear whether the term is being used neutrally. If so, the issue of the moral evaluation of the pornographic is open. If not used neutrally, one moral dispute will be whether some entity is, or counts as, pornographic. The neutral use of "pornography," as defined here, is very similar in meaning, then, to the meaning of "erotic."

The term "erotic" means what arouses, or tends to arouse, sexual desire or LOVE. Hence, all pornography would seem to be erotic (though much or none may arouse love). However, not all the erotic is pornographic. Seeing our juicy strawberry may be erotic but it will not be pornography given our re-

striction of the latter term to denote only sexually explicit depictions of persons.

What about prurience? There are two primary meanings associated with "appeal to the prurient interest." One is what provokes sexual desire *simpliciter.* Thus, what is erotic or pornographic, by definition, will do so. A second meaning is what appeals to unusual or immoderate sexual desires. Whether a given instance of erotica or the pornographic does so will presumably be a contingent matter and vary from person to person.

How then does the obscene fit in? The core meaning of "obscene" is that which is repulsive. What is repulsive (to see, to hear, etc.) will vary somewhat across cultures and among individuals. Some events may be universally repulsive, *e.g.,* a person eating his or her own vomit or excrement, or the TORTURE of a child. Reactions to observing sexual activities often are influenced by the reactor's moral convictions. The tendency to equate the pornographic and the obscene is extremely curious. By definition the erotic and the pornographic tend to arouse sexual desire, a positive attraction toward some object (present or absent) of desire. To be repulsed is to desire to avoid. One may experience a bit of attraction and repulsion at once, *e.g.,* to a fire. Still, it is not obvious that one can *both* be repulsed *on balance* and be positively attracted *on balance* to one object. Hence, it is not obvious that anything can be both pornographic and obscene (in the sense of repulsive). If so, a good deal of public and judicial discussion about such matters is muddled. Of course, something can be pornographic (tending to arouse sexual desire across the adult population) but repulsive to particular individuals.

The core meaning of "obscene" involves no necessary connection with matters of sexuality: understandably, some describe torture, or war as obscene. Since some are repelled by "swear words," or by words denoting sexual organs or sexual activities, understandably, they describe those words as "obscenities" or "obscene."

What has preceded is conceptual sorting. If it is on the right track, the path to a moral evaluation of pornography (its production, dissemination, or restrictions on dissemination) is clearer.

See also: AESTHETICS; CENSORSHIP; CHILDREN; COERCION; CRUELTY; DESIRE; DIGNITY; EXPLOITATION; FEMINIST ETHICS; FITTINGNESS; FREEDOM OF THE

PRESS; HARM AND OFFENSE; HYPOCRISY; LIBRARY
AND INFORMATION PROFESSIONS; MASS MEDIA; PAS-
SION; PATERNALISM; PLEASURE; PUBLIC POLICY; PUR-
ITANISM; RAPE; SEXUALITY AND SEXUAL ETHICS; TOR-
TURE; VIOLENCE AND NON-VIOLENCE.

Bibliography

Copp, David, and Susan Wendell, eds. *Pornography and Censorship.* Buffalo, N.Y.: Prometheus Books, 1983.

Feinberg, Joel. *Offense to Others: Moral Limits to the Criminal Law.* Oxford: Oxford University Press, 1988.

Gubar, Susan, and Joan Huff, eds. *For Adult Users Only: The Dilemma of Violent Pornography.* Bloomington: Indiana University Press, 1989.

Lederer, Laura J., and Richard Delgado, eds. *The Price We Pay: The Case Against Racist Speech, Hate Propaganda, and Pornography.* New York: Hill and Wang, 1995.

MacKinnon, Catherine. *Only Words.* Cambridge, Mass.: Harvard University Press, 1993.

Matsuda, Mari, Charles Lawrence, and Richard Delgado, eds. *Words that Wound: Critical Race Theory, Assaultive Speech, and the First Amendment.* Boulder, Colo.: Westview, 1993.

McElroy, Wendy. *A Woman's Right to Pornography.* New York: St. Martin's, 1995.

Posner, Richard. *Sex and Reason.* Cambridge, Mass.: Harvard University Press, 1992.

Russell, Diana. *Against Pornography: The Evidence of Harm.* Berkeley, Calif.: Russell Publishing, 1994.

Schauer, Frederick. *Free Speech: A Philosophical Enquiry.* Cambridge: Cambridge University Press, 1982.

Strossen, Nadine. *Defending Pornography: Free Speech, Sex, and the Fight for Women's Rights.* New York: Scribner, 1995.

Tisdale, Sally. *Talk Dirty to Me: An Intimate Philosophy of Sex.* New York: Doubleday, 1994.

Tucker, David. *Law, Liberalism, and Free Speech.* Totowa, N.J.: Rowman and Allanheld, 1986.

Williams, Linda. *Hard Core: Power, Pleasure, and the "Frenzy of the Visible."* Berkeley: University of California Press, 1991.

Donald Vandeveer

possibilism

Possibilism is the thesis that the moral status of an act depends on the best possible future acts it would enable the agent to perform. Possibilism contrasts with Actualism, the thesis that the moral status of an act depends on the future acts the agent *would actually* perform.

Since the 1970s, moral theorists have recognized that a present action's status does not depend just on its consequences or on the agent's past acts (such as her making a promise to perform the present act), but also depends in some way on future acts of the same agent. Consider the following abstractly described case:

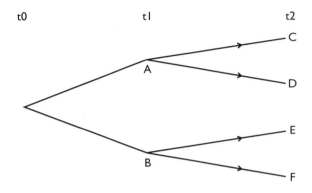

The agent must choose between performing act *A* or act *B* at *t1*. If she performs *A*, she will then have to choose between *C* and *D* at *t2*. On the other hand, if she performs *B*, she will have to choose between *E* and *F* at *t2*. Of the acts at *t2*, *C* is best, *E* is second-best, *F* is third-best, and *D* is worst. Assume that if the agent performs *A* at *t1*, she will actually perform *D* at *t2*, while if she performs *B* at *t1*, she will actually perform *E* at *t2*. Which act ought she to perform at *t1*? The Possibilist says that the agent ought to perform *A*, since performing *A* enables her to perform *C*, the best possible act at *t2*. The Actualist says that the agent ought to perform *B* instead, since *A* would lead her to perform D, the worst act of *t2*, while B would lead her to perform E, a better act. Some theorists, feeling the intuitive pull of both solutions to the agent's dilemma, have attempted to define an intermediate proposal. One type of intermediate solution recognizes multiple levels of obligation, while another type relativizes apparently inconsistent obligations to acts and times. Such proposals often leave it unclear what the agent *really* ought to do.

Even to set up this dilemma involves conceptual difficulties. For example, it must be possible to assess act *D* as worse than act *E*, even though *D* and *E* are not alternatives to each other at *t2*, the time of their possible performance. It must also be possible to define a notion of the intrinsic moral goodness of an act so that the act's *overall* moral status can be understood as a function of its own intrinsic goodness together with the intrinsic goodness of the acts that might or would follow it.

Debates over the issue often become involved in questions of FREE WILL versus determinism. Is it legitimate for moral theory to conceptualize a person's future acts as fixed by her present acts (as Actualism does)? Other equally difficult questions arise. Should she think of her options as acts *A* and *B,* or should she think of her options as *A*-followed-by-*D* and *B*-followed-by-*E,* or should she think of her options as *A*-and-*C, A*-and-*D, B*-and-*E,* and *B*-and-*F* ? If her doing *A* would be followed by her doing *D,* is the sequence *A*-and-*C* genuinely available to her? Suppose the reason she would do *D* if she did *A* is that she would not be brave enough to do *C.* In these circumstances, when Actualism prescribes *B* instead of *A,* is it allowing her to use poor CHARACTER as an excuse for not performing the better action? Theorists have been deeply divided on these issues, and these divisions appear to explain much of the intensity with which the debate between Actualism and Possibilism has been conducted.

See also: ACTION; COMMENSURABILITY; CONSEQUENTIALISM; DUTY AND OBLIGATION; FREE WILL; FREEDOM AND DETERMINISM; IDEALIZED AGENTS; LOGIC AND ETHICS; PERFECTIONISM; PRESCRIPTIVISM; SLIPPERY SLOPE ARGUMENTS; UTILITARIANISM; VOLUNTARY ACTS.

Bibliography

Defenders of Actualism

Goldman, Holly S. "Dated Rightness and Moral Imperfection." *The Philosophical Review* 85 (October 1976): 449–87.

Sobel, J. Howard. "Utilitarianism and Past and Future Mistakes." *Nous* 10 (May 1976): 195–219.

———. "Utilitarian Principles for Imperfect Agents." *Theoria* 42 (1982): 113–26.

Defenders of Possibilism

Aqvist, Lennart. "Improved Formulations of Act-Utilitarianism." *Nous* 3 (September 1969): 299–323.

Feldman, Fred. *Doing the Best We Can.* Dordrecht, Holland: D. Reidel, 1986. Parts 1 and 2.

Goldman, Holly S. "Doing the Best One Can." In *Values and Morals,* edited by A. I. Goldman and Jaegwon Kim, 185–214. Dordrecht, Holland: Reidel, 1978.

Greenspan, P. S. "Oughts and Determinism: A Response to Goldman." *The Philosophical Review* 87 (1978): 77–83.

Thomason, Richmond. "Deontic Logic and the Role of Freedom in Moral Deliberation." In *New Studies in Deontic Logic,* edited by R. Hilpinen, 177–86. Dordrecht, Holland: D. Reidel, 1981.

Intermediate Theories

Jackson, Frank, and Robert Pargetter. "Oughts, Options, and Actualism." *The Philosophical Review* 85 (April 1976): 233–55.

McKinsey, Michael. "Levels of Obligation." *Philosophical Studies* 35 (1979): 385–95.

Goldman [1979] as well as Jackson and Pargetter have discussed issues concerning simultaneous actions that parallel the Actualism/Possibilism debate.

Holly M. Smith (Holly S. Goldman)

postmodernism

The term "postmodernism" has no precise, canonical definition. Its meaning shifts depending on topic and discipline. In this essay, "postmodernism" refers to philosophical works that offer a comprehensive critique of modernism a genealogy of which can be traced to NIETZSCHE (1844–1900) and HEIDEGGER (1889–1976). Thus, the term refers to writers associated with deconstruction, post-structuralism, and certain strands of PHENOMENOLOGY as well.

"Modernism" refers to the ideals and conceptual framework that have informed Western civilization since roughly the end of the Middle Ages. The dominant tendency in philosophical modernism is the gradual development of the notion that some of our ideas provide accurate, objective representations of an independent, external world. Thus, there are unambiguously true answers to central questions regarding the nature of reality, which ultimately form a coherent whole, and reliable methods for answering these questions. The modernist conception of agency asserts that agents employ these representations in forming intentions freely chosen through rational reflection. History is a developmental process of increasing freedom in accordance with reason, the course of which is determined by autonomous human subjects.

Postmodernists claim that cultural transformations in the twentieth century and recent discoveries regarding the instability of linguistic meaning, in work such as that of Jacques Derrida, require the rejection of modernist conceptions of knowledge and agency. The central thesis of postmodern philosophical literature is that our representation of reality is mediated by diverse cultural influences, linguistic indeterminacy, technological change, historical accidents, institutional frameworks, and the vagaries of DESIRE. Thus, human knowledge consists of multiple perspectives with no fixed, independent criteria for choosing between them. Furthermore, moral agents are not autonomous, self-determining rational choosers but are instead the product of those social forces in which they are embedded. Thus, meaning is indeterminate. Multiple, incompatible interpretations of reality are inevitable, and human ACTION is circumscribed and limited by social and historical contexts. This generates the problem of incommensurability—rival perspectives are constituted by differences so substantial that adherents to one perspective may be incapable of recognizing the value and substance of the other. In consequence, our capacity to rationally assess competing points of view is sharply limited, and modernist aspirations to achieve objective, coherent representations of reality and a universal moral code in the service of a progressive, salvific history are no longer credible.

With regard to ethics, conceptions of the "good" and the "right" will themselves be products of multiple, incompatible perspectives resulting in the loss of shared identity and the absence of universal regulative NORMS. Thus, traditional ethical theory has little to say about the practice of ethics since attempts to specify and justify rules of conduct or delineate VIRTUES require general criteria of assessment the existence of which are denied by perspectivism. Furthermore, relying, in part, on Heidegger's critique of Western rationality as bound up with the unconstrained will toward technological domination, postmodernists argue that the dominance of representational patterns of thought in modern civilization has morally disastrous consequences. If there are no general substantive truths regarding how human beings ought to live, and rival points of view are incompatible or incommensurable, then the attempt to articulate universal norms or general descriptions of social reality will in fact only express a partial perspective inappropriate when applied outside their context. When coupled with social POWER, the demand that inquiry must ultimately yield a unified and coherent system of truths results in the imposition of an alien will and the potential for suffering. Thus, attempts to prescribe universal norms or to systematize normative recommendations based on truths about human nature undermine the very pursuit of human freedom central to the modern project.

This charge that reason is implicated in suffering has various characterizations which differ in scope and severity. On the more modest end of the scale, Richard Rorty, although rejecting the comprehensive moral indictment of Western civilization, nevertheless argues that describing others in terms they do not accept inhibits the formation of social identity and generates the helplessness of a life lived on someone else's terms. Others, such as John Caputo, argue that positive formulations of conceptions of the good introduce hierarchies that inevitably produce suffering for those who live by different conceptions of value. Zygmunt Bauman and LÉVINAS argue that limiting a moral perspective to generalizable norms transforms morality into mere conventional behavior, promotes an empty bureaucratic morality, and inhibits our genuine moral responses, which must respond to particular persons in particular situations and be accompanied by a sense of infinite RESPONSIBILITY never satisfied by what is acceptable, expected, or reciprocated.

Furthermore, postmodernists tend to view the suffering caused by these alleged excesses as invisible or concealed. Much of Michel FOUCAULT's (1926–1984) work has been devoted to showing how the application of knowledge in areas such as the PUNISHMENT of criminals, the curing of the ill and the insane, and the regulation of sexuality has produced suffering that is systematically excluded from recognition. Jean-François Lyotard argues that in conflicts between discourses, in the absence of universal criteria to adjudicate the conflict, the imposition of the rules of one discourse inevitably produces victims whose cases are unpresentable in the prevailing discourse, and suffering that has no voice and no name and thus can receive no relief or compensation. This position leads Lyotard to reject consensus as the aim of inquiry or dialogue.

Perhaps most extreme is Lévinas's view that the Western philosophical tradition systematically suppresses genuine moral responsibility. The dominant trend in Western thought is the attempt to achieve the unity of subject and object by bringing all reality under the control of rational categories. Lévinas claims that, on this view, nothing is truly alien to the autonomous subject since rational concepts are the measure of all meaning. However, such a subject must fail to grasp that which resists generalization—the singularity and particularity expressed in the face of another human being. Thus, moral responsibility—responsiveness to this singularity and particularity—is suppressed within the Western tradition. For Lévinas, rationality is inherently violent—assimilating all difference when possible and suppressing what cannot be assimilated.

In consequence, postmodernism will offer the inherent violence and moral blindness of the Western tradition—the inability to respond to "otherness"—as part of the explanation of how the extraordinary commitment to human liberation characteristic of liberal societies could exist side by side with colonialism, imperialism, SLAVERY, and events of mass death such as the HOLOCAUST.

The claim that the most serious wrongs are those that go unnoticed or cannot be articulated defines the problem of ethics for postmodernism—"how to present the unpresentable" as Lyotard says, or how to articulate what cannot be expressed or rationally grounded. The source of the imperative of obligation resists rational representation and can be philosophically grasped only through rhetorical strategies of indirect discourse.

Although postmodernists cannot without self-contradiction offer a set of principles or rules of conduct that would provide a guide to representing the unrepresentable, they do attempt to respond to the opacity of moral claims and our tendency toward moral blindness. All will advocate skepticism, not only toward normative systems that attempt to replace individual, context-sensitive judgment but also toward assertions that express certainty or confidence on moral questions. Rorty advocates an attitude of irony toward one's deepest beliefs, Caputo and Lyotard a sense of one's own inevitable fallibility when addressing moral questions. Because injustice is the product of entrenched representations of social reality that by their very nature exclude opposing points of view, Lyotard and Foucault advocate rampant innovation as our most important moral capacity, the search for new modes of expression that disrupt established convictions and pose new questions. Caputo argues that this constant awareness of the ambiguity of moral notions and the indeterminacy of moral judgment provokes a skeptical attitude that opens up new possibilities of thought and action, perhaps rendering an agent more susceptible to moral claims by promoting the virtues of humility and COMPASSION.

Lévinas radicalizes this view claiming that the ethical relation requires infinite responsibility, accepting the asymmetrical importance of the NEEDS of the other relative to my own and hence the recognition that one's responsibility for others never ends no matter what one has already done and regardless of reciprocation. Thus, Lévinas views the ethical relation as a relation with radical otherness (alterity) that disturbs the coherence of the self, challenging the agent to become other than what she is.

Such a view presupposes that human beings have a basic capacity to respond to the needs of others. However, there is substantial disagreement on how to characterize this capacity, although all agree that moral responsiveness is neither a product of deliberation or argument, nor something that a theoretical justification would secure. Postmodern pragmatists such as Rorty will argue that an aversion to CRUELTY is a product of history and culture, simply the way people firmly entrenched within the liberal tradition have come to view the importance of others. For Caputo, the feeling of being bound by an obligation is a pre-reflective element of human existence fundamental to our awareness of other persons, motivated especially by victims who suffer irretrievable loss. Edith Wyschogrod understands this concern for the other to be grounded in the vulnerability of the body. She argues that narratives of the lives of saints communicate a physical sense of urgency that transforms the moral subject such that desire can operate on behalf of another—a form of radical ALTRUISM.

In any case, fundamental to postmodern ethics is the recognition of the emotional influence concrete, particular persons have on each other unmediated by principles, rationalization, or ideology. To be within the realm of the ethical is to be so captivated by the suffering of other people that ignoring their plight is not an option.

See also: AGENT-CENTERED MORALITY; ALTRUISM; AUTONOMY OF MORAL AGENTS; COMMENSURABILITY; DELIBERATION AND CHOICE; DUTY AND OBLIGATION; FOUCAULT; FREEDOM AND DETERMINISM; GOOD, THEORIES OF THE; HEIDEGGER; IDEALIST ETHICS;

INTENTION; LÉVINAS; MORAL ABSOLUTES; MORAL POINT OF VIEW; MORAL PLURALISM; MORAL REALISM; MORAL RELATIVISM; MORAL SAINTS; MULTICULTURALISM; NIETZSCHE; PHENOMENOLOGY; RATIONALITY VS. REASONABLENESS; RECIPROCITY; RESPONSIBILITY; RIGHT, CONCEPTS OF; SKEPTICISM IN ETHICS.

Bibliography

Bauman, Zygmunt. *Postmodern Ethics.* Oxford: Blackwell Press, 1993.

Caputo, John. *Radical Hermeneutics.* Bloomington: Indiana University Press, 1987.

Derrida, Jacques. *Writing and Difference.* Translated by Alan Bass. Chicago: University of Chicago Press, 1978.

———. "Racism's Last Word." Translated by Peggy Kamuf. *Critical Inquiry* 12 (Autumn, 1985): 290–99.

Foucault, Michel *The Foucault Reader.* Edited by Paul Rabinow. New York: Pantheon Books, 1984.

Heidegger, Martin. *The Question Concerning Technology.* Translated by W. Lovitt. New York: Harper and Row, 1977 [1954].

Lévinas, Emmanuel. *Totality and Infinity.* Translated by Alphonso Lingis. Pittsburgh: Duquesne University Press, 1969 [1961].

———. *Otherwise Than Being, or Beyond Essence.* Translated by Alphonso Lingis. The Hague: Martinus Nijhoff, 1981 [1974].

Lyotard, Jean-François. *Le differend.* Minneapolis: University of Minnesota Press, 1988.

Nietzsche, Friedrich. *On the Genealogy of Morals.* Translated by Walter Kaufmann and R. J. Hollingdale. New York: Random House, 1967 [1887].

Rorty, Richard. *Contingency, Irony, and Solidarity.* Cambridge: Cambridge University Press, 1989.

Wyschogrod, Edith. *Saints and Postmodernism.* Chicago: University of Chicago Press, 1990.

Dwight Furrow

power

A dispositional concept (as opposed to "influence") that identifies the capacity of agents to produce outcomes—to make a difference to the world. We may be concerned with an agent's power to produce a specific outcome or set of outcomes, or with assessing an agent's overall power, or with comparing the power of different agents. In aggregating and comparing power, there is strong disagreement as to what delimiting criterion specifies what is to count as power in (various) social contexts. There are two ways such a delimitation can be made: by delimiting what kinds of outcome are to count (what differences are significant) and how to locate the capacity to produce them (what is to count as being able to make a significant difference).

Many agree with Bertrand RUSSELL (1872–1970) and Max WEBER (1864–1920) who insisted that outcomes be intended. For Russell, power is "the production of intended effects"; for Weber, it is "the probability that an actor in a social relationship will be in a position to carry out his own will, regardless of the basis on which this probability rests." But is INTENTION *sufficient*? What if, like the Stoics, I want only what I can get, or, like a conformist, only what others want, or, like a sycophant, only what (I think) others want me to want? Am I powerful, as opposed to you, if the effects I can intentionally produce are produced because you have threatened or induced me, or if I can produce them only at enormous cost (say by sacrificing my life or what gives it value) or if I can produce nothing but trivial effects (and how are we to decide what is important or trivial here?)? And are the intentions actual or hypothetical? Is power not the capacity to achieve what I might plausibly, but do not actually, want? And is intention *necessary*? Must all power's effects be intended? Can power not be exercised in routine or unconsidered ways, as when, by making investment decisions, I deprive unknown people of work, or provide them with it? Perhaps, rather, the outcomes of power are to be identified as affecting the *interests* (whether positively or negatively) of the powerful and of those their power affects. That the former are advanced only at the expense of the latter is an unduly restrictive assumption found in much of the existing literature on power, even though this is clearly only one possibility.

As for the location of power, some (like Russell) mistakenly equate it with its *exercise* (for example, looking, like Robert Dahl and his behaviorist followers, for the person who prevails in making decisions in situations which involve conflicting INTERESTS) or with the *resources* that back it (for example, measuring the power of states by their military and/or economic resources). But, even among those who correctly see power as a capacity, there is considerable dispute about when it may be said to exist. Some, again like Weber, see conflict and overcoming opposition as essential to it. On this "asymmetric" view, the paradigm use of "power" is "power over"— the securing of compliance of some by others, by means that range from violence and force through manipulation and COERCION to AUTHORITY and rational persuasion. (Whether this last is a form of power is also controversial; if you persuade me, is my mind changed by you or by the reasons you offer me?) Some, like Hannah ARENDT (1906–1975), see it as intrinsically cooperative, as "the human ability not just to act but to act in concert," contrasting with violence and force, and the "command-obedience relationship." On her view, power is "never the property of an individual; it belongs to a group and remains in existence only so long as the group holds together." Others seek to combine both aspects in a more comprehensive view. Yet others see it as an impersonal capacity of social systems to achieve collectively binding goals (Parsons) or reduce complexity (Luhmann), or as the capacity of society to discipline individuals, shaping their discourse and indeed their very desires (Foucault).

Most, however, see power as a capacity of agents, whether individual or collective, but here too there is disagreement over how to interpret that capacity. Does "power" identify what an agent can do under various conditions, or what an agent can do under the conditions that actually obtain? On the first view, you are powerful if you can produce the appropriate outcomes in a wide range of possible circumstances; on the second, only if present circumstances enable you to do so (for example, a particular configuration of voting preferences enables your vote to decide the outcome). The first view identifies an ability that one can deploy across a range of (standard) contexts, the second what one is able to do in a specific time and place. A further view would include as part of power the access to, or the capacity to command, resources, whatever the agent does. On this view, power can include a "passive" component—not only the ability to produce outcomes, but also the ability to secure advantage without effort. On this view, power becomes a generalized index of INEQUALITY.

The truth is that we have diverse reasons for locating and comparing power. We may want to know which actors are in a position to bring about certain desired or feared outcomes, in a range of possible situations, or just in the actual situation. We may want to attribute moral or legal or political RESPONSIBILITY for what is done, or not done, in a particular situation. We may want to evaluate a society, or part of a society, in regard to its distribution of access to advantage and control. Or we may want to explain events or processes in terms of the causal responsibility of particular agents, and thus need to know which agents could do what in given circumstances. These different concerns generate different ways of identifying both capacity and relevant outcomes, and it is probably a mistake to look for a single "objective" conception of power on which all rational persons must agree.

See also: ACTION; AUTHORITY; COERCION; COMPETITION; COOPERATION, CONFLICT, AND COORDINATION; CORRUPTION; DEMOCRACY; DESIRE; ELITE, CONCEPT OF; EQUALITY; FREEDOM AND DETERMINISM; GOVERNMENT, ETHICS IN; INEQUALITY; INTENTION; INTERESTS; OPPRESSION; PROPERTY; RESPONSIBILITY; VIOLENCE AND NON-VIOLENCE.

Bibliography

Arendt, Hannah. *On Violence.* New York: Harcourt Brace, 1970. Quotations from pp. 44, 40.

Dahl, R. A. *Who Governs? Democracy and Power in an American City.* New Haven: Yale University Press, 1961.

Dowding, Keith. *Power.* Minneapolis: University of Minnesota Press, 1996.

Foucault, Michel. *Power.* Edited by James D. Faubrion; translated by Robert Hurley, *et al.* Essential Works of Foucault 1954–1984, vol. 3. New York: The New Press, 2000.

Luhmann, Niklas. *Macht.* Stuttgart: Ferdinand Enke, 1975.

Lukes, Steven. *Power: A Radical View.* London: Macmillan, 1974.

———, ed. *Power: Readings in Social and Political Theory.* New York: New York University Press, 1986.

Morriss, Peter. *Power: A Philosophical Analysis.* Manchester: Manchester University Press, 1987.

Russell, Bertrand. *Power: A New Social Analysis.* London: Allen and Unwin, 1975 [1938]. Quoted from p. 25.

Wartenberg, Thomas. *The Forms of Power: From Domination to Transformation.* Philadelphia: Temple University Press, 1990.

Weber, Max. *Economy and Society.* Edited by G. Roth, and C. Wittich. Berkeley: University of California Press, 1978 [1922]. See especially chapter 10, pp. 941–48. Quoted from p. 53.

Wrong, Denis H. *Power: Its Forms, Bases and Uses.* Oxford: Basil Blackwell, 1979.

Steven Lukes

practical reason[ing]

Based on two premises, one stating that an agent has a certain goal or INTENTION in mind and a second one stating that this agent knows that some particular ACTION is a means to carry out that intention, practical reasoning draws the conclusion that the agent ought practically to carry out this particular action. In sequences of goal-directed argumentation, practical reasoning is a chaining together of the two basic schemes of practical inference represented below, where a is an agent, A is an action, and G is a goal.

> G is a goal for a
>> Doing A is necessary for a to carry out G
>>> Therefore, a ought to do A.
> G is a goal for a
>> Doing A is sufficient for a to carry out G
>>> Therefore, a ought to do A.

The first type of practical inference is called the "necessary condition scheme," and the second type is called the "sufficient condition scheme." Practical reasoning is a goal-driven, knowledge-based, action-guiding kind of argumentation that concludes in a practical imperative of action in relation to the (usually imperfect) knowledge that an agent has of ways and means to proceed in a particular situation. In ethics, practical reasoning is the vehicle for solving casuistical problems of what to do in a particular situation, given that certain goals, policies, or principles have been designated or established as personal commitments to be acted upon by an agent.

The concept of practical reasoning was originally developed by ARISTOTLE (384–322 B.C.E.) and played an important role in ARISTOTELIAN ETHICS, but Aristotle's comments on practical reasoning are scattered and sketchy in his writings, leaving the analysis of the structure of practical reasoning as a fascinating puzzle. Should the conclusion of a practical inference be an ought statement, an action, a must statement, or an imperative? Should the major premise be an intention statement or a want statement? Should the agent of practical reasoning be phrased in the schemes of practical inferences as the first person, "I," or in the third person, "he" or "she"? What is the binding nature of practical reasoning, if it is not a species of deductively valid argument? Leading twentieth-century philosophers have tried to grapple with these puzzling and important questions.

The Binding Nature of Practical Inference

One of the first contemporary writers to draw attention to the Aristotelian notion of practical inference was G. E. M. ANSCOMBE (1919–2001) in her work *Intention* (1957). Perhaps the best introduction to this idea should be given by way of example. Anscombe cites an example given by Aristotle (*Nicomachean Ethics* 1147a5).

> Dry food suits any human.
> Such and such food is dry.
> I am human.
> This is a bit of such and such food.
> Therefore, this food suits me.

This bit of reasoning seems to give the appearance of a deductive inference and hence is often called a "practical syllogism" type of argument. Provided we don't worry too much about the plausibility of a premise that seems to say that hay is a food that suits all humans but soup is not, the argument seems to be of a sort that leads reasonably to its conclusion.

We can see in fact that this particular example has a deductively valid form in first order logic, but that fact, by itself, is unrevealing. What is distinctive about the example is that it represents an agent arriving at a reasonable conclusion to act on the basis of implementing a general policy or rule in particular circumstances. What sort of inference this represents remains highly puzzling.

Some of the examples from Aristotle are deductively valid, meaning that if reasoners accept the premises, they are "forced" to carry out the act recommended by the conclusion unless they want to become committed to a logically inconsistent set of propositions. Yet in other cases, the conclusion does not seem to be "forced" on the practical reasoner. Are there different kinds of practical reasoning then? And what, in general, could it mean to say that inferences of this kind are "valid" or "correct"?

Perhaps more than anyone else, G. H. von Wright has brought out the importance of practical inference as a form of argument appropriate to the humanities as a discipline. In an early work (1963), he discussed this sort of example.

a wants to reach the train on time.
Unless a runs he will not reach the train on time.
Therefore, a must run.

However, in other examples, Wright used the verb 'intends' instead of 'wants' in the major premise, and the term 'sets himself to' instead of 'must' in the conclusion. In the 1963 work Wright claimed that the example above is a valid inference, but later he seems more inclined to think that the premises of a practical inference do not entail behavior and that it is a practical, not a logical, demonstration. In another article (1972), he writes: "Its binding nature stems from the fact that its conclusion declares the intention which an agent is logically bound to have within the teleological frame which in the premises he acknowledges for his prospective action." What is it, then, for a set of propositions to be "binding in teleological frame"?

D. S. Clarke sees practical inference as the vehicle of a kind of means-end deliberation by which agents conclude that they should (practically) do something on the grounds that they want to fulfill a goal in a set of circumstances that is not (entirely) in their control. The practical inference links a means (an action) to the goal, according to Clarke, by directing the agent to carry out a particular action.

An example given by Clarke is an instance of the above framework. I want to keep dry. Taking this umbrella is a means of keeping dry if it rains. It will rain. I may conclude then that I should take the umbrella. Clarke calls the reasoning exhibited above one form of "prudential inference," which he thinks of as a mundane, everyday use of 'ought' distinct from the moral use of 'ought.' But what is a prudential inference? What is the "teleological frame" in which such an inference is binding? Should 'want' or 'intend' be the verb of the major premise? Differences of opinion remain on these questions.

Planning

The basic notions of practical reasoning are centered around the idea that an agent has a certain plan in mind. A *"plan"* may be defined as a set of objectives plus some formulation of means of carrying out these objectives. These objectives may be stated more or less specifically in the plan. In some in-

stances, the objectives may be quite general as formulated by the agent. For example, they may be certain policies that the agent has adopted, or programs or obligations he or she is committed to upholding or carrying out.

Planning comes into play when a creative response to carrying out an intention is required by a situation. But what is planning? Thinking of the term 'strategic planning,' we probably have in mind an agent considering some possible alternative paths of action. This structure represents the agent's knowledge of what is possible in a situation. Practical reasoning fits the missing parts into the collection of means-end sequences that represents the agent's knowledge of what is possible and plausible—in short, the agent's plan of action.

The concept of a plan has achieved recognition in AI (artificial intelligence) as a fundamental tool in script-based reasoning (reasoning based on commonsense knowledge of familiar types of situations). Wilensky has presented a plan-based theory of understanding as a tool for studying problem solving and natural language reasoning for AI. The special aspects of planning highlighted in Wilensky's study are multiple goal planning, resolution of goal conflicts, and the reasoned process of goal abandonment. The kind of goal-directed knowledge structure central to Wilensky's concept of planning is clearly a framework of planning and intelligent deliberation that provides one important teleological framework for practical reasoning. Plans have a means-end coherence that can make actions and goals fit together, which shows how a practical inference can be binding on an agent within the context of his or her plan of action.

Bratman requires that plans should be means-end coherent in the following sense: "They should be filled in with appropriate subplans concerning how I am to do what I plan to do, subplans at least as extensive as I believe is now required to do what I plan." The requirement of extensiveness means that enough steps must be filled in within the projected sequence of action to make a plan feasible and realistic relative to what is known by an agent and to what is possible and plausible in a situation.

Pragmatic Nature of Practical Reasoning

Planning is one pragmatic context in which practical reasoning makes sense as a distinctive kind of reasoning. So construed, it is clearly quite different in nature from theoretical reasoning, like deductive logic. Practical reasoning is knowledge-based, goal-seeking, action-concluding reasoning that binds a conclusion relative to a particular teleological framework as its pragmatic context. Another pragmatic context of practical reasoning is that of advice-giving dialogue where a layperson consults a skilled expert for an opinion on how to solve a problem or carry out an action requiring technical expertise (Diggs). This context is that of two-person, interactive dialogue (reasoning together with another person). Planning (intelligent deliberation) can be more solitary, but often has a dialogic character as well, like debating a problem with oneself.

Practical reasoning is a pragmatic kind of argumentation, best judged in relation to a context of inquiry, problem solving, or issue of discussion. For each argumentation scheme, of either of the two kinds of schemes above, there is a matching set of critical questions of the following form.

1. Are there alternative means of realizing G, other than A?
2. Is A the best (most acceptable) way of realizing G?
3. Is it possible for a to do A?
4. Does a have goals other than G, which have the potential to conflict with a's realizing G?
5. Are there negative side effects of a's bringing about A that ought to be considered?

Practical reasoning is essentially pragmatic because it is not the formal validity of the argument structure that is at issue in evaluating a particular case. Instead, if the two premises of a scheme are satisfied in a situation, a burden of proof is thrown on the critic who rejects the conclusion to pose an appropriate critical question. If the question is relevant, a burden of proof is then shifted back to the agent to reply adequately to the question, in relation to the situation at issue. Practical reasoning is based on burden of proof because of the knowledge-based, practical character of the process of reaching a conclusion on how to act in a particular situation in which the future outcomes of a situation cannot be known or projected with certainty.

Practical reasoning is not a matter of truth or falsehood, but a matter of agents' commitment to propositions that stand in relation to their collective set of commitments representing their position or plan of action, relative to what they know in a given situation. To declare an intention to something can be to commit oneself to general or to specific propositions. But in relation to what an agent knows about a given situation, specific commitments to particular actions then flow, by practical inferences, from these intentions, whether they be abstract (general) commitments, specific commitments, or the two types combined. Robins shows how more abstract intentions can be linked, as commitments, to specific actions contemplated by an agent (see also Bratman and Walton). Thus practical reasoning involves the coherence of an agent's position, his or her collective set of commitments, when that agent plans to act on the basis of what he or she knows in a given situation. Practical reasoning is the coherent chaining together of practical inferences that bring together general commitments of an agent with commitments to specific actions in a particular situation confronted by that agent.

See also: AGENCY AND DISABILITY; ANSCOMBE; ARISTOTELIAN ETHICS; AUTONOMY OF MORAL AGENTS; CASUISTRY; CATEGORICAL AND HYPOTHETICAL IMPERATIVES; COHERENTISM; DELIBERATION AND CHOICE; INTENTION; LOGIC AND ETHICS; MORAL REASONING; OUGHT IMPLIES CAN; *PHRONESIS;* PRACTICAL WISDOM; PRAGMATISM; PRAXIS; PRUDENCE; RATIONAL CHOICE; RATIONALITY VS. REASONABLENESS; SITUATION ETHICS; TELEOLOGICAL ETHICS; THEORY AND PRACTICE.

Bibliography

Anscombe, G. E. M. *Intention.* Oxford: Blackwell, 1957. Cited, pp. 58, 3.

Aristotle. *The Works of Aristotle Translated into English.* Edited by W. D. Ross. Oxford: Oxford University Press, 1928. Cited, p. 275.

Bratman, Michael. "Taking Plans Seriously." *Social Theory and Practice* 9 (1983): 271–88.

———. *Intentions, Plans, and Practical Reason.* Cambridge, MA: Harvard University Press, 1987.

Castañeda, Hector-Neri. "Conditional Intentions, Intentional Action, and Aristotelian Practical Syllogisms." *Erkenntnis* 18 (1982): 239–60.

Clarke, D. S. *Practical Inferences.* London: Routledge and Kegan Paul, 1985. Cited, p. 17.

Davidson, Donald. "Freedom to Act." In *Essays on Free-*

dom of Action, edited by Ted Honderich. London: Routledge and Kegan Paul, 1973.

Diggs, B. J. "A Technical Ought." *Mind* 69 (1960): 301–17.

Kenny, Anthony. *Action, Emotion, and Will.* London: Routledge and Kegan Paul, 1964.

Raz, Joseph, ed. *Practical Reasoning.* Oxford: Oxford University Press, 1978. Includes "On So-Called Practical Inference" by G. H. von Wright (pp. 46–62), first published in *Acta Sociologica* 15 (1972): 39–53.

Robins, Michael H. *Promising, Intending, and Moral Autonomy.* Cambridge: Cambridge University Press, 1984.

Walton, Douglas N. *Practical Reasoning: Goal-Driven, Knowledge-Based, Action-Guiding Argumentation.* Savage, MD: Rowman and Littlefield, 1990.

Wilensky, Robert. *Planning and Understanding: A Computational Approach to Human Reasoning.* Reading, MA: Addison Wesley, 1983.

Wright, G. H. von. *The Varieties of Goodness.* London: Routledge and Kegan Paul, 1963.

———. *Practical Reason.* Ithaca, NY: Cornell University Press, 1983. Includes his 1972 article, "On So-Called Practical Inference." Cited, p. 59.

Douglas N. Walton

practical wisdom

Practical wisdom, a standard translation for the Greek *phronēsis,* is a concept central to ancient ethical thought. It tends to be eclipsed in modern ethical accounts by notions of prudential or instrumental reasoning, and in general by notions of PRACTICAL REASONING that are separable from the ethical character of the agent. Unlike these more neutral cognitive capacities, practical wisdom is intimately linked with virtue and the good life. Though the term PHRONĒSIS can also connote, as in PLATO (c. 430–347 B.C.E.), a more general intellectual ability such as intelligence, understanding, or intellectual expertise, in ARISTOTLE's (384–322 B.C.E.) ethical writings, the term becomes technically coined as the intelligence of the good person, or better, WISDOM, in the sense not of theoretical, but practical wisdom. Indeed for Aristotle, being practically wise is inseparable from having a good CHARACTER. It is a necessary and sufficient condition for mature virtue (NE 1144b30). In later Hellenistic writings, such as those of EPICURUS (341–270 B.C.E.), *phronēsis* (though often translated as "prudence") retains its normative link with good character, and the practically wise person (or sage) is alternatively referred to as *ho sophos* or *ho phronimos.* In THOMAS AQUINAS (1225?–1274) too, *prudentia* (PRUDENCE) retains the normative character of Aristotelian *phronēsis.*

Since the most systematic account of the notion of practical wisdom can be found in Aristotle's writings, it makes sense to turn there for guidance. According to that account, the salient features of practical wisdom are these: Practical wisdom characterizes the good person's deliberation about the promotion of HAPPINESS (*eudaimonia*). Given that virtuous activities will be the primary constituents of the Aristotelian good life, the ends to be promoted will include what we usually associate with moral ends—ends of GENEROSITY, COURAGE, FRIENDSHIP, and TEMPERANCE. Thus while practical wisdom, like the more modern notion of prudence, is concerned with promoting happiness, happiness on the Aristotelian view is itself constituted by moral activity. Accordingly, the reasoning is about how to be good, about how to act finely.

These activities are thought to require an ability to promote not merely the isolated parts of a life, but their overall fit into some nested whole (NE 1140a26–8). It is unlikely that practical wisdom meant deliberation toward what is now sometimes called a life plan. The idea of a life plan seems far too rigid, as if one were to know, in advance of particular circumstances, just what weight more general ends and concerns will bear. Rather, practical wisdom leaves much more to practical judgment than to rule, much more to deliberation about individual cases than to systematic execution of an antecedent plan. But even so, the judgment is not simply about how to promote a single given end, but about how to promote ends that are revisable and defeasible in light of other ends constitutive of character. Practical wisdom requires something of a global point of view.

The revisability of ends is not a claim about the radical choice of ends. That is to say, on the Aristotelian view, the ends a person adopts largely reflect an ongoing habituation of character. This view raises difficult questions regarding the ascription of RESPONSIBILITY and the appropriateness of moral praise and blame. But any such discussion needs to be framed by an open acknowledgment that the habituation of character need be neither a mindless nor involuntary process of being shaped. The development of reflective capacities is a part of that education, culminating in a capacity to exercise virtue in a way that is sensitive to the specific requirements of circumstances. This capacity for specification and alteration of ends is a part of practical wisdom.

As should already be evident, practical wisdom is dependent on perceptual and emotional capacities for discerning morally relevant particulars (1142a15). These are often required for making dispositional ends of character occurrent, *e.g.,* for noticing the appropriate occasions for generosity, for recognizing that now is a moment to show gratitude toward a friend. Equally, they figure in recognizing the means for an end that is now occurrent, for knowing just how to be generous given present resources and rival demands. Aristotle sometimes refers to this related aspect of practical wisdom as practical *nous,* or practical insight. It is a capacity to recognize and evaluate the particular circumstances of action. But there is no indication in Aristotle that such recognitional capacities need be purely cognitive. Sometimes the capacity to notice will be most effective when filtered through the emotions, as when our AN-GER is unleashed or our pity aroused. Through such emotional sensitivities we see and record what might otherwise go unnoticed by the dispassionate intellect; and once it is registered, we go on to make inferences that might not have been made in as compelling a way. The suggestion then is that practical wisdom requires considerable exposure and experience as well as emotional capacities refined by that exposure.

In this view is the implication that practical wisdom replaces rules. To be sure, Aristotle maintains that ethical theory will have certain rules that hold for the most part, summary rules that sum up previous practice and that an agent may rely on in making practical choices. But these summary rules can never guide action in a determinate way. They remain underdetermined with respect to future circumstances and, even when highly specific, guide only to the extent that an agent can recognize the appropriate occasions for application. Yet recognizing the instances cannot itself be a part of formulating the rule. To know a rule, no matter how specific, and to know how to apply it are two different things.

Finally, there is that aspect of practical wisdom that is best thought of as a reflective self-understanding. Those persons who are wise are able to reaffirm their sense of virtue by understanding why it is that a virtuous life is the most meaningful life. This sort of reflection is precisely the sort that Aristotle urges his audience to take on as they listen to and engage in the dialectical method of his lectures. It is a defense of the virtuous life, meant to deepen the convictions of those already enlisted, not to convince those who, like Plato's Thrasymachus, skeptically resist.

But still, the question remains; just how does practical wisdom differ from a more neutral capacity of practical reason? Aren't the capacities described applicable to the scoundrel's deliberations about base ends? Won't such a person have a kind of peripheral vision that brings more than one end to view at a given time, have perceptual capacities for recognizing circumstantial features salient to ends, have the capacity to recast and revise ends as the complexities of circumstances require, and even have the capacity to endorse ends? In what sense does practical wisdom involve a practice of reason that is different from what the nonvirtuous practice in the promotion of their ends? In what sense, if any, is there an excellence of practical intellect peculiar to the virtuous?

These questions are complex, and are ones that Aristotle himself never addresses head-on. He tells us there is a capacity for cleverness (*deinotēs*) that is common to both the virtuous and vicious alike but that falls short of practical wisdom. But just how it falls short—in some more interesting way than that the vicious have bad ends and the virtuous do not—is unclear. Nevertheless, we can try to fill in an answer.

There are two lines to develop. One might concede that practical reason is structurally similar in both cases, but hold that it is differentially valued in different lives. For the vicious it is merely instrumentally valued—a way of promoting POWER, gain, DECEIT, avoidance of RISK or fear. For the virtuous, it is of intrinsic as well as instrumental value. The courageous reason about how to promote victory, but they equally value the reasoning and choice of courageous action even when victory fails.

But there is a problem with this line of approach. Imagine the most resourceful of scoundrels, who has gain or deceit as an external end but who savours the manner and style of profiteering. With ingenuity she achieves her ends and even seems to value reason as an intrinsic good whose artful exercise gives her pleasure. She has made an "art form" of profiteering and has something of an integrated life that works toward that focus. On this approach, she has all it takes to be wise. The same holds for the person who simply adores scheming, independent of the success of her plots. Yet this can't be all there is to practical wisdom. Even if rational activity is valued for its own sake, it has to be valued within a certain kind of life, if there is to be practical wisdom.

This conclusion brings us to the second approach, which I believe is closer to Aristotle's (*cf.*, 1144a29–31). What distinguishes practical wisdom from other deliberative capacities are precisely the ends of virtue that it requires. But we should not understand by this approach an easy division of labor in which virtuous ends are antecedently acquired and practical wisdom aims subsequently at their implementation. Rather, the picture is more fluid. Practical wisdom presupposes habituated ends, but then transforms and deepens them by its grasp. Through its grasp it endorses the ends of virtue as the true ends of a good life. Now this approach is an internalist answer, for it restricts practical wisdom to practitioners; it says only those who are committed to certain ends can be in a position to legitimate their value. This conclusion may seem unsatisfying, but still it is quite different from saying practical wisdom is practical reasoning (or cleverness) externally directed at virtuous ends. For Aristotle's position is that the content of the ends transforms and develops one's practical intellect, so that through the right kind of life one comes to be in a position to grasp the ends that are presupposed. This view seems to be a rather defensible one of what it is to be wise.

See also: ARISTOTELIAN ETHICS; ARISTOTLE; CHARACTER; COURAGE; DELIBERATION AND CHOICE; EPICURUS; *EUDAIMONIA, -ISM;* EXCELLENCE; EXTERNALISM AND INTERNALISM; FRIENDSHIP; GENEROSITY; HAPPINESS; JUSTICE, CIRCUMSTANCES OF; MORAL ABSOLUTES; MORAL DEVELOPMENT; MORAL REASONING; MORAL RULES; *PHRONĒSIS;* PLATO; PRACTICAL REASON[ING]; PRUDENCE; RECIPROCITY; RESPONSIBILITY; SELF-KNOWLEDGE; STOICISM; SYMPATHY; TEMPERANCE; THEORY AND PRACTICE; THOMAS AQUINAS; VIRTUE ETHICS; WISDOM.

Bibliography

Annas, Julia. *The Morality of Happiness.* Oxford: Oxford University Press, 1993.

Aristotle. *The Complete Works of Aristotle.* Revised Oxford translation. 2 vols. Princeton: Princeton University Press, 1984.

———. *Nicomachean Ethics.* Translated by Terence Irwin. Book VI. (Note: Irwin translates *phronēsis* as "intelligence.")

Charles, David. *Aristotle's Philosophy of Action.* Ithaca, NY: Cornell University Press, 1984.

Cooper, John. *Reason and Human Good in Aristotle.* Cambridge, MA: Harvard University Press, 1975.

Dahl, Norman O. *Practical Reason, Aristotle, and Weakness of the Will.* Minneapolis: University of Minnesota Press, 1984.

Dancy, Jonathan. *Moral Reasons.* Oxford and Cambridge, MA: Blackwell, 1993.

Engberg-Pederson, Troels. *Aristotle's Theory of Moral Insight.* Oxford: Oxford University Press, 1983.

Foot, Philippa. *Virtues and Vices.* Berkeley: University of California Press, 1978. See especially the first essay.

Hampshire, Stuart. *Morality and Conflict.* Cambridge, MA: Harvard University Press, 1983. See especially chapter 2.

Inwood, Brad. *Ethics and Human Action in Early Stoicism.* Oxford: Oxford University Press, 1985.

Irwin, Terence. "Aristotle on Reason, Desire, and Virtue." *Journal of Philosophy* 72 (1975): 657–78.

Kraut, Richard. *Aristotle on the Human Good.* Princeton: Princeton University Press, 1989.

Lear, Jonathan. *Aristotle: The Desire to Understand.* Cambridge: Cambridge University Press, 1988.

Nussbaum, Martha C. *The Fragility of Goodness: Luck and Rational Self-Sufficiency in Greek Ethical Thought—The Tragic Poets, Plato, and Aristotle.* Cambridge: Cambridge University Press, 1986. See especially chapters 9 and 10.

———. *Love's Knowledge.* Oxford: Oxford University Press, 1990.

———. *The Therapy of Desire: Theory and Practice in Hellenistic Ethics.* Princeton: Princeton University Press, 1994.

Plato. *Philebus. Republic.*

Richardson, Henry. *Practical Reasoning about Ends.* Cambridge: Cambridge University Press, 1994.

Rorty, Amélie O., ed. *Essays on Aristotle's Ethics.* Berkeley and Los Angeles: University of California Press, 1980.

———. *Essays on Aristotle's Rhetoric.* Berkeley and Los Angeles: University of California Press, 1996.

Sherman, Nancy. *The Fabric of Character: Aristotle's Theory of Virtue.* Oxford: Oxford University Press, 1989.

———. *Making a Necessity of Virtue.* Cambridge: Cambridge University Press, 1997.

———, ed. *Aristotle's Ethics: Critical Essays.* Lanham: Rowman and Littlefield, 1999.

Slote, Michael. *Goods and Virtues.* Oxford: Oxford University Press, 1983. See especially chapter 2.

Thomas Aquinas. *Summa theologica.* 1266–1273. See especially I–II, qq. 56–7.

Wiggins, David. "Deliberation and Practical Reason." In *Essays on Aristotle's Ethics,* edited by Amélie O. Rorty, *supra.*

Williams, Bernard. *Ethics and the Limits of Philosophy.* Cambridge, MA: Harvard University Press, 1985.

Nancy Sherman

pragmatism

America's most distinctive contribution to world philosophy, pragmatism originated in discussions of the Metaphysical Club in Cambridge, Massachusetts, of which Charles Sanders PEIRCE (1839–1914), William JAMES (1842–1910) and Oliver Wendell Holmes Jr. (1841–1935), as well as others, were members. The basic ideas first appeared in print in a series of papers by Peirce in *Popular Science Monthly* 1877–1878. James introduced the term "pragmatism" and made its method more widely known, and Justice Holmes applied it to legal thought. John DEWEY (1859–1952) became a pragmatist under the influence of James's *Principles of Psychology.* F. C. S. Schiller (1864–1937), now generally forgotten, and George Herbert MEAD (1863–1931) contributed to its development, as did C. I. LEWIS (1883–1964) and Charles Morris (1901–1979). Some leading contemporary philosophers continue the pragmatist tradition. Pragmatism developed out of earlier philosophical tendencies under the influence of Darwinism and in turn influenced not only virtually every subfield of philosophy but also many other fields of human endeavor.

The Pragmatic Maxim

First formulated by Peirce, the maxim reads "Consider what effects, that might conceivably have practical bearings, we conceive the object of our conceptions to have. Then our conception of these effects is the whole of our conception of the object" (*Collected Papers,* V. 402). The emphasis here is on "practical bearings"; beliefs are understood to be habits, dispositions to behave in certain ways if the requisite circumstances arise. Accepting this maxim, pragmatists agree in their approach to philosophical matters although they disagree in specific doctrines. All pragmatists reject the Cartesian divorce of the knower from the known, placing the knower as an interacting agent into the world that is known. All

regard inquiry as an ongoing process that depends on the continued existence of a community of inquirers. Pragmatists see their doctrine as mediating between science and religion, THEORY AND PRACTICE, absolutism and SUBJECTIVISM. It is "a philosophy rooted in common sense and dedicated to the transformation of culture, to the resolution of the conflicts that divide us" (Sleeper). Pragmatism's evolving doctrine on truth parallels the development of the theory of the good, sketched below. For Peirce, scientific inquiry is destined to lead, in the indefinitely long run, to one final opinion, the object of which will be reality. James distinguishes between half-truths—those everyday beliefs that, when acted on, do not lead to unpleasant surprises—and absolute truth—the Peircean notion of the final opinion, which lurks in the background as a regulative ideal. Dewey jettisons the idea of an absolute truth. Though he does not eschew the word "truth" in other contexts, when he is concerned with the conditions and results of inquiry, he speaks of warranted assertions and objects of knowledge, and these are as varied as the problems that prompt inquiry.

Ends-in-View, Goods, and Ideals

A theory of the good is not the whole of ethics, but the pragmatic maxim's emphasis on "effects, that could conceivably have practical bearing" suggests that pragmatic ethics begin with a theory of the good. It begins, in fact, with human beings in the situations in which they actually find themselves, *i.e.,* as beings with NEEDS and wants, with intelligence, and with habits and values that are for the most part the results of their social environment. A moral action is an action that is deliberately chosen; it has a purpose, in Dewey's terminology, an "end-in-view." Ends-in-view may be limited to resolving a particular problematic situation—any situation in which we cannot just go on in habitual ways—or they may shape long stretches of our lives, as the aim of getting an education, or a whole life, as in a life devoted to some science or art or humane endeavor.

Peirce insisted that "the only moral evil is not to have an ultimate aim," that is, an aim that can be consistently adopted, recommends itself aside from ulterior motives, is consistent with the agent's free development, and can be maintained regardless of the agent's changing circumstances (*Collected Pa-*

pers, V. 133). What is interesting here is the insistence on the agent's free development, a desideratum shared explicitly by Dewey and implicitly by James as well. Indeed, if anything might be considered an absolute value of the pragmatists it is the growth of individuals. But the very notion of an absolute value is incompatible with pragmatist fallibilism, the ever-present willingness to learn from experience. Peirce believed that truth was the only possible ultimate aim, but that seems to be an insufficient basis for ethics. Peirce lists, however, among the requirements for a life devoted unswervingly to rational inquiry, "interest in an indefinite community," and here again he makes contact with other pragmatists, who are fully aware that the moral life and human flourishing require supportive social conditions.

In any case, whether there is an ultimate value or not, our values have their origins in immediate enjoyments and sufferings; some of these are bodily pleasures and pains, but others are direct responses of disgust, delight, etc., to various situations, real or imagined. These consummatory experiences (Dewey's term) anchor our evaluations and moral and political theories as sense experiences anchor our everyday beliefs and our scientific theories. Evaluation as opposed to immediate valuing (finding that something desired is indeed desirable, appraising something prized as being worth the effort to maintain it, etc.) is the reflection forced on us when our valuings clash, where the conflict may be between things valued by one agent or between the values of different agents. Even within one life choices must be made; the thoughtful agent seeks to find compossible goods in the framework of long-range projects. But values become objective, stable, the basis of obligations, only when there is a community of agents who take an interest in each other's values. This Jamesian conception transforms Peirce's interest in the indefinite community of inquirers into an interest in the members of an ultimately indefinite community of moral agents, seeking not the one ideal of truth, but ever more comprehensive ideals or ends-in-view. Because in our world the ideals of many people are trampled under foot, James's insistence that we are to seek to realize the most inclusive ideals is quite revolutionary. But he warned that revolutionaries must be willing to stake their own lives and reputations on the changes they advocate and that they must always listen for the cries of the wounded they might leave in their wake.

What has been said so far might suggest that pragmatist ethics is simply consequentialist ethics. But even in the hands of James that is not so, for there is no common denominator to which all goods can be reduced. It makes no sense, then, to speak of maximizing the good; James's reference to ever more inclusive ideals must be taken to be, as already suggested, regulative rather than definitive. But pragmatist ethics differs from standard consequentialist theories more deeply than in recognizing the incommensurability of goods. Dewey's starting point is the Peircean idea that inquiry is a response to an unsettled situation, unsettled because habitual action is blocked for reasons that range from moral conflicts to physical obstacles. There is a continuum of problems, not a dichotomy between moral and nonmoral, or between practical and theoretical, problems. Formulating a problem as "moral" or "technical" or some other kind is already a step toward one kind of possible solution and toward eliminating others. A contemplated solution, an end-in-view, becomes a means to dealing with the problem; it determines the relevance of information, reflection (thought-experiments), perhaps experimentation, and ultimately the taking of steps to realize the end-in-view. Once achieved, the reconstructed situation becomes the condition for further development: a means to further ends and a source of new problems. The sharp distinction between means and ends, implicit in Peirce's notion of an ultimate aim, has been shattered. Indeed, the very model of a step-by-step procedure is misleading, for it fails to emphasize that the problem, its envisaged solution, and the means to that solution constantly modify each other.

Values

Because the traditional means-ends dichotomy is rejected in pragmatist ethics, the notion of intrinsic value is abandoned. All values are instrumental because, at a minimum, they guide conduct; all realized values (all situations) are themselves among the means (the causal conditions) for the realization of further values. Beyond denying the means-ends distinction, pragmatists reject the fact-value distinction. They point out first that moral values are simply one species of value, that in any process of inquiry evaluation takes place constantly. As pointed out above, we judge that this information is relevant, these data trustworthy, this procedure reliable. We judge that this problem is worth investigating, this difficulty not be shirked, and so forth. Our so-called factual knowledge rests on a basis of inextricably intertwined facts (observations) and values (evaluations), and the same is true, of course, of our value judgments.

To value something is to take thoughtful measures to bring it about or to preserve it. Comparing different means to the same ends, we evaluate, we establish norms: that these data are relevant, those materials adequate, this institution efficient, that test reliable, etc. Such judgments are grounded in past experience; the more scientific the grounds, the more warranted the evaluation. Sometimes, tragically, we may be forced to conclude that what we value cannot be brought into being or preserved, or only at a cost we are unwilling to pay. Insofar as our evaluations are prospective, they are not simple predictions; rather, they indicate what will happen *only if* certain steps are taken. These steps being taken, one can compare the actual consequences with the end-in-view, thus appraising the latter. A theory of valuation, in contrast to a theory of value, avoids both offering a list of *a priori* ends and accepting all existing desires as equally worthy of satisfaction; it aims rather to determine the conditions of successful practical inquiry. What has been said here might be taken to be a kind of metaethical reflection. But pragmatists will point out that the ethics/METAETH-ICS distinction cannot be maintained. What we recognize as acceptable methods of inquiry, or as sources of AUTHORITY, in ethics will play a decisive role in what practical judgments we accept and whether we cling to them dogmatically or are ready to revise them in the light of experience.

Agents

In turning from questions of valuation to the agents who evaluate and act, pragmatists note that adult agents bring to any problematic situation a number of resources. First, there are the standards and very generalized goals of the community to which the agents belong. To be sure, this conventional morality will be called into question, will be replaced by a reflective morality that is self-imposed even where it agrees with its conventional sources. Second, and to some extent overlapping the first, are

the agent's habits, the total constellation of VIRTUES and vices that make up his or her CHARACTER. To the extent that these habits reinforce each other, the agent has a strong character, for good or evil. Habits, while they have a biological basis, are formed in interaction with the agent's environment, in particular the social environment; hence the overlap of habitual behavior and conventionally moral behavior in the good citizen. Even some of what we take to be immediate moral reactions are actually learned. Though our moral decisions are intensely personal, morality, even reflective morality, is social: agents capable of thoughtful moral choices and intelligent behavior can develop only in a community of such agents. Therefore, the chief practical, *i.e.*, moral, problem in Dewey's opinion is "the establishment of cultural conditions that will support the kinds of behavior in which emotions and ideas, desires and appraisals are integrated" (*Theory of Valuation*, 65).

There is, however, another, more personal side to the involvement of character in moral deliberation. Both James and Dewey make the point that, precisely in the most difficult cases, what is at stake for the choosing agents is less what they are to do than what kinds of persons they are to become. What is at stake here is not simply the question whether one will think well of oneself or not, but what sort of constellation of character traits one will develop if one follows this path or that. Pragmatist ethics here makes contact with contemporary VIRTUE ETHICS.

As already mentioned, pragmatists insist that morality is social. This statement means, on the one hand, that human beings can flourish only in certain kinds of social circumstances, and on the other hand, that many fundamental moral notions are grounded in the social relations in which we stand. To take the latter point first: for pragmatists the point of MORAL RULES, of obligations, of a sense of duty is not only that they make social living possible, but also that living by them we express the social relations in which we stand to each other. If these relations are relations of dominance and OPPRES-SION, then rules will be obeyed resentfully, fearfully. If the relations are those of free and equal moral agents who respect each other, rules will be understood to be beneficial and be obeyed cheerfully. Since no society can survive without laws, pragmatists are vitally interested in the kind of law that prevails in their society. Indeed, pragmatic ethics is social not only in the sense in which all morality is social, but also in not seeing a dichotomy of moral versus political questions. Once again, as in the case of facts and values, or means and ends, pragmatists see a continuum. The important point is that if one sees a dichotomy, if one classifies a problem once and for all as moral or as political, one prevents oneself from even thinking of certain answers, certain ends-in-view. In other words, precisely because morality—in so far as it consists in claims of rights and in impositions of obligations—reflects social relationships, pragmatist ethics aims at creating social conditions in which individuals will flourish not in opposition to, but in harmony with, their fellows.

See also: COMMENSURABILITY; CONSEQUENTIALISM; CONVENTIONS; DEWEY; GOOD, THEORIES OF THE; JAMES; LEWIS; MEAD; MORAL ABSOLUTES; MORAL COMMUNITY, BOUNDARIES OF; MORAL REALISM; PEIRCE; PRACTICAL REASON[ING]; PRACTICAL WISDOM; PRAXIS; RATIONALITY VS. REASONABLENESS; SUBJECTIVISM; THEORY AND PRACTICE; VALUE, THEORY OF.

Bibliography

Dewey, John. *Theory of Valuation.* In his *The Later Works: 1925–1953.* Edited by Jo Ann Boydston *et al.,* vol. 13: 1938–39. Carbondale: Southern Illinois University Press, 1988.

Dickstein, Morris, ed. *The Revival of Pragmatism: New Essays on Social Thought, Law, and Culture.* Durham, NC and London: Duke University Press, 1988.

Flower, Elizabeth, and Murray G. Murphey. *A History of Philosophy in America.* New York: Putnam, 1977. See chapters 10, 11, 14,and 15 in vol. 2.

Goodman, Nelson. Ways *of Worldmaking.* Indianapolis: Hackett, 1978.

Mead, George Herbert. *Mind, Self, and Society: From the Standpoint of a Social Behaviorist.* Edited by Charles W. Morris. Chicago: University of Chicago Press, 1934.

Peirce, C. S. *Collected Papers.* Cambridge: Belknap Press, Harvard University Press, 1931–1958.

Putnam, Hilary. *The Many Faces of Realism.* La Salle, IL: Open Court, 1987.

———. *Pragmatism: An Open Question.* Cambridge, MA: Blackwell, 1995.

Putnam, Ruth Anna. "Creating Facts and Values." *Philosophy* 60 (1985): 187–204.

———. "Weaving Seamless Webs." *Philosophy* 62 (1987): 207–20.

———. "Perceiving Facts and Values." *Philosophy* 73 (1998): 5–19.

Quine, W. V. "On the Nature of Moral Values." In his *Theories and Things.* Cambridge: Harvard University Press, 1981.

Rorty, Richard. *Consequences of Pragmatism.* Minneapolis: University of Minnesota Press, 1982.

Scheffler, Israel. *Four Pragmatists.* London: Routledge & Kegan Paul; New York: Humanities Press, 1974.

Schneider, Herbert W. *A History of American Philosophy.* New York: Columbia University Press, 1946. See chapters 39–42.

Sleeper, R. W. *The Necessity of Pragmatism.* New Haven and London: Yale University Press, 1986. Quoted, pp. 8–9.

White, Morton. *What Is and What Ought to Be Done.* New York and Oxford: Oxford University Press, 1981.

For additional works, see the bibliographies appended to the entries for John Dewey, William James, C. I. Lewis, and C. S. Peirce.

Ruth Anna Putnam

praxis

In Greek and German, the languages to which this word is indigenous, "praxis" has some quite ordinary, broadly descriptive significations, translatable as "practice," (commercial) "affair"—in short, human activity in general. But it has also acquired strong normative connotations, mainly positive in nature, particularly through the Marxian tradition.

ARISTOTLE (384–322 B.C.E.) used "praxis" in a systematic, technical way, distinguishing it from both *theoria,* pure knowing, and *poiesis,* making. Praxis, for Aristotle, involves no material product, but is goal directed and depends on a kind of WISDOM that is not purely intellectual and that must be developed through experience. The subject matter of his writings on ethics and politics, in particular, is this PRACTICAL WISDOM. While Aristotle does not accord to the word "praxis" as central a role in his normative system as "virtue," for example, he always insists that there are objectively better and worse *praxeis;* hence the early relevance of the notion for ethics.

To appreciate the contemporary importance of praxis, we must first look at the flourishing of German thought that begins with Immanuel KANT (1724–1804). The relative importance and even the legitimacy of his distinction between pure (theoretical) reason and practical reason were challenged by his successors. FICHTE (1762–1814) claimed primacy for practical reason, while HEGEL (1770–1831) questioned and claimed to have overcome the theory/practice dichotomy. Hegel identified his epoch as the one in which history's supreme goal—universal freedom—was at last becoming fully actualized. For August von Cieszkowski (1814–1894), a thinker of the Hegelian left, "praxis" named the crucial notion for realizing in fact the universal freedom that Hegel had illusorily asserted to exist already.

The precise locus of society's fundamental practical contradictions was disputed by the Young Hegelians; Ludwig FEUERBACH (1804–1872) claimed that it lay in the domain of RELIGION. Karl MARX (1818–1883) distanced himself from Feuerbach and moved toward first a political and then an economic critique of society. In his brief *Theses on Feuerbach,* he accuses Feuerbach of understanding human agency as too passive and in too purely contemplative a manner and of not viewing it as praxis, which Marx defines as "sensuous human activity." This text has become highly influential.

Although the word "praxis" seldom appears in Marx's later writings, it has been a central term for a number of strands of twentieth-century philosophy. In part, it is a code word for an interpretation of MARXISM that rejects the allegedly more deterministic variety identified with Soviet "orthodoxy"; to stress praxis implies viewing Marxism as an ethical doctrine advocating human action for radical social change. Such change is seen as emancipatory at both the individual and the social levels; on the individual level, successful praxis means overcoming a condition of ALIENATION, while at the social level it means radically altering institutional structures said to perpetuate relationships of dominance and subordination. Many advocates of a philosophy of praxis typically identify some or all of these institutional structures with modern capitalism.

A once influential philosophical movement in former Yugoslavia acquired, through the name of the journal that it initiated, the label of the "praxis group." Before them, Georg Lukács (1885–1971) also employed the term systematically. Antonio Gramsci (1891–1937) wrote "the philosophy of praxis," whenever referring to Marxism, as a precaution against the possible confiscation of his notebooks.

Other philosophers less closely identified with the Marxian tradition have also used the term extensively, usually in the simultaneously descriptive and normative senses used by that tradition itself. Jean-Paul SARTRE (1905–1980), in his later work, uses "praxis" to identify free human activity in general. For the later Sartre, "praxis" thus plays here a role similar to "being-for-itself" in his earlier philosophy, but it gives more emphasis to ACTION and less to mere consciousness. In addition, Sartre's "praxis" has strongly positive normative connotations: through collective action, or "common praxis," it is possible for groups of human beings to overturn the self-created institutional structures that have fettered them. Jürgen HABERMAS also employs, in simultaneously descriptive and normative ways, the "communicative praxis" that he regards as the key to human individual and social emancipation. Enrique Dussel, a "third world" philosopher, explicitly distinguishes between "routine praxis" and the "praxis of liberation" of oppressed peoples.

It is important to distinguish some of the advantages and liabilities of stressing the notion of praxis in an ethical context.

Devaluation of Pure Theory

In general, philosophers who emphasize praxis share the conviction that the Aristotelian ideal of *theoria,* understood as the uninvolved, distanced contemplation of reality by pure consciousness, is at best a false abstraction that implies a way of life that is literally impossible to pursue, at worst an immoral ideal that conduces to self-indulgent behavior that sanctions and reinforces existing social evils. This attitude poses an apparent dilemma for philosophers who advocate praxis, because philosophy has traditionally been considered the contemplative activity *par excellence.* These philosophers, however, urge that philosophy such as theirs is in fact a certain *type* of praxis, theoretical praxis, and that any philosophy that becomes widely known and discussed will inevitably exert profound effects on history and society. In a counter-paradox, they attribute to philosophers who defend pure theory as a possible and valuable ideal a lack of theoretical insight into this inevitability.

Valuation of (Productive) Activity

As a counterpart to the devaluation of pure theory, the advocacy of praxis as an ethical ideal seems to entail placing a high value on productive activity, considered as a kind of human essence. This raises an initial problem. Most praxis philosophers regard typical philosophical accounts of human essence or nature as serving, by setting prior boundaries to all possible change, an ultimately conservative function, which they reject. They argue, on the contrary, that praxis implies no such prior normative limits; at most, it assumes only physical limits that can themselves be vastly extended by TECHNOLOGY. But this reply lays bare a potentially larger issue, namely, whether praxis ought to be conceived on the model of *production,* including production abetted by technological developments. Many philosophers have sharply questioned the ethical value of the ideal of maximizing technological productivity. Praxis philosophers, such as Mihaílo Marković, have countered by identifying praxis as a norm with humanistic values that are not measurable strictly in terms of the quantity and quality of material possessions.

Generality

But this sort of answer points to a conceptual problem that is shared by every formulation of an ethical norm that aspires to such a high level of generality, namely, the problem of developing criteria for distinguishing good from bad or, in this case, emancipatory from alienating praxis. The French mob that took the Bastille (1789), which Sartre uses as illustrating common praxis in its purest form, *may* have been justified in terms both of a grand ethic of history and of humbler ethical considerations; but no one would claim that all would-be revolutionary or counterrevolutionary mobs are equally justified. It is to the theoretical praxis of developing and defending appropriate criteria that ethicists who favor this way of approaching ethical problems need to devote themselves.

See also: HUMAN RIGHTS; HUMANISM; IDEALIST ETHICS; KANT; LIBERTY; LIBERTY, ECONOMIC; MARX; MARXISM; MORAL REALISM; OPPRESSION; POWER; PRACTICAL REASON[ING]; PRACTICAL WISDOM; PRAGMATISM; REVOLUTION; SARTRE; SOCIAL AND POLITICAL PHILOSOPHY; THEORY AND PRACTICE; WISDOM.

Bibliography

Arendt, Hannah. *The Human Condition.* Chicago: University of Chicago Press, 1958. Critique of the modern age for allegedly devaluing classical praxis.

Bernstein, Richard J. *Praxis and Action: Contemporary Philosophies of Human Activity.* Philadelphia: University of Pennsylvania Press, 1971. Praxis in four contemporary philosophical traditions.

Crocker, David A. *Praxis and Democratic Socialism: The Critical Social Theory of Marković and Stojanović.* Atlantic Highlands, NJ: Humanities Press, and Brighton: Harvester Press, 1983. A careful study of two major figures in the Yugoslav movement.

Dallmayr, Fred R. *Polis and Praxis.* Cambridge and London: MIT Press, 1984. Essay collection in political theory.

Dupré, Louis. *Marx's Social Critique of Culture.* New Haven: Yale University Press, 1983. Emphasizes the praxis theme in Marx.

Dussel, Enrique. *Philosophy of Liberation.* Translated by A. Martinez and C. Morkovsky. Maryknoll, NY: Orbis, 1985. Praxis from a "third world" perspective.

Habermas, Jürgen. *Theory and Practice.* Translated by J. Viertel. Boston: Beacon Press, 1974. Translation of *Theorie und Praxis,* 1971.

Lukács, Georg. *History and Class Consciousness.* Translated by R. Livingstone. Cambridge: MIT Press, 1971. Classic of Western Marxism.

Marx, Karl. "Theses on Feuerbach." In *The Marx-Engels Reader,* edited by Robert C. Tucker, 143–45. New York: W. W. Norton, 1978. "Praxis" is translated here as "practice."

Sartre, Jean-Paul. *Critique of Dialectical Reason.* Translated by A. Sheridan-Smith. Atlantic Highlands, NJ: Humanities Press, 1976. Central work of Sartre's later thought.

Schrag, Calvin O. *Communicative Praxis and the Space of Subjectivity.* Bloomington and Indianapolis, IN: Indiana University Press, 1989. A response to postmodern attacks on praxis as subject centered.

William L. McBride

precedent

The requirement that judgments follow precedents, cases previously settled, is well established in law, although the interpretation and justification for this requirement are matters of philosophical dispute. By clarifying the nature of the requirement and its justification in the legal system, we can see better whether there is a similar constraint on moral judgment. Indeed, there seems to be a more fundamental principle that underlies whatever constraints precedents impose in both areas: the principle that we should not judge cases differently without being able to cite a relevant difference between them. This principle generates somewhat different constraints in the two domains because of the different ways we determine cases to be settled, that is, to function as precedents.

In the legal system, judges are required to conform their decisions to earlier decisions by other courts. A case previously decided, especially at the appellate level, remains settled unless it can be shown to rest on a clear mistake of fact or prior law. If it is cited as a precedent for a later case, the judge in that case must be able to distinguish it in order to decide it differently. We can, of course, question why a judge who believes that a previous decision is morally mistaken should nevertheless accept the precedent as a constraint on his present judgment. Perhaps surprisingly, we cannot answer this challenge to the doctrine of precedent by appealing either to the more fundamental principle cited above or directly to the principle that we ought to honor expectations based on the prior decision. If the prior decision was indeed morally mistaken, then the fundamental principle of not deciding cases differently without relevant differences between them is likely to have been violated by that decision, and so the principle cannot call for conforming future judgments to it. In regard to expectations, they will be legitimately formed on the basis of prior legal decisions only once we have justified and adopted the principle of legal precedent, and so they cannot be used directly to justify that principle. (Once other justifications are in place, the need to respect expectations can reinforce them.)

The initial justification for the constraint of precedent in law instead appeals to certain aims of the legal institution and to the place of judges, given the fallibility of their decisions, within the institution. The relevant aims relate to social stability, that is, the creation of a social and economic environment in which stable expectations can be formed, useful ventures risked, and transactions conducted in an orderly and predictable way. For these purposes relevant law must be knowable and judicial decisions predictable. They will be more predictable when judges adhere to earlier decisions of other judges. The CONSERVATISM of the principle, its tendency to maintain the status quo, is justified by appeal to the role of the judge *vis-à-vis* legislators and other judges. Radical change, it can be maintained, ought to be introduced by legislators answerable directly to the electorate. And, given their fallibility and the constraints of time and resources for making decisions in cases before them, judges are more likely to introduce new errors by departing from precedent than to extend old errors by adhering to it, especially when the governing common law derives from whole lines of cases.

Legal scholars often speak of rules created by precedent cases, but these are not strict rules. Even if a seeming rule is stated explicitly in a previous decision and even if the present case falls under the stated conditions of the rule, a judge still has the options of limiting the rule, reformulating it, or rejecting it in favor of some narrower construal. In so doing judges look through the apparent rule to the legal and moral aims served by the prior decision. They must then decide if these aims require a like decision in the present context or whether additional factors present in the new case constitute conflicting values or alter the priorities of the earlier context. The latter question is not relevant when strict rules are literally applied. Thus the constraint of precedent is weaker than the requirement to apply strict rules in decisions.

The institutional considerations that justify the doctrine of legal precedent do not play a similar role when it comes to moral judgment. First, it is not as important that individuals conform their judgments of moral issues to those of other individuals: indeed, initial divergence can be a healthy input to full debate of such issues. Predictability of judgment is not as crucial in the personal domain. Second, there are no moral experts who have mastered a subject area (or institutional history) in the way that legal experts can. Third, there is no division of moral AUTHORITY in the way that we divide the authority of legislators and judges in the legal system. Finally, and related to the above points, there is a value to autonomous moral judgment by individuals that does not apply to legal decisions of judges. For all these reasons, individuals need not and do not consider the judgments of others to settle moral issues, to be settled judgments that operate as constraints on their own MORAL REASONING.

Nevertheless, the fundamental constraint of not judging cases differently without finding relevant differences between them applies in the moral domain as well and demands consistency at least among individual sets of moral judgments. If my judgments are inconsistent, in violation of this constraint, then actions based on them will be self-defeating, in that I will act against values that I pursue in other contexts without any reason for acting differently. My actions toward others will be unfair to them; I will treat people differently who merit the same treatment.

Obeying and applying the constraint, by contrast, provides a way of reasoning to judgments on controversial issues. Indeed, if controversial issues involve conflicting values and if the priorities among such conflicting values change depending on the degree to which they are at stake and on other values that interact with them in broader contexts, then once again the method of reasoning by analogy and difference from settled cases or precedents is applicable where strict or genuine rules (which assume fixed priorities among values) are not. If priorities among values do change in these ways, then we cannot reason simply from one case to another with the same features relevant in the first case (because other factors in the second case may alter their relevance); but we can reason from one case to another with the same relevant features *and* no relevant differences. Relevant differences are those that affect the values at stake and that make differences in other contexts as well.

In practice, the set of one's prior moral judgments in which one retains confidence will function as settled precedents much as in the legal domain. The differences between the domains are that, in the moral sphere, one is not bound by judgments of others, and earlier judgments do not necessarily have priority over later ones. What matters here is not temporal priority, but the subjection of the judgments to fully informed reflection about their origins, outcomes (of acting on them), and consistency with broader sets of judgments. When a new judgment formed on the basis of new experience or reflection conflicts with a previous one and no relevant difference between the objects of the judgments can be found, coherence must be restored; but there is a choice as to whether to revise the earlier or later judgment, a choice that normally does not exist in the legal domain.

Because one is not bound by the moral judgments of others, the constraint of consistency operates first intrapersonally, in relation to the set of one's own judgments, providing a method of reasoning to answers to moral questions that one finds difficult. But it can also provide a method of settling disagreements among individuals, *if* the individuals in question are willing to accept the settled judgments on which they agree as the relevant precedents. In applying the method, we first identify the precedents—

other cases, real or fictional—in which priorities among the values that conflict in the controversial case have been determined to the satisfaction of all parties to the present dispute. We then attempt to identify disanalogies between the present context and these less problematic cases, differences that affect the values at stake and generally make a difference elsewhere. Failing to identify such differences when they exist is again a form of inconsistency, because it is a failure to bring to bear values that are recognized to make a difference among other similar sets of cases. Next, we search for closer analogies or more relevant precedents. If we do not find any relevant differences or closer precedents, then we must judge the controversial issue in the same way as the settled cases or precedents.

See also: ANALOGICAL ARGUMENT; AUTHORITY; AUTONOMY OF ETHICS; AUTONOMY OF MORAL AGENTS; CASUISTRY; CONSERVATISM; DELIBERATION AND CHOICE; FAIRNESS; LEGAL PHILOSOPHY; MORAL POINT OF VIEW; MORAL REASONING; MORAL RULES; NORMS; PERSUASIVE DEFINITION; PRESCRIPTIVISM; PRINCIPLISM; SOCIAL AND POLITICAL PHILOSOPHY; THEORY AND PRACTICE; UNIVERSALIZABILITY.

Bibliography

Alexander, Larry. "Constrained by Precedent." *Southern California Law Review* 63 (1989): 3–64.

Burton, Steven J. *An Introduction to Law and Legal Reasoning.* Boston: Little, Brown, 1985.

Eisenberg, M. I. *The Nature of the Common Law.* Cambridge: Harvard University Press, 1988.

Goldman, Alan. "The Force of Precedent in Legal, Moral, and Empirical Reasoning." *Synthese* 71 (1987): 323–46.

Lyons, David. "Formal Justice, Moral Commitment, and Judicial Precedent." *Journal of Philosophy* 81 (1984): 580–87.

Post, C. Gordon. *An Introduction to the Law.* Englewood Cliffs, NJ: Prentice-Hall, 1963. See chapter VI.

Reynolds, William L. *Judicial Process in a Nutshell.* St. Paul: West, 1980. See chapter 4.

Simpson, A. "The *Ratio Decidendi* of a Case and the Doctrine of Binding Precedent." In *Oxford Essays in Jurisprudence,* edited by A. G. Guest. Oxford: Oxford University Press, 1961.

Sunstein, Cass. "Political Conflict and Legal Agreement." *The Tanner Lectures on Human Values* 17 (1996): 137–249.

Wasserstrom, Richard. *The Judicial Decision: Toward a*

Theory of Legal Justification. Stanford: Stanford University Press, 1961.

Alan H. Goldman

prescriptivism

Ethical theories (in the sense of theories about the meaning and logical properties of MORAL TERMS) fall into two main classes: descriptivist and nondescriptivist. According to descriptivist theories, moral words like "good" and "wrong" resemble ordinary descriptive words like "red" and "rectangular" in that their meaning and their application-conditions are firmly linked, so that to change either is to change the other. Victims of the "descriptive fallacy" (Austin) think that the same has to be true of all words; but this has been shown not to be the case. Historically, the advocates of EMOTIVISM were the first to reject explicitly a descriptivist account of moral words. But the irrationalism that they embraced—the view that no logical canons govern the use of these words—was fairly soon seen not to be a necessary consequence of the rejection of descriptivism. It is possible for there to be logical canons governing nondescriptive speech acts, including even commands: these can be faulted for being self-contradictory, for example. Thus the view that moral judgments can be not, or not wholly, descriptive in their meaning is consistent with the view that there can be a logic which controls their use—*i.e.,* rules governing moral reasoning.

Prescriptivism was the first, and still is the most prominent, attempt to devise a rationalist kind of nondescriptivism, *i.e.,* a theory that insists on the rationality of moral thinking while allowing that the application-conditions of moral words could vary without the words changing their meanings. Two people can mean the same by "wrong" and still differ about what acts are properly called wrong. If this were not so, moral disagreements could not be expressed; for in order to disagree, two people have to mean the same by a proposition affirmed by one but denied by the other.

Prescriptivists (*e.g.,* Hare 1952) took their cue from an observation about imperatives. The application-conditions of imperatives clearly vary independently of their meaning. If I tell someone to shut the door and you tell him not to, we may still be meaning the same by the imperative "Shut the door," which I af-

firm and you negate. But imperatives are nevertheless required by logic to be consistent with one another in the same person's mouth, if that person is not to contradict himself or herself. Most prescriptivists did not completely assimilate moral judgments to imperatives (obviously they are very different in some respects); but in this respect they might be similar. This conclusion is consistent both with the phenomenon just described—that two people can use "wrong" in the same sense while disagreeing as to whether a certain kind of act (*e.g.,* meat eating) is wrong—and with the hope of discovering a logic, or system of reasoning, for answering moral questions.

There could be many kinds of prescriptivism; but the best-known kind is now commonly called *universal* prescriptivism. The name arose from an attempt to differentiate moral judgments from plain imperatives. The latter do not have the feature of UNIVERSALIZABILITY: I can tell one person to do a thing, but tell another not to do it, however similar the people and their circumstances. It is generally thought (by many besides prescriptivists) that this is not so with moral judgments. It was thus tempting to differentiate moral judgments from plain imperatives by analyzing them as universal or universalizable prescriptions or prohibitions. This means that in making a moral judgment one is committing oneself (on pain of being accused of having changed one's mind) to making the same judgment about any situation (actual or hypothetical) having identical nonmoral properties.

The universal prescriptivist theory has been developed by its inventor into a complete account of moral reasoning (Hare 1981 and refs.). He has found formal affinities between this theory and those of KANT (1724–1804) and of UTILITARIANISM. He was thus led to suggest that a synthesis might be found between the two types of theory, generally thought to be antithetical. In order to overcome objections to his theory he has made a number of further moves.

First, since it is generally and rightly held that there *are* standard application-conditions for moral predicates, at least within a given society, and therefore commonly accepted truth-conditions for moral judgments, it is perfectly in order to call moral judgments true or false. Superficially this might seem to be inconsistent with any kind of nondescriptivism; for ethical descriptivism, along with its close allies ethical realism and cognitivism, has often been associated with the view that moral judgments can be called true or false. STEVENSON (1908–1979) coined the term "descriptive meaning" for that *part* of the meaning of moral words which is like the *whole* meaning of ordinary descriptive words: that which *is* governed by truth-conditions, these corresponding to the moral standards current in a given society.

Nondescriptivists, including prescriptivists, can readily allow that there is this element in their meaning and that therefore moral judgments can be called true or false. But they will go on to say that if we think that it is the *whole* of their meaning we shall be in danger of falling into relativism. For if the truth of a moral judgment is assessed by the standards current in a society, and these vary from one society to another, a purely descriptive account of the meaning of moral words will tell us to call true in Rome those moral judgments that the Romans make. It is only by having a part of the meaning of moral judgments (the nondescriptive part) which is independent of these standards that such relativism can be avoided (Hare 1989). And if, unlike the emotivists, we say that this part of the meaning is subject to rules of logic, the way will be open to a nonrelativist, rationalist account of moral thinking. Thus, contrary to what is commonly thought, descriptivism is the enemy, not the ally, of rationalism.

The other common objection to universal prescriptivism receives a closely related answer. The objection is that the utilitarianism which is claimed to be generated by the theory, like older forms of utilitarianism, requires us to hold moral opinions which are highly repugnant to most people's intuitions. To use a hackneyed example, if judicially murdering an innocent man would maximize utility, we ought to do it, according to the theory. Like other utilitarians, the universal prescriptivist can avoid this difficulty by drawing attention, as did PLATO (c. 430–347 B.C.E.) and ARISTOTLE (384–322 B.C.E.), to the undoubted fact that our moral thinking takes place at at least two different levels. In the everyday moral thinking that we practice most of the time, we do appeal to our intuitions, and it is right that we should. For if we tried to perform utilitarian calculations all the time, we should often get them wrong, through lack of information, SELF-DECEPTION, bias, and muddle, especially when in haste or under stress. Paradoxically, we are more likely to hit off the utilitarian ideal by not thinking, normally, as utilitarians; to think intuitively will usually be more conducive to

acting for the best. Utilitarians can therefore justify the cultivation and following of intuitions.

But obviously they have to be the right or the best intuitions; and equally obviously, even if they are the best ones to have, they will sometimes conflict; for we cannot learn very highly specific moral principles, and the rather general ones that are the content of our intuitions are too crude to cope with *all* the complexities of the highly specific situations that we find ourselves in. Even most anti-utilitarian intuitionists have, in their pluralist catalogue of intuitive principles, principles of BENEFICENCE and nonmaleficence; and these will conflict with their other principles as often as the latter conflict with utilitarian prescriptions. Moral conflicts are the source of the tragic dilemmas beloved of writers of fiction, and occur sometimes in real life, in which either to do or not to do some ACTION seems to be wrong.

To cope with these dilemmas and to decide what are the best intuitions to cultivate in general, in ourselves and our children, we need a higher level of thinking (best called *critical*). Most of the serious problems in moral philosophy arise at this higher level. Prescriptivist utilitarians thus have an answer to the allegation of the intuitionists that their theory leads to counterintuitive conclusions. A properly constructed two-level utilitarian prescriptivism would bid us cultivate the very intuitions that the intuitionists appeal to, and act on them in all ordinary situations. The extraordinary situations that appear in the examples of the objectors have to be dealt with by critical thinking; but it is not surprising if the results of this critical thinking can conflict with our intuitions, which were designed to give the best answers in ordinary cases and not to solve problems arising from conflicts between the intuitions themselves.

The answer to this second objection is related to the answer to the first in the following way. Our common intuitions assure us that certain moral judgments are true, because we have learnt certain firm standards, associated with dispositions, to feel strongly about them and to judge and act accordingly. These same standards fix the descriptive meanings of our moral words and therefore what moral judgments we say are true or false. But all this occurs at the intuitive level. If we thought that this was the whole story, we would, like many intuitionists, altogether neglect the problems which call for critical moral thought. This neglect would leave us tied, in making our moral judgments, to the descriptive meanings for the words (the intuitions and standards) in which we were brought up. And these descriptive meanings would vary from one society to another. One society, for example, might think it undoubtedly wrong for wives to disobey their husbands; another might not. Each society would call what it thought, whatever it was, the truth. They could escape from this relativism only by putting their different standards to the test of thinking at the critical level, at which the common logical properties of their shared moral words would discipline their thought and bring it to the same answers.

A third standard objection, based on the alleged difficulty that prescriptivist theories have in accounting for WEAKNESS OF WILL, is discussed under that head.

See also: CATEGORICAL AND HYPOTHETICAL IMPERATIVES; EMOTIVISM; HARE; INTUITIONISM; KANT; LOGIC AND ETHICS; MORAL DILEMMAS; MORAL REALISM; MORAL REASONING; MORAL RELATIVISM; MORAL TERMS; RATIONALITY VS. REASONABLENESS; STEVENSON; UNIVERSALIZABILITY; UTILITARIANISM; WEAKNESS OF WILL.

Bibliography

Austin, J. L. *Philosophical Papers.* Oxford: Oxford University Press, 1961. "Descriptive fallacy," p. 234.

———. *How to Do Things with Words.* Oxford: Oxford University Press, 1962. "Descriptive fallacy," p. 3.

Hare, R. M. *The Language of Morals.* Oxford: Oxford University Press, 1952.

———. *Freedom and Reason.* Oxford: Oxford University Press, 1963.

———. *Moral Thinking: Its Levels, Method, and Point.* Oxford: Oxford University Press, 1981.

———. *Essays in Ethical Theory.* Oxford: Oxford University Press, 1989. Pp. 99–130.

Seanor, D., and N. Fotion, editors. *Hare and Critics.* Oxford: Oxford University Press, 1988.

Stevenson, Charles L. *Ethics and Language.* New Haven: Yale University Press, 1944. His use of descriptive meaning, pp. 67, *ff.*

R. M. Hare

Price, Richard (1723–1791)

Born at Tynton, Glamorganshire, and educated at Dissenting academies, Richard Price became a Dis-senting minister at age twenty-one. After twelve years as a domestic chaplain, he preached primarily at Stoke Newington and Hackney. He married Sarah Blundell, an Anglican, in 1758; they had no children.

Price was an influential actuary, economist, and theologian as well as a moral philosopher and champion of the American and French Revolutions. His papers on "The Doctrine of Chances" (1764, 1765) won him a Fellowship of the Royal Society; his work on life expectancy helped modernize insurance practices. His *Appeal to the Public on the Subject of the National Debt* (1771) influenced William Pitt's (1759–1806) economic policies. His *Observations on the Nature of Civil Liberty, the Principles of Government, and the Justice and Policy of the War with America* (1776) sold 60,000 copies within its first year, and probably encouraged America's decision to declare independence (1776). In *A Discourse on the Love of Our Country* (1789), Price also praised the French Revolution, moving Edmund BURKE (1729–1797) to reply in his *Reflections on the Revolution in France* (1790).

In *A Review of the Principle Questions and Difficulties in Morals* (1758; 2d ed. 1769; 3d ed. 1787), Price defends a rationalist view of ethics, influenced by Samuel CLARKE (1675–1729), against criticisms by the empiricist MORAL SENSE THEORISTS, especially Francis HUTCHESON (1694–1746). The latter had argued that reason cannot give rise to moral ideas because all simple ideas are derived from sense and reflection. Price develops a Platonist theory of the understanding, derived from PLATO's (c. 430–347 B.C.E.) *Theaetetus* and Ralph CUDWORTH (1617–1688), according to which "the faculty within us that discerns *truth,* and that compares all the objects of thought, and *judges* of them, is a spring of new ideas." These ideas include solidity, inertia, substance, accident, duration, space, and power or causation. Price turns HUME's (1711–1776) argument on its head, claiming that since sensation can reveal only constant conjunction, our idea of POWER or causation must come from the understanding. Ideas therefore fall into two categories: those that denote only affections of the mind itself, including both sensory ideas and reflective ideas such as beauty; and those that "denote something distinct from sensation; and imply real and independent existence and truth."

Price examines three pairs of moral ideas to determine which category they belong to: right and wrong, beauty and deformity, and merit and demerit. His main concern is to show that right and wrong are ideas of the understanding. If actions were not right in themselves, our moral perceptions would be arbitrary. Furthermore, no action would really be obligatory, for "intrinsically right" and "obligatory" are the same. But once the thesis that simple ideas must originate in sense is defeated, the main obstacle to the view that right and wrong are "real characters of actions" is removed.

Emotions of approval and disapproval accompany moral perceptions: a right action appears beautiful and a wrong one deformed. But Price denies that these feelings can be explained only by an implanted moral sense. There is an intelligible connection between moral ideas and the attendant feelings: a rational being is *necessarily* pleased by a right action and displeased by a wrong one. Similarly, the ideas of HAPPINESS, truth, and HONOR necessarily move a rational being to desire them for himself and others. Yet because we are imperfectly rational, God has also provided us with "instinctive determinations," including a moral sense, to strengthen our rational intuitions and affections.

Ideas of merit and demerit arise directly from those of right and wrong, for it is right that virtue should be rewarded and vice punished. But the moral motive is the perception of rightness or obligation itself, which moves us directly to action. This does not mean that BENEVOLENCE is not a virtuous motive. Rational, as opposed to instinctive, benevolence "coincides with rectitude." But Price opposes the reduction of all virtue to benevolence. The worship of God, due concern for oneself, GRATITUDE, veracity, and justice are right in themselves.

Virtue requires freedom of the will, which Price defends in *A Free Discussion of the Doctrine of Materialism and Philosophical Necessity* (1778), published correspondence with his friend Joseph Priestly (1733–1804). Priestly argues that freedom of the will requires action without a motive and so without a cause. Price replies that freedom does not require action without a motive as long as the motive is not conceived as a mechanical or physical cause. The cause of free action, and the foundation of morality, is the self-determining agent.

Price's commitment to the value of the self-determining agent also motivated his enthusiasm for the American (1775–1783) and French (1789–1799) Revolutions. In *Observations on Civil Liberty*, Price argues that every human being has a natural right to physical, moral, religious, and civil liberty. Civil liberty exists only in a society whose laws are made by the people themselves, directly or through elected representatives. Indeed, all forms of LIBERTY are forms of self-government, for we act as we like only when the will rules the passions. Like KANT (1724–1804), to whom he is often and justly compared, Price celebrated the revolutions as harbingers of the ultimate triumph of liberty and justice on earth.

See also: CAUSATION AND RESPONSIBILITY; CLARKE; CUDWORTH; FREE WILL; FREEDOM AND DETERMINISM; HUME; HUTCHESON; KANT; LIBERTY; LIBERTY, ECONOMIC; MORAL SENSE THEORISTS; MOTIVES; RATIONAL CHOICE; REVOLUTION.

Bibliography

Works by Price

The Works. Edited by W. Morgan. 10 vols. London, 1815–1816. Includes "Memoirs of the Life of the Rev. Richard Price D.D. F.R.S."

The Correspondence of Richard Price. Edited by W. Bernard Peach and D. O. Thomas. Durham, NC: Duke University Press and Cardiff: University of Wales, 1983. Vol. 1: July 1748–March 1778.

A Review of the Principal Questions in Morals. Oxford: Oxford University Press, 1948 [1758; 1787]. Reprint, with critical introduction by D. D. Raphael, of the 3d, 1787 edition; 1st edition title was *A Review of the Principal Questions and Difficulties in Morals.* Includes "Appendix containing additional notes and a Dissertation on the Being and Attributes of the Deity."

Richard Price and the Ethical Foundations of the American Revolution. Edited by W. Bernard Peach. Durham, NC: Duke University Press, 1979. Contains a critical introduction by the editor. Includes Price's major pamphlets on the American Revolution, including *Observations on the Nature of Civil Liberty, the Principles of Government, and the Justice and Policy of the War with America* (1776); *Additional Observations on the Nature and Value of Civil Liberty and the War with America* (1777); and *Observations on the Importance of the American Revolution and the Means of Making It a Benefit to the World* (1784).

Political Writings. Edited by D. O. Thomas. Cambridge: Cambridge University Press, 1992.

Price, Richard, and Joseph Priestly. *A Free Discussion of the Doctrines of Materialism and Philosophical Necessity, in a Correspondence between Dr. Price and Dr. Priestly.* London: J. Johnson and T. Cadell, 1778. Reprinted New York: Garland, 1978.

Works about Price

Åqvist, Lennart. *The Moral Philosophy of Richard Price.* Upsalla, Sweden: Almquist and Wiksells, 1960.

Cone, Carl B. *Torchbearer of Freedom: The Influence of Richard Price on Eighteenth Century Thought.* Lexington: University of Kentucky Press, 1952.

Cua, Antonio S. *Reason and Virtue: A Study in the Ethics of Richard Price.* Athens: Ohio University Press, 1966.

Hudson, W. D. *Reason and Right: A Critical Examination of Richard Price's Moral Philosophy.* London: Macmillan and San Francisco: Freeman, Cooper, 1970.

Laboucheix, Henri. *Richard Price, theoricien de la révolution Americaine, le philosophe et le socio-logue, le pamphletaire et l'orateur.* Paris: Didier, 1970.

Thomas, D. O. *The Honest Mind: The Thought and Work of Richard Price.* Oxford: Clarendon Press, 1977. Includes extensive bibliography, a complete list of Price's published works, and information on locations of manuscripts of his papers and correspondence.

Thomas, Roland. *Richard Price: Philosopher and Apostle of Liberty.* London: Oxford University Press, 1924. Includes a list of the various editions of Price's published works, and a list, organized by subject matter, of works that were written in direct response to Price.

Christine M. Korsgaard

Prichard, H. A. (Harold Arthur) (1871–1947)

Prichard was the star pupil of the Oxford Realists, was the leader of the Oxford Intuitionists, and did pioneer work in theory of ACTION and ordinary language analysis. His moral philosophy is distinctive, standing as one of three main types of ethical theory, including UTILITARIANISM and CONTRACTARIANISM, recognized in the twentieth century. What is remarkable is that so much influence came from so little published work. Insofar as his influence in ethics derives from publication, it does so from two articles: "Does Moral Philosophy Rest on a Mistake?" (*Mind,* 1912) and "Duty and Ignorance of Fact" (*Proceedings of the British Academy,* 1932).

The message of the first and most seminal article is generally thought to be that one simply intuits ("one just knows," as critics say) moral obligations. More accurately, the mistake is to try to prove what is already known noninferentially in the kinds of actions found in ordinary morality.

The problem of the second article arises out of identifying moral duty with doing what is morally right. What then is the relation of duty to knowledge? Is duty a matter of doing what one *thinks* is right (given what one knows) or what *is* right (given what one should know)? Prichard preferred the first alternative (the "subjective view"), although he spent much effort thereafter arguing with himself and W. D. ROSS (1877–1971) about it. Difficulties in the second ("objective") view are that you can have a duty and not know it (aid a sick relative) or do what is right unknowingly (attend a promised appointment by mistake).

Intuitionism, Realism, Pluralism

Prichard's moral philosophy is usually labeled in textbooks as "moral intuitionism," but that characterization is both too wide and too narrow. If it is considered only as INTUITIONISM, then that invites confusion with the opposing theory held by G. E. MOORE (1873–1958). Moore's theory is utilitarian and teleological. Contributing to the production of a good end, which is intuited, renders any act morally right. Prichard's doctrine is that certain *kinds* of acts themselves are intuited as morally right or wrong. The moral rightness of kinds of acts is entirely underived. Prichard seeks to "sever rightness from goodness," and in that sense is a deontologist. The label "intuitionism" is also too narrow since, although Prichard uses none of the following terms, his moral philosophy includes MORAL REALISM, intuitionism, and pluralism. Moral realism is the doctrine that there exist kinds of acts that are right or wrong of their own nature, independent of human consciousness, such as helping the helpless or punishing those who cannot help what they do. Intuitionism is a type of understanding: a direct apprehension, without inference or further proof, that acts of certain kinds are independently right or wrong. Pluralism means that there are distinct kinds of right and wrong acts, kinds not reducible to a single end of any sort.

Many philosophers attest to the power of Prichard's moral philosophy. Perhaps this is because, for him, the test of any morality (or theory or system) must be a moral one rather than the agreement of agents, coherence, or service to some end.

See also: COMMON SENSE MORALISTS; DEONTOLOGY; DUTY AND OBLIGATION; INTUITIONISM; MORAL PERCEPTION; MORAL PLURALISM; MORAL REALISM; MORAL SENSE THEORISTS; ROSS; SUBJECTIVISM.

Prichard, H. A.

Bibliography

Works by Prichard

Moral Obligation, Essays and Lectures. Edited by W. D. Ross. Oxford: Clarendon Press, 1949. Essays, lectures, short occasional pieces assembled by his friend, W. D. Ross, after Prichard's death; includes three of his four published articles and a note by Ross.

Moral Obligation and Duty and Interest: Essays and Lectures. Introduction by J. O. Urmson. Oxford: Oxford University Press, 1968. Adds the fourth published article, "Duty and Interest," Prichard's inaugural lecture, plus a well-informed introduction by Urmson.

Kant's Theory of Knowledge. Oxford: Clarendon Press, 1909. Prichard's realist critique of Kant.

Knowledge and Perception: Essays and Lectures. Edited by W. D. Ross. Oxford: Oxford University Press, 1950. Prichard's epistemological writings; lectures on the "History of the Theory of Knowledge" helpful in understanding Prichard's own conception of knowledge.

Works about Prichard

Carritt, E. F. *Ethical and Political Thinking.* Oxford: Clarendon Press, 1947. Oxford Intuitionist; Prichard was Carritt's tutor.

Daly, C. B. "Inter-War British Ethics: The Oxford Intuitionists." *Philosophical Studies (Ireland)* 14 (1965): 55–87.

Dancy, J., J. M. E. Moravcsik, and C. Taylor, eds. *Human Agency, Language, Duty, and Value: Philosophical Essays in Honour of J. O. Urmson.* Stanford: Stanford University Press, 1988.

Falk, W. D. "'Ought' and Motivation." *Proceedings of the Aristotelian Society* 48 (1948): 111–38.

———. *Ought, Reasons and Morality.* Ithaca, NY: Cornell University Press, 1986.

Frankena, W. K. "Prichard and the Ethics of Virtue." *Monist* 54 (1970): 1–17.

Hudson, W. D. *Ethical Intuitionism.* New York: St. Martin's, 1967.

Johnson, O. *Rightness and Goodness.* The Hague: Nijhoff, 1969.

Lemos, Ramon M. "Duty and Ignorance." *Southern Journal of Philosophy* 18 (1980): 301–12.

Lucas, J. R. "Ethical Intuitionism II." *Philosophy* 46 (1971): 1–11.

Mabbott, J. D. *An Introduction to Ethics.* London: Hutchinson University Library, 1966.

Mackie, J. L. *Ethics: Inventing Right and Wrong.* Harmondsworth: Penguin, 1977. Criticism of Prichard's type of realism.

Nowell-Smith, P. H. *Ethics.* Harmondsworth: Pelican, 1954. Criticizes Prichard's ethics.

Plamenatz, J. P. *Consent, Freedom and Political Obligation.* 2d ed. Oxford: Oxford University Press, 1968. (1st ed., 1938.)

Price, H. H. "Harold Arthur Prichard, 1871–1947." *Proceedings of the British Academy* 33 (1947): 330–50. A memorial; also an excellent discussion of Prichard's views.

Rees, D. A. "The Idea of Objective Duty." *Proceedings of the Aristotelian Society* 52 (1951–2): 71–94.

Ross, W. D. *The Right and the Good.* Oxford: Clarendon Press, 1930. Close friend and fellow Oxford Intuitionist.

———. *The Foundations of Ethics.* Oxford: Clarendon Press, 1939.

Strawson, P. F. "Ethical Intuitionism." *Philosophy* 24 (1949): 23–33.

Urmson, J. O. "A Defence of Intuitionism." *Proceedings of the Aristotelian Society* 75 (1974–5): 111–19. Able defense that also distinguishes Prichard's position from G. E. Moore's.

Jim MacAdam

pride

Pride is defined along a number of dimensions, most of which are mentioned in the *Oxford English Dictionary*'s rather heavily moralized primary definition: "Pride," the *OED* tells us, is a "high or overweening opinion of one's own qualities, attainments or estate, which gives rise to a feeling and attitude of superiority over and contempt for others; inordinate self-esteem." We may distinguish five dimensions here. One is the loftiness of the prideful person's self-concept (her high opinion of her "qualities"). Another is her high opinion of her accomplishments, possessions, or status ("attainments or estate"). A third is her favorable assessment of her comparative position relative to others ("superiority"). A fourth concerns the warrant for those self-assessments, or lack of it (*e.g.,* "overweening . . . inordinate" SELF-ESTEEM). And a fifth concerns the attitude or feeling she has toward others in the light of such self-assessments (*e.g.,* "contempt").

One obvious philosophical challenge here is to see whether such pride is always a vice, as the definition seems to suggest, or whether it is possible that a virtuous person can appropriately have it. One can of course give various theological accounts of the evil of pride—as it may be involved, for example, in setting oneself "above" God through sin, or in believing oneself to have earned things that come only through God's grace. But theology aside, it is natural to think that some form of pride might be a necessary element of virtue. After all, if the virtuous person is in fact superior to vicious ones and if part of her virtue consists in having knowledge of such things, then it seems as though some dimension of pride is necessarily built into virtuous CHARACTER. How could it be virtuous to deny the truth? Or to ignore the truth? This line of thought makes it difficult to regard HUMILITY and modesty as virtues.

The issue is complicated further by two ways in which pride may be connected to one's identity, or robust sense of self. One is David HUME's (1711–1776) suggestion that the feeling or attitude of pride is a natural PASSION that is intimately bound up with consciousness of oneself and is indispensable for effective moral agency. The other is closely related to HONOR or INTEGRITY and concerns a person's refusal to subordinate or efface her own will or desires or integrity to another. The *OED*'s account of this latter usage is perhaps unduly narrow: "a consciousness or feeling of what is befitting or due to oneself or one's position, which prevents a person from doing what he considers to be beneath him or unworthy of him." But put more generally, pride in this sense refers to an agent's claim of autonomy—a claim that her worth, merit, and life are genuinely her own, that her own will, or desires, or integrity may properly determine her conduct. It does not seem plausible to think that one would want to be without pride in either this sense or Hume's.

For convenience, let us refer to these dimensions of pride, respectively, as those of self-worth, absolute merit, comparative merit, justification (for beliefs about worth and merit), attitudes toward others, and sense of self. And let us be sure to leave open the possibility that pride along all these dimensions might be a good thing, a virtue. That is, let us assume that it is possible in principle to be justifiably proud of one's achievements, or noble in one's proud defiance of an order to kneel.

Indeed, it seems quite sensible to take an Aristotelian approach to the dimensions of pride by noting, first, the way in which people can be *either* deficient *or* excessive along four of the dimensions mentioned (self-worth, absolute and relative merit, and autonomy), given knowledge of the relevant facts. Low self-esteem may be every bit as unwarranted (as inordinate) as an exalted opinion of oneself. Obsequiousness, deference, and self-effacement can be as objectionable as insolence, insubordination, and arrogance. It seems natural to let the truth of the self-assessment in each case determine what counts as the mean between the extremes. If an agent is genuinely exalted, then she will be deficient if she does not have a correspondingly high opinion of herself; if she is entitled to a life of her own, she will be deficient if she does not recognize her claim to it. This is simply "proper pride."

The notion of proper pride is complicated, however, by several factors. First, to recognize one's claim to an autonomous life is not equivalent to actually making that claim. In principle there is room for an argument that agents who actually insist on their ENTITLEMENTS are nonetheless acting objectionably. Perhaps gentleness, CIVILITY, *noblesse oblige* (not to mention PRUDENCE) will require an otherwise unwarranted deference. Proper pride then amounts to holding on to the recognition of the extent of one's autonomy, and the awareness of the justification for yielding it.

Second, from the fact that we should have accurate beliefs about our personal worth and merit, it does not follow that we are justified in publically proclaiming those beliefs, or in encouraging others to believe the truth about us, or even in accepting their public proclamation of it. If I am a wretch and know it, must I wear a badge announcing it? If I am repentant, must I invite public recognition of my sin? If not, then surely the same may be true of EXCELLENCE. If I am exemplary, it is still not settled that proper pride requires me to publish the fact or even overtly to acknowledge it. Proper pride, then, may be consistent with secret pride, modesty, and avoidance of honors. (Hume gives such an argument in his *Treatise of Human Nature* [1737], Book III, Part III, Section II.)

Third, there are knotty problems concerning the attitudes that proper pride should evoke in us—even if we do not let them show. What is the appropriate affective response for you to have to the knowledge that you are wonderful? Surely not dismay, but in addition to wonder, what about delight, triumph, excitement, glory, joy, contempt or PITY for others, amusement, apprehension . . .? This is unsettled terrain in MORAL PSYCHOLOGY.

Finally, there are three general sorts of arguments that are meant to undermine the warrant for important forms of proper pride altogether. One is the attempt to show (usually with premises about causality) that no one deserves credit for being excellent, and thus to the extent that pride involves taking such credit, it is unjustified. Another is the attempt to show (by appeal to egalitarian arguments) that no one is entitled to take pride in comparative or relative advantages. And the third is the attempt to show (by appeal to communitarian or theological arguments) that legitimate claims of personal autonomy are so limited as to render all forms of pride suspect.

It is probably this last sort of argument, particularly as developed by Christians following AUGUSTINE (354–430), that has done the most to identify pride *per se* as a fundamental vice and to marginalize the notions we here have consequently had to call proper pride. In its secular, communitarian version, the idea is that pride typically involves denying the social nature of the self and the social construction of its worth. Pride involves false claims of autonomy from the community; false claims of personal merit; false claims about the intrinsic, objective worth of individuals abstracted from a social order. In its theological version, the idea is that pride typically involves setting oneself apart from God, denying his sovereignty so as to be able to choose, and taking credit for the results of choice. Pride thus involves denying the reality of one's place in the divine order. And since to deny that reality is to repudiate the fundamentals of the faith, pride opens the door to all sorts of other sins. Moreover, it is prompted by a very strong temptation, perhaps the original temptation (*i.e.,* to be like a god). So it is natural to regard pride as the root of all sin.

That sweeping condemnation, however, is no more supportable than a sweeping endorsement of humility. Immanuel KANT (1724–1804), though he condemns some forms of pride, takes pains to distinguish those vicious forms from true, noble pride which (along with appropriate humility) produces the sort of SELF-RESPECT needed to avoid the vice of servility. The general idea here is that we must never regard ourselves, *qua* human beings, as either greater or lesser than other humans. Hume treats pride as a type of immediately agreeable response to the self, a response which is (in proper measure) both agreeable to others and instrumentally good. Friedrich NIETZSCHE (1844–1900) is scornful of humility and connects proper pride with noble character.

Hume's account is perhaps the most interesting, philosophically. In Book II, Part I of the *Treatise,* he gives an account of the nature and origin of pride as a psychological phenomenon, arguing in effect that it is both natural and necessary for human beings in any reasonably hospitable social environment. He says (II, I, vi) that "all agreeable objects [*e.g.,* virtue, beauty, and riches], related to ourselves . . . produce pride" under the following "limitations":

1. *Close relation.* The relation between the agreeable object and our selves will be a close one—specifically, a closer one than is characteristic of simple joy. We may feel joy at merely being at a feast, but unless we have a closer personal connection to it than mere participation we do not feel pride in it. Cases in which one can refer to the object with possessive pronouns ("my feast," "my best friend's feast") are paradigm cases of the necessary sort of close relation.

2. *Rarity.* The object will be uniquely our own, or at least shared with rather few others. Pride typically involves comparisons, and rarity increases the pleasure. Hume says we do not typically feel pride in good health, since it is something "shar'd with such vast numbers."

3. *Discernability.* The object will be "very discernable," not only to ourselves but to others. The reference to others is included because, as Hume argues in Section XI, the original causes of pride and humility "have little influence, when not seconded by the opinions and sentiments of others."

4. *Constancy.* The object and its agreeability will be relatively durable, rather than transient. "What is casual and inconstant gives but little joy, and less pride."

5. *Conformity to a general rule.* The object will be something of a sort that is customarily or conventionally understood to be a source of pride or humility. "For 'tis evident, that if a person full-grown, and of the same nature with ourselves, were on a sudden transported into our world, he wou'd be very much embarrased with every object, and wou'd not readily find what degree of love or hatred, pride or humility, or any other passion he ought to attribute to it."

The question of whether pride is a virtue or a vice is left for Book III, but notice that pride has already been detoxified. Pride is just a form of pleasurable self-consciousness, arising under conditions that are inevitable in agreeable social circumstances. In the abstract it seems quite innocent.

In fact, when Hume turns to the question of pride as a virtue, in Book III, Part III, Section II, he begins with the assumption that since pride is merely a natural passion, the relevant question for morals is to find the point at which it is neither excessive nor deficient. He addresses that question with the methods of CONSEQUENTIALISM, filtered through a moral psychology in which SYMPATHY (the immediate communication of concordant feelings) plays a central role. Pride is an agreeable and very useful feeling, he notes, especially when it is reinforced by others through sympathy. When not reinforced, however, our PLEASURE in it withers. And worse, when others react with distress, ANGER, contempt, or ENVY to our pride, our pleasure in it often turns to distress as well—again through the workings of sympathy. Hume thinks encountering someone who is overtly and obviously proud is always at least a little distressing. If we think their pride is justified, we are humbled, and humility is a disagreeable feeling. If we think their pride is unjustified, we are distressed for other reasons. In short, it is a delicate business. It is good to have proper pride, but our fellows will often not let us have it if we are too overt about it.

Hume's solution is to recommend humility on the outside and proper pride underneath. He says that because self-esteem has such utility for the self, pride is a requisite for good character.

> 'Tis, however, certain, that good-breeding and decency require that we shou'd avoid all signs and expressions, which tend directly to show that passion. We have, all of us, a wonderful partiality for ourselves, and were we always to give vent to our sentiments in this particular, we shou'd mutually cause the greatest indignation in each other, not only by the immediate presence of so disagreeable a subject of comparison, but also by the contrariety of our judgments. (III, III, ii)

This of course raises the issue of HYPOCRISY.

See also: AUGUSTINE; AUTHENTICITY; AUTONOMY OF MORAL AGENTS; CHARACTER; CHRISTIAN ETHICS; CIVILITY; COMPETITION; DIGNITY; EGOISM; ELITE, CONCEPT OF; ENTITLEMENTS; ENVY; EXCELLENCE; FITTINGNESS; FREEDOM AND DETERMINISM; HONOR; HUME; HUMILITY; HYPOCRISY; INEQUALITY; INTEGRITY; MATERIALISM; MERIT AND DESERT; MORAL LUCK; MORAL PSYCHOLOGY; MORAL SAINTS; PASSION; PERFECTIONISM; PRUDENCE; PURITANISM; RESENTMENT; RESPONSIBILITY; SELF AND SOCIAL SELF; SELF-DECEPTION; SELF-ESTEEM; SELF-RESPECT; SUPEREROGATION; SYMPATHY; TEMPERANCE; THEOLOGICAL ETHICS; TOLERATION; VIRTUE ETHICS; VIRTUES; WEAKNESS OF WILL.

Bibliography

Aristotle. *Nicomachean Ethics.* See Book IV, chapter 3, 1123b–1125b.

Baier, Annette. "Hume's Analysis of Pride." *Journal of Philosophy* 75 (1978): 27–40.

———. "Hume on Resentment." *Hume Studies* 6 (1980): 133–49.

Bernard of Clairvaux. *The Steps of Humility.* Cambridge: Harvard University Press, 1940 [c. 1121]. Translation of *De gradibus humilitatus et superbiae.*

Green, William McAllen. *Initium omnis peccati superbia: Augustine on Pride as the First Sin.* University of California Publications in Classical Philology, vol. 13, no. 13. Berkeley: University of California Press, 1949. Survey of Augustine's scattered writings on the subject.

Hume, David. *A Treatise of Human Nature.* 1737. See Book II, Part I for matters of definition and cause; Book III, Part III, Section II, for consideration of pride and humility as virtues.

Kant, Immanuel. *Lectures on Ethics.* 1780. See "Proper Self-Respect."

———. *The Metaphysical Principles of Virtue.* 1797. See "The Elements of Ethics," sections 11 (on servility) and 42 (pride).

Nietzsche, Friedrich. *Beyond Good and Evil: Prelude to a Philosophy of the Future.* Translated by R. J. Hollingdale. Harmondsworth: Penguin, 1973 [1886].

Oppenheimer, Helen. "Pride." "Humility." *S.v. The Westminster Dictionary of Christian Ethics,* edited by James F. Childress and John Macquarrie. Philadelphia: Westminster Press, 1986.

Payne, Robert. *Hubris: A Study of Pride.* Rev. ed. New York: Harper, 1960. Pride in literature.

Rorty, Amélie O. "'Pride Produces the Idea of the Self': Hume on Moral Agency." *Australasian Journal of Philosophy* 68/3 (1990): 255–69.

Lawrence C. Becker

principlism

The term "principlism" has both narrow and broad uses in practical ethics, especially biomedical ethics. In its original, narrow usage, "principlism," a term coined by critics of the position it identifies, referred to an ethical framework with several general and unranked moral principles. More broadly, it has also come to include a wide variety of appeals to moral principles, rules, and other guidelines, including some that have quite specific rules and also rank them. This entry will concentrate on debates in BIOETHICS or biomedical ethics, where this methodological controversy about principles has been especially prominent.

The Nature of Principlism

At the very least, a principlist approach must hold that some general moral action guides or NORMS are central to and perhaps even indispensable in MORAL REASONING. The most general moral action guides, such as utility or respect for autonomy, are often labeled principles, while more specific action guides, such as respect for confidentiality, are often labeled rules. Nevertheless, the terms "principles" and "rules" may be used interchangeably, and the lines between them are often unclear because they reflect different degrees of generality and specificity.

Principlists, even in the narrow sense, differ greatly according to the principles they affirm, how they justify those principles, and how they connect them to concrete cases. Even though, at first glance, principlist approaches might be thought to be nonconsequentialist or deontological (holding that some features of acts make those acts right or wrong independently of their consequences), a framework that affirms only a consequentialist principle of utility would still be principlist. And it could also recognize other principles and rules as binding because adherence to them would maximize utility (rule UTILITARIANISM), or as heuristic rules of thumb that experience has established as useful in identifying acts that contribute to utility (act utilitarianism). Many principlist approaches incorporate consequentialist considerations along with nonconsequentialist ones without deriving one from or reducing one to the other—for instance, a principle of positive BENEFICENCE or utility may be included on equal footing with principles of respect for autonomy and justice.

Tom Beauchamp and James Childress identify four primary principles—respect for autonomy, nonmaleficence, beneficence (including utility), and justice—and several derivative rules—veracity, FIDELITY, PRIVACY, and confidentiality—along with various other rules, such as informed CONSENT. (In attacking this framework, along with William Frankena's *Ethics,* 2d ed. [1973], Danner Clouser and Bernard

Gert [1990] coined the derisive label "principlism." Others have called this framework the "four principles approach" [Gillon 1994].)

In a similar vein, the influential National Commission for the Protection of Human Subjects of Biomedical and Behavioral Research (1978) identified three basic principles that should govern research involving human subjects: beneficence (which includes nonmaleficence), respect for persons, and justice—principles that still guide federally funded research in the United States. In *A Theory of Medical Ethics* (1981), Robert Veatch offers a different list, but one that has substantial overlap: beneficence, contract keeping, autonomy, honesty, avoiding killing, and justice. He also recognizes several moral rules, such as informed consent. And H. Tristram Engelhardt (1995) identifies autonomy and beneficence as principles and then reduces justice to these two considerations; his framework also incorporates several derivative obligations.

Specifying and Weighting Principles

Two basic questions emerge about principles in PRACTICAL REASONING. One is whether broad, general principles can be specified in more concrete rules. For instance, the principle of respect for persons and their autonomous choices might be specified in a rule of informed consent or a rule of truthful disclosure to patients. One version of this approach, building on the work of Henry Richardson, is called "specified principlism" (DeGrazia). As a way to connect general principles to concrete cases that tries to avoid intuitive balancing, specification may still be subject to the charge of arbitrariness because of an excessive appeal to intuition (Arras).

While specification focuses on the meaning, range, and scope of principles, a second question concerns how much weight, or what degree of stringency, different principles have. If moral principles are more than merely advisory or illuminative, then it is important to determine just how binding they are in order to resolve any conflicts that emerge.

Absolutism presents one extreme possibility: absolutists maintain that some moral principles and rules are absolutely binding whatever circumstances arise. But they face irresolvable MORAL DILEMMAS if they recognize more than one absolute principle and those principles came into conflict. As a result, absolutists often carefully specify the meaning, range, and scope of their principles in order to avoid such conflicts (see Ramsey 1968, 1970).

A second possible approach arranges principles in a lexical or serial order. For example, in *A Theory of Medical Ethics* (1981) Robert Veatch assigns all nonconsequentialist principles, such as promise keeping, honesty, and not killing, "lexical priority over the principle of beneficence," a consequentialist principle. However, when nonconsequentialist principles themselves conflict, he employs a "balancing strategy." Thus, while nonconsequentialist principles have "lexical ranking" over the principle of beneficence, they have "coequal ranking" in relation to each other. Critics contend that such a lexical order inevitably breaks down in real-life situations, as do other absolutist approaches.

A third approach—perhaps the one most often associated with principlism—views moral principles as *prima facie* or presumptively binding rather than as absolutely binding or lexically ordered (Beauchamp and Childress). It thus balances various principles when they come into conflict in particular cases. An act is morally right or obligatory insofar as it has the features that, according to the relevant principles, establish moral rightness or obligatoriness. For example, an act is right insofar as it is truthful, wrong insofar as it is a lie. However, a particular act, in particular circumstances, may have features that express some principles while contravening others—for instance, a truthful act may also cause harm or injustice. In such a case, the agent must determine whether one principle or the other is weightier or stronger, a judgment that cannot be made on the basis of prior, abstract formulations. According to its critics, this form of principlism relies excessively on intuition, in spite of whatever procedures it might introduce to reduce the role of intuition in balancing its various principles and rules.

As this survey suggests, principlism covers a wide variety of positions that may differ on which principles are important, what scope and weight they have, and how they can be applied to particular cases, as well as how they can be justified, *e.g.*, by SOCIAL CONTRACT, NATURAL LAW, or revelation—indeed, some critics of narrow principlism may themselves be principlists in the broad sense. Such variety suggests that "principlism" is an umbrella term that may obscure more than it illuminates. And it is not surprising that battles rage among principlists as well as between principlists and their critics.

Major Criticisms of Principlism

Several critics target both broad and narrow principlism, contending that the emphasis on moral principles is misplaced. Some of their criticisms are more effective against some types of principlism than against other types.

First, one type of criticism of principlism holds that moral principles are unnecessary because specific rules and ideals cover the whole moral terrain, that principles are too vague and general to guide ACTION, and that, in the absence of a strong theory, it is not possible to resolve conflicts among principles (Clouser and Gert). However, principlists doubt that all that is important in moral principles, such as respect for autonomy, can be fully captured in such specific rules as don't kill; don't cause pain; don't disable; don't deprive of freedom; don't deprive of PLEASURE; don't deceive; keep your promise; don't cheat; obey the law; and do your duty (Gert, Culver, and Clouser). These rules largely specify the harms that are to be avoided under the general requirement—what others might call a principle—of nonmaleficence, but may not adequately express what many principlists construe as obligations of respect for autonomy, beneficence, and justice. Furthermore, principlists, in the narrow sense, often contend that principles can be further specified to guide action, and they sometimes hold that moral conflicts cannot be fully resolved by theory.

Second, an influential set of criticisms of principlism has emerged from proponents of CASUISTRY and other case-based approaches to practical ethics. Such critics often insist that principles are tyrannical, that moral knowledge is fundamentally particular—*i.e.*, case based—rather than general, and that practical reasoning proceeds by analogy from settled cases, often called paradigm cases, to unsettled ones (Jonsen and Toulmin). In response, principlists often note that principles are important in identifying relevant similarities and differences between cases and, furthermore, that particular case judgments and general principles are dialectically related so that each potentially can modify and correct the other in the pursuit of greater coherence (Beauchamp and Childress).

Third, virtue theorists often contend that principlists concentrate too much on moral problems, quandaries, and dilemmas to the neglect of moral virtue and CHARACTER. Even in particular situations, virtue theorists hold, the moral agent's virtues of discernment and PRUDENCE will be more important than the application of general principles in determining the best course of action. In response to such criticisms, many principlists concede the importance of virtues in the moral life and in moral action, but they further stress that VIRTUES and principles are often correlated, that some principles indicate the value of some traits of character, and that discerning moral agents may still be perplexed about right action in certain situations, which moral principles may help to resolve.

Fourth, some critics charge that principlism is a foundationalist approach that neglects the role of community and tradition in moral reflection. However, principlists are not necessarily foundationalists—indeed, some principlists argue that communities and traditions regularly embody and convey moral principles, just as they pass on settled judgments about cases and seek to engender certain traits of character. And even though some principlists are individualists, who concentrate on respect for autonomy and LIBERTY, many principlists recognize that moral agents are social and that communal values are also important.

Fifth, an influential criticism holds that principlists speak in male voices about male experiences while neglecting women's voices and experiences. According to Carol Gilligan, women tend to concentrate on context, narratives, and relationships of CARE, with their associated responsibilities, rather than on tiers of moral principles, with their logic of hierarchical justification, which men by contrast tend to emphasize. This care perspective offers an important corrective to some principlist approaches by attending to context, narrative, relationships, EMOTION, and the like. However, principlists may respond that care and principles are often complementary; that moral agents often have to determine, in part through principles, how much weight various relationships have when they conflict; and that many feminists (and others) appeal to such principles as justice and respect for autonomy in moral critiques of sexist, patriarchal social structures in science, medicine, and elsewhere.

In both its narrow and broad formulations, principlism stresses the role of general moral principles in moral reasoning, even though it does not necessarily reduce moral reasoning to principled reasoning. Principlists debate which principles are defensible; their meaning, range, and scope; and their weight and strength—all of which significantly affect how they function in practical ethics. In contrast to the first criticism noted above, several other criticisms charge that principlists inadequately attend to other concerns often grouped under narrative ethics—the role of particular cases, tradition and community, the virtues, and care in relationships. Much of the current debate focuses on whether principlism in some form can adequately accommodate these criticisms, as many principlists believe, without surrendering its principles.

See also: APPLIED ETHICS; AUTONOMY OF MORAL AGENTS; BENEFICENCE; BENEVOLENCE; BIOETHICS; CARE; CASUISTRY; CONSENT; CONSEQUENTIALISM; DEONTOLOGY; DUTY AND OBLIGATION; EMOTION; INDIVIDUALISM; INTUITIONISM; JUSTICE, CIRCUMSTANCES OF; LIBERTY; MEDICAL ETHICS; MORAL REASONING; MORAL RULES; NARRATIVE ETHICS; NORMS; PERSONAL RELATIONSHIPS; PRACTICAL REASON[ING]; PRIVACY; PROMISES; SECRECY AND CONFIDENTIALITY; SITUATION ETHICS; SOCIAL CONTRACT; THEORY AND PRACTICE; UTILITARIANISM; VIRTUE ETHICS.

Bibliography

Arras, John D. "Principles and Particularity: The Role of Cases in Bioethics." *Indiana Law Journal* 69 (1994): 983–1014.

Beauchamp, Tom L., and James F. Childress. *Principles of Biomedical Ethics.* 4th ed. New York: Oxford University Press, 1994.

Clouser, K. Danner, and Bernard Gert. "A Critique of Principlism." *Journal of Medicine and Philosophy* 15 (1990): 219–36.

DeGrazia, David. "Moving Forward in Bioethical Theory: Theories, Cases, and Specified Principlism." *Journal of Medicine and Philosophy* 17 (1992): 511–39.

DuBose, Edwin R., Ronald P. Hamel, and Laurence J. O'Connell, eds. *A Matter of Principles: Ferment in U.S. Bioethics.* Valley Forge, PA: Trinity Press International, 1994.

Engelhardt, H. Tristram. *Foundations of Bioethics.* 2d ed. New York: Oxford University Press, 1995.

Gert, Bernard. *Morality: A New Justification of the Moral Rules.* New York: Oxford University Press, 1989.

———, Charles M. Culver, and K. Danner Clouser. *Bioethics: A Return to Fundamentals.* New York: Oxford University Press, 1997.

Gilligan, Carol. *In a Different Voice: Psychological Theory and Women's Development.* Cambridge: Harvard University Press, 1982.

Gillon, Ranaan. "Medical Ethics: Four Principles Plus Attention to Scope." *British Medical Journal* 309 (1994): 184–88.

———, ed. *Principles of Health Care Ethics.* New York: John Wiley and Sons, 1994.

Jonsen, Albert R., and Stephen Toulmin. *The Abuse of Casuistry.* Berkeley: University of California Press, 1988.

National Commission for the Protection of Human Subjects of Biomedical and Behavioral Research. *The Belmont Report: Ethical Guidelines for the Protection of Human Subjects of Research.* DHEW Publication No. (OS) 78–00. Washington, DC: Department of Health, Education, and Welfare, 1978.

Ramsey, Paul. "The Case of the Curious Exception." In *Norm and Context in Christian Ethics,* edited by Gene Outka and Paul Ramsey. New York: Charles Scribner's Sons, 1968.

———. *The Patient as Person.* New Haven: Yale University Press, 1970.

Richardson, Henry. "Specifying Norms as a Way to Resolve Concrete Ethical Problems." *Philosophy and Public Affairs* 19 (1990): 279–320.

Veatch, Robert M. *A Theory of Medical Ethics.* New York: Basic Books, 1981.

———, ed. "Special Issue: Theories and Methods in Bioethics: Principlism and its Critics." *Kennedy Institute of Ethics Journal* 5 (1995): 181–286.

———, ed. "Symposium: Emerging Paradigms in Bioethics." *Indiana Law Journal* 69 (1994): 945–1122.

James F. Childress

privacy

Given the socially active role privacy plays in contemporary controversies related to evolving contours of personhood, there may be some point in not striving for precision in defining privacy before this evolution is further played out. Initially, privacy is better characterized by the contexts in which it is used than by a definition.

The Legal Context

Although privacy has been described in a U.S. Supreme Court decision as a right more fundamental than any of the RIGHTS enumerated in the Bill of Rights, it attracted scant explicit philosophical attention until Charles Fried's 1968 treatment. The Fourth Amendment of the U.S. Constitution guarantees citizens the right to be secure in their persons, houses, papers, and effects against unreasonable search or seizure. The First Amendment affords peo-

ple free exercise of RELIGION and freedom of speech, press, and assembly—freedoms we associate with freedom of CONSCIENCE. In the case of *Stanley v. Georgia* (1969), this amendment was cited as limiting the government's efforts at controlling the contents of thoughts. The Fifth Amendment ensures that people cannot be required to testify against themselves and, along with the Fourteenth Amendment, that they cannot be deprived of life, LIBERTY, and PROPERTY without due process of law.

Two other areas of U.S. law have also evolved in a way protective of privacy. There are in tort law four categories of individual protection:

1. Intrusion upon a seclusion, solitude, or private affairs;
2. Public disclosure of private, embarrassing facts;
3. Public disclosure of a person in a false light;
4. Appropriation of another's name, image, or other aspect of identity, for one's advantage or profit, without that person's consent.

The most controversial treatment of privacy in the law arises in the recent Supreme Court decisions that recognize "procreative rights" as constitutionally protected rights of privacy. Some examples are the relatively unencumbered rights: to choose a marriage partner (*Loving v. Virginia,* 1967); to birth control (*Griswold v. Connecticut,* 1965; *Eisenstadt v. Baird,* 1972; *Carey v. Population Services International,* 1976); to become a parent (*Skinner v. Oklahoma,* 1942); to ABORTION services (*Roe v. Wade,* 1973); and, at least in the setting of a marriage, to unregulated sexual practices (*Bowers v. Hardwick,* 1986). Among those who recognize these rights as *bona fide* privacy rights, there is controversy over whether these rights are primarily attached to people who are part of actual or potential marriage or FAMILY situations, or whether they apply to individuals in intimate contexts irrespective of the potential for marriage (*Bowers v. Hardwick*). (There are contexts in which privacy-related privileges accorded spouses are revoked when third parties are present, including the couple's children.) There is much controversy over whether these rights have constitutional basis on the one hand and whether they actually turn on concern for privacy on the other. Many would argue that these are issues of autonomy and only tangentially raise issues of privacy.

Defining Privacy

Some writers (Laurence Tribe, Tom Gerety, Erving Goffman) have observed that privacy is just as critical to managing "outward dimensions of personality" as it is to fashioning more intimate aspects.

Behavior or relationships can be private and still have a public dimension. Because any act or relationship that is illegal or has important public consequences has a public dimension to it, we will confront situations that are simultaneously public and private. This dichotomy may in part account for why every explicit definition that has been proposed seems controversial.

There are broader and narrower conceptions of privacy. On the most restricted conception of privacy, privacy relates exclusively to information of a personal sort about an individual and describes the extent to which others have access to this information. A broader conception extends beyond the informational domain and encompasses anonymity and restricted physical access. There is an even narrower conception (William Parent), one that limits the range of privacy to personal information that is "undocumented." It would follow from this definition that if everything personal about an individual became publicly documented, there would be no possibility of her losing her privacy, when it would seem as if there would be no possibility of her having any.

Thus far the characterizations draw a sharp contrast between privacy and autonomy. When privacy embraces some aspects of autonomy, it is defined as control over the intimacies of personal identity. At the broadest end of the spectrum, privacy is thought to be the measure of the extent to which an individual is afforded the social and legal space to develop the emotional, cognitive, spiritual, and moral powers of an autonomous agent. An advocate of one of the narrower conceptions can agree about the value of autonomous development but think that privacy as properly defined makes an important but limited contribution to its achievement.

Privacy as an Important Moral Category

Some would argue that the broad range of issues that have been debated under the privacy rubric share some important moral core—like human DIGNITY or full personhood—that makes this range co-herent and that they are not just a medley of concerns classified under the same ambiguous word. Other theorists find no such coherence. Also debated is the distinctiveness or dispensability of privacy as a moral category—the issue of whether privacy claims are inevitably susceptible to defense in terms of moral categories that are more fundamental than privacy and themselves make no reference to privacy.

Privacy is important as a means of respecting or even socially constructing moral personality, comprising qualities like independent judgment, creativity, SELF-KNOWLEDGE, and SELF-RESPECT. It is important because of the way control over one's thoughts and body enables one to develop TRUST for, or LOVE and friendships with, one another and, more generally, to modulate relationships with others. It is important too for the political dimensions of a society that respects individual privacy and that finds privacy instrumental in protecting individual freedom, rights of association, and limitations on governmental control over thoughts and actions. Finally, it has been argued that privacy is important as a means of protecting people from overreaching social (as opposed to legal) pressures and sanctions and is thus critical if people are to enjoy a measure of social freedom.

Much of modern moral theory has ignored private dimensions of people's lives and relationships. It has come up with rules or principles, utilitarian or rights-respecting, that seem better suited to describing social relationships between people who are interchangeable than between people who are intimately related. This would not be a problem if the theories did not purport to be universal and exhaustive of moral understanding, though this has been just what moral theories aim at being.

Two Sorts of Privacy Norms

Social NORMS protecting privacy are of two overlapping sorts. There are social norms that restrict access of others to an individual in a certain domain where the individual is accorded wide discretion as to how to behave in this domain. This sort of privacy promotes private life, individuality, and the integrity of various spheres of life. Then there are social norms that restrict access of others to an individual, but where the behavior carried on in private is rigidly defined by social norms and affords little discretion. Though this sort of behavior is performed in private, is relegated to private life, it does not serve the purpose of promoting a private life. For instance, although defecation is a paradigmatically private activity for an adult in our society, there are many ways of managing this activity in private that would be violative of social norms functioning like taboos. The privacy afforded a person for such an activity does not serve the purpose of self-expression, though perhaps of social definition. This sort of privacy has little to do with having a private life.

Both sorts of norms are privacy norms, and both relate to our practices of showing respect for people, even treating them as sacred, and both are reflections of social structure and symbolism, but their function in other ways is distinct. As a mechanism for showing respect for people, whether our norms lead us to avert our gaze from others' genitals or from their feet is a matter of complete indifference. As a way of promoting private life, the means are not so arbitrary. From the perspective of promoting a private life, a relaxation of the norms that restrict exposure to someone's diary are more violative than would be a relaxation of norms that restrict exposure of activity on the toilet.

Hannah ARENDT (1906–1975) has pointed out that many of the widely shared privacy norms relate to bodily functions and material dependencies that we share with other animals. Stanley Benn has reminded us that often these norms involve notions of shame and impose duties on us not to present certain faces of ourselves in public. So there may be an implicit reason some of our privacy norms express awareness of human distinctiveness and thereby respect for human dignity even when these norms do not provide for private life. Without underplaying this role of privacy norms, we can mark that the privacy norms that enable private life to transpire represent an additional interpretation of what human dignity consists in—an interpretation that emerges in certain sorts of human settings.

See also: ABORTION; AUTONOMY OF MORAL AGENTS; BLACKMAIL; CENSORSHIP; CIVIL RIGHTS AND CIVIC DUTIES; COMPUTERS; DIGNITY; FREEDOM OF THE PRESS; GOVERNMENT, ETHICS IN; HUMAN RIGHTS; JOURNALISM; LEGAL ETHICS; LEGAL PHILOSOPHY; LIBERTY; LIBRARY AND INFORMATION PROFESSIONS; MASS MEDIA; MEDICAL ETHICS; PERSONAL RELATIONSHIPS; PROFESSIONAL ETHICS; PUBLIC AND PRIVATE MORALITY; RIGHTS; SECRECY AND CONFIDENTIALITY; SELF AND SOCIAL SELF; SELF-[entries]; SEXUALITY AND SEXUAL ETHICS; TRUST.

Bibliography

Arendt, Hannah. *The Human Condition.* Chicago: University of Chicago Press, 1958.

Benn, Stanley I. "Privacy, Freedom, and Respect for Persons." In *Privacy,* edited by J. R. Pennock and J. W. Chapman. Nomos, vol. 13. New York: Atherton Press, 1971. One of the first and richest philosophical discussions of privacy; a useful anthology.

Decew, Judith Wagner. "The Scope of Privacy in Law and Ethics." *Law and Philosophy* 5 (1986): 145–74.

Fried, Charles. "Privacy." *Yale Law Journal* 77 (1968): 475–93. The first philosophical treatment of privacy; still unsurpassed in importance. Reprinted in Schoeman, 1984, pp. 203–22.

Gavison, Ruth. "Privacy and the Limits of Law." *Yale Law Journal* 89 (1980): 421–71. Comprehensive and penetrating treatment of legal and philosophical aspects of privacy. Reprinted in Schoeman, 1984, pp. 346–402.

Gerety, Tom. "Redefining Privacy." *Harvard Civil Rights–Civil Liberties Law Review* 12 (1977): 233–96.

Gerstein, Robert. "California's Constitutional Right to Privacy: The Development of the Protection of Private Life." *Hastings Constitutional Law Quarterly* 9 (1982): 385–427.

Goffman, Erving. *The Presentation of Self in Everyday Life.* Garden City, NJ: Doubleday, 1959.

Nissenbaum, Helen. "Protecting Privacy in an Information Age: The Problem of Privacy in Public." *Law and Philosophy* 17/5–6 (1998): 559–96.

O'Brien, David. *Privacy, Law, and Public Policy.* New York: Praeger Special Studies, 1979.

Parent, William. "Recent Work in the Concept of Privacy." *American Philosophical Quarterly* 20 (1983): 341–56. Comprehensive analysis and critique of efforts to define privacy; advocates narrow view.

Polyviou, Polyvois. *Search and Seizure: Constitutional and Common Law.* London: Duckworth, 1982.

Prosser, William. "Privacy." *California Law Review* 48 (1960): 383–423. Definitive treatment of privacy in tort law.

Schoeman, Ferdinand, ed. *Philosophical Dimensions of Privacy.* Cambridge: Cambridge University Press, 1984. Many classic essays on privacy; extensive bibliography.

Tribe, Laurence. *American Constitutional Law.* 2d ed. Mineola, NY: Foundation Press, 1987. Splendid, detailed jurisprudential treatment of privacy in context of constitutional law.

Veyne, Paul, ed. *A History of Private Life.* Cambridge, MA: Harvard University Press, 1987–1989. Invaluable, commissioned essays on private life from pagan Rome to the Renaissance.

Westin, Alan. *Privacy and Freedom.* New York: Atheneum, 1967. One of the very best general treatments of privacy.

Selected Cases

Bowers v. Hardwick, 478 U.S. 1039 (1986).

Boyd v. United States, 116 U.S. 616 (1886). Regards business records that may be incriminating as subject to Fifth Amendment protections.

Carey v. Population Services International, 426 U.S. 918 (1976).

Eisenstadt v. Baird, 405 U.S. 438 (1972). Regards right to privacy as including right of unmarried people to use contraceptives.

Griswald v. Connecticut, 381 U.S. 479 (1965). Establishes a married couple's right to obtain and use contraceptives.

Katz v. United States, 389 U.S. 347 (1967). Establishes that physical intrusion into an individual's property is not necessary condition of invasion of individual's constitutionally protected privacy.

Loving v. Virginia, 386 U.S. 952 (1967).

Olmstead v. United States, 277 U.S. 438 (1928). Noted for the dissenting opinion of Justice Brandeis that took nearly forty years to win constitutional recognition.

Roe v. Wade, 410 U.S. 367 (1973). Recognizes a woman's right to have an abortion during the first trimester of pregnancy as an aspect of her constitutional right to privacy.

Sidis v. F-R Publishing Company, 113 F. 2d 806 (1940). A person in whom the public has a legitimate interest has a diminished level of privacy protection.

Skinner v. Oklahoma, 317 U.S. 535 (1942). Recognizes a constitutional right to bear children.

Stanley v. Georgia, 394 U.S. 557 (1969). Recognizes a right to privately possess pornographic materials in one's home despite legitimate prohibitions on sale or purchase of these materials.

Ferdinand D. Schoeman

private morality

See public and private morality.

professional ethics

We may identify professionals in our society by their special expertise, their provision of important services to clienteles, and their organizations, often self-regulating. Linked to these identifying features, and more pertinent to problems in professional ethics, is their commitment to some overriding value that defines both expertise and service, whether it be health, salvation, the protection of legal RIGHTS, or the provision of public information, knowledge, and education. When these values are threatened, individuals may suffer crises, and they may need the aid of professionals who are expected to protect and further the dominant values to which their professions are committed.

Problems in professional ethics typically arise when the values dominant within particular professions come into conflict with other values in the course of practice. Professionals are likely to perceive these values as dominant where others may not. Commitment to ideals expressing these values constitutes in large part the source of professionals' AUTHORITY and prestige, and such commitment will be reinforced by identification with colleagues and with the INSTITUTIONS in which they practice. These values are reflected in many of the codes of ethics that professionals use to guide their practice. The Code of Professional Responsibility of the American Bar Association, for example, calls for nearly undiluted zealousness in the pursuit of client legal rights and objectives within the law, even when such pursuit conflicts with the interests of nonclients. Various medical codes emphasize the promotion of good health, often without concern for the place of health in the patient's own priorities.

Such codes suggest that professionals may be guided in their practice by special NORMS that express the central values of the profession and that override considerations that might guide the behavior of nonprofessionals in similar contexts of conflict or potential conflict. A question, even a seeming paradox, arises here for moral theory. How can there be such norms? Presumably they would have to be justified by appeal to common moral principles, if the practice accepted within professions is to be accepted by society at large, and yet at the same time they appear to override common moral considerations when in conflict with them. Hence the seeming paradox.

Nevertheless, special professional norms can be logically consistent and morally possible. Ethicists recognize this possibility by distinguishing between the moral content of an action, as judged by ordinary moral criteria or unfettered personal CONSCIENCE, and the authority of agents to act on their judgments of that content. Individuals in institutional or professional roles may lack the authority to act on ordinary moral criteria as they perceive them; or their authority may be augmented in relation to that of others. A good example is that of judges, who must in some cases apply a law with which they morally disagree. Whether professional norms promoting legal rights, health, the provision of news and information, and so on can create similar limitations or augmentations of authority is a fundamental question in professional ethics.

This question is to be answered for each profession by appeal to institutional structure and the place of the professional within that structure. Sometimes it can be shown that an institution that limits professional practice to the pursuit of particular goals or values produces optimal outcomes. Such limitations may be optimal because of the fallibility of moral judgments by individuals, the need for consistency and predictability in the actions of those in professional roles, the importance of the values they are single-mindedly to pursue, their expertise in promoting such values, and the offsetting roles of others within the professions or social institutions in question. Nevertheless, society must remain vigilant and critical of special professional norms, since, when these norms override ordinary moral considerations, INTERESTS of nonprofessionals and nonclients may be sacrificed, and effects on the moral CHARACTER of professionals themselves may be harmful.

Many particular moral issues that cut across professions derive from this fundamental issue. One important problem relates to information and confidentiality. Professionals often cannot serve their clients well unless the clients are completely open in divulging information. They will not be open unless assured that the information will be confidential. But confidentiality, crucial to the promotion of the dominant professional value, may conflict with interests of others and their right to information vital to those interests. The resolution of this issue depends on our ordering of the professional values and norms in relation to the demands of common morality.

Another issue common to several professions is that of divided LOYALTY and the division of authority within the profession. Many individuals in professional roles—for example, engineers, nurses, junior executives, military personnel, police—must act under other authorities. Even those professionals who are not typically issued orders or assignments from others may find that loyalty to clients can come into conflict with loyalty to other individuals or to the broader community. Questions arise as to whether professionals are to obey superiors when their demands seem morally inoptimal or unacceptable, and as to how conflicts of interests are to be avoided or resolved. Once more these questions must be answered in terms of the place of professional norms and values within the broader set of ordinary moral principles.

Some other general problems in professional ethics can be resolved more directly by appeal to broader moral or social theory. One such pervasive problem concerns the distribution or provision of professional services in society. Should this distribution be left to the free market as supplemented by private charity, or should government intervene to create an equal distribution, or one based on need? This question is answered directly by appeal to a broader theory of distributive justice.

The more distinctive issues remain those that derive from special professional norms and value orderings, as illustrated above. The first question that society must ask of each profession is whether it serves its predominant value well; the second question is whether it might serve this value too well.

See also: ACADEMIC ETHICS; AGRICULTURAL ETHICS; ANIMALS, TREATMENT OF; APPLIED ETHICS; AUTHORITY; BIOETHICS; BUSINESS ETHICS; CASUISTRY; COMPUTERS; CORRECTIONAL ETHICS; ENGINEERING ETHICS; FIDUCIARY RELATIONSHIPS; GENETIC ENGINEERING; GOVERNMENT, ETHICS IN; INSTITUTIONS; INTEGRITY; JOURNALISM; JUSTICE, DISTRIBUTIVE; LEGAL ETHICS; LIBRARY AND INFORMATION PROFESSIONS; LOYALTY; MASS MEDIA; MEDICAL ETHICS; MILITARY ETHICS; NURSING ETHICS; POLICE ETHICS; PRECEDENT; PRIVACY; PUBLIC POLICY; SECRECY AND CONFIDENTIALITY; SEXUAL ABUSE AND HARASSMENT; TECHNOLOGY; TRUST; WELFARE RIGHTS AND SOCIAL POLICY.

Bibliography

Baumrin, Bernard, and Benjamin Freedman, eds. *Moral Responsibility and the Professions.* New York: Haven Publications, 1983.

Bayles, Michael D. *Professional Ethics.* Belmont, Calif.: Wadsworth, 1989.

Callahan, Joan C., ed. *Ethical Issues in Professional Life.* New York: Oxford University Press, 1988.

Camenisch, Paul F. *Grounding Professional Ethics in a Pluralistic Society.* New York: Haven Publications, 1983.

Flores, Albert, ed. *Professional Ideals.* Belmont, Calif.: Wadsworth, 1988.

Freidson, Eliot. *Professional Powers: A Study of the Institutionalization of Formal Knowledge.* Chicago: University of Chicago Press, 1986.

Goldman, Alan H. *The Moral Foundations of Professional Ethics.* Totowa, N.J.: Rowman and Littlefield, 1980.

Gorlin, Rena A., ed. *Codes of Professional Responsibility.* Washington, D.C.: Bureau of National Affairs, 1986.

Lebacqz, Karen. *Professional Ethics: Power and Paradox.* Nashville, Tenn.: Abingdon Press, 1985.

Moore, Wilbert E. *The Professions: Roles and Rules.* New York: Russell Sage, 1970.

Alan H. Goldman

promises

The question of promises is divided into two main parts; the first is about the concept of the promise in its true or proper definition, and the second is about the nature, source, and strength of its obligation. An important issue for the theory of promising is whether an answer to the conceptual question will help answer the second, the question of morality.

The Conceptual Question

What one promises is either of two sorts: (a) one's own future action, *e.g.,* to help a friend, or (b) that a certain state of affairs—not in the future—obtains, *e.g.,* the oats are old. The promise of an action (type a) has a formal side (as does the promise of a fact, type b), that being the criteria for the act itself of promising, and also a material side, that being the specific action to be performed as promised. In this regard, there will be times when the speech act "I promise" (or its equivalent) is itself wrong to do, as when one is insincere, and yet the specifically promised action is right to do. So one must distinguish between the act of promising, with the moral quality it has, and the action promised, with the value it has. Promises must be further distinguished on the formal side from such matters as one's vows, firm intentions, resolutions, and plans. The distinction is required because promises must be addressed and communicated (as promisers' acts) to a promisee, whereas vows and so on may be kept private and addressed to oneself alone. The fact that promises are communicated is important. Yet informing another about one's future plans is not sufficient to make a promise. Such a broad conception would allow threats to qualify; one does not promise an action that one believes at the time will be perceived by and for the promisee as harmful overall. Of course threats are sometimes made in promissory language ("I promise, you will suffer!"); but true promises of action are commitments from which one may be *released* by the recipient (but no other) whereas persons threatened will lack a similar POWER over their own or the threatener's position.

It might be thought, if never a threat, that promises are well understood as sorts of reliable assurance about a future state. One may think here of expressions like "I promise that you will be well treated in the hospital," which are a form of reassurance and seem indeed to promise a *future* fact as well. But these are not true promises. What one promises in one's own person must be or appear to be within one's own control or be a settled matter of fact no longer under anyone's control. An apparent promise about the future (but not of one's own future action) is really a prediction, for which one may need to accept some RESPONSIBILITY when it goes wrong. Furthermore, there are lying promises, and persons to whom they are made may be fully aware of the false intent behind them; so the assurance effect (which is what it is) is hardly inevitable when promises are received. However, sincere or not, promises do naturally purport (even as recognized lies) to be good things on which the recipient can place reliance. That is an important aspect of their concept. Promisees, it then may be observed, often have reason against releasing their promisers. On the other hand, if a promisee has no confidence in the promiser, one might say "forget it," even though the performance would be beneficial should it occur. The basic point here is that promisees are thought to gain a *right* grounded in another's formal act—independently, it appears at the moment, of its content—and it is that right which they surrender in releasing the promiser and on which they rely when they have not.

The promise (type b) in which one warrants a present or past state of affairs is a distinct variety and differs from the promise of action, say, to *deliver* oats of a certain age. This promise is more than a simple declaration of factual belief and seeks to communicate one's intent to be understood as undertaking a special responsibility for the truth of what one states. Implicit here is a (factual) claim about one's own prior conduct, *viz.*, that one has done something to verify the fact promised. Of course, a lying promise here is just as possible logically as a lie about one's intentions concerning future action. And there is the added possibility of innocent error, as in "The year was 1065—I promise." Does it make sense to speak of 'releasing' someone from the promise of a fact? (One understands more easily what it means for a promisee to release another from the promise of an action; thereupon, given the release, there is something that no longer requires to be done.) There is a distinction of interest here between two normative powers: releasing someone from an obligation and relieving someone from responsibility for a failure. The power to *release* is the power to eliminate the ongoing obligation of the promiser (it remains that an obligation had obtained), so that a future nonperformance constitutes no failure at all. When one is merely *relieved* of responsibility, the subsequent failure will be nonculpable, even though the obligation to perform had continued. This distinction has relevance here, because the power of release, understood typically as being release from future action, may not extend to promises of fact. Yet given that a promisee can rely on such promises, one is able to say to a promiser, "I'm not going to hold you to that." This comment could be seen as a kind of release from an ongoing responsibility, based on the promise made, to have been factually correct at the time of speaking. Might this promise be 'taken back' by the speaker—as a kind of self-release—before the promisee relies on it? However that may be, the promisee's power of relieving a promiser of responsibility clearly exists respecting both kinds of promise, and so of fact. There is this caution: though release may have been given concerning a promise of action, there may remain other reasons to perform the same action based either on the nature of the act itself or upon a supererogatory ground.

It is impossible to analyze the concept of a promise without reference to obligations undertaken, to RIGHTS given, or powers assumed and employed, for these reside in the formal criteria for the act of promising itself. Yet it seems simplistic to hold that to promise is to undertake an obligation to do something. (Some have found in this idea a conceptual bridge between 'is' and 'ought.') The correct analysis is more elaborate. When Mr. E promises (successfully) Miss Q that he will do *C*, then E brings Q to understand that he intends her to believe, in thus communicating this to her, that he undertakes an obligation (which is to exercise a normative power) to do *C:* thereby, Q is seen to acquire both the right to see *C* done (have the obligation honored) and the power to release or relieve E, should she choose. This explanation allows Miss Q, as promisee, to doubt that a performance will occur, even though Mr. E's undertaking purports of course to be reliable, and her attitude does not as such, even when quite well founded, affect any right that she may have acquired. Also, in this analysis, one's act does not fail to be a promise just because the promisee's interests were misperceived; no doubt in such a case the promiser will be released. Finally, this explanation takes care to exclude cases where, say, by intentionally injuring another, one puts oneself under an obligation to repair the harm. That way of 'undertaking' an obligation is not the exercise of a normative power, even if one's voluntary action had brought about the duty of repair.

The Moral Question

The most important question concerns the moral standing of these normative operations. Is it not a mystery how Mr. E can place himself under a *moral* obligation merely by the exercise of his will with speech? A related basis for perplexity is this: if the normative ground for a promise of action is not essentially connected to the moral quality of its content (a view not excluded here so far), could Mr. E, through a promise that he makes, morally obligate himself to murder Miss Q's ex-boss? Does a promise to do something that is morally wrong create a moral obligation to do it? That would be paradoxical. Does it matter that this 'promise' (though demanded by Miss Q) ought not to have been made? No, for even the insincere promise, which ought not be made, carries an obligation.

Several solutions can be suggested. An easy solution declares that the obligation of the promise is not moral in nature, but always is somehow linguistic or a local nonmoral duty. E then undertakes no moral obligation. But that seems a totally mistaken conception of the promise, for its successful communication (in any context or language) consists in getting the promisee to believe that the speaker intends that this recipient should believe that the promiser is undertaking a moral obligation (through a communicative act). A *moral* sensibility is invoked. That assuredly is how promisers seek to be understood, unless they say otherwise (and such caveats are probably confined entirely to permissive contents, *e.g.,* party attendance). In its grandest form: one has given one's word. Another solution is that the promise as such does carry a moral obligation but it is (or may often be) 'outweighed' by the wrongness of its content, as it might seem regarding Mr. E's promise to Miss Q. But that solution seems generally unacceptable or underdeveloped, for one might, on this notion, regularly morally obligate oneself to perform minor moral transgressions through the promise of them. But in the more serious instance, one might wonder whether Miss Q has secured *any* moral right to support the wrongful death purposed. Finally, one might simply declare it to be an axiom that one cannot promise the impermissible. Yet this seems, without more, to be an arbitrary stipulation.

The question is how content considerations limit promising conceptually and not merely as an act that one may have reason not to perform. Is promising in any way content-dependent? Consider the situation of Mr. E and Miss Q again. If we stay at the (doxastic) level of the analysis given above, we have four useful possibilities to consider: (1) E's own moral belief about a promissory content, *viz.,* a murder; (2) E's belief about Q's belief on the same matter; (3) Q's own moral belief in fact, and (4) her belief about E's belief about the thing she asks him to do. Now possibility (4), it seems clear, is only relevant to the question whether she should ask him to make this promise in the first place and is not relevant to the conceptual question we are asking; she might expect him to reply: "I won't promise that!" Equally, (1) is merely about the appropriateness of promising given one's own belief, and it is possible logically to promise to do that which one thinks one ought not do. That leaves (2) and (3). Possibility (3), *viz.,* Q's own belief in fact, would allow that while Mr. E thinks he has promised, he has not really, because unbeknownst to him Miss Q morally disapproves of its content despite her request. That seems implausible as a conceptual limitation on promising.

Possibility (2) seems right. It is confined to Mr. E's own thinking regarding Miss Q's belief as he seeks to communicate his undertaking of an obligation to her. Here one finds constraint, or content-dependence, in terms of a paradox. If one is trying to create an obligation by communicating this INTENTION to another, then it is paradoxical for the speaker to think that one's addressee will think that what one purposes to do is wrong. Just as a promiser cannot promise to do that which he believes (rightly or wrongly) will be perceived by the promisee as harmful to the promisee overall, so a speaker cannot promise to do that which he believes (rightly or wrongly) will be perceived as immoral by the promisee. Seeking to make the hearer believe a wrong act becomes obligatory is a paradoxical undertaking; the hearer is being asked to understand that she is being given a right to the speaker's wrongdoing. To avoid this paradox one simply says that the moral obligation in action created can exist only when the promisee is thought by the promiser to accept that the content of the promise is freely permissible or already morally obligatory to do. That Mr. E may get this wrong [*re* (3)] is of no direct consequence to the point, or is the fact [*re* (1)] that on his own terms he should refuse her request. Mr. E then promises the deed. Does Miss Q acquire any promissory right to the wrongful death of her boss? Mr. E would probably think, having been asked by her, that Miss Q believes the murder is justified. If so, then, as a conceptual matter, Mr. E can promise her this act, and she has, to some degree, secured a moral right against him to have the deed done. Of course, from a moral point of view there are reasons to say, first, that this commitment ought not to be made and, second, that once it is made, it should not be fulfilled, indeed, that one should be released. On the other hand, if Mr. E thinks she would think (really) that it is wrong to kill her ex-boss, then Mr. E cannot promise the deed. As a function of these considerations, therefore, the obligation of promises is not fully content-independent.

Some have suggested that promises morally obligate only if actual reliance has been placed by the recipient on the performance to come or on the fact warranted. But relying must itself be justified by a right to do so; otherwise it provides little or no basis for another's obligation. Of course, once justified reliance has been placed, a breach of promise would be extra damaging to the moral relationship of the parties, and that fact gives added reason to perform the action. That a promise can create a new obligation from an old permission seems clear, but is it pointless to promise that which one ought to do already, say, to tell the truth? It would seem not, for the promise augments the obligation by giving added reason to fulfil it, when otherwise a lie, say a marginal 'white lie,' might have been justified by considerations that are now no longer sufficient given the promise. To have promised an action establishes an important reason to perform it, though this consideration need not always be decisive. Whether the promise ought to be kept all things considered depends as well on its content and clearly on the extent of the reliance of those with the right to have done so. Hence, some credence must be given to those theorists who hold that the wholly unrelied-upon promise is rather light in weight, especially when its content is not obligatory already. It may even be the kind of obligation—given the absence of reliance—from which one can release oneself by another act of communication with the promisee.

Promising, significantly, is comprehensible only in a community of moral understanding and belief. Just to recognize that a promise has been extended requires the recipient to see that the other intends to be understood as undertaking a moral obligation by communicating this promise. That intention, expressed in that way, producing that understanding, counts as the self-imposition (so both parties will believe) of a moral reason to act as promised. This belief could be false, but its falsity depends ultimately on the results of moral theory; promissory discourse itself presupposes true moral obligations and real rights in the world and, also, a normative power in the hands of those who therewith create (and expunge) rights and obligations. Were there no such power or no true moral belief anywhere, then what promisers seek to produce is really an illusion, establishing no moral reason (or responsibility) for anything.

See also: ACTION; ACTS AND OMISSIONS; BAD FAITH; BARGAINING; CHEATING; COERCION; CONSENT; CONTRACTS; CORRUPTION; DECEIT; DETERRENCE, THREATS, AND RETALIATION; DISCOUNTING THE FUTURE; DUTY AND OBLIGATION; ENTITLEMENTS; EXCUSES; FIDELITY; INTEGRITY; INTENTION; KANT; MORAL RULES; NORMS; PUBLIC AND PRIVATE MORALITY; RESPONSIBILITY; SELF-DECEPTION; SOCIAL CONTRACT; SUPEREROGATION; TRUST; UNIVERSALIZABILITY.

Bibliography

Atiyah, Patrick. *Promises, Morals, and the Law.* Oxford: Clarendon Press, 1981. A defense of reliance and conventionalist theory.

Fried, Charles. *Contract as Promise.* Cambridge, Mass.: Harvard University Press, 1981. A Kantian view of promising in law.

Hudson, W. D., ed. *The Is/Ought Question.* London: Macmillan, 1969. Essays involving debate on promising.

Kant, Immanuel. *Groundwork to a Metaphysics of Morals.* 1785. Several translations; famous example of the lying promise.

Lyons, David. *Forms and Limits of Utilitarianism.* Oxford: Clarendon Press, 1965. Utilitarian difficulties with promising.

MacCormick, Neil. "Voluntary Obligations and Normative Powers." *Proceedings of the Aristotelian Society* (suppl. vol. 46 1972): 59–79. Reliance theory; a reply by Joseph Raz at pp. 80–103.

Prichard, H. A. "The Obligation to Keep a Promise." In *Moral Obligation.* Oxford: Clarendon Press, 1928. Famous essay on the assumption that promising cannot be what it seems.

Rawls, John. *A Theory of Justice.* Cambridge, Mass.: Harvard University Press, 1971. Promising and the fairness principle.

Raz, Joseph. "Promises and Obligations." In *Law, Morality, and Society,* edited by P. Hacker and J. Raz. Oxford: Clarendon Press, 1977. An outstanding essay generally.

Robins, Michael. *Promising, Intending, and Moral Autonomy.* Cambridge: Cambridge University Press, 1984. Use of action theory in excellent book; includes bibliography.

Ross, W. D. *The Right and the Good.* Oxford: Clarendon Press, 1930. *Prima facie* duty and promising.

Searle, John R. *Speech Acts.* Cambridge: Cambridge University Press, 1969. Derives 'ought' from 'is' via the promise.

Warnock, G. J. *The Object of Morality.* London: Methuen, 1971. Connects promising to veracity.

Wright, G. H. von. *Practical Reason.* Ithaca, N.Y.: Cornell University Press, 1983.

Richard Bronaugh

property

Current philosophical discussions of property tend to focus on private property rights, construed as the RIGHTS of private ownership. The leading questions concern the concept of a property right, the general grounds for concluding that such rights are justifiable, and the reasons for thinking that various types of things (*e.g.,* nonrenewable resources; the means of production) either cannot justifiably be owned at all, or can be owned only in specific ways by specific individuals or groups. Questions about public property are usually answered by inference from theories of private property. Questions about particulars (which particular individuals or groups are entitled to which particular property rights) also may have a philosophical dimension, especially in cases of unique objects, or extremely scarce goods.

Traditional accounts of property, such as those discussed by ARISTOTLE (384–322 B.C.E.), Jean-Jacques ROUSSEAU (1712–1778), David HUME (1711–1776), Immanuel KANT (1724–1804), G. W. F. HEGEL (1770–1831), and Karl MARX (1818–1883), often appear to have much broader concerns. They focus on questions of the origin and general rationale for a system of property rights, on its relation to broad political concerns about justice, EQUALITY, and the stability of social orders, on its connection to human NEEDS, self-realization, and OPPRESSION. In particular, the questions that have dominated the debate between socialists and capitalists seem somewhat submerged in the material surveyed below. But all of these broader questions can and have been discussed in terms of the detailed analytical framework described here.

The Concept of a Property Right

It is commonplace to assert that any property right is actually a bundle of rights, organized around the idea of securing, for the right holder, exclusive use or access to a thing. A.M. Honoré, in his article "Ownership" (1961), has given a detailed analysis of the incidents of legal ownership. This analysis, with minor modifications, is now widely followed in philosophical discussions of property rights.

Honoré analyzes the notion of full liberal ownership into these components: rights to possess, use, and manage a thing; the right to the income from its use by others, and the right to the "capital" (*i.e.,* the right to sell it, give it away, consume it, modify it, or destroy it); the power to transmit it to the beneficiaries of one's will; the right to security, or immunity from expropriation. To these rights of various sorts, Honoré adds the following features, typical of full ownership in mature legal systems: absence of a determinate term for the ownership rights, the liability of rights to "execution" for debt, the prohibition of various harmful uses, and the existence of rules defining the residuary character of the rights—that is, rules governing the disposition of property that has been abandoned or otherwise left unowned.

Each of these eleven incidents may occur in a wide variety of forms. Immunity from expropriation, for example, is almost always interpreted loosely enough to allow a considerable amount of taxation and regulation; the prohibition of harmful use, in some legal systems, implies a requirement for productive use; and the rights to alienate and transmit are often severely restricted. Moreover, a great deal of property is owned in ways that are less than "full": a trust, for example, may be arranged so that the owners do not have either management rights or the right to the capital.

Varieties of ownership. How few of the incidents of full ownership need to be present to justify a claim of (a form of) ownership? Are any of the incidents necessary to all such claims? Is any one incident sufficient? Given some set of robustly defined incidents that constitutes a form of ownership, how far can we weaken the definitions of the incidents and still claim to have a form of ownership? These are intriguing conceptual questions with very practical applications. Courts are regularly asked to consider whether to treat partial sets of these incidents as forms of property; professional licenses, welfare benefits, social security benefits, veteran's benefits, and the like have all come under such scrutiny. The attenuated control stockholders have in the management and income of the modern corporation, and the growth of profit-sharing agreements with employees, have raised interesting questions about the ownership of the corporation and thus about the supposed managerial imperative to make money for the owners. A wife or husband whose labor has contributed materially to improving the spouse's earning ability may try (and sometimes succeed) in claiming a property right in the spouse's expected earnings.

These questions are far from settled, but the trend in recent years has been expansionist, in the sense that weaker and weaker subsets of the incidents of full ownership have been held to constitute property rights. Is there any conceptual barrier to concluding, for example, that an immunity from expropriation plus any one of the other rights in the list of incidents constitutes a property right? (See Becker in Pennock.) If not, and if we fail to impose a practical or legal barrier as well, then we may soon find that the concept of property is no longer useful. (See Grey in Pennock.)

The Justification of Property Rights

All of the standard theories of distributive justice give accounts of the general conditions under which private property rights can be justified. Utilitarian theory, for example, predictably holds that property rights are justified if and only if they satisfy the principle of utility (however defined). SOCIAL CONTRACT theory holds that property rights are justified if and only if they satisfy contractarian procedures (however defined). Libertarian theory holds that property rights are justified if and only if people are entitled to claim them, and failing to respect those claims would amount to a violation of people's rights to liberty. And in general, the way one fills in the distributive schema "From each according to her _____, to each according to her _____" will lead to an account of when property rights are in general justifiable. Need, desert, ability, worth, and effort may all be plugged into the schema in various combinations to yield such abstract results about property.

Moreover, there is widespread agreement that all the standard theories of distributive justice, as applied to actual, large-scale human societies, yield the result that property rules are required and that some private property rights are justifiable. But this result is a very weak and indeterminate one—and one that is as changeable as the utilities, agreements, needs, abilities, and efforts that underlie it. Property rights justified on such bases alone seem vulnerable to change in ways that are beyond the control of the RIGHT HOLDERS.

Political and ethical individualists have often been unsatisfied with this state of affairs. Their persistent fascination with John LOCKE's (1632–1704) labor theory of property may be seen as an attempt to remedy that dissatisfaction. Locke was working well within the NATURAL LAW tradition, and it is arguable whether he intended his arguments about property, in *Two Treatises of Government* (1689), as a justification for "original" acquisition. (See Tully, and criticism thereof in Waldron.) Nevertheless, he has very often been construed as having attempted such a justification.

The underlying idea of the Lockean account is that people ought to be entitled to hold, as property, whatever they produce with their own labor—or, as it is sometimes put, that laborers are entitled to the fruits of their labor. Of course, if everything we produce is a "social" product, or if it is produced from materials owned by others, then we will not be able to get this idea going toward a justification of *private* property. But if we imagine ourselves to be working alone with unowned materials, then we may be able to construct an account of how we can come to own what we produce. And if ownership can always be traced to someone's morally justifiable original acquisition, and we can supply a principle of just transfer, then we have a very impressive defense of private property. (See Nozick.)

There are two main lines of argument that one can construct from Locke's text (primarily chapter 5 of the second *Treatise*) to try to get an account of original acquisition. Both of them begin with the notion of SELF-OWNERSHIP. We own our bodies, and by extension our labor. From those premises, the first Lockean argument explores the idea that we somehow come to own whatever is "annexed" to or "mixed" with our labor—strictly, the value our labor adds to the thing. This version has been roundly rejected as impossibly metaphorical and justifying at best the acquisition of the added value, not the thing itself. But more generally (as Robert NOZICK so pointedly puts it), why should we suppose that when we mix our labor with something we come to own anything at all? Why don't we just lose our labor?

Locke himself, it seems, was unsatisfied with the "mixing" argument. He reformulates parts of it repeatedly and eventually produces something quite different—something based on the idea that laborers deserve property rights for their efforts in producing the added value. This argument too has been subjected to searching criticism, most succinctly by Pierre-Joseph Proudhon (1809–1865) who demanded to know why he should be expected to pay someone else in the form of property rights for labor that he, Proudhon, had not asked be performed. Becker (1977) gives reasons for thinking that the argument is sound, but only when it satisfies several stringent conditions: the labor must produce value for others in addition to the laborer; that value must be beyond what the laborer is obligated to produce for others; property rights must be the most appropriate reward for the laborer's efforts; and such rights must satisfy Locke's restriction (or proviso, as Nozick calls it) that enough and as good be left for others.

The Lockean proviso. The right to exclude others from something they may need or want is a right that by definition forecloses opportunities to them, and it appears that the labor argument will never go through (no matter how hard one works) if one's getting a property right would be harmful to innocent people who reject the property claim. So we must find a way to restrict the argument to harmless acquisitions. Locke imagined that, even though any acquisition would foreclose *some* opportunities to the people excluded by it, it would be harmless if it left them with equivalent opportunities. When opportunities and unclaimed goods are abundant, the proviso seems innocuous. But when resources are scarce, or opportunities few, the proviso becomes very stringent. One wonders, for example, whether it could be satisfied in cases in which the owner's property rights put everyone else at a competitive disadvantage, even though, in a formal sense, "enough and as good" remains.

And there is a further wrinkle: the proviso effectively runs with one's title (Nozick; Becker, 1985). One acquires the property right on the condition that having it is harmless. If conditions change, so does the justification for the title. This gives a basis for the same sort of regulatory tinkering with titles that other theories of property rights allow, and which the labor theory was supposed to remedy.

An intriguing argument by David Schmidtz, however, suggests that the proviso is not always a restriction on acquisition (and by extension a condition on one's title): if it can be shown that preserving a significant range of opportunities for others requires excluding them from the thing the laborer has produced (*i.e.,* that privatization of a resource is a social necessity), then the proviso may effectively require acquisition, or operate to strengthen existing titles.

Property and personality. Hegel broached the idea in his *Philosophy of Right* (1821) that the appropriation of things was a necessary feature of the expression of human personality and that the necessity for such expression created an "absolute right of appropriation." These remarks are representative of a persistent, if somewhat tentative and muted, line of thought that tries to ground a general right to acquire property in facts about human nature.

The germ of this idea can be found in ancient STO-ICISM; idealists (and some liberals and libertarians) develop the thought in terms of the conditions necessary for self-realization; anthropologists have debated it in discussions of primitive communism; ethologists and sociobiologists are concerned to explain and draw inferences from the phenomena of territoriality, possessiveness, and aggression. This set of ideas has recently been explored at length by Jeremy Waldron. As he points out, if it could be shown that people have a general right to acquire property and that this right cannot be construed as a purely formal one, the political implications could be very significant. Just how significant would of course depend on what sort of property rights could be shown to be necessary for self-realization. Here the extraordinary cultural diversity in property arrangements throughout human history poses a problem: either we must conclude that most human beings have not been fully self-realized (a dangerously parochial-sounding view), or we must conclude that a general right to property can be implemented in so many ways that its political implications are largely indeterminate.

The Justification of Specific Forms of and Particular Titles to Property

Many issues in APPLIED ETHICS and law raise questions about the sorts of things that can be owned: the sea? the moon? the earth's nonrenewable resources? new forms of life? the algorithms in a computer program? And just as frequently the same issues raise questions about who can own things and what specific bundles of ownership rights are justifiable. Work on such issues is too voluminous and varied to be canvassed here, but interesting theoretical results have come from economics, RATIONAL CHOICE theory, and theories of rights. Much of this work has focused on the grounds for regulating the uses owners may make of their property and their liability for damage caused by permitted uses. But new forms of property (from government ENTITLEMENTS to patents on genetically engineered bacteria) have also had a prominent place in these discussions, as has the continuing controversy between capitalists and socialists over the scope of public ownership. In addition, environmentalist and animal rights movements have raised sweeping questions about previously settled ideas concerning what can justifiably be owned at all, as private or public property. It appears likely, however, that problems concerning distributive justice in intellectual property—patent and copyright—will soon be equally prominent.

See also: AGRICULTURAL ETHICS; ANIMALS, TREATMENT OF; APPLIED ETHICS; COMPUTERS; CONSERVATION; CONTRACTARIANISM; ECONOMIC ANALYSIS; ECONOMIC SYSTEMS; ENTITLEMENTS; ENVIRONMENTAL ETHICS; EXPLOITATION; FORGERY; GENETIC ENGINEERING; GROUPS, MORAL STATUS OF; HEGEL; HUMAN RIGHTS; INDIVIDUALISM; INTERESTS; JUSTICE, DISTRIBUTIVE; LAND ETHICS; LEGAL PHILOSOPHY; LIBERTARIANISM; LIBERTY, ECONOMIC; LOCKE; MARX; MERIT AND DESERT; NATURE AND ETHICS; NEED; NOZICK; OPPRESSION; PLAGIARISM; PRIVACY; PUBLIC POLICY; RATIONAL CHOICE; RIGHT HOLDERS; RIGHTS; SELF-OWNERSHIP; SLAVERY; SOCIAL CONTRACT; SOVIET ETHICAL THEORY; STOICISM; UTILITARIANISM; WELFARE RIGHTS AND SOCIAL POLICY.

Bibliography

Ackerman, Bruce A., ed. *Economic Foundations of Property Law.* Boston: Little, Brown, 1975.

Becker, Lawrence C. *Property Rights: Philosophic Foundations.* London: Routledge and Kegan Paul, 1977. Analysis of standard justifications.

———. "Property Rights and Social Welfare." In *Economic Justice: Private Rights and Public Responsibilities,* edited by Kenneth Kipnis and Diana T. Meyers. Totowa, NJ: Rowman and Allanheld, 1985.

Christman, John. The Myth of Property: Toward an Egalitarian Theory of Ownership. Oxford: Oxford University Press, 1995

Cohen, G. A. *Self-Ownership, Freedom, and Equality.* Cambridge: Cambridge University Press, 1995.

Hegel, G. W. F. *The Philosophy of Right.* Translated by T. M. Knox. Oxford: Clarendon Press, 1942 [1821].

Honoré, A.M. "Ownership." In *Oxford Essays in Jurisprudence,* edited by A. G. Guest. Oxford: Clarendon Press, 1961.

Hume, David. *Treatise of Human Nature.* Edited by L. A. Selby-Bigge. Oxford: Clarendon Press, 1960 [1737]. See also the discussion in his *Enquiry Concerning the Principles of Morals* (1751).

Locke, John. *Two Treatises of Government.* Edited by Peter Laslett. 2d, critical ed. Cambridge: Cambridge University Press, 1967 [1689].

Long, A. A. "Stoic Philosophers on Persons, Property-Ownership and Community." In *Aristotle and After,* edited by R. Sorabji. *Bulletin of the Institute of Classical Studies Suppl.* 68 (1997): 13–32. Discusses the Stoic

concept of *oikeiosis* (psychological appropriation) in connection with the idea that property acquisition is intimately connected with the development of human personality.

Munzer, Stephen. *A Theory of Property.* Cambridge: Cambridge University Press, 1990.

Nozick, Robert. *Anarchy, State, and Utopia.* New York: Basic Books, 1974.

Pennock, J. Roland, and John W. Chapman, eds. *Property.* Nomos, vol. 22. New York: New York University Press, 1980. Includes extensive bibliography. For discussions on whether weak subsets of incidents of full ownership constitute a property right, see Grey, "The Disintegration of Property" and Becker, "The Moral Basis of Property Rights."

Ryan, Alan. *Property and Political Theory.* Oxford: Basil Blackwell, 1984.

———. *Property.* Minneapolis: University of Minnesota Press, 1987. Both of Ryan's works discuss the broader historical and political context; useful bibliographies.

Schmidtz, David. *The Limits of Government.* Boulder, CO: Westview, 1990.

Tully, James. *A Discourse on Property: John Locke and His Adversaries.* Cambridge: Cambridge University Press, 1980.

Waldron, Jeremy. *The Right to Private Property.* Oxford: Clarendon Press, 1988. Includes bibliography that updates Pennock and Chapman.

Lawrence C. Becker

proportionality

The concept of proportionality arises in many places in our moral discourse. We think, for example, that an ACTION that is costly in some important way, as is surgery, might be morally justified if necessary to achieve some significant benefit, but not if necessary only for some trivial one. We can express this belief by saying that the costs of the surgery in the first instance, but not in the second, are proportional to its benefits. Similarly, we may think a given PUNISHMENT, for example, imprisonment, is morally justified in response to a grave offense but not in response to a minor one, and we often express this belief by saying that the punishment's severity is disproportionate to the offense in the latter case, but not in the former.

Philosophers differ over how to determine such proportions. Act-utilitarians tend to identify the punishment that "fits" (is proportionate to) the crime with that punishment imposition of which is optimific, that is, has results at least as good as those of any alternative. Thus, a fifty-dollar fine is proportionate and fitting punishment for littering if and only if any lesser penalty would mean a net loss in utility (owing normally to a loss in deterrence that outweighs the criminal's gain in utility), and any greater penalty would also mean a net loss in utility (owing normally to an increase in the criminal's suffering without any offsetting gain in deterrence). This view is objectionable on several counts: (a) it holds the criminal's fate hostage to others' susceptibility to deterrence; (b) it allows that wildly disparate levels of punishment might, in different times or places, all 'fit' crimes of the same sort; and (c) it accords harms to wrongdoers equal moral weight with harms to their potential victims.

The ancient *lex talionis* (law of retaliation), expressed in the scriptural phrase "An eye for an eye, and a tooth for a tooth", avoids these problems but contains others. The thief might be fined and the kidnapper held against his or her will, but what of the child molester or rapist? An adult offender logically cannot be subjected to child molestation; the rapist cannot be raped without immorality. (Even if one holds the bizarre view that forcing sex on such a person is not unjust [because deserved], the agent who imposes the penalty thereby commits fornication or adultery.)

A modern variant on this traditional view is the indifference theory, which holds roughly that, under the right conditions, we are justified in punishing an offender up to that level of severity at which one would be indifferent between being subjected to the offense and being subjected to the punishment. Some protest that this view does not explain what justifies our imposing such punishment (Honderich). However, this objection misses the theory's point; it is designed not to explain why some level of punishment is permissible, but to determine an upper limit beyond which punishment is impermissible.

While it is uncontroversial that to impose on an offender a disproportionately severe punishment is to treat that person unjustly, it is doubtful whether imposing a disproportionately lenient punishment is an injustice—even if it makes sense to talk of such a punishment. G. W. F. HEGEL (1770–1831) seems to have thought it might violate the offender's right to be punished, but it is odd to think that by committing crimes one acquires new claim RIGHTS against others. KANT (1724–1804) notoriously opposed judicial clemency, insisting that punishments

be meted out according to a strict law of deserts. This view, however, is tied to the thesis that punishment restores some right order of things that the criminal's offense disrupted. This thesis is implausible because it is unlikely that (a) there is a right ordering of things that exists prior to crimes; (b) crimes are wrong because they upset such an ordering; and (c) punishing restores it.

The other sort of proportionality claim we noticed in the surgery example is considerably more problematic. The surgery example might mask this problem if we think of the trade-offs involved as concerning goods and evils of roughly the same type: medical well-being. However, even that concept will comprise aspects as diverse as pain on the one hand and organ-function on the other. When we leave the domain of medicine, the disparity of goods and evils becomes even more striking. Most of us believe it is reasonable to do something that jeopardizes a good FRIENDSHIP in order to save one's health, but disproportionate to do so in order merely to gain a ham sandwich. But in what does this disproportion consist? The charge of incommensurability holds that, unless there is some common currency in which the value of each can find expression or some common scale against which their values can be measured, the comparison lacks meaning or expresses merely a subjective preference that no matter how widely it is shared, lacks objective justification. In response, some have conceded that there can be no *commensuration* of greatly different values, but insist that measurement is not necessary for the making of *comparisons,* as a cardinal scale is not required for ordinal rankings. This approach seems to replace the mathematical computation suggested by understanding proportionality in terms of "commensuration" with a more subjective, intuitive judgment (not necessarily lacking in objective justification).

Proportionality also plays a role in just-war theory and in the principle of DOUBLE EFFECT. By the latter principle, even when only the good and not the EVIL of an action's effects is intended, the action is permissible only if the good effects provide proportional reason to perform the action despite its bad effects. Revisionist moral theologians have proposed a doctrine of proportional reason: the right action is that action which results in the best proportion of good to bad or for which there is greatest proportional reason. They insist that this doctrine is the real meaning behind the principle of double effect or, less implausibly, that it is the grain of truth within that principle. It is hard to know how to interpret this new doctrine. Talk of the "proportion of good to evil" suggests the metric model of proportionality (discussed above), which properly triggers worries about incommensurability. To say the right action is the one for which there is greatest proportional reason is to say merely that one ought to do what one has best reason to do. Here the term 'proportional' is doing no real work and the 'doctrine' appears to be merely a truism.

Some philosophers (Finnis *et al.*) have opened an interesting new approach to proportionality and proportional reason with their suggestion that these concepts are inherently moral. They bid us consider as analogs such cases as that of a wartime bombing raid against a supply depot in enemy territory, a raid that causes civilian casualties in the nearby village. According to the just-war tradition, the raid is justified only if the harm caused is neither intended nor disproportional to the good to be achieved. Rather than construing the relevant proportion the way most would, as requiring us to determine whether the raid is likely to cause more good than evil, Finnis *et al.* suggest that it instead invites us to ask whether those who ordered and executed the bombing would still have done so if the civilian victims had been citizens of their own country, perhaps their own relatives. We should take a negative answer as evidence (though not necessarily conclusive evidence) that in conducting the actual raid, those who ordered and executed the bombing acted wrongly because they acted from an unjust favoritism that counted civilian lives on the enemy side as less worthy of protection than those on their own side.

It is unclear whether this new interpretation of proportionality will be sufficient as it stands. Surely, morality permits people to show many forms of favoritism to their relatives and fellow citizens, so some explanation is needed to show why the favoritism in the bombing case is unjust. Nonetheless, the new interpretation reminds us that in ordinary thought, efficiency is not of direct moral importance. In judging whether the agents in our examples act immorally, we ought to weigh whether their actions do more harm than good only insofar as that deliberation helps us see the actions as careless or in some other way irresponsible. The lesson of Finnis *et al.*

may be that disproportionality matters morally only where it points to vice.

See also: AMNESTY AND PARDON; CASUISTRY; COMMENSURABILITY; CORRECTIONAL ETHICS; DETERRENCE, THREATS, AND RETALIATION; DOUBLE EFFECT; FITTINGNESS; HARM AND OFFENSE; INTENTION; JUSTICE, RECTIFICATORY; MERCY; MERIT AND DESERT; MILITARY ETHICS; POLICE ETHICS; PUNISHMENT; RECIPROCITY; REVENGE; THEOLOGICAL ETHICS; WAR AND PEACE.

Bibliography

Curran, Charles, and Richard McCormick, eds. *Readings in Moral Theology, No. 1.* New York: Paulist Press, 1979. Compiles major sources of proportionalism.

Finnis, John, et al. *Nuclear Deterrence, Morality, and Realism.* Oxford: Oxford University Press, 1987. Treats proportional reason as inherently moral.

Garcia, J. L. A. "Two Concepts of Desert." *Law and Philosophy* 5 (1986): 219–35. Denies justice demands proportional punishment.

Goldman, Alan H. "The Paradox of Punishment." *Philosophy and Public Affairs* 9 (1979): 42–58. Statement of the indifference theory.

Griffin, James. "Are There Incommensurable Values?" *Philosophy and Public Affairs* 7 (1977): 39–59.

Hallett, Garth. "The 'Incommensurability' of Values." *Heythrop Journal* 28 (1987): 373–87. Denies incommensurability.

———. *Christian Moral Reasoning.* Notre Dame, Ind.: University of Notre Dame Press, 1983. Philosophically sophisticated defense of proportionalism.

Hegel, G. W. F. *Philosophy of Right.* Translated by T. M. Knox. Oxford: Oxford University Press, 1952 [1821]. Translation of *Grundlinien der Philosophie des Rechts.* Treats punishment as the criminal's right.

Hestevold, H. Scott. "Justice to Mercy." *Philosophy and Phenomenological Research* 46 (1986): 281–91. Argues that mercifully lenient punishments can be proportional to crime.

Honderich, Ted. *A Theory of Determinism.* Oxford: Oxford University Press, 1988. Analyzes efforts to justify punishment as proportional.

Hoose, Bernard. *Proportionalism.* Washington, D.C.: Georgetown University Press, 1987. Sympathetic review.

Kant, Immanuel. *Lectures on Philosophical Theology.* Translated by Allan Wood. Ithaca, N.Y.: Cornell University Press, 1978 [1783]. Argues that mercifully lenient punishment is immoral because disproportionate.

McCormick, Richard. *Notes on Moral Theology, 1965–1980.* Lanham, Md.: University Press of America,

1981. Annual essays chronicling development of proportionalist theology.

Raz, Joseph. *The Morality of Freedom.* Oxford: Oxford University Press, 1986. Includes intricate defense of value incommensurability.

Sher, George. *Desert.* Princeton, N.J.: Princeton University Press, 1987.

Sinnott-Armstrong, Walter. "Moral Dilemmas and Incomparability." *American Philosophical Quarterly* 22 (1985): 321–27.

Walzer, Michael. *Just and Unjust Wars.* New York: Basic Books, 1977. Influential modern discussion.

J. L. A. Garcia

Protagoras of Abdera (c. 490–c. 421 B.C.E.)

Protagoras was born in Abdera in northeast Greece. According to PLATO (c. 430–347 B.C.E.), he amassed quite a bit of wealth as a professional teacher (*Meno* 91d) and was the first to call himself a Sophist (*Protagoras* 349a). He traveled extensively, visited Athens a number of times, was Pericles's (c. 490–429 B.C.E.) friend, and drew up the laws for the Athenian colony of Thurii. A less credible tradition relates that he was exiled for impiety and his books burned. He was best known for his AGNOSTICISM about the existence of the gods (frag. 4) and for his statement, "man is the measure of all things" (frag. 1).

Since none of Protagoras's surviving twelve fragments deals directly with moral theory, commentators must rely on Plato's accounts of him in the *Protagoras* and *Theaetetus*. Not only is the historical accuracy of these two accounts much disputed, but they are also often thought to be inconsistent.

Morality and the Political Community

In his "Great Speech" in Plato's *Protagoras* (320c–328d), Protagoras argues that cooperative, other-regarding behavior is a necessary condition for political communities as well as for human survival, since survival is not possible apart from such communities. Moral behavior is precisely what is required by and embodied in a community's laws or its system of *nomima kai dikaia* (things that are lawful/customary and just). Although this legal conception of morality requires only minimal regard for the INTERESTS of others, his own preference seems to have been for a community marked by FRIENDSHIP among citizens, an ideal that requires a high level of moral behavior.

Virtually everyone, Protagoras argues, has the capacity for VIRTUES like justice, moderation, and TEMPERANCE, which make a state possible. This moral *arete* (virtue, EXCELLENCE) is taught by parents, nurses, schoolmasters, and the state; and wrongdoers must receive PUNISHMENT that is correctional. Moral *arete* is also what Protagoras claims to teach; and through his teaching his students are able to benefit the community by their leadership and ability to persuade the community to adopt advantageous laws and policies.

While many scholars believe these claims reflect the views of the historical Protagoras, others disagree on grounds that Protagoras and other SOPHISTS were, in fact, only interested in teaching the rhetorical and political excellence (*arete* in a nonmoral sense) necessary for success (Maguire, Adkins). Some scholars have also been troubled by the fact that the *Protagoras* nowhere mentions or alludes to Protagoras's doctrine of relativism.

Moral Relativism

In the section of Plato's *Theaetetus* known as "The Apology of Protagoras" (166a–168c), Socrates attempts to discover a way that Protagoras can defend his view that some are wiser than others in moral or perceptual matters in light of the man-measure doctrine, which claims that all perceptions and beliefs are true. Most commentators hold that Protagoras was a skeptical relativist in ethical matters (Cornford and Kerferd are notable exceptions), for the man-measure doctrine implies that what a community considers just *is* just for it as long as it thinks so. The *Theaetetus* views Protagoras as a relativist, although not a consistent one.

Conclusions

Despite apparent discrepancies, the two dialogues present an essentially consistent portrait of Protagoras. Both the *Protagoras* (which probably reflects the views of the historical Protagoras) and the *Theaetetus* portray him as an individual seriously concerned with political theory; and insofar as this portrait is true, he would have been concerned with moral requirements that secure the existence and advantage of the community. And although his arguments in the *Protagoras* allow him to provide a nonrelativistic ground for a *system* of laws guaranteeing community survival, in neither dialogue was his theory such that he could ground any particular moral requirement or law in anything but community will.

See also: AGNOSTICISM; COLLECTIVE RESPONSIBILITY; COMMUNITARIANISM; COOPERATION, CONFLICT, AND COORDINATION; EXCELLENCE; FRIENDSHIP; MORAL COMMUNITY, BOUNDARIES OF; MORAL RELATIVISM; SKEPTICISM IN ANCIENT ETHICS; SOPHISTS.

Bibliography

Works by Protagoras

Diels, Hermann, and Walter Kranz, comps. *Die Fragmente der Vorsokratiker: Vol. 2.* 6th ed. Berlin: Weidmannsche, 1952. Definitive collection of the fragments in the original Greek.

Freeman, Kathleen, tr. *Ancilla to the Pre-Socratic Philosophers: A Complete Translation of the Fragments in Diels, "Fragmente der Vorsokratiker."* Cambridge: Harvard University Press, 1957 [1948].

Sprague, Rosamond K., ed. *The Older Sophists: A Complete Translation by Several Hands of the Fragments in "Die Fragmente der Vorsokratiker" with a New Edition of "Antiphon" and "Euthydemus."* Columbia, SC: University of South Carolina Press, 1972. English translations of the fragments and ancient testimony.

Works about Protagoras

Adkins, A. W. H. "*Arete, Techne,* Democracy, and Sophists: *Protagoras* 316b–328d." *Journal of Hellenic Studies* 93 (1973): 3–12.

Kerferd, G. B. "Plato's Theory of the Relativism of Protagoras." *Durham University Journal* 42 (1949): 20–26.

———. "Protagoras' Doctrine of Justice and Virtue in the *Protagoras* of Plato." *Journal of Hellenic Studies* 73 (1953): 42–45.

Maguire, Joseph P. "Protagoras . . . or Plato? II. The *Protagoras.*" *Phronesis* 22 (1977): 103–22.

Nill, Michael. *Morality and Self-Interest in Protagoras, Antiphon, and Democritus.* Leiden: Brill, 1985. Analyzes Sophistic views bearing on the issue of reasons to be moral.

Plato. *Protagoras.* See two translations: translated by B. Jowett, extensively revised by M. Ostwald, edited with introduction by G. Vlastos (New York: Bobbs-Merrill, 1956); translation and commentary by C. C. W. Taylor (Oxford: Clarendon Press, 1976).

———. *Theaetetus.* Oxford: Clarendon Press, 1973. Translation and commentary by John McDowell.

Michael Nill

prudence

Prudence traditionally has been characterized as a cardinal virtue, a habitual trait of CHARACTER on which the moral life especially depends. It is the intellectual and moral capacity, developed by following good examples and by practice over a lifetime, to reason well about human action—to distinguish right from wrong action in particular circumstances and to prompt appropriate behavior. Prudence may be generally understood as moral WISDOM resulting in morally correct choices and actions. Although in the modern period the meaning of prudence has been especially associated with fiscal responsibility and even has assumed negative connotations of undue or self-interested carefulness, its classical meaning of good judgment about the whole range of morally significant behavior still persists, especially in CHRISTIAN ETHICS and in traditions of moral thought indebted to ARISTOTLE (384–322 B.C.E.). Although moral philosophy since the Enlightenment, and especially in the modern period, has increasingly abandoned the moral vocabulary and perspective in which the VIRTUES are central, the virtue of prudence plays an important role in the contemporary revival of interest in the moral tradition of virtues and virtue theory.

Prudence and Other Virtues

According to the traditional conception, prudence is essentially related to other moral virtues. Moral virtues are ingrained dispositions to act rightly, developed by practice, just as vices are conceived as tendencies to act wrongly. Virtues are more, however, than merely habitual skills enabling right action; they actually enable the attainment of what it means to be human. They perfect the doer as well as the deed. All things tend toward some end apprehended as good, Aristotle observed, noting that the good toward which humans tend is twofold—active and contemplative. At the contemplative level, the good for humans is the apprehension of truth (and within the Christian tradition, knowledge of God). At the active level, the good is to live a life in accord with reason and virtue. Prudence was conceived as the habitual moral and intellectual capacity that ensured a coincidence between reason and virtue. If the moral virtues are the means toward the achievement of the end of life, prudence guarantees that the means are appropriate and in accord with reason. The exercise of the virtue of COURAGE, for example, requires prudence to avoid the vice of rashness or foolhardiness. A prudent individual has neither too much nor too little regard for dangers or obstacles. One learns what counts as virtue by observing the actions of those who are virtuous, and one develops the ability to act in accordance with virtue by the repeated performance of virtuous actions.

The Western tradition of the four cardinal virtues of prudence, justice, courage, and TEMPERANCE dates back before the time of PLATO (c. 430–347 B.C.E.), whose character Agathon lists prudence as a cardinal virtue in the *Symposium*. These virtues were regarded as the "hinge" (*cardo*) around which the moral life revolved; the virtue of prudence was seen as central to their activity, as their "measure" or their prototype, their prerequisite and their foundation. Antisthenes (c. 445–c. 360 B.C.E.), for example, considered all virtue to be dependent on practical intelligence. Aristotle distinguished PRACTICAL WISDOM (PHRONESIS) from theoretical wisdom (*sophia*) and assigned *phronesis,* or prudence, the role of identifying rational ends for otherwise inchoate desires and of ordering means to the rational achievement of those ends. For the Stoics, to whom virtue consisted in conformity to NATURAL LAW, prudence was the virtue governing moral intelligence, allowing the apprehension of the requirements of reason expressed in nature and governing choices for action in accord with nature. Persistent in these and subsequent accounts of the cardinal virtues is the understanding of the relationship between prudence and the other cardinal virtues as reciprocal. As Joseph Pieper observes, "only one who previously and simultaneously loves and wants the good can be prudent, but only one who is previously prudent can do good."

The Traditional Conception

St. THOMAS AQUINAS (1225?–1274), following the description provided by Aristotle, provides what remains as the fullest account of the role and operation of prudence, especially in the *Summa Theologica,* but also in the *Treatise on Happiness,* the *Treatise on the Virtues,* and his *Commentary on Aristotle's Ethics.* (Thomas departs from Aristotle primarily with respect to the supernatural end—God— toward which Thomas believes prudence is ultimately ordered.) He commonly describes prudence as an application of "right reason to action" (*S.T.,* II-II, q. 47, a. 4) and as "wisdom about human affairs" (*S.T.,* II-II, q. 47, a. 1). To cite Thomas's observations about the nature and activity of prudence is to articulate what might be called the classical or traditional conception of the virtue. For Thomas, as for Aristotle, the virtues of prudence and art "perfect"—complete, make perfect, and enable—the practical intellect, our intellectual ability to deal with contingent truths, the changeable realm of actions that can always be otherwise than they happen to be at any given time. Necessary truths, in contrast, concern the world as it actually is and are apprehended via the "theoretical" aspect of our intellect perfected by the virtue of wisdom.

Whereas art concerns "right reasoning about what is to be made"—the activity of a carpenter or potter is a good example—prudence concerns "right reasoning about what is to be done" (*S.T.,* I-II, q. 57, a. 4). Prudence differs from art, however, because it not only produces the ability to act well, but also presumes the DESIRE; hence its intimate and mutually dependant relation to the other cardinal virtues that order our appetites to the good. An artisan, consistent with art and without being any less skilled, can always choose to introduce a defect into a product, but it is inconsistent with prudence to choose to act contrary to virtue. Thomas takes care to distinguish doing from making because doing not only produces an action but also creates habits within the agent, tendencies to act in good or bad ways. One becomes prudent, temperate, just, and courageous by acting so. Acting contrary to virtue produces a vicious disposition of character. And although one can speak loosely about a prudent investor or ship captain, for example, authentic prudence concerns our actions and orientations as humans. To say that someone is prudent in an unqualified way is to say that he or she is prudent—reasons rightly about how to act—regarding life in general. "Through prudence we deliberate well about matters pertaining to the whole of human life and the ultimate end of human life," Thomas claims (*S.T.,* II-II, q. 47, a. 13).

Prudence is obtained and perfected through practice in deliberation and action, just as the virtue of temperance, for example, is cultivated through rational control of appetites for the various goods toward which humans are naturally inclined. Because prudence is acquired through one's moral experience over a lifetime, it is seldom found in the young (*S.T.,* II-II, q. 47, a. 14). Although there are practical principles and rules-of-thumb reflecting the accumulated moral wisdom of a community or culture to which one can look for guidance in moral decision making, one does not become prudent by a set of moral principles, but rather by practice.

Prudence enables one to do good deeds, the activity in which a good life consists, and to become a good and happy person, the ultimate end toward which humans naturally tend. For a deed to be truly good, Thomas explains, it has to be done in the right way and for the right reasons. Harming someone out of ANGER, for example, would be opposed to justice and temperance as well as to prudence, while harming someone to prevent malicious injury to an innocent victim could well be a prudential, courageous, and just act of virtue. Prudence enables one to act in the right way, for the right reasons, and at the right time. It permits discernment of what is to be done now or in the future on the basis of knowledge of the present situation, past experience, and correct anticipation of consequences. It also presumes an inclination to act virtuously. In short, prudence gives one a sense of moral discernment based on an accurate perspective of reality and an orientation to the good.

Subsidiary Parts of Prudence

The modern understanding of prudence is considerably narrower than its classical conception. For the tradition articulated by Thomas, prudence includes or is related to an array of subsidiary virtues that perfect a wide variety of capacities to judge and to act. Prudence, according to that view, depends on the abilities to take good counsel, to deliberate carefully and well, and to initiate appropriate action, to note just a few. A rich vocabulary was developed to name some of the virtues or habitual dispositions associated with prudence: The habit of *synesis,* equivalent to sagacity, concerns the exercise of good judgment with respect to commonly accepted NORMS of behavior, the perfection of one's ability to evalu-

ate situations as they actually are and to discern some course of action as morally forbidden, commanded, or permitted behavior (*S.T.,* I-II, q. 57, a. 6; II-II, q. 51, a. 3). The virtue of *gnome* perfects the ability to judge what is right when the ordinary rules and guidelines do not apply or appear to be in conflict (*S.T.,* II-II, q. 51, a. 4; I-II, q. 57, a. 6).

Additionally, according to Thomas, no one can be prudent without good habits of "memory, intelligence, and foresight, as well as caution, docility [the ability to take advice], and the like" (I-II, q. 57, a. 6). Shrewdness combined with alertness "to do whatever has to be done" is a part of prudence that Thomas calls solicitude, which enables a person to deliberate as long as necessary to reach a correct judgment, but then to act decisively when action is called for (*S.T.,* II-II, q. 49, a. 9). The development of prudence also depends on the ability to anticipate the future variables of action through the capacity of foresight or providence and to consider the suitability of means to ends in light of the actual circumstances of a situation, which requires circumspection. Caution, although far from being equivalent to prudence, is a necessary adjunct in order to guard against those things that one anticipates will impede virtue or to prepare as well as possible for dealing with unanticipated accidents (*S.T.,* II-II, q. 49, aa. 5–8).

Decline of the Traditional Conception

The classical understanding of prudence still persists, relatively unchanged, although diminished in influence. Joseph Pieper's unabashedly Thomistic discussion of prudence is a good example of modern continuity with that tradition. Its place in moral philosophy has declined, however, with the waning of the influence of the scholastic tradition it informed, with the disappearance of moral consensus in modern culture, and with the decline in religious authority in ethics and politics. Dissertations on the virtue of prudence continue to be written, but until recently, treatments of prudence, as of the other cardinal virtues, have subsisted on the margins of moral philosophical discussion. Most contemporary philosophical discussions of prudence treat it as equivalent to self-interest or carefulness, as in Thomas Nagel's discussions of prudential reasons for ALTRUISM or in discussions of prudential reasons for moral behavior. Such opposition between prudence and virtue was unthinkable within the traditional conception.

The decline of interest in a moral vocabulary concerned with virtue and with prudence in particular can be attributed, in part, to the decline of the Medieval religious view that provided the context in which prudence was considered and to the rejection of Aristotelian science that accompanied it. Enlightenment attempts to ground ethics in something other than revelation, and religious tradition tended to reject or radically reformulate the received moral vocabulary. As early as the Renaissance, however, the very meaning of prudence began to shift as the result of shifting assumptions about the ground for political authority.

Prudence, understood as good judgment about human action, was conceived by Aristotle and Thomas and the traditions they informed as a preeminent political as well as personal virtue. In *The Machiavellian Moment,* which chronicles a shift away from received traditions in political thought, J. G. A. Pocock describes the inherited view of prudence as "nothing less than the ability to make such use of one's experience, and that of others, that good results may be expected to follow." Whether the prince or the people, the few or the many, were best positioned, by virtue of their attainment of prudence, to achieve those good results in the city-state was a matter of considerable debate.

For Donato Giannotti (1492–1573), who argued for the political legitimacy of the *popolo,* the many rather than the few in Venice, prudence was "the reward of those who obey the laws, pool their experience, suffer injuries rather than inflict them." The many excelled in prudence because of their training in OBEDIENCE TO LAW, their variety of practical experience complemented by book learning, and their numbers. For Francesco Guicciardini (1483–1540), on the other hand, "Prudence is, after all, the second virtue of civic aristocracies; it is that ability to act in the present while looking ahead, that exceptional knowledge of affairs possessed by those who have had exceptional opportunities of attaining it."

A shift in the meaning of prudence occurs with an evolving view of prudence as a calculating kind of virtue enabling one to anticipate and to outwit the vagaries of fortune. Prudence had been a prime ingredient in the excellence or the strength of character that enabled the ruler to dominate fortune. Be-

cause of the unpredictability of events, Guicciardini observes, "it is necessary that the governors of states should be men of prudence, vigilantly attentive to the smallest accident, and weighing every possible consequence in order to obviate at the beginning, and eliminate as far as possible, the power of chance and fortune." In this view, the beginnings of the shift toward the modern conception of prudence as almost a vice, as overly careful calculation, and away from the broader classical conception of right reason about how to act, are apparent. By the early eighteenth century, the connotation of prudence as fiscal carefulness is evident in Daniel Defoe's (1660–1731) personification of prudence and probity as the parents of credit (see *The Review,* book 17). Later in the century, Adam SMITH (1723–1790) could characterize prudence as the careful cultivation of self-interest and cite that understanding of prudence as a partially true, if incomplete, account of moral virtue (see his *Theory of Moral Sentiments,* 1759). In short, over the space of a couple of centuries, the meaning of prudence, while still associated with morality in general, no longer was coincident with MORAL REASONING in general. The meaning of prudence has shrunk, at least in the common perception, to concern with self-interest and fiscal responsibility or carefulness. The moral universe in which prudence had once been central had been eclipsed by competing systems and vocabularies.

Renewed Interest

In recent years, however, there has been an increasing interest in reviving and rehabilitating the vocabulary of virtues. Some observers, such as Alasdair MACINTYRE, see an Aristotelian account of the virtues as the only viable alternative to the "endless" moral debates of the modern period (endless, in MacIntyre's view, because competing modern moral theories accurately perceive each other's weaknesses and successfully refute each other). Others, such as Stanley Hauerwas and Gilbert Meilaender, see in virtue theory the possibility of attending more realistically to the actual dynamics of the moral life, which for most of us is more a matter of incrementally developed character, everyday choices and associations, and patterns of how we live our lives than it is a matter of the moral dilemma reasoning so characteristic of modern moral philosophical discussion, if it attends to the moral life at all. As Meilaender observes, what distinguishes virtue talk from its contemporary alternatives is that it is concerned with character and traits of behavior, rather than primarily with "duties, obligations, troubling moral dilemmas, and borderline cases." Its focus is on being, rather than doing. If the virtues become once again a meaningful part of our moral vocabulary, a broad conception of prudence will be a significant feature.

See also: ARISTOTLE; CHARACTER; CHRISTIAN ETHICS; DELIBERATION AND CHOICE; MACINTYRE; MORAL REASONING; NATURAL LAW; *PHRONESIS;* PLATO; PRACTICAL REASON[ING]; PRACTICAL WISDOM; RATIONAL CHOICE; REASONS FOR ACTION; STOICISM; THOMAS AQUINAS; VIRTUE ETHICS; VIRTUES; WISDOM.

Bibliography

Aristotle. *Nicomachean Ethics.* Especially Books I, III, VI.

Butler, Joseph. *The Works of Joseph Butler.* Edited by W. E. Gladstone. 2 vols. Oxford: Oxford University Press, 1897 [1722, 1736]. For "Three Sermons on Human Nature" and *The Analogy of Religion, Natural and Revealed . . .*

Davie, William E. "Being Prudent and Acting Prudently." *American Philosophical Quarterly* 10 (1973): 57–60.

Falk, W. D. "Morality, Self, and Others." In *Collected Papers of W. D. Falk,* 198–231. Ithaca, NY: Cornell University Press, 1986.

Garver, Eugene. *Machiavelli and the History of Prudence.* Madison: University of Wisconsin Press, 1987. Discussion of prudence and rhetoric.

Geach, Peter Thomas. *The Virtues.* Cambridge: Cambridge University Press, 1977. Virtues in general and in particular.

Hauerwas, Stanley. *Vision and Virtue.* Notre Dame, IN: Fides/Claretian, 1974. Attempt to revive the vocabulary of virtue for Christian ethics.

Klubertanz, George P. *Habits and Virtues: A Philosophical Analysis.* New York: Appleton-Century-Crofts, 1965. Description of the connection between habits and virtues and of prudence.

Mabbot, J. D., and H. J. N. Horsburgh. "Prudence." *Proceedings of the Aristotelian Society* 36 (1962): 51–64; 65–76.

MacIntyre, Alasdair. *After Virtue: A Study in Moral Theory.* Notre Dame, IN: University of Notre Dame Press, 1984 [1981]. Argument for an ethics of virtue as alternative to modern moral theory.

McInerny, Ralph. "Prudence and Conscience." *The Thomist* 38 (1974): 291–305.

Meilaender, Gilbert. *The Theory and Practice of Virtue.* Notre Dame, IN: University of Notre Dame Press, 1984. Examination of virtue theory and explication of selected virtues. Quoted from pp. 4–5.

Nagel, Thomas. *The Possibility of Altruism.* Oxford: Clarendon Press, 1970. Reasons for altruism, especially prudential reasons (pt. 2).

Pieper, Joseph. *The Four Cardinal Virtues.* Notre Dame, IN: University of Notre Dame Press, 1966. Thomistic description of prudence, justice, courage, and temperance. Quoted from p. 34.

Pocock, J. G. A. *The Machiavellian Moment.* Princeton, NJ: Princeton University Press, 1975. Analysis of shifting modes of political thought, including descriptions of prudence. Quoted from pp. 24, 310–11, 145, 237.

Thomas Aquinas. *Summa theologica.* Translated by The Fathers of the English Dominican Province. 3 vols. New York: Benziger, 1947 [1266–1273]. See especially material on the cardinal virtues in *S.T.* I-II, qq 49–67. For a Latin edition, Rome: Marietti Editori, 1952; for Blackfriars English and Latin on facing pages, New York: McGraw-Hill, 1964.

———. *Treatise on the Virtues (In General).* Translated by John Patrick Reid. Providence, RI: Providence College Press, 1951. General explication of the virtues, including prudence.

———. *Commentary on the Nicomachean Ethics.* Translated by C. I. Litzinger. Chicago: Henry Regnery, 1964. Explication of Aristotle's remarks on prudence, Books I, III, VI.

Daniel M. Nelson

psychoanalysis

The principal question regarding the relationship between psychoanalysis and ethics is, precisely, the determination of that relationship. There is no question that psychoanalysis, initially and (to a large extent still) focused on the restoration of mental health, normal functioning, and personal well-being, is addressed to matters that cannot be sharply disjoined from broadly eudaimonistic concerns. And yet, in the entire psychoanalytic literature there is no canonical account of the intersection of the technical concerns of the profession and the more general discussion of ethical issues. This point is worth mentioning because of the strong tendency on the part of the psychoanalytic profession, both among the original voices that have inspired the principal schools and the increasingly institutionalized teachings of those schools, to give an explicit and systematic form to their essential doctrines.

There is, for instance, no single sustained discussion of ethics, or of the relationship between psychoanalytic and ethical questions, in the enormous output of either Sigmund Freud (1856–1939) or C. G. Jung (1875–1961). There is a great deal of concern on Freud's part, confirmed by his case studies and his personal letters, regarding the ethics of his professional interventions and of those of his associates; but this concern was never systematized.

It would not be unreasonable to suggest that, ideologically, Freud was strongly motivated by the desire to bring his pioneer disclosures regarding the sexual dimension of human life into line with an enlightened bourgeois ethic, not—except for the impact of that disclosure—radically different from otherwise comparatively conventional views. Roughly, if one construes ethical questions eudaimonistically, then Freud's principal contribution bears on enlarging our sense of the ramified function of psychosexual development in any effective program of self-realization. Historically, it is more the effect of the penetration of Freud's notions into the educative processes of popular culture than the scientific acceptance of his model of psychosexual development that accounts for the considerable accommodation of the Freudian conception among contemporary Western versions of EUDAIMONISM.

Freudian Eudaimonism

There have been some noteworthy efforts, of course, to bring a Freudian or Freudian-like model of psychosexual development into explicit accord with a eudaimonistic ethics. The best-known are those developed by Erik Erikson and Philip Rieff. Both models may be broadly characterized as structuralist, in the sense that they propose relatively invariant developmental sequences for normal maturation that are explicitly psychosexual and at least implicitly eudaimonistic. What is quarrelsome about both is:

(a) that the maturational sequence is construed as distributively uniform, almost without regard for societal cofunctioning or a tolerance for a variety of interfunctioning roles. It is formulated in a linear and unique series of stages, analogically constructed so as to range in parallel ways over the maturation of the members of *Homo sapiens* and the development of culturally trained human persons, and formed

without close attention to historical, cultural, ethnic, gender, and class variability.

(b) that the account thus rendered is then explicitly thought to culminate in an ethically normative stage of development for which there is no comparably explicit biological or biologized analog (the so-called genital ideal).

The conceptual difficulties of these and similar schemata are essentially the same as appear in other structuralist accounts of human developmental processes that are assigned important ethical significance. An example can be found in the theory of MORAL DEVELOPMENT advanced by Lawrence Kohlberg (1927–1987).

Ego Psychology

Underlying all such speculations remains the difficult question of the relationship between membership in *Homo sapiens* and the identification of human creatures as fully formed human persons. Freud's work is noticeably weak in the elaboration of what has come to be called ego psychology, which, broadly speaking, is centered on the full development of the self or person and its protection from all forms of interfering psychopathology. The reason, perhaps, rests with Freud's dynamic model of psychical development—that is, with his primary interest in the functional interrelationships between id, ego, and superego. Freud viewed these distinctions primarily as marking certain dimensions of life occupied with three characteristic "tyrannies": the tyranny of instinct, the tyranny of reality, and the tyranny of social restriction and taboo. Freud was more concerned with detailing the dynamics of causal elements drawn from these three dimensions than he was with elaborating a satisfactory model of individual life or either intra- or inter-societal functioning. Hence, even the elaboration of a relatively canonical model of eudaimonistic functioning, as in Erikson and Rieff, favors a degree of ego psychology that significantly adds to the original emphasis of Freud himself.

The Freudian orientation can be fruitful, however, especially when informed by a more generous sense of the symbiosis of the individual and the societal. Even while it is still construed in terms of psychosexual development, the Freudian orientation can be made responsive to a close study of contingent histories, clearly influenced by the trend toward ego psychology. An example of this appears in Erich Fromm's (1900–1980) *Escape from Freedom* (1941) and his later, explicitly eudaimonistic, ego-psychological ethical treatise, *Man for Himself* (1957).

Difficulties with Eudaimonism

What may be said about all such explorations is that, however sensitized by the specialist studies of the psychoanalysts (of any stripe), the fully normative eudaimonistic programs offered can really claim no scientific privilege with regard to their specifically ethical import, that is, with regard to their authority as a guide in ethical, even self-directed developmental respects. There simply is no reliable conceptual bridge between the development of the members of *Homo sapiens* and that of given persons, or of the development of the members of particular human societies and the normative development of "man," in virtue of which either psychoanalytic or psychological studies could claim a legitimate directive role. There is not, in the entire literature, a single argument of the eudaimonistic sort that is compelling on its face in either of these regards; there is not a single argument drawn from the narrower, more recent literature of professional psychoanalysis, general PSYCHOLOGY, developmental or educational psychology. This finding may seem harsh and contestable. But the fact is that the psychoanalytic literature does not illuminate the stubborn conceptual disjunction between factual studies of human dynamics and the normative (in particular, the ethical) direction of responsible human life. That question, classically raised in the earliest eudaimonistic literature in PLATO (c. 430–347 B.C.E.) and ARISTOTLE (384–322 B.C.E.) has hardly been resolved to this day. It is worth noting that discussants within the psychoanalytic movement who published earlier than Erikson, Rieff, or Fromm—for instance, Heinz Hartmann (1960), R. E. Money-Kyrle, or J. C. Flügel—tend to show greater sensitivity regarding the conceptual issue.

Freud

Freud's characteristic treatment of morality appears most clearly in the *New Introductory Lectures on Psycho-Analysis* (1932). There, Freud treats moral injunctions, restrictions, and the like as linked to the ubiquity of popular RELIGION, which both competes with and goes beyond the efforts of science. Religion is denied authority; "ethical demands" are to be given "another basis," one "indispensable to human society" and linked to human NEEDS, development, and the EVOLUTION of humankind. Freud is quite explicit that the id "knows no judgments of value; no good and evil, no morality." Scientific psychoanalysis proceeds solely and entirely by "the attempt to make the [patient's] unconscious conscious to him."

One can see here the seeds of the dual development of latter-day psychoanalysis. On the one hand, it has increasingly taken the form of a Socratic exercise under professional guidance, pertinent for rational behavior and therapy, but not necessarily ethically informed or focused, or inherently revelatory in ethical terms. On the other hand, it has increasingly turned to the elaboration of the potential ego-psychological themes that yield a model of rationality, mental health, responsible conduct, and a kind of enlightened eudaimonism. In this sense, the incipient ego psychology of Hartmann or of Karen Horney (1885–1952) points the way to an increasingly ramified interpenetration of the ethical and psychoanalytic strands of professional analysis and theory. The usual themes of ego psychology include the protection of the developing ego from psychopathologies that threaten its integrity and normality. The inherent ethical import of technical psychoanalytic work quite naturally centers on whatever contributes to that process.

Two examples may fix the point. In the introduction to her *Neurosis and Human Growth: The Struggle toward Self-Realization,* instructively subtitled "A Morality of Evolution," Horney remarks that "Under favorable conditions man's energies are put into the realization of his own potentialities"; "the problem of morality is . . . different when we believe that inherent in man are evolutionary constructive forces, which urge him to realize his given potentialities." Heinz Kohut is one of the most active of current ego-psychologically oriented psychoanalytic psychiatrists. In his well-known paper "The Future of Psychoanalysis" (1973), he claims that "psychoanalysis is par excellence" the "science of empathy." This "scientific empathy" will not merely contribute, by way of professional expertise, to "the nonconflictual enjoyment of *ego functions*," but will also, through that, facilitate "the broadening and strengthening of this bridge toward the other human being." It will foster, he claims, a functioning society of selves as "the highest *ideal.*" It is difficult to fail to see here the interconnecting of ethical and therapeutic concerns.

Natural-Kind and Functional Distinctions

The single most important conceptual issue here is readily formulated. It is, in fact, invariant for all empirical studies of human existence—whether medical, psychiatric, psychoanalytic, psychotherapeutic, psychological, sociological, anthropological, economic, or historical. It is this: *Homo sapiens* is normally construed as a "natural-kind" distinction; but *person* or *self* is not. By a natural-kind term, one means, in general, a species-wide or classificatory term that conforms, within a critical range of usage at least, with descriptions and explanations that fall under the putatively universal covering laws of nature. "Person" or "self" is a "functional" rather than a natural-kind term. That is, it is a term that favors classifications (even reflexive ones) that conform with human INTERESTS at the cognitive and active level of variable cultures, a term that crosses causal categories without any clear inkling of how to analyze or reduce the resultant distinction in natural-kind terms.

We do not actually know whether the concepts of persons and selves can in principle yield, or can be made to yield in real-world practice, a satisfactory analysis in more fundamental natural-kind terms. There is good reason to think that they cannot. Furthermore, on the usual view, natural-kind distinctions—*Homo sapiens* in particular—do not entail any ethically relevant NORMS or distinctions; although it is in general true that whatever is ethically pertinent surely does not conflict with known empirical facts, particularly with whatever are the law-like regularities of human nature. However, persons or selves are usually taken to be linguistically apt, self-directing, responsible agents capable of effecting changes in the environing world and in themselves, in accord with their intention. Thus it is impossible to free the notion of persons or selves altogether from ethically relevant characterization. In general, then, the eudaimonistic tradition, from the Greeks to contemporary psychoanalysis, has tended to construe the theory of persons, selves, human beings as a theory of a natural-kind distinction. From this, it would straightforwardly follow that a scientific ethic is possible.

A much-debated version of this quarrel takes the form of disputing whether the very concept of mental health is medically or therapeutically defensible by extension from notions of somatic health; whether somatic health is itself an ethically neutral concept; or whether mental health is a hybrid notion, ineluctably combining elements from an extension of somatic health and from eudaimonistic models. The issues clearly remain the same as before. Where somatic health is assigned to persons or to members of *Homo sapiens* insofar as the condition of the body serves the variable functions of contingently encultured persons, the concepts of somatic health cannot fail to be implicitly affected by the prevailing values and norms of particular societies. Whether health can be entirely freed from such a dependency is by no means clear. In effect, there seems to be no way to construe mental health in natural-kind terms rather than in functional terms variably fitted to the practices of different societies. The upshot is that psychoanalytic therapy must be inherently slanted in ethically favored ways.

A corollary finding draws attention to the fact that the practices, habits, INSTITUTIONS, *Sitten* of divergent historical cultures do have ethical or moral significance—descriptively or at the level of the convictions and habits of mind of those who have developed as normal members of particular societies; but it also finds that such "first-order" practices (roughly, the context of the superego of Freudian theory) do not entail any "second-order" or genuinely normative or categorical authority with respect to the legitimation or correction of any first-order practice. Here, one sees the clear sense in which the psychological disciplines cannot be expected to gain a cognitive advantage over the usual efforts of ethical discourse, whether eudaimonistic or not. Again, of course, the natural-kind/functional distinction obtains.

Practical Applications

Apart from this single theoretical issue, it should be said that the psychoanalytic literature is distinguished, in an ethically pertinent way, in terms of at least two principal applications. For one, it has contributed enormously, though at first (certainly in the classical literature) only grudgingly, to altering our perception of HOMOSEXUALITY. Ironically, the conventional view that homosexuality is a practice contrary to nature—hence, morally and legally to be forbidden—corresponds to the "natural-kind" reading of Freud's account of the psychopathology of male homosexuality. It is clear, for instance, from the DSM-III (1987) of the American Psychiatric Association, that psychiatrists and psychoanalysts have not completely resolved their equivocation over the functional or natural-kind classification of homosexuality. Second, psychoanalysis has contributed considerably to the refinement of our notions of insanity, diminished responsibility, and disorders of functioning selves with respect to legal responsibility and volitional and cognitive capacity. In both of these kinds of cases, one cannot fail to see how descriptive psychology contributes to plausible adjustments of would-be ethical constraints, even if it does not permit a direct disclosure of ethically pertinent norms themselves.

Summary

In general, it may be said that Freud tends to oscillate between a view that favors a psychosexually developmental eudaimonism that has distinct ethical overtones (as in treating homosexuality in terms of arrested or regressive development) and a view that regards ethical values as socially generated devices for effective societal functioning, that lack scientific validity. In the latter regard, there is a very strong congruity between Freud's treatment of social values internalized as the superego and Karl MARX's (1818–1883) reduction of such values as ideological and internal necessities local to historically contingent societies. In both, there is a noticeable disinclination to formulate a higher or more objective ethical ideal of "man" freed in some way from the concerns of class conflict or pathology. It remains true, nevertheless, that, in Marx, man is more a social construction; in Freud, there is a structuralist invariance that does permit, more naturally, an elaboration of patterns of development thought to be native to the relatively fixed human species.

See also: CONVENTIONS; *EUDAIMONIA,* -ISM; EVOLUTION; HOMOSEXUALITY; INSTITUTIONS; MEDICAL ETHICS; MORAL DEVELOPMENT; MORAL EDUCATION; MORAL PSYCHOLOGY; MORAL RULES; NEEDS; PSYCHOLOGY; RELIGION; SELF-KNOWLEDGE; SEXUALITY AND SEXUAL ETHICS.

Bibliography

American Psychiatric Association. *Diagnostic and Statistical Manual of Mental Disorders* (DSM-III). 3d rev. ed. Washington, DC: American Psychiatric Association, 1987.

Erikson, Erik. *Childhood and Society.* New York: W. W. Norton, 1950. Classic Freudian formulation of psychosexual development.

Feuer, Lewis. *Psychoanalysis and Ethics.* Springfield, IL: Charles C. Thomas, 1955. Early philosophical overview.

Flügel, J. C. *Men, Morals, and Society.* New York: International Universities Press, 1945. One of the earliest psychologic overviews of psychoanalysis and morality.

Freud, Sigmund. *The Complete Psychological Works of Sigmund Freud.* Edited by James Strachey, *et al.* Standard ed. 22 vols. London: Hogarth Press; Institute of Psychoanalysis, 1953–1954. Quoted from xxii, pp. 168, 74, 68.

Fromm, Erich. *Escape from Freedom.* New York: Rinehart, 1941. Classic specimen of integration of Freudian and Marxist analyses within eudaimonistic conception.

———. *Man for Himself.* New York: Rinehart, 1957. Psychoanalytically oriented eudaimonism.

Hartmann, Heinz. *Psychoanalysis and Moral Values.* New York: International University Press, 1960. Authoritative early Freudian text addressing the relation between psychoanalysis and morality.

Horney, Karen. *Neurosis and Human Growth: The Struggle toward Self-Realization*, pp. 13, 15. New York: W. W. Norton, 1950.

Kohut, Heinz. "The Future of Psychoanalysis." In *The Search for the Self: Selected Writings of Heinz Kohut: 1950–1978,* edited by Paul Ornstein, vol. 2, pp. 663–86. New York: International University Press, 1978 [1973]. Quoted from pp. 678, 684.

Margolis, Joseph. *Psychotherapy and Morality.* New York: Random House, 1968. Overview of concepts of mental health and morality.

———. "The Question of Homosexuality." In *Philosophy and Sex,* edited by Robert Baker and Frederick Elliston, pp. 288–302. Buffalo, NY: Prometheus, 1975. On the medical classification of homosexuality.

———. "The Concept of Mental Illness: A Philosophical Examination." In *Mental Illness: Law and Public Policy.* Vol. 5 of *Philosophy and Medicine,* edited by Baruch A. Brody and H. Tristam Engelhardt, pp. 3–23. Dordrecht: Reidel, 1980. Overview of the philosophical treatment of the concept.

Money-Kyrle, R. E. *Psychoanalysis and Politics.* New York: W. W. Norton, 1961. Early psychoanalytically oriented study.

Rieff, Philip. *Freud: The Mind of the Moralist.* New York: Viking, 1959. Clarification of the genital ideal.

Szasz, Thomas S. *The Myth of Mental Illness.* New York: Hoeber-Harper, 1961. Attack on the concept of mental illness.

Joseph Margolis

psychology

There is no settled literature linking psychology and ethics. There are a great many questions concerning what is sometimes called MORAL PSYCHOLOGY, for example (if one takes the notion generously) regarding such topics as WEAKNESS OF WILL (*akrasia*), freedom and compulsion, RESPONSIBILITY and liability, INTENTION and DOUBLE EFFECT, *mens rea* and diminished responsibility, competence and mental illness, saints and moral monsters, sexual perversion and SUICIDE, volition and deliberation, VIRTUES and vices, and the like. These questions are so complex and must be explored in so many diverging ways that it is impossible to treat them as an orderly array of issues within a well-defined line of professional inquiry: there is no such orderly inquiry.

It is certainly fundamental to the entire range of ethical issues that ethical agents are supposed to be capable of choice and ACTION and competent in relevant ways to choose and act; and it is an essential part of that general assumption that the requisite competence invites an explication in psychological terms at least. In fact, an older literature, concerned with moral responsibility, was much exercised by certain famous disputes regarding freedom and causality or FREEDOM AND DETERMINISM, on the grounds that those joined notions were mutually exclusive. It is fair to say that these disputes have largely dissolved, not so much because of psychologically compelling analyses of the apparent human experience of choice and freedom as of the development of the theory of the sciences, which has put strict determinism and inflexible universal causal laws very much on the defensive. It is certainly true that human deliberation, choice, action, and responsibility are standardly taken to entail alternative real possibilities and the capacity of humans to effectuate intended options among such alternatives. Both the psychology of that capacity and the ontology of a world that supports it are clearly called into play on that commonplace assumption. But there is no clear prospect that the pertinent psychological issues are likely to yield a unified analysis endorsed by the established inquiries of professional psychology. Furthermore, one of the more troublesome aspects of the psychological analysis of notions essential to ethical discourse is just that the relevant concepts are usually already interpreted in ethically tendentious ways and inseparable from such interpretations. Perhaps the most vexed illustration of this sort of complication is afforded by well-known disputes, at once psychological, legal, ethical, and medical, regarding insanity, mental competence, sexual deviance, diminished responsibility, and the like. We shall not pursue these matters here.

Eudaimonism and Related Programs

A more strategically placed line of inquiry linking psychology and ethics concerns questions of PLEASURE and pain, HAPPINESS, self-realization, and human NEEDS. There is a very large literature, of course, concerned with HEDONISM, *apathia, ataraxia,* psychosexual and cognitive stages of maturation, careers functionally congruent with human nature, *eudaimonia,* and the like. All such ethical programs—principally, varieties of UTILITARIANISM, NATURAL LAW doctrines, and EUDAIMONISM (including virtue-centered ethical programs)—tend, insofar as they rely or pretend to rely on psychological dispositions discerned in human beings, to be forms of NATURALISM and essentialism. This finding affords the simplest and most straightforward basis for embedding ethically normative values or criteria in psychologically (or biologically) regular dispositions. The most notorious conflating of these two themes—the psychologically descriptive and the ethically prescriptive—appears, in the utilitarian literature, in Jeremy BENTHAM's (1748–1832) treatment of pleasure and pain as the invariant sources of psychological motivation and, at the same time, as the invariant rational grounds for pertinent choice. It also appears in JOHN STUART MILL's (1806–1873) well-known [alleged?] equivocation on the meaning of "desirable." But the conflating of the descriptive and the prescriptive is not restricted to eighteenth- and nineteenth-century utilitarianism. It is, also, entirely possible to disallow a disjunction between the factual and the normative in "nonnatural" intuitionistic terms, for instance in G. E. MOORE's (1873–1958) account of the good life; but that has the effect, apart from difficulties of another sort, of either precluding empirical psychology or of inventing a subtler form of psychological inspection that is not clearly continuous with the study of natural drives and needs and vulnerabilities.

Two Essential Issues

Behind all these diverse questions loom two closely connected issues, on the resolution of which depends our general overview of the bearing of psychology on ethics. One issue concerns the conceptual relationship between the psychologically apt members of *Homo sapiens* (the biological species) and *persons* or *selves,* the culturally apt agents *of* ethically pertinent reflection and commitment. The other issue concerns the conceptual relationship between the NORMS of ethically appropriate judgment and action, and the drives, dispositions, talents, needs, and capabilities of the precultural animal that comes to function as a person or self, or between norms of the first sort and the specific forms of historically contingent instruction, indoctrination, and habituation that distinguish one human society from another. On the naturalistic view, norms appropriate to the ethical direction of persons are directly discernible in *Homo sapiens* or by construing the formation of persons and selves as the natural development or realization of the teleologically significant aptitudes of *Homo sapiens.* But all known conjectures of this sort have either failed to show that the normal patterns of merely biological or psychological maturation (however strenuous it may be to isolate such patterns) are linearly linked with some ethically normative stage of development (for instance, as with the Freudian conception of the "genital ideal") or have already construed the psychological as fully ethically freighted (for instance, as in construing suicide as, necessarily, clinically pathological). Furthermore, there is no known empirically convincing strategy for deriving ethically normative teleologies from natural biology or psychology. Nevertheless, there can be little doubt that a very large part of the general literature of utilitarianism, eudaimonism, natural law, natural right, and VIRTUE ETHICS are wedded to such a teleologism. It is entirely reasonable to challenge doctrines of these sorts in terms of teleologism, for there is no compelling argument in its favor.

The Constructive Theory of the Self

The deepest challenge linking the two questions just mentioned depends on what may be called the constructive theory of the self (or person). No one holding such a view would deny that human persons are manifested in, and develop from, or simply "are" (as suitably developed), the members of *Homo sapiens.* That is, the constructive theory need not hold that humans (as persons or selves) are merely a collective artifact of cultural history. But the theory maintains that, although the culturally formed capacities of humans are developments—either uniform or diverging—of the fundamental capacities of *Homo sapiens,* nevertheless those abilities are first identified, applied, assessed, and adjusted primarily in accord with norms that, in the same sense, are also constructed and culturally defined.

On this theory, persons or selves do not form natural kinds but only functional or functioning kinds. As a result, it is conceptually impossible to derive virtues, norms, RIGHTS, obligations, or goods for fully formed persons from considerations restricted to the study of *Homo sapiens.* The ethical is not in any way entailed or implicated, therefore, in the psychological. Certainly Greek eudaimonism, Thomistic eudaimonism (at least on the "natural" side), utilitarianism, natural law and natural right doctrines, and evolutionary and virtue ethics have tended to assume a straightforward connection between the two orders or have simply failed to take note of the fact that there is a significant conceptual gap to be closed.

Versions of the constructive theory of selves—spanning the entire range of conservative, liberal, and radical ethical convictions—are chiefly associated with the following: certain threads of MARX's (1818–1883) most radical treatment of PRAXIS (noticeable in Lev Vygotsky's [1896–1934] psychological studies); of NIETZSCHE's (1844–1900) speculations on the will to POWER (as in Michel FOUCAULT's [1926–1984] late analyses of ethical questions); in post-structuralist thinking (as in Louis Althusser's [1918–1990] repudiation of HUMANISM); in Martin HEIDEGGER's (1889–1976) radical conceptions of *Zeitlichkeit* and *Historizität* (as in Hans-Georg GADAMER's development of the idea that man belongs to his historical traditions); and in pragmatist notions of the social formation of the self (as in George Herbert MEAD's [1863–1931] well-known account of the role of the generalized other, and in the recent integration of a number of these strands of thought in Rom Harré's formulation of "personal being"). Clearly, these currents do not converge easily.

Man as Artifact

The consequence of pursuing this line of analysis is not that psychology is no longer pertinent to normative ethics, but that the psychology of "man" is itself a cultural and historical artifact, alterable (within limits undoubtedly) by the discontinuous patterns of life of particular societies. In the Foucauldian vision, for instance, man is exhorted to overcome his "nature" by his own acts—a prospect that would be straightforwardly incoherent on a merely naturalist or essentialist view of man. The "nature" man assigns himself is, on the radical theory, itself an artifact of his historical horizon: he has no fixed nature that he cannot breach. (This is what is meant in the pregnant claim that man has no nature, only a history.) The strategy clearly affects the pertinence of a scientific psychology. Another important finding drawn from this view is that the very provision of ethical codes is construed as no more than a "normalization" of man's psychology or nature within the contingent horizon (*episteme*) favored by the conformist members of a given society.

Descriptive and Normative Discourse

The constructive theory is not inherently conservative or radical in ethical respects. But the usual versions that are either conservative or radical (that is, opposed to familiar or prevailing conservative doctrines) do tend to link human psychology and normative considerations in a logically close way. They do so, so that they treat both the psychology (the "nature" assigned human persons) and their ethical norms as artifacts of the same cultural history. The conservatives argue that human nature remains essentially the same through all historical and cultural change—although not necessarily in an essentialist sense; and the radicals argue that the discontinuities of historical practice yield rather different accounts of "human nature" (*a fortiori,* of ethical norms) even over seemingly continuous stretches of a given people. At the present time, for instance,

Gadamer, Alasdair MACINTYRE, and Charles TAYLOR may well be taken to agree more or less that the history of man tends to exhibit a persistent human nature stabilized through historical and cultural variety; and Foucault stands as perhaps the best-known but by no means the unique representative of the radical thesis.

Natural-Kind and Functional-Kind Terms

That the large claim that "person" and "self" are not natural-kind terms but functional-kind terms (in contrast with "*Homo sapiens*") signifies that the analysis of persons cannot be managed in terms of psychological or other descriptive categories suitably congruent with scientific explanations under covering physical and biological laws. The point of the demurrer is simply that, on the opposed naturalistic view, it would be entirely congenial to claim that the "natural" norms of human life are drawn from a conception of human nature that accords closely with the authority of the empirical sciences. The view of the constructivist, therefore, makes an explicit puzzle of the conceptual connection between any psychologically oriented analysis of human nature and the inference to confirmed ethical norms. In this sense, even Immanuel KANT's (1724–1804) application of the categorical imperative and John RAWLS's liberal conception of the "initial position" are, equally, fatally flawed versions of the same naturalistic conception. In the limit, the "naturalistic" theory claims to find the very enterprise of ethical concern meaningful only in terms of a MORAL REALISM regarding human nature—effectively, an ethics cast in natural-kind terms (as, for instance, in the influential argument offered by David Wiggins). It is fair to say that the implicated dispute is one of the most central of contemporary ethical inquiry, one, therefore, that entrenches the question of the relevance of psychology.

Psychological Consensus and Historical Tradition

The connection between ethics and psychology is also pursued less rigorously within the terms of reference of empirically reflexive affirmations regarding the psychological needs and salient INTERESTS of a particular population. Usually no attempt is made to disjoin the list of such needs and interests first offered in ethically neutral psychological terms from a list of the "normal" or "natural" needs and interests of ethically informed agents. The presumption of a strong consensual convergence—perhaps near-unanimity—ranging over such needs and interests is often taken to fix the substantive concerns of *rationality* (or natural or human reason) in both regards at once. Effectively, it introduces a line of speculation that is distinctly ahistorical or historically naive. It is bound to be culturally tendentious, although it is usually offered in nonrelativistic (sometimes even antirelativistic) terms. In our own time it is usually pressed into the service of liberal or libertarian programs.

Hence, from the view of its critics, reliance on rationality is thought to be incapable of legitimating a clear distinction between an objective ethics and a mere ideological rationalization. Rawls's *A Theory of Justice* is probably the best-known specimen of this contested literature. Precisely the same argumentative options, however, offered in Rawls's account in terms of a reflexively consensual psychology, appear in more collectivist or cultural terms in the strongly historicized accounts of thinkers like Gadamer and MacIntyre, who similarly eschew an essentialized human nature in favor of consensus or tradition. Among such thinkers, a liberal ideology is likely to be replaced by an ideology of traditional values focused on the viability of a functional, somewhat organic society. But the conceptual charge of ideology masquerading as objective ethics appears to be more or less the same and more or less unanswered. There is, therefore, a strong analogy between the psychology/ethics connection and that of cultural history and ethics.

One may even venture to claim that, in a curious way, the first represents the more Kantian tradition in our time and the second, the more Hegelian; and that both converge on the assumption that a moral realism may be empirically, even naively, vindicated. In any case, it is certainly the question of the teleologism of "human nature" and of whether human psychology can be characterized in natural-kind terms that fixes in the deepest sense what may rightly be claimed to be the conceptual resources of any and all forms of ethical naturalism. Shifting from psychology to cultural history, we may or may not supersede naturalism—that, of course, is the very point of disputing whether "person" and "self" are natural-kind terms. But if ethical norms are not natural but only historically prevailing, the prospects of an objective ethics cannot fail to be even more problematic than is naturalism. Kantian *Moralität* ultimately rests on our assumptions about a fixed human nature; and Hegelian *Sittlichkeit* is obscured by its inherent equivocation between a merely descriptive anthropology and the admitted relationship of ethical norms and the concrete data of such an anthropology. The fate of the natural rights tradition depends essentially on the psychologically specified invariances of the first strategy; and the fate of evolutionary ethics depends essentially on the functional stability of distributed societies in accord with the second. Thus: Are CAPITAL PUNISHMENT, suicide, EUTHANASIA, SLAVERY, HOMOSEXUALITY, sexual deviance, war, and related practices in accord with or contrary to the natural law or natural rights appropriately applied to man? And what is the distributed bearing of the conditions of societal or psychological viability on the ethical entitlement or constraint due man? There is no denying a connection between how we characterize "human nature" and how we decide the ethical issues entailed, but there is also no legible path from the one to the other. Again, in our own time, eudaimonism appears to be able to straddle the two strategies: its fate, therefore, is similarly bifurcated.

Summary

Ethics is surely concerned with determining as objectively as possible what norms and criteria creatures of our kind should or could rationally prefer. But our characterization of our own nature (in particular, of our psychological needs, dispositions, interests, and capacities) is not in any obvious or straightforward way determinable independently of actual ethical convictions.

See also: AUTONOMY OF ETHICS; AUTONOMY OF MORAL AGENTS; BIOLOGICAL THEORY; CONSTRUCTIVISM; DELIBERATION AND CHOICE; DESIRE; *EUDAIMONIA*, -ISM; FREEDOM AND DETERMINISM; HAPPINESS; HEDONISM; HUMANISM; INTERESTS; MORAL PSYCHOLOGY; MORAL REALISM; MOTIVES; NATURAL LAW; NATURALISM; NATURE AND ETHICS; NEEDS; NORMS; PAIN AND SUFFERING; PERSON, CONCEPT OF; PHILOSOPHICAL ANTHROPOLOGY; PLEASURE; POWER; PRAXIS; PSYCHOANALYSIS; RATIONAL CHOICE; SELF AND SOCIAL SELF; SELF-[entries]; SEXUALITY AND

SEXUAL ETHICS; VIRTUE ETHICS; VIRTUES; WEAKNESS OF WILL.

Bibliography

Bentham, Jeremy. *An Introduction to the Principles of Morals and Legislation.* 1789. Classic utilitarian text.

Foucault, Michel. *Discipline and Punish.* Translated by Alan Sheridan. New York: Vintage, 1979. Constructivist account of self.

Gadamer, Hans-Georg. *Truth and Method.* Translated by Garrett Barden and John Cumming. New York: Seabury, 1975 [1960]. Hermeneutic account of historicized self.

Harré, Rom. *Personal Being.* Cambridge, Mass.: Harvard University Press, 1984. Constructivist account of persons and selves.

MacIntyre, Alasdair. *After Virtue.* 2d ed. Notre Dame, Ind.: University of Notre Dame Press, 1984. Virtue-centered ethics.

Mead, George Herbert. *Mind, Self, and Society.* Chicago, Ill.: University of Chicago Press, 1936. Pragmatist version of constructive theory of self.

Mill, John Stuart. *Utilitarianism.* 1861. Classic utilitarian text.

Moore, G. E. *Principia Ethica.* Cambridge: Cambridge University Press, 1903. Nonnaturalistic ethics.

Rawls, John. *A Theory of Justice.* Cambridge, Mass.: Harvard University Press, 1971. Formulation of liberal ethics.

Wiggins, David. *Needs, Values, Truth.* 2d ed. Oxford: Basil Blackwell, 1991.

Joseph Margolis

public and private morality

Over the centuries, there has been as much controversy about the meaning of the terms "public" and "private" as there has been about the nature of morality itself (see Dewey). Virtually every person who has written on the subject of morality has employed the distinction between public and private. While these terms do not have a settled meaning, the common element of most usages is that public morality is concerned with the values appropriate for the shared life of a community, especially a political community, whereas private morality is concerned with the values appropriate for the life of the individual person, including the person's FAMILY and sometimes other smaller groups. Controversy has arisen over: whether the values of one domain should be applied to the other domain; whether certain moral concepts from one domain are inappropriate for the other, such as justice in private interactions; and whether there really is, or should be, a separation between the values of these two domains.

Greek philosophers distinguished the private realm of the household from the public realm of the *polis.* The household was that domain of family and slaves where basic needs were met. The *polis* was the realm of freedom where citizens met as equals to discuss the governance of the state. The marketplace was assigned to the private domain since it also dealt with human needs. Early modern liberal theorists distinguished between the private realm of economic transactions and the public governmental sectors, virtually ignoring the household and family. Marxists differed from classical theorists by viewing economic needs as distinctively communal rather than individualistic, hence employing the term "political economy" in a way which previous theorists would have regarded as oxymoronic (see Arendt 1958).

JOHN STUART MILL (1806–1873), epitomizing the modern liberal tradition in *On Liberty* (1859), contended that "there is a sphere of action in which society, as distinguished from the individual, has, if any, only an indirect interest: comprehending all of a person's life and conduct which affects only himself, or if it also affects others, only with their free, voluntary, and undeceived consent and participation." Similarly, in contemporary American constitutional law, one of the chief tasks of law is seen as the protection of PRIVACY, understood as the sphere of RIGHTS governing the behavior that an individual engages in that does not affect anyone except other freely consenting adults. For example, the U.S. Supreme Court has affirmed the right to privacy in cases of birth control decisions, ABORTION, and other reproductive choices. In this private domain no one but the individual should be able to say what is permissible or impermissible conduct. Behavior in the private domain is subject to less constraint than is behavior conducted in public. This makes the private domain the domain of freedom between equal participants, thereby granting to the private domain those freedoms that the Greeks thought to be distinctive of the public realm of the *polis.*

Conscience and Political Affairs

When the household and marketplace are understood as private and the *polis* as public, SOCRATES

(c. 470–399 B.C.E.) is considered to be the first to suggest that the values of private life should have priority over those of the public sphere. In PLATO's (c. 430–347 B.C.E.) *Apology,* Socrates says "a man who really fights for justice must lead a private, not a public, life if he is to survive for even a short time" (32a). The person who moves in the polis must be constantly ready to make compromises; whereas the person who moves only in the household and marketplace can remain a fully principled person. Socrates remained steadfast in claiming that a person could not be truly moral by following the values of public life.

Since Socrates' time, there have been many attempts to argue that the moral values of a private person's CONSCIENCE should have priority over the public values of the group. Henry David THOREAU (1817–1862) was probably the first to provide a carefully detailed argument concerning what is today called the problem of DIRTY HANDS, that is, the problem that effective public action often requires the use of morally questionable political tactics. In "Civil Disobedience" (1849), Thoreau wrote:

> Why has every man a conscience then? I think we should be men first, and subjects afterward . . . The only obligation I have a right to assume is to do at any time what I think right . . . It is not a man's duty, as a matter of course, to devote himself to the eradication of any, even the most enormous, wrongs; he may still properly have other concerns to engage him; but it is his duty, at least, to wash his hands of it, and, if he gives it no thought longer, not to give it practically his support.

Thoreau argued that governments, and other political INSTITUTIONS, managed to get in the way of the commonsense and conscientious reflections of individuals. When involved in public projects, individuals became mere machines, losing their sense of right and wrong. As a result, individuals were blinded to the immorality of such acts as killing another person or contributing in any way to the public institutions that supported such killing. Only when individuals place their consciences clearly above the so-called COMMON GOOD will it be possible for morality to operate properly.

A similar line of argument is developed in con-temporary times for the priority of private conscience over political expediency. Some deontologists argue that politics is by its very nature a questionable moral enterprise. Insofar as politicians must use people as means, and not also as ends, the very nature of political campaigning and lobbying is rendered morally suspect. A similar line of argument is used to show that most capitalistic business practices are also morally suspect.

On the other side of the coin, Thomas HOBBES (1588–1679) is often seen as the main defender of the view that people should not let their private consciences dictate standards for political conduct. In *Leviathan* (1651), Hobbes says:

> The Conscience may be erroneous.
> Therefore, though he that is subject to no
> Civil Law, sinneth in all he does against his
> Conscience, because he has no other rule to
> follow but his own reason; yet it is not so
> with him that lives in a Common-wealth;
> because the law is the publique Conscience,
> by which he hath already undertaken to be
> guided.

In civil society, the public conscience, here understood as the decisions reached collectively through a sovereign authority, is given priority over an individual's own conscientious judgments of what is right or wrong. When individuals attempt to pass judgment on the civil law by reference to their own conscientious judgments, they undermine the ability of the sovereign to provide the peace that all seek. In addition, as the passage above indicates, the individual person is understood to have consented to be subject to the dictates of public morality, and it would be a violation of this agreement to attempt to veto the public's judgments.

Institutional Roles and Personal Values

Some philosophers contend that when an individual person assumes a public role, moral considerations change significantly. Thomas Nagel, for example, argues that if an individual

> takes on a public role, he accepts certain
> obligations, certain restrictions, and certain
> limitations on what he must do. As with any
> obligation, this step involves a risk that he

will be required to act in ways incompatible with other obligations or principles he accepts. Sometimes he will have to act anyway.

But Nagel also admits that there are "basic moral constraints" that hold against individuals as well as against institutions and people in institutions. When these constraints are violated, then "there is no substitution for refusal, and if possible, resistance."

Some other theorists have gone further in arguing that it is immoral to allow any private moral considerations to override the obligations one assumes as a member of an institution. One line of argument contends that private conscience may lead people to act in ways that destroy institutions as well as whole societies, thereby undermining the plausibility of regarding personal values as of overriding concern (see Wand's essay in French). Some have claimed, in addition, that it is immoral for people to introduce their private moral considerations into the realm of business and other nonprivate domains. Those who disregard their public role responsibilities act immorally in that they violate explicit PROMISES or implied TRUST.

Both deontologists and consequentialists have argued that the nature of institutions is such that they, and their members, must be understood to operate under different moral NORMS than exist in the private domain. John Ladd has argued that "certain facets of the organizational ideal are incompatible with the ordinary principles of [personal] morality." Organizations, he contends, have an internal rationality defined by the purposes and goals that make the organization what it is. Organizations are like games such as baseball or chess in which the rules and rationale defining the game "make the activity logically autonomous, *i.e.,* the moves, defenses and evaluations are made independently of external considerations."

Others have argued, to the contrary, that individuals in institutions should not follow different moral standards than they would in private (see May). The individual risks a kind of moral schizophrenia if different standards are applied to these two domains. In any event, it is a mistake to think that the rules of chess, for instance, set *moral* obligations on the individuals who choose to play the game. Similarly, there is no clear reason to think that the existing rules of any organization create over-

riding moral obligations. In addition, those who simply follow institutional rules and fail to exercise independent moral judgment will not have the resources to help steer their institution or society away from the kind of harmful conduct that will tarnish its reputation or risk its destruction.

Challenging the Dichotomy

There are two important challenges to the dichotomy between public and private morality. One view contends that the distinction makes sense only when applied to specific moral categories rather than the whole of morality. Some have argued that justice, for instance, has no place in the private sphere and might even be destructive of private relationships. ARISTOTLE (384–322 B.C.E.) claims that "when men are friends they have no need of justice" (1155a25). And David HUME (1711–1776), in *An Enquiry Concerning the Principles of Morals* (1751), voices one of the most common views of the public nature of justice when he remarks that "the case of families approaches" "such enlarged affections" as to render PROPERTY and justice useless. Hume seems also to think that relations among married persons constitute a domain where justice will not serve a useful purpose because of the strength of the "cement of friendship." And later he argues that the nature of FRIENDSHIP is such that one of its central ingredients, trust, would be destroyed by the application of principles of justice. Critics allege that such claims are based on a naive understanding of the convergence of interests within families, between spouses, and among friends.

Feminist philosophers have recently argued that the very distinction between public and private should be abandoned. It has become common for feminists to argue that the distinction has been used to defend such actions as RAPE and battery in the private sphere of the family and intimate relationships, even though no one would regard these as justified if conducted in the supposedly public sphere of the street (see Nicholson). Feminists contend that the public-private distinction has been exploited for patriarchal political purposes, justifying institutions such as the traditional family and marriage that force women to remain in subordinate status to men and that would not be tolerated in the public space of free men (see Elshtain). Similarly, some continental theorists, most notably postmodernists, contend that the distinction operates to marginalize all those who have not traditionally been well- accepted in the public domain (see Schurmann 1989). Such critiques throw into question the value of maintaining the distinction between public and private morality.

See also: ABORTION; BLACKMAIL; CARE; CIVIL DISOBEDIENCE; CIVIL RIGHTS AND CIVIC DUTIES; COLLECTIVE RESPONSIBILITY; COMMON GOOD; CONSENT; CONVENTIONS; DIRTY HANDS; ETIQUETTE; FAMILY; FEMINIST ETHICS; FRIENDSHIP; GOVERNMENT, ETHICS IN; IMPARTIALITY; INDIVIDUALISM; INSTITUTIONS; MACHIAVELLI; MORAL COMMUNITY, BOUNDARIES OF; PARTIALITY; PATERNALISM; PERSONAL RELATIONSHIPS; PRIVACY; PROFESSIONAL ETHICS; PUBLIC GOODS; RAPE; SELF AND SOCIAL SELF; SEXUAL ABUSE AND HARASSMENT; SEXUALITY AND SEXUAL ETHICS; SOCIAL AND POLITICAL PHILOSOPHY; TRUST; VIRTUE ETHICS.

Bibliography

Arendt, Hannah. *The Human Condition.* Chicago: University of Chicago Press, 1958. See chapter 2.

Aristotle. "Nicomachean Ethics." Translated by W. D. Ross. In *The Basic Works of Aristotle,* edited by Richard McKeon. New York: Random House, 1941. See book VIII.

Dean, Jodi. *Solidarity of Strangers.* Berkeley: University of California Press, 1996.

Dewey, John. *The Public and the Private.* Athens, OH: Ohio University Press, 1980 [1927]. See especially part 1.

Elshtain, Jean Bethke. *Public Man, Private Woman.* Princeton, NJ: Princeton University Press, 1981.

French, Peter A., ed. *Conscientious Actions: The Revelations of the Pentagon Papers.* Cambridge, MA: Schenkman, 1974. See especially the articles by Fotion and Wand.

Greenawalt, Kent. *Private Consciences and Public Reasons.* Oxford: Oxford University Press, 1995.

Habermas, Jürgen. *Moral Consciousness and Communicative Action.* Cambridge, MA: MIT Press, 1990.

Hobbes, Thomas. *Leviathan.* Edited by C. B. Macpherson. New York: Penguin, 1968 [1651]. See especially chapter 29.

Hume, David. *An Enquiry Concerning the Principles of Morals,* Section iii; p. 22. Edited by J. B. Schneewind. Indianapolis, IN: Hackett, 1983 [1751].

Ladd, John. "Morality and the Ideal of Rationality in Formal Organizations." *Monist* 54 (1970): 488–516.

May, Larry. *The Morality of Groups.* Notre Dame, IN: University of Notre Dame Press, 1987.

Mill, John Stuart. *On Liberty.* Edited by Elizabeth Rapaport. Indianapolis, IN: Hackett, 1978 [1859]. See especially chapter 1.

Nagel, Thomas. "Ruthlessness in Public Life." In *Public and Private Morality,* edited by Stuart Hampshire, 89–90. Cambridge: Cambridge University Press, 1978.

Nicholson, Linda. *Gender and History: The Limits of Social Theory in the Age of the Family.* New York: Columbia University Press, 1986. See especially the Introduction.

Plato. "The Apology." In *The Trial and Death of Socrates,* translated by G. M. A. Grube. Indianapolis, IN: Hackett, 1975. See 32a.

Sandel, Michael. *Democracy's Discontent: America in Search of a Public Philosophy.* Cambridge, MA: Harvard University Press, 1996.

Schurmann, Reiner, ed. *The Public Realm: Essays on Discursive Types in Political Philosophy.* Albany: State University of New York Press, 1989. See especially part 3.

Thoreau, Henry David. "Civil Disobedience." In *The Portable Thoreau,* edited by Carl Bode. New York: Viking, 1964 [1849]. For "dirty hands," see pp. 11, 17.

Larry May

public goods

Public goods are those exhibiting common availability. Attempts to make the notion of "common availability" more precise have resulted in diverging definitions; but these have usually involved some subset of the following seven features:

Jointness in supply: if a public good is available to one member of the group for which it is public, then it is freely available to each other member.

Nonexcludability: if anyone is enjoying the good, no one else can be prevented from freely enjoying it without excessive cost to the would-be excluders.

Jointness in consumption: one person's consumption of the good does not diminish the amount available for consumption by anyone else.

Nonrivalness: one person's enjoyment of the good does not diminish the benefits available to anyone else from its enjoyment.

Compulsoriness: if anyone receives the good, no-one else can avoid doing so without excessive cost.

Equality: if anyone receives the good, everyone receives the same amount.

Indivisibility: there can be more than one consumer of the good, and each consumes the total output.

There are entailments between members of this list; but, on the most straightforward reading of them, no two are equivalent. (Thus jointness in supply can be read as entailing nonexcludability, and indivisibility entails jointness in consumption; but the reverse entailments do not hold.) We can see the list as generated by four main questions:

1. Can "free riders" take the good without paying?
2. Does my enjoying the good prevent others from doing so?
3. Have we a choice whether to receive the good?
4. Is it the case that either everyone enjoys the good or no-one does?

Just which combination of features we take to define our conception of a public good depends on which of these questions we are interested in. In what follows, three main problems concerning public goods are distinguished, together with the different conceptions of public goods relevant to them.

First, there is the economist's problem: how can we construct mechanisms for efficiently producing such public goods as defence, a clean environment, traffic regulation, and public health? There are two issues here, and a different sort of publicity is relevant to each. One issue concerns how to describe precisely the conditions under which such goods count as efficiently produced. What makes this a challenge is the unusual consumption characteristics of such goods (labelled "indivisibility" above)—total consumption equals the consumption of each individual rather than the sum of individual consumptions. The other issue, once these conditions are described, is how to construct a mechanism for achieving them. And what makes this issue a problem is a different feature of such goods: their jointness in supply. For goods in joint supply, would-be consumers have an incentive to understate their willingness to pay, and this will result in the failure of a market to provide a mechanism for efficient production. The obvious alternative mechanism is to produce such goods by levying taxes. However, it remains the case that a particular proposal to produce

them at a given level of output and a given cost can be evaluated for efficiency only if we can accurately determine consumers' true preferences: the outstanding economic problem concerns how to do this.

Indivisibility and jointness in supply are independent. (Private viewings of a painting, for example, involve indivisibility but not jointness in supply.) So for the economist's purposes, public goods are best defined as those with both these features. (Notice, however, that, since economic models assume a perfectly calculating self-interest, their results can only approximate the behaviour of people motivated as we actually are. Many people's motivation to pay for a good is affected not only by question 1 but by questions 2 through 4 as well. If so, answering the real-world question concerning the conditions under which certain public goods can be produced will require us to consider to what extent those goods possess each of the seven features identified above.)

To see moral philosophy's interest in public goods, we should turn to a second problem. Under many conditions, goods in joint supply can be such that the failure of a group to cooperate to produce them may be collectively, but not individually, suboptimal from the point of view of self-interest: that is, there can exist a failure to cooperate, without any individual's acting suboptimally from that point of view, even though each individual is self-interested and is worse off without the good than he or she would be paying and getting it. GAME THEORY seeks to spell out the conditions under which this "problem of collective goods" arises. Usually, the problem will centre around questions 1 and 4. If the good is likely to be produced by others, it will be in my INTERESTS to take it without paying; if not, it will be in my interests not to waste my resources paying for a good that will not be produced. But if everyone reasons in this way, no one enjoys the good, even though each would be better off paying and getting it. Clearly, this structure is at the heart of the economist's problem; but it is not itself a problem about mechanisms for efficiently producing such goods. The relevant conception of publicity here is simply that of jointness in supply.

Moral philosophy's interest in the problem of collective goods can be said to have begun with HOBBES (1588–1679), who was the first to give sharp expression to the thought that civil order itself is a collective good for which this problem arises. Moreover, the problem of collective goods is only an instance of a broader one concerning cooperation generally. A failure to cooperate may be collectively, but not individually, suboptimal from the point of view of self-interest when the goods at stake are to be enjoyed privately by each cooperator as well as when they are public. Broadly speaking, this leads moral philosophers to two kinds of questions. One concerns what this problem reveals about the nature of practical rationality. Does it generate an objection to conceiving of rationality in terms of optimizing individual self-interest? It has been argued that the problem shows that, in suitable social circumstances, rationality requires me to optimize not my own interests but those of the group, or that it requires me to constrain my disposition to optimize my own interests by adopting overriding dispositions to cooperate. Thus, it is argued, the requirements of practical rationality coincide with those of morality. The other question concerns whether this problem sheds light on the evolution and, more ambitiously, the point of moral dispositions. Given the advantage to each individual of living in a community of cooperators, this suggests an explanation of the evolution of cooperative dispositions in humans. And if so, perhaps we can draw conclusions concerning the purpose or point of morality, just as we can draw conclusions concerning the function of other adaptations from evolutionary explanations of them.

Our first two problems concerning public goods have focused on questions 1 and 4. With a third problem, questions 1, 2, and 3 become central. This is a specific issue in normative moral philosophy: when is it morally wrong not to pay for goods one enjoys? Most of us think this holds at least of paradigm cases of "free riding," in which individuals help themselves without paying to goods that are available to them only through others' willingness to pay—evading the fares on public transport, for example. A common thought is that this is unfair. But if so, we should be able to say what makes it unfair. There are two questions here: exactly which class of cases exhibits this kind of unfairness; and why should they be thought unfair? Significantly, the complaint of unfairness does not seem to be met by the free rider's insisting that he does not harm anyone else. A satisfactory account of the free rider's unfairness, it seems, must show how action that harms no one can be unfair. Our pair of questions

becomes, under what conditions is it unfair to refuse to pay for nonrival goods that one enjoys, and why?

The answer to this is potentially very important. Among contemporary discussions, a central issue has been whether question 3 governs the obligation to pay for benefits: can I not fairly refuse to pay for *compulsory* goods? It can seem right to say this. It is surely wrong to hold that when benefits are forced on me, I am obligated to pay for them provided only that the institution producing them is justly structured. Nonetheless, several writers have argued that under some conditions there is an obligation to pay for compulsory goods. And if so, then perhaps this argument can ground political obligations to contribute toward certain public goods by recognizing the AUTHORITY of the state. Notice, however, that anyone arguing for such obligations is likely to be seeking the conclusion not simply that it is unfair not to contribute toward sustaining the state, but, more strongly, that individuals may rightly be *coerced* into contributing.

See also: BAIER; BIOLOGICAL THEORY; COERCION; COLLECTIVE RESPONSIBILITY; COMMON GOOD; COMMUNITARIANISM; COOPERATION, CONFLICT, AND COORDINATION; DUTY AND OBLIGATION; ECONOMIC ANALYSIS; EXPLOITATION; FAIRNESS; GAME THEORY; HOBBES; INTERESTS; MATERIALISM; MORAL RULES; NEEDS; PRACTICAL REASON[ING]; PUBLIC HEALTH POLICY; PUBLIC POLICY; RATIONAL CHOICE; RATIONALITY VS. REASONABLENESS; RECIPROCITY.

Bibliography

Axelrod, Robert. *The Evolution of Cooperation.* New York: Basic Books, 1984. An explanation of the strategic dynamics leading to the emergence of cooperation out of an initial situation of noncooperation.

Cowen, Tyler, ed. *Public Goods and Market Failures: A Critical Examination.* New Brunswick: Transaction Publishers, 1992. Anthology of major work on the economic public goods problem.

Cullity, Garrett. "Moral Free Riding." *Philosophy and Public Affairs* 24 (1995): 3–34. Presents an account of the nature and extent of the unfairness of free riding; gives sources for the seven kinds of publicity identified above.

Gauthier, David. *Morals by Agreement.* Oxford: Clarendon Press, 1986. Argues that rationality requires constraining the disposition to optimize self-interest by adopting overriding dispositions to cooperate.

Hampton, Jean. "Free-Rider Problems in the Production of Collective Goods." *Economics and Philosophy* 3

(1987): 245–73. Distinguishes the variety of strategic situations that can yield a game-theoretic problem of collective goods.

Hart, H. L. A. "Are There Any Natural Rights?" *Philosophical Review* 64 (1955): 175–91. Advocates as a source of political obligation a principle of "mutuality of restrictions" (p. 185) according to which those who restrict their liberty in a joint enterprise have a right to a similar restriction on those who benefit.

Nozick, Robert. *Anarchy, State, and Utopia.* New York: Basic Books, 1974. Contains an influential attack (pp. 90–95) on the view that there can be obligations to pay for compulsory goods.

Olson, Mancur. *The Logic of Collective Action.* Cambridge: Harvard University Press, 1965. Prominent study of the conditions under which failures to produce public goods will occur, correlating these conditions with group size.

Simmons, A. John. "The Principle of Fair Play." *Philosophy and Public Affairs* 8 (1979): 307–37. Discussion of the use of Hart's principle to ground political obligations.

Taylor, Michael. *The Possibility of Cooperation.* New York: Cambridge University Press, 1987. Game-theoretic critique of the view that the failure of rational agents to cooperate in the production of public goods, or in collective action more generally, justifies the coercive authority of the state.

Trivers, Robert. *Social Evolution.* Menlo Park, Calif.: Benjamin Cummins, 1985. Chapter 15 gives an influential sociobiological account of the evolution of moral dispositions.

Garrett Cullity

public health policy

Traditionally, "public health" applies only to programs and institutions aimed at protecting or improving the collective health status of the public, in contrast to services that deliver specific benefits to individuals, as in acute medical care. This distinction is difficult to maintain on examination. For example, because access to personal medical services has an impact on public health, public health policy is properly concerned with the financing and distribution of medical services.

Public health policy during the twentieth century has had a profound effect on the level and distribution of well-being. Improvements in the quality of the water supply, nutrition, and sanitation, as well as mass vaccination programs, have dramatically reduced morbidity and mortality from infectious diseases all around the world. Together with family planning measures that have lowered fertility, reducing early death has led to the aging of populations in both developed and developing societies. More recently, public health policies have focused on chronic, degenerative diseases through the regulation of environmental pollution, workplace hazards, and the safety of food, drugs, and consumer products as well as through educational programs aimed at "lifestyle" choices. This progress has been fueled by epidemiological, behavioral, biomedical, and other health-related research. Recent research on the social determinants of health inequalities suggest a profound contribution to population health and its distribution from such factors as the degree of economic and social equality and the effects of racism and gender bias. These factors argue for an expanded, intersectoral public health policy.

Justification and Distributive Justice

Justifying public health policy depends on knowing whether protecting public health is a requirement of justice or merely a matter of serving the public interest. Some libertarian commentators argue that disease and disability are matters of misfortune, not unfairness, and that no one has an obligation, except perhaps an imperfect duty of CHARITY, to contribute to improving the health of others. Even on this view, some public health policies that prevent people from harming the health of others (*e.g.*, environmental regulations or quarantine) count as requirements of justice because they simply enforce RIGHTS to the security of persons and PROPERTY. Similarly, many agree that government is obliged to support public health policies that secure PUBLIC GOODS, like clean air or "herd" immunity from contagious disease through vaccination, since "free riders" make it difficult to obtain such goods through private market mechanisms.

Showing that justice requires more comprehensive public health policies needs an appeal to more robust principles of justice, including welfare rights. Some utilitarians claim that meeting basic health care needs will in general maximize utility, and this result would be sufficient to justify many existing public health policies. Whether this argument yields genuine rights to certain forms of health care is a matter of dispute even among utilitarians. Other commentators conclude that rights to basic health care must be recognized since the absence of disease or disability is a prerequisite for exercising basic liberties, but this line of argument may only yield negative rights to noninterference with one's health. Another line of argument turns on the fact that disease and disability impair opportunity: if society is obliged to take positive steps to protect equality of opportunity, then it will be obliged to pursue public health policies that effectively protect opportunity.

Other issues of distributive justice concern the scope and limits of public health policies. Many people agree that society ought to guarantee a "decent basic minimum" of health care services, but there is little agreement about what that minimum includes. Similarly, some argue that individuals should bear the burden of health costs produced by their own lifestyle choices, but, aside from educational efforts, public health policy ignores this issue of RESPONSIBILITY for health. Social obligations are also constrained by resource limitations: how much is too much to spend on reducing the risk of DEATH or disease? In the context of rapidly rising medical costs, public health policy will have to be guided by acceptable principles for rationing beneficial medical services. Obligations to protect health care are also constrained by concerns about autonomy and PATERNALISM. Public health policy calls for reducing risks to health in the workplace to the level that it is "technologically feasible" to do so, but this obligation means rejecting a mechanism widely used in other contexts for distributing the benefits and burdens of risk taking, namely informed CONSENT. This policy can be justified if the range of choices open to typical workers is part of an unjust distribution of opportunities, undercutting the possibility of meaningful consent. Without such a justification, it may seem as though the government is valuing individual health more highly than it is valued by the individuals it is protecting. Individuals vary in their susceptibility to health risks. Should those at higher risk be made to accept the burdens of their risks? Or should the costs of risk protection be shared as widely as possible? This issue of distributive justice underlies concerns that employer testing and screening programs may penalize certain workers capable of performing the jobs, and it underlies objections to testing for AIDS (acquired immune deficiency syndrome) or its underlying virus, human immunodeficiency virus (HIV), for purposes of health insurance underwriting.

Liberty and Morals

Protecting the public health sometimes conflicts with individual rights to LIBERTY, PRIVACY, and confidentiality. For example, understanding the epidemiology of a disease like AIDS requires accurate information about its incidence and the exposure patterns of the population to HIV. But acquiring this information through mandatory testing or screening may compromise the confidentiality of medical records and can lead to DISCRIMINATION. Though privacy rights and individual liberties are not inviolable when harms to others are involved, public health policy generally permits such measures only when demonstrable health benefits can be achieved in no less intrusive ways.

Sometimes effective public health policy conflicts with the moral values of some groups. For example, explicit sexual education of children is necessary if young people are to understand how to prevent the transmission of AIDS, but such explicit education is thought by some to condone immoral practices. Public health policy thus confronts a central problem in political LIBERALISM: how to protect public health while respecting diversity in a pluralist society.

See also: ABORTION; AGENCY AND DISABILITY; BIOETHICS; CHILDREN AND ETHICAL THEORY; COMMON GOOD; CONSENT; CONTRACTARIANISM; EUTHANASIA; FAMILY; GENETIC ENGINEERING; HUMAN RIGHTS; INTERESTS; JUSTICE, DISTRIBUTIVE; KILLING AND LETTING DIE; LIBERALISM; LIBERTARIANISM; LIBERTY; MEDICAL ETHICS; NEEDS; PATERNALISM; PRIVACY; PUBLIC GOODS; PUBLIC POLICY; REPRODUCTIVE TECHNOLOGIES; RIGHTS; UTILITARIANISM; WELFARE RIGHTS AND SOCIAL POLICY.

Bibliography

Buchanan, Allen E. "Justice: A Philosophical Review." In *Justice and Health Care,* edited by E. Shelp, pp. 3–21. Dordrecht: Reidel, 1983. Surveys the implications of contractarian, libertarian, and utilitarian theories of justice for access to medical services.

Daniels, Norman. *Just Health Care.* Cambridge: Cambridge University Press, 1985. A theory of justice for medical and other forms of health care.

Engelhardt, Tristram. *Foundations of Bioethics.* Oxford: Oxford University Press, 1986. Justice from a libertarian perspective.

President's Commission for the Study of Ethical Problems in Medicine and Biomedical and Behavioral Research.

Securing Access to Health Care: The Ethical Implications of Differences in the Availability of Health Services. 3 vols. Washington, D.C.: GPO, 1983. Vol. 1 is the report; vol. 2 contains articles on the foundations for health policy by the following philosophers: Daniel Brock, Allen Buchanan, Norman Daniels, David Gauthier, Allan Gibbard, and Amy Gutmann.

Norman Daniels

public policy

The public turn in ethics during the last four decades of the twentieth century liberated English-language moral philosophy from its narrow preoccupation with logical positivism and linguistic analysis during the 1930s, 1940s, and 1950s. Philosophers returned to the great issues about the relation of individual and society that had always occupied the best philosophers, from SOCRATES (c.470–399 B.C.E.) to John DEWEY (1859–1952) and Bertrand RUSSELL (1872–1970). This gradual return to substantive issues was driven by both philosophical and political forces, as is perhaps appropriate for a method that encourages movement in both directions between ethics and events.

Within logic and epistemology, by the early 1960s the central positivist dogma that it was both possible and important to classify every true statement dichotomously as either true independently of experience or true because of experience—the analytic/synthetic distinction—had been decisively undermined. Moral philosophers, like other philosophers, no longer assumed that an interest in concrete events was beneath their dignity, and outside their competence, as philosophers. This assumption had earlier required that philosophers restrict themselves exclusively to logic and meaning and leave evidence to scientists. Philosophers in all fields, including ethics, began the reintegration into their arguments of appeals to the evidence of events as well as appeals to the meaning of concepts. This restoration of empirical elements to moral arguments permitted analysis of concrete public policies.

In the United States, in the early 1960s, violent and disturbing events pressed irresistibly from the outside against the artificial walls that were simultaneously being undermined from inside by the critique of the analytic/synthetic distinction. Three specific streams of events forced reconsideration of the questions about the moral obligations, if any, to obey the laws of society that Socrates had raised in PLATO's (c. 430–347 B.C.E.) *Crito*. First, during the mid-1950s, a grassroots movement by African Americans against racist laws in the South was met with brutal violence; the movement responded to the leadership of Martin Luther KING Jr. (1929–1968), and his strategy of non-violent CIVIL DISOBEDIENCE. Second, during October 1962, the leaders of the world's two superpowers knowingly took humanity to the brink of nuclear war during the Cuban missile crisis. Third, the John F. Kennedy (1917–1963) administration introduced American troops into a war in Vietnam. Deep debates raged about the substance of these three issues—civil rights, nuclear deterrence, and foreign military intervention—and about the moral limits on state POWER and the moral limits on the resistance by citizens to what they judged to be immoral laws and policies. On December 27, 1961, the annual meeting of the Eastern Division of the American Philosophical Association sponsored a symposium on "Political Obligation and Civil Disobedience." This symposium signaled that the public turn in contemporary ethics was firmly underway.

In 1971, the establishment of the journal *Philosophy and Public Affairs* gave added respectability to by-then vigorous discussions; five of its first ten articles concerned the morality of war. Then, disturbed by disasters like the famine in 1971 in what is now Bangladesh, philosophers added world hunger and international justice to the list of international questions to be subjected to philosophical analysis. In the mid-1970s political initiatives to constrain foreign policy by respect for HUMAN RIGHTS, which were themselves primarily motivated by moral revulsion against the Vietnam intervention and the alliance with dictatorships in Chile and South Korea, put questions about universal human rights and international law back on the philosophical agenda.

Attention to violations of civil rights had meanwhile evolved into debates about proposed legal remedies like affirmative action, and attention turned to DISCRIMINATION on the basis of sex as well as race. Exclusive concern with the rights of adult humans widened to include questions about responsibilities, if any, toward unborn fetuses (the issues of the legality and morality of ABORTION), toward animals, and toward the natural environment generally. On some issues, such as abortion, philosophical discussion has had little effect on the public debates; on other issues, such as animal liberation, philosophers have had profound influence. On almost all topics, however, attention to the complexities of public policy has reinvigorated and enriched the field of ethics.

In particular, since the ethics of public policy is the ethics of cases that are nonideal—that is, cases that contain disagreements over principles, violations of principles, uncertainties about consequences, fraught histories, mixed MOTIVES, and inadequate INSTITUTIONS—philosophers who pursue it well both inform themselves about matters outside philosophy and collaborate with specialists who understand the other relevant subjects. The principles formulated in this field must be intermediate and synthetic: intermediate between abstract theory and concrete case, and synthetic of conceptual and empirical considerations. Such principles can be formulated not by the mechanical application of completed theory to fixed instance but by doing philosophy in a way that can modify the understanding of both theory and instance.

See also: ABORTION; ANIMALS, TREATMENT OF; APPLIED ETHICS; BARRY; CASUISTRY; CIVIL DISOBEDIENCE; CIVIL RIGHTS AND CIVIC DUTIES; CONVENTIONS; DETERRENCE, THREATS, AND RETALIATION; DISCRIMINATION; DWORKIN; ENVIRONMENTAL ETHICS; EQUALITY; FAMILY; FEMINIST ETHICS; FUTURE GENERATIONS; GAY ETHICS; GOVERNMENT, ETHICS IN; HOMOSEXUALITY; HUMAN RIGHTS; INEQUALITY; INSTITUTIONS; INTERNATIONAL JUSTICE [entries]; KING; LESBIAN ETHICS; MASS MEDIA; NUCLEAR ETHICS; OBEDIENCE TO LAW; POLITICAL SYSTEMS; PUBLIC AND PRIVATE MORALITY; PUBLIC HEALTH POLICY; PUBLIC POLICY ANALYSIS; RAWLS; RIGHT HOLDERS; RIGHTS; RISK ANALYSIS; RUSSELL; SOCIAL AND POLITICAL PHILOSOPHY; THEORY AND PRACTICE; WALZER; WAR AND PEACE; WELFARE RIGHTS AND SOCIAL POLICY.

Bibliography

Barry, Brian. "Editorial." *Ethics* 90 (1980): 317–18.

———. *Political Argument.* 2d ed. New York: Humanities Press, 1990 [1965].

Bedau, Hugo Adam, ed. *Civil Disobedience: Theory and Practice.* New York: Pegasus, 1969. See especially "Letter from Birmingham City Jail" by Martin Luther King Jr. (1963); "The Justification of Civil Disobedience" by John Rawls (1966); and "Civil Disobedience and the Threat of Nuclear War" by Bertrand Russell (1963).

———. "On Civil Disobedience." *Journal of Philosophy* 58 (October 1961): 653–65.

Beitz, Charles R. *Political Theory and International Relations.* 2d ed. Princeton, NJ: Princeton University Press, 1999 [1979].

Bok, Sissela. *Lying: Moral Choice in Public and Private Life.* New York: Pantheon, 1978.

Brown, Peter G., and Douglas MacLean, eds. *Human Rights and U.S. Foreign Policy: Principles and Applications.* Lexington, MA: Lexington Books, 1979.

Brown, Peter G., and Henry Shue, eds. *Food Policy: The Responsibility of the United States in the Life and Death Choices.* New York: Free Press, 1977.

Dworkin, Ronald. *Taking Rights Seriously.* Cambridge: Harvard University Press, 1977.

Fullinwider, Robert K. *The Reverse Discrimination Controversy: A Moral and Legal Analysis.* Savage, MD: Rowman and Littlefield, 1980.

Goodin, Robert E. *Political Theory and Public Policy.* Chicago: University of Chicago Press, 1982.

Held, Virginia. *Rights and Goods: Justifying Social Action.* New York: Free Press, 1984.

———, Kai Nielsen, and Charles Parsons, eds. *Philosophy and Public Action.* New York: Oxford University Press, 1972.

Kavka, Gregory S. *Moral Paradoxes of Nuclear Deterrence.* New York: Cambridge University Press, 1987. See pp. 15–32. Also see his article, "Some Paradoxes of Deterrence" (originally published in *Journal of Philosophy* 75 [June 1978]: 285–302).

Nickel, James W. "Is There a Human Right to Employment?" *Philosophical Forum* 10 (1978–79): 149–70.

———. *Making Sense of Human Rights: Philosophical Reflections on the Universal Declaration of Human Rights.* Berkeley: University of California Press, 1987.

Ruddick, William. "Philosophy and Public Affairs." *Social Research* 47, no. 4 (Winter 1980): 734–48.

Sagoff, Mark. *The Economy of the Earth: Philosophy, Law, and the Environment.* New York: Cambridge University Press, 1988.

Shue, Henry. *Basic Rights: Subsistence, Affluence, and U.S. Foreign Policy.* 2d ed. Princeton: Princeton University Press, 1996 [1980].

Singer, Peter. *Animal Liberation.* 2d ed. New York: New York Review, 1990 [1975].

———. "Famine, Affluence, and Morality." *Philosophy & Public Affairs* 1 (Spring 1972): 229–43.

———. "Philosophers Are Back on the Job." *New York Times Magazine,* 7 July 1974, 6–7; 17–20.

Thompson, Dennis. "Philosophy and Policy." *Philosophy & Public Affairs* 14 (Spring 1985): 205–18.

Walzer, Michael. *Just and Unjust Wars: A Moral Argument with Historical Illustrations.* 2d ed. New York: Basic Books, 1992 [1977].

———. *Obligations: Essays on Disobedience, War, and Citizenship.* Cambridge: Harvard University Press, 1970. See especially "The Obligation to Disobey" (1967).

Wasserstrom, Richard A. "The Obligation to Obey the Law." *U.C.L.A. Law Review* 10 (May 1963): 790–97.

———, ed. *War and Morality.* Belmont, CA: Wadsworth, 1970. Includes most of his "On the Morality of War: A Preliminary Inquiry" (1969).

Henry Shue

public policy analysis

The term "policy analysis" may refer to any thoughtful discussion of issues of PUBLIC POLICY, but, in a more technical sense, it comprises (1) political analysis; (2) means-ends analysis; (3) ethical analysis; and (4) ECONOMIC ANALYSIS. A full consideration of a particular public policy proposal may include all four kinds of policy analysis. Policy analyses typically take the form of advice given to the appropriate political or legal authorities. Policy analyses may be contrasted, then, with institutional and legal analyses, which inquire into the legitimate processes and structures of decision making, that is, who should decide rather than what they should do.

Political analysis is largely the work of consultants who rely on polling data, focus groups, and other opinion research to predict how well different proposals will appeal to the public and "play" to particular constituencies. This kind of analysis also investigates strategies for advancing a policy agenda through legislatures, bureaucracies, and other decision making bodies. Political analysis does not as a rule discuss the merits of or evaluate alternative policy proposals. Rather, it asks if the relevant constituencies can be marshaled in support of a given proposal, how opposing groups can be contained, and how the legal and political apparatus can be manipulated on its behalf. As a result of political analysis, proposals may be "repackaged" or even softened or changed to gain broader acceptance.

Political analysts often suggest ways to bring together groups that may have little in common to support particular policies, for example, the religious right and liberal environmental groups in favoring measures to implement the Endangered Species Act. These analysts may also point to methods—setting up an independent "base-closing" commission, for example—for getting proposals implemented that would be stymied in the usual processes of interest-group politics.

Means-ends analysis constitutes the stock-in-trade of policy think tanks. The analyst evaluates how well a policy or program—often in comparison with an alternative proposal—accomplishes its intended ends. This kind of policy analysis requires careful sociological research into the consequences of particular initiatives. How well did needle-exchange programs work in slowing the spread of AIDS? Do welfare-to-work programs succeed in helping participants hold jobs? Do charter schools improve student performance? How well have job-training programs done in providing high school dropouts with technical skills? To answer these basically empirical questions, the analyst must often assemble data and interpret statistical evidence. In this research, the analyst takes the objective as a given, for example, the goal of reducing air pollution to legislated levels. The analyst then evaluates how well the agency, in this case the Environmental Protection Agency, accomplished the goal. The analysis ends with a report card—for example, a measurement of progress under the Clean Air Act and a discussion of whether or how the agency could have done better at less public and private expense.

Policy analysis of this sort reasons not about ends but only about means to achieve those ends. Critics of governmental programs often use this kind of analysis to demonstrate how expensive public programs can be. The analyst may divide the costs of a program by the results to conclude, for example, that the Fish and Wildlife Service spent hundreds of dollars for each salmon it protected in an area of the Northwest. Critics also use this sort of analysis to display the unintended and sometimes counterproductive consequences of particular policies. It is often said, for example, that by making narcotics illegal, the government encourages a black market, thereby increasing crime. On the other hand, the same kind of analysis may be used to support policies, for example, by showing the success of the "negative income tax" in getting working families out of poverty.

Recently, analysts have emphasized the importance of choosing the right kind of agency to carry out public programs or resolve public controversies. For example, if one asks how a city like Albany can provide housing for the homeless, the answer might be for the municipal government not to create a bureaucracy for the purpose but to contract with the Salvation Army. Analysts have drawn from the private sector conceptions of outsourcing, benchmarking, decentralization, accountability, task forces, and so on and suggested that similar innovations could streamline government. The resulting interest in the public use of civic society—greater reliance on "stakeholder" negotiations, nonprofit organizations, and quasi-public trustee and other *ad hoc* oversight arrangements—has led to some of the most exciting work in policy analysis and political theory today.

Ethical (or normative) analysis concerns the moral appropriateness of the goals of public policy and of the means used to achieve those goals. It takes up questions in political theory such as the extent to which the government is responsible for redistributing wealth among its citizens, for providing EQUALITY of opportunity, or merely for maintaining public safety. Questions in MEDICAL ETHICS, such as those involving cloning, ABORTION, and fetal research, receive a lot of attention, as, of course, do ethical questions central to affirmative action, protections against DISCRIMINATION and harassment, CAPITAL PUNISHMENT, the rights of convicted criminals and suspects, and so on. Ethical analysis typically does not lay down *a priori* conceptions of the goals of our society but infers them from legislation, constitutional and legal analysis, social and cultural history, and the shared moral intuitions of members of society. It marshals these shared values and widely recognized principles into an argument for or against particular proposals, evaluating policies in relation to their underlying goals and principles, often with less attention to their actual outcomes.

Opposing ethical analyses often reflect fundamental disagreements about the appropriate ends of social policy and of the limits of public RESPONSIBILITY for the well-being and behavior of citizens. Perennial debates arise over issues of social equality (for example, public obligations to close the gap between rich and poor), and over PATERNALISM (for example, the prosecution of "victimless" crimes). These discussions exemplify policy—not just ethical—analysis insofar as they address specific programs actually in place or under consideration by legislatures or regulatory agencies. The point of ethical or normative analysis is to weigh these proposals against principles, shared intuitions, and common values associated with various and sometimes competing conceptions of the good society.

Economic analysis covers two altogether different sorts of inquiry. First, macroeconomic analysis seeks to determine the consequences of particular policies on standard economic indicators, such as economic growth, inflation, unemployment, interest rates, the balance of trade, and so on. A typical question for macroeconomic policy analysis would be whether the North American Free Trade Agreement will increase unemployment in the United States. Years ago, macroeconomists reached a fair degree of consensus on such questions as the costs and inflationary effects of environmental regulation. Information of this sort is helpful to policy makers, although often it depends on complex econometric models the nature of which only experts understand.

Second, microeconomic or COST-BENEFIT ANALYSIS offers an approach to policy analysis entirely different from those discussed so far. On this now standard microeconomic approach, public policy and therefore policy analysis seeks to satisfy the preferences of individuals, taken as they come, ranked by the amounts those individuals are willing to pay to satisfy them. Edith Stokey and Richard Zeckhauser, in their influential *Primer for Policy Analysis* (1978), lay out the fundamental assumptions of this method. First, "the purpose of public decisions is to promote the welfare of society." They add that "the welfare levels of the individual members of society are the building blocks for the welfare of society." The measure of these "welfare levels" is found in the amounts individuals are willing to pay to satisfy their preferences. "In the United States we usually take the position that it is the individual's own preferences that count, that he is the best judge of his own welfare."

What is crucial about cost-benefit policy analysis is that it answers the crucial moral and political questions in advance and on A PRIORI grounds. The goal of our society, namely, welfare maximization, is already certain, because it is derived *a priori* from a theory of collective choice, *i.e.,* welfare economic theory, on which this kind of policy analysis is based. On this view, a perfect market in which individuals buy goods and services to maximize their own well-being offers the best method of dealing with environmental, health, education, and other policy concerns. Since such a perfectly competitive market does not exist—since market failure is ubiquitous, especially where environmental goods are concerned—economists trained in the methods of cost-benefit analysis must inform society how to manage resources by centralized methods of efficient allocation.

To determine how a perfectly competitive market

would have allocated resources but for "externalities," PUBLIC GOODS, "transaction costs," "isolation paradoxes," and other sources of market failure, regulatory agencies are to consult economists trained in the art and science of estimating what people are willing to pay for various goods and services. These experts must then use their science to determine how society is to allocate resources to maximize the satisfaction of individuals' preferences. This immense task is often complicated because different sides in political controversies—environmental groups and business groups, for example—may hire their own economists who provide opposing (or "dueling") cost-benefit analyses. There seems to be no agreed upon way to settle disputes of this kind.

To summarize: policy analysis involves both empirical and normative elements. Analysts of an empirical bent examine the consequences of various policies and ways of implementing them—consequences measured against the goals of those programs or against a variety of well-known indicators of economic performance, such as inflation and employment. Analysts whose interests are more normative may look into our social and cultural history, into our shared moral intuitions, or into principles of DEMOCRACY and human equality to understand the legitimate purposes of public policy. Ethical analysis thus deliberates over ends and the conceptual relation to those ends of the means used to achieve them.

In contrast to these other approaches, the cost-benefit or microeconomic approach to policy analysis derives the end of public policy—welfare maximization—from its own theory and then advocates this goal as the rational purpose of collective choice. In this way, it sets up a perfectly competitive market—as distinct from constitutionally mandated political processes—as the model in terms of which governmental agencies should formulate and justify regulatory and other social policies.

See also: BUSINESS ETHICS; CIVIL RIGHTS AND CIVIC DUTIES; COMMON GOOD; CORRECTIONAL ETHICS; COST-BENEFIT ANALYSIS; DELIBERATION AND CHOICE; ECONOMIC ANALYSIS; ENTITLEMENTS; ENVIRONMENTAL ETHICS; GAME THEORY; GOVERNMENT, ETHICS IN; JUSTICE, DISTRIBUTIVE; LIBERTY, ECONOMIC; MEDICAL ETHICS; MORAL REASONING; NEUTRAL PRINCIPLES; POLICE ETHICS; PUBLIC GOODS; PUBLIC HEALTH POLICY; PUBLIC POLICY; RISK ANALYSIS; SOCIAL AND POLITICAL PHILOSOPHY; STAKEHOLDER ANALYSIS; UTILITARIANISM; WELFARE RIGHTS AND SOCIAL POLICY.

Bibliography

Dorf, Michael C., and Charles F. Sabel. "A Constitution of Democratic Experimentalism." *Columbia Law Review* 98 (March 1998): 267–371. Aims "to change the reasons and evidence produced in public debate, and with them the conditions for participation in civic life, so that our disputatious democracy is made both more effective as an instrument of public problem solving and more faithful to its purpose of assuring the self-determination of free and equal citizens" (pp. 288–89).

Freeman, Jody. "Collaborative Governance in the Administrative State." *UCLA Law Review* 45 (1997): 1–98. Argues that policy analysts might well confine themselves to serving coffee to the stakeholders and letting them work out their conflicts collaboratively.

MacRae, Duncan. "Policy Advice and Political Science." In *Advances in Policy Studies Since 1950,* edited by William N. Dunn and Rita Mae Kelly, pp. 125–56. New Brunswick, NJ: Transaction, 1992. "Selection of alternatives of this sort need not involve research expertise; it can be based on a rough preliminary judgment of the expected effects of alternatives, their political feasibility, and their relevance to a client's public arguments" (p. 131).

Majone, Giandomenico. *Evidence, Argument, and Persuasion in the Policy Process.* New Haven: Yale University Press, 1989. "The analyst's job is only to determine the best means to given goals" (p. 21).

March, James G. *A Primer in Decision Making.* New York: Free Press, 1994. This lovely book suggests analysts should "pursue a logic of appropriateness, fulfilling identities or roles by recognizing situations and following rules that match appropriate behavior to the situations they encounter" (p. viii).

Schelling, Thomas C. "Economic Reasoning and the Ethics of Policy." In *Choice and Consequence,* chapter 1, pp. 1–26. Cambridge: Harvard University Press, 1984. A sophisticated and sympathetic statement of the economist's view.

Stokey, Edith, and Richard Zeckhauser. *A Primer for Policy Analysis.* New York: Norton, 1978. The undiluted economic position, *e.g.,* "the purpose of public decisions is to promote the welfare of society" (p. 257). Quotations in text from pp. 257, 263.

Weimar, David, and Aidan Vining. *Policy Analysis: Concepts and Practice.* Englewood Cliffs, NJ: Prentice Hall, 1992. Defines policy analysis as "client-oriented advice relative to public decisions and informed by social values" (p. 4).

White, Louise G. "Policy Analysis as Discourse." *Journal of Policy Analysis and Management* 13/3 (1994):

506–25. "Analysts are not neutral observers, but participants, whose theory and methods help them view the context more systematically. The purpose is to share insights among participants rather than definitively predict behavior or arrive at general truths" (p. 510).

Mark Sagoff

Pufendorf, Samuel, Freiherr von (1632–1694)

The most significant moral and political philosopher of late seventeenth- and early eighteenth-century Europe, Pufendorf was, after Hugo GROTIUS (1583–1645), the main representative of the 'modern' theory of NATURAL LAW. Despite the general oblivion into which they eventually fell, his works had an enormous impact on the development of early modern ethics, political theory, and jurisprudence.

Pufendorf was born into a Saxon pastor's family and educated into an ultra-orthodox Lutheranism whose academic representatives he battled all his life. After attending the universities of Leipzig and Jena, he became the first "professor of natural and international law" at both Heidelberg (1661–1668) and Lund in Sweden (1668–1676), ending his career as royal historiographer and privy councilor successively at Stockholm (1677–1688) and Berlin (1688–1694).

Imprisoned during the war between Sweden and Denmark, Pufendorf composed his first main work, the *Elementa jurisprudentiae universalis* (1660), in a dungeon without the aid of books or notes. It used the "mathematical" method of his Jena professor Erhard Weigel (1625–1699) to integrate Grotius and Thomas HOBBES (1588–1679) into a larger natural law synthesis. Later apologetic for its youthful imperfections, Pufendorf recast and expanded its basic ideas into the monumental *De jure naturae et gentium* (1672) and the much shorter condensation thereof, the *De officio hominis et civis* (1673), which was wildly successful as a textbook throughout Europe. Both these works evoked immediate condemnation from the religious and scholastic establishments, who resented Pufendorf's purported secularism and political LIBERALISM. His important, still untranslated replies to these sometimes vicious attacks were collected under the title of *Eris scandica* (1686).

Pufendorf's achievement emerges against the eclipse of scholastic Aristotelianism, the search for trans-confessional "secular" foundations of moral and political order, and the rise of reductionist physical science. He accepted the challenge of moral skepticism (Pierre Charron [1541–1603], Michel de MONTAIGNE [1533–1592]) but dismissed as failed all efforts to ground the morality of actions in traditional metaphysics or particular religious assumptions. Instead, he developed Weigel's germinal distinction between physical and moral entities into an ontological dualism also found in Gottfried LEIBNIZ's (1646–1716) realms of nature and grace, and in Immanuel KANT's (1724–1804) double aspect theory. By seeing "moral entities" such as RIGHTS, obligations, AUTHORITY, personae, and status as freely "imposed" on physical things through divine or human volition, Pufendorf not only adopted a voluntarist stance in opposition to Grotius and other ethical intellectualists, but also took an important step toward the eventual autonomy of morals.

The main argument of *De jure* begins with a complex adaptation of Hobbes's *a priori* state-of-nature hypothesis. Joined to a less cynical empirical anthropology that nonetheless acknowledges human weakness and self-love, it yields Pufendorf's central Stoic principle that all persons ought to maintain a sociable attitude toward one another. He then applies this supreme moral law to a wide array of empirical circumstances and elaborates a detailed doctrine of duties for the intellectually, religiously, and socially deracinated individuals of early modern nation states that were, themselves, experiencing a legitimation crisis. Many particulars of this doctrine, which William Blackstone (1723–1780) consulted in the eighteenth century, found their way into various nineteenth-century codices of European law.

While detailing HUMAN RIGHTS and duties according to the natural law, Pufendorf originated or clarified a number of now familiar moral concepts. Thus, consistent with his derivation of subjective rights from law-based duties, he transformed the prior Grotian distinction between perfect and imperfect rights (*facultas* and *aptitudo*) into one between perfect and imperfect duties. In so doing, and given his general emphasis on a rule-oriented morality of action (*versus* neo-scholastic and neo-Stoic VIRTUE ETHICS), he not only prepared the way for Christian THOMASIUS's (1655–1728) explicit distinction between legality and morality but also indirectly stimulated the eighteenth-century British emphasis on BENEVOLENCE, SYMPATHY, and other motivational factors. We also find in Pufendorf a clear notion of the so-called heterogeneity of the good (moral *versus* natural), as well as a proto-Kantian conception of human EQUALITY and DIGNITY in terms of our common subjection to (divinely imposed) moral law. Finally, Pufendorf's state, which is the natural outcome of active human cultural and social development, rests on the CONSENT of the governed and also tolerates certain variations in personal belief even while regulating external religious practice.

The early eighteenth century saw innumerable editions and translations of the *De jure* and *De officio*. Of these, the English version of Basil Kennet and the annotated French translations of Jean Barbeyrac (1674–1744), with their occasional Lockean critique, were of particular importance. Gershom Carmichael's (1672–1729) annotated edition of *De officio* became the set text in moral philosophy at Glasgow and thus ensured Pufendorf's impact on the Scottish Enlightenment. In Germany, Pufendorf influenced Thomasius, Christian WOLFF (1679–1754), and Kant. He was also read closely by John LOCKE (1632–1704), Jean-Jacques ROUSSEAU (1712–1778), and various American Founding Fathers, none of whom can be fully understood apart from the natural law tradition he best represented. Indeed, because of his keen sense for fine distinctions, his capacity for complexity, his acute critique of weaknesses in the work of predecessors and opponents, and his encyclopedic efforts to extend his principles to every domain of human activity, Pufendorf's *De jure* may truly be seen as the seventeenth-century "*summa*" of natural law thinking.

See also: ARISTOTELIAN ETHICS; AUTONOMY OF ETHICS; CONSENT; DIGNITY; DUTY AND OBLIGATION; EQUALITY; GROTIUS; HART; HOBBES; HUMAN RIGHTS; JEFFERSON; KANT; LEGAL PHILOSOPHY; LEIBNIZ; LIBERALISM; LOCKE; MONTAIGNE; NATURAL LAW; PAINE; PROPERTY; RIGHTS; ROUSSEAU; SKEPTICISM IN ETHICS; SOCIAL CONTRACT; THOMASIUS; TOLERATION; VOLUNTARISM; WOLFF.

Bibliography

Works by Pufendorf

Gesammelte Werke. Edited by Wilhelm Schmidt-Biggemann. Berlin: Akademie Verlag, 1996–. The first four volumes of this set, which will be the definitive edition, have appeared. Vol. 1: *Briefwechsel* (1966), edited by Detlef Döring. Vol. 2: *De officio* (1997), edited by Gerald Hartung. Vol. 3: *Elementa* (1999), edited by Thomas Behme. Vol. 4: *De jure naturae* (1998; text only, in two parts, with a separate volume of Notes still to come), edited by Frank Böhling.

Kleine Vorträge und Schriften. Texte zu Geschichte, Pädagogik, Philosophie, Kirche und Völkerrecht. Edited and introduced by Detlef Döring. Frankfurt/M: Klostermann, 1995. A collection of important "minor" writings from all phases of Pufendorf's career.

Elementorum jurisprudentiae universalis libri duo = Elements of Universal Jurisprudence, Two Books. 2 vols. Oxford: Oxford University Press, 1931 [1660]. Vol. 1 is a photographic reproduction of the Latin edition of 1672; vol. 2 is an English translation by William Abbott Oldfather.

De jure naturae et gentium libri octo = On the Law of Nature and of Nations, Eight Books. 2 vols. Oxford: Oxford University Press, 1934 [1672]). Vol. 1 is a photographic reproduction of the Latin edition of 1688; vol. 2 is an English translation by Charles Henry Oldfather and William Abbott Oldfather.

De officio hominis et civis juxta legem naturalem libri duo = On the Duty of Man and Citizen According to the Natural Law, Two Books. 2 vols. Oxford: Oxford University Press, 1927 [1673]. Vol. 1 is a photographic reproduction of the Latin edition of 1682; vol. 2 is an English translation by Frank Gardner Moore.

On the Duty of Man and Citizen According to Natural Law. Edited by James Tully and translated by Michael Silverthorne. New York: Cambridge University Press, 1991. Contains an excellent introduction and a brief bibliographical essay.

The Political Writings of Samuel Pufendorf. Edited by Craig L. Carr and translated by Michael J. Seidler. New York: Oxford University Press, 1994. Newly translated selections from the *Elementorum* and the *De jure*.

Samuel Pufendorf's "On the Natural State of Men." Edited and translated by Michael Seidler. Lewiston, NY: Edwin Mellen, 1990 [1675]. Modern edition and translation of this essay from Pufendorf's *Dissertationes academicae selectiores.* Long introduction, explanatory notes, bibliography.

Works about Pufendorf

Behme, Thomas. *Samuel von Pufendorf, Naturrecht und Staat: Eine Analyse und Interpretation seiner Theorie, ihrer Grundlagen und Probleme.* Göttingen: Vandenhoeck and Ruprecht, 1995. A basic introduction.

Denzer, Horst. *Moralphilosophie und Naturrecht bei Samuel Pufendorf.* Aalen: Scientia, 1972. The standard book-length study of Pufendorf's moral and legal thought.

Döring, Detlef. *Pufendorf-Studien. Beiträge zur Biogra-*

phie Samuel von Pufendorfs und zu seiner Entwicklung als Historiker und theologischer Schriftsteller. Berlin: Duncker and Humblot, 1992. Based on extensive archival research, indispensable for future scholarly work on Pufendorf.

Haakonssen, Knud. *Natural Law and Moral Philosophy: From Grotius to the Scottish Enlightenment.* Cambridge: Cambridge University Press, 1996. Very learned, comprehensive, and well-annotated study of the modern natural law tradition, especially in Britain.

Krieger, Leonard. *The Politics of Discretion: Pufendorf and the Acceptance of Natural Law.* Chicago: University of Chicago Press, 1965. An important though controversial interpretation, still the only book on Pufendorf in English.

Palladini, Fiammetta, and Gerald Hartung, eds. *Samuel Pufendorf und die europäische Frühaufklärung.* Berlin: Akademie Verlag, 1996. Based on an international conference held in 1994, this collection presents some of the most recent research on Pufendorf.

Schneewind, J. B. *The Invention of Autonomy: A History of Modern Moral Philosophy.* Cambridge: Cambridge University Press, 1998. See chapter 7, "The Central Synthesis: Pufendorf," 118–40. Places Pufendorf into the wider context of early modern moral and political thought.

Tuck, Richard. "The 'Modern' Theory of Natural Law." In *The Languages of Political Theory in Early-Modern Europe,* edited by Anthony Pagden, pp. 99–119. Cambridge: Cambridge University Press, 1987. An important new interpretation of "modern" natural law theory and its relation to Pufendorf.

Michael J. Seidler

punishment

Attempts to justify punishment, which we may define as the infliction of suffering on an offender for an (alleged) offense, may be divided into two kinds. On one kind of theory, which we may call externalist, punishment is justified, if it is, by the fact that it tends to promote an end to which it is merely a contingently effective means. That aim is, of course, typically crime prevention. If punishment contributes sufficiently effectively to this end, then it is justified; if, as some believe, it does not, then it is an institution that should be abolished and replaced by more effective ones. By contrast, other theories, which we may call internalist, hold that punishment promotes an end to which it is internally, or conceptually, connected, in the sense that the aim of punishment could, as a conceptual matter, not be achieved in any other way.

The most common externalist theories focus on punishment's deterrent, reformative, incapacitative, and denunciatory effects. Individual writers have tended to emphasize one of these effects to the exclusion of the others, but most writers would probably agree that punishment decreases the amount of crime to some degree through all, or most, of these means.

Of them, the most important is perhaps deterrence, and almost all writers on punishment, from PLATO (c. 430–347 B.C.E.) onward, have held that the deterrent effect of punishment is one of its justifying features. Deterrence is often divided into two kinds. The threat of punishment will, it is hoped, deter potential offenders; this is referred to as "general deterrence." It may also be hoped that the actual punishment itself will help to deter from further offenses those who have already offended; this is referred to as "specific deterrence," though it is really a kind of reform. It has understandably proved difficult to document the deterrent effect of punishment with any precision; but though its deterrent effect on potential offenders is probably less than is popularly thought, there seems little reason to think that it is too little to justify the costs involved.

The deterrence theory has often been criticized on the ground that it is inconsistent with our deepest moral convictions, for it does not seem to require that offenders should be given the punishment that they *deserve*. What is required for an effective level of deterrence may well be more or less than that. Indeed, critics have often pointed out that circumstances may conceivably require that one punish innocent people in order to stop an epidemic of crime when one cannot catch the actual culprits; and since we should not find this morally acceptable it follows, they say, that deterrence cannot be our only concern. Deterrence theorists have sometimes replied by holding that, though the *aim* of punishment is indeed deterrence, the means of achieving it should be constrained by other moral considerations, just as the pursuit of our ends in general is constrained by independent moral requirements. In particular, proponents of the deterrence theory may also hold that it is a basic moral principle that people should not be punished more than they deserve, even if doing so would have considerable deterrent effect.

The reform theory has a long history, going back at least to Plato, who thought that reform was the primary aim of punishment. However, the idea of reform, and how to achieve it, have been understood in a number of different ways. The model prisons of the nineteenth century aimed to be places where isolation, labor, and discipline would reform the offender morally and spiritually. They were largely ineffective. More recent attempts at "rehabilitating" offenders have had little more success; and, in any case, in the civilized world at least, most punishments inflicted by the state do not involve imprisonment (fines are by far the most common punishment). Some have thought that inflicting suffering on offenders will bring home to them the wrongness of what they did to their victims. Again, there seems little reason to think that this enlightenment occurs on a significant scale. And how it is supposed to work for such offenses as loitering with intent or speeding is unclear. Perhaps "specific deterrence" is a more plausible hope: the experience of punishment may make the offender more likely to want to avoid it in the future and thus more likely to refrain from crime; but to what extent punishment has this effect is largely unknown. Others, while thinking that it is imperative to reform offenders, have been skeptical that *punishment* can make any significant contribution to this end; we need instead to treat the causes that lie in the PSYCHOLOGY and social background of offenders.

Reform theories have been unfashionable since the 1950s, partly because the attempts at reform have been largely ineffectual. In addition, however, the aim of reforming offenders has seemed to some people morally and politically unacceptable; this is particularly so with those theories which effectively regard the offender as not morally responsible and in need of quasi-medical treatment.

Denunciation theories hold that punishment prevents crime by its vigorous statement that the offense is wrong or illegal, or that it will not be tolerated. These theories are associated with such writers as the sociologist Émile DURKHEIM (1858–1917) and the jurisprudent and historian of law James Fitzjames Stephen (1829–1894). Efforts to demonstrate that the denunciatory force of punishment actually serves to prevent crime to any significant degree have proved fruitless; however, it may be said that it works over the long term and so eludes the normal methods of social science research.

In recent years the incapacitative theory has become increasingly popular (though it was recognized as a legitimate function of punishment by

Hugo GROTIUS [1583–1645] and Jeremy BENTHAM [1748–1842]) and has led to increasingly long prison sentences in the United States and, to a lesser extent, in the United Kingdom. Incarcerated offenders must at least confine their offenses to the prison; and those who are executed can no longer offend at all (though only the United States among Western democracies now executes offenders). However, since most punishments—fines, for instance—have virtually no incapacitative effect, the incapacitative theory provides at most only a partial justification of punishment. (There is also considerable debate about how cost-effective imprisonment is as a method of incapacitation.)

Internalist theories do not see punishment merely as a means to an independent end, such as the prevention of crime; they hold that there is a *conceptual* connection between punishment and its aim. Perhaps the simplest such theory, which we may call the Simple Desert theory, holds that the aim of punishment is just to give offenders what they deserve, namely to make them suffer in proportion to the moral gravity of their offenses. (This theory is often referred to as retributivism, but the word is also often used to cover other, quite different theories and is of doubtful classificatory value.) Unlike externalist theories, internalist theories cannot be criticized on the ground that punishment is unlikely to achieve its aim, for it is conceptually guaranteed that this cannot happen; when the offender is punished, the aim is, *ipso facto,* achieved. Many have objected to such a theory on the ground that it reduces punishment to REVENGE. This objection is not correct, for the theory holds that punishment must be proportional to what the offender morally deserves, and that requirement is no part of the idea of revenge. Others, more plausibly, have held that the theory is incoherent, because it requires that we compare two things—the moral gravity of an offense and the severity of a punishment—that are in fact incommensurable.

Other internalist theories may be able to avoid this last charge. One such theory we may call the Just Distribution theory; it has been attributed to Immanuel KANT (1724–1804), and Friedrich NIETZSCHE (1844–1900) also seems to mention it as one possible "meaning" of punishment. This theory holds that the offender, in committing the offense, has taken unfair advantage of a socially beneficial system of cooperation in which individuals respect the RIGHTS of others so long as their own rights are respected. The offender has thus got an unfair advantage, and justice demands that the situation be rectified. The sufferings, or burdens, that punishment lays on the offender are intended to do this by canceling out the advantage gained from the offense. (The theory therefore gives a tolerably clear sense to the idea that a punishment "annuls" the offense, though this approach is not what HEGEL [1770–1831], with whom this notion is most associated, had in mind. It also, perhaps, cashes such metaphors as that the offender "pays for" the offense.) For punishment to achieve its aim, then, it must be proportional to the unfair advantage that the offender gained from the offense, and here we must know more precisely what is the nature of the unfair advantage that the offender is supposed to have gained from the offense. Some have held that it is the lack of restraint that was enjoyed in committing the offense, others that it is the satisfaction that was gained from the offense, still others that it is simply the benefits of the system of cooperation of which the offender has had a free helping. The major difficulty for this theory has been, then, in specifying the gains that the offender made from the offense in such a way as to justify what seem proportional punishments.

The two internalist theories so far mentioned make punishment unproductive in the sense that no one is expected to be better off when punishment has been administered. Not all internalist theories are like that.

There is, for instance, an internalist reform theory. It holds that the aim of punishment is to reform offenders—but not just in any way. The suffering that offenders undergo in their punishment is to lead them to a penitent understanding of their wrongdoing and a reconciliation with the community from which their wrongdoing has alienated them. The theory is internalist because it holds that only through suffering can an offender acquire a penitent understanding. However, punishment is by no means guaranteed to achieve this aim, and indeed in the real world it seems very rarely to do so; many have felt, therefore, that the theory lacks the contact with the actual world necessary for a theory of punishment.

There is also an internalist denunciation theory, which holds that an offense sends a message that the victim is inferior to the offender. Punishment, in its evident mastery of the offender, is then thought of as the victim "striking back" and thereby countering the message. That many offenses can be thought of in this way—again, loitering and speeding—seems doubtful. Some crimes against the person may well be intended to express a message about the offender (hate crimes, for instance) but it is doubtful whether most are.

We should, lastly, notice that not all writers have indeed been convinced that punishment of offenders by the state can be successfully justified. Emphasizing that the criminal justice system imposes huge costs—moral, political, and financial—and may well contribute little to preventing crime, they have thought that we should abandon punishment altogether, prisons in particular, and explore different ways of resolving the social problems that, they think, lie at the bottom of crime.

See also: ALIENATION; AMNESTY AND PARDON; CAPITAL PUNISHMENT; CORRECTIONAL ETHICS; DETERRENCE, THREATS, AND RETALIATION; EXTERNALISM AND INTERNALISM; FAIRNESS; FORGIVENESS; HARM AND OFFENSE; JUSTICE entries; LEGAL PHILOSOPHY; MERCY; MERIT AND DESERT; MORAL PSYCHOLOGY; OBEDIENCE TO LAW; PAIN AND SUFFERING; POLICE ETHICS; PUBLIC POLICY ANALYSIS; RECIPROCITY; RESENTMENT; REVENGE; SOCIAL PSYCHOLOGY.

Bibliography

Adler, Jacob. *The Urgings of Conscience: A Theory of Punishment.* Philadelphia: Temple University Press, 1991.

Aristotle. *Nicomachean Ethics.* Translated by H. Rackham. Cambridge, MA and London: Harvard University Press and William Heinemann, 1934.

Beccaria, Cesare. *On Crimes and Punishments and Other Writings.* Edited by Richard Bellamy. Cambridge: Cambridge University Press, 1995 [1764].

Bentham, Jeremy. *Introduction to the Principles of Morals and Legislation.* Edited by J. H. Burns and H. L. A. Hart. London: Methuen, 1970 [1789].

———. *Panopticon versus New South Wales.* Edited by J. Bowring. London: Simpkin and Marshall, 1843 [1802].

Braithwaite, John. *Crime, Shame, and Reintegration.* Cambridge: Cambridge University Press, 1989.

Davis, Michael. *To Make the Punishment Fit the Crime: Essays in the Theory of Criminal Justice.* Boulder, CO: Westview, 1992.

Duff, Antony. *Trials and Punishments.* Cambridge: Cambridge University Press, 1986.

———, and David Garland, eds. *A Reader on Punishment.* Oxford: Oxford University Press, 1994.

Durkheim, Émile. *Moral Education: A Study in the Theory*

and Application of the Sociology of Education. Free Press, 1961 [1925].

Finnis, John. *Natural Law and Natural Rights.* Oxford: Clarendon Press, 1980.

Grotius, Hugo. *De jure belli ac pacis.* Translated by A. C. Campbell. London: Walter Dunne, 1901 [1625].

Haan, Willem de. *The Politics of Redress: Crime, Punishment, and Penal Abolition.* London: Unwin Hyman, 1990.

Hart, H. L. A. *Law, Liberty, and Morality.* Oxford: Clarendon Press, 1963.

———. *Punishment and Responsibility: Essays in the Philosophy of Law.* Oxford: Clarendon Press, 1968.

Hegel, G. W. F. von. *Philosophy of Right.* Oxford: Clarendon Press, 1952 [1821].

Honderich, Ted. *Punishment: The Supposed Justifications.* Harmondsworth: Penguin Books, 1971 [1969].

Kant, Immanuel. *The Metaphysical Elements of Justice.* Part 1 of *The Metaphysics of Morals.* Translated by John Ladd. New York: Macmillan, 1965 [1797].

Kleinig, John. *Punishment and Desert.* The Hague: Nijhoff, 1973.

Lacey, Nicola. *State Punishment: Political Principles and Community Values.* London: Routledge, 1988.

McTaggart, J. E. "Hegel's Theory of Punishment." *International Journal of Ethics* 6 (1896): 479–502.

Montague, Philip. *Punishment as Societal Defense.* Lanham, MD: Rowman and Littlefield, 1995.

Moore, Michael. "The Moral Worth of Retribution." In *Responsibility, Character, and the Emotions,* edited by Ferdinand Schoeman. Cambridge: Cambridge University Press, 1987.

Morris, Herbert. *On Guilt and Innocence: Essays in Legal Philosophy and Moral Psychology.* Berkeley: University of California Press, 1976.

Murphy, Jeffrie G., and Jean Hampton. *Forgiveness and Mercy.* Cambridge: Cambridge University Press, 1988.

Nietzsche, Friedrich. *On the Genealogy of Morality.* Edited by Keith Ansell-Pearson. Translated by Carol Diethe. Cambridge: Cambridge University Press, 1994 [1887].

Primoratz, Igor. *Justifying Legal Punishment.* Atlantic Highlands, New Jersey: Humanities Press, 1989.

Sadurski, W. *Giving Desert Its Due.* Dordrecht: Reidel, 1985.

Stephen, James Fitzjames. *A General View of the Criminal Law.* London: Macmillan, 1890.

———. *A History of the Criminal Law of England.* Vol. II. London: Macmillan, 1883.

———. *Liberty, Equality, Fraternity.* Cambridge: Cambridge University Press, 1967 [1873].

Ten, C. L. *Crime, Guilt, and Punishment.* Oxford: Clarendon Press, 1987.

von Hirsch, Andrew. *Censure and Sanctions.* Oxford: Clarendon Press, 1993.

———. *Doing Justice: The Choice of Punishments. Report of the Committee for the Study of Incarceration.* New York: Hill and Wang, 1976.

Walker, Nigel. *Punishment, Danger, and Stigma.* Oxford: Blackwell, 1980.

———. *Why Punish?* Oxford: Oxford University Press, 1991.

Wootton, Barbara. *Crime and the Criminal Law.* London: Sweet and Maxwell, 1963.

———. *Social Science and Social Pathology.* London: Allen and Unwin, 1959.

Zimring, Franklin E., and Gordon Hawkins. *Incapacitation.* Oxford: Oxford University Press, 1995.

Anthony Ellis

puritanism

This article is about small-p puritanism. Capital-P Puritanism had its origin in England in the later sixteenth century; while it gave its name to small-p puritanism and had a major role in spreading its influence, this Puritanism is historically limited, belonging properly to the history of Protestant Christianity (and to the political history of England and its colonies).

The chief characteristic of the puritanism considered here is its denial of the flesh, or of "fleshly pleasures" (all pleasures involving the body), as evil. It has a long lineage, beginning with the Bible (portions of both Old and New Testaments), and is found in the European philosophical tradition in PLATO (c. 430–347 B.C.E.), St. AUGUSTINE's (354–430) *Confessions* (397–401; the source of the interpretation of the expulsion from Eden considered immediately below), and in the modern period, SPINOZA (1632–1677), KANT (1724–1804), JOHN STUART MILL (1806–1873), and Leo Tolstoy (1828–1910). It is also to be found in the traditional Christian baptism ceremony, in which the godparents are required to renounce, in the name of the infant, "the world, the flesh, and the Devil." And consider the following from the Revelation 14:3 and 4 concerning the all-male saving remnant: "the hundred and forty and four thousand, which were redeemed from the earth . . . are they which were not defiled with women; for they are virgins."

Puritanism is perhaps most plainly manifest in the commonly accepted belief that the sin of Adam and Eve was the discovery of sex, symbolized by the serpent and the apple, which put an end to their state of INNOCENCE, seen as sexual innocence, when they were "naked and unashamed." For this discovery they were not only driven from the Garden of Eden, but they also lost their immortality and Adam was forced to work for his living ("by the sweat of his brow"), while Eve, and women ever after, were condemned to endure pain in childbirth. For this sin (the discovery of sexual PLEASURE, understood to be wicked) we are still suffering, so it is understood, and we must still live by the sweat of the brow. A consequence of this story is that labour was, and still is, seen as the ultimate legitimization of PROPERTY, an institution that did not exist in Eden. It is probably also the originating source of the view that there is some kind of moral worth in hard and preferably disagreeable WORK. This approach can be seen (like women's pain in childbirth) as continuing PUNISHMENT for Original Sin, all pleasure since the Fall being regarded as decadent, sinful, or displeasing to God. But it can also be seen as something good in itself ("keeping one's nose to the grindstone"), such hard and painful drudgery being worthy of reward, particularly in material terms—perhaps the only thing that creates such desert.

We see here the reason for the continuing connection between puritanism and the belief that people must work for their livelihood, that the world does not "owe them a living," that no one is to get something for nothing. (St. Paul, noted for his puritanical views, commanded: "If any will not work neither shall he eat" [2 Thessalonians 3:10].) Whatever we get in the way of benefits must be justified by the work we put in, and when we do put work in, then some benefits are justified. This, in turn, is the ultimate source of the view that the social safety net ("government handouts") is somehow immoral and that "welfare" should be replaced with "workfare," such views being tied to the idea of the sacredness of what is believed to be legitimately acquired property.

But let us return to the core of puritanism, the view that the devil is in the flesh, which includes not only sex (look what happened to Sodom and Gomorrah), but even the enjoyment of food, which is never to be eaten for pleasure but only for nourishment. (A parallel for sex is the dictum in Benjamin Franklin's [1706–1790] *Poor Richard's Almanac* [1732–1757], "Use venery for health," made sport of by D. H. Lawrence, one of the notable anti-

puritans, in his *Studies in Classic American Literature* [1959].)

In declaring himself a hedonist (the view that pleasure is the only good, pain the only evil), John Stuart Mill (*Utilitarianism*, chapter 2) insists that he is speaking only of the pleasures of the mind, which he calls the higher pleasures, and not of the pleasures of the flesh—the lower pleasures—said to be shared with beasts. He then writes: "It may be questioned whether anyone who has remained equally susceptible to both classes of pleasures ever knowingly and calmly preferred the lower, *though many, in all ages, have broken down in an ineffectual attempt to combine both*" [italics mine]. In saying (as he does earlier in the chapter) that the pleasures of the flesh are shared with beasts, being nothing but the satisfaction of animal appetites, Mill implies that a gourmet sitting down to his or her favourite dish is comparable to a pig at its trough and that the possibilities for human sexual love-making are comparable to those for the copulation of swine. More absurd still, the italicized clause in the quotation above suggests that any attempt to enjoy both a good dinner and a good book must inevitably lead to some sort of breakdown!

Mill's view strongly recalls one found in Book VI of Plato's *Republic*. The following concludes the relevant passage (Shorey translation):

> Then those who have no experience of wisdom and virtue but are ever devoted to feastings and that sort of thing are swept downward, it seems, and back again to the center, and so sway and roam to and fro throughout their lives, but they have never transcended all this and turned their eyes to the true upper region nor been wafted there, nor ever been really filled with real things, nor ever tasted stable and pure pleasure, but with eyes ever bent upon the earth and heads bowed down over their tables they feast like cattle, grazing and copulating, ever greedy for more of these delights, and in their greed kicking and butting one another with horns and hoofs of iron they slay one another in sateless avidity, because they are vainly striving to satisfy with things that are not real the unreal and incontinent part of their souls. (586ab)

Mill's two main points, (1) that no one who has experienced both sorts of pleasure will choose the "lower" over the "higher," and (2) that the "lower" pleasures are shared with beasts and are not worthy of rational humanity, are both prefigured here. (Plato does not say that you cannot combine the two, but it seems clearly enough implied.)

Spinoza's puritanism is revealed in the opening page of the *Tractatus de intellectus emendatione*, where he says that sensual pleasure enthralls the soul (*animus*) but when gratified leads only to extreme melancholy in which the soul is disturbed and dulled, and in his account of male erotic jealousy (*Ethica,* Book III, Prop. 35), said to involve turning away from the loved one because her image has become associated with another man's "organs of excretion."

Kant, while he has a good word to say for sexual PASSION and ardour in marriage, opposes "unnatural lust" and actually claims (*Metaphysik der Sitten* 425) that masturbation is a worse violation of one's duty to oneself than SUICIDE, which he calls self-murder. Thus:

> The obstinate throwing away of one's life as a burden is at least not a weak surrender to animal pleasure, but requires courage; and where there is courage there is always respect for the humanity in one's own person. On the other hand, when one abandons himself entirely to an animal inclination, he makes himself an object of unnatural gratification, *i.e.* a loathesome thing, and thus deprives himself of all self-respect. (Ellington translation)

Tolstoy is said to have claimed that no decent woman could possibly take pleasure in sex, and his novella *The Kreutzer Sonata* (1890) is a story about the horrors brought on by erotic DESIRE and attachment. Nevertheless he was known to boast about his whoring as a young man, which illustrates the close connection between puritanism and prurience. This association was also evidenced in the publication, designed to provoke both prurient pleasure and disgust, of all the lurid details of President Bill Clinton's indiscrete sexual adventure.

Richard Wagner (1813–1883) appeals to the hand-in-handedness of puritanism and prurience in his very popular opera *Tannhäuser* (1845), the eponymous hero of which commits the ghastly sin of praising erotic love in the sacred precincts of the Hall of Song and before the chaste and virginal Elisabeth, having just come from frolicking with some ladies in the court of Venus (Bacchanale). For this profanation he must go to Rome to beg the Pope's FORGIVENESS, which comes only as he dies, his having caught sight, on his return, of the funeral procession of the pure Elisabeth, who has died to save his soul. Venus continues to appear at intervals throughout the opera, including the final scene, but always vanishes instantly at the mention of anything sacred. (The distinguished tenor Jon Vickers, much to his credit, refused to sing the part on moral grounds.)

The quotation above from the Book of Revelation shows the author claiming that only a few selected male virgins are to be saved—those not "defiled" with women. (The reason that no women are to be saved is presumably that every one of them is an actual or potential defiler of men.) The puritanical view that women bring men low by distracting them from the "higher" things persists. But there has also been, in our history over the last two millennia, a veritable obsession with the virginity and chastity of women, beginning with the "undefiled" mother of Christ, who is alleged to have remained *virgo intacto* even after the birth of her child. This obsession may very well have reached its climax in Victorian England with an influence reaching well into the twentieth century. Not only did virtue for women come, in this period, to mean chastity, but continence (Aristotle's *engkrateia* or moral strength) came to mean not wetting your bed, and TEMPERANCE (Aristotle's *sophrosune* or self-discipline) came to mean total abstinence from alcoholic beverages! The continued obsession with female chastity is revealed in the 1925 edition of *Roget's Thesaurus of English Words and Phrases,* which lists about fifty words or expressions (nearly all clearly gendered) for an immoral or wicked or evil man, but just four for an immoral woman, *viz.* "bad woman," "jade," "Jezebel," and "adulteress," whereupon you are referred to the section on sexual looseness, which gives you "strumpet," "whore," etc.! Apparently the only aspect of bad CHARACTER a woman could be charged with was sexual looseness. Either you were a good woman or a whore. Clearly women had only one proper role in life: to remain virginal until marriage and then to have sex only with their husbands. Apparently nothing else was seen to matter where these mindless beings were concerned.

The dark side of puritanism often amounts to more than mere prurience, for where it is the dominant view, adopted and proclaimed publicly, puritanism is often accompanied by sexual excess in secret. Thus, to give a single example, in Victorian England the demand on the operators of bawdy houses for virgins to defile became so overwhelming that girls of eleven had to be recruited for the purpose. At the present time, while violent PORNOGRAPHY is usually illegal, the ordinary hard-core variety typically portrays sex as wicked, often associated with sin and the Devil, the forbidden and the taboo; and the term "nasty" has come to be the standard term for "sexually exciting." People are in fact "turned on" by the idea of WICKEDNESS, hence by sex that is "really nasty" (which does not imply sadomasochism or violence). This attitude is *inverse puritanism.* Sex, except as licensed in monogamous marriage (where it is not seen as very exciting), is accepted by the inverse puritan as wicked and sinful, but since it is so very pleasurable, delight is taken in the idea of such wickedness and sin, to be drooled over if it is not actually obtainable. If it is not obtainable or there is righteous abstinence, it is often accompanied by a strong desire for the wicked to be punished (consider the Salem witch trials).

Inverse puritanism takes the form, "I don't wanna be good. That's boring. I wanna be bad. That's exciting." Its most extreme form becomes Satanism, which is a kind of morality of anti-morality, and that form is truly evil. The profound irony of inverse puritanism is that the puritan view of things—the Devil is in the flesh—is not rejected but accepted with relish, goodness being seen as a bore, evil as the only exciting thing. In the late twentieth century popular culture has been just loaded with it. Consider the rap and hip-hop subgenres of popular music. Note the bizarre anti-goodness clothing, nose and lip rings, body paint, tatoos, hair styles. This inverse form of puritanism can take relatively harmless forms, as in the common use of the term "really wicked" to mean "unusually good" and "bad girl" to mean "girl who is sexually willing." As well, critics sometimes use the word "bad" to praise a play. Or even lower on the harm scale, "decadent" is commonly used to mean "delicious" in the advertising of packaged foods and in their brand names.

In his *The Birth of Tragedy from the Spirit of Mu-*

sic (1872), NIETZSCHE (1844–1900) describes what he calls the Dionysian (representing fleshly energy) as characterized by lust and CRUELTY (lauded in such later works as *Beyond Good and Evil,* 1886), thereby revealing himself as an inverse puritan. We find this view of the sensual as essentially tied to excess echoed in the dreams of Aschenbach, the puritan protagonist of Thomas Mann's (1875–1955) novella *Death in Venice* (1912). It can also take the form of wild, erotic, religious ecstasy, as in Peter Shaffer's stage play, *Equus* (1973; film, 1977). (The protagonist here is also reacting against the emptiness and meaninglessness of the dominant MATERIALISM of the day.) But sensual pleasure or delight is evil only from the strait-laced puritanical viewpoint, and such excesses are often simply a reaction to this puritan condemnation. Puritanism separates body (transient, mutable, mortal) and soul (eternal) and, except for the religious element, places emphasis on the "rational" as opposed to the feeling or the passionate. But while we are rational, we are also animals. Our souls are embodied, and the denial of the flesh is contrary to our nature. Further, in its stern denial of the flesh and the senses, puritanism drowns all joy, isolates us from one another, and dries up the milk of human kindness.

For anti-puritans, such as William Blake (1757–1827) and D. H. Lawrence (1885–1930), the transient, mutable, and mortal flesh is the source of energy and beauty, the very force of life. Consider Blake's Hell, which represents the carnal in his *The Marriage of Heaven and Hell* (1790). Calling it "hell" is an ironic comment on the puritanism that would condemn it as evil. It is connected with the urgency of the life force, with autonomy, with the rejection of the alleged Divine injunction to reject the flesh. Blake, sounding amazingly modern, aptly referred to this authoritarian and puritanical deity as "Nobodaddy."

See also: CHRISTIAN ETHICS; DESIRE; EPICUREANISM; EVIL; FEMINIST ETHICS; HEDONISM; HYPOCRISY; INNOCENCE; LITERATURE AND ETHICS; MATERIALISM; MERIT AND DESERT; MORAL PURITY; OPPRESSION; PAIN AND SUFFERING; PASSION; PLEASURE; PORNOGRAPHY; PUBLIC AND PRIVATE MORALITY; PUNISHMENT; RELIGION; SELF-CONTROL; SELF-RESPECT; SEX AND SEXUAL ETHICS; TEMPERANCE; WEAKNESS OF WILL; WICKEDNESS; WORK.

Bibliography

Augustine, Saint. *Confessions. The City of God.*

Bible. Portions of the Epistles of St. Paul the Apostle (especially Romans 13:13–14; 1 Corinthians 7; Galatians 5:4; 2 Thessalonians 3:10); The Pentateuch, passim; The Prophets, especially Isaiah 3:16–25; Jeremiah 2; Ezekiel 16 (the metaphor Jerusalem as whore; and surely there are between-the-lines allusions to forbidden sexual carryings-on); Hosea 4:11–19; Revelation. Female sexuality was associated in ancient Israel and Judah with the worship of Ashtoreth, or Asherah, a goddess originally associated with the planet Venus and later with the moon. (Her other, non-Hebrew, Semitic names were Ishtar and Astarte.) She represented the female in all her many aspects, including that of The Great Mother. But the worship of Ashtoreth, usually in conjunction with her consort Baal (a god at different times of different planets), included erotic rites conducted by priestesses. Thus it, and thereby female sexuality itself, became associated with the real abominations, including human sacrifice, of ancient planetary worship. It was this ancient religion that the Jewish prophets, from Moses on, fought so hard to abolish, but whose effort did not succeed until the destruction of Jerusalem and the second Babylonian captivity, when backsliding seemed finally to end. It is in the Jewish rejection of the old religion, which is reflected in the books of the Old Testament, that the common origin of puritanism and misogyny may perhaps be found.

Blake, William. *The Marriage of Heaven and Hell.* [1790]

Dole, Robert. *Le cauchemar américain: essai sur les vestiges du puritanisme dans lamentalité américaine actuelle.* Québec: ULB Éditeur, 1996.

Kant, Immanuel. *Die Metaphysik der Sitten.* Part II. [1797]

Lawrence, D. H. *Sex, Literature, and Censorship.* New York: Viking, 1959. A collection of essays including "Pornography and Obscenity" (1930) and "A propos of *Lady Chatterley's Lover.*"

———. *Studies in Classic American Literature.* New York: T. Seltzer, 1923. The following quotation from this book appears as the epigraph for *Sex, Literature, and Censorship:* "When Adam went and took Eve, *after* the apple, he didn't do any more than he had done many a time before, in act. But in consciousness he did something very different. So did Eve. Each of them kept an eye on what they were doing, they watched what was happening to them. They wanted to KNOW. And that was the birth of sin. Not *doing* it, but KNOWING about it. Before the apple, they had shut their eyes and their minds had gone dark. Now they peeped and pried and imagined. They watched themselves. And they felt uncomfortable after. They felt self-conscious. So they said, 'The *act* is sin. Let's hide. We've sinned.'"

Mill, John Stuart. *Utilitarianism.* [1861] Chapter 2.

Plato. *Republic.* Book VI.

Santayana, George. *The Last Puritan: A Memoir in the Form of a Novel.* [1936]

Spinoza, Benedict de. *De intellectus emendatione.* [Date not known]. *Ethica.* [1677]. Book III.

Steven, Marcus. *The Other Victorians: A Study of Sexuality and Pornography in Mid-Nineteenth-Century England.* New York: Basic Books, 1966.

Tolstoy, Leo. *The Kreutzer Sonata.* [1890]

Babettes gæstebud = Babette's Feast. Nordisk Film, Danske Filminstitut, A-S Panorama Film International, 1987; English subtitled version, Orion Classics, 1988. A film based on a short story by Isak Dinesen and directed by Gabriel Axel, who wrote the screenplay. A powerful portrayal of grim Scandinavian puritanism shattered, to the benefit of all, by the "breaking-out" of a resident French woman.

E. J. Bond

purity

See moral purity.

R

racism and related issues

Racism is the most malign, as well as the most ill-founded, of those social theories that pit groups of human beings against one another. Its destructive consequences are greater and more pervasive than either religious intolerance or nationalism. Because of its sway, millions have been killed, and millions more lead morally and physically impoverished lives. Although Jews and blacks are its most notable recent victims—it was used to justify black SLAVERY, the HOLOCAUST, and apartheid—since its origins are ancient, every racial group has probably at some time suffered from it.

Racism notoriously involves several assumptions. Prominent among these assumptions are that human beings are divided into races; that some of these races are morally, intellectually, or physically superior to others; and that this superiority is due to inherited biological differences. Racism is politically important because it draws a number of purportedly moral claims from these assumptions. These claims vary with the circumstances. Typical of a confident expansive racism is the claim that the superior races have a right to enslave, rule over, lead, control, civilize, or improve the inferior races. When such racism begins to meet serious opposition, it gradually replaces these arrogant claims with arguments designed to protect the advantages of the favored race. Such arguments became prominent after the abolition of slavery; they include the idea that the supe-

rior races have a duty to preserve their purity and a right to protect their privileges by various strategies, notably *de jure* segregation in housing and education and selective restrictions on immigration. When racism is on the defensive, as in late-twentieth-century America, many of its friends attempt a poor subtlety, pretending to desert it and repudiating some of its key moral claims while at the same time arguing that the costs of racial EQUALITY are regrettably too high. They defend various policies that are certain to keep the subjugated races in the lower strata of society where an earlier, bolder racism had confined them. Perhaps the most effective of these policies is institutional racism. In institutional racism the rules of the institution eschew all mention of race but at the same time are designed to unfairly prevent members of the despised races from advancing in the institution. The foes of racism should not lower their guard. If these rearguard actions fail, racism may resort to desperate measures, as it did in Nazi Germany when it erupted with its most maniacal claim: that the superior races have a duty to exterminate the inferior races.

A growing number of biologists have concluded that the concept of race is not useful in their work, and some well-meaning people believe that this finding provides them with a major weapon in their fight against racism. They are mistaken. The failure of biologists to find useful definitions of race in terms of gene pools, or gene frequencies, or by reference to blood types, has little to do with racism's definition of race, which is in terms of gross readily apparent features like skin color and hair texture. Further, the lure of racism has never depended on the strength of its scientific claims. There has always been an air of quackery about these claims. If people took them seriously it was because they wanted to justify the unspeakable but profitable enterprises they were engaged in.

But no reasonable interpretation of racism's scientific claims is enough to justify its moral claims. We do not need to choose between moral theories to see this. No moral theory worthy of serious consideration will countenance racism's moral claims. This is true even of elitist theories, which seem the most likely kind of theory to justify racism. In the *Republic,* for example, PLATO (c. 430–347 B.C.E.) argued that those with the greatest biologically inherited capacity for moral and intellectual attainment should be specially educated to rule. But he never argued that any race—as racism defines race—should rule; nor does what he argued imply, even if racism were right, that intelligence is biologically inherited and strongly correlated to gross, readily apparent features like skin color and hair texture.

This argument would mark a distinction without practical significance if racism's factual claim was not merely that race and intelligence are strongly correlated, but that the members of some races are invariably of low intelligence. Racism used to say that. For example, in a notorious footnote to his essay on "National Character" (1748), David HUME (1711–1776) declared his firm suspicion that all Negroes were of low intelligence. If he were right, an elitist theory like Plato's would justify racist policies. For example, although whites would all have to be carefully tested to see whether they had the intelligence to be rulers, Negroes could be dismissed from consideration on the basis of their race alone. But that all Negroes are of low intelligence is not a reasonable interpretation of racism's claim that there are superior and inferior races. It was not a reasonable interpretation even when Hume vented it. He presumed to base his momentous generalization on evidence that he knew was bound to be both slender and suspect, and cavalierly dismissed counterexamples to it. As I noted, there was always an air of quackery about racism's factual claims. Since Hume, that quackery has become more sophisticated. Although, for example, racism interprets the fifteen-point mean difference between black and white I.Q.s to mean that whites are a superior race, it cannot deny that many blacks have higher scores than many whites and that some blacks have very high scores indeed.

Some people apparently believe that if race and intelligence were strongly correlated, several moral theories, including some nonelitist theories, could justify many racist claims. They argue that the correlation could be used to make statistically reliable predictions of those who should be trained or educated for various positions, and that while such predictions would not be infallible, a society could save itself time and money by acting on them.

This is modern racism's favorite ploy, but it cannot stand scrutiny. Elitist theories like Plato's, which place an enormous premium on matching individuals with the tasks and duties for which nature has best suited them, would reject it as an example of the kind of base injustice moneymakers are likely to perpetrate if they are allowed to rule. Nor would other moral theories with more regard for moneymaking (UTILITARIANISM, for example) pay much more respect to racism's recommendation. Its implementation would arouse the indignation and RESENTMENT of the members of the excluded race, and in the long run, so undermine their SELF-ESTEEM and SELF-RESPECT as to make them a thorn in the side of the society and a burden on its economy.

Although some modern racists bluntly proclaim the morality of using race to make, and act, on statistically reliable predictions about intelligence—as William Shockley has put it, nature has color-coded groups of individuals for intelligence—others repudiate this practice, declaring that individuals should be judged on their merits, though at the same time repeating as often and as loudly as possible that race and intelligence are strongly correlated. This practice is hypocritical, as well as racist, because while it declares allegiance to a recognizable moral principle, it sustains a climate that undermines allegiance to that principle. Someone may object that scientists should be free to study whatever they please, including the possible correlation between race and intelligence. But before blundering about with high-sounding phrases about allowing free play to scientific curiosity, one should remember that there are often more sordid reasons scientists decide to study one thing rather than another. Why indeed is a possible correlation between intelligence and some gross, easily observable feature like skin color so very interesting scientifically? Since study of the possible correlation has involved nothing more significant than tireless attempts to establish it, a reasonable suspicion is that its main interest is to provide the dominant race with specious justifications of its exploitation and disrespect of other races. Nor, after several centuries of slavery, segregation, and stigmatization, which have left the black population in America preoccupied with race and apprehensive about its intelligence, are such studies likely to yield any results worthy of the attention of fair-minded people.

Racism, then, is a patently disreputable theory. It does not attract adherents because of its intellectual appeal, or even less because it is true, but because it is a potent weapon in the COMPETITION over scarce resources. When groups of people with antagonistic interests are racially different, this difference is a convenient and reliable way for each group to distinguish friends from enemies, and an ideal basis for fostering the distrust and contempt for the other that each needs to win the contest. Accordingly, we could abolish racism if we could either abolish groups of people with antagonistic interests; abolish races; or abolish the tendency of these groups to coincide with each other. Each alternative has its advocates.

There are people, for example, who urge the abolition of races. Some of these people mean that all races except the superior race should be exterminated. Although successfully implementing their recommendation would certainly put an end to racism, we can, I think, pass over it without further comment. Others mean to urge miscegenation. This too requires little comment. Although there would be little room for racism in a racially homogenized society, a society could become racially homogenized only after it had already overcome racism.

Marxists are the most prominent advocates of the proposal to abolish racism by abolishing groups with antagonistic interests. They say that this proposal can be accomplished if workers establish a classless society, because classes are the most important groups with antagonistic interests as well as the cause of all important social antagonisms. There are difficulties with this theory. Marxists tell us that the workers will establish a classless society when they sink their differences and unite to overthrow capitalism. This process suggests that they must overcome their racism before they abolish classes. But suppose that they managed to overthrow capitalism before they overcome racism. In that case, we have every reason to believe that the society they would establish after they overthrew capitalism would not be classless.

We are left then with the proposal to curb the tendency of groups with antagonistic interests to coincide with races. While the most important of these groups are the classes of Marx, they also include the various interest groups within society, including professional groups. We can go a long way toward implementing this proposal by a firm commitment to standard principles of liberal justice like fair equality of opportunity. This step must be supplemented with preferential treatment for certain races, such as blacks and American Indians in the United States, for whom the legacy of past racial discrimination has created special handicaps.

Although this proposal probably represents the best way to reduce and ultimately perhaps to eradicate racism, it has its detractors. Many object to fair equality of opportunity. Even more object to preferential treatment. The vehemence and popularity of these objections have led some pessimists to fear that the means I have suggested for ameliorating racism will be successfully resisted by races in the more affluent classes and interest groups. Others have a different worry. These people complain that if the more far-reaching of these means are successful, they will undermine the healthy and stimulating cultural differences that now exist between the races and replace them with a deadening monotony. A third group is more radical. They reject the argument that racial differences become salient only when they coincide with interest groups, suggesting instead that a disposition to racial antipathy, if not for full-blown racism, is built into human nature. On their account, the coincidence of race and interest group is not the result of historical accident, but of racial antipathy. The general implication of these various positions is that the subservient races can be saved only by acquiring the POWER to ensure that they cannot be taken advantage of by others. This implication leads to the various theories of pluralism and separatism and ultimately to the idea that nation-states should coincide with races. This theory is not a reassuring progression, for in the final scenario racism would tend to join forces with the second-most malign force in modern history—nationalism.

racism and related issues

See also: CIVIL DISOBEDIENCE; CIVIL RIGHTS AND CIVIC DUTIES; DISCRIMINATION; ELITE, CONCEPT OF; EQUALITY; EXPLOITATION; FAIRNESS; HOLOCAUST; HYPOCRISY; IMPARTIALITY; INTOLERANCE; JUSTICE, DISTRIBUTIVE; KING; LIBERALISM; MERIT AND DESERT; OPPRESSION; PARTIALITY; POLICE ETHICS; POWER; RACISM, CONCEPTS OF; SLAVERY; TOLERANCE.

Bibliography

Baier, Kurt. "Merit and Race." *Philosophia* 8, no. 2–3 (November 1978): 121–151.

Barzun, Jacques. *Race: A Study in Superstition.* 2d ed. New York: Harper and Row, 1965.

Bracken, H. M. "Essence, Accident, and Race." *Hermathena* no. 116 (Winter 1973): 81–96.

———. *Mind and Language: Essays on Descartes and Chomsky.* Dordrecht: Foris, 1984.

Brotz, Howard, ed. *Negro Social and Political Thought, 1850–1920.* New York: Basic Books, 1966. See especially "The Conservation of Races" by W. E. B. Dubois; "Prejudice Not Natural" and "The Claims of the Negro Ethnologically Considered" by Frederick Douglass; and "Who and What Is a Negro?" by Marcus Garvey.

Goldberg, David, ed. *Anatomy of Racism.* Minneapolis: University of Minnesota Press, 1990.

Gould, Stephen Jay. *Ever Since Darwin.* New York: W. W. Norton, 1977.

Hume, David. "On National Character." In *David Hume: Essays, Moral, Political, and Literary.* Indianapolis: Liberty Fund, 1987, pp. 197–215.

Jensen, Arthur. "How Much Can We Boost I.Q. and Scholastic Achievement?" *Harvard Educational Review* 39, no. 1 (1969): 1–123.

Knowles, Louis L., and Kenneth Prewitt. *Institutional Racism in America.* Englewood Cliffs, NJ: Prentice-Hall, 1969.

Montagu, Ashley. *Man's Most Dangerous Myth: The Fallacy of Race.* 4th ed. Cleveland, OH: World Publishing, 1964 [1942].

Popkin, Richard H. *The High Road to Pyrrhonism.* San Diego, CA: Austin Hill, 1980. See "The Philosophical Bases of Modern Racism," pp. 79–102.

———. "Hume's Racism." *Philosophical Forum* 9, nos. 2 and 3 (1977–1978): 211–26.

Shockley, William. "Dysgenecs, Genticity, and Raciology." *Phi Delta Kappan* (January 1972): 297–307.

Singer, Marcus George. "Some Thoughts on Race and Racism." *Philosophia* 8, no. 2–3 (November 1978): 153–83.

Singer, Peter. "Is Racial Discrimination Arbitrary?" *Philosophia* 8, no. 2–3 (November 1978): 185–203.

Thalberg, Irving. "Justifications of Institutional Racism." *Philosophical Forum* 3, no. 4 (1972): 243–65.

———. "Visceral Racism." *The Monist* 56, no. 1 (1972): 43–63.

Thomas, Laurence. "Sexism and Racism: Some Conceptual Differences." *Ethics* 90 (January 1980): 239–47.

Wasserstrom, Richard. "On Racism and Sexism." In *Today's Moral Problems,* 2d ed., edited by Richard Wasserstrom, pp. 75–105. New York: Macmillan, 1979.

Bernard R. Boxill

racism, concepts of

'Racism' was a name coined by their critics for the theories of racial superiority that came to prominence in early-nineteenth-century Europe (Miles). Today, the word is used more broadly to apply to racially unfair and discriminatory beliefs, actions, desires, projects, persons, groups, social INSTITUTIONS, and practices. When the African American intellectual and activist W. E. B. DuBois (1868–1963) declaimed near its start that the twentieth century's problem was "the problem of the color line," it was racism that gave that line its importance. Racism may also be the reason behind its very drawing.

What Is Racism?

Is there some one thing in which racism consists? Or are there only different kinds or forms of racism—racisms but no racism? Many social thinkers today stress the different forms racism takes, urging a negative answer to the first question and a positive one to the second. However, their position is problematic. If there are different kinds of racism, then what is the thing itself of which they are kinds? What is it that makes each of them a kind of racism? (For discussion, see Goldberg.) Answering these questions need not rest on any strong metaphysical essentialism, and philosophy should help answer them if it is to help us understand, make, and assess accusations of racism.

Social theorists have offered divergent accounts of racism as a belief (D'Souza) or an ideology of racial superiority (Appiah), a social system of racial OPPRESSION (Marable; Ture and Hamilton), racially discriminatory behavior (Flew), racial hate (or contempt or disregard) or other noncognitive mental attitudes (Schmid; Garcia 1997), and a racialized type of sexual or existential psychopathology (Young-

Bruehl; Gordon). Each of these conceptions faces its own problems.

Many identify racism with a belief in racial superiority. However, such belief appears to be neither necessary nor sufficient for racism. It is not necessary because the race-haters who don't rationalize their hatred with ranking beliefs are nevertheless racists. It is not sufficient because individuals may, like Mark Twain's Huckleberry Finn, come to espouse characteristically racist views through no moral or intellectual fault of their own. Appiah persuasively holds that such innocent, "propositional racists" are not truly racists at all. In addition, this approach has difficulty explaining in what sort of inferiority a racist must believe. Usually, it is belief in intellectual or moral inferiority that is treated as definitive of racism. However, these kinds of inferiority, if real, might be thought to help justify race-based deprivation of benefits, emotional repudiation, moral distaste, and perhaps even social DISCRIMI-NATION. Such justifications suggest that when holding these beliefs is wrong and racist, it is because these beliefs rationalize antecedently racist indifference toward, contempt for, hatred of, or victimization of those assigned to a certain racial group.

Some maintain that identifying racism with such beliefs has moral implications. Assuming that what someone believes is not under his or her control in such fashion as to warrant moral condemnation, D'Souza insists that, because racism is simply a belief, it may be condemned only as false or ill-supported, never as immoral. Working from the same assumption, Flew reasons that, because racism is surely a moral offense, it cannot be a matter of belief. The shared assumption behind these opposed arguments, however, is suspect. We can morally condemn someone's belief in something, just as we can condemn that person's action, because that belief results from morally vicious elements in the agent's will.

Identifying racism with a system of social oppression threatens to exonerate powerless, marginalized, ineffectual, or frustrated racists. Racism also faces the challenge of explaining just how individuals and their conduct, attitudes, etc., must be connected to the system if they are to count as racist. It is implausible to say these individuals are racist only if they arise from or exist within such a system. Such a statement means that whether I am racist depends less on what I do, say, and feel than on what others

do and say. However, if no social system is necessary or sufficient for racism, then racism cannot consist in such a system.

The behavioral conception of racism is unclear at crucial points. The form of behavior usually identified as racist is discrimination, but this identification leaves it unclear whether discrimination must impact another person to be racist. Usually the behavior meant is external; so, making racial discriminations in one's mind does not count. However, it is not obvious why mental discriminations should be irrelevant, since some ways of regarding people appear to be racist even if never put into effective action. Moreover, any such account faces difficulty in specifying what distinguishes racist actions from others: Their effects? Their motivation? Their connection to social systems? Whichever it is, these behavioral accounts of racism threaten to self-destruct because the key to racism lodges not in actions themselves but in the inputs, outputs, or contexts that make those actions racist.

The attitudinal approach to understanding racism faces problems in accounting for racism in action and belief, institutional racism, covert racism, unconscious racism, and paternalistic racism. Cautious versions of this approach treat the central case of racism as contempt, indifference, or hostility, but allow that these noncognitive mental attitudes can infect and corrupt an individual's beliefs and external conduct as well as the design and operation of social institutions. It is interesting that this approach supports a promising view of the moral realm, antithetical to act CONSEQUENTIALISM, in which actions are made wrong less by their effects than by the vicious desires, hopes, and choices that constitute their motivational inputs (Garcia 1997).

Some theorists, struck by the ways in which anti-black animosity, in the West especially, has been sexualized, see certain sexual psychopathologies as key to racism. Whatever illumination is shed by concentrating on this connection between race and sex, however, no particular psychological etiology can plausibly be held to be necessary for racism because, again, a vicious race-hater without it would still be a racist. Moreover, if these psychopathological accounts of racism are interpreted deterministically, they threaten to exculpate what we think should be morally condemned.

All these approaches to conceptualizing racism run into problems raised by the phenomenon philosophers call 'MORAL LUCK.' Insofar as we take racism to be a morally unacceptable phenomenon, we think that whether someone or something is racist should be largely independent of chance. We want to hold people (and, sometimes, institutions) responsible, not see racism as a matter of fortune. Thus, it counts against a social system account of racism if the system holds that whether something is racist depends on luck in how things go. Does the system happen to work in such a way that, irrespective of anyone's plans, it specially disadvantages those of a racial group? (See Figueroa and Mills.) Indeed, some versions of this view are committed to holding, implausibly, that even well-intentioned and well-planned anti-racist efforts, such as preferential treatment programs or selfhelp groups for racially oppressed people, are racist if they should prove countereffective—for example, by increasing inter-racial tensions, as some critics of racial preference programs allege. The same objection afflicts other effects-driven accounts, such as conceptions of racism as the exercise of social POWER. Opportunity-luck poses the greatest problem for doxastic conceptions of racism, since what a person believes will largely be a function of the social environment in which that person is raised. For that reason, more sophisticated versions of that approach insist that racism requires holding certain beliefs irrationally, ideologically, self-deceptively, or in some other morally objectionable way. It is constitutive luck that poses special difficulties for mental attitude theories. However, understanding racism as essentially vicious may help here, since vices are most plausibly seen as attitudes and dispositions that are acquired in part through voluntary and morally assessable behavior.

What Is Wrong (Especially, Morally Wrong) with Racism?

Different understandings of what racism is influence different views of what is objectionable in it. Doxastic approaches tend to indict racism especially for being irrational. But in what way need it be irrational? Sometimes, after all, racism can be seen as an understandable (if vicious) mechanism for advancing one group or protecting its interests (Goldberg). So, racism need not be entirely without practical rationality. Is racism economically inefficient? Perhaps it often is. But economic inefficiency cannot

exhaust the moral issue, for there would be something objectionable about racism even if it efficiently used or distributed resources. Is racism socially harmful? Surely, it has been. However, if society were its main victim, then the slave or the victim of lynching would have no more complaint than others. Against this, we usually think that racism is unjust. Yet, if it is unjust, how so? Many approaches treat racism as a violation of justice, as a (Rawlsian) social virtue. A neglected and attractive view is that racism offends against justice as a (perhaps Aristotelian) personal virtue.

What Is Racism?

Racism has been imputed to things of so many different types and for such different reasons as to suggest that there are different types of racism or even that the term is used in different senses. Thus, we find racism in people and their beliefs as well as in their behavior, both individual (*e.g.,* voting) and collective (*e.g.,* the lynch mob), in the design and operation of legal institutions (*e.g.,* SLAVERY and apartheid), and in widespread but informal practices of private life (*e.g.,* residential, marital, and hiring patterns). The reality of both individual and institutional racism seems undeniable, but a good account of racism needs to explain their connection.

More controversially, some claim that racism lies chiefly in the social effects of individual or joint behavior considered in abstraction from that conduct's rationale or purposes; that the principal types of racism are unconscious or covert; that ignoring race is often racist; and that even many anti-racist liberals are racist in their conduct.

Others have asserted that programs of preferential treatment are racist, that forms of same-race favoritism, racial solidarity, or self-segregation among groups recently victimized are themselves forms of racism (Appiah; Kennedy).

From the political left also come denials that recent victims of racism can themselves be racist on the grounds they lack sufficient power, contrary to SARTRE's (1905–1980) famous affirmation of "anti-racist racism." Some on the political right deny that race-based discrimination is racist when statistics show correlation between race and legitimately relevant features. If the powerless cannot be racist, then racism must entail the exercise of power. If statistical inference precludes racism, then racism must be pervasively irrational. If ignoring race can be racist, then racism need not consist in illegitimately attending to race. In this way, each of these and other charges and denials of racism requires defense of such claims about racism's nature and thus ultimately depends on a philosophically articulated and defensible account of that nature.

Racism and Race

If we deny that there really are races, must we deny the existence of racism? An affirmative answer, while tempting, is problematic. Racism can exist and be destructive even if race is only illusion and the racial classifications that racists (and the rest of us) make are all false. (Appiah notes that, as my life may have been ruined because my mother was regarded as a witch, though in reality there are no witches, so it can have been disadvantaged because people classify me as belonging to the black race, even if in fact all racial classification is mistaken.) Whether races are real will in part depend on whether race is best seen as a biological category or whether some meaning can be given to the murky claim that races are "socially constructed." If there are no races, it follows that some judgments and presuppositions crucial to racists are false.

Racial anti-realism would also, however, undermine forms of so-called racial identity (really, self-image) and authenticity. For if no one really is, say, racially black, then an African American who ignores or tries to hide her lineage will not be denying her innermost identity (as some have maintained); and when she proudly comes to think of herself simply as a member of the black race, she will not so much be "raising her consciousness" as mystifying it (Kennedy).

More difficult is determining the causal relationship between race and racism. Does race as a category stem from racism or give rise to it? Logically, racism depends on racial classification. However, it may be that racial classification took the shape and gained the importance it did because of the needs of personal or institutionalized racism (Gordon).

Is Everyone Racist? Is Racism Unavoidable?

Some regard racism in American society as "permanent," and others maintain that everyone is racist in ways they deem almost unavoidable (Bell; Schmid;

Corlett). This doctrine is a despairing one. Whether racism is a social system, an ideology, a belief, a set of motivational attitudes, a form of institutional or individual behavior, a field of discourse, or some additional possibility, there is reason to hope that it can be extinguished. Nor should we accept that racism, a moral evil, is merely an innocent form of that generalization that is a necessary part of human thinking.

We need to face the probability that putting an end to racist discrimination in Western society (and elsewhere) will not suffice to eliminate the continued suffering that centuries of racism among the powerful have wrought throughout the modern world. The poverty, miseducation, demoralization, CORRUPTION, hatred, bitterness, despair, and other setbacks that some racially oppressed people have suffered may survive racism's end and breed their own problems. For that reason, it is important to resist the temptation to use the term 'racism' as a kind of linguistic 'black box' to denominate whatever it is that accounts for the continued plight of victims of past racism. To succumb to that temptation offers the false impression that these deep social problems have some single cause and that we understand what it is and where it is found. Thus, facile accusations of racism can retard both social understanding and social progress.

See also: ACTION; COLLECTIVE RESPONSIBILITY; CONSEQUENTIALISM; CORRECTIONAL ETHICS; CORRUPTION; DISCRIMINATION; ELITE, CONCEPT OF; EQUALITY; GROUPS, MORAL STATUS OF; HATE; INEQUALITY; INSTITUTIONS; JUSTICE [various entries]; MORAL LUCK; OPPRESSION; PATERNALISM; POLICE ETHICS; PRACTICAL REASON[ING]; RACISM AND RELATED ISSUES; RATONALITY VS. REASONABLENESS; RESENTMENT; RESPONSIBILITY; SLAVERY; TOLERATION.

Bibliography

Appiah, Anthony. "Racisms." In *Anatomy of Racism,* edited by D. T. Goldberg, 3–17. Minneapolis: University of Minnesota Press, 1990.

Bell, Derrick. *Faces at the Bottom of the Well.* New York: Basic Books, 1992.

Corlett, J. Angelo. "Analyzing Racism." *Public Affairs Quarterly* 12 (January, 1998): 23–50.

D'Souza, Dinesh. *The End of Racism.* New York: Free Press, 1995.

DuBois, W. E. B. *Souls of Black Folk.* Chicago: McClurg, 1903.

Figueroa, Robert, and Claudia Mills. "Environmental Justice." In *A Companion to Environmental Philosophy,* edited by Dale Jamieson. Oxford: Blackwell, 1998.

Flew, Antony. "Three Concepts of Racism." *Encounter* 75 (July/August, 1990): 63–66.

Garcia, J. L. A. "Current Conceptions of Racism." *Journal of Social Philosophy* 28 (1997): 5–42.

———. "The Heart of Racism." *Journal of Social Philosophy* 27 (1996): 5–45.

Goldberg, David Theo. Racist Culture: Philosophy and the Politics of Meaning. Oxford: Blackwell, 1993.

Gordon, Lewis. *Bad Faith and Antiblack Racism.* Atlantic Highlands: Humanities, 1995.

Harris, Leonard, ed. *The Concept of Racism.* New York: Humanities, 1998.

Kennedy, Randall. "My Race Problem—and Ours." *Atlantic,* May, 1997: 55–66.

Marable, Manning. "Black America: Multicultural Democracy in the Age of Clarence Thomas and David Duke." In *Speaking Truth to Power,* 83–99. Boulder: Westview, 1996.

Miles, Robert. *Racism.* London: Routledge, 1989.

Sartre, Jean-Paul. "Black Orpheus." Translated by John McCombie. In *"What Is Literature?" and Other Essays,* edited by Stephen Ungar, 21–45. Cambridge: Harvard University Press, 1988. Originally published in 1948 as "Orphee Noir."

Schmid, W. Thomas. "The Definition of Racism." *Journal of Applied Philosophy* 13 (1996): 31–40.

Ture, Kwame, and Charles V. Hamilton. *Black Power: The Politics of Liberation in America.* New York: Vintage, 1992 [1967]. Includes new afterwords by the authors. (Kwame Ture was formerly known as Stokely Carmichael.)

Young-Bruehl, Elizabeth. *The Anatomy of Prejudices.* Cambridge: Harvard University Press, 1996.

J. L. A. Garcia

Rand, Ayn (1905–1982)

The American novelist and philosopher Ayn Rand was born Alissa Zinovievna Rosenbaum in St. Petersburg, Russia. The precocious eldest daughter of secular-minded middle-class Jewish parents, she received a formal gymnasium and college education. Growing to maturity during Russia's Silver Age, the period of cultural upheaval that preceded the Bolshevik Revolution, she eventually constructed an original philosophic system that she called OBJECTIVISM, combining epistemological realism, ethical egoism, and libertarian politics with a commitment to *laissez-faire* capitalism. In so doing, she explicitly rejected Russia's religious MYSTICISM and communist materialism alike. Yet, she resembled many of her Russian predecessors in her lifelong opposition to the academic establishment and in her integration of literary art and social criticism with systematic philosophy. And, like them, Rand repudiated the traditional antinomies of Western thought, including mind-body, fact-value, morality-prudence, theory-practice, and reason-emotion.

During her adolescence, Rand was encouraged by the revolt against Tsar Nicholas II (1868–1918) and by the establishment of the Kerensky government, which she hoped would move toward republican rule. With the advent of the Soviets, however, her family suffered great hardship, and her father's pharmacy was nationalized. Adamantly rejecting the view that the individual should be sacrificed by the state for the COMMON GOOD, Rand drew inspiration from the heroic INDIVIDUALISM portrayed by Western novelists and dramatists such as Victor Hugo (1802–1885) and Edmond Rostand (1868–1918). Having decided at an early age to become a writer, she would seek to express a similarly romantic spirit in her own fiction and drama.

In her gymnasium studies, Rand excelled at mathematics and logic. At the University of Petrograd (formerly St. Petersburg), however, she settled on history and philosophy as her areas of concentration. She entered the three-year social science college in the fall of 1921. During this period, Rand was impressed by the work of Fyodor Dostoyevsky (1821–1881) and Friedrich NIETZSCHE (1844–1900). She appreciated Dostoyevsky's literary method of drawing characters as embodiments of principles. And though she rejected Nietzsche's emotionalist-subjectivist "Dionysian" streak, she was deeply affected by his celebration of the "noble soul" and his attacks on altruist morality. Among her college teachers was N. O. Lossky (1870–1965), a distinguished neo-Hegelian thinker who worked within the Russian dialectical tradition of analyzing philosophic and social issues as interrelated aspects of a larger context. In many respects, Rand employs this same dialectical mode of inquiry.

Rand graduated from the University of Leningrad (formerly Petrograd) in 1924, barely escaping the Communist purges, which sent hundreds of "nonproletarian" students to Siberian labor camps and hundreds of "bourgeois" intellectuals into exile. Fascinated by the burgeoning film industry, especially by American movies, she enrolled in the State Institute for Cinema Arts. A monograph she wrote on the film star Pola Negri (1897–1987) was published in 1925 in Leningrad and Moscow, with the author's name given as "A. Rosenbaum." A collection of her essays, *Hollywood: American City of Movies,* was published without her permission in Leningrad in 1926, after she had immigrated to the United States.

Horrified by conditions under the Soviets and contemptuous of traditional Russian culture, Rand resolved to escape. She secured a visa to see relatives in Chicago, and in 1925 left Russia, hoping never to return. In America, she assumed the name Ayn Rand and soon went off to Hollywood, finding work as an extra in the studio of Cecil B. DeMille (1881–1959). On the set of *King of Kings,* she met Frank O'Connor (1897–1979), an actor, whom she married in 1929. When the studio closed, Rand struggled financially, working at odd jobs, but she continued to write fiction in her spare time. Having become a U.S. citizen in 1931, she abhorred the leftist intellectual milieu of America's "Red Decade," which idealized Soviet life. Some of her early stories and film scenarios, later published posthumously in *The Early Ayn Rand* and *Journals of Ayn Rand,* reflect a Nietzschean-inspired rejection of collectivism and religion.

Rand's partly autobiographical first novel, *We the Living* (1936), was set in Russia in the early years of the Soviet regime. It focuses on the destructive effects of totalitarianism on the lives of three talented young people. During World War II, Italian filmmakers produced an unauthorized but largely faithful screen version of the novel. According to some accounts, the fascist authorities eventually suppressed the film when they realized that Rand's message was as anti-fascist in its implications as it was anti-communist.

Rand's second novel, *The Fountainhead* (1943), became a best-seller. Portraying the struggles of an innovative architect, Howard Roark (a character partly inspired by the life and work of Frank Lloyd Wright [1867–1959]), the novel dramatizes the conflict between the creative individual and those who live as "second-hand" parasites on his achievements. Roark was Rand's first full-fledged attempt at "the projection of an ideal man," her explicit literary goal. He was intransigently rational and independent, unwilling to give, or take, the unearned. This brand of EGOISM found expression in all of Rand's literary work—from her futuristic novelette *Anthem* to her

drama *Night of January 16th* to her *magnum opus, Atlas Shrugged.*

After the publication of *The Fountainhead,* Rand met, and exchanged ideas with, many of the leading conservative and libertarian intellectuals of the time, including Albert Jay Nock (1870–1945), H. L. Mencken (1880–1956), Isabel Paterson (1886–1961), Rose Wilder Lane (1886–1968), and Ludwig von Mises (1881–1973). During this period, she also wrote several movie scenarios and screenplays, of which three were successfully produced: *You Came Along* (1945), *Love Letters* (1945), and a film version of her own novel, *The Fountainhead* (1949).

Based on her experience in the film industry, Rand wrote, in 1947, a "Screen Guide for Americans" for the Motion Picture Alliance for the Preservation of American Ideals. The pamphlet urged producers and moviegoers to be wary of the injection of communist ideology into the American cinema. Her profound opposition to communism led her to appear as a "friendly witness" before the House Un-American Activities Committee in 1947. Her testimony focused on the deceptively idealized view of Soviet life presented in such films as *Song of Russia,* a 1943 propaganda effort to gain popular support for the American-Soviet alliance against Hitler.

In the 1940s, Rand also published several essays and labored on a short book, *The Moral Basis of Individualism,* a project she eventually abandoned. Most important, she began planning *Atlas Shrugged,* a novel celebrating "the men of the mind," the creative producers who carry the world on their shoulders. The novel explored the complex interconnections between fields as diverse as epistemology, art, ethics, psychology, economics, education, and human sexuality. Its publication, in 1957, ignited a firestorm of controversy. Leftist commentators blasted its pro-capitalist worldview, while conservatives renounced its atheistic HUMANISM.

The novel presented the outline of a philosophic system, which Rand eventually called "Objectivism." Her ideas soon gave rise to an intellectual movement as fans of her fiction flocked to hear her speak in public forums. This movement was fueled by her earliest followers—notably, Nathan Blumenthal and Barbara Weidman, whom she had met in the early 1950s when they were college students, and who subsequently married. Later, with Rand's enthusiastic approval, Nathaniel, who had taken the surname Branden, formed the Nathaniel Branden Institute (N.B.I.) to sponsor live and taped lectures worldwide in an effort to disseminate Objectivist philosophy.

As Rand appeared on numerous college campuses and on radio and television programs, she began to develop and articulate·her philosophy more systematically. With her associates, she founded a series of publications: *The Objectivist Newsletter* (1962–65), *The Objectivist* (1966–71), and *The Ayn Rand Letter* (1971–76). In addition, Rand wrote regular columns in 1962 for the *Los Angeles Times*. Important essays and speeches that first appeared in these various periodicals were later anthologized in such works as *The Virtue of Selfishness: A New Concept of Egoism* (1964), *Capitalism: The Unknown Ideal* (1967), *The Romantic Manifesto: A Philosophy of Literature* (1971), and *Introduction to Objectivist Epistemology* (1979).

In 1963, Lewis and Clark College in Portland, Oregon, granted Rand the honorary degree of Doctor of Humane Letters (L.H.D.). Yet many intellectuals continued to dismiss her as a reactionary popular philosopher who had spearheaded a movement based on a cult of personality. In 1968, that movement was dramatically sundered by Rand's sudden and mysterious rupture with the Brandens. Years later, it became clear that the break was precipitated by Nathaniel's termination of a long-term extramarital affair with Rand, who was twenty-five years his elder.

Though Rand continued to write and speak, she was estranged from many of her former associates and she became increasingly embittered by the state of the culture. She died in 1982 in New York City.

Rand's ideas substantially influenced aspects of late-twentieth-century political culture and its emphasis on limiting the role of government in economic and social affairs. One of her most prominent admirers is Alan Greenspan, who headed President Ford's Council of Economic Advisers and went on to become chairman of the Federal Reserve Board. Rand's ideas also inspired the founders of the modern Libertarian Party as well as many intellectuals in the libertarian tradition, including Robert NOZICK, Murray Rothbard, Charles Murray, Douglas Den Uyl, Douglas Rasmussen, Tibor Machan, and Eric Mack.

Objectivism is increasingly the subject of academic discussion and scholarship. Various aspects of Rand's thought are dealt with in college texts and in scholarly journals and books. The Estate of Ayn Rand continues to issue edited versions of previously unpublished materials, including her letters, marginalia, journals, and taped-lecture courses. And several organizations have been formed to further interest in her thought: the Ayn Rand Institute; The Objectivist Center (formerly the Institute for Objectivist Studies); and the Ayn Rand Society, an affiliate of the Eastern division of the American Philosophical Association.

See also: EGOISM; HUMANISM; INDIVIDUALISM; LIBERTARIANISM; NIETZSCHE; OBJECTIVISM; SELF-[entries].

Bibliography

Works by Rand

We the Living. New York: Macmillan, 1936. 60th anniversary ed., New York: Dutton, 1995.

The Fountainhead. Indianapolis: Bobbs-Merrill, 1943. 50th anniversary ed., New York: Bobbs-Merrill, 1993.

Anthem. Los Angeles: Pamphleteers, 1946. 50th anniversary ed., New York: Dutton, 1992.

Atlas Shrugged. New York: Random House, 1957. 35th anniversary ed., New York: Dutton, 1992.

The Early Ayn Rand: A Selection from Her Unpublished Fiction. Edited by Leonard Peikoff. New York: New American Library, 1984.

For the New Intellectual: The Philosophy of Ayn Rand. New York: New American Library, 1961. Includes an introductory essay on the history of philosophy, and philosophical excerpts from Rand's fiction.

"*Playboy* Interview with Ayn Rand: A Candid Conversation with the Fountainhead of 'Objectivism.'" *Playboy,* March 1964. Interviewer: Alvin Toffler. Reprinted as a separate monograph: *Ayn Rand: The Playboy Interview.* Poughkeepsie, NY: The Atlas Society, a division of The Objectivist Center, 1999.

The Virtue of Selfishness: A New Concept of Egoism. New York: New American Library, 1964. Essays on ethics and other subjects.

Capitalism: The Unknown Ideal. New York: New American Library, 1967. Essays on politics, economics, and history.

Night of January 16th. New York: New American Library, 1968. Courtroom drama in which a jury selected from the audience for each performance decides the verdict.

The New Left: The Anti-Industrial Revolution. 2d rev. ed. New York: New American Library, 1975. Essays on politics and the history of ideas.

The Romantic Manifesto: A Philosophy of Literature. 2d rev. ed. New York: New American Library, 1975. Essays on the nature and function of art as well as on literature and popular culture.

Philosophy: Who Needs It. New York: Bobbs-Merrill, 1982. Essays on metaphysics, epistemology, ethics, and politics.

The Voice of Reason: Essays in Objectivist Thought. Edited by Leonard Peikoff. New York: New American Library, 1989.

Introduction to Objectivist Epistemology. Enl. 2d ed. Edited by Harry Binswanger and Leonard Peikoff. New York: New American Library, 1990. Originally serialized in Rand's journal *The Objectivist,* 1966–1967. New edition features excerpts from her workshops on epistemology.

The Ayn Rand Column. New Milford, CT: Second Renaissance Books, 1991. Mostly articles written by Rand for the *Los Angeles Times.*

Letters of Ayn Rand. Edited by Michael S. Berliner. New York: Penguin Dutton, 1995. Collection of correspondence, 1926 to 1981.

Ayn Rand's Marginalia: Her Critical Comments on the Writings of over Twenty Authors. Edited by Robert Mayhew. New Milford, CT: Second Renaissance Books, 1995.

Journals of Ayn Rand. Edited by David Harriman. New York: Penguin Dutton, 1997. Rand's notes for her various writing projects.

Russian Writings on Hollywood. Edited by Michael S. Berliner. Marina del Rey, CA: Ayn Rand Institute Press, 1999. Includes translations of Rand's monographs *Pola Negri* and *Hollywood: American City of Movies.*

The Art of Fiction: A Guide for Writers and Readers. Edited by Tore Boeckmann. New York: Plume, 2000. An edited version of Rand's 1958 lectures on fiction writing.

Works about Rand

Branden, Barbara. *The Passion of Ayn Rand.* Garden City, NY: Doubleday, 1986. Biography by a former associate; served as the basis for a *Showtime* cable movie.

Branden, Nathaniel. *Judgment Day: My Years with Ayn Rand.* Boston: Houghton-Mifflin, 1989. Memoir by Rand's closest associate and former protégé. Revised and republished as *My Years with Ayn Rand.* San Francisco: Jossey-Bass, 1999.

Branden, Nathaniel, and Barbara Branden. *Who Is Ayn Rand? An Analysis of the Novels of Ayn Rand.* New York: Random House, 1962. Now out of print, this work includes a biographical essay by Barbara Branden and several essays by Nathaniel Branden on the literary and moral aspects of Rand's work. Nathaniel Branden's essays "The Moral Revolution in *Atlas Shrugged*" and "The Literary Method of Ayn Rand" have been reprinted as separate monographs by The Atlas Society, a division of The Objectivist Center.

Paxton, Michael. *Ayn Rand: A Sense of Life.* Layton, UT: Gibbs Smith, 1998. Companion book to Academy Award–nominated documentary film.

Sciabarra, Chris Matthew. *Ayn Rand: The Russian Radical.* University Park, PA: Pennsylvania State University Press, 1995. Examines Rand's early education and her Russian intellectual roots in relation to her philosophic system.

———. 1996. "Ayn Rand." In *American Writers: A Collection of Literary Biographies, Supplement IV, Part 2: Susan Howe to Gore Vidal,* edited by A. Walton Litz and Molly Wiegel, 517–35. New York: Charles Scribner's Sons, 1996. Reprinted in expanded form as *Ayn Rand: Her Life and Thought.* Poughkeepsie, NY: The Atlas Society, a division of The Objectivist Center, 1999.

———. "A Renaissance in Rand Scholarship." *Reason Papers* 23 (Fall 1998): 132–59. Reviews *Journals of Ayn Rand* and recent scholarship on her work.

———. "The Rand Transcript." *Journal of Ayn Rand Studies* 1, no. 1 (Fall 1999): 1–26. In-depth analysis of Rand's course work at the University of Leningrad, 1921–1924.

Chris Matthew Sciabarra

rape

Although philosophers have not much discussed it, rape has been recognized as a wrong in all the cultures within which they have written. Popular and legal views about the nature of the wrong have, however, changed greatly over time. Two dimensions of the change are of particular note: the specification of just which acts count as rape, along with the identification of those who are wronged by it; and the nature of that wrong.

What Counts as Rape and Who Is Wronged by It?

What is common to acts of rape is sexual intercourse (or possibly some other sexual act) performed by one person on another in the absence of the second person's CONSENT. It typically involves the use of overt force or threats, although it may instead involve COERCION or occur under circumstances in which what we would count as consent could not have been given (as, for example, in statutory rape). It occurs in most if not all cultures, but its incidence varies widely. Nearly all rapists are men, and the overwhelming majority of victims are women, although some victims are young boys or, especially in settings such as prison, men.

The word 'rape' is derived from the Latin *rapere* and originally referred to the carrying off or pillaging of PROPERTY. Gradually it took on a sexual meaning through singling out for particular attention the carrying off of a particular sort of quasi-property, namely women. In European and Euro-American societies women did not acquire most of the RIGHTS associated with legal personhood (*e.g.*, the franchise and the right to bring suit in one's own name) until the twentieth century, and their earlier status, although not precisely that of property, bore important similarities to it. In particular, women were not legally or morally those who were wronged by harms done to them; rather, the injured parties were their fathers or, if they were married, their husbands.

A woman's chastity (virginity prior to marriage and sexual exclusivity after it) was of considerable value, first to ensure her marriageability and later to guarantee that any children she bore were her husband's. Rape drastically reduced a woman's value, thus wronging the man who had a right to benefit from it. (In Athens in the fifth century B.C.E., for example, seduction of a married woman was a worse crime than rape, since more of value was stolen from the husband.) Under SLAVERY in the United States, slave owners were taken to have the right of sexual access to their female slaves, and sexual intercourse forced on slave women by the men who owned them was not considered rape.

More recently, as part of women's fight for legal and moral personhood, there has been a shift toward considering rape as a crime against the woman herself. The harm done is no longer considered as a decrease in the value of something for someone else, but rather as a direct harm to the victim, a harm similar in many ways to the harm done to victims of (other sorts of) assault. With that shift it became possible to think of men and boys as victims of rape, although in many ways the crime remains gendered. Not only are the large majority of victims actually women, but male victims are put in a position (that of being the passive recipient of another's sexual activity) that is culturally encoded as female.

The Role of Consent

Even though women, rather than their husbands or fathers, are now commonly seen as the victims of rape, there are conceptual residues of the earlier view. It is notoriously difficult to obtain a conviction against a rapist who has had a previous sexual relationship with the victim, or against a rapist whose victim is a prostitute or is otherwise regarded as promiscuous according to the standards of the community from which the jury is drawn. In such cases the victim is presumed to have consented, either to the particular man in question or to men in general. The presumption seems an odd one: compare the situation in which the victim of theft has previously given money to the thief or is a philanthropist. The difference in the case of rape comes from the residue of the belief that what is of value is not the woman's autonomy and bodily INTEGRITY, but her chastity, so that the relevant consent is taken to be her presumed earlier consent to the loss of chastity.

Similarly, only very recently have laws begun to change in cases of marital rape, which has been seen as a contradiction in terms: in most states of the United States, for example, rape was legally defined as nonconsensual sexual intercourse with a woman to whom the man was not married. The marriage contract included the right to sexual access, to which the wife was held to have consented at the time of the marriage.

By current criteria, an act of sexual intercourse counts as rape if it was done without consent. (Legally, the *mens rea* for rape refers to the defendant's belief about the victim's consent; questions continue to be raised about the standards of reasonableness to be applied when an alleged rapist believed falsely that his victim had consented.) But if in sexual encounters women are normatively passive and nonagential, consent is likely to be assumed to be tacit (even when a woman is protesting and struggling) or irrelevant (if "good" women are believed always to say no, whatever they may desire). When such assumptions are shared not only by rapists but by those who make up the judiciary, the legal profession, and juries, it can be difficult to demonstrate that a particular act was, in fact, rape.

Problematizing Consent

In some contexts the concept of consent can be seen as relatively unproblematic: the difficulties lie in disproving the presumption of consent in cases of rape. Feminist discussions, however, have raised fundamental questions about the conditions of the possibility of consent. In particular, such discussions have drawn attention to the ways in which INEQUAL-

ITY of POWER undercuts the possibility of consent. Thus, the assumption that consent could not have been freely given in cases of statutory rape is seen as reflecting not only the (likely) ignorance of the child about what was being "consented" to, but also the inequality of power between adult and child. This inequality renders suspicious the assumption that the child's consent was noncoerced, however the adult intended it.

This analysis has been extended to address the element of coercion arguably present in many, if not all, sexual encounters between women and men. The analysis is controversial in large measure because the assimilation of women's status to that of children seems to undercut both the reality and the possibility of female agency: those who in a given situation are regarded as incompetent to consent are unlikely to come to regard themselves as competent to resist. There are, however, inequalities of power that should frequently mitigate the assumption of the noncoerced validity of consent: it may be important, especially outside the legal context, to see consent as admitting of degrees of autonomy by recognizing simultaneously the possibilities for and the constraints on female agency.

Examination of the phenomenon of "date rape" or "acquaintance rape" (that is, rape of a woman by a man she knows, often a man with whom she is socially and perhaps romantically involved) has drawn attention both to the subtle forms of coercion experienced by, especially, young women (*e.g.,* the expectation of sexual favors in exchange for an expensive evening out) and to the systematically mixed messages between men and women concerning consent. As long as normative male sexuality involves conquest and normative female sexuality involves the coy denial of desire, it is difficult to see how such messages can be unmixed, how 'no' can be both meant and understood as 'no.'

The Nature of the Harm of Rape

Rape is a form of assault and carries with it the harm of assault: typically, bodily injury and the psychological harm of having been terrorized. But some rapes, for example those in which coercion rather than physical force is used, may involve no bodily injury. Also, the psychological harm of rape is likely in any case to differ from the harm of other assaults, in large part because the social meaning of rape is distinctive. Even when rape no longer literally devalues a woman, it tends to be experienced, both by the victim herself and by those around her, not only as the ultimate invasion but also as sullying and as obscurely blameworthy. The double cultural associations of sexuality—with intimacy and with sin—make sexual assault psychologically harmful in ways that other assaults are not. For boys and men, the harm of rape includes having been "feminized," that is, having been put sexually in the position of a woman, a position implicitly designated as shameful, in part because it is seen as lacking in agency.

Some feminists have argued that rape is not a sexual crime, but a crime of violence, an expression of hatred or rage directed against a woman *as a woman.* It is, thus, a form of TERRORISM, which victimizes all those who are, because also women, indirectly its target. Such an argument marks an important conceptual shift away from seeing rape as an expression of sexual desire that transgresses conventional bounds—a transgression either because the woman in question "belongs to" another man or because a would-be seducer gets carried away. In making this shift, however, it is important not to lose sight of the explicitly sexual nature of rape as well as the connections between rape and the still normative construction of male sexual desire as aggressive and dominating, as, in fact, misogynist, and female sexual desire as passive and submissive.

The Elimination of Rape

There are two meanings one might have in mind when speaking of the elimination of rape. One is definitional: society might eliminate rape as a category by no longer distinguishing between sexual and other assaults, in part as a response to the peculiar difficulties about consent. Or the elimination of rape might mean the virtual cessation of sexual assault. It is helpful, in coming to understand rape, to consider what would be involved in this second meaning. Crimes like theft, which obviously benefits the criminal, or murder, which obviously harms the victim, would presumably retain their basic motivations—to acquire what one cannot otherwise obtain or to do the gravest of harm to someone one hates—under any conceivable social arrangement, although society may hope to reduce their incidence. Rape, on the other hand, could become incomprehensible.

The defining core of rape is the use of sexual intercourse as an expression of hatred or rage, as a way of debasing and humiliating someone. The existence and the comprehensibility of rape require that male sexual desire be constructed and generally understood in ways that make the prospect of debasing and humiliating someone sexually stimulating. If societal sexual attitudes and the construction of male sexual desire are changeable—and there is no reason to believe that they aren't—then we can imagine a world in which we would simply fail to comprehend rape, because we would fail to comprehend either the sexiness of the violation of personhood or the peculiar aptness of forced sex as an expression of hatred and contempt. The elimination of rape would require not that we eliminate violence but that we cease to find sex inherently violent and violence inherently sexy, and such a change, although enormous, is surely imaginable.

See also: ABORTION; AGENCY AND DISABILITY; AUTONOMY OF MORAL AGENTS; COERCION; CONSENT; CORRECTIONAL ETHICS; DIGNITY; FEMINIST ETHICS; HATE; HONOR; INTEGRITY; MILITARY ETHICS; OPPRESSION; PATERNALISM; PERSUASIVE DEFINITION; POLICE ETHICS; PORNOGRAPHY; POWER; SEXUAL ABUSE AND HARASSMENT; SEXUALITY AND SEXUAL ETHICS; TERRORISM; VIOLENCE AND NON-VIOLENCE; WAR AND PEACE.

Bibliography

Baker, Brenda M. "Consent, Assault, and Sexual Assault." In *Legal Theory Meets Legal Practice,* edited by Anne F. Bayefsky. Edmonton, Alberta: Academic Printing and Publishing, 1988. Legal theory and philosophy of action, focusing on an analysis of consent.

Bar On, Bat-Ami. "Violence against Women: Philosophical Literature Overview and Bibliography." *American Philosophical Association Newsletter on Feminism and Philosophy* 88:1 (1988): 8–13.

Bienen, Leigh. "Mistakes." *Philosophy and Public Affairs* 7 (1978): 224–45. Philosophy of law; continuation of the discussion in Curley (1976).

Brownmiller, Susan. *Against Our Will: Men, Women, and Rape.* New York: Bantam, 1976. History and sociology.

Burgess-Jackson, Keith. "Rape and Persuasive Definition." *Canadian Journal of Philosophy* 25, no. 3 (1995): 415–54. A discussion of the issues surrounding the use by feminists of 'rape' to refer to acts not clearly covered by the term—notably to acquaintance or date rape. The author argues, against those who would delegitimate such usage as persuasive redefinition, that what is at stake are different theories of the nature of rape,

according to some of which such extensions of what is an intrinsically vague term are entirely appropriate.

Clark, Lorenne M. G., and Debra J. Lewis. *Rape: The Price of Coercive Sexuality.* Toronto: The Women's Press, 1977. Legal and political philosophy.

Curley, E. M. "Excusing Rape." *Philosophy and Public Affairs* 5 (1976): 325–60. Philosophy of law; concerns allowing defense against a charge of rape based on a possible mistaken belief in consent.

Davis, Angela. "The Myth of the Black Rapist." In *Women, Race, and Class.* New York: Random House, 1981. Addresses the racist portrayal of black men in the discussions of rape by many white feminists (*e.g.,* Brownmiller 1976).

May, Larry, and Robert Strikwerda. "Men in Groups: Collective Responsibility for Rape." *Hypatia* 9, no. 2 (1994): 134–51. The authors criticize the following views: only the rapist is responsible since only he committed the act; no one is responsible since rape is a biological response to stimuli; everyone is responsible since men and women contribute to the rape culture; and patriarchy is responsible but no person or group. They then argue that, in some societies, men are collectively responsible for rape since most benefit from rape and most are similar to the rapist.

Pomeroy, Sarah B. *Goddesses, Whores, Wives, and Slaves: Women in Classical Antiquity.* New York: Schocken, 1975.

Tong, Rosemary. *Women, Sex, and the Law.* Totowa, NJ: Rowman and Allanheld, 1984. Sociology and legal theory; includes a summary of arguments for and against assimilating rape law to assault law.

Vetterling-Braggin, Mary, and Jane English, eds. *Feminism and Philosophy.* Totowa, NJ: Littlefield, Adams, 1977. The section on rape includes a bibliography and the following essays: "Rape: The All-American Crime" by Susan Griffin; "Rape and Respect" by Carolyn M. Shafer and Marilyn Frye; "What's Wrong with Rape" by Pamela Foa; "Coercion and Rape: The State as a Male Protection Racket" by Susan Rae Peterson.

Naomi Scheman

rational choice

Contemporary rational choice theory is largely the outgrowth of economic approaches to understanding human behavior. It has forerunners in many classical and, especially, English philosophers. Some of its chief findings were presaged in the work of moral and political philosophers from PLATO (c. 430–347 B.C.E.) to JOHN STUART MILL (1806–1873). Thomas HOBBES (1588–1679), David HUME (1711–1776), and the utilitarians make extensive use of rational choice arguments. The central concern of this enterprise is to explain and sometimes to justify individual choices and their aggregation into social choice as grounded in individual incentives, usually, but not always, as represented in individual INTERESTS. The resolute application of the assumption of self-interest to social action and INSTITUTIONS begins with Hobbes.

The contemporary field may be defined by five major areas. The first of these, utility theory, is a theory of value that arguably has ancient origins. Its broad impact has followed its careful articulation roughly from Jeremy BENTHAM (1748–1832) through nineteenth- and twentieth-century economists. The second area is GAME THEORY, which see.

Work in two other areas has been stimulated by discoveries of major problems in the aggregation of individual into collective choices. First, there is the difficulty of aggregating individual preferences into an analogously defined collective preference. Aspects of this problem were seen by the Marquis de Condorcet (1743–1794) and C. L. Dodgson (Lewis Carroll, 1832–1898), but the contemporary understanding dates from Kenneth Arrow's Impossibility Theorem (1951) and Duncan Black's simultaneous work on cyclic majorities. Finally there is the problem of the game theorist's prisoner's dilemma, discovered in some experiments at the Rand Corporation around 1950, and its larger-number analog in the logic of collective action, given its first general treatment by Mancur Olson Jr. (1965). This problem affects groups of individuals who have essentially identical or similar preferences, which could easily be aggregated into at least a partial social preference, so that the group choice need not suffer from Arrow problems. Despite their collective preference for a clearly superior outcome, members of a group reach an inferior outcome if they act from individually rational motivations.

Discovery of these two problems, of preference aggregation and collective action, is essentially the recognition of two fallacies of composition. The first fallacy is to suppose that, if individuals have preferences, then societies or groups of individuals must have preferences of a similar kind. The second is to suppose that, if we all collectively prefer to produce *A* rather than *B,* we will collectively act to produce *A* rather than *B,* just as we would do individually if we were acting on individual preferences. These fallacies pervade much of social thought. Their clear exposure affects our understanding of many issues, often in ways that cast doubt on the coherence of the practical and normative aspirations of many philosophers and other social theorists. In this respect, rational choice theory often seems dispiriting. In many cases it also seems to undercut or even render unintelligible what might have seemed to be straightforward concepts, especially concepts in value theory, strategic interaction, and individual and social choice.

The fifth major area is a part of law and economics. Among the major contributions that have defined this field is the Coase theorem of Ronald Coase (1960).

In addition to these five areas, there are many related areas, including a miscellany of microeconomic analyses and problems as well as discussions of institutions to resolve the aggregation problems. Game theory is discussed elsewhere; here I will address the other four major areas and then briefly mention related areas.

Utility Theory

Traditionally and perhaps commonsensically, utility was seen to inhere in objects, as though the measure of the utility of an object would be the same for everyone. For example, this view is the background for labor theories of value, which hold that the value of anything is a function of the effort put into bringing it about. Against any such theory, we know two things. First, objects that one person values may be worthless to another person. Indeed, without differences in personal valuations there would be no reason for exchange beyond the fact that, say, I might be more efficient at producing some things and you might be more efficient at producing others, so that we could both be better off concentrating our efforts and then exchanging goods. Second, we know that someone might expend enormous effort to produce something of almost no value to anyone. Insofar as utility theory is to serve in the analysis of human choice behavior, it must therefore be subjective.

Much of moral theory is grounded on assumptions that certain values are objective or universal. For example, in his theory of justice, John RAWLS assumes that certain goods and liberties have more or less the same value for everyone. Much of what is good and enjoyable about social life depends on the fact that many of the values that motivate us are not objective or universal. One device for converting even such values to objective status is to put resources for achieving welfare or utility, instead of welfare or utility itself, at the base of theory. Even such a value as LIBERTY may be seen as a resource. Oddly, however, this move seems to make these values—liberties, RIGHTS, and various resources—means rather than basic values in their own right. Yet making them values independent of their effects may cut them free of moral support. This fundamental problem in conceptions of value at the base of moral theories may have been exacerbated by developments in utility theory, which, as is true of other intellectual developments in the twentieth century, seem to take us farther from fundamental resolution rather than closer to it.

Even when it was considered as subjective, the utility of something was commonly conceived to be a cardinal number, so that we could speak of three utiles and so forth. If I value object or experience *A* at three utiles and object *B* at four utiles, one might suppose I must value the pair at seven utiles. But such simple summation is clearly wrong in many cases. For example, I do not rate two identical dinners tonight at twice the value of one dinner. Moreover, I may rate a dinner that combines a variety of items as worth much more than the values I would assign to each of those things alone. The value of the two dinners is less than the sum of the values of the two taken separately because the two identical dinners are *substitutes* for each other and either one fulfills my demand. The value of the combination of foods in a dinner may be greater than the values of the parts taken separately because these parts are *complements* to each other. Hence, if my utility is to have cardinal values, I can define utility only for total states of affairs rather than for pieces of such states. But if I must evaluate whole states of affairs, there may be little point in assigning cardinal values to them. For many purposes it will be sufficient to determine a rank order for alternative whole states of affairs.

Utilitarianism and utility theory developed more or less together from Bentham through F. Y. Edgeworth (1845–1926), whose mathematical developments philosophers did not follow while economists eventually did. Apart from continuing concern with Mill's qualitative differences in pleasures or utilities and with G. E. MOORE's (1873–1958) organic wholes, utilitarian value theory has tended to be stuck with Edgeworth's and Bentham's simple theory of increments of utility that can be added over a

lifetime and across persons. That theory was displaced in economics by the development of ordinal utility theory and by Vilfredo Pareto's (1848–1923) rejection of interpersonal comparisons. Pareto insisted that interpersonal comparisons of utility are without meaning and that they therefore cannot ground a moral recommendation for redistribution. The strict welfarist who agrees with Pareto can only recommend *Pareto improvements:* changes that make someone better off while making no one worse off. If no such improvement is possible, our state of affairs is *Pareto optimal.*

Economists continue to be utilitarian or welfarist while also being Paretian ordinalists. The ultimate achievement of this general approach has been Arrow's impossibility theorem, whose implication is that moral recommendations on social order must be very limited in scope if social choice is to have individualist foundations. Nevertheless, the set theoretic analysis of collective choice following Arrow's work and the game theoretic analysis of social interactions have led to renewed interest by economists in moral and political theory and by philosophers in economic approaches to their issues.

Many economists and philosophers object to subjective utility on the ground that it would have to be an inaccessible mental predicate. We could not measure it or make sense of its causal role in behavior. Revealed preference theory was introduced in economics in the 1930s as a purely behavioral indicator. I reveal my preferences through my choices. Of course, I am unlikely to face enough choices to reveal much of the plausible range of preferences I might have. Moreover, even those who most wish to purge mental terminology from utility theory often have difficulty expressing results in terms that do not imply a mental background of utility.

The Arrow Problem

Condorcet and Dodgson independently noted that majority decision procedures have a troubling flaw. Majorities may prefer *A* to *B*, *B* to *C*, and *C* to *A*. Hence, although each individual voter may be able to rank all candidates consistently, the majority may not be able to rank them but may exhibit preferences that cycle through a choice set. This can be true no matter how large the majority required for decision, so long as it is less than unanimity. For example, 99-percent majorities may exhibit cyclic preferences over 100 candidates.

In some respects, this result should not be surprising. It is merely an instance of the general fact that collectivities need not have the properties of their individual constituents. But the result may trouble democratic theorists and others who wish to give normative justifications for collective decisions. Arrow's General Possibility Theorem, better known and described as his Impossibility Theorem, is that there can be no collective decision rule that meets certain conditions, which are either seemingly innocuous or morally compelling, and that can aggregate individual preference orderings into a social ordering. Hence, not only majority rule but every possible rule is subject to anomalies.

The conditions that Arrow's theorem imposes on aggregations, as simplified in later writings, include the following: O, the ordering condition—the collective choice is a ranking of all states of affairs under consideration; U, the condition of universal domain—our social choice rule must apply to all possible states of affairs; P, the Pareto or unanimity condition—if everyone prefers state x to state y, the social choice must rank x over y. N, nondictatorship—there can be no individual whose ordering is automatically the social ordering; and I, independence of irrelevant alternatives—if individuals' orderings over other alternatives change without affecting their orderings over two or more states, the social ordering over those two or more states must remain unaffected.

The nondictatorship and unanimity conditions may seem morally compelling on their faces. But the other conditions may seem objectionable on various grounds. Our social choice rule need not apply to all possible states of affairs but only to those that come before us. But even a reasonably restricted condition U will suffice to yield impossibilities. Should our social choice meet condition O? We often need no more than to choose a first preference; we do not need a complete ranking of all possible states. But, again, a reasonably restricted condition O may suffice to block apparently good aggregation rules, as simple majority procedures fail in the face of cyclic majorities over first choices only. Finally, condition I has little overt appeal because it is not transparently about anything that matters to us. It effectively entails that the social ordering can be built up out of social orderings over pairs of alternative states.

An election in which the front runner among several candidates wins without facing and defeating each alternative candidate in turn would be ruled out by this condition.

Objections to particular conditions in Arrow's and related theorems of social choice call the entire enterprise into question. Can we stipulate the *a priori* rightness of various procedural rules and then suppose that consequences are acceptable only to the extent that they are consistent with these rules? Axiomatic social choice theory is built on such a supposition. Critics may often suppose that their grasp of the rightness of general consequences of the application of various aggregation rules is better than their grasp of the rightness of the rules themselves. One of the most important lessons to be learned from social choice theory may be the inherent difficulty of making strong claims for the priority of various procedural restrictions when our central concern is with the choices of individuals.

The Arrow theorem itself and much of the ensuing program grows out of the ordinal revolution in value theory. Arrow wanted specifically to assess what scope is left for social choice when individual utility functions are only ordinal and are not interpersonally comparable and additive. Such an assessment is a natural expression of the utilitarian bent of twentieth-century welfare economics. It is not surprising that Arrow's value theory does not fit classical UTILITARIANISM, which was grounded on cardinal, interpersonally comparable, additive utility. But the implications of that value theory for a reconstructed utilitarianism have not been broadly addressed by contemporary philosophers.

Collective Action and Prisoner's Dilemma

You and I may benefit from mutually acting, each at some individual cost, to produce a joint benefit. For example, Hume supposes that we might wish to drain the marsh that borders our properties. Both of us might reckon the benefit of the joint production to be greater than our own individual cost even though neither of us reckons the individual benefit to outweigh the total cost of the joint product. Moreover, each of us might most benefit from letting the other do the other's share while we do nothing. Hence, we have a joint interest in individually bearing half the cost if the cooperation of the other can be made contingent on our own.

If there is a large number of us in the same position with respect to some joint provision, each of us might benefit most by defecting from the cooperation and free riding on the efforts of others. Hence, although we would all benefit from all cooperating, no one of us might have incentive to cooperate.

Unlike the Arrow problem, this problem is fundamentally motivational. It arises despite the fact that many social choice rules would readily produce cooperative action from all parties but that individual incentives work against cooperation. The fallacy of composition that the Arrow theorem points up is the fact that there may be no social preference orderings analogous to individual preference orderings. The fallacy of composition implicit in the logic of collective action is the fact that, while individual interests and motivations to action may be closely tied, collective interests and motivations to action may be quite contrary. In both cases, collectivities are, in important respects, not like the individuals that constitute them.

The odd mismatch of individual incentives and what may loosely be called collective interests is the independent discovery of game theorists, who invented the Prisoner's Dilemma for two persons, and of various philosophers and social theorists who have noted the collective action problem in various contexts (a problem finally articulated cogently in general terms by Olson in 1965).

A specific problem of collective action of central importance in democratic theory is the mismatch between individual incentives and the collective interest in having all citizens vote in elections. If voting entails costs to individuals whereas the benefit from voting is essentially a collective benefit only very weakly dependent on any individual's vote, individuals may find it in their interest not to vote. Evidence from polities in which voting is required and failure to vote is penalized and from those in which there are no penalties for not voting suggests that not voting is a widespread obstacle to popular expression of electoral preferences.

More generally, if political outcomes depend on popular action to inform or influence public officials, we may expect to see strong individual incentives working against democratic representativeness. Hence, the aspirations of DEMOCRACY may falter on Arrow and related problems of the incoherence of aggregation from individual to social choices and,

also, on the disincentive of citizens to act individually in the collective interest.

Law and Economics

The massive field of law and economics is partly driven by the simple application of standard economic theory to legal issues. Much of it, however, is driven by the view that we should make at least the civil law *ex ante* efficient. The foundational argument for this school of thought is the Coase theorem, which says that, subject to certain conditions, the assignment of rights over a productive resource will not affect the actual production from that resource. For example, if I own a piece of land but you can make more productive use of it, I will have incentive to lease my land to your enterprise for a share of your greater profits. The conditions of the theorem are that there are no transaction costs, such as communication, BARGAINING, and litigation costs.

Important implications follow. First, of course, while production might not be affected by a rights assignment, income typically will be. Hence, the main effect of assigning a right over use of some resource to you instead of to me is to give you a greater share of our net benefits from using the resource in the most productive way.

Second, we might suppose that rights assignments would generally be more productive if they were designed to reduce transaction costs. If transaction costs are high, a libertarian first-come-first-served view of property rights might not be generally beneficial because it might block productivity to such an extent as to make all worse off. Unfortunately, this view suggests that rights be assigned to the party who can make best use of the relevant resource, but this rule is implausible. A more plausible move is to design institutions to reduce transaction costs. The scale of these costs is suggested by the fact that the use of civil law is itself a cost of transactions, indeed, a major cost.

Other Issues

There are many efforts to construct alternative value theories not consistent with standard utility theory but largely grounded in a combination of self-interest and other motivations, such as ALTRUISM. There are widespread efforts among economists to apply standard economic analyses, such as price and equilibrium theory, to problems of broad interest to moral and political philosophers. And there is extensive work on the ECONOMIC ANALYSIS of institutional structures and possibilities. All of these efforts would be relevant to addressing, for example, a major missing part of Rawls's theory of justice. His theory specifies what kinds of results we should want to achieve with our political institutions, but it leaves as a separate project the task of devising the relevant institutional structures. What structures would work depends in part on what motivations are likely to work for actual people.

There is also a large body of empirical work on the issues raised by rational choice theory. Much of this work analyzes actual behavior in real contexts and much is experimental, as in gaming experiments. Much of this work attempts to assess to what extent people actually are motivated by something other than self-interest, such as altruism.

See also: ADDITIVITY PROBLEMS; BARGAINING; BARRY; BENTHAM; COERCION; COHERENTISM; COLLECTIVE RESPONSIBILITY; CONSENT; COOPERATION, CONFLICT, AND COORDINATION; COOPERATIVE SURPLUS; DELIBERATION AND CHOICE; DEMOCRACY; DETERRENCE, THREATS, AND RETALIATION; DISCOUNTING THE FUTURE; ECONOMIC ANALYSIS; ECONOMIC SYSTEMS; EQUALITY; FAIRNESS; GAME THEORY; HOBBES; HUME; INDIVIDUALISM; INSTITUTIONS; INTERESTS; INTERNATIONAL JUSTICE: CONFLICT; INTRANSITIVITY; JUSTICE, DISTRIBUTIVE; LIBERTY; JOHN STUART MILL; POLITICAL SYSTEMS; PUBLIC POLICY; PUBLIC POLICY ANALYSIS; RAWLS; RECIPROCITY; REFLECTIVE EQUILIBRIUM; REVOLUTION; RIGHTS; RISK AVERSION; SOCIAL AND POLITICAL PHILOSOPHY; SOCIAL CONTRACT; STRATEGIC INTERACTION; TRUST; UTILITARIANISM; VALUE, CONCEPT OF; VALUE, THEORY OF; WELFARE RIGHTS AND SOCIAL POLICY.

Bibliography

Arrow, Kenneth J. *Social Choice and Individual Values.* 2d ed. New Haven, CT: Yale University Press, 1963 [1951].

Barry, Brian. *Theories of Justice.* Berkeley: University of California Press, 1989. Includes a game theoretic account of theories of distributive justice.

———, and Russell Hardin, eds. *Rational Man and Irrational Society.* Beverly Hills, CA: Sage, 1982. A collection of papers on the Arrow and collective action problems with commentaries; extensive bibliography.

Coase, Ronald H. "The Problem of Social Cost." In *The Firm, the Market, and the Law,* 95–156. Chicago: University of Chicago Press, 1988 (essay first published 1960). One in a collection of important papers on law and economics.

Downs, Anthony. *An Economic Theory of Democracy.* New York: Harper and Row, 1957. On the problem of collective action that undercuts individual incentive to vote.

Eatwell, John, *et al. The New Palgrave: A Dictionary of Economics.* 4 vols. London: Macmillan, 1987. Includes many articles on Arrow's problem, game theory, utility theory, and economists who have made major contributions to these issues; extensive bibliographies.

Hardin, Russell. *Morality within the Limits of Reason.* Chicago: University of Chicago Press, 1988. Applies game theoretic reasoning to utilitarian moral theory.

———. "Rational Choice Theories." In *Idioms of Inquiry: Critique and Renewal in Political Science,* edited by Terence Ball. Albany, NY: SUNY Press, 1987. Discusses differences between game theoretic and microeconomic value theories.

Kavka, Gregory S. *Hobbesian Moral and Political Theory.* Princeton, NJ: Princeton University Press, 1986. A game theoretic analysis.

Mueller, Dennis. *Public Choice II.* 2d ed. Cambridge: Cambridge University Press, 1989. An economist's textbook survey of rational choice theory; extensive bibliography.

Olson, Mancur. *The Logic of Collective Action.* Cambridge, MA: Harvard University Press, 1965. The original treatment of the logic of collective action.

Rawls, John. *A Theory of Justice.* Cambridge, MA: Harvard University Press, 1971.

Samuelson, Paul. "Complementarity: An Essay on the 40th Anniversary of the Hicks-Allen Revolution in Demand Theory." *Journal of Economic Literature* 12 (1974): 1255–89. Account of the development of ordinal utility theory from its beginnings; extensive bibliography.

Sen, Amartya. *Collective Choice and Social Welfare.* San Francisco, CA: Holden-Day, 1970. Survey of the Arrow problem and related issues; extensive (but dated) bibliography.

Russell Hardin

rationality vs. reasonableness

Although both "rationality" and "reasonableness" come from the same Latin root *ratio* ("reason"), some moral philosophers have drawn a sharp distinction between them. According to this distinction, a person is said to be rational if he chooses the most efficient means to his ends, whatever they may be; while, on the other hand, a person is said to be reasonable if he maintains a certain equitable relation between himself and others, a relation characterized by IMPARTIALITY and mutuality of consideration. Thus, reasonableness is directly a moral quality, while rationality is often nonmoral, and it may even be immoral if the agent's ends are exclusively self-interested in ways that go counter to the important INTERESTS or RIGHTS of other persons.

Their Relation to Reason

An initial question concerns how each of these practical qualities is related to reason viewed in the cognitive sense of the power of ascertaining and preserving truth, with its concomitant intellectual procedures and criteria. The relation seems straightforward in the case of rationality, because this involves sound reasoning, inferring, or calculating from some desired end to the means that serve to achieve or maximize that end, whatever it may be. Since means-end reasoning is a species of cause-effect reasoning, in that the end is a desired effect and the means are the actions that are intended to produce or cause the attainment of that effect, the process of reasoning involved in rationality is, broadly speaking, inductive.

The use of reason in the case of reasonableness does not seem to be of this sort. It is indeed true that a reasonable person, aiming to maintain a certain equitableness or mutuality of consideration between herself and others, may need to calculate how this moral end is best achieved. But directly or in itself reasonableness does not involve such means-end inferences; it is rather a characteristic of the end itself. Reasonableness derives from a different use or criterion of reason: logical consistency or the avoidance of self-contradiction. To be reasonable is to accept that what is right for oneself is also right for other persons who are relevantly similar to oneself, so that, at the level of morality where important interests are at stake, it is to accept that other persons, having similar NEEDS or basic interests, have the same rights to their fulfillment as one necessarily wants for oneself. To be unreasonable is thus to contradict oneself, because it consists in holding, on the one hand, that one has certain rights because one has certain needs or interests (where this "because" is that of sufficient reason or condition) and, on the other hand, that other persons who have those same needs or interests do not have those rights. As thus

based on the principle of noncontradiction, reasonableness is an application of deductive inference.

Consistency is also involved in rationality, in the ordering of one's desires and beliefs and in the actions one takes in accordance with them. But such consistency is usually purely intrapersonal (or perhaps also intragroup, where a group may have a common objective), whereas the consistency involved in reasonableness is interpersonal and intergroup, and thus more directly moral. There are also other differences because of the contingent contents allowed by rationality.

Is It Rational to Be Reasonable?

When the ends comprised in rationality are taken to be purely self-interested, its relation to reasonableness raises a problem that has been a perennial preoccupation of moral philosophy: whether it is rational to be reasonable, that is, whether it is in an individual's self-interest to accept and act in accordance with the mutualist, other-regarding requirements of morality. The affirmative answers given by many moral philosophers can be divided into two groups, depending on the view taken of the 'self.' One group, which includes Thomas HOBBES (1588–1679) and David HUME (1711–1776), tries to maintain the original empirical self basically unchanged, with its drive for POWER and possessions. This group incurs various difficulties, including the free rider problem: even if it is in an individual's self-interest to live in a society that maintains the requirements of morality, especially justice, is it not even more in his interest that, while everyone else obeys these requirements, he himself flouts them whenever it is in his interest to do so and he can get away with it? Hobbes's answer that he will not be able to count on getting away with it, especially because of the sovereign's ubiquitous power, is contradicted by the examples of unjust rogues throughout history.

Another group, which includes PLATO (c. 430–347 B.C.E.) and Jean-Jacques ROUSSEAU (1712–1778), contends that the self must undergo change in the direction of "mental health" or similar NORMS. Once this is done, this ideal self's interests will coincide with the requirements of morality. A closely related version of such an approach is that of John RAWLS, who holds that the selves who choose the constitution of their society must operate behind a "veil of ignorance" whereby they are unaware of all their own particular qualities, so that they operate as Kantian "noumenal selves."

This approach also incurs various difficulties. If the "mental health" (or "health of the soul") of which Plato speaks is not to be question-beggingly identified with moral goodness, there is considerable doubt that the mentally healthy person must have the moral commitments that Plato attributes to her. In the case of Rawls there seems to be a similar begging of the question, because, by contra-rationally depriving his individual choosers of all knowledge of their personal qualities, he imposes on them the very FAIRNESS or EQUALITY which it is the purpose of his argument to establish as the system they will "rationally" choose.

The Question of Justificatory Priority

Can the normative or justificatory priority of reasonableness over rationality be defended in a non-question-begging way? It may be argued that this can be done by showing that the principle of noncontradiction, as the first principle of reason, is violated by the person who is egoistically rational, *i.e.,* unreasonable. On the other hand, the reasonable person or group, as such, need not violate the general criteria of means-end rationality.

Hume's Objections and Kantian Replies

The appeal to noncontradiction for grounding moral duties is especially prominent in Immanuel KANT's (1724–1804) first version of the categorical imperative: "Act only on that maxim which you can at the same time will to be a universal law," where "can will" means without self-contradiction. In this and other ways Kant is an upholder of reason in the sense of reasonableness as definitive of morally justified ends, including ultimate ends.

Important objections against this grounding of ultimate ends in reason were presented by Hume. One of his arguments is that because an ultimate or final end is desired for its own sake or "on its own account," no further reason can be given for desiring it, so that "ultimate ends . . . can never, in any case, be accounted for by reason" (*Enquiry,* app. 1). The 'reason' that is here in question is probabilistic or inductive because it is a form of means-end reasoning. The Kantian reply is that the ultimate ends of reasonableness can be accounted for by reason because the moral principle that human beings ought to be treated as having basic rights and hence as ends in themselves can be given a stringently necessary proof, since its denial involves self-contradiction.

A second, closely related argument of Hume is that desired ends move persons to ACTION, but "reason, being cool and disengaged, is no motive to action"; "reason alone can never be a motive to any action of the will" (*Treatise,* 1.3.3). To understand the Kantian reply, at least three points must be noted. First, as against the contrast of "rational" and "reasonable," "rational" can be used in a broader sense to signify whatever is in accord with or established by reason. Second, for Kant as for Hume, reason is a second-order power in that it takes over contents gotten from other sources, including human desires, choices, or actions, and it then critically evaluates or develops these contents on the basis of rational criteria. But Hume confines this rationality to *inductive* reason, including its beginning point in empirical facts. He holds that inductive reason can influence passions and actions by examining their assumptions about what objects exist or what means will be causally efficacious to desired ends. Thus he says, "The moment we perceive the falsehood of any supposition or the insufficiency of any means, our passions yield to our reason without any opposition" (*Treatise,* 2.3.3). On this view even an ultimate end could be irrational if the person who wanted it was making a factual mistake about its constituents or its possibility. But none of this would affect the question of the moral quality of the end; it would not serve to establish what ends morally ought to be desired.

Kant's important addition in this context is to show that *deductive* rationality can also provide criteria for evaluating the rightness of actions and that these criteria apply to ultimate moral ends as well as to means. Reason can "command" the will by setting rational requirements of logical consistency for the universalized maxims of actions that test whether they are reasonable. To say that reason "commands" that these requirements be fulfilled is to say that reason provides the criteria for the rational justificatory adequacy of the maxims in terms of consistency. Whether Kant's consistency test for distinguishing moral from immoral maxims is successful is a further, independent question; but other kinds of consistency tests are also available.

A third point bearing on motivation is that rational persons are motivated to act as reason requires. This is the "internalist" point that motivation is internal to reason. Presumably Hume himself would admit that when acts of deductive mathematical reasoning eventuate in contradictions, the reasoners are motivated to reject such conclusions. Since, in the Kantian doctrine, deductive rational criteria apply to the practical ends that persons set for themselves, their wills can be similarly motivated. In this way reason as reasonableness can move persons to action.

See also: CATEGORICAL AND HYPOTHETICAL IMPERATIVES; CAUSATION AND RESPONSIBILITY; COMMUNITARIANISM; CONSTRUCTIVISM; COOPERATION, CONFLICT, AND COORDINATION; FINAL GOOD; HOBBES; HUME; IMPARTIALITY; INTERESTS; KANT; LOGIC AND ETHICS; MORAL REASONING; MOTIVES; NEEDS; NORMS; PLATO; RATIONAL CHOICE; RAWLS; REASONS FOR ACTION; RIGHTS; ROUSSEAU; SELF-DECEPTION; SELF-KNOWLEDGE; THEORY AND PRACTICE.

Bibliography

Gauthier, David. *Morals by Agreement.* Oxford: Clarendon Press, 1986. Constrained maximizers benefit from cooperation.

Gewirth, Alan. "Can Any Final Ends Be Rational?" *Ethics* 102 (1991): 66–95.

———. "The Rationality of Reasonableness." *Synthese* 57 (1983): 225–47. Reasonableness, based on logically necessary argument, overrides egoistic rationality.

Held, Virginia. "Rationality and Reasonable Cooperation." *Social Research* 44 (1977): 708–44. Uses difficulties of Prisoner's Dilemma to argue for cooperative "social solution" of reasonableness as against competitive rationality.

Hobbes, Thomas. *Leviathan.* 1651. (Many recent editions.) Self-interested individuals, to avoid lethal dangers of anarchy, will accept constraints of morality and a sovereign to enforce them.

Hume, David. *Enquiry Concerning the Principles of Morals.* Edited by L. A. Selby-Bigge. Oxford: Clarendon Press, 1962 [1751]. Honest persons have "inward peace of mind" (section 9, part 2, pp. 282–84).

———. *Treatise of Human Nature.* 1737. (Many recent editions.)

Kant, Immanuel. *Fundamental Principles of the Metaphysics of Morals.* Translated by L. W. Beck. Indianapolis: Library of Liberal Arts, 1959 [1785].

Peters, R. S. "The Development of Reason." In *Rationality and the Social Sciences,* edited by S. I. Benn and G. W. Mortimore, 299–331. London: Routledge and Kegan Paul, 1976. Discusses distinction between rationality and reasonableness in relation to Piaget's account of moral development.

Plato. *Republic.* Mental health is moral virtue (IV. 444).

Rawls, John. "Kantian Constructivism in Moral Theory." *Journal of Philosophy* 77 (1980): 515–72. The reasonable presupposes and subordinates the rational.

———. *A Theory of Justice.* Cambridge: Harvard University Press, 1971. Rational, self-interested persons will choose principles of justice from behind a "veil of ignorance."

Richards, David A. J. *A Theory of Reasons for Action.* Oxford: Clarendon Press, 1971. Reasonableness may conflict with, but is justificatorily prior to, rational choice.

Rousseau, Jean-Jacques. *The Social Contract.* Translated by Donald A. Cress. Indianapolis: Hackett, 1987 [1762].

Sibley, W. M. "The Rational versus the Reasonable." *Philosophical Review* 62 (1953): 554–60. Reasonableness cannot be derived from rationality, but involves judgment by an impartial, sympathetic spectator.

Alan Gewirth

Rawls, John (1921–)

Born and raised in Baltimore, Maryland, John Rawls received his undergraduate and graduate education at Princeton. After earning his Ph.D. in philosophy in 1950, Rawls taught at Princeton, Cornell, the Massachusetts Institute of Technology, and, since 1962, at Harvard, where he is now professor emeritus.

Rawls is best known for *A Theory of Justice* (1971) and for developments of that theory he has published since. Rawls believes that the utilitarian tradition has dominated modern political philosophy in English-speaking countries because its critics have failed to develop an alternative social and political theory as complete and systematic. Rawls's aim is to develop such an alternative: a contractarian view of justice, derived from the tradition of John LOCKE (1632–1704), Jean-Jacques ROUSSEAU (1712–1778), and especially Immanuel KANT (1724–1804).

Rawls carries SOCIAL CONTRACT theory to a "higher order of abstraction" by viewing the principles of justice themselves as the objects of a social contract. Justice is the solution to a problem, which arises in this way: Society, as it is conceived in a liberal DEMOCRACY, is a cooperative venture between free and equal persons for their mutual advantage. Individuals participate in it in order to implement their conceptions of the good life. Cooperation makes a better life possible for everyone by increasing the stock of what Rawls calls "primary goods"—things that it is rational to want whatever else you want, because they are required for any conception of a good life. Primary social goods include RIGHTS, liberties, powers, opportunities, income, wealth, and the social bases of SELF-RESPECT. But society is also characterized by conflict, since people disagree not only about how its benefits and burdens should be distributed, but also about conceptions of the good. Principles of justice are used to evaluate the distributions of benefits and burdens and the INSTITUTIONS that effect them. Rawls's idea is to identify an acceptable conception of justice by asking what principles it would be reasonable for the members of society to agree to, which is to say, what principles would be fair. Accordingly, he calls his account "justice as fairness."

A voluntary cooperative arrangement is fair when the participants agree to the principles that govern their association and when those principles are applied consistently. The task of achieving FAIRNESS in political society is made difficult by two facts. First, society is not actually a voluntary arrangement. We are born into it and have little real choice whether to participate. Second, people are born into different social positions, with different expectations and opportunities. As Rawls sees it, an array of starting places is created by the "basic structure" of society, that is, its political, social, and economic institutions. The effects of one's starting place on one's expectations are pervasive, yet this place is neither voluntarily adopted nor deserved. If society is to approximate a fair voluntary arrangement, then, the principles of justice must govern its basic structure, and the resulting institutions and distributions must be acceptable to each person no matter what social position she is born into.

Rawls therefore proposes that we envision the principles of justice as chosen by members of society themselves in a specially designed standpoint, which he calls "the original position." To guarantee a choice that is both rational and fair, Rawls incorporates special conditions into the original position. First, the parties in the original position are under a "veil of ignorance." They have no knowledge of their individual places in society. They do not know their race, gender, social class, personal characteristics, or conceptions of the good life. They can reason only on the basis of general knowledge. Second, the parties in the original position are mutually disinterested "moral persons." A moral person is characterized by two "moral powers." The first is the capacity for the sense of justice: she can understand, apply, and act from a conception of justice. The second is the capacity to formulate, revise, and rationally pursue a conception of the good. In *A Theory of Justice,* Rawls emphasizes that the parties are motivated to advance their particular conceptions of the good, although they do not know exactly what these conceptions are. In later works, this motive is supplemented by the parties' higher-order desire to exercise the two moral powers. These MOTIVES, together with the restriction on information, guarantee that the parties will serve as unbiased representatives of every member of society when selecting the principles of justice.

The original position is designed to represent the autonomy of citizens in a democracy, and the resulting conception of justice is an ideal one. Rawls believes that the problems generated by the mentally incompetent or ill, and by the noncompliant who refuse to obey the accepted conception of justice, require special principles that should be generated after, and in light of, an ideal conception. Since the principles chosen in the original position are designed to govern the basic structure of a society in which there are no prior claims on PROPERTY or POWER, non-ideal theory is also needed to govern the transition from an unjust society to a just one. These issues are treated separately; we begin by choosing principles for an ideally just society.

It would be best if we could reason directly from the situation of the parties in the original position to a formulation of the principles it would be rational for them to choose. Short of that, we may imagine that various conceptions of justice are proposed to them, among which they choose. In *A Theory of Justice,* Rawls argues that the parties would prefer his own conception of justice to the principle of utility. Rawls's conception of justice consists of two principles:

(i) Each person has an equal right to a fully adequate scheme of equal basic rights and liberties compatible with a similar scheme for everyone.

(ii) Social and economic inequalities are to be arranged so that they are:
   (a) attached to positions and offices open

to all under conditions of fair equality of opportunity.

(b) to the greatest benefit of the least advantaged.

This is a special case of Rawls's "general conception of justice": "All primary social goods are to be distributed equally unless an unequal distribution is to the benefit of everyone." An intuitive argument shows how parties in the original position would arrive at this conception. Because they wish to advance their own conceptions of the good, but do not know what these are, each finds it rational to maximize his share of primary goods. Knowing that this motive will be the same for everyone, each finds it reasonable neither to ask for more nor settle for less than any other. So an obvious initial idea is equal shares. But because the stock of primary goods is not fixed, it is possible that some arrangements would increase the total in ways that make everyone better off, although some more than others. In the absence of irrational ENVY, such arrangements should be acceptable to all. Thus the obvious second step is to agree to the general conception of justice.

To move to Rawls's two principles or "special conception," three additional points are needed. First, Rawls argues for the "difference principle." Among the arrangements that make everyone better off (arrangements that are efficient, or Pareto optimal, relative to EQUALITY), the parties in the original position would prefer those that make the position of the least advantaged members of society as good as possible. Under the difference principle, for example, members of professions requiring unusual talents may claim a higher income only if this arrangement redounds to the advantage of those who will have the lower incomes. Second, Rawls argues for the "priority of liberty." The special conception in effect divides primary social goods into two categories, liberties and opportunities on the one hand, economic goods on the other. Liberties and opportunities must be equal for all, so that it is impossible to trade them for economic gains. This arrangement reflects the preference of moral persons who wish to protect their autonomy, that is, their liberty to advance any conceptions of the good consistent with justice. Finally, Rawls argues that the equal opportunity provision must be understood as a requirement that society take active measures to ensure that opportunities remain open to all members of society.

Otherwise, permissible inequalities will give rise to arbitrary ones over time.

Parties in the original position prefer Rawls's two principles to the principle of utility for a variety of reasons. In *A Theory of Justice,* Rawls gives apparent prominence to the argument that they would find it rational to use the "maximin" rule of choice under uncertainty. Not knowing what their social positions are, eager to advance their particular conceptions of the good, and aware that this exercise is a one-time gamble on which everything depends, the parties try to ensure that even the worst position in society is as good as possible. But in later works, Rawls places more emphasis on arguments from the parties' motivation to exercise the two moral powers. The guarantees of LIBERTY and opportunity embodied in the two principles ensure one's autonomy in formulating, revising, and pursuing one's conception of the good.

Additional points in favor of Rawls's two principles, particularly the difference principle, are drawn from the considerations of "stability" developed in part 3 of *A Theory of Justice.* A conception of justice is stable when it generates its own support. This means that, in a "well-ordered society"—that is, one in which the conception of justice is both publicly acknowledged and successfully implemented—people tend to develop the disposition to act from its principles autonomously and for its own sake. The two principles would be stable for several reasons. Unlike the principle of utility, which may require some persons to have a less good life simply to maximize welfare—that is, so that others may have a better life—the two principles do not require that the worst off members of society be the most benevolent. Since the difference principle allows those favored by nature to make special claims on society only when their gifts are used for the benefit of all, it embodies a conception of RECIPROCITY. Under the two principles, then, no one is asked to accept less than an equal prospect in life because of unfortunate natural endowment or because of the benefit to others. In this sense, all persons are valued as *persons* and are treated as ends in themselves. Because people tend to become loyal to institutions and identified with principles that publicly affirm their worth, the two principles will be stable.

The claim to stability is reenforced by the "congruence" argument also developed in part 3. Congruence is achieved when judgments made from distinct normative standpoints cohere. In Rawls's theory, the right is prior to the good, in two senses. First, the theory of right is developed independently of any particular theory of the good, except for the relatively uncontroversial notion of primary goods. Second, people in a just society are expected to constrain their pursuit of what is good within the limits of the right. We are not to violate justice to pursue good ends, nor to value as good what is intrinsically unjust. But the concepts of the right and the good are distinct, and therefore the question of their congruence arises. We may ask whether a commitment to justice is likely to conflict with our good.

In *A Theory of Justice,* Rawls develops a theory of the good, "goodness as rationality." This theory explains how an individual can move from her existing desires and INTERESTS to a more comprehensive rational plan of life, and it defines a person as happy, and so as leading a good life, when she is successfully executing such a plan. The goodness of ends is defined in terms of their inclusion in a person's rational plan. Rawls argues that most of the standard candidates for human goods—LOVE, FRIENDSHIP, community, culture, and the development of our talents and powers—would turn out to be elements in most rational plans, and so are rationally valued as ends by most persons. Finally, Rawls explains why justice itself is among these human goods—why it is something that, at least in a well-ordered society, the individual has reason to value as an end. Being a just person expresses one's autonomy and reenforces one's ties to the community and one's sense of participation in the culture. For these reasons, we may expect congruence between our judgments of what is right and of what is good for us. Subsequent to *A Theory of Justice,* Rawls called his method of justifying the two principles "Kantian Constructivism." It has two distinguishing features. First, the constructivist regards moral and political philosophy as disciplines that are practical all the way down. The aim is not to discover transcendent truths about an independent moral order, but to provide reasonable principles for solving problems conceived in a practical way. Second, the constructivist solves problems with the aid of a conception of the person whose standpoint represents both an ideal and a problem to which that ideal gives rise. In Kant's own philosophy, the problem is the most general one of what the free rational individual ought to do. Both the ideal and the prob-

lem of freedom are captured by the situation of the negatively free rational agent, who must autonomously choose her own principle of ACTION. The solution rests in showing that this agent would choose to follow the categorical imperative as her principle. Rawls uses the same method, but on a less universal problem: that of generating principles for the basic structure of a liberal democracy. This problem is represented by the situation of the free and equal moral persons in the original position, who must choose principles to govern the terms of their cooperation. Here, the solution rests in showing that they would choose Rawls's two principles.

But Rawls also proposes that the whole argument be checked by a method of "reflective equilibrium," in which all parts of the argument are viewed as revisable. The implications of the principles of justice chosen in the original position should match our most deeply held convictions about what is just. If they do not, we may wish to reconsider our account of what the parties in the original position would choose or even our description of their situation and motives. It is possible that we have not constructed the standpoint from which the solution is to be found correctly, although it is also possible that we will change our minds about what is just. Because it aims at reasonable practical principles rather than theoretical knowledge, the constructivist method yields a tentative result: more reasonable principles may always be found. But at any given moment, REFLECTIVE EQUILIBRIUM may be achieved. If we recognize the ideal of a liberal democracy in the situation of the moral persons in the original position, and if we believe that they would choose Rawls's two principles to govern their association, then Rawls's conception of justice is the most reasonable one for us.

Rawls' second book, *Political Liberalism* (1993), grows out of a problem with the Kantian argument for the stability of justice as fairness in part 3 of *A Theory of Justice.* The stability of a conception of justice requires showing reasonable and rational persons that they have sufficient reason to comply with requirements of justice. The idea of congruence says that it is rational for citizens of a well-ordered society of justice as fairness to act on principles of justice for their own sake. For in doing so citizens enjoy the good of moral community by taking part in a "social union of social unions"; moreover, they realize their nature as free and equal moral persons and thereby realize the supremely regulative good of autonomy. A well-ordered society is then stable since, whatever their different conceptions of their good, citizens all endorse as essential to their good the intrinsic values of autonomy and participation in a community of justice. The problem with this argument is that, because of the basic liberties of CONSCIENCE, thought, and association, people in a liberal society inevitably will have different philosophical, religious, and moral views. Even if all endorse the same liberal principles of justice, they will not accept them for the same reasons. So in a well-ordered society of justice as fairness, it is highly likely that there will be many citizens who, because of their religious, philosophical, and moral views, do not accept autonomy as an intrinsic good. Indeed some, such as liberal Catholics and members of other faiths, might reject autonomy as a conceit of human reason, since it obscures what they regard as the true source of morality and the good in God's will or in an independent order of being. Given that these and other non-Kantian doctrines will be affirmed in a well-ordered society, it is too much to expect that the case for the stability of justice as fairness can rest on the congruence of the Right and the Good. Some other grounds for stability must be located, due to the "fact of reasonable pluralism" of comprehensive doctrines and conceptions of the good.

The primary question of *Political Liberalism* is: How is it possible for there to exist over time a just and stable society of free and equal citizens, who remain profoundly divided by religious, philosophical, and moral doctrines? Rawls's main aim is to show how justice as fairness (or any liberal view) can be affirmed as a public conception of justice by reasonable and rational persons given the fact of reasonable pluralism. Rawls sets forth three primary conditions in response to this question. First, a just and stable society must be regulated by a *political* conception of justice that is generally accepted by the members of society and that is realized in its laws and basic institutions. A political conception is freestanding of the various religious, philosophical, and moral doctrines that exist in society. It is grounded, not in concepts or principles peculiar to any particular doctrine, but in ideas that are shared and implicit in the political culture of a democratic society. Primary among these common doctrines are the idea of free and equal citizens who are reasonable and rational and the idea of social cooperation as involv-

ing not just mutual advantage, but reciprocity and fair terms. A political conception must be freestanding if it is to be justifiable to and serve as a shared public basis for deliberation and justification among people who have different and conflicting doctrines and conceptions of the good. It is necessary for the conception of justice that regulates a liberal society to be justifiable to citizens on terms they can reasonably accept, if citizens are to be respected as free and equal. To carry through this basic idea of liberal and democratic thought, Rawls redefines the basic features of justice as fairness, freeing it from its earlier basis in the Kantian interpretation.

The second feature of a just and stable society is that it must be "stable for the right reasons." This rules out not only stability established on the basis of unjustifiable COERCION, manipulation, or deceit, but also stability founded on a *modus vivendi*, the fortuitous balance of forces among competing conceptions of the good. A well-ordered society is stable for the right reasons when its citizens affirm and want to comply with its principles of justice for moral reasons that are integral to their conscientious beliefs and conceptions of the good. This requires that there be an *overlapping consensus* on the political conception of justice among different religious, philosophical, and moral views. An overlapping consensus exists when the reasonable comprehensive doctrines that gain adherents in a well-ordered society all affirm the liberal political conception of justice, each for the particular reasons implicit in their comprehensive views. So, assuming justice as fairness is the liberal political conception for a well-ordered society, Kantians can affirm it because it realizes autonomy, utilitarians affirm it since they believe it best promotes overall utility under these circumstances, liberal Catholics and others affirm the liberal conception since they see it as part of divine law, and pluralists affirm it because they see the political conception as justifiable on its own terms. Since these and other reasonable doctrines affirm the public political conception for their own reasons, then proponents of these doctrines can accept the liberal conception as compatible with their good.

The third condition of a just and stable society is that its government and its laws must have political *legitimacy*. The need for LEGITIMACY stems partly from the fact that, even in a perfectly just society, some laws and regulations are bound to be occasionally unjust, for no political procedure is perfect.

So, for the sake of stability, citizens need reasons to obey laws they might suspect to be unjust. The *liberal principle of legitimacy* says that coercive political force is legitimate only when exercised according to a constitution whose essentials are reasonably acceptable to all on the basis of their common human reason. This principle implies a *duty of civility:* free and equal citizens, when voting or when exercising political power as government officials, are to act only in ways that can be reasonably justified to others in terms of *the political values of public reason.* Public reason is the reason of free and equal citizens in their capacity as democratic citizens. It is reason that is guided by considerations of the COMMON GOOD among citizens. The common good is specified by the political values of public reason. These considerations promote and maintain the basic interests of free and equal citizens. Among these political values are justice, the public welfare, domestic tranquility, the basic liberties and their priority, economic efficiency and fairness, and so on. These political values are to guide the deliberations of legislators, judges, and administrators in deciding and applying the laws. Moreover citizens, when they vote, have a duty to be able to justify their decisions in terms of the political values of public reason. Laws that cannot be justified in these terms are not legitimate; coercive force of government is then being used in ways that deny citizens their political freedom and that do not respect them as equal citizens. One role of a political conception of justice is to provide "content" to public reason. It is only when a liberal political conception is publicly recognized that the justification of laws in terms of the political values of public reason can be "complete." Public recognition of a liberal political conception is then a condition of the legitimacy of political power in a constitutional democracy.

Rawls's third main book, *The Law of Peoples* (1999), is his account of international justice. (Rawls refers to "peoples" rather than "states," "governments," or "nations," since the latter are simply the political representatives of peoples.) The law of peoples is worked out within political LIBERALISM; it presupposes a politically liberal society, which confronts other societies governed by their own constitutions. Its aim is to provide a basis for the foreign policy of a liberal people, for interacting and cooperating with both liberal and nonliberal peoples. Rawls argues that a liberal people is to cooperate with decent nonliberal people according to the same laws as it recognizes in its relations with other liberal peoples. It is to recognize both liberal and decent peoples as equal members in a society of peoples, respecting their political autonomy and independence. A people is decent so long as it recognizes and respects HUMAN RIGHTS, enforces a common-good conception of justice, and provides some kind of political representation for all its members through a "decent consultation hierarchy." A people does not have to be liberal or democratic to be decent; human rights do not include the full panoply of liberal-democratic rights (such as equal political rights) protected by Rawls's first principle of justice. Instead human rights are the especially urgent rights that must be respected if people are to be treated decently. Rawls lists as human rights the rights to life and to the security of the person, the right to liberty (including freedom from SLAVERY and forced occupation), the right to hold personal property, the right to freedom of conscience sufficient to secure freedom of RELIGION and of thought, and the right to formal equality under law. The right to life includes a right to the means of subsistence: a decent people does not allow its members to starve.

The law of peoples allows a people go to war only in self-defense against a territorial aggressor or in order to defend the human rights of other peoples. A people also has a duty of assistance to other peoples in distress. This includes a duty to provide distressed peoples with economic assistance if they are unable to provide for their own members. The aim of the duty of assistance among peoples is not to create permanent conditions of dependence, but to sustain a people during emergencies or so long as required for them to become self-sufficient and economically independent. Rawls argues for these and other principles on grounds of an original position whose parties consist of representatives for independent peoples. He contends that both liberal and decent nonliberal peoples would agree to the same principles of the law of peoples.

See also: AUTONOMY OF MORAL AGENTS; CATEGORICAL AND HYPOTHETICAL IMPERATIVES; CIVIL RIGHTS AND CIVIC DUTIES; CIVILITY; COMMON GOOD; CONSTRUCTIVISM; CONTRACTARIANISM; COOPERATION, CONFLICT, AND COORDINATION; COSMOPOLITAN ETHICS; DELIBERATION AND CHOICE; DEMOCRACY; ECONOMIC SYSTEMS; EQUALITY; FAIRNESS; GOOD, THE-

Rawls, John

ORIES OF THE; HUMAN RIGHTS; IDEAL OBSERVER; IDEALIST ETHICS; IDEALIZED AGENTS; IMPARTIALITY; INSTITUTIONS; INTERNATIONAL JUSTICE: DISTRIBUTION; JUSTICE, DISTRIBUTIVE; KANTIAN ETHICS; LEGITIMACY; LIBERALISM; LIBERTY; LIBERTY, ECONOMIC; MORAL COMMUNITY, BOUNDARIES OF; MORAL PLURALISM; MOTIVES; OBEDIENCE TO LAW; POLITICAL SYSTEMS; PUBLIC GOODS; RATIONAL CHOICE; RECIPROCITY; REFLECTIVE EQUILIBRIUM; RIGHT, CONCEPTS OF; RIGHTS; RISK AVERSION; SOCIAL AND POLITICAL PHILOSOPHY; SOCIAL CONTRACT; UTILITARIANISM; WELFARE RIGHTS AND SOCIAL POLICY.

Bibliography

Works by John Rawls

"Outline of a Decision Procedure for Ethics." *Philosophical Review* 60 (1951): 177–97.

Review of Stephen Toulmin's *An Examination of the Place of Reason in Ethics* (1950). Philosophical Review 60 (1951): 572–80.

Review of Axel Hägerstrom's *Inquiries into the Nature of Law and Morals* (translated by C.D. Broad; 1953). *Mind* 64 (1955): 421–22.

"Two Concepts of Rules." *Philosophical Review* 64 (1955): 3–32.

"Justice as Fairness." The first version of this paper was published in *Journal of Philosophy* 54 (1957): 653–62. An expanded version appeared in *Philosophical Review* 67 (1958): 164–94. This version is most frequently anthologized. Another revised version was translated into French by Jean-Fabien Spitz as "La Justice comme équité" *Philosophie* 14 (1987): 39–69.

Review of *Philosophy in the Mid-Century: A Survey,* edited by Raymond Klibansky, 1961. *Philosophical Review* 70 (1961): 131–32.

"Constitutional Liberty and the Concept of Justice." In *Justice,* edited by C. Friedrich and John W. Chapman, 98–125. Nomos VI. New York: Atherton, 1963.

"The Sense of Justice." *Philosophical Review* 72 (1963): 281–305.

"Legal Obligation and the Duty of Fair Play." In *Law and Philosophy,* edited by Sidney Hook, 3–18. New York: New York University Press, 1964.

Review of *Social Justice,* edited by Richard Brandt. *Philosophical Review* 74 (1965): 406–9.

"Distributive Justice." The first version of this paper was published in *Philosophy, Politics, and Society,* Third Series, edited by P. Laslett and W. G. Runciman, 58–82. Oxford: Basil Blackwell, 1967. Rawls later published "Distributive Justice: Some Addenda" in *Natural Law Forum* 13 (1968): 51–71. These two essays were combined in a second "Distributive Justice" in *Economic Justice,* edited by E. Phelps, 319–62. London, Penguin Books, 1973.

"The Justification of Civil Disobedience." In *Civil Disobedience,* edited by Hugo Bedau, 240–55. New York: Pegasus, 1969.

"Justice as Reciprocity." (Written in 1958.) In *Mill: Text with Critical Essays,* edited by Samuel Gorovitz, 242–68. Indianapolis: Bobbs-Merrill, 1971.

A Theory of Justice. Cambridge, MA: Harvard University Press, 1971. *A Theory of Justice* has been translated into Chinese, Finnish, French, German, Italian, Japanese, Korean, Portuguese, Spanish, and twelve other languages. For the first of these translations, the German translation of 1975, Rawls made some revisions, which have been incorporated into all the translations. *A Theory of Justice,* revised edition, Cambridge, MA: Harvard University Press, 1999, is a publication of the revised text used for all translations.

"Reply to Lyons and Teitelman." *Journal of Philosophy* 69 (1972): 556–57.

"Some Reasons for the Maximin Criterion." *American Economic Review* 64 (1974): 141–46.

"Reply to Alexander and Musgrave." *Quarterly Journal of Economics* 88 (1974): 633–55.

"The Independence of Moral Theory." *Proceedings and Addresses of the American Philosophical Association* 48 (1974): 5–22.

"A Kantian Conception of Equality." *Cambridge Review* (1975): 94–99.

"Fairness to Goodness." *Philosophical Review* 84 (1975): 536–54.

"The Basic Structure as Subject." The first version was published in the *American Philosophical Quarterly* 14 (1977): 159–65. A revised and expanded version appears in *Values and Morals: Essays in Honor of William Frankena, Charles Stevenson, and Richard B. Brandt,* edited by Alvin Goldman and Jaegwon Kim, 47–71. Dordrecht: Reidel, 1978.

"Kantian Constructivism in Moral Theory: The Dewey Lectures 1980." *Journal of Philosophy* 77 (1980): 515–72.

"Social Unity and Primary Goods." In *Utilitarianism and Beyond,* edited by Amartya Sen and Bernard Williams, 159–85. Cambridge: Cambridge University Press, 1982.

"The Basic Liberties and Their Priority." *Tanner Lectures on Human Values,* Volume 3, 3–87. Salt Lake City: University of Utah Press, 1982.

"Justice as Fairness: Political Not Metaphysical." *Philosophy and Public Affairs* 14 (1985): 223–51.

"On the Idea of an Overlapping Consensus." *Oxford Journal for Legal Studies* 7 (1987): 1–25.

"The Priority of Right and Ideas of the Good." *Philosophy and Public Affairs* 17 (1988): 251–76.

"Themes in Kant's Moral Philosophy." In *Kant's Transcendental Deductions,* edited by E. Förster. Stanford: Stanford University Press, 1989.

"The Domain of the Political and Overlapping Consensus." *New York University Law Review* 64 (1989): 233–55.

Political Liberalism. New York: Columbia University Press, 1993; revised paperback edition, 1996.

"The Law of Peoples." In *On Human Rights: The Oxford Amnesty Lectures, 1993,* edited by Steven Shute and Susan Hurley, 41–82. New York: Basic Books, 1993.

"Reply to Habermas." *Journal of Philosophy* 93/3 (March 1995).

"Fifty Years after Hiroshima." *Dissent* (Summer 1995): 323–27.

"The Idea of Public Reason Revisited." *University of Chicago Law Review* 64 (Summer 1997): 765–807.

Collected Papers. Edited by Samuel Freeman. Cambridge, MA: Harvard University Press, 1999.

The Law of Peoples. Cambridge, MA: Harvard University Press, 1999.

Lectures on the History of Moral Philosophy. Edited by Barbara Herman. Cambridge, MA: Harvard University Press, 2000.

Justice as Fairness: A Restatement. Edited by Erin Kelley. Cambridge, MA: Harvard University Press, forthcoming 2001.

Works about Rawls

Response to *A Theory of Justice* among philosophers, lawyers, political scientists, economists, and others, has been overwhelming. A selection:

Arneson, Richard J., ed. *Symposium on Rawlsian Theory of Justice: Recent Developments. Ethics* 99/4 (1989): 695–944. An issue devoted to work Rawls published after *A Theory of Justice.*

Arrow, Kenneth J. "Some Ordinalist-Utilitarian Notes on Rawls's Theory of Justice." *Journal of Philosophy* 70 (1973): 245–63.

Barry, Brian. *The Liberal Theory of Justice: A Critical Examination of the Principal Doctrines in A Theory of Justice, by John Rawls.* Oxford: Clarendon Press, 1973.

———. *A Treatise of Social Justice.* Vol. 1, *Theories of Justice.* Berkeley and Los Angeles: University of California Press, 1989.

Blocker, H. Gene, and Elizabeth Smith, eds. *John Rawls' Theory of Social Justice: An Introduction.* Athens: Ohio University Press, 1980.

Daniels, Norman, ed. *Reading Rawls: Critical Studies of A Theory of Justice.* Oxford: Basil Blackwell; New York: Basic Books, 1975. Among many noteworthy contributions are H. L. A. Hart's "Rawls on Liberty and Its Priority," which influenced Rawls in "The Basic Liberties and Their Priority"; Thomas Nagel's "Rawls on Justice," to which Rawls replied in "Fairness to Goodness"; and T. M. Scanlon's "Rawls' Theory of Justice."

Freeman, Samuel, ed. *The Cambridge Companion to John Rawls.* Cambridge: Cambridge University Press, 2001. Articles by T. M. Scanlon, T. Nagel, S. Scheffler, J. Cohen, M. Nussbaum, A. Gutmann, F. Michelman, and others.

Harsanyi, John C. "Can the Maximin Principle Serve as a Basis for Morality? A Critique of John Rawls' Theory." *The American Political Science Review* 69 (1975): 594–606.

Nozick, Robert. *Anarchy, State, and Utopia.* New York: Basic Books, 1974. See chapter 7.

Richardson, Henry S., and Paul J. Weithman, eds. *The Philosophy of Rawls: A Collection of Essays.* 5 vols., New York: Garland, 1999.

Sandel, Michael J. *Liberalism and the Limits of Justice.* Cambridge: Cambridge University Press, 1982. One of the most influential communitarian critiques of liberalism, written directly in response to Rawls.

Sen, Amartya. "Equality of What?" *Tanner Lectures on Human Values,* Vol. 1. Salt Lake City: University of Utah Press, 1980.

Symposium on Political Liberalism. Chicago-Kent Law Review, 69:3 (1994). A special issue devoted to Rawls's *Political Liberalism.*

Wellbank, J. H., Denis Snook, and David T. Mason. *John Rawls and His Critics: An Annotated Bibliography.* New York: Garland, 1982.

Christine M. Korsgaard
Samuel Freeman

realism

See moral realism.

reasonableness

See rationality vs. reasonableness.

reason[ing]

See moral reasoning; practical reason[ing]; rationality vs. reasonableness.

reasons for action

The notion of a reason for action is a normative notion; such reasons are relevant to the question of whether actions are rationally allowed, rationally prohibited, or rationally required. The project of justifying morality, for example, is sometimes conceived as the project of showing that there are reasons in favor of moral behavior that are sufficient to make such behavior either rationally allowed or rationally required. "Ought" claims have also often been taken to be logically equivalent to claims about the existence of reasons. Reasons for action are therefore to be distinguished from reasons that causally explain ACTION and also from reasons that make someone's action motivationally intelligible. Causally explanatory reasons might include posthypnotic suggestion or might involve reference to neurochemical processes in the nervous system. Motivationally explanatory reasons might include the fact that an authority told the agent to do something. Some philosophers have held that motivationally explanatory reasons must be regarded by the agent as normative reasons. But the reasons that an agent might offer in order to make an action intelligible could include, for example, excessive ANGER or, relatedly, the fact that the action would hurt a certain other person. Some hold that such reasons might rightly be regarded even by the agent as providing no justification of any sort.

Internal and External Reasons

Among the controversies concerning reasons for action is a debate in which the words "internal" and "external" figure prominently. Internal reasons are held to be ones that must find a corresponding motivation in the agent. Sometimes this "must" is taken as a logical requirement on the existence of internal reasons; the fact that an agent has an internal reason logically entails that the agent has a corresponding motivation. For example, an agent would be held to have an internal reason to take a walk, or to help a stranger, only if that agent had some relevant desire, or adhered to some relevant principle, or was (in the case of helping the stranger) benevolently disposed, or if some other relevant motivational claim were true of the agent. Sometimes the "must" is taken as a normative requirement on agents; failure to be motivated by a reason is logically possible, but counts against the rationality of the agent. For example, some unfortunate agent might be incapable of being moved by the fact that a certain action involves high risk of violent, painful death. One might still claim that such an agent had an internal reason to avoid the action. For this claim can be read as the claim that *if the agent were rational,* then that agent would be motivated to act in accord with it.

Regardless of how one takes the "must" in the definition of "internal reason," external reasons are always taken merely to be reasons that are not internal. That is, they are either reasons that do not logically depend on the motivational state of the agent, or they are reasons that need not find a corresponding motivation even in a perfectly rational agent. The view that all reasons are internal is called "internalism." The dominant view is an internalism that takes the "must" in the definition of "internal reason" as a normative requirement on agents.

Requiring and Justifying Reasons

Reasons for action can be relevant to the determination of the rational status of an action in a number of ways. One important way is by providing a *prima facie* rational requirement. Another is by providing a justification for an action that would otherwise be rationally prohibited. These roles can be called "requiring" and "justifying." Many philosophers take the requiring role as essential and thus hold that all reasons are *prima facie* rational requirements. Often this is done without any recognition of the justifying role. But it has also been held that only justifying is essential and that some justifying reasons do not require action, even when unopposed.

If a reason is "requiring," and therefore provides a *prima facie* rational requirement, then any action that it favors is rationally required, unless there are sufficient countervailing reasons. For example, the fact that an action is very likely to make an agent violently ill presents a *prima facie* rational requirement to avoid that action. If an agent does the action without sufficient countervailing reasons, then that agent is rightly regarded as acting irrationally.

If a reason is "justifying," then it can provide a justification for an action that would, without that reason, be irrational. That is, the presence of a justifying reason can make an otherwise irrational action into a rationally allowed or a rationally required action. For example, it would be irrational for an agent to do something unpleasant and dangerous if there were no justification for doing so. But if such an action would, for example, save the life of someone bitten by a snake, then there would be a justifying reason in favor of the action, and the action would be rationally allowed. Just as a requiring reason presents only a *prima facie* rational requirement, a justifying reason is justifying in virtue of its *capac-*

ity to justify. It need not be strong enough to justify every action to which it is relevant.

The roles of requiring and of justifying are logically distinct. For example, it is logically possible for a reason to play only a justifying role. One can simplify one's account of reasons by holding that the justifying strength and the requiring strength of reasons are always the same. Then one can claim, as many have claimed, that rational action is action based on the preponderance of reasons. For then there will not be any ambiguity in the notion of "strength" that is relevant to what will count as "the preponderance."

It has also been held that not all reasons both require and justify, and that not all reasons have the same strength in both roles. Suppose, for example, that one could save forty children from severe malnutrition by smuggling them food and medicine at high risk of injury and death to oneself. In such a case, there is a very strong requiring reason against smuggling the supplies: that one risks injury and death. It would be seriously irrational to risk injury and death in the absence of countervailing reasons. But in the example there is also a very strong justifying reason in favor of smuggling the food and medicine: that doing so will save many children from serious illness. A question of interest is: Is this justifying reason a requiring reason also, and if so, is it an equally strong requiring reason? Another way of asking this question is: Would it be seriously irrational, or irrational at all, to fail to act so as to save forty children from serious malnutrition, when there were no reasons, or only weak reasons, against saving them? For example, do we regard ourselves as acting irrationally if, instead of preventing malnutrition in forty children by painlessly donating a hundred dollars to UNICEF or Oxfam, we spend the money on a good bottle of wine, or on nothing at all? If the answer is "No," then we have a case in which there are very strong justifying reasons in favor of donating the money, and only weak reasons, or no reasons, against donating it, and yet our action is not irrational.

If the roles of justifying and requiring are sharply distinguished, then the debates between internalists and externalists can be resolved into a number of more pointed debates. It has been argued, for example, that in their requiring role, but not in their justifying role, reasons must find a corresponding motivation in a *rational* agent. And it has been ar-gued that in their justifying role, but not in their requiring role, reasons must find a corresponding motivation in *any* agent.

Universal, Objective, and Subjective Reasons

It is generally accepted that if an agent has a reason to φ in certain circumstances, then any other agent would have the same reason to φ in relevantly similar circumstances. This claim is expressed by saying that reasons are universal. The difference between objective and subjective reasons is independent of the question of universality. Rather, the difference lies in the nature of the circumstances in virtue of which an agent is said to have a reason. If reference to the agent is required in describing these circumstances, then the reason is subjective. Otherwise, the reason is objective. For example, suppose the circumstance under which an agent has a reason to give money to a stranger is: that *the agent* feels benevolently disposed toward the stranger. Anyone who felt benevolently disposed toward the stranger would have this particular reason to give the stranger some money. Thus the reason is universal. But the essential reference to the agent makes this reason subjective. On the other hand, suppose the circumstance under which an agent has a reason to give money to a stranger is: that the stranger is hungry and needs money to get food. In this description of the relevant circumstances there is no reference to the agent, and therefore the reason is objective. Subjective reasons are sometimes called "agent-relative," and objective reasons are sometimes called "agent-neutral."

It has been held that all reasons are objective, that all reasons are subjective, and that there are both sorts of reasons. Internalists who take internalism as a logical requirement on reasons tend to hold that at least some reasons are subjective. For the circumstances that give rise to reasons will, for such philosophers, often depend on the contingent motivational state of the agent. That is, sometimes an agent will have a reason to φ in virtue of *that agent's* relevant desires. On the other hand, internalists who take internalism as a normative requirement on agents are more likely to hold that all reasons are objective. Such philosophers can specify objective circumstances that give rise to reasons and then claim that if an agent is unmoved by those reasons, the agent is, to some degree, irrational. For example, such a philosopher might claim that the fact that smoking causes cancer provides an objective reason for a person to quit smoking. That many smokers are unmoved by this fact may only count against their rationality and not against the claim that they have an objective reason to quit.

See also: ACTION; EXTERNALISM AND INTERNALISM; INTENTION; MOTIVES; NORMS; OUGHT IMPLIES CAN; PRACTICAL REASON[ING]; RATIONAL CHOICE; RATIONALITY VS. REASONABLENESS; SUBJECTIVISM; UNIVERSALIZABILITY.

Bibliography

General

Baier, Kurt. *The Moral Point of View.* Ithaca: Cornell University Press, 1958.

Raz, Joseph. *Practical Reason and Norms.* London: Hutchinson, 1975.

Internal and external reasons

Korsgaard, Christine. "Skepticism about Practical Reason." In *Creating the Kingdom of Ends,* 311–34. Cambridge: Cambridge University Press, 1996.

Williams, Bernard. "Internal and External Reasons." In *Moral Luck,* 101–13. Cambridge: Cambridge University Press, 1981.

Requiring and justifying reasons

Gert, Joshua. "Practical Rationality, Morality, and Purely Justificatory Reasons." *American Philosophical Quarterly* 37, no. 3 (2000): 227–43.

Stocker, Michael. "Agent and Other: Against Ethical Universalism." *Australasian Journal of Philosophy* 54, no. 3 (1976): 206–20.

Universal, objective, and subjective reasons

Nagel, Thomas. *The Possibility of Altruism.* Princeton: Princeton University Press, 1970.

Parfit, Derek. *Reasons and Persons.* Oxford: Clarendon Press, 1984.

Joshua Gert

reciprocity

Generally stated, reciprocity is the practice of making a fitting and proportional return of like for like: of good for good, and EVIL for evil. Beyond this vague characterization, however, reciprocity has no standard definition, and as a social norm it exhibits a wide variety of forms across a wide variety of social interactions. In some settings, it amounts to little more than direct, tit-for-tat exchanges of equal measures of the same thing: a dinner invitation for a dinner invitation; an insult for an insult; an eye for an eye. In other settings the emphasis is on equal measures of different things: money for goods in commercial transactions, or a dinner invitation as a response to a kindness of a wholly different sort. In still other settings, reciprocity is both highly indirect and intricate—as when one donates blood, not in the expectation that the very one who receives the blood will somehow repay the gift, or even in the expectation that one will ever need a transfusion oneself, but rather as a way of participating in an elaborate network of reciprocal social transactions. The idea is that what goes around eventually comes around, in one form or another.

Reciprocity is a complex and robust social norm in every society of record. A large social scientific literature has grown up around this fact, and the norm of reciprocity is central to exchange theory (in anthropology, SOCIOLOGY, and political science), equity theory in SOCIAL PSYCHOLOGY, accounts of reciprocal ALTRUISM in sociobiology, and strategies of RATIONAL CHOICE in political theory and economics. In rational choice theory, for example, Robert Axelrod has shown via computer simulations that tit-for-tat is an extraordinarily robust strategy for solving iterated prisoner's dilemmas and for generating and sustaining social cooperation. And there is empirical work on mediation, negotiation, TRUST building, and tension reduction that also endorses various versions of the tit-for-tat strategy.

In ethics, the concept of reciprocity is most often embedded in discussions of justice, GRATITUDE, and FRIENDSHIP. In all these settings, the notion that one owes a cooperative, beneficent response for the goodwill and helpfulness of others (but owes nothing, or at least not the same thing, to adversaries and free riders) has a strong intuitive hold. The norm of reciprocity has been proposed as part of the justification for principles of distribution and rectification, political and economic equality, filial obligation, OBEDIENCE TO LAW, and obligations to FUTURE GENERATIONS.

Justice

Reciprocity in the form of REVENGE, retaliation, or retribution—*lex talionis*—is obviously an ancient and persistent notion, and its mirror image (returning good for good) has appeal in some distributive contexts. PLATO (c.430–347 B.C.E.), in *Republic* 332, quickly dismisses the idea that justice is a matter of helping friends and hindering enemies, but later (357 *ff.*) takes seriously the contention that the benefit of reciprocal restraint is its central point. He ultimately rejects that notion, but many others, from EPICURUS (341–270 B.C.E.) through Thomas HOBBES (1588–1679) to John RAWLS, David Gauthier, and T. M. Scanlon have seen justice as intimately connected to the mutual advantage of reciprocal transactions and fair play. The notion of PROPORTIONALITY, which is an element of reciprocity, figures heavily in accounts of both distributive and retributive justice.

In some recent discussions (Brian Barry; Allen Gibbard) reciprocity has been treated as the kernel of a fundamental, pre-theoretical concept of "justice as fairness" (Rawls), standing somewhere between the notion of justice as a frank, self-interested arrangement for mutual advantage (Epicurus; Hobbes) and justice as IMPARTIALITY in the pursuit of a supreme principle (KANT; JOHN STUART MILL). The idea is that if and only if others are willing to do the same, it is rational to cooperate in the creation of social INSTITUTIONS designed to reduce conflict, reap the benefits of cooperation and coordination, and manage the distribution of those benefits. This is a natural enough thought, since in the most general sense what the norm of reciprocity regulates is free riding—that is, the extent to which people are allowed to reap the benefits of social cooperation without contributing a fair share to producing those benefits.

Two damaging tendencies have hampered discussions of justice and reciprocity. One is the tendency to restrict the scope of reciprocity to voluntary contexts—to more or less deliberate exchanges between willing participants. The other is to operate with an overly literal interpretation of what counts as a fitting and proportional response. Both these moves limit the extent to which a norm of reciprocity can underwrite a theory of justice.

The scope of the norm. A minority view (Lawrence Becker) holds that the norm of reciprocity covers all of one's interactions with others—that one owes a fitting and proportional return for all the good one receives and not merely for the good actually accepted or invited. The short argument for this wide interpretation of the norm may be put into a series of rhetorical questions: Should we respond to uninvited good by injuring the givers? If not, then should we respond with indifference to the givers? And again if not, then should we respond with unfitting or disproportionate gratitude? If none of the above, the only alternative is to respond with a fitting and proportional return of good, and that is reciprocity.

Most writers have rejected such a wide scope for the norm, arguing instead that at most we owe a return only for the good we have accepted or invited. Given the vast range of goods we receive indirectly from others (from ancestors, from institutions, from people who have no knowledge of us or INTENTION to benefit us) and given our need to have some control over the scope of our obligations (so as not to be hostage to the gifts of busybodies and entrepreneurs), the wide rule appears oppressive if not impossible. And one set of rhetorical questions deserves another: Are we obligated to return the good that a malicious (or clumsy) person does by accident? Are we obligated to return the good that is forced upon us against our will or that we do not want but cannot escape? Such questions frame the view that the scope of the norm of reciprocity should be restricted to voluntary transactions.

Fitting and proportional returns. If reciprocity has a very narrow scope, it may be plausible to hold the view (implicit in some social science accounts) that a fitting and proportional response is typically identical in kind and quantity to the original benefit or harm. But philosophers have generally rejected this narrow conception of FITTINGNESS, not only by rejecting eye-for-an-eye retribution but also by noting that exchanges of identical goods are often pointless and that differentials in the level of sacrifice must also be considered. In general, it seems plausible to hold roughly that the fittingness of a return is determined by what counts as a good to those who receive it, and the proportionality of the exchange is determined by what amounts to an equal marginal sacrifice from both parties. It will not do for me to respond to a good from you by giving you something that is bad for you. But asking more than an equal marginal sacrifice from me puts me at the mercy of your wealth.

Compatibility with benevolence. Problems of scope and fittingness motivate a third line of inquiry about reciprocity: The thought is that there is something fundamentally repugnant about the moral economy of PERSONAL RELATIONSHIPS suggested by the norm. The book-balancing and economizing required by reciprocity seem antithetical to the spontaneous, benevolent, generous, loving, and caring acts held up for admiration by most ethicists. One reaction to the antithesis is to exclude considerations of reciprocity from a wide range of human relationships, especially those already characterized by BENEVOLENCE and LOVE. Another is to regard reciprocity in those cases as a principle of retrospective assessment only, rather than as a motivating one. And still another is to make reciprocity a subordinate consideration, either throughout its entire scope or in particular areas.

Stringency. Is reciprocity a subordinate consideration? What weight should it be given relative to NORMS and ideals about benevolence or justice? In practice, reciprocity typically functions as a requirement—a deontic principle. But practice is not decisive for theory, and it may be that reciprocity is best regarded as an ideal or as merely one of the many valuable characteristics of human interaction. On the other hand, if a general pattern of reciprocity in human transactions is a necessary condition for productive social life, and if that general pattern is unlikely to be sustained without the sanctions of an effective moral requirement, then perhaps its deontic character is justified. The remaining questions of stringency would then concern the relative weight of reciprocity as against other deontic norms, such as LOYALTY, FIDELITY, honesty, and impartiality.

Gratitude

Discussions of gratitude develop the idea of a fitting or appropriate response, especially to benefactors. One of the arguments for obedience to law sketched in Plato's *Crito* is that obedience is an appropriate response for the law's benevolent, parental role. Henry SIDGWICK (1838–1900), in *The Methods of Ethics* (1874), gives a useful general analysis of the problems of defining what gratitude requires. But a warning also emerges from these discussions: Analyses of domination and OPPRESSION give atten-

tion to the way in which a norm of reciprocity, in the presence of significant INEQUALITY, systematically entrenches and deepens differentials of POWER. Crudely put, the argument is that reciprocal exchanges between unequals tend to increase economic inequality and to drive the disadvantaged toward forms of reciprocation that involve subservience.

Friendship

Discussions of friendship also raise the idea that EQUALITY may be a necessary condition for some of the reciprocal relationships that create and sustain productive social life. Such a connection is described by ARISTOTLE (384–322 B.C.E.), in *Nicomachean Ethics* 1155–1172a. He held that reciprocal interactions are at the center of the best sort of friendship and are only possible between equals.

See also: ALTRUISM; BARRY; BENEVOLENCE; BIOLOGICAL THEORY; COMMENSURABILITY; COMMUNITARIANISM; COOPERATION, CONFLICT, AND COORDINATION; DETERRENCE, THREATS, AND RETALIATION; ECONOMIC ANALYSIS; EQUALITY; ETIQUETTE; FAIRNESS; FIDELITY; FITTINGNESS; FRIENDSHIP; FUTURE GENERATIONS; GAME THEORY; GRATITUDE; IMPARTIALITY; INEQUALITY; INSTITUTIONS; JUSTICE, DISTRIBUTIVE; JUSTICE, RECTIFICATORY; MOTIVES; NORMS; OBEDIENCE TO LAW; OPPRESSION; PARTIALITY; PERSONAL RELATIONSHIPS; POLITICAL SYSTEMS; PROPORTIONALITY; PRUDENCE; PUNISHMENT; RATIONAL CHOICE; RATIONALITY VS. REASONABLENESS; RAWLS; REVENGE; SOCIAL PSYCHOLOGY; SOCIOLOGY; STRATEGIC INTERACTION; TRUST.

Bibliography

Aristotle. *Nicomachean Ethics.* Books VIII and IX (1155–1172a). Material on friendship and reciprocity.

Axelrod, Robert. *The Evolution of Cooperation.* New York: Basic Books, 1984. Rational choice theory; sociobiology; tit-for-tat as a cooperative strategy.

Barry, Brian. *A Treatise on Social Justice.* Vol. I: *Theories of Justice.* Berkeley: University of California Press, 1989. Sustained criticism of justice as mutual advantage, including justice as reciprocity.

Becker, Lawrence. *Reciprocity.* Chicago: University of Chicago Press, 1990 [1986]. Includes extensive bibliographic essays.

Blau, Peter M. *Exchange and Power in Social Life.* New York: John Wiley, 1964. Reprinted, with a new introduction, New Brunswick: Transaction Books, 1986. Political theory.

Buchanan, Allen. "Justice as Reciprocity vs. Subject-Centered Justice." *Philosophy & Public Affairs* 19/3 (1990): 227–52. Argument against a conception of justice as either self-interested or fair reciprocity.

Ekeh, Peter P. *Social Exchange Theory: The Two Traditions.* Cambridge: Harvard University Press, 1974. Social theory.

Gergen, Kenneth J., Martin Greenberg, and Richard H. Willis, eds. *Social Exchange: Advances in Theory and Research.* New York: Plenum, 1980. Social psychology.

Gibbard, Allan. "Constructing Justice." *Philosophy & Public Affairs* 20 (1991): 264–79. Explores Rawls as a reciprocity theorist.

Gouldner, Alvin. "The Norm of Reciprocity." *American Sociological Review* 25 (1960): 161–78. Sociology.

Mauss, Marcel. *The Gift: Forms and Functions of Exchange in Archaic Societies [Essai sur le don].* Translated by Ian Cunnison. Glencoe, IL: Free Press, 1954. A classic text in anthropology; published originally as a series of articles, 1923–1924.

Sahlins, Marshall. *Stone Age Economics.* New York: Aldine, 1981. Includes extensive bibliography on anthropology.

Scanlon, T. M. *What We Owe to Each Other.* Cambridge: Harvard University Press, 1999.

Sidgwick, Henry. *The Methods of Ethics.* 7th ed. Chicago: University of Chicago Press, 1907 [1st ed., 1874]. Material on gratitude in Books III and IV.

Simmons, John. *Moral Principles and Political Obligations.* Princeton: Princeton University Press, 1979. Material on gratitude and fair play.

Woozley, A.D. *Law and Obedience.* Chapel Hill: University of North Carolina Press, 1979. Extended commentary on Plato's *Crito,* with a new translation by Woozley.

Lawrence C. Becker

rectificatory justice

See justice, rectificatory.

reflective equilibrium

A "reflective equilibrium" is the end point of a process in which we reflect on and revise our beliefs about something. Alternatively, we can refer to the process or method itself as the "method of reflective equilibrium." The method consists in working back and forth between our considered judgments about particular instances or cases, the principles that govern them, and the theoretical considerations that bear on accepting these considered judgments or principles, revising any of these elements wherever necessary in order to achieve an acceptable coherence among them. We achieve reflective equilibrium when there is coherence among these beliefs—that is, they are not only consistent with, but also provide support or explanation for, each other—and when they are optimally acceptable to us because we are uninclined to revise any of them further.

The method of reflective equilibrium has been advocated as a coherence account of justification in several areas of inquiry, including inductive and deductive logic as well as ethics and political philosophy. On this view, a moral principle or judgment about a particular case (or a rule of inference or a particular inference) would be justified if it cohered with the rest of our beliefs about right ACTION (or correct inferences) on due reflection and after appropriate revisions throughout our system of beliefs. By extension, a person who holds a principle or judgment in reflective equilibrium with other relevant beliefs can be said to be justified in believing that principle or judgment.

This approach to the justification of rules of inductive logic was proposed by Nelson Goodman. Even earlier Goodman and Israel Scheffler had discussed justification more broadly in this way. Goodman's idea was that we justify rules of inference in logic by bringing them into reflective equilibrium with what we judge to be acceptable inferences in a broad range of particular cases.

Drawing on this approach in *A Theory of Justice* (1971), John RAWLS suggested that the principles of justice chosen by rational deliberators in his SOCIAL CONTRACT situation must be in reflective equilibrium with our considered judgments about justice. He also suggested that we should revise the constraints on choice in that situation until we arrive at a contract that yields principles that are in reflective equilibrium with our considered judgments. Thus the method of reflective equilibrium plays a role in both the construction and justification of his theory of justice. Since that suggestion, there has been an extensive literature *pro* and *con* his justificatory claims about the method (as well as *pro* and *con* its use in other areas of inquiry).

Narrow and Wide Reflective Equilibrium

A reflective equilibrium may be *narrow* or *wide.* All of us are familiar with a process in moral deliberation in which we work back and forth between a judgment we are inclined to make about right action in a particular case and the reasons or principles we offer for that judgment. Often we consider variations on the particular case, "testing" the principle against them, and then refining and specifying it to accommodate our judgments about these variations. We might also revise what we say about certain cases if our initial views do not fit with the principles we grow inclined to accept. To the extent that we focus solely on particular cases and a group of principles that apply to them, we are seeking only *narrow* reflective equilibrium. Presumably, the principles we arrive at best "account for" the cases examined. Since others may arrive at different narrow reflective equilibria, containing different principles and judgments about justice, we still face an important question about justification unanswered by the method of narrow reflective equilibrium: which set of beliefs about justice should we accept?

Because narrow reflective equilibrium does not answer this question, it may seem to be a descriptive method appropriate to moral anthropology, not a normative account of justification in ethics. In fact, Rawls suggested that arriving at the principles that match our moral judgments in reflective equilibrium reveals our "moral grammar" and is analogous to uncovering the grammar that underlies our syntactic ability to make judgments about grammatical form. Uncovering a syntax, however, is clearly a descriptive and not justificatory task. Once we can identify the grammar or rules that best account for a person's syntactic competency, we do not ask the question, should that person have this grammar? In ethics and political philosophy, in contrast, we must answer that justificatory question.

Rawls's proposal is that we can achieve real justification in the choice of principles of justice by broadening the circle of beliefs that must cohere. In a *wide* reflective equilibrium, for example, we broaden the field of relevant moral and nonmoral beliefs to include an account of the conditions under which it would be fair for reasonable people to choose among competing principles, as well as evidence that the resulting principles constitute a feasible or stable conception of justice, that is, that people could sustain their commitment to such principles. Our beliefs about justice are justified (and, by extension, we are justified in holding them) if they cohere in such a wide reflective equilibrium.

In *A Theory of Justice,* Rawls's suggestion was that all people might converge on a common or *shared* wide reflective equilibrium that included "justice as fairness," the conception of justice for which he argues. Such agreement would produce a well-ordered society governed by principles guaranteeing equal basic liberties, fair equality of opportunity, and the requirement that inequalities be arranged to make the worst off groups as well off as possible. In his later work, *Political Liberalism* (1993), Rawls believes that justification must accommodate to the unavoidable "fact" that human reason, exercised under conditions of LIBERTY, will yield a pluralism of reasonable comprehensive moral views.

To accommodate to this fact of "reasonable pluralism," Rawls recasts justice as FAIRNESS as a "freestanding" political conception of justice on which people with different comprehensive views may agree in an "overlapping consensus." The *public* justification of such a political conception involves no appeal to the philosophical or religious views that appear in the comprehensive doctrines that form this overlapping consensus. Although there is no convergence on a shared wide reflective equilibrium that contains the political conception of justice, wide reflective equilibrium still plays a critical role in justification. For individuals to be *fully justified* in adopting the political conception of justice, they must incorporate it within a wide reflective equilibrium that includes their comprehensive moral or religious doctrine. It will count as a reasonable view for them only if it coheres with their other beliefs in reflective equilibrium. Over time, people modifying their comprehensive views so that they may accommodate the overlapping consensus, a process that involves both philosophical reflection and the moderating influence of INSTITUTIONS that are governed by the shared conception of justice.

Criticisms of Reflective Equilibrium

Central to the method of reflective equilibrium is the claim that our considered moral judgments about particular cases carry weight, if only initial weight, in seeking justification. This claim is controversial. Some of the most vigorous criticism of it has come from utilitarians, and it is instructive to see why.

A traditional criticism of UTILITARIANISM is that it leads us to moral judgments about what is right that conflict with our "ordinary" moral judgments. In response, some utilitarians accept the relevance of these judgments and argue that utilitarianism is compatible with them. Thus JOHN STUART MILL (1806–1873) argued for a utilitarian foundation for our beliefs about the importance of individual liberty. An alternative utilitarian response to the claim that utilitarianism conflicts with ordinary moral judgments is to dismiss these judgments as pretheoretical "intuitions," perhaps the result of cultural indoctrination. On this view, moral intuitions or judgments should have no evidentiary credentials and should play no role in moral theory construction or justification. Indeed, simply making "coherent" a set of beliefs that have no "initial credibility" cannot produce justification, since coherent fictions are still only fictions.

This criticism has some force, since two standard ways of supplying credentials for initial judgments are not available. One traditional way to support the reliability of these judgments or intuitions is to claim, as eighteenth-century theorists did, that they are the result of a special moral faculty that allows us to grasp particular moral facts or universal principles. Modern proponents of reflective equilibrium reject such mysterious faculties; indeed, they claim moral judgments are revisable, not foundational.

A second way to support the initial credibility of considered judgments is to draw an analogy between them and observations in science or everyday life. This analogy, however, seems to require that we tell some story about why moral judgments are reliable "observations," perhaps something like the causal story we might offer to explain the reliability of observations. Since no such story is forthcoming, proponents of reflective equilibrium must reject the requirement or give up the analogy. They might reject the requirement by suggesting it is premature to ask for such a story in ethics or by claiming that we can provide no analogous causal story for credible judgments we make in other areas, including mathematics or logic.

Another reply to the demand for an account of initial credibility is to claim that alternatives to reflective equilibrium fare no better. For example, a utilitarian, such as Richard BRANDT (1910–1997), argues that we should choose moral principles when they are based on desires that have been subjected to maximal criticism by facts and logic alone, and that we should avoid any appeal to moral intuitions

that might infect this critique. These desires, however, are shaped and influenced by the very same social structures that utilitarians complain have biased and corrupted our moral judgments, undercutting their suggestion that we can step outside our beliefs to arrive at some more objective form of justification.

Other criticisms of reflective equilibrium in ethics have focused on criticisms familiar from discussions in epistemology more generally. These include: complaints about the vagueness of the concept of coherence; worries that people who have different starting points may arrive at different reflective equilibrium points, undercutting the suggestion that critical pressures can produce convergence; complaints that the model overemphasizes and idealizes human rationality, or involves an information burden that cannot be met; general arguments that coherence accounts of justification cannot be divorced from objectionable coherence accounts of truth; and proposals that the method be revised to include the kinds of "conversions" that take place when people fundamentally shift their moral (or scientific) perspectives.

Despite these criticisms, others have argued for a broader understanding of the relevance of the method to practical ethics. For example, a proper understanding of reflective equilibrium can clarify the process used in specifying reasons and principles in practical deliberation. In response to the extensive debate about method in BIOETHICS, when some propose a close attention to cases, others to principles, and still others to theory, the method of wide reflective equilibrium offers the suggestion that all such "methods" should be seen as appropriate to some tasks in ethics and are but parts of a more encompassing method.

See also: BRANDT; COHERENTISM; DELIBERATION AND CHOICE; EQUALITY; FAIRNESS; INEQUALITY; INTUITIONISM; LIBERTY; LOGIC AND ETHICS; METAETHICS; METAPHYSICS AND EPISTEMOLOGY; JOHN STUART MILL; PRACTICAL REASON[ING]; RATIONAL CHOICE; RATIONALITY VS. REASONABLENESS; RAWLS; SOCIAL AND POLITICAL PHILOSOPHY; SOCIAL CONTRACT; THEORY AND PRACTICE; UTILITARIANISM.

Bibliography

Burg, Wibren van der, and Theodoor van Willigenburg, eds. *Reflective Equilibrium: Essays in Honour of Rob-*

ert Heeger. Dordrecht: Kluwer Academic Publishers, 1999.

Daniels, Norman. "Wide Reflective Equilibrium and Theory Acceptance in Ethics." *Journal of Philosophy* 76/5 (1979): 256–82.

———. *Justice and Justification: Reflective Equilibrium in Theory and Practice.* New York: Cambridge University Press, 1996.

DePaul, Michael R. *Balance and Refinement: Beyond Coherence Methods of Moral Inquiry.* New York: Routledge, 1993.

Goodman, Nelson. *Fact, Fiction, and Forecast.* Cambridge: Harvard University Press, 1955.

Rawls, John. *A Theory of Justice.* Cambridge: Harvard University Press, 1971.

———. "The Independence of Moral Theory." *Proceedings and Addresses of the American Philosophical Association* 47 (1974): 5–22.

———. *Political Liberalism.* New York: Columbia University Press, 1993.

Sencerz, Stefan. "Moral Intuitions and Justification in Ethics." *Philosophical Studies* 50 (1986): 77–95.

Stich, Stephan. *The Fragmentation of Reason.* Cambridge: MIT Press, 1990.

Norman Daniels

Reid, Thomas (1710–1796)

Born at Strachan, about twenty miles from Aberdeen, Reid entered Marischal College, Aberdeen, at the age of twelve, receiving his B.A. degree in 1726. He then studied theology, was licensed as a minister in the Presbyterian Church in 1731, and from 1737 to 1751 served the church at New-Machar. In 1751 he was appointed regent in King's College, Aberdeen, where he taught until 1764, the year of the publication of his *Inquiry into the Human Mind on the Principles of Common Sense,* when he succeeded Adam SMITH (1723–1790) as professor of moral philosophy in the University of Glasgow. In 1780 Reid gave up active teaching in order to prepare his philosophical work for publication, publishing the *Essays on the Intellectual Powers of Man* in 1785 and the *Essays on the Active Powers of Man* in 1788.

Reid was the major figure in the Scottish commonsense school of philosophy. He sought to turn back the tide of SUBJECTIVISM and skepticism that he saw in HUME (1711–1776) as the logical outcome of the theory of ideas set forth by DESCARTES (1596–1650). If we have immediate access only to ideas, we end up, Reid contended, exchanging the world of objects for the impressions of sense, the objective moral order for feelings of approval or disapproval. Against this skepticism and moral subjectivism, Reid set himself to rebuild philosophy on the firm foundation of the beliefs of common sense. His major contributions were in epistemology, metaphysics, and philosophy of mind. His work on human action, freedom, and morality is also of considerable importance.

Reid held that the actions for which we are morally responsible are those we do as a result of *freely* willing to do them. A free act of will is one that the agent causes, where 'cause' is used in its strict sense implying that the cause is an agent who has power to produce the act of will, power not to produce it, and exerts its power. No agent can be caused to cause an act of will, for then, given the cause, the agent would lack power not to cause that act of will. Reid therefore denied the view of HOBBES (1588–1679) and LOCKE (1632–1704) that freedom is consistent with the will being necessitated by prior beliefs, judgments, and desires. On the other hand, Reid held that, were we not influenced by MOTIVES, power over the will would result in capricious acts. Motives that act directly on the will and do not require the use of reason (apart from selecting the best means to the satisfaction of some end determined by desire) he called "Animal Principles of Action." Motives in which reason makes judgments about ends as well as means, he called "Rational Principles of Action." The two rational principles that influence a person's actions are rational self-love (a regard for one's own greatest good) and a regard for duty. Reid's moral theory is elaborated in the context of his discussion of the rational principle of action that consists in a regard for duty.

As a member of the moral sense school, Reid contended that by nature we possess a cognitive power the exercise of which results not only in our ideas of right and wrong, of moral worth and fault, but also in our judgments that "this conduct is right, that is wrong; this character has worth, that demerit." Judgments of right, wrong, and indifferent are directed at actions; judgments of moral worth or demerit are directed at agents. Some actions (action-types) are immediately perceived by our moral faculty to be right or wrong. The related moral judgments—Reid called them "first principles of moral reasoning" and held them to be necessary truths—form the starting point for MORAL REASONING, the process of reasoning from self-evident moral principles to conclusions that certain actions (particular or general) are morally right (obligatory), wrong, or indifferent. "Thus we shall find that all moral reasoning rests upon one or more first principles of morals, whose truth is immediately perceived without reasoning, by all men come to years of understanding." Because circumstances and consequences vary, the moral character of a particular action is always a contingent matter. Sometimes we can be certain that a particular action is right or wrong, but often we must rely on a judgment of what is most likely. Reid gave as an example the case of the magistrate who knows that he ought to promote the good of the community, but is uncertain as to which course of action will yield that result, and so must depend on probable judgment.

Reid held a *deontological* theory of morals. He held, that is, that the moral character of an action often depends on features of the action other than the good or bad consequences that will (or likely will) result from the performance of the action. But Reid did not think that the consequences of an action were never relevant to its moral character. For example, one of the first principles of morality he mentions is: "We ought to prefer a greater good, though more distant to a less; and a less evil to a greater." It is not only foolish, against our interest, to choose the lesser immediate good over the greater but more distant good, it is also *morally wrong*. So, although clearly opposed to the view that conduciveness to our own greatest good is either the definition of duty or the single mark of its presence, Reid did think it *a mark* of the presence of duty. But there are other marks of duty.

Reid distinguished duties that relate to duty in general (for example, our duty to use the best means we can to be well informed as to what our duty actually is) from those that relate to the different branches of duty and those that determine precedence when duties conflict. He cited the following different branches of duty: a duty to secure our own good upon the whole; our duty to BENEVOLENCE (with respect to various groups: FAMILY, friends, one's community, etc.); our duty to venerate God (provided we believe in his existence and perfection); our duty to act toward another in the way we believe to be right for that person to act toward us were our circumstances reversed; and our duty to comply with the "intention of nature" as far as it appears to us in the human constitution. Our instincts and appetites are clearly intended by nature to ensure our preservation. Other principles of action, Reid believed, also reveal nature's intention. He claimed that the fact that we have benevolent affections toward others shows "that the author of our nature intended that we should live in society, and do good to our fellow-men as we have opportunity." Seeing that nature has designed us for these ends, Reid concluded that we have a duty to act in a way that fosters these ends.

Apart from the difficulty of determining that a principle of action is ours by nature, rather than acquired, and the difficulty of inferring the end for which such a principle of action was implanted in us, there is the larger problem of concluding that we *ought* to pursue ends because they *are* ends for which nature has designed us. Reid could appeal to God, the author of our nature, and our duty to obey him, as the ground of our obligation to act agreeably to the intention of nature. But this conclusion would be to deduce the present principle from the duty to God. Reid's view is that it is self-evidently wrong to act against our nature.

Although the principles of morality are not themselves in conflict, they may lead to a conflict in action, one principle supporting a given action, another principle supporting a contrary action. Thus, our duty to benevolence may support an action of GRATITUDE that the principle of justice forbids (Reid's example). So, if we are to reach unequivocal judgments as to the rightness or wrongness of a particular action, there must be axioms that dictate which principle should take precedence. Reid did little toward setting forth such principles, being content to note that justice takes precedence over gratitude, and gratitude preference over unmerited GENEROSITY. Between the two rational principles of action, self-love and duty, he thought no actual conflict would occur in a morally governed universe. But between the two, he undoubtedly thought duty to be supreme.

When Reid tells us that the moral sense is part of our constitution and that by which we both acquire moral ideas and perceive that certain actions are right and others wrong, he does not mean that from childhood we are all able to see the self-evidence of the first principles of morals; nor does he mean that each of us will be able to make these judgments even when we come "to years of understanding." He likens the progress of the powers of the mind to the progress of the body from infancy to maturity. Their

Reid, Thomas

development is the work of nature, work that "may be greatly aided or hurt by proper education. It is natural to man to be able to walk, or run, or leap; but, if his limbs had been kept in fetters from his birth, he would have none of those powers." Hence, proper instruction and practice are necessary for the development of our powers, and the moral sense faculty is no exception. It is only by practice and instruction that persons come to see the self-evidence of the principles of morality.

Reid held that the property of being our duty is an indefinable, intrinsic aspect of certain action-types. In apparent conflict with this view was his claim that the moral rightness of an action depends on its being done from a sense of duty. He resolved this apparent conflict by distinguishing the moral character of the action considered abstractly from the moral worth of the agent in performing that action. The former is inherent in the action. "No opinion or judgment of an agent can in the least alter its nature." But the moral worth of the agent in performing the action depends entirely on the motive in performing it. When an action is done from a bad motive we "figuratively impute to the action" the badness that is properly imputed to the agent. It is thus only in a figurative sense that the moral character of an external action depends on the motive from which the agent acts. Whether the action is itself good or bad, the agent who performs it deserves moral approbation for performing it only if the agent believed the action to be right and was influenced in performing it by that belief.

Although motives influence actions, Reid held that they are not causes, for they are not agents endowed with active power. Animal desires, however, directly influence the will and may, on occasion, be so strong as to render the agent unfree and, therefore, not morally responsible for his or her action. Reid likened rational motives to advice and argument, leaving the agent free to act from them or to yield to the animal motives. He saw human freedom, the agent's power over the determination of the will, as nature's gift to enable humans to cast their lot with reason and morality when the rational and animal principles propose contrary courses of action.

See also: BENEVOLENCE; COMMON SENSE MORALISTS; DEONTOLOGY; DUTY AND OBLIGATION; FREE WILL; FREEDOM AND DETERMINISM; GENEROSITY; GRATITUDE; INTUITIONISM; METAPHYSICS AND EPISTEMOL-OGY; MORAL REASONING; MOTIVES; NATURAL LAW; SUBJECTIVISM.

Bibliography

Works by Reid

The Philosophical Orations of Thomas Reid. Translated from the Latin by Shirley Darcus Sullivan. Edited by D. D. Todd. Carbondale: Southern Illinois University Press, 1989. Includes Todd's extensive bibliography of works by and about Reid.

Philosophical Works. 8th ed. Hildesheim: Georg Olms, 1967 [1895]. Includes notes and supplementary dissertations by William Hamilton; introduction by Harry M. Bracken.

Works about Reid

Grave, S. A. *The Scottish Philosophy of Common Sense.* Oxford: Clarendon Press, 1960.

Kuehn, Manfred. *Scottish Common Sense in Germany, 1768–1800.* Montreal: McGill-Queen's University Press, 1987.

Lehrer, Keith. *Thomas Reid.* London: Routledge, 1989.

Marcil-Lacoste, Louise. *Claude Buffier and Thomas Reid: Two Common-Sense Philosophers.* Montreal: McGill-Queen's University Press, 1982.

William L. Rowe

relationships

See friendship; personal relationships.

relativism

See moral relativism.

religion

When viewed abstractly, religion poses two sorts of problems in relation to ethics. It may, in the first place, claim to be the authoritative source of moral truths or requirements, even to the extent of claiming that the only possible grounding of morality is in religion. Second, it may hold that a religious life provides new or more effective or better motives for living a moral life than morality itself does—or alternatively, as in antinomianism, reasons a moral life need not be lived. Conversely it has been claimed that morality requires certain religious truths, such as that there is a God or an afterlife, in order for it to be satisfactorily established.

Religion as a Source of Moral Value or Moral Truth

'Religion' may be understood as 'natural religion,' the supposed product of reason or of natural piety, enshrining belief in the existence of God, and of an afterlife, and maintaining a morality based on intuition or CONSCIENCE or universal CONSENT or the recognition of the NATURAL LAW. The deism of Edward Herbert, Baron of Cherbury (1583–1648), for instance, claimed to identify and establish such a religion. The philosophical issues that this position raises for ethics are akin to those of deriving moral truths or injunctions from reason or custom.

More acute philosophical problems arise when religion embraces the claim that we possess a divine revelation that has come through God's appointed messengers or directly from God himself. Supposing that the problem of how any purported revelation is to be authenticated to be solved, any such revelation is regarded by some, like John LOCKE (1632–1704) as a republication or popularization of the conclusions of reason about morality. Others regard revelation as disclosing truths, including moral truths, not otherwise known. It is difficult, however, to maintain that a revelation makes known *all* moral truths, and in fact few have gone so far. There must be some point of contact or overlap between natural and revealed morality; otherwise how would the revealed morality engage with the everyday moral concerns of humanity?

The degree of any such overlap will determine whether the revelation gives entirely new knowledge, or merely emphasizes, clarifies, and builds on what is known apart from itself, by natural law for example. Matters are made more complicated if the giving of the revelation is regarded as part of a process of renewing and clarifying human moral awareness.

One powerful reason for looking to religion to support morality has been the fear of SUBJECTIVISM and relativism in ethics and the belief that only by grounding morality in the will of God can the necessary invariance and objectivity be ensured. It is frequently said, for example, that if ethics is not derived from the will of God then "everything is permitted." For similar reasons religious morality has

tended to be unsympathetic to noncognitivism in ethics. An interesting exception is R. B. Braithwaite's adoption of noncognitivism in both ethics and religion; he regarded the symbolism of the latter as a psychological spur to the former.

Kant

Immanuel KANT's (1724–1804) philosophy provides a special case of the relation between religion and morality, one in which morality largely supplants the role of religion. By his appeal to human autonomy, the capacity of each human mind to become a "law making member of the kingdom of ends," Kant in effect cut off an appeal to the moral AUTHORITY of any empirical religion or revelation, arguing that such a claim would be "heteronomous" and thus not authentically moral. For Kant religion becomes, in essence, nothing other than the morality of the rational human being, who regards all duties as divine commands. God's existence is not proved, or provable, by the theoretical reason, but is and must be recognized by the PRACTICAL REASON. Thus (rational) humanity requires God for moral fulfillment, but God does not require humanity to be morally obedient.

This subordination of religion to morality was challenged by Rudolf Otto (1869–1937), among others, on the grounds that it failed to do justice to the distinctiveness of religion, which is, in essence, a feeling of awe-struck dependence on the divine.

Since Kant, the claim that an authoritative religious morality infringes on human autonomy and so is 'infantile' has been frequently heard. But the claim is not an altogether clear one. By 'autonomy' may be meant simply the normal, adult decision making processes. Alternatively, it may refer to the purity of moral MOTIVES, or to preparedness not to pass responsibility to a higher authority but to take individual RESPONSIBILITY. It may, again, equate to 'conscientiousness,' or to the need for morality to be unselfish. It is difficult to see how a morality that is in part derived from religion need, of necessity, compromise autonomy in all of these senses.

Just as for Kant the existence of God is a postulate of the pure practical reason, and so religion is subordinated to morality, so those who have viewed religion with less favor, but who have been within the same broad intellectual tradition as Kant, have thought of religion, and particularly of an afterlife of rewards, as a projection of the alienated human consciousness. Karl MARX (1818–1883), Ludwig FEUERBACH (1804–1872), and Sigmund Freud (1856–1939) were all sympathetic to arguments of this kind. But these arguments all appear to suffer from the flaw of supposing that a causal explanation of religion is sufficient to discredit it.

Religion and Utilitarianism

Kant was both a supporter of religion and an opponent of UTILITARIANISM. But there is no necessity about such a position. In fact modern secular utilitarianism derived in part from the natural theology of William PALEY (1743–1805). There could be a religious utilitarianism in which the commands of God are treated in rule utilitarian fashion. In principle, the commands could even be taken as rules that must be followed without exception because an omniscient and all-good God knows that exceptionless obedience will in fact maximize human satisfaction.

Opposition, 'Non Conformity', Dissent

There is also a tradition in which religion and 'worldly' morality are opposed to each other, and this opposition has, historically speaking, taken a variety of forms. Examples include: (1) A distrust of the body and a withdrawal from society, in sects or religious orders or as individual hermits and holy men. (2) The creation of taboos placed on various places, or times, or activities, or substances (*e.g.,* alcohol). (3) The development of moral attitudes (and sometimes of codes) that are at odds with current, 'easy' morality. Occasionally there has been opposition to the way in which worldly morality has compromised religion, *e.g.,* PASCAL's (1623–1662) *Provincial Letters* (1656–1657) with their powerful indictment of the Jesuits. Others have argued that conventional morality is a sham, and those who practice it are hypocrites. (4) Antinomians have claimed that their spiritual status frees them from any moral obligation except that of love to God.

Human Nature

Religions have also been a source of conflicting views of human nature. Some thinkers, *e.g.,* AUGUSTINE (354–430), have regarded human nature as fallen and deeply flawed, incapable of pleasing God until renewed by divine grace. Even when renewed, human beings have no prospect of perfection in this life. Others, *e.g.,* Pelagius (c. 360–c. 420), have stressed the natural capacity of even fallen men and women to please God, who provides grace to assist them. And others, *e.g.,* those in the Wesleyan tradition, have held out the prospect of sinless perfection in this life.

The Euthyphro Dilemma

While there is a diversity of possible relationships between religion and morality, there is one common basic problem, that of the relative priority of each. Part of PLATO's (c. 430–347 B.C.E.) *Euthyphro* raises a question that is a dilemma for some religions. Suppose that morality is (in whole or in part) commanded by God or by some appropriate religious authority. Is the command obligatory *because* it is commanded by God, or does God command it because it is good or true?

Each horn of this dilemma brings difficulties. If we answer that God's commands are obligatory because God issues them, we appear to subordinate morality to God's command and to open the door to theological VOLUNTARISM of the sort that has been countenanced by, for example, WILLIAM OF OCKHAM (c. 1285–1349). But the other horn of the dilemma appears to compromise God's sovereignty, making it subordinate to some supreme moral value or values.

But perhaps the dilemma is artificially constructed. If moral values are metaphysically necessary, as Ralph CUDWORTH (1617–1688) believed, then there is no logical alternative to them, and God's sovereignty is not compromised. Alternatively, if God is essentially good, and hence *could* not be subordinated to some good principle nor be capable of whimsically commanding what is wicked, the dilemma may also be avoided.

A similar problem may be formulated in terms of the reasons humans have for obeying God's commands. Ought a person to obey God because God is all powerful and hence capable of inflicting punishment for nonobedience? If so, then religion is a matter of PRUDENCE, and the motive for obedience is selfish. Yet if we ought to obey solely because God's commands are morally good, the reference to God seems irrelevant. But again the problem may be in the formulation of the dilemma. There are other possible reasons God ought to be obeyed. Perhaps we must obey because God is the creator and owner of everything and therefore has the right to command.

Religion as a Moral Motivator

One of the many things that the slogan "morality depends on religion" might mean is that only religion can provide the necessary motivation to live a sincere moral life. The source of such moral strength could be gratitude to God for his goodness (as in the Christian doctrine of grace), or it could be fear of eternal PUNISHMENT. Whether moral behavior is changed in this way is a matter of detailed and difficult empirical research, though it is a commonplace that religion has produced both saintliness and immoral fanaticism. Some, for example Augustine, have claimed that only one kind of DESIRE, namely love for God and neighbor, is the proper or acceptable moral motivator.

There are formal similarities between religious and secular moralities. For example, for both a secular utilitarian and a religious *agape*ist, no action is without moral significance. For both a secular deontologist and a divine command theorist, there may be actions that are morally indifferent—that are not obligations or are not commanded by God. And to secular acts of heroism there corresponds the view of some religious moralists that there are actions that are above and beyond the command of God, acts of SUPEREROGATION.

See also: AGNOSTICISM; ATHEISM; AUTONOMY OF ETHICS; AUTONOMY OF MORAL AGENTS; BUDDHIST ETHICS; CHRISTIAN ETHICS; CONFUCIAN ETHICS; CONSCIENCE; HINDU ETHICS; HYPOCRISY; ISLAMIC ETHICS; JEWISH ETHICS; MORAL RELATIVISM; MORAL SAINTS; NATURAL LAW; PHILOSOPHY OF RELIGION; PRACTICAL REASON; SHI'ISM; SUBJECTIVISM; SUFISM; SUNNISM; TAOIST ETHICS; THEISM; UTILITARIANISM; VOLUNTARISM.

Bibliography

Anscombe, G. E. M. "Modern Moral Philosophy." *Philosophy* 33 (1958): 1–19.

Augustine, Saint. *De civitate Dei (The City of God)*. 413–26. See especially i.20, 25; xvi.32.

Flew, Antony. *God and Philosophy*. London: Hutchinson, 1966. Argues for the independence of morality from religion.

Hare, John E. *The Moral Gap*. Oxford: Clarendon Press, 1996.

Helm, Paul, ed. *Divine Commands and Morality*. Oxford: Oxford University Press, 1981. Modern discussions of the role of divine commands in ethics.

Kant, Immanuel. *Religion within the Limits of Reason Alone*. New York: Harper, 1960 [1793].

Kierkegaard, Søren. *Fear and Trembling*. Translated by W. Lowrie. Princeton: Princeton University Press, 1945 [1843].

Nielsen, Kai. *Ethics without God*. London: Pemberton, 1973. Argues for a secular ethic.

Outka, Gene, and J. P. Reeder, eds. *Religion and Morality*. New York: Doubleday Anchor, 1973. An anthology of contemporary articles.

Quinn, Philip L. *Divine Commands and Moral Requirements*. Oxford: Clarendon Press, 1978. A defense of a divine command theory of ethics.

Ramsey, I. T., ed. *Christian Ethics and Contemporary Philosophy*. London: S.C.M. Press, 1966. An anthology of contemporary articles.

Thomas Aquinas. *Summa theologiae*. 1266–73. See especially Ia 19; I IIae 91, 93, 94.

Paul Helm

religion, philosophy of

See philosophy of religion.

reproductive technologies

As medical research in human reproductive technology and genetics makes possible the manipulation of many steps in human reproduction, it also raises novel ethical issues and introduces new dilemmas in APPLIED ETHICS. In some instances, technology has been modified to meet ethical objections.

Five Categories of Reproductive and Genetic Technologies (RGTs)

One cluster of technologies assists conception in couples who cannot conceive naturally. Examples are sperm treatments, injection of sperm into eggs (ICSI), hormonal stimulation of ovulation, egg retrieval by various routes, fertilization in the laboratory (in vitro fertilization, or IVF) and transfer of an embryo into a uterus (ET or ER). A second cluster of technologies provides donor sperm, donor egg, or the use of another woman's uterus when any of these is missing or nonfunctional. Examples are artificial insemination by donor (AID or DI), donor egg or sperm combined with IVF, and the misnamed "surrogacy," in which a woman gestates a fetus to be raised by others. A third cluster manipulates egg or embryo in the laboratory for such purposes as sex detection, analysis of chromosomes or genes, embryo freezing, cloning by embryo splitting or nuclear transplantation, or GENETIC ENGINEERING. A fourth cluster diagnoses or corrects defects in a fetus through prenatal diagnosis or fetal surgery. A fifth detects genes in babies and adults via such procedures as genetic screening, genetic fingerprinting, chromosome mapping/sequencing—"the genome project."

Categories of Ethical Issues

Natural/unnatural. The Vatican has objected to most RGTs (see Congregation for the Doctrine of the Faith 1987): unnatural procreation, such as conception outside the human body, is considered wrong. Permitted in some Catholic hospitals is gamete intrafallopian transfer (GIFT), a modification of IVF in which eggs are retrieved from ovaries, put in layers separate from sperm in a catheter, and injected into fallopian tubes so that (when GIFT succeeds) fertilization occurs inside the body.

One response calls the Catholic prohibition a NATURALISTIC FALLACY, *i.e.,* that only what is natural is right. A second response is to claim that manipulation is an important aspect of human nature—that it even may be a *duty* to use human (God-given?) ingenuity to harness nature for human benefit, particularly to improve the defective genetic makeup of humans.

Moral status of the embryo. At the center of RGT debates is the unresolved issue of whether an embryo from the moment of conception is a person with full HUMAN RIGHTS and thus entitled to protection. Morally problematic, therefore, are: IVF because so many created embryos fail to implant; freezing of or alteration to embryos; prenatal diagnosis because it might lead to ABORTION.

The position of professional organizations such as the American Society for Reproductive Medicine (formerly, American Fertility Society) is that the human embryo "is entitled to profound respect, but does not possess full human rights," that any obligations to embryos can be outweighed by such moral duties as care to infertile couples. To such organi-

zations, embryo research is necessary to improve IVF and lessen embryo loss in the future. Some recommend that human embryos be created specifically for this research, because otherwise insufficient "surplus" embryos are available.

The slippery slope. Although commonly considered to be a fallacy, the slippery slope argument—that a morally acceptable position can, sometimes without anyone's realizing it, change incrementally into less and less acceptable positions—seems to describe the development of RGTs from the 1970s through the 1990s. IVF with couples' own gametes has been extended to the use, first of donor sperm, then of donor egg, next of a gestator's uterus, and then to the proposal that all couples reproduce by IVF for quality control of their embryos. The prenatal diagnosis of profound disabilities has been extended to sex determination; the categories for which a pregnancy is considered "high risk" are expanding; routine screening of all pregnant women via ultrasound and through blood tests for alpha-fetoprotein is increasing. For screening of adults in the workplace and for insurance, geneticists are sequencing genes to detect "predispositions" to diseases that exhibit ambiguous familial transmission, such as diabetes, alcoholism, schizophrenia, and homosexuality (Henefin in Cohen and Taub; Committee on Assessing Genetic Risks).

One response to those who are concerned about these situations as slippery slopes is that physicians and scientists can and do draw lines. Some clinics do not allow surrogate gestators for IVF or prenatal diagnosis for sex selection; many will not use IVF in nontraditional families; most scientists are against cross-species fertilization or cloning of humans. A second response is that these extensions of IVF and of genetic testing are desirable and should be encouraged, to lead us "up" to positive consequences that will relieve human suffering (Bonnicksen; Robertson 1994).

Autonomy and governmental regulation. Proponents of RGTs argue that the right to PRIVACY and the right to determine what happens to one's own body should permit anyone to choose to sign up for any procedure. To them, government *may not* interfere with reproduction. As for clinics and laboratories, physicians' groups argue for setting their own guidelines because outsiders do not understand the clinical situation; such groups believe, instead, that marketplace competition and the threat to physicians of lawsuits suffice to protect the public (Bonnicksen; U.S. Congress).

Opponents of RGTs counter that in exercising one's RIGHTS, one may not infringe on anyone else's rights, *e.g.,* the rights of children produced or of women used as surrogates or egg donors. Some argue that regulation is necessary to promote safety, efficacy, and informed CONSENT. In 1990, legislation mandating an interdisciplinary regulatory body was passed in the British Parliament (Human Fertilisation).

The right to reproduce. First, is there such a right? According to Robertson (1994), the U.S. Constitution protects married couples' rights to reproduce by sexual intercourse, and from this follows the right to reproduce noncoitally and to get assistance from donors and surrogates. If such a right exists, is it a liberty right or a claim right? Robertson argues that couples have a liberty right, "a right against state interference with or prohibition of their actions to create, store, transfer, donate and possibly even to manipulate . . . embryos . . . for the purpose of rearing as their child."

As for claim rights, infertile couples and their advocates argue that insurance companies (or the government in countries with national health services) ought to cover the costs of infertility treatments.

Opponents hold that at the most there is a liberty right for noninterference with sexual intercourse, but that any rights for external creation and manipulation are overridden by other ethical concerns, especially the rights of the created entities. To them, a claim right to infertility treatment could exist only if underpopulation were a problem.

Purpose of medicine. Authors raise such questions as: Is infertility a disease (Shannon in Baruch *et al.*)? Is providing a child to an infertile couple analogous to giving eyeglasses to the nearsighted or insulin to a diabetic, and hence an appropriate function of medicine in relieving symptoms, although not curing an underlying disease? But if having a child is a cultural value or a personal desire, should medicine respond?

Does the practice of IVF encourage technological "fixes" at the expense of infertility prevention? Do some patients accept high-tech solutions when simple corrections (such as education about fertile periods or curing an infection) might lead to pregnancy? To what risks should medicine put nonpatients, for example, women who risk hormonal stimulation of ovulation because their husbands have low sperm counts, or because they donate eggs to other women or for research?

If gene therapy becomes possible, should it be used only for treatment because enhancement of desired traits is unethical (Daniels in Murray, Rothstein, and Murray)? And, finally, how "commercial" is it ethical for the practice of medicine to become?

Safety; risk/benefit analysis. Do some RGTs cause more physical or psychological harm than good? Proponents say: IVF is safe because the percentage of defective children conceived that way is no higher than in the general population; 95 percent of the time surrogacy is a positive experience for both the contracting couple and the surrogate herself; prenatal diagnostic methods (chorionic villus sampling, amniocentesis, ultrasonography) add but a tiny risk of miscarriage; abortion of a defective fetus saves medical and custodial resources plus personal suffering; and genetic engineering, once developed, will be cost-effective by making persons normal who otherwise would be genetically disabled. Psychological benefits include relief of infertile couples' unhappiness and of women's fears about having to care for handicapped children.

Opponents point to data showing that IVF pregnancies are more likely to be ectopic and that IVF children are more likely to be premature with low birth weight, often from multiple pregnancies with their accompanying health risks for both mother and babies (Launslager in Basen, Eichler, and Lippman). In 1998, the U.S. media documented an octuplet and a septuplet pregnancy after high doses of fertility drugs without IVF; each produced seven living babies. Strong reactions from ethicists and the general public emphasized the high cost of intensive care nurseries, health risks, and the mothers' adamant pro-life stances.

Other risks posed are that children of surrogate arrangements may suffer if they consider their mothers to have "sold" them; that, without sufficient experimentation, we cannot know to what extent genetic engineering of eggs or embryos is risk-free; and that genetic screening of adults may result in undue stigmatization, unemployment, and loss of insurance. Feminists have pointed out physical risks to women from egg retrieval techniques and hormonal stimulation in IVF, including permanent menstrual irregularity, premature menopause, ovarian cysts, and ovarian cancer (Baraldi in Basen, Eichler, and Lippman; Fillion in Basen, Eichler, and Lippman; "Fertility Market"; Rowland).

Efficacy. How effective are RGTs? Results of genetic screening and prenatal diagnosis may give false positives or false negatives or may be misinterpreted. Failure may occur at each step of IVF: hormone stimulation has a 25 percent failure rate; egg retrieval and laboratory fertilization each yield a 12 percent failure; establishment of full-term pregnancy shows a 75 percent failure rate ("Fertility Market"; Rowland; U.S. Congress). Often unsuccessful are preimplantation diagnoses including embryo sex detection, fetal surgery, and flushing embryos out of egg donors' uteruses. Yet should not people have the choice (given our cultural approval of gambling and our sporting ethos) to elect low success treatments? Many consider the reward high enough to warrant the gamble: "You'll never forgive yourself if you don't try."

Informed consent. Are RGT consumers vulnerable to advertising and questionable consent procedures? For example, some IVF clinic brochures exaggerate success rates (U.S. Congress). Pregnant women have difficulty refusing amniocentesis and even more difficulty refusing ultrasound, blood screening, and Caesarean sections. The legal response here is that pregnant women are incompetent to make decisions about their fetuses (Henefin in Cohen and Taub); that medicine decides by proxy in the best interests of the future child. Occasionally, informed consent is elaborate: Most IVF patients are asked to sign detailed forms about the disposition of their not-yet-created "surplus" embryos, especially after the United Kingdom reported 52,000 abandoned frozen embryos in mid-1995 (Robertson 1996b).

Human experimentation. A related objection is that many RGTs have been developed without adequately controlled experiments to test safety and efficacy. Techniques developed in livestock research are often used with humans in a trial-and-error approach. Public concern about transfer to humans arose after a February 1997 report that a ewe had been cloned in Scotland after 276 attempts to transfer a nucleus from one of her adult body cells into an enucleated sheep egg. In the next few years several other methods for cloning domestic animals were patented. The possibility of human cloning generated much media attention and many ethics debates in the press and published books (Pence; Silver).

In human IVF, procedures can be improperly labelled "no longer experimental" or "clinical application" and thus avoid evaluation by review boards; review by in-house boards may be only perfunctory (Bonnicksen). Until recently no registry of IVF clinical results existed in the United States (U.S. Congress).

Some counterarguments are that patients (once informed) should be "permitted to choose" an untested procedure; that any "monsters" created or any excessively high rate of, say, cancer or spontaneous abortion, would inevitably come to medicine's attention; and that it may be impossible to design an ethical human experiment with RGTs.

Children as products. Who owns an embryo/fetus/child? What kind of ownership is implied when an IVF clinic allows patients to choose for their extra embryos: scientific experiments, freezing to use later (with options for disposal), donation to another couple, or destruction? Is surrogacy "baby-selling" (treating a child as a commodity)? Are children products to be perfected (Daniels in Murray, Rothstein, and Murray)? How defective should a fetus be to be aborted (Basen, Eichler, and Lippman; Purdy)? Conversely, is it "fetal abuse" to refuse prenatal diagnosis? Does selecting a child's sex promote its HAPPINESS by making it more wanted, or does it reinforce sex role stereotyping (Holmes in Callahan)?

Do grandparents and children need genetic intergenerational continuity? If so, then technologies that use donor eggs, donor sperm, donor embryos, or surrogates are *per se* wrong. Is adoption more acceptable (even though it, too, raises questions about roots and intergenerational responsibilities) because the child already exists?

Confidentiality/secrecy. A host of issues here includes whether: to contact family members to trace inheritance of a bad gene; to tell employers or insurers the results of genetic tests; to tell children that they came from a surrogate mother or a donor egg or sperm. By 1996, Austria, New Zealand, and Sweden had laws for disclosure of parentage to children at age eighteen, but many other nations reaffirmed strict confidentiality, although some do mandate collection of "nonidentifying genetic information." If children come from donor gametes and are not told, will they be harmed by being raised in an atmosphere of secrecy?

Allocation of resources and social justice. Do RGTs demonstrate wise use of medical and research dollars? Some argue that using some $1.75 billion each year to produce IVF babies for the benefit mainly of upper-middle-class white couples cannot be justified. A World Health Organization report estimated that infertility could be prevented in 1,000 couples for the cost of just one IVF baby. Some even consider the sequencing of the human chromosomes in the genome project an especially unwise use of resources.

On the other side are the arguments that ridding the world of genetic disease would save society tremendous rehabilitative and custodial costs, and that couples who have the money should be permitted to spend it as they choose.

Raising unique issues of social justice is the Human Genome Diversity Project initiated by the international Human Genome Organization in 1994. Anthropologists and geneticists are collecting blood and tissue samples from some 700 indigenous peoples worldwide to preserve cell lines and genes. Some ethicists argue that this project is neocolonialism, exploiting ethnic groups for a resource of current value, with the goal of patenting cells or genes.

Compromising/commercialization of science and medicine. In gene-splicing, genome sequencing, and cloning, has the lure of corporate profits and the consequent secrecy before patenting gene sequences enticed scientists into abandoning the primary ethic of scientific research: open communication and cooperation? Have there been unethical links between academia and private industry? Do we all gain because more knowledge accumulates with COMPETITION, or have financial incentives taken priority over patient well-being? And is some knowledge in the RGT area potentially so dangerous that it would be better never to obtain it?

In what some call the Fertility Industry, by 1996 the 300 plus IVF clinics in the United States were estimated to conduct a $500-million-a-year business. The growing demand for eggs from young donors has fostered misleading advertisements and "finders' fees" ("Fertility Market"). A few IVF clinics sell limited money-back guarantees to carefully selected clients: a part of the larger-than-usual prepayment will be refunded if patients fail to become pregnant or miscarry early in pregnancy.

Opportunity for errors and misconduct. Laboratory and clinical techniques in RGTs are so complicated that technicians can make errors inadvertently. Eggs, embryos, and sperm can get lost or mislabelled. In IVF, such errors can result, for example, in sperm from one couple being used to fertilize eggs from another or in embryos being implanted in the wrong uterus. Mothers have given birth to twins with two fathers. In high-volume, commercially motivated practices, clinicians may be tempted to replace lost or nonviable eggs, sperm, and embryos with viable ones from other couples. From 1991 to 1995 at the University of California at Irvine some forty or more eggs and embryos were donated without permission; the university first fired and then "bought off" the whistle-blowers (Robertson 1996a, 1996b).

Potential profits in genetic testing and genetic engineering have already tempted the biotechnology industry to market tests before they are perfected or based on sound scientific data, and to market them directly to patients rather than through the medical system. Accurate DNA fingerprinting requires intricate care; in addition to failing to detect technical errors, laboratory directors may be influenced by their attitudes toward the case in court.

Eugenics. Is it wrong to attempt to improve humankind genetically? Who defines "improve"? Are we tampering with EVOLUTION, *i.e.,* is there some "wisdom" to evolution? Is negative eugenics (eliminating the unfit) ethically acceptable, while positive eugenics (creating the fit) is unacceptable? Or *vice versa*? Those opposed to negative eugenics cite the Nazi program of *Vernichtung des lebensunwerten Lebens* (destruction of unworthy life) (Glazier in Basen, Eichler, and Lippman). Will genetic engineering increase prejudice against people who are nonwhite, or disabled, or short? Or in a slippery slope argument—one condition may be clearly disabling, but others, only partially so—where do we draw the line between the correction of defects and cosmetic improvement? Is it an argument against IVF that it exposes embryos to the possibility of genetic manipulation? And finally, is the genome project especially questionable because it may trigger personal eugenic decisions or make eugenics more "scientific" than in the 1930s?

Feminist Analysis

History. In the early 1980s some feminists began raising unique issues about the effect of RGTs on the personhood, roles, and stereotyping of women. Members of this network (established in 1985 and named FINRRAGE for Feminist International Network of Resistance to Reproductive and Genetic Engineering) published journal articles and books and started a journal, *Issues in Reproductive and Genetic Engineering,* before other feminists began to argue a more libertarian view. The debate continues.

Positions. FINRRAGE members were among the first to question safety, efficacy, and informed consent and to advocate prevention of infertility (Appendix C in Basen, Eichler, and Lippman). Further, they view IVF and other RGTs as elitist and discriminatory procedures that give too much power to doctors (Basen, Eichler, and Lippman; Rowland). German FINRRAGE members are concerned about the revival of eugenic thinking in their country. However, the root argument is that RGTs reinforce the cultural stereotype that procreation is the primary role of women in society and that the sole worth of women lies in their biological capacity (Shannon in Baruch *et al.*). Some believe that RGTs stem from a patriarchal conspiracy to control the one function of women over which men hitherto have had little control.

Many liberal feminists support RGTs—with some caveats—as offering "choices" to women. To them, as long as a woman is fully informed and knows risks and success rates, she should be allowed to choose donor egg, surrogacy, or whatever. They see the forbidding of risk-taking behavior as the paternalistic attitude that women cannot make decisions (Baruch *et al.*; Andrews in Cohen and Taub; Purdy). This position's main criticism of RGTs is lack of access, *i.e.,* that RGTs generally are not, but should be, available to lesbians, single women, the poor, persons with disabilities, and ethnic minorities.

Commissions and Studies

A unique development in applied ethics is that, by 1989, thirteen governments on four continents had appointed commissions to discuss the RGTs (especially clusters 1 through 3). The first report from such a commission, the Warnock Report (Warnock) in the United Kingdom, has been a model for many others. In 1985, British IVF practitioners set up an interdisciplinary regulatory body, the Voluntary Licensing Authority, to implement one Warnock Report recommendation. Renamed the Interim Licensing Authority in 1989, it came officially under the government as the Human Fertilisation and Embryology Authority in 1991.

The government of Canada created the Royal Commission on New Reproductive Technologies in 1989 to examine the implications of RGTs and to recommend policies. Unlike most commissions, it gave considerable attention to the impact on women. Its final report in 1993 made 293 recommendations (Basen, Eichler, and Lippman; Canada). In 1995 Canada's Ministry of Health declared an interim moratorium on nine applications of RGTs. By mid-1999, Parliament had not yet discussed the Ministry's proposed prohibitions and regulatory scheme.

In the United States, the Ethics Advisory Board of the Department of Health, Education, and Welfare published a report on IVF in 1979; the President's Commission for the Study of Ethical Problems in Medicine and Biomedical and Behavioral Research reported on human genetic engineering in 1982. Each advised governmental regulation; by 1998 their recommendations had not been implemented. In the 1980s the Congressional Office of Technology Assessment conducted studies assessing RGTs, and some American physicians' professional societies composed ethics statements (*e.g.,* American Fertility Society). In 1996, President Clinton appointed a new National Bioethics Advisory Commission to address such issues as human-gene patenting, genetic privacy, and protection of human subjects. In March 1997 he asked the Commission to investigate the ethics of human cloning; their report in June concluded that federal law should ban human cloning (Pence).

Most governmental commissions, studies, and opinion polls have assessed what citizens were ready for and have thus extracted an "ethos" rather than provided moral guidance.

See also: ABORTION; APPLIED ETHICS; BIOETHICS; CASUISTRY; CHILDREN AND ETHICAL THEORY; CONSENT; DOUBLE EFFECT; EXPLOITATION; FAMILY; FEMINIST ETHICS; FUTURE GENERATIONS; GENETIC ENGINEERING; HOLOCAUST; HUMAN RIGHTS; JUSTICE, DISTRIBUTIVE; LIBERTY, ECONOMIC; LIFE, RIGHT TO; MEDICAL

ETHICS; NATURALISTIC FALLACY; NATURE AND ETHICS; NEGLIGENCE; PATERNALISM; PRIVACY; PUBLIC HEALTH POLICY; RIGHTS; RISK; RISK ANALYSIS; SECRECY AND CONFIDENTIALITY; SLIPPERY SLOPE ARGUMENTS; TECHNOLOGY; TECHNOLOGY AND NATURE.

Bibliography

American Fertility Society. Ethics Committee. *Ethical Considerations of Assisted Reproductive Technologies. Fertility and Sterility* 62, no. 5, suppl. 1 (1994). See also *Fertility and Sterility* 65, no. 5, suppl. 1 (1997).

Andrews, Lori B. 1999. *The Clone Age: Adventures in the New World of Reproductive Technologies.* New York: Henry Holt and Company. Drawing on her personal experience, a legal expert on the RGTs exposes ethical and legal quandaries in clinics, ethics committees, and lawsuits.

Baruch, Elaine, *et al.,* eds. *Embryos, Ethics, and Women's Rights: Exploring the New Reproductive Technologies.* New York: Harrington Park Press, 1988. Mixed, mostly feminist, arguments on IVF, surrogacy, prenatal diagnosis. See especially *"In Vitro* Fertilization: Ethical Issues," by Thomas A. Shannon, pp. 155–65 (lucid anti-IVF arguments).

Basen, Gwynne, Margaret Eichler, and Abby Lippman, eds. *Misconceptions: The Social Construction of Choice and the New Reproductive and Genetic Technologies.* 2 vols. Hull, Quebec: Voyageur Publishing, 1993–1994. Strong feminist anti-RGT views; analysis of procedures of Canadian Royal Commission.

Bonnicksen, Andrea L. *In Vitro Fertilization: Building Policy from Laboratories to Legislatures.* New York: Columbia University Press, 1989. How physicians, patients, policy makers, and the public can call limits and assume responsibility. Good bibliography.

Callahan, Joan C., ed. *Reproduction, Ethics, and the Law: Feminist Perspectives.* Bloomington: Indiana University Press, 1995. See especially "Choosing Children's Sex: Challenges to Feminist Ethics," by Helen Bequaert Holmes, pp. 148–77.

Canada. Royal Commission. *Proceed with Care: Final Report of the Royal Commission on New Reproductive Technologies.* Canada: The Commission, 1993.

Cohen, Sherill, and Nadine Taub, eds. *Reproductive Laws for the 1990s.* Clifton, N.J.: Humana, 1989. Most authors emphasize choice, access. See especially "Alternative Modes of Reproduction," by Lori B. Andrews, pp. 361–403 (feminist arguments that are pro-RGTs, especially surrogacy); "Prenatal Screening," by Mary Sue Henefin *et al.,* pp. 155–83.

Committee on Assessing Genetic Risks, Institute of Medicine. *Assessing Genetic Risks: Implications for Health and Social Policy.* Washington, D.C.: National Academy Press, 1994.

Congregation for the Doctrine of the Faith. *Instruction on Respect for Human Life in Its Origin and on the Dignity of Procreation: Replies to Certain Questions of the Day.* Vatican translation. Boston, Mass.: St. Paul Editions, 1987.

"The Fertility Market." *New York Times.* Series of four front-page articles, 7–10 January (1996).

Holmes, Helen Bequaert, ed. *Issues in Reproductive Technology.* New York: Garland Publishing, 1992. Also New York: New York University Press, 1994. See especially "Part 3: Cryopreservation of Human Embryos," pp. 193–244, and Part 5: "New Perspectives on Contract Pregnancy," pp. 297–421.

Human Fertilisation and Embryology Act. London: Her Majesty's Stationers Office, 1990.

The Human Genome Initiative and the Impact of Genetic Testing and Screening Technology. Special issue of *The American Journal of Law and Medicine* 17, nos. 1 and 2 (1991).

Murray, Thomas H., Mark A. Rothstein, and Robert F. Murray Jr., eds. *The Human Genome Project and the Future of Health Care.* Bloomington: Indiana University Press, 1996. See especially "Medicine, Gene Therapy, and Society," by William J. Polvino and W. French Anderson, pp. 39–57; "The Implications of the Human Genome Project for Access to Health Insurance," by Deborah A. Stone, pp. 133–57; "The Human Genome Project and the Distribution of Scarce Medical Resources," by Norman Daniels, pp. 173–95.

Pence, Gregory E., ed. *Flesh of My Flesh: The Ethics of Cloning Humans.* Lanham, Md.: Rowman and Littlefield, 1998. Thirteen well-argued positions, including the recommendations of the U.S. National Bioethics Advisory Commission.

Purdy, Laura M. *Reproducing Persons: Issues in Feminist Bioethics.* Ithaca: Cornell University Press, 1996. Feminist arguments generally favorable to RGTs.

Reproductive Technologies. Special issue of *The Journal of Medicine and Philosophy* 21, no. 5 (1996).

Robertson, John A. *Children of Choice: Freedom and the New Reproductive Technologies.* Princeton: Princeton University Press, 1994. A "right to reproduce" analysis.

———. "Eggs, Embryos, and Professional Ethics." *Chronicle of Higher Education* 5 January (1996a): A64.

———. "Legal Troublespots in Assisted Reproduction." *Fertility and Sterility* 65, no. 1 (1996b): 11–12.

Rowland, Robyn. *Living Laboratories: Women and Reproductive Technologies.* Bloomington: Indiana University Press, 1992. Good collection of data and anti-RGT feminist arguments.

Silver, Lee M. *Remaking Eden: Cloning and Beyond in a Brave New World.* New York: Avon Books, 1997.

U.S. Congress. House of Representatives. Subcommittee on Regulation, Business Opportunities, and Energy. *Consumer Protection Issues Involving In Vitro Fertilization Clinics.* Washington, D.C.: GPO 1989. Serial No. 101–5. Hearing proceedings; IVF descriptive and promotional brochures; results from survey of ninety-six U.S. clinics.

Warnock, Mary. *A Question of Life: The Warnock Report on Human Fertilisation and Embryology*. Oxford: Basil Blackwell, 1985.

Helen Bequaert Holmes

resentment

The two most important studies of the relationship between resentment and ethics were made by Friedrich NIETZSCHE (1844–1900) and Max SCHELER (1874–1928). Both believe that resentment played a determining role in historically central value inversions in Western ethics. For Nietzsche, resentment was the motive for elevating many values that are considered distinctively *moral* (most of which derive from CHRISTIAN ETHICS). For Scheler, resentment was the source of more recent moral value inversions (humanistic ethics and relativism). Because it elevates false idols that are inimical to achieving human EXCELLENCE, they both see resentment's value inversions as disastrous for humanity. Both believe that resentment corrupts CHARACTER in ethically invidious ways and that overcoming it is a minimum condition for living an ethically viable life. They offer a powerful critique of resentment—showing that it leads to SELF-DECEPTION, self-hatred, and an inability to grasp and respond to higher values. In addition, both examine key necessary conditions for the phenomenon of resentment and thus contribute to full comprehension of the concept.

Analysis of the Phenomenon

Nietzsche's primary discussion of resentment appears in *On the Genealogy of Morals* (1887), especially Essay One. Nietzsche takes resentment to be an essential feature of a reactive type of morality he calls "slave morality," to which he contrasts "noble morality." Noble morality is self-affirming and active—expressing vitality, PASSION, and enthusiasm. Its adherents' joy derives from their own achievements. Slave morality, on the other hand, is essentially reactive, always at war with a hostile world, negating whatever it experiences as different or alien. Its adherents' joy derives from rejecting others' achievements. The key to the resentment-based slave morality is *felt impotence,* an experienced inability to successfully embody the POWER, SELF-CONTROL, and grace of the exemplars of noble morality. Exemplars of slave-morality hate the success of noble types and feel indicted by their own failures. This hatred fuels their negativity and invariably produces self-hatred, which Nietzsche regards as self-poisoning. They cannot acknowledge their failures, however, and systematically deceive themselves about their own worth by creating compensatory oppositional values that they can embody.

For noble morality, good is the defining value; whatever expresses or contributes to the noble's success and strength is experienced as good. Its conception of "bad" is an afterthought, reserved for features that undermine strength and achievement. For slave morality, "evil" is the defining value (and it calls evil all the traits that noble morality takes to be good) while "good" is the secondary notion, defined as whatever opposes the values it seeks to stigmatize. Noble morality thus has no concept of EVIL; this is created only by resentment-based slave moralities. Correlatively, slave-morality has no genuinely affirmative concept of good; everything it takes to be good is posited reactively to convince its adherents that they possess some value. Thus, weakness is rechristened as goodness of heart; cowardice becomes HUMILITY, abjection becomes obedience, impotence becomes FORGIVENESS, and resentment itself becomes justice. In addition, Nietzsche claims that resentment-filled persons are unable to achieve a balanced, just vision of the world and also exhaust themselves in making their enemies pay for their "sins." Noble types, on the other hand, maintain a just assessment of and respect for even those who harm them and also celebrate their enemies as worthy opponents.

Thus, for Nietzsche, resentment is repressed hatred for those who are more successful and stronger, hatred that unbalances the character of resentful persons, turning them against themselves in self-hatred, hatred that seeks to punish and wreak vengeance on its enemies, which it does by inverting their values, causing them to doubt their own strengths and VIRTUES and creating a mendacious system of values that is embraced only because it opposes the values of noble morality. The values many people regard as *moral* values (*e.g.,* BENEVOLENCE, meekness, SYMPATHY, doing duty for duty's sake, asceticism, ALTRUISM, and retributivism) derive from this inversion of values.

Scheler's major discussion of resentment appears

in his book, *Ressentiment* (1912). He defines resentment as the repression of negative emotions that undermines people's capacity to apprehend higher values because the positive emotions essential to perceiving them are inhibited or blocked. Resentment derives from a demand for REVENGE that, because of weakness or fear, is not expressed; thus, a sense of powerlessness is a precondition for resentment, and it is typically a reaction to a prior perceived insult or transgression. Scheler notes that resentment can be overcome if either the transgression is forgiven or if the revenge is expressed actively. As the hatred becomes more fully repressed, its victim passes through a series of other-directed stages—malice, the impulse to detract, and spite—that culminate in resentment. The scope of these attitudes can become so universal that they target everyone. Antagonism suffuses the entire outlook of resentment's victims, undermining their capacity to apprehend higher values. Hatred fixes attention on lower (or negative) values, leading resentful people to take lower values for higher ones. Scheler claims that such value-delusions are never completely convincing; hints of the truly higher values remain, but the resentful person does not respond to them. The negativity of resentment often becomes so intense that the resentful person's impotence will trigger self-hatred, dissolving all sense of SELF-ESTEEM. Self-hatred and impotence thus reinforce each other. Resentful people reject higher values because they feel incapable of realizing them. Lower, suspect values are substituted for them.

Scheler argues for an objective hierarchy of value: the lowest values are sensory values; then life-values; then cultural values like truth, beauty, and justice; and the highest are spiritual values. He thinks that everyone has access to this hierarchy through their emotions (*e.g.,* LOVE or preferring); emotions are the doorways to the realm of value like the senses are doorways to the perceived world. Different people may be drawn to different areas of the hierarchy, and the specific values to which each individual is most attuned define his or her value-essence. Different cultures also typically cultivate different sectors of the hierarchy. These different devotions allow both people and cultures to broaden their grasp of the hierarchy by co-experiencing each other's value-essences. Love provides the clearest insight into higher values. The highest values are often revealed through the actions and demeanor of personal mod-

els. Hatred blocks the insight love can provide and focuses attention on lower, or even negative, values instead. Because resentment's lifeblood is hatred (for the transgressor, for one's own impotence, for a world that allows such transgressions to occur), it powerfully inhibits its victim's capacity to grasp higher values. Hatred also displaces individuals from their own value-essences, thus corrupting their ability to achieve their best possibilities.

Scheler notes that certain social groups are more prone to resentment than others either because their social positions are experienced as inherently humiliating or because they are socially powerless. For example, in a society in which formal EQUALITY is a declared right, but substantive economic INEQUALITY is the rule, resentment among the poor will be common. Also, social conditions that encourage people to define their own value only in relation to others (*e.g.,* comparative grading on a curve) invite resentment because they undermine self-esteem. For Scheler, clear insight into one's own self-value is an important shield from resentment. Also, certain social relations inherently invite resentment, *e.g.,* the older generation's relation to the younger; the mother-in-law's relation to her son's new wife; younger brothers' relationships to older ones. The aged must renounce their positions of AUTHORITY without rancor to avoid resentment; the mother-in-law must accept the new affections of her son and entrust him to the new wife's care to escape resentment; the younger brother must either forgive the older brother's bullying or gain enough courage to fight back in order to overcome his natural resentment.

The two major arguments offered by both Scheler and Nietzsche to criticize resentment are that it leads to disastrous historical consequences for humanity through the value inversions it produces and that it leads to the ethical corruption of the individuals who succumb to it.

Value Inversions

One of Nietzsche's goals in *On the Genealogy of Morals* is to question the value of moral values. This task is part of his more general project of a revaluation of all values. He associates "morality" (narrowly construed) with the experience of evil, guilt, bad conscience, retributive PUNISHMENT, asceticism, and the rejection of life (*i.e.,* life as it really is on this earth) more generally. Ordinary language provides the term "moralistic" to describe those who embody such experiences; in their hands values becomes weapons of TORTURE against both others and themselves. Resentment is not only a determinant of the inversion of slave morality over noble morality, but it also plays a central role in the elevation of guilt, asceticism, and life-negation as essential elements in the moralistic stance. As possible alternatives to this moralistic orientation, Nietzsche offers the noble mode of evaluation, the INNOCENCE of becoming, continuous but gradual self-perfection through a stylization of character, the free spirit, great health, rising above the impulse to punish and blame, and life-affirmation. He extols a wide range of alternative virtues that constitute an entirely different ethical universe than this moralistic one.

The elevation of slave morality is one element of the rise of these moralistic values. Nietzsche notes that noble morality has occasionally reasserted itself historically (especially in the Renaissance) and that current humanity is a battleground between the two types of morality. Christianity's elevation of meekness, poverty, humility, pity, and self-abnegation is the most dramatic example of resentment's attempt to assert the dominance of moralistic values. Not only does Nietzsche find these values contemptible, he believes they undermine humanity's capacity and will to achieve its highest and best possibilities. It turns humanity against life and its own desire to perfect itself. Moralism is thus deeply problematic because it militates against humanity's highest possibilities and distracts people with a false sense of achievement. Nietzsche seeks to provide a path by which humanity can make something glorious out of its all-too-human nature, but moralistic values demean humanity and prevent it from embracing that task.

Scheler is also critical of many features of "morality," but he rejects Nietzsche's sweeping critique of Christianity. He tries to show that key Christian virtues are resentment-free and even satisfy Nietzsche's own standards of value. For example, although Christian love does offer itself to others, it does so in the spirit of Nietzsche's gift-giving virtue—full of spiritual riches and vitality, secure in an inner bliss, sufficiently overflowing to be able to give to others without any diminution in itself. Christian love grasps the highest value possibilities of its recipients rather than offering pity for their suffering.

Scheler acknowledges that some ways of "serving" others are motivated by the self's sense of emptiness and need, but he insists that this motive is not characteristic of Christian love. Scheler also argues that the Christian willingness to "turn the other cheek" is not a sign of weakness or a desire to shame the other, but simply a refusal to adopt any "reactive" stance, an insistence that one's orientation to the other must derive from one's own value-essence, not from any harms the other may inflict. It rises above the urge for retribution in the way Nietzsche recommends. Even Christian asceticism can be motivated by a love of something higher than the body (without denigrating the body's value), rather than a more reactive hatred of the body. Scheler suggests that the former is the ideal Christian form of asceticism. He acknowledges that Christianity has allowed itself sometimes to oppose life, to ignore that spirit is rooted in life, but he believes this lapse occurred because Christianity embraces values higher than life.

Scheler claims that a number of more recent trends in ethics—*e.g.,* humanitarianism and relativism—result from value-inversions produced by resentment. He defines humanitarianism as a feeling for humankind as a presently existing collective (not for the value-essences of individual persons or for humanity's highest possibilities) that seeks to increase its general welfare through equalitarian social arrangements. These are justified by claiming that each person is equally valuable because each exemplifies humanity in general. Scheler criticizes this stance for several reasons. The goal of the humanitarian is improvement on the lower dimensions of value (sensory values) (not on humanity's highest possibilities); it targets only what is superficially important in human life (pleasure/pain), not its ethical core. In addition, humanitarian love is a mere feeling—typically passive—often spread by infection at the sight of others' suffering; such love does nothing to nourish their ethical achievement. (Often it relieves the guilt of the humanitarian without doing any real good for the recipient.) Scheler thus suggests that humanitarian love ignores higher possibilities in favor of lower ones. It displaces a more affirmative, enhancing love for the value-essences of individuals. Its equalitarianism ignores differences of talent and merit, weakens the quality of education, and levels-down the benefits of higher culture. Instantiating the abstraction "humanity" pales beside the actual sense of unity and ethical inspiration produced by actual social groups, like families and professional associations. Scheler concludes that humanitarianism betrays a secret hatred of the higher possibilities of humanity by focusing exclusively on the lowest common denominator.

Scheler also claims that relativism and the view that values are merely subjective is largely a function of resentment toward higher values. What easier way to reject the force and challenge of higher values than to regard them as relative to a culture or a historical era or to dismiss them as mere matters of taste? The resentful person cannot bear the lowering of self-value that serious objective values would imply, and instead of striving to achieve them, he or she dismisses their possibility. Not only do relativists sidestep the force of higher values, they deny their sense of inferiority to model persons, who successfully embody higher ideals. They thus reject the very idea of objective good in order to avoid acknowledging their own mediocrity. Scheler believes that relativists resent higher human beings, just as Nietzsche thought priests and Christians resented them.

Personal Corruption

The second major argument against resentment offered by Nietzsche and Scheler is that it poisons or corrupts personal character. Nietzsche laments its ability to turn people away from their distinctive individual virtues—from the higher possibilities they could realize—to an obsession with debunking others' virtues. It causes people to dwell on others' flaws rather than their own possibilities. Moreover, the self-hatred it produces weakens people's self-esteem and self-respect, making them less capable of the self-discipline and COURAGE needed to cultivate their talents. Still further, to the extent that resentment succeeds in substituting lower values for higher ones, it allows people to deceive themselves about their actual accomplishments. The hatred and negativity that constitutes resentment easily disseminates by infection, thus multiplying the threat of CORRUPTION. Additional character flaws typically accompany resentment: the incapacity to adopt a measured, balanced perspective, general WEAKNESS OF WILL, and excessive vulnerability to slights and insults. To counteract these flaws, Nietzsche celebrates the virtues of justice (giving each perspective its due), strength (the ability to organize one's drives

and marshal one's resources to achieve great things), and hardness (resistance to pettiness and self-pity), as well as gift-giving virtue (allowing others to draw freely on one's resources without asking for or wanting anything in return). Indeed, the whole constellation of virtues Nietzsche embraces is developed to overcome the corrupting influence of resentment.

Scheler worries that resentment will blind people to higher values and render them incapable of realizing their value-essences. Resentment substitutes false or lower values for the higher ones to which individuals are naturally drawn. He also agrees with Nietzsche's claim that resentment corrodes self-esteem. Without such self-esteem people cannot will their own best possibilities or experience the enriching power of ethical models. (Scheler believes that ethical models are the main vehicles by which individuals' value-essences are broadened.) Self-hatred accentuates the lowest possibilities of those it victimizes, producing an endless cycle that is hard to break. Finally, resentment's hatefulness expands beyond the initial transgression and transgressor to embrace everyone that might be associated with or responsible for its disadvantaged position. It slanders anyone to whom it cannot feel superior. Scheler notes that the best cure for resentment is a recovery of responsiveness to one's higher possibilities and of the strength to realize them; often this recovery is enabled by the love other people offer. Their affection can sometimes shatter the self-reinforcing cycles of resentment by restoring self-esteem and contact with genuinely higher values.

See also: ABSURD, THE; ALIENATION; ANGER; CHARACTER; CHRISTIAN ETHICS; CORRUPTION; DECEIT; DETERRENCE, THREATS, AND RETALIATION; DISCRIMINATION; EGOISM; ELITE, CONCEPT OF; EMOTION; ENVY; ETHICS AND MORALITY; EXCUSES; GUILT AND SHAME; HARM AND OFFENSE; HATE; HISTORY OF WESTERN ETHICS 10, 11: NINETEENTH- AND TWENTIETH-CENTURY CONTINENTAL; HUMANISM; HYPOCRISY; IMMORALITY; INEQUALITY; MORAL RELATIVISM; NIETZSCHE; OPPRESSION; PAIN AND SUFFERING; PHENOMENOLOGY; POSSIBILISM; PRIDE; PUNISHMENT; RACISM AND RELATED ISSUES; REVENGE; SCHELER; SELF-[entries]; SLAVERY; SUBJECTIVISM; WEAKNESS OF WILL.

Bibliography

Bittner, Rüdiger. "Ressentiment." In *Nietzsche, Genealogy, Morality,* edited by Richard Schacht, 127–38.

Berkeley: University of California Press, 1994. Argues that resentment is less strategic than Nietzsche believes; suffering itself produces the inversion of values; the sufferer is less responsible for it.

Dostoevsky, Fyodor. *Notes from Underground.* Edited and translated by Michael R. Katz. New York: W.W. Norton, 1989 [1864]. Perhaps the best literary study of the resentment mentality. Traces the origins and development of the condition (Part II) and offers a synchronic, in-depth examination of it (Part I).

Nietzsche, Friedrich. *On the Genealogy of Morals.* Translated by Walter Kaufmann and R. J. Hollingdale. New York: Random House, 1967 [1887].

Reginster, Bernard. "*Ressentiment,* Evaluation, and Integrity." *International Studies in Philosophy* 27/3 (1995): 117–24. Examines the character flaw resentment produces, concluding it is a form of self-deception.

Scheler, Max. *Ressentiment.* Edited by Lewis Coser; translated by William Holdheim. New York: Free Press of Glencoe, 1961 [1912].

Solomon, Robert. "One Hundred Years of *Ressentiment.*" In *Nietzsche, Genealogy, Morality,* edited by Richard Schacht, 95–126. Berkeley: University of California Press, 1994. Raises questions about Nietzsche's evaluation of resentment primarily on the grounds that it is the source of the experience of injustice, which Solomon believes is the foundation for the concept of justice.

Strawson, P. F. "Freedom and Resentment." In *Freedom and Resentment and Other Essays,* 1–24. London: Methuen, 1974. A lecture delivered in 1962.

Sugarman, Richard Ira. *Rancor against Time: The Phenomenology of Ressentiment.* Hamburg: Meaner, 1980. Discusses Nietzsche and Scheler and offers some additional original insights.

William R. Schroeder

responsibility

"Responsibility" is used to mean many different things. There is a discernible pattern to these meanings.

First there is what may be called causal responsibility. Someone may say, for instance, that the short circuit was responsible for the fire. Normally, this statement would simply mean that the short circuit caused, or helped cause, the fire.

Then there is what may be called personal responsibility. It is useful to distinguish two main types of personal responsibility, prospective and retrospective. If someone were to say that the lifeguard is responsible for the swimmers' safety, this statement would normally be taken to mean that it is the lifeguard's duty to ensure the swimmers' safety. Here we have a case of personal responsibility that is prospective (in the sense that what the person in question is responsible for lies in the future). To bear prospective responsibility for something, then, is to have a responsibility—that is, a duty, or obligation, in virtue of some role that one fills—to see to it that that thing occurs or obtains.

Retrospective responsibility is quite different. If someone were to say that the lifeguard is responsible for the swimmers' deaths, this statement would not normally be taken to mean that it is the lifeguard's duty to ensure the swimmers' deaths. On the contrary, the deaths to which reference is made lie in the past, not the future, and the lifeguard's responsibility is tantamount to a sort of blameworthiness. Far from consisting in having a duty that remains as yet unfulfilled, the lifeguard's responsibility concerns having failed to fulfill a duty. But retrospective responsibility need not concern this. It may be positive, rather than negative, and constitute a sort of praiseworthiness rather than blameworthiness, as when a generous donor is said to be responsible for a charity's success.

Personal responsibility, whether prospective or retrospective, can be of many different sorts. One's role may be defined by virtue of moral, legal, or some other sort of rules (such as the rules of chess), and so one may incur prospective responsibility that is moral, legal, or of some other kind. Similarly, praise and blame may express moral, legal, or some other sort of approval or disapproval, and so one may incur retrospective responsibility that is moral, legal, or of some other kind.

It may be a mistake to assert that all responsibility is either causal or personal. In recent years considerable attention has been paid to the question of whether collectives (such as corporations) may bear responsibility for some things. This question has usually been raised with respect to retrospective responsibility, but it arises in the context of prospective responsibility also. Often, the issue has been one of legal liability. Here, perhaps, no problem of categorization exists, since corporations are often treated as persons, from the legal point of view, and so the question may be seen to concern personal, retrospective responsibility of the legal variety. But often the issue is treated as a moral one, and here it is not so clear what should be said, since it is surely problematic to think of corporations as persons on a moral par with individuals. The main options appear to be these, given that the question is not a legal one. If Company X is said to be responsible for a certain mishap, then either (1) this statement is a misleading way of merely attributing causal (and not moral) responsibility for the mishap to some event in which Company X was involved, or (2) this statement is a disguised way of attributing personal moral responsibility to some key individuals in Company X for the mishap, or (3) this statement is an attribution of moral responsibility to Company X for the mishap, an attribution that is not wholly reducible to an attribution of moral responsibility to one or more individuals. The third option is difficult to support, although it has had its proponents.

It is necessary to draw a further distinction between two types of retrospective moral responsibility. Passive praise- or blameworthiness attaches to a person who is worthy of being judged in a certain way. The judgment need never be overtly expressed, but it will be accurate just in case the individual's moral standing has been enhanced (in which case praise is appropriate) or diminished (in which case blame is appropriate) by virtue of his or her having acted in a certain way. Such responsibility is distinct from active praise- or blameworthiness, which is a matter of someone's deserving to be treated in a certain way (for example, rewarded or punished). Very often, it is thought that passive praise- or blameworthiness is a precondition of active praise- or blameworthiness. For example, retributivists (of one sort) hold that one deserves to be punished for some action only if one is passively blameworthy for that action (that is, only if one is morally at fault in acting, so that one's moral standing has been diminished to some extent by one's action). It is on the basis of this thesis that some have objected to strict liability, which, on one understanding, involves the practice of holding persons ready for PUNISHMENT for certain legal offenses even when they are not passively morally blameworthy for committing these offenses.

Sometimes individuals are said to be responsible persons (period), rather than responsible for something. This view attributes to them a measure of moral maturity. Two types of such maturity may be distinguished. In one sense, one is a responsible person if one has a certain capacity: the capacity to make a reasonable assessment of one's prospective responsibilities (duties, obligations) and thereby to

incur retrospective responsibility for one's actions. If one is not a responsible person in this sense, one is "nonresponsible." In another sense, one is a responsible person if one takes one's prospective responsibilities seriously and endeavors to fulfill them. If one is not a responsible person in this sense, one is "irresponsible."

Henceforth, this article will concentrate on issues surrounding personal, retrospective, moral, passive responsibility. Philosophers have concerned themselves with what is needed and what suffices for such responsibility. Two distinct conditions have been suggested.

The First Condition: Freedom

A common assumption is that, for someone to be morally responsible (retrospectively and passively) for some action, that person must have performed that action freely. Just what goes into such freedom has been a matter of considerable controversy. The central idea is that the person in question must have enjoyed some measure of control—that the action was "up to" him or her—but, beyond that, there is little that is not subject to dispute.

There is a venerable argument to the effect that this condition of moral responsibility is impossible to satisfy, and hence that such responsibility is never incurred. The argument involves the notion of determinism (roughly, the thesis that every event has a cause) and may be put as follows (where "event" is to be construed broadly and covers, in particular, decisions, actions, omissions, and their outcomes, since moral responsibility for each of these is commonly thought possible):

1. If determinism is true, then no one is ever free with respect to any event.
2. If determinism is false, then no one is ever free with respect to any event.
3. Determinism is either true or false.

Hence:

4. No one is ever free with respect to any event.
5. One is morally responsible for an event only if one is or was free with respect to it.

Hence:

6. No one is ever morally responsible for any event.

Premise 5 just states the precondition for moral responsibility that is at issue. Premise 3 is taken to be a logical truth. The rationale for premise 1 is this: if an event *C* causes an event *E*, then *C* is, under the circumstances, sufficient for *E*; if so, then *E* was not avoidable; hence, if determinism is true, then no event is avoidable; if an event is not avoidable, then no one is free with respect to it; hence, if determinism is true, no one is free with respect to any event. The rationale for premise 2 is this: if an event occurs uncaused, then it occurs at random; if so, then no one is free with respect to it; hence, if determinism is false, some events occur with respect to which no one is free; the only events that escape this are those that are caused despite the falsity of determinism; but with respect to these events, the rationale for premise 1 applies; hence, if determinism is false, no one is free with respect to any event.

Some philosophers have accepted this argument. Others have rejected the first premise, claiming that the truth of determinism is compatible with there being freedom of ACTION. Still others have rejected the second premise, claiming that an action that is not caused by any event may still be in an agent's control. (FREEDOM AND DETERMINISM is discussed more fully elsewhere in this encyclopedia.)

More recently, premise 5 has been challenged. Harry Frankfurt has claimed that it is possible that one should be morally responsible for what one has done, even though one could not have done otherwise. Suppose, for example, that Peter and Paul are mortal enemies. Some acquaintances carry Peter, asleep, into Paul's room and lock him in. Paul is asleep, too. Peter awakes first and, though surprised at his surroundings and unaware that he is locked in, resolves to remain in Paul's room; for he wants to annoy Paul, and he knows that he will succeed in doing so simply by being present in Paul's room. Paul then awakes and, as predicted, is annoyed. It has been argued that Peter is morally responsible for Paul's annoyance even though he could not have done other than annoy Paul.

This conclusion can be attacked from a number of points of view. It is worth noting, however, that there is perhaps room for accepting the conclusion and yet denying that this is tantamount to a rejection of premise 5. This premise implies that, if Peter did not act freely, then he is not morally responsible for what he did. The case undermines this claim, however, only if acting freely requires being able to do other than that which one does. But there is reason to think that this is not true and that, for example, Peter did freely annoy Paul even though he could not have done otherwise. If this is so, the case poses no threat to premise 5.

This premise has come under attack from another perspective, though. Robert Adams has recently argued that there are certain sins that are involuntary, and hence with respect to which one is not free, but for which one may yet be to blame. Examples would be the sins of CRUELTY, thoughtlessness, cowardice, lack of compassion, subscription to the Nazi ethic, and so on, where these sins are understood not as a matter of acting in a certain way (cruelly, thoughtlessly, and so on)—something that may well be under one's control—but of being a certain way, that is, of having certain inclinations, desires, or beliefs—something that may well not be under one's control. And Adams's point is that, whether or not these phenomena are under one's control, one is certainly to blame for them, and freedom is not a precondition of moral responsibility.

There are two main ways to avoid Adams's conclusion. One is to deny that the phenomena are not under one's control. ARISTOTLE (384–322 B.C.E.), for example, thought all our vices (and VIRTUES) to be under our control, at least indirectly; that is, he thought that, even if we have now reached a point at which certain character traits are beyond our control (not in terms of acting on them, but in terms of ridding ourselves of them or of acquiring them), still there was a time when we could have acted in such a way as to prevent our having them (if they are vices that we now have) or to produce them in ourselves (if they are virtues that we now lack). It is debatable how plausible this position is. The other way to resist Adams's conclusion is to deny that we are responsible for our virtues and vices (or at least for those that never were even in our indirect control). Nevertheless it may be that we are to be praised or blamed for these character traits, in a sense of "praise" and "blame" that does not impute responsibility for these traits.

An argument very similar to, but importantly different from, the argument given at the outset of this section has recently received attention. The end of the argument can be put in exactly the same way as in the first argument. That is:

1488

4. No one is ever free with respect to any event.
5. One is morally responsible for an event only if one is or was free with respect to it.

Hence:

6. No one is ever morally responsible for any event.

The difference lies in the rationale for statement 4. Here the claim is that 4 is true, not because of any general considerations concerning causation or the lack of it, but simply because of the fact that luck is ineliminable from our lives, given the way we and the world are constituted. Thus we now have the following premises leading to 4:

1*. Luck is an element in the occurrence of any event.
2*. If this is so, then no event is in anyone's control.
3*. If this is so, then no one is free with respect to any event.

In support of premise 1*, cases of the following sort are commonly cited. John throws his dagger at George and kills him, the blade piercing the latter's heart. Johannes throws his dagger at Georg in like fashion but, because of a strong wind that suddenly arises, fails even to wound Georg. This case dramatizes the fact that, in all our actions, what we succeed in doing is in large measure not up to us but, as it is often said, up to nature. It was just luck that there was no wind to prevent George's death while there was one to prevent Georg's. Or again, Jean is on the threshold of throwing his dagger at Georges but suddenly succumbs to a sneezing fit; Georges luckily survives. The more one thinks about it (independent of any question of determinism), the more one sees that luck permeates our lives, eroding whatever control over our actions we may have thought we had; whence premise 2*. Such control is the essence of the sort of freedom that is at issue in this context; whence premise 3*.

But this argument is unacceptable. The role of luck in our lives can (and should) be acknowledged without our throwing in the towel regarding moral responsibility. Either premise 2* is to be denied or premise 3* is, depending on how the phrase "in anyone's control" is to be understood. If the phrase means "in anyone's control to any extent," then 2*

is to be denied; if it means "in anyone's complete control," then 3* is to be denied. The point is that, while there is no event that is in anyone's complete control (in the sense that the occurrence of any event will always hinge to some degree on factors beyond anyone's control), many events are (or would appear to be) in someone's control at least to some extent, and to this extent there is freedom with respect to that event and thus moral responsibility for it remains a possibility. For example, while George's death was not in John's complete control, it was (apparently) in his control to some extent—to the extent to which his throwing the dagger was in his control.

Another problem arises here, though. It may be argued that, even if George's death was in John's control to some extent, it would still not be appropriate to blame him for it. After all, there is nothing to distinguish John from Johannes in this regard, for each did the same; it was simply that nature intervened in the one case but not the other. But inasmuch as Johannes clearly is not to blame for Georg's death (for Georg did not die), John cannot be to blame for George's death. One response to this intriguing problem is this: while it may be agreed that Johannes is not to be blamed for Georg's death, still he is to be blamed for his attempt to kill Georg, and in this he differs not at all from John. True, John is to blame for George's death, but a distinction should be drawn between being to blame for more things and being more to blame. While John is to blame for more things than Johannes, he is no more to blame. Even so, each is to blame to some degree, and moral responsibility is thus not eliminated.

What of Jean, though? He seems to be morally on a par with both John and Johannes, yet he never even made an attempt to kill Georges; he was interrupted by the sneezing fit. Clearly then (it may be argued), Jean is not to blame at all, and if John and Johannes are morally on a par with him, then they are not to blame after all.

To this challenge there are two main responses (other than agreement). Either one might deny that Jean is morally on a par with the others; or one might claim that Jean is to blame for something. If one takes the latter tack, what would be the thing for which Jean might be to blame? One candidate is this: being such that he would have attempted to kill Georges, had he not been interrupted by the sneezing fit. And here Jean is no different from John and Johannes.

Finally, just what sort of freedom or control might be thought necessary for moral responsibility has been a subject of some controversy. Some philosophers (such as Michael J. Zimmerman) propose a fairly thin account of this, involving one's being in a certain sense the source of one's action. Others propose richer accounts, involving such matters as "reasons-responsiveness" (see John Martin Fischer) or volitional control coupled with autonomy (see Ishtiyaque Haji). Whatever the proper account may be, it is worth noting a distinction between two types of freedom, each of which may initially appear necessary for moral responsibility. This distinction can best be drawn out by a familiar example. Suppose that Bonnie holds up a bank. She does so by pointing a gun at Tess, a teller, and ordering her to hand over all the money in her till. Tess does so. The questions here are these: Did Tess hand over the money freely? And is she morally responsible for doing so? One's initial reaction to both questions is likely to be: "No, of course not." One may be tempted to add to this that the negative response to the first question is the ground for the negative response to the second. It is not clear on reflection, however, that this is the best assessment of the case. While there certainly is a sense in which Tess unfreely handed over the money—she was strongly coerced, after all—there is clearly also a sense in which she freely handed it over; for she had a choice in the situation (a decidedly unpleasant one, to be sure) and, we may assume, she made the right one. Indeed, in virtue of this fact, it may well be appropriate to praise her for what she did (she kept calm; she did not endanger other people present; and so on), and this would seem to imply that she is responsible for her action after all. It thus seems that the sort of freedom necessary for moral responsibility (if, indeed, any sort of freedom is necessary) is that which Tess exemplified rather than that which she failed to exemplify.

The Second Condition: Belief and Intention

It is sometimes maintained that freedom is not just necessary but also sufficient for moral responsibility. But this statement seems clearly false, for a certain mental condition would also appear necessary. Tom, a three-year-old child, has a choice as to whether or not to torment the cat; if he makes the wrong choice, that is no reason to blame him—to scold him, yes, but scolding is properly understood in this context as an educative device and not as an imputation of moral responsibility.

What is it that Tom lacks? The obvious response is that he lacks any awareness of the moral character of his action and is therefore not to be blamed for it. This response suggests that one is morally blameworthy for an event only if one was aware that one was doing moral wrong with respect to it. But many would object to this claim as posing too strong a condition. First, to be aware that one is doing wrong requires that one is indeed doing wrong. But can one not be to blame even if one does no wrong, as long as one believes (mistakenly, of course) that one is doing wrong? Secondly, however, it may be said that even such belief, rather than awareness, constitutes too strong a requirement; for, after all, in many cases blameworthiness for an action is incurred due to thoughtlessness—we talk of culpable ignorance, of culpable inadvertence, of NEGLIGENCE—and here it is the very lack of awareness of the moral character of the action that appears to render the agent blameworthy for the action.

There is a great deal of plausibility to both objections. The first objection, if successful, appears to require a modification to the traditional account of justifications and excuses. J. L. Austin (1911–1960), whose account of this matter has often been taken as standard, suggests that one may escape blame for an action in one of two ways, either by having had a justification for performing it (in which case one did no wrong in performing it) or by having an excuse for having performed it (in which case one was not justified in performing it but one is still not to blame for it). On this view, if one did not do wrong, one has incurred no blameworthiness. The first objection implies that this view is mistaken.

The challenge posed by the second objection is this. If freedom of action is necessary but not sufficient for moral responsibility, and a belief concerning wrongdoing is not necessary, what besides freedom is needed? Surprisingly, there has been very little discussion of this issue in the literature. It is not easy to see what the answer should be.

A third objection, initially less plausible than the first two, is this. It is not possible to have the belief in question; that is, one cannot do something while believing that what one is doing is morally wrong. Many philosophers, from PLATO (c. 430–347 B.C.E.) and Aristotle to R. M. HARE, have argued for this claim. While the claim, which many have rejected, certainly seems at odds with common experience, its plausibility may grow on reflection. For example, many alleged examples (drawn from common experience) of doing something that one believes at the time to be morally wrong reveal themselves on inspection to be better characterized as cases of doing something that one believes at the time to be held by others to be morally wrong (or prohibited or condemned for some other reason).

Perhaps, though, this much can be said. Freedom of action conjoined with a belief that what one is doing is morally wrong does suffice for moral blameworthiness. What of the corresponding thesis concerning praiseworthiness? Does freedom of action conjoined with a belief that what one is doing is morally right suffice for moral praiseworthiness? There is reason to reject this thesis, even if one accepts its counterpart concerning blameworthiness. The reason is that one may believe that what one is doing is right and yet this belief may be wholly incidental to one's purpose. For example, Rebecca may rescue Donna from drowning in the river, and she may believe that this action is the morally right thing to do; however, if Rebecca rescues Donna not for the reason that it is right but because she anticipates a sizable reward, then she would appear to forfeit the praise that would otherwise be her due. If this is so, it seems that one must intend to do what is right (indeed, intend to do it because it is right), and not simply believe that what one is doing is right, if one is to be praised for what one does.

Finally, mention must be made of the relevance of mental disorders to moral responsibility. It is commonly assumed that, if one is genuinely mentally disturbed when one performs an action, then one cannot be to blame for it. But this assumption is far too sweeping. While kleptomania may furnish an excuse for theft, it surely furnishes no excuse for rape; similarly, while exhibitionism may furnish an excuse for exposing oneself, it surely furnishes no excuse for theft. There must be some intimate connection between the mental disorder and the offense for an excuse to be in the offing. Even then, we must proceed cautiously. If Karl steals some items from a grocery store, and it is then discovered that he suffers from kleptomania, why think that he therefore has an excuse for his action? One answer is that, given his condition, Karl could not help himself. It is not obvious, though, that this answer is correct. Was Karl impelled by his disorder to steal, as one is impelled to kick out by a well-placed tap on the kneecap? This seems unlikely. More accurate would seem to be the claim that Karl's disorder rendered it very difficult, rather than impossible, for him to resist the impulse to steal. But if there was still the possibility of resistance, should Karl be excused for failing to resist? If so, on what grounds? Perhaps the answer is that Karl is not to be excused after all; for he recognized that what he was doing was wrong, and he knew that he could have resisted. Or perhaps the answer is that Karl is relevantly similar to Tess who, although she could have resisted Bonnie's threat, reasonably believed that she did not do wrong in not doing so; if so, then, like Tess, Karl has an excuse. However this issue is to be resolved, the most important point to note is the following. If a mental disorder furnishes an excuse, it appears to do so by way of excuses already accounted for. That is, it appears to do so because it occasions the absence of one or the other of the two conditions already acknowledged as likely to be necessary for moral responsibility—freedom and belief (or some other kind of mental state). If this observation is accurate, then we may say, along with Joel Feinberg, that when it comes to furnishing EXCUSES, there is nothing special about mental disorders.

See also: AGENCY AND DISABILITY; AGENT-CENTERED MORALITY; AUTONOMY OF MORAL AGENTS; CASUISTRY; CAUSATION AND RESPONSIBILITY; CHARACTER; COERCION; COLLECTIVE RESPONSIBILITY; CONSCIENCE; CONSEQUENTIALISM; DELIBERATION AND CHOICE; DUTY AND OBLIGATION; EMOTION; EXCUSES; FATE AND FATALISM; FREE WILL; FREEDOM AND DETERMINISM; GROUPS, MORAL STATUS OF; GUILT AND SHAME; HARE; HART; HOLOCAUST; INNOCENCE; INTENTION; INTRANSITIVITY; MERIT AND DESERT; MORAL LUCK; NEGLIGENCE; PRESCRIPTIVISM; PUNISHMENT; REASONS FOR ACTION; SELF-CONTROL; STOICISM; VOLUNTARY ACTS; WEAKNESS OF WILL; WICKEDNESS; WILLIAMS.

Bibliography

Adams, Robert Merrihew. "Involuntary Sins." *Philosophical Review* 94 (1985): 3–31.

Aristotle. *Nicomachean Ethics.* Books II and III.

Austin, J. L. "A Plea for Excuses." *Proceedings of the Aristotelian Society* 57 (1956–7): 1–30.

Feinberg, Joel. *Doing and Deserving.* Princeton: Princeton

University Press, 1970. Essays on several topics concerning responsibility.

Fischer, John Martin. *The Metaphysics of Free Will.* Oxford: Blackwell, 1994.

————, and Mark Ravizza. *Responsibility and Control: A Theory of Moral Responsibility.* Cambridge Studies in Philosophy and Law. Cambridge: Cambridge University Press, 1998. General discussion of moral responsibility.

Frankfurt, Harry G. "Alternate Possibilities and Moral Responsibility." *Journal of Philosophy* 66 (1969): 829–39.

French, Peter A. *Collective and Corporate Responsibility.* New York: Columbia University Press, 1984.

Glover, Jonathan. *Responsibility.* London: Routledge and Kegan Paul, 1970. Extended treatment of responsibility.

Haji, Ishtiyaque. *Moral Appraisability: Puzzles, Proposals, and Perplexities.* Oxford: Oxford University Press, 1998. General discussion of moral responsibility.

Hare, R. M. *The Language of Morals.* Oxford: Oxford University Press, 1952.

Hart, H. L. A. *Punishment and Responsibility.* Oxford: Oxford University Press, 1968. Essays on several topics concerning responsibility.

Nagel, Thomas. *Mortal Questions.* Cambridge: Cambridge University Press, 1979. Includes an essay on moral luck.

Plato. *Meno.* Especially pp. 77b–78b.

Schlossberger, Eugene. *Moral Responsibility and Persons.* Philadelphia: Temple University Press, 1992. Extended attack on freedom as a necessary condition of moral responsibility.

Smith, Holly. "Culpable Ignorance." *Philosophical Review* 92 (1983): 543–71.

Williams, Bernard. *Moral Luck.* Cambridge: Cambridge University Press, 1981.

Zimmerman, Michael J. *An Essay on Moral Responsibility.* Totowa, NJ: Rowman and Littlefield, 1988. General discussion of moral responsibility; extensive bibliography.

Michael J. Zimmerman

responsibility, collective

See collective responsibility.

retaliation

See deterrence, threats, and retaliation.

retributive justice

See justice, rectificatory.

revenge

The desire for revenge is a powerful motivation in human affairs. Collective revenge manifests itself in retaliatory wars, gang reprisals, public lynchings. Instances of individual revenge arising out of romantic disharmony, family disagreements, property disputes, personal and professional conflict are diverse and legion. Revenge is a persistent literary theme from the plays of Aeschylus (525–c. 456 B.C.E.) to recent popular and feminist fiction. Yet the nature and morality of revenge have received scattered attention in Western philosophy.

Revenge is a form of retaliation, a return of injury for injury, bad for bad. Not all retaliation in kind is revenge. Retaliation in kind can be strategically motivated, as in the return of force to repel an attack or reprisals aimed at deterrence. In contrast, the point of retaliation that is revenge is the satisfaction of paying someone back for a perceived insult or injury to oneself or to another with whose INTERESTS or cause one identifies. Payback retaliation need not be premeditated (although it very often is). A spontaneous angry retort can be revenge; but an utterly blind response to provocation is not.

Revenge often invokes the idea of payment on both sides. An act of revenge is a requital, a *repayment* of insult or injury. Revenge is also often said to be exacted: the subject is *made to pay.* The essential payback element of revenge is typically vindictive and malicious. However, some nonvindictive acts are called revenge where the agent regards them *post facto* as payback. "Revenge" may mean little more than evening a score in the context of friendly grudge matches; and revenge in this sense might even be had (rather than taken) unwittingly. There are also common, but nevertheless marginal, uses of "revenge" in which the core notion of retaliation is weak or absent. Reversals such as electoral victories that bring satisfaction at another's expense are called revenge. The satisfaction of seeing one's adversaries suffer the effects of their own conduct is sometimes regarded as revenge—indeed very sweet revenge since one has the satisfaction without the RESPONSIBILITY. (Consider also, "Success is the best revenge.") Revenge seeks the satisfaction of payback retaliation; but analogous satisfaction without retaliation is not really revenge.

The recompense side of many acts of revenge is broadly retributive: the subject is thereby made to pay for the insult or injury. This broad sense of "retributive" does not imply any offense or wrongdoing on the subject's part. Illegitimate grievances can give rise to revenge. Revenge can be taken for humiliations or injuries (unfavorable reviews, sporting defeats, judicial punishments) that are not offenses or wrongs, nor necessarily perceived as wrongs by those taking revenge. Insults or injuries for which revenge is taken may *also* constitute offenses or wrongs, and because wrongs are *avenged,* revenge and vengeance are often wrongly equated. Revenge should also be distinguished from PUNISHMENT that is inflicted for an offense or a wrong. Moreover, even in the broad sense of "retributive" outlined above, retribution and revenge are differently conceived. The retributive aspect of many acts of revenge is a matter of *making someone pay* on account of an insult or injury (whether or not also a wrong); but revenge is essentially retaliation, more precisely, it *is paying someone back.*

Acts of revenge have an intended subject who is being repaid for an insult or injury for which they are believed (however implausibly) to be responsible. Revenge can be misdirected (shooting the messenger); indirect (A takes revenge on B by harming B's family); indiscriminate (shooting into a crowd in response to being taunted, or trying to get even with one's community or even with society in general by causing public mayhem). Nevertheless, even where misdirected, indirect, or indiscriminate, revenge is always paying (someone) back. Simply hitting out over an insult or injury—taking out one's frustration, ANGER, or RESENTMENT on the nearest or easiest target (kicking the cat)—is not revenge.

Revenge is a form of RECIPROCITY, motivated by the (arguably) natural resentment of humiliation, insult, or injury. Yet as a rationale of ACTION, revenge is now widely regarded as morally improper. For instance, state punishment is sometimes defended as deterring antisocial individual and collective acts of revenge. Retributivist punishment is commonly characterized by its critics as 'institutionalized revenge'; for their part, advocates of retributivist punishment are usually anxious to distinguish retribution from revenge. Usually it is vindictive, malicious revenge (and not friendly grudge matches and the like) that is morally criticized. Those (*e.g.,* Kantians, virtue theorists, religious ethicists) who emphasize the moral significance of MOTIVES, and of the character traits from which actions flow, will particularly condemn malicious revenge as the exercise of a vice.

A number of familiar objections to revenge can be levelled from the point of view of various ethical theories—consequentialist, contractarian, and modern versions of NATURALISM—that emphasise the strategic justification of acts, roles, rules, and policies. For instance, to seek satisfaction from revenge can lead to frustration, compounding the resentment that the revenge was intended to relieve. The pursuit of revenge can become self-destructive; revenge seekers can lose perspective, become consumed by resentment or hatred. Revenge is characterized as 'getting even', but those bent on revenge often inflict disproportionate harm. Familiar modes of revenge, *e.g.,* vilification, destruction of PROPERTY, and personal injury, also inflict unjust harm. Further, innocent parties can become targets of misdirected revenge, can be used as means of revenge, or can get caught in the cross fire. Instances of revenge can evolve into relentless cycles of injury followed by payback retaliation. These sometimes escalate into vendettas involving codes of revenge or vengeance. Such codes retain the logic of injury followed by payback retaliation, but can lack otherwise characteristic or typical features of both revenge and vengeance. Burdensome duties of revenge (vengeance) can be imposed on individuals in the absence of any independently motivated desire on their part to inflict or accept retaliation. Within a code of revenge (vengeance) a prescribed individual may be required to avenge a prescribed offense by harming a prescribed subject. The agent may act with great reluctance, feeling no genuine malice and believing that the subject does not really deserve what is inflicted other than in the sense that it is mandated by the code. Of course individuals can, and often do, identify with and internalize particular codes of revenge (vengeance), and they are genuinely affronted by a specified offense that they maliciously avenge. Nevertheless, for an individual to shirk a socially or culturally imposed duty of revenge (vengeance) is a cause of public shame and sanction. For good reasons, acts of individual and collective vengeance are considered part of an older, more primitive morality, now properly replaced by public standards and institutions of justice. While highly morally significant as objections to revenge, the above points are nevertheless contingent or suggestive of individual or collective vengeance.

The desire for revenge is grounded in notions of SELF-ESTEEM and reputation. HONOR is frequently identified as the source of the desire for revenge. Particular conceptions of honor can of course mitigate against revenge where, *e.g.,* in CHRISTIAN ETHICS turning the other cheek is considered the more honorable course. Nonetheless, such conceptions require that a very real and understandable desire for revenge be curbed and controlled. So, why is restraint *eo ipso* the better course? An instrumentalist-inspired answer is the claim that greater satisfaction is gained by keeping one's temper in the face of insult or injury. A virtue-oriented perspective will condemn the resort to violent revenge as a form of incontinence. However, both these replies primarily address retaliation in anger and violence; they are not principled rejections even of malicious revenge. (Consider "Revenge is a dish best eaten cold.")

Arguably the motivation of all revenge can be characterized as morally shabby insofar as it derives satisfaction from another's suffering, not for any instrumental value of the suffering but just for the sake of suffering. Even so, people do not invariably consider even malicious revenge shameful. On the contrary, they sometimes boast of taking revenge or (where PRUDENCE dictates secrecy) wish that they could do so. Some revenge stories can be very amusing. Some instances of revenge can evoke the kind of empathy and vicarious satisfaction that would be highly morally inappropriate responses to, *e.g.,* envious or spiteful acts. However, we need to recognise that revenge often gains positive moral impetus from its close association with vengeance; and that it is the desire to avenge a wrong, and not the desire for revenge, that is grounded in moral indignation and a sense of injustice. Francis Bacon (1561–1626) remarked that the "most tolerable sort of revenge is for those wrongs which there is no law to remedy." It is noteworthy that this degree of moral SYMPATHY derives from the association of revenge with avenging a genuine wrong. In contrast, there is nothing intrinsically morally appropriate about repaying an indignity or injury in kind. Some such acts are relatively harmless; but many are harmful or unjust.

See also: AMNESTY AND PARDON; ANGER; CORRECTIONAL ETHICS; DETERRENCE, THREATS, AND RETALIATION; FORGIVENESS; GUILT AND SHAME; HARM AND OFFENSE; HATE; HONOR; INTERESTS; JUSTICE, RECTIFICATORY; MERCY; MOTIVES; PACIFISM; PRIDE; PROPORTIONALITY; PUNISHMENT; REASONS FOR ACTION; RESENTMENT; SELF-DEFENSE; SELF-ESTEEM; STRATEGIC INTERACTION; SYMPATHY; TERRORISM; VIOLENCE AND NON-VIOLENCE; WAR AND PEACE; WEAKNESS OF WILL.

Bibliography

Aeschylus. *The Oresteian Trilogy.* Translated by Philip Vellacott. Harmondsworth: Penguin, 1956. Dramatic representation of murder and vengeance within the royal family of Argos, revolving around the question of the relation of justice to vengeance.

Bacon, Francis. "Wild Justice." In his *Essays Civil and Moral.* London: Ward, Lock, [1597]. Argues that revenge is inferior to pardon; self-destructive; anti-social; usurps the law's role.

Elster, Jon. "Norms of Revenge." *Ethics* 100 (1990): 862–85. Discusses proximate and ultimate causes of social norms of revenge.

Hamlin, Alan P. "Rational Revenge." *Ethics* 101 (1990): 374–81. Reply to Elster.

Kleinig, John. *Punishment and Desert.* The Hague: Martinus Nijhoff, 1973. Distinguishes revenge and vengeance; revenge and punishment.

Murphy, Jeffrie G., and Jean Hampton. *Forgiveness and Mercy.* Cambridge: Cambridge University Press, 1988. See especially chapter 3. Discussion of revenge and "retributive hatred."

Njál's Saga. Translated by Magnus Magnusson and Hermann Palsson. Harmondsworth: Penguin, 1960 [c. 1280]. Sections 122–29 of this medieval Icelandic saga starkly illustrate the dynamics of a violent blood feud and the duties imposed by a code of revenge.

Smith, Adam. *The Theory of the Moral Sentiments.* London: H. G. Bohn, 1853 [1759]. Discusses resentment and its relation to the desire for revenge.

Wallace, Gerry. "Wild Justice." *Philosophy* 70 (1995): 363–75. Clear analysis of the nature and morality of revenge.

Weldon, Fay. *The Life and Loves of a She-Devil.* London: Hodder and Stoughton, 1983. Tale of relentless revenge.

Suzanne Uniacke

revolution

Revolution—in the sense that is relevant here—is an attempt at a thorough transformation of a society or cluster of societies (the Russian Revolution), initiated by the seizure of state POWER from the old regime, and carried on by deliberately implementing measures designed to yield social INSTITUTIONS and practices radically distinct from those that obtained prior to the seizure of power.

Is any revolution justified if it uses violence—if it involves killing or injuring people or forcing them into submission to attain the revolution's ends? Setting aside the question of whether PACIFISM is justified, the only right answer is both answers: sometimes revolutions are justified and sometimes not. It depends on the ends of the revolution, on whether nonrevolutionary options are genuinely viable and are less harmful than the alternatives, on the extent and level of violence involved, on the evilness of the old order. Revolution is sometimes morally justified and may even in certain circumstances be justified in regimes that are in some sense democratic (Nielsen 1982).

What will be discussed here is not that broad question, but whether individuals, and most particularly workers, are justified in engaging in revolutionary activity (sometimes violent) with the end-in-view of making a socialist revolution where such a revolution is feasible and where the replacement of capitalism by socialism is, everything considered, a desirable thing, not likely to be obtainable except by revolution. If an individual is aware of these circumstances and if she is a person of moral INTEGRITY, must or (more weakly) should she be a revolutionary when she is in a position to so act to any good effect? On the admittedly contentious assumption that socialism is very desirable, can it be shown that individual workers, or individuals sympathetic to their cause, should struggle for socialism when it is not likely to come through resolute electoral politicking, and when its attainment, however desirable, is fraught with risks for the individuals who engage in such a struggle (Elster)? When, if ever, are the risks of revolution morally and rationally justified?

Some philosophers claim that the socialist revolution presents a "collective action" problem. Suppose we are a group of workers thinking about whether we should struggle for a socialist transformation of society. Suppose we conclude that the revolution, if successful, will have benefits that clearly outweigh the losses, on balance; and further, let us assume that the revolution is necessary to bring about these general benefits. But we can also see that the benefits (the goods) coming to the working class

are collective goods. Each member of the working class will enjoy these goods, regardless of whether or how much he contributed to the revolution and regardless of whether he incurred any costs through participating in it.

The standard free rider problem arises if workers are for the most part rational egoists whose overriding concern is to protect and pursue their own personal INTERESTS. What would motivate workers into not being free riders on the revolution when the revolution promises, and reasonably so, results that they would genuinely like? Beyond that, what reasons, if any, can be given them to be rationally so motivated (Miller)?

Suppose it is agreed that socialism would improve the life of workers. Even if that is so, the triumph of socialism might benefit individual workers even though they take no active part in the struggle. In revolutionary struggles, the risks for workers are predictable and considerable; and most workers (plain people who are neither saints nor heroes) might well say that, while they strongly agree with the ends of the revolution, they will stand aside from revolutionary action. They will refuse to become revolutionaries out of individual self-interest, for it is not literally true that they have nothing to lose but their chains. They, as well as members of their families, could lose their jobs; they could be blacklisted; they could be ostracized; they could be beaten up and—when things get really tough—they could be tortured or even killed. To publicly join the working class in a revolutionary situation, one risks a lot and needs very good reasons indeed, even if a worker, for taking that risk.

Karl MARX (1818–1883) thought that to become revolutionaries, workers need a certain CHARACTER, a character that he believed was repeatedly exemplified by workers in their struggles and was reinforced by these struggles. The most dramatic exemplification of this sort of character was produced by the workers in the Paris Commune of 1871. The character that was needed, one that was admired and encouraged by Marx, was the character that united hatred of oppressors with concern for the oppressed; truculence, where their interests are basically opposed, with a positive desire to cooperate elsewhere; discipline with creativity and a tolerance for risks (Miller). Having such a cluster of character traits is especially valuable; when workers know their own class interests, such traits will motivate a commitment to a course of active support for a socialist revolution, even when the motivation is not a distinctively moral motivation. But such support does require an extensive subordination of (at least immediate) self-interest. Suppose a rational person asks himself: why should I so sacrifice my self-interest? Why should I take such a risky course? If there were some magical way of bringing about socialism without RISK I should indeed welcome it, but why should I risk my neck and my family's neck to achieve it, particularly when participating is a very risky business indeed?

Where the risks are considerable, the reliance on *purely moral motivations* is indeed unstable. For that reason Marxists have generally been reluctant to rely on them. However, given the situation above, what could revolutionaries do but *moralize* by telling workers it is their duty to fight for the revolution? But such an appeal is not only foreign to the Marxist tradition, it provides, psychologically speaking, a very weak and unstable motivation for revolutionary activity.

A Marxian Motivation for Revolution

The underlying problem is how or whether we can make such risk-taking acceptable to workers. It has been argued that Marx sought a stable motivation for revolution that is rooted neither in personal self-interest nor a broadly based ALTRUISM, but rather in the kind of limited reciprocal altruism that accompanies class solidarity (Miller). The fight for socialism might not be motivated by justice—an equal concern for the interests of all—but by a desire to uphold working class interests as the interests of, if not all, then at least the vast majority of humankind. Such a motivation is also powerfully rooted in a hatred of oppressors and in a determination not to be degraded and abused or to allow others close to one to be abused or forced into an impoverished life.

Revolutionary mechanisms. What mechanisms are at work that produce class-conscious concerns strong enough to support a socialist revolution? The way in which productive forces develop as capitalism evolves makes labor increasingly cooperative and interdependent. Workers are no longer isolated. Differences in ethnic background, race, and social affinities slowly break down as workers with different backgrounds are thrown together. Moreover, in modern industry, there are far fewer highly differentiated skills that set some workers apart from (and not infrequently against) other workers. As capitalism develops, according to some arguments, it becomes increasingly apparent to workers that they must sink or swim together. Industrial development creates new forms of interaction among workers that lead to broadened and more determined cooperation in resistance. In time, this cooperation could very well lead to a revolutionary combination.

Modern capitalism develops in such a way that there is an ever greater concentration of power—the ownership and control of the means of production—in fewer and fewer hands. Moreover, there is a growing trend toward an international corporate capitalism. As Marx argued in *Capital* (1867–95), the way the industrial revolution progresses both helps and compels the working class to cooperate. That notwithstanding, it is at least arguable that, in most major Western industrial societies, the capitalist classes are now in better control than they were in Marx's time. They now possess more highly efficient means of surveillance and are better coordinated. When the situation is seen in global terms, the struggle will be multifaceted and sometimes disguised, but it will also be both prolonged and bitter. Backed only by moral motivations, workers may be beset by cynicism and world weariness. But workers, especially in emerging countries, will have been palpably and unrelentingly harmed. This harm, when combined with some victories or partial victories in their struggles with the capitalist class, will strengthen their will to struggle. They will also come to see the capitalist class as their class enemies and resolve to resist and fight them. These attitudes must be strong if the workers are to win. In seeing the bourgeoisie as their enemies rather than as objects of equal concern and respect, the working class will be drawn together in a common struggle against what it perceives to be the foe (and indeed *is* the foe, if Marxist class analysis is accurate). It is easier to rally people to a common struggle against an enemy than to appeal to distinctively moral conceptions. Humanitarian motives will not carry the psychological punch that is necessary to make and sustain a revolution.

Sources of revolutionary motivation. If the foregoing argument is accurate, we do not (*pace* Allen Buchanan) need to show that individual rational self-interest is necessary to motivate workers for the risky business of fighting for socialism (Buchanan

1979). When people traditionally help one another, perhaps initially in ways that involve little or no self-sacrifice, they will typically come to care for each other. As the RECIPROCITY continues and becomes more deeply embedded and more extensive, the goals of community and fraternity will grow more important and the caring will deepen and extend. When that community and fraternity is attacked, it is plausible to expect that that caring will motivate more substantial sacrifices and that the effect will be cumulative.

Marx thought that a certain understanding of the world, a thorough class consciousness and its accompanying class solidarity, is essential for a firm revolutionary motivation. He believed that this class consciousness will be widespread among workers only under certain circumstances. To have the proper revolutionary motivation, people must have a well-developed hatred of OPPRESSION and an angry contempt for oppressors. They should still be, as most revolutionaries are, caring people who engage in reciprocity naturally and uncalculatingly. They should, of course, take note of what is going on. And they should not continue to cooperate no matter what others do. Their capacity for caring and reciprocity must be strong enough for them to be able to make sacrifices, even for those who are outside the circle of their personal acquaintances. But their caring must not obliterate their capacity to hate and to act resolutely against oppressors. Marx predicted that these are the people who have stable revolutionary motivations. Without such people, there will be no socialist revolution.

Causes and Reasons: The Moral Basis for Revolutionary Activity

The account above has at least roughly specified the kinds of things that are stable *causes* of people's coming to have revolutionary motivations. To revolt, one need not act out of respect for the moral law, or respect for persons, or because one knows that certain moral principles are true. What *makes* people have concern for others and what, under certain circumstances, *makes* some people capable of sustained and dangerous revolutionary activity is much more mundane. To assess the moral relevance of this we need to distinguish between *causes* and *reasons* (Peters; Toulmin). It is important to make this distinction even if all reasons are also causes. (Another way of putting it would be to refer to a distinction between *explanatory* reasons and *justificatory* reasons. See Baier and Bond.) It is one thing to say that a person keeps his PROMISES because he was taught to do so. It is another thing again to say that he keeps his promises because he believes in universalization and that a world in which no one kept promises would be a dreadful world indeed.

The previous sections show the conditions that would produce staunch socialist revolutionaries. But these conditions are *causes* only; what is needed to *justify* revolutionary motivation is to give *reasons* sufficient to justify such activity. We want to discover not only what *makes* people revolutionaries, but what would *justify* their actions. These reasons are also likely to be causes, even though the conceptual and moral distinction between causes and reasons remains. What reasons would be *justifying* reasons?

Assuming socialism rather than capitalism is justifiable, it does not follow that individual workers would be justified in putting themselves at considerable risk by struggling for socialism. *Three* questions arise: (1) what justifies the set of practices that constitute socialism; (2) what will justify the claim that an individual should fight for socialism; and (3) what *makes* individuals fight for socialism? Some skeptics think that there is insufficient motivation for revolutionary struggle. They believe that there *can* be justifying reasons for socialism, even though there are no reasons that will be decisively justifying reasons for individual workers to struggle for socialism.

It may be true that the struggle for socialism is supererogatory. If so, there can be no obligation to engage in revolutionary struggle. Revolutionary acts may well be supererogatory acts, but there can still be justificatory reasons for supererogatory acts. One is not obliged to do everything one has reason to do or is justified in doing (HART). Not everything we ought to do is something we have an obligation or duty to do. There are supererogatory acts we ought to do that we have no obligation or duty to do. Thus, it may be the case that a worker ought to struggle for a socialist revolution even though she has no duty or obligation to do so.

The question remains what *justificatory* reasons, as distinct from purely *explanatory* reasons, can be given for a worker to actively struggle for socialism. Miller has given us reasons for *predicting* that, as capitalism develops, more and more workers will struggle for socialism. But these reasons are *explanatory* reasons.

If the justificatory reasons are meant to show a worker, as a rational egoist, that he should struggle for socialism, then Allen Buchanan is right in that no such justification can be given (Buchanan 1982). Under these assumptions, to show a worker who is a rational egoist that he should struggle for socialism is like trying to show him that he should be moral. If a person does not care for others and has no commitment to FAIRNESS, then in some circumstances we cannot show him that acting as a person of principle must be the prudent thing to do (Nielsen 1989). We can hardly give the proletarian rational egoist, on grounds *he* would deem relevant, justifying reasons to engage in the struggle for socialism, for in many circumstances PRUDENCE would not dictate such a course of action. Moreover, if the individual's rationality is to maximize his expected utility, then rationality does not require him to join the struggle, either.

There is no trick at all, however, in showing someone why she should respond as a person of moral principle *if* she is resolved to be fair. Similarly if we (where that 'we' includes most workers) care about others, have a strong sense of solidarity and reciprocity, are courageous and resolute, and indeed value these things, then we can give justificatory reasons for individual workers to struggle for socialism when the workers see that socialism is desirable. In such circumstances, what explains revolutionary motivation can also be used in justifying it.

If we believe that caring, solidarity, honoring and engaging in reciprocity, COURAGE, and resoluteness are VIRTUES greatly to be prized, then, on some perfectly reasonable empirical assumptions, we can justify the socialist revolutionary activity of workers or indeed of anyone else. Workers who struggle for their own emancipation and the emancipation of others are justified in so acting.

See also: CIVIL DISOBEDIENCE; COLLECTIVE RESPONSIBILITY; COOPERATION, CONFLICT, AND COORDINATION; DEMOCRACY; DETERRENCE, THREATS, AND RETALIATION; ECONOMIC SYSTEMS; FAIRNESS; GROUPS, MORAL STATUS OF; MARX; MARXISM; MORAL POINT OF VIEW; MOTIVES; OBEDIENCE TO LAW; OPPRESSION; PACIFISM; POLITICAL SYSTEMS; POWER; PRUDENCE; REASONS FOR ACTION; REVENGE; RISK; SUPEREROGATION; VIOLENCE AND NON-VIOLENCE; WORK.

Bibliography

Baier, Kurt. *The Moral Point of View.* Ithaca, NY: Cornell University Press, 1958. See chapter 6.

Bond, Edward J. *Reason and Value.* Cambridge: Cambridge University Press, 1983. See chapter 2.

Buchanan, Allen E. *Marx and Justice.* Totowa, NJ: Rowman and Littlefield, 1982. Passages noted, see pp. 86–102.

———. "Revolutionary Motivation and Rationality." *Philosophy and Public Affairs* 9 (1979): 59–82.

———. "Marx, Morality, and History." *Ethics* 98 (1987): 104–36.

Cohen, Gerald A. *History, Labour, and Freedom.* Oxford: Clarendon Press, 1988.

Elster, Jon. *Making Sense of Marx.* Cambridge: Cambridge University Press, 1985. Important work in analytical Marxism, containing a discussion of revolutionary motivation. Passages noted, pp. 100–1.

Hart, H. L. A. "Legal and Moral Obligation." In *Essays in Moral Philosophy,* edited by A. I. Melden, 82–107. Seattle: University of Washington Press, 1958.

Holmstrom, Nancy. "Rationality and Revolution." *Canadian Journal of Philosophy* 12 (1983): 305–26.

Miller, Richard. *Analyzing Marx.* Princeton, NJ: Princeton University Press, 1984. Central discussion of revolutionary motivation; cuts against the stream. Passages noted, pp. 63–76.

Nielsen, Kai. "On Justifying Violence." *Inquiry* 25 (1982): 16–35.

———. *Why Be Moral?* Buffalo, NY: Prometheus, 1989. Limits of justification, reasons, and causes.

Peters, R. S. *The Concept of Motivation.* London: Routledge and Kegan Paul, 1958. Reasons, causes, and motivation.

Shaw, William. "Marxism, Revolution, and Rationality." In *After Marx,* edited by T. Ball and J. Farr. Cambridge: Cambridge University Press, 1984.

Taylor, Michael, ed. *Rationality and Revolution.* Cambridge: Cambridge University Press, 1988. Classic articles on revolutionary motivation and rationality.

Toulmin, Stephen. "Reasons and Causes." In *Explanation in Behavioural Sciences,* edited by Borger and Cioffi, 1–41. Cambridge: Cambridge University Press, 1970.

Kai E. Nielsen

Ricoeur, Paul (1913–)

The work of Paul Ricoeur in ethical theory marks the passage of classical PHENOMENOLOGY in this area toward an account both more metaphysically and more institutionally oriented. *Philosophie de la volonté* (1950, 1960), his massive two-volume investigation on the philosophy of the will, is one of the last major works of the school of French existential phenomenology comprised by the writings of Jean-Paul SARTRE (1905–1980), Maurice Merleau-Ponty (1908–1961), Simone DE BEAUVOIR (1908–1986) and Mikel Dufrenne. Like those writers, Ricoeur's analysis of the will in the first volume, *Le voluntaire et l'involuntaire,* centers on the context of MORAL REASONING, linking the problem of moral reasoning to the analysis of existential embodiment. Like his existential predecessors, Ricoeur understands the problem of the relation between ACTION and PASSION dialectically, explicating the foundations of rational action by means of the protocols of phenomenological motivation. His analysis likewise reveals the lingering influence of Max SCHELER's (1874–1928) theory of values, albeit transformed beyond the latter's commitments to an ahistorical INTUITIONISM.

In the second volume, *Finitude et culpabilité,* Ricoeur deepens the initial phenomenological descriptions in claiming that ethical theory ultimately requires an analysis of an original fault at the heart of human finitude, the opening of culpability, a domain properly approached through the explication of the symbolic and the mythological. While such admittedly neo-Fichtean considerations concerning the gulf between the finite and the infinite may be held to be transcendentally necessary for understanding the origins of the ethical, Ricoeur also recognized they could not be sufficient to account for the rationality underlying moral claims. If the formal account of obligation can be captured thereby, the specific content of moral theory itself escapes the description of transcendental origins. An adequate post-Kantian account of morality would also need to capture the possibility of conflict between wills, the conflict of interpretation, and the ensuing undeterminability afflicting the judgments of moral theory. Hence, the inevitability of hermeneutics for ethics.

While this account leads Ricoeur to align himself with G. W. F. HEGEL (1770–1831) in centering on the problem of recognition as fundamental to the intersubjective domain, generating an ethics of freedom as respect for the second person, and repeating, thereby, the incorporation of objective spirit as the institutional background and guarantee of ethical decision—he does so without following Hegel in the subsumption of particular wills beneath that of the general ("The Problem," 1978). For the first, Ricoeur returns to the problem of intersubjectivity in Edmund HUSSERL (1859–1938); for the second, he brings the analogical presentation that functions in intersubjective recognition together with the analogical play underlying transcendental imagination and presentation in general. The former provides the guarantee of freedom in preserving the differences between interpretations. The latter, in explicating the narratological structure of reason itself, provides an account of the generation of NORMS (as the schematization of the moral) and an account of their critique by disclosing the play of possibility within narrative variation (*Time and Narrative,* 1985–1988). As in Ricoeur's epistemological writings, therefore, it is the imagination that binds, both as the source of values and the space of alterity, which makes possible their critique.

See also: CRITICAL THEORY; DE BEAUVOIR; EXISTENTIAL ETHICS; FICHTE; FREE WILL; HEGEL; HUSSERL; INTUITIONISM; METAPHYSICS AND EPISTEMOLOGY; NARRATIVE ETHICS; PHENOMENOLOGY; SARTRE; SCHELER; SUBJECTIVISM; TRANSCENDENTALISM; VOLUNTARY ACTS.

Bibliography: Works by Ricoeur

Philosophie de la volonté I: Le voluntaire et l'involuntaire. Paris: Aubier, 1950. Translated by Erazim V. Kohak into English as *Freedom and Nature.* Evanston, IL: Northwestern University Press, 1966.

Philosophie de la volonté II: Finitude et culpabilité. Paris: Aubier, 1960. Vol. 1, *L'homme fallible;* vol. 2, *La symbolique du mal.* Translated into English by Charles A. Kelbley as *Fallible Man.* New York: Fordham University Press, 1986; and by Emerson Buchanan as *The Symbolism of Evil.* Boston: Beacon Press, 1969.

"The Problem of the Foundation of Moral Philosophy." Translated by David Pellauer. *Philosophy Today* (Fall 1978).

Time and Narrative. Translated by Kathleen McLaughlin, and David Pellauer. 3 vols. Chicago: University of Chicago Press, 1985–1988.

Stephen H. Watson

right, concepts of

The word "right" can be used either as an adjective or as a noun, for it is idiomatic to speak of the right ACTION or the right to free speech. The German noun *Recht* can refer either to the legal or moral standard of rightness (*objektives Recht*) or someone's right to something (*subjektives Recht*). There seems to be no word in classical Greek marking the concept of a right. The Latin *jus* began by meaning what is right or in accordance with justice and only later took on another meaning that can be accurately translated as "a right."

The concept of a right arose gradually from Roman jurisprudence, especially the dictum that justice consists in giving each his or her own, and from the Stoic philosophy of NATURAL LAW. The first philosopher to define the concept of a moral right was probably WILLIAM OF OCKHAM (c. 1285–c. 1349), who notes that *jus* sometimes refers to a POWER to conform to right reason. Thus, he conceives of a moral right as a power of acting in conformity to the natural law. To possess a right is to have a faculty or capacity of acting rightfully in some manner; to act in this way is to exercise this right. The owner of a car has the ability of driving it rightfully whenever she wishes; if anyone lacking this property right drives the car without the owner's permission, his act violates the moral law. While Ockham conceives of a right as a power of acting, Thomas Holland (1835–1926) takes a right to be a power of causing another to act. He defines a right as a power of influencing the acts of another by the force of society. The creditor's right to repayment consists in the creditor's power of causing, by means of legal sanctions or the informal social pressures of morality, the debtor to repay the loan. Although both Ockham and Holland conceive of rights in terms of power, both distinguish between might and right. Ockham limits any right to power exercised within the limits of the natural law; Holland distinguishes between causing another to act by using one's own brute force and influencing the acts of another via the force of society regulated by the rules of law or morality.

Thomas HOBBES (1588–1679) conceives of a right not as a power, but as a LIBERTY. One has a liberty of doing something if and only if one has no obligation not to do so. To say that one has the right of SELF-DEFENSE is simply to say that one has no duty to refrain from using force to defend oneself from an attack, and to say this is not to deny that one may also have a duty to defend oneself. H. L. A. HART (1907–1992) suggests that we would not speak of "a right" to self-defense unless one had the liberty of refraining from, as well as using, force against an attacker. Moreover, any full right to self-defense would include duties of others not to prevent one from exercising one's liberty of using or not using force against an attacker. Paradigmatically, a right consists of a bilateral liberty with a protective perimeter of duties. Although Hobbes can explain what distinguishes one's rights from one's duties, for duties oblige while rights consist in the absence of an obligation, Hart can also explain how it is that a right of one person imposes duties on second parties.

Many philosophers identify rights with the duties they imply. John Austin (1790–1859) holds that a right is a relative duty. "The creditor has a legal right to be repaid by the debtor" simply asserts that the debtor has a legal duty to the creditor to repay the debt. JOHN STUART MILL (1806–1873) similarly conceives of a moral right as a relative moral duty. The questioner's right to be told the truth consists in the answerer's moral duty to answer truthfully. This duty is owed to the questioner because it is she who will be harmed in the event that the answerer fails to answer truthfully.

Joel Feinberg argues that what is left out by any reduction of rights to duties is the process of claiming, for it is this activity that is distinctive of and most valuable in any right. He defines a right as a valid claim. To have a claim to something is to be in a position to demand it as one's due, for example to claim one's seat at the theater by presenting one's ticket. A valid claim is one justified by the relevant rules. Legal rights are validated by legal rules; moral rights are claims justified by the principles of an enlightened CONSCIENCE. Rights are important because they give the right holder standing to demand, not merely petition for, performance of the duties they imply.

Wesley Hohfeld (1879–1918) shows that in legal language the expression "a right" is used indiscriminately to refer to legal liberties, claims, powers, or immunities. It is worthy of note that although moral philosophers have conceived of rights as powers, liberties, or claims, none has defined a moral right as a moral immunity. Hohfeld argues that in the strictest sense a legal right is a single legal claim held by one person against another person.

Carl Wellman denies that a simple claim could

constitute a right and conceives of a right as a complex structure of liberties, claims, powers, and immunities. He shows that Hohfeld's conceptions can be applied to moral rights by identifying moral analogues of legal liberties, claims, powers and immunities. What unifies a cluster of such elements into a single right is the way in which the system of Hohfeldian elements, if respected, confers dominion on the right holder in face of some second party in some potential confrontation. Thus, he conceives of a right as a system of dominion.

Not all conceptions of rights can be interpreted in Hohfeldian terms. John Salmond (1862–1924) conceives of a right as a protected interest. Rights are valuable because the content of any right is some interest or good of the right holder. But not every interest constitutes a right; only an interest protected by a legal or moral rule is a genuine right. Presumably the rule protects the interest by imposing on others at least a duty not to damage that interest and sometimes even a duty to promote it. The difference between this conception and Hart's protected choice conception of a right illustrates the traditional distinction between an interest and a will theory of rights. While the former conceives of rights as giving some special place to human INTERESTS, the latter conceives of rights as providing some distinctive legal or moral standing to the will of an agent.

Robert NOZICK believes that to identify rights with interests of any kind is to fundamentally misconceive their moral relevance. Interests identify goals of human action; rights limit the morally permissible ways in which one may act to promote those goals. Thus, rights are side constraints on the pursuit of interests, whether these concern one's own welfare or that of another. Ronald DWORKIN similarly conceives of rights as imposing limits on morally permissible actions. Since his paradigms are the political rights of the citizen held against the state, he argues that the point of a right is to give the individual some special protection against wrongful state action. Any unjustified treatment of the individual by society is wrongful. Although social utility justifies most governmental actions, it fails to justify any act that infringes a right. Thus, a right is an individual trump over social goals in the moral justification of political action.

Joseph Raz also believes that what is definitive of rights is their role in PRACTICAL REASONING, but he takes that role to be linking interests to duties. A right should not be identified with some correlative duty, for rights are logically prior to duties and a right may imply more than one duty or various duties under varying circumstances. A right is a reason for one or more persons to bear one or more duties. But rights are not ultimate self-evident reasons; they are in turn grounded on human interests. Accordingly, Raz conceives of a right as an interest-based reason for some duty or duties.

The concept of a right is now clearly distinguishable from the concept of right action, but conceptual connections might remain. Could one conceivably have a right to do what is wrong? On some conceptions of rights this question cannot even arise. If a right is a relative duty, for example, it is not the right holder who exercises the right by acting; the right holder enjoys her right when the duty bearer acts to fulfill the correlative duty. If a moral right is a power of acting in conformity to the natural law, then obviously one cannot have any right to act in violation of that moral law. One might, however, have a moral right to do what is legally wrong or a legal right to do what is morally wrong. It is when one conceives of a right as a naked unilateral liberty (Hobbes) or a protected bilateral liberty (Hart) that the logical relation between a right and its rightful exercise becomes most controversial. Since a moral liberty of acting in some manner consists in the absence of any moral obligation to refrain from such action, it would seem that one could not have any moral right to do what is morally wrong. One naturally assumes that any morally wrong act must violate some moral obligation; and if so, one could not have any moral liberty of performing this action. But is it true that the only reason any act could be morally wrong is that it violates some moral duty or obligation? Some acts may be wrong because they are morally indecent or because they violate moral standards other than the strict dictates of duty. Any plausible conception of a liberty-right will define a moral liberty in terms of some quite limited concept of a moral duty. This definition will then suggest that there might be a moral right to do what is wrong, for it will leave room for moral standards of conduct other than the performance of one's moral duties.

It is important to distinguish carefully between the very different concepts of rights used in ethical theory and moral debate because their logical properties are very different. We see this clearly as we examine the conceptual connections, if any, between rights and right action. Other conceptual issues at least as important are how, if at all, any right implies one or more duties and what sorts of beings one can meaningfully say possess a right.

See also: CIVIL RIGHTS AND CIVIC DUTIES; COMPARATIVE ETHICS; CONSCIENCE; DEONTOLOGY; DUTY AND OBLIGATION; DWORKIN; ENTITLEMENTS; FAIRNESS; HART; HOBBES; HUMAN RIGHTS; INTERESTS; LEGAL PHILOSOPHY; LIBERTY; JOHN STUART MILL; MORAL RULES; NATURAL LAW; NEEDS; NOZICK; RIGHT HOLDERS; RIGHTS; SOCIAL AND POLITICAL PHILOSOPHY; WALZER; WELFARE RIGHTS AND SOCIAL POLICY; WILLIAM OF OCKHAM.

Bibliography

Austin, John. *Lectures on Jurisprudence.* London: John Murray, 1885 [1863]. See vol. 1, chapters 12, 15, 17.

Dworkin, Ronald. *Taking Rights Seriously.* Cambridge: Harvard University Press, 1977. See chapter 7.

Feinberg, Joel. *Social Philosophy.* Englewood Cliffs, NJ: Prentice-Hall, 1973. See chapters 4–6.

Golding, Martin P. "The Concept of Rights: A Historical Sketch." Chapter 4 of *Bioethics and Human Rights,* edited by E. and B. Bandman. Boston: Little, Brown, 1978.

Hart, H. L. A. *Essays on Bentham.* Oxford: Clarendon Press, 1982. See chapter 7.

Hobbes, Thomas. *Leviathan.* New York: Dutton, 1950 [1651]. See chapter 14.

Hohfeld, Wesley Newcomb. *Fundamental Legal Conceptions.* New Haven: Yale University Press, 1919.

Holland, Thomas E. *Elements of Jurisprudence.* Oxford: Clarendon Press, 1924. See chapters 7, 8.

Martin, Rex, and James W. Nickel. "Recent Work on the Concept of Rights." *American Philosophical Quarterly* 17 (1980): 165–80.

Mill, John Stuart. *Utilitarianism.* Chapter 5, vol. 10 of his *Collected Works,* edited by J. M. Robson. Toronto: Toronto University Press, 1969 [1861].

Nozick, Robert. *Anarchy, State, and Utopia.* New York: Basic Books, 1974. See chapter 3.

Raz, Joseph. *The Morality of Freedom.* Oxford: Clarendon Press, 1986. See chapter 7.

Salmond, John William. *Jurisprudence.* 6th ed. London: Sweet and Maxwell, 1920. See chapter 10.

Wellman, Carl. *A Theory of Rights.* Totowa, NJ: Rowman and Allenheld, 1985.

William of Ockham. *Opus nonaginta Dierum.* In volume 2 of his *Opera politica,* edited by R. F. Bennett and H. S. Offler. Manchester: Manchester University Press, 1963 [1330].

Carl Wellman

right holders

Are ABORTION and the withdrawal of life-support systems from irreversibly comatose patients immoral violations of the right to life? Some moral philosophers deny this view on the ground that fetuses and irreversibly comatose patients are not human beings in the sense that would qualify them for the possession of RIGHTS. But what is this sense? More generally, what kinds of beings are possible right holders? The possibility in question is conceptual. Given the most adequate conception of a right, what qualification must something have to be capable of possessing a moral right?

Henry J. McCloskey (1925–2000) argues that because exercising a right, acting on the basis of one's right, is essential to the concept of a right, only a being capable of acting could possess a right. Because in exercising one's rights one must call on one's moral capacities, only moral agency fully qualifies one as a right holder. Children, even infants, are also possible possessors of rights by virtue of their potential agency. An irreversibly comatose patient who has lost both actual and potential moral agency has become incapable of holding rights. Plants and even animals possess neither actual nor potential moral agency and therefore are not possible moral right holders. Although its officers can have moral rights to act on behalf of an organization, the organization cannot have any rights because organizations as such are incapable of moral decision and ACTION.

Carl Wellman holds that the essential function of a right is to determine the proper allocation of dominion (freedom and control) between a right holder and some second party in a possible confrontation. Because only an agent could exercise freedom or control, only agents are possible right holders. Normal adult humans are clearly moral agents and thus paradigm moral right holders. Although infants cannot be right holders because they lack agency, children gradually acquire the capacity to possess rights as they develop their capacities for moral action. The mentally limited can possess only limited rights depending on their degree and kind of capacity for moral action. Because human fetuses, dead persons, animals, and groups are not moral agents, these kinds of beings are not possible moral right holders.

Some philosophers believe that one can accept the thesis that only moral agents can possess moral rights without limiting possible right holders so narrowly. Although the action of a corporation may be constituted by the actions of its officers, as when its board votes to reduce pollution, one must distinguish between the several individual acts of voting of the members of the board and the corporate act of deciding to reduce pollution. Because the latter is really an action, organizations are moral agents and are possible moral right holders. Moreover, the highest level of moral agency may not be required to exercise a right. For example, a normal adult exercises her moral right to SELF-DEFENSE, not only when she deliberately fights off an attacker, but also when she strikes back instinctively without the slightest moral reflection. Hence, many nonhuman animals possess moral agency in a sense robust enough to qualify them for the possession of moral rights.

Neil MacCormick distinguishes between two kinds of theories of rights, those that say that a right consists in the preeminence of one's will over that of others and those that hold that a right consists in having one's interest protected by the duties of others. He rejects the former because it implies that very young children, who have not yet acquired moral agency, cannot possess any moral rights, a conclusion inconsistent with the clear fact that from the moment of birth a child does have a moral right to be cared for and nurtured. Therefore, he infers that to have a right is to have an interest, a component of one's well-being, valuable enough to impose duties on others at least not to injure and often to protect and advance that interest. Because even neonates have INTERESTS, children of all ages can possess moral rights. An interest theory of rights is also more congenial to the rights of groups than a will theory. Although one can argue plausibly that corporations make decisions and engage in action, it is much harder to explain how unorganized groups as a whole act. Still, it seems clear that a colonial people might have an interest in political independence and an ethnic minority an interest in the preservation of its language. They could have a moral right to self-determination or to education in their own language respectively if it is the possession of some important interest that makes one a possible moral right holder.

Joel Feinberg holds that to have a right is to be in a position to make a valid claim. This view seems to imply that infants could not have any rights because they are incapable of claiming anything as due to themselves, but he believes that clearly even babies do have rights. Babies' rights are possible because they can be represented by their parents or guardians claiming on their behalf. The question then is, "what kind of beings can be represented as claimants?" Feinberg concludes that only a being with interests can be a right holder for two reasons: others cannot speak for anything that lacks interests because it has nothing on behalf of which to speak, and a right holder must be capable of being benefitted in itself but only a being with interests can be benefitted or harmed. Because children have interests, they can have moral rights. Unborn children (fetuses) are possible right holders because the interests they will have in the future can be protected by moral duties before birth; dead persons can have moral rights because interests they had while alive, such as interests in their reputation or that their heirs acquire their estates, survive their deaths. Animals are also possible right holders because they have interests in having food and not being caused to suffer. Species of animals cannot have any rights, even a right to survive; although each member of the species might have an interest in its own survival, the species is merely a class of animals incapable of having any interests. Plants and natural objects, such as trees or lakes, are not possible right holders because interests presuppose desires or aims and they have no conative life at all.

Even if one grants that it is the capacity to have interests that renders one capable of having moral rights, controversy remains about what kinds of beings are possible right holders. If interests presuppose desires and to desire anything one must believe that it has some desired property, then some argue that nonhuman animals lack interests because beliefs presuppose concepts and they lack any language in which to conceptualize desired objects. Conversely, one can argue that only interests in some weaker sense are required for the possession of rights. Surely animals and possibly even plants have interests, things or conditions that are good or harmful for them, in some significant sense. Similarly, there are debates both about the nature of organized and unorganized groups and about the kinds of interests that might be those of the group as a whole rather than interests of its individual members.

A third sort of theory holds that only persons are possible moral right holders. Mary Anne Warren defines personhood in terms of psychological traits such as consciousness, rationality, self-motivated activity, the capacity to communicate, and self-awareness. As far as we know, only normal human beings possess personhood in the full sense. Although it is difficult to determine exactly when in its development a human organism becomes a person, probably it is after its birth. Hence, only normal human beings could possess full moral rights. Children can have increasingly strong moral rights as their psychological capacities mature. A human fetus could possess at most very weak moral rights by virtue of its psychological resemblance to a normal person.

A. I. Melden (1910–1991) also maintains that only persons can have moral rights, but he denies that personhood can be defined in purely psychological terms. Only a normative conception of personhood could explain our possession of rights. Persons must be capable of joining their lives together in a network of moral relationships. For example, when one person makes a promise to another, they become related by a complex set of mutual rights and obligations. It is not merely that the promisee has a right to performance and the promisor an obligation to keep her promise. Under some circumstances, the promisee ought to release the promisor; and if the promisor fails to keep her promise, then she acquires an obligation to make amends. The content of these variable moral relationships depends on how the promise fits into their respective lives and on what is required to sustain the moral network joining those lives. Children can have moral rights because of the ways in which their lives are joined morally with the lives of adults. Even infants can have moral rights. They do not become persons as they mature morally; a baby and the adult she will become are one and the same person. Animals are not possible moral right holders because they lack normative personhood.

What is it about persons that commands our respect and explains their moral rights? Some philosophers assert that it is because they have a very special sort of value, inherent value, that they ought to be respected as ends in themselves. Tom Regan argues that UTILITARIANISM cannot explain our moral rights because it regards persons as merely receptacles of pleasures or other intrinsic values. Human beings have moral rights because they have an inherent value that makes it wrong to harm one person as a means of increasing the total amount of value in the universe. But what gives a person this inherent value? It is that each person is the subject of a life that is more or less valuable for that individual. This theory can explain why it is that marginal human beings, such as newborn babies or the severely mentally enfeebled, are capable of having moral rights; they have lives that can go better or worse for them. Regan goes on to argue that many animals are also subjects of a life. If being the subject of a life confers inherent value on normal human beings, then presumably marginal humans and at least some animals also have inherent value and are, therefore, possible moral right holders.

Is it only human beings and animals similar to humans in being subjects of a life that have inherent value? To assume this view might be to adopt an arbitrary subjective homocentric view of nature according to which nature and natural objects are mere means to human ends, not ends in themselves. The natural sciences suggest a more objective ecocentric viewpoint. The natural world in which we live is a vast ecosystem composed of more limited ecosystems in which various species of biological organisms interact with each other within an environment of nonliving natural objects. The individual lives of human and nonhuman animals can have no value or existence independent of nature as a whole. Environmentalists can argue that nature as a whole and the natural objects, such as trees or rivers, that make it up should be recognized as beings with inherent value and capable of having moral rights.

Another kind of theory holds that membership in the moral community qualifies a being for the possession of moral rights. Annette Baier explains that to assert that someone has a moral right is to say that at least one other person has an obligation to the right holder and that there is or should be a socially recognized means for the right holder or her proxy to take appropriate action should that obligation be neglected. Also, one possesses a right by virtue of some social role, for example as a teacher or a student, that relates one to some duty bearer. Because rights are essentially social, only members of a moral community can possess moral rights. Although very young children are incapable of claiming their moral rights, they are members of our moral community and parents or guardians can take appropriate action as their proxies. Past persons remain members of our moral community for some years as demonstrated by the ability of those who survive them to enforce their last will and testament. Conversely, future persons are already members of our moral community and possible moral right holders because our obligation to preserve a fair share of natural and cultural resources for them can be claimed by living proxies.

Martin Golding argues by a different route that only members of a moral community can possess moral rights. The expression "a right" is a forensic term used by a right holder or someone speaking on her behalf to claim something from some second party. Presumably, in claiming a right one is demanding some good for oneself, but how could one justify one's claim to some duty bearer? This justification would be possible only if the second party recognizes that good as good for herself also. Thus, every moral right is grounded on some shared good, and more generally, moral rights presuppose a social ideal of the good life that defines a moral community. Hence, children, who are members of our moral community, can have moral rights, but animals could possess moral rights only if their welfare is included in our social ideal. Like Baier, Golding believes that dead persons and FUTURE GENERATIONS are possible right holders because they are also members of our moral community.

Jeffrie Murphy suggests that the language of rights performs two different functions. One function, stressed by Immanuel KANT (1724–1804), is to mark out the special kind of treatment morally appropriate to rational persons. Only a moral agent could possess such autonomy rights. But there is another function of rights talk recognized by JOHN STUART MILL (1806–1873) when he observed that to assert that one has a right is to say that society ought to defend one's claim to the possession of something. Any being that ought morally to be protected by law could possess this kind of moral right. Murphy denies that these rights are grounded on social utility and maintains that they are justified by a Rawlsian hypothetical SOCIAL CONTRACT. Although very young children and mentally retarded persons are incapable of possessing any autonomy rights, they could possess social contract rights because rational persons, were they to make a social contract, would choose legal INSTITUTIONS to protect the interests of these classes of persons. Because rational persons would judge that suffering is bad, they would probably also choose legal institutions to protect animals. But works of art are not possible right holders; although they ought morally to be protected, this protection is because of their value for us, not for their own sakes.

A few moral philosophers have rejected this conclusion. The esthetic value of works of art makes them intrinsically, not merely instrumentally, good. Hence, at least the most precious works of art ought to be protected by society for their own sakes, not merely because of their value for us. They conclude that works of art are possible moral right holders. Others regard this view as a *reductio ad absurdum* of the theory that what qualifies a being for the possession of moral rights is that it ought morally to be protected by society.

It is illuminating to distinguish between primary and secondary qualifications for the possession of rights in any moral philosophy. Although Feinberg's theory of rights as valid claims seems to imply that only beings capable of making moral claims could have moral rights, he insists that infants can have moral rights. Moral rights are possible here because infants can have interests, and thus, representatives can make moral claims on their behalf. In his theory, the capacity to make claims is the primary qualification and the capacity to have interests is the secondary qualification for being a possible moral right holder. In MacCormick's interest theory of rights, however, having interests is the primary qualification for the capacity to possess rights. Melden's theory of rights implies that personhood is the primary qualification for the possession of rights. But he extends the range of possible right holders beyond the class of normal adult humans by introducing the secondary qualification of personal identity so that infants, who have not yet developed personhood, are possible right holders. More often, moral philosophers introduce the secondary qualification of potentiality to explain how neonates or fetuses can possess moral rights even though they lack some primary qualification such as personhood or moral agency. Alan GEWIRTH argues that the primary qualification for the possession of moral rights is prospective purposive agency because morality essentially concerns action. In order to explain how infants, mentally deficient persons, and even some animals can be moral right holders, he appeals to the secondary qualification of PROPORTIONALITY rather than mere potentiality. Any being can possess moral rights in proportion to the degree of its prospective purposive agency.

Do these theories of the possible possessors of moral rights apply to legal rights also? Some philosophers, such as MacCormick and Feinberg conceive of legal and moral rights as essentially similar. Presumably their theories would imply that the qualifications for the possession of legal and moral rights are very much the same. Other philosophers point to an essential difference between legal and moral rights. Whereas the former are conferred by some legal system, the latter exist independently of any social institutions. Although Christopher Stone doubts that natural objects could have moral rights, he believes that there could be environmental legal rights. The law could confer rights on natural objects by empowering some guardian to institute legal actions in the name of a natural object, specifying that courts must take injury to that object into account when granting relief and requiring that the relief must run to the benefit of the object. He argues that these conditions could be satisfied in the case of natural objects such as trees or rivers. Therefore, it may be that some kinds of beings could possess legal rights even if they are not possible possessors of moral rights.

See also: ABORTION; AGENCY AND DISABILITY; ANIMALS, TREATMENT OF; AUTONOMY OF MORAL AGENTS; CAPITAL PUNISHMENT; CHILDREN AND ETHICAL THEORY; CIVIL RIGHTS AND CIVIC DUTIES; COLLECTIVE RESPONSIBILITY; CONSENT; DESIRE; DUTY AND OBLIGATION; ENTITLEMENTS; ENVIRONMENTAL ETHICS; EUTHANASIA; EXPLOITATION; FUTURE GENERATIONS; GEWIRTH; GROUPS, MORAL STATUS OF; HUMAN RIGHTS; INFANTICIDE; INTENTION; INTERESTS; KILLING/LETTING DIE; LEGAL PHILOSOPHY; LIBERTY; LIFE, MEANING OF; LIFE, RIGHT TO; MEDICAL ETHICS; MORAL COMMUNITY, BOUNDARIES OF; MORAL PSYCHOLOGY; NATURE AND ETHICS; NEEDS; OPPRESSION; PERSON, CONCEPT OF; PROPORTIONALITY; RIGHT, CONCEPTS OF; RIGHTS; SELF-DEFENSE; SELF-OWNERSHIP; SOCIAL CONTRACT; THOMSON; WELFARE RIGHTS AND SOCIAL POLICY; WORK.

Bibliography

Baier, Annette. "The Rights of Past and Future Persons." In *Responsibilities to Future Generations,* edited by Ernest Partridge, 171–83. Buffalo, NY: Prometheus Books, 1981.

Feinberg, Joel. *Rights, Justice, and the Bounds of Liberty.* Princeton, NJ: Princeton University Press, 1980. See chapters 7–10.

Gewirth, Alan. *Reason and Morality.* Chicago: University of Chicago Press, 1978. See especially pp. 121–24 and 141–44.

Golding, Martin P. "Towards a Theory of Human Rights." *The Monist* 52 (1968): 521–49.

MacCormick, Neil. "Children's Rights: A Test-Case for Theories of Right." *ARSP* 62 (1976): 305–17.

McCloskey, Henry J. "Moral Rights and Animals." *Inquiry* 22 (1979): 23–54.

Melden, A. I. *Rights and Persons.* Oxford: Basil Blackwell, 1977. See especially chapter 6.

Murphy, Jeffrie G. "Rights and Borderline Cases." *Arizona Law Review* 19 (1977): 228–41.

Regan, Tom. *The Case for Animal Rights.* Berkeley: University of California Press, 1983. See especially chapter 8.

Stone, Christopher D. "Should Trees Have Standing?—Toward Legal Rights for Natural Objects." *University of Southern California Law Review* 45 (1972): 450–501.

Warren, Mary Anne. "On the Moral and Legal Status of Abortion." *The Monist* 57 (1973): 43–61.

Wellman, Carl. *Real Rights.* New York: Oxford University Press, 1995. See chapters 4 and 5.

Carl Wellman

rights

The claiming of rights is one of the strongest ways of demanding protection of persons' INTERESTS. At the same time, many aspects of the appeal to rights are intensely controversial. The controversies bear not only on the normative and substantive issues of who has rights to what but also on basic conceptual issues.

Hohfeld's Distinctions

The standard starting point for dealing with the conceptual issues is Wesley N. Hohfeld (1879–1918), who saw that the phrase "a right" was used with different meanings in the legal literature. To avoid the resulting confusion, he distinguished four meanings of this phrase. He viewed rights as legal relations having "jural correlatives" and "jural opposites," but his typology can also be extended to other spheres of rights. First, if A has a *claim-right* to X against B, then B has a correlative *duty* to A to refrain from interfering with A's having or doing X, or, in some situations, a duty to give X to A or to help A to have or do X. Thus, A has a claim-right to life against B and all other persons in that they have a correlative duty to refrain from taking A's life; and if B has promised to meet A at the bookstore at noon, then A has a claim-right against B that B meet him there and then, and B has a correlative duty to meet A as promised.

Second, if A has a *liberty-right* (or *privilege*) to X against B, then B has a correlative *no-right* (*i.e.,* no claim-right) that A not do X. Hence A has no duty to refrain from doing X; but also, in contrast to the case of claim-rights, B has no duty to refrain from interfering with A's doing X. Thus, if A and B spontaneously engage in a footrace, each has a liberty-right to win the race if he can—neither has a duty to refrain from winning it—and each has no right that the other not win. The liberty-right is hence the opposite of a duty, just as the no-right is the opposite of a claim-right.

Third, if A has a *power* (or *power-right*) to X with regard to B, then A is in a legal or other justified position to effect a change in some relevant status of B, and B has a correlative *liability* to undergo this change. Thus a religious official has a power-right to perform a marriage ceremony between a man and a woman, so that their legal status is changed from being unmarried to being married to each other.

Fourth, if A has an *immunity* (or *immunity-right*) to X against B, then A is free or exempt from B's legal or other justified POWER or control with regard to X, and B is under a correlative *disability* to affect the legal or other relevant status of A. Thus, A has an immunity to being forced to testify against himself in a criminal case, and the state has a correlative disability to force him to testify. The immunity is the opposite of a liability, and the disability is the opposite of a power (or power-right).

These distinctions clarify many of the diverse usages of the phrase 'a right'; but they also leave many conceptual problems unresolved. For example, what do all these types of 'rights' have in common? Hohfeld said they are all "legal advantages"; but this definition is vague. Other problems arise from the very sharpness of his distinctions. To deal with these problems, one suggestion has been that rights must be viewed not as diverse Hohfeldian types taken separately but rather as "bundles" of these types taken together, with one or another type being the "core" and the others the "periphery."

The Elements of Claim-Rights

Despite the possible interconnections between Hohfeld's types, it is generally agreed that claim-rights are the most important kind of rights, especially because of their stringency as entailing strict duties to forbear or assist. The general structure of a claim-right is given by the following formula:

A has a right to X against B by virtue of Y.

There are five main elements here: first, the *subject* (A) of the right, the right holder; second, the *nature* of the right, what being a right consists in or what it means for someone to have a right; third, the *object* (X) of the right, what it is a right to; fourth, the *respondent* (B) of the right, the duty bearer, the person or group that has the correlative duty; and fifth, the *justifying ground* (Y) of the right.

The Problem of Redundancy

This formula with its elements helps to elucidate some of the chief conceptual problems that have been raised about rights. One is the problem of redundancy, which takes two forms. The first form concerns the relation between the subject's rights and the respondent's duties. Since rights and duties are correlative, this problem is taken to mean that the right of A against B is the "same relation" as (or, as Hohfeld said, is "equivalent" to) the duty of B to A. But if they are the "same relation," then isn't one of them redundant?

A main answer is that claim-rights and strict duties have objects that differ in valuational content. Rights are justified claims to certain benefits, the support or protection of certain interests of the subject or right holder. Duties, on the other hand, are justified burdens on the part of the respondent or duty bearer: they restrict her freedom by requiring that she conduct herself in ways that directly benefit not herself but rather the right holder. But burdens are for the sake of benefits, and not conversely. Hence duties, which are burdens, are for the sake of rights, whose objects are benefits, so that rights are the justifying reasons for duties. Thus, rights and duties are distinct, and neither is redundant.

In opposition to this answer, it is sometimes contended that the objects of rights are not always benefits to the right holder. Examples are the right to smoke excessively and the right to have a promise to oneself kept that will benefit not oneself but only some third party. There are at least three replies: (a) The right to smoke and to engage in other self-harming actions may be taken as species of the right to freedom, which is in general a good to the right holder. Thus the objects of rights are general goods for the right holder, even if all their specific varieties may not be good for her. (b) Rights would not be *claimed* unless the claimant *thought* there was some value in her having the object of the right. (c) In the case of third-party beneficiaries, the person to whom a promise is made also has an interest in the promise's being kept, so that to this extent she too derives benefit from it.

These considerations lead to a second form of the problem of redundancy. In the formula given above, the object (*X*) of the right—the object consisting in certain benefits or interests—seems to do most or all of the work for which the right is invoked, so that the concept of rights is again declared to be redundant. For if what is so important about rights is the support or protection of certain benefits or interests, then why isn't such protection sufficient; why do we also need rights to these interests?

There are several answers. All involve that rights, especially when they are moral, provide certain indispensable normative additions to simply having or being protected in certain interests or benefits. To begin with, A's having a moral right to *X* adds to his having *X*, or his being protected in having *X*, the important qualification that there is strong justification both for his having *X* and for his being protected in having *X*. This justification, moreover, is of a special sort, in that, when A has a right to *X*, this means that he is personally entitled to have *X* as his due, as what belongs personally to him, so that it is normatively necessary that A be protected in having or doing *X*.

Rights as Normatively Necessary Personal Entitlements

These aspects of personal entitlement and normative necessity bear on three specific relations among the elements of rights distinguished above. First, rights are normatively necessary in the relation between the subject and the object, in that the subject has personal PROPERTY in, and thus justified personal control over, the object, so that it is personally owed to him as his due and for his own sake, not because it adds to overall utility. Second, rights are also normatively necessary in the relation between the subject and the respondent, in that the former is in a position to make a justified personal claim or demand, not merely a request or a plea, against the latter for the support or protection of his having the object of his right. In this way the respondent has duties that are personally owed to the subject. Third, rights are normatively necessary in the relation between the subject and the object, on the one hand, and the justifying ground, on the other, in that this ground supplies the warrant or title, and thus the necessitating premise, for the object's being personally owed to the subject and hence for the requirement that the subject have, and be protected in having, the object to which he has a right. In view of these stringent aspects of normative necessity, the question arises whether rights can ever be overridden. This question will be discussed below.

The Nature of Rights

These three diverse relations between the subject, on the one hand, and the respondent, the object, and the justifying ground, on the other, also have a direct bearing on the conceptual question of the nature of a right. Two different theories focus on different elements in the structure of a right given above. The "benefit theory" emphasizes the relation between the subject and the object of rights. Since the object consists in certain benefits or interests of the subject, the benefit theory holds that for a person to have a right is for him to be the directly intended beneficiary of someone else's performance of a duty or, in a further version, that some projected benefit or interest of his is a sufficient ground for other persons' having duties. The "choice theory," on the other hand, emphasizes the relation between the subject and the respondent of rights. The theory holds that to have a right is to be in a justified position to determine by one's choice how other persons (the respondents) shall act.

Each theory is plausible, but each also incurs difficulties. It has been held that the choice theory does not explain how children and mentally deficient persons may have rights; but this objection could be taken care of by the consideration that such persons can be represented by other persons who make claims for them. Another, perhaps more serious difficulty for the choice theory is that it implies that subjects may waive their rights; but some rights, such as those provided by the criminal law or by welfare legislation, cannot be waived. On the other hand, it seems to follow from the benefit theory, unlike the choice theory, that animals have rights, since they have certain interests and thus are capable of being benefited. Some thinkers have endorsed this conclusion and have used it to reject the choice theory. At the same time, however, the choice theory has the distinct advantage that it views the right holder as an active claimant on her own behalf and thus as having an indispensable element of autonomy and DIGNITY, in contrast to the passive recipience that the benefit theory seems to attribute to right holders. This defect of the benefit theory can, however, be substantially remedied if it can be shown that a full justification of the theory involves that all morally justified rights have, as their most general objects, the fulfillment and support for each right holder of the necessary conditions of action and of generally successful action. This point will be further discussed below. It seems, then, that despite the possible divergences of the benefit and choice theories, the most acceptable account of the nature of rights must involve some combination of the two theories that incorporates the strong points of each while omitting its negative features.

The Nature of Moral Rights

The justifying ground of legal rights consists in the statutes and other provisions of positive municipal law. But it is also often said that persons have certain rights even if these are not recognized or enforced by positive laws, such as when it is asserted that slaves have a right to be free. In such cases the having in question, like the rights themselves, is moral, not legal.

There are two different views on the nature or existence of moral rights. On one view, for such rights to exist means that, while they fulfill certain moral criteria, they are embodied in positive laws or other social rules. On another view, moral rights exist or are had even when they are not so embodied;

it is sufficient that they fulfill or derive from justified moral principles or other morally relevant considerations. Against this latter view it is objected that because of the diversity and conflicts of moral principles, there would be no way of definitively determining whether anyone has moral rights, in contrast to the determinate answers provided by positive laws. This point is often adduced in criticism of the undisciplined proliferation of right-claims that are invoked by various protagonists in political and legal controversies. But against the former, positivist view it is objected not only that it incurs the same difficulty of ascertainment when it seeks to evaluate positive laws by moral criteria, but also that it makes unintelligible the recognized practice of appealing to rights even when they are not embodied in positive laws or ongoing social rules, and even in opposition to such laws and rules. Against the specifically legal positivist view it is further objected that it does not provide for those moral rights that, by general agreement, are not and should not be embodied in positive laws, such as the rights, in ordinary interpersonal relations, not to be lied to and not to be subjected to broken PROMISES, as well as the rights of children to receive loving care from their parents.

The Justifying Ground of Moral Rights

To ask who has what moral rights to what is to ask a normative and substantive question, not only a conceptual one, although conceptual considerations also figure in the answers one gives. If, for moral rights to exist, they must be justified by sound moral principles or other morally relevant grounds, where do we look for such principles or grounds? An important emphasis has been that human beings have interests. But not all interests generate rights. In view of the normative necessity involved in rights, it would seem that the interests that ground them must also involve necessity. Such necessity could be obtained if the interests consisted not in contingent, dispensable desires or goods, but rather in the goods that are necessary for human ACTION or for having general chances of success in achieving one's purposes by action.

For such a general grounding of general moral rights to be successful, the necessary conditions of action and of generally successful action would have to be carefully specified. The two main such conditions are freedom and well-being. Freedom is the procedural necessary condition of action; it consists in controlling one's behavior by one's own unforced choice while having knowledge of relevant circumstances. Well-being is the substantive necessary condition of action; it consists in having the general abilities and conditions needed for achieving one's purposes. Since the agency-needs that are here called "necessary" pertain not only to bare action but also to generally successful action, the necessity in question can accommodate the varying degrees in which practical abilities and conditions are needed for action. Thus, well-being falls into a hierarchy of goods ranging from life and physical integrity to education and opportunities for acquiring wealth and income. According to the general substantive theory here sketched, all actual or prospective agents have equal moral rights to freedom and well-being, and their having these rights is grounded in their enduring needs for the necessary conditions of their action and generally successful action. An argument can be given for the moral principle that grounds this thesis.

Moral Rights as Solely Negative

According to one libertarian view, all moral rights are negative: they set absolute "side constraints" on actions in that their correlative duties require refraining from actions that interfere with persons' freedom. A difficulty with this view is that it cannot handle conflicts of rights. Suppose A is going to murder B, and the only way to prevent this is for C to steal the car of D, who is entirely innocent in relation to A's murder project. Here the absolute rights not to be murdered and not to be stolen from come into unresolvable conflict.

To deal with such cases, it has been suggested that rights construed as side constraints should be supplemented by "consequential analysis" that trades off the lesser badness of infringing one right by the greater badness of infringing another. A related suggestion is the general idea presented above that rights fall into a hierarchy according to the degree of their objects' needfulness for action, so that the right not to be stolen from is overridden by the right not to be murdered when these rights are in conflict.

Such a procedure has been called a "utilitarianism of rights." But this phrase is misleading if it implies a constant readiness to interfere with rights for the sake of regularly achieving some sort of weighted minimization of rights violations. A "utilitarian" approach of this sort is different from considerations that are restricted to wide disparities in degrees of importance between the interests that are the objects of the respective rights, as in the above example.

What, however, of situations where the rights that are in conflict have objects that are of the same degree of importance? A recurrently adduced example is the one in which a casual bystander can save ten innocent persons from being murdered only if she murders one of the persons herself. It has been suggested that, since the function of rights is to protect justified personal interests and since the interests in this example are on a par, the rights theorist must seriously consider participating in this abominable project.

The rejection of such participation can, however, be justified on grounds of rights. For the rights to life of the nine other innocent persons do not extend to the right to life of the tenth person. In general, if a person has a right to X, then he has a right to anything else Y that may be necessary for his having X, *unless* someone else already has a right to that Y, *and* Y is as important for action as is X. For example, if Jones is starving and cannot obtain food by his own efforts, while Smith has abundant food, then Jones's right to life overrides Smith's property right in the food, so that Jones has a right to as much of Smith's food as he needs in order to prevent starvation. But if Smith has only enough food to prevent his own starvation, then Jones does not have a right to it because Smith's not starving is as important for his action as Jones's not starving is for his. It is for such a reason that the nine other innocent persons do not have a right that the tenth person be murdered in order to prevent their being murdered. Hence, if the casual bystander were to murder the tenth person, she would be violating that person's right to life, while if she were to refrain from the murder, she would not be violating the others' rights to life, since they do not have a right that the tenth person be murdered in order to prevent their murder.

Positive Rights

A second view of the contents of moral rights is that they are positive as well as negative. If the ultimate justifying ground of rights is the needs of agency, including well-being, then positive welfare rights are justified when persons cannot fulfill their needs of well-being by their own efforts so that positive assistance by other persons is required, in cases ranging from relief of starvation to provision of educational resources. As in the case of negative rights, the application of the positive-rights model requires consideration of degrees of needfulness for action, so that, for example, taxation that removes a relatively small part of affluent persons' wealth is justified and is not a violation of the taxed persons' rights, if this tax is needed in order to prevent other persons' starvation or to provide opportunities for education. More than in the exclusively negative theory of rights, the positive theory requires recourse to institutional, especially state, provision for various rights, as against leaving such provision solely to individual initiative. Thus on this view moral rights are social and economic as well as political and civil.

Utilitarianism and Rights

UTILITARIANISM raises two kinds of questions for theories of rights. One is whether it can "accommodate" rights, *i.e.,* whether the requirements of rights can be justified by the utilitarian principle that the rightness of actions is to be determined by consequentialist considerations about the maximizing of total or average utility. It has been contended that utilitarianism can require that special protection be provided for the special interests and NEEDS that are the objects of rights. A chief reply to this thesis is that, since the aim of utilitarianism is ultimately aggregative, to maximize utility, the distributive protections provided by even the most important rights would be at best only contingently maintained, since the rights could be overridden whenever the maximization of utility required this.

A second question about the relation of utilitarianism to rights goes in the reverse direction. Even if utilitarianism cannot adequately accommodate rights, is this always a fault? Isn't it also true that rights cannot accommodate utilitarianism, in that the insistence on individual rights may block the fulfillment of important communal goals? This question underlies the charge, which goes back at least to Jeremy BENTHAM (1748–1832) and Karl MARX

(1818–1883), that rights are egoistic because they involve claims for the fulfillment of individual interests, so that they may operate to submerge the values of community or society.

Two replies can be given to this charge. The first relies on the thesis sketched above about the varying degrees of importance or needfulness of the objects of rights. Thus the theory of rights may allow for the exercise of eminent domain where an important community project like the building of a new public school requires that some persons be forced to give up their property rights in their houses at a certain location (with due compensation). But the theory cannot allow, for the reasons indicated above, that an innocent person be killed in order to prevent certain even severe harms from befalling the community as a whole.

A second reply is that HUMAN RIGHTS, which are universally distributed moral rights, require of each person that he act with due regard for other persons' interests as well as his own. For since, in principle, each person has human rights against all other persons, every other person also has these rights against him, so that he has correlative duties toward them. The concept of human rights thus entails a reciprocal universality: each person must respect the rights of all the others while having his rights respected by all the others, so that there must be a mutual sharing of the benefits of rights and the burdens of duties. The human rights hence involve mutuality of consideration and, thus, a kind of ALTRUISM rather than EGOISM. By requiring mutual aid where needed and practicable, the human rights make for social solidarity and a community of rights.

See also: ALTRUISM; ANIMALS, TREATMENT OF; CIVIL RIGHTS AND CIVIC DUTIES; COMMUNITARIANISM; CONSEQUENTIALISM; CONTRACTS; CORRECTIONAL ETHICS; DELIBERATION AND CHOICE; DEONTOLOGY; DUTY AND OBLIGATION; DWORKIN; EGOISM; ENTITLEMENTS; *EUDAIMONIA,* -ISM; FREEDOM AND DETERMINISM; GEWIRTH; HUMAN RIGHTS; INTERESTS; KANT; LIBERTARIANISM; LIBERTY; LIFE, RIGHT TO; MARX; MORAL RULES; NEEDS; NORMS; NOZICK; POLICE ETHICS; PROMISES; PROPERTY; PUBLIC POLICY; RECIPROCITY; RESPONSIBILITY; RIGHT, CONCEPTS OF; RIGHT HOLDERS; SOCIAL AND POLITICAL PHILOSOPHY; TELEOLOGICAL ETHICS; THOMSON; UTILITARIANISM; WELFARE RIGHTS AND SOCIAL POLICY.

Bibliography

Becker, Lawrence C. *Property Rights: Philosophic Foundations.* London: Routledge and Kegan Paul, 1977. Arguments for and against rights to private property.

Bentham, Jeremy. *A Critical Examination of the Declaration of Rights.* In *Bentham's Political Thought,* edited by Bhiku Parekh. New York: Barnes and Noble, 1973. Classic condemnation of natural rights as antisocial nonsense.

Campbell, Tom. *The Left and Rights: A Conceptual Analysis of the Idea of Socialist Rights.* London: Routledge and Kegan Paul, 1983. Socialism not antithetical to rights.

Dworkin, Ronald. *Taking Rights Seriously.* Cambridge, Mass.: Harvard University Press, 1977. Rights as "trumps."

Feinberg, Joel. *Rights, Justice, and the Bounds of Liberty.* Princeton, N.J.: Princeton University Press, 1980. Importance of rights; their relation to claims.

———. *Social Philosophy.* Englewood Cliffs, N.J.: Prentice-Hall, 1973. Analysis and conflict of rights.

Finnis, John. *Natural Law and Natural Rights.* Oxford: Clarendon Press, 1980. Rights account for the requirements of practical reasonableness.

Flathman, Richard E. *The Practice of Rights.* Cambridge: Cambridge University Press, 1976. Rights are adversarial; communitarian objections.

Gewirth, Alan. *Reason and Morality.* Chicago: University of Chicago Press, 1978. Rights based on necessary conditions of action.

———. "Why Rights Are Indispensable." *Mind* 95 (1986): 329–44. Answers conceptual and moral objections against rights.

Hart, H. L. A. "Are There Any Natural Rights?" *Philosophical Review* 64 (1955): 175–91. Derives natural rights from special moral rights.

———. *Essays on Bentham: Studies in Jurisprudence and Political Theory.* Oxford: Clarendon Press, 1982. Argues for the choice theory.

———. *Essays in Jurisprudence and Philosophy.* Oxford: Clarendon Press, 1983. Includes criticisms of utilitarianism, Nozick, and Dworkin on rights.

Hohfeld, Wesley N. *Fundamental Legal Conceptions as Applied in Judicial Reasoning.* New Haven and London: Yale University Press, 1964 [1919]. Classic fourfold typology.

Lyons, David, ed. *Rights.* Belmont, Calif.: Wadsworth, 1979. Good collection, including Lyons's "Rights, Claimants, and Beneficiaries" (pp. 58–77), which argues for the benefit theory.

Martin, Rex, and James W. Nickel. "Recent Work on the Concept of Rights." *American Philosophical Quarterly* 17 (1980): 165–80. Extensive bibliography.

Marx, Karl. *On the Jewish Question.* In *The Marx-Engels Reader,* edited by Robert C. Tucker, 26–52. New York: W. W. Norton, 1978. "Rights of man" are egoistic (unlike "rights of the citizen").

Melden, A. I. *Rights and Persons.* Berkeley and Los Angeles: University of California Press, 1977. Rights based on personhood.

Nozick, Robert. *Anarchy, State, and Utopia.* New York: Basic Books, 1974. Rights as absolute side constraints; against "utilitarianism of rights."

Raphael, D. D., ed. *Political Theory and the Rights of Man.* London: Macmillan, 1967. Historical and analytic essays.

Rawls, John. *A Theory of Justice.* Cambridge, Mass.: Harvard University Press, 1971. Rights based on ideal contract.

Raz, Joseph. *The Morality of Freedom.* Oxford: Clarendon Press, 1986. Individual freedom based on rights.

Ritchie, David G. *Natural Rights: A Criticism of Some Political and Ethical Conceptions.* London: George Allen and Unwin, 1894. Historical and critical; rights based on social utility.

Sen, Amartya. "Rights and Agency." *Philosophy and Public Affairs* 11 (1982): 3–29. Discusses "goal rights system" wherein the fulfillment or nonfulfillment of rights is included in the consequential evaluation of states of affairs.

Shue, Henry. *Basic Rights: Subsistence, Affluence, and U.S. Foreign Policy.* Princeton, N.J.: Princeton University Press, 1980. Basic rights include subsistence as well as security and liberty.

Sumner, L. W. *The Moral Foundation of Rights.* Oxford: Clarendon Press, 1987. Argues against natural-law and contractualist theories of rights and for consequentialist theory.

Thomson, Judith J. *The Realm of Rights.* Cambridge, Mass.: Harvard University Press, 1990. Examines what rights are and which rights there are.

Tuck, Richard. *Natural Rights Theories: Their Origin and Development.* Cambridge: Cambridge University Press, 1979. History of rights theories from twelfth to seventeenth centuries.

Waldron, Jeremy, ed. *Theories of Rights.* Oxford: Oxford University Press, 1984. Good introduction and bibliography.

Wellman, Carl. *A Theory of Rights.* Totowa, N.J.: Rowman and Allanheld, 1985. A right is a complex structure of legal positions having a central core.

———. *Welfare Rights.* Totowa, N.J.: Rowman and Allanheld, 1982. Examines grounds of ethical welfare rights.

Wolgast, Elizabeth H. *Equality and the Rights of Women.* Ithaca, N.Y.: Cornell University Press, 1980. Women's rights based not on egalitarian reasoning but on distinctiveness and interdependence.

Alan Gewirth

rights, human

See human rights.

risk

A risk is a likelihood of injury, damage, or loss. Thus, the concept comprises two elements: the normative judgment of a possible event or condition as *adverse* plus the *chance* or *probability* that it will come about. The magnitude of a particular risk is often thought of in terms of the severity of the potential harm weighted by the probability of its occurrence. A low probability of a serious harm may thus be seen as equivalent, in magnitude of risk, to a higher probability of a less serious harm. It may then be suggested that the acceptability of a given risk is determined by its magnitude and hence that risks of equal magnitude are, or ought to be, equally acceptable (or unacceptable).

This way of thinking may be misleading, however, in at least three ways: (1) It suggests an often unattainable degree of precision in estimating the probabilities of the events that concern us. (2) It suggests commensurability of harms of very different sorts (loss of home, sight, life, loved one) that may occur in very different ways (during recreation, due to storm or earthquake, intentional or negligent actions of others, etc.). These and many other factors are morally and psychologically relevant to individual and societal judgments of acceptability. (3) It suggests that it makes sense to think in terms of a general level of acceptable risk for a person and/or for a society. But to look for a general level of acceptable risk is like looking for a general fair price. Price for what? No risk is acceptable if it does not bring with it some benefit—and it matters both whether those who bear the risk *consent* to bear it and whether they themselves reap the benefit.

Consent

Scarcely any activity can be carried on that does not impose some risk on someone—often not (only) on the agent, but on others. We are not morally required to obtain the explicit CONSENT of everyone potentially at some risk from an act (such as driving to work or turning on the furnace) before we may perform it. Some risks, though, such as medical research, may not be imposed without the explicit informed consent of those potentially at risk. There may be risks it would be morally impermissible to impose even with informed consent. It is not clear how we should distinguish cases in which consent is required from cases in which it is not (and from cases, if any, for which it may not suffice).

It is also difficult to determine what, if anything, should count as consent in situations in which direct consent is unfeasible or unreasonable. There are serious limits to the justificatory force of such notions as implicit or hypothetical consent to risk. Inferring implicit consent by workers to workplace risks, for example, presupposes that workers are fully informed of the hazards they face, that they have reasonable alternatives available if they find the risks unacceptable, and thus that they are satisfied with the wage/risk packages they currently get. Each of these assumptions is subject to serious question. To extrapolate from labor market behavior to other areas of life and infer implicit consent to risks of "equal magnitude" compounds the problem. Similarly, insofar as the moral significance of consent derives from respect for the autonomy of those whose consent is sought, appeals to hypothetical consent may be poor substitutes for the real thing. Providing for meaningful participation in the decision making process by those potentially at risk may more fully respect their autonomy. (Purely self-imposed risks raise issues of whether there are duties to the self that may be violated and of the justifiability of PATERNALISM.)

Justice

Risks resulting from an activity or policy may be borne wholly or largely by some members of a community, while the benefits are shared equally, or enjoyed entirely, by persons other than those at risk. In such cases, it may be possible (obligatory) to compensate in some way those who bear the risks (and perhaps to compensate further those for whom the risk turns out badly) so that the INTERESTS of those at risk are not sacrificed either for the COMMON GOOD or for the benefit of others. (Questions would remain as to whether prior consent to such a risk compensation package would be required.)

The requirements of justice may differ depending on whether those who would be at risk from an activity already bear a disproportionately larger or smaller share of risks or are antecedently worse or better off in other ways than those who would benefit. How much weight one believes such considerations ought to have will depend in part on one's general moral views—the relative importance one attaches to individual RIGHTS, the general welfare, and social EQUALITY, for example. Equity considerations arise between local communities, regions, and nations as well as between individuals or groups within a community. They present special difficulties when they arise between generations.

It is not clear what our moral obligations are in cases in which those potentially at risk do not yet exist. We cannot ask their consent, and it does not seem reasonable to ascribe rights to persons who do not exist—and who may or may not exist, depending in part on our decisions. Yet it does not seem morally acceptable to ignore the potential effects of our policies on FUTURE GENERATIONS. The question, then, is how these considerations should enter into our decisions.

Facts and Values

Because the concept of risk involves two elements—chance and adversity—some propose that decisions concerning risks involve two fundamentally different sorts of activity: (1) measurement or estimation of risk; and (2) evaluation of its acceptability. The first is thought to be factual, objective, and scientific, while the second is normative, subjective, and personal or political. Many practitioners and theorists of risk assessment insist that their function is restricted to measurement, while evaluation is the job of individuals and/or the policy makers who represent them. Others argue that there are normative and subjective elements present throughout the process—beginning with the judgment that a possible outcome is adverse and hence its possibility constitutes a risk, and continuing with judgments as to how conservatively to estimate probabilities, how to frame risks (whether in terms of probability of adverse or favorable outcome, what comparisons and alternatives to represent in characterizing the nature and magnitude of risk, and so on). They maintain that the factual and evaluative components of risk decisions are inextricably intertwined, and hence that the widely accepted division of labor in the decision process is ill-conceived.

See also: COERCION; COMMON GOOD; CONSENT; DISCOUNTING THE FUTURE; ENVIRONMENTAL ETHICS; FUTURE GENERATIONS; GENETIC ENGINEERING; HARM AND OFFENSE; INDIVIDUALISM; INTERESTS; NEGLIGENCE; PATERNALISM; PUBLIC POLICY; PUBLIC POLICY ANALYSIS; RATIONAL CHOICE; RISK ANALYSIS; RISK AVERSION; TECHNOLOGY.

Bibliography

Anderson, Elizabeth. "Values, Risks, and Market Norms." *Philosophy and Public Affairs* 17 (1988): 54–65.

Douglas, Mary, and Aaron Wildavsky. *Risk and Culture: The Selection of Technical and Environmental Dangers.* Berkeley: University of California Press, 1982.

Fischhoff, Baruch, *et al. Acceptable Risk.* Cambridge: Cambridge University Press, 1981. Cognitive psychology.

Fletcher, George P. "Fairness and Utility in Tort Theory." *Harvard Law Review* 85 (1972): 537–73.

Fried, Charles. *An Anatomy of Values: Problems of Personal and Social Choice.* Cambridge, Mass.: Harvard University Press, 1970. See chapter 11, "Imposing Risks on Others."

Gibson, Mary, ed. *To Breathe Freely: Risk, Consent, and Air.* Totowa, N.J.: Rowman and Allanheld, 1985. Interdisciplinary anthology; bibliographies.

Humber, James M., and Robert F. Almeder, eds. *Quantitative Risk Assessment.* Biomedical Ethics Reviews, 1986. Clifton, N.J.: Humana Press, 1987. Interdisciplinary anthology; bibliographies.

Kahneman, Daniel, Paul Slovick, and Amos Tversky, eds. *Judgment under Uncertainty: Heuristics and Biases.* Cambridge: Cambridge University Press, 1982. Cognitive psychology.

Kasperson, Roger E., and Jeanne X. Kasperson. "Determining the Acceptability of Risk: Ethical and Policy Issues." In *Risk: A Symposium on the Assessment and Perception of Risk to Human Health in Canada.* Ottowa: Royal Society of Canada, 1983. Proceedings of a conference held 18–19 October 1982. Reprinted as CENTED Reprint no. 41. The CENTED reprint series (Worcester, Mass.: Center for Technology, Environment, and Development) contains many fine papers on ethical and policy issues in risk assessment and hazard evaluation.

Krimsky, Sheldon, and Rosemary Chalk, eds. *Technical and Ethical Aspects of Risk Communication.* Special Issue, *Science, Technology, and Human Values,* 12 (1987).

Lowrance, William. *Of Acceptable Risk: Science and the Determination of Safety.* Los Altos, Calif.: William Kaufmann, 1976.

MacLean, Douglas, ed. *Values at Risk.* Totowa, N.J.: Rowman and Allanheld, 1985. Interdisciplinary anthology; bibliographies.

Nelkin, Dorothy, and Michael S. Brown. *Workers at Risk.* Chicago: University of Chicago Press, 1984.

Rescher, Nicholas. *Risk: A Philosophical Introduction to the Theory of Risk Evaluation and Management.* New York: University Press of America, 1983.

Risk Analysis: An International Journal. New York: Plenum, 1980–. Official publication of the Society for Risk Analysis; published four times yearly.

Sagoff, Mark. "On Markets for Risk." *Maryland Law Review* 41 (1982): 755–73.

Schelling, T. C. "The Life You Save May Be Your Own." In *Problems in Public Expenditure Analysis,* edited by Samuel Chase. Washington, D.C.: Brookings, 1968.

Starr, Chauncey. "Social Benefit versus Technological Risk." *Science* 165 (1969): 1232–38. This article is commonly held to have inaugurated the current "risk debate" and the risk analysis and assessment industry.

Stevenson, Leslie. "Defense Policies and the Evaluation of Risk." *Social Theory and Practice* 14 (1988): 215–34.

Tversky, Amos, and Daniel Kahneman. "The Framing of Decisions and the Psychology of Choice." *Science* 211 (1981): 453–58.

Mary Gibson

risk analysis

Nearly every important decision in life involves a RISK of losing something of value. Risk analysis is a process of identifying these possible adverse consequences and figuring out what to do about them. It includes estimating the magnitude of different risks, along with the costs and benefits of trying to reduce them. How bad are the risks we face? Should we accept and live with them, try to mitigate them in particular ways, or try to eliminate them altogether? Risk analysis can be part of the process of deciding whether to invest in a new weapons system for the nation or new tires for your car. It is part of deciding whether to get a medical checkup or whether it is wise to sit in the sun, eat less beef, or drink more wine. Depending on one's situation, inclinations, and access to information, a risk analysis can be intuitive or formal, and it can play a stronger or weaker role in determining what one does.

Although risk analysis of some sort is something most people do frequently, the term is usually reserved for more formal analyses of important PUBLIC POLICY decisions, where the possible adverse consequences include risks to public health and safety or environmental degradation. In these contexts, too, risk analysis has been done for as long as the public has been concerned about threats to health and safety from disease, pollution, wars, or technologies, but it came to be identified as such after 1960, during a period when there was broad social support in the United States and other industrially developed countries for increasing government regulations aimed at protecting public health and safety.

Between 1965 and 1980, the U.S. Congress enacted more than thirty major laws, which established or strengthened at least a dozen regulatory agencies, for the purpose of managing occupational, consumer product, environmental, transportation, and other sources of risk. This attention to risk led to the growth and greater influence of public advocacy groups, some of which argued that stricter regulations were needed in this or that area, while others protested that regulation had gone too far and cost too much. It also prompted engineers and scientists to develop methods of risk analysis that could improve the quality of these complex policy decisions.

Managing the risks of public health and safety and of the environment has proven to be a controversial activity, and some ethical concerns that focus on the methods and use of risk analysis are at the heart of many of the controversies. These concerns are well illustrated in the heated debates over the safety of nuclear power plants of the 1970s and 1980s. While the Nuclear Regulatory Commission was considering safety regulations that would have added significant costs to what was turning out to be a marginally profitable industry, some risk analysts and nuclear engineers, while admitting that a small risk of a serious accident at a nuclear reactor would inevitably exist, began to argue that most nuclear reactors were nevertheless safe enough at that time. They considered the levels of risk that people seemed willing to accept in other areas, as revealed in consumer behavior, and they analyzed these data to estimate the public's willingness to pay for general risk reduction. Their claim that nuclear power was already safe enough was based on an argument that its risks were lower than other risks that people found acceptable and that the cost of reducing these risks further was greater than most people were willing to pay. Those who were demanding additional safety at nuclear power plants were thought either to have an irrational fear of risk or to be pursuing some political agenda through the regulatory process. With arguments like these on the table, the debates about risk analysis came to focus on the question: How safe is safe enough?

Part of the problem in finding a socially acceptable answer to this question is cognitive. Research shows that most people find it difficult to think clearly and consistently about risk and probability, and it is especially hard to compare different risks directly in a coherent way. It is easy to be confused— and experts disagree—about the significance of low levels of exposure to a harmful substance. For these reasons, one may question the value of arguments that use data about consumer willingness to pay for optional safety features in automobiles or preventive medicines, which may or may not be based on a clear assessment of the risks involved, to support general conclusions about socially acceptable tradeoffs between risk and benefit.

In response to problems involved in trying to find indicators in consumer behavior of socially acceptable risk levels, some other researchers asked people directly about their attitudes toward different risks. One purpose of this research was to find out why public risk perceptions differed so significantly from expert assessments. When people are asked directly about their attitudes toward risks, it turns out that their responses tend to express not only their beliefs about expected levels of mortality and morbidity, as expert assessments do, but these responses also express "subjective dimensions" or attitudes toward different qualities of risk. A number of these determinants of perceived risk can be expressed in two subjective dimensions: the degree to which a type of risk is familiar or new, and the degree to which the source of risk evokes feelings of dread. The latter dimension is in turn a function of properties like the involuntariness of the risk, the potentially catastrophic nature of the harms, ignorance about the mechanisms relating cause to effect, and latency between cause and effect. The risks of nuclear power in particular rank very high on these subjective dimensions, a fact that is taken to explain why in surveys where people were asked to rank a large number of risks in order of severity, many people ranked nuclear power risks as the worst, even though these same people estimated the expected number of annual fatalities from nuclear power as among the lowest of all the risks they were comparing.

Risk managers must therefore decide how to allocate resources devoted to reducing risk between risks judged to be worst by experts and those of greatest concern to the public. Risk analysts must in turn ask whether they should be trying to identify and measure subjective dimensions of risk or restrict the scope of their analyses to estimating only consequences like expected fatalities, morbidity, envi-

ronmental impacts, and other "objective" costs and benefits.

Answers to these questions depend on what one takes to be the proper role or use of risk analysis. Several expert studies sponsored by the National Academy of Sciences (NAS) have addressed this issue by trying to distinguish risk assessment from risk evaluation. They would like to interpret risk analysis or assessment as a relatively value-free, objective, scientific undertaking that can contribute important information to risk management and public policy decisions, which quite properly must take broader questions of value into account. The argument in favor of such an approach is simply that it is useful, when confronting large, important, and complex decisions, to try to disaggregate them into components that can be analyzed separately. The subjective dimensions of risk belong in the evaluative process, where their importance can be properly considered, but these issues should be separated from the more objective enterprise of identifying possible harms and estimating their probabilities, which is the proper focus of risk analysis.

As the experts who wrote these NAS reports were aware, however, the issue of making risk analysis a value-free enterprise is not so simple. Analysis must begin by identifying which risks to study and what to count as a risk, an exercise that usually requires making value judgments. Suppose, for example, that you are interested in reducing occupational risks, and you learn that exposure to a certain chemical acts synergistically with tobacco smoke to produce cancer rates in workers exposed to both that are higher than the aggregate of each independent risk. You must decide whether this risk should be included in an analysis of occupational risks, or whether you can ignore it in your study because it is a risk to smokers only, and not a risk to workers. A choice like this obviously involves making ethical judgments.

More important than these issues of identification, however, are problems caused by uncertainties that pervade risk analysis. Consider, for example, the problem of analyzing risks to a population exposed to low doses of radiation or to some possibly carcinogenic chemical. In the absence of direct epidemiological evidence of the risks involved, we may have to rely on studies of animals exposed to high levels of the substance. Experts disagree about the most accurate way to extrapolate risks from animals to humans and from high doses to low doses, and these disagreements reflect uncertainties that can lead to analyses in which risk estimates differ by up to several orders of magnitude. The NAS studies recommend that risk analyses include these uncertainties by reporting their conclusions as ranges rather than numbers. But this solution is not always feasible, so the question then arises whether the analyst should take the most conservative number, his or her estimate of the best number, some average of different expert opinions, or some other number. In any event, the risk analyst must often make important value judgments.

A third class of ethical issues that are not easily detached from scientific risk analyses have to do with the distribution of risks, costs, and benefits. Public policies must be concerned with distributive justice, but issues of justice are often best treated explicitly, by separating them from the process of risk analysis. Other kinds of distributive issues, however, are not so easily avoided in risk analysis. For example, consider a situation in which an average individual in an exposed population has a $1/n$ chance annually of suffering an adverse consequence. This level of individual risk can be distributed across a population in many different ways. To take just two possibilities: $1/n$ individuals in the population will with certainty suffer the consequence each year, or there is a $1/n$ chance that the entire population will suffer the consequence in any year. Taking the perspective of the population as a whole, the former possibility involves no risk at all, while the latter might be a catastrophic risk. It is clearly an important ethical consideration to determine whether and how risk to the group is to be balanced against risk to an average individual within the group, and balancing the risks as seen from these different perspectives can require changing the level of risk exposure to the individual or to the group.

We cannot eliminate the possibility of adverse consequences from activities we deem to be socially desirable. Many of the ethical issues surrounding risk analysis can be seen as asking how we should be measuring and responding to these risks, but at least one concern raises a different sort of question. Some people are bothered by the assumptions of most risk analyses that all our values are comparable and measurable on a single scale. This concern is especially high when the chosen scale of measurement is money, for then the values of human life and health and natural treasures appear to be treated as goods with a price. The question raised by this concern is not whether ethical judgments must be made in the process of risk analysis; rather, it is whether ethical issues are involved in even thinking about some possibilities as appropriate subjects of risk analysis.

See also: APPLIED ETHICS; CONSEQUENTIALISM; COST-BENEFIT ANALYSIS; ENGINEERING ETHICS; ENVIRONMENTAL ETHICS; JUSTICE, DISTRIBUTIVE; LIBERTY, ECONOMIC; LOGIC AND ETHICS; NUCLEAR ETHICS; PUBLIC HEALTH POLICY; PUBLIC POLICY; PUBLIC POLICY ANALYSIS; RATIONAL CHOICE; RISK; RISK AVERSION; SELF-DECEPTION; SOCIAL AND POLITICAL PHILOSOPHY; SUBJECTIVISM.

Bibliography

Ames, Bruce, Renae Magaw, and Lois Swirsky Gold. "Ranking Possible Carcinogenic Hazards." *Science* 236 (17 April 1987): 271–80. Describes a framework for comparing different risks, which includes comparing technological carcinogens against naturally occurring carcinogens.

Douglas, Mary, and Aaron Wildavsky. *Risk and Culture.* Berkeley: University of California Press, 1982. Defense of a cultural theory that argues that differences in attitudes toward risk are strongly determined by the structure of one's culture or subculture.

Fischhoff, Baruch, Stephen Watson, and Chris Hope. "Defining Risk." *Policy Sciences* 17 (1984): 123–39. A clear description of the subjective dimensions of risk perception; argues for the need to include these aspects in a conception of risk analysis.

Keeney, Ralph, and R. Winkler. "Evaluating Decision Strategies for Equity of Public Risks." *Operations Research* 33 (1985): 955–70. The nature of different distributions of risk, and an attempt to prove that greater equity and risk reduction can be incompatible.

MacLean, Douglas, ed. *Values at Risk.* Totowa, NJ: Rowman and Allanheld, 1983. Articles by philosophers exploring the ethical dimensions of risk analysis.

National Academy of Sciences Committee on Risk and Decision Making. *Risk and Decision Making: Perspectives and Research.* Washington, DC: National Academy Press, 1982. An influential study of risk analysis in government agencies; argues for a distinction between risk assessment, which should be value-free, and risk evaluation, where ethical issues are properly considered.

Schelling, Thomas. "The Life You Save May Be Your Own." In *Choice and Consequence.* Cambridge: Harvard University Press, 1984. An important contribution to the development of a revealed preference theory for acceptable risk; shows how economic behavior can be used to reveal attitudes toward risks in general.

Shrader-Frechette, Kristin. *Risk and Rationality.* Berkeley: University of California Press, 1991. A sustained discussion by a philosopher of technological risk, risk analysis, and ethical issues.

Slovic, Paul, Baruch Fischhoff, and Sarah Lichtenstein. "Rating the Risks." *Environment* 21 (1979): 14–39. Reports the influential research into risk perception that explains how subjective factors determine which risks people regard as the worst risks we face.

Starr, Chauncey. "Social Benefit Versus Technological Risk." *Science* 165 (1969): 1232–38. Argues that economic data can show how the public makes tradeoffs between the risks and benefits of a technology; important implications for the early discussions of nuclear power and for interpreting the question, "How safe is safe enough?"

Douglas MacLean

risk aversion

Choices in an uncertain world often involve a risk of losing something of value. You can keep your money safely in the bank, or you can invest it in the stock market, where you can gain more but also take the chance of losing it. You can join the family business or try your luck at becoming a successful artist. Some people prefer to play things safe; others would rather take a risk for the chance of greater gain. Any theory of RATIONAL CHOICE must take account of such attitudes toward risk and uncertainty.

The attitude toward risk that is supposed to be by far the most common and explain much economic behavior is *risk aversion,* which can be defined as an unwillingness to take an actuarially fair bet or, alternatively, as a willingness to give up some expected benefits in order to avoid accepting a risk of loss. To illustrate, suppose a person is offered the following gamble: if a fairly tossed coin lands heads, she wins $1,000; and if it lands tails, she wins nothing. The expected value of this gamble, $500, is the sum of the product of each possible outcome multiplied by the probability of that outcome. A person is risk averse in this situation if she would prefer some amount less than the expected value of the gamble (say $450) with certainty to the gamble. (A person who is indifferent between the expected value and the gamble is risk neutral, and a person who prefers the gamble to the expected value with certainty is risk preferring.) The degree of a person's risk aversion for money in this range can be measured by varying the outcomes or the probability of winning

and seeing how these changes affect her preferences. Thus, the probability of winning can be increased until she is indifferent between choosing the gamble and choosing to take $500 with certainty, or the amount she wins can be increased until she is indifferent between a gamble at even odds and $500 with certainty.

In the formal theory of rational choice, a utility function is a way of representing a preference ordering. The shape of a person's utility function for some good such as money is completely determined by her attitude toward risk. A utility function for money, for example, can be represented as a graph, with amounts of money plotted on the x-axis and utility values on the y-axis. Assuming that more money is always preferred to less, risk aversion with respect to money would be represented by a utility function that is constantly increasing but concave toward the x-axis. Greater risk aversion would be represented by a more steeply concave utility function.

Risk aversion, or a concave utility function, also represents diminishing marginal utility for increases in money. Thus, if a person is risk averse for money, the gain in utility of each $100 she receives is less than the gain of the previous $100. Another way to characterize risk aversion for the gamble described above, therefore, is to say that for the risk averse person the $500 she might lose in the gamble represents greater utility than the $500 she might win. Of course a person might have a different attitude toward risk, which would be represented by a utility function with a different shape. A straight line would represent risk neutrality, and a convex utility function would represent risk preference. A person's utility function for some good could also be more complicated. An S-shaped utility function for money, for example, would represent risk aversion at some levels of wealth and risk preference at others.

In economics, risk aversion is supposed to explain such phenomena as why people with similar qualifications receive lower salaries as tenured professors than they do working in industry, where their jobs and incomes are less secure; or why investors demand higher returns on investments with greater risk, such as stocks, than on investments with lower risk, such as treasury bonds. More generally, the concept of profit is frequently linked to risk aversion in economic theory, where profit is regarded as a premium necessary to offset prevailing attitudes of risk aversion and coax out the supply of socially desirable risk bearing.

Risk aversion also explains why most people think it is reasonable and are in fact willing to buy insurance to protect themselves and their families from ruinous loss. One might be tempted to think that a homeowner who buys fire insurance shows a willingness to gamble, because he is willing to make a bet with his insurance company that his home will burn in the next year. If he loses the bet, his loss is the cost of the premium. Homeowners are willing to accept this bet, moreover, at less than fair odds, because the insurance companies set premium rates that can pay their losses while also covering their costs and returning a profit. The expected monetary value to the homeowner of purchasing insurance is thus less than the expected value of not being insured. But in fact, a willingness to buy insurance shows risk aversion, because the disutility of the expected loss of one's home, without insurance, is much greater than the disutility of paying the premium. Insurance markets allow risk averters to spread the risk of serious loss among all policyholders, which reduces the risk of serious loss to each of them in exchange for accepting the certain loss of the premium payment. Stock markets, futures markets, and many other economic institutions are likewise mechanisms for spreading or shifting risk, which allow risk averters to engage in productive economic activities without accepting all the risks involved.

However important the assumption that risk aversion characterizes most human behavior is in economics, some experimental studies of individual choice claim to show that most people tend to have a different and more complicated attitude toward risk. These studies suggest that people do not generally express a risk attitude toward different possible outcomes, such as different levels of wealth, which people might realize through their choices, but instead adopt a reference point from which they evaluate prospects in terms of expected gains and losses. According to these studies, most people express risk aversion with respect to perceived gains, and risk preference with respect to prospects for avoiding perceived losses. Thus, when asked to choose between a prospect of gaining $500 with certainty and a gamble with equal chances of gaining $1,000 or nothing, most people prefer the risk averse alternative of $500 with certainty. But when

asked to choose between a prospect of losing $500 with certainty and accepting a gamble with equal chances of losing $1,000 or nothing, most people prefer the gamble to the sure thing. To make matters worse, the reference point is not objectively determined and may be influenced by different framings or descriptions of identical prospects. Some prospects can be framed in terms of either gains or losses, according to where the reference point is set. If attitudes toward risk are determined more by perceived gains and losses than by outcomes, then this fact raises serious issues for assessing the rationality of risk averse attitudes, and more generally for reconciling behavioral theories of human choice with normative theories of rational choice.

Risk aversion also has important connections to theories of justice and EQUALITY. One utilitarian argument in favor of equalizing the distribution of important goods such as money, for example, is based on the assumption of individual diminishing marginal utility for such goods. If this assumption is generally true (and given some further assumptions about the shape and comparability of utility functions), then the overall aggregate of utility will be increased by redistributing goods such as money from those who have more to those who have less, or in the direction of greater equality. The connection between the assumption of diminishing marginal utility and risk aversion is that both concepts are expressed by the concavity of individual utility functions. Since attitudes toward risk define a utility function, then according to this theory, these attitudes are necessary to support this utilitarian argument for equalizing the distribution of goods. If people were in general risk neutral or risk preferring, then this kind of utilitarian argument for equality would not be available.

In John RAWLS's nonutilitarian theory of justice, inequalities in the distribution of basic social goods such as wealth and income must be justified by a "maximin" rule of social choice. This rule, which is expressed in Rawls's difference principle, says that the basic structure of social INSTITUTIONS in a just society should be arranged so that representative individuals who are made worst off by inequalities are nevertheless better off than the worst off would be under any alternative arrangement. Some of Rawls's critics charge that the difference principle is unreasonably risk averse. Decision theorists usually defend maximin rules of choice as reasonable only in situations of uncertainty, *i.e.,* situations where one has no idea about the probabilities of various outcomes. Where one can make a reasonable assessment of probabilities, a maximin principle seems in most cases to be an unreasonably cautious rule of choice. It is one thing to be risk averse, but it is something quite different to be willing to forgo any amount of expected benefits in order to avoid the worst possible outcome, no matter how improbable that outcome may be. Rawls, however, does not defend the maximin rule or the difference principle as a principle of reasonable risk aversion. He argues instead that the difference principle is the most reasonable principle of justice that can be chosen under fair conditions, by people who do not know in advance what their situation or INTERESTS will be, including their attitudes toward risk.

See also: BUSINESS ETHICS; ECONOMIC ANALYSIS; ECONOMIC SYSTEMS; EQUALITY; INEQUALITY; INTERESTS; JUSTICE, DISTRIBUTIVE; LIBERTY, ECONOMIC; LOGIC AND ETHICS; NEEDS; RATIONAL CHOICE; RISK; RISK ANALYSIS; UTILITARIANISM.

Bibliography

Arrow, Kenneth J. *Essays in the Theory of Risk-Bearing.* Chicago: Markham Publishing, 1971. A thorough, formal treatment of risk aversion in the theory of rational choice in economics.

Bernoulli, Daniel. "Specimen theoriae novae de mensura sortis." *Commentarii Academiae Scientiarum Imperiales Petropolitanae* 5 (1738): 175–92. Translated by Louise Sommer as "Exposition of a New Theory on the Measurement of Risk." *Econometrica* 22 (1954): 23–36. This essay is usually cited as the first statement of the concept of risk aversion. Bernoulli proposed a solution to the so-called St. Petersburg paradox by suggesting that the utility of money decreases as a function of wealth.

Broome, John. "Utilitarianism and Expected Utility." *The Journal of Philosophy* 84 (1987): 405–22. Explores the connection between risk aversion and decreasing marginal utility; describes some puzzles about uncertainty for utilitarian theory.

Friedman, M., and L. J. Savage. "The Utility Analysis of Choices Involving Risk." *Journal of Political Economy* 56 (1948): 279–304. This essay was one of the first formal treatments of risk attitudes in the theory of rational choice.

Harsanyi, John. "Morality and the Theory of Rational Behavior." In *Utilitarianism and Beyond,* edited by Amartya Sen and Bernard Williams, 39–62. Cambridge: Cambridge University Press, 1982. Harsanyi defends a social theory of rational choice and risk aversion, which he uses to criticize Rawls's maximin principle.

Kahneman, Daniel, and Amos Tversky. "Prospect Theory: An Analysis of Decision Under Risk." *Econometrica* 47 (1979): 263–91. Describes an emprically based behavioral theory of choice that includes discussion of the idea that attitudes toward risk vary according to whether outcomes are perceived as gains or losses.

Luce, Robert Duncan, and Howard Raiffa. *Games and Decisions.* New York: John Wiley, 1957. This classic work in decision theory gives a clear description of the formal theory of rational choice in chapter 2; discusses rational attitudes toward risk and uncertainty in chapter 13.

Ramsey, Frank P. "Truth and Probability." In *The Foundations of Mathematics and Other Logical Essays,* edited by R. B. Braithwaite, 156–98. London: K. Paul, Trench Trubner, 1931. Ramsey developed the method for measuring a person's utility and subjective probability for different outcomes by examining the person's preferences for different gambles.

Rawls, John. *A Theory of Justice.* Cambridge, Mass.: Harvard University Press, 1971. Rawls's discussion of the difference principle of justice for justifying inequalities in basic goods, and his interpretation of the maximin criterion of choice in a theory of justice are discussed in chapters 2 and 3, and especially in section 28.

Sidgwick, Henry. *The Methods of Ethics.* 7th ed. London: Macmillan, 1907 [1874]. Sidgwick gives a clear statement of the connection between utilitarianism, theories of justice, and the concept of diminishing marginal utility in book IV, chapter 1.

Douglas MacLean

Ross, W[illiam] D[avid] (1877–1971)

Distinguished scholar and influential moral philosopher. As a scholar Ross oversaw the Oxford translations of ARISTOTLE's (384–322 B.C.E.) works, published between 1908 and 1931. His own translations of the *Metaphysics* and the *Ethics* form an important part of this monumental project. Further Aristotelian scholarship includes his *Aristotle* (1923), which many still regard as the definitive overall exposition of Aristotle's thought available in English. In addition Ross wrote important studies of PLATO (c. 430–347 B.C.E.) (*Plato's Theory of Ideas,* 1951) and KANT (1724–1804) (*Kant's Ethical Theory,* 1954).

Ross's influence as an original thinker stems largely from two works in moral philosophy: *The Right and the Good* (1930), and *Foundations of Ethics* (1939). The former sets forth the broad outlines of his ethical theory; the latter, while it restates this theory, also contains Ross's replies to some of the major criticisms occasioned by the earlier work.

Ross's theory is intuitionistic. There are, he thinks, certain normative and evaluative propositions that are self-evidently true. Some of these propositions concern what is right, others, what is good. In both areas Ross is pluralistic. There is no one normative truth concerning what is right, and there is no one evaluative truth concerning what is good.

Ross's position regarding the good was strongly influenced by G. E. MOORE (1873–1958), especially the latter's *Principia Ethica* (1903). In this work Moore argues that the word 'good,' when used to mean "what is good in itself," names an indefinable, objective property. Ross agrees with Moore and agrees further when he argues for a plurality of intrinsic goods. Where Moore and Ross differ is over the correct list of these goods, with Ross naming knowledge, virtue and PLEASURE as the three great intrinsic goods, while Moore insists on a separate place for beauty.

While he follows Moore regarding the good, Ross diverges sharply form Moore's views regarding the right. In *Principia,* Moore maintains that "'right' does and can mean only 'cause of a good result'." Ross argues that 'right' does not mean anything of the kind and is in fact, like 'good,' the name of an indefinable, objective property. In this respect, as in others, Ross's thought was greatly influenced by the third member of the twentieth century's British intuitionists, H. A. PRICHARD (1871–1947).

Like Prichard, Ross believes we know that certain *kinds* of acts are morally right or morally wrong. More precisely, kinds of acts are known to be *prima facie* right or wrong (right or wrong, that is, in the absence of overriding considerations). For example, we know, according to Ross, that it is *prima facie* right to keep a promise and *prima facie* wrong to lie. In cases where rules of *prima facie* duty conflict, however, Ross is skeptical about the possibility of moral knowledge.

Although Ross's positive views are deeply colored by Moore's and Prichard's, he made important contributions of his own, not the least of which were his sustained, trenchant criticisms of ethical SUBJECTIVISM and UTILITARIANISM.

See also: ARISTOTLE; DUTY AND OBLIGATION; GOOD, THEORIES OF THE; INTUITIONISM; KANT; MOORE; MORAL PLURALISM; MORAL REALISM; MORAL RELATIVISM; PRICHARD; UTILITARIANISM.

Bibliography

Ross, W. D. *The Right and the Good.* Oxford: Oxford University Press, 1930.

———. *The Foundations of Ethics.* Oxford: Oxford University Press, 1939.

Tom Regan

Rousseau, Jean-Jacques (1712–1778)

Moralist, social theorist, essayist, composer, and novelist.

Background

Rousseau was born in Geneva to an artisan father and a mother from a wealthy family. His mother died at his birth. His father fled Geneva to avoid arrest after a dispute with a wealthy landowner, abandoning him at the age of ten to be raised by others. At sixteen Rousseau ran away from Geneva and began a series of travels and adventures that took him through the Savoy, Lyons, Paris, and Venice. His aspirations to literary success led to his first stay in Paris (1741), during which he began to make the acquaintance of the major figures of the French Enlightenment. When success arrived, it brought controversy and turmoil. His *Discourse on the Sciences and Arts* (1750) and *Discourse on the Origin of Inequality* (1755) earned him immediate recognition and a notoriety that culminated in 1762 with the publication of *Émile* and *On the Social Contract.* He was forced to flee Paris when both of these works were condemned, and shortly thereafter the works and their author were also banned from Geneva. His final years were difficult, in part because he thought himself the victim of persecution. He died in Ermenonville. The details of Rousseau's life are chronicled in his autobiographical *Confessions* (written c. 1770), and the later *Dialogues: Rousseau, Judge of Jean-Jacques* (1776) and *Reveries of a Solitary Walker* (written c. 1778).

The major works in social theory that Rousseau published in his lifetime include the *Discourse on the Sciences and Arts, Discourse on the Origin of*

Inequality, Discourse on Political Economy (1755), *On the Social Contract,* and *Émile.* Though many interpreters have found surface inconsistencies between these works, read together they do present a unified social theory. The *Discourse on the Origin of Inequality* provides a diagnosis of the ills of contemporary social life; *Émile,* a treatise on education, offers a psychological solution by describing the formative process that would render an individual immune to the corrupting influence of modern society; and *On the Social Contract* sketches a political solution to be found in the establishment of the right sort of democratic order. (Other important works beyond the scope of this essay are *Letter to D'Alembert on the Theater* [1758], *La Nouvelle Héloïse* [1761], *Letters Written from the Mountain* [1764], *Project for the Constitution of Corsica* [written 1765], and *Considerations on the Government of Poland* [written 1771].)

The First and Second Discourses

Written in response to questions published by the Academy of Dijon, the first two discourses constitute an attack on the supposed enlightenment of modern society. The *Discourse on the Sciences and Arts* denies that the restoration of the arts and sciences has contributed to the purity of morals, arguing that the luxury and refinement associated with progress in the arts and sciences corrupt tastes and distract from the cultivation of virtue. The *Discourse on the Origin of Inequality* advances these critical themes and develops the MORAL PSYCHOLOGY that is the basis of much of Rousseau's social theory. He sees social life as marked by inequalities of wealth and POWER and OPPRESSION by the privileged, and the very structure of social relations as a source of conflict. Individuals are driven by passions they cannot control, foremost among which is *amour-propre*—the tendency to value oneself above others and to distinguish oneself. These passions lead to the social vices of vanity, ENVY, duplicity, a consuming ambition, subservience to the opinions of others, etc. The question of the second *Discourse* is, "What is the origin of inequality among men, and is it authorized by natural law?" Rousseau maintains that the inequalities that seem inevitable in all social life are produced by social and political INSTITUTIONS, arguing that they are minimal in the state of nature. But his larger aim is the parallel thesis that individ-

ual vices and the disorders of social life are not due to inherent features of human PSYCHOLOGY; rather, they are caused by the relations of dependence and subordination that become formalized through the establishment of social and political institutions, and by the conflicts that they engender (both within and between individuals).

While a critique of society, the second *Discourse* thus "defends the cause of humanity" in that it attempts to reconcile the vices of individuals and disorders of social life with the natural goodness of humanity. ("Men are wicked . . . however man is naturally good.") It achieves these aims through a hypothetical account of the development of civilization, intended to show how the CORRUPTION of the present could have evolved from a state of nature in which these vices were absent. Rousseau criticizes earlier theorists for failing to distinguish what is original from what is social in our nature and for projecting the qualities of the social onto the natural individual. Like HOBBES (1588–1679), he depicts the original state of nature as a presocial condition in which individuals are completely independent and self-sufficient; but unlike Hobbes, he views it as tranquil. The rudimentary level of cognition keeps needs simple and easily satisfied, and since the instinct toward self-preservation is moderated by natural pity, it does not produce enduring conflict. Society develops as a kind of accident, with the FAMILY as the first and most harmonious form, followed by the discovery of agriculture and metallurgy, division of labor, the institution of PROPERTY, and the formal establishment of law and government. The introduction of more complex social and political forms increases relations of dependence among individuals and allows natural differences to translate into inequalities of power and privilege. Changes in social interaction in turn give rise to new forms of self-consciousness and new passions, transforming self-love, innocuous in the state of nature, into *amour-propre,* which is the source of the social vices.

An important theme that emerges is that our natural motivational structure (when left to develop without guidance) does little to prepare us for social life. Socialization both brings about and requires a radical transformation of the individual. The question that the *Discourse* raises is whether it is possible to prevent the process of socialization from deforming the individual. Both *Émile* and *On the Social*

Contract address this question, the former exploring a solution that focuses on the individual, the latter a solution that focuses on social institutions.

Émile

Rousseau's work on education is a philosophical novel whose central characters are the pupil, Émile, the tutor, Jean-Jacques, and Sophie, who appears in the final book as the woman Émile is to marry. It traces a scheme of individual development that is structurally parallel to the hypothetical development of civilization of the second *Discourse* and an education that respects the natural pattern of growth in human faculties. *Émile* describes the formation of an individual for whom the eventual transformation into a social individual would not be disfiguring. He must be an individual raised first of all to live for himself, suited to the job of living rather than of occupying a specific social station.

Jean-Jacques isolates Émile from certain kinds of social influence so that he will model the independence and self-sufficiency of the "natural" individual of the second *Discourse*. Specifically, Jean-Jacques must maintain an appropriate balance between Émile's needs and desires and his power to satisfy them; prevent him from acquiring concepts of domination and the extraction of services as the fundamental mode of relating to others; make him indifferent to the opinions, prejudices, and tastes of those with whom he associates; and retard the emergence of the passions, then direct their growth, so as to forestall the appearance of *amour-propre* and leave Émile capable of BENEVOLENCE and a sense of justice. Jean-Jacques's principal technique is to structure Émile's environment so that it creates an immediate interest in doing what is good and never presents incentives to vice. Émile is to be attracted to good by its perceived advantage, and the limits imposed on his conduct are to come from the necessity of things (inherent possibility and impossibility), and not the commands or AUTHORITY of other human beings. In this way Émile will experience the greatest freedom and lack of restraint throughout his youth and will not find virtue and interest to be in conflict; he will come to act as reason prescribes, without the authority of reason as his motive. But the shaping of Émile's desires and passions and his insensibility to opinion, in conjunction with the fact that he has never experienced the direction of reason as tyran-

nical, prepare him for eventually guiding himself by the authority of his own reason.

Aside from Émile's attachment to his tutor, Jean-Jacques defers significant social relationships as long as possible. Émile's passage into society begins in late adolescence, primarily with his introduction to sexuality, love, and marriage (the appearance of Sophie). By this time a core self exists that serves as a foundation onto which social ties may be built without deforming the individual. Because of the virtuous habits that have been established affectively in his earlier youth, Émile will be receptive to the self-restraint and maxims of reason required for social life and will be able to take on the duties of citizenship in an autonomous fashion.

On the Social Contract

Despite Rousseau's indictment of contemporary societies, he accepts the necessity of social life and recognizes that it is required for the perfection of the higher human faculties. *On the Social Contract* is a theory of political legitimacy that explores the extent to which the disorders described by the second *Discourse* can be rectified institutionally, by a democratic order in which all citizens actively participate in determining the conditions of their association. The problem set by *The Social Contract* is to find a form of association that confers the benefits of social life but avoids its disorders, by preserving the freedom, independence, and EQUALITY of the state of nature. Rousseau's solution is for all individuals to place themselves in common under the direction of the general will. The tensions apparent here with Rousseau's earlier emphasis on independence are partially resolved through an understanding of the key concept of the "general will" and of the active role of citizens in determining its content. The general will is the will of society as a whole concerning matters of common interest, and it takes the form of properly enacted laws. For a law resulting from political deliberation to be truly general and thus to count as a legitimate exercise of sovereignty, it must be "general in its object as well as in its essence"—it must benefit and burden all citizens equally and be directed at the COMMON GOOD (which is formed out of shared INTERESTS of individuals). The general will is to be determined through the actual operation of a properly structured political process in which all participate equally. A commitment to abide by the general will thus preserves independence and equality because the SOCIAL CONTRACT makes all citizens equally sovereign and subject, and benefits all equally. Moreover, citizens obey only laws they have chosen for themselves and are never subject to the private will of another.

The large part of *The Social Contract* develops the implications of Rousseau's theory of sovereignty and elaborates a theory of the political institutions required to determine and give effect to the general will. Rousseau's overall attitude toward DEMOCRACY is somewhat ambiguous, due in part to the distinction that he draws between sovereignty and government—that is, between legislative and executive power. He clearly held a democratic theory of sovereignty, which placed in the hands of all citizens supreme legislative authority as well as the power to elect government officials and in general to oversee the administration of the law. But he thought that an enlightened individual was needed to draft the system of legislation that the sovereign enacts, and favored an elective aristocracy as the best governmental form for the administration of law. Though there is some interpretive disagreement over how Rousseau would divide political power between the legislative and executive functions, one can conclude that his aim was a system of institutions conducive to the maintenance of the general will. He thought that LIBERTY was best preserved in an egalitarian state and espoused a social ideal of virtuous citizens united by shared mores, common interests, and ties of affection. Rousseau was not optimistic about the possibility of actualizing these ideals, for he recognized that democratic decisions can be unenlightened and that the private and factional interests of citizens will tend to subvert the general will. The success of his institutional solutions would seem to require the very individual psychology that they would have the aim of creating. But whether or not Rousseau's solution to his initial problem is ultimately satisfactory and fully consistent, *The Social Contract* is of lasting importance to democratic theory.

See also: COMMUNITARIANISM; CONTRACTARIANISM; DEMOCRACY; EQUALITY; HOBBES; INEQUALITY; LIBERTY; MORAL DEVELOPMENT; MORAL EDUCATION; MORAL PSYCHOLOGY; NATURAL LAW; PRIDE; SOCIAL AND POLITICAL PHILOSOPHY; SOCIAL CONTRACT.

Bibliography

Works by Rousseau

Oeuvres complètes. Edited by Bernard Gagnebin and Marcel Raymond. 5 vols. Bibliothèque de la Pléiade. Paris: Gallimard, 1959–1995. The standard French edition.

The Collected Writings of Rousseau. 8 vols. Edited by Roger D. Masters and Christopher Kelly. Hanover and London: University Press of New England, 1990–1998. An English edition of Rousseau's works.

The Confessions. In *The Confessions and Correspondence, Including the Letters to Malesherbes.* Vol. 5 of *The Collected Writings of Rousseau.* Translated by Christopher Kelly. Edited by Christopher Kelly, Roger D. Masters, and Peter G. Stillman. Hanover and London: University Press of New England, 1995 [1781–1788].

Constitutional Project for Corsica. In *Political writings: containing The Social Contract, Considerations on the Government of Poland, Constitutional Project for Corsica, Part I.* Translated and edited by Frederick Watkins. Madison: University of Wisconsin Press, 1986 [1765].

The Discourses and Other Early Political Writings. Edited and translated by Victor Gourevitch. Cambridge/New York: Cambridge University Press, 1997. Contains the first and second *Discourses* [1750; 1755], *Essay on the Origins of Language* [1852], and replies to critics. Includes an extensive bibliographical essay.

Émile, or On Education. Translated by Allan Bloom. New York: Basic Books, 1979 [1762].

Politics and the Arts: Letter to M. d'Alembert on the Theater. Translated by Allan Bloom. Ithaca: Cornell University Press, 1968 [1758].

The Reveries of a Solitary Walker. Translated by Charles E. Butterworth. New York: Harper and Row, 1979 [1782].

The Social Contract and Other Political Writings. Edited and translated by Victor Gourevitch. Cambridge and New York: Cambridge University Press, 1997. Contains *On the Social Contract* [1762], *Discourse on Political Economy* [1755], selections from *The Geneva Manuscript,* and *Considerations on the Government of Poland* [1782]. Includes an extensive bibliographical essay.

Works about Rousseau

Cohen, Joshua. "Reflections of Rousseau: Autonomy and Democracy." *Philosophy and Public Affairs* 15, no. 3 (1986): 275–97.

———. "The Natural Goodness of Humanity." In *Reclaiming the History of Ethics,* edited by Andrews Reath, Barbara Herman, and Christine Korsgaard. Cambridge and New York: Cambridge University Press, 1997.

Cranston, Maurice. *Jean-Jacques: The Early Life and Work of Jean-Jacques Rousseau, 1712–1754; The Noble Savage: Jean-Jacques Rousseau, 1754–1762;* and the third volume of his biography, *The Solitary Self: Jean-Jacques Rousseau in Exile and Adversity.* Chicago: University of Chicago Press, 1982, 1991, 1997.

Dent, N. J. H. *Rousseau.* Oxford: Blackwell, 1988.

Derathé, Robert. *Jean-Jacques Rousseau et la science politique de son temps.* Paris: J. Vrin, 1970.

Durkheim, Émile. *Montesquieu and Rousseau: Forerunners of Sociology.* Translated by Ralph Manheim. Ann Arbor: University of Michigan Press, 1960.

Ellenberg, Stephen. *Rousseau's Political Philosophy: An Interpretation from Within.* Ithaca: Cornell University Press, 1976.

Fralin, Richard. *Rousseau on Representation.* New York: Columbia University Press, 1978.

Gildin, Hilail. *Rousseau's Social Contract.* Chicago: University of Chicago Press, 1983.

Hendel, Charles H. *Jean-Jacques Rousseau: Moralist.* 2 vols. New York: Library of Liberal Arts, 1962.

Melzer, A.M. *The Natural Goodness of Man.* Chicago: University of Chicago Press, 1990.

Miller, James. *Rousseau: Dreamer of Democracy.* New Haven: Yale University Press, 1984.

Neuhouser, Frederick. "Freedom, Dependence, and the General Will." *The Philosophical Review* 102, no. 3 (1993): 363–95.

Shklar, Judith N. *Men and Citizens: A Study of Rousseau's Social Theory.* 2d ed. Cambridge: Cambridge University Press, 1985.

Starobinski, Jean. *Jean-Jacques Rousseau: Transparency and Obstruction.* Translated by Arthur Goldhammer. Chicago: University of Chicago Press, 1988.

Wokler, Robert. *Rousseau.* Oxford: Oxford University Press, 1995.

Andrews Reath

Royce, Josiah (1855–1916)

A preeminent American philosopher, Royce was a metaphysical thinker whose central concern was to provide an ontological grounding for MORAL REASONING. Giving voice to the moral idealism that one can garner from Immanuel KANT (1724–1804), Johann Gottlieb FICHTE (1762–1814), and Ralph Waldo EMERSON (1803–1882), Royce saw himself as fulfilling the pragmatist concern for action, for acknowledgment of the temporality of human experience, and for the concrete embodiment of the ideas we utilize in our continuing interpretation of the meaning of human experiences. Starting with a deliberate phenomenological stance, Royce was preoccupied with the temporalism that arose from the Kantian legacy (see Lowenberg). At the end of his career, Royce appropriated C. S. PEIRCE (1839–1914) in his thesis that ethical concerns are essentially communal because they structure the inherently social individuality we each express. Gabriel Marcel (1889–1973), the preeminent French philosopher, saw Royce as providing the bridge between German idealism and twentieth-century existentialism.

Royce's course of philosophic development found its expression in four major works.

The first major work, *The Religious Aspect of Philosophy* (1885), sees moral philosophy as entailing both a priority of 'ought' to 'is,' and a conception of morality concerned with MOTIVES.

The World and the Individual (1901), generally regarded to be his central work, sought to establish an idealist ontology in which the notion of 'The Absolute' was arguably not that of G. W. F. HEGEL (1770–1831), but more probably patterned after Emerson's Oversoul. Royce espoused a voluntaristic idealism that develops the concept of the self as an ultimate social reality in touch with a communally encompassing Reality, one that we all share but in which we "cannot be devoured by a barren Absolute."

The Philosophy of Loyalty (1908), perhaps Royce's best known work, may be read as an attempt to provide Kantian moral FORMALISM with a principle of concrete content. This proposal comes closest to the kinds of specific ethical injunctions Royce proposed. These injunctions result in an ethics of self-realization that is ontologically grounded while it seeks, within the primacy of motivation and the autonomy of the will, to pragmatically coalesce motives with the consequent actions that are necessary to its fulfillment.

The Problem of Christianity (1913), explains the meaning of an 'atonement ethic' (already anticipated in *The World and the Individual*). Incorporating the Christian doctrine of Atonement into moral philosophy, Royce developed his continuing attempt to reconcile the polarities of the human experience—individuality and sociality. The ethic of 'vicarious atonement' incorporates the intrinsic temporal structure Royce saw in the fabric of human existence: individual acts are rooted in a historic process, the MORAL DEVELOPMENT of the future. Redeeming the wrongs of the past provides a more fruitful impetus to the ongoing moral development of the human community. The notion of 'historic community' thus replaces any notion of 'causality' in moral discourse. Ideally, morally committed individuals take up their inheritance as presenting a task framing the scope of their own efforts to contribute to what can be rendered out of it.

Royce's moral commitment was to an ethical view of human existence and to the need to recognize that moral struggles, epitomized in individual moral commitments, are part of a historic process out of which forms the ethical inheritance of FUTURE GENERATIONS.

See also: COMMUNITARIANISM; EMERSON; EXISTENTIAL ETHICS; FICHTE; FORMALISM; IDEALIST ETHICS; KANT; LOYALTY; METAPHYSICS AND EPISTEMOLOGY; MORAL REASONING; MOTIVES; PEIRCE; PRAGMATISM.

Bibliography

Works by Royce

The Religious Aspect of Philosophy. Boston, 1885.
The World and the Individual. 2 vols. Peter Smith, 1976 [1901]. See vol. 1, p. 415; vol. 2, p. 343.
The Philosophy of Loyalty. New York: Macmillan, 1908.
The Problem of Christianity. 2 vols. New York: Macmillan, 1916 [1913].

Works about Royce

Clendenning, John. *The Life and Thought of Josiah Royce.* Madison: University of Wisconsin Press, 1985.
Fuss, Peter. *The Moral Philosophy of Josiah Royce.* Cambridge: Harvard University Press, 1965.
Kuklick, Bruce. *Josiah Royce: An Intellectual Biography.* Indianapolis, IN: Bobbs-Merrill, 1972.
Lowenberg, J., ed. Introduction to *Fugitive Essays by Josiah Royce.* Cambridge: Harvard University Press, 1925.
Mahowald, Mary Briody. *An Idealistic Pragmatism: The Development of the Pragmatic Element in the Philosophy of Josiah Royce.* The Hague: Martinus Nijhoff, 1972.
Marcel, Gabriel. *Royce's Metaphysics.* Translated by Virginia Ringer and Gordon Ringer. Chicago: Henry Regnery, 1956 [1918–1919]. Reprint, Westport, CT: Greenwood, 1975.
Sherover, Charles M. "Royce's Pragmatic Idealism and Existential Phenomenology." In *Pragmatism Considers Phenomenology,* edited by Robert S. Corrington, Carl Hausman, and Thomas M. Seebohm. Washington, DC: University Press of America, 1987.
Smith, John E. *Royce's Social Infinite: The Community of Interpretation.* New York: Liberal Arts Press, 1950.
———. *The Spirit of American Philosophy.* Oxford: Oxford University Press, 1963.

Charles M. Sherover

Russell, Bertrand [Arthur William] (1872–1970)

One of the most influential thinkers of the twentieth century. Enormously productive, Russell made significant contributions to logic and the foundations of mathematics, the theory of knowledge, the philosophy of science, and almost every branch of philosophy. He was also renowned for the graceful and witty style in which he expressed his ideas. His reputation is primarily based on books and articles written between 1903 and 1921—*The Principles of Mathematics* (1903), *Philosophical Essays* (1910), *Principia mathematica* (3 vols., 1910–1913, with A. N. Whitehead), *The Problems of Philosophy* (1912), *Our Knowledge of the External World* (1914), "The Philosophy of Logical Atomism" (1918), *Mysticism and Logic* (1918), *Introduction to Mathematical Philosophy* (1919), and *The Analysis of Mind* (1921). During the period between the two world wars he wrote numerous books of a nontechnical nature on political, social, historical, and religious topics. Russell's popular books—of which *Marriage and Morals* (1929) is probably the most famous, and the magnificent history of the nineteenth century, *Freedom and Organization 1814–1914* (1934), is the most unjustly neglected—brought him a huge worldwide audience. Not since VOLTAIRE (1694–1778) has there been a philosopher with such an impact on the thinking of educated people throughout the world. Like Voltaire, Russell was the target of a great deal of abuse and persecution, which culminated in the annulment of his appointment at the City College of New York in 1940 by a bigoted judge who found that Russell's presence would be a menace to the "health and morals" of students. Russell's work was, however, fully appreciated by scholarly societies. In 1908 he was elected a Fellow of the Royal Society and in 1950 he was awarded the Nobel Prize for Literature. In making the award the Nobel committee cited Russell as "one of our time's most brilliant spokesmen of rationality and humanity."

Russell was a passionate advocate of certain moral positions, but he also repeatedly addressed himself to metamoral issues. In his first important essay on the subject, "The Elements of Ethics" (1910), he defended an objectivism closely akin to that of G. E. MOORE's (1873–1958) *Principia ethica* (1903). "*Good* and *bad*," he wrote, "are qualities which belong to objects independently of our opinions, just as much as *round* and *square* do; and when two people differ as to whether a thing is good, only one of them can be right, though it may be very hard to know which is right." Russell was not unaware of the wide appeal of the familiar arguments for SUBJECTIVISM—the "divergence of opinion" on moral questions and the difficulty of "finding arguments to persuade people who differ from us in such a question." He did not then regard these arguments as having any logical force. "Difficulty in discovering the truth," he wrote, "does not prove that there is no truth to be discovered." Russell totally rejected the comparison of moral disagreement with a difference in taste. "As a matter of fact," he observed, "we consider some tastes better than others: we do not hold merely that some tastes are ours and other tastes are other people's."

"The Elements of Ethics" was published in the first edition of *Philosophical Essays* (1910). In a preface to the 1966 edition, Russell explained that he no longer believed in "objective values" as he did when the essay was originally published. "The Elements of Ethics" had also been reprinted in 1952 in *Readings in Ethical Theory,* a book edited by Wilfrid Sellars and John Hospers. Russell added a footnote there in which he explained that the change in his views was originally due to SANTAYANA's (1863–1952) criticisms in his *Winds of Doctrine* (1913), adding that he "found confirmation" for his later position "in many other directions." It is worth pointing out that the abandonment of the objectivity of values occurred at about the same time as the rejection of Platonism and the synthetic *a priori.*

The first of Russell's anti-objectivist views was stated in a posthumously published paper entitled "Is There an Absolute Good?" According to Alan Ryan, the paper was probably written in 1922 and read to "The Society" ("the Apostles") at Cambridge in March of that year. Russell here proposed what has come to be known as the "error" theory, which is primarily associated with the writings of John Mackie (1719–1981). Moore, writes Russell, "is

right, I think, in holding that when we say a thing is good we do not *merely* mean that we have towards it a certain feeling, of liking or approval or what not. There seems to me no doubt that our ethical judgments claim objectivity." Our moral judgments *claim* objectivity, but there is no such objectivity and hence all our moral judgments are false. Moore was both right and wrong—he was right about what we *mean.* In calling something good we do ascribe an objective characteristic to it, but no such objective characteristic exists. Russell did not seem to realize that this theory involves a wild paradox. It implies that if, for example, we assert that the Nazi persecution of the Jews was EVIL, what we say is just as false as the assertion that it was a good thing. It is surely most implausible to maintain that all moral judgments are false. What is not implausible is the view that the ordinary person vaguely holds the metamoral theory that goodness and badness are objective characteristics and this *meta*moral theory is mistaken.

The error theory does not reappear in Russell's later writings. In all of them he defends what he calls "the doctrine of the subjectivity of values." In direct contradiction to what he maintained in the 1910 paper, Russell wrote in 1955 that "in a universe devoid of sentience" nothing would have value. "The fundamental data of ethics" are "feelings and emotions, not percepts" (*Human Society in Ethics and Politics*). In the 1922 paper, he had held that Moore was at least right about what we *mean* by ethical predicates. This view is now also repudiated. "There are no facts of ethics" (*Power,* 1938) and hence ethical judgments do not possess any property "analogous to truth." From the 1930s on, Russell became convinced that, grammatical appearances notwithstanding, ethical judgments are not statements or assertions at all, but *expressions* of DESIRE. "A judgment of intrinsic value," he writes in *Power,* "is to be interpreted, not as an assertion, but as an expression of desire concerning the desires of mankind. When I say 'hatred is bad,' I am really saying: 'would that no one felt hatred.' I make no assertion; I merely express a certain type of wish." It is evident that Russell here advocates a position that is very similar to the emotive theory of the logical positivists, but it was arrived at independently.

In several places Russell discusses and rejects "psychological hedonism," by which he means the view that everybody does, and inevitably must, pursue his own pleasure and nothing else. Psychological HEDONISM is false both because what we frequently desire is not PLEASURE but certain objects (*e.g.,* food when we are hungry), and also because not all desires are selfish. Human beings often desire the welfare of others—their children, friends, and animals. The objects of their desires may even lie "wholly outside their own lives." This point is important to the understanding of moral judgments because what they express are "impersonal" desires. If I say that freedom of speech is a good thing, my statement is a genuine moral judgment if it expresses my desire for everybody's freedom, not just my own. In this connection Russell also observes that the philosophers who stressed the "universality" of moral principles were in a sense quite right. This universality, however, does not consist in any *a priori* character or logical necessity. What is universal is the *object of the desire* expressed by a moral judgment. "This wish, as an occurrence, is personal, but what it desires is universal. . . . It is this curious interlocking of the particular and the universal which has caused so much confusion in ethics" (*Religion and Science,* 1935).

The main reason for favoring the subjectivity of values is not the *actual* moral disagreement among people but the *undecidability* of disputes about values. In ethics there is not, Russell writes, as in science "a recognized technique for resolving disagreements" (*Human Society in Ethics and Politics*). It is true that we cannot prove to a color-blind man that grass is green, but there are various ways of showing him that he lacks a certain power of discrimination. In the case of values, on the other hand, "there are no such ways." If three people argue, one saying "The good is pleasure," the second "The good is pleasure for Aryans and pain for Jews," and the third "The good is to praise God and glorify Him forever," they cannot, as people engaged in scientific dispute, "appeal to facts," for facts, it seems obvious, "are not relevant to the dispute" (*Power*).

In the discussions of the 1930s, Russell did not express any misgivings about the soundness of his subjectivism in ethics, but from 1945 on he repeatedly stated that his theory was somehow unsatisfac-

tory. The main reason seems to have been that he thought he was doing more than just expressing his own desire when taking up his various moral positions. "While my own opinions as to ethics do not satisfy me," he wrote in 1945, "other people's satisfy me still less" ("A Reply to My Critics"). Over ten years later, in the course of replying to Philip Toynbee's review of *Why I Am Not a Christian,* Russell confessed that although he finds his own views "argumentatively irrefutable," they nevertheless seem to him "incredible," adding that he does not know the solution.

See also: CIVIL DISOBEDIENCE; DESIRE; GOOD, THEORIES OF THE; HEDONISM; LOGIC AND ETHICS; MORAL ABSOLUTES; MYSTICISM; PACIFISM; PLEASURE; RELIGION; SANTAYANA; SUBJECTIVISM; VALUE, CONCEPT OF.

Bibliography

Works by Russell

"Is There an Absolute Good?" *Russell: The Journal of the Bertrand Russell Archives* 6 (1986–1987). Introductory note by Alan Ryan.

"The Elements of Ethics." In *Readings in Ethical Theory,* edited by Wilfrid Sellars and John Hospers. New York: Appleton-Century-Crofts, 1952.

The most detailed defenses of Russell's subjectivism are found in his *Religion and Science* (1935); *Power* (1938); "Reply to My Critics" in *The Philosophy of Bertrand Russell,* edited by Paul Arthur Schilpp (Evanston: Northwestern University Press, 1944; 5th ed., La Salle, Ill.: Open Court, 1989); *Human Society in Ethics and Politics* (1955). In the last, he combines his subjectivism with a utilitarian account of "right."

Works about Russell

Ayer, A. J. *Bertrand Russell.* New York: Viking, 1972.

Edwards, Paul. "Russell, Bertrand Arthur William." In *The Encyclopedia of Philosophy,* edited by Paul Edwards. New York: Macmillan, 1967. See the section on "Ethics and the Critique of Religion."

Monro, D. H. "Russell's Moral Theories." *Philosophy.* 1960.

Ruja, Harry. "Russell on the Meaning of 'Good'." *Russell: The Journal of the Bertrand Russell Archives.* 1984.

Paul Edwards

S

saints, moral

See moral saints.

Santayana, George (1863–1952)

Spanish-born American philosopher. "The first principle of my ethics is relativity," wrote Santayana in 1940 (*"Apologia pro mente sua"*). Perhaps the best statement of this relativism is the section of his essay on Bertrand RUSSELL (1872–1970) in *Winds of Doctrine* (1913; chapter IV, section 4) in which he criticizes the intuitionist ethics that Russell then shared with G. E. MOORE (1873–1958) and that Russell abandoned partly as a result of this critique. Santayana effectively endorses the Moorean claim that the key concepts in ethics are those of intrinsic good and bad (though he seldom mentions the latter) and agrees that these are real indefinable qualities we encounter in our experience of the world. However, he thinks it absurd to suppose that they are there independently of our awareness of them. Rather, they are features of things as they must present themselves to someone whose will is directed toward or away from them. Rational moral thinking is an attempt to bring into clearer focus, develop the internal logic of, and grasp the practical demands imposed by the values proper to one's own will.

Thus nothing is good or bad in itself in the sense of being so apart from a will directed toward or away from it; yet these are real qualities or essences present in the world as presented to us. (This is almost the view that they are secondary qualities, though Santayana's final position can only be understood in the context of the theory of essences of *Realms of Being* [1927–1940].) The idea is not that a man who says that something is good *means* that it stands in a certain relation to himself. Rather he usually *means* that it possesses that quality inherently. But the philosopher should realize that it only has this quality of goodness for a mind with a will with a certain definite bent.

One who realizes the relativity of values should develop a certain tolerance of divergent ethical opinion and respect the opposed activities of others as being directed at what is as truly good for them as what he pursues is for him. However, Santayana was strongly opposed to a LIBERALISM that puts all values on a par. Each must promote his own values, but his battle on their behalf should be conducted with chivalry to those in pursuit of alternative, equally valid values of their own. However, no system of values can be fully actualized unless there is a unified culture in which it is cherished, and Santayana often criticized the liberal ideal as one of a society in which no values are adequately sustained.

From *The Life of Reason* (1905–1906) onward, Santayana distinguished three main types of morality: prerational, rational, and postrational. (A morality of the second kind is only an aspiration; all we actually have is the idea of it, which Santayana calls rational ethics.) A prerational morality is that of a society whose moral principles reflect judgments of value stemming from a variety of more or less fundamental human needs, but it has no conscious overall rationale and is often in conflict with itself. A postrational morality is a way of life, arising from disillusion with what life at large may offer, in which everything is organized around the pursuit of some one single liberating goal (*e.g.,* PLEASURE, knowledge, mystical detachment, salvation). A rational morality would be one in which the maximum of human impulses could find their satisfaction and in which the claims of each were adjusted (or if necessary denied) so that they harmonized with those of the others. For a rational morality no object of DESIRE would be other than good in itself, but it might have to give way to the good of reason. Thus reason is the pervasive—if seldom very successful—impulse toward a form of life in which every known impulse (one's own dormant impulses and those of others included) that one can represent to oneself in imagination can find its good, so far as the impulse can be brought into harmony with that of others.

As a philosopher, Santayana refused to side with one moral outlook against another, but his allegiance was mainly to rational ethics, and the extent to which this outlook has been developed in various aspects of human life was the theme of *The Life of Reason.* In his later work (from 1927 onward), however, he turned his attention more toward a postrational morality in which a spiritual life of pure intuition is the dominant aim. His hope, however, was for a rational morality in which this spiritual life is given a prominent place.

It is likely to be objected today that Santayana's belief, that ethical relativism shows that we should ascribe a value worthy of some respect to the object of every impulse, is confused and that the proper conclusion is that value can only be ascribed from a particular MORAL POINT OF VIEW. But Santayana's position is subtler than such criticism would recognize. He shares the view of William JAMES (1842–1910) and Josiah ROYCE (1855–1916) that to realize in imagination how the world presents itself to one with values other than one's own is necessarily to achieve some sympathy with those values. For the icons of those alien values in one's own mind must have some influence on one's attitudes. Thus concrete realization of the truth of relativism will lead to mutual respect between those who have different moral outlooks. As Santayana sees it from his own

moral perspective, however, such mutual respect goes too far when individuals and societies are so influenced by this truth that they fail to cherish, promote, and protect the values proper to their own dispositions.

See also: EXTERNALISM AND INTERNALISM; GOOD, THEORIES OF THE; INTUITIONISM; JAMES; MOORE; MORAL IMAGINATION; MORAL POINT OF VIEW; MORAL RELATIVISM; MYSTICISM; RATIONAL CHOICE; ROYCE; VALUE, THEORY OF.

Bibliography

Works by Santayana

The Works of George Santayana. Edited by Herman J. Saatkamp. 19 vols. projected. Cambridge: MIT Press, 1986–. Collected works.

The Life of Reason; Or, The Phases of Human Progress. 2d ed. 5 vols. New York: Scribner's, 1922 [1905–1906].

Realms of Being. 1 vol. ed. New York: Cooper Square, 1972 [1927–1940]. *The Realm of Essence. The Realm of Matter. The Realm of Truth. The Realm of Spirit.*

Scepticism and Animal Faith: Introduction to a System of Philosophy. New York: Scribner's, 1923.

Works about Santayana

Lachs, John. *George Santayana.* Boston: Twayne, 1988.

Munitz, Milton Karl. *The Moral Philosophy of Santayana.* New York: Humanities Press, 1958.

Schilpp, Paul Arthur, ed. *The Philosophy of George Santayana.* Library of Living Philosophers, vol. 2. Evanston, IL: Northwestern University Press, 1940. Critical essays; autobiography; reply; bibliography.

Singer, Beth J. *The Rational Society: A Critical Study of Santayana's Social Thought.* Cleveland, OH: Press of Case Western Reserve University, 1970.

Sprigge, Timothy L. S. *Santayana: An Examination of His Philosophy.* London: Routledge and Kegan Paul, 1974.

Timothy L. S. Sprigge

Sartre, Jean-Paul (1905–1980)

French philosopher, novelist, and dramatist. Born June 21, 1905, in Paris, Jean-Paul Sartre was educated at the lycées Henri IV and Louis-le-Grand in Paris and at the École Normale Supérieure. After several years teaching in lycées, interrupted by a year at the French Institute in Berlin (1933), military service, and nearly a year in a concentration camp after the fall of France in 1940, he devoted the rest of his life to philosophical, literary, and political activity, including editing the review *Les Temps modernes,* which he founded (1945) with Simone DE BEAUVOIR (1908–1986) and Maurice Merleau-Ponty (1908–1961). He refused the Legion of Honor (1945) and the Nobel Prize (1964). He died in Paris on April 15, 1980.

It is now common to divide the ethical theory of Jean-Paul Sartre into three phases: (a) his vintage existentialist ethic of AUTHENTICITY of the 1940s and 1950s; (b) his dialectical ethic of the 1960s; and (c) the ethic of the "we" that he was in the process of formulating at the time of his death. His first ethic is most fully articulated and has had the greatest philosophical influence.

Ethic of Authenticity

"Authenticity," Sartre claims, "consists in having a true and lucid consciousness of the situation, in assuming the responsibilities and risks that it involves, in accepting it in pride or humiliation, sometimes in horror and hate" (*Anti-Semite and Jew,* 1946). Some have claimed that the only existentialist "virtue" is authenticity. This claim is true to the extent that Sartre insists we have no human nature that might serve as a moral norm, but only a human condition (we are born, find ourselves in a maze of *de facto* conditions, including our consciousness that throws us beyond these conditions, and we die). We are thus free in the sense of being "other" than and temporally "beyond" our conditions. Yet we are free only *in a situation;* consciousness-freedom does not float above its conditions (facticity) but constitutes them as facticity by its very move beyond them (transcendence): the rock appears too steep only in regard to my project of scaling it.

The basis of Sartrean ethics, then, is ontological—the "inner distance" by which consciousness "transcends" its facticity, conferring on facticity whatever meaning it has by subsuming it into consciousness. We are thus "responsible" for our situation, whatever it may be. This RESPONSIBILITY, though ontological in that it characterizes us as constitutors of a "world" of meanings and values, slips into the moral realm when linked with authenticity and BAD FAITH.

The same nonself-coincidence that grounds our freedom also makes possible a "truncated igno-rance," an "ignorance which knows better," that Sartre called "bad faith." This is the major form of inauthenticity: denial of the freedom and responsibility that mark our ontological condition as human. Thus, the "perfect waiter" who imitates the gestures and solicitude of his ideal, without acknowledging his freedom-responsibility in sustaining this behavior, lives in bad faith. Consciousness is always "ahead" of itself; human reality always (prereflectively) comprehends more than it (reflectively) knows. The waiter is responsible for his ignorance; he is trying to be what he is in the way a stone is a stone, that is, in the thing-like manner of being-in-itself.

"A man can always make something out of what is made of him" (*Between Existentialism and Marxism*). This is the maxim of Sartrean humanism. That same freedom (coextensive with consciousness) that brings the givens of our situation into the purview of our project enables us to alter their significance if we so choose. Inauthenticity takes either of two forms. One collapses our transcendence into facticity like the perfect waiter. Such is the nature of all determinisms. By denying the specificity of consciousness as transcendence, they reduce being-for-itself to being-in-itself, culture to nature. The other kind of inauthenticity evaporates facticity into transcendence, the past into the future, the givens of a situation into our projective interpretations. In both cases there is an unwillingness to live the *tension* generated by our freedom-in-situation. Conversely, the choice of just such a tension, of freedom as the basis of whatever meaning or value inhabits our world, of the contingency of our projects and all they entail—this is existentialist authenticity. Like Sartre's image of the writer, Jean Genet, we can be neither pure subject nor pure object but must "have the courage to go to the limits of ourselves in both directions at once" (*Saint Genet,* 1952).

Authenticity, creatively living this contingency of our ongoing choices, is thus more an ethical *style* than a content. Indeed, to pin it down to a determinate content would solidify it into the realm of the in-itself, where, according to Sartre, traditional ethical principles and moral maxims obtain. Such value commitment exhibits what Sartre calls "the spirit of seriousness," another form of bad faith. And yet he counsels us to choose freedom. Indeed, he insists that "the actions of men of good faith have, as their ultimate signification, the quest of freedom itself as such," that is, the willing of "freedom for freedom's sake in each particular circumstance" (*Existentialism Is a Humanism,* 1946). Sartre's defense of this claim is disputed, but it rests on the ontological thesis that freedom (consciousness) is the source of all value and that in choosing anything, we, by that fact alone, choose freedom. Sartre's additional claim that "I cannot take my freedom for an end [in the sense just described] unless I take that of others for an end" (*Existentialism Is a Humanism*) raises the claim of human community and calls for a new, dialectical ethic of disalienation and RECIPROCITY.

Dialectical Ethic

Sartre understood that the "situation" that human reality constitutes is social (but not necessarily Hobbesian) in nature, and that one cannot be free in any concrete sense unless the socioeconomic conditions that mediate interpersonal relations facilitate rather than deflect positive *reciprocity* among agents. This understanding led to a series of essays and unpublished collections of notes that develop the premise that ethics was both inevitable and impossible in a capitalist and neo-colonialist age such as ours: inevitable because the norm of absolute freedom is implicit in every human act (*praxis*); impossible because material scarcity and the class struggle that responds to it harden this norm into the inertia of traditional values and reiterated imperatives—the very alienation of "integral man" (*praxes* recognizing one another as such) that now emerges as Sartre's ethical ideal. This phase was the period of his "amoral realism" when he advocated "direct action" as counterviolence against a system that institutionalizes violence and EXPLOITATION.

Ethic of the "We"

The breaks between Sartre's ethics are not sharp. The posthumously published *Notebooks for an Ethics,* written in 1947–1948 and elaborating the ethic of authenticity, stresses the value of fraternity and positive reciprocity advocated in the second ethic. *Being and Nothingness* (1943) already announces the project of "freeing the whole 'Us' from its object-state by transforming it into a We-subject." But only in his last years did Sartre undertake the formulation of his third ethic, which focused on the "interpenetration" of consciousnesses in what he calls relations of "fraternity" ("Last Words," 1980). This undertaking, which grappled with the conflict between fraternity and violence in a society of material scarcity, was cut short by his death.

See also: ABSURD, THE; ALIENATION; AUTHENTICITY; BAD FAITH; CAMUS; DE BEAUVOIR; EXISTENTIAL ETHICS; FREEDOM AND DETERMINISM; HUMANISM; PRAXIS; RECIPROCITY; SELF-DECEPTION; SITUATION ETHICS.

Bibliography

Works by Sartre

Anti-Semite and Jew. Translated by George J. Becker. New York: Schocken, 1948 [1946]. Most extensive discussion of authenticity, inauthenticity. (Passage quoted in text of article is from p. 90.)

Being and Nothingness. Translated by Hazel E. Barnes. New York: Philosophical Library, 1956 [1943]. Translation of *L'Être et le néant.* Phenomenological ontology grounding his ethics of authenticity (p. 422).

Between Existentialism and Marxism. Translated by John Mathews. New York: William Morrow, 1974. Interviews and essays from his dialectical period. (Quotation is from p. 35.)

"Existentialism Is a Humanism." Translated by Philip Mairet. In *Existentialism from Dostoevsky to Sartre,* edited by Walter Kaufmann, 287–311. Cleveland, Ohio: World Publishing, 1956 [1946]. Translation of *L'Existentialism est un humanisme;* responsibility as social (pp. 307, 308).

"The Last Words of Jean-Paul Sartre." Translated by Adrienne Foulke. *Dissent* (Fall 1980): 397–422. Sketch for an ethic of the "We" (p. 414).

Notebooks for an Ethics. Translated by David Pellauer. Chicago: University of Chicago Press, 1992. Posthumously published notes for an ethic of authenticity. [Translation of *Cahiers pour une morale,* written 1946–1947.]

Saint Genet, Actor and Martyr. Translated by Bernard Frechtman. New York: George Braziller, 1963 [1952]. Genet as model of existential good faith (p. 599).

"Entretien." With Michel Sicard. *Obliques,* no. 18–19 (1979): 9–29. Elements of his third ethic.

Works about Sartre

Anderson, Thomas C. *The Conditions and Structure of Sartrean Ethics.* Lawrence: Regents Press of Kansas, 1979. Dependable analysis of Sartre's arguments.

———. *Sartre's Two Ethics: From Authenticity to Integral Humanity.* Chicago: Open Court, 1993.

Barnes, Hazel E. *An Existentialist Ethics.* New York: Vintage, 1967. Original essay inspired by Sartre.

Bell, Linda A. *Sartre's Ethics of Authenticity.* Tuscaloosa: University of Alabama Press, 1989. Reconstruction of the first ethic.

de Beauvoir, Simone. *The Ethics of Ambiguity.* Translated by Bernard Frechtman. New York: Citadel, 1964 [1947]. Classic commentary on and development of Sartre's theses.

Flynn, Thomas R. *Sartre and Marxist Existentialism: The Test Case of Collective Responsibility.* Chicago: University of Chicago Press, 1984. The aporiae of an existentialist social ethic.

Jeanson, Francis. *Sartre and the Problem of Morality.* Bloomington: Indiana University Press, 1980 [1947]. Early, classic study.

Kruks, Sonia. "Sartre's *Cahiers pour une morale.*" *Social Text,* no. 13/14 (Winter/Spring 1986): 184–94.

Stone, Robert, and Elizabeth Bowman. "Dialectical Ethics: A First Look at Sartre's Unpublished 1964 Rome Lecture Notes." *Social Text,* no. 13/14 (Winter/Spring 1986): 195–215.

Thomas R. Flynn

scepticism

See skepticism in ethics; skepticism in ancient ethics.

Scheler, Max [Ferdinand] (1874–1928)

Max Scheler was born in Munich on August 22, 1874, to a Jewish mother and Lutheran father. He taught philosophy at Jena, Munich, and Cologne universities. After a dramatic life, he died in Frankfurt on May 19, 1928.

In Europe, Asia, and the Americas, Scheler's *Formalism* (1913/16) is considered to be foundational on four accounts:

1. It is the first attempt to put ethics on a phenomenological footing.

2. It argues that, while formal laws of logic hold among values as formal objects, such laws fail in value experience. In this, Scheler's work is the culmination of a long, albeit neglected tradition first articulated by Blaise PASCAL (1623–1662): that our innermost feelings have, independently of reason, a logic of their own.

3. It appears to disprove a general assumption which reached its apogee in KANT (1724–1804) that feelings are chaotic and need to be brought under the control of reason.

4. It questions whether imperatives and definitions of the moral good can improve the moral status of humanity.

In Scheler's view, values, like any other phenomena, are instantaneous givens (*noemata*) in particular acts of consciousness. Just as colors are given in acts of seeing, values are given in feelings. Moreover, values are experienced prior to any other data in consciousness. This view implies a basic tenet in *Formalism:* whatever "ought" to be, or to be done, must already have gone through an experience of its value, no matter how unnoticed. Therefore, the determination of emotive experience is indispensable for the clarification of moral comportment, the "person," and the origin of moral experience in value feelings: man's *ordo amoris.* Values, like colors, have no existence unless they occur on substrates, but they are, nevertheless, independent of the latter. Thus, the value "holy" may occur with a person or a fetish, just as the color "green" may occur with a stone or a lawn.

The origin of moral experience lies in the essence of LOVE, the *ordo amoris* of the human being. It resembles a "crystal," says Scheler, reflecting the order of ranks in the spectrum of values toward which love is directed, or not directed as in all forms of HATE and RESENTMENT. Initially, values are "*a priori* felt" equally by all human beings in this hidden order of the human "heart," before values become objects of conjecture, judgment, *etc.,* in the domain of reason and everyday life. Nonetheless, in practice, the *ordo amoris* is always refracted in each individual person's moral life, in individual directions of intentions, acts, and deeds. In this point *Formalism* departs from Kant's categorical imperative as well as from all universalism found in the history of ethics. In their stead, Scheler reinstates what he refers to as the "value of all values," *i.e.,* the individual person. He reinstates as well the significance of the "call of the hour" (*kairos*), no matter how grave or trivial moral situations may be in which the call imposes itself on the person.

According to Scheler, there are five different contents in ("material") value ranks, arranged in two groups, from lowest to highest. First, those relative to life: (1) PLEASURE, (2) utility, and (3) life values; and second, values of the person: (4) those of the mind (justice, beauty, cognition of truth) and (5) the value of holiness. Good and EVIL do not belong to these ranks because they "ride on the back" of realizing in acts of preferring (or rejecting) higher (lower) values. "Preferring" originates in the person's "heart" or moral tenor rather than in the will or in reason. Moral goodness, then, appears in any "call of the hour" of a person's value realizations stemming from the moral tenor's pristine preferring, say, of values of the person, like justice, over sensual pleasure values. The emotive order of values is also reflected in all negative values: physical pain is sharply distinguished from the personal injuries like injustice and pangs of CONSCIENCE. The former are reasonably manageable, the latter are not.

Whereas in *Ideas I* (1913) HUSSERL (1859–1938) elaborated on acts of consciousness in general, Scheler in *Formalism*, independently of Husserl, elaborated on the individual's execution of acts: the "person." For, in practice, there is no consciousness without being "in person." And every person has his or her own "qualitative direction" of acting out acts, making the person morally irreplaceable, the value of all values, indifferent to race and gender and pure temporality.

This view bears on moral experience in two ways: First, as an "embodied" person, act-executions span all five value ranks. Second, since the person is bearer of all values, to each rank there corresponds an ideal "model person." In ascending order, they are: the master in the art of living, the leader of civilization, the hero, the genius, and the saint. They are the most effective and hidden vehicles in education and history. As pure exemplars, however, they have, like values, no existence of their own, but occur only with individual persons in multiple variations that, in turn, are the result also of social, cultural, and historical conditions. Each imperfect person, and group, is drawn to one such personal paradigm, owing, however, always to the latter's pure exemplarity.

The person, then, is not primarily rational and volitional (Kant), but rather a being of love (*ens amans*), tacitly drawn toward ever higher values. This is the *a priori*, hidden power of love. Notwithstanding value deceptions (*e.g.*, in resentment feelings), the order of values remains as translucent as light is in darkness. This conclusion is reflected in the net result of *Formalism*: that all persons ought to be equal as to lower value ranks (*e.g.*, equal distribution of material goods) but, as to higher values, all persons are, in their individual uniqueness, different and unequal. For DEMOCRACY "on earth" does not preclude aristocracy "in heaven."

While the person varies in every act individually as well as by dint of the group a person belongs to, and while good and evil echo value realizations, the dynamic becoming of personhood in every act is further illustrated by four social forms of human togetherness: the mass, the life community, society, and the collective personality. In ascending order, there is ever more personalization of the individual endowed with both self- and CO-RESPONSIBILITY. This personalization leads Scheler to envision the morally highest person, the "holy man," (*e.g.*, Christ) as pure exemplarity of man's *ordo amoris* whose unsurpassable historical effects are not the result of works, accomplishments, or success, but realized through the pure value being of the person.

See also: HUSSERL; IDEALIZED AGENTS; MORAL SAINTS; PASCAL; PHENOMENOLOGY; VALUE, THEORY OF.

Bibliography

Works by Scheler

Gesammelte Werke. Bern: Francke Verlag, 1954–1985; Bonn: Bouvier Verlag, 1985–1997. The original, complete German edition of fifteen volumes prepared by Maria Scheler from 1954–1969 and by Manfred S. Frings from 1970–1997.

Formalism in Ethics and Non-Formal Ethics of Values: A New Attempt Toward the Foundation of an Ethical Personalism [Der Formalismus in der Ethik und die materiale Wertethik. Neuer Versuch der Grundlegung eines ethischen Personalismus]. Translated by Manfred S. Frings and Roger L. Funk. Evanston, IL: Northwestern University Press, 1973. First published in German in Edmund Husserl's *Jahrbuch für Philosophie und phänomenologische Forschung*, 1913/1916. Translation of Bd. 2, 5th rev. ed., of the *Gesammelte Werke.*

The Nature of Sympathy [Wesen und Formen der Sympathie]. Translated by Peter Heath. Hamden: Archon Books, 1970 [1923]. Translation of Bd. 7 of the *Gesammelte Werke.*

Person and Self Value: Three Essays, with an introduction, edited, and partially translated by Manfred Frings. Dordrecht: Martinus Nijhoff, 1987. Contains *Shame and Feelings of Modesty* (1957); *Repentance and Rebirth* (1917); *Exemplars of Person and Leaders* (1957). Translations made from vols. 5 and 10 of the German collected edition.

Ressentiment. Translated by William W. Holdheim. 3d

ed. Edited by Manfred S. Frings. Milwaukee: Marquette University Press, 1994 [1915].

Works about Scheler

Barber, Michael D. *Guardian of Dialogue: Max Scheler's Phenomenology, Sociology of Knowledge, and Philosophy of Love.* Lewisburg: Bucknell University Press; London: Associated University Presses, 1993.

Blosser, Philip. *Scheler's Critique of Kant's Ethics.* Athens: Ohio University Press, 1995. Contains list of American dissertations on Scheler.

Bosio, F. *Invito al pensiero di Scheler.* Milan: 1995. Contains list of international translations.

Frings, Manfred S. "The Background of Max Scheler's 1927 Reading of *Being and Time:* A Critique of a Critique through Ethics." *Philosophy Today* (May 1992): 99–113.

———. *The Mind of Max Scheler: The First Comprehensive Guide Based on the Complete Works.* Milwaukee: Marquette University Press, 1997. Contains up-to-date list of English translations and of the Collected Works.

———. "The *Ordo amoris* in Max Scheler." In *Facets of Eros,* edited by F. J. Smith and E. Eng 40–61. The Hague: Martinus Nijhoff, 1973.

———. *Person und Dasein: Zur Frage der Ontologie des Wertseins.* Phaenomenologica 32. The Hague: Martinus Nijhoff, 1969. An in-depth study of Scheler's ethics and Heidegger's *Being and Time.*

Kelly, Eugene. *Max Scheler.* Boston: Twayne, 1977.

———. "*Ordo amoris:* The Moral Vision of Max Scheler." *Listening* 21 (1986): 226–42.

———. *Structure and Diversity: Studies in the Phenomenological Philosophy of Max Scheler.* Phaenomenologica 141. Dordrecht: Kluwer Academic Publishers, 1997.

Spader, P. H. "A Change of Heart: Scheler's *Ordo amoris,* Repentance and Rebirth." *Listening* 21 (1986): 188–96.

———. "The Possibility of an *A priori* in Non-formal Ethics of Values." *Man and World* 9 (1976): 153–62.

———. "The Primacy of the Heart: Scheler's Challenge to Phenomenology." *Philosophy Today* 23 (1983): 223–29.

Sweeney, R. "The Affective *A priori.*" In *Analecta Husserliana, III,* 80–97. The Hague: Reidel, 1974.

Vacek, E. "Scheler's Phenomenology of Love." *The Journal of Religion* 62 (1982): 156–77.

Wojtyla, Karol [Pope John Paul II]. "The Acting Person." In *Husserliana X,* edited by Anna-Teresa Tymien-iecka. Dordrecht: Kluwer Academic Publishers, 1979.

———. *Primat des Geistes.* Stuttgart: Seewald Verlag, 1979. With an introduction by Manfred S. Frings. Contains the Pope's habilitation-thesis work on Scheler's

ethics as well as various ethics essays on Scheler and Kant.

Manfred S. Frings

Schelling, Friedrich Wilhelm Joseph von (1775–1854)

Along with FICHTE (1762–1814) and HEGEL (1770–1831), Schelling was a principal post-Kantian, German Idealist philosopher. His major initial contribution was a philosophy of nature that provided an "objective idealism" to complement Fichte's "subjective idealism." His early work culminated in the "identity philosophy" of the early 1800s, presented in dialogue form in *Bruno* (1802). Here the traditional metaphysical opposites of subject/object, ideality/reality, and spirit/matter were absorbed into the "absolute." The realm of nature and the fields of history, RELIGION, and art were shown to be powers (*Potenzen*) of the absolute as it develops through time.

It is not surprising that Schelling should have advanced to the problem of good and EVIL. That problem lies at the heart of his philosophical endeavors, even those focusing on philosophy of nature or "physics." This attention becomes clear early on in a text that is variously attributed to Hölderlin (1770–1843), Hegel, and Schelling (who were friends and roommates at Tübingen University during the early 1790s), namely, the "Oldest Program Toward a System in German Idealism" (1796–1797). The "Program" begins with the words "an ethics," and it asserts that "the whole of metaphysics will in the future be subsumed under *moral philosophy.*" It argues further that "this ethics will be nothing else than a complete system of all ideas, or, what comes to the same, of all practical postulates." As for Schelling himself, his master's thesis of 1792 had dealt with the problem of "the oldest philosophemes concerning the origin of human evil."

If the problem of good and evil required a long incubation period in Schelling's development, however, that is because the opposites of good and evil could not be unproblematically absorbed into the absolute: whereas God might be both subject and object, ideality and reality, spirit and the secular world, and whereas he might act in nature and history alike, he clearly could not be peremptorily designated as the primal ground of evil. After 1806, when Schelling came into contact with Franz von Baader (1765–1841) and seriously studied the works of Jakob Böhme (1575–1624), ethical questions—principally that of radical evil and the absolute—came to occupy center stage in his thought.

Schelling's 1809 *Treatise on Human Freedom* contains his most daring formulations of the principal questions of traditional ethics and moral philosophy. Schelling rejects the tradition that prevails from AUGUSTINE (354–430) through LEIBNIZ (1646–1716), according to which evil is a mere lack in being, an absence of the good—an interval, as it were, in the great chain of being. He also repudiates DESCARTES'S (1596–1650) and Fichte's subjective idealisms and SPINOZA's (1632–1677) pantheism, all of which he regards as lifeless systems lacking a basis in nature. (To be sure, the rejection of Spinoza, to whom Schelling's early philosophy of nature is indebted, is only half-hearted.) A system of reason must be monistic rather than dualistic, Schelling avers, even though his own efforts to elaborate such a system consistently fail to establish a convincing monism. A monism must do more than merely postpone the problem of evil; it must do more than merely displace the problem "one point farther down the line, without resolving it." Schelling concerns himself with evil as a possibility of creation, an actuality in human history, and a necessity concealed in the ground (*Grund*) of the divine essence or absolute itself.

However, it becomes impossible for Schelling to prevent the possibility of evil from penetrating to the very core of the divine essence; it also proves to be impossible to distinguish the "eternal deed" of divine creation from the "eternal deed" of Adam's sin and fall; finally, it proves to be impossible to heal the split within the divine essence between "ground" and "existence," or between the "will of love" and the "will of the ground." Schelling's first strategy is to identify a point of "absolute indifference" that would be prior to both existence and ground in God, a point at which good and evil would appear, not as opposites, but as a simple, unified disjunction. Nevertheless, Schelling himself suspects that such a strategy resembles the dialectical legerdemain—a kind of logical sleight-of-hand—that he criticizes in his contemporaries. He suspects that absolute indifference (which, in any case, in his nature philosophy defines not God but *death*) is itself merely a displacement of the problem of evil "one point farther

down the line," rather than a resolution of it. His second strategy is to envisage a point at which the "will of love" achieves ultimate unity within the bifurcated essence of God. Nevertheless, he argues that such love, which begins as languor and languishing (*die Sehnsucht*), will produce a "final and total divorce" between good and evil, a "scission of forces" in the absolute, by means of a *crisis* that expels evil rather than reconciles it to its source. Yet to extrude evil seems once again, inevitably, merely to postpone the realization that the possibility, actuality, and necessity of evil lie in divinity.

Martin HEIDEGGER (1889–1976) argues in his courses on Schelling that in the 1809 treatise Schelling's ontotheology, that is, the metaphysical system that is embedded in theological postulates, struggles valiantly—but in vain—to survive its gravest challenge. If failures are often more instructive than apparent successes, however, Schelling's importance for every discussion of the problem of radical evil in our own time—whether on the divine or the human scenes—cannot be gainsaid.

See also: AUGUSTINE; EVIL; FICHTE; GOOD, THEORIES OF THE; HEGEL; IDEALIST ETHICS; NATURE AND ETHICS; PHILOSOPHY OF RELIGION; SPINOZA; SUBJECTIVISM.

Bibliography

Works by Schelling

Historisch-kritische Ausgabe. Edited by H. Krings and W. Jacobs. Stuttgart: Frommann-Holzboog, 1976–. Projected to be eighty volumes; by the end of the year 2000, this edition approached the end of the 1790s in Schelling's work.

Sämmtliche Werke. 14 vols; edited by Karl Schelling. Stuttgart and Augsburg: J. G. Cotta'scher, 1856–1861. The standard edition. Because of its antiquity, this edition is quite rare.

Ausgewählte Werke. Darmstadt: Wissenschaftliche Buchgesellschaft, 1980–. Photographic reproductions of most of the major writings found in the *Sämmtliche Werke.* See especially *Schriften von 1806–1813,* which contains the 1809 *Treatise on Human Freedom,* pp. 275–360 (corresponding to vol. 7, pp. 333–416 of the *Sämmtliche Werke*).

Treatise on Human Freedom. Edited by Horst Fuhrmans. Stuttgart: Reclam, 1964. An excellent, inexpensive edition.

Treatise on Human Freedom. Translated by J. Gutmann. Chicago: Open Court, 1936 [1809].

Treatise on Human Freedom. Translated by Priscilla

Hayden-Roy. In *Philosophy of German Idealism,* edited by Ernst Behler. New York: Continuum, 1987. A more recent translation.

Works about Schelling

Baumgartner, Hans Michael. *Schelling: Einführung in seine Philosophie.* Freiburg-im-Breisgau: Karl Alber, 1975. Includes an excellent bibliography.

Coble, Don Kelly. "Inscrutable Intelligibility: Intelligible Character and Deed in Kant, Schelling, and Musil." Diss. DePaul University, 1999.

Heidegger, Martin. *Schelling's Treatise on the Essence of Human Freedom.* Translated by Joan Stambaugh. Athens: University of Ohio Press, 1985 [1971].

Jaspers, Karl. *Schelling: Grösse und Verhängnis.* Munich: R. Piper, 1955.

Kirchhoff, Jochen. *Schelling in Selbstzeugnissen und Bilddokumenten.* Reinbek bei Hamburg: Rowohlt, 1982. An excellent introductory study with bibliography.

Krell, David Farrell. "The Oldest Program Toward a System in German Idealism." *The Owl of Minerva* 17 (1985): 3–19.

———. "The Crisis of Reason in the Nineteenth-century: Schelling's Treatise on Human Freedom (1809)." In *The Collegium Phaenomenologicum: The First Ten Years,* edited by John Sallis *et al.,* pp. 13–32. Dordrecht, Holland: Kluwer Academic, 1988.

Portmann, Stephan. *Das Böse—die Ohnmacht der Vernunft: Das Böse und die Erlösung als Grundprobleme in Schellings philosophischer Entwicklung.* Meisenheim am Glan: Anton Hain, 1966.

David Farrell Krell

Schiller, [Johann Christoph] Friedrich von (1759–1805)

German playwright, poet, historian, and essayist. Best known for such historical dramas as *Don Carlos* (1787), *Wallenstein* (1796–99), *Maria Stuart* (1800), and *Wilhelm Tell* (1804); and for such poetry as the "Ode to Joy" (1785), the text used in the fourth movement of Beethoven's (1770–1827) Ninth Symphony (1823). Schiller's place in the history of philosophy rests on a series of essays written in the 1790s in which he explored connections between ethical and aesthetic ideals. In these essays, especially *On Grace and Dignity* (*Über Anmut und Würde,* 1793) and the *Letters on the Aesthetic Education of Mankind* (*Briefe über die ästhetische Erziehung des Menschen,* 1795), Schiller sought to bridge what he perceived as the undesirable gulf between moral sentiment and PRACTICAL REASON in KANT's (1724–1804) ethics. In the *Letters,* in particular, he argued that the development of both sensibility and rationality by aesthetic education is a necessary prerequisite for moral and political progress. By so arguing, Schiller set the stage for even greater incorporation of AESTHETICS into ideals of individual and collective conduct in subsequent idealist and romantic writers.

Schiller's main works on ethics and aesthetics had been preceded by the "Kallias" letters, a correspondence with Christian Gottfried Körner (1756–1831) in January and February of 1793. In the correspondence, Schiller attempted to tighten the analogy between the beautiful and the morally good found in Section 59 of Kant's *Critique of Judgment* (1790). Kant had argued that the beautiful could be taken as the symbol of the morally good because of analogies between aesthetic and moral *judgment*—each is disinterested, free, and universally valid. Schiller extended the analogy to the *objects* of these judgments by arguing that the beautiful is "freedom in appearance," or actually offers a sensible intuition of autonomy. However, he also subjected morality itself to aesthetic constraints by arguing that virtuous action must appear beautiful, that duty must seem as if it is inclination.

Schiller did not publish the Kallias letters, but they prepared the way for a more direct critique of Kantian ethics in his next work, *On Grace and Dignity.* Here Schiller attempted to correct what he regarded as Kant's neglect or even suppression of moral feeling. He argued that grace in conduct, the appearance of a natural harmony between agents' principles and their inclinations rather than a forcible domination of the latter by the former, is itself a central component of our ideal of virtue. Although individual *actions* in which reason must forcibly dominate inclination may be virtuous, Schiller argued, a virtuous *agent* is one whose actions do not generally have to take this form: "Not *virtues* but *virtue* is [our] precept, and virtue is nothing other than an inclination to duty." Schiller conceded, however, that such grace was an ideal that could not always be attained; and that where it could not, we would have to settle for DIGNITY, which he defined as the expression of a "sublime disposition" to rule our inclinations through "moral force" or "freedom of spirit."

Kant replied to Schiller's critique in his *Religion within the Limits of Reason Alone* (1793). Instead of emphasizing Schiller's concession that dignity rather than grace may be a more attainable ideal for human beings, Kant tried to minimize disagreement with Schiller by asserting that any outward appearance of conflict between an agent's will and inclination is only evidence of a "hidden *hatred*" of the moral law. This reply, however, shows that Kant was still primarily interested in the character of an agent's maxim rather than in the harmony between maxim and inclination. His doctrine of an imperfect duty to self-perfection in the *Metaphysics of Morals* (1797) suggests a deeper appropriation of Schiller's position.

Schiller's philosophical *magnum opus,* the *Letters on Aesthetic Education,* is a complicated work, influenced by ROUSSEAU (1712–1778), Moses Mendelssohn (1729–1786), and FICHTE (1762–1814) as well as Kant. In the *Letters,* Schiller maintained that aesthetic education could overcome fundamental problems in contemporary politics (paradigmatically, the French Revolution's turn to terror) as well as bridge the divide between reason and sensibility in the metaphysics of morals. Schiller suggests at least four different levels on which aesthetic education could prepare for an improvement in human conduct. First, the experience of beauty can refine or energize the characters of individual agents, as their circumstances of action may require (Letters 16–17). Second, an aesthetic education can maximize agents' sensitivity to particular situations as well as their rational grasp of general principles. Both of these features are prerequisites of sound practical reasoning (Letters 11–14). Third, it can show us that our conceptualization of any particular situation is not automatically imposed on us from without but must itself be constructed by us (Letters 21 and 25). This too is an important recognition for MORAL REASONING. Finally, an aesthetic education can introduce us to a realm of "semblance" (*Schein*) where we can freely reconcile nature and reason in ways we cannot always count on in the nonaesthetic realm (Letters 26–27). The first of these points is a traditional theme in MORAL PSYCHOLOGY. The last of them threatens to undermine Schiller's entire argument by driving an insuperable wedge between the realm of the aesthetic and the real world where moral and political action must take place. But the other two claims suggest points of fundamental importance in what one might call moral epistemology.

See also: AESTHETICS; ANALOGICAL ARGUMENT; AUTONOMY OF MORAL AGENTS; DIGNITY; DUTY AND OBLIGATION; FICHTE; IDEALIST ETHICS; KANT; LITERATURE AND ETHICS; MORAL EDUCATION; MORAL PSYCHOLOGY; MORAL REASONING; PRACTICAL REASON[ING]; RATIONALITY VS. REASONABLENESS; ROUSSEAU; VIRTUE ETHICS.

Bibliography

Works by Schiller

Sämtliche Werke. Edited by Eduard von der Hellen. Säkular Ausgabe. Stuttgart: Cotta, 1904–1905.

Werke. Edited by Julius Petersen and Gerhard Fricke. Nationalausgabe. Weimar: H. Böhlaus, 1943–.

Briefwechsel zwischen Schiller und Körner. Edited by Ludwig Geiger. Stuttgart: Cotta, 1895–1896 [1793].

Briefe. Edited by Fritz Jonas. Stuttgart: Deutsche Verlagsanstalt, 1892–1896.

On the Aesthetic Education of Man: In a Series of Letters. Translated by Elizabeth M. Wilkinson and L. A. Willoughby. Oxford: Clarendon Press, 1967 [1795]. Includes extensive Bibliography, introduction, commentary, glossary of terms.

Works about Schiller

Beiser, Frederick C. *Enlightenment, Revolution, and Romanticism: The Genesis of Modern German Political Thought.* Cambridge, MA: Harvard University Press, 1992.

Cassirer, Ernst. *Freiheit und Form: Studien zur deutschen Geistesgeschichte.* Darmstadt: Wissenschaftliche Buchgesellschaft, 1961 [1916]. See especially pp. 262–302.

Ellis, J. M. *Schiller's Kalliasbriefe and the Study of His Aesthetic Theory.* The Hague: Mouton, 1969. Has extensive bibliography.

Guyer, Paul. *Kant and the Experience of Freedom.* Cambridge: Cambridge University Press, 1993. Chapter 3.

Henrich, Dieter. "Beauty and Freedom: Schiller's Struggle with Kant's Aesthetics." In *Essays in Kant's Aesthetics,* edited by Ted Cohen and Paul Guyer, 237–57. Chicago: University of Chicago Press, 1982 [1957]. Translation of "Der Begriff der Schönheit in Schillers Ästhetik."

Kerry, S. S. *Schiller's Writings on Aesthetics.* Manchester: Manchester University Press, 1961.

Menzer, Paul. "Schiller und Kant: Zum 150 Todestage Friedrich von Schillers am 9. Mai 1955." *Kant-Studien* 47 (1955–56): 113–47; 234–72.

Miller, R. D. *Schiller and the Ideal of Freedom: A Study of Schiller's Philosophical Works with Chapters on Kant.* Oxford: Clarendon Press, 1970.

Wessell, Leonard P. *The Philosophical Background to*

Friedrich Schiller's Aesthetics of Living Form. Frankfurt a. M.: Peter Lang, 1982. Includes extensive bibliography.

Wilm, Carl Emil. The Philosophy of Schiller in Historical Relations. Boston: John W. Luce, 1912.

Paul Guyer

Schopenhauer, Arthur (1788–1860)

Born on February 22, 1788, in Danzig, Schopenhauer went to school in Hamburg, Gotha, and Weimar (1809–1811). He studied at the University of Göttingen, the University of Berlin, attending lectures by FICHTE (1762–1814) and Schleiermacher (1768–1834), and in 1813 he was awarded the degree of doctor of philosophy (Jena). During the period 1814–1818 he wrote *The World as Will and Idea* (1818). In 1820–1832, he was a lecturer at the University of Berlin. After 1833, he lived in Frankfurt, where he died on September 21, 1860.

Ethics is concerned with investigating the moral aspect of human ACTION and especially with finding the moral basis for such action. For Schopenhauer, there are two steps in this investigation: an analytical step and a metaphysical step.

The analytical step is concerned with understanding the nature of actions that may be said to have a moral quality (*i.e.,* good or EVIL). For Schopenhauer, all such actions are the product of two factors: MOTIVES and CHARACTER. Motives include everything known to have the power to bring about action. Motives belong to the category of causes and, like mechanical causation, biological stimuli, and indeed every kind of causality, make necessary that which is conditioned by them. Actions are thus necessary. Freedom of action is therefore not possible.

Motives, however, produce action through the medium of character. It is through character that the Will (the metaphysically fundamental "blind drive" or force implicit in every thing) is expressed, and through the Will that action receives its moral qualities. Character has the following features: it is empirical (can be known only through experience), it is individual (different in everyone), it is constant (stays the same throughout one's whole life), and its main elements are inborn. Character becomes morally significant through the Will, specifically, through the freedom of the Will. In so far as character is

regarded as this extratemporal Will, it is called "intelligible" character. In it resides the RESPONSIBILITY, and guilt, for actions.

The metaphysical step of ethical reflection explains intelligible character (as the source of good and evil) in the framework of a grandly designed metaphysics of Will. Will, which in the form of intelligible character gives actions their moral quality, is the essence of man (and all beings). In itself, Will is blind drive, without "Idea" or ideational "representation" (*Vorstellung*). But in human beings, it appears as Body accompanied by "Idea." Since all appearances are bound by the forms of time, space, and causality, and the principles of becoming and decay, so too it is for human beings as embodied ideational Will: we are individuals who are subject to suffering and DEATH and who have to rely on our embodiedness for the satisfaction of our needs. In nature we strive after preservation and growth as individuals, without regard for other individuals; we are originally egoistic. We hold that our own bodily individuality is our essential nature as human beings and see in all other individuals *the same* essential nature. But with the power of our ideational capacity we can see through this deceptive identification of essence with the appearance of individuality, looking through the basis for our deception (through *ma-ya*, the veil of the illusory phenomenal world), and thus overcoming the EGOISM from which evil action stems.

The disregard of one's own individuality and the recognition of an independent nature in all other individuals results in freely willed rectitude, and in love for humankind, in its highest form, *compassion*. Only those whose character is capable of compassion proceed to perfection.

Schopenhauer's ethics has roots in antiquity, in Christianity, in the moral teachings of KANT (1724–1804), and in ancient Indian philosophy. A main difference between Schopenhauer's ethics and the ethics of a large part of the Western tradition is in Schopenhauer's rejection of the view that good actions depend on reason. Moral action is not irrational, according to Schopenhauer; but it is not accomplished primarily by knowledge, but through immediate intuition. The importance of Schopenhauer's philosophy, and particularly Schopenhauer's ethical reflection, lies in its emphasis on an intuitionistic morality of compassion.

See also: CAUSATION AND RESPONSIBILITY; CHARACTER; CHRISTIAN ETHICS; EGOISM; FICHTE; FREE WILL;

FREEDOM AND DETERMINISM; INDIA; INTUITIONISM; KANT; METAPHYSICS AND EPISTEMOLOGY; MOTIVES; RESPONSIBILITY.

Bibliography

Works by Schopenhauer

Sämtliche Werke. Edited by Julius Frauenstädt, Arthur Hübscher, and Angelika Hübscher. Vierte Aufl. 7 vols. Mannheim: Brockhaus, 1988.

Works in English. Edited by Will Durant. Abridged ed. New York: F. Unger, 1906?

The World as Will and Idea. Translated by R. B. Haldane and J. Kemp. 8th ed. 3 vols. London: Kegan Paul, Trench and Trubner, 1907? [1818]. Translation of *Die Welt als Wille und Vorstellung.* Also translated by E. F. J. Payne, as *The World as Will and Representation* (Indian Hills, CO: Falcon's Way, 1958).

On the Basis of Morality. Translated by E. F. J. Payne. Indianapolis, IN: Bobbs Merrill, 1965. Introduction by Richard Taylor.

Essay on the Freedom of the Will. Translated by Konstantin Kolenda. New York: Liberal Arts, 1960.

Complete Essays of Schopenhauer. Translated by T. Bailey Saunders. New York: Willey, 1942.

Works about Schopenhauer

Hamlyn, David W. *Schopenhauer: The Arguments of the Philosophers.* London: Routledge and Kegan Paul, 1980.

Hübscher, Arthur. *Denker gegen den Strom.* 2. Aufl. Bonn: Herbert Grundmann, 1982.

Magee, Bryan. *The Philosophy of Schopenhauer.* Oxford: Oxford University Press, 1983. Includes bibliography.

Malter, Rudolf. *Arthur Schopenhauer: Transzendentalphilosophie und Metaphysik des Willens.* Stuttgart-Bad Canstatt: Frommann-Holzboog, 1991.

———. *Der eine Gedanke: Hinführung zür Philosophie Arthur Schopenhauers.* Darmstadt: Wissenschaftliche Buchgesellschaft, 1988.

Rudolf Malter
[translated by Candice Horne]

Schweitzer, Albert (1875–1965)

Born in Alsace, Schweitzer died at the medical station he established at Lambarene, Gabon. His learning had rare breadth, earning him international recognition in philosophy, theology, music, and medicine. His outlook combined Indian, Christian, and German thought. Although an idealist in viewing thoughts and ideas (a *Weltanschauung*) as requisite for civilization (*Kultur*), he could not regard his own life as complete unless he put his principles into practice.

Philosophy of Civilization

Like many other thoughtful scholars, Schweitzer worried about civilization, feeling personally out of step with its main stream. World War I (1914–1918) presaged a doom that was confirmed for Schweitzer by the world's greed and frivolity and the lack of an ethical (rather than aesthetic, historical, or material) *Weltanschauung*. His philosophy of civilization therefore forms the context for his ethical views. Schweitzer's insistence that civilization is ultimately ethical marks an important distinction between individual cultures and civilization. Civilization is universal, binding all humanity, whereas cultures are particular and distinctive. Civilization is essentially ethical because only ethical ideas can transcend the parochialism of aesthetic, material, and historical conditions.

Schweitzer's main thesis about civilization, so defined, is that we have lost any coherent sense of it along with our sense of the ethical; that is, we lack a viable *Weltanschauung*. While this thesis is mainly historical (compare Spengler, HUSSERL, Toynbee, WEIL, MACINTYRE, ANSCOMBE, *et al.*), it is also normative. Just as a target is necessarily something to aim at, civilization is something to achieve.

For Schweitzer the restoration of civilization depends in part on the guidance of philosophy. He recognizes two sorts of philosophy: philosophy of nature, which is based in experience, focused on practical action, and derived from appreciation of the world around us; and dogmatic philosophy, which is speculative and academic. Dogmatic philosophy has created the crisis; philosophy of nature, with the Stoics and SPINOZA (1632–1677) as acknowledged forerunners, is needed to resolve it, by providing a viable *Weltanschauung*. Schweitzer's insistence that philosophy based on the natural world entails ethical ideas sets him apart from most contemporary naturalists, just as his NATURALISM sets him apart from most moralists.

Ethics

Schweitzer articulated two distinctive ethical ideas. One is a fundamental principle sufficient to ground civilization; the other concerns what sort of life is worth living.

His fundamental principle is reverence for life, from which he derives the fundamental ethical duty of affirmation of life and the secondary principle that good fortune entails additional obligations. Schweitzer carried reverence for life to the point of refusing to kill flies in his hospital, but he does not require such an interpretation by others. The principles seem not to entail universal precepts (duties in the Kantian sense), and since Schweitzer explicitly recognizes necessity as justifying killing, he does not even condemn all HOMICIDE. Acknowledging this, Schweitzer incorporated a mystical basis for his commitments, claiming to have been led rationally into MYSTICISM.

For Schweitzer, the primary ethical problem is to find a life worth living, one congruent with essential human nature. Such a life will serve civilization, the greatest human achievement. It will, therefore, be guided by reverence for life. One cannot ignore aesthetic, material, and historical values; nonetheless they must give way if one is to fulfill one's real self. One can achieve nothing without both enthusiasm and sacrifice. For Schweitzer, medical work in AFRICA required sacrificing many of the occasions and amenities that might have furthered his love of music, his social connections, and his material comfort.

Schweitzer's ethics transcends words. Words are important; indeed, since philosophy can revitalize civilization, words to express and convey such revitalizing ideas have a greater role than most contemporary philosophers would allow. But personal practice is even more important than words and thoughts. Although Schweitzer continued to write and lecture, the last decades of his life were devoted primarily to medicine in Africa rather than to the tasks he assigned to philosophers.

See also: AFRICA; DUTY AND OBLIGATION; *EUDAIMONIA*, -ISM; HUMANISM; LIFE, RIGHT TO; MARCUS AURELIUS; MULTICULTURALISM; MYSTICISM; NATURALISM; PACIFISM; PRACTICAL REASON[ING]; SPINOZA; STOICISM; THEORY AND PRACTICE; VIOLENCE AND NON-VIOLENCE.

Bibliography

Works by Schweitzer

Christianity and the Religions of the World. Translated by Johanna Powers. New York: Henry Holt, 1939.

Goethe: Five Studies. Translated by Charles R. Joy. Boston: Beacon Press, 1961.

Indian Thought and Its Development. Translated by Mrs. Charles E. B. Russell. London: A. and C. Black, 1936.

Memoirs of Childhood and Youth. Translated by Kurt and Alice Bergel. Syracuse: Syracuse University Press, 1997.

Out of My Life and Thought: An Autobiography. Translated by A. B. Lemke. New York: Henry Holt, 1990.

The Philosophy of Civilization. Translated by C. T. Campion. London: A. and C. Black, 1923. Vol. I: *The Decay and Restoration of Civilization.* Vol. II: *Civilization and Ethics.*

The Quest of the Historical Jesus: A Critical Study of Its Progress from Reimarus to Wrede. Translated by William Montgomery. New York: Macmillan, 1901.

A Friendship in Letters. With Alice Ehlers. Translated and edited by Kurt and Alice Bergel. New York, London: University Press of America, 1991.

Works about Schweitzer

Brabazon, James. *Albert Schweitzer: A Biography.* New York: Putnam, 1975.

Clark, Henry. *The Philosophy of Albert Schweitzer.* London: Methuen, 1964.

Cousins, Norman. *Albert Schweitzer's Mission: Healing and Peace.* New York: Putnam, 1985.

Kraus, Oscar. *Albert Schweitzer: His Work and His Philosophy.* A. and C. Black, 1944. Introduction by A. D. Lindsay. A good short critical examination of Schweitzer's philosophy.

Murray, John Middleton. *The Challenge of Schweitzer.* London: Jason Press, 1948. An orthodox Christian criticism of the main claims of *Civilization and Ethics.*

Spiegelberg, Herbert. "Good Fortune Obligates: Albert Schweitzer's Second Ethical Principle." *Ethics* 85 (1975): 227–34.

Newton Garver

Scotus, John Duns

See Duns Scotus, John.

secrecy and confidentiality

All of us have secrets and most of us keep them for others. Generally we find the practice of secrecy readily understandable and largely noncontroversial. On some occasions, however, people outside the ambit of a secret may have a legitimate interest in the secret information; under such circumstances the practice of secrecy becomes morally problematic.

This situation is all the more true because of a fundamental asymmetry of POWER built into the very structure of secrecy. P may not know that she has a legitimate interest in secret information, or even that such secret information exists (or the identities of the people who possess it). In such a case P is not in a position to press her claim to be let in on the secret, and the decision whether to keep the secret or divulge it to P is made by an interested party: the secret holder. If Q holds money to which P has a legitimate claim, P can press that claim before a neutral court; but if Q secretly holds information to which P has a legitimate claim, only Q is in a position to decide whether to share it.

Personal Secrets

Secrecy raises distinct though overlapping moral questions in private life, professional practice, and politics. In private or personal life, the rationale for keeping secrets flows in the first instance from the very nature of PRIVACY itself: for any of a variety of reasons I may not want you to know certain things about my life (my intimate habits, my own thoughts, my past, my salary), and the same motivations that lead us to respect privacy justify the practice of first-personal secrecy. At the same time, all of us experience the need to share personal information for practical reasons, or for confessional reasons, or simply because we like or are intimate with another person. As Bruce Landesman has argued, this combination of the fundamental human NEEDS to maintain a sphere of privacy, on the one hand, and to share information with our fellows, on the other, justifies the practice of what we may call second-personal secrecy, *i.e.,* sharing our secrets with confidants who will themselves maintain them.

In second-personal secrecy, as in the case of professional and political secrecy, two types of moral complications typically arise. The first occurs when the only way to keep a secret (to which, we will assume, one is legitimately entitled) is through deception. This dilemma will arise, for example, when one is directly asked about secret information in a situation where simply saying "I know but I won't (can't) tell you" is precluded. The second complication occurs when A entrusts B with a secret that A is arguably not entitled to keep or (alternatively) that A is not entitled to expect B to keep. For example, A may confide in B that he or she is a child abuser or has committed a crime. An important value will be offended whether B keeps the secret or violates it.

Professional Confidence

Situations of this second kind typically characterize confidentiality dilemmas in professional ethics. Should a journalist reveal a source when the source is needed to testify in a criminal defense? Should a physician warn the spouse or lover of an HIV-positive patient to engage only in safe sex? Should a lawyer rectify a client's fraud? What distinguishes these cases from nonprofessional cases is not the singularity of the dilemmas, but that we might resolve them differently than we would in nonprofessional life. For it is typically asserted that professional obligations of confidentiality are stronger than personal obligations. The professional obligations are backed not only by the two reasons that justify second-personal secrecy in private life (respect for the basic human need to share information in a relatively invulnerable setting and respect for a trust-relationship), but also by additional weighty reasons.

This additional justification of confidentiality can be spelled out in a two-step argument. The first step says that professionals should keep confidences because carrying out their professional duties requires them to dig out information that will be tendered only in confidence. This argument is an instrumental one: confidentiality is justified because it is necessary to do the job. The second step says that the job is important: journalists point to the importance of a free and vital press in a democracy; physicians, to the value of health and, perforce, of life itself; lawyers, to the centrality of vigorous and informed representation in the adversary system; business managers, to the virtues of a competitive market system; and so on.

The second step of this argument will tell a tale about the profession that is either consequentialist or nonconsequentialist in character. The lawyer may justify the adversary system either because it gets at the truth or because it is essential to honoring the DIGNITY of litigants; doctors can understand ministering to health in consequentialist terms of pain reduction or in nonconsequentialist terms of showing respect for individual physical integrity.

When the argument takes a consequentialist turn, we will have to compare the benefits of keeping confidences with the benefits of revealing them in problem situations, and then it is unclear how well the two-step argument succeeds. In the wake of the well-known *Tarasoff* case (in which a psychiatrist kept confidential a client's threat to kill a woman—which the client subsequently did), the psychiatric profession urged that the benefits of encouraging disturbed individuals to seek help outweigh the benefits of permitting psychiatrists to warn potential victims of dangerous clients. But why should we believe this claim? Characteristically, such arguments will turn on hard-to-verify and largely unexplored empirical premises.

If, on the other hand, a plausible nonconsequentialist defense of professional activity can be made, it might be possible to argue that the two-step argument for confidentiality implicates values that trump social utility and therefore should not be weighed in a flat-footed manner against the benefits of disclosure. In that case the argument for a strong duty of confidentiality will be more persuasive.

Political Secrecy

Political secrecy is as old as politics itself, and it is virtually impossible to imagine politics without it. Yet it is undeniable that the practice of political secrecy is troubling. This is because of the asymmetry of power discussed above: the government not only keeps secrets, but by classifying information makes it impossible for citizens to evaluate the government's decisions about what to keep secret. In this way secret policies are facially inconsistent with government accountability.

In *Perpetual Peace* (1795), KANT (1724–1804) proposed as a "transcendental condition of public law" that any actions affecting the RIGHTS of other people must be capable of full publicity; else they are illegitimate. But why? Kant suggests that a policy that cannot withstand publicity must be unjust, but this argument is unpersuasive, since the policy may instead merely be unpopular: it sometimes happens that just policies are unpopular. Alternatively, the publicity condition may be defended as a version of the UNIVERSALIZABILITY test: if everyone can adopt a policy as a maxim, it can withstand full publicity. However, it is often impossible to formulate public policies as individual maxims. Think, for example, of the policy of progressive taxation; it makes no sense to ask what would happen if everyone adopted progressive taxation as their maxim. In such cases

the publicity condition requires a rationale independent from universalizability.

Though the problem of providing that rationale is a difficult one, the intuitive force of Kant's position is obvious: secrecy may be out of place in an open and democratic society—perhaps even in a closed and undemocratic society—and thus the necessity of secret policies ought to be demonstrated by arguments stronger than "the government knows best what its citizens shouldn't know at all." Unlike the personal and professional cases, it may be that the presumption lies against political secrecy rather than with it.

See also: BLACKMAIL; BUSINESS ETHICS; CIVILITY; DECEIT; DIGNITY; ETIQUETTE; GOVERNMENT, ETHICS IN; INTEGRITY; JOURNALISM; LEGAL ETHICS; LIBRARY AND INFORMATION PROFESSIONS; MEDICAL ETHICS; PERSONAL RELATIONSHIPS; POWER; PRIVACY; PROFESSIONAL ETHICS; PUBLIC AND PRIVATE MORALITY; PUBLIC POLICY; TRUST.

Bibliography

Bok, Sissela. *Lying: Moral Choice in Public and Private Life.* New York: Pantheon, 1978.

———. *Secrets: On the Ethics of Concealment and Revelation.* New York: Pantheon, 1983.

Kant, Immanuel. "Von der Einhelligkeit der Politik mit der Moral . . . = Of the Harmony Which the Transcendental Concept of Public Right Establishes Between Morality and Politics." 2d appendix to *Zum ewigen Frieden = Perpetual Peace,* in *On History,* edited by Lewis White Beck. Indianapolis, IN: Bobbs-Merrill, 1957 [1795]. Also found in *Kant's Political Writings,* 2d ed., edited by Hans Reiss, Cambridge: Cambridge University Press, 1991.

Landesman, Bruce. "Confidentiality and the Lawyer-Client Relationship." In *The Good Lawyer: Lawyers' Roles and Lawyer's Ethics,* edited by David Luban. Totowa, NJ: Rowman and Allanheld, 1983.

Luban, David. "The Publicity Principle." In *The Theory of Institutional Design,* edited by Robert E. Gordon. Cambridge: Cambridge University Press, 1996.

Wigmore, John Henry. *Evidence in Trials at Common Law.* Edited by John T. McNaughton. Boston, MA: Little, Brown, 1961. See vol. 8.

David Luban

self and social self

The debate in ethics and social philosophy as to whether the self is fundamentally a social or individual being has taken center stage in the last three decades of the twentieth century, but has its roots in discussions dating back to the Greeks. It was addressed in explicit terms by nineteenth-century German philosophers and again in the earlier part of the twentieth century by English and American Hegelians and pragmatists as well as by Marxists and existentialists. A brief look at this history is helpful for putting into perspective the contemporary debates between individualistic and communitarian approaches to the sociality of the self.

In different ways, PLATO (c. 430–347 B.C.E.) and ARISTOTLE (384–322 B.C.E.) both hold the view that the individual is fundamentally a social and political being. While regarding the tripartite soul as constitutive of a single individual, Plato argues in the *Republic* that the state, through its educative and socializing functions, plays an important role in shaping this individual psyche. In addition, he follows his teacher SOCRATES (c. 470–399 B.C.E.) in seeing the dialogical interaction among individuals as decisive in forming the knowledge base and, in turn, the possibilities of virtue, for each individual. Aristotle's famous dictum that the human being is a *zoon politikon,* or a social and political animal, likewise gives central place to the idea that people are fundamentally members of a political community, which helps them develop their CHARACTER and their particular excellences or VIRTUES.

This conception resonated through parts of medieval thought but receded in the modern period in the face of perspectives that focused on the individual self as the locus of self-consciousness and of rationality. René DESCARTES'S (1596–1650) radically individuated *cogito* and LEIBNIZ'S (1646–1716) monads are illustrative of this emphasis. So too are the liberal individualist theories of Thomas HOBBES (1588–1679) and John LOCKE (1632–1704) and their associated SOCIAL CONTRACT approaches to the formation of the state, in which individual selves concerned with their own self-interest are said to reason that they would be better off associating in states rather than remaining isolated in a precarious state of nature. This liberal individualist theory was in turn criticized in the nineteenth-century by G. W. F. HEGEL (1770–1831), Ludwig FEUERBACH (1804–1872), and Karl MARX (1818–1883), who also were concerned to oppose the INDIVIDUALISM found in Immanuel KANT (1724–1804) and more radically in FICHTE (1762–1814).

The theories of Hegel and Marx can be viewed as direct antecedents of some of the more recent approaches to the self and the social self. In his *Phenomenology of Mind* (1807), and in his system of absolute spirit as well, Hegel develops an interactive model of consciousness and a social conception of the origin and nature of knowledge. In his renowned account of "the master-slave dialectic," which in turn influenced later thinkers as diverse as Marx, Sigmund Freud (1856–1939), Jean-Paul SARTRE (1905–1980), Simone DE BEAUVOIR (1908–1986), Franz Fanon (1925–1961), Charles TAYLOR, and many others, Hegel proposes that a self needs to be recognized by another in order to be itself and that such reciprocal recognition is what distinguishes humans from animals and makes SELF-KNOWLEDGE possible. Karl Marx, in some important ways influenced by the writings of Feuerbach before him, develops this Hegelian theme further in his account of alienated labor, in criticizing capitalistic economic forms as separating individuals from each other and thereby alienating them from themselves as social beings. In *The German Ideology* (written 1845–1846) and the "Theses on Feuerbach" and other writings, Marx argues that under capitalism, the truly social and interdependent nature of people's economic relations to each other are disguised by the idea that we are separate and individual selves concerned only for ourselves and freely choosing to contract with whomever we please. By contrast, Marx proposes in his "Theses on Feuerbach" that the individual is in fact "an ensemble of social relations."

The Hegelian and Marxist approaches to the sociality of the self were taken up by the British idealists, including F. H. BRADLEY (1846–1924), with his conception of the relations between individuals as not external but rather internal ones, *i.e.,* relations that constituted the individuals as who they are within a social whole; and T. H. GREEN (1836–1882), in his emphasis on positive freedom and the availability of the conditions for individuals' choices, as an essential supplement to the purely negative freedom from restraint characteristic of LIBERALISM. Certain leading figures in American PRAGMATISM too, especially John DEWEY (1859–1952), supplemented their individualist approaches with a recognition of the importance of political community and the socialization accomplished through the educational process for the development of the self. George Herbert MEAD (1863–1931) went even further in this direction in his analysis of the function of social roles in the determination of individual character. These views in turn had some impact on the SOCIAL PSYCHOLOGY of the postwar period, which emphasized the importance of roles and practices in the socialization of the person in addition to (or in place of) the earlier psychoanalytical emphasis on individual MOTIVES and drives, or the behaviorist emphasis on individual behaviors in response to external, often physical, stimuli. In a different tradition, drawing on both continental and classical modes of thought, Hannah ARENDT (1906–1975) subsequently drew attention to the ways in which individuals show themselves to others through speech and action in the context of political community, thereby in some ways hearkening back to the Greek conception of the individual as *zoon politikon.*

The contemporary philosophical discussion of the self and the social self emerges from this general background, but also more specifically in reaction to two dominant individualist approaches, characteristic of the mid-twentieth century. One was the continental school of thought of existentialism, especially in the early work of Martin HEIDEGGER (1889–1976) and of Jean-Paul Sartre, with its emphasis on the role of individual projects and choices in the formation of an individual's mode of being. Especially in Sartre's *Being and Nothingness* (1943), other persons are understood as literally other to a person's self-consciousness, which is conceived as radically individuated. The second individualist approach, this one mainly Anglo-American, was in fact the liberal individualism noted above, now in updated form as a theory centering on individuals understood as free, rational choosers, who pursue life plans and individual goals and who might choose to cooperate with others for their own ends, but are not fundamentally understood as social beings.

In the recent debates on this topic, which date largely from the late 1960s, the first critiques were given by theorists influenced by the earlier theories of Marx and of Marxists such as Georg Lukács (1885–1971)and Rosa Luxembourg (1871–1919), insofar as these theories provided the initial framework for the movements of the "new left." Thinkers like Herbert Marcuse (1898–1979), Jurgen HABERMAS, and the Yugoslav Praxis school (*e.g.,* Mihailo Markovic and Gajo Petrovic) enunciated a humanistic social perspective that emphasized the liberation of the individual from ALIENATION, in the con-

text of social interaction and the NORMS of an egalitarian and democratic community. These foci were taken up by second generation thinkers, such as Carole Pateman, Frank Cunningham, and Carol Gould, who sought to emphasize the sociality of individuals and the elaboration of new forms of participatory DEMOCRACY (in this way also influenced by the work of C. B. Macpherson). The criticism of abstract individualism by these thinkers (and by Charles Taylor in his critique of "atomism") was directed against both the older liberal individualism and the existentialist versions, but sought to retain a strong conception of the individuality of the self and its development while putting considerably more weight than these earlier approaches on social cooperation (and the INSTITUTIONS that foster this cooperation) as necessary for individual self-development. The social ontologies constructed by these thinkers emphasized the role of interaction in the constitution of the self and complemented the earlier Marxist emphasis on historically changing forms of practical activity and on the social and economic conditions of life as a framework for ethics. Important in this later context too was a critique of domination by others (as supplementary to economic EXPLOITATION) and the establishment of supportive relations of RECIPROCITY and mutuality, if the individual is to be free. (It may be noted that a conception of reciprocity subsequently came to play a significant role in Anglo-American ethics as well, as discussed, for example, by Lawrence Becker.)

The critique of liberal individualism was also taken up, especially in the context of the appropriation of John RAWLS's *A Theory of Justice* (1971), by communitarian theorists like Michael Sandel, Michael WALZER, and Alasdair MACINTYRE, who in various ways criticized Rawls's work as based on a conception of individual agency without an adequate social component. Sandel focused on a critique of Rawls's conception of agency as transcending any given life plan, where identity is incorrectly seen, he argues, as independent of our various engagements with others in practices, traditions, and other preexisting involvements. Walzer placed weight on individuals' membership in the political community and in a plurality of lesser groupings as providing frameworks for action and criteria for diverse senses of justice appropriate to each community or type of grouping and interaction. MacIntyre more radically rejected the liberal individual framework altogether and argued for an older conception of virtue that emphasized the necessity for character to be developed within a stable community.

These and other communitarian approaches focused not only on the relational nature of the individual but on participation in an ongoing political community as conditions for one to be a full person. More recently, attention has shifted to membership in a particular culture and to cultural identity as crucial to the self as a social being. The writings of Charles Taylor played a key role in this new context, with his account of the recognition of cultures in a multicultural framework and the issue of whether cultures can make a claim to survive as such. Other theorists have also argued for the important role played by ethnicity or nationality in the constitution of the identity of a person.

Another crucial thread in the self and social self debate, also emerging from the late sixties and being elaborated up to the present, is provided by feminist theorists. In philosophy, the earlier emphasis on women's EQUALITY came to be supplemented by a concern with difference as a crucial category for understanding the OPPRESSION of women. The concept of difference (whether explicitly or only implicit in the work of Simone de Beauvoir, Carol Gould, Alison Jaggar, Iris Young, Seyla Benhabib, Elisabeth Spelman, Martha Minow, and many others, and in more postmodernist forms influenced especially by the French feminisms of Luce Irigaray, Hélène Cixous, and Julia Kristeva), has been used to call attention to the various social relations in which women stand to men, to other races and ethnicities, and to society, as well as the differences among women and between women and men. In this way, "difference" can be used to posit a view of the female self, not as separate from male selves (though some postmodern French feminist theorists or radical feminists have used the concept in this way), but rather as interrelated with others, and to call attention to the diversity of the oppressive social relations in which women may find themselves.

The relationality of women also came to be theorized directly in an emphasis on CARE and on mothering (*e.g.,* in Virginia Held, Sara Ruddick, Caroline Whitbeck, Carol Gilligan, and Joan Tronto), which, it was argued, has been omitted from traditional male theories of ethics and politics, in their exclusive concern with abstract justice and individual RIGHTS.

The female experience of caring and concern, and women's focus on relationships and taking responsibility for them, has suggested a new model of the person and new directions for understanding our moral obligations. There have also been efforts recently to extend this understanding to political community and international ethics as well.

Largely because of the success of the arguments by many of the theorists above, it has by now become practically a truism in philosophy that the individual is to various degrees a social being. Even conservative libertarians and RATIONAL CHOICE theorists seem willing to grant some important measure of sociality to individuals. Yet crucial questions and differences of views remain: Is it correct to say that the individual is formed by his or her social relations? What happens to agency, choice, and autonomy on such a view? Should we instead regard individuals as capable of choosing and changing their social relations? But doesn't this return us to the old liberal idea of fully formed individuals whose relations are external to who they are? And isn't this latter idea perhaps simply reflective of contemporary practices in advanced industrial society and thus relative to a particular social and historical formation?

Indeed, an array of positions seems possible on the difficult question of the sociality of the self, including though not limited to the following: (1) the self as a product of social circumstances, as a set of relations, or as fundamentally to be understood as a member of a community; (2) the self as both choosing its relations and formed by them (in some way to be specified); or (3) the self as free chooser who needs only to cooperate with others for its own purposes.

What finally is the impact on ethics (both individual and social) of a conception of the social self? By way of summary, we may take note of a variety of suggestions, some by now rather obvious: (1) An emphasis on caring or RESPONSIBILITY for others versus traditional views of individual rights or of justice (though it may also be argued that these rights themselves depend on structures of reciprocal recognition among persons). (2) Related to this, a concern with reciprocity and mutuality, rather than simply the pursuit of individual self-interest or egoistic approaches to ethics. Further, the supplementation of conceptions of autonomy (if not their replacement) with more relational, and possibly contextual, approaches. Connected to this point, too, the issue of whether moral responsibility can pertain to groups or collectives in addition to individuals, and, in political philosophy, whether we can talk of group rights in addition to individual ones. (3) An emphasis on people's circumstances and their socialization in understanding their actions and in reforming society (and eliminating crime). (4) In a related way, an emphasis on social institutions and practices rather than simply individual self-improvement and good action (or action in accordance with moral principles), in order to achieve justice and a better society; here, living in the right sort of community becomes crucial. (5) An emphasis on obligations that one owes to the community as a whole (in a more complex way than the earlier focus on the performance of social roles—"my station and its duties") rather than simply performing one's duties to other individuals. (6) On some views also, a focus on relations to particular others, *e.g.*, in one's FAMILY or nation, because of one's existing ties and relations to them, rather than simply on one's universal obligations to individuals generally. (7) Finally, in political philosophy, an emphasis on forms of social cooperation, on dialogue and deliberation, and on the codetermination of common INTERESTS in new democratic contexts, in place of or at least supplementary to, the traditional emphases on meeting individual preferences, avoiding conflict, and making decisions by COMPROMISE or by voting, or, if necessary, by even more adversarial means.

See also: ALIENATION; AUTONOMY OF MORAL AGENTS; CARE; CHARACTER; COLLECTIVE RESPONSIBILITY; COMMUNITARIANISM; COMPROMISE; COOPERATION, CONFLICT, AND COORDINATION; COOPERATIVE SURPLUS; CULTURAL STUDIES; DEMOCRACY; EQUALITY; EXCELLENCE; EXISTENTIAL ETHICS; EXTERNALISM AND INTERNALISM; FAMILY; FEMINIST ETHICS; FORMS OF CONSCIOUSNESS; GROUPS, MORAL STATUS OF; HUMANISM; INDIVIDUALISM; LIBERALISM; LIBERTARIANISM; LIBERTY, ECONOMIC; MORAL COMMUNITY, BOUNDARIES OF; MOTIVES; MULTICULTURALISM; NORMS; OPPRESSION; PERSON, CONCEPT OF; PERSONAL RELATIONSHIPS; PRAGMATISM; PSYCHOANALYSIS; PUBLIC AND PRIVATE MORALITY; RATIONAL CHOICE; RECIPROCITY; SELF-[entries]; SOCIAL AND POLITICAL PHILOSOPHY; SOCIAL CONTRACT; SOCIAL PSYCHOLOGY; VIRTUES.

Bibliography

Aboulafia, Mitchell. *The Mediating Self: Mead, Sartre, and Self-Determination.* New Haven: Yale University Press, 1986.

Arendt, Hannah. *The Human Condition.* Chicago: University of Chicago Press, 1958.

Becker, Lawrence C. *Reciprocity.* Chicago: University of Chicago Press, 1990 [1986].

Benhabib, Seyla. "The Generalized and Concrete Other." In *Feminism as Critique,* edited by Seyla Benhabib and Drucilla Cornell. Minneapolis: University of Minnesota Press, 1988 [1987].

Bradley, F. H. *Appearance and Reality.* Oxford: Oxford University Press, 1930 [1893].

———. *Ethical Studies.* Oxford: Oxford University Press, 1927 [1876].

Cixous, Hélène, and Catherine Clément. *The Newly Born Woman.* Translation, by Betsy Wing, of *Jeune née.* Minneapolis: University of Minnesota Press, 1986 [1976].

Cunningham, Frank. *Democratic Theory and Socialism.* Cambridge: Cambridge University Press, 1987.

de Beauvoir, Simone. *The Second Sex.* Translated by H. M. Parshley. New York: Alfred A. Knopf, 1953 [1949].

Dewey, John. *The Public and Its Problems.* New York: Holt, 1927.

Fanon, Franz. *The Wretched of the Earth.* New York: Grove Press, 1963.

Gilligan, Carol. *In a Different Voice.* Cambridge, MA: Harvard University Press, 1982.

Gould, Carol C. *Marx's Social Ontology.* Cambridge, MA: MIT Press, 1978.

———. *Rethinking Democracy: Freedom and Social Cooperation in Politics, Economy, and Society.* Cambridge: Cambridge University Press, 1988.

———. "The Woman Question: Philosophy of Liberation and the Liberation of Philosophy." In *Women and Philosophy,* edited by Carol C. Gould and Marx W. Wartofsky. New York: G. P. Putnam's, 1976 [1974].

Green, T. H. *The Works of Thomas Hill Green.* 3 Vols. Edited by R. L. Nettleship. London, 1885–1888.

Habermas, Jürgen. *Communication and the Evolution of Society.* Translated by Thomas McCarthy. Boston: Beacon Press, 1979.

———. *Knowledge and Human Interests.* Translated by Jeremy Shapiro. Boston: Beacon Press, 1971.

Hegel, G. W. F. *The Phenomenology of Mind.* Translated by J. B. Baillie. London: George Allen and Unwin, 1949 [1807].

Heidegger, Martin. *Being and Time.* Translated by J. Macquarrie and E. Robinson. New York: Harper and Row, 1962 [1927].

Held, Virginia. *Feminist Morality: Transforming Culture,*

Society, and Politics. Chicago: University of Chicago Press, 1993.

Irigaray, Luce. *This Sex Which Is Not One.* Translated by Catherine Porter. Ithaca: Cornell University Press, 1985.

Jaggar, Alison M. *Feminist Theory and Human Nature.* Totowa, NJ: Rowman and Allanheld, 1983.

Kittay, Eva Feder, and Diana T. Meyers, eds. *Women and Moral Theory.* Totowa, NJ: Rowman and Littlefield, 1987.

Kristeva, Julia. *The Kristeva Reader.* Edited by Toril Moi. Oxford: Blackwell, 1986.

Lukács, György. *History and Class Consciousness.* Translated by R. Livingstone. Cambridge, MA: MIT Press, 1971.

MacIntyre, Alasdair. *After Virtue.* Notre Dame, IN: Notre Dame University Press, 1984 [1981].

Macpherson, C. B. *Democratic Theory: Essays in Retrieval.* Oxford: Oxford University Press, 1973.

———. *The Political Theory of Possessive Individualism: Hobbes to Locke.* Oxford: Oxford University Press, 1962.

Marcuse, Herbert. *Eros and Civilization: A Philosophical Inquiry into Freud.* New York: Vintage Books, 1962 [1952].

———. *One-Dimensional Man: Studies in the Ideology of Advanced Industrial Society.* Boston: Beacon Press, 1964.

Markovic, Mihailo. *From Affluence to Praxis.* Ann Arbor: University of Michigan Press, 1974.

Marx, Karl. *Economic and Philosophic Manuscripts of 1844.* Edited by D. J. Struik. Translated by M. Milligan. New York: International Publishers, 1964.

———. *Grundrisse: Foundations of the Critique of Political Economy.* Translated by Martin Nicolaus. New York: Vintage Books, 1973.

———. *The Marx-Engels Reader.* Edited by R. Tucker. New York: W. W. Norton, 1972.

Marx, Karl, and Friedrich Engels. *The German Ideology.* Parts I and III. Edited by R. Pascal. New York: International Publishers, 1939 [written 1845–1846].

Mead, George Herbert. *Mind, Self, and Society.* Chicago: University of Chicago Press, 1967 [1934].

Minow, Martha. *Making All the Difference: Inclusion, Exclusion, and American Law.* Ithaca: Cornell University Press, 1990.

Pateman, Carole. *Participation and Democratic Theory.* Cambridge: Cambridge University Press, 1970.

———. *The Sexual Contract.* Stanford: Stanford University Press, 1988.

Petrovic, Gajo. *Marx in the Mid-Twentieth Century.* Garden City, NY: Doubleday Anchor, 1967.

Rawls, John. *A Theory of Justice.* Cambridge, MA: Harvard University Press, 1971.

———. *Political Liberalism.* New York: Columbia University Press, 1993.

Ruddick, Sara. *Maternal Thinking.* Boston: Beacon Press, 1989.

Sandel, Michael. *Liberalism and the Limits of Justice.* Cambridge: Cambridge University Press, 1982.

Sartre, Jean-Paul. *Being and Nothingness: An Essay on Phenomenological Ontology.* Translated, with an introduction, by Hazel E. Barnes. New York: Philosophical Library 1956 [1943].

Spelman, Elisabeth. *Inessential Woman: Problems of Exclusion in Feminist Thought.* Boston: Beacon Press, 1988.

Taylor, Charles. "Atomism." In *Philosophy and the Human Sciences: Philosophical Papers,* vol. 2. Cambridge: Cambridge University Press, 1985, pp. 187–210.

———. *Multiculturalism and the "The Politics of Recognition."* Edited by Amy Gutmann. Princeton: Princeton University Press, 1992.

Tronto, Joan. *Moral Boundaries: A Political Argument for an Ethic of Care.* New York: Routledge, 1993.

Walzer, Michael. *Obligations.* Cambridge, MA: Harvard University Press, 1970.

———. *Spheres of Justice: A Defense of Pluralism and Equality.* New York: Basic Books, 1983.

Wartofsky, Marx W. *Feuerbach.* Cambridge: Cambridge University Press, 1977.

Whitbeck, Caroline. "A Different Reality: Feminist Ontology." In *Beyond Domination: New Perspectives on Women and Philosophy,* edited by Carol C. Gould. Totowa, NJ: Rowman and Littlefield, 1983.

Young, Iris. *Justice and the Politics of Difference.* Princeton: Princeton University Press, 1990.

Carol C. Gould

self-control

ARISTOTLE (384–322 B.C.E.) tells us that self-control (*enkrateia*) and its contrary (*akrasia*) "are concerned with that which is in excess of the state characteristic of most men; for the [self-controlled] man abides by his resolutions more and the [akratic] man less than most men can" (*Nicomachean Ethics* 1152a25–27). Although he limits the sphere of self-control and *akrasia* (want of self-control, WEAKNESS OF WILL) to "pleasures and pains and appetites and aversions arising through touch and taste" (1150a9–10), both self-control and *akrasia* have come to be understood much more broadly. Self-control may be exhibited in the successful resistance of actual or anticipated temptation in any sphere. Temptations having to do with sexual activity, eating, drinking, smoking, and the like are tied to touch and taste. But we may also be tempted to work less or more than we judge best, to gamble beyond the limits we have set for ourselves, to spend more or less on gifts than we believe we should, and so on.

As a first approximation, self-control is a power exhibited in behavior that conforms with the agent's better judgment in the face of actual or anticipated temptation, and self-controlled individuals are agents possessed both of significant motivation to conduct themselves as they judge best and of a robust capacity to do what it takes so to conduct themselves in the face of such temptation. People devoid of self-control are at the mercy of whatever desires happen to be strongest—even when those desires clash with their better judgments.

Self-control may be either regional or global, and it comes in degrees (see Rorty 1980a). A scholar who exhibits remarkable self-control in adhering to the exacting work schedule that she deems best for herself may be weak-willed about smoking. She is self-controlled in one "region" of her life and weak-willed in another. Furthermore, some self-controlled individuals are more self-controlled than others. Agents possessed of self-control in all regions of their lives would be especially remarkable, if, in every region, their self-control considerably exceeded that of most people.

Aristotle views the self-controlled agent as a person whose "desiring element" is "obedient" to his "reason" or "rational principle," though less obedient than the temperate person's (1102b26–28). A person "is said to have or not to have self-control," Aristotle writes, "according as his reason has or has not the control (*kratein*), on the assumption that this is the man himself" (1168b34–35). Given his contention that "reason more than anything else is man" (1178a7; *cf.*, 1166a17, 22–23; 1168b27ff.; *cf.*, Plato, *Republic* 588b-592b), Aristotle's identification of self-control with control by one's "reason" is predictable.

One may instead take a more holistic view of human persons, according to which the *self* of self-control is to be identified with the *human being*, broadly conceived. Even when one's passions and emotions run counter to one's better judgments, they are rarely plausibly regarded as alien forces. A conception of self-controlled individuals as people who characteristically are guided by their better judgments even in the face of strong competing motivation leaves it open that EMOTION and PASSION

have a significant place in the self of self-control. Self-controlled people need not be Stoic sages. Their feelings, emotions, and appetites can inform their conceptions of the good life, their systems of values, and their better judgments. The better judgments that self-control serves in a particular self-controlled person may often rest, for example, on a principle of PRACTICAL REASONING that measures the importance of the INTERESTS of others on the basis of his or her emotional ties to them. The traditionally tight connection between self-control and better judgment leaves room for a great variety of lifestyles among self-controlled agents. What we judge best depends significantly on what we want, value, and enjoy; and most consistent collections of pro-attitudes can be well served by self-control.

Self-control and its opposite can figure in the etiology of overt action at a variety of junctures. Imagine, with Aristotle, that the production of intentional action is roughly divisible into four stages: assent to the major premise of a practical syllogism; assent to a minor premise; assent to a conclusion; action. Amélie Rorty (1980b) has observed that *akrasia* may break in at any of these locations, manifesting itself, for example, in an agent's endorsement of a certain major premise, or in a failure to draw a warranted conclusion. Similarly, self-control may be exhibited, for example, in an agent's keeping a proper premise in focus or drawing a warranted conclusion.

Looking beyond even the "major premises" of Aristotelian practical syllogisms, we notice that people may accept principles concerning the acceptance, rejection, and modification of their beliefs, emotions, values, preferences, or desires. Acceptance of such principles may sometimes take the form of better judgments. For example, Ann may judge it best to assess her desires and preferences from an impartial perspective and to identify with or modify them accordingly, Bob may judge it best to monitor his values with a view to keeping them in line with those of his spiritual leader, and so on. People who are self-controlled in these spheres will conduct themselves in accordance with the principles they accept.

There is ample evidence that motivation often exerts a biasing influence on what we believe, as in cases of SELF-DECEPTION (see Mele). Suppose Ann assents to the principle that it is best not to allow what she wants to be the case to determine what she believes is the case. She may be in a position to exercise self-control in resisting a natural tendency toward motivationally biased belief. Out of a concern to be an unbiased believer about important issues, Ann may endeavor to scrutinize relevant data in an objective way, seek out the advice of experts, and so on.

It is generally recognized that we have some control over whether particular emotions result in action. However, there is room for self-control as well in bringing our emotions themselves into line with relevant better judgments. We may stem an embarrassing flow of SYMPATHY for a character in a film by reminding ourselves that he is *only* a character. The man who regards his ANGER at his child as destructive may dissolve or attenuate it by vividly imagining a cherished moment with the child. The timid employee who believes that she can muster the COURAGE to demand a much-deserved raise only if she becomes angry at her boss may deliberately make herself angry by vividly representing injustices she has suffered at the office. These are instances of *internal* control. Many emotions are subject to *external* control as well—control through one's overt behavior. Ann defeats mild depression by calling her brother. Bob overcomes modest fears by visiting his coach for an inspirational talk.

In normal agents, a capacity for self-control is not a mental analogue of brute physical strength. We learn to resist temptation by promising ourselves rewards for doing so, by vividly imagining undesirable effects of reckless conduct, and in countless other ways. Our powers of self-control include a variety of skills—and considerable savvy about which skills to use in particular situations.

"Orthodox" exercises of self-control serve the agent's better judgment. There are also unorthodox exercises. Young Carl has decided to join some friends in breaking into a neighbor's house, even though he judges it best on the whole not to do so. Experiencing considerable trepidation, Carl tries to steel himself for the deed. He succeeds in mastering his fear, and he proceeds to pick the lock. Seemingly, Carl exercised self-control in the service of a decision that conflicts with his better judgment.

The existence of unorthodox exercises of self-control does not preclude there being a tight connection between self-control and better judgment (Mele 1995). Donald Davidson has argued that any interpretable human agent is largely rational, in the sense that her beliefs, intentions, and the like generally cohere with one another and with her behav-

ior. If this conclusion is true, we should expect this rationality to manifest itself in the purposes people have in exercising self-control. Even if the frequency with which self-controlled agents attempt to exercise self-control in support of their better judgments were not to exceed that of other agents, the former agents, owing to their greater powers of self-control, would tend to succeed more often. To be sure, owing to their greater powers, self-controlled agents may also have a greater rate of success in *unorthodox* exercises of self-control. But given the presumption that every interpretable agent is generally rational in Davidson's sense, interpretable agents who make attempts at self-control will tend to do so much more often in support of their better judgments than in opposition to them. As a little arithmetic would show, greater success in the more limited domain of unorthodox self-control is insufficient to counterbalance the effects of greater powers of self-control in the much broader domain.

See also: ANGER; AUTONOMY OF MORAL AGENTS; COURAGE; DESIRE; EMOTION; EXTERNALISM AND INTERNALISM; HATE; INTERESTS; MOTIVES; NEEDS; PASSION; PLEASURE; PRACTICAL REASON[ING]; RISK; SELF-DECEPTION; SITUATION ETHICS; STOICISM; STRATEGIC INTERACTION; TEMPERANCE; WEAKNESS OF WILL.

Bibliography

Aristotle. *Nicomachean Ethics.* In *Works of Aristotle,* edited by W. D. Ross, vol. 9. London: Oxford University Press, 1915.

Bigelow, John, S. Dodds, and R. Pargetter. "Temptation and the Will." *American Philosophical Quarterly* 27 (1990): 39–49.

Charlton, William. *Weakness of Will.* Oxford: Basil Blackwell, 1988.

Davidson, Donald. "Incoherence and Irrationality." *Dialectica* 39 (1985): 345–54.

Kennett, Jeanette, and M. Smith. "Frog and Toad Lose Control." *Analysis* 56 (1996): 63–73.

Mele, Alfred. *Irrationality: An Essay on Akrasia, Self-Deception, and Self-Control.* New York: Oxford University Press, 1987.

———. *Autonomous Agents: From Self-Control to Autonomy.* New York: Oxford University Press, 1995.

Plato. *The Republic.* In *The Dialogues of Plato,* translated by Benjamin Jowett. 4th ed. Oxford: Clarendon Press, 1953.

Rorty, Amélie. "Akrasia and Conflict." *Inquiry* 22 (1980a): 193–212.

———. "Where Does the Akratic Break Take Place?" *Australasian Journal of Philosophy* 58 (1980b): 333–46.

Watson, Gary. "Skepticism about Weakness of Will." *Philosophical Review* 86 (1977): 316–39.

Alfred R. Mele

self-deception

In a wide sense, *self-deception* refers to (a) *activities* of evading significant truths or topics, and (b) resulting *states* of ignorance, false, or unwarranted beliefs or lack of clear consciousness. In a narrow sense, *self-deception* refers to a special case of such activities and states that is describable as a form of lying—lying to oneself. No one doubts that self-deception in the wide sense is a common phenomenon, but questions have been raised about its nature and moral significance. And philosophers have questioned whether self-deception in the narrow sense is possible at all.

In a typical case of deceiving others by lying to them, one individual who knows a truth purposefully gets a second individual to believe the opposite—a falsehood. But can self-deceivers literally lie to themselves—purposefully persuade themselves into believing what they simultaneously know (and hence believe) is false? Yes, according to Jean-Paul SARTRE (1905–1980) and Raphael Demos (1892–1968), who hold that people can deceive themselves by directing their attention to a false belief while ignoring both contrary evidence and the activity of disregarding evidence. Other philosophers, however, find this answer paradoxical and challenge the analogy with interpersonal deception. They ask, Does it make sense to describe one person as believing and disbelieving the same thing at the same time? Can a person discern the truth and then willfully ignore it in order to sustain a contrary belief? Is the truth perhaps discerned unconsciously and automatically kept from consciousness, as Sigmund Freud (1856–1939) suggested, and if so, is self-deception an unintentional process rather than, as the expression suggests, a purposeful activity? Does this process divide the personality so that there is not really one "self" that is simultaneously deceiver and deceived?

Answers to these questions provided by epistemologists and philosophers of mind are important in understanding the moral issues concerning self-deception. Yet these issues can be sketched using the wide sense of *self-deception,* assuming it is clear that self-deceivers can have suspicions about painful truths or topics and then evade detailed and unbiased reflection about them.

In what ways and to what extent is self-deception morally harmful? Is it sometimes morally permissible or even desirable to evade unpleasant truths and problems? Are we responsible for harm done through self-deception if we are not fully aware of what we are doing? How does self-deception relate to fundamental values such as honesty, truthfulness, INTEGRITY, SELF-RESPECT, rationality, and LOVE? If self-understanding is required for meaningful life, as SOCRATES (c. 470–399 B.C.E.) suggested ("the unexamined life is not worth living"), then does self-deception thwart prospects for self-fulfillment and rational living? M. W. Martin has grouped responses to these questions into four main categories, depending on the moral perspective and type of cases emphasized: inner HYPOCRISY, AUTHENTICITY, moral ambiguity, and vital lies.

Inner Hypocrisy

Joseph BUTLER (1692–1752) used "inner hypocrisy" to refer to self-deceit about moral obligations, wrongdoing, and CHARACTER. Seeking to maintain a flattering self-image or to avoid onerous duties, self-deceivers refuse to acknowledge their wrongdoing and vices, making themselves guilty of willful moral neglect. In gray areas of morality, such as how much kindness is owed to others, self-deceivers make selfish and biased judgments. In clear-cut areas of moral duty, they disregard obligations and engage in rationalization in order to excuse their moral failings. Butler viewed this self-deception as immoral in three ways: (1) it supports wrongdoing, WEAKNESS OF WILL, and avoidance of moral reform; (2) it fosters dishonest self-images and constitutes hypocrisy with respect to ourselves and others; and (3) it distorts moral judgment, thereby corrupting CONSCIENCE and undermining integrity. Self-deception is capable of warping entire value perspectives, as was emphasized by Max SCHELER (1874–1928) in his study of *ressentiment* (repressed hatred) and George Orwell (1903–1950) in his study of "doublethink" (self-contradictory reasoning) in *1984* (published 1949).

Authenticity

The authenticity perspective attacks virtually all self-deception, not just self-deception about immorality. Existentialist philosophers elevate authenticity to a supreme value, defining it as avoiding self-deception and exercising autonomous reasoning. Sartre condemned self-deceivers as cowardly scum who refuse to recognize their freedom and who in BAD FAITH flee RESPONSIBILITY for their actions, values, and interpretations of the world. Friedrich NIETZSCHE (1844–1900) criticized self-deceivers for not daring to confront harsh truths about DEATH, our will to POWER, and the human (rather than divine) origin of values. Søren KIERKEGAARD (1813–1855) explored how self-deception erodes individuality and religious authenticity.

Moral Ambiguity

This perspective challenges whether self-deceivers are clearly or fully responsible for their self-deception and its consequences. In his influential treatise, *Self-Deception* (1969), Herbert Fingarette based this challenge on a comprehensive theory of consciousness and personal identity. To deceive oneself is to disavow a threatening reality—to refuse to identify oneself as the person engaged in the world in a particular way and to support one's preferred identity through selective attention. Disavowal undermines voluntary agency and this calls into question responsibility. In particular, neurotic self-deceivers erode their capacities for agency, making it difficult to assess how far they are blameworthy for the harm they cause. R. G. Collingwood (1889–1943) foreshadowed Fingarette's approach and like him was influenced by Freud's theory of unconscious psychological defense. Mary Haight raised doubts about holding self-deceivers responsible given general uncertainties about the extent of human freedom.

Vital Lies

Self-deception can be life-giving and helpful in coping with problems. It may contribute to SELF-ESTEEM, FRIENDSHIP, love, and community, as suggested by psychologists (see Taylor and Lockard and Paulhus) and playwrights (*e.g.,* Henrik Ibsen [1828–1906] in *The Wild Duck* and Eugene O'Neill [1888–1953] in *The Iceman Cometh*). Contrary to Sartre, self-deception is sometimes morally permissible, desirable, and rational, according to F. C. S. SCHILLER (1864–1937), John King-Farlow, Amélie Rorty, Robert Audi, and Béla Szabados.

Self-Fulfillment

Yet a fifth perspective might be distinguished that emphasizes how self-deception can undermine personal integrity and self-realization, whether or not these characteristics are viewed as primary moral values, as F. H. BRADLEY (1846–1924) held. The ideas of false consciousness and self-alienation developed by G. W. F. HEGEL (1770–1831) and Karl MARX (1818–1883) have been used to criticize social structures and economic forces that distort self-understanding and prevent individuals from realizing their true needs.

Whichever perspective proves most helpful in dealing with particular instances and general tendencies, caution must be used in ascribing self-deception. When atheists like Sartre and Nietzsche accuse theists of self-deception and vice versa, the concept of self-deception becomes a rhetorical weapon, rather than a tool for understanding moral character and conduct.

See also: ALIENATION; AUTHENTICITY; BAD FAITH; BUTLER; CHARACTER; CONSCIENCE; DECEIT; DUTY AND OBLIGATION; HYPOCRISY; INTEGRITY; KIERKEGAARD; MORAL ATTENTION; MORAL PSYCHOLOGY; NIETZSCHE; PSYCHOANALYSIS; RESENTMENT; RESPONSIBILITY; SARTRE; SCHELER; SECRECY AND CONFIDENTIALITY; SELF-KNOWLEDGE; SELF-RESPECT; WEAKNESS OF WILL.

Bibliography

Ames, Roger T., and Wimal Dissanayake, eds. *Self and Deception.* Albany: State University of New York Press, 1996.

Butler, Joseph. "Upon the Character of Balaam"; "Upon Self-Deceit." In his *Fifteen Sermons,* 1722.

Collingwood, R. G. *The Principles of Art.* Oxford: Oxford University Press, 1958. Discussion of "corrupt consciousness."

Demos, Raphael. "Lying to Oneself." *Journal of Philosophy* 75 (1960): 588–95.

Dilman, İlham. *Freud and the Mind.* Oxford: Blackwell, 1984. Chapter 6 explores Freud's work on self-deception.

————, and D. Z. Phillips. *Sense and Delusion.* New York: Humanities Press, 1971. How self-deception threatens meaningful life.

Elster, Jon, ed. *The Multiple Self.* Cambridge: Cambridge University Press, 1986. Essays by psychologists and philosophers including David Pears, Donald Davidson, Amélie Rorty.

————. *Sour Grapes: Studies in the Subversion of Rationality.* Cambridge: Cambridge University Press, 1983. Social and Marxist themes about biased ideology.

Fingarette, Herbert. *Self-Deception.* London: Humanities Press, 1969. Expanded edition, Berkeley: University of California Press, 2000. Masterful study.

Haight, M. R. *A Study of Self-Deception.* London: Humanities Press, 1980. Insights into the divided self.

Hegel, G. W. F. *The Phenomenology of Spirit.* 1807.

Kierkegaard, Søren. *The Sickness Unto Death.* 1849. Self-deception and religious despair.

King-Farlow, John, and Sean O'Connell. *Self-Conflict and Self-Healing.* Lanham, MD: University Press of America, 1988. Practical orientation combining philosophy and psychotherapy.

Lockard, Joan S., and Delroy L. Paulhus, eds. *Self-Deception: An Adaptive Mechanism?* Englewood Cliffs, NJ: Prentice Hall, 1988. Unified presentation of major psychological perspectives.

Martin, Mike W. *Self-Deception and Morality.* Lawrence: University Press of Kansas, 1986. Four moral perspectives.

————, ed. *Self-Deception and Self-Understanding: New Essays in Philosophy and Psychology.* Lawrence: University Press of Kansas, 1985. Essayists include R. Audi, M. R. Haight, H. Fingarette, J. King-Farlow, R. Bosley, B. Szabados; extensive bibliography.

McLaughlin, Brian P., and Amélie Rorty, eds. *Perspectives on Self-Deception.* Berkeley: University of California Press, 1988. Twenty-four new essays.

Mele, Alfred R. *Irrationality: An Essay on Akrasia, Self-Deception and Self-Control.* Oxford: Oxford University Press, 1987. Shows the philosophical relevance of experimental psychology.

————. "Recent Work on Self-Deception." *American Philosophical Quarterly* 24 (1987): 1–17. Main approaches to the paradoxes.

Nietzsche, Friedrich. *Basic Writings of Nietzsche.* Translated by Walter Kaufman. New York: Modern Library, 1968. Scattered insights into the good and bad of self-deception.

Pears, David. *Motivated Irrationality.* Oxford: Oxford University Press, 1984. Advanced study of self-deception and weakness of will.

Pines, Christopher L. *Ideology and False Consciousness.* Albany: State University of New York Press, 1996.

Sartre, Jean-Paul. *Being and Nothingness.* Translated by Hazel E. Barnes. New York: Washington Square, 1966 [1943]. Classic discussion in chapter on "Bad Faith," pp. 86–116.

Scheler, Max. *Ressentiment.* Translated by William W. Holdheim. Edited by Lewis A. Coser. New York: Schocken, 1972 [1915]. Neitzsche-inspired exploration of how self-deception distorts values.

Schiller, F. C. S. *Problems of Belief.* New York: Doran, 1924. Defends some self-deception as necessary for well-being.

Steffen, Lloyd H. *Self-Deception and the Common Life.* New York: Peter Lang, 1986. Comprehensive treatise and bibliography.

Szabados, Béla. "The Morality of Self-Deception." *Dialogue* 13 (1974): 24–34. Innovative study of moral issues.

Taylor, Shelley E. *Positive Illusions.* New York: Basic Books, 1989. Psychological study of healthy and creative self-deception.

Mike W. Martin

self-defense

Self-defense is the least controversial use of force, including lethal force, by one person against another. Those who are near-pacifists concerning the use of force by individuals or by nations often believe that purely self-defensive fighting can be permissible. Many who hold a conservative position on ABORTION make an exception when the pregnant woman's life is threatened, believing the circumstances to be, or to be sufficiently like, self-defense. The use of force in genuine self-defense is most commonly accepted as morally and legally justified (permissible or right), rather than excusable (wrong but pardonable). Self-defense is also widely held to constitute a particularly strong justification: it is an exception to the moral and legal prohibition of HOMICIDE. Self-defense is also thought of as a positive right (some even consider it a duty).

However, there is no corresponding philosophical consensus about the nature and limits of justified self-defense. Its justification proves more complex and difficult than is commonly supposed, and most recent philosophical accounts are regarded, for varying reasons, as problematic. Differences arise over three basic issues: the characterization of acts of self-defense; the right of self-defense and the limits and extensions of this right; and the justification of self-defense and the limits of justified self-defense.

Self-defense is most often characterized as the use

of force in warding off an attacker or an aggressor. Justified acts of self-defense are typically like this characterization. However, it is possible, as an aggressor, to defend oneself against someone who is retaliating in self-defense. Paradigmatically, acts of self-defense involve the use of force in resisting, warding off, or repelling a direct active threat. Thus, the use of force in self-defense is distinguishable from other acts of self-preservation (*e.g.,* taking another's blood or food supply in an emergency) in which the use of force is essentially aggressive rather than defensive. Force used in self-defense is also distinguishable from force used against a nonthreat in the course of self-defense (where, *e.g.,* I deflect a missile to a bystander or use a bystander as a shield). Nevertheless, disagreement can arise over the conditions under which someone is a threat such that the use of force against them is self-defense. For instance, acts of self-defense are commonly held to repel present force, and "present" is usually interpreted so as to allow for anticipation of a blow. But it is open to dispute just how imminent the threat must be for anticipatory force to be self-defense, as distinct from a preemptive strike. Further, self-defense is possible against a conditional threat (*e.g.,* one posed by duress); but the use of preventative force against an indirect threat (*e.g.,* against the instigator of a "contract" on one's life) would not normally be regarded as self-defense. There is general agreement that one acts in self-defense in warding off an involuntary active threat (*e.g.,* an insane person wielding a knife). But the use of force against a passive threat—someone who threatens one not as an agent, but as an object might—is problematic. It seems natural to say that I act in self-defense in, say, deflecting someone who has been thrown at me or who will crush me by falling on me. This may or may not also extend to my repelling someone who is suffering from a highly contagious disease. But the use of force in removing someone who is, say, stuck in an escape route, can seem insufficiently a case of resisting, warding off, or repelling its subject to be self-defense. The use of force against someone whose mere existence or presence endangers one (*e.g.,* a competitor for limited air) is highly dubious as claimed self-defense. A variety of conceptually difficult and disputed examples lies on the boundary of self-defense and the broader category of so-called necessity.

Self-defense is often cited as a justification. The fact that particular force is used in self-defense is relevant to its justification, but it does not settle the matter. Acts of self-defense are not always morally or legally justified. One can, for instance, act in self-defense against a just threat (*e.g.,* against those who are defending themselves against one's own wrongful attack). For this reason, most justifications of self-defense consider that the moral background of the situation is relevant to whether someone under threat has a right of self-defense in the circumstances. (That force is used in self-defense by someone who is in the wrong may or may not be a mitigating factor.) A minority view, held most notably by Thomas HOBBES (1588–1679), regards the individual's right of self-defense as a very strong natural right, limited only by necessity, that persists irrespective of the rights and wrongs of the conflict.

Traditional NATURAL LAW accounts—by, for example, Hugo GROTIUS (1583–1645), Samuel PUFENDORF (1632–1694), and John LOCKE (1632–1704)—agree with Hobbes in grounding the individual's right of self-defense in the instinct of self-preservation. Unlike Hobbes, they regard this instinct as insufficient to establish a right of self-defense. The individual's right of self-defense is usually taken, in natural law accounts and also more widely, to be an aspect of other basic HUMAN RIGHTS such as the right to life and the right to LIBERTY. These more general RIGHTS are not limited only by necessity: they are constrained, for instance, by the equal rights of others, which means that there is no positive right to use force on an unoffending person in order to protect or preserve oneself. (Such force might nevertheless be morally defensible, or excusable, under certain conditions.) However, one has a positive right to resist, forcefully if necessary, someone who poses an unjust threat to one's life or other legitimate INTERESTS. The right of self-defense is a positive right directly to resist, ward off, or repel unjust harm. This positive right depends on there being a moral asymmetry between oneself as an unoffending person, and someone who poses a threat.

Recent accounts of self-defense differ over the relevance, explanation, and implications of this purported asymmetry. Someone who is an unjust aggressor is commonly said to forfeit certain rights. This forfeiture is often taken as crucial to the justification of the use of force against a person in self-defense. Despite the problems associated with the notion of forfeiture in this context (THOMSON;

Uniacke), unless one adopts Hobbes's view that individuals have a right of self-defense against legitimate force, the positive right of self-defense requires some account of the moral disparity between the parties. (There are problem cases in which, due to reasonable mistake of fact, both parties to a conflict seem to have a right of self-defense. Uniacke discusses ways in which such cases might be resolved.)

An appeal to forfeiture of rights as part of the justification of self-defense implies that, contrary to a very strong recent philosophical trend, human rights such as the right to life are not possessed equally by individuals simply *qua* human beings or persons: such rights are also conditional on one's conduct or on how one stands in relation to others. Accounts differ over the type of conduct or relationship that could imply the forfeiture of basic rights such as the right not to be killed. Those who seek to justify self-defensive force as punitive regard the aggressor's moral culpability as necessary to such forfeiture. Such accounts obviously require a separate justification of self-defense against nonculpable aggressors, *e.g.,* the insane. (Alternatively, self-defense against nonculpable aggressors might be regarded as excusable.) A basic objection to this approach is that the right of self-defense is essentially a right of *defense,* not a type of private PUNISHMENT. A complete unitary justification of self-defense as a right of defense against an unjust threat needs to account for the conditions under which one person is an unjust threat to another. While an unjust threat need not be culpable, self-defense against some nonculpable threats, and against passive threats, poses deep challenges for the provision of such an account.

A theory of forfeiture or abrogation of rights is relevant to the justification of self-defense because there is a very strong moral (and legal) constraint against inflicting harm on other persons. I have no positive right to kill or injure an unoffending person even if my life depends on it. (Where the use of such force can be justified as the lesser evil, I wrong the person who is harmed all the same.) But harm inflicted on an unjust threat in self-defense does not seem to wrong its victim. We need to bear in mind, however, that the fact that someone lacks a right to life, or parity in respect of that right, does not give me a positive right to kill that person. What grounds a positive justification of self-defense is that it directly resists, wards off, or repels otherwise irreparable unjust harm. This justification provides a more plausible basis from which to extend the right of self-defense to the right (sometimes the duty) to defend others (including strangers) than does the instinct of self-preservation.

Most accounts limit the right of self-defense in terms of the conditions of necessity and PROPORTIONALITY. (An alternative view, with the same substantive implications, construes the right of self-defense as limited by necessity and regards proportionality as a requirement of BENEVOLENCE.) One is entitled to use the degree of force that is necessary in the circumstances to resist or ward off the threat: I am not justified in, say, shooting to kill if I can easily repel an attacker by less violent means. The harm one foreseeably inflicts in self-defense must also be proportionate to the harm with which one is threatened: I may not use lethal force to prevent someone, say, from stepping on my toe even if this action is, in the circumstances, the only way of stopping her. Necessary and proportionate force are also necessary conditions of the legal right of self-defense. Disagreement can arise about what constitutes proportionate force, and why. For instance, threatened kidnap and RAPE are commonly thought to justify the use of lethal force if necessary. This justification might be because the victims of such harms are often in danger of being physically injured or killed; or it might be because these harms are believed in themselves sufficiently serious to warrant lethal force. Some maintain that the use of lethal force in defense of PROPERTY can be justified; but many will accept that this justification is so only insofar as one's life or physical safety is also threatened. Another contentious issue is the basis on which the judgments of necessity and proportionality, and indeed the prior judgment that one is under threat, are made. The standard usually invoked in coming to a view about the justification of particular acts of self-defense is what it was reasonable for the agent to believe in the circumstances. Some instances of purported self-defense, and of the use of unnecessary or disproportionate force, raise challenging questions about the nature of justification and excuse (Uniacke).

Those who believe, with THOMAS AQUINAS (1225?–1274), that a private person cannot permissibly kill anyone intentionally, need to justify foreseen killing in self-defense as unintended homicide under the conditions of the doctrine of DOUBLE EF-

FECT. (Grisez offers a complex analysis.) Critics of this view argue that genuinely self-defensive homicide can be justified, intended killing (Uniacke).

To have a right of self-defense against an unjust threat does not necessarily justify the use of self-defensive force, all things considered. We have rights that it can be wrong for us to exercise in particular circumstances; and the use of force in self-defense might be unjustified, for instance, where the means of self-defense would intentionally or incidentally inflict serious harm on unoffending third parties.

See also: ABORTION; BECCARIA; DETERRENCE, THREATS, AND RETALIATION; ENTITLEMENTS; EXCUSES; GROTIUS; HOBBES; HOMICIDE; INTERNATIONAL JUSTICE: CONFLICT; JUSTICE, CIRCUMSTANCES OF; LIFE, RIGHT TO; LOCKE; NATURAL LAW; PACIFISM; PROPORTIONALITY; PUFENDORF; PUNISHMENT; SITUATION ETHICS; THOMAS AQUINAS; THOMSON; VIOLENCE AND NON-VIOLENCE; WALZER; WAR AND PEACE.

Bibliography

Fletcher, George P. "Punishment and Self-Defense." *Law and Philosophy* 8 (1989): 201–15.

———. "Defensive Force as an Act of Rescue." *Social Philosophy and Policy* 7 (1990): 170–79.

Grisez, Germain. "Toward a Consistent Natural Law Ethics of Killing." *The American Journal of Jurisprudence* 15 (1970): 64–96.

Grotius, Hugo. *The Rights of War and Peace.* Translated by William Whewell. Cambridge: Cambridge University Press, 1853 [1625]. See pp. 61–68.

Locke, John. *The Second Treatise of Government.* Rev. ed. Edited by Peter Laslett. Cambridge: Cambridge University Press, 1961 [1689]. See book 2, chapters 2–5.

McMahan, Jeff. "Self-Defense and the Problem of the Innocent Attacker." *Ethics* 104 (1994): 252–90.

Montague, Phillip. "Self Defense and Choosing between Lives." *Philosophical Studies* 40 (1981): 207–19.

Pufendorf, Samuel. *On the Duty of Man and Citizen According to Natural Law.* Translated by Michael Silverthorne. Cambridge: Cambridge University Press, 1991 [1673]. See book 1, part 5.

Thomas Aquinas. *Summa Theologiae.* Blackfriars edition, vol. 38. London: Eyre and Spottiswood, 1966 [c. 1270]. 2a 2ae 64, article 7.

Thomson, Judith Jarvis. "Self-Defense." *Philosophy and Public Affairs* 20 (1991): 283–310.

Uniacke, Suzanne. *Permissible Killing: The Self-Defence Justification of Homicide.* Cambridge: Cambridge University Press, 1994.

Wasserman, David. "Justifying Self-Defense." *Philosophy and Public Affairs* 16 (1987): 356–78.

Suzanne Uniacke

self-esteem

Self-respect and self-esteem are often treated as synonymous terms, but it is important, as some philosophers have noted, to distinguish two modes of self-assessment, one usefully called SELF-RESPECT and the other, self-esteem. The distinction is important because it helps us understand the relationships between certain evaluative attitudes and concepts that are crucially related to these two modes of self-assessment.

The distinction between the two concepts is best made out in terms of what it is for a self-evaluative person to lack self-respect on the one hand and self-esteem on the other. A self-evaluative person might lack the ability to tolerate him- or herself, and this kind of negative assessment is crucial to understanding a range of emotions related to such an assessment. On the other hand, one might have the ability to tolerate oneself on reflection but nonetheless find oneself lacking in some qualities prized from one's own point of view. This negative assessment is a different kind, and it too is crucial to understanding a range of emotions related to it. What should be clear is that one might have self-respect but lack self-esteem, that is, one might be able to tolerate oneself but still believe that one lacks highly prized qualities that would add to one's sense of worth.

What is it, then, to have self-respect or self-esteem? To answer this question, we need to distinguish all things considered self-assessments and role-relative assessments. All things considered self-assessments are overall assessments we make of ourselves as persons, whereas role-relative assessments are assessments we make of ourselves only in terms of our filling some role where succeeding or failing in that role does not dictate the outcome of our overall assessment of ourselves as persons. Though how we fill a certain role, say, whether we are good parents, might factor into our overall assessments of ourselves as persons, it need not, and often does not; for example, whether we are very good at tennis does not usually factor into such judgments. The primary focus here is on self-respect and self-esteem as they relate to our overall assessment of ourselves as persons. To have respect for oneself as a person, then, is to value certain qualities in persons in a way that is necessary to one's ability to have even minimal tolerance for persons from one's own point of view and to believe that one has these qualities. Call these qualities in terms of which a self-evaluative person is able to tolerate him or herself R-qualities. To have self-esteem, on the other hand, is to value certain qualities in persons that are not necessary to one's ability to tolerate oneself but are nonetheless highly prized from one's own point of view. Call these qualities in terms of which a self-evaluative person is able to have a higher sense of self-regard beyond that of mere tolerance E-qualities.

For a more extensive understanding of these concepts, we need an understanding of how each concept is related to other concepts, especially to concepts of emotions, of human well-being, and of good CHARACTER. The comments offered here are only suggestive.

Consider both positive and negative emotions related to self-assessment: PRIDE, HUMILITY, and shame. The proper understanding of these emotions is sometimes distorted by conflating the distinction between self-respect and self-esteem. When a self-evaluative person believes that he or she is in possession of the requisite R-qualities, we expect a certain pattern of emotional response to judgments of self-appraisal. Consider the positive EMOTION of pride. When a self-evaluative person believes that he or she possesses the requisite R-qualities, we do not expect pride to issue from such an assessment. To believe oneself to possess R-qualities is to believe oneself to meet minimal standards for self-affirmation, but pride is an emotional response that reflects the belief that one exceeds such standards. To make sense of pride, then, we need to employ the notion of E-qualities. It is only when a person believes that he or she possesses some degree of these qualities that pride makes sense as a pattern of emotional response. Humility, on the other hand, is a pattern of emotional response that is consistent with the positive evaluation that one believes oneself to meet minimal standards for self-affirmation, but the kind of response is made vivid only when seen as including the belief that one lacks qualities superior to those found in merely tolerable persons. When shame is a response to overall rather than mere role-relative self-assessment, it reflects repudiation of the person one takes oneself to be. Unlike humility, then, shame

is an emotional response that is inconsistent with believing that one has the relevant R-qualities, let alone E-qualities. The distinction between the two modes of self-assessment also serves to illuminate the fact that shame is an emotion of self-concealment in a way that humility and pride are not. That humility is not an emotion of self-concealment is reflected in the fact that false pride is inconsistent with humility, and false pride contains an element of self-concealment, sometimes through SELF-DECEPTION. What allows the humble person to avoid the desperation for self-concealment is a requisite level of positive self-regard, but this is missing from the person experiencing shame. The humble person can look persons worthy of respect in the eye, but the shameful person cannot tolerate the eyes of even minimally worthy persons.

Self-respect and self-esteem also function differently in human well-being, especially in terms of how important personal relationships are to a good life. Finding oneself worthy of respect, as meeting minimal standards of approval by self and others, seems fundamental to the psychological health of any self-evaluative person. The reason for this need is that it is difficult for a self-evaluative person to find him- or herself worthy of the good things of life when plagued by a consciousness lacking minimal positive regard. But a person might avoid this affliction, yet be denied access to other important goods, because of a lack of self-esteem. Being friends with those one admires rather than merely tolerates would be quite difficult without self-esteem, especially where FRIENDSHIP is a peer relationship. And, of course, the point generalizes to all other peer relationships, where others are held in high regard. Mere tolerance does not make for depth in PERSONAL RELATIONSHIPS, whereas esteem deepens possibilities even where it narrows them.

The qualities necessary for self-respect seem best conceived negatively in terms of aversions, that is, they are qualities apart from which one has a deep aversion to oneself and, if protracted, to life itself. Yet believing oneself to have these qualities does not provide one with reasons for living, even for a self-evaluative person, but for avoiding ways of life that are inconsistent with minimal self-affirmation. Self-respect, then, can give us reasons for living one way rather than another only when we have reasons for living that are grounded in other concerns. On the other hand, the qualities necessary for self-esteem seem best conceived positively, as attached to goods that do give us positive reasons for living. It is the deeper personal relationships and projects that jumpstart our lives and keep us going, and it is the qualities central to such relationships and projects that tend to be the bases for high self-regard.

Together these thoughts indicate that self-respect and self-esteem might be best understood as related to different sets of VIRTUES, the set for self-esteem being more extensive than the set for self-respect. If this view is true, then there are difficulties for those conceptual schemes that require the doctrine of the unity of the virtues. Reflection also reveals that there are difficulties for those schemes that insist on some most fundamental virtue, such as justice or LOYALTY. The Kantian tradition insists on the primacy of justice, yet Dante reserved the deepest recesses of hell for those guilty of betrayal, indicating the primacy of loyalty. Neither view seems terribly plausible, for it is anything but clear how to judge either the respect or the esteem due to persons who vary in different degrees in terms of their FAIRNESS and loyalty. One might reserve respect for the bare capacity for agency, as the Kantians do, and maintain that esteem varies with virtue. But the issue will remain how to vary esteem, degree of regard, with degree of virtue, and it is anything but clear that there is some linear path along which our considered judgments regarding self-esteem are to run.

Finally, self-esteem seems far less egalitarian than self-respect, because respect, due to its concern for minimal and hence baseline criteria for self-approval, does not admit much of degree. Self-esteem, on the other hand, seems a perfect fit for the notion that we could be both better and worse than we happen to be. Only by conceiving some qualities as adding to one's worth can a self-respecting person think of self-improvement as possible. But what can be added to the worth of persons can be subtracted and value thereby diminished. If we focus only on self-respect, we miss this important nonegalitarian message. Perhaps the tendency to focus on one concept in abstraction from the other explains the distortions of both Kantian and Aristotelian moral theories.

See also: ARISTOTELIAN ETHICS; CHARACTER; EMOTION; *EUDAIMONIA,* -ISM; GUILT AND SHAME; HUMILITY; KANTIAN ETHICS; MERIT AND DESERT; NEO-KANTIAN ETHICS; PERSONAL RELATIONSHIPS; PRIDE; SELF-DECEPTION; SELF-KNOWLEDGE; SELF-RESPECT; VIRTUE ETHICS; VIRTUES.

Bibliography

Deigh, John. "Shame and Self-Esteem." *Ethics* 93 (1983): 225–45.

Dillon, Robin S., ed. *Dignity, Character, and Self-Respect.* New York: Routledge, 1995.

Harris, George W. *Agent-Centered Morality: An Aristotelian Alternative to Kantian Internalism.* Berkeley: University of California Press, 1999.

Hill Jr., Thomas. *Autonomy and Self-Respect.* Cambridge: Cambridge University Press, 1991.

———. *Dignity and Practical Reason in Kant's Moral Theory.* Ithaca: Cornell University Press, 1992.

Kant, Immanuel. *Groundwork of the Metaphysics of Morals.* Translated by H. J. Paton. New York: Harper Torchbooks, 1964 [1785].

———. *Lectures on Ethics.* Translation by Louis Infield. New York: Harper and Row, 1963. (Translation of *Eine Vorlesung Kant's über Ethik . . .* , 1775–80.)

Rawls, John. *A Theory of Justice.* Cambridge, MA: Harvard University Press, 1971.

Rorty, Amélie O., ed. *Explaining Emotion.* Los Angeles: University of California Press, 1980.

Sachs, David. "How to Distinguish Self-Respect from Self-Esteem." *Philosophy and Public Affairs* 10, no. 4 (1981): 346–60.

Taylor, Gabriele. *Pride, Shame and Guilt: Emotions of Self-Assessment.* Oxford: Clarendon Press, 1985.

George W. Harris

selfishness

See egoism.

self-knowledge

"Know thyself" is not simply a particular kind of epistemological injunction but a normative one as well, and for that reason indicates that some knowledge is more important than other knowledge. Whether there can be a kind of knowledge that is of the self and whether, if there is such knowledge, it has a kind of privileged status over other forms of knowledge are issues hotly contested in the philosophy of mind. In ethics, the injunction to self-knowledge implies a RESPONSIBILITY to know things about oneself that are relevant to the issue of how to live both rightly and well. Of course, the injunction implies that there are some things about oneself that are important to know and that one can know these things. From the ethical perspective, then, the issue of the necessity and hence the possibility of self-knowledge is limited, in a broad sense, to the practical domain.

It would seem that getting a grip on the importance of self-knowledge would depend on getting a grip on what knowledge of the self is about and, of course, theories of what the self is about: a simple substance directly available through introspection, a substance knowable only through its properties, a noumenal substance unavailable to experience but ontologically prior to the possibility of any experience whatever, a complex function of a neurological system, or a social construct largely the function of a social and political environment. But is it really true that we must settle such metaphysical issues before we can make sense of improving our knowledge of ourselves? Must we have knowledge of what the metaphysical status of a person is before we can in some sense know another person both intimately and well? And if there is a sense in which we can know others both intimately and well without settling metaphysical accounts, what is to stop us from knowing ourselves both intimately and well? In fact, knowing ourselves without knowing what a self is seems to be just the kind of knowledge that is so important to the issue of how to live.

If knowledge of the metaphysical status of the self is not so important to living both rightly and well, then what is it about oneself that is so important to know? Why, more specifically, is knowledge of these things so important? How can one know these sorts of things about oneself? And what kinds of obstacles are there to such knowledge?

There is a kind of self-knowledge that is indicated when we say that we are in touch with ourselves. To be in touch with ourselves in this sense is to know with some degree of accuracy a number of things: what is important to us, what our priorities are in regard to those things that are important to us, what our MOTIVES are, how we appear to others, and what our strengths and weaknesses are in regard to our CHARACTER. To be in touch with ourselves, then, is to know a great deal about both our personality structure and our character. Although knowing these things about ourselves is often quite difficult, knowing them is nonetheless crucial to our ability to live both rightly and well from our own points of view. Without this knowledge, we are unable to regulate and maintain the kinds of persons we want ourselves to be in relationship to the other things we

care about, and we are unable to appreciate ourselves for the persons we in fact are. For most of us, it is important that we are not fools, fakes, philistines, personally insensitive, boorish, overbearing, unfair, cowardly, gullible, unintelligent, cruel, given to betrayal, selfish, lazy, utterly mediocre, ugly, or tone deaf. Hence, it is important to us that we are in fact wise, genuine, tasteful, respectful and sympathetic, polished, considerate, fair, courageous, savvy, intelligent, kind, loyal, other-regarding, resourceful, excellent in some regards, passably attractive, and that we sing on key. To be mistaken about these kinds of things regarding ourselves is an error we think very important to avoid. One way to think about self-knowledge, then, is to think of it as not being mistaken about these sorts of things about oneself: more generally, it is not being mistaken about the kind of person one is.

Knowing how not to be mistaken about the kind of person one is is to possess the skills and the VIRTUES of self-knowledge. What are those skills and virtues? Perhaps the first is the capacity to take criticism from others. Because others often know things about us that we do not know about ourselves, learning what they know about us is often essential to our knowing the kinds of persons we are. If we are to know whether we are fair or kind, we must be attentive to the critical responses of those to whom we could be unfair or cruel; to be assured that we are not philistines or boorish, we must be open to the criticism of those who are tasteful and polished; to avoid utter mediocrity, we must make ourselves pupils of those who are excellent; and so on. But to whom does one go for critical assessment of the kind of person in general one is? ARISTOTLE (384–322 B.C.E.) would have said to one's friends. Why? Because a friend is an equal, not just in some respect but as a person. Having friends that will criticize us in appropriate ways, then, is crucial to self-knowledge, which makes the skill of choosing our friends essential to the task. Moreover, any ethical account of self-knowledge assumes that the particular skills of self-knowledge are accessible to us only when we have some robust sense of the kind of person we would like to be like. Without such a sense, we will choose bad friends, get unreliable criticisms, and fail to learn what we need to from others in order to know ourselves. The possession of these skills, then, presumes some self-knowledge already. If we lack this more basic self-knowledge and its skills, we might consult a therapist instead. In any event, there is much about ourselves that we can know from the critical responses of others.

But how and by what means does one gain self-knowledge through one's own observations? Recent philosophical work on the emotions provides some guidance in this regard. Robert C. Roberts has recently argued that there are similarities between emotions and perceptions, and that one important similarity between them is that just as there can be perceptual errors there can be emotional errors. For example, just as one can misperceive that a stick partly in the water is crooked rather than straight, one can misperceive that a friend is angry when he is simply perplexed. More importantly, we can misperceive ourselves because of certain kinds of emotional errors. We can misperceive a situation emotionally because we are factually in error; we can misperceive the importance of a situation because our emotional response is incommensurate with the values at stake in a situation; we can misperceive one emotional response for another; and we can misperceive the object of our emotion.

Knowing something about the cognitive and affective structure of various emotions and knowing the patterns of our own emotional responses can help us gain valuable knowledge about ourselves. Suppose, for example, that I want to know whether I am a committed philosopher and intellectual. Others have told me so, but perhaps they are flatterers; still others have denied that I am, but perhaps they are resentful. How can I settle this for myself through my own observations? I claim to take pride in doing philosophy well, but do I? Is there something that can be known about the structure of the emotion of PRIDE together with some information about myself that might help me answer these questions myself? Suppose I find myself being resentful at the accomplishments of others when they are equal to or greater than my own. Being in tune with my emotions in this regard would alert me to a misplaced value. RESENTMENT of similar accomplishments of others should lead me to question whether my priorities are what I have led myself to believe they are, and reflection should reveal a distorted emotional picture of my own values. Knowing this, I can take the necessary steps of self-regulation and become more like the kind of person I most want to be.

Similar kinds of analysis might be available for answering other questions about ourselves. In fact, careful observation of the patterns of my emotional response might correct my beliefs about the kind of person I think I want to be. Should I persistently find myself admiring good teachers and repulsed by the effects of political posturing, I might revise my longstanding plan for a political career because my emotions bring into better focus the kind of person I most want to be like. What are the patterns of behavioral response indicative of a person with a certain pattern of emotional response, and do we have the behavioral responses indicative of the emotions we attribute to the kind of person we most want to be like? An extensive study of the emotions and their structure as they relate to good character promises to provide us an invaluable set of tools for gaining self-knowledge.

Emotional obtuseness aside, there other obstacles to self-knowledge. On the most optimistic accounts the obstacles are primarily confined to SELF-DECEPTION and weakness of will. Just what self-deception is is a matter best discussed elsewhere, but whatever it is the injunction to know ourselves includes the commitment to stand on guard against it. KANT (1724–1804) seems to have thought that the possibility of self-deception regarding the kind of person one is is so pervasive that we cannot ever know whether we are self-deceived or not. Since his conclusion is largely a function of his metaphysical views on what a self is, we must find those views mistaken if we are to take the task of self-knowledge seriously, as he, somewhat inconsistently, held that we should. Similarly, if we are to know ourselves, we must cultivate the COURAGE to take seriously the criticisms of others, to be in tune with ourselves, and to live an examined life. On the more moderate views of the possibility of self-knowledge, self-revelation is possible but often only through extensive psychoanalysis. Freudian views of the formation of the self are prominent at this point on the philosophical spectrum. At the extreme end are the pessimistic views of POSTMODERNISM that variously proclaim the death of the self or at least its hopeless fragmentation in postmodern society.

See also: CHARACTER; COGNITIVE SCIENCE; EMOTION; FRIENDSHIP; INTERESTS; MORAL ATTENTION; MORAL IMAGINATION; MORAL PERCEPTION; MOTIVES; NEEDS; PRIDE; SELF AND SOCIAL SELF; SELF-

CONTROL; SELF-DECEPTION; SELF-ESTEEM; WEAKNESS OF WILL.

Bibliography

Aristotle. *Nicomachean Ethics.* Translated by M. Ostwald. Indianapolis: Bobbs-Merrill, 1962.

Cassam, Quassim, ed. *Self-Knowledge.* New York: Oxford University Press, 1994.

Harris, George W. *Agent-Centered Morality: An Aristotelian Alternative to Kantian Internalism.* Berkeley: University of California Press, 1999.

Kant, Immanuel. *Groundwork of the Metaphysics of Morals.* Translated by H. J. Paton. New York: Harper Torchbooks, 1964 [1785].

Martin, Mike W., ed. *Self-Deception and Self-Understanding: New Essays in Philosophy and Psychology.* Lawrence: University Press of Kansas, 1989 (1985).

Mele, Alfred R. *Irrationality: An Essay on Akrasia, Self-deception, and Self-control.* New York: Oxford University Press, 1987.

Nozick, Robert. *The Examined Life.* New York: Touchstone, 1989.

Plato. *Collected Dialogues.* Edited by E. Hamilton and H. Cairns. Princeton: Princeton University Press, 1961. See especially *Charmides* and *Laches.*

Roberts, Robert C. "Feeling One's Emotions and Knowing Oneself." *Philosophical Studies* 77 (1995): 319–38.

Stocker, Michael, and Elizabeth Hegeman. *Valuing Emotions.* Cambridge: Cambridge University Press, 1996.

George W. Harris

selflessness

See altruism.

self-ownership

John LOCKE (1632–1704), libertarians, and others have held that agents are self-owners in the sense that they have private property rights over themselves in the same way that people can have private property rights over inanimate objects. This private ownership is typically taken to include (1) *control rights* over (power to grant and deny permission for) the *use* of their persons (*e.g.,* what things are done to them); (2) *rights to transfer* the rights they have to others (by sale, rental, gift, or loan); and (3) *tax immunities* for the possession and exercise of these rights (so that, unlike renters, for example, they owe no payment for these rights). The property rights in question are *moral* rights and need not be legally recognized. Thus, a country that allows involuntary SLAVERY fails to recognize the (moral) self-ownership of the slaves.

Self-ownership, like private ownership in general, is a bundle of RIGHTS that can vary in strength. *Full* self-ownership (which is how self-ownership is usually understood) involves a maximal set of property rights over oneself comparable to the maximal set involved in the private ownership of inanimate objects. Partial forms of self-ownership leave out some of these rights. At the core of self-ownership is *control self-ownership,* the right to control the *use* of one's person (but not necessarily any right to transfer this right to others, or any tax immunity for the possession or exercise of this right). Something like control self-ownership is arguably needed to recognize the fact there are some things (*e.g.,* various forms of physical contact) that may not be done to an individual without his or her CONSENT, but which may be done with that consent. Endorsement of control self-ownership, however, does not require the endorsement of full self-ownership. And even if rational agents are full self-owners, there is the further question of what sort of ownership, if any, other sentient beings (animals, children, etc.) have.

Some Common Misunderstandings about Full Self-Ownership

Full self-ownership is often held to have implications that it in fact does not have. It is sometimes held to entail, for example, that one owns one's entire *body.* This implication does not follow automatically, since it depends on whether the self-owning being is identical with his or her body. If the being in question is a mental being that need not occupy a body to exist (*e.g.,* a Cartesian soul), then self-ownership alone does not guarantee ownership of the body.

Full self-ownership is sometimes thought to guarantee that the agent has a certain basic *liberty of action,* but this is not so. For if the rest of the world (natural resources and artifacts) is fully ("maximally") owned by others, one is not permitted to do anything without their consent (since it involves the use of their PROPERTY). The protection that self-ownership affords is a basic protection against others doing certain things to one, and not a guarantee of LIBERTY. But even this protection may be merely formal. For a plausible thesis of self-ownership must allow that some rights (*e.g.,* those that imprisonment violates) may be lost as a result of past injustices committed by an agent. Hence, if the rest of world is owned by others, then anything one does without their consent violates their property rights, and as a result of such violations one may lose some or all of one's rights of self-ownership. This point shows that, because agents must use natural resources (occupy space, breathe air, etc.), self-ownership on its own has no substantive implications. It is only when combined with assumptions about how the rest of the world is owned (and the consequences of violating those property rights) that substantive implications follow.

It is often supposed that full self-ownership gives one property rights in one's *products,* but this is so only if the products are part of oneself (*e.g.,* an improvement in one's ability to do mental arithmetic). For any products that involve natural resources involve materials that may belong to others, and a person who makes something from stolen materials may not own the product. Again, it all depends on how the rest of the world is owned.

The Ownership of the External World

Libertarianism is sometimes (and increasingly) understood as the thesis of full self-ownership. So understood, a distinction can be made between *right-libertarianism* and *left-libertarianism,* depending on the stance taken on how natural resources are owned. Right-libertarianism (the traditional form of LIBERTARIANISM) holds that natural resources are initially unowned and typically may be appropriated without the consent of, or significant payment to, others. It holds, for example, that whoever first discovers, or first mixes her labor with, a natural resource owns that resource as long as certain minimal conditions hold (*e.g.,* Locke's "enough and as good for others"). Left-libertarianism, by contrast, holds that natural resources are owned by the members of society in some egalitarian sense, so that appropriation is legitimate only with their consent or with a significant payment to them. For example, according to *joint ownership,* all decisions about the use of natural resources are made by some collective decision-making procedure (Grunebaum). According to an *equal market share* conception, agents must pay the *market rent* (based on demand and

supply) for any rights they claim over natural resources, and these rents are divided equally among agents (Steiner). This latter view has the advantage of permitting agents to use and appropriate natural resources without the consent of others as long as an appropriate payment is made to the members of society. (Under joint ownership one is not permitted to do anything without the consent of others.) There are, of course, many other possible conceptions of the ownership of natural resources that can be combined with full self-ownership, and the plausibility of the full theory will depend crucially on the plausibility of the conception of natural resource ownership invoked. (For discussion, see, for example, Cohen.)

Objections to Full Self-Ownership

Some authors object that the very notion of self-ownership is incoherent on the grounds that agents are not the kinds of things that can be owned, or on the grounds that the notion of *full* self-ownership is radically indeterminate. To the first point it can be replied that agents have the right to control the use of their person in various ways and that such rights constitute a form of ownership rights. To the second point it can be replied that, although there is some indeterminacy in the notion of full ownership of anything, there is no particular indeterminacy in the notion of full self-ownership.

The following four objections can be raised to the implications of full self-ownership. One objection is that it permits voluntary enslavement. For agents have not only the right to control the use of their person, but also the right to *transfer* that right (by sale or gift) to others. Many authors—such as Locke, Rothbard (1982), and Grunebaum—deny that the rights over oneself are so transferable (typically on the grounds that it undermines one's autonomy). Those who defend the right of self-enslavement—Steiner, for example—defend it on the grounds (roughly) that the right to *exercise* one's autonomy is more fundamental than the *protection or promotion* of one's autonomy.

A second objection to full self-ownership is that it denies that individuals have any (enforceable) obligation to perform actions that help the needy (except through voluntary commitment). Some authors who endorse a form of self-ownership—such as Locke and Grunebaum—hold that one's rights of self-control are limited by an obligation to provide aid to others when the aid is necessary for basic survival. Those who reject this obligation typically do so on the grounds that it induces a form of partial slavery.

A third substantive objection to full self-ownership is that it includes a right to make gifts of one's services and that such gifts (like gifts of money and material objects), when given from members of an older generation to members of a younger generation, can significantly disrupt the conditions of equality of opportunity. Those who defend the right of gifts of personal services emphasize how gifts are an essential part of intimate PERSONAL RELATIONSHIPS. They also insist that if a person has the right to perform an action for his own benefit, then he also has the right to perform it for someone else's benefit.

A fourth objection to full self-ownership is that (like rights in general) it can lead to inefficient outcomes. Where there are externalities or PUBLIC GOODS (such as police protection), each person may be better off if some of each person's rights are infringed (*e.g.,* if each person is required to provide service each week on a police patrol). Given the problems generated by prisoners' dilemmas and other kinds of market failure, in large societies it will typically be impossible to get people's consent to perform such services. But many would argue that it is nonetheless just to coerce them into providing services (in violation of full self-ownership) as long as everyone benefits appropriately. The crucial difference here concerns the ultimate basis for the rights of self-ownership. Those who endorse the *choice theory* (rights protect choices) will deny, and those who endorse the *interest theory* (rights protect INTERESTS) will hold, that infringements are permissible when they benefit the agents appropriately.

It should be kept in mind that, even if some of the rights of full self-ownership are rejected, a partial form of self-ownership may nonetheless be plausible.

See also: ABORTION; ANIMALS, TREATMENT OF; AUTONOMY OF MORAL AGENTS; CHILDREN AND ETHICAL THEORY; COERCION; CONSENT; CONTRACTS; CORRECTIONAL ETHICS; ENTITLEMENTS; EQUALITY; GROUPS, MORAL STATUS OF; HARM AND OFFENSE; INDIVIDUALISM; JUSTICE, DISTRIBUTIVE; JUSTICE, RECTIFICATORY; LAND ETHICS; LIBERTARIANISM; LIBERTY; LIFE, RIGHT TO; LOCKE; MARXISM; OBJECTIVISM; PATERNALISM; PRIVACY; PROPERTY; RAND; RIGHT HOLDERS; RIGHTS; SELF-CONTROL; SELF-DEFENSE; SLAVERY; SUICIDE; TORTURE; WORK.

Bibliography

Becker, Lawrence C. *Property Rights: Philosophic Foundations.* Boston: Routledge and Kegan Paul, 1977.

Christman, John. *The Myth of Property.* New York: Oxford University Press, 1994.

Cohen, G. A. *Self-Ownership, Freedom, and Equality.* Cambridge: Cambridge University Press, 1995.

Grunebaum, James. *Private Ownership.* New York: Routledge and Kegan Paul, 1987.

Kymlicka, Will. *Contemporary Political Philosophy.* New York: Oxford, 1990.

Locke, John. *Two Treatises of Government.* Edited by Peter Laslett. New York: Cambridge University Press, 1960 [1690].

Nozick, Robert. *Anarchy, State, and Utopia.* New York: Basic Books, 1974.

Rothbard, Murray N. *For a New Liberty: The Libertarian Manifesto.* Rev. ed. New York: Collier Books, 1978.

———. *The Ethics of Liberty.* Atlantic Highlands, NJ: Humanities Press, 1982. Reprinted, with a new introduction by Hans-Hermann Hoppe, New York: New York University Press, 1998.

Steiner, Hillel. *An Essay on Rights.* Cambridge, MA: Blackwell, 1994.

Waldron, Jeremy. *The Right to Private Property.* New York: Oxford University Press, 1988.

Peter Vallentyne

self-respect

Moral reflection often makes use of the idea of self-respect. To say, for example, that a person has no self-respect is to criticize that person's CHARACTER; and to say of an act that no self-respecting person would do it is a strong condemnation. To argue that an institution tends to undermine the self-respect of a person or a group of people is typically to raise a moral objection to that institution. These familiar facts have led philosophers to consider a variety of questions about self-respect, and some moral theorists have given the idea of self-respect a central role in their work.

Among the main questions raised by contemporary philosophers are these: (1) What is self-respect, and how is it distinguished from related notions such as SELF-ESTEEM, PRIDE, and self-confidence? (2) Is the idea substantive or formal? That is, is there a fairly specific content to the idea of a self-respecting person (like the idea of a kind or honest person), or is the idea more open-ended (like the idea of a righteous or conscientious person)? (3) Is the idea subjective or objective? That is, is it sufficient for having self-respect that one has certain self-regarding feelings, attitudes, and beliefs, regardless of whether one judges oneself correctly and behaves morally; or is it also necessary that one meet external standards of correct judgment and/or moral conduct? (4) What are the relations between self-respect and RIGHTS? For example, could there be no self-respect in a community that did not acknowledge rights? Does self-respect require valuing and standing up for one's rights? (5) How are self-respect and respect for others related? For example, can one respect oneself but not respect others, or vice versa? Are the dependencies, if any, conceptual or psychological? Does maintaining one's self-respect require being respected by others or believing that the basis of self-respect is a quality valued by others? (6) Is there a basic duty to respect oneself that is analogous to the duty to respect others? (7) Is self-respect a primary good relevant to assessing the justice of social INSTITUTIONS?

Moral philosophers who give self-respect a central place in their work typically do so in two distinct ways. Some argue that morality requires that we maintain our self-respect and that consequently certain acts are morally required and others are prohibited. Other philosophers argue that self-respect is an important good to anyone who has it, and on this basis they support institutions and policies that affirm persons' self-respect and object to those that undermine self-respect. The first line of argument is prominent in KANT's (1724–1804) ethics, and the second is central in RAWLS's theory of justice.

One of Kant's formulations of the supreme moral principle states that one must treat the humanity, or rational nature, of every person (including oneself), as an "end in itself." From this point Kant argued not only for duties of respect to others but also for the duties to oneself associated with "proper self-respect." The latter include duties to avoid drunkenness, SUICIDE, servility, making oneself a sexual object, and more generally, unrestrained indulgence of inclinations. Fulfilling such duties, Kant maintained, is a necessary condition of fulfilling duties to

others. Various twentieth-century philosophers have argued along similar lines that a proper self-respect requires affirming one's moral EQUALITY, refusing to tolerate without protest the denial of one's rights, and seeking to avoid self-harm, SELF-DECEPTION, and WEAKNESS OF WILL. Underlying many of these arguments is a conception of self-respect as an attitude and conduct appropriate to full recognition of one's own moral rights.

In the work of John Rawls and his commentators, the question is not "What must the agent do to be self-respecting?" but rather "How can basic social institutions be designed so that they will foster self-respect in citizens?" Self-respect then is conceived not as a moral ideal for individuals to strive for but as a "primary good," an asset likely to be desirable to rational agents whatever their projects. Self-respect, according to Rawls, "includes a person's sense of his own value, his secure conviction that his conception of his good, his plan of life, is worth carrying out" and also "a confidence in one's ability, so far as it is within one's power, to fulfill one's intentions." He argues that "justice as fairness" is superior to UTILITARIANISM insofar as it better affirms and promotes such self-respect. Similarly, others have argued that specific policies, such as affirmative action, must be assessed according to their effect on the self-respect of minorities.

Rawls's conception of self-respect has been criticized on the grounds that it fails to distinguish self-respect from self-esteem. Self-esteem is generally taken to be a positive self-evaluation based on perceived merits, such as talents and achievements, whereas self-respect, in its narrower sense, is often viewed as an appropriate recognition and response to one's status as a person with rights and responsibilities. David Sachs makes the distinction by noting that: (a) one can have excessive or unwarranted self-esteem but not too much or unwarranted self-respect; (b) maintaining one's self-respect is a ground for self-esteem, but not the reverse; (c) a person may have little or no self-esteem ("he is proud of nothing") even though his self-respect is intact ("he has his pride"); but (d) it is difficult to imagine a socialized rational human being who utterly lacks self-respect. Regarding the last, Sachs says: "Were there to be such a person, he would not find it a reason for resentment that persons ignore, capriciously or even blankly ignore, what they know to be his wishes. . . . Nor would he be averse to submitting to anything on the ground that it was degrading. Also he would not resent or be indignant about the flaunting of any rights he possessed; not, that is, for the reason that rights of his were being flaunted."

Some writers, unlike Sachs, do not regard recognition of one's rights as essential to self-respect. On one account, for example, the central elements are independence, tenacity, and SELF-CONTROL (Telfer). Other accounts stress the importance of setting and living by one's own standards (Hill) or standards implicit in projects one identifies with and regards as worthy (Massey).

See also: AUTONOMY OF MORAL AGENTS; CHARACTER; DIGNITY; EGOISM; EQUALITY; GUILT AND SHAME; HONOR; HUMILITY; KANT; PATERNALISM; PRIDE; RAWLS; RESPONSIBILITY; SELF-CONTROL; SELF-DECEPTION; SELF-ESTEEM; SELF-KNOWLEDGE; SELF-OWNERSHIP; SUBJECTIVISM; WEAKNESS OF WILL.

Bibliography

Boxill, Bernard. "Self-Respect and Protest." *Philosophy and Public Affairs* 6 (1976): 58–69.

Darwall, Stephen L. "Two Concepts of Respect." *Ethics* 88 (1977): 36–49.

Deigh, John. "Shame and Self-Esteem: A Critique." *Ethics* 93 (1983): 225–45.

Downie, R. S., and Elizabeth Telfer. *Respect for Persons.* London: Allen and Unwin, 1969.

Feinberg, Joel. "The Nature and Value of Rights." *Journal of Value Inquiry* 4 (1970): 263–77.

Green, O. H., ed. *Respect for Persons.* Tulane Studies in Philosophy, vol. 31. New Orleans, LA: Tulane University Press, 1982. See especially "Self-Respect and Respect for Others: Are They Independent?" by David Sachs (p. 109–28).

Hill Jr., Thomas E. *Autonomy and Self-Respect.* Cambridge: Cambridge University Press, 1991.

Kant, Immanuel. *Lectures on Ethics.* Translated by Louis Infield. New York: Harper and Row, 1963 [1780]. See especially "Proper Self-Respect" and "Duties to Oneself".

Martin, Mike W. *Everyday Morality.* Belmont, CA: Wadsworth, 1989. See pp. 75–121.

Massey, Stephen. "Is Self-Respect a Moral or a Psychological Concept?" *Ethics* 93 (1983): 246–61.

———. "Kant on Self-Respect." *Journal of the History of Philosophy* 21 (1983): 57–74.

Rawls, John. *A Theory of Justice.* Cambridge, MA: Harvard University Press, 1971. For passage cited, see p. 440.

Sachs, David. "How to Distinguish Self-Respect from Self-Esteem." *Philosophy and Public Affairs* 10, no. 4 (1981): 346–60. For citation, see p. 352.

Telfer, Elizabeth. "Self-Respect." *Philosophical Quarterly* 18 (1968): 114–21.

Thomas, Laurence. "Morality and Our Self-Concept." *Journal of Value Inquiry* 12 (1978): 258–68.

Thomas E. Hill Jr.

Seneca, Lucius Annaeus ["the Younger"] (c. 4 B.C.E.–65 C.E.)

Roman philosopher born in Spain. Having been Nero's (37–68 C.E.) tutor and then a prominent adviser, particularly in the earlier and better part of the reign, Seneca was ordered by the Emperor to take his own life. A playwright as well as a Stoic moral philosopher and moralist, he has had a widespread influence on European thought. Because he lacks theoretical originality and rigour of argument he is not a moral philosopher of the first rank but, as Martha Nussbaum in particular has shown, he writes penetratingly of human weaknesses and depravity, offers a training in moral virtue adapted to the nature of the particular individual, and relates his theses to questions and objections. Quintilian (c. 35–100 C.E.) remarked (*Institutio Oratoria* X.1.129) that he was "not sufficiently thorough in philosophy, but exceptional as an outspoken critic of vices."

Seneca's best-known work, the *Epistulae Morales* or *Letters on Conduct* (63–65), was nominally addressed to a young friend, Lucilius. The 124 letters are extremely repetitive: Fronto (c. 95–166), in his *Letters,* said that they "set forth the same opinion a thousand times in one dress after another."

One prominent theme, perennial for Seneca, is that of *apatheia* or freedom from passions. J. B. Lightfoot observes that *apatheia* is the twin sister of the Epicurean *ataraxia* or serenity. In the ninth letter, Seneca suggests that the ideal of *apatheia* is best presented to Romans as that of an invulnerable mind, beyond all suffering.

Seneca's weaknesses and strengths, and his general view of emotions or passions as requiring extirpation, appear clearly in a much earlier work, *On Anger,* written between 41 and 51. He so defines ANGER that a remark such as "She kept her anger entirely under control, and acted constructively" would be incoherent: anger for him is essentially out of control, for he sees it as the result of the surrender of one's reason. "Emotion is not a matter of being moved by impressions received, but of surrendering oneself to them and following up the chance movement" (II.3.1). There is also a tendency to write as though a vivid description of one instance or form of something is applicable to all. "Anger," says Seneca at the beginning of the work, "is all excitement and impulse," and there follows an account of an extreme form:

> Raving with a desire that is utterly inhuman for instruments of pain and reparations in blood, careless of itself so long as it harms the other, it rushes onto the very spear-points, greedy for vengeance that draws down the avenger with it.

The accounts by PLATO (c. 430–347 B.C.E.) of the "anger-like" element in the *psuche* (*Republic* 439–44) and by ARISTOTLE (384–322 B.C.E.) of anger (*Nicomachean Ethics* IV.5), in both cases as able and needing to be under rational control, show the shallowness of Seneca's claim that anger, if stronger than reason, is uncontrollable by it, and if weaker not needed by it (I.8.5). Yet Seneca's achievement in *On Anger* of "put[ting] all the faults of anger on show" (III.5.3) and providing a therapy for it is a considerable one from which much of practical value may be learnt.

Striving for invulnerability, like the extirpation of such passions as anger, requires SELF-KNOWLEDGE and arduous training: "it helps to know one's illness and to suppress its power before it spreads . . . Fight with yourself" (III.10.4, 13.1). Nothing should strike one as unexpected or upsetting: the mind, therefore, should be strengthened by contemplating in advance the scale not only of what does happen but of what could happen (Letter 91; cf. 107). Himself extremely wealthy, Seneca did not forbid wealth but urged that one should both train oneself to do without it and think of it as about to vanish (18). One must also develop a readiness to die (26), and Seneca did so with conspicuous success, as is shown by Tacitus's (c. 55–120) account of his SUICIDE.

Seneca scorned to excess any philosophy that was not practical and did not assist human beings in their wretchedness (48) to live conformably to their nature by overcoming fear, desire, and passion (see also 88 and 108). His letters are not as good a Roman source for systematic STOICISM as Book III of the *De finibus* of CICERO (106–43 B.C.E.), but are noteworthy for such striking sayings as "treat your inferior as you would wish to be treated by your superior" (this in a discussion of relations with slaves, 47) and, in a discussion of FRIENDSHIP, "you should live for another if you wish to live for yourself" (48).

This latter precept, however, which is offered as essential if one is to "live happily" (*beate vivere*), suggests what is true, that Seneca's account of the life that deserves an ultimate congratulation has too little concern for the welfare of others for their own sake. "[Seneca's] ideal of purity and integrity . . . is . . . more than a little egocentric" (Nussbaum). His moral system is humane, and he affirms a common humanity (for example, in *On Favours*, written after 56, when he is describing the virtues that slaves have shown: III.18–28); but we do not find a consistent emphasis on disinterestedness or recognition of the possibility of a constructive LOVE of one's neighbour. Seneca's advocacy of inner invulnerability and of moderation relies in part on the contemplation of transience and the greatness of the universe. His references to God or gods are not coherent (compare the ends of Letters 65 and 53).

See also: ANGER; ARISTOTLE; CICERO; EPICUREANISM; EPICURUS; FRIENDSHIP; GOLDEN RULE; NEO-STOICISM; PAIN AND SUFFERING; PASSION; PLATO; PRACTICAL REASON[ING]; SELF-KNOWLEDGE; SLAVERY; STOICISM; SUICIDE; VIRTUE ETHICS; WEAKNESS OF WILL.

Bibliography

Editions of works by Seneca

Ad Lucilium epistulae morales. Edited by Richard M. Gummere. Loeb ed. 3 vols. 1917–1925.

Letters. Edited by L. D. Reynolds. Oxford: Oxford University Press, 1965. The full text.

Letters from a Stoic. Translated by Robin Campbell. New York: Penguin, 1969. Selections from the letters with useful introduction, based on *Letters* 1965.

Moral and Political Essays. Edited and translated by John M. Cooper and J. F. Procopé. Cambridge: Cambridge University Press, 1995. Has a good general introduction to Seneca and to Stoicism. Translations given in text of extracts from *On Anger* are from this edition.

Dialogues. Edited by L. D. Reynolds. Oxford: Oxford University Press, 1977.

Moral Essays. (Twelve books on moral subjects.) Translated by J. W. Basore. Loeb ed. 3 vols. 1928.

Works about Seneca

Arnold, E. Vernon. *Roman Stoicism.* Cambridge: Cambridge University Press, 1911.

Griffin, Miriam T. *Seneca: A Philosopher in Politics.* Oxford: Oxford University Press, 1976.

Lightfoot, J. B. "St. Paul and Seneca." In his edition of *Saint Paul's Epistle to the Philippians.* 2d ed. London: Macmillan, 1879. See p. 272*f.*

Motto, Anna Lydia. *Seneca.* New York: Twayne, 1973.

Nussbaum, Martha C. *The Therapy of Desire.* Princeton, NJ: Princeton University Press, 1994. Chapters 9–12 discuss Seneca, with particular reference to the extirpation of the passions. Chapter 11, on Seneca's treatment of anger, with attention to three modern instances, is excellent. (Sentence quoted, p. 436.)

Reynolds, Leighton Durham, Miriam T. Griffin, and Elaine Fantham. "Annaeus Seneca, Lucius." In *Oxford Classical Dictionary,* 3d ed., edited by Simon Hornblower and Antony Spawforth, pp. 96–98. Oxford: Oxford University Press, 1996. See for Seneca's works and rhetorical style, and an account of his life.

John Howes

sexual abuse and harassment

Sexual abuse and harassment are relatively recent legal and moral concerns. They both involve sexual advances or actions that occur against the wishes of the person toward whom they are directed or in situations in which that person is either incompetent to consent or where CONSENT was given under conditions that are reasonably seen as coercive. The recent attention these topics have received has come primarily from concern with institutionalized POWER inequalities as these affect various social groups.

Women in the Workplace

Men as well as women can experience sexual harassment, and women as well as men can be guilty of it. Male-instigated, heterosexual harassment, however, is not only the most common, but, given the nature of gender INEQUALITY, the only sort whose implications systematically go beyond the individuals immediately affected.

As Catherine MacKinnon argues in her groundbreaking study, such harassment in the workplace is a form of sex—*i.e.,* gender—DISCRIMINATION. Rather than being an aberration, it is the consequence of the power inequality between men and women, along with the sexiness that is ascribed both to inequality itself and, relatedly, to the tacit job descriptions of many traditionally women's jobs. Sexual harassment has consequences for the workplace EQUALITY even of women who are not the immediate victims of it, making it difficult for women to see themselves and to be seen by others as competent and as appropriately in control. Through the intertwined social constructions of gender and of sexuality, women are defined not as independent, assertive, and competent, but as normatively subordinate and vulnerable, and they are characterized by their real or perceived accessibility to sexual advances. Since sexual harassment both depends on and reinforces these attitudes, it affects men and women very differently, whether they experience it directly or not.

Students

Beginning in the 1970s, sexual harassment of students by teachers has increasingly come to be seen as a major problem in colleges and universities, and many schools have drafted policies to deal with it. The problem can be identified in a number of quite different ways. It can be seen to lie in the pressing of unwanted sexual advances by anyone on anyone else, made worse by the use of threats or inappropriate PROMISES. Thus, anyone can sexually harass anyone else, though only some have ready access to such things as grades to be used as bribes and retaliations. On such a view the power difference between teachers and students is only contingently relevant: should a student have some means of bribing or threatening a teacher or another student for failing to respond to sexual advances, the situation is, on this view of the matter, precisely analogous to the more usual one.

Alternatively, inequalities of power can be seen as intrinsic to the problem of sexual harassment in a number of ways. Teachers can be seen as standing in a position of RESPONSIBILITY toward their students that is incompatible with becoming sexually involved with them. Again, this view is especially clear in the situation of female student and male teacher. It is difficult, given the continuing sexism at all levels of education, for female students to believe that they are taken seriously for their academic abilities and, consequently, to take themselves seriously. To discover that a trusted teacher is interested in them sexually will almost inevitably lead to their questioning not only his opinion of them as students but that of other instructors as well. As closely associated as the roles are in our cultural mythology (in fact, in part because of this association), the roles of teacher and lover don't typically work to the benefit of the student.

A further relevance of inequalities of power is to the issue of consent. Definitions of sexual harassment refer to unwanted sexual advances, but actual implementation of policies often recognizes the need to distinguish between what is—and comes later to be seen—as in people's real interest and what they may at the time consent to. The relevant notion of consent seems to be counterfactual: would the student have consented in the absence of the teacher's power? When the answer is no, students may later come to see the relationship as one that, even if they initiated it, was not in their real interest, and schools are increasingly concluding that the responsibility in such cases lies with faculty.

Sexual harassment may also occur outside of one-on-one relationships, through sexually suggestive or demeaning language or images that create a climate of intimidation. Problems arise around the extent to which rights to freedom of expression can be curtailed in the interest of eliminating systematic inequalities of access; the strongest arguments in favor of restrictions are those that justify some curbs on the expression of the more powerful in cases in which such expression when unregulated serves systematically to suppress expression on the part of the less powerful.

Clients and Patients

The sort of incompatibility many believe to obtain between the roles of teacher and lover is more widely believed to obtain between the roles of clinician or therapist or counselor, and lover, so much so that in some cases such sexual relationships are held to constitute RAPE. They are consistently proscribed in codes of PROFESSIONAL ETHICS. The inequalities of power and the dependence that characterize the client/clinician relationship are such that the argument that a sexual involvement can be in—or at least not against—the client's interests is usually taken not only to be unsound but also not to be in good faith, and such involvement is typically regarded as an abuse of power and responsibility. Not only are the conditions for autonomous consent arguably absent

in such cases, but the clinician has entered into a relationship in which the client's real interests and needs, rather than the satisfaction of sexual desire on the part of either or both of the parties, appropriately govern her or his actions.

Children

Sexual abuse of children has a longer history of attention, although one that is difficult to track, in part because of the changing definition of childhood. The sort of sexuality prevalent in fifth-century B.C.E. Athens and extolled by PLATO (c. 430–347 B.C.E.) was between adult men and adolescent boys. Jeremy BENTHAM (1748–1832) wrote at intervals throughout his life in (utilitarian) defense of what he called "pederasty," by which he meant sexual activity between adult, usually married, men and adolescent boys. When he considers all the things that people might conceivably find wrong with such activity, the youth of the boys is not among them, since it was not regarded as impairing their ability to be consenting sexual partners.

Similarly, incest, which we now think of nearly exclusively as child sexual abuse by an older family member (or by someone in a nonfamilial position of trust), used to be identified in a way that made the age of the participants irrelevant to the wrong and that made responsibility and agency mutual. (Consider what is probably the most famous example of incest: Oedipus and Jocasta.) When incest and pederasty were regarded as wrong (and incest almost universally was), the reasons had nothing to do with children. Rather, certain sexual acts, or any sexual acts between certain people, were seen as wrong, independently of any concern about the authenticity of consent.

Freud (1856–1939) drew attention to the sexual abuse of children, only, notoriously, to pull away from acknowledging its prevalence in favor of attributing many of the reports of it to children's fantasies. But since his writing there has been increasing concern about the abuse of power and responsibility involved in adults' sexual behavior toward children. Such behavior, for the most part committed by men against girls, is not uncommon: the taboo concerning it has functioned more to keep it secret than to inhibit it. Aside from the harm it causes, the wrongness of child sexual abuse lies in the inability of children to consent in any meaningful way to an adult who has what seems to be unlimited power over them concerning behavior they cannot understand. And, unlike the teacher/adult student situation, where concerns with empowerment usually preclude a paternalistic response, third parties are increasingly expected to be alert to and to report cases of suspected child sexual abuse.

Empowerment is not, however, irrelevant to discussions of child sexual abuse. It is argued, for example, that children are capable of distinguishing between forms of touching that are appropriate and those that are not, and that they need to be allowed and encouraged to protest if they are touched in ways that make them uncomfortable. That is, although children may not be in a position to consent to sexual activity, they are in a position to *dissent from* it, and acquiring the ability and the right to say no on the basis of how something feels to them may be not only protective but also empowering.

Here, as elsewhere in discussions of sexual harassment and abuse, differences in perspective affect the definition of what is abusive, and, in ways that have been deeply controversial, analyses of these phenomena have given definitional and epistemic privilege to the less powerful. It is primarily for this reason that, as we currently understand these terms, their history is so recent: when epistemic privilege either resides with the more powerful or is detached from any particular perspective, these phenomena are literally invisible.

See also: ACADEMIC ETHICS; BLACKMAIL; BRIBERY; CENSORSHIP; CHILDREN AND ETHICAL THEORY; COERCION; CONSENT; DECEIT; DETERRENCE, THREATS, AND RETALIATION; DISCRIMINATION; FEMINIST ETHICS; INEQUALITY; MEDICAL ETHICS; OPPRESSION; PATERNALISM; POWER; PROFESSIONAL ETHICS; PROMISES; RAPE; SEXUALITY AND SEXUAL ETHICS; WORK.

Bibliography

Breines, Wini, and Linda Gordon. "The New Scholarship on Family Violence." *Signs* 8 (1983): 490–531. A review essay including a section on incest.

Davis, Nancy (Ann). "Sexual Harassment in the University." In *Morality, Responsibility, and the University,* edited by Steven M. Cahn, 150–76. Philadelphia: Temple University Press, 1990. The author argues that the legal definition of "sexual harassment" (in the United States) is inappropriate to guide university policies, since in targeting behavior that appropriately calls for punishment, it either misdescribes or renders invisible pervasive, systemic, and profoundly destructive forms of behavior that call for education (in particular of faculty) rather than punishment.

Finkelhor, David. *Child Sexual Abuse: New Theory and Research.* New York: Free Press, 1984. Sociology.

Herman, Judith Lewis, and Lisa Hirschman. *Father-Daughter Incest.* Cambridge: Harvard University Press, 1981. Social psychology; based on clinical work.

Hughes, John C., and Larry May. "Sexual Harassment." *Social Theory and Practice* 6 (1980): 249–80. Political and legal philosophy.

MacKinnon, Catharine A. *Sexual Harassment of Working Women.* New Haven: Yale University Press, 1979. Social and legal theory; defines sexual harassment as sex discrimination.

Masson, Jeffrey. *The Assault on Truth.* 2d ed. New York: Penguin, 1985. Argues that Freud's theory of infantile sexual fantasy covered up the prevalence of actual child sexual abuse.

Neu, Jerome. "What Is Wrong with Incest?" *Inquiry* 19 (1976): 27–39. Questions the justification and meaning of the incest taboo.

Paetzold, Ramona, and Bill Shaw. "A Postmodern View of 'Reasonableness' in Hostile Environment Sexual Harassment." *Journal of Business Ethics* 13 (1994): 681–91. The authors argue for and against requiring, in order for a sexual harassment claim on grounds of a hostile work environment to be actionable, that a "reasonable person" would regard the environment in question as hostile. The "postmodern" position holds that the requirement of "reasonableness," even when qualified as referring to a "reasonable woman," appears value neutral but in fact valorizes masculinist notions of rationality while rendering illegitimate (because unreasonable) many of the plaintiff's responses that crucially inform her perception that the environment in question is hostile. The counterposition holds that the reasonableness standard is not, or at least need not be, discriminatory and that it is required to separate spurious from genuine claims. The rejoinder holds that such attempts at separation, working as they do from a perspective specifically not that of the plaintiff, are in fact part of the problem and that the fears around crediting plaintiffs' perspectives are ill-founded.

Rush, Florence. *The Best Kept Secret: Sexual Abuse of Children.* Englewood Cliffs, NJ: Prentice Hall, 1980. Cultural and social theory.

Russell, Diana E. H. *The Secret Trauma: Incest in the Lives of Girls and Women.* New York: Basic Books, 1986. Sociology.

———. *Sexual Exploitation: Rape, Child Sexual Abuse, and Sexual Harassment.* Newbury Park, CA: Sage, 1984. Sociology.

Tong, Rosemary. *Women, Sex, and the Law.* Totowa, NJ: Rowman and Allenheld, 1984. Sociology and legal theory.

Wise, Sue, and Liz Stanley. *Georgie Porgie: Sexual Ha-*

rassment in Everyday Life. London: Pandora, 1987. Ethnomethodology.

Naomi Scheman

sexuality and sexual ethics

There are five logically distinct questions that can be asked about sexual activity. First, we can inquire about the moral quality of a sexual act. Is it morally obligatory, morally permissible, supererogatory, or morally wrong? Second, we can examine a sexual act's nonmoral quality: does it provide PLEASURE (nonmoral goodness) or is it tedious, boring, and unenjoyable (nonmoral badness)? A phenomenon deplored (or celebrated) in literature and film is that a disparity often exists between what is morally permissible in our sexual behavior and what is satisfying. Third, we can ask about the legality of sexual activity: is it legally permissible or prohibited? This varies by jurisdiction. Fourth is the pragmatic evaluation of sexual acts. Some sexual acts are medically and psychologically safe or have desired consequences; others are medically or psychologically unsafe or have undesired consequences. Finally, sexual acts can be evaluated as biologically or psychologically natural or unnatural (perverted). It is important to keep these distinctions in mind.

The Dangers of Sex

In sexual activity our flawed bodies and infantile fantasies are exposed to scrutiny. We can be dominated by the other's physical strength, POWER, or beauty as much as by our own desires. Further, in seeking the pleasure of the body and the comfort of intimacy, we become vulnerable to betrayal, jealousy, and sorrow. Thus there is reason to think that sexual ethics is important. When we acknowledge the potential consequences of sexual behavior—the effect of a child's existence on its parents, FAMILY, and the population it joins; the cultivation or reinforcing of pernicious habits; the transmission of deadly disease—the imperative to judge sexual behavior morally becomes even more clear.

It is one thing to argue that morally evaluating sexual behavior is important, and another to argue that sexual ethics must be restrictive. Yet, given the psychological nature and potential consequences of

sexuality, it could be claimed that sexual activity is *prima facie* morally wrong, is always in need of justification, or must be avoided unless stringent conditions are met. Perhaps, then, we can understand the hostility of the world's religions to sex. AUGUSTINE (354–430) provides a sharp example: "A man turns to good use the evil of concupiscence . . . when he bridles and restrains its rage . . . and never relaxes his hold upon it except when intent on offspring, and then controls and applies it to the carnal generation of children . . . not to the subjection of the spirit to the flesh in a sordid servitude."

Immanuel KANT (1724–1804) had equally unkind words for sex: "Sexual love makes of the loved person an Object of appetite. . . . Taken by itself it is a degradation of human nature." Sexual DESIRE, because it focuses on the body, is ever prone to the objectification of its target. As a powerful urge and hence motivator to manipulation and deception, sexual desire approaches another person as an instrument, without regard for the other's subjectivity or ends. Thus the quest for sexual pleasure is permissible only when anchored in, or subordinated to, other more valuable goals: LOVE, marriage, procreation.

This grim, conservative characterization of sexuality and the restrictive sexual ethics it implies are rejected by those who think that sexual desire is not intrinsically sinful or selfish. Sexuality is a natural bonding mechanism that, through the power to produce pleasure, forges a psychological joint interest out of two independent interests. At least, the self-interested drive for sexual pleasure can, either by its nature or by proper education, expand into a drive for the satisfaction of another's desire. Further, sexual pleasure is a good thing in itself, one of the few intense and delectable joys life offers. Its achievement ought to be encouraged and appropriate arrangements devised to make sexual activity less likely to lead to evil consequences. There is nothing about a virtuous life lived well that excludes seeking sexual pleasure for its own sake.

Are There Special Ethical Principles for Sex?

If the possible consequences and risky psychological nature of sexuality imply that sexual ethics is important and restrictive, they also suggest that there might be special moral principles that apply discretely to this area of life. *Sui generis* sexual ethics makes sense if sexuality plays a unique role in human life. Sex is by far the primary way to reproduce humans. If procreation has significance precisely as a couple's contribution to God's ongoing work of creation, sexuality is supremely important and must be governed by restrictive rules, which might apply only here. The significance of sexuality, however, might be little different from the significance of eating, breathing, sleeping, and defecating; all are instigated by the needs of the natural body. If the desire for sexual pleasure is little different from the desire for food, sexual behavior is to be constrained by moral principles that apply to behavior in general: the ethics of sex is no more (or less) important than the ethics of anything else.

Often, in the popular mind, "ethics" is something that applies primarily to sexual behavior. In a weak sense, then, there is a *sui generis* sexual ethics, if there is no ethics other than the sexual. This view is shallow, yet it possesses an intriguing grain of truth. Freudians and others have suggested that sexual personality resides at the core of moral personality: how we perceive and behave toward sexual partners both influences and is a mirror image of how we perceive and interact with people more generally. The education of sexuality provides a foundation or pattern for acting—morally or immorally—in the world. The failure to learn to control the pursuit of sexual pleasure undermines the achievement of a virtuous CHARACTER. Perhaps fostering bad sexual habits or noxious patterns of sexual behavior even destroys the capacity for love. But all this means is that sexual ethics is restrictive and important, if not the centerpiece of morality, not that sexual ethics is *sui generis.*

If sexuality is assessed in utilitarian terms, by calculating the costs and benefits of sexual activity to participants and society, no *sui generis* sexual ethics is possible. Such an ethics must be deontological. Causing needless pain and treating people unfairly are often considered intrinsically and irreducibly wrong; injustice is wrong because it is injustice, not because it is a species of something else that is wrong. If sexual activity is objectifying and selfish, except when purified by love or marriage, its wrongness follows from the wrongness of objectification and selfishness. These moral faults are hardly confined to sexual behavior. A *sui generis* sexual ethics is possible only if there are sexual acts that are intrinsically and irreducibly wrong, not as instances of

selfishness, DECEIT, harm, and so forth, but wrong as sexual acts. Could sexual acts be morally wrong in their own right?

Consider contraceptive heterosexual acts. One could argue that this practice is morally wrong on consequentialist grounds (it weakens the family and the social fabric) or on the grounds that these sexual acts tend to be exploitative or degrading, insofar as such acts overemphasize the goal of pleasure. But if contraceptive sexual acts are wrong for these reasons, they are not wrong because they are sexual. A multitude of similar examples supports the conclusion that "the fact that an act is sexual in itself never renders it wrong or adds to its wrongness if it is wrong on other grounds" (Alan Goldman). Yet perhaps coercing someone into a sexual act is morally worse than coercing someone into other types of acts (giving up money), due to the special psychological and social nature of sexuality: RAPE can elicit shame and be especially humiliating, in contrast to a mugging. If so, a *sui generis* sexual ethics might be possible if, from the fact that an additional contribution to the total wrongness of an act is made by the act's being sexual, it follows that the act is wrong, in part, because it is sexual.

The Morality of Sexual Behavior

Applied sexual ethics explores the VIRTUES and vices of a wide assortment of activities: ABORTION, contraceptive intercourse, acquaintance rape, making and viewing PORNOGRAPHY, engaging in sexual harassment, sexual objectification, casual sex, adultery, prostitution, HOMOSEXUALITY, sadomasochism, and intergenerational sex. Each of these activities raises its own special questions. But there are four general debates concerning the details of the morality of sexual behavior.

One debate is between a NATURAL LAW approach to sexuality and a secular outlook that is derivable from either Kantian themes or UTILITARIANISM. The sexual liberal emphasizes autonomous choice, self-determination, freedom, respect for persons, and pleasure, in contrast to a tradition that justifies a more restrictive sexual ethics by invoking a Grand Scheme to which human action must conform or by appealing to Reason, which detects modes of human behavior that are contrary to human nature. To a standard list of reasons a sexual act might be morally wrong—it is dishonest, coercive, manipulative, selfish, cruel, dangerous, or unfair—some add "unnatural."

The sexual ethics of THOMAS AQUINAS (1225?–1274) are central in the Natural Law tradition. Sexual acts can be morally wrong, according to Aquinas, in two different ways. First, "when the act of its nature is incompatible with the purpose of the sex act [procreation]. In so far as generation is blocked, we have unnatural vice, which is any complete sex act from which of its nature generation cannot follow." Aquinas gives four examples: "the sin of self-abuse," "intercourse with a thing of another species," acts "with a person of the same sex," and acts in which "the natural style of intercourse is not observed, as regards the proper organ or according to other rather beastly and monstrous techniques." Second, sexual acts can be morally wrong even if natural; in these cases, "conflict with right reason may arise from the nature of the act with respect to the other party," as in incest, rape, seduction, and adultery. For Aquinas, sexual sins in the first category are the worst: "unnatural vice flouts nature by transgressing its basic principles of sexuality, [so] it is in this matter the gravest of sins." Kant, too, asserts that masturbation and homosexuality are morally wrong because they are unnatural: "Onanism . . . is abuse of the sexual faculty. . . . By it man sets aside his person and degrades himself below the level of animals. . . . Intercourse between *sexus homogenii* . . . too is contrary to the ends of humanity." The masturbator, as well as the homosexual, "no longer deserves to be a person."

In response to such Natural Law claims, one might suggest that there is no easy equivalence between an act's morality and its naturalness. Fellatio, cunnilingus, anal intercourse, mutual masturbation, and consensual sadomasochism, even if unnatural, can be performed with Christian "charity" and hence not be morally wrong. The paradigmatically immoral sex act is not buggery or bestiality, but rape. Regardless, nonprocreative sexual activity might be natural to human beings: not only because there may be a genetic foundation for, say, homosexuality, but also because the plasticity of human desire and the variety of acts we enjoy performing result from our developed brains. Homosexuality might even be one of the ways humans were fashioned by a God following a principle of plenitude.

A second debate is about whether, in the absence of harm to third parties, the fact that two people engage in a sexual act voluntarily is sufficient for satisfying morality. Sexual activity between two persons might be harmful to one or both participants; a moral paternalist would claim that it is wrong for X to harm Y, or for Y to allow X to harm Y, even when both X and Y consent to their activity. Consent is not sufficient. But a restrictive sexual ethics is more commonly justified by claiming that only in a committed relationship is sexual activity morally licit.

On one view, the fact that participation in a sexual act is voluntary means that the persons are being treated as ends and not merely used. Consent is sufficient, since each person is respecting the other as an autonomous agent capable of making up his or her mind about the activity's value. On the other view two mutual uses, even when consensual, do not "cancel" each other to create a virtuous act. Kant and Karol Wojtyla (Pope John Paul II) take this position; voluntarily allowing oneself to be used sexually by another makes an object of oneself. For Kant, sexual activity avoids treating a person merely as a means only in marriage, since here both persons have surrendered their bodies and souls to each other and have achieved unity. For Wojtyla, "only love can preclude the use of one person by another," since love is a unification of persons resulting from a mutual gift of the selves. But the thought that love is the justifying ingredient has immediate application to homosexuality: gay and lesbian sexual activity seems permissible if it occurs within loving, monogamous homosexual marriages. Further, the appeal to love makes defending the use of contraception easier if sex acts, even the nonprocreative, express and bolster the love spouses have for each other.

A third debate is over what "voluntary" means. Whether consent is only necessary or also sufficient, any moral principle that relies on consent to make moral distinctions among sexual events presupposes a clear understanding of consent: what it is, how to recognize it, how to distinguish the genuine from the bogus. Participation in sexual activity ought not to be coerced or occur in response to threats, nor should it depend on deception or ignorance of that to which one is consenting. But this platitude leaves things wide open. Does the presence of *any* kind of pressure put on one person by another amount to COERCION that negates consent, so that the subsequent activity is morally wrong? In some cases it might be reasonable to say that some pressures do not count as coercion or that some pressures are coercive but not morally objectionable. (On problems with "consent" in sexual contexts, see Wertheimer.)

Questions about consent to sex are analogous to those that arise in medicine, business, and law. How *specific* must consent be in order that a person engage voluntarily in subsequent sexual behavior? Because consent is opaque, when one person agrees "to have sex" with another the first has not necessarily consented to any sensual caress or coital position the second has in mind. How *explicit* must consent be? Can consent be reliably implied by nonverbal behavior; may we take nonverbal cues as decisively showing that another has consented to sex? How *informed* must consent be? Does one partner have an obligation to warn the other that their anticipated sexual activity is medically dangerous?

Bertrand RUSSELL (1872–1970) wrote, back in the 1920s, that "the intrusion of the economic motive into sex is always . . . disastrous. Sexual relations should be a mutual delight, entered into solely from the spontaneous impulse of both parties." In this vein, Russell reflected on the sexual activity of married couples: "the total amount of undesired sex endured by women is probably greater in marriage than in prostitution." Russell's observation about marital sex was prophetical. In objecting to the economic pressure experienced by women to acquiesce to the sexual demands of their husbands, Russell voiced something close to Robin Morgan's feminist definition of rape: "Rape exists any time sexual intercourse occurs when it has not been initiated by the woman, out of her own genuine affection and desire. . . . How many millions of times have women had sex 'willingly' with men they didn't want to have sex with? . . . How many times have women wished just to sleep instead or read or watch the Late Show? . . . Most of the decently married bedrooms across America are settings for nightly rape." The woman who is nagged into sex by her husband worries that if she says "no" too often, he will abandon her, which she fears for economic, social, and psychological reasons. Women will be free to refuse sex to men only when they are the economic and social equals of men. (But maybe we should also acknowledge an ethics of CARE: the wife is not so much raped by her husband as she has performed a supererogatory sex-

ual act, generously giving in to his impatient wishes instead of satisfying her desire to watch television.)

A fourth debate concerns the extent to which effects on third parties figure into moral evaluations of sexual behavior and what effects on third parties count as harm. Is a person harmed if he or she experiences nausea when seeing two homosexuals kiss in public? Is a spouse harmed by the infidelity he or she knows nothing about? A narrow notion of harm generates a less restrictive sexual ethics than does a broad notion; here utilitarians such as JOHN STUART MILL (1806–1873) and H. L. A. HART (1907–1992) square off against James Fitzjames Stephen (1829–1894) and Lord Patrick Devlin (1905–1992). Utilitarian sexual ethics can, in any event, be restrictive *or* permissive, depending on the truth of empirical assertions about the consequences of sexual behavior (or about the consequences of trying to prevent sexual behaviors). In addition to depending on contestable notions of well-being, the empirical claims underlying utilitarian judgments are difficult to verify. Nevertheless, a case can be made that a *prima facie* right to engage in sexual activity can be derived from Mill's utilitarianism. Utilitarian reasons for a right to engage in sex do exist: the value of pleasure *per se* and its role in the good life, and the contribution shared pleasure makes to the value of PERSONAL RELATIONSHIPS. Private, consensual sexual activity creates much good and, if harm to third parties is avoided, no bad, and on this score would be blessed by utilitarianism.

The Nature of the Sexual

Conceptual philosophy of sex analyzes sexual desire, sexual pleasure, sexual sensation, sexual thought, sexual act, sexual perversion, sexual arousal, sexual INTENTION, and sexual satisfaction. What makes a feeling a sexual sensation? What makes a desire a sexual desire? Further, which of these concepts is logically prior to the others, in the sense that the analysis of other concepts depends on its analysis? Shall we understand a sexual act in terms of the sexual desire that gives rise to it, or in terms of the sexual pleasure that the act is performed to provide? Other conceptual questions have to do not with what makes an act sexual, but with what makes it the type of sexual act it is. These derivative sexual concepts, whose definition in part refers to sexuality, include rape, prostitution, homosexuality, objectification, harassment, and pornography.

"Sexual activity" is an intriguing concept; it is difficult to state the conditions that are necessary for an act to be sexual. Consider proposal 1, that sexual acts are those that involve contact with a sexual body part. But flirting visually, talking over the phone, and sending e-mail messages can be sexual even though no contact is made with a sexual body part. It seems that contact is not necessary. Further, touching a breast or the genitals is sexual when done by lovers, but not when done during a cancer or gynecological exam. So contact with a sexual body part is not sufficient. "Sexual body part" might be logically dependent on "sexual activity," not the other way around.

Proposal 2 is that he procreative nature of sexual activity might be employed analytically instead of normatively. Sexual acts, on such a view, can be analyzed as those having procreative potential in virtue of their biological structure. That is, sexual acts are (i) acts that are the kind of act that could result in conception plus (ii) acts that are psychologically or physiologically the antecedents or concomitants of sexual acts so defined. (The second clause is required to be able to include, say, kissing within the sexual.) This analysis is too narrow, for there are acts we ordinarily call sexual that have no connection with procreation (anal intercourse). Acts that occur between people who have the same sexual anatomy would not count as sexual, since none of these acts are procreative. Many sexual perversions (fondling shoes) are sexual even though they bear no substantial resemblance to coitus or its concomitants. And masturbation, when performed by a person at home alone, is neither a procreative act nor a precursor of coitus.

Proposal 3 suggests that perhaps sexual acts are those that produce sexual pleasure: holding hands is sexual when sexual pleasure is produced; procreative (and nonprocreative) acts are sexual when they produce sexual pleasure. Robert Gray thinks that "any activity might become a sexual activity" if sexual pleasure is derived from it, and "no activity is a sexual activity unless sexual pleasure is derived from it." "Sexual act" is here logically dependent on "sexual pleasure." But if pleasure is the mark of the sexual, pleasure cannot be the gauge of the quality of sex acts. This analysis conflates what it is for an act to be a nonmorally good sexual act with what it is

for an act to be sexual *per se,* which might not produce any pleasure.

Proposal 4 asks, can we rely on intentions or purposes to distinguish the sexual from the nonsexual? A lifeguard's pressing her mouth against the mouth of a swimmer would be sexual if her intention were to derive sexual pleasure; it is not sexual if she intends to revive the swimmer. Yet the intention to experience or provide sexual pleasure is not necessary for an act to be sexual: a heterosexual couple engaging in coitus, both parties intending (taking the advice of Augustine) only that she be impregnated and not concerned with sexual pleasure, is engaging in a sexual act.

Intentions are plausibly irrelevant in making sexual acts sexual. A rapist might force someone into a sexual act to get sexual pleasure from it, or to humiliate his victim, or assert his masculinity and dominance (say, in prison), or all three. From the fact that in some cases the rapist primarily intends to degrade his victim, to exert power over her or him, it does not follow that the act is not sexual. The rapist might have chosen a sexual act deliberately as an effective method to humiliate, believing that his victim will in forced sex experience shame. Fully consensual sexual acts, too, have many uses—to show affection, to make money, to dissipate excess energy, to kill time—so the purpose one has in engaging in sex cannot be that which distinguishes sexual from nonsexual acts.

Proposal 5: another attempt is to define sexual activity in terms of a logically prior notion of sexual desire. Alan Goldman has approached the analytic task this way, offering the following definitions: "Sexual desire is desire for contact with another person's body and for the pleasure which such contact produces; sexual activity is activity which tends to fulfill such desire of the agent." Goldman acknowledges that not all physical touches are sexual: if a parent's cuddling his or her baby comes from a desire to show affection, and not from a desire for the pleasure of physical contact itself, then the parent's act is not sexual. That is, if the desire that precipitates the act is not sexual, neither is the act. If so, a woman who performs fellatio for the money she earns is not performing a sexual act. The act does not fulfill the sexual desire "of the agent," for, like the baby-cuddling parent, the woman has no sexual desire to begin with. The prostitute's contribution to this act of fellatio might be called, instead, a "rent-accumulating" act, since it tends to fulfill her desire to have shelter.

Social Constructionism

Maybe all the acts we think of as sexual have no common denominator and the conceptual project is doomed from the start. There are good reasons for this view. Acts involving the same body part are sometimes sexual, sometimes not. Some touches are deemed sexual in one context or culture but not in others. The fragrances, mannerisms, and costumes that are sexually arousing vary from place to place and time to time. Bodily movements acquire meaning, as sexual or as something else, by existing within a culture that attaches meaning to them. There are, if this view is right, only variable social definitions of the sexual. The history of human sexuality is primarily the history of our customs and "discourse" about sex, as Michel FOUCAULT (1926–1984) might have put it. We create social things by using words. There really is no such item as masturbatory insanity or nymphomania—no medical condition, no psychological character trait, no underlying pathology. Such things "exist" only because we have picked out some behaviors and made up a word for them, not because they have, like Mars, an existence independent of our language, our observations, and our evaluations. Similar considerations apply to "perversion," "philanderer," and "homosexuality."

Such is the view known as social constructionism. As Robert Padgug expresses the thesis, "the very meaning and content of sexual arousal" varies so much among genders, classes, and cultures that "there is no abstract and universal category of 'the erotic' or 'the sexual' applicable without change to all societies." Nancy Hartsock has elaborated this claim: "We should understand sexuality not as an essence or set of properties defining an individual, nor as a set of drives and needs (especially genital) of an individual. Rather, we should understand sexuality as culturally and historically defined and constructed. Anything can become eroticized."

The claim that "anything can become eroticized" implies that our preferred or desired sexual partners, positions, and activities are strongly under the control of cultural forces. (Adrienne Rich thinks that the eroticization of heterosexuality for women is socially engineered.) It might very well be true that "anything" can be linked to sexual arousal and pleasure; after all, unusual items bring paraphiliacs sexual joy. If so, however, there is a sexual common denominator, an essential even if narrow core: a culturally invariable experience of sexual arousal and pleasure. Hence there is a universal category of the sort Padgug and Hartsock deny. We need to distinguish the dubious thesis that sexuality *per se* is socially constructed from the more plausible thesis that the sexual derivatives (prostitution, homosexuality, pornography) are socially constructed.

Perhaps we cannot analytically distinguish the sexual and nonsexual because the sexual is inextricably wrapped up with our existence and identities as embodied and gendered creatures. It is understandable, then, that a sexual ethics might apply not merely to discrete sexual performances but also to any behavior of a person that could impinge on or interact with his or her nature as a (sexual) being. A sexual ethics might tell us when and with whom it is permissible to touch another person's genitals with the intention of producing pleasure; in what cases the impersonal touching of the genitals ought not to become a pleasurable touching; and in what circumstances one may make the touching of genitals one's profession and contribution to society. Sexual ethics can thus be seen as a large portion of ethics and as a significant area for education. But this fact does not make sexual ethics *sui generis,* even if this ethics is important. Nor need it be restrictive: if identity and gender are sexual, that could be just as much reason for a relaxed as for a restrictive sexual ethics. But let's not get overly sentimental about sex. Margaret Farley sermonizes that "more and more theorists are coming to the conclusion that sexual desire without interpersonal love leads to disappointment and . . . meaninglessness." At last someone is catching up with those theorists who have concluded that sexual desire *with* love leads to disappointment and meaninglessness. Indeed, it is not farfetched to think that everything leads to disappointment and meaninglessness. It is not sex, with or without love, that allows us to avoid our fate.

See also: ABORTION; AUGUSTINE; CARE; CENSORSHIP; CHILDREN AND ETHICAL THEORY; COERCION; CONSENT; DECEIT; DESIRE; EMOTION; *EUDAIMONIA,* -ISM; EXPLOITATION; FAMILY; FEMINIST ETHICS; GAY ETH-

ICS; GENETIC ENGINEERING; HEDONISM; HOMOSEXU-
ALITY; KANTIAN ETHICS; LESBIAN ETHICS; LITERA-
TURE AND ETHICS; LOVE; LOYALTY; NATURALISM;
NATURALISTIC FALLACY; NEEDS; OBJECTIVISM; PAUL;
PERSONAL RELATIONSHIPS; PLEASURE; PORNOGRA-
PHY; PSYCHOLOGY; PUBLIC HEALTH POLICY; PURI-
TANISM; RAPE; RELIGION; REPRODUCTIVE TECHNOL-
OGY; RUSSELL; SELF-CONTROL; SEXUAL ABUSE AND
HARASSMENT; THOMAS AQUINAS; TRUST; VOLUN-
TARY ACTS.

Bibliography

Augustine. *On Marriage and Concupiscence.* In *Works,* vol. 12. Edinburgh: T. and T. Clark, 1874. Early Christian sexual ethics. Quotation is from book 1, chapter 9.

Baker, Robert, and Frederick Elliston, eds. *Philosophy and Sex.* 2d ed. Buffalo, NY: Prometheus, 1984. See also the 1st ed. (1975) and, for a comparison of the two, A. Soble, *Teaching Philosophy* 8/3 (1985): 250–51.

Baker, Robert B., Kathleen J. Winiger, and Frederick A. Elliston, eds. *Philosophy and Sex.* 3d ed. Amherst, NY: Prometheus, 1998.

Davis, Murray. *Smut: Erotic Reality/Obscene Ideology.* Chicago: University of Chicago Press, 1983. Explores Jehovanist, Naturalist, and Gnostic philosophies of sex.

Farley, Margaret. "Sexual Ethics." In *Encyclopedia of Bioethics,* edited by W. Reich, vol. 4, pp. 1575–89. New York: Free Press, 1978. A history of sexual ethics.

Foucault, Michel. *The History of Sexuality. Vol. 1: An Introduction.* New York: Vintage, 1978. *Vol. 2: The Use of Pleasure.* New York: Pantheon, 1985. *Vol. 3: The Care of the Self.* New York: Vintage, 1986. History of sex by a central proponent of social constructionism.

Goldman, Alan. "Plain Sex." *Philosophy and Public Affairs* 6/3 (1977): 267–87. Reprinted in *Philosophy of Sex,* edited by A. Soble, 1st ed., 119–38; 2d ed., 73–92; 3d ed., 39–55. Conceptual analysis of "sexual activity" and "sexual desire"; Kantian sexual ethics. Quotations are from Soble, 3d ed., pp. 40, 49.

Gray, Robert. "Sex and Sexual Perversion." *Journal of Philosophy* 75/4 (1978): 189–99. Reprinted in *Philosophy of Sex,* edited by A. Soble, 1st ed., 158–68; 3d ed., 57–66. Conceptual analysis of "sexual perversion" and "sexual act." Quotation is from Soble, 3d ed., p. 61.

Hartsock, Nancy. *Money, Sex and Power: Toward a Feminist Historical Materialism.* New York: Longman, 1983. A feminist-Marxist theory of gender and sexuality. Quotation is from p. 156.

Herman, Barbara. "Could it Be Worth Thinking About Kant on Sex and Marriage?" In *A Mind of One's Own,* edited by L. Antony and C. Witt, 49–67. Boulder: Westview, 1993. Explores similarities between Kant's sexual philosophy and feminism.

Kant, Immanuel. *Lectures on Ethics.* Translated by Louis Infield. New York: Harper and Row, 1963 [1780]. Sexual metaphysics and ethics. Quotations are from pp. 163, 170.

MacKinnon, Catharine. *Toward a Feminist Theory of the State.* Cambridge, MA: Harvard University Press, 1989. A feminist legal and social analysis of heterosexuality, rape, and pornography.

Mappes, Thomas. "Sexual Morality and the Concept of Using Another Person." In *Social Ethics,* 5th ed., edited by T. Mappes and J. Zembaty, 163–76. New York: McGraw-Hill, 1997 [1985]. An exploration of libertarian sexual ethics.

Mayo, David. "An Obligation to Warn of HIV Infection?" In *Sex, Love, and Friendship,* edited by A. Soble, 447–53. Amsterdam: Editions Rodopi, 1997. Argues that persons who are HIV positive have no moral duty to reveal that fact to sex partners.

Morgan, Robin. *Going Too Far: The Personal Chronicle of a Feminist.* New York: Random House, 1977. Quotation is from pp. 165–66 ("Theory and Practice: Pornography and Rape" [1974]).

Noonan, John. *Contraception: A History of Its Treatment by the Catholic Theologians and Canonists.* Enlarged ed. Cambridge, MA: Harvard University Press, 1986 [1965]. History of philosophical and theological arguments surrounding contraception.

Nussbaum, Martha C. "Objectification." *Philosophy and Public Affairs* 24/4 (1995): 249–91. Reprinted in *Philosophy of Sex,* 3d ed., edited by A. Soble, 283–321. Analyzes seven types of sexual objectification.

Padgug, Robert. "Sexual Matters: On Conceptualizing Sexuality in History." *Radical History Review* 20 (Spring/Summer, 1979): 3–23. Reprinted in *Forms of Desire,* edited by E. Stein, 43–67. Marxist social constructionism of sexuality. Quotation is from Stein, p. 54.

Posner, Richard. *Sex and Reason.* Cambridge, MA: Harvard University Press, 1992. Elaborates an economic model of sexual behavior.

Primoratz, Igor, ed. *Human Sexuality.* Aldershot, England: Dartmouth, 1997. Reprints important philosophical essays, 1970–1996.

Rich, Adrienne. "Compulsory Heterosexuality and Lesbian Existence." In her *Blood, Bread and Poetry: Selected Prose, 1979–1985,* pp. 23–75. New York: Norton, 1986. A classic item of feminist social philosophy; originally published 1980.

Russell, Bertrand. *Marriage and Morals.* London: George Allen and Unwin, 1929. Still worth reading. Quotations are from pp. 121–22.

Scruton, Roger. *Sexual Desire: A Moral Philosophy of the Erotic.* New York: Free Press, 1986. A conservative Kantian theory of sex. See Martha Nussbaum's review, "Sex in the Head," *New York Review of Books* (18 December 1986): 49–52.

Shelp, Earl, ed. *Sexuality and Medicine.* 2 vols. Dordrecht: D. Reidel, 1987. Essays in biomedical ethics and the philosophy of sex.

Soble, Alan , ed. *The Philosophy of Sex.* 1st ed., Totowa, NJ: Rowman and Littlefield, 1980. 2d ed., Savage, MD: Rowman and Littlefield, 1991. 3d ed., Lanham, MD: Rowman and Littlefield, 1997.

———. *The Philosophy of Sex and Love.* St. Paul, MN: Paragon House, 1998. An introductory, single-author textbook designed for philosophy courses.

———. *Sexual Investigations.* New York: New York University Press, 1996. Sexual ethics, politics, and conceptual analysis.

Stein, Edward, ed. *Forms of Desire.* New York: Routledge, 1992. Collection of essays defending and criticizing social constructionism.

Thomas Aquinas. *Summa theologiae.* 60 vols. Cambridge: Blackfriars, 1964–1976 [1265–1273]. Quotations are from vol. 43, 2a2ae, q. 154, aa. 1, 11, 12.

Vannoy, Russell. *Sex without Love: A Philosophical Exploration.* Buffalo, NY: Prometheus, 1980. Argues that sexual activity is morally and nonmorally sound without being attached to love.

Wertheimer, Alan. "Consent and Sexual Relations." *Legal Theory* 2 (1996): 89–112. Consent is a normative, not an empirical, notion.

Wojtyla, Karol [Pope John Paul II]. *Love and Responsibility.* New York: Farrar, Straus and Giroux, 1981. A Kantian-catholic sexual ethics. Quotation is from p. 30.

Alan Soble

Shaftesbury, [Anthony Ashley Cooper] 3rd Earl of (1671–1713)

Grandson of the famous Restoration Whig politician. Shaftesbury's work in ethics and AESTHETICS profoundly influenced philosophers throughout the eighteenth-century. His great work, *Characteristics,* went through eleven editions from 1711 to 1790, and affected thinkers in England and on the Continent, including HUTCHESON (1694–1746), HUME (1711–1776), VOLTAIRE (1694–1778), Diderot (1713–1784), ROUSSEAU (1712–1778), KANT (1724–1804), and the German Romantics. SIDGWICK (1838–1900) wrote that its appearance "mark[ed] a turning-point in the history of English ethical thought."

In opposition to the seventeenth-century NATURAL LAW tradition that preceded him, Shaftesbury's ethics was notable for its psychological focus. Shaftesbury developed the CAMBRIDGE PLATONISTS' idea that morality centers on what is internal to the moral agent—on CHARACTER, motive, and sentiment; and he did so in a modern idiom that captured the attention of philosophers of the eighteenth century. Moreover, Shaftesbury's ethics were "internalist" in an even deeper sense: he held not only that what *has* ethical features is fundamentally internal (*e.g.,* a motive), but that a necessary condition of *its having* ethical features depends on internal, psychological considerations as well. In Sidgwick's words: "Shaftesbury is the first moralist who distinctly takes psychological experience as the basis of ethics."

Characteristics is composed of six treatises, only one of which, "An Inquiry Concerning Virtue or Merit," is a work in systematic moral philosophy. Its title clearly announces that Shaftesbury's is an ethics of virtue rather than law. "It is . . . by affection merely," he wrote, "that a creature is esteemed good or ill." Indeed, according to Shaftesbury, whether an act is right or wrong cannot be determined independently of the "affections" from which it arises: "Whatsoever is done through any unequal affection is iniquitous, wicked, and wrong. If the affection be equal, sound, and good . . . this must necessarily constitute what we call equity and right in any action."

The passions and affections form a system or "economy," both within an individual person, the "self-system," and in the natural interrelation and reciprocation of individual human psyches in larger wholes, including that of the whole species. These economies can be balanced, ordered, and harmonious when the various affections are properly adapted to each other, or out of balance when they are not. Shaftesbury argues that the self-system can be in harmony only when it is properly adapted to the species-system. It is simply our psychological nature to have affections adapted to the good of the whole, including affections *directed toward* the good of others (and potentially the whole), whose promptings must be heeded if an individual's mind is to be properly balanced.

So far, Shaftesbury's view may appear to differ little, except for its emphasis on *psychological* system, from any ethics resting on a natural teleology. What made his view distinctive was his insistence on a natural human capacity for cultivated aesthetic sensibility, which, when combined with the rational capacity for self-reflection, enables human beings to contemplate the order or disorder of their own affections. When they do, he thought, human beings naturally respond agreeably to harmoniously ordered affection and are repelled by dissonant characters. "The mind, which is spectator or auditor of other minds, cannot be without its eye and ear, so as to discern proportion, distinguish sound, and scan each sentiment or thought which comes before it. . . . It feels the soft and harsh, the agreeable and disagreeable in the affections; and finds a foul and fair, a harmonious and a dissonant. . . . Nor can it withhold its admiration and ecstasy, its aversion and scorn."

Further, there are places where Shaftesbury suggests that moral beauty simply consists in being such as would be approved by a properly cultivated (but natural) sentiment. Thus: "if there be no real amiableness or deformity in moral acts, there is at least an imaginary one of full force. Though perhaps the thing itself should not be allowed in Nature, the imagination or fancy of it must be allowed to be from Nature alone." He coined the phrase "moral sense" to refer to this sensibility when it engages character and motive, thereby initiating the tradition of moral sentimentalism found in Hutcheson and Hume.

Affections that are properly ordered and adapted to the good of the whole are "natural" or "equal" and worthy of esteem. "Virtue or merit" requires more, however, than properly ordered affections; it requires *self-ordered affections*—a *self-created* or *self-maintained harmony*. Any sensible creature can be good, but virtue or merit "is allowed only to . . . a creature capable of forming general notions of things, . . . [of] the very actions themselves, and the affections of pity, kindness, gratitude, and their contraries" by reflection, and who can thereby maintain the beauty and order of the creature's own soul through his or her moral sense. Here Shaftesbury introduces an idea which was absent from later moral sentimentalists such as Hutcheson and Hume, but which would loom large in a tradition including BUTLER (1692–1752), Rousseau, and Kant: moral agency requires the capacity for moral self-determination.

Precisely how Shaftesbury's MORAL PSYCHOLOGY functions at this point is a delicate matter. Moral sense confirms the motivation of "equal" affections, but it does not directly motivate virtuous actions. Nor does the judgment of moral sense directly create or recognize an *obligation* to virtuous ACTION. The obligation to virtue, for Shaftesbury, derives from what he believed to be the rationally conclusive motive to virtue consisting in the fact that having a virtuous character is most in the individual's own in-terest. Still, that this is so is not independent of moral sense and the harmony of character to which it responds.

So why does virtue or merit require *self-maintained* harmony? In some respects, Shaftesbury anticipates Kant's ideas. Although he supposes obligation to consist in a motive of self-interest, that is because he supposes the latter to be a rationally conclusive motive, and he thinks, like Kant, that obligation can be understood only in these terms. In Treatise III of *Characteristics*, "Soliloquy, or Advice to an Author," and in his philosophical notebooks, Shaftesbury develops a conception of autonomy or authorship as involving the self-imposition of (obligatory) rational MOTIVES. Moreover, he accepts some version of the doctrine that rational beings have a special dignity by virtue of the capacity for autonomy. But while he anticipates Kant in these respects, his major reason for thinking that virtue must involve self-created beauty is aesthetic. Our response to the beautiful is really a response to *the beautifying*—to mind. We can admire the natural beauty of well-composed affections of nonrational creatures, but in doing so we are really admiring their composer—God. Only rational creatures have, like God, the capacity to create beauty in accordance with their own sense of it. Real virtue is character in whose beautifying principle virtuous people themselves share.

See also: AESTHETICS; AGENT-CENTERED MORALITY; AUTONOMY OF MORAL AGENTS; BUTLER; CAMBRIDGE PLATONISTS; CHARACTER; EXTERNALISM AND INTERNALISM; HUME; HUTCHESON; INTUITIONISM; KANT; MERIT AND DESERT; MORAL SENSE THEORISTS; MOTIVES; SELF-KNOWLEDGE; VIRTUE ETHICS; VOLTAIRE.

Bibliography

Works by Shaftesbury

Characteristics of Men, Manners, Opinions, and Times. New York: Bobbs-Merrill, 1964 [1711]. 2 vols. in one; reprint of 2d, revised edition, John M. Robertson, ed. London, 1714.

The Life, Unpublished Letters, and Philosophical Regimen of Anthony, Earl of Shaftesbury. Edited by Benjamin Rand. London: Swan Sonnenschein, 1900. The "Regimen" comprises Shaftesbury's Notebooks.

Second Characteristics, or the Language of Form. Edited by Benjamin Rand. Cambridge: Cambridge University Press, 1914 [1712].

Complete Works, Selected Letters, Posthumous Writings.
Stuttgart: Frommann Holzboog, 1981–. Translated
into German with English original; edited, translated,
with comments, by Gerd Hemmerich and Wolfram
Benda.

Works about Shaftesbury

Darwall, Stephen L. "Obligation and Motive in the British
Moralists." In *Foundations of Moral and Political Philosophy,* edited by Ellen Frankel Paul. Oxford: Blackwell, 1989.

———. *The British Moralists and the Internal 'Ought':
1640–1740.* Cambridge: Cambridge University Press,
1995. See chapter 7.

Grean, Stanley. *Shaftesbury's Philosophy of Religion and
Ethics.* Athens: Ohio University Press, 1967.

Klein, Lawrence E. *Shaftesbury and the Culture of Polite-
ness: Moral Discourse and Cultural Politics in Early
Eighteenth-Century England.* Cambridge: Cambridge
University Press, 1994.

Schneewind, J. B. *The Invention of Autonomy: A History
of Modern Moral Philosophy.* Cambridge: Cambridge
University Press, 1998. See pp. 295–309.

Sidgwick, Henry. *Outlines of the History of Ethics.* Boston, MA: Beacon Press, 1964 [1886].

Trianosky, Gregory. "On the Obligation to Be Virtuous:
Shaftesbury and the Question Why Be Moral?" *The
Journal of Philosophy* 16 (1978): 289–300.

Uehlein, Frederich A. *Kosmos und Subjectivität.* Frei-
burg/München: Karl Albert, 1976.

Stephen Darwall

shame

See guilt and shame.

Shī'ism

Historically, the division that later constitutes the
Sunnī and Shī'a credal formulations in ISLAM stems
from disagreement arising among early Muslims
over succession after the death of the Prophet Muḥammad. Less than three decades after the Prophet's
death, succession issues come under closer scrutiny,
especially after bloody civil wars destabilized the
community of believers. The key figure is 'Alī, the
cousin and son-in-law of the Prophet Muḥammad.
'Alī, according to the Sunnīs, is the fourth deputy
(khalīfa) to the Prophet; and according to the Shī'a
he is the first apostolic leader (imām). Mu'āwiya, the
governor of Syria, opposed him and refused to

pledge loyalty to 'Alī unless the latter avenged the
murder of the third caliph, 'Uthmān, a kinsman of
the governor. Diplomacy failed to salvage matters,
resulting in a clash between 'Alī and Mu'āwiya that
irretrievably split Islam into political sects that are
legitimated by theological claims. Those who considered 'Alī to be justified in his actions against a
rebellious governor considered themselves to be
shī'a, a term that simply meant being a "partisan"
of 'Alī.

Later, this ideological split develops into a full-
fledged doctrinal ideology in which Shī'ism also acquires a religious sensibility. The Shī'a argue that
'Alī was more deserving of being the legitimate
leader (imām) after the Prophet. In fact, he was designated to this office by the Messenger of God himself. However, he was robbed of his claim when the
information about his leadership was unlawfully
suppressed by senior Companions for reasons of expediency and POWER. For most of the Shī'a, the
reign of the first three caliphs after Muḥammad is
illegitimate and at best tolerable under duress. Hereditary succession vested in the household of the
Prophet (ahl al-bayt) through the line of 'Alī and his
wife, Fāṭima, constitutes legitimate temporal and
spiritual AUTHORITY. The murder of 'Alī's son, Ḥusayn, by the Ummayyad leader, Yazīd, only consoli-
dated the claim of the Shī'a that a pious and righteous imāmate, was the only proper alternative to
monarchy. Starting from 'Alī, the Shī'a identify a
succession of twelve hereditary imāms that constitute the spiritual constellation of the main branch of
the Shī'a, called the "Twelvers" (ithna 'ashariyya).
The last of the twelve imāms, Muḥammad al-Mahdī,
went into major occultation around 939 (329, Islamic calendar) and will remain in that condition as
long as God wills, to finally return as the righteous
guide (mahdī) before the end of time. Other sub-
divisions of the same pedigree constitute the Zaydīs,
who follow Zayd al-Shāhid, the son of the fourth
imām 'Alī al-Sajjād (d. 712; 95, Islamic calendar).
Another group, the Ismā'īlīs, consider Ismā'īl, and
hence the apellation, the son of the sixth imām Ja'far
al-Ṣādiq (d. 757; 140, Islamic calendar) to be the
legitimate successor to his father. Today the Ismā'īli
community is led by the Āgha Khān.

The Islamic Republic of Īrān provides *de facto*
leadership for the mainstream Twelver Shī'īs. With
the advent of the 1979 revolution in Īrān, under
stewardship of the Āyatullāh Rūḥullāh Khumaynī

(d. 1989), Shī'ite theology has taken a more activist turn, ending a long spell of political quietism. Khumaynī argued that waiting for the arrival of the messianic guide (mahdī) led to the intolerable situation in which the religious law (sharī'a) was effectively suspended, which in turn paved the way for despotism, tyranny, and ungodly secular governance to triumph. In order to halt this deterioration, he gave a more dynamic interpretation to the doctrine of the "governance or authority of the jurist" (wilāyat al-faqīh). Under this dispensation the jurist acts as the custodian of the law until the reign of justice under the messianic imām is restored. Although this interpretation was contested by some clerical quarters, it became the centerpiece of the modern theocratic establishment and constitutional arrangement in modern Īrān.

See also: AUTHORITY; ISLAM; ISLAMIC ETHICS; LEGITIMACY; SUNNISM.

Bibliography

Dabashi, Hamid. *Theology of Discontent: The Ideological Foundations of the Islamic Revolution in Iran.* New York: New York University Press, 1993.

Nasr, Seyyid Hossein, Hamid Dabashi, and Seyyid Vali Reza Nasr. *Shi'ism: Doctrines, Thought, and Spirituality.* New York: State University of New York Press, 1988.

Sachedina, Abdulaziz Abdulhussein. *Islamic Messianism: The Idea of Mahdi in Twelver Shi'ism.* Albany: State University of New York Press, 1981.

Ṭabāṭabā'ī, 'Allāmah Sayyid Muúammad Ḥusayn. *Shi'ite Islam.* Translated, edited, and with an introduction and notes by Seyyid Hossein Nasr. London: George Allen and Unwin, 1975.

Ebrahim Moosa

Sidgwick, Henry (1838–1900)

English moral philosopher. Sidgwick was the author of *The Methods of Ethics* (1st ed., 1874), regarded by a number of astute commentators as "the best treatise on moral theory that has ever been written" (Broad). Naturally not all philosophers agree with that assessment. What is striking is how many do; no other work has ever elicited a similar assessment from so many. Of course *The Methods* is nowhere near as well known or as widely read as such acknowledged classics as Plato's *Republic,* Aristotle's *Nicomachean Ethics,* or Mill's *Utilitarianism* (1861). It is long, it is technical, its argument is complicated. It is, in short, a *treatise.*

In addition to *The Methods,* Sidgwick published a *History of Ethics* (1883), a classic of its genre; wrote treatises on political economy and on political theory; and published *Practical Ethics* (1898), a collection of essays. Five other books were published posthumously, from essays and fully written lectures, in accordance with plans he had laid out in advance.

Sidgwick taught at Trinity College, Cambridge, from 1859 on, and was Knightbridge Professor of Moral Philosophy from 1883. His work, with its emphasis on the importance of respecting and examining common sense and the ordinary senses of terms, was instrumental in resurrecting the philosophy of common sense stemming from Thomas REID (1710–1796). The "ordinary language movement"—though not some of the turns it sometimes took—traces from the influence of Sidgwick. Sidgwick was active in the affairs of his college and especially active in promoting higher education for women. Thus he played a leading role in the founding of Newnham College (1871). He also took an active interest in psychical research and was one of the founders of the Society for Psychical Research in 1882. He engaged in this research in the same spirit of cautious, disinterested, fair-minded inquiry exhibited in his philosophical works. He was never an advocate, always a judge. Although he had a reputation as a conversationalist and wit, these characteristics are rarely visible in his writing, which is marked by caution and circumspection, a dedication to examining all sides of a subject and never asserting more than is warranted by a careful sifting of the evidence. These traits were also manifested in his dealings with public questions, and he displayed a decidedly unusual capacity to enter into the minds and thinking of those who held views contrary to his own. Brand Blanshard (1892–1987) has characterized Sidgwick as "the exemplar of objectivity in thought, of clear and passionless understanding. The light he threw on his subject was uniquely uncolored by feeling, prejudice, or desire." It was "pure white light!" Blanshard added that of all the persons he had "known or read about," Sidgwick is "the nearest approximation to the genuinely reasonable man" (*Monist*). These characteristics are especially manifest in *The Methods,* which is the reason that many readers have found it dull and failed to stay the course. Sidgwick himself said that his *Methods* was "an attempt to introduce precision of thought into a subject usually treated in a too loose and popular way, and therefore . . . cannot fail to be somewhat dry and repellant" (*Henry Sidgwick: A Memoir*), and he expressed the thought that "the real progress of ethical science . . . would be benefitted by an application to it of the same disinterested curiosity to which we chiefly owe the great discoveries of physics" (*Methods*).

Sidgwick conceived of ethics as "inquiry into the principles and method of determining what is right and wrong in human action, the content of the moral law, and the proper object of rational choice and avoidance" (*Misc. E.*). His two other treatises fit into a general plan of exploring the whole of practical philosophy. Sidgwick regarded economics and politics as being essentially normative, with ethics as the foundation of both. In these works as in others he is closely concerned with methods of reasoning to practical conclusions and for arriving at basic principles. *The Methods of Ethics* is not only his single most important work, it also contains the foundations of his system of philosophy, which his premature death prevented him from working out in detail. Method was the major concern in many of his works.

On Sidgwick's view the ultimate aim of philosophy is to coordinate theoretical and practical philosophy and to "connect fact and ideal in some rational and satisfactory manner" (*Phil.*). Accordingly, his aim is to systematize, coordinate, make consistent and coherent, clarify and make precise, the main data of the subject and bring it into line with a theory that would explain this data and in turn be supported and clarified by this process. This is the procedure he followed in ethics and in his treatment of philosophy itself. In his view, philosophy "uses primarily . . . the dialectical method, *i.e.,* the method of reflection on the thought which we all share, by the aid of the symbolism which we all share, language" (*Phil.*). This is the method of *The Methods of Ethics*.

For a long time Sidgwick was regarded as the last of the outstanding utilitarians of the nineteenth century and *The Methods* as "the last authoritative utterance of traditional utilitarianism." This assessment is not wholly wrong, but it is largely so. Sidgwick's aim in *The Methods* was not to establish

UTILITARIANISM, although it does look that way. His aim was to explore impartially the methods of ethics, that is, the procedures used in common life to determine what ought to be done. He finds and distinguishes three: EGOISM (or egoistic hedonism), INTUITIONISM, and utilitarianism (universalistic HEDONISM). In Book 1 he makes a number of distinctions important for the subject, including the crucial distinction between a *method* and a *principle*—thus emphasizing that his primary concern is with the *methods,* not the principles, of ethics. Book 2 is devoted to a dispassionate examination of egoism as a method of ethics, that is to say, as a method of determining what one ought to do by taking one's own ultimate good as the ultimate aim of action. In the process he brings out the difficulties in applying hedonism—the idea that PLEASURE is what is ultimately good—in a way that has not been matched since. Book 3 is devoted to exploring intuitionism, or the morality of common sense, as Sidgwick conceived of it, since he believed that implicit acceptance of some form of intuitionism is characteristic of common sense morality. He distinguished three forms of intuitionism: "perceptual," which involves judging particular cases intuitively, without reference to consequences; "dogmatic," in which general rules are taken as what is known intuitively; and "philosophical," in which only certain very abstract principles, having no immediate or obvious application to conduct, are judged intuitively to be sound. Dogmatic intuitionism corresponds to the morality of common sense. Sidgwick's detailed and comprehensive examination of common sense morality (the morality, he says, that is his own as much as it is anyone's) is the greatest achievement of its kind since the work of Aristotle. Sidgwick concludes that despite the pervasive character of common sense morality, in cases of perplexity it is inadequate to provide practical guidance, and therefore inadequate by itself as a method of ethics. He concludes also that common sense morality is "unconsciously utilitarian," in the sense that when such practical difficulties arise, common sense unconsciously resorts to the utilitarian method to resolve them.

The utilitarian method is examined in Book 4 and does not itself come off unscathed. Sidgwick raises questions, along with other problems, about the differences that obtain in applying the utilitarian method in a society of utilitarians and in a society not made up of utilitarians, a distinction not heretofore thought of. He concludes that, despite the problems connected with the use of the intuitionist method, utilitarians must recognize that they themselves are imbued with common sense morality and that the latter, despite its defects, cannot be changed rapidly or by decree or by the mere application of a theory.

In his examination of intuitionism, Sidgwick finds some abstract principles that he concludes are genuinely self-evident. One is the principle of justice: what is right for one person must be right for every similar person in similar circumstances (the principle that in the mid-twentieth century was rechristened the principle of UNIVERSALIZABILITY). Another is the first principle of egoism, and a third is the principle of rational BENEVOLENCE. It is Sidgwick's view that the principle of rational benevolence, together with the principle of justice, is a self-evident principle (in the process he distinguishes and discusses four criteria for genuine self-evidence) lying at the basis of utilitarianism. Thus he regards utilitarianism as resting on an intuitional basis. The problem he finds, however, which is discussed in the concluding chapter of *The Methods,* is that of reconciling the apparently self-evident first principle of rational egoism with the apparently self-evident first principle of rational benevolence. This problem, that of the Dualism of the Practical Reason, in which PRACTICAL REASON by valid reasoning seems irrevocably at odds with itself, is one that plagued Sidgwick all his life; although he never gave up hope of finding a solution for it, he had not found one at the time of his death. In somewhat different terminology, the problem is one of reconciling self-interest and duty, and is one that has existed in ethics from its inception. In Sidgwick's *Methods* it takes on a technical form in which the problem is even more pronounced.

What was Sidgwick's main aim in *The Methods*? J. B. Schneewind argues that "The main line of argument . . . is an attempt to show how the apparently self-evident axioms are involved in the systematization of our moral knowledge. . . . The central thought . . . is that morality is the embodiment of the demands reason makes on practice under the conditions of human life, and that the problems of philosophical ethics are the problems of showing how practical reason is articulated into these demands," and if Schneewind's idea is not the whole truth it is certainly part of it.

See also: BENEVOLENCE; COMMON SENSE MORALISTS; EGOISM; GOLDEN RULE; GOOD, THEORIES OF THE; HAPPINESS; HEDONISM; INTUITIONISM; JUSTICE, CIRCUMSTANCES OF; METAETHICS; MORAL PERCEPTION; MORAL SENSE THEORISTS; MORAL TERMS; NATURALISTIC FALLACY; PLEASURE; PRACTICAL REASON[ING]; REID; UNIVERSALIZABILITY; UTILITARIANISM.

Bibliography

Works by Sidgwick

The Methods of Ethics. 7th ed. London: Macmillan, 1907 [1874]. Publication history: 1st ed., 1874; 2d ed., 1877; 3d ed., 1884; 4th ed., 1890; 5th ed., 1893; 6th ed., 1901; 7th ed., 1907. The 7th edition has been reprinted several times and is the standard edition cited. Sidgwick died before completing the revisions for the 6th edition. It, and the 7th, were seen through the press by E. E. Constance Jones. The 2d and 3d editions were accompanied by *Supplements,* detailing "for the use of purchasers of the first edition" the "numerous alterations and additions" made. An index appeared for the first time in the 4th edition, the work of Constance Jones. Quoted from p. *vi.*

The Principles of Political Economy. 1st ed. London: Macmillan, 1883. 2d ed., 1887; 3d ed., 1901. Among its other merits, a pioneering work in welfare economics. The 3d edition was prepared for the press by John Neville Keynes, a logician and economist, with the assistance of his son, John Maynard Keynes.

Outlines of the History of Ethics for English Readers. London: Macmillan, 1886. 2d ed., 1888; 3d ed., 1892; 4th ed., 1896; 5th ed., 1902. Still regarded by some as the finest short history of ethics ever written.

The Elements of Politics. 1st ed. London: Macmillan, 1891. 2d ed., 1898; 3d ed., 1908. Especially valuable for its careful working out of "the 'individualistic minimum' of governmental interference."

Practical Ethics: A Collection of Essays and Addresses. London: Swan Sonnenschein, 1898. Contains a brilliant essay on "Unreasonable Action." The last work published by Sidgwick in his lifetime. Contains some fascinating casuistical studies, with an emphasis on the importance, in dealing with such questions, of "middle axioms," as distinct from "ultimate principles." Reprinted, with an introduction by Sissela Bok (New York: Oxford University Press, 1998), with different pagination. (See citation for Bok; for a review, see Schultz.)

Philosophy, Its Scope and Relations. London: Macmillan, 1902. Cited as *Phil.* A course of lectures. Quoted from pp. 30, 49.

Lectures on the Ethics of T. H. Green, H. Spencer, and J. Martineau. London: Macmillan, 1902. In some ways, nicely supplements *The Methods.*

The Development of European Polity. London: Macmillan, 1903. A companion work to the *Politics,* put together from fairly full lecture notes.

Miscellaneous Essays and Addresses. London: Macmillan, 1904. Quoted from p. 249.

Lectures on the Philosophy of Kant and other Philosophical Lectures and Essays. London: Macmillan, 1905. Contains Sidgwick's epistemological essays and his groundbreaking essay, "The Philosophy of Common Sense."

"Some Fundamental Ethical Controversies." *Mind* 14, old series, no. 56 (1889): 473–87. The closest thing we have to a commentary on *The Methods* written by Sidgwick himself.

Essays on Ethics and Method, edited by Marcus G. Singer. Oxford: Clarendon Press, forthcoming. Contains the three essays mentioned above—"Some Fundamental Ethical Controversies" (1889), "Unreasonable Action" (1893), and "The Philosophy of Common Sense" (1895)—and twenty-seven others.

The Works of Henry Sidgwick. 15 vols. Bristol, England: Thoemmes Press, 1996. Sidgwick's complete works, including previously uncollected essays and reviews.

The Complete Works and Selected Correspondence of Henry Sidgwick. 2d ed. Edited by Bart Schultz, with J. M. Wilkins, Belinda Robinson, Andrew Dakyns. Past Masters Series. A CD-ROM. Charlottesville, VA: Intelex, 1999 (1997).

Henry Sidgwick: A Memoir. Arthur Sidgwick and Eleanor Mildred Sidgwick. London: Macmillan, 1906. Contains numerous excerpts from Sidgwick's letters and a journal he kept for a number of years. An absorbing book, coauthored by his brother and his widow. For passage quoted, see p. 295. Cited as *Mem.*

Works about Sidgwick

Albee, Ernest. *A History of English Utilitarianism.* London: George Allen and Unwin, 1901. In the three chapters on Sidgwick, traces out the changes in some of the more important doctrines and chapters from one edition of *The Methods* to another.

Blanshard, Brand. *Reason and Goodness.* London: George Allen and Unwin, 1961. See esp. pp. 90–91.

———. *Four Reasonable Men: Marcus Aurelius, John Stuart Mill, Ernest Renan, Henry Sidgwick.* Middletown, CT: Wesleyan University Press, 1984. Pp. 181–243 are on Sidgwick; for passage quoted, see p. 181; see also pp. 242–43.

Bok, Sissela. Introduction to Sidgwick's *Practical Ethics,* pp. *v–xix.* New York: Oxford University Press, 1998. For a review, see Schultz.

Broad, C. D. *Five Types of Ethical Theory.* London: Kegan Paul, 1930. Quoted from p. 143.

———. "Henry Sidgwick." In *Ethics and the History of Philosophy,* 49–69. London: Routledge and Kegan Paul, 1952.

Daurio, Janice. "The Role of the Distinction between

Method and Principle and the Place of Common Sense Morality in Henry Sidgwick's *The Methods of Ethics.*" Ph.D. diss., Claremont Graduate School, 1994. UMI Dissertation Services. An excellent work, which contains among other things a useful and ample bibliography of recent writings on Sidgwick.

———. "Sidgwick on Moral Theories and Common Sense Morality." *History of Philosophy Quarterly* 14/4 (1997): 425–45. Reprinted in *The Philosopher's Annual,* edited by P. Grim, K. Baynes, and G. Mar, 20 (1997): 49–67.

Donagan, Alan. Review of Schneewind. *Ethics* 90 (1980): 282–95.

Edgeworth, F. Y. *New and Old Methods of Ethics.* London: James Parker, 1877. A monograph-length discussion by an acute thinker who pioneered in applying mathematics to economics.

Frankena, William K. "Sidgwick, Henry." In *An Encyclopedia of Morals,* edited by Vergilius Ferm, 539–44. New York: Philosophical Library, 1956. A penetrating and perceptive article, which should be better known.

Harrison, Ross. Review of Schultz. *British Journal for the History of Philosophy* 4 (1996): 203–6.

———. "Henry Sidgwick." *Philosophy* 71 (1996): 423–38.

Havard, William C. *Henry Sidgwick and Later Utilitarian Political Philosophy.* Gainesville: University of Florida Press, 1959.

Hayward, F. H. *The Ethical Philosophy of Sidgwick.* London: Swan Sonnenschein, 1901. The first actual commentary, this little-known work is worth seeking out for its uncommon insights and bibliographical notes.

The Monist. 58 (July 1974): entire issue. An issue devoted to Sidgwick, with essays by, among others, Blanshard, Schneewind, D. D. Raphael, W. K. Frankena, Stephen Darwall, Gertrude Ezorsky, and Peter Singer. Quoted at p. 349.

Moody-Adams, Michele M. Review of Schultz. *Victorian Studies* 35 (Autumn 1885): 149–50.

Mullins, T. Y. "Sidgwick's Concept of Ethical Science." *Journal of the History of Ideas* 24 (1963): 584–88.

Rashdall, Hastings. "Professor Sidgwick's Utilitarianism." *Mind* 10, old series (1885): 200–26. Many journal discussions of *The Methods* appeared; this one is on the 3d ed. Rashdall sent an earlier version of this discussion to Sidgwick before the completion of the 3d edition. Sidgwick revised the 3d edition partly in light of the original version of this essay, which then had to be rewritten. Many readers have complained that Sidgwick's style of writing is stodgy and boring. They might be interested in Rashdall's unquestionably disinterested assessment of that: "*The Methods of Ethics* has long been recognized as a philosophical classic. It is one of those works of which it is safe to prophesy that no advance in philosophical doctrine will ever render them obsolete. It is not merely a piece of acute and subtle philosophical criticism but a work of art with a unity and beauty of its own as much as a dialogue of Plato or of Berkeley. And nothing is so well calculated to increase the reader's admiration for Prof. Sidgwick's literary skill as a comparison of the successive revisions to which he has subjected it. Every edition represents a nearer approach to artistic perfection" (p. 200).

Rayleigh, Lord. "Some Recollections of Henry Sidgwick." *Proceedings of the Society for Psychical Research* 45 (1938–1939): 162–73. Recollections by a friend.

Rothblatt, Sheldon. *The Revolution of the Dons: Cambridge and Society in Victorian England.* London: Faber and Faber, 1968. See especially chapter 4.

Schneewind, J. B. *Sidgwick's Ethics and Victorian Moral Philosophy.* Oxford: Clarendon Press, 1977. The definitive work, if any philosophical work can be definitive, on Sidgwick and the period covered. The bibliography is unrivaled, though unfortunately it is not annotated and does little to single out works specifically on Sidgwick. (For reviews, see Donagan, M. Singer, and Skorupski.)

Schneewind, J. B., and Bart Schultz. "Henry Sidgwick, 1838–1900." In *The Cambridge Bibliography of English Literature,* 3d ed. Cambridge: Cambridge University Press, 1999. An extensive bibliography, with some unfortunate omissions.

Schultz, Bart, ed. *Essays on Henry Sidgwick.* Cambridge: Cambridge University Press, 1992. The first book of its kind. Contains essays by, among others, John Deigh, Alan Donagan, William Frankena, Russell Hardin, T. H. Irwin, J. L. Mackie, David Brink, J. B. Schneewind, Nicholas White, Stefan Collini, and James T. Kloppenberg. The introduction, by the editor, is especially fine, informative and acute. (For reviews, see Harrison, Moody-Adams, Skorupski, M. Singer, and P. Singer.)

———. Review of Sissela Bok's introduction to reprint edition of Sidgwick's *Practical Ethics. Ethics* 109 (1999): 678–84.

———, ed. "Sidgwick 2000." *Utilitas.* Projected for publication in November 2000. To contain several articles by various writers.

Shaver, Robert. "Sidgwick's False Friends." *Ethics* 107 (1997): 314–20. A brief account of a rather obscure point in Sidgwick, with useful references to other discussions.

Singer, Marcus G. Review of Schneewind. *Nous* 16 (1982): 339–50.

———. Review of Schultz. *Philosophy and Phenomenological Research* 59 (1999): 533–37.

Singer, Peter. Review of Schultz. *Ethics* 104 (1994): 631–33.

Skorupski, J. Review of Schneewind. *Philosophical Quarterly* 29 (1979): 158–69.

———. "Clearly Undecided." *Times Literary Supplement,* July 10, 1992: 24–25. Review of Schultz.

Slater, John. "The Importance of Henry Sidgwick." In *The Works of Henry Sidgwick,* vol. I, *v–liv.* Bristol, England: Thoemmes Press, 1996. The introduction to Sidgwick's complete works.

Sorley, W. R. "Henry Sidgwick." *International Journal of Ethics* 11 (1900–1901): 168–74. A sample of one of the many memorial notices that appeared after Sidgwick's death, by Sidgwick's successor as Knightbridge Professor of Moral Philosophy.

Sverdlik, Steven. "Sidgwick's Methodology." *Journal of the History of Philosophy* 58 (1985): 537–53.

Thomson, Joseph John. "Henry Sidgwick." In his *Recollections and Reflections,* 293–300. New York: Macmillan, 1937.

Marcus G. Singer

Singer, Marcus G. (1926–)

The moral philosophy of Marcus Singer represents an anti-skeptical vision of moral discourse and practice according to which there are basic moral truths, expressible as moral principles that are capable of being known. Hence, one main task of moral inquiry is to discover such principles and explore the possibilities of their proof.

Singer was born in New York City and served in the U.S. Army Air Forces, 1944–1945. He graduated from the University of Illinois with an A.B. degree in 1948 and earned a Ph.D. degree in philosophy from Cornell University in 1952. In 1952, Singer accepted a teaching position in the Department of Philosophy at the University of Wisconsin, Madison where he taught until 1994. He was president of the American Philosophical Association, Central Division, 1985–1986.

Singer's principal work, *Generalization in Ethics* (1961), is primarily an elaboration and defense of a normative moral theory that takes the familiar question, "What if everyone did that?" as central to rational moral thought and discussion. According to Singer, this question is associated with the so-called *generalization argument* (GA): If everyone were to do that the consequences would be undesirable; therefore, no one ought to do that. This argument, expressed as a moral principle (with some refinements added) says: If the consequences of everyone's doing some action A would be undesirable (on the whole), while the consequences of no one's doing A would not be undesirable (on the whole), then no one has the right to do A (without a justifying reason). Although Singer defends other moral principles, he claims that the generalization argument principle has a central role to play in ethical thought and argumentation because it "serves as a test or criterion of the morality of conduct, and provides the basis for moral rules" (*Generalization*).

Another moral principle that is given extensive treatment and plays a fundamental role in Singer's moral theory is the *generalization principle* (GP): What is right (or wrong) for one person to do is right (or wrong) for all similar persons in similar circumstances. He argues that this principle (often called the principle of UNIVERSALIZABILITY) is a presupposition of all MORAL REASONING and, when properly interpreted, is neither morally useless nor trivial in the context of moral argumentation.

Singer's elaboration and defense of these principles involves a good deal of ingenuity, subtlety, and attention to detail. For instance, he argues that in cases in which GA is invertible—*i.e.,* in cases where the consequences of everyone's doing some act would be undesirable while the consequences of no one's doing that act would also be undesirable—the principle is not applicable because the situation is described too generally for purposes of moral evaluation. In defense of GA, Singer explains the conditions of its correct application, shows how it can be applied to specific cases, defends it against various charges, and criticizes opposing moral principles. Additionally, Singer attempts to justify GA by deriving it from other principles featured in his theory. One such principle is the *principle of consequences* (C): If the consequences of some individual S doing *A* would be undesirable, then S does not have the right to do *A* (without a justifying reason). Singer claims that C is a necessary presupposition of moral reasoning, which provides the basis for a generalized version of the principle (GC): If the consequences of everyone's doing *A* would be undesirable, then not everyone has the right to do *A*. GC together with GP provide the premises for deriving GA. This argument sparked a flurry of articles debating the validity and soundness of the attempted deduction.

Although the most general aim of *Generalization in Ethics* is to "determine, through the examination of these principles, how moral judgments can rationally be supported, how moral perplexities can be resolved, and how moral disputes can rationally be settled" (*Generalization*), the book also contains an illuminating discussion of the distinction between and relations among moral principles and MORAL RULES, an argument against duties to oneself, an extensive and influential interpretation and defense of Immanuel KANT's (1724–1804) categorical imperative, and a critique of ethical relativism.

Singer's moral theory, featuring GA, is often classified as a version of UTILITARIANISM—a kind of indirect version that focuses on the values of the consequences of a type of action being performed by a specified class of individuals in determining the deontic status of concrete particular actions of the specified type. (Direct versions focus on the values of the consequences of individual actions being evaluated.) Like utilitarianism, Singer's moral theory takes the values of consequences (specifically, their undesirability) as the most fundamental morally relevant feature in determining the rightness and wrongness of actions, though, as Singer has argued, there are important differences between his view and familiar versions of utilitarianism. For instance, GA does not bid one to perform actions whose general performance would maximize HAPPINESS, nor does it bid one to perform actions whose general performance would minimize unhappiness. Indirect versions of utilitarianism are supposed to differ from direct versions in having more plausible implications regarding the morality of concrete actions. One area of controversy is whether Singer's view, with its focus on the question of what would happen if everyone did some type of action, differs in its normative implications from a view whose focus is on the question of what would happen if this particular act were to be performed. According to some critics there is no difference and hence GA is extensionally equivalent (equivalent in all its normative implications) to C.

Since the publication of *Generalization in Ethics,* Singer has continued to elaborate, extend, and in some ways modify his earlier views. His writings also include important work on the moral philosophies of JOHN STUART MILL (1806–1873) and Henry SIDGWICK (1838–1900) as well as articles in the areas of SOCIAL AND POLITICAL PHILOSOPHY, philosophy of law, and American philosophy and on such topics as the GOLDEN RULE, racism, and institutional ethics. Singer is currently at work on a book tentatively entitled, "Justification and Proof in Ethics."

See also: CATEGORICAL AND HYPOTHETICAL IMPERATIVES; CONSEQUENTIALISM; GOLDEN RULE; IMPARTIALITY; KANT; KANTIAN ETHICS; MORAL REASON-

Singer, Marcus G.

ING; MORAL RELATIVISM; MORAL RULES; RACISM AND RELATED ISSUES; SIDGWICK; SKEPTICISM IN ETHICS; SLIPPERY SLOPE ARGUMENTS; UNIVERSALIZABILITY; UTILITARIANISM.

Bibliography

Works by Singer

Generalization in Ethics: An Essay in the Logic of Ethics, with the Rudiments of a System of Moral Philosophy. New York: Alfred A. Knopf, 1961. Passages quoted are from pp. 9 and 6.

"The Golden Rule." *Philosophy* 38 (1963): 293–314.

"Moral Skepticism." In *Skepticism and Moral Principles,* edited by C. L. Carter, 77–108. Evanston: New University Press, 1973.

"The Principle of Consequences Reconsidered." *Philosophical Studies* 31 (1977): 391–409.

"Actual Consequence Utilitarianism." *Mind* 86 (1977): 67–77.

"The Paradox of Extreme Utilitarianism." *Pacific Philosophical Quarterly* 64 (1983): 242–48.

"Universalizability and the Generalization Principle." In *Morality and Universality: Essays on Ethical Universalizability,* edited by Nelson Potter and Mark Timmons, 47–73. Dordrecht: D. Reidel, 1985.

"Imperfect Duty Situations, Moral Freedom, and Universalizability." In *Moral Philosophy: Historical and Contemporary Essays,* edited by William C. Starr and Richard C. Taylor, 145–69. Milwaukee: Marquette University Press, 1989.

"Mill's Stoic Conception of Happiness and Pragmatic Conception of Utility." *Philosophy* 75/291 (January 2000): 25–47.

Essays on Ethics and Method, edited by Marcus G. Singer. Oxford: Oxford University Press, 2000. Collection of essays on Sidgwick.

The Ideal of a Rational Morality. Oxford: Oxford University Press, forthcoming. A collection of essays in which Singer explores a variety of issues in metaethics, normative ethics, and social philosophy.

Works about Singer

Lyons, David. *Forms and Limits of Utilitarianism.* Oxford: Oxford University Press, 1965. Chapters 1–3 contain an extended defense of the extensional equivalence thesis while the appendix is devoted to Singer's derivation of GA.

Nakhnikian, George. "Generalization in Ethics." *Review of Metaphysics* 17 (1964): 436–61. A detailed critique of Singer's derivation of GA. Also contains useful discussions of various critiques by other philosophers of Singer's derivation.

Sobel, J. Howard. "Generalization Arguments." *Theoria* 31 (1965): 32–60. Critical of Singer's no conflict thesis, according to which C and GA can never conflict.

Thomas, Sid B. "The Status of the Generalization Principle." *American Philosophical Quarterly* 5 (1968): 174–82. An interpretation and defense of GP.

Verdi, John J. "In Defense of Marcus Singer." *The Personalist* 58 (1977): 208–20. Defends Singer's view against various objections, including Sobel's criticism of the no conflict thesis.

Mark Timmons

situation ethics

Generally stated, situation or "contextual" ethics claims that the context or circumstances ought to determine a moral choice and action. The position emerged in Christian communities during two decades following World War II. It was defined primarily against "legalism"—the heteronomous determination of right conduct by conformity to codes of MORAL RULES prescribed by moral authorities. In Europe it was promoted by Roman Catholic authors, some of whom found affinity with strands of Protestant writings. The position was officially condemned by the Vatican Holy Office in 1956. In North America it was propagated widely by Joseph Fletcher, in his *Situation Ethics* (1966), and by other Christian writers. No author identified with the position has published a rigorously developed philosophical theory and defense; the literature is mostly practical and often rhetorical, or couched in particularly Christian terms.

Situation ethics has affinities with identifiable ethical trends in philosophy and religious thought. It differs from classic CASUISTRY, which is also "situation"-oriented, in that it eschews the use of classifications and distinctions in the analysis of circumstances, does not invoke the principle of DOUBLE EFFECT, and is not based on a metaphysics, as classic Catholic casuistry was based on the theory of NATURAL LAW. In Fletcher's book, LOVE is the basic or ground term and reality, but it functions in a variety of ways as he develops his themes. For Paul Lehmann, "humanizing" is the aim of action. It affirms MORAL RELATIVISM of a general sort, and most particularly in its polemic against "absolutism." The influence of PRAGMATISM is evident, and in some writings existentialist writers have had influence. "Personalism" is invoked, primarily to counter the perceived impersonalism of "absolutist" and "legalistic" ethics. Perhaps its closest philosophical affinity is with act-UTILITARIANISM; only the end justifies the means and it seems that there are few moral restraints on means that can be used to achieve a desirable outcome. Little attention is given, however, to procedures for calculating probable consequences. There are similarities to *Kathekontic* ethics of STOICISM and of recent Christian proposals, but good outcomes appear to be more significant than right or fitting relationships. Situation ethics has not provided a philosophical defense of its implied position on the fact/value problem; it seems to adhere to a kind of perceptual intuition of the right act once the agent has formed a configuration of what are deemed to be the morally relevant facts of a case.

Situation ethics preempted discussions in Christian communities for a decade or two. All APPLIED ETHICS, whether religious or philosophical, address choices possible in classes of cases or in individual circumstances; a "situational" component is necessarily considered. Polarized discussions occurred that were prompted more by moral anxieties than by intellectual interests. The term fell into oblivion as attention was gained by more sophisticated analyses of how particular moral choices are to be made.

See also: APPLIED ETHICS; CASUISTRY; CHRISTIAN ETHICS; CONSCIENCE; DOUBLE EFFECT; EXISTENTIAL ETHICS; INTUITIONISM; LOVE; MORAL REALISM; MORAL REASONING; MORAL RELATIVISM; MORAL RULES; PRAGMATISM; PRESCRIPTIVISM; THEORY AND PRACTICE; UTILITARIANISM.

Bibliography

Fletcher, Joseph. *Situation Ethics: The New Morality.* Philadelphia: Westminster, 1966.

Ford, John C., and Gerald Kelly. *Contemporary Moral Theology.* 2 vols. Westminster, Md.: Newman Press, 1958. Vol. 1, pp. 104–40, is a report and discussion of situation ethics in the Roman Catholic Church.

Gustafson, James M. "Context versus Principles: A Misplaced Debate in Christian Ethics." *Harvard Theological Review* 58 (1965): 171–202. An analysis of the issues; published during the peak of interest in situation ethics.

Lehmann, Paul. *Ethics in a Christian Context.* New York: Harper and Row, 1963.

Ramsey, Paul. *Deed and Rules in Christian Ethics.* New York: Scribner's, 1967. Pp. 49–103 and 145–225

contain polemics against Paul Lehmann's "contextual" ethics and Fletcher's situation ethics.

James M. Gustafson

skepticism in ancient ethics

Ancient skeptical arguments, their status, and their effects are all strikingly and interestingly different from their modern counterparts.

As early as the fifth century B.C.E. the SOPHISTS challenged the idea that ethics is simply a matter of fact, like other facts in the world. They made a distinction between 'nature' (*phusis*) and 'convention' (*nomos*). As the Greeks became aware of ethical differences among societies, it became common to claim that, while, for example, fire burns both in Greece and in Persia, because that is its nature, the fact that Greeks and Persians disagree about justice shows that justice does not in this way have a nature and is not part of the natural world. Rather, Greeks have one set of conventions about justice, while Persians have another. All values come in this way to be thought of as a product of human convention.

This view is, however, not one clear position but several. The nature/convention distinction can be drawn in several places, because while nature standardly means the natural world independent of humans, the convention side varies widely. *Nomos* ranges from established law through sanctioned custom down to arbitrary convention; which position is meant will make an enormous difference. That morality is a matter of law would not lead to alarming results, such as loss of confidence in its AUTHORITY, which would seem appropriate if it has no surer basis than mere convention. Relativism, the reaction to the thought that morality is not an immutable part of the natural world but rather the product of changeable human INSTITUTIONS, was not a skeptical position at all (see below). The main relativist was PROTAGORAS (c. 490–c. 421 B.C.E.); two extensive sections of Plato's (c. 430–347 B.C.E.) dialogues *Protagoras* and *Theaetetus* discuss Protagoras's value relativism. PLATO presents Protagoras with a confused view; unfortunately we cannot tell whether this presentation is accurate or represents Plato's hostility. And while Plato has several interesting defenses of objectivity in other areas, in that of values he does not argue but simply gives a consciously rhetorical statement that values are objective.

Although ARISTOTLE (384–322 B.C.E.) in *Nicomachean Ethics* V discusses issues of nature and convention, true skepticism does not emerge until the Hellenistic period. It took two forms: the skeptical phase of Plato's Academy, and the Pyrrhonists. Both schools share the fundamental assumptions of ancient skepticism. The skeptic attacks not just knowledge, but all the beliefs of others. The skeptic does not show beliefs to be false, but argues that, at least on disputed matters, there is as much to support one side as the other and claims that finding this to be so is followed by suspension of judgment (*epochē*) and detachment. And the skeptic attacks beliefs of all kinds; thus morality is never attacked from an allegedly firmer, 'scientific' basis.

The Skeptical Academy

The skeptical heads of the Academy, notably Arcesilaus (315–241 B.C.E.) and Carneades (214–129 B.C.E.), argued purely against others' views, putting forward none themselves. They did not themselves argue against commonsense acceptance of the reality of values; for this argument would have to be done from certain premises (*e.g.,* about justification) and they held no such premises *in propria persona*. Rather, they argued to *epochē* about all other philosophers' theories of morality. We do not have many of these arguments, but we do have two responses by Arcesilaus to a common anti-skeptical objection: if you assent neither to any beliefs of your own nor to anyone else's about values, what is your 'criterion of action'—that is, how do you determine whether you are doing the right thing or not? For HAPPINESS requires a criterion; if you lack it your life will lack shape and direction. Sextus Empiricus (c. 150–c. 225), in *Against the Professors* (*M*) VII 158, says that Arcesilaus provided such a criterion: 'the reasonable' (*to eulogon*), following which will lead to achievement (the Stoic term for a fully virtuous action). For happiness is achieved through intelligence, intelligence lies in achievements, and an achievement is what, when it is done, has a reasonable defense. This argument has often been regarded as *ad hominem* against the Stoics, whose terminology it uses; but it does not go from clearly Stoic premises to a conclusion that embarrasses the Stoics. However, if it is Arcesilaus's own argument, then his skepticism seems compromised; he is asserting that in ACTION we should do what seems reasonable,

but skeptics cannot assent to beliefs of this kind, which they find eminently disputable.

In another passage (Plutarch, *Against Colotes, 1122 A–D*), Arcesilaus argues that action is possible for the skeptic who suspends judgment, for action does not require assent. Action requires only that the situation strike one in a certain way and that one react to this (in ancient terms, action requires appearance and impulse, but not assent to the belief expressing the content of the appearance). This, however, would appear to explain only mechanical or instinctive action or to reduce all action to such. Moreover, we seem again to have Arcesilaus assenting to a view of his own. How do we reconcile this with the claim that 'the reasonable' is the criterion of right action?

It is often thought that Arcesilaus did not successfully meet the objection that the skeptic must, inconsistently, assent to some things in order to act. However, Arcesilaus frequently stresses *nature* as guiding our lives, and there is an *obiter dictum* to the effect that in argument he would often be led naturally to say things normally implying assent. This observation suggests that he had a consistent position. To act in a rationally grounded way, we would have to assent to various beliefs about values. Skeptical argument, however, gets us to a state of detachment about these beliefs. But we act anyway, since our nature leads us to act even in the absence of assent to any beliefs.

Still, is Arcesilaus not compromising his skepticism in assenting to theses about, for example, reasonableness? No; for he is not assenting to them at all. Rather, as a result of much argument he now finds himself with these views; he naturally expresses what seems to him the best view but, being skeptically detached, does not assent to this.

This position is coherent and interesting, and suggestive of HUME (1711–1776) in its claim that our nature will support us, nonrationally, in various persistent habits of action which appear to require belief, even when belief is removed.

The Pyrrhonists

In the first century B.C.E., as the Academy's skepticism grew weaker, there was a radical breakaway movement led by Aenesidemus, which harked back to the semi-legendary figure of Pyrrho (c. 360–270 B.C.E.), who wrote and taught nothing but was regarded as a founding figure of radical skepticism. Some of Aenesidemus's arguments survive in the later compendium of Pyrrhonist arguments put together by Sextus Empiricus. Pyrrhonist arguments about value are found in the Tenth Mode and in sections on ethics in Sextus's shorter work (*Outlines of Pyrrhonism,* hereafter cited as *PH*) and the longer one (*Against the Professors,* hereafter cited as *M*).

The Ten Modes, which derive from Aenesidemus, are argument schemata to be applied skeptically to lead to *epochē*. The Tenth, which we have in three sources, 'especially concerns ethics.' Sextus, in our fullest version, singles out five factors relevant to our beliefs about values (call these persuasions): lifestyle, custom or habit, laws, mythical belief, and dogmatic philosophical theories; then he systematically produces conflicts between all these factors. These are evidence for conflict of beliefs about value: the same thing appears good to people of one persuasion, bad to those of another. And since the thing can't *be* both good and bad, we see that if we think it good, this is only because of our persuasion; and since people of another persuasion disagree, our belief has no more rational support than its contradictory. Once in this state, we will in fact suspend belief on the matter and feel detached from commitment to the belief.

This is a standard application of the method of showing that we have 'conflicting appearances,' used in the other Modes and other skeptical arguments. Just as equally good arguments on both sides of a question cancel each other out and leave a person detached from both, likewise if something appears to a person good from one point of view and bad from another and there is nothing rationally to choose between the two points of view, a person is left detached from both appearances. This is the only skeptical argument that applies to commonsense value beliefs as opposed to the result of argument. Individual arguments resulting from filling in examples of valued things and persuasions in the argument schema will depend for their force on the plausibility of the examples. Sextus's own examples are unfortunately not at all convincing; he fails to see that to detach us from a belief we need persuasions that are as acceptable to us as our own, not outlandish or bizarre ones. The fact that other people's persuasions are very different from ours has in itself no power to shake our confidence in ours; indeed it often produces the reverse effect. Cases where we really will be led to suspend belief are much rarer than the skeptics assume; they fail to establish a general presumption that ethical values give rise to unhealable conflict and hence *epochē*.

Philo of Alexandria, one source for the Tenth Mode, adds two arguments, more limited and unique in antiquity. One is that dispute in ethics differs from that in other areas in being chronic even among the experts. The other is a forerunner of the argument that disagreement about value is to be explained by differences in upbringing and background, not vice versa.

In *PH* III and *M* XI, Sextus retails many arguments against ethical philosophers. They center on two points: there is widespread philosophical disagreement over the definition of 'good,' 'bad,' and so on (*PH* III 169–78; *M* XI 21–41); and there is also disagreement over what things are good or bad (*PH* III 179–234; *M* XI 43–109). (There are also subsidiary arguments directed against the positions of particular schools.) Sometimes argument is directly pitted against argument; sometimes against intuitive belief. Always the aim is to detach us from belief by convincing us that the belief has as much going against it as for it, so that we are equally convinced both ways. Again, the arguments vary in their ability to convince and do not establish that values are always problematic in this way nor that ethical argument must always be inconclusive.

Strangely, in the longer work there is a minor strain of arguments to *relativism* (*M* XI 69–78; 114–18), which seem to derive from Aenesidemus (cf. *M* XI 42–44). These undertake to show that nothing is good for everyone and that one should retreat to claiming that one's 'private' good is good for oneself. This confusion is inexplicable; relativism leaves one with beliefs different from one's original ones, whereas skepticism detaches one from all beliefs.

The Pyrrhonists claim that the skeptic's detachment will result in *ataraxia,* tranquillity. We are troubled by holding value beliefs, both because they expose us to uncertainties about obtaining and keeping the things we value and also because the mere commitment to something's being valuable exposes us to anxiety. (For we are always exposed to arguments that will convince us that we are wrong.) Thus only the skeptic about values is tranquil and thus happy (*PH* III 235–38; *M* XI 110–67). This will hardly convince those who do not identify happiness with tranquillity. But the Pyrrhonists arguably improve over Arcesilaus as to how the skeptic can act without assenting to any beliefs. They say that the skeptic will follow the appearances where an appearance is the content of the relevant belief but is not assented to as true or false. Even when not prepared to make a claim of truth about value, I can act on a conviction about it which survives the demonstration that I have no rational grounds for belief. Thus the skeptic will retain the content of whatever ethical beliefs have been instilled into him or her. And the skeptic will share with others whatever goods and evils do not depend on belief (hunger, cold, etc.). Skeptics will differ from non-skeptics only in their inner attitudes to the convictions they act on.

See also: PROTAGORAS; SKEPTICISM IN ETHICS; SOPHISTS.

Bibliography

The Sophists and Plato

Guthrie, W. K. C. *The Sophists.* Cambridge: Cambridge University Press, 1971. Chapter 4 on the *nomos/phusis* antithesis is useful.

Kerferd, G. B. *The Sophistic Movement.* Cambridge: Cambridge University Press, 1981. Chapter 10 is useful.

Plato. See *Gorgias* for an exposition of the *nomos/phusis* contrast in the person of Callicles. *Protagoras* and *Theaetetus* contain accounts of Protagoras's position and Plato's response.

Ancient Skepticism

Annas, Julia, and Jonathan Barnes. *The Modes of Scepticism.* Cambridge: Cambridge University Press, 1985. Provides a general introduction to ancient skepticism and its differences from modern. It also contains translation of and comment on all the skeptical Modes. Chapter 13 contains the Tenth Mode in the versions of Sextus *PH* I 145–63, Diogenes Laertius IX 83–84, and Philo *de Ebrietate* 193–202.

Annas, Julia. "Doing without Objective Values: Ancient and Modern Strategies." In *Ethics,* ed. by Stephen Everson, pp. 193–200. Cambridge: Cambridge University Press, 1998. Companions to Ancient Thought, 4. Discusses the Tenth Mode and other Pyrrhonist strategies and responses in ethics.

Ioppolo, A.-M. *Opinione e scienza.* Naples: Bibliopolis, 1986. Discusses Arcesilaus's arguments and position.

Maconi, H. [Discussion review of Ioppolo]. *Oxford Studies in Ancient Philosophy* 6 (1988): 231–53.

Plutarch. *Against Colotes* in vol. 14 of the *Moralia,* translated by B. Einarson and P. De Lacy. Loeb Classical Library. Cambridge, MA: Harvard University Press.

Sextus Empiricus. *Outlines of Scepticism.* Translated by Julia Annas and Jonathan Barnes. Cambridge: Cambridge University Press, 1994.

Sextus Empiricus. *Against the Ethicists.* Translated and with commentary by Richard Bett. Oxford: Oxford University Press, Clarendon Library of Later Ancient Philosophy, 1997.

Striker, Gisela. "Sceptical Strategies." In *Doubt and Dogmatism,* edited by M. Schofield, M. Burnyeat, and J. Barnes. Oxford: Oxford University Press, 1980. Discusses Arcesilaus's arguments as part of a wider discussion of skeptical argument.

Julia Annas

skepticism in ethics

There is no single canonical formulation of moral skepticism, yet there are at least two doctrines that deserve to be regarded as skeptical about morality as such: a denial that there are actually any moral requirements, and a skepticism about the rationality of compliance with morality.

Skepticism about the existence of requirements could be expressed by saying, in words used by Immanuel KANT (1724–1804), that morality "is a mere phantom of the brain" or a "chimerical idea without any truth." It is therefore more sweeping than its name suggests, for it is a skepticism about moral VIRTUES, vices, goods, and bads as well as requirements, duties, and obligations. Of course, the skeptic would concede that most of us *believe* that we are subject to moral requirements, but denies that there are *in fact* any moral requirements. There are many imaginable moral standards, and we nonskeptics take it that some but not all of them are credible. We subscribe to some of them, and some of them have currency in our society in that they are socially enforced and transmitted from generation to generation in the culture. Yet the skeptic claims that *there are no* true or appropriately justified or otherwise credible standards that correspond to actual moral requirements. A weaker skepticism would merely *doubt* that there are any credible standards that correspond to actual requirements.

There are two ways to understand the skeptic's claim, which reflect different conceptions of the nature of moral standards: (a) On an "epistemic" conception, moral standards are conceived to be propositions with a truth-value, and the skeptical thesis is taken to be the denial that any moral standard is true. An anti-skeptical theory, such as INTUITIONISM, would have to provide evidence or an argument to show to the contrary that there are true moral standards. (b) On a "practical" conception, moral standards are regarded as rules or NORMS, and rules are regarded as having no truth-value and therefore as not being propositions. The skeptical thesis is taken to be the denial that any moral standard has a justification of a sort that would entail the existence of a moral requirement to comply with it. By way of analogy, the rules of hockey, such as the rules governing various penalties for rough play, are presumably not things we evaluate as true or false, but we can evaluate them as suitable or not, given the goals of COMPETITION in the sport. Given these goals, we may decide that certain imaginable rules would be better or more rational than the rules actually in force. Of course, there is no body with AUTHORITY to "give force" to a moral rule as such, but on the practical conception, a norm or rule corresponds to an actual moral requirement just in case it has an appropriate justification. Practical theories attempt to explain the justification of moral standards in a way that makes use of a conception of PRACTICAL REASON or of RATIONAL CHOICE. There are many different theories that attempt this kind of justification, such as Kantian theories, rational choice theories (Brandt), and certain contractarian theories (Gauthier).

On both conceptions, defeating the skeptic requires showing that certain moral standards are justified. On an epistemic conception, it requires finding evidence or an argument that certain standards are true. On a practical conception, it requires developing a criterion for the rational validation of moral standards and supporting the thesis that standards that meet the criterion correspond to actual moral requirements. The skeptic's underlying doctrine can therefore be expressed as the denial that any moral standard is or could be justified in a way that would show it to correspond to an actual moral requirement.

Certain putative justifications seem clearly irrelevant. The skeptic need not deny the psychological and sociological reality of moral beliefs or attitudes. She ought to concede that some of us have systematically structured beliefs as to what morality asks of us, and that some of us have moral views that are coherent both among themselves and with our other

beliefs. The skeptic ought also to concede that a person's subscription to certain moral standards might have a kind of prudential justification, due to the circumstances of her life, as would obtain, for example, if the social enforcement of the standards were especially efficient. Yet, the skeptic would deny that either of these concessions undermines her skepticism.

Skepticism about moral requirements is not typically derived from skeptical arguments. For example, it is not typically a corollary of a more general skepticism about all standards of justification. There is no special form of argument, the defeat of which would mean the defeat of skepticism. However, skepticism is often supported by citing (a) the alleged existence of persistent and fundamental differences of moral belief; (b) the absence of an effective and widely accepted method for testing our moral beliefs, comparable to the methods of science; and (c) the absence of a method for establishing our moral beliefs by any process of reasoning comparable to the methods of mathematics. In addition, some philosophers have thought that (d) there are no moral requirements if there is not FREE WILL; and some have thought that (e) there are no moral requirements if there is no God.

David HUME (1711–1776) is often regarded as a skeptic, but there is controversy about his views. J. L. Mackie (1917–1981) argued that there are no "objective values." Contemporary noncognitivists, such as A. J. AYER (1910–1989), Charles STEVENSON (1908–1979), and R. M. HARE in his early writings, are also plausibly described as skeptics.

Skepticism about the rationality of compliance is sometimes expressed by the challenge, "Why be moral?" We can distinguish conceptually between the existence of a moral requirement and the existence of a reason to comply with it, and a skeptic about compliance may concede the existence of moral requirements. The skeptic's thesis is that *even if* there are moral requirements, there may be no reason for anyone to comply with them. This form of skepticism is typically motivated by the observation that morality often requires a person to act in ways that are not to his personal advantage. Of course, reasons of advantage may be available for conforming to morality in various circumstances, such as circumstances in which the social enforcement of a societal moral code is especially efficient. Yet skepticism about compliance holds that the existence of a reason to comply is not guaranteed. A weaker version would hold that the existence of a *sufficient* reason to comply is not guaranteed.

We may take the skeptic to be concerned with the rationality of compliance with the true or maximally justified moral code, if there is one. And we may take her to be concerned with the rationality of individual morally required acts, not merely with the rationality of a morally virtuous state of CHARACTER. Her thesis implies that a plausible conception of practical reason or rational choice, if combined with the claim that an action is morally required, would not entail that there is a reason to perform the action. Accordingly, her thesis is inconsistent with "internalism about reasons," the claim that being subject to a moral requirement entails having a reason to comply with it. Yet it is stronger than simply the denial of internalism. For the skeptic would claim that neither the proposition that a moral standard is justified in a way which shows that there is a moral obligation to comply with it, nor the proposition that an agent is fully rational, nor the conjunction of these propositions with general facts about human PSYCHOLOGY and the circumstances of human social existence entails that the agent has a reason to comply with the standard.

METAETHICS studies, among other things, the two forms of skepticism described above, namely, skepticism about requirements and skepticism about compliance, and theories that attempt to defeat them. Some anti-skeptical theories, such as Kantianism, attempt to defeat both skeptical doctrines at once. Hence, Kant argues that if morality is "something real," then the supreme principle of morality is a requirement to act only on maxims that pass a Categorical Imperative test. He attempts to ground this principle in the thesis that any fully rational agent would act only on such maxims, assuming the agent to be free of the effects of nonrational motivation. The Kantian claim that compliance with the supreme principle is essential in this way to full rationality purports to answer both forms of skepticism. Other theories treat the skeptical challenges separately. For example, a moral sense theory might hold that certain moral standards can be justified epistemically, through perception, in a manner analogous to the manner in which empirical observational propositions can be justified. But it would leave the rationality of compliance as a separate issue, to be addressed in a MORAL PSYCHOLOGY. It is

a matter of controversy whether either of the two central skeptical positions can be defeated.

A variety of other positions might be described as skeptical about morality. Different schools of thought take different doctrines to state central truths about morality, and each school would take the denial of what it regards as a central truth to express a skepticism. For example, the claims that moral requirements are not "categorical" and that they are not "overriding" could be described as forms of skepticism, even though, depending on how they are interpreted, they may not entail either of the two major skeptical doctrines. It may be best to reserve the label "skepticism" for these two major doctrines, for each of them is a skepticism about morality as such, about the very existence of requirements or their rational AUTHORITY.

See also: AUTHORITY; AYER; CATEGORICAL AND HYPOTHETICAL IMPERATIVES; CONTRACTARIANISM; EXTERNALISM AND INTERNALISM; HARE; HUME; KANTIAN ETHICS; METAETHICS; MORAL ABSOLUTES; MORAL REASONING; MORAL RULES; MORAL SENSE THEORISTS; NORMS; PRACTICAL REASON[ING]; RATIONAL CHOICE; RATIONALITY VS. REASONABLENESS; SKEPTICISM IN ANCIENT ETHICS; STEVENSON.

Bibliography

Ayer, A. J. *Language, Truth, and Logic.* London: Victor Gollantz, 1946 [1936].

Brandt, Richard B. *A Theory of the Good and the Right.* Oxford: Oxford University Press, 1979.

Copp, David. "Moral Skepticism." *Philosophical Studies* 62 (1991): 203–33.

Copp, David, and David Zimmerman, eds. *Morality, Reason, and Truth: New Essays on the Foundation of Ethics.* Totowa, NJ: Rowman and Allanheld, 1984.

Gauthier, David. *Morals by Agreement.* Oxford: Oxford University Press, 1986.

Hare, R. M. *The Language of Morals.* Oxford: Oxford University Press, 1952.

Harman, Gilbert. *The Nature of Morality: An Introduction to Ethics.* Oxford: Oxford University Press, 1977.

Hume, David. *A Treatise of Human Nature.* Edited by P. H. Nidditch. Oxford: Oxford University Press, 1978 [1737].

Kant, Immanuel. *Grounding of the Metaphysics of Morals.* Translated by James W. Ellington. Indianapolis, Ind.: Hackett, 1981 [1785]. Pagination in this edition follows the standard, Prussian Academy edition. For passages quoted in this article, see pp. 445–49.

Mackie, J. L. *Ethics: Inventing Right and Wrong.* Harmondsworth: Penguin, 1977.

Nagel, Thomas. *The View from Nowhere.* Oxford: Oxford University Press, 1986.

Nielsen, Kai. "Why Should I Be Moral?" In *Introductory Readings in Ethics,* edited by W. K. Frankena and J. T. Granrose, 473–92. Englewood Cliffs, NJ: Prentice Hall, 1974.

Snare, Francis. "Three Sceptical Theses in Ethics." *American Philosophical Quarterly* 14 (1977a): 129–36.

———. "The Empirical Bases of Moral Scepticism." *American Philosophical Quarterly* 21 (1977b): 215–25.

Stevenson, Charles L. *Ethics and Language.* New Haven: Yale University Press, 1944.

Williams, Bernard. *Ethics and the Limits of Philosophy.* Cambridge, MA: Harvard University Press, 1985.

David Copp

slavery

This subject has generated a vast literature; but as moral philosophers we are concerned mainly with the arguments used to attack or defend the institution. Such arguments shed some light on the theory of moral argument in general and have therefore been much used as examples to rebut particular theories, especially UTILITARIANISM and its opponents (see RAWLS). What view we take of these examples will depend on whether we see LIBERTY as an 'absolute value' or whether we derive its value from the consequences it has. For our present purposes slavery can be defined as a status in which (a) the slave is denied certain legal and political RIGHTS enjoyed by ordinary citizens, such as appeal to the courts for redress of wrongs, the vote, and liberty to change abode or employment; and (b) the slave is legally the PROPERTY of some particular person (or body—which may be the state itself), to be used as that person wishes just like any other property. The precise details of the status will vary from one society to another, and to that extent the term "slave" is vague.

If human beings were morally better than nearly all of them are, the institution of slavery need not have the appalling consequences (in the form of misery for the slaves and degradation of their owners) that it has almost universally had (see Patterson, Elkins, and B. Franklin, cited in Finley). And even granted these evils, it could perhaps be claimed that slavery has also produced *some* countervailing benefits, certainly to the slave owners and their society

and maybe even to the slaves. It goes without saying that in all actual societies these benefits have come nowhere near compensating for the harms, except in negligibly rare cases. But the mere logical possibility that the consequences might in imagined cases be different, so that the balance of EVIL over good was reversed, has seemed to some philosophers to afford an argument against utilitarianism. For do not our intuitions rebel against the thought that slavery could be justified even in these fantastic cases?

In order to understand this issue, it is necessary to have a clear picture of the structure of moral thinking. At the everyday intuitive level it is highly desirable for us to have the conviction that slavery is wrong. And this in turn is because people who have other people in their POWER will more often than not exploit and maltreat them, subjecting them to atrocious punishments and using them as expendable human fuel if there is an economic advantage to be so gained. And we also think it, and ought to think it, shameful that one human being should be treated by another in this way: one party is denied the opportunity, and the other the incentive, to realize full human potential, and so both are degraded.

These intuitions are the ones we ought to have. But the intuitive level of thinking is not self-sustaining. There may be rare cases in which the value of liberty to a person is in conflict with some other value, even to that person. To resolve such conflicts, intuitions, which have generated them, do not suffice. And even if there were no such conflicts, we should need a kind of thinking that could assure us that the intuitions we have grown up with are the best ones. Slave owners had other intuitions, for example about the sanctity of property rights. PASCAL (1623–1662) may be right that the heart has reasons that reason knows nothing of (*Pensees* iv); but this is a deficiency in reason, which demands a remedy. He should ask why the heart's reasons are good reasons, and why other reasons (sometimes equally heartfelt) are bad ones. To discover *why* we ought to have these intuitions, it is necessary to ask what good comes of accepting these as reasons: that is, why it is better to have learnt to accept them than not. And it is hard to see how else this question could be answered than by appeal to the consequences of having them. If human nature were such that the consequences of a general acceptance of slavery were harmless or even beneficial, we ought

slavery

not to have the intuitions that we have. But it is as certain as it could be that this is not so.

See also: CIVIL RIGHTS AND CIVIC DUTIES; COERCION; CONSEQUENTIALISM; DIGNITY; DISCRIMINATION; EQUALITY; HUMAN RIGHTS; INTUITIONISM; JEFFERSON; LIBERTY; LIFE, MEANING OF; LIFE, RIGHT TO; MORAL ABSOLUTES; POWER; PRESCRIPTIVISM; PROPERTY; RACISM AND RELATED TOPICS; RACISM, CONCEPTS OF; RIGHTS; UTILITARIANISM.

Bibliography

Elkins, S. M. *Slavery.* Chicago: University of Chicago Press, 1959.

Finley, M. I., ed. *Slavery in Classical Antiquity: Views and Controversies.* Cambridge: Cambridge University Press, 1960.

———. *Ancient Slavery and Modern Ideology.* London: Chatto and Windus, 1980. See B. Franklin's comments, p. 100.

Hare, R. M. "What Is Wrong with Slavery." *Philosophy and Public Affairs* 8 (1979): 103–21. Reprinted in *Essays on Political Morality* (1989) and in *Applied Ethics,* ed. by Peter Singer (1986), both Oxford: Oxford University Press.

Patterson, O. *The Sociology of Slavery.* London: MacGibbon and Kee, 1967.

———. *Slavery and Social Death: A Comparative Study.* Cambridge: Cambridge University Press, 1982.

Rawls, John. *A Theory of Justice.* Cambridge, MA: Harvard University Press, 1971. See esp. 158 *f.;* 248.

Westermann. *The Slave Systems of Greek and Roman Antiquity.* Philadelphia, Pa.: American Philological Society, 1955.

Wyatt-Brown, Bertram. [Review of Patterson, *Slavery and Social Death*]. *Society* (March–April 1984).

R. M. Hare

slippery slope arguments

The so-called slippery slope argument (SSA) is often deployed in moral, political, and legal contexts in order to cast doubt on the wisdom of introducing changes in the *status quo.* It is thus a favorite weapon of social conservatives and a perpetual thorn in the side of reformist liberals. In brief, the argument asserts that if we allow an ACTION or policy *A,* which is either morally permissible or at least neutral, then we will be led by a series of gradual steps to action or policy *Z,* which is assumed to be an unacceptable result. It is then claimed that if we wish to avoid the morally evil result *Z,* we must reject *A* as well, since *A* is said to lead inevitably or ineluctably to *Z.* The argument is often used with regard to new developments in science and TECHNOLOGY and is thus very much at home (though obviously by no means exclusively so) in the domain of biomedical ethics. For example, critics of in-vitro fertilization (IVF) have claimed that allowing IVF for infertile married couples (policy *A*) will inevitably lead to the breakdown of the traditional FAMILY and thus of civilization as we know it (result *Z*). Although SSAs are often dismissed as mere fallacies in several logic texts, more sympathetic observers contend that the argument can be a legitimate and, given appropriate circumstances, a powerful argumentative device.

Formulations of the Argument

Different kinds of slippery slope arguments project different kinds of trajectories leading from *A* to *Z:*

Conceptual slope arguments. The distance between *A* and *Z* is often occupied by a gray zone in which the grounds for applying a vague term are unclear because the differences between adjacent points on the slope are very small. Thus, it is sometimes argued in the ABORTION controversy that between conception (point *A*) and birth (point *Z*) there is no "magic moment" in which a fetus becomes suddenly and conspicuously transformed from a "nonperson" into a "person." Since any effort to draw a line—*e.g.,* at "quickening," or viability—is bound to be arbitrary, it is held that we should treat embryos as human beings or persons from the moment of conception, hence making abortion morally impermissible.

Dangerous precedent arguments. Here it is claimed that making an isolated and arguably unobjectionable exception to a rule will set a precedent for making other, possibly objectionable, exceptions to the rule. Consider the rule against physician-assisted suicide (PAS). It is often argued that in allowing an exception to this rule, *A,* which would for example permit only cases of voluntary PAS when the patient is terminally ill, in great pain, mentally competent, etc., one thereby sets a precedent that would make the rejection of further exceptions to the rule, for example that voluntary PAS is permissible even if the person is not in great pain, difficult to sustain. A chain of such precedents would then make the rejection of a clearly objectionable exception to the rule, Z (*e.g.,* the involuntary EUTHANASIA of the mentally infirm), impossible to sustain; thus, it is argued that we should not allow exception A in the first place.

Causal slopes. Even in cases where a clear-cut conceptual difference exists between policy A (*e.g.,* voluntary PAS in strictly limited cases) and policy Z (killing elderly residents of nursing homes without their consent), an opponent of A might argue that allowing A will cause events B, C, D, . . . Z to happen, and therefore we should not allow A. In other words, notwithstanding their conceptual differences, various social and empirical features of the world will conspire to bring about Z once we allow A. Thus, one might argue that allowing A will bring about a gradual lessening of respect for human life, which, in conjunction with other factors (*e.g.,* scarce resources) will lead to involuntary active euthanasia of 'unproductive' and 'burdensome' members of society.

Mixed slippery slope arguments. In real life, classical SSAs tend to incorporate elements of all the above varieties. Thus, in response to a proponent of PAS who holds that it should be allowed but only in cases where it is voluntary and the patient is terminally ill and experiencing intractable pain (policy A), an opponent of A typically argues that people won't, in fact, be able or willing to draw a clear line between A and closely related policies, such as PAS for nonterminal patients with mental illness who are leading horrible lives or direct killing by physicians when patients are too debilitated to kill themselves (illustrating the conceptual SSA). This inability to draw a clear line will, it is claimed, lead to a more lenient attitude toward killing all sorts of patients not contemplated under policy A (illustrating the causal SSA). Consequently, we should reject A in favor of the present rule against PAS because that rule does give us a reliable stopping point, whereas A (and all the other points on the slope toward which A leads) cannot do that (illustrating the dangerous precedent SSA).

Rational versus Effective Breaking Points

Bernard WILLIAMS has introduced an important distinction between proposed breaking points on the slope that are rationally justified and those that will be effective in preventing more slippage. He points out that sometimes a reasonable distinction can be made between adjacent points on the slope that may nevertheless not be effective. For example, it could be argued that a clear distinction can be drawn between PAS and direct physician killing, but that it will in fact be difficult to hold the line at PAS due to various empirical factors (*e.g.,* once inured to PAS, society will want to extend the "right to die" to competent patients who, due to physical infirmity, cannot kill themselves). Conversely, Williams argues that a proposed breaking point might be effective without being rationally justified by a clear-cut distinction between two adjacent points on the slope. For example, in the debate over embryo experimentation, many governmental commissions have favored a fourteen-day cutoff point after which continued experimentation would not be allowed. Although this point coincides with a significant developmental marker (the advent of the so-called primitive streak), it is hard to argue that a fifteen-day-old embryo suddenly possesses crucial human characteristics that it lacked the day before. Nevertheless, legislation could draw the line separating permissible from forbidden research precisely at fourteen days, not for rationally defensible reasons but rather for reasons of policy, and this line might well prove to be durable and highly effective.

Criticizing Slippery Slope Arguments

Some critics portray SSAs as examples of logical fallacies whose faulty reasoning would infect them no matter what the context in which they were deployed. Sometimes there is force to this claim. For example, some uses of the SSA commit what Govier calls the "fallacy of assimilation"—*i.e.,* arguing that because the difference between any two contiguous points on a continuum stretching from A to Z is minute and insignificant, there cannot be a significant difference between A and Z. Thus, just because we cannot mark a significant distinction between A and B, M and N, or Y and Z, this doesn't mean that there isn't a significant distinction between A, a completely bald man, and Z, a man with a full head of hair (or between a conceptus and a newborn baby).

A more context-dependent approach to criticizing SSAs would focus on some crucial elements bearing on the alleged badness or unacceptability of Z or on the likelihood of A actually leading to Z.

Thus, one way of criticizing an SSA would be to deny that Z is all that bad. If the critic claimed, for example, that allowing PAS only for terminal illness would inevitably lead to PAS in nonterminal cases, such as patients with amyotrophic lateral sclerosis (ALS, or "Lou Gehrig's disease"), the proponent of a change in the law could respond that such a result wouldn't be so bad, that it would in fact be welcome (but then it would be hard for this person to claim at the start that we should permit PAS only in terminal cases). Another tactic available here would be for the proponent of A to claim that although A does have undesirable consequences, maintaining the present rigid rule will have consequences that are even worse (*e.g.,* forbidding PAS will only serve to drive the practice underground, where it cannot be effectively regulated).

The other main line of criticism in this more pragmatic vein is to claim that the predicted (admittedly bad or horrible) results simply won't materialize for one reason or another. As Gorovitz puts it, a person starting out walking east from Kansas will eventually fall into the Atlantic ocean, *unless he stops at some point!* Thus, one can claim that various procedural safeguards can be built into A to effectively guard against slipping down to Z. In the case of PAS these safeguards might include such procedures as required committee review of all proposed PAS cases. Or one could claim that the future is uncertain and the predicted bad consequences are only speculative, whereas the bad consequences of not allowing A (*e.g.,* the continued pain and suffering of dying AIDS patients) are imminent and predictably certain.

These pragmatic challenges to slippery slope arguments reveal how context-dependent such arguments are. In some instances, an SSA can advance highly plausible claims that should, at the very least, throw the burden of proof back on the proponent of a change in the *status quo.* In other cases, an SSA can be used in illicit and demagogic ways to silence one's opponents and cut short a potentially fruitful debate on the likely consequences of a proposed change. Although some slippery slope arguments qualify as being formally invalid, most are either more or less plausible depending on the circumstances.

See also: ABORTION; ANALOGICAL ARGUMENT; APPLIED ETHICS; BIOETHICS; CONSEQUENTIALISM; CONSERVATISM; EUTHANASIA; GENETIC ENGINEERING; LIBERALISM; LIFE, RIGHT TO; LOGIC AND ETHICS; MEDICAL ETHICS; MORAL REASONING; PERSON, CONCEPT OF; PRAGMATISM; PRECEDENT; PUBLIC POLICY; RATIONALITY VS. REASONABLENESS; REPRODUCTIVE TECHNOLOGIES; SOCIAL AND POLITICAL PHILOSOPHY; TECHNOLOGY; WILLIAMS.

Bibliography

Gorovitz, Samuel. "Progeny, Progress, and Primrose Paths." In *Doctors' Dilemmas: Moral Conflict and Medical Care.* New York: Oxford University Press, 1982. Assesses SSAs in context of new reproductive technologies.

Govier, Trudy. "What's Wrong with Slippery Slope Arguments?" *Canadian Journal of Philosophy* 12 (June 1982): 303–16. Influential taxonomy and evaluation of SSAs.

Lamb, David. *Down the Slippery Slope: Arguing in Applied Ethics.* London: Croom Helm, 1988. Emphasizes distinction between the clarity of conceptual line drawing and the complexities encountered in the real world.

Schauer, Frederick. "Slippery Slopes." *Harvard Law Review* 99 (1985): 361–83. SSAs should be viewed skeptically, but they are not necessarily invalid. Empirical factors can invest them with considerable force in appropriate circumstances.

Van der Burg, Wibren. "The Slippery Slope Argument." *Ethics* 102 (October 1991): 42–65. Provides a taxonomy of SSAs and distinguishes the various moral and legal contexts in which they might be usefully employed.

Walton, Douglas. *Slippery Slope Arguments.* Oxford: Clarendon Press, 1992. Probably the best overall treatment of SSAs; favors a more pragmatic approach.

Williams, Bernard. "Which Slopes Are Slippery?" *Making Sense of Humanity,* 213–23. Cambridge: Cambridge University Press, 1995.

John D. Arras

Smith, Adam (1723–1790)

Scottish economist and philosopher. Although numbered among the most influential philosophers of all time, continuously acclaimed by politicians, economists, and social scientists generally, Adam Smith has suffered undeserved neglect within his chosen profession of philosophy. Recently, interest in his moral philosophy has revealed significant insights into two topics of major contemporary interest: MORAL DEVELOPMENT and moral deliberation.

Smith was born, and raised by his mother, in Kirkcaldy, Scotland. After studying under Francis HUTCHESON (1694–1746) at the University of Glasgow, he attended Balliol College, Oxford. He spent two terms delivering public lectures at the University of Edinburgh and then accepted a chair at the University of Glasgow. His most significant works grew out of the lectures delivered at Glasgow. The first was in moral theory: *The Theory of Moral Sentiments* (1759). During his lifetime Smith's reputation rested mainly on that work. He resigned the chair at Glasgow after a dozen years and devoted more than a decade to travel and writing. The product was the *Wealth of Nations* (1776). This work was the subject of immediate and continuing acclaim, not the least from his fellow philosopher and lifelong friend, David HUME (1711–1776). Until his death Smith devoted himself to the duties of a minor government post and to preparing later editions of both these books. Smith never married. He was buried in Cannongate Churchyard, Edinburgh.

Smith espoused, as had Hutcheson and Hume, a dispositional analysis of moral properties. On this view practices, acts, dispositions, attitudes, etc., are right or wrong depending on how an appropriately situated spectator would react to them. If the spectator would approve of them, they are right; if the spectator would disapprove, they are wrong. The distinctive character of Smith's contributions to this style of moral theory bear mainly on moral development and moral deliberation.

Moral Development

For Smith, as for psychologists of the twentieth century such as Sigmund Freud (1856–1939), Gordon Allport, and Lawrence Kohlberg (1927–1989), the capacity for moral judgment and moral ACTION is a faculty acquired in a multistep interactive process. Through moral development people achieve the capacity to govern their own behavior by subordinating the spontaneous impulses of PASSION to considerations of what are or should be the sentiments of others. That process can be divided into three phases that, for convenience, might be labeled the life of PLEASURE, the life of emulation, and the life of virtue.

The life of pleasure is peculiar to the very young. Among infants, behavior is reflex: their actions are determined entirely by internal and external stimuli. Very young children exercise no control over their conduct, nor are they conscious of themselves as agents.

Smith believed that the only effective instrument of MORAL EDUCATION among the very young is swift and painful discipline administered by parents. In this way the child is at once made sensitive to the response of others to its own behavior; made conscious that its own past action was the indirect cause of its own present discomfort; and required to include the evident preferences of others among the considerations according to which it will attempt to direct its future conduct. Thus the child begins to achieve a degree of self-government and to apply less self-interested criteria in directing its conduct. When the child emerges from the life of pleasure, the greatest danger is vanity—the tendency to pretend to qualities and talents that deserve the praise of others. Effective guidance at this point involves identifying the sham and encouraging young people to be more diligent in attaining the qualities to which they now only pretend.

The dominant theme in the life of emulation is respectability. Here individuals strive to measure up to the image projected by respected and influential people in the community as they praise and blame the conduct of others. Public opinion becomes the standard of self-government. But, as anyone who surveys public opinion discovers, much to the disgust of moralists, praise is accorded to the possession of riches and blame to its lack. People embarked on a life of emulation, guided by the standard of public opinion, imitate the behavior of the rich, aping their manners and deportment, not as a measure calculated to advance their net worth but simply because the rich are believed to deserve their deference. This disinterested admiration and emulation of the wealthy is the famous "desire of bettering our own condition" that served as the main engine of commerce in the *Wealth of Nations*.

In Smith's view, the great majority of people never develop beyond a life of emulation. Most are caught up in imitating the rich. Those few who are rich realize full well how little extra convenience their possessions afford and how great an expense their maintenance exacts. Their chief preoccupation is to display elegant and graceful airs. In this way they sustain the admiration and deference of those of lesser rank. Some in the lesser ranks are foolish enough to devote their lives to amassing treasure and fortune only to discover, usually after sacrificing health, friends, and DIGNITY, that the game is not worth the candle. Those at the bottom of the social ladder are truly unfortunate. Their poverty condemns them not only to lives of misery but also to the neglect and scorn of their neighbors.

Occasionally a few of the middle rank abandon the life of emulation for more solid recognition than the cool esteem they have been able to manage in the shadow of an unreformed peerage. The final phase of moral development begins when a person affirms that the dispositions and behavioral patterns of the middle rank are approved, not because they put one in mind of the rich, but because they are right and just. It is at this point that moral deliberation commences.

Moral Deliberation

As indicated above, Smith espoused a dispositional analysis of moral properties. One of the key challenges that such an approach must address is how a coincidence is assured between what the actor is motivated to do and what the spectator is motivated to approve.

Hume proposed an aesthetic solution to this challenge. Actors, motivated mainly by self-interest, form systems of cooperation that afford benefits to themselves and others as well. Spectators, beholding such systems, are put in mind of the good life with which those systems are associated. Practices, actions, and dispositions are seen as symbols of a happy life. In that way they evoke the spectator's approval. While Hume's solution illuminates the life of emulation quite well, Smith found it an insufficient account of moral judgments. Smith proposed a more complex sociological solution to the challenge of reconciling the motivations of actor and spectator, a solution that combined improvements on two of Hume's key concepts—SYMPATHY and the impartial spectator.

The function of sympathy is to reconcile a disparity between actor and spectator. The perspectives taken by the actor and the spectator are separated by a gulf that must be bridged if judgment is to take place. Sympathy, imagining oneself in the situation of the other, bridges that gulf. Hume was content with sympathy of this kind, often called empathy. This sort of sympathy is exercised by the spectator alone. Spectators empathize by considering how they would react if presented with the same situation as actually confronts the actor.

Although sufficient in scientific and aesthetic con-

texts, empathy does not suffice in a practical context where actor and spectator take quite different INTERESTS in the situation that confronts the one but not the other. There, an affective gulf must also be bridged lest the cool indifference of the spectator alienates the actor and the violence of the actor offends the spectator. Here, too, sympathy is required to bridge the gulf, although sympathy of a different sort. Here, what is required is that both actor and spectator attune the interest they take in the actor's situation until the two are in sufficient concord to permit them to sustain one another's company. The process by which that concord of sentiment is negotiated among the parties resembles the bargaining of a marketplace.

Just as estimating the relative magnitude of visual objects by their apparent magnitude can easily lead to distortion when we are situated at unequal distances from the objects, so estimating the relative importance of situations of practical consequence by the way we respond to them is liable to distortion where we take radically different levels of interest in that situation. So also, just as we compensate for the former type of distortion by imagining how the objects would appear from a position equally removed from both, so we compensate for distortion in our moral deliberations by imagining how we would respond were we to take a level of interest in the situation that is mutually supportable by both actor and spectator. The persona embodying that unbiased temperament is the supposed impartial spectator.

The disposition of the impartial spectator is not a fixed prototype discovered by reflection. Neither is it invariant across cultures or times. Rather, the impartial spectator is an equilibrium of temperament negotiated over the course of lifetimes of interaction with others in the capacities of both actor and spectator. It represents as intimate and as shared a temperament as circumstances permit and wit suggests. The impartial spectator is the optimum degree of interest that people can reasonably be expected to take in a situation in view of their common aspiration of sustaining a community among themselves. That aspiration is sufficient to prompt them to seek a concord of sentiment with their fellows and to restrain their reactions to within the narrow limits permitted by an impartial disposition. In this way the coincidence of the motivations of actors and spectators is assured.

Smith's reputation as a champion of "economic

man" is due mainly to the efforts of those economists and politicians who sought to enlist his authority in support of their policy agendas. A sensitive reading of the full range of Smith's writings reveals that a more interesting and profound vision informed his work as a whole. The picture of the good life that Smith entertained was devoted neither to self-indulgence nor vaulting ambition, qualities often associated with "economic man." Instead, it was marked by "self-command," by moderation of one's actions in accordance with the sentiments of the supposed impartial spectator. That emphasis on self-restraint is more reminiscent of the normative theories of the Roman Stoics than of the egoism either of Thomas HOBBES (1588–1679) or Bernard MANDEVILLE (1670–1733).

See also: CHILDREN AND ETHICAL THEORY; DELIBERATION AND CHOICE; ECONOMIC ANALYSIS; ECONOMIC SYSTEMS; HUME; HUTCHESON; IDEAL OBSERVER; IDEALIZED AGENTS; IMPARTIALITY; MORAL DEVELOPMENT; MORAL EDUCATION; MORAL PSYCHOLOGY; MORAL REASONING; PASSION; PLEASURE; PRACTICAL REASON[ING]; RAWLS; SELF-CONTROL; SOCIAL AND POLITICAL PHILOSOPHY; SOCIAL CONTRACT; STOICISM; SYMPATHY.

Bibliography

Works by Adam Smith

Works and Correspondence of Adam Smith. Edited by D. D. Raphael and A. S. Skinner. Glasgow Edition. 6 vols. Oxford: Oxford University Press, 1976–1980. Definitive, critical edition. Included are the following titles: *The Theory of Moral Sentiments* (1759), edited by A. L. MacFie and D. D. Raphael; *An Inquiry into the Nature and Causes of the Wealth of Nations* (1776), edited by R. H. Campbell and A. S. Skinner; *Essays on Philosophical Subjects* (1795), edited by W. P. D. Wightman and J. C. Bryce; *Lectures on Rhetoric and Belles Lettres* (1783), edited by J. C. Bryce; *Lectures on Jurisprudence,* edited by R. L. Meek, D. D. Raphael, and P. G. Stein; and *Correspondence,* edited by E. C. Mossner and I. S. Ross.

Works about Adam Smith

Campbell, T. D. *Adam Smith's Science of Morals.* London: Allen and Unwin, 1971.

Harman, Gilbert. "Moral Agent and Impartial Spectator." Lawrence: Lindley Lecture, University of Kansas, 1986.

Lindgren, J. Ralph. *The Social Philosophy of Adam Smith.* The Hague: Nijhoff, 1973.

Morrow, Glenn R. *The Ethical and Economic Theories of Adam Smith.* New York: Longmans, Green, 1923.

Raphael, D. D. "The Impartial Spectator." In *Essays on Adam Smith,* edited by A. S. Skinner and T. Wilson, 83–99. Oxford: Oxford University Press, 1975.

J. Ralph Lindgren

social and political philosophy

The philosophical examination of political and social INSTITUTIONS should be distinguished both from empirical inquiry and from polemics on behalf of particular causes. Unlike the empirical investigator, political philosophers are interested in more than the causal explanation of events in the political and social realm, even when such explanations are embedded in complex explanatory theories about the nature of political reality. In addition, political philosophers are concerned with clarifying and evaluating the basic normative principles presupposed by political and social institutions. Unlike ideologists, political philosophers attempt to provide a reasoned evaluation of such principles. Of course, it may be, as some critics charge, that what passes for political philosophy really is nothing over and above disguised ideology. However, such a dismissal of the claims of political philosophy to a kind of rationality and objectivity hardly is self-evident and requires philosophical defense since it itself makes claims which purport to be objective and hence more than mere ideology.

While political and social philosophers are concerned with examining and evaluating political and social institutions, there are significantly different conceptions of the kind of examination which is philosophically appropriate or even possible, and on the relevance of such examination for social and political practice. Thus, linguistic analysts, whose views have been most influential in the mid-twentieth century, tend to view political and social philosophy primarily, if not exclusively, as a second-order activity. On their view, the job of the political philosopher is not to make political recommendations, even of a highly general and theoretical sort, but rather to stand back and clarify the language used by participants in political and social life. On a radically different conception, other political philosophers, such as ARISTOTLE (384–322 B.C.E.) or G. W. F. HEGEL (1770–1831), attempt to justify political and social institutions by embedding them in a complex metaphysics or a psychology of human nature.

The conception of political philosophy advanced by the linguistic analysts arguably is too narrow, even by their own lights. At the very least, substantive argument in political philosophy can elicit the implications of our political and social commitments and present us with the choice of either accepting the implications of our views or revising them. On an even broader view, suggested by writers such as John RAWLS and Norman Daniels, definitions and logical analyses of concepts are justified only by their function within a broader theory. On this view, political justification consists in revising our principles until they are in harmony with the substantive judgments about actual cases to which we are most firmly committed after reflection. Political justification consists of continual readjustment of both our principles and our judgments about concrete cases until they are maximally coherent, in what has been called broad REFLECTIVE EQUILIBRIUM. Still other views of justification ground basic principles on requirements of IMPARTIALITY and reason, as argued by Immanuel KANT (1724–1804) and later writers in the Kantian tradition.

Accordingly, while linguistic analysis of concepts might often be a useful tool of clarification, the classic texts in the field, as well as many important contemporary works, go well beyond analysis of concepts and attempt to evaluate NORMS, ideals, and principles. Such texts also often appeal to conceptions of human nature, to psychological or sociological generalizations, and sometimes to metaphysical claims of various sorts, which are not always carefully separated from the evaluation of political and social principles. While such empirical or metaphysical premises do not strictly entail normative conclusions, they may lend rational support to such conclusions in less direct fashion. The justification of such independent claims often goes beyond the bounds of political and social philosophy, and is ultimately empirical or, in the case of metaphysical assumptions, more broadly philosophical in nature. Nevertheless, such empirical and metaphysical claims often play a significant role in the complex kind of argument which characterizes much of the best of political and social philosophy, and arguably can provide rational support along with other kinds of premises for normative conclusions in political theory.

Although the nature of justification in political and social philosophy is controversial, as is the scope of the field itself, it will be useful to conceive of the field broadly as the clarification and justification of principles underlying social and political practices. While the discussion will focus on issues in and approaches to political and social philosophy, these fields also can be conceived of as a body of classic works, such as PLATO's (c. 430–347 B.C.E.) *Republic,* Aristotle's *Politics,* Thomas HOBBES's (1588–1679) *Leviathan* (1651), and John LOCKE's (1632–1704) *Second Treatise* (1689). However, an examination of the issues discussed by political philosophers and approaches taken to them is presupposed by any list of classic works, since they are among the criteria for inclusion on the list in the first place. The activity of political and social philosophy ranges from discussion of highly theoretical analyses of the nature of RIGHTS, EQUALITY, rationality, and human nature to more recent work in APPLIED ETHICS on such issues as affirmative action, CENSORSHIP and PORNOGRAPHY, FEMINIST ETHICS, and the morality of nuclear deterrence. Rather than surveying work on a wide range of substantive issues, most of which are covered elsewhere in this encyclopedia, the discussion here will focus on fundamental points of difference among various approaches to political and social thought. While not exhaustive, it should help in identifying and examining major theoretical differences among political and social philosophers.

Different general approaches to political and social philosophy can be examined more closely by looking at their application to a specific problem. Among the political institutions which philosophers have attempted to evaluate, the state, because of its POWER and importance, surely is primary. Is there any *moral* justification for such an institution? What, if anything, *morally* supports its claims to AUTHORITY over individual citizens? Are there *moral* limits to that authority? An examination of various approaches to this set of issues can help clarify fundamental differences among political philosophies.

Justification of the State

Contractarian individualism. Perhaps the most influential modern philosophical analysis of the state was that of Thomas Hobbes. Although different commentators have advanced importantly different interpretations of Hobbes's work, Hobbes seems to have seen the state as a solution to a kind of "prisoner's dilemma," a situation in which individually rational action by each agent leads to a worse result than otherwise would be possible through cooperation. In particular, Hobbes tried to justify the state by showing why we would be worse off without it in a nonpolitical state of nature. Hobbes's theory does not presuppose that such a state of nature actually existed, although Hobbes himself may have regarded international affairs, sovereign nations uncontrolled by a higher world government, as a kind of state of nature. Rather, we can follow contemporary social contract theorists in thinking of the state of nature as a hypothetical construct which forces us to work out our view of what life would be like in the absence of political institutions such as the state.

The essence of Hobbes's thought is that in the absence of the coercive power of the state, life would be "nasty, brutish, and short." Human beings, on his view, are basically egoistic, and, given the lack of resources sufficient to satisfy all desires, would constantly be at each others throats, or at least would have to assume all others were potential enemies and act accordingly. As a result, cooperation becomes impossible, since each agent has no reason to trust others to cooperate. The only solution, Hobbes seems to have thought, is for each individual to enter a covenant, or SOCIAL CONTRACT, whereby each gives up all power to a coercive state or sovereign. The sovereign, who must have all power (since any power left to individuals would simply regenerate the war of all against all which characterized the state of nature), guarantees peace and security by enforcing laws, which Hobbes tends to view as commands backed by threats.

While this is only a sketch of a complex theory which can be interpreted in a number of plausible ways, it has certain key elements that have been extraordinarily influential. Hobbes can be read as attempting to show that there is a justification for the state by deriving it only from assumptions about individuals, their motivation, their situation in a world of scarcity, and the requirements of rationality. On this reading, he avoids appeal to controversial moral principles, to any conception about what the good life is for human beings, or to such metaphysical notions as the commands of the Deity or the divine rights of rulers. While his own assumptions are hardly indisputable, they set the tone for much of

subsequent political thought by trying to derive the justification of collective political institutions from a conception of individual motivation and rationality. Thus, while later writers such as Locke, Jean-Jacques ROUSSEAU (1712–1778), and Kant, and in our day, Rawls and David Gauthier, differ from Hobbes in important ways, sometimes by arguing for binding pre-contractual moral rights and obligations, they too adopted much of his methodology.

For example, John Locke also attempted to show that rational individuals in a state of nature would enter a social contract to create the state. Once again, the state of nature and the ensuing social contract are best viewed, not as actual historical events, but as hypothetical constructions designed to illuminate the reasoning underlying justified political institutions. But unlike Hobbes, Locke argues that moral principles do apply in the state of nature, and in particular that persons possess natural rights to life, LIBERTY, and PROPERTY, that it would be wrong to violate. The state is formed in order to protect those rights, which are never ceded by the parties to the contract. Thus, on a plausible reading, the Lockean argument is that rational individuals would give up only enough of their natural authority to allow the state to more efficiently protect their rights, but would be irrational to give up all the rights themselves. Hence, the purpose of the state, in Locke's view, is to protect individual rights, and its power is limited by the rights individuals retain.

Although Hobbes and Locke differ enormously in the range of authority they cede to the state, and in the assumptions about morality with which they start, they both view the individual as the atom of political analysis. Each attempts to justify political institutions by showing that the formation of such institutions is rational from the point of view of a pre-politically situated rational individual. In this respect, they set the tone for an important strand of individualist political morality; individualist in that it is the pre-political (hypothetical) individual who is the starting point for analysis. The state's function is to provide peace and security or, at most, to protect the rights of the individual. It is for individuals to determine for themselves what their own good is. Contemporary writers on a variety of subjects, such as Rawls on justice or Gauthier on the contractual foundations of morality, while they differ enormously from earlier writers in this liberal individualist tradition, continue to develop some of the building blocks of this approach by appealing to what can be accepted by rational individuals in a hypothetical position of fair or uncoerced social choice.

Critics of contractarian individualism. Of course, the idea of justifying the state through appeal to a social contract has its critics, from both within and without a broader range of individualist theories. *Utilitarian* thinkers going back at least to David HUME (1711–1776) have regarded even the hypothetical contract as theoretically unnecessary and misleading conceptual baggage. On their view, institutions such as states, and particular legal systems or laws within the state, are to be justified by their social utility. Some contractarian thinkers might reply that UTILITARIANISM provides insufficient protection for individual rights, since it permits sacrifice of the individual to achieve the greater good of the community. Utilitarians can respond to that in a variety of ways, perhaps by arguing that rights are not 'natural' even in the sense of having a justification independent of human INTERESTS but really are nothing but rules which it is socially useful to enforce. Other utilitarians might respond in a more uncompromising fashion that if the sacrifice of rights really would benefit a greater number of persons or advance the aggregate of human interests, then the sacrifice is justified.

Whether a utilitarian kind of ethic might prove ultimately defensible remains a controversial topic. We can note here only that utilitarian theories, like contractarian approaches to the state, tend to take individuals and their preferences as fundamental. Just as the contractarian attempts to justify the state by appeal to rational individual choice, so the utilitarian appeals to the rationality of individual preference satisfaction. Perhaps the most acute criticism of the contractualism of writers such as Hobbes and Locke, and of contemporary theorists such as Rawls, is that the entire approach rests on a harmful fiction: that of the isolated pre-political individual.

According to *perfectionist* thinkers, the justification of human institutions lies in how they contribute to some conception of human flourishing or EXCELLENCE. To a thinker such as Aristotle, the distinctive human good or excellence is exercise of rationality, particularly rational interaction and discourse. Since such discourse can be carried out only within a community, humans are political animals. We achieve or fulfill our humanity only within a

community, and participation in political life within such a community constitutes our good. Thus, the political community, the *polis,* is both natural in that it is the kind of setting in which we would live in the absence of interfering conditions, and desirable since it is necessary for human flourishing. To an Aristotelian, the idea of a pre-political person making rational choices about social contracts is incoherent since it is only through participation in political communities that we become fully rational in the first place.

Later writers who have stressed the idea of human flourishing within traditional practices sometimes adopt a historicist position to the effect that the canons of justification themselves are intelligible, or at least applicable, only from within a perspective defined by the practices and traditions of a particular community. According to such *perspectivist* views, the idea of a pre-social, atomistic individual living in a nonpolitical state of nature really serves an ideological function. In particular, by hiding (perhaps even from themselves) their liberal biases under the guise of laws of human nature or postulates of rationality, liberal contractarians in effect smuggle in highly controversial political assumptions under the guise of ground rules for political discussion. For example, Locke may be accused of elevating a kind of possessive acquisitiveness, actually characteristic of individuals raised in capitalistic competitive societies, into a fundamental human characteristic. More recently, critics who stress the role of communal values and practices in directing individual development have charged that Rawls has chosen a value-laden and metaphysically dubious individualistic conception of the self to serve as an allegedly neutral cornerstone of his theory of justice. Indeed, just as Rawls has criticized the utilitarians for ignoring the value of the individual in pursuit of overall social good, communitarian critics of Rawls have accused him in characterizing the self of abstracting from all individual differences, thereby ending up with an impoverished conception of the self from which all individuality is purged.

Such charges may or may not be acceptable. Rawls for one, has defended his conception of the self as a politically appropriate point of departure for discussion in a pluralistic society rather than a metaphysical account of the person.

What these ongoing debates illustrate, however,

are the great methodological differences among political and social philosophers. Thus, even in discussing the justification of such a fundamental political entity as the state, political and social philosophers differ widely in their approaches. Even among representatives of what can loosely be called the liberal individualist tradition, some appeal to the social utility of practices and institutions while others argue on a contractarian basis or appeal to fundamental human or natural rights. To those who see human institutions evolving from practices and traditions, both liberal individualistic approaches are suspect. Both take for granted the individual as the unit of analysis, while Hegelians, Marxists, communitarians, and a whole range of theorists who may be called perspectivists maintain that individuals are not a common unit of analysis but themselves are the product of social contexts, practices, and institutions. To talk about individuals in abstraction from the particular social, economic, or historical context in which they are embedded is to risk elevating a characteristic of persons found in a particular time or place into a universal principle of morality or rationality.

The liberal individualist, however, can reply that perspectivism runs the danger of extreme relativism; no basis is left for criticism of any one perspective or tradition from an objective external point of view. Moreover, the claim that justification is coherent only within the framework of a tradition or a set of practices itself seems to be made from a broader perspective, since it purports to be about such practices from the outside, and so arguably presupposes a kind of justification which goes beyond the limits of perspectivism itself.

Political and social philosophers not only examine the basis of political institutions such as the state, but also attempt to formulate and defend criteria for evaluating institutions and practices that arise within the state. Particular attention has been paid to the development and criticism of theories of social justice, the exploration of the scope and limits of individual liberty and the nature and justification of individual rights, and to the examination of various kinds of claims made on behalf of equality. Underlying many of these discussions, however, are fundamental differences in approach to basic values. Many political philosophers now consider the issue of the alleged priority of the right over the good to be among the most important.

The Right and the Good

While political philosophers investigate and argue about the content of substantive political principles, such as those of social justice or equality of opportunity, their perspectives often reflect more general differences in approach. For example, one major division exists between those who take the notion of the right as fundamental to ethical justification and those who take the notion of the good as morally fundamental. According to the former, principles of right conduct or justice set limits to how individuals may pursue the good. As Rawls puts it in *A Theory of Justice,* "Justice is the first virtue of social institutions as truth is of systems of thought." To such theorists, the individual generally is conceived of as a freely choosing being. The function of political institutions is to allow expression to that freedom and autonomy. Hence, it becomes crucial to protect individual rights and personal autonomy. Those philosophers who take pursuit of the good as fundamental may also value autonomy and individual rights, but normally only as means for achieving the good. To the deontological thinkers who give priority to the right, reducing such basic values to mere means to an end devalues their status as fundamental norms, and makes our rights vulnerable to attack on the grounds that in "special" situations, as defined by the powerful, they must give way to some conception of the public good or interest.

In the utilitarian tradition, political and social institutions are evaluated in terms of their effects on promoting human welfare, HAPPINESS, or satisfaction. Perfectionists will emphasize the consequences of such institutions for achievement of an ideal of human fulfillment or excellence. On either view, opponents fear, rights and autonomy are values only so long as they are effective means to the good in question.

Although views of theorists within each group vary significantly, and views among representatives of different approaches can overlap, as when the good is *identified* with promotion of human autonomy itself, a difference in theoretical approach often will underlie differences in substantive political disputes. For example, proponents of a religious ideal of the human good, which they hold takes precedence over all questions of justice and rights, may not hesitate to impose it upon those they regard as unbelievers or heretics. On the other hand, it has been argued that a too-exclusive focus on individual rights ignores elements of a common morality and a sense of community that must be acknowledged if any human group is to be more than a set of isolated atomistic individuals, each exclusively preoccupied with its own concerns.

Some recent defenders of LIBERALISM, such as Bruce Ackerman and Ronald DWORKIN, have argued, following a line of thought developed earlier by JOHN STUART MILL (1806–1873), that the state must be *neutral* with respect to conceptions of the good. On that view, the state is not to officially support or impose a conception of the good life, a religious ideal, a code of sexual morality, or a conception of human excellence, except to prevent actual harm to others, or perhaps to prevent avoidable offense under certain especially restricted conditions. According to a popular version of such a doctrine, what goes on between consenting adults in private is nobody's business but their own. Such a view would imply, for example, that unless it can be shown that the distribution of pornography has a clear tendency to lead to harmful acts, such as sex crimes, the sale or distribution of pornography, however immoral, should not be legally prohibited. Critics might reply that the relationships pictured in pornography are inherently degrading and destructive of the very values that constitute a decent community and respectful relations among its citizens. Such values, on their view, might well justify censorship of pornography in the name of preserving the good life for a community.

Thus, different conceptions of the relationship between the right and the good might lead to quite different views on applied issues. The dispute over censorship of pornography illustrates how disagreement among philosophers over fundamental theoretical issues can lead to substantive disagreement at the level of concrete political and social issues as well.

Other philosophers, including some feminist writers, might reject the dualism of the right and the good entirely, and replace it with an ethics of CARE, in which concern for human relationships in particular contexts in paramount, or maintain that the idea of OPPRESSION, rather than the distribution of rights and goods, should be paramount in normative political analysis. Moreover, some theorists, perhaps influenced by post-modern critiques of notions such as impartiality, neutrality, and objectivity, question

the appeal to impartial reason underlying liberal INDIVIDUALISM, but such far reaching critiques seem to be in danger of undermining the very tools of critical analysis on which the rationality of their own position depends.

Human Nature

It is difficult to discern how a political philosophy claiming any degree of generality of application could avoid making either direct or indirect commitments about human nature. This is clearly true of many of the classic texts. Thus, Plato's conception of rule by an intellectual elite rests in significant part on his belief that most persons are incapable of participating effectively in government. It is difficult to see how such an assumption could be reconciled with belief in DEMOCRACY within the framework of a single consistent political theory. Similarly, Hobbes's case for an absolute sovereign is supported by his view of human nature as primarily egoistic. Proponents of democracy make assumptions about human nature as well, as when Mill argues that participation in the democratic process is an effective means of improving our rational faculties, so that we become fit to govern by governing. Indeed, writers who see humanity as malleable to environmental influences, and who deny the existence of any "fixed" human nature, are themselves committed to a view of (a malleable) human nature which is as much in need of defense as any other conception.

Even views which self-consciously attempt to avoid any presuppositions about human nature may not be successful in such an attempt, or have difficulty in remaining neutral in this area. Thus, Rawls has suggested that his conception of the self as a choosing agent, which is to be conceptualized apart from its abilities, capacities, and other individual characteristics, is not a metaphysical account of the self but a reasonable starting point for political discussion. However, such an assertion seems difficult to reconcile with Rawls's intuitive argument that we do not deserve the rewards that flow from use of our natural assets since we do not deserve the assets. We may not need to deserve such natural assets in order to deserve the rewards that flow from their exercise if they are inherent to the self to begin with. Rather, their exercise and the rewards people are willing to provide to stimulate productive performance, can themselves be seen as justifiable expressions of autonomy and selfhood.

Do all conceptions of human nature function only ideologically to prop up each author's favorite position? While that question is itself a debatable one within political philosophy, it is by no means clear that conceptions of human nature cannot be rationally supported or criticized. Often examination of such conceptions will involve empirical as well as philosophical considerations. Thus, the recent arguments of sociobiologists that evolutionary theory not only fails to rule out a genetic basis for human ALTRUISM, but instead may actually explain the biological basis for it, surely counts against the Hobbesian conception of human nature as egoistic, even if we take into account that what the sociobiologists mean by "altruism" is quite different from what ethical theorists mean by it. Even if altruism in the sociobiological sense refers to a (not necessarily intended) loss in ability to reproduce or pass on one's own genes, and altruism in the ethical sense has to do with conscious sacrifice of interests, it may be that biological altruism is causally related to tendencies to behave altruistically in the ethical sense.

While it is difficult to see how commitment to some conception of human nature can be altogether avoided in political philosophy, such commitments are highly controversial. Moreover, as we have seen, these commitments raise issues which overlap in a variety of different areas ranging from biological and social scientific accounts of the nature-nurture controversy to metaphysical theories of the self. Accordingly, while accounts of human nature sometimes are uncritically presupposed by political philosophers, they in fact raise a particularly challenging and fundamental set of issues within political philosophy itself.

Achievement in Political Philosophy

What does political philosophy contribute to our understanding of political and social institutions and practices? Do political philosophers make *progress* on the issues they discuss? For example, are we closer now to understanding the requirements of social justice than we were when Plato wrote *The Republic*? Are works of political and social philosophy merely sophisticated pleas for the author's own ideology disguised in the rhetoric of rational discourse?

These questions raise a variety of complex philosophical issues of their own, which cannot be treated exhaustively here. However, perhaps a few observations about what we can learn from political philosophy might help not only to place them in a broader context but also to indicate directions for further thought about them. To begin with, we might ask first if we view political philosophy as an attempt to provide answers to questions, just as we might expect, say, physics to constitute a set of answers to questions about the nature of physical reality. On this conception, the philosopher who advances a theory of justice is trying to provide us with an answer to the question "What is justice?"

On such a conception, political philosophy would be making progress if subsequent generations of philosophers were getting closer and closer to the correct theory of justice. Political philosophy would be more than mere ideology because it would conform to standards of rational discourse and aim at truth rather than merely persuasion.

There are difficulties with such a view, however. For one thing, there are few achievements in political philosophy that are not philosophically controversial. Classic texts such as *The Republic, The Politics, The Second Treatise of Government* (1689), *The Social Contract* (1762) and, in our own day, *A Theory of Justice* (1971) are commonly regarded as fundamentally flawed by critics who at one and the same time regard them as important contributions to the field. Moreover, later works are not always regarded as improvements on earlier ones; the notion of cumulative gains over time may not be applicable to political and social philosophy. Finally, as we have seen, political philosophers do not agree even on a common methodology or on a common set of normative principles with which to approach political and social issues.

On the other hand, the notion of progress is not entirely absent from the field either. Contemporary political philosophers may be more methodologically sophisticated than their predecessors and have more tools of logical and empirical analysis at their command. Major weaknesses of earlier achievements have been identified and can be addressed by later theorists. For example, anyone writing within the utilitarian tradition today can have access to literature which explicates central problems in utilitarian thought, ranging from difficulties with protection of individual rights to problems of securing cooperation in a utilitarian society, that were perhaps not as

social and political philosophy

clearly understood by early generations of utilitarian theorists. Progress, then, can consist in clearer understanding of problems with different approaches, greater sophistication in developing solutions, and greater logical rigor in evaluating them.

Moreover, we need to be careful in applying standards to political and social philosophy that we do not apply elsewhere. Thus, theories advanced in the natural and social sciences are not final answers presented as beyond intellectual challenge but rather they elicit criticism and stimulate further inquiry as well. It can be argued that great achievements in political philosophy function in a similar fashion. Even if they do not constitute unchallengeable answers to specific questions, they can constitute visions of political ideals, elucidations of basic principles underlying our thought, or critical challenges to conventional political thought. In such cases, they too stimulate criticism and elicit further inquiry. Indeed, one can argue that it is the *process* of political philosophy which is at least as important or valuable as any "answers" that may emerge from it.

Nevertheless, the position that some political theories are more defensible than others and come closer to constituting the best answers currently available remains defensible. At the very least, political and social philosophers have presented powerful and theoretically interesting arguments on a variety of topics in their area of study. Views which purport to show that such arguments are merely disguised ideological rhetoric whose only value is persuasive are hardly self-evident and themselves require philosophical defense of a rigorous sort. Whether the view of political philosophy as intellectual investigation of, and attempts to resolve, a particular set of problems can be sustained, however, remains a major philosophical issue itself. Regardless of the outcome of that debate, political and social philosophers have made great progress not only in clarifying the normative political and social issues before us but also in teaching us a kind of political humility by bringing to light the intellectual difficulties standing in the way of any political orthodoxy that claims to be beyond rational challenge.

See also: AUTHORITY; AUTONOMY OF MORAL AGENTS; BARRY; CARE; COHERENTISM; COMMON GOOD; COMMUNITARIANISM; CONSERVATISM; CONVENTIONS; DEMOCRACY; DWORKIN; ELITE, CONCEPT OF; EQUALITY; EXCELLENCE; GOOD, THEORIES OF THE; GOVERNMENT, ETHICS IN; HAPPINESS; HEGEL; HOBBES; HUMAN RIGHTS; HUME; IMPARTIALITY; INDIVIDUALISM; INSTITUTIONS; KANT; KANTIAN ETHICS; LEGITIMACY; LIBERALISM; LIBERTARIANISM; LIBERTY; LIFE, RIGHT TO; LOCKE; MACINTYRE; MARX; MARXISM; JOHN STUART MILL; NATURAL LAW; NEUTRAL PRINCIPLES; NORMS; NOZICK; OPPRESSION; PERFECTIONISM; PLATO; POLITICAL SYSTEMS; POWER; PROPERTY; PSYCHOLOGY; PUBLIC GOODS; PUBLIC POLICY; PUBLIC POLICY ANALYSIS; RATIONAL CHOICE; RAWLS; REFLECTIVE EQUILIBRIUM; RIGHTS; ROUSSEAU; SOCIAL CONTRACT; SOCIAL PSYCHOLOGY; SOCIOLOGY; UTILITARIANISM; WELFARE RIGHTS AND SOCIAL POLICY.

Bibliography

Ackerman, Bruce A. *Social Justice and the Liberal State.* New Haven, CT: Yale University Press, 1980.

Barry, Brian. *Justice as Impartiality.* New York: Oxford University Press, 1995.

Benn, Stanley, and R. S. Peters. *The Principles of Political Thought: Social Foundations of the Democratic State.* New York: Free Press, 1965. Originally published as *Social Principles of the Democratic State.* Remains one of the most comprehensive yet intelligible treatments of the major issues in social and political philosophy.

Daniels, Norman, ed. *Reading Rawls: Critical Studies of A Theory of Justice.* Oxford: Basil Blackwell; New York: Basic Books, 1975.

Dworkin, Ronald. *Taking Rights Seriously.* Cambridge: Harvard University Press, 1977.

Gauthier, David. *Morals by Agreement.* Oxford: Oxford University Press, 1986.

Gewirth, Alan. *Reason and Morality.* Chicago: University of Chicago Press, 1978. A sophisticated attempt to develop a proof of a basic principle of morality and examine its implications for practice.

Hampton, Jean. *Political Philosophy.* Boulder, CO: Westview Press, 1997.

Kymlicka, Will. *Contemporary Political Philosophy: An Introduction.* Oxford: Clarendon Press, 1990.

MacIntyre, Alasdair. *After Virtue.* 2d ed. Notre Dame, IN: University of Notre Dame Press, 1984. A stimulating and erudite critique of the idea that normative ethics and political philosophy can have a rational foundation apart from particular historical traditions and practices.

Nozick, Robert. *Anarchy, State, and Utopia.* New York: Basic Books, 1974. An attempt to defend libertarian principles along lines which are primarily Lockean in character; contains interesting remarks on justification in political philosophy.

Popper, Karl. *The Open Society and its Enemies.* Princeton, NJ: Princeton University Press, 1950. Also subsequent editions. A critique of what the author regards as the totalitarian implications of Platonic political theory.

Rawls, John. *A Theory of Justice.* Cambridge: Harvard University Press, 1971. A major contribution not only to our understanding of social justice, but also to the methodology of theorizing about justice and related values in political thought.

———. *Political Liberalism.* New York: Columbia University Press, 1993. Rawls's attempt to present liberalism and his own principles of justice as a "political" rather than a "comprehensive" theory; that is, one that attempts to develop common presuppositions of democratic cooperation in a society divided on fundamental issues rather than claim objective truth.

Sher, George. *Beyond Neutrality: Perfectionism and Politics.* New York: Cambridge University Press, 1997. A sympathetic but critical evaluation of the liberal defense of state neutrality toward the good and a defense of a limited form of perfectionism.

Simmons, A. John. *Moral Principles and Political Obligation.* Princeton, NJ: Princeton University Press, 1979.

Simon, Robert L., ed. *Blackwell Guide to Social and Political Philosophy.* New York: Blackwell, 2001.

Young, Iris Marion. *Justice and the Politics of Difference.* Princeton, NJ: Princeton University Press, 1996. Argues, from a postmodern and feminist perspective, that eliminating oppression of diverse social groups rather than distributive justice should be the central focus of inquiry in political and social theorizing about justice.

Robert L. Simon

social contract

The label 'social contract' is applied to a wide variety of theories concerning legitimate government, justice, and political obligation. It is not easy to say, however, what features or family resemblances might justify their all having this label in common. In fact, as will become evident from the following discussion, the more "theoretical" such theories become, the less contractual (or even social) they may appear to be. It is true that they all address questions of social organization and social justice; it is true that some notion of agreement among moral agents (often a very metaphorical or attenuated notion of it) is central to them all. But that is hardly enough to give adequate definition to a distinctive and unitary class of theories.

Historically, at least from the High Middle Ages through the end of the eighteenth century, the rise of philosophical interest in various notions of social contract ran roughly parallel to the shift away from hereditary, feudal, theological, or communitarian concerns with status (one's station and its duties) toward egalitarian, democratic, secular, and individualistic concerns with autonomy. Philosophically, one of the foundational elements of this shift toward autonomy is the conviction that, at least in some areas of their lives, people can create and incur morally binding obligations only through their CONSENT or agreement, and what is more, under certain conditions can nullify existing moral requirements by refusing or repudiating them. This historic shift, then, is from a conception of the moral life in which one's station and its duties are largely *imposed* (by God, by hereditary rank, by nature) and cannot be altered by the individual, to a conception in which they are largely *chosen* by the individual. In Sir Henry Maine's (1822–1888) famous phrase, it is a shift "from status to contract."

For present purposes, let us call the philosophical kernel of this shift "the contract idea," and use it to illuminate the differences between various forms of social contract theory. Perhaps the wide range of their differences can be understood in terms of the ways in which they define (*or dispense with*) various elements of the contract idea: autonomy, consent, agreement, refusal.

(It may be noted that the contract idea can in principle be the basis for a comprehensive ethical theory as well as a social contract account of political obligation, social organization, government, and justice. That is, it can yield a deontological alternative to utilitarian, Kantian, and perfectionist ethical theories. Such a comprehensive social contract account would hold, as a normative rather than a descriptive matter, that what is right is simply what people agree is right, or consent to accept as right. This position is a form of VOLUNTARISM, distinguished from other comprehensive theories by the fact that its substantive account of right is derived ultimately from mutual agreement rather than, for example, from a theory of human good.)

Varieties of Social Contract Theories

Actual vs. hypothetical. Perhaps the most striking division in the class of social contract theories is the one between its actual and hypothetical versions. In terms of the contract idea, we may formulate the distinction in this way:

Suppose matters of consent and refusal are construed much as the law of CONTRACTS might construe them if it omitted the complications introduced by "objective" standards of agreement and doctrines of unconscionable bargains and constructive or quasi-contract. That is, suppose we require the *actual* consent or refusal (express, tacit, or implied) of *actual* people who know what they are doing and who are not being coercively or fraudulently manipulated into doing it. Suppose we require a genuine "meeting of minds" in a genuine agreement. And suppose we are willing to let such agreements stand, however impulsive, irrational, or unfortunate they are. If so, then the social contracts we contemplate will have to be actual contracts.

However, if we construe matters of consent and refusal along the lines implicit in the legal notion of unconscionable contracts and the law of quasi-contracts (restitution or unjust enrichment), then we will get a very different sort of theory. That is, we will not require actual consent at all, but will enforce those obligations that we imagine people would have consented to if they had had the choice. And we will not enforce any putative obligations that we imagine people would have refused, had they had the choice. If we take that course, then the social contracts we contemplate will be hypothetical. Just how hypothetical will turn on how far we are willing to depart from hypotheses about what actual people would do in actual situations and move instead to hypotheses about what abstract or idealized moral agents would do under abstract or idealized conditions. Recent versions of social contract theory have been very hypothetical.

Several things push people toward hypothetical versions of social contract theory. For one, it is commonly asserted that the concept of an actual contract is virtually inapplicable to large-scale societies. It is arguable whether many people ever seriously consider their relation to law and government in this way, under conditions in which they can effectively refuse to participate in the enterprise. David HUME's (1711–1776) well-known analogy of the impressed seaman makes the point vividly. Imagine a man who is drugged, brought on board a ship, and awakened only when the ship is a hundred miles from land. He is then offered a choice: consent to ship's rules, or swim. His "consent" in that case proves nothing, and that case is like the situation most of us face. When we come to moral consciousness, the only viable option we have is to stay on board—at least for quite some time. In the meantime, our consent means nothing. John LOCKE's (1632–1704) efforts to save

actual social contracts with the notion of tacit consent seem beside the point, at least for fundamental questions about consent to an entire social or legal structure.

Even in more restricted contexts, however, such as obedience to particular laws (see below), there are reasons for moving away from the idea of actual contracts. To the extent that we question whether, in practice, people's actual consent or refusal is likely to be well-informed and unmanipulated, we may question whether it can satisfy the contract idea at all. And just as we are willing to substitute our judgment of what is in a child's best interests for the judgment of the child, we may want to insist that only under certain (often hypothetical) knowledge and autonomy conditions will consent reflect a person's "real" preferences or choices. We will then have reason to contemplate what people would consent to under those special conditions, rather than what they actually do in real time under real conditions.

As critics of hypothetical versions of social contract theory have pointed out, however, a hypothetical contract is no contract at all. ("Not worth the paper it is not written on.") It is questionable whether the notion of contract has a function here at all, except a heuristic one designed to reveal what reasons there might be for holding various views about moral requirements. In hypothetical contract accounts, the existence of the moral requirements seems to be tied only to the existence of such reasons, rather than to the existence of anything resembling a contract.

In defense of the hypothetical approach, we may again call attention to the law of contracts and how even there the elements of the contract idea often become attenuated. In adjudicating contract disputes, we may look first for unmistakable, overt signs of mutual consent—an offer by one party that is accepted by another. But we will often have to construe rather ambiguous behavior. (If I clap my hands and shout for joy, have I accepted the deal?) And we will become embroiled in many disputes about what each party to the contract actually understood it to mean—for example, with respect to unforeseen situations not discussed at the time of the agreement. To sort this out, we may well have to resort to some assumptions about what people *would* have agreed to *if* they had confronted that situation in making a given contract. Thus, we may resort to constructing accounts of agreements, or contracts, that are quite hypothetical. The first step away from the actual here is to say that what matters is not a conscious meeting of minds but rather an underlying, latent similarity (agreement) in views about how the contract should be understood. The second step is to appeal to such agreement among ordinary or reasonable people generally rather than between the actual parties to the contract. If this sort of hypothetical notion of agreement is enforceable in the law of contracts, perhaps it is rash to cast doubt on the warrant for attaching the contract label to hypothetical social contract theories.

Obedience to law. At least three basic uses for social contract arguments in political theory are commonly distinguished: one of them is to justify obedience to legitimate government or valid law; another is to establish the LEGITIMACY of an existing putative government or an existing putative law; and a third is to address questions about the general conditions under which any government (or social institution) may be considered to be legitimate, its laws valid, and its claims for obedience just.

"Contract of obedience" arguments, such as the one explored by Socrates in PLATO's (c. 430–347 B.C.E.) *Crito,* assume the legitimacy of the existing government, the validity of its laws, and perhaps even a general (presumptive) obligation to obey the law. They then argue that consenting to a law or set of laws, especially when combined with the acceptance of benefits flowing from government, creates a special or conclusive obligation to obey. It also follows, however, from another part of the contract idea, that a genuine refusal to participate in or accept benefits from a government would remove the burden of obedience. Socrates alludes to this by noting that he had had the option (before his conviction) of giving up his Athenian citizenship. His not leaving Athens can only be considered an indication of consent to its laws if he was in fact free to make his refusal effective in that way.

There are many interesting theoretical questions here. The usual questions about the interpretation of consent and refusal arise, and we may be moved to give them an objective or hypothetical cast—holding, perhaps, that only acts of consent or refusal that are in some sense rational are to count as morally effective. The pressure toward hypothetical contract theory, in other words, can be felt even at this very concrete level. In addition, of course, we need

to know how overt, conscious, and deliberate the acts must be. Is tacit or implied consent enough to count? From what behavior may such consent be inferred?

Moreover, to the extent that we hold a substantive doctrine of NATURAL LAW, natural RIGHTS, or duty, the scope of these contract of obedience arguments will be limited. On such accounts, for example, agents are typically not able to escape the moral force of prohibitions on murder, cannibalism, theft, incest, and so on simply by leaving societies that prohibit them. And our consenting to make laws to enforce such prohibitions, while it may be necessary for public order, will be morally superfluous; our consent does nothing to create the moral obligations. In other words, to the extent that we imagine individual autonomy to be restricted by natural or externally imposed law, the role of contract will be reduced.

There is a further complication. It is arguable whether an individual's consent should be regarded as effective—morally binding—unless it is embedded in a general social practice of obedience. Just as an ordinary contract is typically bilateral, surely a social contract must be genuinely social. If something breaks down cooperative schemes of obedience in a particular region of the law, the continued existence of obligations derived from consent is thrown into doubt. People engaged in certain forms of CIVIL DISOBEDIENCE (*e.g.,* passive resistance on a massive scale) may hope to undermine the effectiveness of consent in this way.

Legitimation. Historians of social contract theory (*e.g.,* Barker or Gough), speaking of developed theories rather than isolated arguments, place its beginnings in the High Middle Ages, and claim that it was, at first, addressed to the question of establishing the legitimacy of particular governments. Such "contract-of-government" arguments, as they have been called, typically assumed the legitimacy of a given *form* of government, and then considered how to establish the legitimacy of a particular sovereign (*e.g.,* from among several contenders for a throne), a particular constitution for a given sovereign (*e.g.,* Magna Charta), or a particular set of governmental INSTITUTIONS.

In a weak form, which might well have been attractive during the High Middle Ages and Renaissance, a social contract argument of this type might have been purely epistemological. Legitimacy could be seen as a matter of divine right, natural right, or sheer POWER. But since those things are often in dispute (among warring factions), we need a way of determining which side is correct. Social contract is then an alternative to trial by combat. The argument would be that general or social consent to be governed by some particular sovereign, constitution, or set of institutions is the best indicator of the presence of the factor (divine will, natural right, effective power) which at bottom makes political AUTHORITY legitimate. And the reverse is true as well: general or social refusal to be governed is a sign of the absence of the legitimating factor. This weak form of contract of government arguments can coexist nicely with everything from the most unbending version of divine right accounts of legitimacy to the most hardheaded contemporary versions of political realism.

The strong form of contract of government arguments is that general, social consent constitutes (rather than indicates) legitimacy and that general, social refusal destroys legitimacy. On this view, government actually *derives* its just powers from the consent of the governed (Jefferson). Giving an account of why this might be so, however, requires a theory addressed to the concerns that have virtually defined social contract theory since the seventeenth century: Under what conditions is government of any sort able to create morally binding obligations on its citizens? And more generally, what are the principles of justice that legitimate our fundamental social and political institutions? The contract idea has been brought to bear powerfully on those issues. As follows:

Origination. The most ambitious and fundamental form of social contract arguments begins at the (conceptual) point of origin: with nothing granted about the legitimacy of a particular form of government; with nothing granted about whether any government at all could ever be legitimate; with nothing granted about whether autonomous individuals would even choose to gather themselves into a society, or a "people." It then proposes that only the contract idea can account for (legitimate) communities, social institutions, and governments; only institutions satisfying the contract idea can create morally binding obligations on the individuals whose lives they direct. It assumes, to paraphrase Jean-Jacques ROUSSEAU (1712–1778), that government has no "natural" authority, and that might does not make right. It then argues that actual or hypothetical

consent to be governed creates the possibility of legitimate government, and that the character of the consent determines the form any legitimate government must take. The reverse also follows, and provides an opening for anarchism: actual or hypothetical refusal to be governed would make all political authority illegitimate.

The intellectual warrant for these theories is a function of the warrant for the notion of autonomy embedded in the contract idea and the strength of competing accounts. In Western philosophy, theories of divinely granted rights to rule and doctrines of natural aristocratic rights to rule have long had minimal credibility. Social contract's main competitors are now UTILITARIANISM (roughly: the best form of government is the form that governs best to maximize aggregate welfare); wholesale rejections of the notions of legitimacy and justice in favor of a "realistic" or "scientific" or "pragmatic" view (roughly: there is no legitimacy or justice other than that imposed by might); and various right-based theories of justice such as Robert NOZICK's or Ronald DWORKIN's (roughly: there is a criterion of right that is not derived exclusively from utility, power, or consent, and conformity to what is right is at least a necessary condition of legitimacy or justice).

Current Social Contract Theories

At least three versions of social contract theory have been pursued vigorously in contemporary philosophy. One owes its inspiration to Locke, another to Thomas HOBBES (1588–1679), and the third to Immanuel KANT (1724–1804). Rousseau's account, with its emphasis on the notions of community, COMMON GOOD, and general will, has not inspired as much contemporary attention. Individualists tend to think Rousseau undercuts the contract idea altogether; communitarians tend to read Rousseau for reasons unrelated to advancing social contract theory.

The Lockean tradition. In the second of Locke's *Two Treatises of Government* (1689) there is the outline of a social contract theory that remains a very powerful political force. It aims to stay as close as possible to the notion of actual consent and refusal. It insists that human beings are by nature free, subject only to respecting others' natural rights, and with the moral authority to enforce their own. It holds that the only thing that can create a government with moral authority over its subjects is their consent to be subject to it; their consent to be governed. It holds that the only necessity for such government is a practical one: as a practical matter, we cannot manage to protect our rights and respect others' without the coordination and COERCION provided by a government. It holds that the recognition of this practical necessity is the only reason for which people would consent to be governed, and that therefore the sole purpose of government must be to protect people's natural rights.

There are three central theoretical challenges for such a theory. One is to defend the notion of natural freedom or autonomy for humans, squaring it with claims that some humans are incompetent to rule themselves. This problem is usually addressed by arguing against doctrines of divine or natural authority, and then giving a developmental account of autonomy (often emphasizing the ability to reason) and a justification for paternalistic interventions in aid of it. The difficult matter of accommodating the need for reliance on experts, especially in highly technical matters concerning PUBLIC POLICY, remains.

A second theoretical challenge is to defend the idea that actual political societies can be organized in terms of the actual consent and refusal of individuals. Is it plausible to suppose that civil society generally got started in this way? Is it plausible to think that contemporary societies reflect (or could reflect) the actual consent of their members? This problem calls forth speculation about the prehistoric origins of human governments; accounts of tacit, implied, or imputed consent; defenses of majority rule; and reflections on the extent to which democratic political processes elicit expressions of genuine consent or refusal.

The third challenge is to specify the natural rights or other NORMS that limit human autonomy and define the purposes of government. Locke speaks of rights to life, LIBERTY, PROPERTY, and paternal authority. Thomas JEFFERSON (1743–1826) says life, liberty, and the pursuit of HAPPINESS. What rights should be on the list? Are they all "negative" in character—that is, rights to be left alone? Or are some of them positive or welfare rights? Should things other than rights be on the list? NEEDS and INTERESTS, perhaps? This plunges the theory directly into the deepest thickets of normative ethics.

These challenges faced by the Lockean line of social contractarians are formidable ones. It has become commonplace to heap scorn on the notion of tacit consent, to be cynical about the extent to which popular consent is manipulated, to point out the ways in which all large-scale political processes are oppressive, and to cast doubt on the very possibility of human autonomy. The Lockean arguments are resilient, however, and continue to be pursued, especially by philosophers with a direct concern with public policy and democratic institutions.

Rational choice arguments and the Hobbesian tradition. Among the most recent developments in social contract theory is a line of argument that owes its inspiration, if not origin, to a certain reading of Hobbes. It is a version of hypothetical contract theory that tries to pull itself up by its bootstraps. In its purest form it begins with the assumption that human autonomy is complete; there are no prior moral constraints at all on the parties to the contract. It assumes that what we want to know is whether it would be rational for completely autonomous agents to bind themselves by agreements that limit their autonomy (such as social compacts to establish governments). It assumes that the most challenging and rewarding way to consider the question is by defining rationality as narrowly as possible—that is, simply as the ability to find and choose the course of action, in any given situation, that will maximally satisfy the agent's own interests. It places as few prior conditions as possible (and no overtly "moral" ones) on the interests that agents might want to pursue. It then asks itself whether ideally rational agents would choose to make binding agreements with each other—or what comes to the same thing, choose to enter into and remain in cooperative endeavors with others. This general approach to the cooperation problem is by way of RATIONAL CHOICE theory. Its connection to social contract theory has been explored provocatively by economists (Harsanyi, Buchanan, and Tullock), and David Gauthier has given it an explicit and detailed contractarian development.

There are many challenges faced by this rational choice form of CONTRACTARIANISM. Two fundamental ones are these: First, since the motivation for this form of contractarianism is so closely linked to the need to solve the problems known collectively as "prisoner's dilemmas" (discussed in detail elsewhere in this encyclopedia), it must genuinely solve those problems. Second, it must persuade us that the behavior of rational agents (in the narrow sense of rational), operating in a moral vacuum, establishes something that helps answer at least some of the traditional questions of social contract theory. No consensus has yet emerged on its success with these problems, but Russell Hardin has perhaps indirectly done the most to show its promise by arguing for the rationality of government and other powerful social institutions in a way quite similar to a Hobbesian social contract theory.

Kantian constructivism. An enormous body of comment, criticism, and revivified interest in social contract theory has grown up around the work of John RAWLS since the publication of his book, *A Theory of Justice,* in 1971. Rawls's theory is described in detail in a separate article in this encyclopedia. Some brief remarks on the general, "constructivist" line of argument are appropriate here, however. More may be found in the article on CONSTRUCTIVISM.

The most striking aspect of Rawls's approach is its reconceptualization of the project of social contract theory, and the method employed to pursue that project. Rawls calls it Kantian constructivism. It takes as common ground a vague, general conception of justice as fairness in the context of a cooperative, reciprocal scheme for mutual advantage and a list of "primary" goods necessary for every rational life plan. It adopts a thin definition of rationality (as above), and a number of assumptions about the general nature of the "moral powers" and motivations of autonomous moral agents. The fundamental question it addresses concerns the basic structure of society—not the traditional questions of obedience and origination described above, but rather the question of the principles that social institutions must satisfy in order to be just. The question is given a contractarian answer in the sense that the answer is to be found by discovering what principles of justice autonomous agents would *choose,* or agree on. (This may, but need not, turn out to be a familiar set of principles from some other theory of justice.) The choice must be made under conditions consistent with the background conception of FAIRNESS. For Rawls, this means that the agents cannot be allowed to make use of (to "know") the special circumstances of their own situations to manipulate the contract in their favor. He imagines the choice being made behind a "veil of ignorance" about all the particular details of one's life: one's sex, race, social class, education, religion—even one's conception of the good.

The idea is to characterize a procedure whose outcome (in the form of the principles chosen) we can accept as definitive of justice for the basic structure of society. (Compare Jürgen HABERMAS's notion of an "ideal speech" situation and "discourse ethics.") It is already clear that Rawls's articulation of this approach to contractarianism is a landmark in the history of social contract theory. Like the other approaches described here, it faces formidable challenges. It has been charged with circularity; with bias toward deontological and liberal theories of justice; with adopting an incomprehensibly abstract notion of autonomous choice.

In terms of method, some philosophers have come to prefer an alternative proposed by T. M. Scanlon, first in an article, and now in a book. Scanlon proposes that we construct the account of justice not in terms of what greatly IDEALIZED AGENTS would choose from behind a veil of ignorance, but rather in terms of what "we" who are willing to consider these things in good faith, without morally irrelevant bargaining advantages, could not reasonably reject.

See also: AUTHORITY; AUTONOMY OF MORAL AGENTS; CIVIL DISOBEDIENCE; CIVIL RIGHTS AND CIVIC DUTIES; COERCION; COLLECTIVE RESPONSIBILITY; COMMON GOOD; COMMUNITARIANISM; CONSENT; CONSTRUCTIVISM; CONTRACTARIANISM; CONTRACTS; CONVENTIONS; COOPERATION, CONFLICT, AND COORDINATION; DEMOCRACY; DWORKIN; ECONOMIC SYSTEMS; FAIRNESS; GAME THEORY; GOVERNMENT, ETHICS IN; HABERMAS; HOBBES; HUME; IDEALIST ETHICS; IDEALIZED AGENTS; INDIVIDUALISM; INSTITUTIONS; JEFFERSON; KANT; LEGITIMACY; LOCKE; NATURAL LAW; NOZICK; OBEDIENCE TO LAW; PATERNALISM; POLITICAL SYSTEMS; PUBLIC GOODS; PUBLIC POLICY; RATIONAL CHOICE; RAWLS; RECIPROCITY; REFLECTIVE EQUILIBRIUM; RIGHTS; ROUSSEAU; SOCIAL AND POLITICAL PHILOSOPHY; STRATEGIC INTERACTION; THEORY AND PRACTICE; UTILITARIANISM.

Bibliography

Atiyah, Patrick. *Promises, Morals, and Law.* Oxford: Clarendon Press, 1981.

Barker, Ernest, ed. *Social Contract: Essays by Locke, Hume, and Rousseau.* Westport, CT: Greenwood Press, 1980 [1947]. Contains classic material on social contract, together with Barker's historical introduction.

Barry, Brian. A Treatise on Social Justice. Vol. I: *Theories of Justice.* Berkeley: University of California Press, 1989. Sustained criticism of justice as mutual advantage (exchange; contract), including justice as reciprocity.

Buchanan, James. *The Limits of Liberty: Between Anarchy and Leviathan.* Chicago: University of Chicago Press, 1975.

Buchanan, James, and Gordon Tullock. *The Calculus of Consent.* Ann Arbor: University of Michigan Press, 1962.

Dworkin, Ronald. *Taking Rights Seriously.* Cambridge, MA: Harvard University Press, 1977.

Gauthier, David. *Morals by Agreement.* Oxford: Clarendon Press, 1986.

Gough, J. W. The Social Contract: A Critical Study of Its Development. Oxford: Clarendon Press, 1957.

Hampton, Jean. *Hobbes and the Social Contract Tradition.* Cambridge: Cambridge University Press, 1986.

Hardin, Russell. *Morality within the Limits of Reason.* Chicago: University of Chicago Press, 1988. Reasons for thinking that an appreciation of our intellectual limitations and the need for strategic interaction is decisive in showing the need for social conventions and stable institutions.

Harsanyi, John. "Cardinal Utility in Welfare Economics and in the Theory of Risk-Taking." *Journal of Political Economy* 61 (1953): 434–35. Early step in constructivist theory..

Hobbes, Thomas. *Leviathan.* New York: Dutton, 1950 [1651].

Kavka, Gregory S. *Hobbesian Moral and Political Theory.* Princeton, NJ: Princeton University Press, 1986.

Lesnoff, Michael. *Social Contract.* Atlantic Highlands, NJ: Humanities Press, 1986. Historical survey and critique.

Locke, John. *Two Treatises of Government.* Edited by Peter Laslett. 2d, critical ed. Cambridge: Cambridge University Press, 1967 [1689].

Nozick, Robert. *Anarchy, State, and Utopia.* New York: Basic Books, 1974.

Patemen, Carole. *The Problem of Political Obligation: A Critical Analysis.* London: John Wiley, 1979.

Pitkin, Hannah. "Obligation and Consent." *American Political Science Review* 59; 60 (1965; 1966): 990–99; 39–52.

Rawls, John. *A Theory of Justice.* Cambridge, MA: Harvard University Press, 1971.

Rousseau, Jean-Jacques. *The Social Contract and Discourses.* Translated by G. D. H. Cole. New York: E. P. Dutton, 1950 [1762; 1755].

Scanlon, T. M. "Contractualism and Utilitarianism." In *Utilitarianism and Beyond,* edited by Amartya Sen and Bernard Williams. Cambridge: Cambridge University Press, 1982.

———. *What We Owe to Each Other.* Cambridge, MA: Harvard University Press, 1999. Development of the idea that the appropriate test for constructivist principles of justice is best stated negatively, as the requirement that such principles be ones that we cannot reasonably reject.

Simmons, A. John. *Moral Principles and Political Obligations.* Princeton, NJ: Princeton University Press, 1979.

Lawrence C. Becker

social psychology

Ethics, Psychology, and Theoretical Autonomy

Social psychology investigates "how the thought, feeling, and behavior of individuals are influenced by the actual, imagined, or implied presence of others" (Allport). At first glance, such inquiry appears directly relevant to ethics; while ethical reflection is not easily characterized, few would deny that it centrally concerns social judgment and behavior. Yet Western analytic ethics, the tradition I consider here, has largely ignored social psychology.

This is not merely benign neglect. Following MOORE (1873–1958), philosophers have studiously avoided what he termed the NATURALISTIC FALLACY (Moore; cf. Darwall, *et al.*)—the inappropriate use of descriptive claims to adjudicate normative questions—and employing empirical PSYCHOLOGY in ethical reflection seems to stray dangerously near this uncertain terrain. But not everyone believes that Moorean caution requires ethics to be, as Nagel suggested, an "autonomous" discipline; some philosophers assert that empirical psychology may inform ethical reflection without undermining its distinctively normative character (*e.g.*, Flanagan; Railton). I will not here attempt to resolve disputes about the theoretical AUTONOMY OF ETHICS. Instead, I will describe some striking experimental results, in the hope that discussion regarding the relevance of empirical psychology to ethical reflection may become better informed.

The study of human social behavior is an enormous field, encompassing a multitude of methodologies and problematics, but I will confine myself to reporting, with little attention to interpretive controversy, some representative results in experimental social psychology. While any such editorial decisions are debatable, I hope this focus on the experimental tradition is a defensible one; philosophers, like all of us, are well able to engage in acute social observation, but philosophy is not noted for its systematic observation of behavior in controlled contexts. Accordingly, experimental social psychology may be among the most enlivening forms of social inquiry for philosophical ethics to encounter.

The psychology I describe is further limited to "situationist" approaches to circumstantial influences on cognition and behavior. Of course there are other areas of interest in experimental social psychology: emotions and the cross cultural study of EMOTION (*e.g.,* Ellsworth); attitudes, prejudice, and stereotyping (*e.g.,* Eagly and Chaiken); and group dynamics (*e.g.,* Baron *et al.*). But the situationist experimental tradition encompasses some of the most provocative results in the behavioral sciences—results that may provide very fertile materials for ethical reflection.

Social Cognition

The study of cognition has been a central preoccupation of modern social psychology. In a seminal study, Kahneman and Tversky (1937–1996) asked two groups of subjects to estimate the probability that a particular individual in a sample of 100 was employed as an engineer; one group was told the population "base rate" was 70 lawyers and 30 engineers, while the other group was given the opposite distribution, 30 lawyers and 70 engineers (Kahneman and Tversky). When presented with no further information, subjects typically made appropriate use of the base rate, *e.g.,* assessing the probability to be 30 percent that a randomly selected individual in the first group was an engineer. But when subjects were also presented with "thumbnail descriptions" of the individuals their predictions were to target, they apparently neglected the base rate. In one example, subjects presented with a profile designed to be "totally uninformative" about a target individual's profession (*e.g.,* "high ability," and "well liked") typically estimated the probability to be 50 percent that the individual was an engineer, *regardless* of whether the group they considered had a 70 percent or 30 percent representation of engineers. In as much as estimates were approximately the same in either base rate condition, it seems fair to conclude that subjects neglected the base rate when faced with the uninformative personality profile. This is especially striking because the subjects themselves seemed aware that the "uninformative" information was valueless: their 50 percent estimate reflects no more confidence than they presumably

would have had in the outcome of a coin toss. As Kahneman and Tversky put it, attention to "worthless" information may cause useful information to be "ignored." In particular, it may be that "personal" information of dubious value has exaggerated salience when compared with valuable "statistical" information.

Kahneman and Tversky's work raises issues concerning "ecological validity": to what extent do experimental phenomena have analogs in "naturalistic" contexts outside the laboratory? Variations on Kahneman and Tversky's protocol suggest that their results are to some extent an artifact of experimental design. In one variant, Schwarz and colleagues found that subjects made better use of the base rate when told that the uninformative personality sketch was computer generated than they did when told it was written by a psychologist. Apparently, information from psychologists is more highly regarded than that generated by computer; thus subjects exhibit greater base rate neglect when confronted with what they believe to be higher quality information. Given the communicative setting of a psychology experiment, it seems quite reasonable to take the deliverances of psychologists seriously; accordingly, Kahneman and Tversky's demonstration of base rate neglect may in substantial measure be understood as subjects quite properly following what Schwarz calls "the rules of cooperative conversational conduct." Although some communicative conventions result in laboratory errors, they may reflect quite serviceable strategies for the cognitive demands of everyday life.

To address concerns regarding ecological validity, investigators search for "real world analogs" of experimental results. For example, Kahneman and Tversky discovered that experimentally induced failures to appreciate "regression to the mean" have analogs in the work behavior of experienced flight instructors, who may eschew "positive reinforcement" on the grounds that praising a trainee's exceptional performance often "causes" the trainee to perform less well on the subsequent trial. But this sort of regression is just what they should expect, insofar as less-than-exceptional performances are more common than exceptional ones!

While controversies regarding ecological validity are widespread, some distinguished commentators (*e.g.,* Nisbett and Ross) argue that there is no shortage of naturalistic analogs for the "cognitive biases" repeatedly demonstrated in the lab. Indeed, Schwarz need not be unsympathetic to the work of Kahneman and Tversky, for their dialogue underscores a central lesson of social psychology: small changes in circumstance may make large differences in how we think and act.

Perhaps the most ethically significant research on cognitive shortcomings concerns the "fundamental attribution error" identified by Ross, Nisbett, and others (*e.g.,* Ross; Nisbett and Ross; Gilbert and Malone). The attribution error, as Nisbett and Ross describe it, is a tendency to attribute the causes of behavior to the actor's dispositions and "ignore powerful situational determinants of behavior." For example, people may make confident personality assessments based on behavioral evidence of quite dubious value: Fleming and Darley found that subjects believed the "real life" personality of an actor to be consistent with his behavior in a film clip, even when the role in question required the actor to portray extremely violent behavior.

Conversely, people may make overconfident behavioral predictions based on impressions of personality, as in what Ross and Nisbett term the "interview illusion." They report that assessments based on one-hour hiring interviews have been found to correlate with subsequent measures of job performance at a level hardly distinguishable from chance (.10), while subjects expect correlations markedly above chance (.59). Attribution theory suggests a diagnosis of this tendency: managers take interview performance as evidence supporting attribution of reliable dispositions, which in turn are expected to support confident behavioral predictions. Apparently, people make confident judgments about what others are "really like" based on scanty evidence; unsurprisingly, some of the resultant behavioral expectations are disappointed.

While some commentators (*e.g.,* Epstein and Teraspulsky; Wright and Mischel) argue that social psychologists have overstated the extent to which laboratory attribution errors are reflected in "real world" problems in social judgment, it seems quite reasonable to conclude that people experience marked difficulty in this regard, given the surprise and disappointment that often characterize our social interactions. Such difficulties in social perception, we shall see presently, are due in part to the unexpectedly potent influence of situational variation on behavior.

Situational Influences on Helping Behavior

Much social psychological research was provoked by the 1964 murder of Kitty Genovese in Queens, where thirty-odd witnesses failed to intervene or call police, despite the fact that Genovese's screams were audible for over thirty minutes. In a protocol designed to investigate the interaction of group size and helping behavior, Latané and Darley pumped thick clouds of artificial smoke into a waiting room occupied by volunteers for an experiment. When subjects were alone, 75 percent promptly reported the smoke to experimenters, but when subjects waited with two passive experimental "confederates" assigned by investigators to pose as subjects, only 10 percent reported it. In another manipulation, Latané and Darley found that 70 percent of bystanders offered help to the victim of a staged accident when alone, as opposed to 7 percent in the company of an unresponsive confederate. The "group effect" has been replicated repeatedly: the presence of numerous bystanders may inhibit individual helping behavior (Latané and Nida). This is a striking finding: we might fairly expect to see people act more confidently and effectively in groups—just the opposite of what much experimental work suggests. One explanation of this disquieting phenomena is "diffusion of responsibility": the more people present in a crisis, the greater the extent to which each individual feels "it's not up to me" to intervene.

Whatever the explanation, bystander effects illustrate the central finding of situationist experimental social psychology: the extraordinary power of situational factors to influence cognition and behavior (Ross and Nisbett; Haney and Zimbardo). Two aspects of this phenomenon are of particular interest: (1) *Unexpectedness:* Situational stimuli often impact behavior in ways that defy our customary predictive strategies. (2) *Insubstantiality:* Non-coercive, seemingly insignificant situational factors may have a powerful impact on behavior. Of course, unexpectedness and insubstantiality interact: situational influences are often unexpected precisely because they seem so insubstantial.

Isen and Levin provided an especially elegant demonstration of these points. In their study, an experimental confederate posing as a shopper dropped a file of papers in front of callers leaving a mall phone booth. The manipulation was simple: some callers had found a dime (at that time, the cost of a phone call) experimenters had planted in the phone's coin return slot; for other callers, no dime was planted. The effect on helping behavior proved remarkable (after Isen and Levin):

	HELPED	DID NOT HELP
DIME FOUND	14	2
NO DIME FOUND	1	24

If a subject finds a dime, they'll very likely help; if they don't, they very likely won't. Contrary to what habits of dispositional attribution lead us to expect, the difference in situation has more impact here than any differences in personal characteristics—unless we are to suppose that the compassionate very regularly lucked into a dime and the callous very regularly didn't, an extraordinary coincidence indeed.

Darley and Batson conducted another classic experiment in this vein. Their subjects performed tasks at two separate sites. The behavior of interest occurred when subjects walked from one site to the other, and passed an experimental confederate posing as the victim of a health crisis. Before leaving the first site, subjects were told either that they were running late ("high hurry"), right on time ("medium hurry"), or a little early ("low hurry"); thus members of each group experienced a different degree of time pressure while traveling from one site to the next. Helping behavior varied markedly with degree of hurry: 63 percent offered help in "low hurry," 45 percent offered help in "medium hurry," and only 10 percent offered help in "high hurry." As in Isen and Levin, a rather innocent situational variable had a potent impact on helping behavior. But these results are even more unsettling than Isen and Levin's, since here "the stakes are high"—the victim appeared to be suffering a real crisis, rather than the inconvenience of a few dropped papers. Helping behavior, one begins to suspect, is distressingly variable with situational variation; we may begin to wonder if morally important dispositional structures, such as those implicated in compassion, are highly defeasible.

Situational Influences on Destructive Behavior

Experimental manipulations may also induce harming behavior, as was shown in perhaps the most famous of all social-psychological studies, Milgram's (1933–1984) "obedience experiments."

Subjects acted as "teacher" in what was purported to be a study of PUNISHMENT and learning. Teachers were asked by the experimenter to give a remotely administered "test" to an experimental confederate "learner" hidden from their view in another room, and to punish wrong answers with realistic-seeming simulated shocks. Shock "intensity" was increased with each wrong answer, and as shock "punishments" increased in intensity, the learner responded with increasingly vehement protests (Milgram, 1974): *e.g.,* "I can't stand the pain. Let me out of here!" If the teacher balked, the experimenter "firm[ly]" but "not impolite[ly]" insisted they continue (Milgram, 1974). In standard permutations, approximately two-thirds of subjects were fully obedient: they complied with the experimenter's directives until they were asked to stop administering shocks (experiment 5; Milgram, 1974).

The compliant subjects were not blindly obedient, or willfully sadistic; instead, they experienced unbearable stress, as this report shows:

> I observed a mature and initially poised businessman enter the laboratory smiling and confident. Within 20 minutes he was reduced to a twitching and stuttering wreck, who was rapidly approaching a point of nervous collapse. He constantly pulled on his earlobe, and twisted his hands. At one point he pushed his fist into his forehead and muttered: "Oh God, let's stop it." And yet he continued to respond to every word of the experimenter, and obeyed to the end.
> (Milgram, 1963)

Such reports depict obedient subjects not as cruel, but suggestible; verbal manipulation resulted in their acting against their scruples even when they were extremely reluctant to do so. The fact of human malleability, not human CRUELTY, is the lesson we should learn; indeed, the extent of obedience varied markedly with variations of the experimental protocol. For example, in the "touch-proximity" condition, where the teacher administered punishment by pressing the learner's hand onto a "shock plate," obedience dropped to 30 percent (Milgram, 1974). When the "experimenter" was absent during the experiment and instructed the teacher by phone, obedience dropped to 20.5 percent (1974). Milgram's experiments show not only that bad behavior may be all-too-easily situationally induced, but also that bad behavior may be ameliorated (and, one hopes, good behavior induced) by the appropriate situational manipulation.

Of course it is hardly surprising that human beings, social creatures that they are, will go to considerable lengths to conform, especially with someone they believe to be an authority. Milgram's protocol is indebted to the "conformity paradigm" of his mentor Solomon Asch (1907–1996). In a classic series of studies, Asch found 75 percent of subjects were willing to avow perceptual judgments they knew to be grossly erroneous in order to secure conformity with a group of experimental confederates unanimously asserting the erroneous judgment. Subjects evinced considerable stress, as did Milgram's obedients, but Milgram's results are more startling, because the mortal implications of the Milgram situation must have seemed far weightier to subjects than the "going along to get along" we find in Asch. Indeed, we must note just how surprising Milgram's studies were at the time he performed them. When Milgram (1974) asked college students, psychiatrists, and "middle class" adults to predict their own behavior in the experiment, no individual predicted that they would be fully obedient in the role of a subject acting as "teacher"; when asked to predict the behavior of others, those surveyed typically predicted that less than 1 percent of subjects would be fully obedient.

It is important to place Milgram's results, and the incredulity we may experience upon first hearing them, into historical context. As Milgram (1974) and others (*e.g.*, Kelman and Hamilton) have noted, his stylized experimental paradigm bears substantial similarities to the destructive obedience displayed by many Germans in the Third Reich (1933–1945). This similarity should certainly give pause to anyone questioning the ecological validity of the Milgram experiments. More importantly, Milgram's work may illuminate the question of how ordinary people are induced to commit atrocities even when the inducements are not explicitly coercive, for he demonstrated the situationist lessons of unexpectedness and insubstantiality in the starkest terms: seemingly minor situational influences may effect grotesque moral failings.

Such experiments may also be thought to exhibit moral failings on the part of the investigator; some observers argue that Milgram abused his subjects

(see Miller *et al.*). Indeed, this complaint may apply to many social psychology experiments, since they often involve DECEIT and manipulation. But the proper treatment of human subjects is not a question for this article; while the moral status of experiments like Milgram's may be disputable, the importance of their results is not.

Another controversial experiment in the tradition of Milgram is the Stanford Prison Experiment, in which student volunteers were randomly assigned the role of "prisoner" or "guard" in a simulated campus "prison." The situational effect on subjects selected for "normalcy" (Zimbardo *et al.*; Haney and Zimbardo) was appalling.

"Guard A" prior to start of experiment:

> As I am a pacifist and non-aggressive individual I cannot see a time when I might guard and or maltreat other living things.

"Guard A" on day five:

> The new prisoner . . . refuses to eat his sausage . . . we throw him into the hole ordering him to hold sausages in each hand. We have a crisis of authority. . . . I decided to force feed him, but he wouldn't eat. I let the food slide down his face. I didn't believe it was me doing it. I hated myself for making him eat but I hated him more for not eating. (Zimbardo *et al.*)

Concerns about escalating brutality led experimenters to terminate the scheduled two-week experiment after only six days. The "guards" were volunteers and had not been instructed (much less coerced) to perpetrate cruelties; once more, the situational "input" seems remarkably insubstantial when compared with the behavioral "output." Accordingly, investigators Haney and Zimbardo remember their results as "shocking and unexpected." The common complaint that behavioral scientists are merely in the business of "demonstrating the obvious" seems quite inapplicable to the tradition we have discussed.

Ethics and Psychology: A Rapprochement?

How might the study of ethics be informed by these striking demonstrations? I will be content to ask some questions. (1) How should demonstrations of cognitive biases affect our thinking on moral evaluation? Are we ever justified in concluding that a person is in circumstances that approximate ideal conditions for moral judgment? (2) How should the existence of attribution errors affect our thinking on CHARACTER assessment? Can we ever be confident of such assessments? (3) How should the extraordinary power of situational stimuli affect our understanding of agency and RESPONSIBILITY? Are we ever responsible for our actions, or is all our behavior primarily attributable to situational factors? (4) How should acknowledging the "power of the situation" affect our conceptions of VIRTUES like honesty, TEMPERANCE, and COURAGE, which we often think of as substantially resistant to the vagaries of circumstance?

To some moral philosophers, these seem pressing and provocative questions. But as I said at the outset, to others they seem questions safely ignored, on the grounds that ethics cannot without distortion be constrained by empirical inquiry. Conversely, prominent ethical theorists such as BRANDT and Gibbard have engaged empirical psychology, as have their colleagues in epistemology (Goldman), and the philosophy of mind (Churchland). With these efforts as background, interdisciplinary work in ethics and psychology became more influential during the 1990s. Writers like Flanagan and Becker argued for increased "psychological realism" in ethics, and their work orchestrated fruitful encounters between ethics and scientific psychology. In this spirit, Flanagan, Railton, and Doris began to apply the lessons of experimental social psychology to critical discussion of VIRTUE ETHICS, an influential approach to ethical thought in the last third of the twentieth century (*e.g.*, McDowell; FOOT; WILLIAMS). At the twentieth century's end, the outcome of these discussions was undecided, but the disciplinary barriers between ethics and social psychology had begun to suffer serious scrutiny.

See also: ANALOGICAL ARGUMENT; AUTHORITY; AUTONOMY OF ETHICS; AUTONOMY OF MORAL AGENTS; CASUISTRY; COGNITIVE SCIENCE; CORRECTIONAL ETHICS; CRUELTY; CULTURAL STUDIES; EMOTION; GROUPS, MORAL STATUS OF; HOLOCAUST; JUSTICE, CIRCUMSTANCES OF; MEAD; MORAL EDUCATION; MORAL IMAGINATION; MORAL PERCEPTION; MORAL REALISM; MULTICULTURALISM; NARRATIVE ETHICS; NATURALISTIC FALLACY; OBEDIENCE TO LAW; PSYCHOLOGY; PUNISHMENT; RESPONSIBILITY; SELF AND SOCIAL SELF; SITUATION ETHICS; SOCIAL AND POLITICAL PHILOSOPHY; SOCIOLOGY; VIRTUE ETHICS; VIRTUES.

Bibliography

Allport, Gordon W. "The Historical Background of Social Psychology." In *The Handbook of Social Psychology,* 3d ed., edited by Gardner Lindzey and Elliot Aronson, vol. 1, 1–46. New York: Random House, 1985.

Asch, Solomon E. "Opinions and Social Pressure." *Scientific American* 193 (1955): 31–35.

Baron, Robert S., Norbert L. Kerr, and Norman Miller. *Group Process, Group Decision, Group Action.* Buckingham: Open University Press, 1992.

Becker, Lawrence C. *A New Stoicism.* Princeton, NJ: Princeton University Press, 1998. Cited, p. 124.

Brandt, Richard B. *A Theory of the Right and the Good.* Oxford: Oxford University Press, 1979.

Churchland, Paul M. *Matter and Consciousness.* Cambridge, MA: MIT Press, 1984.

Darley, John M., and C. Daniel Batson. "From Jerusalem to Jericho: A Study of Situational and Dispositional Variables in Helping Behavior." *Journal of Personality and Social Psychology* 27 (1973): 100–8. Cited, p. 105.

Darwall, Stephen L., Allan Gibbard, and Peter Railton. "Toward *Fin de siècle* Ethics: Some Trends." *Philosophical Review* 101 (1992): 115–89.

Doris, John M. "Persons, Situations, and Virtue Ethics." *Noûs* 32 (1998): 504–30.

Eagly, Alice H., and Shelly Chaiken. *The Psychology of Attitudes.* Fort Worth, TX: Harcourt, Brace, Jovanovich, 1993.

Ellsworth, Phoebe C. "Sense, Culture, and Sensibility." In *Emotion and Culture: Empirical Studies in Mutual Influence,* edited by H. Markus and S. Kitayama, 23–50. Washington, DC: American Psychological Association, 1994.

Epstein, Seymour, and Laurie Teraspulsky. "Perception of Cross-Situational Consistency." *Journal of Personality and Social Psychology* 50 (1986): 1152–60.

Flanagan, Owen J. *Varieties of Moral Personality.* Cambridge, MA: Harvard University Press, 1991. Cited, p. 32.

Fleming, John H., and John M. Darley. "Actors and Observers Revisited: Correspondence Bias, Counterfactual Surprise, and Discounting in Successive Judgments of Constrained Behavior." *Social Cognition* 11 (1993): 367–97. Cited, p. 380.

Foot, Philippa. *Virtues and Vices.* Berkeley and Los Angeles: University of California Press, 1978.

Gibbard, Allan. *Wise Choices, Apt Feelings: A Theory of*

Normative Judgment. Cambridge, MA: Harvard University Press, 1990.

Gilbert, Daniel T., and Patrick S. Malone. "The Correspondence Bias." *Psychological Bulletin* 117 (1995): 21–38.

Goldman, Alvin I. *Epistemology and Cognition.* Cambridge, MA: Harvard University Press, 1986.

Haney, Craig, and Philip Zimbardo. "The Past and Future of U.S. Prison Policy: Twenty-Five Years After the Stanford Prison Experiment." *American Psychologist* 53 (1998): 709–27. Cited, pp. 709–10.

Harman, Gilbert. "Moral Philosophy Meets Social Psychology: Virtue Ethics and the Fundamental Attribution Error." *Proceedings of the Aristotelian Society* 99 (1999): 315–31.

Isen, Alice M., and Paula F. Levin. "Effect of Feeling Good on Helping: Cookies and Kindness." *Journal of Personality and Social Psychology* 21 (1972): 384–88. Cited, p. 387.

Kahneman, Daniel, and Amos Tversky. "On the Psychology of Prediction." *Psychological Review* 80 (1973): 237–51. Cited, pp. 241–43; 250–51.

Kelman, Herbert C., and V. Lee Hamilton. *Crimes of Obedience: Toward a Social Psychology of Authority and Responsibility.* New Haven and London: Yale University Press, 1989.

Latané, Bibb, and John M. Darley. *The Unresponsive Bystander: Why Doesn't He Help?* New York: Appelton-Century Crofts, 1970. Cited, pp. 46; 47–48; 59–60.

Latané, Bibb, and Steve Nida. "Ten Years of Research on Group Size and Helping." *Psychological Bulletin* 89 (1981): 308–24. Cited, p. 320.

McDowell, John. "Virtue and Reason." *Monist* 62 (1974): 330–50.

Milgram, Stanley. "Behavioral Study of Obedience." *Journal of Abnormal and Social Psychology* 67 (1963): 371–78. Cited, p. 377.

———. *Obedience to Authority.* New York: Harper and Row, 1974. Cited, pp. 56; 21; 56–61; 35; 59–62; 27–31; 1–2.

Miller, Arthur G., Barry E. Collins, and Diana F. Brief. "Perspectives on Obedience to Authority: The Legacy of the Milgram Experiments." *Journal of Social Issues* 51 (1995): 1–19. Cited, pp. 10–12.

Moore, G. E. *Principia Ethica.* Cambridge: Cambridge University Press, 1903. Cited, pp. 9–10.

Nagel, Thomas. "Ethics as an Autonomous Theoretical Subject." In *Morality as a Biological Phenomenon,* edited by Gunther S. Stent, 198–205. Berkeley and Los Angeles: University of California Press, 1980.

Nisbett, Richard E., and Lee Ross. *Human Inference: Strategies and Shortcomings of Social Judgment.* Englewood Cliffs, NJ: Prentice Hall, 1980. Cited, pp. 11, 31.

Railton, Peter. "Made in the Shade: Moral Compatiblism and the Aims of Moral Theory." *Canadian Journal of Philosophy,* Supple. Vol. 21 (1995): 79–106.

Ross, Lee. "The Intuitive Psychologist and His Shortcomings." In *Advances in Experimental Social Psychology* 10, edited by L. Berkowitz, 173–220. San Diego, CA: Academic Press, 1977.

Ross, Lee, and Richard E. Nisbett. *The Person and the Situation.* Philadelphia: Temple University Press, 1991. Cited, p. 136–38.

Schwarz, Norbert. *Cognition and Communication.* Mahwah, NJ: Lawrence Erlbaum Associates, 1996. Cited, pp. 18–23; 87.

Williams, Bernard. *Ethics and the Limits of Philosophy.* Cambridge, MA: Harvard University Press, 1985.

Wright, Jack C., and Walter Mischel. "Conditional Hedges and the Intuitive Psychology of Traits." *Journal of Personality and Social Psychology* 55 (1988): 454–69.

Zimbardo, Philip G., *et al.* "The Mind Is a Formidable Jailer: A Pirandellian Prison." *New York Times Magazine,* April 8, 1973: 38–60. Cited, pp. 38; 53–56.

John M. Doris

social self

See self and social self.

sociobiology

See biological theory.

sociology

The writings of sociology's three most important classical theorists, Émile DURKHEIM (1858–1917), Max WEBER (1864–1920), and Karl MARX (1818–1883), reveal considerable ambiguity about the place of ethics in sociological inquiry. Despite the fact that their work imparts a clear moral immediacy and a deep concern for the nature and direction of the societies in which they lived, these men insisted on the separation of ethical considerations from sociological discourse. Most sociologists today share that view. Genuine science, they hold, must avoid all judgments about such matters as the justice or injustice of particular institutional arrangements and modes of social organization.

Durkheim argued that sociology could attain the rank of a positive and empirical discipline only by avoiding all normative judgments. But he saw it as no violation of this position for the sociologist to pronounce upon what was desirable for the health or well-being of a society. Durkheim believed that shared moral values helped create social solidarity and contribute to the integration of individuals into society. The sociologist, he argued, could ascertain scientifically the appropriateness of a given set of moral values or a given social practice for a particular society. According to Durkheim, there can be no absolute standards of morality; what is desirable depends on what is required by one or another society.

Durkheim's claim that scientific sociology can pronounce on matters of ethics was one that Weber resolutely opposed. He emphasized the "absolute heterogeneity" of facts and values, and insisted that the social scientist can deal only with the factual side of the dichotomy. Weber's doctrine of value-freedom recommended that the sociologist behave as if he or she were a moral skeptic, uncommitted to any moral viewpoint. The sociologist may explain the existence of an institutional arrangement but must make no judgment about whether it is just or unjust.

In presenting the results of his or her research, Weber held, the sociologist must segregate any value-judgments that are made. Statements of ideals, of what the sociologist personally believes should be the case, do not belong to scientific inquiry. It is not only that empirical statements and value-judgments are logically different kinds of propositions, argued Weber, but the latter have an inferior epistemological status. Empirical statements are, in principle, demonstrable, while value-judgments are not. Consequently, value-judgments must be excluded from the realm of sociology.

Like Durkheim and Weber, Marx was ambiguous about the relation of ethics and sociology. His work did explicitly address the moral dimensions of modern capitalist society, and he obviously wanted to bring about a more desirable social order. But Marx considered such concepts as RIGHTS and justice to be ideological constructions that could have no critical content for evaluating social arrangements. Consistent with his general position, he argued that ethical principles always reflect the dominant economic relationships in a society. Just as with RELIGION, art, science, and other forms of "consciousness," philosophical thinking about morality is valid only for those material conditions of which it is a reflection. Moral ideas function as NORMS within a given mode of production, and thus the only applicable standard

of rights or of justice is the one inherent in the existing economic system. Ethical values are mere mystifications of the basic economic and social relations which produce them and which they reflect.

Consequently, Marx did not criticize capitalism in terms of some set of ethical standards that transcend a particular society. This is not to deny, of course, that he objected to the way control over the means of production was distributed in capitalist societies, and to the callousness and complacency of people who would tolerate a system in which many persons lived in misery and unfreedom. Certainly, his whole system of thought is pervaded by a general concern with good and evil. But the very notion of an impartial or disinterested standpoint from which social institutions could be evaluated was, for Marx, an ideological illusion.

Durkheim, Weber, and Marx agreed about the fundamental importance of ethical values in social life. Durkheim stressed their function in providing for social integration, and Weber saw them as giving meaning and purpose to individual life, while Marx conceived of ethical values as functioning to support a particular social order and to serve as a mask for class INTERESTS. And each of these classical thinkers was deeply concerned about the achievement of humane and morally acceptable social arrangements. But none of them ever attempted to rationally justify a particular set of ethical values or principles as superior to all others; Durkheim and Weber because this was ruled out by methodological prohibitions, and Marx because of his conviction that all talk about rights and justice was ideologically tinged and to be avoided at all costs.

Most sociologists today have been schooled in the tradition of value-neutrality. There is, however, no consensus about whether a value-free sociology is either possible or desirable. The dominant position—especially in empirical areas of research—sees sociological inquiry as directly analogous to inquiry in the natural sciences. The task of sociology is to investigate and explain social reality without any moral assumptions or commitments. Sociology is to be either analytic or empirical and descriptive, not ethical and prescriptive.

Many other sociologists hold that sociological inquiry is shaped unavoidably by moral considerations. They argue that different sociological perspectives are themselves rooted in particular ethical assumptions and commitments about, for example, the nature of human beings and the relationships between individuals and larger collectivities. Ethical concerns, they insist, also influence the selection of research topics and the application of sociological knowledge, as well as the sociologist's position regarding the Weberian split between description and evaluation. Some of these sociologists are forthright in stating their own value-preferences, but most share the view that ethical principles and standards cannot be rationally justified.

Sociologists combine empirical descriptions of social life and value-preferences in a number of different ways. With regard to their view of human nature, a conception of human agency broadly associated with Talcott Parsons's (1902–1979) "general theory of action" was long dominant in sociology. From this functionalist perspective, individuals are seen as being both positively motivated and socially constrained by moral values. Through the mechanism of socialization, individuals come to learn and internalize the dominant moral values. This assures that they will be motivated to meet the requirements imposed on them by the imperatives of their society, and that there is created the normative consensus necessary for social order.

Sociologists in the functionalist tradition today follow Parsons in giving society priority over the individual. Their emphasis is on the NEEDS and interests of society, and they are concerned with individuals only insofar as their conduct contributes to the health and optimal functioning of society. Every agent is seen as having the duty to act in terms of the dominant societal norms and values—whatever these may be. The appropriateness of any particular system of ethical standards and principles is determined entirely by its consequences for the functioning of the society. There can be no universal, rational justification for these standards and principles.

Partly in opposition to this emphasis on society and its needs, symbolic-interactionism, exchange theory, ethnomethodology, and a dramaturgical approach all focus on the purposeful, reasoning, goal-directed, individual actor. Some of these sociologists describe individual conduct as being guided entirely by considerations of private interest, and others portray a social world in which people's performances count above all else. Human motivation is seen as essentially amoral and people's actions as being oriented toward the achievement of social approval, POWER, prestige, wealth, or other sources of satis-

faction. At the level of collectivities, social life is conceived of in terms of competing groups striving to maximize their own interests. Since individuals and groups are assumed to pursue advantage on the basis of their available resources, COERCION, manipulation, and EXPLOITATION are seen as inevitable in social life.

Sociologists emphasizing the centrality of interests and conflict presume their own capacity to discern the underlying motivations of individuals and groups, as well as the extent to which their interests are realized. Whether focusing on the individual, the group, or the wider society, these sociologists see ethical principles as having only an instrumental value in serving different interests. Apart from their utility in the struggle for domination, such principles are completely arbitrary and unjustifiable.

A communitarian approach to sociological inquiry rejects the doctrine of private interest and explicitly combines explanatory and normative concerns. Somewhat like the consensus theorists, this perspective conceives of individual and group behavior as being regulated by ethical values. But in opposition to the position of value-neutrality espoused by the consensus sociologists, a communitarian approach is open in advocating how people ought to live and how they ought to order their society. Central to this position is the notion of a COMMON GOOD that is prior to, and characterizable independent of, the summing of individual desires and interests. Ultimate AUTHORITY is seen as rooted in the community at large, and every person ought to be ready to sacrifice his or her own individual interests for the sake of the common good. Self-fulfillment is achieved through contributions to the larger community and the common good.

In contrast to the functionalist consensus tradition, where the dominant moral norms and values are accepted by the sociologist as given, it is the community itself that determines the appropriateness of norms and values to its unique circumstances and its substantive traditions, practices, and institutional arrangements. There is, according to these communitarian sociologists, no independent perspective from which different traditions, practices, and arrangements can be assessed or evaluated.

Another value-based approach is CRITICAL THEORY, especially as represented in the work of Jürgen HABERMAS. Like the communitarians, Habermas is highly critical of self-interest theories and of value-neutral inquiry. In common with the consensus theorists, Habermas gives priority to moral values in examining social interaction. But in opposition to all the other positions examined thus far, Habermas is concerned to escape normative relativism. He argues that moral principles and normative judgments *are* capable of being rationally justified in the same manner as empirical propositions. The rational assessment of these principles and judgments, says Habermas, requires what he terms the "ideal speech situation." In a fully emancipated society, with symmetrical chances for all members to participate in unrestrained discourse, argues Habermas, consensus about both facts and values is equivalent to a justified validity.

Although Habermas defends the possibility of offering rationally grounded judgments about the justice of laws, distributive arrangements, and the like, such judgments require the realization of the ideal speech situation. Research rooted in a critical perspective helps identify structural and cultural obstacles to non-distorted communication and rational consensus. But in the absence of the actual realization of the ideal speech situation, Habermas is unable to specify the substantive outcomes of collective discourse. Thus, he must remain silent about those moral principles that ought to govern a just or humane society.

Relativism is also rejected by a type of sociological inquiry that integrates sociology and philosophical ethics. Here, too, the claim is that normative statements about moral issues are as fully capable of rational justification as explanatory ones about social life. But instead of requiring the realization of the ideal speech situation, as does Habermas, this normative sociology holds that fundamental ethical principles can be justified by appeal to certain needs common to people everywhere. Normative sociology aims not only to explain how various societal patterns and regularities come about, but also to specify the kinds of social, political, and economic arrangements required by justified ethical principles. This approach to sociological inquiry attempts to identify discrepancies between what is and what ought to be, and to suggest societal changes to reduce or eliminate these discrepancies.

See also: COMMON GOOD; COMMUNITARIANISM; CONVENTIONS; CRITICAL THEORY; CULTURAL STUDIES; DURKHEIM; ECONOMIC SYSTEMS; GROUPS, MORAL STATUS OF; HABERMAS; INDIVIDUALISM; INSTITUTIONS; MARX; MORAL RELATIVISM; MULTICULTURALISM; POLITICAL SYSTEMS; PRINCIPLISM; SKEPTICISM IN ETHICS; WEBER.

Bibliography

Alexander, Jeffrey C. *Theoretical Logic in Sociology.* Vol. 1. Berkeley: University of California Press, 1982.

Bellah, Robert N., *et al. Habits of the Heart.* Berkeley: University of California Press, 1985.

Durkheim, Émile. *Essays on Morals and Education, 1904–1920.* London: Routledge and Kegan Paul, 1979. Edited and with an introduction by W. S. F. Pickering.

Etzioni, Amitai. *The New Golden Rule.* New York: Basic Books, 1996.

Haan, Norma, *et al.,* eds. *Social Science as Moral Inquiry.* New York: Columbia University Press, 1983.

Habermas, Jürgen. *The Theory of Communicative Action.* Vol. 1. Translated by Thomas McCarthy. Boston: Beacon Press, 1984.

Marx, Karl. *Das Kapital.* 1867–1895.

Miller, Richard W. "Reason and Commitment in the Social Sciences." *Philosophy and Public Affairs* 8 (1979): 241–66.

Parsons, Talcott, and Edward Shils, eds. *Toward a General Theory of Action.* Cambridge: Harvard University Press, 1951.

Phillips, Derek L. *Toward a Just Social Order.* Princeton, NJ: Princeton University Press, 1986.

———. *Looking Backward: A Critical Appraisal of Communitarian Thought.* Princeton: Princeton University Press, 1993.

Turner, Jonathan. *The Structure of Sociological Theory.* Chicago: Dorsey Press, 1986.

Wardell, Mark L., and Stephen P. Turner, eds. *Sociological Theory in Transition.* Boston: Allen and Unwin, 1986.

Weber, Max. *The Methodology of the Social Sciences.* 1903–1917. Translated and edited by Edward A. Shils and Henry A. Finch. Glencoe, IL: Free Press, 1949.

Derek L. Phillips

Socrates (c. 470–399 B.C.E.)

Socrates was the son of a (probably) middle-class stonemason. He performed his military service as an infantryman in the Peloponnesian War (431–404 B.C.E.). His philosophical activities and his suspected impiety resulted in his trial and execution (described in Plato's *Apology* and *Phaedo*).

The Evidence on Socrates

Socrates wrote no philosophical works of his own, and our evidence on his views comes primarily from the works of PLATO (c. 430–347 B.C.E.) and Xenophon (c. 435–354 B.C.E.), in which Socrates is introduced as a speaker. Many questions arise about the historicity of Plato and Xenophon. The following assumptions are reasonable:

1. Plato's dialogues can be ordered chronologically on internal evidence, with a fair degree of reliability, on the basis of style, literary form, and philosophical content, into early, middle, and late groups. The early group includes *Apology, Euthyphro, Crito, Laches, Charmides, *Lysis, *Euthydemus, *Protagoras, *Gorgias*. The middle group includes *Meno, Phaedo, Symposium, Republic*. The late group includes *Theaetetus, *Phaedrus, Philebus, Statesman, Laws*. (This list includes only the dialogues of ethical interest. An asterisk marks those whose place in Plato's development is most disputed.)

2. The early group of dialogues can reasonably be regarded (with some qualifications about the *Protagoras* and *Gorgias*) as an accurate account of the historical Socrates. In the middle and late groups, Plato works out his own views in response to Socrates, and sometimes in criticism of him. (Presumably the early dialogues also express Plato's views at the time when he agreed with Socrates.)

3. In these early dialogues, Socrates holds and defends a moral position of his own; he does not confine himself to pointing out inconsistencies and confusions in his interlocutors.

Two points support this preference for Plato's account:

(a) ARISTOTLE's (384–322 B.C.E.) comments, especially on Socratic ethics, support Plato's account. (See *Nicomachean Ethics* 1144b28–30, 1145b22–7, *Magna moralia* 1182b15–23, *Metaphysics* 987a29–b7, 1078b17–31, *Topics* 183b1–8.)

(b) Moral philosophers after Socrates were not dependent on Plato for their knowledge of Socrates; the Socratic schools of CYNICS and CYRENAICS disagreed vigorously with each other about Socratic doctrine. The account in Plato's early dialogues explains why both Cynics and Cyrenaics thought they were Socratics.

The Main Questions about Socrates

Socrates was tried, condemned, and executed for impiety and for "corrupting the young men" by undermining their belief in conventional morality (*Apology* 19b, 23b, 24b). He regarded the charges as wholly unjustified; he claimed to reform and improve both his own moral outlook and other people's. He devoted his life to cross-examining other people about virtue; he urged them to pay attention to their souls (*i.e.*, to their moral beliefs and characters), not to wealth, POWER, and other external advantages of less importance than one's soul (*Apology* 29d–30b). He believed that examining one's life and one's conception of virtue was the best way to progress toward virtue (*Apology* 38a).

After his trial and condemnation, Socrates shows why he thinks his inquiries into virtue are morally important. He refuses the opportunity to escape into exile and to avoid the death penalty; and to justify himself, he appeals to the results of his moral inquiries. He argues that:

(a) he follows the same method of argument that he has always followed;
(b) his method of argument shows that it is always in our interest to be just rather than unjust;
(c) it is unjust to harm anyone;
(d) attempting to escape would be harming the city; and
(e) hence he will not attempt to escape (*Crito* 46b–50a).

Socrates believes that his method justifies substantive and controversial moral claims. He thinks he can show that—contrary to any doubts about the rationality of being moral—we always have overriding reason to accept morality. This argument introduces us to the 'Socratic Paradoxes,' the counterintuitive claims that fascinated and provoked moral philosophers throughout the history of Greek ethics (Cicero, *Paradoxa stoicorum* 4).

1. We are virtuous if and only if we are happy.
2. We have virtue if and only if we have knowledge.

Socrates believes that his method of argument supports these paradoxes and the practical conclusions he draws from them.

Socratic Method

The normal Socratic dialogue is a cross-examination (*elenchos*) in which Socrates eventually convinces an interlocutor that the interlocutor does not really know what he initially supposed he knew. Characteristically, the conversation sets out from an attempt to define a virtue (*Laches* 190bc, *Charmides* 159a, *Euthyphro* 5cd, *Apology* 29d–30a). The interlocutor proposes several candidate definitions and eventually the participants agree that they do not know what the virtue is.

In seeking a definition, Socrates wants an answer to his question "What is bravery (justice . . . etc.)?" He is not asking for the meaning of the word "bravery" (and hence does not want the type of definition that might appear in a dictionary). He wants a single account of, say, bravery that applies to all and only brave people and actions, and shows what is brave about each of them. This account will provide a 'standard' or 'pattern' by reference to which we can judge whether someone's actions display the virtue or not (*cf. Euthyphro* 6de).

The sort of answer that Socrates seeks for the VIRTUES will describe a persistent trait or state of a person—not simply a pattern of behavior (*Laches* 192ab). He assumes that if we examine our assumptions about virtuous people, we will understand and improve our views about which actions are virtuous. The *elenchos* makes progress because it uncovers our shared assumptions about a virtuous person, and uses these to correct some of our initial assumptions about particular virtues.

Socrates secures agreement on these points:

1. A virtue must be 'fine' (*kalon*) and beneficial. Mere fearlessness, for instance, cannot be bravery, since it might sometimes lead us to take foolish risks. (*Laches* 192cd, *Charmides* 160e–161b).

2. A virtue must include knowledge; without this we will not choose what is fine and beneficial (*Laches* 192d).
3. Each virtue is identical to knowledge of good and EVIL (*Laches* 196d, 198d).
4. All the virtues are really identical to the same knowledge (the 'unity of virtue,' *Laches* 198d, *Protagoras* 329cd, 349a–c, 359a–360e).

Agreement on the third point seems especially open to challenge. We might think knowledge is insufficient for virtue, for two reasons: (a) I might know that *x* is virtuous, but still see no overriding reason to be virtuous; I can misuse my knowledge (*Hippias Minor* 375d–376b, Aristotle, *Metaphysics* 1025a1–13); and (b) If I believe I have overriding reason to be virtuous, I may still act irrationally in choosing what I know to be worse; in that case I act incontinently, displaying WEAKNESS OF WILL (*akrasia, Protagoras* 352a–c, Aristotle, *Nicomachean Ethics* 1145b22–7).

Socrates seeks to answer these two objections, by defending two further claims:

5. We all want our own HAPPINESS (*eudaimonia*), and we do everything that we do for the sake of happiness (*Euthydemus* 278e, 280b).
6. Virtue is necessary and sufficient for happiness (*Crito* 48b, *Charmides* 174bc, 175e, *Gorgias* 470e, 507a–c).

A defense of these last two claims will answer the objections to the third, for if they are true, and we believe they are true, we will want to be virtuous.

Happiness and Reason

Socrates assumes without much argument that all our rational ACTION aims at happiness, because happiness is a suitable ultimate end to explain action and DESIRE. We do not think the mere appeal to a desire is enough to explain an action (*Gorgias* 467c–468c). We understand the action once we explain it with reference to a desire for some explanatory end, and ultimately to some self-explanatory end. Socrates claims that happiness is the only self-explanatory end (*Euthydemus* 278e, *Meno* 77b–e, *Lysis* 219b–220b). With every other end, it is reasonable and appropriate to ask, "And why did you want that?" and such a chain of questions comes to an end only when we reach happiness.

Socrates believes that

(a) all desires that explain voluntary action (*cf. Protagoras* 352d, 355a) must be rational desires; and

(b) all of an agent's rational desires must be ultimately focused on the agent's happiness.

In defending (a), he rules out the possibility of incontinence; in defending (b), he defends some form of EGOISM.

Desire and Action

To maintain that we always act on our rational desires, Socrates must refute the common view that sometimes we believe *x* is better than *y*, but still choose to do *y*, because we have a non-rational desire to do *y* that is stronger than our rational desire to do *x*.

Socrates argues against this view by claiming that it leads to absurd results. He makes two assumptions:

1. HEDONISM is true and we believe it is true; we all believe that pleasantness is just the same as goodness (*Protagoras* 353c–354e).
2. We always pursue the maximum overall PLEASURE.

Now the intuitive view of incontinence claims, according to Socrates, that

3. though A knows that *x* is better than *y*, A chooses *y*.

By (1) and (2), this amounts to

4. though A knows that *x* is pleasanter than *y*, A chooses *y* because A believes that *y* is pleasanter than *x*.

But (4) seems to imply unintelligibly inconsistent beliefs about *x* and *y* (*Protagoras* 355b–e).

This argument is open to dispute. First, it relies on a disputable hedonist claim (see further below).

But in any case, (2) is questionable. We do not seem to believe that (*e.g.*) taking revenge now will yield greater pleasure overall than we would obtain if we kept our temper; if we did believe that, we would not regard our action as incontinent. In assuming (2), Socrates seems to assume something that a believer in incontinence ought not to concede without argument.

Socrates' argument against incontinence helps to show why he believes that knowledge is sufficient for virtue, and in particular why he takes seriously the analogy between a virtue and a craft (*technê*) such as shoemaking, navigation, or medicine (*Charmides* 165c–e, *Euthydemus* 288d–292e, *Protagoras* 356c–357e). We might think the analogy breaks down at a crucial point; experts in a craft are free to misuse their craft-knowledge or to leave it unused, but it is essential to virtuous people that they perform the virtuous action on the right occasion. Socrates is aware of this apparent disanalogy between craft and virtue (*Hippias Minor* 375d). But he does not think it is a real disanalogy. Virtuous people do not misuse their knowledge; but this is not because virtue is anything more than knowledge, but because no one has any motive for misusing the sort of knowledge that virtue is. For, in Socrates' view, virtue is simply the knowledge of what promotes the agent's happiness; and when we have this knowledge, we will not misuse it (since there is no such thing as incontinence).

Eudaimonism

To show that virtue is simply the knowledge of what promotes the agent's happiness, Socrates must defend his assumption that all of an agent's rational desires are ultimately focused on the agent's happiness; then he must show why virtue is the knowledge of what promotes the agent's happiness.

Socrates takes it to be uncontroversial that "doing well" (*eu prattein*) or "being happy" (*eudaimonein*; *Euthydemus* 278e, 280b, 282e) is what we all want, and that anything else we want is something we want only for the sake of our happiness. He assumes that the question, "How am I to live?" (*cf. Laches* 187e–188a, *Gorgias* 492d, 500c) is the same as the question "How am I to be happy?" (*Gorgias* 472cd).

Socrates assumes the truth of a form of egoism (insofar as he claims that I have overriding reason to pursue my own interest) and more specifically of

EUDAIMONISM (insofar as he connects my interest to my happiness). Some version of this eudaimonist assumption is almost universal in Greek ethics, but Socrates does not face all the questions it raises. Our view of its plausibility will be affected by our view of the nature of happiness.

The use of the English "happiness" to render *eudaimonia* should not be taken to imply that *eudaimonia* must consist in "feeling happy"—in a feeling of pleasure or contentment. As Socrates' assumptions about *eudaimonia* suggest, he need not have anything more definite in mind than "doing well" or "welfare." Greek moralists, hedonists and non-hedonists alike, assume that some argument is required if one wants to claim that happiness is identical to pleasure; those who take eudaimonism for granted do not thereby take hedonism for granted. Still, if Socrates is to be justified in claiming that virtue is necessary and sufficient for happiness, he needs some further account of what happiness consists in (Aristotle, *Nicomachean Ethics* 1095a17–22).

Though Socrates does not directly face these questions about happiness, some of his remarks suggest three different conceptions of happiness that he might have in mind: happiness as pleasure (hedonism), happiness as the satisfaction of feasible desires (an adaptive conception), and happiness as fulfillment of one's nature.

Happiness as Pleasure

In the *Protagoras,* Socrates seems to identify happiness with the maximization of pleasure over pain (353b–354e). He argues: when we take an unpleasant-tasting medicine or force ourselves to face some danger we feel like running away from, we expect the "painful" course of action to yield more pleasure than pain, and the "pleasant" course of action to yield more pain than pleasure, when their total effects are considered.

Socrates argues that if we think *x* is better on the whole than *y,* we think so because we think *x* yields more pleasure on the whole than *y.* He might well be right to assume that thinking *x* good is connected with finding *x* pleasant; but he hardly justifies the strong hedonist claim that *x*'s goodness consists in, and is explained by, *x*'s pleasantness.

We might challenge the strong hedonist claim by suggesting that Socrates has got the relation be-

tween goodness and pleasantness the wrong way round. Perhaps our finding *x* pleasant depends on our thinking *x* good; hence, the good person will take pleasure in good things and the bad person in bad things. On this view, an appeal to pleasure provides no neutral test of which person is better off. In the *Gorgias* (497d–500a), Socrates seems to recognize the force of this objection, and both Plato and Aristotle find it cogent.

Happiness as Satisfied Desire

In the *Gorgias,* Socrates suggests a conception of happiness that includes two claims:

1. If we have satisfied our desires, we are happy.
2. If we adapt our desires to the resources available for satisfying them, and we satisfy these desires once we have adapted them, we are happy (*Gorgias* 492d–494a).

In (2), Socrates explains how he interprets (1). Suppose I have very extravagant desires, requiring large external resources, but lack the external resources to satisfy them. I can still—in Socrates' view—be happy without acquiring large external resources. For if I adapt my desires to the available resources, the fulfillment of these adapted and feasible desires is happiness. If the crucial feature of happiness is the fact that my desires are satisfied—and not the fact that these particular desires, or a large number of desires, are satisfied—then the adaptive strategy seems reasonable.

If we accept this adaptive conception of happiness, then we can explain why some apparent harms are not genuine harms. We may think we are much better off with a large supply of external resources (providing opportunities for expanding and satisfying desires), and that we are much worse off if we lose these resources. Socrates argues that such a loss is no real harm; for if we adapt our desires to our reduced resources, we can still be no less happy than we would have been if we had satisfied the desires requiring larger resources.

Happiness as Fulfillment of Nature

Sometimes Socrates assumes that life is not worth living with an unhealthy body (*Crito* 47de, *Gorgias*

505a), and argues by analogy that it is not worth living with a corrupt and diseased soul. He seems to assume that happiness requires more than satisfied desire. For it seems quite possible for rational agents with a bodily disease to adapt their desires to accommodate their disease, and then to satisfy their adapted desires; but Socrates cannot consistently allow that this satisfied condition is happiness, if he thinks health is necessary for happiness. He apparently assumes that without bodily health, say, I am not fulfilling my natural capacities, and that this fact by itself shows—contrary to the hedonist and the adaptive conception—that I am not happy.

This conception of happiness as fulfillment of one's natural capacities strongly influences Plato, Aristotle, and the Stoics. Though Socrates might be taken to suggest it, he does not see any conflict with an adaptive conception.

Why Virtue Is Sufficient for Happiness

Socrates' main argument to show that virtue is sufficient for happiness relies on the claim that virtue is sufficient for the proper use of all the ordinary goods (wealth, health, strength, etc.). Socrates infers that it is sufficient for happiness, and that therefore the ordinary goods are not really goods at all (*Euthydemus* 280b–281b). His argument assumes that no particular level of ordinary goods is necessary for happiness, and that the virtuous person's use of whatever ordinary goods may be available is all that matters for happiness.

Can Socrates defend this assumption by appeal to one of his three conceptions of happiness?

The hedonist conception raises difficulties. For it seems reasonable to assume that larger external resources offer greater pleasures. If we are to show that this assumption is false, we need to know more about the connection between pleasure and goodness (*cf. Gorgias* 504e–505b).

The adaptive conception suggests a partial defense of Socrates. I might suppose that if I cheat, I can get the money I think I need to satisfy my desires, and hence to secure my happiness. An adaptive account implies that this argument is mistaken. If I forgo an ordinary good, I simply need to adapt my desires to the new circumstances, and I will not necessarily forgo any happiness; hence, the mere fact that virtuous people lose ordinary goods does not show that they lose happiness. But Socrates does not show that an adaptive attitude is sufficient for the sorts of actions that we normally expect from a virtuous person. We do not expect a just person to be totally indifferent to the INTERESTS of others; but an adaptive conception of happiness does not seem to preclude indifference to their interests.

The third conception of happiness as fulfillment of nature allows a defense of Socrates' claims about virtue, if he can show that virtuous action fulfills our nature better than vicious action does. Socrates does not develop such an argument (but *cf. Gorgias* 506b–507c).

Socrates is confident that justice and morality are always in our interest. He insists that a just person will allow nothing to count against doing the just action, no matter what the cost may be (*Apology* 28b). If Socrates were to choose an ordinary good over the just course of action, he would be choosing an action that is bad for him, and he refuses to do this; that is why he refuses to propose an alternative to the death penalty (*Apology* 37b–e). But his views about happiness and virtue do not show that he has good grounds for his confidence.

See also: ARISTOTLE; CHARACTER; CYNICS; CYRENAICS; DESIRE; EGOISM; *EUDAIMONIA*, -ISM; HAPPINESS; HEDONISM; PLATO; PLEASURE; SOPHISTS; STOICISM; VIRTUE ETHICS; VIRTUES; WEAKNESS OF WILL.

Bibliography

Primary Sources

Plato. *Complete Works.* Edited by J. M. Cooper and D. S. Hutchison. Indianapolis: Hackett, 1997. Translations of most of Plato's dialogues.

———. *Euthyphro, Apology, and Crito.* Edited by J. Burnet. Oxford: Clarendon Press, 1924.

———. *Protagoras.* Translated by C. C. W. Taylor. Oxford: Clarendon Press, 1976.

———. *Gorgias.* Edited by E. R. Dodds. Oxford: Clarendon Press, 1959.

———. *Gorgias.* Translated by T. Irwin. Oxford: Clarendon Press, 1979.

Secondary Sources

Gosling, J. C. B., and C. C. W. Taylor. *The Greeks on Pleasure.* Oxford: Clarendon Press, 1982. Chapters 2–4.

Guthrie, W. K. C. *A History of Greek Philosophy.* Vol. 3. Cambridge: Cambridge University Press, 1969.

Irwin, T. H. *Plato's Ethics.* Oxford: Oxford University Press, 1995. Chapters 2–8.

Socrates

Kraut, Richard. *Socrates and the State.* Princeton, NJ: Princeton University Press, 1984.

Penner, T. "The Unity of Virtue." *Philosophical Review* 82 (1973): 35–68.

Santas, G. *Socrates.* London: Routledge and Kegan Paul, 1979.

Vlastos, Gregory. "Socrates." *Proceedings of the British Academy* 74 (1988): 89–111.

——. *Platonic Studies.* 2d ed. Princeton, NJ: Princeton University Press, 1981. See chapter 10, "The Unity of the Virtues in the *Protagoras.*"

——. "Socrates on *Acrasia.*" *Phoenix* 23 (1969): 71–88.

——. *Socrates: Ironist and Moral Philosopher.* Ithaca: Cornell University Press, 1991.

——. *Socratic Studies.* Cambridge: Cambridge University Press, 1994.

——, ed. *The Philosophy of Socrates.* Garden City, NY: Doubleday, 1971.

T. H. Irwin

Sophists

The Sophists were a group of theorists and professional teachers active in Greece during the second half of the fifth century B.C.E. Although some of them were polymaths sharing an interest in natural philosophy with the pre-Socratics, their primary focus was on moral, social, and political issues and rhetoric. Their importance for the development of Greek moral theory was considerable, as was their influence on contemporary writers like Thucydides (c. 460–c. 399 B.C.E.) and Euripides (480 or 484–406 B.C.E.). But despite their common interests, the Sophists were not members of a school bound by allegiance to a certain set of beliefs.

The term 'Sophist' is related to *sophos* (wise), a Greek word frequently applied to poets and statesmen thought to have PRACTICAL WISDOM based on superior understanding of the divine and the human. Indeed, PLATO (c. 430–347 B.C.E.) has PROTAGORAS (c. 490–421 B.C.E.), the earliest Sophist, link his instruction with that of poets (*Protagoras* 316c–e). This propaideutic role of the Sophists made them controversial and often suspect, for generally neither their style nor their ideas were traditional. Aristophanes (c. 448–388 B.C.E.) in the *Clouds,* a comic parody which (in some respects misleadingly) casts SOCRATES (c. 470–399 B.C.E.) as a prototypical Sophist, portrays Sophistic thought and education as a dangerous innovation that promotes moral decline and the triumph of worse arguments over better ones.

The most famous Sophists were Protagoras, Gorgias, Prodicus, and Hippias. Others generally included on this list by scholars are Antiphon, Lycophron, Thrasymachus, Callicles, Critias, Alcidamas, Euthydemus, and two anonymous authors: Anonymus Iamblichi and the author of the *Double Arguments* (*Dissoi Logoi*). The list itself is controversial: Lycophron and Alcidamas were active in the fourth century; it is not certain that Callicles was a historical figure; scholars are undecided about whether this Antiphon is to be identified with Antiphon the Orator; Critias was not a teacher, and most recent commentators are now inclined to attribute his Sophistic fragments to Euripides. Some scholars have also noted similarities between the Sophists and Socrates, although it would be misleading to identify him as a Sophist.

Evidence and Interpretive Difficulties

Many difficulties confront anyone studying the ethical views of the Sophists. With few exceptions, only short fragments remain from the many books and treatises whose titles have been preserved. The only substantial surviving texts of relevance to ethical questions are Prodicus's *Choice of Heracles;* the papyrus fragments of Antiphon's *On Truth* which were discovered and published early in the twentieth century; and the two anonymous treatises mentioned above. Scholars must thus reconstruct Sophistic views in large part from reports of later writers, especially Plato. In numerous dialogues such as *Protagoras, Gorgias, Hippias Major, Hippias Minor,* and the first book of the *Republic,* Plato discusses and almost always rejects the views of the Sophists. It is clear that his philosophical agenda and disagreements with the Sophists may have seriously distorted his accounts of their views; at the very least it is difficult to determine to what extent the views of the Sophists expressed in his dialogues are historically accurate. Scholarly attitudes toward Plato have thus strongly influenced modern interpretations of the Sophists. Whereas partisans of Plato have tended to view them as enemies of reason and truth who were merely interested in winning arguments, Plato's detractors have praised them as empiricists, positivists, democrats, and liberals. The most recent scholarship has been more balanced in assessing the Sophists and Plato's view of them.

Although a noncontroversial account of the overall moral views of individual Sophists is impossible, we can at least delineate the issues they discussed and debated. Factors which significantly influenced their analyses include traditional Greek views of the benefits and importance of *nomoi* (laws, customs) as the foundation for civilized life, a growing awareness of cultural diversity, and tensions between a moral or nonmoral understanding of *arete* (EXCELLENCE, virtue).

Legal Conception of Morality

Origins of society, law, and morality. A number of Sophists argued that human beings once lived in something like a Hobbesian state of nature, but were forced to band together as a political unit for convenience and for protection against injury either from wild animals or other human beings. Legal and moral prescriptions (*nomima kai dikaia*: things that are legal—conventional, customary—and just) arose then precisely when political communities were established.

This legal conception of morality involves three major points: (l) moral prescriptions are embodied in laws requiring other-regarding, cooperative behavior among citizens; (2) these prescriptions are a necessary condition for the existence of political communities and hence for human survival; and (3) they are products of human agreement or convention. This is essentially the view offered by Protagoras in his "Great Speech" (*Protagoras*, 322c–328d). Although some commentators argue that the Great Speech does not represent the views of the historical Protagoras, it is clear that other Sophists held these ideas. In Plato's *Republic* (358c–360d), Glaucon refers to Sophistic views when he talks about those who argue that the origin of political communities is a compact entered upon by those desiring laws to protect their interests and physical well-being. Lycophron (frag. 3) also believed, at least implicitly, in a compact in which the laws become the "guarantor of mutual justice," as did Critias (frag. 25).

Reasons to obey laws. All Sophists appear to have believed, consciously or unconsciously, that the proper criterion for action is rational self-interest. Those who were proponents of the legal conception

of morality thus argued that the laws should be obeyed because they were beneficial for the individual citizen and the community as a whole—and not because morality requires it or because the citizens had entered into a compact. In addition to Protagoras's argument that they are needed for political communities, the Anonymus Iamblichi, for example, argues that in law-abiding societies, men can live in peace and security and can trust each other in an environment that is free from factional strife and respectful of each individual's INTERESTS (7.1–12). This argument relies on RECIPROCITY: mutual benefits and mutual acts of justice secure the benefits everyone wants. Another approach was to argue for the benefits individuals receive from exercising *arete*: love of friends, community honors and admiration (Prodicus in the *Choice of Heracles*).

Objections and Alternatives to Law as Morality

Other Sophists found three major weaknesses in such law-based notions of morality. First, the laws of actual communities do not protect the weak. Speaking as a disillusioned moralist, Thrasymachus argues that the *nomima kai dikaia* of a political community merely represent the advantage of the most powerful individual or group in the state (*Rep.* 338c–339a). However overstated, this view does undermine the legal conception of morality for all but ideal political communities.

Second, obeying laws is not always beneficial to agents. In fragment 44A, Antiphon argues that infractions against nature (*physis*) always result in injury or harm to agents, but not infractions against the law (*nomos*), and thus it is beneficial for agents to disobey the law when they can escape notice in doing so. The *nomos-physis* antithesis (convention *vs.* nature, man-made *vs.* NATURAL LAW) was commonly appealed to in fifth-century thought. Antiphon uses *physis* as a term for self-interested human nature. Even if he himself did not accept this immoralist position or adopt self-interest as his criterion for action as some have argued, his objection to defenders of the legal conception of morality cannot be successfully countered by Protagorean arguments. A more extreme form of IMMORALISM was adopted by Callicles, who in Plato's *Gorgias* (482d–484a, 491e–492c) argues that justice consists in obeying the higher law of *physis* which sanctions the pursuit of POWER and PLEASURE by the strong. This extreme immoralism finds no parallel in other Sophistic texts; and since there is no other evidence for Callicles, Plato may have created him to show how such views might arise out of the inadequacies of Sophistic thought, particularly that of Gorgias, who trained his students for success in political life, but did not, it appears, teach them moral *arete* (*Meno* 95c).

Third, (most) laws lack universal validity. As Hippias noted, laws are mere products of human agreement, are subject to change, and can impose artificial and unnecessary restrictions on natural human tendencies or abilities (Plato *Protagoras* 337c–d; Xenophon *Memorabilia* IV.iv.14–25). Hippias is no immoralist, however: for him, valid laws would be those grounded in *physis*, that is, those which are universally accepted. Protagoras is susceptible to this type of objection: although he could ground a system of laws that guarantees community survival, he cannot ground any specific law in anything but human agreement.

Ethical Ideals

Those Sophists adopting the legal conception of morality understood morality to mean obeying the laws. Among the VIRTUES required of citizens are justice, piety, and moderation/temperance (*Protagoras* 322e–323a); but although these virtues require discipline, they are not yet seen as inner qualities of the soul as Plato makes them. Presumably they represent the kind of action required by the laws, but evidence for Sophistic views of virtue is meager. However, insofar as proponents of the legal conception of morality like Protagoras and the Anonymus Iamblichi tended to think in terms of well-functioning states marked by FRIENDSHIP among citizens, a high level of virtue was needed. Their model for the superior and wise citizen was one who benefited the state by persuading the citizens to adopt advantageous courses of action (*Theaetetus* 167b–c). Although the community of citizens was broadly understood, there is no indication that they argued that all members of the community should share in citizenship.

Among those who objected to the legal conception of morality, Hippias and Antiphon presented a particularly promising approach to moral theory by arguing that *physis* recognizes no distinctions between barbarians and Greeks or between people of noble or lowly birth. But there is no indication that they concluded from this that people have a moral obligation to treat everyone, including slaves, equally. Nor can we say what conclusions, if any, Alcidamas drew from his claim that God made no one a slave (scholiast at Aristotle *Rhetoric* 1373b).

Also noteworthy is Antiphon's focus on the agents of action, an emphasis which shifted discussion of virtues away from the political sphere to the individual. For example, he discusses the inadvisability of hoarding money (frags. 53, 53a, 54) and indulging in immediate pleasures (frag. 58). In fragments 58, 59, 60, and 61, he argues that discipline and self-mastery are necessary for the successful pursuit of the good life. However, although successful pursuit requires a certain inner state, the actual components of the good life are traditional and external: wealth, possessions, health, honors, and a good reputation (frags. 45, 54). Nevertheless, Antiphon seems to have gone farther than any other Sophist in characterizing the good for persons.

Importance and Legacy

The fact that Plato not only attempted to refute Sophistic views, but also used them as springboards for his own philosophical positions, testifies to their importance. The Sophistic belief that *arete* was teachable led to the Socratic/Platonic doctrine of virtue as knowledge, as well as to Plato's adoption of Protagoras's enlightened view that PUNISHMENT of wrongdoers should be educational, not retributive. One of the major projects of Plato's moral theory was to demonstrate that morality is good for one's soul, thereby resolving the Sophistic conflict between *nomos* (morality) and *physis* (self-interest). Antiphon prepared the way for this project by focusing on the agents of action and the good for persons and by indicating that the resolution of the conflict depends on showing that wrongdoing always harms the agent.

Perhaps the most important contribution of the Sophists was methodological: They explored moral issues through rational argumentation without ultimate appeals to myth or RELIGION. And although Plato finds fault with their emphasis on rhetorical skills, it is arguable that at least some of the Sophists practiced a method of question and answer similar to the Socratic elenchus (*Protagoras* 339 ff.). This method was related to or synonymous with antilogic, a system of opposing one *logos* or account to another one in order to point out inconsistencies. Such a method is a powerful tool in the search for rational answers to social, political, and moral issues.

See also: COMMUNITARIANISM; CONVENTION; COOPERATION, CONFLICT, AND COORDINATION; EXCELLENCE; FRIENDSHIP; IDEALIST ETHICS; IMMORALISM; MORAL COMMUNITY, BOUNDARIES OF; NATURAL LAW; NORMS; OBEDIENCE TO LAW; PLATO; PRACTICAL WISDOM; PRESCRIPTIVISM; PROTAGORAS; RECIPROCITY; SOCRATES.

Bibliography

Diels, Hermann, and Walter Kranz, comps. *Die Fragmente der Vorsokratiker, Vol. 2.* 6th ed. Berlin: Weidmannsche, 1952. Definitive collection of the fragments in the original Greek.

Freeman, Kathleen, tr. *Ancilla to the Pre-Socratic Philosophers: A Complete Translation of the Fragments in Diels, "Fragmente der Vorsokratiker."* Cambridge, MA: Harvard University Press, 1957 [1948].

———. *The Pre-Socratic Philosophers: A Companion to Diels, "Fragmente der Vorsokratiker."* 2d ed. Reprint. Cambridge, MA: Harvard University Press, 1966.

Guthrie, W. K. C. *The Sophists.* Cambridge: Cambridge University Press, 1971. A classic overview with extensive bibliography.

Kerferd, G. B. *The Sophistic Movement.* Cambridge: Cambridge University Press, 1981. A good, recent overview.

Nill, Michael. *Morality and Self-Interest in Protagoras, Antiphon, and Democritus.* Leiden: Brill, 1985. Analyzes Sophistic views bearing on the issue of reasons to be moral.

Romilly, Jacqueline de. *The Great Sophists in Periclean Athens.* Translated by Janet Lloyd. Oxford: Clarendon Press, 1992. Tr. of *Les grands Sophistes dans l'Athènes de Périclès,* Editions de Fallois, 1988.

Sprague, Rosamond K., ed. *The Older Sophists: A Complete Translation by Several Hands of the Fragments in "Die Fragmente der Vorsokratiker" with a New Edition of "Antiphon" and "Euthydemus."* Columbia: University of South Carolina Press, 1972. English translations of the fragments and ancient testimony.

Michael Nill

Soviet Ethical Theory

The Early Period

The beginning of the 1920s was marked by lively discussion among Soviet ethical theorists of the "Darwinian Marxism" of Karl Kautsky (1854–1938). Kautsky had attempted to plug the "ethics gap" in Marxist theory by means of the Darwinian hypothesis sketched in *The Descent of Man* (1871). According to this hypothesis, "social instincts" had a survival value for intraspecific struggle that had established them firmly in pre-human animals. For Kautsky, this provided an adequate naturalistic ground for the otherwise inexplicably powerful sense of moral obligation in human beings. The attempt had only limited theoretical success: its stress on *biological* factors generated theoretical tension with the Marxist stress on *historical* factors, including the "class nature" (*klassovost'*) of moral obligation. In any case, this was one of the unsettled philosophical debates which Joseph Stalin (1879–1953) closed off in 1931, when he dismissed and denounced the leading Soviet philosopher of the period, A.M. Deborin (1881–1964), for, among other offenses, "holding erroneous Kautskyan views in ethics."

The Withering Away of Morality

It was widely assumed among Soviet theorists in the late 1920s that, with the "building of socialism," certain elements of the ideological superstructure—RELIGION, in the first instance, but also law and morality—would "wither away." Many theorists considered expressions like 'socialist law' and 'socialist morality' to be oxymorons. They regarded morality in general, and the idea of duty in particular, as "bourgeois." In consequence, they tended to focus their theoretical attention on other areas of philosophy—dialectics, philosophy of science, the critique of "bourgeois" thinkers—which they considered more promising (than ethics) for Marxist analysis.

The Stalinist Legacy

Stalin changed all that, introducing a series of measures to codify Soviet law and strengthen such social INSTITUTIONS—formerly slated for withering away—as the FAMILY and the school. The Stalin Constitution (1936) was heralded as the "moral code of Soviet society." The Stalinist rapprochement of law and morality continued through the 1980s: to be a moral person is to obey the laws of the Soviet state and to despise and denounce violators of those laws. That morality can be developed by a code of law is a quite un-Marxist claim: it implies that an element of the ideological superstructure can directly modify human conduct, regardless of what economic base is operative. A similarly un-Marxist assumption with respect to morality has come to the fore in discussion (since the 1960s) of socialist morality as an "instrument of social control."

From the early 1930s until 1950, theoretical discussion and philosophical critique of ethical issues was crowded out by ideological celebration of the superiority of socialist morality and ideological abuse of "bourgeois morality." Curiously, it was Stalin's widely discussed essay on "Marxism and Linguistics" (1950) that, by admitting the existence of social and cultural realities (such as language) that were a part neither of superstructure nor base, opened up a limited theoretical space for the relatively independent development of socialist morality and Soviet ethical theory.

After Stalin

The turn to serious work in ethical theory was not appreciably advanced by Nikita Khrushchev's (1894–1971) de-Stalinization campaign of 1956, accompanied as it was by a massive "re-Leninization" of Soviet society and ideology. However, a second move by Khrushchev—the promulgation of a very un-Marxist document grandiosely labeled "The Moral Code of the Builder of Communism" (1961)—opened the floodgates not only to detailed interpretation and defense of the Code's twelve principles, but also to increasingly professional work in ethical theory, a process which has run parallel to the increasing professionalization of Soviet philosophy generally between the 1960s and 1991.

"The Simple Laws of Morality and Justice"

A central question, raised in a 1916 polemic between G. V. Plekhanov (1856–1918) and L. I. Aksel'rod (1868–1946), on the one side, and Iu. O. Martov (1873–1923), on the other—and broached again in the mid-1960s—concerns what Karl MARX (1818–1883) had called "die einfachen Gesetze der Sittlichkeit und Gerechtigkeit." From comments Marx made in a letter (November 4, 1864) to Frederick ENGELS (1820–1895), it appears that this was a theoretically unserious insertion, for tactical reasons, in Marx's inaugural address to the First Inter-

national. Marx, clearly, did not view the "simple laws of morality and justice" as transcending the class-relativity of moral NORMS and judgments. Yet, Marx had *said,* and had repeated in 1870 after the outbreak of the Franco-Prussian War, that such "simple laws" should govern the relations not only among individuals but also among nations. Plekhanov concluded that Imperial Germany, by violating the neutrality of Belgium (which it had a treaty obligation to respect) had, in August 1914, broken just such "simple laws" and thereby earned the moral condemnation of Marxists. Lenin (1870–1924) and Trotsky (1879–1940) followed Martov in ridiculing such claims as inconsistent with the class-nature of morality, insisting that *all* of the combatants in World War I were capitalists and imperialists whose policies and actions were *equally* reprehensible to serious Marxists.

In any case, the "Moral Code of the Builder of Communism" is filled with simple norms—norms not specific to either "proletarian" or "bourgeois" morality—*e.g.,* "honesty and truthfulness, moral purity, [and] modesty . . . ; mutual respect in the family." (Other, more partisan and controversial, aspects of the "Moral Code" will be noted in the sequel.) During the 1980s, Soviet ethical theorists have placed increasing emphasis on the "universally human" (*obshchechelovecheskie*) or "all-human" (*vsechelovecheskie*) aspects of morality. This represents a move away from the theoretical position of Marx, Engels, and Lenin in the direction of common sense; and it can be "justified" (following the lead of Plekhanov and Aksel'rod) by an appeal to Marx's comments—however unseriously they may have been meant—about the "simple laws of morality and justice."

Leninist Instrumentalism

Soviet ethical theory is not only Marxist, it is also Leninist, and its Leninism is expressed in a pervasively instrumental view of morality as (1) a *means* to facilitate the building of a future communist society as *end;* and (2) more generally, as an instrument of "social control." Lenin had declared in 1920 that morality is "what serves to destroy the old exploiting society and to unite all toilers around the proletariat, which is building a new, communist society," adding "Our morality is wholly subordinated to the interests of the class struggle of the proletariat," and summing up: "At the foundation of communist morality lies the [present] struggle for the strengthening and [future] completion of communism."

Soviet ethical theorists still quote these Machiavellian pronouncements often and approvingly. But they now claim that much more needs to be said to define and clarify the nature of socialist morality. This is true enough, but much of what is most important is still passed over in silence. Soviet theorists explicitly embrace the powerful future orientation of both Marx and Lenin, but they are reticent about the corollary of that future orientation, namely, the devaluing of the present and overvaluing of the future, the instrumentalizing of present persons for the sake of the communist future. Present persons, viewed as means, may be either facilitating or obstructive of the future end. One of the modes of obstruction which Khrushchev found intolerable was large-scale crime against socialist (*i.e.,* state and public) PROPERTY. In 1961, the year of the promulgation of the "Moral Code," he introduced the death penalty for non-violent crimes, crimes not against persons but only against property. The Soviet state, between 1961 and 1988, took the *lives* of some 500 of its citizens, persons whose only crime was to have taken or misused the *property* of the state. What is of particular relevance in the present context is that even under the conditions of *glasnost'* ("openness," initiated by Mikhail Gorbachev in 1985), no Soviet ethical theorist has ventured to break the deafening theoretical silence which surrounded this topic until the early 1990s.

"Marxist Humanism"

Despite repeated and insistent claims that Soviet ethical, social, and legal principles are "humanistic," there has been a conspicuous failure to recognize that the HUMANISM in question—like Marx's own—is a future-oriented "humanism of ideals," fully compatible with the instrumentalizing of living persons for the sake of a future end, fully compatible even with "transitional totalitarianism." Such a humanism stands in sharp contrast to a present-oriented "humanism of principles." Only the latter precludes as morally unacceptable the instrumentalizing of living persons for the sake of "building socialism" or achieving the communist ideal (see Kline). A parallel distinction, equally ignored by Soviet ethical theorists, is that between a (present-oriented) morality of *rights* and a (future-oriented) morality of *emancipation* (see Lukes). It is clear that the dominant Marxist-Leninist approach has always been sweepingly negative toward a humanism of principles or a morality of RIGHTS. Thus, the familiar insistence on the "humanism" of Soviet law and morality turns out to involve a rhetorically impressive but theoretically empty claim.

A welcome move in the direction of both a morality of rights and a humanism of principles was made in 1988 by Ivan T. Frolov (1929–1999), although Frolov used neither of these expressions. Admitting that Marxist-Leninist ethical theory was a relatively undeveloped discipline, he stressed that it would need to be developed in such a way as to provide a theoretical guarantee that humanistic ends would never again be pursued by recourse to anti-humanistic means. In the published version of this address, Frolov's strong statement is slightly weakened, referring only to the "necessity for the complete harmony of humane (*gumannye*) means with the humanistic (*gumanisticheskie*) ends to be realized [through those means]."

Devotion to Communism, Collectivism, Altruism

Principle 1 of the "Moral Code" is "devotion (*predannost'*) to the communist cause." This turns out to mean, as many Soviet commentators have made clear, "devotion to the U.S.S.R. and its ruling Communist Party," which in turn means—as Scanlan puts it—"unquestioning obedience to [the] state authority [of the moment]." Principle 11, which urges an "uncompromising attitude toward the enemies of communism," requires "love toward one part of humanity and hostility toward another [part]"—which offers "ample evidence of an anti-humanist spirit."

Principle 5 enjoins collectivism, which Soviet ethical theorists standardly equate with ALTRUISM, opposing both to EGOISM or self-interest. The matter is not so simple. Consider the case of a Soviet accountant who has reason to suspect that a fellow employee is embezzling substantial state funds and is thus subject, if apprehended, to the death penalty. Given the severity of PUNISHMENT for a crime against property, ordinary altruism might well motivate the accountant to conceal his suspicions and even, if necessary, help the culprit avoid apprehension. Collectivism would clearly require that he denounce his fellow employee forthwith. And if he did so, his conduct might well be motivated by self-interest: he could be rewarded, for timely denunciation of his co-worker, with money, public recognition, and professional preferment.

Value Theory

Soviet Marxist-Leninist value theory may be said to have sprung fullblown—in a highly un-Marxist fashion, since no *individual* theorist is supposed to play a significant part in the development of theoretical disciplines—from the brow of V. P. Tugarinov (1898–1978), who, in a series of works, the first of which appeared in 1960, set out the principles of this new "science." Tugarinov's theory is naturalistic and relativistic, interpreting values as the products of social acts of valuing, acts which in turn serve to satisfy NEEDS and INTERESTS. The question of the objectivity and validity of values remains obscure, as does the question of whether, and if so in what sense, value judgments are cognitive and hence characterizable as 'true' or 'false'. Tugarinov's work stirred up strong resistance among Soviet Marxist-Leninists. Most notable of these was O. G. Drobnitsky (1933–1973), who sensed a Nietzschean "irrationalism" in the talk about values, and called the "problem of values" a pseudo-problem. He dismissed value theory as an abortive attempt to elevate the "logic of feeling" to the status of a quasi-theory. Value-consciousness (*tsennostnoe soznanie*) is for Drobnitsky a defective form of rational Marxist-Leninist knowledge of the laws of historical development. Values, he insists, are properties of "social objects" and should be studied not by philosophers but by social psychologists, who will investigate "scientifically" the ways in which values are produced and reproduced (see Fleischer).

Tugarinov's approach prevailed in the face of Drobnitsky's objections. But with the talk about Marxist-Leninist value theory there was a good deal of breathless apologia for the "values of Soviet society" and the "values unique to the Soviet socialist way of life." Certain of the ideological claims of Soviet value theorists, such as that the "absolute value" of human life has long been recognized in Soviet institutions and practice, ring hollow against the massive instrumentalizing of human life through recourse to the death penalty for crimes against socialist property.

Recovery of the Past

The past dozen years have seen a remarkable rediscovery and (generally positive) reassessment by Soviet philosophers of earlier Russian thinkers such as Vladimir Soloviev (1853–1900), Lev Shestov (1866–1938), and Nicholas Berdyaev (1874–1948), who had previously been dismissed with such abusive epithets as "reactionary, idealistic, and mystical." There have also been solid and serious studies of the history of Western ethical theory. In the address cited above, Frolov declared: "We are turning to the traditions of world philosophy, including Russian philosophy. We are studying the works of outstanding Russian philosophers who were previously neglected, such as V. Soloviev, N. Fyodorov, N. Berdyaev and, of course, the works of L. Tolstoy and F. Dostoevsky." As Frolov was surely aware, Soloviev and Fyodorov offered trenchant criticisms of the Marxists of their day, and Berdyaev, in the first decade of the twentieth century, sharply criticized the Marxist class-theory of morality.

Frolov's mention of Tolstoy (1828–1910) and Dostoevsky (1821–1881) is especially interesting in the light of Iuri Davydov's fascinating and controversial book. Davydov drew the immediate wrath of Soviet hard-liners, both for his aloofness from Marxist-Leninist positions (Davydov fails to discuss either communist morality or the communist ideal) and for his sympathetic treatment of the moral, and also *religious,* views of Tolstoy and Dostoevsky. He argues that these giants of "classical Russian literature" were also the formulators of a "classical moral philosophy" which established—against both Schopenhauerian pessimism and Nietzschean amoralism—the absolute moral distinction between good and EVIL, celebrating the moral VIRTUES of self-denial and sacrificial LOVE.

Davydov is perhaps the most extreme example of a more general move on the part of Soviet ethical theorists away from the rigidly Marxist-Leninist positions of earlier years toward a more capacious ethical theory. Another striking case is that of Mil'ner-Irinin (1911–1989), whose ethical treatise, composed in the early 1960s, is still considered too controversial for Soviet publication. Two chapters from the book were included in a collective volume (see Bandzeladze) and a complete German translation has recently appeared. The author moves away from Marxist-Leninist CONSEQUENTIALISM and instrumentalism in the direction of a quasi-Kantian deontological position, tinged with religious imagery and rhetoric, that places central stress on the principles of CONSCIENCE and "humaneness," in a sense remote from the future-oriented Marxist-Leninist "humanism of ideals" and close to a present-oriented and rights-oriented "humanism of principles."

The theoretical shift between the 1920s and the 1980s was dramatic. In the early Soviet period, both morality and ethical theory were expected to wither away with the building of socialism. In the 1980s, the Soviet approach to ethical theory, no longer narrowly Marxist-Leninist, was being supplemented, and in some cases, supplanted by more traditional ethical positions drawn from both Russian and Western sources.

Post-Soviet Developments

The dramatic collapse of the Soviet Union in late 1991 brought to a sudden end the Marxist-Leninist ideological and philosophical monopoly in such fields as ethical theory. The ensuing process of normalization and the move toward pluralism and professionalism was accompanied by an almost total erosion of the powerful influence of Marxism-Leninism on ethical theory. Several striking developments of the 1990s are listed below. None of them would have been imaginable before the mid-1980s.

- Republication of the works of such major Russian thinkers as the brilliant conservative Konstantin Leont'ev (1831–1891), of such major treatises as Vladimir Soloviev's *Opravdanie dobra* (Justification of the Good, 1897), and publication of Russian translations of such previously ignored or abused Western figures as Søren KIERKEGAARD (1813–1855), Friedrich NIETZSCHE (1844–1900), Max WEBER (1864–1920), and Martin HEIDEGGER (1889–1976)—in every case accompanied by extensive and sympathetic commentary.
- Publication of the Russian text of Trotsky's impassioned defense of state terrorism ("Their Morals and Ours," 1938), and of the first Russian translations of the important critical responses of John DEWEY (1859–1952) in 1938 and Jean-Paul SARTRE (1905–1980) in 1947–48 to this text. A. A. Guseinov provided judicious critical commentary.
- The founding in 1989 by Guseinov and R. G. Apressyan of the Center for Studies in Nonviolence, connected with the Institute of Philosophy. The Center has organized a number of national and international conferences and workshops, publishing several volumes of papers and proceedings.
- The powerful Marxist-Leninist orientation toward the remote historical future and the corollary instrumentalizing of present persons was belatedly subjected to acute criticism. Iu. N. Davydov laid much of the blame for the inhumanities of the Soviet period on an obsessive "love of the distant future" and an implicit rejection of "love of neighbor." Public intellectual Gelian Prokhorov blamed the related focus on attaining the "radiant future of communism" with the attendant denial of ordinary human decency in the present. Vitaly Korotich, editor of *Ogonek,* the leading Russian journal of the *glasnost'* period, made a parallel point, stressing the difficulty of moving from the "morality of hatred" of the Soviet period to a "morality of [brotherly] love" in the post-Soviet period.
- The long silence among ethical theorists about the Soviet recourse to the death penalty for crimes against (socialist) property was finally broken, first by legal scholars and public intellectuals, then by ethical theorists. Such executions were in fact suspended late in 1988, although major economic criminals were still subject *de jure* to the death penalty until January 1997. Recently published statistics place the total number of executions for the period 1961–1988 at more than 20,000, of which between 400 and 600 were for crimes against *property.*

Recent Russian work in ethical theory has moved, on the one hand, toward greater theoretical generality, exploring the ontological grounding of moral values and principles, and, on the other, toward the specificity of various areas of applied ethics and the attempt to develop a Russian equivalent of the "Protestant work ethic."

Soviet Ethical Theory

See also: ALTRUISM; AUTHORITY; BIOLOGICAL THEORY; CAPITAL PUNISHMENT; COLLECTIVE RESPONSIBILITY; DARWIN; ECONOMIC SYSTEMS; ENGELS; HISTORIOGRAPHY; HUMANISM; MACHIAVELLI; MARX; MARXISM; MORAL RELATIVISM; NATURALISM; NIETZSCHE; OBEDIENCE TO LAW; POLITICAL SYSTEMS; PRINCIPLISM; PROPERTY; REVOLUTION; SCHOPENHAUER.

Bibliography

Primary Sources

Bandzeladze, G. D., ed. *Aktual'nye problemy marksistskoi etiki: Sbornik statei.* (Current Problems of Marxist Ethics: A Collection of Articles.) Tbilisi: Izd. Tbilisskogo gosudarstvennogo universiteta, 1967. Notable for three controversial articles: "Etika—nauka o dolzhnom" (Ethics—The Science of What Ought to Be), and "Etika, ili printsipy istinnoi chelovechnosti: Printsip sovesti" (Ethics, or The Principles of True Humaneness: The Principle of Conscience), both by Mil'ner-Irinin; and "Osnovnoi vopros etiki kak filosofskoi nauki i problema nravstvennogo otchuzhdeniia" (The Fundamental Question of Ethics as a Philosophical Science and the Problem of Moral Alienation), by P.M. Egides.

———. *Etika: Opyt izlozheniia sistemy marksistskoi etiki.* (Ethics: An Attempt to Expound a System of Marxist Ethics.) 2d ed. Tbilisi: Sabchota Sakartvelo, 1970.

Davydov, Iu. N. *Etika liubvi i metafizika svoevoliia: Problemy nravstvennoi filosofii.* (The Ethics of Love and the Metaphysics of Willfulness: Problems of Moral Philosophy.) Moscow: Molodaia gvardiia, 1982. For passages cited in this article, see pp. 6, 237, 258, 262, 272.

Drobnitskii, O. G. *Problemy nravstvennosti.* (Problems of Morality.) Moscow: Nauka, 1977.

Frolov, Ivan T. "Perestroika: filosotskii smysl . . ." (Restructuring: its philosophic meaning . . .) *Voprosy filosofii* no. 2 (1989): 19–23. Address to a plenary session of the World Philosophy Congress, Brighton, England, August 1988. Passages quoted are from pp. 21 and 22.

Guseinov, A. A., and G. Irrlitts. *Kratkaia istoriia etiki.* (A Short History of Ethics.) Moscow: Mysl', 1987. From Homer and the pre-Socratics to Hegel and Feuerbach; appendix contains Russian translations of brief selections from the works of Aristotle, Augustine, and Kant.

Lenin, Vladimir Ilich. *Sochineniia.* 5th ed. Moscow, 1958–1965. For passages quoted, see vol. 41, pp. 311, 313.

Marx, Karl, and Frederick Engels. *Karl Marx, Friedrich Engels Werke.* Berlin: Dietz, 1961–1966. The standard recent edition. For passage cited here, see vol. 16, p. 13.

Mil'ner-Irinin, Ia. A. *Ethik.* Edited by Peter Ehlen. Munich: Berchmans, 1986 [1963]. A German translation of the author's *Etika, ili printsipy istinnoi chelovechnosti,* which was distributed "for purposes of discussion" in a printing of 60 copies in Moscow, 1963. Commentary by Helmut Dahm.

Tugarinov, V. P. *O tsennostiakh zhizni i kul'tury.* (On the Values of Life and Culture.) Leningrad: Izd. Leningradskogo universiteta, 1960.

———. *Teoriia tsennostei v marksizme.* (The Theory of Values in Marxism.) Leningrad: Izd. Leningradskogo universiteta, 1968.

Secondary Sources

DeGeorge, Richard T. *Soviet Ethics and Morality.* Ann Arbor: University of Michigan Press, 1969. Includes Bibliography, through 1968, of Soviet works in ethical theory and Western commentaries.

Ehlen, Peter. *Die philosophische Ethik in der Sowjetunion: Analyse und Diskussion.* Munich: Anton Pustet, 1972. Includes Bibliography of Soviet works in ethical theory through 1971.

Fleischer, Helmut. *Wertphilosophie in der Sowjetunion.* Berlin: Berichte des Osteuropa-Instituts an der freien Universität Berlin, 1969. Passages cited here are on pp. 69, 73, 75, 87, 95.

Grier, Philip T. *Marxist Ethical Theory in the Soviet Union.* Dordrecht: Reidel, 1978. Includes Bibliography, through 1977, of Soviet works in ethical theory and Western commentaries.

Kline, George L. "Was Marx an Ethical Humanist?" *Studies in Soviet Thought* 9 (1969): 91–103.

Lukes, Steven. *Marxism and Morality.* Oxford: Oxford University Press, 1985. See especially chapter 6, "Means and Ends." For passages cited here, see pp. 29, 35, 70.

Scanlan, James P. *Marxism in the USSR: A Critical Survey of Current Soviet Thought.* Ithaca, NY: Cornell University Press, 1985. See chapter 7, "Philosophy of Morality." Passages quoted here are on pp. 291–92.

Post-Soviet Sources

This list is not intended to be comprehensive, but only to give some idea of the scope, variety, and seriousness of recent Russian work in this field.

Apressyan, R. G., *Ideia morali i bazovye normativnoeticheskie programmy* (The Idea of Morality and Basic Normatively Ethical Programs). Moscow: Institut Filosofii, 1995.

Apressyan, R. G., ed. *Moral' i ratsional'nost'.* (Morality and Rationality.) Moscow: Institut Filosofii, 1995. Essays by Apressyan, Guseinov, and other Russian authors, as well as Russian translations of essays by R. M. Hare, Onora O'Neill, Alan Montefiore, and other Western authors.

Apressyan, R. G., and A. A. Guseinov, eds. *Entsiklopedicheskii slovar' po etike.* (Encyclopedic Dictionary of Ethics.) Moscow: Gardariki, 2001. On schools, movements, and classical texts, but not individual thinkers. Major attention to the Indian, Chinese, and Islamic traditions.

Davydov, Iu. N. "Veber i Bulgakov: Khristianskaia askeza i trudovaia etika." (Weber and Bulgakov: Christian Aceticism and the Work Ethic.) *Voprosy filosofii* no. 2 (1994): 54–73.

Guseinov, A. A. "Zur Geschichte und aktuellen Situation der Ethik in der Sowjetunion." *Studies in Soviet Thought* 42 (1991): 195–206.

Iudin, Boris, ed. *Vvedenie v bioetiku* (Introduction to Bio-ethics). Moscow: Progress-Traditsiia, 1998.

Kuznetsova, G. V., and L. V. Maksimov. *Priroda moral'-nykh absoliutov.* (The Nature of Moral Absolutes.) Moscow: Nasledie, 1996.

Meleshko, E. D. *Filosofiia neprotivleniia L. N. Tolstogo.* (L. N. Tolstoy's Philosophy of Nonresistance.) Tula: Izd. TPGU im. Tolstogo, 1999.

Solov'ev, E. Iu. *I. Kant: Vzaimodopolnitel'nost' morali i prava.* (Kant: The Mutual Complementarity of Morality and Law). Moscow: Nauka, 1992.

George L. Kline

Spencer, Herbert (1820–1903)

Born in Derby, England. Within his lifetime Spencer was both acclaimed as one of the world's great philosophers and dismissed as an evolutionist whom time had passed by. His multivolume *magnum opus, The Synthetic Philosophy* (1860–1896), includes Spencer's major work in moral theory, *The Principles of Ethics* (1892–1893). Also of importance to his moral and political theories are the early systematic work, *Social Statics* (1851; revised edition in 1892), and *The Man Versus the State* (1884). Spencer described his moral theory as "rational utilitarianism." He attempts a synthesis of four elements: the general HAPPINESS principle as the ultimate standard of conduct; the rejection of this principle as useless and even self-defeating as a proximate guide to conduct; a general conception of EVOLUTION as leading to ever more complexly interrelated heterogeneous units; and a specific conception of human moral and social evolution from a "militant" phase to an "industrial" phase.

For Spencer, all moral theorists must ultimately defend their prescriptions on the basis of general happiness; the implicit premise of "pessimists" and "optimists" alike is that life is worth living if and only if it yields a "surplus of agreeable feeling." However, both within and across individuals, pleasures are in-commensurable; and to this double incommensurability must be added mankind's ignorance of the means of *directly* promoting general happiness. Nevertheless, since general happiness would be achieved were individuals to attain their own happiness, and individuals are best able to identify and achieve their own happiness (albeit, by progressively finding egoistic pleasures in altruistic pursuits), the *indirect* means to the greatest happiness is the establishment of the social conditions which enable individuals to pursue their own happiness. The crucial condition is justice, *i.e.,* respect for the law of equal freedom. Equal freedom implies the joint ownership of the earth, but full private ownership of self and the products derived from one's leasing of portions of the earth. In the ideal society, complete justice is crowned by a spontaneous BENEFICENCE reflective of full adaptation to the social state.

Successful adaptation and functioning within one's environment is signaled and rewarded by PLEASURE, while pain signals and punishes maladaption and dysfunction. Since evolution moves toward complete adaptation, without conscious design, humanity evolves toward the greatest aggregate pleasure. This process requires that each receive and suffer the good and bad results of chosen actions. However, this "positive" element in the freedom formula is qualified by the "negative" element that each is to respect a like freedom in others. Humanity must adapt to this qualification, which is needed to secure the mutual gains of social existence (including those deriving from increasing specialization).

The dictates of "absolute ethics," namely, complete equal LIBERTY and the reconciliation of EGOISM and ALTRUISM, will be feasible only in a future world in which a peaceful, contractual, "industrial" social order and the psychological changes it brings are realized. We are still evolving from an earlier "militant" stage in which survival depended upon success in warfare and in which the individual was appropriately subordinated to the group. Since even the most peaceful nations still face external enemies, "relative ethics" requires that individuals be sacrificed in defensive wars, though such warfare reverses the social and psychological changes conducive to evolution toward equal liberty and portends at least the temporary "re-barbarization" of mankind.

See also: ALTRUISM; BIOLOGICAL THEORY; COMMENSURABILITY; DARWIN; EGOISM; EVOLUTION; HAPPI-

NESS; LIBERTY; MORAL DEVELOPMENT; MORAL EDU-CATION; SELF-OWNERSHIP; UTILITARIANISM.

Bibliography

Primary Sources

A System of Synthetic Philosophy. 10 vols. New York: Appleton, 1900–1902 [1860–1896].

The Man Versus the State. Indianapolis, IN: Liberty Classics, 1981 [1884]. Includes six additional essays in political ethics.

The Principles of Ethics. 2 vols. Indianapolis, IN: Liberty Classics, 1978 [1893].

Social Statics. New York: Robert Schalkenbach Foundation, 1970 [1851]. The original text.

Secondary Sources

Doherty, G., and T. S. Gray. "Herbert Spencer and the Relation Between Economic and Political Liberty." *History of Political Thought* 14 (1993): 475–90.

Gray, T. S. *The Political Philosophy of Herbert Spencer.* Aldershot: Avebury, 1996.

———. "Is Herbert Spencer's Law of Equal Freedom a Utilitarian or a Rights-Based Theory of Justice?" *Journal of the History of Philosophy* 26 (1988): 259–78.

History of Political Thought 3 (1982). Contains articles by J. Gray, W. Miller, J. Paul, and H. Steiner on Spencer's moral and political thought.

Sidgwick, Henry. *Lectures on the Ethics of T. H. Green, Mr. Herbert Spencer and James Martineau.* London: Macmillan, 1902.

Smith, George. "Herbert Spencer's Theory of Causation." *Journal of Libertarian Studies* vol. 5 no. 2 (Spring 1981). Emphasizes the role of Spencer's idea of causation within his system of ethics.

Taylor, M. W. *Men Versus the State.* Oxford: Clarendon Press, 1992. Highly informative study of Spencer and his Individualist allies; good bibliography.

Weinstein, D. *Equal Freedom and Utility: Herbert Spencer's Liberal Utilitarianism.* Cambridge: Cambridge University Press, 1998. Spencer as indirect utilitarian; good bibliography.

———. "Equal Freedom, Rights and Utility in Spencer's Moral Philosophy." *History of Political Thought* 11 (1990): 119–42.

Eric Mack

Spinoza, Baruch de (1632–1677)

Latin form: Benedictine de Spinoza. The son of Sephardic Jews who had migrated from Portugal to Amsterdam to escape the Spanish Inquisition, Spinoza was taught Hebrew from childhood and Latin in early youth. By his early twenties he had earned the respect of experts in Biblical studies, in medieval Jewish philosophy, and in the new post-Aristotelian natural science and philosophy. He openly contended that the Amsterdam synagogue should tolerate radical reinterpretations of traditional religion in the light of the new science; but the synagogue, seeking to regain the religious life it had been compelled to compromise in Portugal, in 1656 solemnly expelled him. He left Amsterdam, living at first at Rijnsburg, and later at Voorburg and the Hague. He attracted the friendship of a small but distinguished group of liberal Dutch Protestants. His chief occupation was philosophical study and research, the results of which he communicated to his friends by manuscripts and letters. He partly supported himself by grinding optical lenses, but was also helped by the generosity of his richer friends, who would have given him more if he would have accepted it. Never in robust health, he died in 1677.

Spinoza published only two books during his short life: in 1663, an exposition *more geometrico* of the first two parts of René DESCARTES's (1596–1650) *Principia philosophiae* (1644), and in 1670, anonymously, the *Tractatus theologico-politicus.* The latter was ferociously denounced by the orthodox; and it was legally banned in 1674, although it continued to be reprinted. He therefore withheld his masterpiece, *Ethics, Demonstrated in Geometrical Order,* arranging that friends publish it promptly after his death, together with a selection from his correspondence and two unfinished works, the early *Tractatus de intellectus emendatione* and the late *Tractatus politicus.*

Spinoza's views about ethics derive from the radical implications he perceived in new natural science and philosophy. In the *Tractatus theologico-politicus* he set out those implications for traditional Judaism and Christianity. Although the inspired teachers of both—Moses and Jesus—proclaimed that God is infinite and caused by nothing else, they identified God with a supernatural creator of nature because they were imaginatively convinced that nature, being finite, must be caused by something beyond it. On the other hand, the philosophers of the new natural science—Francis Bacon (1561–1626) and Descartes—while teaching that nature is infinite and conserved, declined to draw the heretical conclusion that the power of nature must be "itself the divine power and excellence (*virtus*)," and that the divine power must in turn be "the very essence of God himself."

Divine inspiration, or prophecy, Spinoza concluded, must itself be a natural process, although its explanation eludes us. It is the nonrational power by which prophets, Jewish or (like Balaam) non-Jewish, solve difficult practical problems confronted by their societies. Prophets find ways out of dangerous individual situations that reason cannot find; but reason confirms such of their religious and ethical teachings as are universal. The universal teaching of all prophets reduces to some or all of the same seven essentials: that God, the infinite being, exists; that God is one; that God is omnipresent and omniscient; that God is supreme and bound by no law; that the true worship of God consists in justice and CHARITY, or LOVE of one's neighbour; that all who so worship God are saved; and that God condones the sins of the penitent.

The prophets express these essentials according to their imaginative limitations, which are not inspired. Thus, Moses and Jesus, imagining that God has made human beings in his image, express the inspired truth that living justly and charitably is the true worship of God by the falsehood that God himself is just and charitable, and wills that human beings be as he is. Inspired solutions of particular social problems have no universal significance. Many of the laws laid down by Moses were not universal; being designed solely to ensure that the ancient Jewish state prospered, they bound only the members of the Jewish state, and only while it existed.

The first of the five Parts of the *Ethics* establishes the essence of God or nature; and the last four Parts have to do with the things following from that essence that "can lead us, by the hand as it were, to cognition of the human Mind and its highest blessedness." Each of the five Parts is set out in geometrical order: axioms and definitions are laid down without proof; and "propositions" or theorems are then systematically shown to follow from them by ordinary deductive reasoning. It is tempting to suppose that Spinoza offers the axioms as self-evident (*per se nota*) in either the Aristotelian or the Cartesian sense, because his undefined primitive expressions are those of medieval philosophy, as modified and supplemented by Descartes. But the temptation must be resisted. As he must have

known, neither Aristotelians nor Cartesians would accept his axioms as self-evident. More importantly, by warning readers (in II, 11 schol.) that they will find much to give them pause, and begging them "to continue with [him] slowly, step by step," he himself gives notice that the truth of what he writes will not become evident to them until, having mastered it as a whole, they see that it alone solves the major problems of philosophy.

In *Ethics* I and II, God or nature is presented as an infinite being consisting of every attribute that constitutes an infinite essence. The only two such attributes accessible to human beings are extension and thought. As extended, nature is an infinite three-dimensional plenum, in which a complex internal motion, whose quantity is eternally conserved, makes it possible to distinguish finite bodies of varying complexity. This internal motion is not introduced into a quiescent mass, but is eternally necessitated by nature's own laws of *immanent* causation. Those laws are such that the system of finite bodies is deterministic: its state at any given time necessitates all its later states according to laws of *transient* causation.

As constituted by the attribute of thought, nature immanently causes an infinite complex idea (the infinite idea of God), the causal structure of which (its "order and connection") is identical with that of extended nature. Both as thinking and as extended, God or nature is one and the same substance: that is, one and the same causal system. The laws of that system are expressible in terms of each of its attributes, and in no other way. Its attributes, which are really distinct, each "constitute" the same substance, in the sense that it is in principle possible to lay down a rule for transforming the expression of the laws of nature in terms of any one of them into its expression in terms of any other.

Not only is nature-as-thinking the same causal system as nature-as-extended, it adequately and so truly represents nature-as-extended—and as constituted by every other attribute. However, since the attributes constituting human beings are extension and thought, and are the only ones accessible to them, the others can be disregarded in considering Spinoza's ethics. Just as each human being, body and mind, is defective as a causal system, because it partly depends on external causes for its continued existence, so each human mind is inadequate as a system of representative thoughts or ideas, and its inadequacies are supplied in the infinite idea of God by ideas external to it.

Finite bodies and minds, as Spinoza conceives them, are functional: they are tendencies of finite patterns of motion and rest, or finite patterns of ideas, to persist in being. Such tendencies are distinct from the sets of component bodies and ideas in which they are found. As found in different sets of component bodies at different times, such tendencies may increase and decrease in their power to persist; for example, the pattern of motion and rest in the components of a healthy and mature human body tends more effectively to persist than it will do in those of the same body in extreme old age.

Good and EVIL, according to Spinoza, are relative to things. God is absolutely good: since he is completely self-caused and independent, nothing can conceivably benefit or harm him. Finite things are otherwise: as tendencies to persist, what is good for them is what contributes to their persistence, and what is evil is what hinders it. Given what God or nature is, all finite things will undergo some evil relative to them, and some will undergo far more evil than good. From the point of view of God, that is as it should be: that millions were murdered by the Nazis and Stalinists is no less necessary and desirable than that others benefited from works of MERCY and charity. The highest state of mind to which human beings can aspire is *acquiescentia:* a state of mental quiet or rest in which, no matter what the relative evil of their own lot, they accept God or nature as absolutely good—that is, love God without wishing their love to be returned.

How would human beings live if they were as free, that is, as rational, as in favorable conditions they can be? Although, in the causally determined course of nature, virtually no human individuals in fact so live, working out what so living would be, which will necessarily be accompanied by parallel changes in one's body's tendencies to act, is the chief contribution philosophy can make to ethical practice. Free human beings each desire their own good directly, and hence "act, live, and conserve their being from the foundation of seeking their own advantage (*proprium utile*)."

What is this foundation? Alexandre Matheron and others have recently challenged the view, still prevalent among English-speaking commentators, that it is psychological EGOISM—that people in every individual situation necessarily do what they believe will result in their own advantage. What emerges from Spinoza's own treatment in *Ethics* IV is that, since human beings can effectively seek their own advantage only in cooperation with others, the foundation of seeking their own advantage must be the general conditions of effective cooperation. Those conditions are both individual and political. Individually, free human beings will offer cooperation to others by being benevolent and peaceable (except to those who behave malevolently and aggressively) and by being willing to make and keep agreements to carry out common projects with others who show themselves trustworthy. Politically, they will support political INSTITUTIONS to the extent that their laws are, or promise to become, for the good of all citizens. In contrast with his near-contemporary Thomas HOBBES (1588–1679), Spinoza held that "sedition, wars and contempt or violation of laws are to be imputed, not to the wickedness of subjects, but to the depraved condition of government (*imperii*). For citizens are made, not born."

To the egoist objection that seeking one's advantage according to such dictates will in some individual situations result in disadvantage, Spinoza simply replied that if it were reasonable for anybody to behave uncooperatively when it is advantageous, the absurd conclusion would follow that everybody would reasonably do so, and hence that nobody would reasonably cooperate in good faith. From this it is evident that he conceived seeking one's own advantage as seeking conditions of life that are generally to one's own advantage; and he reasoned that those conditions are the same for all, and require each to accept the occasional disadvantages of keeping faith for the sake of the indispensable advantages of cooperation.

Spinoza embarrasses many of his admirers by concluding *Ethics* V with an examination of "those things which pertain to the Mind's existence without relation to the body." That he should do so nevertheless makes perfect sense, given that he has proved (as he believes) that some of the ideas an active human mind has of its own essence are adequate, that all adequate ideas are eternally in God's infinite intellect, and that finite minds are not finite substances, but simply ideas in God's infinite intellect. His theory of immortality is as unusual as it is unorthodox, but it is not incoherent.

See also: CHRISTIAN ETHICS; CLARKE; COMMON GOOD; COOPERATION, CONFLICT, AND COORDINA-

TION; DESCARTES; EGOISM; *EUDAIMONIA, -*ISM; FICHTE; GAME THEORY; GOVERNMENT, ETHICS IN; GRATITUDE; HOBBES; HUME; JEWISH ETHICS; NATURAL LAW; OBEDIENCE TO LAW; SCHELLING; SCHWEITZER; THEOLOGICAL ETHICS.

Bibliography

Works by Spinoza

Spinoza Opera. Edited by Carl Gebhardt. 4 vols. Heidelberg: Carl Winter, 1924–1926. The standard edition.

The Collected Works of Spinoza. Edited and translated by Edwin Curley. Princeton, NJ: Princeton University Press, 1985–. Vol. 1 contains the early works, *Ethics,* and correspondence to June 1665. Vol. 2 will contain *Tractatus theologico-politicus, Tractatus politicus,* and the remainder of the correspondence. Valuable as a critical edition, it should long remain the standard English translation.

A Spinoza Reader: The Ethics and Other Works. Edited and translated by Edwin Curley. Princeton, NJ: Princeton University Press, 1994. Contains a lengthy introduction by Curley.

The Political Works. Translated by A. G. Wernham. Oxford: Clarendon Press, 1958. Valuable as a critical edition of the Latin texts, with a lively translation. Contains part of *Tractatus theologico-politicus* and all of *Tractatus politicus.*

Works about Spinoza

Allison, Henry. *Benedict de Spinoza: An Introduction.* Rev. ed. New Haven: Yale University Press, 1987.

Bennett, Jonathan. *A Study of Spinoza's Ethics.* Cambridge: Cambridge University Press, 1984. A radical but stimulating interpretation.

Curley, Edwin. *Behind the Geometrical Method: A Reading of Spinoza's "Ethics."* Princeton, NJ: Princeton University Press, 1988.

Donagan, Alan. *Spinoza.* Chicago: University of Chicago Press, 1989.

Harris, Errol E. *Salvation from Despair: A Reappraisal of Spinoza's Philosophy.* The Hague: Martinus Nijhoff, 1973.

Joachim, H. H. *A Study of Spinoza's "Ethics."* Oxford: Oxford University Press, 1901. A classic treatment from the point of view of Oxford absolute idealism.

Matheron, Alexandre. *Individu et communaute chez Spinoza.* Paris: Editions de Minuit, 1969. A modern classic; an unrivaled treatment of Spinoza's ethical and political theories based on a lucid analysis of their metaphysical and epistemological grounds.

Pollock, Frederick. *Spinoza: His Life and Philosophy.* London: C. Kegan Paul, 1880. The pioneering study of Spinoza in English, still fresh in its approach.

Alan Donagan

sport

Sport is not only a major feature of contemporary American and Western culture but also a practice which raises a variety of philosophical issues. Among the most important philosophical issues raised by sport are the nature of sport, the value of sport, and the ethic that should govern participants in sport. However, a host of additional philosophical questions can be raised about sport as well, including the relation of sport to art, the relation of sport to play, the cultural role of sport, and the implications of sport for understanding the nature of persons. In addition, specific policy issues often are raised by sport, such as the permissibility of the use of performance enhancing drugs in athletic competitions, and the nature of gender equity in sport.

With regard to the nature of sport, some philosophers offer what have come to be called formalist accounts of what it is to be a sport, while others emphasize the role of social CONVENTIONS. Philosophers who tend to identify sports as games of physical skill which are distinguished by their constitutive rules are called formalists. On the other hand, their critics tend to emphasize the role that informal social conventions rather than formal rules play in determining what is appropriate sporting behavior, as well as in distinguishing one sport from another, and from activities outside the realm of sport as well. Contrary to Wittgenstein's well-known suggestion that games bear only a family resemblance to one another, formalists, such as Bernard Suits, have offered plausible definitions of "game" and have shed a good deal of light on the relationship between sport, play, and games, while conventionalists have done much to illuminate the social context in which sport takes place. These debates may be viewed as more than different attempts to stipulate a definition of "sport"; rather, they amount to justifications of different theoretical approaches, each of which claims to offer a better understanding of sport and a more defensible set of normative implications. Thus, formalists are more likely to claim that cheaters can't win because they don't really play the game, since on their view the game is defined by its constitutive rules which are the very rules the cheater presumably violates. Conventionalists reply that this is too ideal a conception of sport (to cite a frequently debated example, surely pitcher Gaylord Perry was playing baseball when he threw the illegal spitball).

Other philosophers have offered accounts of why so many people find sport fascinating, whether as participants or spectators, and why sport plays such a major role in our society. For example, sport may be seen as an outlet for aggression or as a way of reinforcing dominant values of the culture in which it is embedded. Radical critics of organized sport have argued, primarily from the left, that sport reflects and perhaps functions to support what they regard as the excessive competitiveness built into market societies. However, critics of such reductive accounts reply that they omit crucial features inherent to sport. For example, standards in sport can contradict rather than reflect or support existing values, as when concern for EXCELLENCE in sport and belief in objective standards for measuring it can contradict a more general acceptance of mediocrity or scepticism about objectivity. Nonreductive theories tend to stress the intrinsic value of the challenge provided by COMPETITION in sport as sufficient explanation, as well as a justification, for its hold upon us.

Perhaps the fundamental set of issues examined by philosophers of sport concerns the importance, value, and justification of such activities as sport, games, and especially competition in athletics. Competitive sport, particularly organized athletic competition, can be criticized not only for particular abuses within particular practices, such as recruiting violations in intercollegiate athletics, but also for their competitive nature itself. Thus, athletic competition is sometimes seen by its critics as an egoistic practice in which competitors are taught to win for themselves at the expense of others. The emphasis on competitive success, which is defined as winning, turns contests into zero-sum games in which opponents are reduced to obstacles to success rather than seen as persons in their own right.

Proponents of competitive sport may reply that such a hostile account might apply to degenerate forms of athletic competition, but are not generally applicable to competitive sports and athletics. It has been argued, for example that athletic competition is a significantly cooperative, or at least a mutually advantageous activity, in which competitors agree to present mutually acceptable challenges to each other simply for the sake of pursuing excellence in the sport in question. On this view, athletic competitors treat each other as persons by honoring the framework of RIGHTS and obligations that makes a competitive contest possible. To the extent that competitive sport, at its best, provides a worthy challenge to both mind and body, exhibits aesthetic qualities, and calls for the exhibition of such values as dedication, COURAGE, and excellence, it can be defended as one of those human activities which is valuable in itself, over and above its consequences and origins.

In addition to studying the morality of competition in sport, philosophers of sport have also examined the kind of behavior that is appropriate to competitors within sport. For example, how is the notion of being a good sport, or the idea of sportsmanship, to be understood? While some writers argue that what counts as being a good sport varies with the intensity of the competition being played, others look for more unitary conceptions. Thus, is being a good sport one thing at the level of recreational sport—perhaps, as some have suggested, requiring GENEROSITY toward opponents, and quite another in highly competitive contests where only basic FAIRNESS and allegiance to the rules can plausibly be expected of competitors? Or are there other values such as ALTRUISM toward opponents and respect for the traditions of the game which apply at all levels of sport?

Formalists often tend to set standards of behavior for players that are stricter than the conventions that often apply in practice. For example, some formalists have suggested that committing fouls for strategic advantage, such as fouling in order to stop the clock in basketball, are forms of CHEATING since they involve intentional violation of mutually acceptable rules. Conventionalists tend to reply that strategic fouls are acceptable since this form of rules violation is part of the conventions that players use in interpreting and applying the official rule book. Some formalists respond that, even though penalties for strategic fouls are part of the rules, such fouling is not permissible any more than crimes are allowed by the law simply because legal penalties are prescribed for them, conventions to the contrary notwithstanding. Still other formalists argue that the penalties for strategic fouls are not analogous to punishments in the criminal law, but are more like the price charged for a permissible activity. On this view, strategic fouling is permissible, even on formalist grounds, since the rules setting penalties for such fouls should not be understood on the model of criminal sanctions. This debate, along with explications of such notions as being a good sport, are part of attempts by philosophers of sport to subject the behavior of athletes within competition to an ethical critique and to develop ethical standards that should apply to competitive sport.

In addition to more general questions about the ethic of competitive sport, specific practices within sport often raise issues that overlap with and illuminate related areas in ethics, AESTHETICS, and metaphysics. Consider, for example, whether athletes ought to be permitted to take drugs, such as anabolic steroids, in order to enhance performance in athletic competition despite the risk of serious side effects. Libertarians might argue that if competent and informed athletes think the chance of gain in performance is worth the risk, it is no one's business but their own. On the other hand, it can be replied that to allow some to use such drugs coerces others into becoming users to remain competitive, cheapens the value of excellence in sport, and sanctions a practice that could not be agreed to by rational impartial competitors under fair conditions of choice. The examination of sport also raises questions about our culture and its conception of the kind of persons we should emulate. Why, for example, are leading athletes often regarded as heroes, particularly by the young? Is such adulation misplaced or is there a moral component to sport, perhaps the idea of meeting challenge and demonstrating excellence, that makes such identification not only natural but perhaps justifiable? Are the qualities necessary for success in athletics instances of *moral* VIRTUES, or are they merely instrumentally effective in the pursuit of fame and fortune?

Clearly, many basic issues of ethics and social philosophy are involved in the attempt to formulate and defend answers to basic questions about the nature and value of sport, and the features of proper conduct within athletic competition. The philosophy of sport, by examining broader questions about the proper role of sport in human life, as well as by analyzing the nature of sport and its implications for public life, contributes not only to our understanding of such basic philosophic notions such as autonomy, equality, competition, and excellence, but also to our understanding of a particularly rich and fascinating set of human practices.

See also: ACADEMIC ETHICS; ALTRUISM; ANGER; ANIMALS, TREATMENT OF; AUTONOMY OF MORAL AGENTS; BRIBERY; CHEATING; CIVILITY; COMPETITION; CONSENT; CONVENTIONS; COOPERATION, CONFLICT, AND COORDINATION; CORRUPTION; COURAGE; CRUELTY; EGOISM; EQUALITY; ETIQUETTE; EXCELLENCE; EXCUSES; EXPLOITATION; FAIRNESS; FORMALISM; HONOR; HUMILITY; MERCY; PERFECTIONISM; PERSON, CONCEPT OF; PRIDE; PROPORTIONALITY; RISK; SELF-CONTROL; VIOLENCE AND NON-VIOLENCE; VIRTUES.

Bibliography

Arnold, Peter J. *Sport, Ethics and Education.* London: Cassell, 1997.

Callois, Roger. *Man, Play, and Games.* Translated by Meyer Barash. New York: Free Press of Glencoe, 1961.

Fraleigh, Warren P. *Right Actions in Sports: Ethics for Contestants.* Champaign, IL: Human Kinetics, 1984.

Gerber, Ellen W., and William J. Morgan, eds. *Sport and the Body: A Philosophical Symposium.* Philadelphia: Lea and Febiger, 1979.

Huizinga, John. *Homo ludens.* London: Routledge and Kegan Paul, 1950.

Hyland, Drew. *The Question of Play.* Lanham, MD: University Press of America, 1984.

Journal of the Philosophy of Sport. Published annually for the Philosophic Society for the Study of Sport. Champaign, IL: Human Kinetics, 1974–.

Kretchmar, R. Scott. *Practical Philosophy of Sport.* Champaign, IL: Human Kinetics, 1994.

McNamee, M. J., and S. J. Parry. *Ethics and Sport.* London: Routledge, 1998.

Morgan, William J. *Leftist Theories of Sport: A Critique and Reconstruction.* Urbana: University of Illinois Press, 1994.

Morgan, William J., and Klaus V. Meier, eds. *Philosophic Inquiry in Sport.* 2d ed. Champaign, IL: Human Kinetics, 1995.

Osterhoudt, Robert G. *The Philosophy of Sport: An Overview.* Champaign, IL: Stipes, 1991.

Postow, Betsy, ed. *Women, Philosophy, and Sport: A Collection of New Essays.* Metuchen, NJ: Scarecrow Press, 1983.

Simon, Robert L. *Fair Play: Sports, Values, and Society.* Boulder, CO: Westview Press, 1991.

Suits, Bernard. *The Grasshopper: Games, Life, and Utopia.* Toronto: University of Toronto Press, 1978.

Weiss, Paul. *Sport: A Philosophic Inquiry.* Carbondale: Southern Illinois University Press, 1969.

Robert L. Simon

Staël, Madame de (1766–1817)

Full name: Anne Louise Germaine Necker, Madame de Staël, Baronne de Staël Holstein. French Revolutionary activist and Romantic theorist. Staël's *Lettres sur Rousseau* (1788), condemning women's "domestic slavery" and claiming that her fellow-Genevan ROUSSEAU (1712–1778) committed suicide, confirmed her early fame as daughter of Louis XVI's finance minister. Between exiles, she influenced French policy in 1791–1792, co-writing speeches for the Minister for War, in 1795–1802, when the Constitution of the Year III was elaborated in her salon, and in 1814–1817, as political mentor of the Doctrinaires. She co-wrote the *Rapport* that made WOLLSTONECRAFT (1759–1797) dedicate *The Rights of Women* (1792) to Talleyrand (1754–1838).

Staël's works list 146 items. Her main political tracts, from the *Réflexions sur la paix* (1794) through *Des circonstances actuelles* (1798) to the *Considérations sur la Révolution française* (1818), rework MONTESQUIEU (1689–1755) in particular to establish the liberal two-Revolutions model, dismissing the Old Regime, Reign of Terror (1793–1794), and Napoleon (1769–1821) together as three forms of despotism. Staël's companion Benjamin Constant (1767–1830) based his "two liberties" distinction on her writings, countering the Terror's quasi-totalitarian SOCIAL CONTRACT with praise of negative LIBERTY; Constant's "lying to a murderer" controversy with KANT (1724–1804) also echoes Staël's life. Presciently, Staël later rejected simple negative liberty as a trap which imprisons women in the *oikos,* constructing an alternative model quite close to Hannah ARENDT (1906–1975): silent peoples produce leaders who represent them, authorized by public credit and speaking in the nation's voice. This nation-genius symbiosis, a new twist to theories of representation, combines Protestant credit and social contract traditions, tracing public credit in finance, politics, and art. Countless Romantics and nationalists draw on this model of national genius, developed by Staël notably in her novel *Corinne ou l'Italie* (1807); and this middle path between corporatism and molecular INDIVIDUALISM, the two fashions of the 1790s, also has some resemblance to modern communitarian discourse.

Privately, *De l'influence des passions* (1796) is a Stoic's response to Revolutionary faith in reason, though Staël favors Idéologue empiricism as late as *De la littérature* (1800), a history of literature as a social phenomenon anchored in a new theory of human perfectibility. A Socinian Calvinist, Staël briefly leans toward quietism around 1806–1810; in contrast to 1796, these works see the passions as divinely inspired, and suffering as ennobling. *De l'Allemagne* (1810, 1813), read among others by the Transcendentalists, the French Eclectics, and JOHN STUART MILL (1806–1873), builds from Kant an answer to UTILITARIANISM and empiricism, bridging heart and head: "the necessary in all things has something revolting when the possessors of the superfluous determine it." Staël nuances Kant by contrasting moralities of justice and CARE, much like recent FEMINIST ETHICS; her biography weakened her belief in perfect systems. In 1795, she lied to the murderers. Two later concerns mark this religious shift in Staël's view of the individual in society: her struggle against the slave trade, 1814–1817, and her *Réflexions sur le suicide* (1812), repudiating her frequent early mentions of SUICIDE and, incidentally, sketching out DURKHEIM's (1858–1917) sociogenic analysis. Before 1812, Staël had treated suicide, like divorce or citizenship, simply as another inalienable right under threat from Napoleon.

Three factors add interest to Staël's eclectic work: her movement between contemporary British, French, and German philosophies, and her impact around Europe and America; her first-hand knowledge of Europe's different institutions, from Old Regime to Republic, Empire and Restoration, from London to Moscow; and her gender, which shapes every page she wrote. Few women of comparable public fame have so fully elaborated a system of public and private ethics, censored though it was, at so important a period in the history of thought. In the 1970s, first-generation feminists accused Staël of selling out, but her CENSORSHIP by her own son, no less, and fifteen years in exile remind us that words are cheaper today than they were after 1793.

See also: ARENDT; CARE; COMMUNITARIANISM; DURKHEIM; FEMINIST ETHICS; INDIVIDUALISM; KANT; LIBERTARIANISM; LIBERTY; LITERATURE AND ETHICS; MONTESQUIEU; PERFECTIONISM; PUBLIC AND PRIVATE MORALITY; REVOLUTION; ROUSSEAU; SLAVERY; SOCIAL CONTRACT; STOICISM; SUICIDE; TRANSCENDENTALISM; UTILITARIANISM; WOLLSTONECRAFT; WOMEN MORAL PHILOSOPHERS.

Bibliography

Works by Germaine de Staël

Oeuvres complètes. Edited by A. de Staël. 17 vols. Paris: Treuttel and Würtz, 1820–1821. Still unreplaced, but Staël's son revised her style and censored her political texts.

De l'Allemagne. Edited by the comtesse J. de Pange and S. Balayé. 5 vols. Paris: Hachette, 1958–1960 [1810, 1813]. The book Napoleon pulped. Subsequent critical editions include Staël's *Ecrits de jeunesse, De la littérature, Delphine, Dix années d'exil,* and theater.

Correspondance générale. Edited by B. W. Jasinski. Paris: Pauvert, Hachette, Klincksieck, 1960–. Indispensable.

Des circonstances actuelles qui peuvent terminer la Révolution. Edited by L. Omacini. Genève: Droz, 1979 [1798]. Staël's main treatise on political philosophy, unpublished until 1906.

Madame de Staël: Écrits retrouvés. Cahiers staëliens, No 46. Edited by J. Isbell with S. Balayé. Paris: Société des Études staëliennes, 1994–1995. Identifies 146 Staël texts and publishes 29 new ones, groundwork for a second *Oeuvres complètes.*

Ten Years of Exile. Translated by Avriel H. Goldberger. De Kalb: Northern Illinois University Press, forthcoming. Translation of *Dix années d'exil* (1821).

An Extraordinary Woman: Selected Writings of Germaine de Staël. Translated and with an introduction by Vivian Folkenflik. New York: Columbia University Press, 1987.

Madame de Staël on Politics, Literature, and National Character. Translated and edited by Morroe Berger. Garden City, NY: Doubleday, 1964.

Corinne, or, Italy. Translated and with an introduction by Avriel V. Goldberger. New Brunswick, NJ: Rutgers University Press, 1987 (1807).

Delphine. Translated and with an introduction by Avriel V. Goldberger. DeKalb: Northern Illinois University Press, 1995 (1802).

Works about Staël

Balayé, Simone. *Madame de Staël: Ecrire, lutter, vivre.* Genève: Droz, 1994. Articles by today's leading Staël scholar, on liberty, relations with power, public opinion.

Balayé, Simone, and J.-D. Candaux, eds. *Le Groupe de Coppet.* Genève and Paris: Slatkine-Champion, 1977. Articles on Staël and Kant, Schlegel, nationalism, psychology.

Cahiers staëliens. Paris: Société des Études staëliennes, 1962–. Published annually; articles and book reviews.

Gutwirth, M., A. Goldberger, and K. Szmurlo, eds. *Germaine de Staël: Crossing the Borders.* New Brunswick, NJ: Rutgers University Press, 1991. Articles on liberty, revolution, suicide, nationalism.

Hofmann, E., and A.-L. Delacrétaz, eds. *Le Groupe de Coppet et la Révolution française.* E. Lausanne and Paris: Institut Benjamin Constant-Touzot, 1988. Articles on Staël and the politics of history, the passions, civil war, perfectibility.

Isbell, John C. *The Birth of European Romanticism: Truth and Propaganda in Staël's De l'Allemagne.* Cambridge: Cambridge University Press, 1994. Staël's text read as liberal propaganda anchored in a totalizing philosophy of history. See p. 135 for Kant's truthful victim.

———. "Le Contrat social selon Benjamin Constant et Mme de Staël, ou la liberté a-t-elle un sexe?" *Cahiers de l'Association internationale d'Etudes françaises* (May 1996): 439–56. Staël's credit-social contract theory.

Kloocke, K., ed. *Le Groupe de Coppet et l'Europe, 1789–1830.* Lausanne and Paris: Institut Benjamin Constant-Touzot, 1994. Articles on nationalism, moral education, despotism.

Madame de Staël et l'Europe. Paris: Klincksieck, 1970. The first of six Colloques de Coppet; three others follow. Articles on Staël and the Year III (1795), England, suicide.

Szmurlo, Karyna, "Madame de Staël." In *A Critical Bibliography of French Literature,* Vol. I, *The Nineteenth Century,* edited by David Baguley. Syracuse, NY: Syracuse University Press, 1994, pp. 51–69. Useful annotation.

John Claiborne Isbell

stakeholder analysis

The literature of management and business ethics during the last quarter of the twentieth century is replete with references to "stakeholder analysis" and a "stakeholder theory" of managerial decision making. Debates have considered whether "stakeholder thinking" accurately describes specific individuals, organizations, or corporate legal requirements. Some have suggested that "stakeholder analysis" provides a *normative* principle—in contrast with a *descriptive* one—for guiding managers.

The decision-making task is described as systematically identifying parties affected by organizational decisions (*e.g.,* customers, employees, suppliers, investors, communities) and taking the INTERESTS and RIGHTS of these parties seriously. The "stakeholder approach" is frequently contrasted with more conventional models of managerial decision making in which managerial attention is principally focused on the investor, with secondary attention to customers and employees. So-called "constituency statutes" passed during the 1980s in a majority of American states have permitted corporate boards of directors to consider not only stockholders but a wider set of stakeholders in their deliberations.

It is often suggested, moreover, that *ethical* values enter management decision-making through the gate of stakeholder analysis. Thus, business ethics can be interpreted as essentially a proposal to set aside more conventional management paradigms in favor of a stakeholder paradigm. This proposal is questionable, but to understand why, it is first necessary to define the term "stakeholder" and then to distinguish between two importantly different ideas with which it can be associated: analysis and synthesis.

Defining "Stakeholder"

The term "stakeholder" appears to have been invented in the early 1960s as a deliberate play on the word "stockholder" to signify that there are other parties who have a "stake" in the decision making of the modern, publicly held corporation besides those holding equity positions. R. Edward Freeman defines the term as follows: "A stakeholder in an organization is (by definition) any group or individual who can affect or is affected by the achievement of the organization's objectives."

Examples of stakeholder groups (beyond stockholders) are employees, suppliers, customers, competitors, governments, and communities. Another metaphor with which the term "stakeholder" is associated is that of a "player" in a game like poker. One with a "stake" in the game is one who plays and puts some economic value at risk.

Analysis and Synthesis

The decision making process of an individual or an organization, once an issue or problem presents itself for resolution, includes such steps as gathering, sorting, weighing, integrating, deciding, and acting on relevant information. Stakeholder analysis, strictly speaking, includes the first two of these steps in relation to information about stakeholders, but does not go beyond them to weighing, integrating, and eventually deciding. In a stakeholder analysis of several options available to a decision maker, the affected parties for each available option are identified and the positive and negative implications for each stakeholder group are clarified. But questions having to do with weighing and integrating this information in order to make a decision remain to be

answered. These steps are not part of the *analysis* but of the *synthesis*.

Stakeholder analysis may give the initial appearance of being a complete decision making process, while in fact it is only a *segment* of a decision making process. It is the opening phase that awaits the crucial application of the moral (or nonmoral) values of the decision maker. To be informed, therefore, that an individual or an institution regularly makes stakeholder analysis part of its decision making or takes a "stakeholder approach" to management is to learn little about the ethical character of that individual or institution. It is to learn that stakeholders are regularly identified in relation to proposed courses of action, and perhaps further that the implications for each stakeholder are identified as well; but it is not to learn *why and by what criterion a decision will be made*. Stakeholder analysis is, as a practical matter, morally neutral. It is, therefore, a mistake to see it as a substitute for normative ethical thinking.

What has been called "stakeholder synthesis," on the other hand, goes further into the sequence of decision making steps to include weighing the significance of the available options for the affected stakeholders and making a normative judgment that integrates the information into a decision. The critical point is that stakeholder synthesis involves moving from stakeholder identification to a normative response or resolution of the problem presenting itself.

Different Kinds of Synthesis

We can imagine decision makers doing "stakeholder analysis" for different underlying reasons, not always having to do with ethics. A politician or a management team, for example, might be careful to take positive and (especially) negative stakeholder effects into account for no other reason than that offended stakeholders might resist or retaliate (*e.g.,* through political action or economic boycott). It may not be *ethical* concern for stakeholders that motivates and guides such analysis, so much as concern about potential impediments to the achievement of strategic objectives. Thus, effects on relatively powerless stakeholders may be ignored or discounted in the synthesis and eventual decision. MACHIAVELLI (1469–1527) is often interpreted as having advocated such a discounting of the least powerful.

In this more "Machiavellian" kind of synthesis, at least as it applies to business organizations, stakeholders outside the stockholder group are viewed instrumentally, as factors potentially affecting the overarching goal of optimizing stockholder interests. They are taken into account in the decision making process, but as external environmental forces, potential sources of either good will or retaliation. (It should be emphasized that managers who adopt this stakeholder approach are not necessarily *personally* indifferent to the plight of stakeholders who are "strategically unimportant." The point is that, *in their role as managers,* with a fiduciary relationship that binds them as agents to principals, their basic outlook subordinates other stakeholder concerns to those of stockholders. Managers rely upon market and legal forces to secure the interests of those whom strategic considerations might discount.)

Unlike mere stakeholder *analysis,* this kind of synthesis goes beyond simply *identifying* stakeholders. But is it an adequate rendering of the *ethical* component in managerial judgment? One answer is that this kind of synthesis falls short not because it is *im*moral, but because it is *non*moral. The idea is that *moral* concern would avoid injury or unfairness to those affected by one's actions because injury and unfairness are wrong, regardless of the retaliatory potential of any aggrieved parties.

Thus the move from analysis to synthesis in discussions of the stakeholder concept is not necessarily a move toward ethics. And the explanation has to do with the possibility of according merely an instrumental status to stakeholder groups other than stockholders. But if we were to treat all stakeholders non-instrumentally, by strict analogy with stockholders, would we then have arrived at a more ethically satisfactory form of stakeholder synthesis?

What Makes a Synthesis Ethical?

In contrast to a "Machiavellian" posture toward stakeholders, one can imagine a management team processing stakeholder information by giving the same care to the interests of, say, employees, customers, and local communities as to the economic interests of stockholders. This kind of commitment to stakeholders might involve trading off the economic advantages of one group against those of another, *e.g.,* in a plant closing decision. On this impartial way of integrating stakeholder analysis with decision making, all stakeholders are treated as having equally important interests, deserving joint "maximization" (what decision theorist Herbert Simon refers to as "satisficing"). It is tempting to call this "stakeholder utilitarianism," but strictly speaking, *maximization* of stakeholder interests is only one approach to impartial synthesis. A Rawlsian "contractarian" synthesis might be another approach.

An impartial view, in contrast to the Machiavellian view of stakeholder synthesis, considers stakeholders apart from their instrumental, economic, or legal clout. It does not think of them merely as what philosopher John Ladd calls "limiting operating conditions" on management attention. On the impartial view, the word "stakeholder" carries with it, by the deliberate modification of a single phoneme, a dramatic shift in managerial outlook. Some would say a shift from *amoral* to *moral.*

Nevertheless, it has been argued that such an approach to stakeholder synthesis is incompatible with widely held moral convictions about the special fiduciary obligations owed by management to stockholders. At the center of the objection is the belief that the obligations of agents to principals are either stronger or different in kind from those of agents to third parties.

The Stakeholder Paradox

Managers who would pursue an *impartial* stakeholder synthesis face resistance from those who believe that a *partial* orientation to stockholders is the only *legitimate* one for business to adopt, given the economic mission and legal constitution of the modern corporation. This anomalous situation has been referred to as the Stakeholder Paradox: *It seems essential, yet illegitimate, to guide corporate decisions by ethical values that go beyond partial or instrumental stakeholder considerations to impartial ones.*

The term "paradox" is used because there appears to be an ethical problem no matter which approach management takes. Morality seems to both forbid and demand a partial (as against impartial) mindset. The issue arises from management's *fiduciary* duty to the stockholder, essentially the duty to keep a profit-maximizing promise. An impartial stakeholder synthesis, in the eyes of some, cuts managers loose from certain well-defined obligations of stockholder accountability and leads to a *betrayal of trust.* Critics claim that this *dilutes* the fiduciary obligation to stockholders (extending it to customers, employees, suppliers, etc.) and thereby threatens the "privacy" of the private sector organization. If corporate responsibility is modeled on public sector INSTITUTIONS with IMPARTIALITY toward all constituencies, the provider of capital loses status.

The stakeholder paradox seems to invite an account of corporate responsibility that (a) avoids surrendering moral relationships between management and stakeholders as the "Machiavellian" view does, while (b) not interpreting obligations to stakeholders as fiduciary obligations (thus protecting the uniqueness of the principal-agent relationship between management and stockholder).

Perhaps management has no additional *fiduciary* relationships to non-stockholder constituencies, but there may still be morally significant *nonfiduciary* obligations surrounding any fiduciary relationship (see the table below). Such *nonfiduciary* obligations are not merely contingent, as on the "Machiavellian" model. They are direct (or "categorical" in Kant's terms), but they are not rooted in a *fiduciary* relationship.

DIRECT MANAGERIAL OBLIGATIONS	Fiduciary	Non-Fiduciary
Duties to Stockholders	X	
Duties to Other Stakeholders		X

A Principle for Stakeholder Synthesis

The responsibilities of management toward stakeholders may best be understood as extensions of the obligations that *stockholders themselves* would be expected to honor in their own right. No one can expect of an *agent* behavior that is ethically less responsible than he would expect of himself. I cannot (ethically) *hire* done on my behalf what I would not (ethically) *do* myself. (We might think of this principle as a formal requirement of consistency in business ethics [and professional ethics generally]: *Investors cannot expect of managers (more generally, principals cannot expect of their agents) behavior that would be inconsistent with the reasonable ethical expectations of the community.*)

This principle does not, of course, resolve me-

chanically the *prima facie* ethical conflicts that managers face. But it does suggest that such challenges are of a piece with those that face us all. It suggests a stakeholder synthesis different from both the partial and the impartial, a synthesis that both management and institutional investors might apply to policies and decisions.

The way out of the stakeholder paradox may lie in understanding the CONSCIENCE of the corporation as a logical and moral extension of the consciences of its principals. It is not an *expansion* of the list of principals, but a gloss on the principal-agent relationship itself. Whatever the structure of the principal-agent relationship, neither principal nor agent can claim "moral immunity" from the basic obligations that apply to any human being (or human organization) toward other members of the community.

Stakeholders have a morally significant relationship to management, but that relationship is different from a fiduciary one. Management may never have promised customers, employees, suppliers, etc., a "return on investment," but management is nevertheless obliged to take seriously its extra-legal obligations not to injure, lie to, or cheat these stakeholders *quite apart from* whether it is in the stockholders' interests.

The conscientious corporation maintains its private economic mission, but in the context of fundamental moral obligations owed by any member of society to others affected by that member's actions. Recognizing such obligations does *not* thereby transform an institution into a public one. Private institutions, like private individuals, can be and are bound to respect moral obligations in the pursuit of private purposes.

As we think through the *proper* relationship of management to stakeholders, fundamental features of business life must undoubtedly be recognized: that corporations have a principally economic mission and competence; that fiduciary obligations to investors and general obligations to comply with the law cannot be set aside; and that abuses of economic POWER and disregard of corporate stewardship in the name of business ethics are possible.

But these things must be recognized as well: that corporations are not solely financial institutions; that fiduciary obligations go beyond short-term profit and are in any case subject to moral criteria in their execution; and that mere compliance with the law can be unduly limited and even unjust.

Understanding that stakeholder analysis is different from stakeholder synthesis, and that stakeholder synthesis can take many forms, some of which are more plausible than others, may help to carry ethical thinking into action with more discipline—and quality—than is found in popular accounts of the task.

See also: APPLIED ETHICS; BUSINESS ETHICS; CHEATING; COMPETITION; CONSCIENCE; DELIBERATION AND CHOICE; DUTY AND OBLIGATION; ECONOMIC ANALYSIS; ENVIRONMENTAL ETHICS; FAIRNESS; FIDUCIARY RELATIONSHIPS; IMPARTIALITY; INSTITUTIONS; INTERESTS; PARTIALITY; POWER; PROFESSIONAL ETHICS; PROMISES; PROPERTY; PUBLIC AND PRIVATE MORALITY; RIGHT HOLDERS; RIGHTS; RISK; SOCIAL CONTRACT THEORY; TRUST; UTILITARIANISM.

Bibliography

Berle, A., and J. Means. *The Modern Corporation and Private Property.* New York: Macmillan, 1933. Rev. ed., New York: Harcourt, Brace, and World, 1968.

Boatright, John. "What's So Special about Shareholders?" *Business Ethics Quarterly* 4 (no. 4, October 1994): 393–407. This issue of *Business Ethics Quarterly* contains several articles on stakeholder analysis.

Beauchamp, Thomas, and Norman Bowie, eds. *Ethical Theory and Business.* 6th ed. Englewood Cliffs, N.J.: Prentice Hall, 2001. Contemporary essays and theoretical overview.

The Caux Round Table Principles for Business. The Caux Round Table, 1994. Copies can be obtained from the CRT web site: ⟨http://www.cauxroundtable.org⟩.

Freeman, R. Edward. *Strategic Management: A Stakeholder Approach.* New York: Pitman, 1984.

Goodpaster, Kenneth E. "Business Ethics and Stakeholder Analysis." *Business Ethics Quarterly* 1 (no. 1, January 1991): 53–74.

Goodpaster, Kenneth E., and Thomas E. Holloran. "In Defense of a Paradox." *Business Ethics Quarterly* 4 (no. 4, October 1994): 423–29. A direct response to the Boatright article cited above.

Ladd, John. "Morality and the Ideal of Rationality in Formal Organizations." *The Monist* 54 (1970): 488–516.

Ruder, David S. "Public Obligations of Private Corporations." *University of Pennsylvania Law Review* 114 (1965): 209–29.

Stone, Christopher. *Where the Law Ends: The Social Control of Corporate Behavior.* New York: Harper and Row, 1975. Legal perspective on corporate responsibility.

Kenneth E. Goodpaster

Stevenson, Charles L[eslie] (1908–1979)

American moral philosopher. Charles Stevenson produced the most fully developed emotivist theory of his time. Most of his writings are contained in two works: *Ethics and Language* (1944) and *Facts and Values* (1963). Stevenson's theory starts from the assumption that science is marked by agreement and morality by disagreement, and is further shaped by the acceptance of two distinctions. The first is the fact/value distinction: beliefs do not logically entail acceptance of attitudes, and value discourse does not report facts or express beliefs. The second is the distinction between normative ethics and METAETHICS. Normative ethics recommends conduct as right or wrong and evaluates individuals as virtuous or vicious. It also tries to support these judgments. To make a moral judgment is to moralize. Moralizing is non-scientific. Metaethics, by contrast, is a detached, scientific, and value-free analysis of what we are doing when we moralize. Its purpose is not to recommend or plead a case but to gain clarity about the function and meaning of value terms and the ways in which value judgments may be supported. According to Stevenson, moralizing is outside the province of philosophy; philosophy is scientific and so confined to metaethical analysis.

Although Stevenson shares with other early emotivists a positivist outlook, his version of emotivism was not developed primarily as a response to the verificationist worry that moral language, like metaphysical language, might be nonsensical and meaningless. Metaethical analysis, Stevenson insists, starts from an examination of everyday, real life ethical problems, yet his picture of the normative standpoint is Deweyean. According to Dewey, the occasion of moral deliberation is an excess of preferences. Rejecting the idea of fixed ends valued for their own sake, DEWEY (1859–1952) claims that means and ends 'name the same reality.' Deliberation is not just a matter of finding the best means to a given end, but the dramatic rehearsal of the possible consequences of satisfying desires with a view to determining which desire to privilege or temporarily take as an end in view.

Stevenson modifies Dewey's claims in two ways. First, he adapts the Deweyean picture to the interpersonal case in which two or more people have opposing desires or attitudes. He thus stresses the dynamic role of normative language in social contexts as a social instrument for altering, redirecting, sustaining, and encouraging the attitudes and conduct of others. Second, and more importantly, he claims that normative disagreements, whether personal or interpersonal, are characterized by disagreement in attitude as opposed to disagreement in belief. The former consists in a clash of attitudes both of which cannot be satisfied; the latter in an opposition of beliefs both of which cannot be true. Dewey, along with most other ethicists, Stevenson says, assumed that normative disagreement is a species of disagreement in belief and thus incorrectly classified normative ethics as a branch of science. Although normative disagreements are typically accompanied by disagreement in belief, their distinctive feature is disagreement in attitude.

Recognition of this affects the analysis of the function and meaning of normative discourse. Normative terms are dynamic. Their function is not to describe, report, or convey information but to express the attitudes of the speaker and to invite others to share these attitudes. Accordingly, value terms possess a special kind of meaning especially suited to these two dynamic functions—emotive meaning—although value terms usually possess descriptive meaning as well. Stevenson adapts Ogden's and Richards's causal or pragmatic theory of meaning, claiming that emotive meaning is a dispositional property of terms, their tendency, "arising from the history of their usage, to express attitudes of speakers and to evoke those of . . . hearers."

Disagreement in attitude gives direction and unity to moral arguments, determining what beliefs are relevant and when the arguments will terminate. According to Stevenson, any belief about any matter of fact can count as a relevant reason in support of a value judgment as long as the speaker considers it likely to alter attitudes. What counts as a good reason is a normative issue. The relationship between beliefs (reasons) and attitudes (the conclusion) is causal, not logical: beliefs may change a person's attitudes but only if that person already has prior attitudes toward those beliefs. While arguments in support of a belief may be valid or invalid, standards of validity are inapplicable to value arguments themselves. Validity is connected with truth and, strictly speaking, value judgments lack truth value.

Support for value judgments thus includes the use of rational and persuasive methods. The choice of what methods to use in a moral argument, Stevenson claims, is itself a normative issue. It is to moralize about the methods of the moralist. The aims of moral discourse (to secure agreement or not), and so the issue of when a value discussion terminates, are also normative issues as is the emotive meaning a person attaches to the descriptive meaning of value terms. As normative issues, these are not the concerns of the metaethicist. This explains why Stevenson never sharply distinguishes between moral and other value discourse. Value discourse and argumentation share features distinguishing them from scientific language. But what distinguishes the moral from other normative viewpoints is itself a normative issue; and we can decide that issue on either rational or persuasive grounds.

See also: ANALYTIC PHILOSOPHY AND ETHICS; DEWEY; EMOTIVISM; HISTORY OF WESTERN ETHICS: TWENTIETH-CENTURY ANGLO-AMERICAN; LOGIC AND ETHICS; METAETHICS; MORAL REALISM; MORAL REASONING; MORAL TERMS; NORMS; PRESCRIPTIVISM.

Bibliography

Works by Charles L. Stevenson

Ethics and Language. New Haven, Conn.: Yale University Press, 1944.

Facts and Values: Studies in Ethical Analysis. New Haven: Yale University Press, 1963. Collection of ten previously published articles plus "Retrospective Comments." Includes the early, influential article, "The Emotive Meaning of Ethical Terms" (*Mind* 46 (1937): 14–31) as well as "The Emotive Conception of Ethics and Its Cognitive Implications" (*Philosophical Review* 59 (1950): 291–304).

"Brandt's Questions About Emotive Ethics." *Philosophical Review* 59 (1950): 528–34.

"Ethical Fallibility." In *Ethics and Society: Original Essays on Contemporary Moral Problems,* edited by Richard T. DeGeorge, 197–217. Garden City, N.Y.: Doubleday, 1966.

Works about Stevenson

Brandt, Richard B. "The Emotive Theory of Ethics." *Philosophical Review* 59 (1950): 305–18.

———. "Stevenson's Defense of the Emotive Theory." *Philosophical Review* 59 (1950): 535–40.

Cavell, Stanley. *The Claim of Reason.* Oxford: Oxford University Press, 1979. "An Absence of Morality," part 3, chapter 10, is a penetrating criticism of Stevenson's conception of 'morality.'

Darwall, Stephen. "Moore to Stevenson." In *Ethics and the History of Western Philosophy,* edited by Robert J. Cavalier, James Gouinlock, and James P. Sterba, pp. 366–98. New York: St. Martin's Press, 1989.

Falk, W. D. "Guiding and Goading." *Mind* 62 (1953): 145–69.

Hudson, W. D. *Modern Moral Philosophy.* Garden City, N.Y.: Doubleday, 1970.

MacIntyre, Alasdair. *After Virtue.* Notre Dame, Ind.: University of Notre Dame Press, 1981.

Ogden, D. K., and I. A. Richards. *The Meaning of Meaning.* London: Routledge and Kegan Paul, 1923.

Robinson, Richard, H. J. Paton, and R. C. Cross. "The Emotive Theory of Ethics." *Proceedings of the Aristotelian Society, suppl.* 22 (1948): 79–140.

Satris, Stephen. "The Theory of Value and the Rise of Ethical Emotivism." *Journal of the History of Ideas* 43 (1982): 109–28.

Toulmin, Stephen. *An Examination of the Place of Reason in Ethics.* Cambridge: Cambridge University Press, 1950. Especially chapters 3, 4.

Urmson, J. O. *The Emotive Theory of Ethics.* Oxford: Oxford University Press, 1969.

Warnock, G. J. *Contemporary Moral Philosophy.* London: Macmillan, 1969.

Charlotte Brown

Stewart, Dugald (1753–1828)

Prominent in the Scottish Enlightenment in the student generation after David HUME (1711–1776), Adam SMITH (1723–1790), and Adam Ferguson (1723–1816), Stewart was educated at Edinburgh and served there as professor, first of mathematics, then of moral philosophy. He made a distinctive contribution to the line of moderate empiricism that stretches from Thomas REID's (1710–1796) common sense to C. I. LEWIS's (1883–1964) PRAGMATISM by exploring the role of formal systems and the activity of the knower in organizing experience. His unified program is grounded in an empirical PSYCHOLOGY which acknowledges the wholeness of human emotional and intellectual response as well as the capacities to frame and pursue ends. It examines private moral judgment and moral philosophy which, in the Enlightenment sense, includes political economy, jurisprudence, history and SOCIOLOGY.

Stewart faults rationalist reliance on self-evident truths as misunderstanding the mathematical model. Mathematical definitions (axioms) are arbitrary starting points among alternatives, limited only by criteria of coherence and simplicity; once assigned empirical reference, certainty is lost. Empirical knowledge, starting from observed constant (not necessary) conjunctions, is strengthened by increasing evidence and broader unifying generalizations open to prediction, test, and experiment. Definitions now come at inquiry's end, but empirical knowledge, though indefinitely corrigible, is never more than probable.

Stewart faults narrow empiricism for overlooking talents and capacities that mark man as intelligent, active, and social. These allow him to plan, to invent, and to learn in distinctively human ways; selective attention, hypotheses, perceived similarities are already at work in the registration of experience. Stewart's version of Common Sense, his substitute for innate ideas, points to original and active powers that structure knowledge and make inquiry intelligible. These indispensable conditions of belief include a belief in the continuity of the self, in the general reliability of memory, in the uniformity of nature (that tomorrow will be sufficiently like today to support generalizations), in an objective world where even perceiving is referential and judgmental, and in the power of framing prudential and moral judgments. Such laws or principles are not substantive.

Beyond particular prudential judgments, we can frame a general idea of HAPPINESS, a life good on the whole, in the light of which we may act or postpone or plan. Such happiness is complex, modified by differences in temper, imagination, habit, the ability to discriminate and learn from experience, and specific opportunities. But languages build in a distinction between judgments of interest and those of right and wrong quite apart from utility. The latter are attended by emotions of PLEASURE and pain and estimates of the agent's INTENTION, but their focus is on actions and they are cognitive and objective. Moral judgment takes place in a context of systems of belief; of vastly differing levels of culture and science and historical development; exigencies of war, scarcity, tyranny; and in changing INSTITUTIONS which make understandable divergent views of such matters as usury, theft, political assassination. Man's morality is expressed in society and there can best be efficacious. The larger task of philosophy is to discern those general lessons that may better ensure moral progress—from strife to social concord and wealth—and strengthen us to act on the conviction that prejudice, SLAVERY, and CORRUPTION must gradually give way, and thus realize the benevolent design.

Stewart's influence was considerable, not only through his eloquent lectures (JAMES MILL [1773–1836] and Walter Scott [1771–1832] were among his hearers), but in his liberal sympathies: for freedom and DEMOCRACY; broader educational opportunities (for women also); relaxing church control over educational and cultural life. He influenced French philosophy from Destutt de Tracy (1754–1836) and Royer-Collard (1763–1845) to Victor Cousin (1792–1867); and American philosophy from Thomas JEFFERSON (1743–1826) and Benjamin Rush (1745–1813) to the Cambridge pragmatists; and a wider public through his essays on moral progress for the *Encyclopedia Britannica*.

See also: COMMON SENSE MORALISTS; JEFFERSON; MORAL SENSE THEORISTS.

Bibliography

Works by Dugald Stewart

Collected Works. 11 vols. Edited by William Hamilton and John Veitch. Edinburgh, 1854–1860.

Works about Stewart

Segerstedt, Torgny T. *The Problem of Knowledge in Scottish Philosophy,* n.s., no. 6. Lunds Universitets Arsskrift, 1935.
Stenson, Sten. "History of Scottish Empiricism from 1730–1856." Dissertation. Columbia University, 1952.

Elizabeth Flower

Stoicism

The label "Stoic ethics" is used to refer to the moral doctrines of a school of philosophy that existed for at least five centuries. Historians of philosophy usually distinguish three periods: the early Stoa (so called after the Painted Colonnade, *stoa poikile*, in Athens, where the founders used to teach), from its founding around 300 B.C.E. down to the middle of the second century B.C.E.; the middle Stoa, represented mainly by Panaetius (c. 180–109 B.C.E.) and Posidonius (c. 135–51 B.C.E.); and the late Stoics of the Roman Empire. Far from adhering to a rigid orthodoxy, the Stoa was known for internal debates and differences of opinion among its prominent members. Thus, the adjective "Stoic" is no more precise than, say, "Kantian" or "Cartesian"; its use can be justified, however, not only by the fact that so many philosophers officially professed adherence to the school, but also by the impression, arising from our ancient sources, that there was indeed a core of common views, shared by members of the school, such that to abandon any of these would be to abandon Stoicism.

The central doctrines were presumably established by the first three heads of the school: Zeno of Citium (342–270 B.C.E.), its founder; Cleanthes of Assos (c. 300–220 B.C.E.), Zeno's immediate successor; and Chrysippus of Soloi (c. 280–207 B.C.E.), who was credited with having provided Stoicism with what was seen as its impressive systematic unity. The works of all three are lost, apart from a few brief fragments. What have survived are some more or less coherent accounts from authors such as CICERO (106–43 B.C.E.), SENECA (c. 4 B.C.E.–C.E. 65), EPICTETUS (c. 55–c. 135), historians of philosophy or doxographers such as Diogenes Laertius (second century C.E.) and Stobaeus (fl. C.E. 500); in addition, there are quotations and paraphrases in philosophical authors such as the Academic Plutarch (c. 46–120) and the Aristotelian commentator Alexander of Aphrodisias (second to third centuries) who discuss Stoic views in various contexts.

Any account of Stoic philosophy will therefore be a speculative reconstruction, open to doubts and modifications, and unlikely to represent exactly the theories of any individual member of the school. What follows is an attempt to describe the common core, corresponding perhaps most closely to the doctrines as developed by Chrysippus.

Early Stoicism

Zeno, and all Stoics after him, saw themselves as followers of SOCRATES (c. 470–399 B.C.E.) in their ethics. It is indeed easy to recognize that they held and defended some of Socrates' most famous theses, best known to us from PLATO's (c. 430–347 B.C.E.) early dialogues. Examples are the claim that virtue is sufficient for HAPPINESS, that it consists in some kind of knowledge or expertise, and as corollaries, the claims that all moral failures are due to error and that WEAKNESS OF WILL is, strictly speaking, impossible. But the Stoics were writing more than a century after Socrates, and philosophy had become considerably more technical and sophisticated in the fourth century. Hence, while Socrates seems to have defended his convictions mainly by dint of confounding those who disagreed with him and exposing the incoherence of their moral beliefs, the Stoics felt the need to provide systematic arguments in support of the Socratic positions they wished to defend.

The final good. The theoretical framework of EU-DAIMONISM, developed by Plato and his students and most explicitly set out in the opening chapters of ARISTOTLE's (384–322 B.C.E.) *Nicomachean Ethics,* was evidently taken over by all the Hellenistic schools. At the beginning of the third century, then, a systematic ethics was expected to begin from an argument to establish what was to count as the FINAL GOOD, the end of all ACTION, or happiness (*eudaimonia*), and to work out the consequences of such a conception for the conduct of life.

The Stoics held that the end was "a consistent life" or "a life in agreement with nature"—these two formulae were apparently regarded as equivalent. The argument for this thesis was based on their metaphysics of nature. According to Stoic doctrine, nature is a rational being that permeates the universe in the form of a divine "breath" (*pneuma*) and rules the world by a rational plan in every one of its parts, so that everything that exists or happens must be considered to be determined by nature. "Nature," "reason" (*logos*), "Zeus," "fate," "providence," and "god" were all names of this one divine entity. Natural things form a hierarchy, with inanimate objects at the bottom and rational animals at the top. The best and most admirable thing in the world is divine reason, which manifests itself in the natural order of the universe.

Now according to the Stoics, a thing is good if it is a perfect exemplar of its kind. But since the perfection of rationality is not only different in kind, but also superior to perfections of all other sorts, the Stoics said that the term "good" should, strictly speaking, be reserved for the perfection of reason, and its opposite, "bad" or "evil," for the respective contrary, whatever goes against reason. Human beings are endowed with rationality and therefore occupy a place in the natural hierarchy just below god or nature herself. The human good, therefore, will consist in the perfection of human reason, and will count as a good in the strict sense. The best way to achieve perfect rationality will be to conform to the rational order of the universe, and such "agreement

with nature," being the perfect state of human reason, will count as human virtue. This, then, is "what all action in life ought to be referred to"—the final good for man. The "ought" here is probably best understood as an indication that nature intends human beings to pursue this goal: the rational order of the universe was also described by the Stoics as the will of Zeus, or the law of nature.

Virtue. From the two propositions that human virtue is rational perfection and that reason is perfected by obeying the law of nature, the Stoics inferred that virtue is the human good, and that the goal of life must be living in agreement with nature. Up to this point the identification of virtue with obedience to the law of nature might seem to be a mere verbal maneuver. It remains to be shown that there is a connection between the perfection of reason and virtue as ordinarily understood, so as to include, for example, the four cardinal virtues of COURAGE, TEMPERANCE, justice, and WISDOM. Here the Stoics seem to have introduced their celebrated doctrine of *oikeiosis*—"appropriation" or "familiarization" with one's self and others. They argued that nature has provided the human being, just like every other animal, from birth with a sense of its own self and the capacity to recognize and pursue those things that will foster and preserve its life, as well as to avoid things that will harm or destroy it. Humans also have a natural feeling of familiarity with other members of the species and hence a tendency to care about the preservation and well-being of their FAMILY, friends, and rational animals in general.

The first of these "impulses" would foster self-regarding behavior such as looking after one's health and strength, getting food and shelter, acquiring material wealth, and also developing one's capacities for reasoning and trying to acquire knowledge—ways of acting that one might not ordinarily describe as being morally valuable. The second "impulse," however, was described as the foundation of justice, based on respect for others and the desire to help fellow human beings seen as belonging to one, at least in kind. Following these two natural impulses toward self-preservation and toward CARE for others would lead a human being to pursue and avoid things in a systematic, orderly way that can be described as "appropriate conduct." But a person who led a "natural life" in this sense would not yet be considered virtuous. Virtue is not only a matter of acting correctly, but first and foremost a matter of acting for the right reasons, and, according to the Stoics, virtue must be based on knowledge, not instinct. The person who does the right thing from instinct, or for the wrong reason, does not display virtue. After all, non-rational animals are made by nature to behave in the ways appropriate to *their* nature, but they cannot attain virtue.

In order to distinguish the aims set by nature for the natural impulses from the higher end of conformity with nature's will, the Stoics introduced a number of terminological distinctions. Since the terms "good" and "bad" were reserved for virtue (rational perfection) and its opposite, the objects of the natural impulses, such as health, wealth, friends, and family, were to be called "natural advantages" or "preferred"; their opposites "against nature" or "dispreferred." The decision to pursue or avoid objects that are natural advantages or disadvantages was called "selection," as opposed to "choice," which would consist in aiming at real goods, that is, virtue. Health, wealth, friends, etc. were said to have "selective value," but not to be goods. In fact, the scale of real goods and evils comprised only virtue and vice, so that the "natural" things were to be described as completely indifferent. Actions aimed at attaining the natural advantages or avoiding their opposites were "appropriate," as opposed to "right," which was reserved for virtuous action aimed at agreement with nature.

Given this terminology, the Stoics described a human being's ideal development toward virtue as follows. In the early stages of life, the human child does not yet possess reason. His actions are guided by the natural impulses, which lead him to pursue and avoid things that are in accordance with his nature or against it, selecting things that have selective value, and rejecting those that have selective disvalue. By the time reason comes to take control of the natural impulses—at about age fourteen—a person is able to recognize that his natural and appropriate conduct exhibits a kind of rational order that is itself far more valuable than the objects pursued in his individual actions. He comes to realize that goodness consists in perfect rationality, and thereupon makes it his ultimate aim to live according to the rational order of nature, of which human conduct is only a minor part. He will therefore cease to value natural advantages in their own right, and continue to pursue them only in order to achieve agreement with nature and thus perfect his rationality.

The switch from the pursuit of natural aims to an exclusive interest in rational agreement with nature marks the transition to virtue. The virtuous person—the sage, as the Stoics would say—is the one whose every action is informed by his insight into the will of Zeus and whose only desire is to conform to nature's law. The sage's knowledge of NATURAL LAW is said to derive from observation and reflection upon the way nature has organized the universe, and human beings in particular. He will therefore continue to follow the pattern he had adopted instinctively under the guidance of the natural impulses, but his reasons for doing so will have changed. Since his knowledge was assumed to determine the wise man's conduct, it could be identified with the knowledge of good and EVIL that Socrates had held to be virtue.

Moral psychology. The Stoics relied upon their psychological theory to support the claim that the sage's knowledge will be sufficient for virtue, and sufficient for happiness as well. They rejected the Platonic and Aristotelian thesis that EMOTION and reason are distinct sources of motivation within the human soul, and insisted that after the advent of reason, human action was determined by reason alone. A decision to act is constituted by assent to a "rational impression" (an articulate thought) that presents the agent with the description of some action to be done or avoided, for example, "I should take a walk now." Assent is in the agent's power in the sense that she can either give or withhold it, and hence human beings are responsible for what they do.

The rightness or wrongness of an action depends upon whether the proposition or impression to which the agent assents is true or false. The sage will assent only to true impressions, and hence will infallibly follow the will of nature. Now since no human mind can foresee the exact course of events as planned by universal nature, the wise person often will be guided by her observation of general but not exceptionless rules, such as that nature normally intends human beings to preserve their health, look after their children, partake in the administration of their community, and the like. It is reasonable or probable, but not certain, that she should pursue those aims and attain them. Hence, the propositions to which she assents will often have the form "it is reasonable for me, as a human being, to do *X*." In fact, "appropriate action" was defined as "what, when done, has a reasonable justification."

Since things that can reasonably be expected to happen may not actually occur, the sage will not always attain the results she is trying to achieve. She may, for example, try to preserve her health, but still fall ill. Nevertheless, she will have succeeded in doing what is reasonable; and as her aim was ultimately to follow nature's will, and she is convinced that whatever happens as a result of nature's plan must be good, she will not be disappointed. The virtuousness of her actions depends only upon the rightness of her intentions, and is not diminished by external failure.

By contrast, people who are not wise—"fools," as the Stoics called them—are likely to be misled by PASSION or emotions. These "affections of the soul" were declared by the Stoics to be impulses caused by or consisting in erroneous assent, given to propositions to the effect that some object other than virtue or rationality is good or bad. The phenomenon of weakness of will, described by Aristotle and Plato as a case of conflicting desires in the soul, did not indicate the presence of other sources of motivation besides reason. Rather, it should be seen instead as a case of reason wavering between conflicting impressions. Ordinary humans are liable to fall into the error of thinking that the objects of the natural impulses are good, their opposites bad. This will lead them to assent to the corresponding impressions—say, "it is good for me to acquire wealth"—and hence to pursue delusive goods with an intensity that may make them impervious to rational considerations. They will be prone to act unreasonably, and furthermore, since their plans will often be thwarted by nature, their lives will be full of conflicts and misery. The only way, then, to save a person from unhappiness will be to rid her of the passions altogether, so that her only desires and aversions are directed toward what is truly good—nature's law—or truly evil—disagreement with nature.

Happiness. Stoics, like other Hellenistic philosophers, used to describe their ideal of human perfection in terms of the sage. On the one hand, to say what the sage will do is simply a graphic way of telling us what human beings can do or ought to do. On the other hand, putting these claims together in the portrait of the sage provided a vivid model that could serve as an inspiration for aspiring Stoics. Wisdom, or virtue, is the final stage of human development if everything happens as it should. Once a person has freed herself from the tendency to give in to seductive impressions and has discovered the true notion of the good, she will achieve peace of mind (*ataraxia*) and serenity in the realization that all that really matters is in her power. Since virtue is the only good, and it is in her power, everything that is beyond her control will appear to her as a matter of indifference—not in the sense that she will not continue to follow the path of "selecting" what contributes to a natural human life, but in the sense that she will be content with whatever nature has ordained, knowing that all that counts is her rational attitude, and that nature has arranged everything in the best possible way. The passions that trouble the souls of ordinary people will have been left behind. In their place, the sage will experience "ways of being well affected" (*eupatheiai*). Unlike the passions, these are directed at real goods and evils, and consist, for example, in eagerness in the pursuit of virtuous action, or elation at the thought of nature's perfect rationality. On the negative side, there will be caution in the avoidance of moral wrongdoing, but neither grief nor PITY—after all, whatever happens, even the death of one's dearest relatives and friends, is part of nature's plan and must be good, whether we can understand it or not.

A person who has reached this stage will have achieved happiness, according to the Stoics, by all the criteria philosophers had come up with for the final good. She will have all that she desires, since her desires are only for the good; and she will lack nothing, since virtue is the only thing anybody needs in order to act in agreement with nature. All her actions, whether momentous or trivial, will have the one quality that makes them real goods—being based on knowledge of nature's law, and done with the intention of agreeing with nature.

The Stoics did not claim that this ideal was often realized. On the contrary, there were disputes as to whether a truly wise person had ever existed. The founders of the school did not claim such distinction for themselves, and the only candidate on whom there seems to have been agreement was, once again, Socrates. But they insisted that the ideal was possible and indeed prescribed by nature, so that it should in principle be in each person's power to reach it if that person tried seriously enough.

Later Developments

During the third and second centuries B.C.E., Stoicism became the most influential school of philosophy, but its leaders also had to refine and defend their doctrines in the light of acute and ingenious objections from the Academic skeptics, who challenged such fundamental assumptions as that it is possible to acquire the knowledge needed for virtue, that the natural impulses will lead one to morally appropriate conduct, or that virtue is the only human good. One of the main stumbling blocks seems to have been the Stoic distinction between "preferred" and "dispreferred" things said to be indifferent, on the one hand, and real goods and evils on the other. The critics argued that if anything has any value, it must ultimately contribute to the final good, and hence cannot be indifferent.

At the end of the second century, the Academy lost its critical vigor, and the Stoics turned their interest more to the detailed application of their doctrine in everyday life than to its epistemological or metaphysical foundations. An exception may have been Posidonius, who is said to have abandoned the rationalist psychology of the earlier Stoics in favor of the Platonic model because he found it impossible to explain the existence of evil in the world on the basis of orthodox Stoic assumptions. But Posidonius's main interest seems to have been in fields other than ethics. Panaetius, a philosopher who spent much of his life in Rome, wrote mostly about the so-called "appropriate actions," obviously the most practical part of Stoic ethics. Cicero claims to be following him closely in his book *De officiis* ("On Duties"), and so we are relatively well informed about some of his work. It may have been Panaetius's idea to expand the theory of familiarization to one's self by including not only the natural tendencies toward self-preservation and development of capacities common to all human beings, but also consideration of individual talents and action appropriate to a given social role or position. He is also said to have promised to deal with the interesting problem—no doubt raised by the Academics—of whether egoistic and social values (utility and moral goodness, as Cicero puts it) may conflict. The answer, of course, was to be that such conflict is impossible; but according to Cicero, Panaetius did not fulfill his promise, and Cicero's own attempt to fill the gap does not go very far.

It was probably the lawyer and statesman Cicero (in his book *De legibus*, "On Laws") who introduced the theory of natural law into legal debates, arguing that the written laws of a human community would be just only if they were in agreement with the higher law of nature's reason, as described by the Stoics. With this step, reason's law, which had primarily been seen as guiding an individual's actions, also became the yardstick of human legislation.

The Stoics of the imperial age—Seneca, Epictetus, and MARCUS AURELIUS (121–180) usually did not discuss or question the metaphysical underpinnings of Stoicism, but concentrated instead on the task of spelling out ways of achieving the wisdom that promises happiness for the Stoic sage. They showed great psychological subtlety and ingenuity in developing specific techniques for acquiring the kind of detachment from bodily and external things that is essential to the Stoic conception of virtue, and the submission to nature's will that lets the ideal Stoic sustain all sorts of calamities with perfect equanimity. The accent had evidently shifted from Panaetius's and Cicero's concern with appropriate action, whether public or private, to self-improvement as a way to salvation. Stoicism thus became a kind of inward-directed and unworldly morality that obviously held great appeal for the early Christians.

But as a school of philosophy it was eclipsed by the renewal of interest in the great classics, and the eventual domination of neo-Platonism on the one hand, and Christian thought on the other.

However, the portrait of the Stoic sage as a person concerned only with virtue and completely unaffected by external events, together with the idea of a moral law ordained by reason as the ruler of the universe, has proved throughout the history of philosophy to be one of the most attractive and influential conceptions of both morality and human happiness.

See also: ARISTOTELIAN ETHICS; CICERO; COSMOPOLITAN ETHICS; EMOTION; EPICTETUS; EPICUREANISM; *EUDAIMONIA,* -ISM; FAIRNESS; FATE AND FATALISM; FINAL GOOD; FITTINGNESS; FREEDOM AND DETERMINISM; GOOD, THEORIES OF THE; HAPPINESS; HISTORY OF WESTERN ETHICS 3 (HELLENISTIC), 4 (ROMAN); MARCUS AURELIUS; NATURAL LAW; NATURALISM; NEO-STOICISM; PASSION; *PHRONESIS;* PRACTICAL WISDOM; RATIONALITY VS. REASONABLENESS; SELF-KNOWLEDGE; SENECA; SKEPTICISM IN ANCIENT ETHICS; VIRTUE ETHICS; WEAKNESS OF WILL; WISDOM.

Bibliography

Works by Stoics

Arnim, I. von, comp. *Stoicorum veterum fragmenta.* 4 vols. Reprint. Stuttgart: Teubner, 1964 [1903–1906]. The standard edition of the fragments of the early Stoics; commonly abbreviated SVF. The 4th volume is an index by M. Adler (1924).

Long, A. A., and D. N. Sedley, tr. and comps. *The Hellenistic Philosophers.* 2 vols. Cambridge: Cambridge University Press, 1987. A collection of fragments in new translations, ordered by topic, with a concise commentary. Vol. 2 contains the original texts of the fragments, along with an excellent annotated Bibliography for recent works (most in the form of articles) on Stoic ethics.

The following bilingual Loeb editions contain the most important of the longer sources.

Cicero, Marcus Tullius. Loeb Classical Library. Cambridge, MA: Harvard University Press. See *De finibus* (On ends), books III and IV—an outline of Stoic ethics followed by a critique; *De officiis* (On duties); *De legibus* (On laws), book I; *Tusculanae disputationes* (Tusculan disputations), books III and IV, for the theory of the passions; *De fato* (On fate) for the problem of determinism and free will.

Diogenes Laertius. *Lives of Eminent Philosophers.* Book VII. Loeb Classical Library. Cambridge, MA: Harvard University Press.

Epictetus. *Discourses* and *Manual* (Handbook). Loeb Classical Library. Cambridge, MA: Harvard University Press.

Marcus Aurelius. *The Communings with Himself* (Meditations). Loeb Classical Library. Cambridge, MA: Harvard University Press.

Seneca. *Epistulae morales* (Letters to Lucilius) and *Moral Essays* (Dialogi). Loeb Classical Library. Cambridge, MA: Harvard University Press.

Secondary Sources

Forschner, M. *Die stoische Ethik.* Stuttgart: Klett-Cotta, 1981. Reprinted, Darmstadt, 1995. A more comprehensive recent account.

Inwood, Brad. *Ethics and Human Action in Early Stoicism.* Oxford: Clarendon Press, 1985. Stoic moral psychology and theory of action.

Inwood, Brad, and P. Donini. "Stoic Ethics." In *The Cambridge History of Hellenistic Philosophy,* edited by Keimpe Algra *et al.,* pp. 675–738. Cambridge: Cambridge University Press, 1999.

Long, A. A. *Stoic Studies.* Cambridge: Cambridge University Press, 1996.

Gisela Striker

strategic interaction

We commonly undertake actions that make sense only when seen as responses to or functions of the actions that we expect others to take. For example, we can negotiate urban sidewalks at rush hour by tacitly coordinating with thousands of other pedestrians. Or a parent threatens a child with being sent to bed early in the expectation that the threat alone will cause a change of behavior by the child. Or, in an example of David HUME (1711–1776), I cooperate with you to drain the bit of marshy land between us.

These are all instances of strategic interaction. They differ in important ways but they are similar in that, in each of them, the benefits to us from our own actions depend on the actions of others. Often, we would have preferred to act differently if we had known that others would act as they then do. Even more often, of course, we would prefer that others act differently in order that our own action might then produce what we think to be the best of all possible outcomes from our interaction.

In strategic interaction, what I choose is a strategy or an ACTION rather than an outcome. Of course, it is typically my concern for outcomes that guides me in selecting my strategy, but I commonly cannot directly choose an outcome because any possible outcome is a result not only of my choice of strategy but also of your action and perhaps actions of many others.

A grasp of strategic interaction can lead to clarifying insights about social interaction, for example, in the explanation of social order. It can also severely undercut standard action theory with its sometime supposition that an individual's action will have a determinate result. And it can inform debates in moral theory. Let us consider these in turn after first canvassing the range of forms that strategic interaction can take.

Classes of Interaction

The two modal forms of pure strategic interactions are conflict and coordination. In a case of pure conflict, if one of us gains, the other must lose. In a case of pure coordination, you and I wish to do exactly the same thing in some sense, although we might not care which of several things it is that we both do. For example, we want both to drive on the left or both on the right, but not one of us left and the other right.

There is another very large class of interactions that combines elements of both of these. We face partial conflict and partial coordination problems. The most important of all such interactions—called mixed-motive games in GAME THEORY—is simple exchange, in which: I most would like to have what I have plus what you have; I next most would like to have what you have while giving up what I have; I next most would like to keep what I have while you keep what you have; and, finally, I would least like to give up what I have while you keep what you have. If you have analogous preferences, and if my stealing what you have is blocked, we might readily succeed in exchanging with each other, and we could therefore both be better off. Exchange has the structure of the prisoner's dilemma game (discussed in CO-OPERATION, CONFLICT, AND COORDINATION), which is therefore a pervasive game in our lives.

There are many other mixed-motive games. Indeed, virtually all real world games are probably mixed-motive, but often there is a dominant element of either conflict or coordination. For example, in warfare, the dominant element might be conflict, but there might still be reasons for coordinating on not using particularly hideous strategies such as poison or biological warfare.

In addition to these basic forms of interaction, we can be involved repeatedly in the same or a similar interaction with someone or some group, or we can interact once only with someone. Hence, we may have incentives from iteration of our interaction that change the way we would choose in a single, one-shot interaction that held no expectation of further interaction with that partner or those partners. In many contexts, iteration is fundamentally important. For example, in the discussion of promise-keeping below, it follows that I have a far stronger incentive to keep PROMISES to those with whom I am involved in ongoing relationships than with strangers. In a sense, we can import the external influence of future interactions into our interaction of this moment to change its incentives to us.

Social Order

The three major classes of theories of social order are conflict, cooperation or exchange, and shared value theories. In the conflict theories, as associated with Thrasymachus in PLATO's (c. 430–347 B.C.E.) *Republic,* it is supposed that order depends on enforcement by a powerful government. In the exchange theories, following from the Scottish Enlightenment vision of Adam SMITH's (1723–1790) economics, we achieve order because it is in our interest to truck and barter with each other. In the shared value theories of certain anthropologists and of the French sociologist Émile DURKHEIM (1858–1917), it is supposed that order comes about spontaneously because we share values and we all work toward joint ends.

The peculiarity of the first two of these three schools of thought is that they are grounded in a vision of strategic interaction, but that vision is limited to a single one of the possible forms of strategic interaction discussed above (and in COOPERATION, CONFLICT, AND COORDINATION). The shared value school seems oblivious of the problem of strategic interaction. One might suppose that the conflict and exchange visions are grounded in suppositions that one of the three general forms of interaction is modal, that is to say, it is the form that dominates our interactions in general.

Oddly, however, the form of strategic interaction that is surely modal in this sense is that of coordination. For example, in the standard case of the driving convention, we need not share values with each other, face real conflict between each other, or have any prospect of entering exchange with each other. Yet we desperately want to achieve a workable social order that allows you to get where you are going and me to get where I am going without our colliding with each other. All that we genuinely want or expect is successful coordination on this limited matter. I may dislike everything you want to do that brings you onto the road with me, and you may oppose everything I want to do at the end of my trip. What is centrally important to all of us while we are driving, however, is merely to have others stay out of our way.

Arguably, for the largest part of our problem of social order, such simple coordination is the core issue. Hume presented the first extensive account of coordination theory, much of it in the footnotes of book 3 of his *A Treatise of Human Nature* (1739–1740), as discussed below. In a modern, large-scale liberal society, coordination is overwhelmingly important for the simple reasons that we have few direct dealings with most people and therefore cannot be exchanging with them and that we are not in substantial conflict with many of them. Yet, it would be silly to claim that we share important values to such a degree that we simply agree on all major issues. Indeed, there may be some need of government CO-ERCION to stop us from imposing our own values on others, as, for example, many fundamentalist religious believers might often wish to impose their values and as many others might wish to impose their relatively specific policy values, as in time of divisive war.

Social order can be regulated by coordination even when the coordination is unequal in the sense that one group has a superior position and yet the group in the inferior position submits to the coordination. Hierarchical societies and unequal gender roles are often supported even by those who are worse off in them. Often no one need be coerced to submit to inferior outcomes because there is no way a single member of the inferior group might beneficially act against the social order. The social order might not be as potent in motivating people as the driving convention is, but it still might be sufficient. Edna Ullmann-Margalit calls such NORMS of hierarchy and INEQUALITY "norms of partiality." To break such a norm may virtually require group coordination on opposition or even rebellion. Such coordination runs against the logic of collective action, which suggests that each individual might prefer to let others rebel and to benefit from their action rather than take the risk of participating in the collective action.

Action Theory

In a typically complex choice context, you might choose a strategy that includes among its possible outcomes some that are dismal or even reprehensible. The very same strategy, however, might also include among its possible outcomes one that is the best of all possible outcomes that could result from any choice you might make in the circumstances. It is incoherent to say you choose one of those outcomes directly. You merely choose to do what has the chance of producing a very good outcome or avoiding a very bad one.

Consider a grand—but real, not fanciful—example: the effort of the World Health Organization (WHO) to eliminate smallpox. This sounds like a morally good action—of course, the reason it is morally good is that it saved hundreds of millions of people from the gruesome effects of smallpox. Unfortunately, WHO's actions also made it possible for the world to suffer the worst epidemic in human history, because almost no one is any longer vaccinated against smallpox and virtually everyone would be vulnerable to an epidemic that started from the accidental or terrorist release of some of the extant stores of the virus (Preston).

The leaders of the WHO effort clearly wanted the very good outcome of eradication of the worst disease of human experience; they did not want the dreadful result of the worst epidemic of human experience. Their actions, however, were the virtually necessary steps in enabling *both* these outcomes. Their actions turned out to be sufficient, in the context of others' actions, to accomplish their intended goal of eliminating smallpox in the wild. They were not sufficient to eliminate stores of the virus in the former Soviet Union and the United States.

In general, an individual's action in social contexts can have a large panoply of possible results, and which of these materializes depends on the actions of potentially large numbers of other actors. The possibilities that might follow from my action this moment might range from disastrous to wonderful, with most of the likely results being merely okay or somewhat better or worse than the status quo. But, because disaster can follow (I merely drove to the store to buy food for dinner, but I unintentionally killed a pedestrian on the way), strategic interaction is inherently clouded with RISK. Ordinary action in even the most deliberately simplistic examples of action theory also faces this problem. For example, when I flip the switch that turns on a light, I may cause a short that sets the building on fire and destroys many lives. One might suppose that such a problem is itself an instance of strategic interaction, because it results, perhaps, from the botched work of an electrician or of the employees who manufactured the switch.

Moral Theory

The most heated debate in moral theory over the past couple of centuries has focused on a peculiar difference between an ethics of the right and an ethics of the good, or between DEONTOLOGY, especially Kantian moral theory, and CONSEQUENTIAL-

ISM, especially UTILITARIANISM. In deontology, the focus is commonly on actions that are judged to be right or wrong *tout court*. In consequentialism, the focus is on outcomes or consequences that are judged to be good or bad—or, more accurately, better or worse. This is a difference that makes no sense in pragmatic or rational choice, in which all actions are merely means to ends that are judged better or worse than ends that would follow from alternative actions. Typically, one consequence is better for me than another if it entails greater welfare for me. One might roughly characterize utilitarianism, which is the principal branch of consequentialist ethics, as a moral theory that extends this principle of pragmatic choice to the welfare of all rather than merely to the welfare of the actor.

That the difference between deontological and utilitarian ethics might be severe is suggested by the account above of strategic interaction in various classes of games. In these games, individual actions are essentially choices of strategies, and outcomes to each individual are the result of the choices of strategies of all. To evaluate the strategies, which are tantamount to actions, independently of the outcomes to which they might be expected to lead would make no sense in either pragmatic or utilitarian moral choice. Yet, this is typically what is stipulated in deontological ethics, with perhaps a constraint to allow actions to block grievous outcomes. Strategies per se do not have a moral valence. They are merely means, and they could be labeled with entirely value-free labels, such as number 1, 2, 3, and so forth.

Some arguments for a morality of rules for action suppose that rules can be correctly specified for an ideal world, such as the world of Kant's kingdom of ends, and that these rules should then be followed even in our less than ideal world. At the abstract level, this seems to be either sleight of hand or a fundamental misunderstanding. At the practical level, however, it is execrable. For example, in the ideal world, it would be wrong to lie to anyone. In the Nazi world of the German industrialist Oskar Schindler and the French pastor André Trocmé (Hallie 1979), lying to protect Jews from extermination was surely not wrong but right. In an ethics of virtue, it might even count as supererogatory—beyond the call of duty. For Kant, it was wrong. He grotesquely insisted that one should not even lie to an intended assassin about where the assassin's target happens to be (Kant [1797] 1909). This partic-

ular claim can be dismissed as silly or mistaken, as it is by many Kantians. But the principle that grounds its deduction must be rejected as fallacious. Actions or action-types are generally not moral *per se* but only contingently.

Other arguments for a morality of rules (including the rule-utilitarian branch of utilitarianism) suppose that there are epistemological reasons for people to follow rules rather than to assess consequences. For example, individuals commonly lack relevant causal understandings even to choose actions well by their consequences. Hence, they should learn rules for action rather than try to produce good results by ad hoc choices of actions. Such arguments have against them that it is hard to see how one could know that a rule is generally apt to be good even when one could not assess whether its specific applications would be good.

F. A. Hayek (1960: 54–70) and G. E. Moore (1903: 158) have argued that broadly accepted rules have typically survived evolution through a process of social selection that suggests that they are well adapted to our circumstances. Hence, such rules can be seen to be generally correct. Against this view, one might claim that, while they might have had adaptive qualities, a large fraction of all major social rules ever followed were amoral or even immoral on almost any universal principles of morality. Very many of them regulate nothing more than mere matters of taste. Many of them are racist, exclusionary, hierarchical, static, vicious, and so forth. The fact that they were socially selected did not imbue them with any moral qualities.

No rule-utilitarian has given a credible analysis of how we are to know that some rules are better than direct consideration of consequences in determining good consequences. JOHN STUART MILL ([1861] 1969) supposed that, for the ordinary run of humankind, perhaps teaching moral rules as essentially inviolable would be better on the whole than trying to teach them to act from consideration of consequences. Mill did not go further and say that the simplistic rules were therefore morally right, merely that they were a good means to achieving good outcomes for many people.

In some rule-utilitarian arguments and in Kant's theory, the conclusion in favor of a particular rule for action defines that rule as morally right. Neither kind of argument would be at all compelling for pragmatic choice. Much of game and rational choice theory might be read as an effort to establish best strategies or rules for action. The implication of such efforts is that no particular rule for strategy choice in a general interaction with others *whose actions are not yet determined* could plausibly be thought to be rationally right.

The moral judgment of many actions makes easy enough sense because it can be supposed that those actions have particular implications or consequences. For example, it seems relatively uncontroversial that abusing a child is wrong and it hardly matters whether one is speaking of the action by the actor or of its consequence for the child. It is not so clearly uncontroversial to say that it would be wrong not to vote in a democratic election or even that it would be wrong to kill someone. The latter action is sometimes tricked up as an issue of murder, with the instant conclusion that it would be wrong to murder someone. In this statement of the problem, however, the morality of the action has largely been included in the definition of the action. Murder is wrongful killing. If it were not wrongful, it would merely be killing.

Hume's Moral and Political Theory

Hume lacked the vocabulary of strategic action and game theory for his presentation, but he used such reasoning throughout his account of moral and political theory (Hardin). He saw the significance of conflict, exchange, and coordination, and he placed them and their differences at the center of his theory. He has often been criticized for getting parts of that theory wrong, but when we keep our focus on the strategic structure of the issues as he defines them, we can see that many of those criticisms are wrong. His theory might nevertheless be misguided, but it is not subject to many of the commonplace claims of inconsistency or incoherence.

Hume divides moral problems into five categories. These are small-number conflict, small-number exchange or cooperation, large-number conflict, large-number exchange, and large-number coordination. Consider the small-number—indeed, often dyadic—cases. Small-number conflict is BENEFICENCE. It is not in my interest to give alms to the poor, but I may do so out of beneficence. Small-number exchange is generally in my interest and is therefore not a major moral problem except possibly in promising (as discussed below). Hume does not

discuss small-number coordination, but this is no significant oversight. Most of us can handle coordination with each other to meet for lunch and other mutually desired activities.

Standard individual-level moral problems fit into Hume's system straightforwardly. For example, promising can be used to coordinate (as on our meeting for lunch) or to organize exchange over time (as when you do something for me today in exchange for my promise to do something reciprocal for you tomorrow). Promising might also be gratuitous, with no value to the promiser, so that it can be a matter of conflict of INTERESTS. Such promises, however, did not interest Hume and probably should not often interest anyone. Coordination promises are also not a major problem for morality. Even keeping exchange promises is primarily motivated by interests and not morality (*A Treatise of Human Nature,* 3.2.5). This is clearly true of the exchange promises we make to those with whom we expect and wish to be dealing well into the future. If we do not keep such promises, we will not be able to benefit from further exchanges with such people.

Turn to large-number interactions, which are often matters of political more than moral philosophy. Hume discounts concern with large-number conflict because he thinks any effort at distributive justice must necessarily produce more harm than good (Hume's *An Enquiry . . .* [1751], 3.2; and Hardin). Perhaps he was not entirely wrong to exclude distributive justice in an era when the state had little capacity to manage it.

Large-number exchange is for Hume merely the problem of justice as order. The law is used to determine rules for exchange of PROPERTY and many other things that regulate our lives in productive ways. Each of us *de facto* gives up certain opportunities—which become illegal—in order to get all others to give up those opportunities.

Large-number coordination allows us to live with each other successfully even though we need not care much about each other. Hume speaks of successful coordination as the adoption or following of a convention, such as the convention on primogeniture or monarchical succession. The fundamental rule of the road (to drive right or to drive left) is a compelling convention that does not require legal enforcement for the simple reason that we would almost never see it in our interest to drive on the wrong side of the road against drivers who are coordinating on our normal practice. Hence, in this and in many other contexts, we do not need government for much of the detail of daily life but only for large-scale structuring of our possibilities.

A major forerunner of Hume in grasping the strategic structure of social order was Thomas HOBBES (1588–1679). Hobbes is often held to have argued that society is regulated by a contract, which implies an exchange theory of social order. The central part of his argument, however, is that order is to be secured only by our universal coordination on a single government or sovereign. Once we coordinate on it, that government has the POWER thereafter to coerce us individually to keep our order.

Hence, Hobbes's account combines the traditional conflict theory with a limited but fundamentally important element of the coordination theory. We might instructively divide these two in the following way. The problem we face is one of pervasive conflict of interest. I want the goods you produce as well as my own, and you want mine plus your own. But our resolution of this pervasive problem is through coordination, a coordination that works for the simple reason that we have no interest in opposing it or engaging in severe conflict with each other once our coordination has been effective in putting a sovereign in power. More generally, we might say that it is our ongoing coordination on an extant sovereign that enables that sovereign to sustain order.

Concluding Remarks

The influence of game theory in contemporary social science and philosophy derives from the fact that it provides a wonderfully lucid schema for describing and cataloging strategic interactions. It is sometimes criticized or even dismissed for its supposition that all action is based on self-interest. That criticism is wrong. Game theory (and also RATIONAL CHOICE) can represent interactions based on any principle of choice of outcomes, including purely altruistic principles. Valuations or principles of choice merely determine individuals' orderings of outcomes. My ranking of one outcome over another can follow from, for example, the fact that *you* are better off in the first. Game theory then works with these orderings, sometimes with weightings that can convert the orderings to cardinal values.

Cardinal values are very commonly used in game theoretic analyses, especially when outcomes at is-

sue are valued in something like monetary value or interest. Although this may be a common form that values in applied game theory take, it is merely one of the kinds of values games can represent. Strategic interaction is, of course, not restricted to monetary issues or even to interests. It is a central part of our lives whenever we must interact, directly or indirectly, openly or subtly, with others, which is essentially in every aspect of our social lives.

If social life is fraught with strategic interaction in such manifold and important ways, then we might expect our moral theories to deal with such problems. It seems natural for utilitarianism to deal with them because, in a sense, it is a generalization from individual choice for the sake of the individual chooser to individual and collective choice for the sake of all. Some moral theories are apt to have greater difficulty in accommodating themselves to the problems of strategic interaction.

See also: ALTRUISM; BARGAINING; BENEFICENCE; CHEATING; COHERENTISM; COLLECTIVE RESPONSIBILITY; CONSEQUENTIALISM; CONTRACTS; CONVENTIONS; COOPERATION, CONFLICT, AND COORDINATION; DEONTOLOGY; DETERRENCE, THREATS AND RETALIATION; DURKHEIM; GAME THEORY; GROUPS, MORAL STATUS OF; HOBBES; HUME; INEQUALITY; INTERESTS; INTERNATIONAL JUSTICE: CONFLICT; INTRANSITIVITY; JUSTICE, DISTRIBUTIVE; JOHN STUART MILL; MOTIVES; NEEDS; NORMS; PERSONAL RELATIONSHIPS; PROMISES; RATIONAL CHOICE; RECIPROCITY; REVENGE; RISK; RISK ANALYSIS; SMITH; SOCIAL AND POLITICAL PHILOSOPHY; SOCIAL CONTRACT; UNIVERSALIZABILITY; UTILITARIANISM; WAR AND PEACE.

Bibliography

Hallie, Philip P. *Lest Innocent Blood Be Shed.* New York: Harper, 1979. An account of the protection of Jews in Nazi controlled France.

Hardin, Russell. *Morality within the Limits of Reason.* Chicago: University of Chicago Press, 1988. Chapter 2 applies game theoretic reasoning to a Humean moral theory. See especially at pp. 40–41.

Hayek, Friedrich A. *The Constitution of Liberty.* Chicago: University of Chicago Press, 1960. Reprinted, Chicago: Regnery, 1972.

Hobbes, Thomas. *Leviathan.* Edited by C. B. Macpherson. London: Penguin, 1968 [1651].

Hume, David. *A Treatise of Human Nature.* Edited by L. A. Selby-Bigge and P. H. Nidditch. 2d ed. Oxford:

Oxford University Press, 1978 [1739–1740]. See p. 523.

———. *An Enquiry Concerning the Principles of Morals.* In his *Enquiries,* edited by L. A. Selby-Bigge and P. H. Nidditch, 3d edition, 167–323. Oxford: Oxford University Press, 1975 [1751]. For section alluded to, see p. 194.

Kant, Immanuel. "On a Supposed Right to Tell Lies from Benevolent Motives." In his *Critique of Practical Reason and Other Works on the Theory of Ethics,* edited by Thomas Kingsmill Abbott. 6th ed. London: Longman's, 1909 [1797].

Mill, John Stuart. *Utilitarianism.* In his *Essays on Ethics, Religion and Society,* vol. 10 of *Collected Works of John Stuart Mill,* edited by John M. Robson. Toronto: University of Toronto Press, 1969 [1861].

Moore, G. E. *Principia Ethica.* Cambridge: Cambridge University Press, 1903.

Preston, Richard. "The Demon in the Freezer." *New Yorker* (12 July, 1999): 44–61. An account of the elimination of smallpox in the wild and its preservation in many laboratories.

Ullmann-Margalit, Edna. *The Emergence of Norms.* Oxford: Oxford University Press, 1977. A strategic analysis of norms.

Russell Hardin

Suárez, Francisco (1548–1617)

The most original of the Late Scholastics, Suárez was born into a distinguished family in Granada. He entered the Society of Jesus in 1564 and was ordained in 1572. Devoting his life to the study of theology, he taught throughout Spain, in Rome, and from 1597 until 1615 as the professor at Coimbra. His philosophical writings engage the subject with a free and critical spirit and, being the work of genius, have independent interest. The tenth of his fifty-four supremely erudite *Metaphysical Disputations* (1597) examines transcendental good; the eleventh, EVIL. He discussed ethical and moral matters in the posthumously published *On Charity* (1621), *On the Ultimate End of Man and Happiness* (1628), and *On the Goodness and Badness of Human Actions* (1628). He contributed to the philosophy of law, society, and government in *On Laws and God the Legislator* (1612). In a reply to James I of England, *Defense of the Catholic and Apostolic Faith* (1613), he argued against the divine right of kings. He was pontifically honored as the Eximious Doctor.

Following THOMAS AQUINAS (1225?–1274), Suárez took as good for a thing that which perfects the thing. Good for humans is, properly, what in itself befits human essence. This "honest" good he distinguished from the useful, delectable, or morally worthy. For Suárez, the pleasurable or consequentially beneficial may be contrary to human nature, and only deliberate actions are morally right or wrong. His view was that an act's moral value depends on conditions which are internal to the agent, but what makes something good or bad is independent of an agent's attitudes. He claimed further that even God cannot will the good for humans to be other than it is, since human nature cannot be other than it is; and he wrote that human good is not so because it agrees with reason, but that it agrees with reason because it is good. Still, he affirmed that, in the end, all value issues from God, the only true being, absolute creator and supreme legislator.

HAPPINESS or the state of human fulfillment is eternal beatitude. For Suárez, the good life, the life conducive to happiness and lived in agreement with reason, is governed by laws—adequately promulgated, just, and relatively permanent prescriptions. While stressing that moral value is presupposed and not produced by any law, he argued for a system of rules enforced through reward and PUNISHMENT, on the grounds that people are weak and subject to temptation. This corpus of NATURAL LAW is in principle available to all. First moral truths, being divinely inscribed in reason, are self-evident; from them all other natural precepts can be clearly deduced. Thus, Suárez incorporated in an Aristotelian framework elements of a legalistic approach to ethics, centered on the determination of the worth of act-types.

Humans tend essentially toward association in families and larger groups. Accordingly, Suárez found the foundations of society and government in nature and finally in God. But he also held that legitimate rule requires common CONSENT; for humans are born naturally free, and God gives political AUTHORITY to freely established self-sufficient communities aimed at the COMMON GOOD. Since only the community as a whole is endowed with this power, Suárez introduced a second contract to delegate it and institute a specific form of government. Here he delimited a considerable jurisdiction for positive civil law, asserting that effective government must dictate NORMS which, though compatible with moral truth, do not follow from it. Unlike "honest value," positive value results from an act of will:

what is commanded by civil law is made good by the command. Nevertheless, he was clear that it is an honest good that subjects obey their legitimate rulers. Similarly, he held that political POWER is bestowed on communities originated in free contract, and he thus combined a recognition of personal autonomy with the doctrine that authority comes from God.

Suárez was a man attuned with his times, separating the moral and spiritual jurisdiction of the Church from the material jurisdiction of civil government. Commentators have emphasized his economic or utilitarian conception of the state. All the same, he upheld the preeminence of ecclesiastic authority in cases of conflict between material and spiritual concerns. His treatment of PROPERTY relations, central to his understanding of good government and the common good, reveals the extent to which he submitted the pursuit of material prosperity to moral constraints. Like most Scholastics, he believed that everything is by nature common. Yet he considered the assignment of productive goods to individuals to be a permissible institution of positive law. But an owner ought not to dispose of something superfluous, if someone else needs it to survive with DIGNITY. So, he concluded, owners are mere administrators of their surplus wealth, and they become thieves if they fail to distribute their surplus among the needy.

Christian charity is indeed difficult to reconcile with acceptance of the coexistence of opulence and extreme poverty. The duty to love one's neighbor drove Suárez, as it had many of the Church Fathers, toward austere socialism. He denounced the desire for individual gain, and built self-denial, discipline, and solidarity into the very constitution of the social order. He maintained that, in any system of government, under threat of rightful and possibly violent deposition by the community, political power must be exercised for the common welfare and never against it. Moreover, he defended the overriding claim of the community, when in need, over any citizen's property or life, adding that subjection to communal interest and authority is necessary for individual flourishing. Toward the end of his life, Suárez was able to know of the relatively successful Jesuit *reducciones* in Paraguay, organized in 1610 around the communal ownership of goods.

Scholars have connected these Suárecian doctrines with latter-day MARXISM. However, it is perhaps more informative to focus on the ethical underpinnings of his politics, and, consequently, to underscore his divergence not only from Protestant INDIVIDUALISM but also from historicist communism. In fact, much remains to be learned here and elsewhere from the unjustly neglected writings of this brilliant thinker, a fully entitled participant in the timeless conversation of philosophy.

See also: ALTRUISM; ARISTOTLE; AUGUSTINE; AUTONOMY OF MORAL AGENTS; CHARITY; CHRISTIAN ETHICS; COMMON GOOD; COMMUNITARIANISM; LEGAL PHILOSOPHY; MERIT AND DESERT; MORAL RULES; NATURAL LAW; OBEDIENCE TO LAW; PRESCRIPTIVISM; PROPERTY; PUNISHMENT; SOCIAL AND POLITICAL PHILOSOPHY; SOCIAL CONTRACT; THEOLOGICAL ETHICS; THOMAS AQUINAS; WELFARE RIGHTS AND SOCIAL POLICY.

Bibliography

Works by Francisco Suárez

Opera omnia. Edited by D. M. André, *et al.* 28 vols. Paris: Luis Vives, 1856–1878. Incomplete and in need of revision; the only edition of the collected works since the seventeenth century.

De legibus. Edited by L. Pereña, *et al.* 6 vols. Critical edition. Madrid: Consejo Superior de Investigaciones Cientificas, 1971–1977 [1612].

Selections from Three Works of Francisco Suárez, S. J. Edited by James B. Scott. 2 vols. Oxford: Oxford University Press, 1944. The second volume contains English translations from *On Laws* (1612), *Defense of the Faith* (1613), and *On Charity* (1621).

The Metaphysics of Good and Evil According to Suárez. Metaphysical Disputations X and XI and Selected Passages from Disputation XIII and Other Works. Translation, with introduction, notes, and glossary by Jorge J. E. Gracia and Douglas Davis. München: Philosophia Verlag, 1989. English translations with an extensive introduction, notes, a glossary, several indexes, and a bibliography.

Works about Suárez

Ceñal, R. "Los fundamentos metafísicos de la moral según Suárez." *Revista de Filosofía (Madrid)* 7 (1948): 721–35. Suárez on moral and natural good.

Copleston, F. *A History of Philosophy.* New York: Doubleday, 1963. Introductory exposition of Suárez's philosophy in vol. 3, chapters 22, 23.

Elorduy, E. "La soberanía popular según Francisco Suárez." In *Francisco Suárez "Defensio fidei" III,* edited by L. Pereña, *xiii–cci.* Madrid: Consejo Superior de

Investigaciones Científicas, 1965. Extensive study of Suárez on political authority introducing a critical edition of *Defense of the Faith,* book III, chapters 1–9.

Hamilton, B. *Political Thought in Sixteenth-Century Spain.* Oxford: Oxford University Press, 1963. Suárez and three other late scholastics (Vitoria, de Soto, and Molina) on natural law and the social order.

Iturrioz, J. "Bibliografía Suareciana." *Pensamiento* 4 (1948): 603–38. Useful Bibliography in a special issue commemorating Suárez's fourth centenary.

Santos, C. "Bibliografía Suareciana de 1948 a 1980." *Cuadernos Salmantinos de Filosofía* 7 (1980): 33–37. Update of Iturrioz's Bibliography in an issue that includes articles on Suárez's ethics.

Wilenius, R. *The Social and Political Theory of Francisco Suárez.* Helsinki: Societas Philosophica Fennica, 1963. Survey of Suárez's social philosophy.

Jorge Secada

subjectivism

There are different sorts of subjectivism: (1) subjectivism about personal good, (2) subjectivism about PRACTICAL REASON, (3) subjectivism about moral requirement, and (4) subjectivism about evaluative judgments. Subjectivism about personal good, subjectivism about practical reason, and subjectivism about moral requirement are quite different from, and potentially inconsistent with, subjectivism about evaluative judgments.

Subjectivism about personal good includes a family of theories. Each of these holds that personal good—a person's welfare or well-being, or what is best in terms of that person's self-interest—depends on the attitudes of the person, or, we might say, on the attitudes of the subject. One such theory holds that a person's good is constituted by the net enjoyment she or he gets. Another such theory holds that a person's good is constituted by the extent to which his or her desires are fulfilled.

Those are different theories. Of course, normally people enjoy having their desires fulfilled. Nevertheless, in some cases, people do not derive enjoyment from the fulfillment of their desires. For example, they may get no enjoyment from the fulfillment of some of their desires because they never find out these desires are fulfilled. Likewise, people can enjoy believing their desires are fulfilled although their beliefs are in fact false. So increasing people's enjoyment and increasing the fulfillment of their desires do not necessarily go hand in hand.

Still, the theory that personal good resides in enjoyment and the theory that personal good resides in DESIRE fulfillment are alike in being subjective views about personal good. Whether something brings you enjoyment depends on contingent and variable facts about you as a subject. Whether something fulfills your desires also depends on contingent and variable facts about you as a subject. Hence, both of these theories maintain that whether something constitutes a benefit to you depends on contingent and variable facts about you as a subject.

Subjectivism about practical reason is the view that all reasons for ACTION ultimately depend upon an agent's subjective (contingent and variable) desires. This is supposed to be true not only of so-called motivating reasons—*i.e.,* the reasons that as a matter of fact do bring the agent to act. It is also supposed to be true of good REASONS FOR ACTION—*i.e.,* normative reasons determining how people *should* act.

Suppose we accept the subjectivist thesis that what good reasons there are for an agent to do something depend on (and vary with) the agent's desires. Suppose we also accept the thesis that an agent cannot be morally required to do what she has no reason to do. If we maintain these two theses, then we must also accept the subjectivist view of moral requirement. This holds that whether an agent is morally required to do a certain act depends on whether the agent has desires that this act would fulfill.

Subjectivism about moral requirement is highly suspect. It seems to allow agents to reject any requirement simply by denying they have any desire that would be fulfilled by their compliance with the requirement. Yet morality seems to have an authority independent of and superior to the agent's desires. When someone has no desire that compliance with a moral requirement would fulfill, this seems to count against him, not against the requirement. Subjectivism about moral requirement reverses the order of AUTHORITY. This is counterintuitive.

If we therefore reject subjectivism about moral requirement, we have to decide which premise is mistaken in the above argument for this kind of subjectivism. Rejecting the second premise, some philosophers maintain that what one is morally required to do does not depend on what one has reason to do. Rejecting the first premise, other philosophers hold that good reasons for action do not depend on the agent's desires.

The argument against subjectivism about good reasons for action need not, however, refer to moral reasons. We might well hold that agents have good reasons for action that simply do not depend on their motivations. For example, the reason I have for taking vitamins does not seem to depend on whether I care about my long-term health or good. This reason seems to be a prudential or self-interested one, rather than a moral one. Indeed, our own long-term good seems to present us regularly with good reasons for action which do not depend on our present desires. Such reasons can conflict not only with our present desires but also with our moral obligations to other people.

However, as has long been argued, once we accept that there can be self-interested reasons that do not depend on an agent's desires, there seems little sense in denying that there can be moral reasons that also do not depend on an agent's desires. Once we have taken one step away from thinking all good reasons depend on something subjective, what bar is there on taking further steps?

Subjectivism about evaluative judgments has been popular with many of the same people who hold one or more of the kinds of subjectivism outlined above. Subjectivism about evaluative judgments insists there is some necessary connection between the meaning of evaluative judgments and the attitudes of the speaker. One kind of subjectivism about evaluative judgments says that evaluative judgments *describe* the speaker's attitudes. Another kind says that evaluative judgments *express* the speaker's attitudes. These are quite different theories, as will be explained below.

The view that evaluative judgments describe the speaker's attitudes is sometimes called 'old-fashioned subjectivism' and sometimes called 'descriptive subjectivism.' On this view, when I say "Embryo research is morally right," I am simply reporting that I have a positive attitude toward embryo research. When someone else says "Embryo research is morally wrong," that person is reporting the opposite attitude toward embryo research.

But this kind of subjectivism has few philosophical defenders. For it cannot explain why we take a person who says "*X* is right" and someone else who says "*X* is wrong" to be disagreeing with one another. To onlookers, they certainly seem to be disagreeing. And the things they go on to say to one another—such as "No, you are mistaken" or "We cannot both

be correct"—indicates that they take themselves to be disagreeing with one another. Yet, according to descriptive subjectivism, these two speakers are not disagreeing at all, nor need one of them be wrong. One is simply saying that he has a certain attitude about something, and the other is saying she has a different attitude about the same thing. Clearly, they could both be entirely right about what their own attitudes are. What each says could be perfectly true. And yet the speakers themselves, as well as onlookers, understand their moral judgments to be contradicting one another. Descriptive subjectivism does not seem to do justice to the meaning of evaluative judgment.

A different subjectivist view about evaluative judgment is that such judgments *express* attitudes. This view used to be known as EMOTIVISM, but now is usually called expressivism. The simplest form of this view holds that the meaning of (for example) my moral judgment that embryo research is right is *not* 'I approve of embryo research,' but rather 'Hurrah embryo research.' Similarly, the simplest form of the theory maintains that the meaning of someone else's moral judgment that embryo research is morally wrong is 'Boo embryo research.'

One advantage of expressivism over old-fashioned subjectivism is that expressivism does not take apparently conflicting evaluative judgments to be about different things—and therefore to be *actually* consistent. Expressivism locates the disagreement between the speakers in their attitudes and associated desires. The speakers are not (making or intending to make) factual claims about their different attitudes—they are instead expressing different attitudes toward whatever they are evaluating. And if expressivists are correct that the evaluative judgments really amount merely to 'Hurrah *X*' or 'Boo *Y*,' then this helps explain why so many people who say that evaluation is subjective say also that evaluative judgments cannot be literally true or false.

There are a number of reasons why philosophers have found expressivism attractive. One is that expressivism does without something many have suspected to be merely mythical—namely, truth as predicated of evaluative judgments. Another is that it explains the supposed 'internal' connection between motivation (alias desire) and sincere evaluative judgment. As an example of evaluative judgment, consider again moral judgment. The claim is often made that the internal connection between moral judgment and motivation is supposed to be that anyone judging sincerely that everyone ought morally to behave in a certain way must be motivated (to some extent) to behave in that way. If expressivists are right that certain words can be applied appropriately only when an attitude of approval is expressed, and other words only when an attitude of disapproval is expressed, then there can be no surprise that motivation is internal to sincere moral judgment.

Just what the connection between evaluative judgment and motivation is, however, is controversial. A society typically will fall apart unless at least most of the people in it are motivated to do what they judge they morally ought to do. Hence, all societies with which we are familiar are ones where most people are (at least to some extent) motivated to do what they judge they morally ought to do. We therefore have good reason to expect that at least most people will be so motivated. But this does not entail that evaluative concepts other than moral ones imply motivational commitments such that you cannot use them unless you have certain motivations. It does not even imply that moral concepts cannot be applied unless the speaker has certain motivations.

Expressivism has been developed with impressive sophistication. Yet disquiet about it continues. Many philosophers think that we really cannot do without the concept of truth in evaluative discourse, and that such truth can be conceived of in a way that does not have weird metaphysical implications.

Whether expressivism or some other form of subjectivism about evaluative judgment turns out to be sustainable, subjective theories of evaluative judgment sit very uneasily with the subjectivist views about personal good and reasons for action outlined earlier. Both descriptive subjectivism and expressivism connect the speaker's judgments with her own motivations necessarily. But they do *not* necessarily connect the speaker's judgments with anyone else's motivations, not even with those of the person about whom a judgment is made.

For example, if I judge that you would benefit from a certain outcome, then, according to descriptive subjectivism, I am stating that I favor this outcome when I focus on your own good. According to expressivism, I am expressing such favor (not stating that I have it). But in neither case am I indicating anything about your subjective states. On both descriptive subjectivism and expressivism, my judgment that you would benefit from the outcome in question does not entail that I believe it would bring you PLEASURE or fulfill your desires. I can favor the outcome for your own sake and yet not accept any subjectivist theory of personal good.

The same can be held of judgments about good reasons for action. If I say that you have a good reason to quit drinking, then, according to old-fashioned subjectivism, I am stating that, in at least one respect, I favor your quitting. According to expressivism, I am instead expressing such favor. What I may or may not think is that your quitting connects up with your subjective motivation. I may, after all, approve of your quitting and yet neither approve of your motivations nor accept a subjectivist theory of good reasons for action.

See also: AUTONOMY OF ETHICS; AUTONOMY OF MORAL AGENTS; AYER; BRANDT; DESIRE; DUTY AND OBLIGATION; EGOISM; EMOTIVISM; EXTERNALISM AND INTERNALISM; GOOD, THEORIES OF THE; HAPPINESS; HUME; INDIVIDUALISM; INTERESTS; JOHN STUART MILL; MORAL RELATIVISM; MORAL RULES; MOTIVES; NEEDS; OUGHT IMPLIES CAN; PARTIALITY; PLEASURE; PRACTICAL REASON[ING]; PRESCRIPTIVISM; REASONS FOR ACTION; STEVENSON; UTILITARIANISM; WILLIAMS.

Bibliography

On Personal Good

Crisp, Roger. *Mill on Utilitarianism.* London: Routledge, 1997. Ingenious discussion of the arguments against subjectivist accounts of personal good.

Mill, John Stuart. *Utilitarianism.* (1861) Chapter 2. The classic statement of the view that personal good is net pleasure, with pleasures ranked in terms of quality as well as quantity.

Parfit, Derek. *Reasons and Persons.* Oxford: Oxford University Press, 1984. See especially Appendix I. Excellent outline of the main subjectivist and objectivist views about personal good.

Sumner, L. W. *Welfare, Happiness, and Ethics.* Oxford: Oxford University Press, 1996. Superb presentation of the arguments for a subjectivist account of personal good.

On Good Reasons For Action

Brandt, Richard B. *A Theory of the Good and the Right.* Oxford: Oxford University Press, 1979. See part 1. Argues that if our ordinary language concept of 'rational agent' cannot be defined as follows, we should stipulate

subjectivism

a new 'reforming definition' such that we use this term to mean someone whose desires would survive exposure to all relevant empirical facts and correct logical reasoning.

Hume, David. *Treatise of Human Nature.* (1740) Book II, part III, section III. Holds that desire cannot be irrational: "Reason is, and ought only to be, the slave of the passions, and can never pretend to any other office than to serve and obey them."

Parfit, Derek. "Reasons and Motivation." *Proceedings of the Aristotelian Society,* Supplemental vol. 71 (1997): 99–130. Preeminent defense of the view that good reasons for action are not provided by the agent's desires.

Williams, Bernard. "Internal and External Reasons." In *Rational Action,* edited by Ross Harrison. Cambridge: Cambridge University Press, 1980. Reprinted in Williams's *Moral Luck* (Cambridge: Cambridge University Press, 1981). Argues that all good reasons for action must be rationally derivable from the agent's subjective motivations.

On Evaluative Judgment

Ayer, A. J. *Language, Truth and Logic.* London: Gollancz, 1936. Chapter 6. Early development of expressivist theory of evaluative judgment.

Blackburn, Simon. *Spreading the Word.* Oxford: Oxford University Press, 1984. Chapter 6. Influential modern presentation of expressivism.

Gibbard, Alan. *Wise Feelings, Apt Choices.* Cambridge, MA: Harvard University Press, 1990. Systematic development of expressivism.

Hooker, Brad, ed. *Truth in Ethics.* Oxford: Blackwell, 1996. See the following three articles: David Wiggins: "Objective and Subjective in Ethics, With Two Postscripts on Truth." Proposes that 'subjective' and 'objective' be defined as follows: Morality is subjective if it appeals to a standard founded on human sentiment. Morality is objective if in enough cases the explanation of moral beliefs points to considerations whose cumulative force leaves us no room to deny the truth of these moral beliefs. Crispin Wright: "Truth in Ethics." A claim is true if it is assertible in some state of information and remains true no matter what new information comes along. Michael Smith: "Internalism's Wheel." Extremely helpful discussion of the role played by the idea that there must be some necessary connection between motivation and moral judgment.

Stevenson, Charles L. *Ethics and Language.* New Haven: Yale University Press, 1944. Sustained development of expressivist theory of evaluative judgment.

Brad Hooker

suffering

See pain and suffering.

suicide

"There is but one truly serious philosophical problem," wrote Albert CAMUS (1913–1960), "and that is suicide." While in the twentieth century suicide has largely been treated as a medical or psychiatric matter, the conceptual, epistemological, and ethical problems it raises have reemerged as right-to-die issues that direct attention to the individual's role in his or her own death.

Conceptual Issues

The term "suicide" carries extremely negative connotations. However, there is little agreement on a formal definition. Some authors count all cases of voluntary, intentional self-killing as "suicide"; others include only cases in which the individual's *primary* INTENTION is to end his or her life. Still others recognize that much of what is usually termed "suicide" is neither wholly voluntary nor involves a genuine intention to die: suicides associated with depression or other mental illness, for example. Many writers exclude cases of self-inflicted death which, while voluntary and intentional, appear aimed to benefit others or to serve some purpose or principle—for instance, Socrates' drinking the hemlock, Captain Oates's walking out into the Arctic blizzard to allow his fellow explorers to continue without him, or the self-immolation of war protesters. These cases are usually not called "suicide," but "self-sacrifice" or "martyrdom," terms with strongly positive connotations. However, attempts to differentiate these positive cases often seem to reflect moral judgments, not genuine conceptual differences. Cases of death from self-caused accident, self-neglect, chronic self-destructive behavior, victim-precipitated HOMICIDE, high-risk adventure, and self-administered EUTHANASIA—which all share many features with suicide but are not usually termed such—cause still further conceptual difficulty.

Consequently, some authors claim that it is not possible to reach a rigorous formal definition of suicide, and that only a criterial or operational approach to characterizing uses of the term can be successful. Nevertheless, conceptual issues surrounding the definition of suicide are of considerable practical importance in policy formation, as for instance in coroners' practices in identifying causes of death, insurance disclaimers, psychiatric protocols, religious prohibitions, and laws either prohibiting aiding or abetting suicide, or permitting physician assistance in suicide.

Ethical Issues

Much of the extraordinarily diverse discussion of suicide in the history of Western thought has been directed to ethical issues. PLATO (c. 430–347 B.C.E.) acknowledges Athenian burial restrictions (the suicide was to be buried apart from other citizens, with the hand severed and buried separately) and, in the *Phaedo,* reports the Pythagorean view that suicide is categorically wrong. But he also accepts suicide under various conditions, including shame, extreme distress, poverty, unavoidable misfortune, and "external compulsions" of the sort imposed on Socrates by the Athenian court. In the *Republic* and the *Laws,* respectively, Plato obliquely insists that the person suffering from chronic incapacitating illness or uncontrollable criminal impulses *ought* to allow his life to end or cause it to do so. ARISTOTLE (384–322 B.C.E.) held more generally that suicide is wrong, claiming that it is "cowardly" and "treats the state unjustly." The Greek and Roman Stoics, in contrast, recommended suicide as the responsible, appropriate act of the wise man, not to be undertaken in emotional distress but as an expression of principle, duty, or responsible control of the end of one's own life, as exemplified by Cato the Younger (95–46 B.C.E.), Lucretia (sixth century B.C.E.), and SENECA (c. 4 B.C.E.–C.E. 65).

Although Old Testament texts nowhere express general disapproval of suicide, Josephus (37–100) rejects it as an option for his defeated army. Clear prohibitions of suicide appear in Judaism by the time of the Talmud, often appealing to *Genesis* 9:5, "For your lifeblood I will demand satisfaction." Nor does the New Testament condemn suicide. There is evident disagreement among the early Church Fathers about its permissibility, especially in one specific circumstance: while some disapproved, Eusebius (c. 264–340), Ambrose (d. 397), and Jerome (c. 342–420) all hold that a virgin may kill herself in order to avoid violation. While Christian values clearly include patience, endurance, HOPE, and submission to the sovereignty of God, values which militate against suicide, they also stress willingness to sacrifice one's life, especially in martyrdom, and absence of the fear of death. Some early Christians (*e.g.,* the Circum-

cellions, a subset of the rigorist Donatists) apparently practiced suicide as an act of religious zeal: suicide committed immediately after confession and absolution, they believed, permitted earlier entrance to heaven. In any case, with the assertion by AUGUSTINE (354–430) that suicide violates the commandment "Thou shalt not kill" and is a sin greater than any that could be avoided by suicide, the Christian opposition to suicide became unanimous and absolute.

This view of suicide as morally and religiously wrong intensified during the Christian Middle Ages. THOMAS AQUINAS (1225?–1274) argued that suicide is contrary to the NATURAL LAW of self-preservation, injures the community, and usurps God's judgment "over the passage from this life to a more blessed one." By the High Middle Ages, the suicide of Judas, earlier viewed as appropriate atonement for the betrayal of Jesus, was seen as a sin worse than the betrayal itself. The Enlightenment began to question these views; Thomas More (1478–1535) incorporated euthanatic suicide in his *Utopia* (1516); John Donne (1572?–1631) treated suicide as morally praiseworthy when done for the glory of God (as, he claimed in *Biathanatos* [1608, published posthumously 1647], was the case for Christ); David HUME (1711–1776) mocked the medieval arguments, justifying suicide on both autonomist and beneficent grounds; and later thinkers like Mme. de STAEL (1766–1817) (though she subsequently reversed her position) and Arthur SCHOPENHAUER (1788–1860) construed suicide as a matter of human right. Throughout this period, other thinkers insisted that suicide was morally, legally, and religiously wrong: for instance, John Wesley (1703–1791) said that suicide attempters should be hanged, and William Blackstone (1723–1780) described suicide as an offense against both God and the king. Immanuel KANT (1724–1804) used the wrongness of suicide as a specimen of the moral conclusions the categorical imperative could demonstrate. In contrast, the Romantics tended to glorify suicide, and Friedrich NIETZSCHE (1844–1900) insisted that "suicide is man's right and privilege."

The volatile discussion of the moral issues in suicide ended fairly abruptly at the close of the nineteenth century. This was due in part to the insistence of Émile DURKHEIM (1858–1917) that suicide is a function of social organization, and also to the views of psychological and psychiatric theorists, developing from Jean Esquirol (1772–1840) to Sigmund Freud (1856–1939), that suicide is a product of mental illness. These new "scientific" views reinterpreted suicide as the product of nonvoluntary conditions for which the individual could not be held morally responsible. The ethical issues, which presuppose choice, reemerged only in the later part of the twentieth century and continue with full force into the twenty-first.

Is suicide *morally* wrong? Both the historical and contemporary discussions exhibit certain central features. Consequentialist arguments tend to focus on the damaging effects a person's suicide can have on FAMILY, friends, coworkers, or society as a whole. But, as a few earlier thinkers saw, such consequentialist views would also recommend or require suicide when the INTERESTS of the individual or others would be served by suicide. Deontological theorists have tended to treat suicide as intrinsically wrong, but are typically unable to produce support for such claims that is independent of religious assumptions. Contemporary ethical argument has focused on such issues as whether the individual hedonic calculus of self-interest, where others are not affected, provides an adequate basis for choices about suicide; whether life has intrinsic value sufficient to preclude choices of suicide; and whether it is possible, on any ethical theory, to show that it would be *wrong*, rather than merely imprudent, for the ordinary, nonsuicidal person, not driven by circumstances or acting on principle, to end his or her life.

Among religious moralists, Christian thinkers variously assert that divine commandment categorically prohibits suicide, that suicide repudiates God's gift of life, that suicide ruptures covenental relationships with other persons, or that suicide defeats the believer's obligation to endure suffering in the image of Christ. With the exception of ISLAM and Judaism (though Judaism venerates the suicides at Masada and accepts *kiddush hashem,* self-destruction to avoid spiritual defilement), other world religions (for example, Hinduism and Shinto) do not uniformly prohibit suicide, and there has been no similar tradition of discussion of the issues in suicide in nonwestern cultures.

Many traditional societies exhibit institutionalized suicide practices: for example, the *suttee* of a Hindu widow, expected to immolate herself on her husband's funeral pyre; the *seppuku* (or *hara-kiri*) and *junshi* of traditional Japanese nobility; and the Eskimo practice of voluntary abandonment of the elderly. The Vikings held that suicide, as a form of violent death, guaranteed entrance to Valhalla. The Maya recognized a goddess of suicide, Ixtab, and held that those who hanged themselves went to the Maya heaven. The view that suicide is intrinsically and without exception wrong is associated most strongly with post-Augustinian, especially medieval Christianity, surviving into the present; this absolutist view is not by and large characteristic of other schools of thought.

Epistemological Issues

Closely tied to conceptual issues, the central epistemological issues raised by suicide involve the kinds of knowledge available to those who contemplate killing themselves. The issue of what, if anything, can be known to occur after DEATH has, in the West, generally been regarded as a religious issue, answerable only as a matter of faith; few philosophical writers have discussed it directly, despite its clear relation to theory of mind. Some writers have argued that, since we cannot have antecedent knowledge of what death involves, we cannot knowingly and voluntarily choose our own deaths; suicide is therefore always irrational. Others reject this move, instead attempting to establish conditions for the rationality of suicide. Still other writers examine psychological and situational constraints on decision making concerning suicide: for instance, the depressed suicidal individual is described as seeing only a narrowed range of possible future outcomes in the current dilemma, the victim of a kind of "tunnel vision" constricted by depression; and the possibility of preemptive suicide in the face of deteriorative mental conditions like Alzheimer's disease is characterized as a problem of having to use that very mind which may already be deteriorating to decide whether to bear deterioration or die to avoid it.

Public Policy Issues

With some exceptions, recent discussion of epistemological issues in suicide has tended to eclipse the somewhat older discussion of ethical issues. It is often, though uncritically, assumed that, if a person's suicide would be "rational," it ought not be interfered with or prohibited. However, this raises policy issues about the role of the state and other institutions in the prevention of suicide.

In the West, both church and state have historically assumed roles in the control of suicide. In most European countries, ecclesiastical and civil law imposed burial restrictions on the suicide and additional penalties, including forfeiture of PROPERTY, on the suicide's family. In England, suicide remained a felony until 1961. Suicide is now decriminalized in the United States and in England, primarily to facilitate psychiatric treatment of suicide attempters and to mitigate the impact on surviving family members; but in most jurisdictions, aiding or abetting another person's suicide remains against the law. However, while neither U.S. nor English law prohibits suicide, neither recognizes it as a right, and there is considerable pressure from right-to-die groups in favor of recognizing a right to self-determination or "self-deliverance" in terminal illness. These policy issues raise two factual questions: whether permissive attitudes toward rational suicide, for example in terminal illness, would engender more nonrational suicide, as in love-sick adolescents; and whether these attitudes would engender more callous attitudes within a cost-conscious medical establishment about ending the lives of the elderly or terminally ill.

These slippery slope arguments have not been developed in adequate empirical detail, and counter-arguments are also often presented—for instance, that more open attitudes toward suicide would reduce psychopathology by allowing more effective counseling. The general issue of whether governmental institutions should intervene in suicide, and if so under what conditions, is becoming increasingly complex. There have been considerable advances in the epidemiological study of suicide, in the identification of risk factors, including biological and genetic markers, and in forms of clinical treatment. Suicide prevention professionals welcome increased funding for education and prevention measures targeted at youth and other populations at high risk of suicide. Nevertheless, philosophers and bioethicists are increasingly alert to the more general theoretical issues suicide raises. Particularly relevant to policy discussions is the contention of some contemporary writers that suicide will become "the preferred way of death," since it allows control over the time, place, and circumstances of dying, and that it will grow increasingly acceptable and appropriate as the likelihood of otherwise dying of prolonged deteriorative illness in advanced age continues to increase. Opponents hold that, as medical capacities for pain control improve, the call for physician-assisted suicide will decrease; proponents claim that interest in assisted dying is not so much about avoiding pain as it is about autonomy, the right to chose one's own way of dying. Camus's conclusion that suicide is morally wrong is under heavy debate; but his dictum that it is a "truly serious philosophical problem" can hardly be challenged.

See also: AGENCY AND DISABILITY; ALIENATION; AUTONOMY OF MORAL AGENTS; CAMUS; CAUSATION AND RESPONSIBILITY; CONSEQUENTIALISM; DEATH; DEONTOLOGY; *EUDAIMONIA,* -ISM; EUTHANASIA; GUILT AND SHAME; HOMICIDE; HOPE; HUMAN RIGHTS; HUME; INTENTION; KANT; KILLING/LETTING DIE; LIFE AND DEATH; LIFE, MEANING OF; LIFE, RIGHT TO; MEDICAL ETHICS; MORAL ABSOLUTES; NURSING ETHICS; PAIN AND SUFFERING; PATERNALISM; PUBLIC HEALTH POLICY; PUBLIC POLICY; RATIONALITY VS. REASONABLENESS; REVENGE; SELF-RESPECT; SENECA; STAEL; STOICISM; THEOLOGICAL ETHICS; VOLUNTARISM; WOLLSTONECRAFT.

Bibliography

Several influential articles, not cited separately, are contained in anthologies listed below.

Alvarez, A. *The Savage God: A Study of Suicide.* London: Weidenfield and Nicolson, 1971. Includes historical essay and study of Sylvia Plath.

Anderberg, Thomas. *Suicide: Definitions, Causes, and Values.* Lund, Sweden: Lund University Press, 1989.

Baechler, Jean. *Suicides.* Translated by Barry Cooper. New York: Basic Books, 1979.

Battin, Margaret Pabst. *Ethical Issues in Suicide.* 2d ed. Prentice Hall, 1995 (1982). Trade title, *The Death Debate* (1996).

Battin, Margaret Pabst, and Ronald W. Maris, eds. "Suicide and Ethics." *Suicide and Life-Threatening Behavior* 13, no. 4 (Winter 1983). Issue devoted to papers by contemporary moral theorists on suicide.

Battin, Margaret Pabst, and David J. Mayo, eds. *Suicide: The Philosophical Issues.* New York: St. Martin's Press, 1980. Collection of classic essays on conceptual, moral, and epistemological issues, psychiatry, and law.

Battin, Margaret P., Rosamond Rhodes, and Anita Silvers, eds. *Physician-Assisted Suicide: Expanding the Debate.* New York; London: Routledge, 1998. Essays.

Beauchamp, Tom L., ed. *Intending Death: The Ethics of Assisted Suicide and Euthanasia.* Upper Saddle River, NJ: Prentice Hall, 1996. Essays.

Brody, Baruch A., ed. *Suicide and Euthanasia: Historical*

and Contemporary Themes. Dordrecht: Kluwer, 1989. Collection of scholarly essays on classical philosophy, Jewish casuistry, early Christianity, Renaissance, reformation, and Enlightenment thought, plus contemporary essays.

Camus, Albert. *The Myth of Sisyphus.* Translated by Justin O'Brien. New York: Vintage, 1955 [1942].

Clemons, James T. *What Does the Bible Say About Suicide?* Minneapolis, MN: Augsburg Fortress, 1990.

Daube, David. "The Linguistics of Suicide." *Philosophy and Public Affairs* 1 (1972): 387–437. Classic paper.

Donne, John. *Biathanatos.* Edited by Michael Rudick and M. Pabst Battin. New York: Garland, 1982 [written c. 1608]. Modern spelling critical edition.

Durkheim, Émile. *Suicide: A Study in Sociology.* Translated by J. A. Spaulding and G. Simpson. New York: Free Press, 1951 [1897]. Sociological classic.

Emanuel, Linda L., ed. *Regulating How We Die: The Ethical, Medical and Legal Issues Surrounding Physician-Assisted Suicide.* London; Cambridge, MA: Harvard University Press, 1998. Essays.

Fedden, H. Romilly. *Suicide: A Social and Historical Study.* London: Peter Davies, 1938. Classic study.

Hume, David. *Two Essays.* 1826 [1777]. "On Suicide."

Humphrey, Derek. *Final Exit: The Practicalities of Self-Deliverance and Assisted Suicide for the Dying.* Eugene, OR: Hemlock Society, 1991; New York: Dell, 1992.

Kant, Immanuel. *Lectures on Ethics* [1780]. *Fundamental Principles of the Metaphysic of Morals* [1785]. *Critique of Practical Reason* [1788]. *Metaphysics of Morals: Pt. II of Metaphysical Principles of Virtue* [1797].

Landsberg, Paul-Louis. *The Experience of Death and the Moral Problem of Suicide.* Translated by Cynthia Rowland. New York: Philosophical Library, 1953 [1951].

Novak, David. *Suicide and Morality: The Theories of Plato, Aquinas and Kant and Their Relevance for Suicidology.* New York: Scholars Studies, 1975.

Perlin, Seymour. *A Handbook for the Study of Suicide.* Oxford: Oxford University Press, 1975.

Prado, Carlos. *The Last Choice: Preemptive Suicide in Advanced Age.* Westport, CT: Greenwood Press, 1990.

Shneidman, Edwin S., and Norman L. Farberow, eds. *Clues to Suicide.* New York: McGraw-Hill, 1957. Anthology assembled by the founders of contemporary suicidology.

Sprott, S. E. *The English Debate on Suicide: From Donne to Hume.* La Salle, IL: Open Court, 1961.

"Symposium on Physician-Assisted Suicide." *Ethics* 109/3 (1999): 497–642.

Weir, Robert F., ed. *Physician-Assisted Suicide.* Bloomington; Indianapolis: Indiana University Press, 1997. Essays.

Werth, James L. *Rational Suicide? Implications for Mental Health Professionals.* Washington, DC: Taylor and Francis, 1996.

Zucker, Marjorie B., ed. *The Right to Die Debate: A Documentary History.* Westport, CT; London: Greenwood Press, 1999. Sourcebook of primary documents.

Margaret Pabst Battin

Sunnīsm

The term Sunnī is shorthand for *ahl al-sunna wa 'l-jamā'a,* literally meaning the "folk who follow the tradition and the united community." It is a common perception to view Sunnīsm as the "mainstream" sect in ISLAM. On closer examination, it may prove to be more diverse than being a monolith. Sunnīsm emerges as a middle-of-the-road compromise that navigated the divisions of early sectarian conflicts within Islam. Much of the sectarian divide stems from political disputes expressed in the language of theology. The seeds for the earliest political fragmentation were sown by the civil war (*fitna*) during the reign of 'Alī (c. 600–661), the fourth successor after the Prophet Muḥammad. This conflict spawned both extremist and passivist political theologies. The "Secessionists" (*Khawārij*) declared anyone who committed a major sin to be an infidel (*kāfir*). On the other hand, another group called the "Postponers" (*Murji'a*) left the judgment of the acts of sinners to the divine court and were reluctant to excommunicate believers. Rationalist tendencies influenced by various strands of Hellenic philosophy, the most famous being the Mu'tazila, emphasized monotheism in the most uncompromising terms. The latter group were often in conflict with Aḥmad bin Ḥanbal (780–855), an influential jurist-theologian of Baghdad, and his later followers.

It was Ibn Ḥanbal who gave the Mu'tazila and their patrons among the Abbassid caliphs stiff opposition for proposing a state-sponsored pro-Mu'tazila creed. In the end, it led to the ninth-century Inquisition (Miḥna) and the persecution of Ibn Ḥanbal for not following the official state doctrine. In essence, it was a conflict between two kinds of rationalities in early Islam. The Ḥanbalīs advocated a strict scripture-based teaching that had anthropomorphism and literalism as distinguishing characteristics. The Mu'tazila drew on a mixture of Stoic and Aristotelian propositions in their presentation of RELIGION. The Ḥanbalīs claimed to represent the pedigree of authentic Arabicity in its doctrines and resisted the mixing of any foreign ideas, as they suspected the Mu'tazila of doing. During the

Inquisition, the conflict centered on the Qur'ān. The Mu'tazila claimed that the Qur'ān was the created speech of God, whereas the Ḥanbalīs maintained that it was the eternal and uncreated speech of God. Just as God has the eternal attribute of knowledge, so does his revealed speech also share the same quality. For the Mu'tazila, only God's essence was eternal and all other attributes were contingent.

A former Mu'tazila scholar, Abū 'l-Ḥasan al-Ash'arī (c. 873–c. 936), broke rank with his former schoolmen and placed his skills as a dialectical theologian in the service of explicating the primitive Ḥanbalī belief. It was al-Ash'arī who first systematized a core doctrine that can be identified as the proto-Sunnī belief. He constructed an intellectual middle ground among the contentious doctrines mentioned above and made dialectical theology an acceptable method for theologians. The "middle ground" meant that he showed how he differed with the Mu'tazila, Khawārij and Shī'a, all of whom al-Ash'arī severely critiqued. For the Ash'arī version of Sunnism, the essential beliefs are that God acts in the world and re-creates it at every instant in time. In theory, Ash'arism denies causation and potentialities in favour of the direct efficacy of God in the production of events. Human beings acquire the will to act in history, but God creates and produces all acts. God's omnipotence and unfettered power to act defines Ash'arī VOLUNTARISM. EVIL, in addition, was the product of God's will, the Ash'arīs argued, much to the chagrin of the Mu'tazila. Another school, that of Abū Manṣūr al-Māturīdī (d. 944), differed in some respects from Ash'arism and maintained that evil did not take place with the good pleasure of God. Māturīdī also allowed greater room for human efficacy. In the later development of this school, the absolute efficacy of human will was emphatically stated. Asha'rism did play a critical role in structuring the doctrine of the Sunnī theological tradition. However, Sunnī is a flexible umbrella term that includes Ḥanbalīs and Māturīdīs and some other less well known theological tendencies.

See also: ARISTOTELIAN ETHICS; EVIL; FATE AND FATALISM; FREEDOM AND DETERMINISM; ISLAM; ISLAMIC ETHICS; STOICISM; VOLUNTARISM.

Bibliography

Fazlur Rahman. *Islam.* Chicago: University of Chicago Press, 1966.

Abū 'l-Ḥasan 'Alī b. Ismā'īl al-Ash'arī. *Kitāb al-Luma' fī 'l-Radd 'alā Ahl 'l-Zaygh wa 'l-Bida'.* Edited by Richard Joseph McCarthy. Beirut: Imprimeria Catholique, 1953.

Ebrahim Moosa

supererogation

Although the concept of supererogation has a long philosophical history, thanks to its relevance to Church doctrine, twentieth-century fascination dates to the publication of J. O. Urmson's "Saints and Heroes" in 1958. Urmson objected to ethical theories which classify all acts as either forbidden, merely permissible, or obligatory, pointing out that this threefold classification fails to capture saintly and heroic acts. Saintly and heroic acts are not obligatory (nor, usually, are they forbidden); and to classify them as merely permissible is to miss their special goodness. What is needed, Urmson suggested, is another category: that of supererogatory acts. Ethical theory needs to distinguish sharply, he argued, between acts which go beyond duty, and acts required by duty.

His position is not without its dissenters. Probably the most historically interesting anti-supererogationist view is that taken by many in the Reformation who, in denouncing the institution of Indulgences, criticized not only the corruption of that institution but the doctrine of supererogation on which it rested. They rejected the position developed by THOMAS AQUINAS (1225?–1274) and others that there is, thanks to the Saints, a superabundance of merit which is the "property" of the Church and can be transferred to others. Among their reasons for rejecting it was their belief that there are no acts that are beyond duty. There is no surplus of merit, LUTHER (1483–1546) and CALVIN (1509–1564) held, and so nothing to be transferred.

The anti-supererogationist views taken in the Reformation were buoyed by religious beliefs, such as that we are dependent on—and in no way deserving of—God's grace and MERCY. No matter what we do, it is "not enough," and thus cannot possibly be *more* than enough. Twentieth-century critics, concerned not with medieval Church doctrine but with Urmson's claim that ethical theories need a special category of supererogatory acts, question the utility of the "base-line" approach to ethics (according to which everything below the line is strictly required, and everything above is strictly beyond duty). The strongest of the contemporary anti-supererogationist views is offered by Christopher New, who defends UTILITARIANISM without the qualifications to allow room for the supererogatory that rule-utilitarianism facilitates. We have a duty, he suggests, to do whatever act (of those open to us) will produce the most good. True, heroic and saintly acts may not be open to those of us who are weak or cowardly; but, New suggests, we have a duty to be, and to become, as good as we possibly can, and to try to become saintly and heroic.

Elizabeth Pybus advances a similar but slightly weaker thesis. She holds that we have a duty to be as good as we possibly can, but does not defend the utilitarian thesis that we ought to do whatever act will produce the most good. Emphasizing ideals and VIRTUES and the variety of ways in which these can be exemplified, she holds that we all have a duty to be, for example, courageous, but points out that this does not entail that we all have a duty to do the same courageous acts.

It is helpful to see how KANT's (1724–1804) distinction between perfect and imperfect duty provides a reply to Urmson's thesis, and motivates either Pybus's position or a slightly weaker view. Kant's ethics arguably constitutes a counterexample to Urmson's claim that without expanding the threefold classification of acts to recognize a separate category of supererogatory acts, ethics fails to capture the phenomena of the heroic and saintly. Kant's imperfect duties are duties to adopt certain ends, specifically the HAPPINESS of others and one's own perfection. Indirectly, they require one to perform some acts or other of a general type—to help others and to develop one's talents—but they do not specify exactly what one is to do. In Kant's scheme, acts which most contemporary ethicists would classify as supererogatory are not really beyond duty, since one must perform some such acts, though they are not required one by one either. They are ways of "fulfilling" imperfect duties. ('Fulfill' needs scare quotes since the duties are never discharged, but rather are to guide and direct one all one's life.)

If one accepts this, and goes on to say that we have a duty to strive to be as virtuous as possible, the view is very much like Pybus's; alternatively, one could leave more open-ended just what degree of commitment the requirement to adopt these ends entails and thus take a slightly weaker anti-supererogationist position.

Their differences aside, these alternative views raise the question of whether the category of supererogatory acts is crucial to ethical theory. Do we need to draw a line, in ethical theory, between those acts which are morally required and those which it would be good to do, but which one is in no way required to do?

Disagreements on this will depend partly on what one thinks our duties are: is it that we are morally required to do only a minimum (possibly, but not necessarily low), such that all good deeds beyond that minimum are essentially optional? Those who hold that we are obligated to do as much good as we possibly can or to try to be as good as we possibly can (New) will respond in the negative, as will Kantians who maintain that we have an imperfect duty to improve ourselves morally and that this duty precludes drawing a line and saying, "This much is required; anything more is optional" (Baron).

The disagreement can be traced to metaethical differences, as well. Many of those who believe that ethics does need to recognize a category of the supererogatory construe duty on a legalistic or institutional model, holding that it is part of the concept of duty that we have a right to demand that others fulfill their duties. Others distance themselves from this view but tacitly assume (as does Heyd when he claims that a refusal to do a favor cannot be criticized as morally wrong since one can ask for a favor but never claim it as one's due) that x cannot be wrong unless it wrongs someone. Those who construe 'duty' more broadly tend to be less sympathetic to the view that a line can and should be drawn, in ethical theory, between duty and the supererogatory.

Urmson's arguments reflect these and other disagreements. Here are some of the arguments he offers in defense of his claim that our "moral code"—and that term is revealing—must distinguish between morality's basic requirements and "the higher flights of morality."

(1) We need to know precisely what our duties are, and such precision is not possible with respect to alleged duties to help others.

(2) It is imperative that people not fall below a minimum of decency; but if more than that minimum is presented to us *as* mor-

ally required, we will be less willing to abide by morality's minimal requirements.

(3) It is preferable that people be free from pressure, including moral pressure; it is best, therefore, that our duties be kept to a minimum.

To reply: (1) is based on an assumption that many philosophers (*e.g.,* Kant) reject, the assumption that all duties are such that we may, indeed should, exact them like debts. In addition, as New has argued, the "precision test" is open to question. New also points out that (2) is a dubious psychological claim; it is no less likely that loftier expectations would yield better conduct. But (3) merits more serious consideration. One might reply that the fact that *x* is a duty for S does not entail that it is appropriate to pressure S to do *x,* so (3) is beside the point. But (3) can be recast, and indeed has been by Heyd and others. The point, they suggest, is that moral constraint (with or without pressure to conform) limits freedom. Since the notion of a duty does entail moral constraint, it is desirable to keep our duties to a minimum. This argument has found favor with many philosophers; it hinges, however, on the assumption that moral constraints limit freedom, an assumption that some, notably Kant, would reject.

Urmson's article was influential both in that it convinced many readers that ethical theories which do not have, and cannot accommodate, a category of supererogatory acts are *ipso facto* defective, and in the interest it generated in related questions. Related questions include the following:

(a) What are the necessary and sufficient conditions for an act's being supererogatory?

(b) At what point can we say that we have done enough, that the rest is beyond duty?

(c) What ethical theories can best accommodate the supererogatory?

On (a), there are disagreements as to whether an act must, to qualify as supererogatory, be performed from altruistic MOTIVES or whether, as Heyd contends, the motive need not be altruistic as long as the INTENTION is. Alternatively, one might argue that motive and intention are both irrelevant. Another issue concerning (a) spills over into (b): Must the act involve considerable self-sacrifice to be supererogatory?

Disagreements on (b) abound, particularly within discussions in APPLIED ETHICS, such as the debate over our obligations to alleviate poverty. Peter Singer advocates a very high cutoff and has sparked considerable dissent. The more popular (and personally less demanding) views favor drawing the line fairly low, and often appeal to the desirability of keeping moral requirements from "limiting our autonomy." They reject the suggestion that to qualify as supererogatory the act must involve self-sacrifice, and maintain that non-spectacular acts, such as those of doing a small favor for a neighbor, should qualify.

Regarding (c), rule-utilitarianism is often held to be especially suited to accommodate the supererogatory, the idea being that utility is maximized not by requiring individuals to do all they can to maximize utility—since the burden would generate unhappiness for each of them—but rather by requiring something less onerous. Deciding just what degree of BENEFICENCE should be required has thus been a task for rule-utilitarians: at what point is too much asked of people, so that the disutility of having to conform to demanding MORAL RULES (or disutility generated by morale problems) lowers the net utility?

One other issue, closely related to (a) and (b), deserves mention: What grounds the claim that, despite being so very good, supererogatory acts are not obligatory? Is it, as some familiar arguments suggest, (just) that many people are incapable of living up to tougher demands, that is, that they cannot perform many supererogatory acts? If we could all be saints or heroes, would there cease to be a need for the category of the supererogatory? Heyd argues that the need would remain. Even if we could all be saintly and heroic, it is preferable, he maintains, to regard a range of good deeds as beyond duty. In support of his claim, he cites the value of being free from moral constraints. He thus defends "unqualified supererogationism": its value is not contingent on human limitations.

See also: ALTRUISM; BENEFICENCE; CHARITY; CHRISTIAN ETHICS; DUTY AND OBLIGATION; EXCELLENCE; FORGIVENESS; GRATITUDE; INTENTION; KANT; MERCY; MORAL SAINTS; PERFECTIONISM; UTILITARIANISM.

Bibliography

Baron, Marcia. *Kantian Ethics Almost Without Apology.* Chapters 1–2. Ithaca, N.Y.: Cornell University Press, 1995.

Feinberg, Joel. "Supererogation and Rules." *Ethics* 71 (1961): 276–88. Reprinted in his *Doing and Deserving.* Princeton, N.J.: Princeton University Press, 1970.

Fishkin, James S. *The Limits of Obligation.* New Haven, Conn.: Yale University Press, 1982.

Heyd, David. *Supererogation.* London: Cambridge University Press, 1982.

Hill, Thomas E., Jr. "Kant on Imperfect Duty and Supererogation." *Kant-Studien* 62 (1971): 55–76. Reprinted in his *Dignity and Practical Reason in Kant's Moral Theory.* Ithaca, N.Y.: Cornell University Press, 1992.

Mellema, Gregory. *Beyond the Call of Duty: Supererogation, Obligation, and Offence.* Albany: State University of New York Press, 1991.

Montague, Phillip. "Acts, Agents and Supererogation." *American Philosophical Quarterly* 26 (1989): 101–11.

New, Christopher. "Saints, Heroes and Utilitarians." *Philosophy* 49 (1974): 179–89.

Pybus, Elizabeth. "Saints and Heroes." *Philosophy* 57 (1982): 193–200.

Singer, Peter. "Famine, Affluence and Morality." *Philosophy and Public Affairs* 1 (1972): 229–43.

Urmson, J. O. "Saints and Heroes." In *Essays in Moral Philosophy,* edited by A. I. Melden, pp. 198–216. Seattle: University of Washington Press, 1958. Reprinted in *Moral Concepts,* ed. Joel Feinberg, pp. 60–73. London: Oxford University Press, 1970.

Marcia Baron

sympathy

This altruistic emotion belongs to a cluster that includes LOVE, concern, compassion, and fellow-feeling, emotions that are naturally expressed in conduct that is caring, helpful, or benevolent. Sympathy presupposes a capacity for empathy, the ability to share imaginatively and to identify with another's feelings, perceptions, cares, or commitments. (The German *Mitleid* brings this out). In addition, it is essentially altruistic, a responsive other-regarding stance: we delight in the joys and triumphs or feel sorrow at the disappointments and suffering of others for their *own* sake. While sympathy is one of the passions, something we passively undergo, it also includes an active component, a readiness to respond with good will toward another—in case of suffering, through helping behavior, through sharing or easing another's pain. To be seen as "merely sympathetic," that is, as feeling sympathy without in the least being moved toward benevolent action, is typically a rebuke, implying that one is deficient in sympathy itself. Whatever the depth of our empathetic response, then, if we are sympathetic, we will also attend to the well-being of the other and be disposed toward helpful action.

Historical Sketch

David HUME (1711–1776) and Arthur SCHOPENHAUER (1788–1860) give sympathy a central role in ethics. And this altruistic trait or EMOTION is clearly esteemed in our folk morality. But the classic philosophers who have set the terms for modern debate in moral theory either exclude sympathy from a central role—as with Thomas HOBBES (1588–1679) and Immanuel KANT (1724–1804)—or, like JOHN STUART MILL (1806–1873), they give it a somewhat precarious status.

The Hobbesian tradition discounts ALTRUISM generally, arguing that any apparently unselfish sympathy can be more accurately described as disguised self-interest. This tradition has become powerfully fused with an economic or market model of human motivation that underlies much of the contemporary discussion in economics, PSYCHOLOGY, and ethics. This model accords primary theoretical status only to the self-interested MOTIVES of "pre-social" atomic individuals. Adam SMITH (1723–1790), who is generally credited with discovering the structural dynamics of a competitive, capitalistic economy, had a more generous and pluralistic view of motivation, claiming not only that sympathy is a natural sentiment co-existing with more selfish springs of action, but that it is universal:

> [Even] the greatest ruffian, even the most hardened violator of the laws of society, is not altogether without it.

In one well-known passage, Kant identifies emotions or feelings as mere inclinations. Morally speaking, however altruistic they may be, they are to be disregarded, for like brute impulses, they are fickle, independent of the deliberative will, and subversive of the ideals of autonomy and rationality:

> there are . . . many persons so sympathetically constituted that without any motive of vanity or selfishness they find an inner satisfaction in spreading joy, and rejoice in the contentment of others which they have made possible. But I say that however dutiful and amiable it may

be, that kind of action has no true moral worth.

Sympathy fares much better in the tradition of Jeremy BENTHAM (1748–1832) and Mill. The goal of conduct for utilitarians is clearly altruistic—to maximize the well-being of others, to alleviate suffering—and its method requires of the moral agent a capacity for sympathy in the initial tallying of pleasures or pains, of NEEDS or preferences, of benefits or burdens. Utilitarians appeal to this natural sentiment, asking only that we expand the range of its application to others beyond our immediate or provincial circles, and indeed, Bentham urges, to all creatures that can suffer, including animals.

But sympathy's role can become compromised to the extent that the IDEAL OBSERVER conducting the required tally of preferences or needs must be a sort of impersonal bureaucrat working out sums and balances and delivering administrative policy edicts. Sympathy is typically an immediate responsiveness to the needs of particular persons. Insofar as UTILITARIANISM requires a more abstract and impersonal calculative attention to a universe of potential or actual plaintiffs, it may seem to encourage a moral stance at odds with such personalized sympathetic response. In addition, it may seem that imaginatively taking in the condition of more and more petitioners from the vast world of sufferers necessarily dilutes our capacity to feel sympathy toward any one sufferer in particular. Acting for the good of too many, we may become emotionally numb, and at last morally incapacitated. Nevertheless, even the detached bureaucratic utilitarian can plausibly calculate that encouraging sympathy among members of a community and between conflicting communities will make the world a better place. And for self-protection, invoking rule-utilitarian considerations, she may even sensibly limit the amount that relatively distant others can claim of her time.

A constructive account of the moral significance of sympathy must face the objections presented by these dominant traditions. In addition, it must face the popular association of sympathy or altruism with Christian ideals of self-abnegation and self-sacrifice. In a humanistic age of self-realizing or acquisitive INDIVIDUALISM, these apparently self-denying ideals become easy targets of ridicule. Overall, then, we confront in our theories a package of philosophical and cultural presumption promoting a secular ethics based on the pillars of reason and autonomy, or on some balance of individual RIGHTS and social welfare, an ethics that orphans the more tender altruistic sentiments. Sympathy, like personal charm, may be agreeable and even socially useful. But its moral import, on this packaged view, is either precarious or rejected outright.

Hume and Schopenhauer are notable exceptions to this story of neglect. For Hume, sympathy permits us to recognize and respond approvingly to virtue in others. It is the "mechanism" whereby we sorrow in the plight of others and are moved to respond benevolently; or alternatively, whereby we rejoice in the HAPPINESS of others and are moved to celebrate their good fortune. Sympathy is fundamental to the intrinsic sociability of our lives:

> The epithets sociable, good-natured, humane, merciful, grateful, friendly, generous, beneficent, or their equivalents, are known in all languages, and universally express the highest merit which human nature is capable of attaining. (*Enquiry*)

As the enabling vehicle for sociable ties, sympathy becomes activated in the FAMILY, notably in the relationship between parent and child. And through its extension to more distant others, it contributes to the general pleasures of good company and to the obvious social benefits of gentle and cooperative public enterprise.

Hume saw such sympathetic connectedness not only as socially useful, but also as a condition of our SELF-ESTEEM or appropriate PRIDE. For only as sympathy is mutually reciprocated, only as the worth of our deeds or CHARACTER becomes acknowledged through the response of sympathetic others, can we maintain an adequately lively, healthy sense of self-worth. Against the presumption that sympathy must involve an unhappy self-denial, on Hume's view, reciprocally sympathetic relationships form the necessary context for nourishing and sustaining selves, selves capable of any interest whatsoever.

Schopenhauer praised sympathy or compassion as the highest of moral VIRTUES, an instance of the selfish "will to live" turning against itself, breaking through the separateness that divides one person from another. He too was sensitive to the subtle relationship between sympathy and self-identity, arguing that moral sympathy cannot be merely my assimilation of another's pain as my own. In fact, such a conflation of self and other would make altruism impossible. Without an appropriate distinction between my own pain and the pain of the other, my sympathetic response, whatever its beneficial consequences, would be primarily self-regarding, a response to my *own* pain, rather than to that of the sufferer.

Objections and Replies

We have alluded to a number of obstacles that an account of sympathy as a moral emotion must confront, for example, the suspicion that sympathy is antithetical to a strong sense of autonomous self-worth. This could be called the *autonomy objection.* But as Hume suggests, sympathy is not properly conceived as self-abnegation, and the development of autonomy may in fact presuppose a fundamental sociability, built on our capacity for reciprocal sympathy.

Then there is the *mere sentiment objection,* which can be broken into two strands. How reliable or steady is sympathy as a moral motivator? And if sympathy is just a "brute feeling," how can a conflict of such sentiments be resolved without recourse to something—say, reason—which transcends such instinctual responsiveness? Love, sympathy, and compassion are typically among the most steady of motivators within family and friendships—at least as reliable as reason, which itself can be vacillating. Perhaps a solid principle of PRACTICAL REASON could reinforce such natural motivators. This would *join* reason and sentiment in a mutually supportive enterprise. Commitments based on love, relationships grounded on sympathetic responsiveness, kindness springing from the heart, are not self-evidently at *odds* with reason. Must a Kantian respect for the moral law—no doubt on its own ground a worthy enough moral trait—rule out other grounds for moral response? Must our sense of "the moral" have a single root? Why must one side against Hume or Schopenhauer, denying the altruistic emotions an honorific moral status?

Absent a legislative or adjudicative role for reason, in either a Kantian or utilitarian guise, a moral theory built on our capacity for sympathy needs a mechanism for reinforcing sympathies that might otherwise falter, for deciding when sympathy may be an inappropriate response, for weighing sympathies in conflict situations, and for balancing, when necessary, the claims of sympathy against other moral claims—perhaps those of justice. Here, as Annette Baier persuasively argues, Hume provides the sensible and necessary notion of a reflective, self-correcting sympathy, a sympathy that can gaze critically on itself, on its context, and on its object. This notion, if accepted, will considerably diminish the "mere sentiment" charge, for it allows sympathy a self-critical role, a reason-like ability to impartially adjudicate conflicting moral claims.

The *particularist objection* maintains that a moral response must by definition be mediated by appeal to a universal law or principle, tacit or articulated. Native sympathetic impulses lack specifically moral worth to the extent that the agent has not framed the situation as an instance where a generalized rule or principle applies. Morality is tied first to the faculties of judgment or reason rather than to action or responsiveness. Yet to assume that a moral emotion or response is essentially identified by its (presumed) implicit or declared motivating principle defies a number of intuitions. We believe, for example, that encouraging sympathy, kindness, and helping behavior in children is encouraging moral growth, even when it is clear that such children lack the capacity to be motivated by abstract principles of duty, justice, or utility.

The market model of individual self-interested pursuit highlights what we could call the *rational egoist objection.* Despite the self-interested picture of human motivation that can emerge through some familiar mapping of the public world of market, legal, and military COMPETITION, surely within the world of family and intimate relationships, *bona fide* examples of spontaneous and appropriate sympathy abound. To deny them moral title seems arbitrary. We can better suppose that the world we enter as infants and share as children is a social matrix of sympathetic caregivers within which selfish, altruistic, and morally neutral sentiments have roughly equal *prima facie* footing. Why assume that our early capacity for unselfish reciprocal sympathy should on maturity vanish, leaving in its place an adult devoted exclusively to self-interested pursuits?

Further Questions

Recent years have seen a marked revival of philosophical interest in the moral sentiments, including sympathy. Thus, we have Annette Baier's striking defense of Hume as a virtue theorist and "a women's moral theorist." Compassion and the altruistic virtues generally are defended by a wide range of writers, including Lawrence Blum and Richard Taylor. A marked expansion of the range of topics deemed fitting for moral investigations is also evident. Among many, here are some of the questions this literature can prompt: How can sympathy be usefully distinguished from adjoining or overlapping emotions like compassion, CARE, CHARITY, or pity? What are its typical distortions (for example, sentimentality or servility)? Is sympathy gender-biased, a "women's virtue," as the work of Carol Gilligan and others might suggest? To what extent is sympathy the keystone of a broadly utilitarian framework? What role might sympathy play in a reconstructed Kantianism? And finally, what are the concrete historical settings (familial, educational, economic, political) that encourage or discourage the development of the altruistic emotions?

See also: ALTRUISM; AMNESTY AND PARDON; ANIMALS, TREATMENT OF; BENEFICENCE; BENEVOLENCE; BENTHAM; CARE; CHARITY; COMPETITION; EGOISM; EMOTION; EUTHANASIA; FAMILY; FORGIVENESS; FRIENDSHIP; GENEROSITY; HUME; LOVE; MERCY; JOHN STUART MILL; PAIN AND SUFFERING; PASSION; PERSONAL RELATIONSHIPS; RECIPROCITY; SCHOPENHAUER; TOLERATION; UTILITARIANISM.

Bibliography

Baier, Annette. *A Progress of Sentiments: Reflections on Hume's Treatise.* Cambridge: Harvard University Press, 1991.

———. "Hume, the Women's Moral Theorist?" In *Women and Moral Theory,* edited by Eva Kittay and Diana T. Meyers, 37–55. Totowa, NJ: Rowman and Littlefield, 1987.

Baron, Marcia W. *Kantian Ethics Almost Without Apology.* Ithaca, NY: Cornell University Press, 1995. A generous interpretation of Kant's views on sympathy, going beyond the narrow account found in Kant's *Foundations.*

Blum, Lawrence A. *Friendship, Altruism, and Morality.* London: Routledge and Kegan Paul, 1980. A groundbreaking study of connections between altruistic emotion and morality; excellent Bibliography.

Gilligan, Carol. *In a Different Voice.* Cambridge: Harvard University Press, 1982. A much discussed study which links the contrast between the ideal of moral care (or sympathy) and the ideal of justice (or moral principle) to differences in gender.

Hume, David. *Enquiry Concerning the Principles of Morals.* New York: Liberal Arts Press, 1957 [1751]. Quoted at section II.

———. *A Treatise on Human Nature.* Edited by L. A. Selby-Bigge. Oxford: Clarendon Press, 1888 [1737]. Contains a classic discussion of the ethics of sympathy; see especially book 3.

Kant, Immanuel. *Foundations of the Metaphysics of Morals.* Translated by Lewis W. Beck. New York: Bobbs-Merrill, 1959 [1785]. Quoted from p. 14. And see Baron, *supra.*

Mercer, Phillip. *Sympathy and Ethics.* Oxford: Oxford University Press, 1972. Subtitle: A Study of the Relationship Between Sympathy and Morality with Special Reference to Hume's *Treatise.*

Noddings, Nell. *Caring: A Feminist Approach to Ethics and Moral Education.* Berkeley: University of California Press, 1984. A rich account of the ethics of care in interpersonal and pedagogic relationships.

Scheler, Max. *The Nature of Sympathy.* Translated by Peter Heath. London: Routledge and Kegan Paul, 1954 [1913]. A phenomenological account which claims that in true sympathy the separateness of the other is fully acknowledged.

Schopenhauer, Arthur. *On the Basis of Morality.* New York: Bobbs-Merrill, 1965 [1842]. A classic critique of Kant and defense of sympathy or compassion as the proper basis of morality.

Smith, Adam. *The Theory of Moral Sentiments.* In *British Moralists,* edited by L. A. Selby-Bigge. New York: Bobbs-Merrill, 1964 [1759]. Quoted at part 1, section 1, chapter 1.

Taylor, Richard. *Good and Evil.* New York: Macmillan, 1970. Easily accessible discussion of love, compassion, and a morality of aspiration rather than duty.

Edward F. Mooney

T

Taoist ethics

Early Taoism has had an incalculable influence on the development of Chinese philosophy and culture. Second in influence only to the Confucian school, the classical Taoist philosophers in many ways have been construed as both a critique on and a complement to the more conservative, regulatory precepts of their Confucian rivals. And when Buddhism entered CHINA in the second century C.E., Buddhist adepts appropriated many of the concepts of indigenous Taoism as a sympathetic vocabulary through which to express a fundamentally foreign system of thought. In so doing, they made Buddhist ideas more palatable to the Chinese audience, but at the same time also set Buddhism on a course of irrevocable sinicization.

Philosophical Taoism is often called "Lao-Chuang" philosophy, referring directly to the two central and most influential texts, the *LAO TZU* (or *Tao-te-ching*) and the *CHUANG TZU,* both of which are composite and were probably compiled in the fourth and third centuries B.C.E. Beyond these two texts, we might include the syncretic *Huai Nan Tzu* (c. 140 B.C.E.) and the *Lieh Tzu,* reconstituted around the fourth century C.E., as part of the traditional Taoist corpus.

Taoism has often been construed as an anarchic critique on the constraining conventionalism of Confucian morality. It has frequently been characterized in terms of passivity, femininity, quietism, spirituality—a doctrine embraced by artists, recluses, and religious mystics. Confucianism, by contrast, has been cast in the language of moral precepts, VIRTUES, imperial edicts, and regulative methods—a doctrine embodied in and administered by the state official. This difference has been articulated through a plethora of distinctions: feminine versus masculine, heterodox versus orthodox, mystical versus mundane, anarchy versus top-down regulatory government, other-worldliness versus this-worldliness, rebellion versus political authority, nature versus culture, personal creativity versus social responsibility, and so on. Paralleling the assumption of gender traits that promotes a sexist reductionism in our own culture, the injudicious application of this *yin-yang*-like contrast to Taoism and Confucianism tends to impoverish our appreciation of the richness and complexity of these two traditions. Used in such a heavy-handed way, it obfuscates the fundamental wholeness of both the Confucian and Taoist visions of a meaningful human existence by imposing an unwarranted conservatism on classical Confucianism and an unjustified radicalism on Taoism.

How then should the Taoist critique on Confucianism be understood? There is a common ground shared by the teachings of classical Confucianism and Taoism in the advocacy of self-cultivation. In general terms, both see life as an art rather than a science. Both express a "this-worldly" concern for the concrete details of immediate existence rather than exercising their minds in the service of grand abstractions and ideals. Both acknowledge the uniqueness, importance, and primacy of the particular person and the person's contribution to the world, while at the same time stressing the ecological interrelatedness and interdependence of this person with his or her context.

Wherein do they differ then? For the Taoists, the Confucian penchant for reading the "constant *tao*" myopically as the "human *tao*" is to experience the world at a level that generates a dichotomy between the natural and human worlds. The argument against the Confucian seems to be that the Confucians do not take the ecological sensibility far enough, defining self-cultivation in purely human terms. It is the focused concern for the overcoming of ego-self and the spiritual extension and integration in the human world that gives classical Confucianism its sociopolitical and practical orientation.

But from the Taoist perspective, "overcoming self" is not simply to redefine the limits of one's concerns and responsibilities within the confines of the human sphere. This only results in an extended "ego-self" with the same kind of limitations and attachments that one is seeking to transcend. That is, instead of *personally* being "disintegrated" with the world, it is the human being *as a species* that is disintegrated. The Taoists do not reject human society and culture as such; rather, they reject the notion that human experience occurs independent of the natural world, and that the whole process of existence can be reduced to human values and purposes. They reject the pathetic fallacy implicit in the earliest Confucian humanism which gives the human being special status in the world, a status that ultimately serves to "dis-integrate" even an integrated social world from nature as a whole. The Taoist, observing that the human being has a natural as well as a social environment, insists that the Confucian model for self-cultivation be opened up from sociopolitical order to cosmic order, from the emulation only of human exemplars to the emulation of natural order broadly. As classical Confucianism evolves, it responds to this Taoist challenge, and extends its human-centered vision to locate the human experience within the cosmos more broadly.

To turn to Taoist moral philosophy specifically, ethics would refer to "ethos" in the classical sense of "character"; it would involve not simply moral judgments, but the total CHARACTER of the person in his or her social and natural environments. This total character is the changing lineaments of habit and disposition that include not only what might be deemed "good" or "moral" but the full complement of the qualities which constitute the personal, social, and natural fabric of one's existence. (Thus, no clear separation between ethics, SOCIAL AND POLITICAL PHILOSOPHY, and environmental philosophy exists in this tradition.) Importantly, in the immanental and ecological cosmology of Taoism, the ethos is always experienced and interpreted from some particular perspective. Appealing to the vocabulary of Taoism itself, this then is the basis of the polar and correlative relationship between *tao* as environment or field, and *te* as individuated particular or focus. *Tao* is the defining conditions—the context or environment—for the particular *te*. Given that perhaps the core Taoist text—the *Tao-te-ching*, or "Classic of *tao* and *te*"—takes its name from these two concepts, an exploration of Taoist philosophy might well begin from a closer examination of *tao* and *te*, and of their relationship.

There is a problem in using "ethos" as an equivalent for *tao*. *Tao* is perhaps most frequently translated as the "Way." "Ethos" quite adequately captures the determinate and intelligible order of our various environments—the "way" or "mode" of existence. However, *tao* is not only the "how," but also the "what." That is to say, *tao* is ontologically categorial: it is both the perceived order of the cosmos, and the vital energy or *ch'i* in which this order is expressed. The myriad things are perturbations of hylozoistic energies which coordinate themselves to constitute the harmonious regularity which is *tao*. *Tao* produces the myriad things, and the myriad things constitute the *tao*.

More also can be said about *te* as particular perspectives or foci on the ethos we call *tao*. *Te* is frequently translated as "virtue" in the sense of "potency," "capacities," "strength," or "influence." If we think of particular phenomena in relationship to their environments, they register varying degrees of impact on the character of their contexts as a function of their own particular potencies. *Te*, or "virtue," is the full range of the ways and the qualitative degrees by which a phenomenon alters and contributes to the character of its world. Having said this, it must be clear that any "ethical" judgments in the narrow sense are going to be derived from aesthetic sensibilities—the intensity, INTEGRITY, and appropriateness that one detail has for its environing elements as interpreted from some particular perspective.

To the extent that Taoism is prescriptive, it is so not by articulating rules to follow or by asserting the existence of some underlying moral principle, but by describing the conduct of an achieved human being—the sage, the consummate person, the authentic person—as a recommended object of emulation. The model for this human ideal, in turn, is the orderly, elegant, and harmonious processes of nature. Throughout the philosophical Taoist corpus, there is a "grand" analogy established in the shared vocabulary used to describe the conduct of the achieved human being on the one hand, and the harmony achieved in the mutual accommodations of natural phenomena on the other.

It is interesting that the Taoists create, or at least popularize, a new terminology for the consummate human exemplar—the *chen jen*. The common translation—True Man or Real Man—belies the fact that *chen* etymologically implies both "authenticity" and "transformation." That is, whatever the human exemplar might be, he or she is one who is able to express personal integrity and uniqueness in the context of a transforming world. "Authentic Person" would thus perhaps be a better rendering for *chen jen*.

The choice of "authentic" to translate *chen* is calculated. With the same root as "author," it captures the primacy given to the contribution of the particular person. It further registers this contribution as what is most fundamentally "real" and "true." It is because of the primacy of the "authorship" of the "authentic person" in creating human order that "there must be the Authentic Person before there can be authentic knowledge." The claim made here at the beginning of *Chuang Tzu* 6 is that a "knower" does not simply cognize a pre-existing reality. Rather, one participates actively in the "making real" or "realization" of one's world through one's own "self-disclosure" (*tzu-jan*). "Knowing" for the Taoist, in addition to being cognitive, is profoundly experiential and performative. It is precisely because the Authentic Person must "author" the world to "know," or better, to "realize" it, that this term *chen* has at once metaphysical and epistemological significance. *Chen* as what is "authentic" is both what is "real" and what is "true."

There is need for further refinement. When we say "self-disclosure" (*tzu-jan*), we must bear in mind that "self" is always "in context." It is an individuated focus in the ecological process of existence which is dependent upon and ultimately reflects in itself, the full consequence of nature. The Authentic Person has an interdependence and mutuality with all environing conditions such that *one's* own disclosure and *their* disclosures are mutually entailing. The Authentic Person is both transforming and transformed in that, as one's contribution impresses itself on and conditions the *tao,* so the *tao* conditions the expression of one's own insistent particularity.

We can make this profile of the consummate exemplar more concrete by referring to the texts. The *Tao-te ching* is primarily a *political* treatise. As such, it is the portrait of the ruler who, emulating the regularity of nature, sets broad political and social conditions for the pursuit of personal realization. The sage-ruler is thus referred to as the "model of the world" under whose organization the people are at leisure to pursue their own realization.

The concerns of the *Chuang Tzu* are somewhat different. Instead of focusing on the sage-ruler and the manifestation of his personal enlightenment in the appropriate government of the state, the *Chuang Tzu* concerns itself with the realization of the particular person, assuming perhaps that enlightened government is simply a natural extension of the enlightened person. The most salient features of this enlightened person—the Authentic Person—that can be abstracted from the Taoist texts are the following. First, the Authentic Person through modeling human conduct on the rhythm and cadence of natural change, is able to realize an integration and continuity with the process of change as a whole. A recognition of the mutuality one shares with one's environments leads to a reconciliation of opposites: a transcending of the self/other distinction and a freedom from the desires, attachments, and dichotomous values that are generated from the notion of a discrete self (that is, reconciliation of "this/that," "good/bad," "right/wrong," "life/death," and so on). This "deconstruction of polar opposites" is pervasive, and can be illustrated in the androgynous ideal of the *Tao-te-ching.* In chapter 28, it describes "one who knows masculinity and yet preserves femininity" as "the river gorge of the world" to which all repair. Another example of this deconstruction of polar opposites is the *tao-te* or "field-focus" relationship. As we have seen, *te* as a focus in the *tao* is a unique particular with its own integrity and character. But when viewed as a perspective on *tao* which entails all of its environing conditions as integral to itself, the focus/field distinction is deconstructed. *Chuang Tzu* 1 observes: "If you look at things in terms of how they differ, the gap between liver and gall is as great as the distance from Ch'u to Yüeh; if you look at them in terms of their sameness, everything is continuous."

The consummate person in Taoism is characterized by a seeming indifference to worldly conditions, reflective supposedly of the relative and arbitrary nature of value judgments. This attitude is frequently misunderstood. It is sometimes construed as a passivity, a quietism, and a resignation, when it is perhaps better seen as a relaxation of conventional value judgments through an attitude of tolerance and accommodation. It is certainly not the case that Taoism eschews value judgments. This point can be made through a discussion of what perhaps is Taoism's central normative concept, *wu-wei*.

Tao has been described as an emerging pattern of relatedness perceived from the perspective of an irreducibly participatory *te,* or particular. The perceived order is an achievement, not a given. Because *tao* is an emergent, "bottom-up" order rather than something imposed, any interpretation of *tao* that would reduce it to preexisting laws or principles that discipline the natural world in some necessary way would be problematic. This being the case, the question is: what is the optimal relationship between *te* and *tao,* between a particular and its environing conditions? The Taoist response is the self-dispositioning of particulars into relationships which allow the fullest degree of self-disclosure and development. In the Taoist literature, this most appropriate action is perhaps most often described as *wu-wei,* formularistically translated "non-action." Those translators who seek to avoid the passive and quietistic implications of the translation, "non-action," generally render it as "not acting willfully" or "acting naturally." Of course, any attempt to thus define *wu-wei* as "natural action" and to distinguish it from "unnatural action" (*yu wei*) will give rise to the perennial question that haunts most interpretations of Taoism: if all is *tao,* and *tao* is natural, what is the source, the nature, and the ontological status of unnatural activity?

To answer this question, we might want to consider the philologically similar term, "anarchy," as a more appropriate translation of *wu-wei,* describing as it does the negation of the authoritarian determination of one thing by another. *Wu-wei,* then, is the negation of that kind of "making" or "doing" which requires that a particular sacrifice its own integrity in acting on behalf of something "other," a negation of that kind of engagement that makes something false to itself.

The sympathy between *anarchy* and *wu-wei* that lies in their common reference to activity performed in the absence of coercively determinative constraints would certainly recommend "anarchy" as a translation for *wu-wei.* But there is also an important difference. Anarchy describes the fundamental relationship between a particular and a determinative principle—an *archē.* Because the *archē* is a "beginning"—that which determines without itself being determined—there is an ontological disparity between the *archē* and the particular that makes their relationship dualistic.

Wu-wei, by contrast, does not describe the dualistic relationship between principle and particular, but the polar relationship that obtains between two particulars. In human terms, the personal integrity that must be sustained in the project of self-disclosure requires an awareness that uncoordinated action between oneself and the elements of one's environment not only deprives environing particulars of their possibilities, but further, impoverishes one's own. *Wu-wei* describes a productively creative relatedness. *Wu-wei* activity "characterizes"—that is, produces the character or ethos of—an aesthetically contrived composition. There is no ideal, no closed perfectedness. Ongoing creative achievement itself provides novel possibilities for a richer creativity. *Wu-wei* activity is thus fundamentally qualitative: an aesthetic category and only derivatively an ethical one. The distinction between *wu-wei* and *yu-wei* activity is not made by appeal to some fixed principle or standard. But because there is no invariable structure to provide a science of "correct" relatedness, this does not mean that there is no basis for making value judgments. *Wu-wei* can be evaluated on aesthetic grounds, allowing that some relationships are more *wu-wei* than others. Some relationships are more successful than others in maximizing the creative possibilities of oneself in one's environments.

This classical Taoist aesthetic, while articulated in these early texts with inimitable flavor and imagination, was, like most philosophical anarchisms, too intangible and impractical to ever be a serious contender as a formal structure for social and political order. In the early years of the Han dynasty (beginning about 200 B.C.E.), there was an attempt in the *Huai Nan Tzu* to encourage the Taoist sense of *ethos* by tempering the lofty ideals with a functional practicability. It appropriates a syncretic political framework as a compromise for promoting a kind of practicable Taoism—an anarchism within expedient bounds. While historically the *Huai Nan Tzu* fell on deaf ears, it helped to set a pattern for the Taoist contribution to Chinese culture across the sweep of history. Over and over again, in the currency of anecdote and metaphor, identifiably Taoist sensibilities would be expressed by inspiring a range of theoretical structures and social grammars, from military strategies to the dialectical progress of distinctively Chinese schools of Buddhism to the constantly changing face of poetics and art. It can certainly be argued that the richest models of Confucianism, represented as the convergence of Taoism, Buddhism and Confucianism itself, were an attempt to integrate the Confucian concerns with human community with the broader Taoist commitment to an ecologically sensitive humanity.

See also: BUDDHIST ETHICS; CHINA; CHUANG TZU; COMPARATIVE ETHICS; CONFUCIAN ETHICS; LAO TZU.

Bibliography

Primary Sources

Chuang-tzu: The Seven Inner Chapters and Other Writings from the Book of Chuang-tzu. Translated by A. C. Graham. London: Allen and Unwin, 1981.

Lao Tzu: Texts, Notes, and Comments. By Ch'en Ku-ying. Translated by Rhett Young and Roger T. Ames. San Francisco: Chinese Materials Center, 1977.

Tao Te Ching. Translated by D. C. Lau. Harmondsworth: Penguin Books, 1963.

Yuan Dao: Tracing Dao to Its Source. D. C. Lau and Roger T. Ames, translators. Classics of Ancient China. New York: Ballantine, 1998.

Secondary Sources

Ames, Roger T. *The Art of Rulership: A Study in Ancient Chinese Political Thought.* Honolulu: University of Hawaii Press, 1983.

———. "The Common Ground of Self-Cultivation in Classical Taoism and Confucianism." *Tsing Hua Journal of Chinese Studies,* n.s. 17, no. 1, 2 (1985): 65–97.

———. "Is Political Taoism Anarchism?" *Journal of Chinese Philosophy* 10 (1983): 27–47.

———. "Putting the *Te* Back Into *Taoism.*" In *Nature in Asian Traditions of Thought: Essays in Environmental Philosophy,* edited by J. Baird Callicott and Roger T. Ames. Albany: State University of New York Press, 1989.

Chang, Chung-yuan. *Creativity and Taoism: A Study of Chinese Philosophy, Art, and Poetry.* London: Wildwood House, 1963.

Feng, Yu-lan. *Chung-kuo che-hsüeh shih hsin-pien.* Peking: Peoples Press, 1983. Vol. 2.

Giradot, N. J. *Myth and Meaning in Early Taoism.* Berkeley: University of California Press, 1983.

Graham, A. C. *Disputers of the Tao.* LaSalle, Ill.: Open Court, 1989.

———. "Taoist Spontaneity and the Dichotomy of 'Is' and 'Ought.'" In *Experimental Essays on Chuang-tzu,* edited by Victor H. Mair. Honolulu: University of Hawaii Press, 1983.

Hall, David L. "Process and Anarchy—A Taoist Vision of Creativity." *Philosophy East and West* 28 (1978): 271–85.

———. *The Uncertain Phoenix: Adventures Toward a Post-Cultural Sensibility.* New York: Fordham University Press, 1982.

Hall, David L., and Roger T. Ames. Thinking from the Han: Self, Truth, and Transcendence in Chinese and Western Culture. Albany: State University of New York Press, 1998.

Huai-Nan Tzu: Philosophical Synthesis in Early Han Thought. Translated by Charles LeBlanc. Hong Kong: Hong Kong University Press, 1985.

Izutsu, Toshihiko. *A Comparative Study of the Key Philosophical Concepts in Sufism and Taoism.* Tokyo: Keio Institute of Cultural and Linguistic Studies, 1967. Vol. 2.

Lieh-tzu. *The Book of Lieh Tzu.* Translated by A. C. Graham. New York: Columbia University Press, 1990 (1960).

Needham, Joseph. *Science and Civilisation in China.* Cambridge: Cambridge University Press, 1954. Vol. 2.

Schwartz, Benjamin I. *The World of Thought in Ancient China.* Cambridge, Mass.: Harvard University Press, 1985.

Roger T. Ames

Taylor, Charles (1931–)

Canadian philosopher. Taylor was born in Montreal, educated at McGill University and All Soul's College, Oxford, where he received his doctorate in 1961. He returned to Montreal, where he taught at the Université de Montréal and McGill. From 1976 to 1981 he was Chicele Professor of Social and Political Theory in the University of Oxford. He then taught at McGill University until his retirement in 1998.

Taylor's unique contribution to philosophy in the twentieth century arises largely from his ability to integrate some of the best elements of the "continental" and "analytic" traditions. While the major sources of his philosophical thinking can be found in G. W. F. HEGEL (1770–1831), Martin HEIDEGGER (1889–1976), and Maurice Merleau-Ponty (1908–1961), Taylor retains the commitment to clarity of expression and ordinary language associated with the philosophical culture of Oxford in the 1950s. As a result, he has consistently succeeding in taking ideas that are very far from the philosophical mainstream and presenting them in ways that demand serious consideration. As an active public intellectual, he has similarly succeeded in bringing sophisticated, and often very subtle, philosophical ideas to bear on concrete political issues in Canada and beyond.

Taylor's philosophical influence stems from four major philosophical interventions. First, his "Interpretation and the Sciences of Man" (1971) provided the classic statement of the "interpretivist" or hermeneutic position in the English-language debate over the methodological status of the social sciences. Second, his *Sources of the Self* (1989) developed a theory of modernity that radically reconceptualized the relationship between Enlightenment rationalism and Romanticism. Third, his theory of personal identity, and in particular his conception of *strong evaluation,* provided an important and influential alternative to instrumental or desire-based theories of value. Finally, a series of papers, culminating in *Multiculturalism and 'The Politics of Recognition'* (1992), came to be regarded by many as the most sophisticated expression of the "communitarian" position in the liberalism-communitarianism controversy.

The key idea informing Taylor's philosophy is his rejection of what he calls the "formal" conception of rationality, a view which he takes to have dominated philosophy in the modern period. According to Taylor, rationality is not about following a set of procedures; it is about providing the most "perspicuous articulation." What counts as perspicuous, ultimately, is determined by the extent to which a particular articulation puts one in touch with the substantive moral goods that inform one's thinking. Thus the products of reason—everything from cultural practices to philosophical systems—are different expressions, more or less indirect, of a set of underlying moral commitments.

This analysis leads Taylor to the conclusion that most philosophers in the modern period have failed to understand, much less articulate, the deeper sources of their own thought. For instance, he regards "formal" ethics in the Kantian or utilitarian style as an attempt to gerrymander a system of rules that will generate the "right" answers, *i.e.,* the answers that everyone *already* believes to be correct. Similarly, he views political LIBERALISM as an attempt to gerrymander a system of RIGHTS or a theory of justice that will produce the "right" outcomes. In both cases, theorists engage in a perverse sort of SELF-DECEPTION, pretending that they do not already know the answers to the questions they pose. But when these moral sources are forgotten or denied, it can generate unnecessary rigidities—a punitive moral code, enforced by guilt, or a purely negative conception of individual liberties. Progress, in Taylor's view, can occur only if everyone acknowledges the substantive goods that motivate their more specific doctrinal commitments. Once individuals begin to acknowledge their underlying moral motivations, they can attempt to achieve a more perspicuous articulation of these sources. This process of dialogue and recognition will lead to convergence on certain key moral sources, but still leave room for pluralism among the substantive conceptions of the good that are endorsed in the culture. This recognition also makes possible the mutual understanding and respect necessary for peaceful coexistence and exchange.

In his major work, *Sources of the Self,* Taylor develops this idea into a strikingly original thesis about the status of cultural modernity. Again, the dominant conception of modernity in the West has been formalist. This is most obvious in theories influenced by Max WEBER (1864–1920), who regarded the process of modernization as one of rationalization. Taylor chooses instead to regard modernity as a particular configuration of substantive goods that have acquired prominence under specific historical conditions in the West. Furthermore, he claims that these values are not fully compatible with one another, and that the tension between them is largely responsible for the fragile and dynamic character of modern societies.

Thus, Taylor regards typical Enlightenment values (normally explained as the product of a "disenchanted" view of nature, or an instrumentalization of social relations) as the expression of an underlying "affirmation of everyday life" and a commitment to the good of efficacy. At the same time, he regards the Romantic rejection of Enlightenment rationalism as no more than the expression of a different set of values, one that emphasizes self-creation and individual expression. Modern cultures arise precisely from the tension between these commitments. The great figures of the European philosophical tradition—Immanuel KANT (1724–1804), Hegel, and in some respects Karl MARX (1818–1883)—generated excitement precisely because they promised to reconcile or synthesize these rival goods in new and unexpected ways.

This analysis of modernity radically changes the terms of the debate over modernity and postmodernity. It suggests that anti-modernists who align themselves with counter-Enlightenment Romanticism are just as much a part of "modern" society as those whom they criticize. The debate over POST-MODERNISM is just one more cycle in the cultural dynamic that *constitutes* the identity of modern societies and individuals. According to this view, postmodernists are quintessentially modern philosophers; they simply refuse to acknowledge the deeper—ultimately moral—sources of their personal and philosophical commitments. Their fear of normativity is just another facet of the self-imposed inarticulacy that they share with their Enlightenment brethren.

Taylor's commitment to the work of articulating—and thereby renewing—the moral sources of modern culture is also evidenced in his activities as a public intellectual. In Quebec, Taylor has been well known as a political commentator for over thirty years, through newspaper and magazine writing, and later through frequent television appearances. He first came to public attention in 1965 through an unsuccessful campaign for federal office, in which he ran as the Social-Democratic candidate against Canadian Prime Minister-elect Pierre Elliott Trudeau. Of dual French-English parentage, Taylor has a long-standing commitment to the goal of accommodating Quebec nationalism within the framework of Canadian federalism. He has been one of the most articulate proponents of "asymmetric federalism," a constitutional model designed to allow Quebec greater autonomy without radically decentralizing the Canadian federation. At the same time, Taylor has vigorously criticized the Anglophone minority in Quebec for using the language of individual rights and equality to resist accommodating the legitimate collective aspirations of Francophones. As a result,

his views carry considerable authority on both sides of the often highly polarized linguistic divide.

Of Taylor's early work, the most important is his scholarly treatise on Hegel (a condensed version of the larger work, *Hegel* [1975], was published as *Hegel and Modern Society* [1979]). The larger work did an enormous amount to revive interest in Hegelian ideas at a time when there was very little sympathy for German idealism in the Anglo-American philosophical community. The most important contribution to Hegel scholarship made by this work involved Taylor's attempt to situate Hegel within a philosophical tradition that he referred to as "expressivism." This analysis drew out connections between Hegel's thought and the more general currents of German Romanticism that were widely overlooked or misunderstood.

See also: COMMUNITARIANISM; CRITICAL THEORY; CULTURAL STUDIES; FORMALISM; HEGEL; HUMANISM; INDIVIDUALISM; INTEGRITY; LIBERALISM; MORAL PLURALISM; MULTICULTURALISM; POSTMODERNISM; RATIONALITY VS. REASONABLENESS; SELF-KNOWLEDGE; SOCIAL AND POLITICAL PHILOSOPHY; SOCIAL PSYCHOLOGY; SOCIOLOGY.

Bibliography

Works by Charles Taylor

The Explanation of Behaviour. London: Routledge and Kegan Paul, 1964.

Hegel. Cambridge: Cambridge University Press, 1975.

Hegel and Modern Society. Cambridge: Cambridge University Press, 1979.

Human Agency and Language. Philosophical Papers Vol. 1. Cambridge: Cambridge University Press, 1985. Includes "Interpretation and the Sciences of Man" (1971).

Philosophy and the Human Sciences. Philosophical Papers Vol. 2. Cambridge: Cambridge University Press, 1985.

Sources of the Self: The Making of the Modern Identity. Cambridge, Mass.: Harvard University Press, 1989.

The Malaise of Modernity. Toronto: Anansi, 1991. Republished as *The Ethics of Inarticulacy.* Cambridge, Mass.: Harvard University Press, 1992.

Multiculturalism and "The Politics of Recognition." Edited by Amy Gutmann. Princeton: Princeton University Press, 1992.

Reconciling the Solitudes. Montreal: McGill-Queen's University Press, 1993.

Philosophical Arguments. Cambridge, Mass.: Harvard University Press, 1995.

Works about Taylor

Tully, James, ed. *Philosophy in an Age of Pluralism: The Philosophy of Charles Taylor in Question.* Cambridge: Cambridge University Press, 1994.

Joseph Heath

technology

ARISTOTLE (384–322 B.C.E.) pointed out in Book III of the *Nicomachean Ethics* that one can deliberate only about what is within one's power to do. Technologies such as gene splicing and nuclear fission were not within the power of the Greeks, so there was no ethical deliberation about them until centuries later. Throughout history, technology (knowledge associated with the industrial arts, applied sciences, and various forms of engineering) has opened new possibilities for actions. As a result, it has also raised new ethical questions.

Most of these questions have not generated new ethical concepts; instead they have expanded the scope of existing ones. For example, because hazardous technologies threaten those who live nearby, ethicists have expanded the notion of "equal treatment" to include "geographical equity"—equal treatment of persons located at different distances from dangerous facilities.

Because new developments force the expansion of ethical concepts, those who investigate technology and ethics need both technical and philosophical skills. To assess the ethical desirability of using biological (*versus* chemical) pest control, for example, one must know the relevant biology and chemistry, as well as the economic constraints on the choice. Although such factual knowledge does not determine the ethical decision, it constrains it in important and unavoidable ways.

Since policymakers evaluate virtually all technologies, at least in part, by methods such as benefit-cost or benefit-risk analysis, knowledge of economics is essential for informed discussions of technology and ethics. Philosophers investigate both the ethical constraints on developing or implementing particular technologies and the ethical acceptability of various economic and policy methods used to evaluate technology.

Philosophical questions about technology and ethics generally fall into one of at least five categories:

(1) conceptual or *metaethical* questions; (2) *general normative* questions; (3) *particular normative* questions about specific technologies; (4) questions about the ethical *consequences* of technological developments; and (5) questions about the ethical justifiability of various *methods* of technology assessment.

Examples of (1) are: "How ought one to define 'free, informed consent' to risks imposed by sophisticated technologies?" Or "How ought one to define 'equal protection' from such risks?" Examples of (2) are: "Does one have a right, as Alan GEWIRTH argues, not to be caused to contract cancer?" Or "Are there duties to future generations potentially harmed by various technologies?" Examples of (3) are: "Should commercial nuclear power licensees, contrary to the Price-Anderson Act, be subject to strict and full liability?" Or "Should the United States continue to export banned pesticides to developing nations?" Examples of (4) are: "Would development of a plutonium-based energy technology threaten civil liberties?" Or "Would deregulation of the airline industry result in less safe air travel?" Examples of (5) are: "Does benefit-cost analysis ignore noneconomic components of human welfare?" Or "Do Bayesian methods of technology assessment ignore the well-being of minorities likely to be harmed by a technological development?"

The leading philosophical issues concerning technology and ethics are the following:

How to Define Technological Risk

Engineers and technical experts tend to define 'technological risk' as a probability of physical harm, usually as "average annual probability of fatality." Philosophers and other humanistic critics claim both that technological RISK cannot be defined purely quantitatively, and that it includes more than physical harm. Instead, they argue that technology often threatens other goods, such as civil liberties, personal autonomy, or RIGHTS such as due process.

The technologists argue for a quantitative definition of risk, claiming that we need a common denominator for evaluating diverse technological hazards. They also claim that it is impossible to evaluate nonquantitative notions, such as the technological threat to DEMOCRACY. Those who oppose the quantitative definition argue not only that it excludes qualitative factors (like equity of risk distribution) affecting welfare, but also that the nonquantitative factors are sometimes more important than the quantitative ones. Hence, they argue, for example, that an equitably distributed technological risk could be more desirable than a quantitatively smaller one (in terms of probability of fatality) that is inequitably distributed.

How to Evaluate Technologies in the Face of Uncertainty

Whether one technological risk is quantitatively greater than another, in terms of average annual probability of fatality, however, is often difficult to determine. Most evaluations of technology are conducted in the face of probabilistic uncertainty about the magnitude of potential hazards. Typically, this uncertainty ranges from two to four orders of magnitude. It arises because the developments most needing evaluation, *e.g.,* biotechnology, are new. We have limited experience with them and hence limited data about their accident frequency.

How should one evaluate technologies whose level of risk is uncertain? According to John Harsanyi, the majority position is that, in such situations, one should either use subjective probabilities of experts, or assume that all uncertain events are equally probable. The desirable technological choice is then the one having the highest "average expected utility," as measured by the probability and utility of the outcomes associated with each choice. Critics of the majority position, like John RAWLS, maintain that it has all the flaws of UTILITARIANISM. It fails, they say, to take adequate account of minorities likely to be harmed by high-consequence, low-probability risks. Rawls argues instead that we should use a maximin rule in situations of probabilistic uncertainty. Such a rule, like the difference principle, would direct us to avoid the outcome having the worst possible consequences, regardless of its alleged probability.

Critics of the Rawlsian position claim that it is irrational to choose so as to avoid worst-case technological accidents. They claim that taking small chances with technology often brings great economic benefits for everyone. Opponents of the majority Bayesian position respond, however, that such benefits are neither assured nor worth the risk, and that the subjective probabilities of experts often exhibit an "overconfidence bias" that there will be no serious accidents or negative health effects from a given technology.

Technological Threats to Due Process

Ethicists also charge that technology threatens due-process rights. To the extent that hazardous technologies cause (what Judith THOMSON calls) "incompensable risks," like DEATH, due process is impossible because the victim cannot be compensated.

One of the most controversial due-process debates concerns commercial nuclear fission for generating electricity. Current U.S. law limits liability of the nuclear licensees to less than three percent of total possible losses in a catastrophic accident. Critics maintain that this law (the Price-Anderson Act) violates citizens' due-process rights. Defenders argue that it is needed to protect the industry from possible bankruptcy, and that a catastrophic nuclear accident is unlikely. Supporters of the law respond that if a catastrophic nuclear accident is unlikely, then industry needs no protection from bankruptcy caused by such an event.

How Safe Is Safe Enough?

Because a zero-risk society is impossible, philosophers and policymakers debate both how much risk is acceptable and how it ought to be distributed. The distribution controversies raise all the classical problems associated with utilitarian *versus* egalitarian ethical schemes. Conflicts over how much technological risk is acceptable typically raise issues of whether the public has certain welfare rights, like the right to breathe clean air. The controversies also focus on how much economic progress can be traded for the negative health consequences of technology-induced risks.

Philosophers are particularly divided about how to evaluate numerous negligible risks, from a variety of technologies, that together pose a serious hazard. Small cancer risks that are singly harmless, but cumulatively and synergistically harmful, provide a good example of such cases. They raise the classical ethical problem of the contributor's dilemma. This dilemma occurs because the benefit of avoiding imposing a single small technological risk is imperceptible, although the cumulative benefit of everyone's doing so is great. Some philosophers view such small risks as ethically insignificant, while others claim they are important. Those in the latter group argue that agents are responsible for the effects of *sets* of acts (that together cause harm) of which their individual act is only one member.

Consent to Risk

The sophistication of many technologies, from genetically engineered organisms to the latest nuclear weapons, makes it questionable whether many individuals understand them. If they do not, then it is likewise questionable whether persons are able to give free, informed CONSENT to the risks that they impose. Critics of some contemporary technologies point out that those persons most likely to take technological risks (*e.g.*, blue-collar workers in chemical or radiation-related industries) are precisely those who are least able to give free, informed consent to them. This is because they are often persons with limited education and no alternative job skills.

Those who claim that both workers and the public have given consent to technological risks use notions like "compensating wage differential" to defend their position. They say that, since workers in hazardous technologies receive correspondingly higher pay because of the greater risks that they face, they are compensated. Likewise, they maintain that accepting a risky job constitutes a form of consent. They also claim that society's acceptance of the economic benefits created by hazardous technologies constitutes implicit acceptance of the technologies.

In response, more conservative ethicists argue both that ECONOMIC ANALYSIS does not show the existence of a compensating wage differential in all cases, and that mere acceptance of a job in a risky technology does not constitute consent to the hazard, especially if the worker has no other realistic employment alternatives. They also argue that acceptance of the benefits of hazardous technologies does not constitute acceptance of the technologies themselves since many people are inadequately informed about such risks.

See also: APPLIED ETHICS; BAIER; BIOETHICS; BUSINESS ETHICS; COLLECTIVE RESPONSIBILITY; COMPUTERS; CONSENT; COST-BENEFIT ANALYSIS; ECONOMIC ANALYSIS; ENGINEERING ETHICS; ENVIRONMENTAL ETHICS; EQUALITY; FUTURE GENERATIONS; GENETIC ENGINEERING; GEWIRTH; GOVERNMENT, ETHICS IN; NATURE; NUCLEAR ETHICS; PUBLIC HEALTH POLICY; PUBLIC POLICY; PUBLIC POLICY ANALYSIS; RAWLS; REPRODUCTIVE TECHNOLOGIES; RESPONSIBILITY; RISK; RISK ANALYSIS; SOCIAL AND POLITICAL PHILOSOPHY; THOMSON; UTILITARIANISM; WELFARE RIGHTS AND SOCIAL POLICY.

Bibliography

Baier, Kurt, and Nicholas Rescher, eds. *Values and the Future: The Impact of Technological Change on American Values.* New York: Free Press, 1969. Philosophical analysis of problems associated with technological development.

Durbin, Paul T., ed. *Philosophy and Technology.* Boston: Kluwer, 1985–. Annual publication of the Society for Philosophy and Technology. Essays, many of which deal with ethics and technology, written from a variety of philosophical perspectives.

Ellul, Jacques. *The Technological Society.* Translated by John Wilkinson. New York: Knopf, 1964. General overview of problems associated with technology; widely viewed as anti-technology.

———. *The Technological System.* Translated by Joachim Neugroschel. New York: Continuum, 1980. General overview of problems associated with technology; widely viewed as anti-technology.

Goodpaster, Kenneth, and Kenneth Sayre, eds. *Ethics and the Problems of the 21st Century.* South Bend, IN: University of Notre Dame Press, 1979. Original philosophical essays on various problems associated with technological development.

Harsanyi, John C. "Can the Maximin Principle Serve as a Basis for Morality? A Critique of John Rawls's Theory." *American Political Science Review* 59, no. 2 (1975): 594–605.

Jonas, Hans. *The Imperative of Responsibility.* Chicago: University of Chicago Press, 1985. Criticism of contemporary technological society and proposals for reform.

Kasperson, Roger, and Mimi Berberian, eds. *Equity Issues in Radioactive Waste Management.* Boston: Oelgeschlager, 1983. Descriptive analysis of equity issues related to radwaste management.

MacLean, Douglas. *Values at Risk.* Totowa, NJ: Rowman and Allanheld, 1984. Consideration of the ethical problems posed by issues of nuclear security and deterrence.

MacLean, Douglas, and Peter Brown, eds. *Energy and the Future.* Totowa, NJ: Rowman and Allanheld, 1983. Essays on ethical issues associated with energy technologies.

Rescher, Nicholas. *Unpopular Essays on Technological Progress.* Pittsburgh: University of Pittsburgh Press, 1980. Widely ranging essays on a variety of topics related to technology.

Shrader-Frechette, Kristin. *Nuclear Power and Public Policy.* Boston: Reidel, 1983. Criticism of nuclear technology on grounds that it violates various ethical principles.

———. *Science Policy, Ethics, and Economic Methodology.* Boston: Reidel, 1984. Analysis of problems with benefit-cost methods and proposals for amending them.

———. *Risk Analysis and Scientific Method.* Boston: Reidel, 1984. Analysis of problems associated with assessment of technological risk assessment and proposals for amending them.

Thomson, Judith Jarvis. *Rights, Restitution, and Risk.* Cambridge, MA: Harvard University Press, 1986. Treats a variety of ethical issues related to technological risk.

Kristin Shrader-Frechette

technology and nature

Technology consists of tools, machines, COMPUTERS, techniques, and systems of control and production of which humans are essential parts. The first major moral question about TECHNOLOGY is whether any technological device or system is in itself good or bad. If it is bad or evil, as Martin HEIDEGGER (1889–1976) suggests, then its use could be considered to be bad, and thus one should not use it. If it is good, as Buckminster Fuller (1895–1983) insists, then presumably it should be used. But technology may be value neutral; or it could be either good or bad depending on how it is used.

The second major question is whether the manifestations and development of technology are autonomous. If technology is autonomous and develops independently whatever choices humans make, then whether technology is in itself good, bad, or value neutral, human use of technology and participation in technological systems can be said to be as good, bad, or value neutral as the technology itself is. In this case, involved humans cannot be morally praised or blamed because the manifestations of technology they are involved in develop independently of their choices. It would thus be unrealistic to say that humans should choose one as opposed to another course of technology, because such choosing plays no role in whether the results are good or bad.

The common sense view is that technology is neutral and non-autonomous. This is expressed in the maxim: Guns don't kill people, people do. A gun is neither good nor bad in itself, but its use can be either good or bad depending on whether one uses it for good or bad purposes. Humans then can be morally praised and blamed for developing and deploying some branches of technology and suppressing others. Moral discussions of technology concern whether the results of its use are good or bad. Moral imperatives, and praise and blame, are addressed and allocated to humans on the basis of their voluntary and directive participation in technological systems that are perceived to have either good or bad results.

In other words, the common sense view of technology as value neutral is well adapted to a straightforward utilitarian ethics.

The major opposition to a utilitarian view of technology is based on a distinction between the natural and the artificial, with technology being seen as unnatural because tools, machines, computers, techniques, and technological systems are artifacts of human devising. This distinction depends on taking humans to be not part of nature. Thus, for example, houses humans build are not natural, while nests birds build are. Such a view of the unnaturalness of human artifacts is often supported by supernatural religions such as the Judaic, Christian, and Muslim. Human products can be treated as having moral value above the natural as does Judaism; or as morally bad and to be avoided, as does Catholicism with respect to birth control, ABORTION, and gene splicing technology. Technology is sometimes presented as absolutely good or bad according to the declaration of God. The only argument against this is to oppose supernaturalism itself.

The general naturalistic, scientific view in opposition to supernaturalism is that humans and human technology are parts of nature that are good or bad according to their use, which leads again to utilitarian ethics. The third major moral question is what to do in the face of human ignorance about the results of utilizing and developing technology. The Industrial Revolution (of the late eighteenth and the nineteenth centuries) was the result of millions of individual choices about the development and deployment of technology, and most people in the West think the general results are good. But if use of fossil fuels results in an increase of carbon dioxide in the atmosphere that changes the world's climate adversely, then everyone will think the results are very bad. No one chooses or anticipates most bad results of technology, nor is anyone responsible for the overall systemic good results. We tend to praise heroes of the Industrial Revolution, but they could not have anticipated its massive effects. Then who, if anyone, is to blame for its bad effects?

If our choices of technology are made in ignorance of worldwide and long-range results that may be either bad or good, then even if we should choose the good, how can we? And even if we are morally bound to blame those who make choices that lead to bad results, how can we, given that they sincerely believed their choices would lead to good results? These problems of ignorance and of distributive and extensive RESPONSIBILITY are among the most difficult in ethics.

The ethics of technology can be linked with EN-VIRONMENTAL ETHICS in two ways. Some argue that good technological choices can be made if they are informed by a knowledge of ecology, and that these choices should be made with the goal of maintaining worldwide ecological balance. Then technology as a whole becomes a form of conservationist resource management, and the good is what maintains balance.

Others argue that humans do not and perhaps cannot understand the complex ecology of the planet, and so should not interfere. Technology is then evaluated as good or bad on the basis of whether it disrupts worldwide ecological balance. Because it is based on our ignorance of future results, this hands-off-nature view can lead to the claim that we should reject all technology.

But humanity is distinguished by technology. Humans are tool-making animals. All human social orders are based on techniques for the control and manipulation of both materials and other humans. What is good and bad and what should and should not be done in human societies is intimately linked to their technological systems. MORAL DILEMMAS arise when ethical NORMS are based in both scientific common sense UTILITARIANISM and religious supernatural absolutism. This explains why many ethical problems about technology are unresolved.

See also: ANIMALS, TREATMENT OF; BIOETHICS; BIOLOGICAL THEORY; BUSINESS ETHICS; COLLECTIVE RESPONSIBILITY; COMPUTERS; CONSERVATION ETHICS; DOUBLE EFFECT; ECONOMIC ANALYSIS; ENGINEERING ETHICS; ENVIRONMENTAL ETHICS; EXPLOITATION; FUTURE GENERATIONS; GENETIC ENGINEERING; LEOPOLD; LIFE AND DEATH; MEDICAL ETHICS; MYSTICISM; NATURALISM; NATURE AND ETHICS; NUCLEAR ETHICS; PUBLIC HEALTH POLICY; PUBLIC POLICY; REPRODUCTIVE TECHNOLOGIES; TECHNOLOGY; THOREAU; UTILITARIANISM.

Bibliography

Durbin, Paul T., ed. *Technology and Responsibility*. Dordrecht: Reidel, 1988.

Ellul, Jacques. *The Technological Society*. New York: Alfred A. Knopf, 1967.

Ferré, Frederick. *The Philosophy of Technology*. Englewood Cliffs, NJ: Prentice Hall, 1988.

Fromm, Erich. *The Revolution of Hope: Toward a Humanized Technology*. New York: Harper and Row, 1968.

Fuller, Richard Buckminster. *Operating Manual for Spaceship Earth*. Carbondale: Southern Illinois University Press, 1969.

Gouldner, Alvin W., and Richard A. Peterson. *Notes on Technology and the Moral Order*. Indianapolis, IN: Bobbs-Merrill, 1962.

Heidegger, Martin. *The Question Concerning Technology, and Other Essays*. New York: Garland, 1977.

Husserl, Edmund. *The Crisis of European Sciences and Transcendental Phenomenology: An Introduction to Phenomenological Philosophy*. Evanston, IL: Northwestern University Press, 1970.

Jonas, Hans. *The Imperative of Responsibility: In Search of an Ethics for the Technological Age*. Chicago: University of Chicago Press, 1984.

Lipscombe, Joan, and William Williams. *Are Science and Technology Neutral?* London; Boston: Butterworth, 1979.

Mander, Jerry. *Four Arguments for the Elimination of Television*. New York: William Morrow, 1978.

Mesthene, Emmanuel G. *Technological Change, Its Impact on Man and Society*. New York: New American Library, 1970.

Mitcham, Carl, and Robert Mackey, eds. *Philosophy and Technology: Readings in the Philosophical Problems of Technology*. Reprint. New York: Free Press, 1983.

Pot, Johan Hendrik Jacob van der. *Steward or Sorcerer's Apprentice? The Evaluation of Technical Progress: A Systematic Overview of Theories and Opinions*. Translation by Chris Turner of Bewertung des technischen Fortschritts; foreword by Alexander King. 2 vols. Delft: Eburon Publishers, 1994.

Taviss, Irene. *Our Tool-Making Society*. Englewood Cliffs, NJ: Prentice Hall, 1972.

Winner, Langdon. *Autonomous Technology: Technics-out-of-control as a Theme in Political Thought*. Cambridge: MIT Press, 1977.

Richard A. Watson

teleological ethics

The term "teleological" comes from the Greek word *telos* for goal or aim. The idea of teleological ethics in recent usage has been understood, most fundamentally, as standing in contrast with "deontological" approaches to ethics. Deontological moralities require people or societies sometimes to act in disregard of and even against good consequences, *e.g.,* by forbidding the killing of an innocent person even if that is the only way one can prevent a greater loss of human life. Teleological theories, by contrast, are all supposed to accept some version of the idea that the end (always) justifies the means.

In addition, the notion of a teleological ethics is generally thought to embrace two rather different kinds of approaches to morality (or ethics): ancient VIRTUE ETHICS and modern-day CONSEQUENTIALISM (including UTILITARIANISM). However, the widespread assumption that these two forms of ethics have something in common that distinguishes them from deontological theories is subject to great, if not insuperable, difficulties that threaten the very idea of a fundamental distinction between teleology and DEONTOLOGY.

In the first place, the idea that (act-)utilitarianism and (act-) consequentialism are teleological is something of a stretch. True, utilitarians like Henry SIDGWICK (1838–1900) often speak of HAPPINESS or PLEASURE as a/the rational (final) end of human action and also hold that the morality of any action is determined by how much happiness or pleasure it yields. But none of this entails that the agent who acts rightly must *aim* at the general happiness or indeed at happiness at all. If the best consequences for human happiness will actually be achieved by an agent's concerning himself only with his own FAMILY or by his refusing even to think about using certain deontologically forbidden means to certain good ends, then it will be permissible and even obligatory for him to disregard the "goal" of universal happiness. In that case, utilitarianism is more properly regarded as a consequentialist view than as a teleological one; and indeed the modern-day tendency, initiated by Elizabeth ANSCOMBE (1919–2001), to dwell on the consequentialist, rather than on the teleological, character of utilitarianism, PERFECTIONISM, and the like, shows, I think, an implicit recognition of the inaccuracy of regarding these views as necessarily prescribing that people should have universal happiness or any other particular good as their goal or aim in life.

By the same token, the indiscriminate application of the term "teleological" to all ancient forms of virtue ethics is also problematic. To be sure, ARISTOTLE (384–322 B.C.E.) not only begins the *Nicomachean Ethics* by saying that happiness or EUDAIMONIA is a reasonable ultimate end of all human action, but also subscribes to a metaphysical form of teleology according to which all (living) things aim for ends or goals that are dictated by their natures. This might then understandably lead one to suppose that Aristotle thinks of the human virtue(s) he describes in Books II through V of the *Ethics* as *character traits required for individual human happiness,* and that he is perhaps even an ethical egoist who holds that the virtuous, rational individual aims for her own happiness in all her actions. But in fact this gives a distorted picture of Aristotle's view in the *Ethics,* and we can take the first step toward seeing this if we recognize that Aristotle conceives of happiness or *eudaimonia* as consisting mainly in acting virtuously (over a long life).

If *eudaimonia* is to be understood in terms of living virtuously, then, upon pain of circularity, virtue cannot also be understood as what contributes to or is required for *eudaimonia.* And indeed there is a great deal of evidence in the *Ethics* that Aristotle rejects the latter idea and instead understands virtue in intuitionist terms. The virtuous individual is someone who, without the benefit of formulas or rules, "sees" what is just or courageous and, therefore, noble in various situations and, without a struggle or mental reservations, acts accordingly. Situational facts about what is just or courageous would then function as the ground floor of Aristotelian ethics, with happiness being understood in terms of virtue, rather than *vice versa.*

Moreover, Aristotle often describes the virtuous person (*e.g.,* the soldier who risks his life for his country) as someone who acts "for the sake of the noble," and this seems to rule out the idea that (rational) virtue consists in seeking one's own happiness. Certainly, in a fashion rather typical of ancient virtue ethics, Aristotle sometimes argues that, in doing what is noble (for its own sake), we invariably are better off than if we had been the sort of person able or likely to do otherwise (accordingly, even someone who dies bravely in battle will have had a better life than a coward who lives longer). But, again, this only means that virtuous actions contribute or are requisite to our happiness, not that our happiness is their goal. (Aristotle may be in some important sense a *eudaimonist,* but it seems a mistake to think of him as an ethical *egoist*.) In that case, the idea that ARISTOTELIAN ETHICS is unambiguously *teleological* is mistaken or at least dubious, and this conclusion is further strengthened by considering the seemingly deontological character of some parts of Aristotle's thinking.

Aristotle says, for example, that the just individual will distribute goods in accordance with virtue or merit, and there is no suggestion here that this injunction might sometimes be ethically suspended or superseded in the name of overall good consequences. Moreover, certain sorts of actions—*e.g.,* adultery and matricide—are said to be always wrong, and such absolute prohibitions seem to place Aristotle with the deontologists and against the consequentialists, once again, therefore, calling the whole teleological/deontological distinction into question.

Does this mean that we have no use for the idea of a teleological ethics? Not quite. The problems we have encountered come from the assumption that ancient virtue ethics and modern consequentialism are (most) usefully classed together and the assumption that teleology and deontology exhaust the possibilities for ethics. But if, in line with etymology, we were to conceive teleological ethics more narrowly as the sort of ethics that prescribes certain goals or purposes for agents, then we could avoid the just-mentioned assumptions and still have a useful distinction. After all, some forms of ethics—*e.g.,* various forms of the "self-realization" ethics so characteristic of British neo-Hegelianism—do seem to tell the agent consciously to strive for or seek certain goals, and it might be useful to be able to distinguish such views from approaches to morality that don't require particular purposes in agents (even if they do require the agent somehow to produce good results or consequences).

Alternatively, we might reserve the term "teleological" for forms of ethics that derive from or accompany a teleological metaphysics or (philosophy of) science, and this narrow usage would also, I think, escape the difficulties that a more overarching construal of teleology appears to create. But such more specific or narrower usages do render the idea of teleological ethics less important as a classificatory notion, and it may even be possible that future philosophy encyclopedias will not feel the same need to explain the notion that they certainly have felt up till now.

See also: ANSCOMBE; ARISTOTELIAN ETHICS; CHRISTIAN ETHICS; CHU HSI; CONSEQUENTIALISM; DEONTOLOGY; DUTY AND OBLIGATION; ECONOMIC SYSTEMS; *EUDAIMONIA*, -ISM; EXCELLENCE; FINAL GOOD; GOOD, THEORIES OF THE; INTUITIONISM; LIBERALISM; MACHIAVELLI; NIETZSCHE; PERFECTIONISM; PRACTICAL REASON[ING]; PUNISHMENT; RIGHTS; SIDGWICK; VIRTUE ETHICS; VIRTUES; UTILITARIANISM; VOLUNTARISM.

Bibliography

Annas, Julia. *The Morality of Happiness.* New York: Oxford University Press, 1993.

Anscombe, G. E. M. "Modern Moral Philosophy." *Philosophy* 33 (1958): 1–19.

Aristotle. *Nicomachean Ethics. On the Parts of Animals.*

Bales, R. Eugene. "Act-Utilitarianism: Account of Right-Making Characteristics or Decision-Making Procedure?" *American Philosophical Quarterly* 8 (1971): 257–65.

Bradley, F. H. *Ethical Studies.* 1876.

Hurka, Thomas. *Perfectionism.* New York: Oxford University Press, 1993.

Railton, Peter. "Alienation, Consequentialism, and the Demands of Morality." *Philosophy and Public Affairs* 13 (1984): 134–71.

Sidgwick, Henry. *The Methods of Ethics.* 1874.

Michael Slote

temperance

Philosophical work on temperance, one of the four traditional cardinal VIRTUES, has a lengthy history. Yet many puzzles about the nature and scope of the virtue remain. There is still good reason to ask, as SOCRATES (c. 470–399 B.C.E.) did in Plato's *Charmides,* what temperance is and with what things it is concerned.

PLATO (c. 430–347 B.C.E.), in his *Republic,* portrays temperance (*sophrosune*) as a virtue of the soul as a whole. In this, it resembles justice but differs from the two remaining cardinal virtues, WISDOM and COURAGE, which Plato locates, respectively, in the reasoning and HONOR-loving parts of the soul. The soul of the temperate person is characterized by the harmonious relations among its three parts, with "reason" as the acknowledged and effective leader.

ARISTOTLE (384–322 B.C.E.), in his *Nicomachean Ethics,* identifies temperance as a mean between insensibility (*anaisthesia*) and self-indulgence (*akolasia*). The former vice, he observes, is rare, consisting as it does of a disposition to take less delight in pleasures than one should. For this reason, he says, temperance is commonly opposed simply to self-indulgence. Both traits are concerned specifically with a certain class of bodily pleasures—sex, food, drink, and the like, or what Aristotle terms the pleasures of touch. They are derivatively associated with a class of pains, those that may arise from the lack or want of pertinent pleasures.

Aristotle distinguishes temperance from continence or SELF-CONTROL (*enkrateia*). Both temperate and continent persons are disposed "to do nothing contrary to the rule for the sake of bodily pleasures"; but the latter, unlike the former, must occasionally struggle against "bad appetites." The desires and feelings of the temperate person are in perfect agreement with his rational principle. And since the moral virtues imply the presence of the *right* rule or principle, the desires and feelings of temperate agents never miss the mark. Temperate individuals desire the pleasures *that* they ought, *when* they ought, and *as* they ought. Continent agents are typically successful in *resisting* temptation; temperate individuals are not even *subject* to temptation.

If Aristotle's position seems excessively restrictive, his requirements on temperance may be relaxed along either or both of two dimensions—knowledge and inclination. Must a temperate agent recognize in each case what he ought to desire? And must his desires always fall in line?

Henry SIDGWICK (1838–1900) observes in his *Methods of Ethics* (1874) that "our common idea of Virtue includes two distinct elements, the one being the most perfect ideal of moral excellence that we are able to conceive for human beings, while the other is manifested in the effort of imperfect men to attain this ideal." Since human beings, as they actually are, do not always know what they ought to do, and do not always desire in accordance with their assessment of the desired items, any account of the virtues that successfully treats them as traits of actual human beings must allow for cognitive and motivational imperfections. Perhaps it can safely be said, with James Wallace, that certain traits of a person count as virtues when they are "developed . . . to a noteworthy degree."

If we grant that a temperate person may occasionally have pertinent desires that do not hit the mark, even his own mark, as it were, Aristotle's distinction between temperance and continence or self-control must be revised. Perhaps temperate individuals are characterized by a remarkable conformity of appetite to judgment or reason, whereas continent persons, though they are subject to temptation rather more often, are exceptionally good at resisting.

Though, for Aristotle, temperance and self-control are concerned with the same class of pleasures and pains, recent literature on self-control gives that trait a much broader range of application. According to accounts of self-control defended by Gary Watson and Alfred Mele, the trait can be exhibited in the mastery of any sort of motivation that competes for the determination of behavior with the agent's better judgment.

A similarly broad conception of the domain of temperance violates traditional distinctions between temperance and courage. Courage is displayed in (among other things) the mastery of fear. So is self-control on Watson's and Mele's accounts, provided that the fear inclines the agent toward behavior that her better judgment recommends against. But temperance and courage, traditionally conceived, are concerned with distinct ranges of motivation.

Recent accounts of temperance tend to be less exclusive than Aristotle's about the proper objects of the virtue. G. H. von Wright treats PLEASURE in general as the special object of temperance. For James Wallace, temperance, as the polar opposite of self-indulgence, is concerned with "*easy* pleasures and amusements—ones that require no particular effort or sacrifice to secure and enjoy." Obviously, not all such pleasures are bodily pleasures.

Wallace suggests that, "characteristically, the self-indulgent person is unwilling or unable to forego an immediate pleasure when considerations indicate that he should." We may say that it is characteristic of temperate persons, in contrast, to be both willing and able to forego immediate pleasures for the sake of what they deem greater goods. Following Aristotle, we may plausibly add that the desires of temperate persons for immediate pleasures are characteristically in line with their better judgments. This may explain the willingness of these agents to forego these pleasures when they compete with greater goods.

The approximate account of temperance just sketched fails for at least two reasons. First, it places excessive emphasis on immediacy. Someone may exhibit temperance on Monday in irrevocably declining an invitation to an orgy scheduled for Saturday; and a self-indulgent person may self-indulgently accept. Second, it is overly inclusive. Someone whose desires for immediate pleasures are in perfect harmony with his better judgments about pleasure, but only because he accepts the principle that he ought always to pursue the temporally nearest pleasure, surely does not count as temperate. Conformity of one's desires for pleasure to one's better judgments about pleasure is not sufficient for temperance.

One might attempt to resolve the latter problem by limiting the better judgments in our tentative account of temperance to judgments that *correctly* gauge the value of the pertinent pleasures. But, *by his own standards,* the better judgments of the voluptuary who consistently acts as his conception of the good directs *do* correctly gauge the value of the pleasures that he pursues. A Platonist may appeal to higher, agent-independent standards of value in arguing that this voluptuary is not temperate. However, even a thoroughgoing relativist about the good can maintain that some conceptions of the good leave no room for temperance—for example, a conception that recommends the pursuit of whatever pleasure happens to be nearest and that breaks ties by appealing, say, to intensity. (Roughly this conception is characteristic of Aristotle's *akolastos,* the self-indulgent person.) Temperate persons display moderation in their pursuit of immediate appetitive pleasures; our voluptuary does not. The suggestion that the latter is temperate strikes us as absurd precisely because part of what it *means* to say that someone is temperate is that she seeks and enjoys appetitive pleasures only in *moderation.* That the voluptuary is not temperate is a pronouncement of ordinary usage of the word 'temperance' and does not depend upon any particular theory of the good.

This is not to say that a hedonist cannot be temperate. Epicurus (341–270 B.C.E.), in his "Letter to Menoeceus," writes:

> When . . . we maintain that pleasure is the end, we do not mean the pleasures of profligates and those that consist in sensuality, . . . but freedom from pain in the body and from trouble in the mind. For it is not continuous drinkings and revellings, nor the satisfaction of lusts, nor the enjoyment of fish and other luxuries of the wealthy table,
>
> which produce a pleasant life, but sober reasoning, searching out the motives for all choice and avoidance, and banishing mere opinions, to which are due the greatest disturbance of the spirit.

Plainly, someone who seeks the life of Epicurean pleasure would be well served by temperance.

It is tempting to suppose that temperance entails giving appetitive pleasure a modest place in one's hierarchy of values, and that a combination of an appropriate modesty condition with the requirement that a temperate person be strongly disposed to desire pleasures in accordance with her better judgments yields necessary and sufficient conditions for possession of the virtue. However, the supposition is problematic. Someone who satisfies the second requirement but who places appetitive pleasure near the top of her system of values might count as temperate. Perhaps she simply does not care for appetitive pleasures normally deemed excessive or evil. Though she gives appetitive pleasure a high evaluative ranking, her desires and behavior might be of the sort characteristic of temperate persons. Conversely, someone who satisfies the second requirement and places appetitive pleasure at or below the middle of his hierarchy of values might often desire and act as voluptuaries do. Consider a hypothetical person who values only knowledge, artistic expression, appetitive pleasure, and money—in that order. Keeping his priorities straight need not preclude his often desiring and acting intemperately.

Temperance is plausibly regarded as entailing a supranormal conformity of one's appetites to one's better judgments. The trait is legitimately distinguished from self-control; and even if Aristotle was overly demanding in drawing the line at *perfect* conformity, the notion of judgment/appetite conformity is central to a proper distinction. One might try to provide the remainder of an adequate account of temperance by constraining the conception of the good or the system of values that supports the pertinent better judgments. An alternative approach is behavioral. One might defend an account of the distinctive observable features of temperate action and then attempt to combine it with a judgment/appetite conformity principle to produce an attractive characterization of temperance. On this approach, the virtue might be analyzed, roughly, as a supranormal disposition to pursue appetitive pleasures in moderation as a consequence of a tendency to desire them in accordance with one's better judgment.

This sketch of an analysis correctly suggests that an agent may fail to have temperance for either of the following two reasons. Her moderate behavior might not characteristically be due to a noteworthy conformity of her appetites to her better judgment: she might, for example, be continent rather than temperate. Or she might satisfy the conformity condition and yet not characteristically behave moderately as a result: perhaps she is a voluptuary who holds that satisfaction of appetites is a very great good.

Peter Geach once warned his readers that temperance, far from being an exciting topic, "is a humdrum common-sense matter" and that the considerations that recommend the trait "are not such as to arouse enthusiasm." However humdrum temperance may be, it poses a significant challenge to the philosophical analyst, as is amply demonstrated by the absence in the literature of an unproblematic account of the virtue.

See also: ARISTOTLE; COURAGE; EMOTION; EPICUREANISM; HEDONISM; PASSION; PHILOSOPHY OF RELIGION; PLATO; PLEASURE; SELF-CONTROL; SEXUALITY AND SEXUAL ETHICS; STOICISM; THOMAS AQUINAS; VIRTUES; WEAKNESS OF WILL.

Bibliography

Aristotle. *Nicomachean Ethics.* In vol. 9 of *Works of Aristotle,* edited by W. D. Ross. London: Oxford University Press, 1915. Passages cited: 1109a; 1119a; 1107b; 1118a–b; 1151b–1152a; 1102b; 1144b.

Epicurus. "Letter to Menoeceus." In *Epicurus: The Extant Remains,* translated by Cyril Bailey, 82–93. Oxford: Clarendon Press, 1926.

Foot, Philippa. "Virtues and Vices." In her *Virtues and Vices and Other Essays in Moral Philosophy,* 1–18. Berkeley: University of California Press, 1978.

Geach, Peter. *The Virtues.* Cambridge: Cambridge University Press, 1977.

Mele, Alfred. *Irrationality: An Essay on Akrasia, Self-Deception, and Self-Control.* New York: Oxford University Press, 1987.

———. *Autonomous Agents: From Self-Control to Autonomy.* New York: Oxford University Press, 1995.

North, Helen. *Sophrosune: Self-Knowledge and Self-Restraint in Greek Literature.* Ithaca, NY: Cornell University Press, 1966.

Plato. *The Dialogues of Plato.* Translated by Benjamin Jowett. 4th ed., vols. 2, 3. Oxford: Clarendon Press, 1953. See especially *The Republic* (see 442 b–d) and *Charmides.*

Sidgwick, Henry. *The Methods of Ethics.* 7th ed. New York: Macmillan, 1907 [1874]. See p. 225.

Thomas Aquinas. *Basic Writings of St. Thomas Aquinas.* Edited by Anton Pegis, vol. 2. New York: Random House, 1945. See *Summa Theologica,* I–II, Questions 55–61.

Wallace, James. *Virtues and Vices.* Ithaca, NY: Cornell University Press, 1978.

Watson, Gary. "Skepticism about Weakness of Will." *Philosophical Review* 86 (1977): 316–39.

Wright, G. H. von. *The Varieties of Goodness.* London: Routledge and Kegan Paul, 1963.

Alfred R. Mele

terrorism

There are two central philosophical questions about terrorism: What is it? And what, if anything, is wrong with it?

The definitional question is essentially irresolvable by appeal to ordinary language alone since terrorism as a concept is not "ordinary" in even the way that INTENTION, guilt, and dishonesty are. Nor is it a technical term belonging to some science; its natural home is in polemical, ideological, and propagandist contexts. Even so, there are certain contours to the confused public outcry about terrorism which can give a purchase for conceptual analysis. The success of any such analysis must be judged both by its degree of fit with such contours and its contribution to specific and more general moral debates about violence.

Definitions abroad in the theoretical literature fall into several groups stressing different aspects of the phenomena commonly referred to as terrorist:

(a) *The effect of extreme fear, either as intended or as achieved.* Definitions stressing this element are influenced by the reference to terror in the word itself and by certain aspects of the history of its use.

(b) *An attack upon the State.* Here all violent internal attacks upon the State are regarded as terrorist, and the State's own employment of violence cannot be terrorist.

(c) *The strategic purposes for which violence is used, such as publicity-seeking.*

(d) *The supposedly random or indiscriminate nature of terrorist violence.*

(e) *The nature of the targets of violence.*

(f) *Secrecy in the use of violence.*

Some definitions combine a number of these emphases, others are more austerely concentrated. Hughes defines terrorism as "a war in which a secret army . . . spreads fear," thus drawing on (a) and (f); Paskins and Dockrill say it is "indiscriminate war of evasion," which combines (d) and a version of (b); Wardlaw speaks of political violence "designed to create extreme anxiety and/or fear in a target group larger than the immediate victims with the purpose of coercing that group into acceding to the political demands of the perpetrators," thus combining (a) and (c). Coady concentrates upon the idea that terrorist violence is targeted upon noncombatants or innocents, so stressing (e).

This last emphasis catches a central logical and moral aspect of common discourse employing the term since terrorism is frequently objected to because "the innocent" are attacked. It also gives a handle for serious ethical discussion by linking terrorism to moral argument about war. In addition, there are reasons of theoretical utility favoring a definition which is relatively uncommitted on the specific purposes of terrorist violence. If we treat terrorism as the tactic of violent attacks upon noncombatants, we can leave it an open empirical question for which purposes it is used.

The element of fear in (a) raises complex issues. There are parallel reasons for excluding it as a purpose since attacks upon noncombatants may be made not to terrorize but for publicity value, for "symbolic" reasons, or merely to strike the only blow possible. On the other hand, the publicity or symbolic effect will usually operate and be expected to do so through the fear generated by the violence; the third sort of case is perhaps best treated, in its pure form, as exceptional.

Some general reference to purpose is in any case required to make it clear that the tactic of terrorism has a political rather than a merely personal or criminal orientation. Spectacular criminal outrages, with no political motivations, are often enough called terrorist in the media because they frighten people and vividly set their perpetrators at odds with the State, but the major interest of terrorism, both theoretically and morally, lies in its political orientation. Ter-

rorist acts will be illegal but their significance is deeper and more disturbing than, say, a revenge bombing of a police station by criminals. When criminals operate on a scale and with ambitions that bring them into the political arena, then the matter is different, as is illustrated by the Colombian drug syndicates of the 1980s.

If we define terrorism as the tactic of intentionally targeting noncombatants with lethal or severe violence for political purposes, we will capture a great deal of what is being discussed with such passion and we can raise crucial moral and political questions about it with some clarity. We might narrow the definition in certain respects by incorporating a reference to the idea that the attacks or threats are meant to produce political results via the creation of *fear,* and we could widen it by including noncombatant PROPERTY as a target where it is significantly related to life and security.

Such a definition will not require secret armies nor the idea of indiscriminate violence. Terrorism does not have to be indiscriminate, in the sense of random or irrational, but it will deliberately violate the normal discriminations favoring noncombatant immunity.

This way of proceeding ties the widespread moral revulsion against terrorism to the fundamental prohibition in just war theory against violation of the RIGHTS of noncombatants. It also helps to raise sharply the moral analogies between the State's use of violence against non-legitimate targets, either in State-to-State warfare or against its own citizens, and the political violence of non-State agencies against similarly illegitimate targets. A genuine case can be made in support of the common accusation of the insurgent that States, too, use terrorism. This should do nothing to excuse its use by revolutionaries, but it does point to a certain HYPOCRISY in much common indignation about terrorism. Those who think that the State terrorism of the World War II saturation bombing raids was justified by some argument of necessity, or other overriding moral considerations, cannot refuse to look at such arguments when mouthed by revolutionaries.

A difficulty with this definitional approach is that the concept of noncombatant needs clarification, especially for the case of revolutionary violence. Its moral significance also needs to be established against certain natural objections. We cannot enter fully into either of these here, but the distinction between combatant and noncombatant is clearly more difficult in subversive war than "normal" war. In "normal" war, the immunity of noncombatants is a basic principle, because our justification for using lethal violence is specified by the need to deal with those who are prosecuting the EVIL which gives us just cause. "Combatants" is the technical term for such agents and will include those who do so under duress, such as conscript soldiers, and agents without uniforms, such as spies and certain politicians. (Its connotations are both wider and narrower than "guilt" because one at least hesitates to ascribe guilt to the quaking conscript, and many who do not prosecute the evil are guilty of approving it.) In formal war, there are plenty of problem applications of the concept, but informal war increases such problems for familiar reasons. Nonetheless, some revolutionaries do try to make the discriminations both in their theory and propaganda and in their practice.

It is important from the point of view of morality and often of long-term political objectives not to identify people as combatants too readily. Both revolutionaries and governments lose support by slaughtering village administrators and killing peasants or destroying villages on suspicion, not to mention the difficulties created for postwar reconstruction by such policies. A genuine reluctance to harm noncombatants will be exhibited in the reluctance to classify people as combatants even where this involves a degree of real RISK to one's life and cause.

This point about reluctance has another implication for the definition of terrorism. If terrorism is defined in terms of violent attacks upon noncombatants, then certain actions or policies which will not strictly count as terrorist can nonetheless be carried out in a terrorist spirit because they show indifference to the welfare of noncombatants. If a grenade and machine gun attack is made against soldiers on duty in a crowd of civilians when it could have been made when they were alone, it would be understandable to describe the attack as terrorist simply because the civilian casualties were eminently avoidable. If the avoidability is sufficiently stark, it may be difficult to see the deaths and injuries as unintentional, but, in some cases, they may be unintended but culpably reckless.

This suggests that the definition of terrorism might be extended somewhat, while keeping much the same focus, by including acts which are not sufficiently concerned with avoiding harm to noncom-

batants. Another expansionary suggestion would be to define terrorism in terms of any breach of the *jus in bello* so that the refusal to give quarter to combatants or the mutilation of corpses, for instance, would be terrorist. The first suggestion has more merit than the second, though both would make reasonable analytical and ethical tools. The second has the defect that there is room for even more debate about the other rules of war than the central dictum about noncombatant immunity.

Even if we are unimpressed by the need for some form of noncombatant immunity, there remains an important moral problem for terrorist policies in that they face serious criticism in purely tactical terms, since it is by no means clear that terrorism can be expected to work. This is partly because it is sometimes obscure what goals are being pursued, but even where this is relatively clear, it is often doubtful whether there is any reasonable prospect of success. This is also true for goals provided by the view of terrorism as "expressive" (of despair or righteous ANGER, perhaps), since the point of expression cannot be disconnected from the realistic possibilities of audience recognition.

Finally, it is important to stress that acts of political violence may be very wrong even where they are not terrorist. Perpetrators of an unjust war or an unjust REVOLUTION do a great wrong even where they do not kill or endanger noncombatants. Nazi troops who shoot down armed Jewish resisters do evil even where they respect noncombatant immunity. In certain cases, where the rationale for resort to violence is sufficiently bizarre, we may find the attribution of combatant status too absurd to take seriously. Given a fantastic enough ideology, even attacks upon magistrates, police, or politicians may be as terrorist as attacks upon postmen or office workers.

See also: CIVIL DISOBEDIENCE; COERCION; DETERRENCE, THREATS, AND RETALIATION; HARM AND OFFENSE; HOMICIDE; INNOCENCE; INTERNATIONAL JUSTICE: CONFLICT; LIFE, RIGHT TO; MILITARY ETHICS; PACIFISM; REVENGE; REVOLUTION; SECRECY AND CONFIDENTIALITY; VIOLENCE AND NON-VIOLENCE; WAR AND PEACE.

Bibliography

Coady, C. A. J. "The Morality of Terrorism." *Philosophy* 60 (1985): 47–70. Philosophical analysis and ethical discussion.

Fotion, Nicholas, and Gerard Elfstrom. *Military Ethics.* Boston; London: Routledge and Kegan Paul, 1986. Philosophical and ethical material with a pronounced utilitarian orientation.

Frey, R. G., and Christopher W. Morris, eds. *Violence, Terrorism, and Justice.* Cambridge: Cambridge University Press, 1991. Excellent collection, with problems to do with terrorism as one focus.

Hughes, Martin. "Terrorism and National Security." *Philosophy* 57 (1982): 5–26.

Laquer, Walter. "Reflections on Terrorism." *Foreign Affairs* 65 (1986): 86–100. Makes some interesting observations about the relative insignificance of terrorism as a political problem despite its high public profile.

———. *Terrorism.* Boston: Little, Brown, 1977. One of many books and articles by this author on various aspects of terrorism. Another is *The Age of Terrorism* (Boston: Little, Brown, 1987). Basically historical and political analysis.

Luper-Foy, Steven, ed. *Problems of International Justice: Philosophical Essays.* Boulder, CO: Westview Press, 1988. See especially "Understanding Terrorism" by Robert K. Fullinwider; and "Terrorism: A Critique of Excuses" by Michael Walzer.

Murphy, Jeffrie G. "The Killing of the Innocent." *The Monist* 57 (1973): 527–50. Discusses, *inter alia*, the philosophical basis of the moral objection to killing noncombatants.

Paskins, Barrie A., and M. L. Dockrill. *The Ethics of War.* London: Duckworth; Minneapolis: University of Minnesota Press, 1979.

Primoratz, Igor. "What Is Terrorism?" *Journal of Applied Philosophy* 7 (1990): 129–37.

Simpson, Peter. "Just War Theory and the I.R.A." *Journal of Applied Philosophy* 3 (1986): 73–88.

Teichman, Jenny. "How to Define Terrorism." *Philosophy* 64 (1989): 505–17.

———. *Pacifism and the Just War.* New York; Oxford: Blackwell, 1986. Has philosophical discussion of innocence, noncombatance; chapter 9 is on "Terrorism and Guerilla War."

Walzer, Michael. *Just and Unjust Wars.* New York: Basic Books, 1977. History and philosophy. Chapter 12 is on terrorism; there is much discussion throughout of noncombatant immunity.

Wardlaw, Grant. *Political Terrorism.* Cambridge; New York: Cambridge University Press, 1982. An unusually balanced discussion of modern forms of terrorism and the appropriate political responses to them. The author is a criminologist.

Wilkinson, Paul. *Political Terrorism.* London: Macmillan, 1974. This was Wilkinson's first shot at the topic, but he has elaborated considerably on the issues since, most notably in his later book, *Terrorism and the Liberal State* (London: Macmillan, 1986). Vigorous political science, occasionally marred by some oversimplification.

Young, Robert. "Revolutionary Terrorism, Crime and Morality." *Social Theory and Practice* 4 (1977): 287–302.

C. A. J. Coady

theism

Theism is the belief that God exists, where God is thought of as the unique, all-good, all-powerful, all-knowing immaterial person who created, or otherwise explains the existence of, the universe. Theism is usually distinguished from polytheism, belief in many gods, and from deism, belief in God as an impersonal first cause. It is often understood as the common core of the major monotheistic religions, Christianity, ISLAM, and Judaism, but it can also be understood as a philosophical thesis in its own right, independent of the claims of any historical religions. Theism is a metaphysical thesis, not an ethical one, but it bears on ethics in respect of several important issues: the nature of God, the content of ethics, and the relation between God and ethics.

The Nature of God

The God of theism is held to be perfectly morally good. This raises a number of philosophical questions, the most obvious being, "What does it mean to say that God is perfectly morally good?" Does it mean that God violates none of his duties? If so, what are these duties, to whom does God owe them, and why is God subject to them? Or does it mean that God has all the VIRTUES and none of the vices? If so, are these the same as human virtues and vices, or is there a different set of virtues and vices, applicable only to God? However theists answer these questions, they have to tread carefully. Answers that make God's goodness too different from human goodness become hard to understand as goodness at all. On the other hand, answers that make God's goodness too similar to human goodness risk diminishing God as an object of worship, and make theism more vulnerable to the problem of EVIL.

Quite separate from the question of *what it means* to say that God is good is the question of *whether* God is good. According to David HUME (1711–1776), the evil and suffering we observe in the world around us raise these questions for the theist: "Is [God] willing to prevent evil, but not able? then is he impotent. Is he able, but not willing?

then is he malevolent? Is he both willing and able? Whence then is evil?" This 'problem of evil' is the greatest challenge to theism, and can be posed in a simple argument:

1. If an all-good and all-powerful God existed, then little or no evil would exist.
2. But much evil exists.
3. Therefore, no all-good and all-powerful God exists.

As the passage from Hume suggests, the idea behind premise (1) is that an all-good being would want to prevent evil, and an all-powerful being would be able to prevent evil, so if an all-good and all-powerful being existed, it would not allow any evil to exist. According to premise (2), much evil exists, whether "natural evils" such as the suffering caused by famine and disease, or "moral evils" caused by wicked human choices, such as crime and war.

Importantly, this argument's conclusion does not deny the existence of all gods, but only the God of theism, who is supposed to be all-good as well as all-powerful. In response, some have accepted a reduced theism, concluding that God's goodness can be preserved only by conceiving of God's power as limited. Classical theists, on the other hand, have rejected the argument by denying one or the other of the premises. Some have challenged (2), arguing that, contrary to appearances, there is little or no evil in the world. Many more have challenged (1), arguing with Leibniz (1646–1716) that God allows moral evil as a necessary condition of human freedom, or with Irenaeus (c. 120–202) that God allows natural evil as a necessary condition for moral and spiritual development.

The Content of Theistic Ethics

We might suppose that a substantial metaphysical commitment such as theism would bring equally substantial ethical commitments in its train, but this is not obvious. Consider first the practical content of morality: Do theists prohibit SLAVERY? It depends on their view of human society. Do theists permit polygamy? It depends on their understanding of sexuality, LOVE, and marriage. Do theists eat pork? It depends on whether they take God to have forbidden it. On these and many other points, the moral

codes held by theists have varied widely and depend more on the distinctive claims of particular theistic religions than on theism itself.

Consider next the ethical theories which give a reflective account of practical morality. Again, we find diversity. Among Christian theists, for example, we find deontological or divine command theories (ABELARD [1079–1142], WILLIAM OF OCKHAM [c. 1285–c. 1349]), consequentialist theories (Berkeley [1685–1753], PALEY [1743–1805]), and NATURAL LAW or teleological theories (AUGUSTINE [354–430], THOMAS AQUINAS [1225?–1274]). These accounts are all theistic, so their differences are best explained by other differences in philosophy, theology, or cultural context.

That said, one can make a few high-level generalizations. Most theistic ethical theories have been: (a) objective rather than subjective, viewing the truth about ethics as independent of human opinion; (b) absolutist rather than relativist, holding that certain types of acts, such as idolatry, are never permissible, regardless of one's situation (though which types of acts these are will depend on the theory considered); and (c) non-sceptical rather than sceptical, holding that God allows us enough knowledge of right and wrong for practical purposes.

These may be explained as merely coincidental features of particular theistic systems, but they may also be explained by the fact that theism in general has resources for rejecting the SUBJECTIVISM, relativism, and scepticism that dog so many purely naturalistic accounts. It is interesting to note that some naturalistic ethical theories attempt to avoid such undesirable implications by making use of a hypothetical IDEAL OBSERVER, who resembles God in knowing all the relevant non-moral facts, and in being perfectly impartial and sympathetic.

The Relation between God and Ethics

Philosophical questions also arise concerning the metaphysical, epistemological, and motivational relations between the God of theism and the realm of ethics. As a matter of metaphysics, if God created the universe, did he also create ethical values and obligations? Do good and right depend for their existence on God's willing? PLATO's (c. 430–347 B.C.E.) dialogue, *Euthyphro,* presents the theist with an apparent dilemma on this subject. Assuming that God wills what is right, we may ask: does God will the right because it is right? Or are things right simply because God wills them? If we answer 'yes' to the first question, we imply that ethical values such as rightness exist independently of God's will and that God must submit to them. This appears to diminish God's power and sovereignty. But if we answer 'yes' to the second question, we imply that ethical values depend on God's will and would have been different if God had willed differently. This appears to makes ethics contingent and God's willing arbitrary. Some theists reply that regarding ethical values as independent of God's will does not diminish God, either because these ethical values depend on another aspect of God himself, such as his nature, or because ethical truths are logically necessary, and no more diminish God's sovereignty than do logically necessary mathematical truths. Other theists have replied that regarding ethical values as contingent on God's will does not make them contingent or arbitrary, either because God's willing is logically necessary, or because God has sufficient non-moral reason for willing as he does.

Does belief in God give us reason to believe in ethics? Some have held that theism gives us an epistemological reason to hold or obey certain ethical beliefs, as the all-knowing God has revealed to us ethical truths which we might not have known otherwise. Others have held that theism gives us a motivational reason, as God will reward us for acting rightly and punish us for acting wrongly. Of course, such relations might run the other direction, too, as ethics might give us some reason for believing theism. Some, such as C. S. Lewis (1889–1963), have held that it gives us an epistemological reason, as in a moral argument for the existence of God. Others, such as KANT (1724–1804), have held that it gives us a PRACTICAL REASON, with God being a necessary postulate for the practical reasonableness of ethics.

The Similarity between Ethical Judgments and Theistic Judgments

Many philosophers have noticed another sort of relation between judgments about God and judgments about ethics, namely, one of similarity. Because such judgments do not seem straightforwardly empirical or conventional, both have been regarded as semantically or epistemologically problematic in similar ways. Empiricist critics have therefore urged that both ethical judgments and religious judgments

be interpreted as expressing feelings or attitudes instead of descriptive statements. Just as some ethical naturalists have replied that judgments about ethics can be vindicated in terms acceptable to empirical NATURALISM, some religious naturalists have replied that judgments about God can be similarly vindicated. And just as ethical non-naturalists have rejected the demand that ethical judgments be vindicated in naturalistic terms, many reformed epistemologists have rejected the demand that judgments about God be vindicated in terms acceptable to naturalism, with its empiricist presuppositions and barely concealed anti-religious bias.

See also: ABELARD; AGNOSTICISM; ATHEISM; AUGUSTINE; AUTONOMY OF ETHICS; CHRISTIAN ETHICS; CONSEQUENTIALISM; EVIL; HUME; ISLAM; JEWISH ETHICS; LEIBNIZ; METAPHYSICS AND EPISTEMOLOGY; MORAL ABSOLUTES; MORAL RELATIVISM; NATURALISM; PALEY; PHILOSOPHY OF RELIGION; RELIGION; SUBJECTIVISM; TELEOLOGICAL ETHICS; THOMAS AQUINAS; WILLIAM OF OCKHAM.

Bibliography

Adams, Marilyn M., and Robert M. Adams. *The Problem of Evil.* Oxford: Oxford University Press, 1990. A representative collection of essays on the problem of evil.

Beaty, Michael, Carlton Fisher, and Mark Nelson, eds. *Christian Theism and Moral Philosophy.* Macon, GA: Mercer University Press, 1998. A collection of essays illustrating the diversity of Christian theistic approaches to ethics.

Helm, P., ed. *Divine Commands and Morality.* Oxford: Oxford University Press, 1981. A collection of important essays for and against the divine command theory.

Hume, David. *Dialogues Concerning Natural Religion.* Edited and with an introduction by N. K. Smith. Indianapolis, IN: Bobbs-Merrill, 1947 [1779]. A classic source of arguments against theism. See p. 198 for passage quoted.

Kant, Immanuel. *Critique of Practical Reason.* Translated by Lewis White Beck. Indianapolis, IN: Bobbs-Merrill, 1956 [1788]. Kant's main work on ethics, including his discussion of God as a postulate of 'pure practical reason.'

Mavrodes, G. 'Religion and the Queerness of Morality.' In *Rationality, Religious Belief, and Moral Commitment,* edited by R. Audi and W. Wainwright. Ithaca, NY: Cornell University Press, 1986. An accessible moral argument for a theistic world-view.

Lewis, C. S. 'Right and Wrong as a Key to the Meaning of the Universe.' In *Mere Christianity.* New York: Macmillan, 1952.

Mill, John Stuart. *Theism.* In *Collected Works of John Stuart Mill,* edited by J. M. Robson, vol. X. Toronto: University of Toronto Press, 1969, 429–89. A classic critical discussion of theism.

Plantinga, Alvin. *God, Freedom and Evil.* Grand Rapids, MI: Eerdmans, 1974. Includes a lucid and influential response to the problem of evil.

Plato. *Euthyphro.* In *Plato: The Collected Dialogues,* translated by Lane Cooper, edited by Edith Hamilton and H. Cairns. Princeton, NJ: Princeton University Press, 1961. The original source of the 'Euthyphro problem.'

Swinburne, R. *The Coherence of Theism.* Oxford: Clarendon Press, 1993. A powerful exposition of theism. See especially chapters 9, 11, and 15.

Mark T. Nelson

theological ethics

Any ethical doctrine that makes theistic assumptions is theological. The ethical theories characteristic of the traditions of Judaism, Christianity, and ISLAM are thus theological. However, ethics can be religious without being theological. Because Theravāda Buddhism does not make theistic assumptions, its ethical thought is religious but not theological. There are theological versions of most of the standard ethical views. So, for example, the NATURAL LAW theory of THOMAS AQUINAS (1225?–1274) is theological because Aquinas thinks that natural law depends upon God's eternal law. And the UTILITARIANISM of William PALEY (1743–1805) is theological because Paley is a divine command theorist.

There are also theological virtue theories. They often differ with their secular counterparts over which traits of CHARACTER count as VIRTUES. Unlike ARISTOTLE (384–322 B.C.E.), for example, Aquinas holds that obedience to God is the greatest of the moral virtues. In the *Summa theologiae* (1266–1273), he argues that "properly speaking, the virtue of obedience, whereby we contemn our own will for God's sake, is more praiseworthy than the other moral virtues, which contemn other goods for the sake of God." The Aristotelian virtue of magnanimity seems to be akin to the Christian vice of PRIDE and directly opposed to the Christian virtue of HUMILITY. And even when theological and secular virtue theories agree that a certain trait is a virtue, they often offer different accounts of it. Thus, while for Aristotle death on the battlefield is the highest expression of COURAGE, for Aquinas suffering martyrdom is its highest expression. Important recent work

in VIRTUE ETHICS that stems from traditions of Christian theology has been done by Alasdair MACINTYRE and by Stanley Hauerwas and Charles Pinches.

A form of theological ethics that has been prominent in Christianity and Islam but less important in Jewish traditions is theological VOLUNTARISM. According to this view, morality depends, at least in part, on God's will. In CHRISTIAN ETHICS, theological voluntarism often assumes that this dependence is specifically on the divine will as promulgated by divine commands, and so the position has come to be known as divine command ethics. Divine command theories are found in the Franciscan ethics developed by John DUNS SCOTUS (c. 1266–1308) and WILLIAM OF OCKHAM (c. 1285–1347). Andrew of Neufchateau (c. 1340–1400), another Franciscan, conducted the lengthiest and most sophisticated known medieval defense of an ethics of divine commands. Both Martin LUTHER (1483–1546) and John CALVIN (1509–1564) endorsed the divine command conception. It is also to be found in the ethical theory of William Paley and in the distinctively Christian ethics of Søren KIERKEGAARD (1813–1855).

The last three decades of the twentieth century saw a revival of philosophical interest in divine command ethics. Among those who have contributed significantly to this revival are Robert M. Adams, Janine M. Idziak, and Philip L. Quinn. Both the attractive features and the points of vulnerability of theological ethics stand out in particularly sharp relief in the case of divine command ethics, and for that reason the remainder of this article will focus on this particular variety of theological ethics.

Divine command ethics is best understood as an account of the deontological part of morality that concerns duty or obligation. Moral deontology's chief concepts are moral requirement (obligation), moral permission (rightness), and moral prohibition (wrongness). On a divine command conception, actions are morally wrong just in case and only because God forbids them; actions are morally right just in case and only because God does not forbid them; and actions are morally obligatory just in case and only because God commands them. Contemporary divine command theorists disagree about how to conceive of the precise relation between, for example, being morally wrong and being forbidden by God. On one view, the property of being morally wrong is identical with the property of being forbidden by God; on another, the former property is distinct from but supervenes on the latter. A third view is that God's forbidding an action causes it to be morally wrong.

Monotheists of all stripes should, at least initially, be sympathetic to an ethics of divine commands. Judaism, Christianity, and Islam share the view that the Hebrew Bible has authority in religious matters. Both Exodus 20:1–17 and Deuteronomy 5:6–21, which recount the revelation of the Decalogue, portray God as a commander, instructing the Chosen People about what they are to do and not to do by commanding them. It seems natural enough to suppose that the AUTHORITY of the Decalogue depends on the fact that it is divinely commanded. It is possible, of course, to understand these divine commands as nothing more than God's emphatic endorsement of a moral code whose truth is independent of them. Being omniscient, God would know such moral truths, and being supremely good, God would want to communicate them to the Chosen People. On this view, commands are God's way of transmitting important moral information to humans. But it is also possible to understand the truth of the moral code expressed by the Decalogue as dependent on the divine commands.

Moreover, there are other stories in the Hebrew Bible on which an argument to the conclusion that the deontological status of at least some actions depends on divine commands can be based. These stories recount the incidents commonly described as the immoralities of the patriarchs; they are cases in which God commands something that appears to be morally wrong. The most famous of them is the divine command to Abraham, recorded in Genesis 22:1–2, to sacrifice his son Isaac. According to a medieval exegetical tradition, Abraham did no wrong in consenting to slay Isaac and would have done no wrong if he had slain Isaac. Thomas Aquinas explains that,

> when Abraham consented to slay his son, he did not consent to murder, because his son was due to be slain by the command of God, Who is Lord of life and death: for He it is Who inflicts the punishment of death on all men, both godly and ungodly, on account of the sin of our first parent, and if a man be the executor of that sentence by Divine authority, he will be no murderer any more than God would be.

In other words, Thomas thinks that, because Abraham would have been carrying out a death sentence imposed by God if he had slain Isaac in obedience to the divine command, he would not have committed a murder and so would not have done wrong if he had killed Isaac.

Andrew of Neufchateau reaches a similar conclusion. He argues that there are actions, such as HOMICIDE, which, when examined by natural reason, seem to be wrong but are not necessarily sins with respect to God's absolute POWER. Abraham, he says, "wished to kill his son so that he would be obedient to God commanding this, and he would not have sinned in doing this if God should not have withdrawn his command." In other words, for Andrew, because God's absolute power determines whether a homicide is a sin, Abraham would not have sinned and so would have done no wrong if he had killed Isaac in obedience to the divine command.

What the two medieval exegetes share is the conviction that the slaying of Isaac by Abraham, which would be wrong in the absence of the divine command, would not have been wrong and, indeed, would have been obligatory, given its presence, if it had not been withdrawn. And it is hard to see how Thomas or Andrew could resist the conclusion that any divinely commanded homicide would be obligatory. Lordship over life and death and absolute power, which are the divine attributes they take to explain why God's command to kill Isaac imposes an obligation on Abraham, would be properties of God even if divine commands to kill were numerous. So it seems that the considerations mobilized to defend Abraham against the charge of immorality can be generalized to support the conclusion that whether any action is morally obligatory depends on whether it is divinely commanded.

Divine commands play an important part in Christian ethics. It is a striking feature of the ethics of LOVE set forth in the New Testament that love is commanded. In one Gospel Jesus says: "You shall love the Lord your God with your whole heart, with your whole soul, and with all your mind. This is the greatest and first commandment. The second is like it: You shall love your neighbor as yourself" (Matthew 22:37–39). Similar commands are reported in the Gospels of Mark and Luke. In his last discourse, recorded in John's Gospel, Jesus tells his followers that "the command I give you is this, that you love one another" (John 15:17). This is a divine command if, as orthodox Christians believe, Jesus is God the Son. Hence, the foundational documents of Christianity teach that the distinctively Christian ethics of love (*agape*) of neighbor is expressed in the form of a divine command.

In *Works of Love* (1847), Søren Kierkegaard gives two reasons for thinking that *agape* must be a matter of duty or obligation. His discourse on Matthew 22:39 draws a sharp contrast between erotic love (*eros*) and FRIENDSHIP (*philia*), on the one hand, and Christian love of neighbor, on the other. Both erotic love and friendship play favorites; love of neighbor is undiscriminating. Kierkegaard says

> Therefore the object of both erotic love and of friendship has preference's name, "the beloved," "the friend," who is loved in contrast to the whole world. The Christian doctrine, on the contrary, is to love the neighbor, to love the whole human race, all people, even the enemy, and not to make exceptions, neither of preference nor of aversion.

But our spontaneous affections will not move us to love everyone without distinction. Love of neighbor must therefore be a duty in order that we can be motivated to it by our sense of duty. What is more, erotic love and friendship are mutable because they depend on characteristics of the beloved and the friend that can change, while love of neighbor is supposed to be invulnerable to changes in its objects. If the beloved loses the traits that made him or her erotically attractive, erotic love withers; if the virtuous friend turns vicious, friendship dies. Love of neighbor must remain unchanged even when such changes occur. If it is to do so, it cannot depend on the ways in which mutable features of the neighbor naturally attract or repel us.

According to Kierkegaard, it can have the independence of these features it needs only if it is obligatory, for only then can it derive from a stable commitment to doing what one is obliged to do. It is in this way, he says, that "this *shall,* then, makes love free in blessed independence. Such a love stands and does not fall with the contingency of its object but stands and falls with the Law of eternity—but then, of course, it never falls." So, for Kierkegaard, Christian love of neighbor must be a dutiful love because only a love motivated by a sense of duty can be both

extensive enough to embrace everyone without distinction and invulnerable to alterations in its objects. And what makes love of neighbor a duty is a divine command.

An ethics of divine commands thus has roots in the scriptures of the monotheistic religions and has been developed by means of philosophical and theological reflection on those scriptures. Such an ethics ought to seem attractive to people within the religious communities that regard such scriptures and the traditions of thought that interpret them as normative. There are, however, serious objections to divine command ethics, and they may undercut or even eliminate the attractiveness.

One objection is that divine command ethics is either useless or unacceptably divisive in a religiously pluralistic society. Jeremy BENTHAM (1748–1832) presses the point about uselessness. He says

> We may be perfectly sure, indeed, that whatever is right is conformable to the will of God: but so far is that from answering the purpose of showing us what is right, that it is necessary to know first whether a thing is right, in order to know from thence whether it be conformable to the will of God.

If Bentham's view is correct, divine command ethics is of no practical use because we can never learn what is right by first learning that something is conformable to God's will and then inferring that it is right.

But, of course, most divine command theorists will disagree with Bentham and argue that we can sometimes learn that something is conformable to God's will from sources such as revelation and then use this information to determine that it is right. If the appeal to revelation is allowed against Bentham, however, the fact that religiously pluralistic societies contain rival views about what, if anything, has been revealed and competing claims about what, if anything, has been divinely commanded must be taken into account. When it is, it seems that allowing the appeal will be divisive because it introduces religious controversy into ethics and eliminates the prospect of coming by rational means to agreement on moral principles. It is worth noting that, if this is a successful objection to divine command ethics, parallel objections will succeed against other forms of theological ethics. For in a religiously pluralistic society, there are also disagreements about what virtues and vices there are and what natural laws, if any, hold.

A divine command theorist can say three things in response to this objection. First, religious disagreement does not inevitably give rise to disagreement about moral principles. A divine command theorist and a nonreligious Kantian can agree on the principle that torturing the innocent is always morally wrong. They will, to be sure, disagree about why it is always wrong. The divine command theorist will say that it is wrong because God forbids it, and the Kantian may say that it is wrong because it is a failure to treat the humanity in another as an end in itself. But disagreement in the metaphysics of morals is consistent with overlapping consensus at the level of moral principle. Second, not all moral disagreement is divisive. A Kierkegaardian Christian may think that Mother Teresa was only doing her duty toward her neighbor as specified by the Love Commandment, while one of her secular admirers believes that much of the good she did was supererogatory. But if they agree that she did a great deal of good, their disagreement about whether some of it was supererogatory is not apt to be particularly divisive. And third, introducing religious considerations into ethics does not destroy prospects for rational agreement that would otherwise exist. The history of modern secular ethical theory gives us no reason to expect that agreement on a single comprehensive ethical theory will ever be achieved in a climate of free and rational moral inquiry.

Another objection may reveal a way in which divine command ethics is vulnerable that is not shared by other forms of theological ethics. Its main claim is that divine command theories make morality unacceptably arbitrary. One way of developing the objection is to note that divine command ethics conjoined with ATHEISM implies a kind of moral NIHILISM. If there were no God, there would be no divine commands and, in particular, no divine prohibitions. Hence, according to divine command ethics, if there were no God, nothing would be morally wrong. In other words, given divine command ethics, Ivan Karamazov was right in thinking that if there were no God, everything would be permitted. But surely, the objection goes, murder would still be wrong and would not be morally permitted even if God did not exist.

Ralph CUDWORTH (1617–1688) spells out the arbitrariness objection in a different way. He takes it to be a consequence of divine command ethics that "nothing can be imagined so grossly wicked, or so foully unjust or dishonest, but if it were supposed to be commanded by this Omnipotent Deity, must needs upon that Hypothesis forthwith become Holy, Just and Righteous." Consider some grossly wicked and foully unjust action, for example, torturing an innocent child to death. According to divine command ethics, if God were to command a person to torture an innocent child to death, it would be obligatory for the person to torture the child to death. But surely, the objection in this form goes, it would not be obligatory to torture the child to death even if God were to command it.

One sort of reply to these objections rests on an appeal to the theological doctrines of divine necessary existence and essential perfect goodness. Because God exists and is perfectly good in every possible world, there is no possible world in which God commands grossly wicked and foully unjust actions and no possible world in which God fails to forbid them. In short, the divine essence constrains the divine will. So the counterfactual that everything would be permitted if there were no God is trivially true in virtue of a necessarily false antecedent, and the counterfactual that torturing the innocent would be obligatory if God were to command it is also trivially true because, it being impossible for God to command torture of the innocent, its antecedent is impossible. A difficulty with this reply is that it seems to undercut what Thomas Aquinas and Andrew of Neufchateau say about the case of Abraham and Isaac. If God cannot command grossly wicked and foully unjust actions, then it would seem that God not only does not but also cannot command Abraham to slay Isaac.

Another reply to the objections insists that God does in fact forbid murder and torture of the innocent and so they are wrong, but allows that there are possible worlds in which there are no divine commands and everything is permitted, and possible worlds in which, torture and killing of the innocent having been divinely commanded, they are obligatory. This is probably the line that would be taken by extreme Ockhamists who want morality to depend on the absolute power of God and place few limits on divine absolute power, though it is disputed whether it is the view of Ockham himself; and this is the view that Cudworth and others find so objectionable.

Those who raise the arbitrariness objection against divine command ethics are likely also to object to any form of theological ethics that makes morality depend on something about God that could have been different. Thus, for example, if what character traits are virtues depends on God's purposes for humans and those divine purposes could have been different, then there will be an arbitrariness objection to theological virtue ethics. The only form of theological ethics acceptable to friends of what Cudworth thinks of as eternal and immutable morality would be one that makes morality depend on something about God that could not have been different. If there is no plausible form of theological ethics that satisfies this condition, then the friends of eternal and immutable morality will, even if they are theists, insist that morality is independent of God.

See also: AGNOSTICISM; ATHEISM; BENTHAM; CALVIN; CHRISTIAN ETHICS; CUDWORTH; DUNS SCOTUS; DUTY AND OBLIGATION; HUMILITY; ISLAMIC ETHICS; JESUS OF NAZARETH; JEWISH ETHICS; KIERKEGAARD; LOVE; LUTHER; MACINTYRE; NATURAL LAW; PALEY; PHILOSOPHY OF RELIGION; PRIDE; THEISM; THOMAS AQUINAS; VIRTUE ETHICS; VOLUNTARISM; WILLIAM OF OCKHAM.

Bibliography

Adams, Robert Merrihew. *Finite and Infinite Goods: A Framework for Ethics.* New York; Oxford: Oxford University Press, 1999. Develops a divine command account of moral obligation within a framework of theistic Platonism according to which God is the Good.

Andrew of Neufchateau. *Questions on an Ethics of Divine Commands.* Edited and translated by Janine Marie Idziak. Notre Dame, IN: University of Notre Dame Press, 1997 [1514]. Medieval defense of divine command ethics. See p. 91.

Bentham, Jeremy. *An Introduction to the Principles of Morals and Legislation.* New York: Hafner, 1948 [1789]. Contains criticism of divine command ethics. See p. 22.

Cudworth, Ralph. *A Treatise Concerning Eternal and Immutable Morality.* New York: Garland, 1976 [1731]. Criticizes divine command ethics. See pp. 9–10.

Hauerwas, Stanley, and Charles Pinches. *Christians Among the Virtues: Theological Conversations with Ancient and Modern Ethics.* Notre Dame, IN: University of Notre Dame Press, 1997. A defense of theological virtue ethics by a leading Protestant moral theologian (Hauerwas) and one of his former graduate students (Pinches).

Idziak, Janine Marie, ed. *Divine Command Morality: Historical and Contemporary Readings.* New York: Edwin Mellen Press, 1979. Contains a useful bibliography.

Kierkegaard, Søren. *Works of Love.* Edited and translated by Howard V. Hong and Edna H. Hong. Princeton, NJ: Princeton University Press, 1995 [1847]. Defends a distinctively Christian divine command ethics of love. See pp. 19 and 39.

MacIntyre, Alasdair. *Three Rival Versions of Moral Enquiry: Encyclopedia, Genealogy, and Tradition.* Notre Dame, IN: University of Notre Dame Press, 1990. A defense of Thomistic virtue ethics by a leading Roman Catholic moral philosopher.

Quinn, Philip L. *Divine Commands and Moral Requirements.* Oxford: Clarendon Press, 1978. Develops several versions of an ethics of divine commands.

Thomas Aquinas. *Summa theologiae.* Translated by Fathers of the English Dominican Province. Westminster, MD: Christian Classics, 1981 [1266–1273]. See I–II, q. 94 and q. 100 and II–II, q. 104.

Philip L. Quinn

theory and practice

The idea that some things are fine in theory but do not work in practice was already an "old saying" when KANT (1724–1804) wrote about it in 1793. Kant, who was annoyed that a man named Garve had criticized his ethical theory on this ground, responded by pointing out that there is always a gap between theory and practice. Theory provides general rules but it cannot tell us how to apply them—for that, practical judgment is needed. "[T]he general rule," said Kant, "must be supplemented by an act of judgment whereby the practitioner distinguishes instances where the rule applies from those where it does not." This means that those who lack judgment might be helpless, even though they know a lot of theory. "There are doctors and lawyers," Kant explains, "who did well during their schooling but who do not know how to act when asked to give advice."

The point is especially important for the kind of absolutist ethic that Kant defends. Kant held that MORAL RULES have no exceptions; on his way of thinking, we may *never* lie, we may *never* break a promise, and so on. This is a clear example of an ethic that seems not to work in practice, for sensible people recognize that, in extreme circumstances, even very serious rules may have to be broken.

But the "gap" that Kant identifies has often been exploited to soften the impact of such harsh precepts. Traditional CHRISTIAN ETHICS, for example, says (like Kant) that SUICIDE is always wrong; but because judgment is required to determine which acts count as suicide, casuists have been able to excuse various sorts of self-destruction (and, not coincidentally, avoid consigning the deceased to hellfire) by classifying them as something else. Thus the hero who sacrifices herself to save others is not a suicide, nor is the man who kills himself while blind with grief, as he lacks the required rational INTENTION. It might be thought that such gaps could be closed by adding further principles to the theory—for example, principles that specify more closely what counts as suicide and what does not. Similarly, one might make the rules against lying and promise-breaking more complicated by adding clauses to specify circumstances under which those actions would be permitted. But, as Kant observed, one could never add enough complications. Gaps will always remain.

Kant noticed one way that theory and practice come apart, but there are others. Many ethical ideals are endorsed even though they are unattainable. The Jains of India, for example, believe that one should never harm any living creature. Jain priests carry brooms to sweep the ground before them as they walk to avoid crushing bugs beneath their feet. But, for practical reasons, ordinary Jains cannot do this, and they inevitably kill. Christians believe that we should love our neighbors as ourselves, although no one can actually manage such a stunning feat of BENEVOLENCE.

What good is an ideal, one might ask, if it cannot be put into practice? Such ideals might be understood as goals toward which we should strive, even if we can never fully realize them. The fact that we cannot live up to the ideals might be taken as revealing morally unfortunate limitations in our circumstances or in ourselves. They also express moral reasons: the fact that a course of conduct would bring us closer to the ideal is a reason in its favor.

For general ethical theories such as UTILITARI-ANISM, the gap between theory and practice poses an especially acute problem. Utilitarianism, perhaps the most influential ethical theory of the past 200 years, says that we should do whatever will have the best consequences for everyone affected by our actions, where everyone's welfare counts as equally important. This may sound nice in theory, but critics have pointed out that no one is willing to adopt such

an ethic in practice. For one thing, none of us regards everyone's welfare as equally important. On the contrary, we naturally pay special attention to our own NEEDS and to the needs of our friends and FAMILY. For another thing, the utilitarian ethic is too demanding—it would require that we use almost all of our resources to help others. We could not, for example, spend money on new clothes, concert tickets, automobiles, and the like while third-world children do not have enough to eat.

Some utilitarian philosophers are unmoved by such complaints. They counter that if we are unwilling to live according to the utilitarian standard, that shows there is something wrong with us, not with the standard. Others, such as R. M. HARE, take a more flexible approach. In theory, Hare says, the right thing to do is whatever maximizes utility. However, it would be ruinous if people went about calculating utility all the time. Therefore, it is not wise to ask people to guide their conduct by referring directly to the principle of utility. For practical purposes, people need simple, easy-to-apply rules of thumb. The question for utilitarian calculation, therefore, is: what simple rules would it be best to promulgate? Considering the circumstances of ordinary life and the facts of human nature, the best set of rules that has any chance of acceptance would be fairly close to the rules of moral common sense. Such rules would not only permit but would encourage people to be especially concerned for their family and friends; and they would demand charitable contributions only a little in excess of what normally generous people are willing to give. By this method of reasoning, the demands of utilitarian theory are brought closer to the practices of ordinary life.

If utilitarianism seems to demand too much, other theories seem to demand too little. The leading alternative to Kant's view and utilitarianism is SOCIAL CONTRACT theory, which sees moral demands as based upon agreements of mutual benefit. Each of us has much to gain from associating with other people, but if our interactions are to be profitable, certain rules must be followed—rules that require us to be truthful, to keep our bargains, not to harm one another, and so on. Morality arises when each of us agrees to follow these rules, on the condition that others do so as well.

Contract theory, however, implies that we have fewer duties than conscientious people generally acknowledge, and this is another way that theory and practice can come apart. How, on such a theory, could we have obligations to mere animals or to mentally impaired humans? After all, they are not able to participate in agreements of mutual benefit. To handle this problem, contract theorists have sometimes suggested that our duties to such individuals are only "indirect" duties—that is, duties owed not to them but to the (unimpaired) people who care about them. I should not mistreat your dog or your handicapped child because it is part of my agreement with you. (Presumably, though, orphans and strays are fair game?) Moreover, on some versions of contract theory, our charitable obligations turn out to be so small they are virtually nonexistent. Thus, Jan Narveson holds that, because I would have nothing to gain from a social rule that required me to contribute to the maintenance of children halfway around the world, I have no obligation to help them.

Considering these difficulties, it is not surprising that, despite Kant's defense, many people continue to believe that ethical theories are useless in practice. Contemporary philosophers who work in APPLIED ETHICS, particularly in BIOETHICS, often say this. Part of the problem is that every general ethical theory seems flawed, for reasons such as we have mentioned. But even setting that aside, the precepts of ethical theory seem too neat and abstract to be of any use in dealing with real cases, which are messy and particular.

Is this a fair complaint? Suppose it were said that physics is irrelevant to automobile mechanics, because a mechanic cannot "apply" the principles of physics to determine what is wrong with a car. Or that biology is irrelevant to medicine because a physician cannot "apply" the principles of biology to diagnose a patient's illness. Such remarks would seem very odd. Certainly, the highest-level laws of physics are not of much use to the auto mechanic; nevertheless, cars obey physical laws, and a working knowledge of scientific principles is often useful. The same may be said of the physician's knowledge of biology: while a good doctor needs to know a lot more than biology, in many instances a working knowledge of biology might be critical.

The relation of ethical theory to practice might be like the relation between biology and medicine. Just as fundamental research in biology may sometimes concern matters distant from the physician's problems, fundamental issues in ethical theory might

sometimes seem far from issues of practical choice. Moreover, as in medicine, practical judgment in ethics may require more than theoretical knowledge, and theory may be more useful in some instances than in others. But this does not mean that ethical theory is useless in practical decision-making, any more than biology is useless in medicine. In both areas, Kant's remark might be apt: "No-one can pretend to be practically versed in a branch of knowledge and yet treat theory with scorn, without exposing the fact that he is an ignoramus in his subject."

See also: APPLIED ETHICS; CASUISTRY; CONSEQUENTIALISM; IDEALIST ETHICS; IMPARTIALITY; JAINISM; KANT; METAETHICS; MORAL ABSOLUTES; MORAL REALISM; MORAL REASONING; MORAL RULES; PARTIALITY; PHRONESIS; PRACTICAL REASON[ING]; PRACTICAL WISDOM; PRAGMATISM; PRAXIS; PRINCIPLISM; SOCIAL CONTRACT; UTILITARIANISM.

Bibliography

Hare, R. M. *Moral Thinking: Its Levels, Method and Point.* Oxford: Oxford University Press, 1981.

Kant, Immanuel. "On the Common Saying: 'This May Be True in Theory, But It Does Not Apply in Practice.'" Translated by H. B. Nisbet. In *Kant: Political Writings,* edited by Hans Reiss. Cambridge: Cambridge University Press, 1970 [1793].

Narveson, Jan. *Moral Matters.* Lewiston, NY: Broadview Press, 1993.

"Theories and Methods in Bioethics: Principlism and Its Critics." *Kennedy Institute of Ethics Journal* 5 (September 1995).

James Rachels

Thomas Aquinas, Saint (1225?–1274)

Born in Roccasecca, Italy, Thomas received his first education at Montecassino, where he was sent at the age of five. As a teenager he went to Naples, where he studied the liberal arts and later joined the Order of Preachers founded by St. Dominic (1170–1221). Like the Franciscans, the Dominicans were a mendicant order. Thomas studied at Cologne under Albert the Great (1137?–1280), editing his teacher's lectures on ARISTOTLE's (384–322 B.C.E.) *Ethics.* From 1252, he studied theology at Paris and was a *magister regnans* there from 1256 to 1259. He spent the next ten years in Dominican houses in Italy, but was called to Paris for a second professorate, 1269–1272, to take part in the Latin Averroist (after Averroës, or IBN RUSHD [1126–1198]) controversy. Thomas's views on the compatibility of Aristotle and Christianity met opposition but eventually were to prevail. He spent his last years in Italy, dying on March 7, 1274, in Fossanova.

Although he was primarily a theologian and wrote many works of moral theology, Thomas Aquinas is also of importance for moral philosophy. (Moral theology assumes as principles the truths of Christian revelation, which are held by faith; moral philosophy appeals only to what can be known in principle by anyone, believer or nonbeliever.)

Thomas's fundamental philosophical orientation was Aristotelian, and the *Nicomachean Ethics* is his chief guide in moral philosophy. He wrote a commentary on this text, probably in 1271, at the same time he was composing the second or moral part of the *Summa theologiae*. In the Aristotelian fashion, Thomas begins moral philosophy with the end, the human good, that which is sought in any human action. Human actions deliberately undertaken for the sake of an end form the subject matter of moral philosophy.

The distinction between human acts and acts of a man is Thomas's version of Aristotle's function or *ergon* approach. When is an act a human act? Acts performed by men and by no other entity are *per se* human. This is not simply a matter of distinguishing between activities that can be truly ascribed to Socrates and those truly ascribed to his dog. There are activities true of Socrates which are not true of him *qua* man. That he should fall when pushed, that he grows and takes nourishment, that he feels fear and DESIRE, that he sees and hears—all these are true of Socrates, but they are not peculiar to men. It is the activity peculiar to men that Thomas means by the human act. Activities which are true of man and other things as well are called by contrast acts of a man.

Rational activity is peculiar to man. To perform this activity well will make a man a good man. (The going well of acts of a man do not make a man a good man.) Insofar as "rational activity" is an analogous term, bearing a plurality of ordered meanings, there is a plurality of senses of doing rational activity well. Since doing something well is the perfection or virtue of that activity, the human good consists of an orderly plurality of VIRTUES.

An activity can be called rational either essentially or by way of participation. The activity of reason itself is what is meant by essential rational activity; any other activity which can be guided by reason is rational by participation. This is the basis for the distinction between intellectual and moral virtues.

Essential rational activity is subdivided according to the distinction between theoretical and practical reasoning. These differ in their ends. The theoretical use of the mind aims at the perfection of its own activity, a perfection which is called truth. When we use our minds practically, our aim is to direct other activities to the good of the agent. The virtues of theoretical intellect are those we find in Aristotle: understanding, science, and WISDOM. The virtues of the practical intellect are art and PRUDENCE, based on the distinction between making and doing. Art aims at the good of the artifact; prudence at the good of the agent. The good artist is not by that fact a good man, but to be prudent or practically wise is to be a good man.

The moral virtues reside in appetite as amenable to the guidance of PRACTICAL REASON. Thomas's psychology is Aristotelian; he distinguishes between the concupiscible and irascible appetites so that TEMPERANCE and COURAGE emerge as the chief moral virtues. Justice is a moral virtue too, but its seat is not an appetite consequent on sense perception, as the concupiscible and irascible are, but intellectual appetite or will. The will needs rational direction with respect to the good of others, and its habitual response to such direction is justice. The four cardinal virtues—prudence, justice, temperance, and courage—command the structure of the moral part of the *Summa theologiae*.

Ultimate end. Like Aristotle, Thomas observed that, if it is the case that every human act is undertaken with an eye to an end, the ends and acts are of an unthinkable multiplicity. The universal statement about human acts thus does not entail a single end of all that men do. If such an overriding end of human life is to be maintained, it must be argued for. Aristotle moves toward it by way of clustering the ends of some actions under the end of a commanding or superior action, as in the variety of actions called military or medical or building. The general, the physician, and the master builder direct subordinate acts and their ends to a superordinate end. Is it possible so to cluster all human acts, seeing them as subordinate to an overriding ultimate end?

In his commentary on the *Nicomachean Ethics*,

Thomas analyses Aristotle's argument as a *reductio ad absurdum*. If whatever we do is aimed at some further end, we can never achieve what we set out to do. This renders acting for an end absurd. But the desire of the end is natural, and nature cannot be absurd, since it is the product of the Prime Mover.

In the *Summa*, Thomas's argument is somewhat different. Is it the case that all human agents seek the same ultimate end? The question presupposes, of course, that all human agents seek an ultimate end. That they do follows from what Thomas means by ultimate end. He first distinguishes between what he calls the *ratio finis ultimi*, the formal notion of ultimate end, and then the thing or things which are taken to satisfy that notion. The formal notion of ultimate end is the comprehensive fulfillment of all my desires, my complete and perfect good. The material ultimate end is where I see that notion satisfied.

Thomas takes it to be part of the logic of human action that it is undertaken for some purpose. A sign of this is the linking of moral and responsible action. The moral realm comes into view when the question "Why are you doing that?" is relevant. The answer will be the aim or end of acting so. The end need not be something different from the action itself, however. To engage in theoretical thinking is an end in itself. The comprehensive human good comprises the ends of all the virtues, no one of which is sufficient for human fulfillment, not even that which is highest, contemplation, the perfection of the highest activity of theoretical reason. Like Aristotle, then, Thomas sees virtuous activities as what truly satisfy or save the notion of ultimate end.

It should be stressed that the human good is a COMMON GOOD. Politics, concern with the good shared by members of a community, is the architectonic practical science for Thomas as for Aristotle. Men are naturally social, born into families, able to survive only if nurtured and trained; to speak of the good or fulfillment of such beings is inevitably to give priority to goods shared with others, common goods.

Since Thomas as a Christian holds that our ultimate end is felicific union with God in the next life, must not Aristotle's ultimate end become penultimate for him? Thomas distinguishes between an imperfect HAPPINESS achievable in this life and the perfect happiness of the next. He even suggests that Aristotle himself was aware of the imperfection of his sketch of the perfect good available to living men

(*Nicomachean Ethics* 1101a20). Since Thomas too holds that the happiness achievable by us in this life is imperfect, he has no quarrel with Aristotle.

Natural law. Just as there are certain self-evident starting points of theoretical reasoning, so too are there of practical reasoning. It is these universal precepts of practical reason that Thomas means by NATURAL LAW. Just as civil law commands, so does practical reason command the agent. The moral task is to bring about the integration of the agent, making his lower appetites amenable to reason's perception of the agent's complete good. Only when the goods of sense appetite are rationally ordered to the good of the agent as such are they humanly good.

Prior to such rational direction, there are natural inclinations to such goods as food and drink, sex, knowledge, companionship. We do not choose to have these inclinations; they are part of what we are. The moral task is to bring the desires for these goods under the comprehensive good of the agent. Initial and sweeping judgments taken to be inescapably true make up natural law. That we should do good and avoid EVIL, that is, rationally direct our lives to what fulfills us and avoid the opposite, is self-evident. That our desire for food and drink and sex will contribute to our good only if they are guided by reason is also taken to be evident. Such judgments, expressed as precepts, are the principles which govern the moral order (*e.g.*, be temperate, be just, be courageous).

To be effective, they must be particularized, and the more practically helpful the precept, the more open to exceptions it is. The vast majority of moral judgments are true only for the most part. Only the fundamental and universal precepts of natural law are absolutes. No moral theory can reach the singular as such. But actions are singular. It is prudence, the virtue of practical intellect, which presupposes the good disposition of sense appetite, that enables us to judge well in the singular case.

There is scholarly disagreement on every aspect of Thomas's moral theory, not least the relation of it to Aristotelian doctrine. Some Thomists deny the very possibility of a natural ethics. Scholars like Gauthier hold that Thomas fitted Aristotle into the Procrustean bed of his religious beliefs. The nature of Thomas's teaching on natural law is variously understood. What is beyond dispute is that the views of Thomas Aquinas form a constant element in ethical discussion, and it is difficult to imagine a discussion in moral philosophy which does not refer, positively or negatively, to his writings.

See also: ARISTOTLE; CHRISTIAN ETHICS; COMMON GOOD; COURAGE; FINAL GOOD; IBN RUSHD; NATURAL LAW; PHILOSOPHY OF RELIGION; PRACTICAL REASON[ING]; PRUDENCE; TEMPERANCE; THEOLOGICAL ETHICS; THEORY AND PRACTICE; WISDOM.

Bibliography

Works by Thomas Aquinas

Commentary on the Nicomachean Ethics. Translated by C. I. Litzinger. Chicago: Henry Regnery, 1964.

Disputed Question on Evil. Translated by Jean Oesterle and John Osterle. Notre Dame, IN: University of Notre Dame Press, 1991.

Sententia libri ethicorum. Vol. 46 of *Sancti Thomae de Aquino opera omnia,* edited by R. A. Gauthier. Leonine ed. Rome: Liberia Editrice Vaticana Roma, 1969.

Summa theologiae. Westminster, MD: 1982 [1266–1273]. First and second parts of the Second Part.

Works about Aquinas

Donagan, Alan. "Thomas Aquinas on Human Action." In *The Cambridge History of Late Medieval Philosophy.* Cambridge: Cambridge University Press, 1982.

Finnis, John. *Natural Law and Natural Right.* Oxford, 1980.

Gauthier, R. A. *L'Ethique à nicomaque.* 2d ed. Louvain: Nauwelaerts, 1970. See the introduction to Book 1.

MacIntyre, Alasdair. *Whose Justice? Which Rationality?* Notre Dame, IN: University of Notre Dame Press, 1988. Chapters 11 and 12.

Maritain, Jacques. *Neuf leçons sur les notions premières de la philosophie morale.* Paris: Téqui, 1951.

McInerny, Ralph. *Ethica thomistica.* Washington, DC: Catholic University Press, 1982.

Ralph McInerny

Thomasius, Christian (1655–1728)

German jurist, educator, philosopher, and journalist. Thomasius is widely viewed in German scholarship as the major philosophical writer of the opening phase of the German Enlightenment. No one claims that he was a great philosopher. But he has a place in the history of moral philosophy because of his pioneering attempt to separate the domain of morality from that of law.

Previous NATURAL LAW writers ("lawyers") had seen morality as simply one aspect of what is required by law. It is what is required of all people by the natural law, in contrast to what God requires of special groups, like the Jews, Christians, and Muslims, or what sovereigns require of their subjects. Since law generally has to be backed by sanctions, morality has to be considered as enforceable. This is true at least of what the lawyers called "perfect duties." But there is one class of exceptions to the enforceability principle. Acts required as "imperfect duties" are acts required by what some of the lawyers called the law of love. This law is not enforceable; but performance of such actions calls for GRATITUDE from beneficiaries. Thomasius reworked this distinction.

A translation of the title of his first book on the subject (published 1692) gives a fair idea of its general scope: "Of the Art of Loving Rationally and Virtuously, as the sole means to attain to a happy, gallant, and enjoyable Life; or Introduction to the Doctrine of Morals." Thomasius propounds the view that the good life consists in the kind of enjoyable tranquillity advocated by EPICURUS (341–270 B.C.E.). The only means to attaining this kind of tranquillity, he argued, is reasonable LOVE—of which there are two kinds:

(a) Particular love is directed at some people rather than others, because of certain features, such as their age, sex, or looks. It gives rise to the personal connections that enhance our lives. Of course, it cannot be enforced, but when it is expressed, the recipient owes gratitude to the agent.

(b) Universal love gives rise to a number of VIRTUES, and, whether one feels it or not, it is owed to all persons equally, as is the exercise of its virtues. There are two peculiarities of universal love. Although we are all obligated to have it, no one can be compelled to; and no one owes gratitude for its expression.

Thomasius thus presented the idea of a realm of action in which people can have obligations for which no sanction is possible, where the actions are nonetheless so ordinary and so widely needed that no gratitude is called for as a return. He called this realm the realm of morality, and contrasted it sharply with the realm of justice. Justice for him is the domain of law. It involves actions which people ought to do from love but can be compelled to do if love is absent.

In his later work on natural law, Thomasius elaborated on the distinction between law and morals and added new thoughts about how external propriety differs from both. If his way of drawing the distinctions has not endured, his claim that there is a sphere of right action not called for by law or by politeness has become a central feature of the modern conception of morality.

See also: EPICURUS; FITTINGNESS; GRATITUDE; LEGAL ETHICS; LEGAL PHILOSOPHY; LOVE; NATURAL LAW; OBEDIENCE TO LAW.

Bibliography

Works by Christian Thomasius

Einleitung zu der Vernunft-Lehre. 1691. A practical logic aimed at showing how to discover truth.

Von der Kunst Vernünftig und Tugendhaft zu lieben . . . Oder, Einleitung zur Sitten-Lehre. 1692. A guide to the principles of a happy and loving life.

Von der Artzeney wider die unvernünftige Liebe . . . Oder: Ausübung der Sitten-Lehre. 1696. More detailed advice on how to live, quite opposed to the views of the previous book which Thomasius advised readers to throw away.

Fundamenta juris naturae et gentium. 1705. Treatise on natural law. None of Thomasius's books have been translated into English.

Works about Thomasius

Beck, Lewis White. *Early German Philosophy.* Cambridge, Mass. 1969. See especially pp. 247–56. Excellent brief overview of Thomasius's life, work, and importance in German thought. As Beck's bibliography (pp. 526–27) indicates, there is almost nothing in English on Thomasius.

Bloch, Ernst. "Christian Thomasius, a German Scholar Without Misery." In his *Natural Law and Human Dignity* (translation of *Naturrecht und menschliche Würde* by Dennis J. Schmidt), 281–314. Cambridge, Mass.: MIT Press, 1986 [1961].

Schneewind, J. B. *The Invention of Autonomy.* Cambridge: Cambridge University Press, 1998. Chapter 8.

Schneiders, Werner. *Naturrecht und Liebesethik.* Hildesheim, 1971. A magisterial and exhaustive study of Thomasius as moral and political thinker in the tradition of ethics of love. Extensive bibliography.

Wolff, Hans M. *Die Weltanschauung der deutschen Aufklarung.* Bern: Francke Verlag, 1949. Chapter 1.

Wundt, Max. *Die deutsche Schulphilosophie im Zeitalter der Aufklärung.* Hildesheim, 1964 [1945]. A long chapter on Thomasius as the major figure in the first stage of the German Enlightenment.

J. B. Schneewind

Thomson, Judith Jarvis

American philosopher, long-time professor of philosophy at the Massachusetts Institute of Technology. Thomson writes in the areas of philosophy of mind, philosophy of ACTION, philosophy of law, and moral philosophy. Her style is characterized by clear, probing arguments and an abundance of memorable examples which never fail to stimulate reflection and deepen one's understanding of the issue under discussion.

Most of Thomson's published works deal with some central issue of moral RIGHTS and seek to lay bare the structure of an argument or principle. She has, on more than one occasion, remarked that, even though moral philosophy requires a theory of rights, there was no satisfactory theory. Her *The Realm of Rights* (1990) fills this void and provides an instrument by which Thomson reassesses her earlier works. Among these instruments is the Trolley Problem which presents a narrow set of exceptions in which it is permissible to infringe a right. While there are circumstances in which it is permissible to infringe a right, there are considerations which are relevant. Among them: seeking a waiver from the rightholder, compensating for any loss that the person may suffer, apologizing or explaining to the person the reason for the infringement.

Thomson first examined this dilemma in her article "Killing, Letting Die, and the Trolley Problem" (1976). The brakes on a trolley fail. Ahead lie two tracks: on one track is a single workman and on the other track, five workmen. The driver of the trolley can turn it to the track where there is one, or to the track where there are five. Whoever is on the chosen track will be killed. The intuition is that it is permissible to steer the trolley toward the one. Philippa FOOT, from whom Thomson borrowed this example, claims that it is permissible to turn the trolley to the one because the negative duty not to kill five is more stringent than the negative duty not to kill one. So the driver not only may, but must, turn the trolley toward the one.

Suppose instead that the trolley driver faints and a passenger takes over the controls. If he does nothing, he kills no one; but if he turns the trolley, he kills either one or five. The conflict for the passenger is between the negative duty not to kill one and the positive duty to save five. This is the same conflict as that faced by a transplant surgeon deciding whether to kill one patient to provide organs for five others. It is impermissible for the surgeon to proceed since she would violate a negative duty not to kill. However, our intuition is that it is permissible for the passenger to intervene and turn the trolley. Why? Thomson considers a number of possibilities in which it could be said that the five have a greater claim than the one. Having a greater claim explains why a surgeon may not operate on one patient to provide organs for five others: the potential organ donor has a greater claim against anyone who would kill him, for it is his body and in some sense he owns it. But there seems to be no plausible account of why it could be said of the five trolley workmen that they have a greater claim than the one. Consider, Thomson says, "Bystander at the Switch." Bystander's role is the same as that played by the passenger in the previous example. But in throwing the switch, Bystander causes a better distribution of harm for those who are threatened. The trolley will cause harm whether or not Bystander intervenes. Thomson concedes that it is not clear why it is permissible to deflect harm from the five to the one, but she thinks that it is permissible.

In reconsidering this problem in *The Realm of Rights,* Thomson says that there must be something about the workmen's situation which accounts for the intuition. Suppose that the workmen had agreed that, in the event of a runaway trolley, it would be permissible to divert the trolley from the many to the one because in this way each has a greater chance to survive. This is so because the jobs are assigned by lottery, meaning each worker has a greater chance of being in the work detail of five than of working alone. Further, each had agreed to the method of selection without knowing whether he would be working alone or with others. If the trolley must be turned, the single worker faces certain death, but is bound by his prior agreement. This solution seems to make it obligatory that the trolley be turned toward the one since he waived

his right by agreeing to the work assignment process.

In *The Realm of Rights,* Thomson revisits the issue for which she may be best known. Her article, "A Defense of Abortion" (1971), exposed the weakness of arguments which attempt to prove that abortion is always impermissible because the fetus has a right to life. Consider the following analogy: A famous concert violinist, unconscious and suffering from kidney failure, will die unless a suitable host is found whose kidney function he can share while his own kidneys repair themselves. The Society of Music Lovers kidnaps a suitable host and has the attachment made. Upon awakening from the procedure, the host is told that she must remain attached to the violinist until his kidneys heal because the violinist has a right to live and were he disconnected he would die.

Thomson argues convincingly that detaching oneself from the violinist does not infringe the violinist's right to life. That right constrains others from killing him unjustly—a negative right—but it does not impose a duty on anyone else to permit him the use of her body to preserve his life. Analogously, a fetus's right to life does not require that the pregnant woman provide it with what it needs for its life.

The violinist argument justifies abortion in the limited class of cases that involve coerced pregnancy. Providing a number of additional examples, Thomson argues more generally. Suppose sperm floats in the air like pollen; even with the best pollen screen, a person seed enters from outside and begins to grow in your rug. Suppose also that a burglar enters your dwelling by squeezing through the burglar bars and in so doing injures himself. According to Thomson, one is required neither to allow the person seed to develop nor to give aid to the injured intruder.

Thomson's argument for a more general defense is more problematic than the limited defense involving the violinist. Sperm does not float in the air like pollen; neither do fetuses enter uteruses as burglars enter dwellings. A fetus, in coming to exist, does not violate one's rights in the way a burglar does. Despite their difficulties, these examples raise interesting questions about the exercise of CARE and the attribution of RESPONSIBILITY—issues of great importance which have not had the attention due them. For example, if exercising care does not succeed in preventing loss or harm, is it permissible to compel another to bear the cost? This seems to be the issue raised by the defect in the pollen screen: the manufacturer of the screen may be liable, but is the fetus culpable when it exists because contraception fails?

On the issue of responsibility, Thomson claims that a child has a right only if certain conditions obtain: The parents do not try to prevent pregnancy, do not abort the fetus, do not put the child up for adoption. This account seems to clash with some of the arguments made in *The Realm of Rights*. On the issue of whether the child has a right which is independent of legal or social practices, Thomson seems to answer in the affirmative, taking it as given that there are fundamental rights. Whether *infants* have claims against others that they not be killed, or otherwise exposed to harm, is not made explicit even in *Rights;* but Thomson *is* explicit that *fetuses* do not have rights because they are not persons.

"[A] fertilized egg, a very early embryo, is not a person at all." Arguably, this is the view that did the moral work in the abortion article even though the argument is meant to proceed with the opposite assumption. There has been no change in her position on abortion from the early article to the book twenty years later. Thomson's arguments lack a full account of the notion of potentiality. While she claims that her theory of rights can accommodate how individuals come to possess them, none of the ways in which one usually comes to possess a right—gift, purchase, promise, permission, or legislation—explains how a fetus which lacks the right to life could come to possess it. The right to life, or the cluster of rights which is denoted by that description, is a fundamental right. It is no wonder that those opposed to abortion remain unmoved by the 1973 United States Supreme Court decision, *Roe vs. Wade*.

Thomson's discussions of rights have made a major contribution to moral philosophy, political philosophy, and the philosophy of law. And, as indicated above, she has raised important issues in "Defense" that remain to be explored.

See also: ABORTION; CARE; DUTY AND OBLIGATION; FOOT; KILLING/LETTING DIE; LIFE, RIGHT TO; PERSON, CONCEPT OF; PRIVACY; RESPONSIBILITY; RIGHT HOLDERS; RIGHTS; SOCIAL AND POLITICAL PHILOSOPHY.

Bibliography

Works by Judith J. Thomson

"A Defense of Abortion." *Philosophy and Public Affairs* 1/1 (1971): 47–66. Widely anthologized. And see next listing.

"Rights and Deaths." *Philosophy and Public Affairs* 2/2 (1973): 146–59. This issue also contains "The Rights and Wrongs of Abortion: A Reply to Judith Thomson," by John Finnis, 117–45.

"Preferential Hiring." *Philosophy and Public Affairs* 2/4 (1973): 364–84.

"The Right to Privacy." *Philosophy and Public Affairs* 4/4 (1975): 295–314. In the same issue, see "Thomson on Privacy," by Thomas Scanlon, 315–33.

"Self-Defense and Rights." 1976 Lindsey Lecture at University of Kansas.

"Killing, Letting Die and the Trolley Problem." *Monist* 59 (1976): 204–17.

"Some Rumination on Rights." *University of Arizona Law Review* 19 (1977).

Acts and Other Events. Ithaca, NY: Cornell University Press, 1977.

"Rights and Compensation." *Nous* 14 (1980): 3–15.

Rights, Restitution and Risks. Edited by William Parent. Cambridge, MA: Harvard University Press, 1986. Collection of Thomson's essays, including those cited above. Quoted passage is from page 291.

The Realm of Rights. Cambridge: Harvard University Press, 1990.

"Self-Defense." *Philosophy and Public Affairs* 20/4 (1991): 283–310.

Thomson, Judith J., and Gilbert Harman. *Moral Relativism and Moral Objectivity.* Oxford: Blackwell, 1996.

Thomson, Judith J., and Gerald Dworkin, eds. *Ethics.* New York: Harper and Row, 1968.

Calvin G. Stewart

Thoreau, Henry David (1817–1862)

Like his friend and teacher Ralph Waldo EMERSON (1803–1882), Thoreau wrote no works of moral philosophy as it is most commonly construed. He is best known for the night he spent in the Concord jail and for the two years (1845–1847) he spent alone at Walden Pond in a cabin he built by himself. The book *Walden* contains his account of those years. It was published in 1854, seven years after the conclusion of that experiment, and it is widely recognized as one of the masterpieces of American writing. The journal he kept almost daily for twenty-four years has also come to be regarded as itself a major document of American intellectual history.

Thoreau's impact on our thinking about the ethical realm can be assessed in terms of at least six different trajectories within his thought.

1. The extremity and spiritual violence of his opposition to SLAVERY and to the Mexican War, as contained in his famous essay, "Civil Disobedience" (1849) and in his much less famous "A Plea for Captain John Brown" (1859);
2. his modification of Emerson's post-Kantian concern for the conditions of thinking, reading (or interpretation), and originality (*Walden,* chapter III, paragraph 3);
3. his revisions of a Platonic insight into the permanent and the transitory and his effort to overcome the philosophical disrespect for the body and its senses (II, 21; XI, 7);
4. the project of living at Walden itself and of writing *Walden,* which is intended, among other things, as an account of a crisis in a philosophical or ethical life;
5. his radicalizing of Emerson's repudiation of social morality, amounting at times to a repudiation of morality itself;
6. his attempt to revise Christian scripture and experience, rendering them less isolating and less constricting to the human imagination.

Thoreau disclaimed any general moral significance for his writing and for his other enterprises: "I came into this world, not chiefly to make this a good place to live in, but to live in it, be it good or bad." ("Civil Disobedience," paragraph 19) And again: "I do not mean to prescribe rules to strong and valiant natures, who will mind their own affairs whether in heaven or in hell" (*Walden,* I, 21). But if Thoreau sought only to follow "the faintest but constant suggestions" of his own genius, he knew this path to be inseparable from the desire to "speak somewhere without bounds, like a man in a waking moment, to men in their waking moments" (XI, 7; XVIII, 6). As in a prophetic vision, he saw a connection between the despairing lethargy of everyday life—disguised as its hectic round of business—and the *de facto* acceptance in the North of slavery and of a war of conquest against Mexico.

Thus the ferocity of his shame at being a citizen of a slave-holding and imperialistic nation blended, from time to time, with the ecstasies and anxieties of the "private business" that he went to Walden to transact (I, 32). *Walden* often exhibits an acute sense that the possibilities of resolving Thoreau's private crises of faith, depression, art, and ambition are closely tied to some hope of resolving or exacerbating the nation's crises of tyranny and cultural self-degradation. This gives to *Walden* what sometimes appears to be a Romantic or late adolescent cast, which some readers have used to dismiss or disparage it. Beyond this fervor, there is also the specific ambition—elucidated by Stanley Cavell—to compose a nation's scripture. This means more than that Thoreau is sometimes to be found in attitudes of devotion and prophetic denunciation: Cavell claims further that *Walden* seeks the redemption of a people and its words by one another.

Such redemption has less to do with an idealization or canonization of our words than with a reconception or revaluation of them. It is meant to free us for a reinvestment of value in our world as much as in our words. The first feature of our condition to which we must awaken is our growing deadness to the words that express what we care about. In the nineteenth century, these words were still primarily either the words of RELIGION or words whose life was fatally constricted by the spirit of religion: "There are such words as *joy* and *sorrow,* but they are only the burden of a psalm, sung while we believe in the ordinary and the mean" (XVIII, 16). Thoreau shares with NIETZSCHE (1844–1900) and with MARX (1818–1883)—a year younger than Thoreau—a sense that religion infects almost every aspect of our lives, perhaps most especially the lives of those who imagine that they are opposing it.

Thoreau's concern is not just for the distance of our words from the things and moments of highest worth. He is equally concerned with the distance of our words from everyday matters and from our common human functions. He describes this as the remoteness of "the language of our parlors" from the kitchens and the workshops that must supply the nerve and sustenance of what we say to one another: "How can the scholar, who dwells away in the Northwest Territory or the Isle of Man, tell what is parliamentary in the kitchen?" (XIII, 8). (Like many men who raise issues which might be conceived as undermining a society's gender roles, Thoreau had little to say about the empirical women who occupied these roles. His interest in the speech of the kitchen did not, apparently, lead him to speculate about the lives of those who were doing most of the cooking.)

Thoreau calls for a philosopher whose daily life

will be—like that of SOCRATES (c. 470–399 B.C.E.)—an occasion for wonder and admiration. "To be a philosopher is not merely to have subtle thoughts but so to love wisdom as to live according to its dictates, a life of simplicity, independence, magnanimity and trust" (I, 19). Thoreau's call for a life which is truly philosophical—or truly economical—is motivated as much by his epistemology as by his ethics. Our objectivity and our IMPARTIALITY are equally threatened by our life of luxury or rather of false necessities: "None can be an impartial or wise observer of human life but from the vantage ground of what *we* should call voluntary poverty" (I, 19). Thoreau was well aware that such voluntary poverty can be the prerogative only of those who are not actually poor. Accordingly, he addressed himself to those "who are said to live in moderate circumstances" (I, 50).

Such questions about need and luxury form one of the many links between *Walden* and PLATO's (c. 430–347 B.C.E.) *Republic*. Thoreau is all but perfectly explicit about his wish to inherit Plato's project (cf. III, 10). Indeed, *Walden* can be taken as an effort to construct what Plato called a "city of words" (*Republic* 592a–b), and to demonstrate that this city contains the possibility of the best life for the just human being. And like Plato's philosopher-ruler, Thoreau must descend from the realm of his highest values to the realm of the Cave. But Thoreau returns from Walden not in order to rule but to be imprisoned: "Under a government that imprisons any unjustly, the true place for a just man is also a prison" ("Civil Disobedience," 22). The just man returns to the cave of society not to obey its laws, much less to make them, but to keep watch over its behavior. The social organism is still full of movement and purpose, but it has the life of a deranged animal or a machine that is running amok.

The absence of the sound of philosophical conversation from *Walden* does not signify the impossibility of philosophy but Thoreau's sense of our unreadiness for it. For Thoreau, the perception of injustice and of the fact that "our whole life is startlingly moral" (XI, 10) must precede the possibility of public conversation or dialectic. We lack the common points of departure for an ethical discourse that is both communicable and coherent. As ARISTOTLE (384–322 B.C.E.) or J. L. Austin (1911–1960) might have put it, we do not possess a usable understanding of the "origins [*archai*]" of our ethical reflec-

tions, because we have not had the right sort of upbringing. In Thoreau's words: "our education is sadly neglected" (III, 12). He thus writes for those he calls "poor students" (I, 2), that is, for those who can acknowledge the poverty of what they know. Echoing Socrates, he tells us that our growth requires the remembering of our ignorance. But he also reminds us that, given the way we now live, we may not be able to afford such SELF-KNOWLEDGE: "[Our] labor would be depreciated in the market" (I, 6). There is much that remains instructive in Thoreau's call for philosophy, as well as in his doubts about whether the call could be justly or safely heeded. The circumstances in which he wrote are perhaps not as different from ours as we would like to think.

See also: CHRISTIAN ETHICS; CIVIL DISOBEDIENCE; EMERSON; GANDHI; IMPARTIALITY; KING; LEGAL PHILOSOPHY; MARX; MATERIALISM; MORAL EDUCATION; MORAL SENSE THEORISTS; NATURALISM; NATURE AND ETHICS; NIETZSCHE; PLATO; RELIGION; SELF-KNOWLEDGE; SLAVERY; SOCRATES; TRANSCENDENTALISM; WAR AND PEACE.

Bibliography

Works by Henry David Thoreau

The Variorum Walden. Edited by Walter Harding. New York: Washington Square Press, 1963. Very useful explanations of references and background.

Walden and Other Writings. Edited by William Howarth. Modern Library College ed. New York: Random House, 1981. Good selection, including "A Plea for Captain John Brown" (1859).

The Journal of Henry David Thoreau. Edited by Bradford Torrey and Francis Allen. Salt Lake City, Utah: Gibbs M. Smith, 1984. Paperback reprint of the 1906 edition.

The Writings of Henry David Thoreau. Edited by Elizabeth Witherall, *et al.* Princeton, N.J.: Princeton University Press, 1981–.

Works about Thoreau

Anderson, Charles R. *The Magic Circle of Walden.* New York: Holt, Rinehart and Winston, 1968. Good introduction to the thought of *Walden*.

Boswell, Jeanetta, and Sarah Crouch. *Henry David Thoreau and the Critics.* Metuchen, N.J.: Scarecrow Press, 1981. A useful bibliography.

Cavell, Stanley. *The Senses of Walden.* An expanded edition. San Francisco: North Point Press, 1980. Explores Thoreau's relation to Romanticism, to Kant, and to post-Kantian thought. Offers terms for thinking about Thoreau's relation to philosophy.

Dolan, John, ed. *The Thoreau Quarterly.* Interdisciplinary quarterly edited by a philosopher. See especially articles related to Cavell's *Senses of Walden* in volume 14 (Summer-Fall 1982) and volume 16 (Fall 1984).

Dombrowski, Daniel. *Thoreau the Platonist.* New York: Peter Lang, 1986. Useful evidence about Thoreau's reading.

Harding, Walter. *The New Thoreau Handbook.* New York: New York University Press, 1980. A useful bibliography.

Miller, Perry. *Consciousness at Concord: The Text of Thoreau's Hitherto Lost Journal (1840–1841).* Boston: Houghton Mifflin, 1958. Polemic but still useful confrontation with Thoreau, by one of the most important historians of American literature.

Myerson, Joel. *Critical Essays on Henry David Thoreau's Walden.* Boston: G. K. Hall, 1988. Contains interesting selection of nineteenth-century reviews (by George Eliot, Horace Greeley, and others) and twentieth-century essays.

Paul, Sherman. *The Shores of America: Thoreau's Inward Exploration.* Urbana: University of Illinois Press, 1958. Still one of the major statements about Thoreau's enterprise.

Sanborn, Frank B. *Henry David Thoreau.* New York: Chelsea House, 1980 [1882]. Reprint of 1882 memoir and intellectual biography. Illuminating.

Shanley, J. Lyndon. *The Making of Walden with the Text of the First Draft.* Chicago: University of Chicago Press, 1957. Essential material on Thoreau's methods of composition.

Timothy Gould

threats

See deterrence, threats, and retaliation.

toleration

Toleration is intentionally allowing, or refraining from preventing, actions which one dislikes or believes to be morally wrong. Questions of toleration arise in circumstances which are characterized by diversity, coupled with dislike or disapproval. These circumstances serve to distinguish toleration from LIBERTY, and from indifference, where there need be no reference to dislike. Moreover, toleration requires that the tolerator have POWER to intervene, but refrain from using that power. Acquiescence due to ignorance of a practice is not sufficient for toleration. Often, and particularly in the liberal tradition, toleration is thought to be a moral ideal, not a value neutral concept; but understanding toleration in this way generates a serious problem about its justification—it is difficult to explain why it should be considered a moral ideal where the thing tolerated is believed to be morally wrong, for thinking something morally wrong implies thinking it right to prevent it. And how can it be right to tolerate, or allow, something which is believed to be morally wrong? This question raises three issues of central importance: What is the justification of toleration? What are its proper limits? And can it be defended as a virtue or only as a *modus vivendi*?

In the history of political philosophy, questions of toleration arose most often in connection with religious matters, and here toleration was often advocated on prudential or pragmatic grounds. It was invoked in circumstances where refusal to tolerate would result in civil disorder, and thus it was often seen as merely a police matter, rather than a matter of profound moral principle. However, a prudential justification of this sort is somewhat uncertain and precarious, for considerations of public order do not invariably dictate a policy of toleration, but can lead to repression or even persecution of religious heterodoxy. Thus, nonprudential justifications were also employed, and, prior to the growth of LIBERALISM, these often took the form of appeals to the INTEGRITY of the individual and respect for individual CONSCIENCE, particularly in religious matters. Similarly, conservative respect for tradition has generated a justification of toleration as good in itself. However, it is with liberalism that such nonpragmatic accounts of toleration are most closely associated, and here the desire to justify toleration as a moral ideal, rather than a requirement of expediency, is to be explained by liberal commitment to diversity.

This desire to explain the value of toleration as a moral ideal has issued in two major justifications within liberalism: the first links toleration to state *neutrality.* The second links toleration to *autonomy* or *respect for persons.* The neutrality-based justification urges that the state should be neutral between competing conceptions of the good life: it should neither prescribe nor proscribe moral or religious values, but should merely provide a neutral arena within which people are free to pursue a plurality of ways of life. Sometimes this justification is associated with moral and religious skepticism. The belief here is that, since there are no truths in morality or religion, there are no grounds for state interference with any chosen way of life. However, it is not clear that such a grounding will reliably dictate policies of toleration. The view that one way of life is as good as another may be associated not with pluralism and toleration, but with repression and even persecution.

A further problem with this justification is that the concept of neutrality is itself ambiguous. In particular, it is not clear what the adoption of a policy of neutrality will require of the state. For example, neutrality may be understood either as an intentional concept or as a causal one, and practices of toleration will differ depending on which interpretation is adopted. Understanding neutrality as an intentional concept simply requires that the state not act with the aim of favoring any one group; but if we understand neutrality in a causal way, we are committed to ensuring that all groups are given an equal opportunity to flourish. The latter may, of course, mean providing extra help to weaker groups. This ambiguity renders the neutrality principle difficult to apply. Moreover, if we are to advocate a policy of neutrality, we need a clear criterion for establishing its scope. States are not required to be neutral between everything which individuals may want to do, but only between their differing conceptions of the good. This raises problems about how to differentiate between the area of the right (where the state may legitimately intervene), and the area of the good (where state intervention is not justifiable). Many writers have doubted whether a clear and uncontroversial distinction between the right and the good is available. Finally, and perhaps most importantly, it is not clear that the principle provides an argument for toleration rather than simply a restatement of its desirability.

Faced with these difficulties, some philosophers have sought to ground toleration in a principle of respect for persons as rational and autonomous beings. We show respect for others by tolerating their moral and religious beliefs, even though we think those beliefs to be misguided and wrong. The principle of respect for persons, which has its origins in the moral philosophy of KANT (1724–1804), both grounds and limits toleration. It dictates that actions which are disapproved of should be tolerated except where they fail to show respect for persons as autonomous agents. However, just as the neutrality principle was ambiguous, and therefore difficult to apply, so the principle of respect for persons relies crucially upon a clear understanding of what autonomy amounts to. In some cases, the principle fails to give a clear answer to questions about what should be tolerated. For example, some writers have construed the principle as dictating a policy of extensive toleration of pornographic material, whereas some feminist writers urge that PORNOGRAPHY fails to show respect for women and therefore should not be tolerated.

These considerations draw attention to the ambiguities inherent in the concepts of neutrality and autonomy. However, it is also argued that, however interpreted, neutrality and autonomy cannot, in the end, provide justifications of toleration as a virtue, but only pragmatic defences of it. The point is this: if neutrality and autonomy are understood as central concepts of liberalism, then the justifications of toleration which they generate will themselves be ones which have appeal only to those already sympathetic to liberalism. On the other hand, if neutrality and autonomy are understood as transcending liberalism itself, then they cannot justify toleration as a virtue at all, but only as practical means by which people with diverse and conflicting conceptions of the good may be enabled to live together in relative peace. In the final analysis, liberalism will have difficulty in steering a path between the imposition of its own conception of the good on others, and a merely pragmatic defense of toleration as a *modus vivendi*.

See also: AESTHETICS; AUTONOMY OF MORAL AGENTS; COMMUNITARIANISM; COMPROMISE; CONSCIENCE; CONSERVATISM; CULTURAL STUDIES; DISCRIMINATION; GAY ETHICS; GOOD, THEORIES OF THE; GOVERNMENT, ETHICS IN; GROUPS, MORAL STATUS OF; HOMOSEXUALITY; IDEALIST ETHICS; IMPARTIALITY; LESBIAN ETHICS; LIBERALISM; LIBERTARIANISM; LIBERTY; JOHN STUART MILL; MORAL PLURALISM; MORAL RELATIVISM; MULTICULTURALISM; NEUTRAL PRINCIPLES; OPPRESSION; PARTIALITY; PATERNALISM; POLITICAL CORRECTNESS; RACISM AND RELATED ISSUES; RIGHT, CONCEPTS OF; SKEPTICISM IN ETHICS; SOCIAL AND POLITICAL PHILOSOPHY.

Bibliography

Heyd, David, ed. *Toleration: An Elusive Virtue*. Princeton, NJ: Princeton University Press, 1996. Essays on pluralism, liberalism, and defences of toleration in modern moral and political philosophy.

Horton, John, and Susan Mendus. *Aspects of Toleration.* London: Methuen, 1985.

King, Preston. *Toleration.* London: George Allen and Unwin, 1976. Includes extensive bibliography.

Locke, John. *Epistola de Tolerantia.* 1689–1692. Letter concerning toleration; a classic text on religious toleration.

Mendus, Susan. *Justifying Toleration: Conceptual and Historical Perspectives.* Cambridge: Cambridge University Press, 1988. Essays in the history of political philosophy.

Mill, John Stuart. *On Liberty.* 1859. The most important justification of toleration in the liberal tradition.

Milton, John. *Areopagitica.* 1644.

Newman, Jay. *Foundations of Religious Tolerance.* Toronto: University of Toronto Press, 1982. Material on relativism and pluralism.

Rawls, John. *Political Liberalism.* New York: Columbia University Press, 1996.

Wolff, Robert Paul, Barrington Moore, and Herbert Marcuse. *A Critique of Pure Tolerance.* Boston: Beacon Press, 1969. Essays.

Susan Mendus

torture

Torture is the deliberate infliction of violence, and through violence, severe mental and/or physical suffering upon individuals. It may be inflicted by individuals or groups and for diverse ends, ranging from extracting information, confession, admission of culpability or liability, and self-incrimination to general persuasion, intimidation, and amusement. Torture may also be inflicted out of love of CRUELTY, but it can be distinguished from sadism, in that it need not involve sexual overtones or motivation.

Organs of the state may resort to torture, quite apart from and in addition to what must be conceded to be its recurrent use in ordinary police interrogations. In the past, with official sanction, torture was sometimes an overt instrument of state policy; today, when most state constitutions bar it, it exists in places as a covert instrument of policy enforcement, aimed at eliminating or intimidating political opponents. In this regard, its use seems often to be counterproductive, through fostering increased opposition and zeal among those whose opposition the torturers are trying to eliminate and those who come to learn of the torturers's activities.

Conceptually, interesting questions arise. Can torture involve mental suffering alone? Or must it involve physical pain? What if, through graphic description, one produces more anxiety and distress in someone than repeatedly striking them would produce? If this is torture, so that "mental cruelty" might so qualify, then is not torture going to turn out to be more widespread and deeply embedded in ordinary life than we usually suppose? Again, how much suffering, and over what duration, turns the infliction of violence into torture? Is twisting a person's arm torture? What about twisting their arm for six hours? And what of the case of the young person who yearns powerfully throughout his youth for parental affection and who is knowingly and repeatedly denied it? Can deliberate deprivation, or deliberate frustration of deep-seated, relatively intense desires, be torture, if only it persists?

(We sometimes use the word "torture" to refer to activities or experiences that we find unpleasant, as when we say of sitting through a colleague's lecture that it was torture or "pure" or "sheer" torture. With expressions such as these, the term "torture" no longer refers essentially to violence and the infliction of pain; it can be used, *e.g.,* to pick out how boring or stifling or deadening a lecture it was. The connotation is still negative, but the intimate connection with violence and pain is severed.)

Morally, while theorists of all stripes condemn torture, deontologists and utilitarians have typically disagreed over a number of points in connection with it. Three of these are much discussed.

First, can torture be proscribed, absolutely? Torture is a horrific thing, a barbarity that, in addition to the PAIN AND SUFFERING involved, is an affront to and an assault upon human DIGNITY. Those wedded to certain absolute RIGHTS or exceptionless duties; those committed to the view that moral EVIL may never be done that good may come; those who elevate some view about treating people as ends to the supreme principle of ethics; these deontologists typically hold that it would always be wrong to torture someone, no matter what may befall others as a result and no matter how numerous these others may be. Torture is proscribed absolutely, and this (act-) consequentialists/utilitarians cannot typically endorse. For while they accept that torture is an assault upon human dignity and is nearly always wrong, they do not accept, *a priori,* that circumstances could never arise in which torture was right. They almost certainly will estimate the probability of such circumstances arising as very slight indeed; but even this is typically enough to make them demur at an *absolute* prohibition.

Of course, some utilitarians today, on grounds of utility, build into their theories rules or principles that bar direct appeals to consequences on a case-by-case basis. We are, they think, more likely for all kinds of reasons to produce best consequences if we act on the strength of such rules and principles, rather than try to think through cases in the heat of the moment. Nevertheless, these thinkers usually envisage a level of critical thinking, undertaken in a "cool hour," on which direct appeals to consequences are permissible, either with respect to particular cases or with respect to exceptions to the rules and principles by which we try to live our lives in the usual run of cases. At this level, a case for torture could be justified, depending upon a full assessment of all the various consequences and an intense scrutiny both of the victim's plight and the plight of others (if the torture is not carried out).

The sort of case usually discussed in this connection is that of an enemy soldier captured in battle who refuses to reveal the point of an impending attack, which information could then be used to help save the lives of one's own soldiers. If one regards the war in which one's side is engaged to be just, would it be permissible to torture this enemy soldier to extract the information? Would it make a difference if the torture were slight and/or of brief duration? If the number of lives to be saved on one's side were large? If the number of lives to be saved on both sides were great? It is not difficult to believe that even quite ordinary people who are not enamored of UTILITARIANISM may well think that circumstances *could* be described in which they would agree to trade the torture of a single individual for the lives of some larger number.

A case that arises here as elsewhere for deontologists is whether it is permissible, by doing what is forbidden, to prevent other and more numerous instances of the forbidden act from occurring. Would it be permissible to torture someone in order to prevent other and more numerous acts of torture? Of course, since (act-) consequentialists/utilitarians embrace a tradeoff position from the outset, this case, construed as one of preventing greater evil, is less problematic for them.

Second, what kind of person could torture an-

other? What kind of CHARACTER could such a person have? Deontologists damn the torturer as evil and corrupt, and so, too, typically, do utilitarians. But, here, utilitarians press a further point: what one allows or is prepared to see happen is as much a part of one's character as what one does. If there are things that it would never be right to do, no matter what befalls others and no matter how numerous these others are, then why is the plight of these others not to be traced to how one decided to act and so to be treated as relevant to the assessment of one's character? Can one really, effectively, remove oneself from RESPONSIBILITY for what happened to them, because one decided one way rather than another? Since deontologists will try to resist this line of argument by denying that what befalls others as a result of not torturing someone *can* be laid at their door, morally important questions of responsibility turn upon the success of this attempt.

Put differently, torturing someone has consequences, but so, too, does not torturing someone, and, in the case above, not torturing someone has the consequence that other and more numerous people are tortured. If one could have prevented this and did not, is what befalls these others to be laid at one's door, even though one does not oneself torture anyone? Clearly, it would be very much to the advantage of the deontologist here if, in the much larger debate to do with acting and not acting or acting and omitting, it turned out that omissions were not causes.

Third, what makes torture wrong? (Act-) consequentialists/utilitarians usually take themselves to be on strong ground here: torture is wrong because of the suffering it produces. Nothing, as it were, comes between the suffering and the wrongness. The case the deontologist mounts, they insist, is more problematic. For it seems distinctly odd to say that what is wrong with pouring boiling water over someone is that it violates some right not to be tortured or some duty not to be treated as a means or that it fails to exemplify some virtue on the part of the agent. What is wrong with the act is the agony and screaming it produces. In this way, (act-) consequentialists/utilitarians need no firmly grounded theory of rights or duties, no philosophical theory of the VIRTUES to account for the wrongness of the act. Of course, nothing in all this prejudges the attempt, for example, to ground a theory of rights, and such attempts are today rife.

See also: ACTS AND OMISSIONS; COERCION; CONSEQUENTIALISM; CORRUPTION; CRUELTY; DEONTOLOGY; DIGNITY; EVIL; HARM AND OFFENSE; HUMAN RIGHTS; MILITARY ETHICS; PAIN AND SUFFERING; POLICE ETHICS; RIGHTS; TERRORISM; UTILITARIANISM; VIOLENCE AND NON-VIOLENCE; WAR AND PEACE.

Bibliography

Amnesty International. *Torture in the Eighties.* New York: Amnesty International, 1984.

Armistice International. *La Torture, instrument de pouvoir. fleau a combattre.* Paris: Le Seuil, 1984.

Brady, James A., and Newton Garver, eds. *Justice, Law, and Violence.* Philadelphia: Temple University Press, 1991.

Crelinsten, R. D., and A. P. Schmid, eds. *The Politics of Pain: Torturers and Their Masters.* Boulder, CO: Westview Press, 1995.

Downie, R. S., and R. M. Hare. "The Ethics of Medical Involvement in Torture." *Journal of Medical Ethics* 19 (1993): 135–41.

Frey, R. G., and C. Morris, eds. *Violence, Terrorism, and Justice.* Cambridge: Cambridge University Press, 1991.

Langbein, John H. *Torture and the Law of Proof.* Chicago: University of Chicago Press, 1977.

Levin, Michael. "The Case for Torture." In *Elements of Argument,* ed. by Annette T. Rottenberg. 2d ed., pp. 434–36. New York: St. Martin's Press, 1988.

Peters, Edward. *Torture.* Expanded ed. Philadelphia: University of Pennsylvania Press, 1997.

Ruthven, Malise. *Torture: The Grand Conspiracy.* London: John Murray, 1978.

R. G. Frey

tragedy

Tragedy (*tragōidia*) is a form of dramatic performance that was of central importance in the ethical life of ancient Athens; it provided moral paradigms for younger citizens and, for the city as a whole, insight into tensions and conflicts contained in its scheme of ends. The art form attracted the interest of the ancient philosophers, being sharply attacked by PLATO (c. 430–347 B.C.E.), defended and theoretically described by ARISTOTLE (384–322 B.C.E.). Since these descriptions, together with the surviving corpus of Athenian tragic dramas, appeared to later playwrights and philosophers to capture something important about human life, tragedy continued to have a productive existence, both as a literary dramatic form and as the subject of philosophical theorizing. But one should bear in mind that most of the later history is in some sense a continuation of or commentary on what was found significant in Athenian tragedy.

Tragedies in ancient Athens were performed at major civic religious festivals attended by the entire citizen body, and probably by women and (in some cases) by foreigners as well. Attending a tragic festival was not at all like going to the theatre in modern times. The aims of diversion, fantasy, and escape, so central to the modern experience, were less prominently acknowledged than the goals of social insight and ethical awareness. Dramas were regularly assessed for their ethical content; during the fifth century B.C.E., the tragic poets were considered to be (along with the epic poets Homer and Hesiod) the primary ethical teachers of the young. Aristophanes' (c. 448–c. 388 B.C.E.) comedy *Frogs,* produced in 405 B.C.E., shows Athens, in a time of crisis, searching for a moral leader. The characters quickly decide that the solution must be to bring back from the underworld one of the three great dead tragic poets—Aeschylus (c. 525–c. 456 B.C.E.), Sophocles (c. 496–c. 405 B.C.E.), and Euripides (480 or 481–406 B.C.E.). The plot, from then on, concerns which one will be chosen; the eventual contest between Aeschylus and Euripides focuses on ethical issues above all, and treats style as a vehicle of ethical content.

Despite the keen interest later theorists have shown in giving definitions of tragedy and the tragic, it is difficult (and perhaps not terribly important) to find any clear unity among even the members of our small surviving group of tragedies. The extant plays are usually concerned with stories drawn from ancient myth, though one (Aeschylus' *Persians*) concerns a recent historical event. In formal metrical terms, all show an alternation between an iambic trimeter (more strictly constrained than the trimeter used in ancient comedy) and lyric metres of great variety. In the surviving plays, there is always a chorus, which usually both plays a role in the action and comments lyrically upon it. The number of individual roles is restricted by conventional limitations on the number of actors (first two, later three). Actors and chorus wore masks. Music and dance clearly played a large part in the total experience, but we know little about these elements. It is important to bear in mind that tragedy was above all a performance. There were scripts available for reading by the end of the fifth century, but the civic and communal nature of performance dominated citizens' responses even to what was read.

Tragic plots usually focused on some crisis in the life of a hero or heroine, generally involving a reversal of fortunes. The crisis was treated seriously: humor is rare. But the reversal may be in either direction, and a number of the most admired tragedies (including Aeschylus' *Eumenides,* Sophocles' *Philoctetes,* and Euripides' *Alcestis*) have happy endings. Tragedies were performed in groups of three by the same poet, often with thematic links, followed by a "satyr play" (of which Euripides' *Cyclops* is our only surviving complete example) containing grotesque lampooning of tragic seriousness.

The name *tragōidia* means "goat-song"—but the meaning of *that* meaning is disputed. Nietzsche, for example, connected it with the goatlike satyrs who form the chorus of the satyr play, and hypothesized that in early times all tragic choruses were composed of satyrs (which Nietzsche connected with untrammeled sexual energy). Others, Walter Burkert, for example, have connected it with ritual sacrifice, arguing that tragedy, like sacrificial ritual, explores the fragile boundaries of the civilized, the thin line that divides civilized animal sacrifice from the ritual slaughter of humans. More recently, John J. Winkler has linked the name with other evidence that tragedy was closely connected with the civic education of the "ephebes"—young men on the verge of puberty, about to embark on their customary period of military service. Arguing from the evidence of vase-painting that the tragic chorus may have been composed of such young men, Winkler tentatively suggests that the "goat-song" may refer to the bleating sound of the breaking male voice (described elsewhere in those terms). The issue is not likely to be settled any time soon.

Plato, in the *Republic* and the *Laws,* attacks tragedy as an art form unsuitable for the education of young citizens in the ideal city. Although some of his negative arguments apply generally to all artistic representing (*mimēsis*), he also has arguments directed specifically against what he takes to be the ethical stance implicit in tragic form. Tragic plots, he argues (and some epic plots as well), hold the reader's interest by suggesting that accidental reversals of fortune are extremely important for good people. They show good people expressing emotions such as fear of the loss of a city or a loved one, and grief when such losses have come to pass. The audience, in its turn, is encouraged to feel pity for the hero—and, insofar as the hero has been presented as a good and exemplary person, to emulate, in their thoughts about their own lives, the hero's fear and grief. In this way, tragedies teach—falsely, according to the *Republic*—that a good person is not self-sufficient, that reversals in fortune have serious ethical significance.

Aristotle's ethical writings hold that certain sorts of reversals in fortune do affect the ethical quality of a good person's life. Misfortune cannot, he holds, make a good person become bad or do vicious actions. (In this way he may be more optimistic than some tragedies, especially those of Euripides.) But it can remove a relationship of LOVE or FRIENDSHIP that is constitutive of a person's conception of the good life; and in other ways it can deprive a person of instrumental means to the performance of virtuous actions. This means that, for him, tragic reversals can be of serious ethical importance, showing a barrier between being good and success at leading a fully good life. The tragic poets' emphasis on such reversals is not misguided, on this view, but ethically informative. Moreover, the central tragic emotions of pity and fear can be ethically correct responses to the perception of the situation of human goodness in the world. Aristotle's *Poetics* indicates that tragic action is a source of information about EUDAIMONIA, the good human life; and that our interest in tragic representation is an interest in learning (chapter 4).

Aristotle defines tragedy as:

the representation (*mimēsis*) of a serious and complete action having size, in pleasant style, this being done separately for each kind of style in the different parts, performed by actors and not told through report, accomplishing, through pity and fear, a *katharsis* of experiences of this kind. (*Poetics* 1449b24–28)

This well-known definition was intended less to constrain future poets than to provide the basis for an informed and self-conscious critical analysis; it has generated an enormous amount of controversy and debate. Most mysterious is the reference to *katharsis,* nowhere else clearly explained. Renaissance theorists saw *katharsis* as a moral "purification"; nineteenth-century materialists as a medical "purgation" of accumulated humors. More recently, critics have focused closely on the ordinary nontechnical meaning of the word, "clearing up," "cleaning up," and have suggested that *katharsis* refers to the clarification or illumination concerning human life that the audience achieves in and through its emotional responses to the reversals displayed. They have connected *katharsis* with Aristotle's claim elsewhere (chapter 4) that people attend to representations for the sake of learning. On this account, Aristotle, by defending (as he also appears to elsewhere) a cognitive role for the emotions, would be differing with Plato not only about the ethical importance of fortune, but also about the way in which we gain understanding of the good. Other central concepts of Aristotle's theory of tragedy, such as "reversal" (*peripeteia*), "recognition" (*anagnōrisis*) and "missing-the-target" or "error in action" (*hamartia*) can be analyzed in a way that connects them closely with these ethical concerns.

The subsequent history of both tragedy and theories of tragedy shows the tremendous influence of Aristotle's theory, though often in garbled form. Because for Christian authors the word *hamartia* came to be the word for "sin," Aristotle's notion of tragic "missing-the-target"—which he distinguished explicitly from a defect or flaw of CHARACTER—came to be understood as the notion of a "tragic flaw," and it was held that each tragic hero or heroine must have a flaw, and fall on account of it. Obsessive interest in Aristotle's casual remark that tragedy usually takes place in the span of a single day generated the normative doctrine of the "unities" of time and place, which imposed constraints on later dramaturgy.

Among later theories of tragedy, the most philosophically interesting are those of HEGEL (1770–1831), SCHOPENHAUER (1788–1860), and NIETZSCHE (1844–1900). Hegel argues, with reference to Sophocles' *Antigone,* that tragedy shows the clash of two opposing claims of right, each of which is given by one of the protagonists a too narrow and too exclusive emphasis. Antigone is right to value the family, and Creon the state; each is wrong not to acknowledge the claim of the other. The drama, Hegel argues, points the way to a higher synthesis, in which both opposing claims are harmoniously acknowledged. Schopenhauer, by contrast, offers a more pessimistic reading: the purpose of tragedy is to confront the spectator clearly with the horror, in-

justice, and arbitrariness of life, in such a way as to quiet the will to live.

Nietzsche's *The Birth of Tragedy* (1872) offers a striking reinterpretation of the history and significance of Athenian tragedy, and also connects Greek tragedy with fundamental NEEDS in human life. According to Nietzsche, human life exhibits two fundamental "drives" or "tendencies," each of which he connects with the name of a Greek god. The Apollinian tendency is the drive or need to impose order on the chaotic flux of our experiences, carving things up and drawing clear boundaries. Nietzsche connects this tendency with conceptualization and intellectual reflection; in art, with sculpture. The Dionysian is a drive connected with erotic energy and the will to live. It seeks, frequently, an exuberant disorder and the breaking down of clear boundaries. It is manifested in intoxication, in sexual activity, in the art of the dance. Nietzsche claims that, in tragedy, the Greeks created a remarkable synthesis of these two forms, mixing the energy of the body with the clarity of the intellect. In so doing, they found for their entire community a way of affirming life, including both the body and rational activity, in the face of an awareness of the terrible arbitrariness of the world, the absence of any intrinsic moral order. In much of Nietzsche's subsequent work, he sought to recover for his contemporary world, which was living through the crisis of the "death of god," a parallel affirmation; and, referring ahead to his own *Thus Spoke Zarathustra* (1883–1885), he wrote, "*incipit tragoedia*"—"The tragedy begins."

Dramas calling themselves tragedies have been written in many times and places, by writers as diverse as SENECA (c. 4 B.C.E.–C.E. 65), Corneille (1606–1684), Racine (1639–1699), Shakespeare (1564–1616), Lessing (1729–1781), SCHILLER (1759–1805), and Goethe (1749–1832). The description "tragic" has also been applied to works in other genres, such as novels and histories, usually on account of an ethical resemblance. One can frequently find links, either formal or ethical, that make these works in some way continuous with the ancient theatre. But it is not always illuminating to press the questions, "Is *X* really a tragedy? Does *X* really fit the best definition of tragedy?"—since, clearly, the ancient form depended on historical conditions that are unrealizable today, and since such questioning frequently distracts the critic from more concrete and revealing questions, such as, "What precisely are the formal and ethical characteristics of the particular work?" "In what social and historical circumstances did it arise?" Nonetheless, the ethical power of the visions of life embodied in the surviving Greek dramas continues, appropriately, to exercise a considerable influence on the imaginations of both poets and philosophers.

See also: AESTHETICS; ARISTOTLE; CHARACTER; CRITICAL THEORY; EMOTION; *EUDAIMONIA,* -ISM; HEGEL; LITERATURE AND ETHICS; MORAL LUCK; MORAL SAINTS; NARRATIVE ETHICS; NIETZSCHE; PLATO; SCHOPENHAUER.

Bibliography

Aristotle. *The Poetics of Aristotle.* Translated by S. Halliwell. Chapel Hill: University of North Carolina Press, 1987. Includes notes by the translator.

Burkert, Walter. "Greek Tragedy and Sacrificial Ritual." *Greek, Roman, and Byzantine Studies* 7 (1966): 87–121.

Butcher, S. H. *Aristotle's Theory of Poetry and Fine Art.* New York: Dover, 1951.

Cooper, Lane. *The Poetics of Aristotle, Its Meaning and Influence.* New York: Cooper Square, 1963.

Else, Gerald F. *Aristotle's Poetics: The Argument.* Cambridge, Mass.: Harvard University Press, 1957.

Halliwell, Stephen. *Aristotle's Poetics.* Chapel Hill: University of North Carolina Press, 1986. A large critical discussion, distinct from the translation above.

Hegel, G. W. F. *Hegel on Tragedy.* Edited by A. and H. Paolucci. New York: Dover, 1975.

Hume, David. *Four Dissertations.* 1757. "Of Tragedy."

Kaufmann, Walter. *Tragedy and Philosophy.* New York: Doubleday, 1968.

Kitto, H. D. F. *Form and Meaning in Drama.* London: Methuen, 1956.

Knox, Bernard. *The Heroic Temper: Studies in Sophoclean Tragedy.* Berkeley: University of California Press, 1964.

Nietzsche, Friedrich. *The Birth of Tragedy.* Translated by W. Kaufmann. New York: Viking, 1976 [1872].

Nussbaum, Martha C. "Aristotle." In *Ancient Writers: Greece and Rome,* edited by T. J. Luce, 377–416. New York: Scribner's, 1982.

———. *The Fragility of Goodness: Luck and Ethics in Greek Tragedy and Philosophy.* Cambridge: Cambridge University Press, 1986.

———. "Introduction" to Euripides' *The Bacchae,* translated by C. K. Williams. New York: Farrar, Straus, and Giroux, 1990.

———. "The Transfigurations of Intoxication: Nietzsche, Schopenhauer, and Dionysius." *Arion* NS 2 (1991).

Pickard-Cambridge, A. W. *The Dramatic Festivals of Athens.* 2d ed. Oxford: Oxford University Press, 1968.

Plato. *Republic. Laws.*

Quinton, A.M. "Tragedy." *Proceedings of the Aristotelian Society* Supplementary Volume 34 (1960).

Schopenhauer, Arthur. *The World as Will and Representation.* Translated by E. J. Payne. New York: Dover, 1969 [1818]. Translation of the 3d ed., 1859.

Silk, M. S., and J. P. Stern. *Nietzsche on Tragedy.* Cambridge: Cambridge University Press, 1981.

Steiner, George. *The Death of Tragedy.* New York: Knopf, 1961.

Taplin, O. *Greek Tragedy in Action.* Berkeley: University of California Press, 1978.

Winkler, John J. "The Ephebes' Song: Tragōidia and Polis." *Representations* 11 (1985): 26–62.

Martha C. Nussbaum

transcendentalism

The movement of American thinking and writing dubbed "transcendentalism" emerged in New England in the 1830s and flourished until the American Civil War (1861–1865). This informal grouping of writers and thinkers included Ralph Waldo EMERSON (1803–1882), Margaret Fuller (1810–1850), Bronson Alcott (1799–1888), James Marsh, and Henry David THOREAU (1817–1862). But the vitality of this moment in American culture stirred other writers as well. The cultural shock of transcendentalist originality affected some interesting if little-remembered figures such as the philosophical theologian Frederick Hedge (later a professor of philosophy at Harvard) and the poet Jones Very (1813–1880). But the movement also affected poets like Walt Whitman (1819–1892) and Emily Dickinson (1830–1886), and, hence, transcendentalism can be said to figure in the creation of an American tradition of poetry. So powerful was the transcendentalist strain that it affected even those, like Nathaniel Hawthorne (1804–1864) and Herman Melville (1819–1891), who were suspicious of what seemed to be its otherworldly and utopian extravagance.

In recent years, scholars and critics have scrutinized the links between the transcendentalists and their politics, but the ethics of transcendentalism has received little attention. The sweeping views and the imperative mood of transcendentalist writing have not fallen on receptive ears. Moreover, transcendentalism's apparent lack of a rigorous philosophical method, coupled with attempts to evoke the monumental facts of human consciousness and society, have led most historians of philosophy to regard it primarily as a literary or quasi-religious movement. Transcendentalist writing has seemed to produce its greatest accomplishments in literary forms (such as Thoreau's *Walden* [1854] or Emerson's *Essays* [1841, 1844]), and it has seemed to remain too close to the Protestant and Unitarian crises that presided over its origins.

A core of issues can nevertheless be excavated that remain potentially vital and instructive. The transcendentalist movement took its name from KANT's (1724–1804) problematic of the transcendental employment of ideas. Rather than seeking a transcendent something—or someone—beyond any human experience, transcendental (or critical) philosophy seeks the conditions under which our knowledge and experience of ordinary objects become possible. According to Emerson's influential reading, Kant had discovered "forms . . . through which experience was acquired" that were not themselves acquired by experience. He described the tendency of Kant's transcendentalist followers to grant to these "imperative forms . . . all authority over our experience" ("The Transcendentalist," 93).

It is not easy to characterize the shift by which an epistemological faithfulness to the conditions of our experience becomes an ethical demand. Yet nothing is more characteristic of the transcendentalist writers and poets. And the impulse to trace such a movement lies at the heart of Emerson's own effort to characterize transcendentalism as a species of idealism:

> The materialist respects sensible masses, Society, Government, social art and luxury, every establishment, every mass, whether majority of numbers, or extent of space, or amount of objects, every social action. The idealist has another measure, which is metaphysical, namely the rank which things themselves take in his consciousness, not at all the size or appearance. . . . He does not respect labor, or the products of labor, namely property, otherwise than as a manifold symbol, illustrating with wonderful fidelity of details the laws of being; he does not respect government, except as it reiterates the law of his mind; nor the church, nor charities, nor arts, for themselves; but hears, as at a vast distance what they say, as if his consciousness would speak to him

through a pantomimic scene. ("The Transcendentalist," 89)

Emerson ascribes to idealism the idea that the rank that the world assumes in our consciousness can provide us with the true measure of the order and value that things and INSTITUTIONS possess for us. He assimilates to MATERIALISM the tendency to take things and institutions at face value—in the order and the degree of reliability that they most immediately present to us. Despite this characteristic mixing of terms of value with terms of ontology, it is still something of a surprise to read on to the next paragraph:

> From this transfer of the world into the consciousness, this beholding of all things in the mind, follow easily his whole ethics. It is simpler to be self-dependent. (89–90)

A present-day philosopher is likely to be suspicious of any effort to derive an ethics from the facts of human consciousness, much less from facts that seem designed to carry so large a metaphysical load.

We see here even more clearly than in Emerson's influential "Self-Reliance"—written in the same period—his double conviction that the ethics of idealism follow directly from its metaphysics of consciousness. However religious the language, the central strand of transcendentalist ethics becomes visible as the demand for self-dependence or self-reliance. If anything constitutes the unity of a movement as multiform as transcendentalism, it is this confidence that the realization of the "transfer" of consciousness is already a step toward such an ethics of self-dependence. It is difficult in our time to share this confidence, and equally difficult to fathom its sources.

Several elements of the transcendentalist account seem worth singling out:

(1) The transfer into consciousness is occurring constantly in all human beings. At its truest pitch, the transfer is meant to occur spontaneously, but the spontaneity is anything but assured. In most human beings, the capacity for such spontaneity is obscured and slumbering. Such a capacity must be awakened and clarified, and the struggle for such an awakening occurs against the dominant weight of custom and conformity and against the individual's own wish for passivity and self-stultification. Human beings pre-

fer to interpret the transfer as if it were dictated by the natural system of things and values that appears to them to constitute the material world.

(2) The insistence on the true nature and direction of the "transfer" is an implicit correction of an initial falsity in the human being's conception of its place in the world. Human beings begin their lives as children and, understandably, they begin by seeking their good from others. This natural tendency persists in us, until it becomes the source of an inveterate mistake about the source of the truest value. This moral mistake is cognate with our epistemological mistake about the independent reliability of the world. The transcendentalists were confident that human beings will learn to locate themselves within all the forms of human dependence and passivity.

What transcendentalists meant by the moment of ethical realization is less the achievement of any particular ethical result than the dawning awareness of the powers of the soul. This awareness constitutes the individual's chance for an ethical life at all. Whatever the self-dependence of consciousness may come to mean, it begins as the exact correlative of the dependence of the world on my consciousness. This is not initially an occasion for epistemological self-congratulation but for an ethical realization. This is the moment where individuals become aware of themselves as having already located the source of the world's value elsewhere than in the active self. They have located themselves and their needs in a world that has already been conceived as the source of stability and hence of what passes for value.

Becoming aware of the true direction of the transfer, or transformation, of world into consciousness is the first step away from my dependence on the world and toward my willingness to rely on my self in all its insubstantial transitoriness. Accordingly, while the initial step toward the ethical substance of the human world seems inward, this awareness immediately manifests itself as a demand for the revolution of the outward forms of the world: in RELIGION, politics, education, literature, and even in the up-bringing of children. As the child seeks its good from parental indulgence, so the religious sensibility of the age seeks to have its faults overlooked rather than its sins forgiven. In politics, the role of representative government becomes to adjudicate—or rather to inflate—the different forms of need prevailing in the different levels of social class. The common denominator of politics is the POWER of the rich, the needs of the masses, and, in every sector, the sentiment of the mob, which needs to make itself heard in order to believe in its right to be satisfied. (It substitutes the right to be placated for the right to be satisfied.)

A hallmark of the transcendentalist program is a kind of reciprocity between the inward seriousness of the spirit and the commitment to the reform of the conditions of human experience and utterance, in religion, literature, politics, and the social world. Transcendentalism influenced the movement to abolish SLAVERY in the United States, and many, like Thoreau, Emerson, Fuller, and Alcott, played significant roles in that movement. Margaret Fuller indeed saw both inner and outer connections between those "signs of the times" that insisted on the abolition of slavery and those that insisted on the emancipation of women (cf. *Woman in the Nineteenth Century* [1845], first entitled "The Great Lawsuit"). She was one of the first to demonstrate the empty viciousness of the theory that based the political suppression of women on their physical or mental or economic incapacity. If by nothing else, she argued, such a theory was vitiated by the demands that slavery placed on African American women and the demands that the capitalist factory system placed on working-class women. Fuller even took an interest in the effects of the penal code and the penitentiary as they worked out their effects on their primarily working-class victims.

Fuller also did the most to document that the transcendentalist imperative went to the heart of social and political issues of feminism. She diagnosed the eagerness of men to discharge their obligations to self-dependence by counting the number of people who are compelled to depend on them. She demolished the arguments that the INTERESTS of women were adequately represented by men in the realm of politics. Indeed, she heaped scorn on the idea that one gender or class of human beings could interpret the NEEDS of another gender or class. Apart from the dangers of self-interested delusion, she suggests that it is part of the self-dependence of the self that it learn to interpret its own needs. An individual must not be deprived of the right to determine whether her needs are shaping the demands of her desires, or forming the ground of political action, or suggesting the direction of her further education.

While less insistent on economic rights than some other feminists, she described the depth of interaction between the life of the marketplace and the life of inward fervor: "The women, shut out from the market place, made up for it at the religious festivals. For human beings are not constituted that they can live without expansion. If they do not get it in one way, they must in another or perish" (149). At such moments, she anticipates Max WEBER (1864–1920) and parallels the explorations of the young Karl MARX (1818–1883). As in the FAMILY, so in the factory, transcendentalists discerned that it was not the accomplishments of living and working together—of social production—but the accumulation of PROPERTY (called "private") that counted the most in the substance of human affairs.

Margaret Fuller's criticism and her translations of Goethe (1749–1832) were exemplars of transcendentalist ambition and accomplishment. Perhaps more even than Emerson, she saw the role of criticism in the nineteenth century as intensifying ethically, as well as culturally: "The critic, then, should be not merely a poet, not merely a philosopher, not merely an observer, but tempered of all three" (70). The critic is not fundamentally an outsider to the family of genius but rather, as she strikingly remarks, the younger brother of genius (70). The critic's powers of analysis are not antithetical to the powers of creation; rather they are essential to telling the story of that creation and providing us with the elements of creativity's new ordering of the world.

As with Emerson and Thoreau, for Fuller, the ethical impulse of the critic and artist are not something added on the work of art—like a motive or a moral. The ethical elements of potential awakening and growth are part of the medium in which the work is to be received. The ethical element is part of the substance at once of the work and of its eventual audience. Ethics is not a realm that can be separated without cost from the realm of art and literature, any more than it can be separated from the other realms of philosophy and the other departments of human life. The separations and exclusions that we have come to expect in modern life and in the contemporary university were, to the transcendentalists, signs of ALIENATION and weakness.

See also: EMERSON; EXCELLENCE; EXISTENTIAL ETHICS; FEMINIST ETHICS; IDEALIST ETHICS; INDIVIDUALISM; KANT; LITERATURE AND ETHICS; MATERIALISM; METAPHYSICS AND EPISTEMOLOGY; MORAL SENSE THEORISTS; MYSTICISM; NATURALISM; PERFECTIONISM; PROPERTY; RELIGION; SLAVERY; SOCIAL AND POLITICAL PHILOSOPHY; SOCIAL CONTRACT; THEOLOGICAL ETHICS; THOREAU; WORK.

Bibliography

Works by transcendentalists

Emerson, Ralph Waldo. *The Writings of Ralph Waldo Emerson.* Edited by Tremaine MacDowell, with an introduction by Brooks Atkinson. New York: Modern Library, 1951. (See for citations given in this entry.)

Fuller, Margaret. *American Romantic: A Selection from Her Writings and Correspondence.* Edited and with an introduction and notes by Perry Miller. Ithaca, N.Y.: Cornell University Press, 1963. (See for citations given in this entry.)

———. *The Letters of Margaret Fuller.* Edited by Robert N. Hudspeth. 6 volumes. Ithaca, N.Y.: Cornell University Press, 1983–1995.

———. *Woman in the Nineteenth Century.* Facsimile of the 1845 edition, with an introduction by Madeleine B. Stern, textual apparatus by Joel Myerson. Columbia: University of South Carolina Press, 1980.

Miller, Perry, ed. *The Transcendentalists.* Cambridge, Mass.: Harvard University Press, 1950.

Works about transcendentalism

Anderson, Quentin. *The Imperial Self: An Essay in American Literary and Cultural History.* New York: Knopf, 1971.

Cavell, Stanley. *In Quest of the Ordinary.* Chicago: University of Chicago Press, 1988.

———. *The Senses of Walden.* Expanded edition. San Francisco: North Point Press, 1981.

Chevigny, Bell Gale. *The Woman and the Myth: Margaret Fuller's Life and Writings.* Old Westbury, N.Y.: Feminist Press, 1976.

Ellison, Julie. *Delicate Subjects: Romanticism, Gender, and the Ethics of Understanding.* Ithaca, N.Y.: Cornell University Press, 1990.

Flower, Elizabeth, and Murray G. Murphey. *A History of Philosophy in America.* Vol. 1. New York: Putnam's, 1977.

Goodman, Russell. *American Philosophy and the Romantic Tradition.* Cambridge: Cambridge University Press. 1990.

Gould, Timothy. "Henry David Thoreau." In *Routledge Encyclopedia of Philosophy,* Edward Craig, general editor. Vol. 9, 388–92. New York: Routledge, 1998.

———. *Hearing Things: Voice and Method in the Writing of Stanley Cavell.* Chicago: University of Chicago Press, 1998.

———. "Ralph Waldo Emerson." In *Encyclopedia of Aes-*

thetics, edited by Michael Kelley. Oxford: Oxford University Press, 1998.

Kuklick, Bruce. *Churchmen and Philosophers: From Jonathan Edwards to John Dewey.* New Haven: Yale University Press, 1985.

Packer, Barbara L. "The Transcendentalists." In *The Cambridge History of American Literature,* vol. 2, 1820–1865. Sacvan Bercovitch, general editor, Cyrus R. K. Patel, associate editor. Cambridge: Cambridge University Press, 1994.

Zwarg, Christina. *Feminist Conversations: Fuller, Emerson and the Play of Reading.* Ithaca, N.Y.: Cornell University Press, 1995.

Timothy Gould

transitivity

See intransitivity.

trust

There are remarkably many views on trust, some of which make it the central focus in trust relations but most of which make trustworthiness, usually implicitly but sometimes explicitly, the central problem. For those who see trustworthiness as central, trust is typically not a moral term. For some writers, however, it is a moral term, either through its implications for virtue or CHARACTER or through the presumption of an obligation to trust. I will discuss conceptions of trust according to which it is justified if and only if the trusted party is thought to be trustworthy in the relevant way. Such trust is cognitive; it is in the family of the terms knowledge and belief.

Trustworthiness

The range of reasons another person might be trustworthy with respect to some trust is large. Among the modal reasons, that is, reasons that characterize large clusters of cases, is, first, that the trusted has an interest grounded in the larger relationship with the truster to be trustworthy. For example, because I generally value my ongoing relationship with you and would like to continue that relationship, I have an interest in living up to your trust in me on some matter. That is, to some extent, I encapsulate your interest indirectly in mine for causal reasons. Of course, other INTERESTS might sometimes trump, and then this ground for trust may fail. In an ongoing relationship, it is common that each party has occasion to depend on the other, so that their relationship is likely to be one of mutual trust. The fact that you depend on me to some extent then gives me additional reason to trust you when I depend on you.

Second, you may genuinely take my interests as to some extent your own because, say, you love me or you are my good friend. Hence, you directly encapsulate my interests.

Let us call these instances of strong trust. They have in common that the trusted in some way takes the interests of the truster as her own—therefore the truster trusts. A third case is also potentially quite strong. You might have a strong moral or other disposition to be trustworthy, perhaps especially in any context in which you have given someone reason to trust you.

The current social scientific literature on trust includes one additional category that we might call weak trust and yet another category that involves little more than inductive expectations. Weak trust is what I might have for you if you are a role holder in an institution or a profession and if I believe that you are monitored in your behavior to make sure you serve the interests of clients such as me, or I believe that the socialization of such professionals as you is effective in making you want to serve clients' interests (Barber).

Trust that is little more than inductive expectations is the expectation that a person, organization, or public official will act in your interest, but without your having any knowledge of an incentive structure that might motivate the person, organization, or official. The bulk of the currently large literature on trust in government involves nothing more than such inductive expectations for typical citizens. One might sooner call it confidence than trust.

In the vernacular, people use the term trust much more loosely to mean almost anything that involves an expectation. For example, people say, "I trust that the sun will shine today." This is a trivializing use of the term. Less trivializing are claims that people trust organizations, the government, a professional whom they do not actually know very well, people of a particular ethnic group or nationality, random strangers, and so forth. In each of these uses of the term, the meaning and content of trust clearly is different from the strong uses above. At least in some of these cases, however, one might meaningfully suppose that the relevant actors have reasons to be trustworthy, such as the strong organizational and reputational incentives noted above to behave in the way that a client expects or that serves the client's interests. The client's knowledge of such people is likely to be far more restricted than is our knowledge of close associates whom we trust in the strongest sense, but it need not be defective knowledge.

Typically, the range of a claim of trust is restricted. I will trust you only over certain matters and not over everything. For example, Count Vronsky in Tolstoy's *Anna Karenina* could be trusted to repay his gambling debts but he could not be trusted with Karenin's wife. Claims of trust therefore commonly have the three-part form, A trusts B with respect to matters *X*. One or another of these parts might be left implicit, but few genuine trust relationships work fully with only two of the parts.

Finally, we will generally want someone to be competent to do what we might entrust to her and to have the proper motivation to do it. In all visions of trust, both these elements seem important, although competence is often at best implicit in many discussions.

Trust As Relational

A standard thesis in relational contract theory holds that all exchange is relational. Similarly, virtually all trust is relational. We seldom genuinely trust someone with whom we have neither direct prior relations nor indirect relations that might be grounded in reputational effects on our relations with others. (The role of reputation is not merely in telling us how someone did behave in the past but even more in giving her incentive to behave well in order to maintain a good reputation.) If this is the way trust works, then it is, again, a cognitive term (in some accounts, trust is held to be noncognitive; see Becker and perhaps Rotter). To say I trust you is to say, in part, that I know relevant things about you. Among these things are your competence and your incentive or other motivation to act cooperatively with me.

Bernard WILLIAMS (in Gambetta) and many others suppose that trust is necessarily possible only in the context of "thick relationships" in which we all know each other very well and have ongoing, fairly intensive dealings with each other. Somewhat more generally, I can have an ongoing relationship with you even though we are both part of a large, loosely interrelated society and not part of a close-knit community. The incentive I have to be trustworthy toward you in such a relationship is encapsulated interests.

Generalized Trust

Some writers suggest that trust is a disposition (Rotter) and even that many people have generalized trust in essentially the randomly selected other person or in certain kinds of institutions, such as government and its agencies. In a truly generalized trust, there would be no B; A would simply trust any and everyone. This is implausible for people who have survived very long. But many people may have a, perhaps learned, disposition to be optimistic about the likely cooperativeness or trustworthiness of others. Survey research on American views of trust suggest that such optimism has been in decline in recent decades.

If I have a learned disposition to be optimistic about others, I will take risks on people fairly readily and I will therefore soon learn who is and who is not likely to be trustworthy. Indeed, if I move into a community in which trust is generally violated, I will soon learn not to trust. If I have a learned disposition to be pessimistic, however, I will take far fewer risks and I will therefore learn much less about who is and is not trustworthy. If I now move into a community in which trust is generally fulfilled, I will be very slow to adjust my expectations and to benefit from the change just because I will not often take the risks that would give me the knowledge that risk-taking would pay off in this community.

Obligation of Trustworthiness

Many academic discussions of trust run trust and trustworthiness together in making claims about trust that could plausibly apply to trustworthiness but that make no sense when applied to trust. Writers therefore sometimes transfer any moral approbation that might apply to trustworthiness to trust. But one could trust as a matter of cold rational assessment without any moral residue.

If there were a law to govern trust relations, it might seem to be analogous to laws of promise-keeping, as in contract law. But that means that it would be a law of trustworthiness, not a law of trusting. We need law to constrain the promiser to do what is promised, not to constrain the person to whom a promise is made. The contingently difficult issue in a trust relationship is whether *you* will live up to *my* trust. If I promise, I have an obligation; if I trust, you seemingly have one. It would be odd, however, to say you ought to be legally obligated to fulfill my trust just because I have trusted you. That would mean I could unilaterally impose a legal obligation on you that you had not chosen to take upon yourself in the way you might take on a contractual obligation to fulfill a contract or promise.

A law of trust would therefore merely be the law of promise-keeping as restricted to any instance in which one person promises or contracts to fulfill another's trust. Of course, there are trust relationships in which the trusted person promises to fulfill a trust, but there are many others in which trust is merely grounded in expectations and assessments that are not backed by PROMISES.

Trust and Society

A major part of the current discussion of trust is about its purported effect on making society run well socially (Barber, Govier, and Luhmann), economically (Fukuyama), and politically (Warren). We might all want a good, well-ordered, working society and yet wonder how important trust is in achieving it. It is very difficult to establish causal claims, and most of this literature seems to be speculative. Most of it is also, again, about trustworthiness more than about trust. If we know that someone is trustworthy (for any reason: encapsulated interests, moral commitments, or other), we generally can therefore trust her. Society might work relatively well because government agencies (Hardin in Warren), professionals (Barber), and other INSTITUTIONS are trustworthy, perhaps without our being in a position to know that they are. Hence, we may not genuinely trust and yet society may work well.

It is interesting that the contemporary worry with declining trust in democratic government runs counter to traditional liberal views that citizens should distrust government. The traditional worry was that officials must often have interests of their own that interfere with their serving the interests of citizens, so that we require institutional safeguards to block their CORRUPTION, self-seeking, and so forth. Those safeguards may be stronger today than at the time that, say, the U.S. Constitution was drafted (in 1787) by liberals who deeply distrusted government. Nevertheless, it seems likely that citizen wariness is still justified. The current worry is that government cannot work as well if citizens actively distrust it, in part because citizen participation is sometimes required for government success. For example, police effectiveness may depend on citizen willingness to report crimes and suspicious behaviors.

Trust and distrust in this arena appear to be epistemologically asymmetric. We can know enough (the simple liberal theory that public officials must often have interests contrary to those of citizens in general) to ground distrust, but we cannot know enough to ground trust. As typical citizens, we do not have ongoing relations with public officials, we do not know much about their institutional safeguards or their incentive structures more generally, and we cannot sensibly believe that they are mostly very strongly morally motivated (although many of them may be). The correct epistemological stance is therefore to distrust and to reckon ourselves unable to trust government. We might, from general experience, suppose that a particular government is benign and we might therefore have substantial confidence that it serves us well. But that is merely to say that we have inductive expectations that it will continue to serve us well. It is not clear that more than this is actually needed for democratic government to work (Hardin in Warren).

There appear to be significant differences in the forms of trust relationships in different cultures. Arguably, different forms work better for different organizations of the economy and society (Fukuyama). In some cases, what might be organized by ongoing relationships of trust in one context might be organized by the force of NORMS, with their sanctions, in another context (Cook and Hardin). Strong norms of communal LOYALTY might even block the development of separate trust relationships, so that certain entrepreneurial forms of economic organization would be difficult.

In our personal relations, trust might be very important. In general, however, in a complex society we might suppose that the nature and quality of various institutions enables them to substitute for reliance on trust with respect to those with whom we do not have ongoing relationships in which to ground trust or whom we do not and cannot know well enough to judge them trustworthy. We may be confident in the workings of our institutions without claiming that we trust them in any sense beyond confidence grounded in their performance—insofar as we know enough to judge their performance.

Trust As a Reductive Term

Trust is a term that appears to be very hard to define; it has manifold apparent meanings in both vernacular and scholarly discussions. People often treat it as a primitive as though they know it when they see it. It is essentially a reductive term. It is not a primitive that we know by direct apprehension, as the color blue may be to the ordinary person who does not treat it as a problem in optics. Trust is reducible to some set of other elements, including RISK, expectations, and assessments of the motivations and competence of the trusted. In the encapsulated interest view, the motivational assessments are about the interests of the trusted to act in the interests of the truster. In a dispositional view of trustworthiness, trust is grounded in assessments of the disposition of the trusted. Because trust is typically grounded in a reading of the other party, it can be misplaced, as it often is.

Perhaps because trust involves a complex array of elements, there is no distinctive term for trust, either in the verb or the noun form or both, in many languages. For example, the nearest formulation for "I trust" in French is probably "*j'ai confiance*"—I have confidence. Hence, we could not so readily make the distinction, made above, between trusting a government and merely having confidence in it in French.

See also: ALIENATION; AUTHORITY; BAD FAITH; BARGAINING; BLACKMAIL; BRIBERY; CARE; CHARACTER; CHEATING; COMMUNITARIANISM; CONSCIENCE; CONTRACTS; CONVENTIONS; CORRUPTION; DECEIT; DEMOCRACY; ECONOMIC SYSTEMS; FAIRNESS; FAMILY; FIDELITY; FIDUCIARY RELATIONSHIPS; FRIENDSHIP; GOVERNMENT, ETHICS IN; HONOR; HOPE; INTEGRITY; INTERESTS; LEGITIMACY; LOVE; LOYALTY; MOTIVES; NEGLIGENCE; PARTIALITY; PERSONAL RELATIONSHIPS; POLICE ETHICS; POLITICAL SYSTEMS; PRIVACY; PROFESSIONAL ETHICS; PROMISES; PRUDENCE; RECIPROCITY; RISK AVERSION; SECRECY AND CONFIDENTIALITY.

Bibliography

Baier, Annette. "Trust and Antitrust." *Ethics* 96 (1986): 231–60. An influential discussion.

Barber, Bernard. *The Logic and Limits of Trust.* New Brunswick, NJ: Rutgers University Press, 1983. A treatment of trust of professionals.

Becker, Lawrence. "Trust As Noncognitive Security about Motives." *Ethics* 107 (1996): 43–61.

Coleman, James S. *Foundations of Social Theory.* Cambridge, MA: Harvard University Press, 1990. Chapter 5 presents a rational choice theory of trust.

Cook, Karen S., and Russell Hardin. "Norms of Cooperativeness and Networks of Trust." In *The Emergence of Norms,* edited by Karl-Dieter Opp and Michael Hechter. New York: Russell Sage Foundation, 2000.

Fukuyama, Francis. *Trust: The Social Virtues and the Creation of Prosperity.* New York: Free Press, 1995. A widely read account of cultural differences in patterns of trust and of their significance in explaining differences in social and economic order.

Gambetta, Diego, ed. *Trust: Making and Breaking Cooperative Relations.* Oxford: Blackwell, 1988. A diverse, multidisciplinary collection on trust.

Govier, Trudy. *Social Trust and Human Communities.* Montreal: McGill-Queens University Press, 1997. A broad philosophical treatment of the morality of trust relations.

Hardin, Russell. *Trust and Trustworthiness.* New York: Russell Sage Foundation, forthcoming. A general account of the roles of trust and trustworthiness.

Luhmann, Niklas. *Trust: A Mechanism for the Reduction of Social Complexity.* In his *Trust and Power,* 4–103. New York: Wiley, 1980. A sociological theory of the rise of trust and its significance in modern societies.

Macauley, Stewart. "Non-Contractual Relations in Business: A Preliminary Study." *American Sociological Review* 28 (February 1963): 55–67. An influential early work on relational contract theory.

Rotter, Julian B. "Interpersonal Trust, Trustworthiness, and Gullibility." *American Psychologist* 35 (1980): 1–7. An important psychological account of trust.

Warren, Mark E., ed. *Democracy and Trust.* Cambridge: Cambridge University Press, 1999. A rich collection of papers on its topic.

Russell Hardin

Tufts, James Hayden (1862–1942)

Born 9 July 1862 in Monson, Massachusetts, Tufts was educated at Amherst College (A.B., 1884), at the Yale Divinity School (B.D., 1889), and in Germany (Ph.D., Freiburg, 1892). He taught philosophy at the University of Michigan from 1889 to 1891, and at the University of Chicago from 1892 to 1930. At Chicago, Tufts also held a number of administrative positions and served as editor of *The Interna-*

tional Journal of Ethics from 1914 to 1931. He died in Berkeley, California, on 5 August 1942.

Tufts wrote that his initial interest in philosophy was "with studies in its history." Early in his years at Chicago, he shifted his focus to ethics because "as I came to gain a clearer view of the important tendencies of the time, I thought the ethical changes the most significant" (*Selected Writings*). This ethical focus remained primary throughout his career, coloring both his university work and his practical efforts for organizations like Hull House and the Chicago City Club. Tufts also served on various statewide committees that addressed problems of WORK, housing, and illness; and, in 1919–1920, he headed the board of arbitration that oversaw the men's clothing industry for the Chicago area. Working with his University of Chicago colleagues, John DEWEY (1859–1952) and George Herbert MEAD (1863–1931), Tufts helped to develop a school of social PRAGMATISM that applied the methods and results of expanding social science to the problems of modern society.

Tufts's work reflected the impact of Darwinian thought on Western ideas of the nature and meaning of human life. "We are living to-day," he wrote in 1914, "in the century of Darwin" (*Selected Writings*). Darwinism had, for Tufts, three aspects. First, it emphasized the embodiment of human life, the seamless connection between the animal and the spiritual elements of our existence, and the natural roots of moral conduct. Second, it made history the record of emergent, natural organisms as they attempt to adapt to the challenges of living. In this process of adaptive growth, the mind is a tool to solve problems and to establish the values by which we ought to live. Tufts also saw in Darwinism the recognition that we are fundamentally social in nature and that our basic moral goods are social as well. He wrote of a kind of social debt that we all acquire through the collective efforts of centuries of earlier humans. We can repay this debt only to those with whom we come into contact, and to those who are to follow us, by deliberate efforts to advance the COMMON GOOD.

Commitment to this evolutionary world-view undergirded Tufts's belief that it is necessary to reconstruct our social inheritance. He explored with particular care the career of ideas and INSTITUTIONS. Reconstructing the former involves rethinking our conceptions of social and moral ideas like 'equality'

and 'democracy' that arose as solutions to problems at an earlier time when contexts and possibilities were different. As we move into the future, Tufts wrote, DEMOCRACY should come to mean that "every one so far as ability, and character, and the common weal allow, should share in the fuller life which human genius, through its conquests over nature, and human will, through cooperation in organized institutions, are making possible" (*Selected Writings*). We thus cannot continue to be satisfied with only formal claims that are not translated into actual EQUALITY. The ideal of equality functioned particularly strongly in the classroom since, as Tufts wrote, equal education "holds out to the common man and his children the one sphere of equality in the conditions that enter into every citizen's life, which is open under our system" (*Selected Writings*).

Tufts emphasized that the reconstruction of these and other concepts is part of a larger task of social reconstruction. This larger process integrated institutional reconstruction as well. Institutions, for Tufts, were modifiable human creations that were aimed at advancing our vision of a good society. Institutions as such include families and corporations, hospitals and religious congregations, transportation systems and schools. All of these institutions, and numberless others, arose in the course of human struggles and are to be evaluated and modified based upon their ongoing ability to solve social problems.

Tufts continually emphasized the importance of cooperative democracy to advancing the common good. He saw communitarian efforts as the true focus of the religious life, writing of the need to turn RELIGION away from concerns with ritual, MYSTICISM, and personal salvation, and toward fostering human community and "the spirit of service to mankind" (*Selected Writings*). Similarly, his moral interest was not in inculcating current standards of personal morality but in advancing public morality by educating the young to discover better standards that will meet our changing conditions.

Tufts's social and moral viewpoint in general is melioristic, maintaining that the conditions existing at any moment may be bettered with effort. By recognizing our part in the human family and thinking of life as an opportunity for service, Tufts believed that we could accomplish cooperatively what individuals cannot accomplish alone. Such commitment is without guarantees. There is just faith, an element that Tufts considered essential to moral life. "Faith in the possibility of regenerating society," he wrote, "not by miracle, but by the great and profound agencies of larger vision of life's true values and of love to mankind, has a place in a better world-order." The meliorism that Tufts advocated thus emphasized that "it will make a great difference whether we believe that as things have been, so they must always continue to be, or whether we have faith that human nature can improve, that nations as well as individuals may have a change of heart" (*Selected Writings*).

See also: COMMON GOOD; COMMUNITARIANISM; CO-OPERATION, CONFLICT, AND COORDINATION; DARWIN; DEMOCRACY; DEWEY; EQUALITY; EVOLUTION; FAMILY; FUTURE GENERATIONS; INSTITUTIONS; LIFE, MEANING OF; MEAD; MORAL COMMUNITY, BOUNDARIES OF; NATURE AND ETHICS; PRACTICAL REASON[ING]; PRAGMATISM; PUBLIC AND PRIVATE MORALITY; RELIGION; SOCIAL AND POLITICAL PHILOSOPHY; SOCIOLOGY; WORK.

Bibliography

Works by James Hayden Tufts

Our Democracy: Its Origins and Its Tasks. New York: Henry Holt, 1917. *The Real Business of Living.* New York: Henry Holt, 1918. *The Ethics of Cooperation.* Boston: Houghton, 1918. These three wartime volumes describe the nature and potential of American society.

Education and Training for Social Work. New York: Russell Sage Foundation, 1923. The preparation of social workers.

America's Social Morality: Dilemmas of the Changing Mores. New York: Henry Holt, 1933. The moral strains of contemporary life.

Selected Writings of James Hayden Tufts. Edited by James Campbell. Carbondale: Southern Illinois University Press, 1992. Contains the most important of Tufts's numerous articles and reviews; biographical and thematic introduction; complete annotated bibliography. Quoted from pp. 1, 162, 137, 309, 273, 263.

Tufts, James Hayden (and John Dewey). *Ethics.* New York: Henry Holt, 1908; revised, 1932. Tufts's most influential volume; discusses social history (Tufts); moral theory (Dewey); and current problems (Tufts).

Manuscript depositories: Amherst College Library; Regenstein Library, University of Chicago; Morris Library, Southern Illinois University, Carbondale.

Works about Tufts

Diner, Steven J. *A City and Its Universities.* Chapel Hill: University of North Carolina Press, 1980. The role of the university in social reform activities.

Feffer, Andrew. *The Chicago Pragmatists and American Progressivism.* Ithaca, NY: Cornell University Press, 1993. A consideration of broader reform questions.

Rucker, Darnell. *The Chicago Pragmatists.* Minneapolis: University of Minnesota Press, 1969. Exploration of the intellectual mood at the University of Chicago.

James Campbell

U

universalizability

This is the name given to a feature of moral judgments acknowledged in one form or another by most thinkers. But its precise nature and definition, and the implications it has for MORAL REASONING, are disputed. The main dispute concerns whether it is a purely logical feature which holds in virtue of the meaning of the words, or whether to acknowledge it is to embrace a substantial moral principle. A related dispute is about whether, if it is a purely logical or formal feature, it can have any bearing on substantial disputes about moral issues, as some have claimed. Others put this claim out of court on the ground that formal, logical theses cannot in principle have substantial consequences. But the examples of mathematics and of logic itself have persuaded others that formal theses can at least have relevance to substantial issues, when combined with other more substantial premises.

To understand what the feature is, we must first distinguish carefully, as many do not, between the notions of universality and generality. These words are often used very loosely, as if they meant the same; and the confusion goes back at least to ARISTOTLE's (384–322 B.C.E.) use of the corresponding expression *kath' holou*. KANT (1724–1804) also was unclear as to which of these two different features his categorical imperative required moral principles to have. For clarity, it is necessary to tighten up the terms to mark an important distinction.

Let us then use '*general*' as the opposite of '*specific*,' while allowing *universal* terms and propositions to be, on occasion, highly specific and therefore not general (Hare 1972). The principle that one ought never to tell lies is thus both universal and general; but the principle that one ought never to tell lies to someone who is seriously ill unless one knows that to tell the truth would endanger his life is much more specific, and could be made even more so by the addition of further detailed specifications, without ceasing to be universal. Many discussions of universalizability assume that the thesis that moral judgments are universalizable, and thus involve universal principles, means that these principles have to be highly general and simple; but this is not so. The second of the two principles just cited is still just as universal as the first, though much more specific. It applies to *all* cases answering to the description it gives, and this uses only universal terms. The thesis of universalizability allows both to count as moral principles.

A full definition of 'universal' is beyond the scope of this article; but the following will perhaps suffice for our purposes. A predicate (one- or many-place) is universal if and only if it can be defined without reference to any individual a, other than of the form 'like a' or 'unlike a'. Thus 'like the Paris meter rod in length' can be a universal term, but 'married to Jill' cannot. However, 'married to' is itself a universal term (a two-place universal predicate). The failure to understand this has been a source of confusion, as we shall see. A proposition or principle is universal if and only if the predicates it contains are all universal, and the subject-terms (except those preceded by 'like' or 'unlike,' as above) are all universally quantified variables, and never individual constants. Thus, 'For all x and y, if x is married to y, x ought to have no secrets from y' is a universal principle; but 'Jack ought to have no secrets from Jill' is not. It might be universaliz*able* if its holder were prepared to make it so by deriving it from the former principle in conjunction with the premise 'Jack is married to Jill'; but if he refused, and said he was just prescribing for the case of himself and Jill, not because of any universally specifiable relation between them, then the principle he was appealing to would not be universal, and therefore not a moral one, if the thesis of universalizability holds.

Many have been confused enough to think that the thesis rules out the former principle as moral; this would mean that one could not have moral duties to one's wife. It would also mean that one could not have a moral duty to keep *one's own* PROMISES that did not extend to a duty to keep *everybody's* promises. That everybody ought to keep *his* (or her) *own* promises is, however, a universal principle, and therefore not debarred by the thesis from being a moral one.

These distinctions made, the thesis of universalizability can be stated as follows.

(1) A principle is not a moral principle unless it is universal in the sense defined above. Note that this is intended as a necessary condition for being a moral judgment, not a sufficient one. There are nonmoral principles which are universal in the sense defined, for example aesthetic ones (Hare 1963). A definition of 'moral' (not to be attempted here) would have, therefore, to stipulate further conditions (Hare 1981).

(2) There are also singular moral propositions like 'Jack ought now to tell Jill the whole truth.' These can be moral if they are universaliz*able* (see above). The author of them must be prepared to embrace some universal principle, even if only of the form 'In all cases just like this case in all their universal nonmoral properties, the following ought to be done.' Another way of putting this is to say that anyone who makes a moral judgment is committed, on pain of being said to have changed his mind, to making a similar judgment about all cases identical in their nonmoral universal properties, whatever in-

dividuals occupy the several roles in them. In other words, to say that there are two cases identical in all their universal nonmoral properties, but one of them having a moral property and the other not having it, is to contradict oneself.

A related feature of moral properties is that they are *supervenient* on nonmoral properties—though unfortunately the word 'supervenient,' while having a clear sense in moral philosophy, has been borrowed for their own purposes by workers in other fields and used in senses which they have not always clearly defined (Hare 1984a). Older philosophers used to express a similar point by saying that acts, if right or good, are so because of right- or good-making properties, themselves distinct from the properties of being right or good.

The definition given avoids problems about the *range* or *domain* over which the universal quantification implicit in a moral judgment has to extend, and also problems about alleged *stages* of universalization (Mackie 1977; see Hare 1984b). The range extends to anyone or anything answering to the description, in properly universal terms, given in the judgment, whatever substitutions are made for the individual references; so the only stage relevant to moral argument is Mackie's last stage (Seanor). This condition is so severe that it has been questioned whether people who make moral judgments think themselves bound by it. Can they not, for example, make moral judgments intending them to apply only to members of *their own* FAMILY or tribe or race or species? The answer is that they cannot, if the judgments are moral ones.

To see this, consider the case of someone who thinks that it is wrong to cause suffering to members of his or her own species, but not wrong to cause it to members of other species. There are several ways in which this could be a moral judgment without breaching the thesis. He could, for example, say that there was a universal duty of species-loyalty which all members of any species owe to each other, but not to any other being. Or alternatively he could say that his own species has certain universal properties not shared by others, so that their situations are different in morally relevant respects. For example, saying insulting things to humans may cause them suffering, but insulting horses does not cause the horses to suffer; so only the former is wrong. That these moves can be made is consistent with the thesis, and therefore not an objection to it.

Once these irrelevant moves are out of the way, it is hard to see how anybody could refuse to extend his moral judgments to all situations identical in their universal properties. Suppose that I claim to think that it is morally all right for me, just for fun, to hang this cat up by its tail, but deny that it would be all right for someone else, in identical circumstances, to hang me up by my tail, if I had one and were in all other respects like this cat, suffering in just the same way (which is not too difficult to imagine). Those who understand the words will say that I am guilty of a logical inconsistency—that I cannot know what 'morally all right' means. For if there were no other difference, how could there be a moral difference?

If this is correct, then someone who was trying to convince me that it would not be all right to do this to the cat could argue by asking me whether I was prepared to universalize the judgment that it was all right. If not, then I could not be making a moral judgment about the situation. At this point I could escape by refusing to make any moral judgment at all about anything. But if I were not a consistent amoralist, it is hard to see how I could successfully state the moral principle according to which I differentiated those situations about which I was prepared to make moral judgments from those about which I was not. For this differentiating principle could not, without breaching the universalizability condition, include reference to the interests of myself, this individual. But unless it did this, it would not distinguish the cases in which I wanted to be allowed to do things to others from those in which I did not want others to do the very same things to me (Hare 1981).

Two possible counter-moves have to be considered. The first would be for me to claim that the case in which I had a tail and suffered like the cat is a hypothetical one, and that being nonactual is a morally relevant characteristic. But this move is ruled out by the same argument as before: someone who said that the difference between actual and hypothetical situations made a moral difference would be said not to understand what the moral words meant. It is an essential logical feature of moral argument that we can demand that people make the same moral judgments about hypothetical situations as about qualitatively identical actual ones (Hare 1981).

Nor will it do to cite some arbitrarily chosen feature of my actual situation (*e.g.,* the fact that I do not have a tail), and pronounce it to be a morally relevant difference between my situation and the cat's. For the crucial move was to ask whether I thought it all right to do that to me, if I were in the *cat's* situation; and that would include having a tail (Hare 1963).

The thesis of universalizability provides, then, a powerful weapon in moral argument. But it will not prevail all on its own. We need in addition at least the following supports. Our opponent has to have abjured consistent amoralism. He has to be able to represent to himself accurately, in all its intensity, the situation of his proposed victim with the latter's preferences. This requirement of true representation is what makes facts relevant to moral decisions. And he has to envisage *himself* in that very position and prescribe for it universally.

Nevertheless, it may well be asked how, if universalizability provides such a powerful weapon, it can be a merely logical thesis. For this reason and others, some have denied that it can be (*e.g.,* Rabinowicz). Certainly the GOLDEN RULE was, as a matter of history, propounded by religious teachers as a substantial, not a logical, commandment. But logical arguments do sometimes provide powerful weapons. If we are asking whether all ravens are black and then find one which is not, it is the logic of quantification, in conjunction with this fact, that compels us to answer our question negatively. In the same way, if I am wondering whether to accept that it is all right, as a universal principle, to make cats suffer by hanging them up by their tails, this is also a logically compelling counter-instance, at least *ad hominem*. Logic does not compel me to hold that it is not all right for it to be done to me in that situation if I am a cat; but *if* I hold this, it compels me to abandon the universal principle.

However, universalizability does not by itself enforce IMPARTIALITY or equal treatment. It is consistent with holding, as a universal principle, that everybody ought to act in his (or her) own sole interest; and it is consistent with similarly holding that people with great houses are entitled to rack-rent the peasants on their estates. Such principles are universal in the required sense. But the question is, not whether such principles can be consistently formulated, but whether those who hold them will go on *prescribing* or *willing* their application to hypothetical cases in which they are the sufferers, when they have fully represented to themselves their own situations in such cases. They will not, unless they believe that the INEQUALITY, or each person's selfish pursuit of his own ends, is an independent ideal to be followed for its own sake, no matter how much they themselves suffer. This, the 'fanatical' move, has too many ramifications to be discussed here (but see Hare 1981).

See also: AESTHETICS; ANIMALS, TREATMENT OF; CATEGORICAL AND HYPOTHETICAL IMPERATIVES; DISCRIMINATION; EQUALITY; FAMILY; GOLDEN RULE; GROUPS, MORAL STATUS OF; HARE; IMPARTIALITY; INEQUALITY; INTERESTS; KANT; LOGIC AND ETHICS; MORAL ABSOLUTES; MORAL COMMUNITY, BOUNDARIES OF; MORAL IMAGINATION; MORAL REASONING; MORAL RELATIVISM; MORAL RULES; MORAL TERMS; NEEDS; PARTIALITY; PRESCRIPTIVISM; PRINCIPLISM; PROMISES; RATIONALITY VS. REASONABLENESS; SINGER.

Bibliography

Hare, R. M. *Freedom and Reason.* Oxford: Oxford University Press, 1963. For passages cited, see pp. 139ff.; 106f.

——. "Principles." *Proceedings of the Aristotelian Society* 72 (1972–1973). Reprinted in his *Essays in Ethical Theory.* Passage cited, p. 1ff.

——. *Moral Thinking.* Oxford: Oxford University Press, 1981. For passages cited, see pp. 55ff.; 184ff.; 113; 170ff.

——. "Supervenience." *Proceedings of the Aristotelian Society* suppl. 58 (1984a). Reprinted in his *Essays in Ethical Theory.*

——. "Rights, Utility and Universalization: A Reply to John Mackie." In *Utility and Rights,* edited by R. G. Frey. Minneapolis: University of Minnesota Press, 1984b. Reprinted in Hare's *Essays on Political Morality.*

——. *Essays on Political Morality.* Oxford: Oxford University Press, 1989.

——. *Essays in Ethical Theory.* Oxford: Oxford University Press, 1989.

Hoche, Hans-Ulrich. "Die Goldene Regel: Neue Aspekte eines alten Moralprinzips." *Zeitschrift für philosophische Forschung* 42 (1978). English translation in *Contemporary German Philosophy,* translated and edited by J. C. Evans, *et al.* (University Park: Pennsylvania State University Press, 1982).

——. "Zur logischen Struktur von 'Goldene Regel'-Argumenten in Sinne Hares." *Kant-Studien* 74 (1983).

Mackie, J. L. *Ethics: Inventing Right and Wrong.* Harmondsworth: Penguin, 1977. See chapter 4.

——. "Rights, Utility and Universalization." In *Utility and Rights,* edited by R. G. Frey. Minneapolis: University of Minnesota Press, 1984.

Rabinowicz, W. *Universalisability.* Dordrecht: Reidel, 1979. Passage cited, see p. 19.

Seanor, D., and N. Fotion, eds. *Hare and Critics: Essays on Moral Thinking.* Oxford: Oxford University Press, 1988. Passage noted, pp. 268ff.

R. M. Hare

utilitarianism

A prominent, compelling, and controversial theory about the fundamental basis of morality, utilitarianism holds that human conduct should promote the interests or welfare of those affected.

Utilitarian appraisal of behavior may be compared with the widely accepted theory of "rational choice" that ranks alternatives solely by their promotion of the agent's own long-term INTERESTS. Equivalent to "ethical egoism," that conception of RATIONAL CHOICE implies that the interests of others may be ignored except as they happen to merge or conflict with interests of the agent. By contrast, utilitarianism is impartial as to persons affected and holds that similar effects on one's own or any other individual's welfare provide equal reason for action. Utilitarianism may thus require self-sacrifice to promote greater benefits for others. This suggests that the theory unites the concept of rational choice with the moral ideal of IMPARTIALITY.

As an ethical theory, utilitarianism should be distinguished from narrower normative standards, such as the national interest (a standard that ignores the interests of outsiders), and must be considered apart from psychological theories with which it is sometimes associated, such as the claim that human motivation is irremediably selfish ("psychological egoism").

Although utilitarian elements are evident in various ethical traditions, the theory first gained prominence in the late Enlightenment. It has frequently served as the ideological basis for political, economic, and social reforms.

Jeremy BENTHAM (1748–1832) developed the first thoroughgoing utilitarian system of the modern era, focusing on problems of institutional structure, PUBLIC POLICY, legislation, and political administration. He championed a vast array of reforms, ranging from an overhaul of penal law to democratization of the parliamentary system. JOHN STUART MILL (1806–

1873) maintained the utilitarian tradition of social criticism and institutional reform, but also emphasized problems of personal conduct, the value of justice and LIBERTY, and the importance of human potentiality, individuality, and moral sensibility. With insight and rigor (but less attention to political morality), Henry SIDGWICK (1838–1900) framed a utilitarian criterion that served as a model for later theorists.

Bentham suggested that opposition to utilitarian ideas reflects bias, entrenched interest, superstition, or confusion. Mill saw the need to argue for as well as clarify utilitarianism. He offered a "proof" of "the principle of utility," which commentators have regarded as an embarrassing failure, given Mill's stature as a logician. Mill's proof primarily defended the claim that HAPPINESS is the ultimate good, which is only half of the utilitarian theory. Nonutilitarians sometimes accept this part of the theory while denying the other half, that morality calls for the maximal promotion of any such value.

Following Bentham (and with the notable exception of J. S. Mill), utilitarians have typically been skeptical about moral judgments referring to moral RIGHTS and obligations, for these judgments seem to presuppose principles that are independent of utility and at odds with its commitment to promotion of the general welfare. But utilitarians have increasingly been concerned to accommodate and to account on utilitarian grounds for such moral convictions.

Criticism of utilitarianism, variations on it, and alternatives to it have flourished in recent years. Some of these developments are sketched in the discussions below.

A utilitarian theory may be seen as combining (1) a conception of "intrinsic" value, or fundamental good, which says how consequences are basically to be appraised, with (2) a view about the relation between "rightness" and "goodness," *i.e.,* between morally required or defensible conduct and the intrinsic value that can be realized. Utilitarianism encompasses a wide range of theories along both of these dimensions.

Individual Good

Viewed in this way, utilitarianism holds that the ultimate good is the good of individuals, and that this is determined by empirical facts about their welfare. Other things can have value, but only insofar as they promote or otherwise contribute to the good of individuals.

Ethical "hedonism" is one theory about such value. HEDONISM claims that intrinsic value uniquely attaches to a distinct element or aspect of conscious experience called "pleasure," the quantity of value being determined by that feature's intensity and duration. According to Bentham's hedonistic utilitarianism, the rightness or wrongness of an act is determined solely by its probable instrumental value, or in other words by the amount of PLEASURE it can be expected to bring about, less the "pain" (the quantity of unpleasant experience) it can be expected to cause, as compared with what would otherwise happen.

Hedonism claims that value attaches to pleasure however it might arise. This would include sadistic pleasures, gotten from causing others pain, as well as any pleasure that a rapist derives from his act. Critics argue that no value attaches to such pleasures, at least no value that could justify or give moral reason for the actions.

Bentham's hedonistic theory of value was enmeshed within a complex hedonistic theory of motivation and behavior. He held that the term "pleasure" refers to a distinct element of conscious experience which results from realizing a desire, and the prospect of which motivates action; and that "pain" refers to a correspondingly unwelcome element of experience which motivates aversive behavior. But the various linkages in his theory appear to admit many exceptions. We do not always like what we get when we get what we had wanted, for we can be mistaken about what we shall like; so "pleasure" does not always result from realizing a desire. More importantly here, because liking what we get is not always accompanied by a common and distinct feeling, it seems impossible to analyze welcome experience by reference to the sort of element that Bentham called "pleasure." Bentham's hedonism thus seems to presuppose a false picture of human PSYCHOLOGY. Ethical hedonism requires reconstruction. It needs first to explain what "pleasure" refers to, and then to show that basic value always attaches to that particular element of conscious experience and to nothing else.

Any plausible conception of individual good must be concerned with welfare over the long term. It needs to distinguish more from less important interests, to identify real but unrecognized interests, and to expose illusory interests. Hedonism does so in terms of a balance of "pleasure" over pain. Partly for reasons that have been suggested, many theorists believe that hedonism is an inadequate conception of individual good.

An alternative approach is "eudaimonistic" utilitarianism, which regards personal happiness as the sole intrinsic good, but, unlike hedonism, sees it as something other than the maximum balance of pleasure over pain in the long run. Mill suggested such a theory. Although he retained a hedonistic framework, he distinguished "higher" from "lower" pleasures and held that the "quality" of pleasure always counts more than its quantity. This seems to mean that something other than pleasure constitutes or contributes to human happiness and accordingly to intrinsic value. Mill held that these qualitative distinctions are determined, not by our individual aims and aspirations, but rather by the informed preferences of competent, experienced, and knowledgeable individuals.

Traditional utilitarianism assumes that individual good is some more or less complex function of interests whose determination requires no further judgments of value. Some critics of traditional utilitarianism hold, on the contrary, that individual good cannot be equated with welfare, so conceived, but involves other elements possessing independent value, such as individual autonomy or DIGNITY. Other departures from traditional utilitarianism are noted below.

Rightness and Goodness

The second principal dimension of utilitarian theories concerns the precise relation they see between right conduct and the promotion of intrinsic value. "Utility," or the property of promoting intrinsic good, can be ascribed to various things. These range from acts through social rules and INSTITUTIONS to moral attitudes. Utilitarian theories differ with respect to what they regard as the principal object of the utilitarian test.

"Act utilitarianism" applies the criterion of utility directly to specific acts done by particular individuals. It approves as morally right only acts that promote welfare as much as can be done on the particular occasion, given the alternative actions that are available to the agent. It holds that moral precepts (except the principle of utility itself) merit respect just to the degree that such an attitude would maximize the performance of "optimific" acts (right conduct under the act utilitarian criterion).

Although Bentham and Mill have often been considered act utilitarians, the evidence is equivocal. They attached instrumental value to practices and principles, which they sometimes suggested determine right conduct. Their theories were of course framed before act utilitarianism was distinguished from alternatives.

Sidgwick's principle is more clearly act utilitarian. For half a century, theorists such as G. E. MOORE (1873–1958) followed Sidgwick's interpretation of utilitarianism, until it began to be seen as just one among a range of theories predicated on the promotion of welfare.

Various theories (which may be called "indirect utilitarianism") hold that right conduct is fundamentally determined by maximally useful general patterns of behavior within a community. "Rule utilitarianism" holds, for example, that right conduct is the conduct that is permitted by useful rules, *i.e.*, rules that are or would be useful when they are generally accepted or universally complied with. Other types of indirect utilitarianism have been proposed, such as "motive utilitarianism," which applies the utilitarian test directly to behavioral dispositions and indirectly to acts (it is as yet unclear how such a theory defines right conduct).

Indirect utilitarianism gained prominence for a variety of reasons. Some hold that rule utilitarianism reflects the inherent logic of moral reasoning by requiring direct reference to rules, such as "Tell the truth" and "Keep your promises," that are not overtly utilitarian. Some hold that deliberately following act utilitarianism is counter-productive because of the leeway it leaves for the influence of ignorance, bias, and temptation on individual judgment, and that acting on moral dispositions or complying with a limited set of simpler rules is more conducive to welfare promotion on the whole.

Some theorists claim that rule utilitarianism squares better than does act utilitarianism with common understandings about morality, such as firm and widely held considered convictions about moral obligation. A general feature of morality, as commonly conceived, is that moral requirements constitute minimal standards of decent behavior, given by a limited set of simple rules. This allows for the possibility of "supererogation," self-sacrificing conduct "above and beyond the call of duty," that is morally valued but not mandated. Unlike rule utilitarianism, act utilitarianism requires that we always act "optimifically," promoting good as much as possible. Act utilitarianism leaves no room for SUPEREROGATION.

It would seem that innumerable variations are possible on the utilitarian theme, and it is unclear whether any particular variety constitutes the most faithful or most plausible interpretation of utilitarianism. The maximal promotion of utility, for example, may well require a mixed strategy, one that theoretical work has not yet identified.

Consequentialism

Just as utilitarianism encompasses a family of theories, differentiated from one another by their conceptions of individual good, it constitutes just one branch of an extended family that has come to be called "consequentialism." Consequentialist theories are, like utilitarianism, dedicated to the promotion of good consequences either directly or indirectly, but the nonutilitarian branches of CONSEQUENTIALISM deny that the value of consequences is determined solely, or possibly at all, by the welfare of individuals.

(It should be noted that philosophical usage varies. Sometimes the term "utilitarian" refers to the wider class of consequentialist theories, and sometimes it refers specifically to hedonistic versions.)

Nonutilitarian consequentialists sometimes claim that utilitarianism is insensitive to some basic values that are neither constituents of nor reducible to individual welfare. They may claim, for example, that individual good involves personal conditions other than welfare, such as knowledge; that some basic value essentially involves relations between persons, such as FRIENDSHIP; or that some basic value is realized in impersonal conditions, such as natural beauty.

Nonconsequentialists judge conduct somewhat differently. "Deontological" or "Kantian" theorists claim that the morality of conduct is, more or less, independent of consequences. A deontologist may hold, for example, that one has obligations that derive from independent moral principles.

Variations among consequentialist theories, including utilitarianism, are sometimes emphasized along dimensions other than the two that have so far been discussed (their conceptions of value and of the relation between rightness and goodness). Theories hold that right conduct is determined, directly or indirectly, either by actual or by probable consequences. For example, we can distinguish "actual consequence" from "probabilistic" versions of act utilitarianism. The former requires that conduct truly be optimific—that it have consequences that are as good as can be brought about—whereas the latter requires conduct that can most reasonably be regarded as optimific, given the available evidence, which might be misleading. Actual consequence act utilitarianism readily explains how one can be mistaken about the morality of an act because of factual ignorance. Probabilistic act utilitarianism endorses a version of the idea that right conduct follows the moral decisions made by conscientious moral agents. Indirect theories can likewise be developed in terms of actual or probable consequences.

Interpersonal Comparisons of Utility

The contrast drawn earlier between utilitarianism and rational choice may be taken further. Just as one's own personal interests can sometimes conflict, in which case "rational self-interest" requires the sacrifice of some interests for the sake of greater long-term personal benefits, the long-term, overall interests of different individuals can conflict, in which case utilitarianism requires that the welfare of some persons be sacrificed in order to realize greater aggregate benefits. For example, although utilitarians have consistently opposed exploitative social institutions, such as chattel SLAVERY, their theory would condone enslaving or otherwise exploiting individuals whenever that would maximize total benefits, overall, by generating greater advantages for the beneficiaries.

Critics accordingly claim that a purely "aggregative" principle like utilitarianism neglects a "distributive" dimension of sound social morality: morality cares not only about the size of the benefits pie but also how it is divided among persons.

Before considering this substantive moral objection to the soundness of utilitarianism, we should note a problem which, if it is not soluble, would suggest that the theory is useless, at best.

Critics and champions of utilitarianism agree that the theory presupposes the possibility of "interpersonal comparisons of utility." Principles of rational choice take for granted the idea of an act's utility for a given individual, comprising the advantages that would accrue to a particular person from a given choice, less the disadvantages that would accrue to that same person from that same choice. Utilitarianism assumes that the advantages and disadvantages accruing to different individuals can be added together to determine overall utility. This presupposes that there is, at least in principle, some way of equating units of benefit and of burden, not just for one person, but interpersonally.

Some deny that interpersonal comparisons of utility are possible, even in principle. If that is true, utilitarian principles lack determinate implications for many situations where the interests of different individuals are affected by choices. It would lack solutions for a central, if not the single most important, class of moral problems.

Such skepticism was originally directed against hedonistic theories, on the ground that pleasures and pains, being "private" or "internal," could not be subject to public measurement. Skeptics charge more generally that utilitarians have failed to develop a comprehensive basis for interpersonal comparisons of utility, even in principle. However, because we often make rough and ready comparisons between the effects of decisions on different persons, utilitarians continue to suppose that interpersonal comparisons of utility are generally possible.

Social Justice

To return to the issue of "distribution": Utilitarians and their critics often see it as concerning the proper role of egalitarian considerations. Critics frequently claim that a maximizing principle like utilitarianism represents only one aspect of morality, which must be supplemented and sometimes constrained by the requirement that individuals' net benefits be equalized.

Utilitarians have, however, traditionally championed institutional changes promoting social EQUALITY, on the ground of "diminishing marginal utility," *i.e.,* that, as a matter of fact, overall benefits are best promoted by allocating resources to those with fewer resources. Critics respond that utilitarianism's commitment to egalitarian justice is based entirely on contingent matters of fact and is limited accordingly. Utilitarians reply, on the one hand, that equality is a substantively ambiguous social ideal and, on the other, that utilitarianism embodies the unambiguous

conceptual core and most fundamental requirement of egalitarianism by insisting that all interests of all individuals be taken fully into account and thus that no class be specially favored or disfavored. If critics reply that unequal treatment requires moral justification, utilitarians respond that their principle provides the necessary justification.

These arguments leave us with the initial questions, what (if any) kind of equality is mandated by morality, and whether utilitarianism concurs. Answers have long awaited promising theories of social justice.

A most important recent development is John RAWLS's work, which is offered as an alternative to utilitarianism. Rawls provides both a theory about how principles of justice can be justified and a multifaceted argument leading to a distinctive set of general principles, which may be characterized as a severely qualified egalitarianism. The principles apply only to the basic institutions of a society and concern how typical members of the various social stations can reasonably be expected to fare, in the long run, as measured by allocations of certain socially distributable goods. According to Rawls, justice condemns institutions that benefit some at others' expense, and it regards certain rights or liberties as "inviolable." An adequate appraisal of utilitarianism must now consider this theory and the literature it has generated.

But theories of "distribution" do not exhaust the topic of justice, and problems of "distribution" are more pervasive than the foregoing discussion might suggest. These matters are discussed below.

Corrective Justice

Theorists since ARISTOTLE (384–322 B.C.E.) have separated issues of "distributive" from "corrective" justice. One concerns the proper basis for allocating benefits and burdens; the other concerns the moral response to substandard conduct, ranging from NEGLIGENCE to injustice.

Theories of corrective justice offer answers to such questions as, "When should restitution be required, and when is punishment justifiable?" In this context, discussions generally focus on legal PUNISHMENT.

Utilitarians have long argued that legal punishment can never be justified by the felt need for retaliation but only by the value of its consequences compared with alternative measures. They have typically supposed that punishment can sometimes be justified because its use can discourage harmful conduct. Not only can the persons punished be influenced, but others also can be dissuaded from engaging in such conduct by the risks of suffering the prescribed punishment.

One who disagrees need not demand "an eye for an eye." Because utilitarianism evaluates the act or practice of punishment solely in terms of its utility, the theory implies that punishment may be imposed without regard for the individual's culpability. Critics hold, on the contrary, that punishment is justifiable only if it is justly deserved because of the individual's past wrongdoing.

Critics believe that this problem represents a much larger and more serious class of difficulties for utilitarianism, not all of which concern punishment. Because utilitarianism evaluates acts and practices solely by utility, its logic implies that it condones the deliberate use of legal punishments against innocent persons whenever that would maximize aggregate benefits by somehow preventing some worse evil.

Utilitarians may defend their view by claiming that the theory has no such applications in the real world, for which alone moral theory is intended. They argue that the side-effects and risks involved in punishing innocent persons militate against such practices.

By similar reasoning, it can also be shown that utilitarianism would in various conceivable circumstances license practices such as TORTURE—practices regarded by some as absolutely unjustifiable. Utilitarians may claim, however, that extreme measures are sometimes justified, when the stakes are high enough, and that no ethical theory provides plausible grounds for absolute prohibitions to the contrary.

Rights and Obligations

These last examples suggest one respect in which "distributive" issues cannot be confined to the realm of "distributive justice" as that is usually conceived. Claims about rights and obligations often concern the morality of burdening some in order to benefit others or the distribution of goods such as freedom or special consideration.

To take a less charged example, promising places one under a special obligation, which is owed to a specific person or persons. Promising limits one's moral freedom, for one requires special justification not to perform as one has promised. The mere personal inconvenience of keeping one's promise provides no justification. One owes special consideration to the person to whom one has promised.

The distributive aspect of promising is suggested if we imagine that one must choose between keeping and breaking a promise, where the net effects are that keeping the promise would benefit the promisee and breaking it would benefit some other person equally. A critic of utilitarianism may argue that the moral choice is clear: the promise should be kept.

Suppose, now, that breaking the promise would benefit some third person more than keeping it would benefit the promisee. This means that keeping the promise would have some "marginal disutility." Critics may argue further that the mere marginal disutility of keeping a promise cannot justify breaking it. The obligation to keep one's promises can be overridden by important countervailing considerations, but not by the mere opportunity to do some greater good. The same is said to be true of other obligations to particular persons, such as to friends and to certain benefactors.

Act utilitarians reply that PROMISES have special significance just because they explicitly license others' expectations about one's behavior. Breaking promises frustrates those expectations and causes further inconvenience because promisees make plans based on the expectations generated by the promises. So act utilitarians argue that the characteristic disutility of breaking promises explains the kernel of truth in the idea that promising creates a special obligation. By contrast, rule utilitarians argue that promising, by generating reliance and cooperation, is a very useful practice whose requirements accordingly merit our respect. Similar considerations presumably apply to other perceived obligations.

Critics also argue that rights prohibit others from treating us in certain ways, even when such treatment would maximize utility. They argue, for example, that others and specifically governments are not justified in restricting freedom in order to promote the general welfare. This applies with special force to "paternalistic" intervention, designed to serve the interests of those whose freedom is infringed.

Utilitarians reply that paternalistic intervention is suspect precisely because it often mistakes others' interests and is accordingly counter-productive. They may claim more generally that perceived moral rights concern especially important interests which require protection from others' adverse conduct. Such interests come to be seen as legal or moral rights when they are protected through legal enforcement or by widely shared convictions that intervention requires special justification.

Agent-Relativity

Critics have recently formulated objections to utilitarianism in terms of so-called "agent-relative" aspects of morality. One such claim, using an example mentioned before, is that certain ways of treating people, such as torture, cannot be justified even when the act possesses the requisite instrumental value. The "agent-relative" version of this argument claims that special moral significance attaches to what one does as distinct from what one can bring about. The argument claims that ends, however good, don't always justify the means that are necessary to achieve them.

The argument just sketched assumes that consequences are evaluated on a neutral, impartial, or "impersonal" basis. A variation on the argument claims that the appraisal of consequences and the moral evaluation of conduct relative to them cannot be impersonal but depend at least in part on the agent's specific point of view.

A somewhat similar idea is that a utilitarian conception of morality cannot be integrated with the outlook of a normal individual. People who would not normally be regarded as immoral, amoral, or excessively self-centered have important attachments and commitments that are incompatible with the neutral, impartial, impersonal outlook of utilitarianism. Internalizing a utilitarian outlook would require one to be impartial between one's own and others' interests, and would involve an impossibly detached attitude toward one's own most significant commitments.

Utilitarians may reply that such reasoning underestimates the utility of significant commitments and of the dispositions they presuppose, as well as the disutility of abandoning commitments that give shape and meaning not only to one's own life but also to the lives of others who are essentially involved.

Relation to Ordinary Moral Judgment

Utilitarians are critical of prevailing moral attitudes, but differ in their approaches to it. These dif-

ferences might be explained by different "metaethical" views, *i.e.,* about the character and foundations of moral judgment.

Most utilitarians believe that moral principles are either justified or unjustified, and of course that their principle survives critical appraisal. Among these theorists, some believe that moral principles cannot be justified on purely abstract theoretical grounds and that justified principles must account for, or to some degree accommodate, ordinary moral judgments that there is no independent reason to discount. Ordinary moral judgments have no comparable importance to other theorists, including, at one extreme, those who believe that there is adequate abstract theoretical support for the utilitarian conception of morality and, at the other extreme, those who believe that moral views express arbitrary attitudes which are not subject to critical appraisal. Theorists with either of these last two views about the character and foundations of moral judgment would be least inhibited in rejecting moral convictions that seem inconsistent with the theory.

Moral requirements concern what ought or ought not to be done. As a foundation for moral requirements, utilitarianism applies only to those who can be held responsible for their behavior. If, as we tend to assume, humans alone are such "moral agents," then the scope of utilitarianism is limited accordingly. The same applies to all other moral theories that purport to ground moral requirements. But, because animals other than humans have interests, utilitarianism differs from many theories in requiring that we humans take the interests of nonhuman as well as of human beings fully into account.

Conclusion

It is understandable that utilitarianism remains at the center of controversy within theoretical ethics, accepted by many theorists and rejected by many others. If familiar views on either side of the controversy appear implausible, we can describe alternatives which are not so easily discredited. Utilitarianism is not confined to Benthamic hedonism, just as deontological theories do not necessarily insist that morality is defined by a simple set of traditional taboos. It is difficult to suppose that rights and obligations lack foundations, or that underlying values do not include individual well-being. How to understand that value, and how the good of the individual may be linked with the good of others, remain central issues. Modern utilitarians and their critics have enriched our understanding of the issues by revealing new dimensions to morality.

See also: ALIENATION; ALTRUISM; ANIMALS, TREATMENT OF; BENEVOLENCE; BENTHAM; COMMON GOOD; CONSEQUENTIALISM; COOPERATION, CONFLICT, AND COORDINATION; COSMOPOLITAN ETHICS; COST-BENEFIT ANALYSIS; DECEIT; DETERRENCE, THREATS, AND RETALIATION; DUTY AND OBLIGATION; ECONOMIC ANALYSIS; EGOISM; EQUALITY; *EUDAIMONIA, -ISM;* EXCUSES; FINAL GOOD; GOOD, THEORIES OF THE; GREEN; HAPPINESS; HEDONISM; IMPARTIALITY; INDIVIDUALISM; INEQUALITY; INTEGRITY; INTERESTS; JUSTICE (various entries); KANTIAN ETHICS; JOHN STUART MILL; MOORE; MORAL RULES; MORAL SAINTS; NATURALISTIC FALLACY; NEEDS; PARTIALITY; PATERNALISM; PLEASURE; POLITICAL SYSTEMS; PROMISES; PRUDENCE; PUBLIC POLICY; PUBLIC POLICY ANALYSIS; PUNISHMENT; RATIONAL CHOICE; RAWLS; REASONS FOR ACTION; RESPONSIBILITY; RIGHTS; SIDGWICK; SLAVERY; SOCIAL CONTRACT; SUPEREROGATION; SYMPATHY; TELEOLOGICAL ETHICS; TORTURE; VALUE, THEORY OF; WILLIAMS.

Bibliography

Bentham, Jeremy. *An Introduction to the Principles of Morals and Legislation.* Ed. by J. H. Burns and H. L. A. Hart. London: Athlone Press, 1970 [1789]. The recent definitive edition, in *The Collected Works of Jeremy Bentham,* general editor, J. H. Burns. Many good inexpensive editions are available. Classic source of utilitarian theory and its application.

Brandt, Richard B. *Ethical Theory.* Englewood Cliffs, N.J.: Prentice-Hall, 1959. The standard modern discussion of utilitarianism and related issues, chapters 12–19.

———. *A Theory of the Good and the Right.* Oxford: Clarendon Press, 1979. An important recent version of utilitarian theory.

Mill, John Stuart. *Utilitarianism.* Ed. by J. M. Robson. Toronto: University of Toronto Press, 1969 [1861]. The recent definitive edition, in *The Collected Works of John Stuart Mill,* general editor, F. E. L. Priestley. Many good inexpensive editions are available. The second classic source of utilitarian theory.

Moore, George Edward. *Ethics.* Oxford: Oxford University Press, 1912. The standard modern presentation of hedonistic act-utilitarianism. See chapters I, II, and VII.

Scheffler, Samuel, ed. *Consequentialism and Its Critics.* New York: Oxford University Press, 1988. An excellent anthology treating current issues.

Sidgwick, Henry. *The Methods of Ethics.* 7th ed., 1907. Indianapolis: Hackett Publishing Company, 1981. Book IV is the third classic source of utilitarian theory.

Smart, J. J. C., and Bernard Williams. *Utilitarianism: For and Against.* Cambridge: Cambridge University Press, 1973. Important recent discussions.

David Lyons

value, concept of

Value in general may best be glossed as that which is worth having, getting, or doing. So glossed, to say that something has value (is valuable) is to say either that it is a thing or a property that is itself worth having, getting or doing, or that it possesses some property or properties that make it so. Value, thus understood, is essentially *relational, i.e.,* it is value *for* some person(s) or other living being(s). Most obviously, it belongs to anything that is necessary for, or a contribution to, some living being or beings' thriving, flourishing, fulfillment, or well-being, starting with what is necessary for growth and survival. This will include, for all living beings, the physical equipment and the environment (in the broadest sense) required for living and functioning as an animal or plant (consider roots and soil) of a particular kind, and for human beings (and perhaps some other animals) whatever contributes to their well-being in the sense of HAPPINESS, living well, or *EU-DAIMONIA* (the human good). (The internal relation between the concept of value and the concept of the good is here clearly revealed.)

There is an important distinction to be made between something that is *valuable as an end* (something worth having, getting, or doing for its own sake), and something that is *valuable as a means* to acquiring, keeping, preserving, or doing something that is valuable for its own sake or valuable as an end. This will include the avoidance, prevention, or removal of something evil (something bad for some living being or beings). (We could call this "disvalue" or "negative value," if we needed a term.) For value as a means, we could use the term "instrumental value," but this term is perhaps best avoided, for our linguistic habit is to contrast instrumental value with intrinsic value, and the latter (as is claimed immediately below) is a dubious or at least a problematic notion.

The relational account of value given above is seriously challenged if there is such a thing as *intrinsic* value, or the value that a thing can have in its own right, quite independently of the value it has or could have as a contribution to the good of any living being, and many philosophers have explicitly or implicitly claimed intrinsic value in this sense for some things. PLATO (c. 430–347 B.C.E.), for instance, claimed such value for the Idea of the Good, KANT (1724–1804) claimed it for "the good will" which "shines like a jewel in its own light" and is "the only thing in the world that is good without qualification." G. E. MOORE (1873–1958) claimed it for beauty. Intrinsic value has also been claimed for life and for existence itself (*vs.* sheer nothingness). Some argue that happiness has intrinsic value (is an intrinsic good) in this sense, that the existence of a happy person is intrinsically valuable; hence, that the more happy people there are in the world, the more intrinsic value the world contains.

It is important to notice that, in every case, whatever is said to possess intrinsic value in this sense is something *worth there being,* even if from no point of view (hence, it is paradoxically inferred, from every point of view), and, where action is possible, or even conceivable, an end to be sought or preserved or treated as an object of high regard, even veneration. This shows that even this alleged intrinsic value is closely related to value in the sense of our original gloss (above). This conception of intrinsic value, however, seems not to exist in the common human understanding. In believing, for instance, that God is good, most ordinary people understand this to mean that He is beneficent, or at least not indifferent or maleficent, that He is concerned with our good, or at least that He is just.

True, it is difficult simply to dismiss the view that *persons* have intrinsic value. After all, the view first put forward by Kant, that persons should never be treated merely as means but always also as ends, or what is commonly called respect for persons, is a necessary ingredient of any civilized morality. Kant based his (implicit) claim that persons had intrinsic value on the grounds that, as rational beings, they were possible subjects of a good will. However, we do not need this apparatus to explain the centrality of respect for persons, which is surely better understood in terms (however hedged and elaborated) of treating other persons as we would ourselves be treated. Such an understanding of the matter would seem to carry a great deal more weight than the obscure notion of intrinsic value.

There are many kinds of value: economic value, exchange value (price), aesthetic value, medicinal value, hedonic value (PLEASURE), moral value, and so on indefinitely—probably not a denumerable list. Some of these, *e.g.,* medicinal value, have value as a means ("instrumental value"), others have value as ends (*e.g.,* aesthetic value, hedonic value), *i.e.,* as partly constituting or contributing to the flourishing of some living organism or organisms, especially human beings. Those which have value as ends may also be called "goods." Where the value in question is valuable as a means, we say it is "good for" something, specifying the valuable end, *e.g.,* "Acetaminophen [U.K.: paracetamol] is good for relieving headaches and reducing fevers" [both evils, or negative values]. Some goods, *e.g.,* health of the body, are valuable (have value, are values) both as means and as ends.

Clearly, it is values that provide us with REASONS FOR ACTION or abstention (reasons for choice). Simply expressed, to say that there is a reason for choosing some course of action (or inaction) is to say that there is something of value or worth to be gained or preserved by it, while to say that this particular course of action is the one to take or, in other words, that this is what, all things considered, we ought to do, is to say that there is more of value or worth to be gained or preserved by this course of action (including the prevention or elimination of evils) than by any other. It is important to recognize that this understanding of value does not commit us to any narrow EGOISM. It is not ruled out, for instance, that the well-being of another individual person, or of the community at large, should be a value *for me.* Indeed, this may well be true for all of us.

The account of value given here may be (has often been) challenged on the grounds that, since value is not something (an object, property, or relation) that can exist in the natural world, and since we can make no sense of the notion of a "non-natural" object, property, or relation, values and value-judgments are either purely subjective or merely conventional. This view is reinforced by the fact that some value judgments, especially moral judgments (a species of value judgment), are highly contested, or in dispute, or differ from culture to culture, a fact that leads one to suppose that consensus can never, even in principle, be reached. Thus, one may be led either to a relativist or to a non-cognitivist account of value. (This is the modern source of the alleged fact/value distinction.)

Value relativity can take two forms, cultural relativism and subjective relativism. On the cultural relativist view, because cultures vary over place and time, and different things are seen as, regarded as, or taken to be values in different cultures, there are no universal human values. Nevertheless, from within the perspective of a particular culture, the values of that culture are *taken* as universal; they are not *seen* as relative. (Only the "enlightened" recognize them as such.) Two different conclusions can be drawn from this. The first is that, since in order to have practical relevance a value must be seen as universal, and since none in fact *is* universal, there are no real values, only supposed ones. The second is that, yes, there are real values, but only from within the perspective of a particular culture or tradition; the only real values are those recognized within the culture or tradition, and they have validity only for those within that cultural perspective or who subscribe to that tradition. This view ignores the fact that the values of a particular culture or tradition can be challenged not only from outside that culture or tradition, but from within it, on the grounds that they are not conducive to, or are inimical to, well-being, and that is a universal consideration.

According to subjective relativism, everyone has his or her own personal values, which he or she creates for himself or herself, and no one may impose his or her values on anyone else. Whereas for the cultural relativist, value is strictly a *local* matter, for the subjective relativist it is purely a *personal* matter. This appears to make some sort of sense for personal preferences (*e.g.,* clothing, length of hair, entertainment, marriage or the single life), but if we are to have a community at all, some at least of its values, including its moral values, must be shared, and there are some things, *e.g.,* health, which are clearly valuable for every individual person, and where it would be absurd to suppose that there could be individual variance. And even where personal preferences are concerned, while different things may be agreeable or disagreeable to different persons, the value of *being agreeable* is clearly common to all.

There is a sense of the word "value" that is non-evaluative, a sense that is not used in making value judgments, but rather in stating or attempting to state anthropological, sociological, or psychological facts. Thus, we may speak of the values of a particular culture or tradition, meaning by that the things that are held valuable, or are valu*ed* within that culture or tradition. And we can speak of some individual's personal values, meaning the set of that person's beliefs or convictions about what is truly valuable. But nothing about what actually is valuable follows from any such statement, only about what is believed to be so. It might be added that, if values amount to nothing more than value-beliefs (valu*ings*), none better than any other, they cannot justify but can at best explain actions, unlike personal preferences, which do constitute one kind of value.

On the non-cognitivist account of value, value judgments contain an inescapable emotive or imperative element, used to express an attitude or commitment which not all may share, and thus they are incapable of being true or false. Values, this view supposes, cannot be anything real beyond personal attitudes or commitments, even if these are universalized commitments to principle, seen as valid for

everybody. But there is an internal incoherence in supposing such commitments to be universalizable, for I cannot both universalize my own commitments (see them as valid for all humankind) and see the differing commitments of others as equally valid when they are held with equal sincerity.

An alternative to both relativism and non-cognitivism (what might be called cognitivist anti-realism), is that value judgments are *meant and understood* as objective by whoever makes them, and many who hear or read them, but that this is a systematic error. The notion of value, especially moral value, it is said, is at best a useful invention for the purpose of social cohesion, and general acceptance is the only kind of objectivity a value could have. (This is the view of J. L. Mackie [1917–1982].) Ironically, social cohesion seems to be a value within this scheme, and not an invented one.

There are no doubt insuperable objections to NATURALISM—it eliminates the element in value judgments which gives them their attitudinal (for or against) and gerundive (to be chosen, or not to be chosen) implications, and to non-naturalism—values are "queer" objects, relations, or properties that are "part of the fabric of the universe." There is no need, however, in order to account for these implications, and to eliminate any would-be reference to the non-natural ("queer"), to resort to relativism, non-cognitivism, or any form of anti-realism. The gloss given at the beginning of this article both accounts for the attitudinal and gerundive implications of value judgments, and is perfectly consistent with the objectivity of value(s) without postulating any "queer" objects, properties, or relations.

Another common view, according to which value would be purely subjective, is that value for anyone (only human beings are considered) is a function of *de facto* DESIRE. Something has value for me if and only if I happen to desire it. But the truth is that desire cannot create value. I may get what I want and find it to be worthless or even an EVIL (something bad for me), a negative value. This applies even to hedonic value, where, although different people enjoy or take pleasure in different things, the proof of the pudding is in the eating. Oscar Wilde (1854–1900) is reported to have said: "Life contains two kinds of bitter disappointment—the first is not getting what you want; the second is getting it." This contains much wisdom. The discovery, *e.g.,* through eating the pudding, that something possesses hedonic value for oneself may generate future desires for it. But the desire for the never-yet-eaten pudding cannot create hedonic value!

Nor can I create value by willing it. We sometimes use the expression "conferring value on" to mean the same as "valuing." But to value something is simply to suppose it to have value, and this supposition may prove false. Some philosophers have adapted the word "valorize" (originally signifying "to raise or fix the price of [a commodity, etc.,] by artificial means, esp. by government action"—*Concise Oxford Dictionary,* 8th ed.) to signify this alleged conferring of value on things, something which is supposed to magically make them valuable or give them worth for the conferrer. In this they have copied the French, who have adapted the French word "valoriser" (originally meaning to develop the economy of a region or to enhance the value of a product by improving it) to signify this same magical trick of creating value by willing it. It is possible to raise prices or to improve a product, but it is no more possible to make something valuable by willing it than it is by desiring it. Either a thing is valuable in one way or another, or for one person or another, or it is not; and if we don't know which, we have to find out—in the case of the pudding by sampling it, in the case of acetaminophen by testing it. And is it possible to deny that a headache, for example, is evil or undesirable in itself (a negative value) for the person who suffers it, even if, in a particular case, it is an evil necessary to prevent or alleviate some greater one? Or that pleasure in the sense of pleasant or agreeable activities or experiences, however much these may vary from person to person or from time to time, is a good (a positive value), even if some pleasures are not to be indulged because they are evil in some other regard, whether in their nature (what they are pleasure *in*) or their consequences? One may debate, or one may be in doubt, as to whether something possesses value, and, where it is not simply a matter of personal liking or disliking (which cannot be questioned), opinions may continue to differ; but in every case, including personal likes and dislikes (preferences), it still can only be a matter of discovery (coming to know, finding out), not of invention.

Objection may be taken to the gloss on value given in the opening sentence of this article on the grounds that it is naturalistic, or that if it is not naturalistic it is circular. A naturalistic account of value would be one that identified it with some "natural" object, property, or relation, one that is empirically observable, or otherwise explicable in non-evaluative terms, thus taking the evaluative element out of value. This is certainly not true of "worth having, getting, or doing," but it might be objected that the account given turns naturalistic with the attempt to tie value to growth and survival and to *eudaimonia.* But the account above does not say that the concept of value is to be *understood* in these terms, but rather that certain things, and only those things, *are* worth having, getting, or doing. And, it seems, *eudaimonia* (to say nothing of the word "worth") is itself an evaluative term, since two of its rough synonyms are living well and well-being.

Does this mean, then, that the account is circular? No, for one could consider it circular only on the grounds that it contained a value element that should not have appeared in the gloss; but without such an element, the account would be naturalistic! Of course if it is held that if an account is "value-free," then it is naturalistic and therefore inadequate because it leaves value out, and that if it contains a value element, it is circular, and for that reason unacceptable, then it would follow that no account can be given at all. I think that dilemma has been avoided here, for the gloss given does not eliminate the value element (and hence it is not naturalistic), but it does attempt to explain (or unpack) what value is in a way that is not revealed by the word "value" standing on its own, and hence it is not circular, or at least not viciously so.

Moral values present a special and perhaps more difficult case than other kinds of value. What are thought to be moral VIRTUES, or how a particular virtue, *e.g.,* COURAGE (perhaps at one time essentially a military virtue), is understood, vary over time and place, as do questions of what is morally obligatory or morally wrong or morally permissible. But is it really possible to deny that courage, honesty, and GENEROSITY are virtues (possess moral value in this sense), or that CRUELTY is a vice? Can one, barring moral NIHILISM, help but admire a person for being brave or honest or generous or kind? Or can one, in real life terms, again barring moral nihilism, fail to accept that not causing unnecessary or unwarranted hurt or pain, or not failing (unless it is unavoidable) to discharge the duties attached to one's social roles (*e.g.,* parent, teacher, doctor, friend), or aiding the distressed when one is uniquely in a position to do so, are morally obligatory or required (possess moral value in this sense)? Why are certain qualities of CHARACTER virtues, and why are some acts or abstentions morally required, thus possessing moral value? If the account of value in general above is correct, this can be only because these qualities of character and these acts or abstentions are necessary for, or are a contribution to, the thriving or flourishing of human beings living together in community; while if a quality of character is vicious, or a kind of act or omission is morally wrong (a moral transgression), thus possessing negative moral value, that can be only because it is destructive of this thriving or flourishing.

See also: AESTHETICS; COMMON GOOD; CONVENTIONS; CULTURAL STUDIES; DESIRE; EMOTIVISM; GOLDEN RULE; GOOD, THEORIES OF THE; HAPPINESS; HEDONISM; INDIVIDUALISM; INTRANSITIVITY; MERIT AND DESERT; MORAL ABSOLUTES; MORAL REALISM; MORAL RELATIVISM; MULTICULTURALISM; NATURALISM; NATURALISTIC FALLACY; PLEASURE; REASONS FOR ACTION; SUBJECTIVISM; VALUE, THEORY OF.

Bibliography

Audi, Robert. *Practical Reasoning.* London: Routledge, 1989.

Bond, E. J. *Reason and Value.* Cambridge: Cambridge University Press, 1983.

———. *Ethics and Human Well-Being.* Oxford: Blackwell, 1996. Chapters 5 (Practical Reason and Value) and 6 (Moral Value).

Gaus, Gerald F. *Values and Justification.* Cambridge: Cambridge University Press, 1990.

Grice, Paul. *The Conception of Value.* Oxford: Clarendon Press, 1991.

Nerlich, Graham. *Values and Valuing.* Oxford: Clarendon Press, 1989.

Wiggins, David. "Truth, Invention and the Meaning of Life." Originally published in 1976; reprinted in his *Needs, Values, Truth: Essays in the Philosophy of Value.* Oxford: Blackwell, 1987.

Intrinsic value

Beardsley, Monroe C. "Intrinsic Value." *Philosophy and Phenomenological Research* 26 (1965): 1–17.

Chisholm, Roderick. "Intrinsic Value." In *Values and Morals,* edited by A. Goldman and J. Kim. Dordrecht: Reidel, 1978.

Korsgaard, Christine M. "Two Distinctions in Goodness." *Philosophical Review* 92 (1983): 169–95.

Moore, G. E. "The Conception of Intrinsic Value." In his collection of essays, *Philosophical Studies.* London: Routledge, 1922.

———. *Principia Ethica.* Cambridge: Cambridge University Press, 1903. See especially pp. 83–85.

———. "A Reply to My Critics." In *The Philosophy of G. E. Moore,* edited by Paul Arthur Schilpp. Evanston, IL: Northwestern University Press, 1942.

Ross, W. D. *The Right and the Good.* Oxford: Clarendon Press, 1930. Chapters 4 and 5.

Cultural relativism

Benedict, Ruth. *Patterns of Culture.* London: Routledge, 1935.

MacIntyre, Alasdair. *After Virtue.* 2d ed. London: Duckworth, 1985.

———. *Whose Justice? Which Rationality?* London: Duckworth, 1988.

Sumner, William Graham. *Folkways: A Study of the Sociological Importance of Usages, Manners, Customs, Mores, and Morals.* Boston: Ginn, 1907. Benedict and Sumner present the simple or unsophisticated cultural relativism of the earlier part of the twentieth century. For a more complex, contemporary view, which, although it applies principally to ethics, is of quite general application to rationality and value in general, see the following:

Non-cognitivism and anti-naturalism

Barnes, W. H. F. "A Suggestion About Value." *Analysis* 1 (1933): 45–46.

Hare, R. M. *The Language of Morals.* Oxford: Oxford University Press, 1952.

Stevenson, Charles L. *Facts and Values.* New Haven: Yale University Press, 1963. Stevenson was the foremost proponent of the emotive theory of value. This is a collection of his earlier papers.

Naturalistic accounts of value

Dewey, John. *Theory of Valuation.* Chicago: University of Chicago Press, 1939.

Lewis, C. I. *An Analysis of Knowledge and Valuaton.* LaSalle, IL: Open Court, 1946.

Monro, D. H. *Empiricism and Ethics.* Cambridge: Cambridge University Press, 1967.

Perry, Ralph Barton. *General Theory of Value: Its Meaning and Basic Principles Construed in Terms of Interest.* New York: Longmans, Green, 1926.

Cognitivist anti-realism

Mackie, J. L. *Ethics: Inventing Right and Wrong.* Harmondsworth: Penguin Books, 1977.

Value as a function of desire

Beehler, Rodger. *Moral Life.* Oxford: Oxford University Press, 1978.

Foot, Philippa. "Reasons for Action and Desires." First published 1972; reprinted in her *Virtues and Vices.* Oxford: Oxford University Press, 1979.

Nagel, Thomas. *The Possibility of Altruism.* Oxford: Oxford University Press, 1970.

Taylor, Richard. *Good and Evil.* New York: Macmillan, 1970.

Williams, Bernard. "Internal and External Reasons." First published 1979; reprinted in his *Moral Luck.* Cambridge: Cambridge University Press, 1981.

Wright, G. H. von. *The Varieties of Goodness.* London: Routledge, 1963.

E. J. Bond

value, theory of

In the last hundred years a *general theory of value* attempted to unify all normative fields from ethics and AESTHETICS to social and religious philosophy. Even when the general theory receded, its language and the way it formulated methodological issues remained standard for most of twentieth-century moral philosophy. Its influence dissipated only when use of the term "value" became so commonplace as to lose all determinate significance.

"Value" had always suggested some comparative process of assessing or measuring. For example, BENTHAM (1748–1832) headed a chapter "Value of a Lot of Pleasure, how to be measured." It could also refer to some satisfying experience or the object upon which that experience was directed, although the term "good" had usually filled that role. Economic theory invoked both aspects: a commodity had some "use value" which gave it entry into the market, while "exchange value" was presumed to explain the interchange of commodities and the movement of prices. (Earlier explanations looked to a labor theory of exchange value, later ones to the PSYCHOLOGY of demand and DESIRE.) The rise of such a complex theory of value in this special field was a clear response to the importance of markets in modern industrial economy. The theory looked away from the specific features of the objects evaluated to relational properties of exchange and its general determinants.

Other aspects of modern life prompted a general idea of value. A broadened area of individual choice—among commodities, occupations, residence, marriage partners, ideas, patterns of life—raised problems of preferential choice and its criteria. Some moral philosophers even argued that "better than" was the fundamental ethical concept, and "good" should be defined in terms of it.

Darwinian EVOLUTION opened a new chapter for general value theory. Those who opposed locating human beings within the scheme of animal development sought a distinctive spiritual property to pit against the natural world that science studied. This dichotomy of nature and spirit was particularly explored in German philosophy. R. H. Lotze (1817–1881) fashioned value as an ultimate category, A. Ritschl (1822–1889) applied it to the nature of the divine, and W. Windelband (1848–1915) and H. Rickert (1863–1936) separated the methodologies of scientific and humanistic fields. General value theory was worked out in technical detail in the Vienna school associated with BRENTANO (1838–1917), Meinong (1853–1920), and Ehrenfels (1859–1932). During the first decade of the twentieth century, in the United States, the idealist approach was advanced particularly by W. M. Urban (1873–1952), who took value to be the feeling aspect of conative processes giving meaning to the object for the subject. H. Münsterberg (1863–1916), even further, saw any imposing of order in the universe as a value act. The naturalistic approach, accepting mankind's place in the evolutionary scheme, welcomed a general idea of value for a different reason: it could be used to explore the continuities in the growth and diversification of different normative fields from the basic initial efforts of group survival; DARWIN (1809–1892) had outlined such a view for ethics in *The Descent of Man.* R. B. PERRY (1876–1957) mapped this kind of theory, using *interest* as selective action for the fundamental meaning of value.

For both sides, *value* (in the sense of intrinsic value) became a fundamental property or quality of a thing or situation or human attitude; there was agreement on its singularity and its generality, but not on how it was to be analyzed or what philosophical status to assign to it. DEWEY (1859–1952) provided a dissenting voice in these early debates: in his view, the basic idea was simply appraising or evaluating; this called for analysis of its processes, but intrinsic value meant little more than finding something attractive; it was not a unique quality with special philosophic import. For philosophy generally, value theory became an established branch: *axiology* was listed as distinct, alongside *ontology*. Indeed, the ideal realm of value might have a slight edge over that of being, for it provided the criteria by which *what is* can be judged.

With the general concept enthroned, ethics became only one species, that concerned with moral values, as others were with aesthetic, religious, social, economic, etc. As the generic term "value" began to absorb the specific "good," ethics turned chiefly to "right" and "obligation" and "virtue." This accentuated the already strong Kantian trend in modern ethics, with its stress on moral law and virtue. Perhaps the most serious effect of general value theory on ethics was that methodological issues became formulated in a wholesale way, for value as a whole. A question about the nature of value expected a single answer about value as such: emotive or volitional or cognitive. Value had to be either unverifiable or verifiable (if the latter, intuitive or empirical). Value judgments were either absolute or relative. This high level of abstraction—wholesale answers rather than contextually pluralistic ones—together with the sharply separated treatment of value from fact, characterized a great part of the stream of books on value theory throughout the century.

Explorations of value moved in different directions. UTILITARIANISM and economic theory had already stimulated the development of the logic of preference and decision theory, in both individual and social choice. This now included both formal deontic and preference systems, statistical studies, and designed experiments (*e.g.,* risk-taking, voting behavior). In methodological questions of verifiability, the simplistic contrast of cognitivist or voluntarist or emotivist was found early in the emotive theory of ethics. This influential school took value utterances to be emotional expression or persuasive effort; it began with the use of the language of ethics, but in fact was governed by the sweeping separation of fact and value that characterized positivism. Greater progress became possible when distinctions were made among constituent concepts. For example, C. I. LEWIS (1883–1964) brought value down from its generic position to comparable status with obligation. He then found it possible to regard value, as satisfaction, to be verifiable, but obligation in the sense of right-ness to be regulative for all knowledge, not merely for morality.

Scientifically oriented theories of value during the century followed Perry's lead, though seeking a more definite bio-psychological base than *interest:* for example, attempting to sharpen *pleasure* (familiar hedonism, sometimes with Freudian backing, as in Parker); *purposive action* (construed in the light of a specific psychology, as in Pepper); and similarly for desire, wish, even impulse and appetite and drive and need, and occasionally a picture of holistic organic response.

The phenomenological analysis, whether in its general philosophical or in its scientific psychological approach, attempted not so much to explain value as to give it clearer characterization in the experiential field. Nicolai HARTMANN's (1882–1950) extensive treatment ended with a separate domain of value essences that are intellectually sensed; they are many, not one, and may even include antinomic values. On the other hand, Köhler's (1887–1967) Gestalt inquiry proposed *requiredness* as the unitary experiential feature of value, whatever its special area (whether the necktie matches the shirt or the action is morally proper). More recent phenomenologists stress rather the vast value variety revealed in direct experience. Existentialist treatments, as in SARTRE (1905–1980), focused on the critical moment of present decision, as the values stabilized in past decision call for constant reaffirmation or recasting in the freedom of the now; even to invoke a reason in deliberation is an active present choice.

Linguistic philosophy played a crucial role in the outcome of value theory. While many studies simply continued philosophical controversies compounded with varying views of signification, some, like Everett Hall, tried to find from an ideal language of value a categorial value structure of the world. The central weight of linguistic philosophy (Oxford or ordinary language analysis), however, had a dissolving effect on value theory. The concept of value had found little use in England (as contrasted with Germany, Scotland, America) and the effort of ordinary language analysis was to explore varied linguistic contexts of traditional usage, not constructed abstract ideas. Indeed, it not only used the older ethical terms, but even diversified them: for example, "ought" was differently analyzed in "I ought," "You ought," "He ought," showing different functions (decision, advice, assessment).

While the idea of value was thus being trimmed in philosophy, it grew formidably in the social sciences, beginning with the mid-century. Stimulated by the rise of global interests after World War II and the exhibition of differences in cultures, INSTITUTIONS, national ideologies, as well as by historical changes, social sciences began to recognize the dynamic role of attitudinal diversity in social differences. The very generality and looseness of the concept of value admirably fitted this entry into an arena in which the narrower language of ethics had been avoided as "subjective." Values thus became part of the subject matter of scientific investigation, quite apart from the perennial issue of whether science itself made ethical assumptions. Anthropologists, because they had long been mapping cultural patterns and differences, led the way (*e.g.,* the Harvard Values Studies of Five Cultures), but value studies became widespread also in sociology, political science, SOCIAL PSYCHOLOGY, and education.

Other NEEDS and INTERESTS, both of understanding and of action, fed into the stream. The social sciences had become increasingly interested in whole-society features: for example, whether societies were cooperative or competitive or individualistic, repressive or tolerant, militaristic or peaceful. The startlingly rapid transformation of Germany under Nazism turned attention to causal conditions of democratic and authoritarian patterns as well as conditions generating value change. The importance of studying value transformations grew with the accelerated changes in all countries throughout the world. For a time, the need for clearer national policies prompted the development of "policy science" alongside the social sciences. In education, different schools of thought emerged regarding the cultivation of values in the young.

Methodologically, social scientists now employed the idea of value in two ways. Its simpler use was *descriptive.* The scientist sought to exhibit the value-attitudes of the group under study, as an effort to map its behavior more systematically. But fairly often, the term was reserved for a special *explanatory* or even *justificatory* role. To learn the values of a people would tell us why they behaved the way they did, and why they felt justified in behaving that way: for example, explain differences in national policies by differing *ideologies,* clusters embodying different value assumptions fused with factual beliefs. The values of a people thus gave rational form to their conduct and policies. The two uses of the concept, when distinguished and kept apart, raised no special theoretical difficulties. On the whole, then, the concept of value may be credited with helping social science overcome traditional contrasts of subjectivity and objectivity that had hindered the extension of scientific inquiry into social life; it also helped break down traditional field barriers. At the same time, however, it had become so extended and so commonplace that most of the general questions originally raised about value lost significance.

The rise of APPLIED ETHICS in the last third of the twentieth century has added to the same effect. Particular practical problems called for analysis in terms of specially relevant rather than general concepts and greater attention to contextual differences rather than broad unities. This leaves little prompting to work on a general theory of value as such. Generality is likely to be found, if at all, in the processes of comparison and the methodology of evaluation, as providing instruments for use in special contexts.

See also: AESTHETICS; BENTHAM; CULTURAL STUDIES; DARWIN; DEWEY; ECONOMIC ANALYSIS; EMOTIVISM; EXISTENTIALISM; GOOD, THEORIES OF THE; HARTMANN; INTRANSITIVITY; LEWIS; MULTICULTURALISM; NATURALISM; NATURALISTIC FALLACY; PERRY; PHENOMENOLOGY; PSYCHOLOGY; SARTRE; UTILITARIANISM; VALUE, CONCEPT OF; VOLUNTARISM.

Bibliography

Dewey, John. *Theory of Valuation.* Volume 13 in *John Dewey: The Later Works, 1925–1953.* Edited by Jo Ann Boydston. Carbondale: Southern Illinois University Press [1939]. Interpretation of value as appraisal.

Eaton, Howard O. *The Austrian Philosophy of Value.* Norman: University of Oklahoma Press, 1930. One of the founding schools of general value theory.

Edel, Abraham. *Exploring Fact and Value.* Science, Ideology, and Value II. New Brunswick, N.J.; London: Transaction Books, 1980. Various aspects of value and value-fact relations.

———. "The Concept of Value and Its Travels in Twentieth-Century America." In *Values and Value Theory in Twentieth-Century America: Essays in Honor of Elizabeth Flower,* edited by Ivar Berg and Murray G. Murphey. Philadelphia: Temple University Press, 1988. Traces growth of the value concept over the century in philosophy and social science.

Friedman, Bertha B. *Foundations of the Measurement of Values, the Methodology of Location and Quantification.* Teachers College, Columbia University, Contributions to Education, No. 914. New York: Bureau of Publications, Teachers College, Columbia University,

1946. Contains a rich comparative survey of definitions and theories.

Hall, Everett W. *What Is Value? An Essay in Philosophical Analysis.* London: Routledge and Kegan Paul, 1952. Goes from analysis of value to structural categories of the world.

Hartmann, Nicolai. *Ethics.* Translated by Stanton Coit. 3 vols. New York: Macmillan, 1932. Translated from the German original of 1926. The most comprehensive of the phenomenological treatments of value. Volume 2 is a detailed analysis of moral values.

Kluckhohn, Clyde, *et al.* "Values and Value Orientation in the Theory of Action." In *Toward a General Theory of Action,* edited by Talcott Parsons and Edward A. Shils. Cambridge, Mass.: Harvard University Press, 1951. The initial analysis of value in launching the Harvard Values Studies of values in five cultures, under direction of John M. Roberts, Clyde Kluckhohn, and Evon Z. Vogt. The many works issuing from these studies compared values in family, law, music, property, myth, physiological reaction, intercultural reaction, etc. The studies had a pioneering role in the contemporary social science investigation of values.

Kluckhohn, Florence Rockwood, and Fred I. Strodtbeck. *Variations in Value Orientations.* Evanston, Ill.: Row, Peterson, 1961. Contrasts in whole-cultural value attitudes.

Köhler, Wolfgang. *The Place of Value in a World of Facts.* New York: Liveright Publishing, 1938. Brings the methods of Gestalt psychology to analysis of value as a phenomenon.

Laird, John. *The Idea of Value.* Cambridge: Cambridge University Press, 1929. A study of the value concept and its emergence from the history of ethical theories.

Lepley, Ray. *Verifiability of Value.* New York: Columbia University Press, 1944. A sympathetic view of the thesis that value judgments are verifiable.

————, ed. *Value: A Cooperative Inquiry.* New York: Columbia University Press, 1949. Essays by many of the diverse writers on value theory of that period, characterized by wide disagreements.

————, ed. *The Language of Value.* New York: Columbia University Press, 1957. Linguistic analyses of value and their theoretical implications.

Lewis, C. I. *An Analysis of Knowledge and Valuation.* La Salle, Ill.: Open Court, 1946. A basic methodological treatise, channeling value and rightness along divergent paths, and defending the verifiability of value.

Münsterberg, Hugo. *The Eternal Values.* Boston; New York: Houghton Mifflin, 1909. A philosophical idealism finding values constitutive in our very conception of a world.

Parker, DeWitt H. *The Philosophy of Value.* Ann Arbor: University of Michigan Press, 1957. An expanded hedonism, enriched by aesthetic and Freudian concepts.

Pepper, Stephen C. *The Sources of Value.* Berkeley; Los Angeles: University of California Press, 1958. Theory of value based on a broadened psychological concept of purposive behavior.

Perry, Ralph Barton. *General Theory of Value: Its Meaning and Basic Principles Construed in Terms of Interest.* New York: Longmans, Green, 1926. The work that most definitively established a discipline of general value theory in the first half of the twentieth century.

Rescher, Nicholas. *Introduction to Value Theory.* Englewood Cliffs, N.J.: Prentice-Hall, 1969. Gives special attention to the logical aspects of preference, social choice, and decision. Excellent bibliography.

Taylor, Paul W. *Normative Discourse: A Modern Study in General Theory of Value Using the Technique and Approach of Contemporary Philosophical Analysis.* Englewood Cliffs, N.J.: Prentice-Hall, 1961. How ordinary language analysis turns general theory into paths of contextual detail.

Urban, Wilbur Marshall. *Valuation, Its Nature and Laws, Being an Introduction to the General Theory of Value.* New York: Macmillan, 1909. The foundational work in general value theory from an idealist perspective in early twentieth-century America.

Wright, G. H. von. *Norm and Action.* On logics of choice and action, obligation and preference.

Abraham Edel

vices

See virtues.

violence and non-violence

Definitions of 'violence' are controversial and fluid. In central uses of the term, people or governments act 'violently' when they intentionally or predictably damage others, inflicting upon them serious harm or injury whose effects are prolonged or irreparable. In central cases of violence, it is people who are damaged. However, it is also possible, and some believe equally serious, to act violently toward non-human animals and the natural world.

In central cases, violence is wrought upon bodies; murder, beating, and burning are clear instances. Harm to minds, psyches, or souls is apprehended as violent by analogy with physical injury and mutilation. While physical damage is paradigmatic of violence, it does not follow that psychological damage is of lesser consequence. Repeated humiliation can be as lastingly injurious as physical beating. In some clear and central instances of violence—for example, RAPE and TORTURE—physical and psychological damage are inseparable. The primacy of the physical is conceptual; to learn the concept of violence is to appreciate what it means to inflict physical damage on another, to violate and mutilate bodies.

Violence is typically inflicted by one person upon another without the other's CONSENT. But it is possible to inflict violence upon oneself—SUICIDE and protracted hunger strikes are clear examples—and possible to consent to violence upon oneself, for example, in chosen martyrdom. It is also possible to do violence to one person by violating another—for example, by forcing one person to watch another being tortured. Violence centrally involves actively injuring another; but neglect which is deliberately or predictably damaging is understood, by analogy, as violent. Although active injuring is conceptually primary, if judged in terms of actual damage and lasting harm, neglect may be as seriously violent as assault.

Violence is coercive, but not all COERCION is violent—that is, intentionally or predictably damaging. Forcefully wresting a knife from a child, pinning an attacker against the wall, or knocking a gun from an assailant's hand are coercive but non-violent acts. Typical "non-violent" strategies like boycotts and strikes are clearly meant to coerce. The fact that effective non-violent coercion frequently provokes retaliatory violent response does not render the original coercion violent, although it does suggest that it is often difficult to draw a sharp line between violence and non-violence.

Violence almost always involves pain, but the infliction of pain may not be violent. Ordinary medicine, for example, administering injections, provides uncontroversial examples of non-violent infliction of pain. Even deliberately inflicting damage may not be violent if the infliction is clearly intended to benefit its victim. Chemotherapy performed at an informed patient's request is an example of non-violent infliction of damage. However, the infliction of pain and, even more, of damage are presumptive of violence; hence, the inflictor should stand ready to spell out the benefits accruing to the afflicted person and the particular grounds of her or his consent.

The relation between violence and morality is complex. There are clear examples of undeniably violent practices in which people who consider themselves moral conscientiously participate—for example, war-making and CAPITAL PUNISHMENT. Many scientists have argued that human violence is deeply rooted in our animal past, that violence is nearly inevitable in human—or at least male-dominated—societies, and that attempts to live non-violently are psychologically costly, perhaps especially for men. Serious thinkers have celebrated the psychological benefits of acting violently to states, oppressed people, or men. Many morally "ordinary" people act violently toward others without apparent apology or remorse. Much racial violence and violence against women is seen by its perpetrators to be "natural" as well as morally permissible. Similarly, some parents, corporate executives, and imperialists, while they may defend violent practices on utilitarian or other moral grounds, also believe that they are *entitled* to violate children, workers, or weaker countries. These and other violent people may base their right to violence on property rights over the people (or animals, or nature) they violate or on "natural," divine, or social hierarchies that render them superior to the violated. Or they may claim that they are acting for state or corporate interests which needs no further justification.

Although many people act violently without moral qualms, violence—the deliberate or predictable harming, injuring, mutilating, or killing of others without compensatory benefit to *them*—is also often taken to be paradigmatic of EVIL. Violent actions seem emblematic of the human impulses and practices which morality is meant to defeat. At the least, violent acts are *prima facie* wrong.

Typically, people charged with violence will redescribe their act so that its "violent" character disappears. Someone who kills a terminally ill person in excruciating pain denies that her act, intended only to benefit its victim, can be called truly damaging or injurious. A pregnant woman explains that, in her metaphysical view, a fetus in the early months of development is not yet a person (and is not a living animal) and therefore is not yet an object of injury or damage.

In the most problematic cases, people simultaneously acknowledge the violence of their acts, appreciate the evil of violence, and continue to act violently. They must then account for and justify apparently immoral actions. Justifications for violence often take a utilitarian form. For example, a government, while lamenting the need to use armed force against its people, predictably injuring some of them, defends its actions in terms of the need for order and the goods which disorder makes impossible. Similarly, most civil societies maintain armed police despite the likelihood of excessive and accidental as well as defensive police violence, persuaded both of the virtues of order and of ineradicable human criminality, greed, and aggression. Proponents of capital punishment and other forms of retributive violence argue that only violent retaliation fits certain seriously violent crimes. Many people who deplore violence claim that, in certain circumstances, only determined, deliberate violent action can prevent worse violence from occurring. Wars are standardly defended in this manner, and just war theorists provide a model for sustained and serious reflection on violence by its supporters. Many participants in revolutionary violence defend their actions by underlining the violence inflicted by the tyrannical, exploitative, or racist governments they combat.

Many people who defend violence nonetheless agree that violence is both *prima facie* wrong and emblematic of evil. Accordingly, they claim that they resort to violence only as a last and desperate resort after non-violent struggle has failed. They would agree that a person, collective, or state that aims to act morally will also aim to act non-violently and should work to establish the social and political conditions in which non-violence is possible. This would require, at the least, assessing actions, strategies, and policies in terms of their potential violence and selecting, in the light of other moral goods, the least violent among them. In this minimal sense, 'non-violence' is intrinsic to morality.

More strictly, the term 'non-violence' is commonly used to refer to coercive but noninjurious, nondamaging ways of fighting—of protecting the vulnerable, maintaining civil order, rescuing the assaulted, redressing injustices, and resisting tyranny. The two best-known creators of the theory and practice of non-violent action are Mohandas K. GANDHI (1869–1948) and Martin Luther KING, Jr. (1929–1968). In recent decades, many ethicists have attempted to identify characteristics of 'non-violent' societies and relationships which shape, but are not limited by, experiences of battle and conflict. To take only one example, the "ethic of care" delineated by Carol Gilligan is said to rest on the premise of non-violence. Although definitions and theories of non-violence are very much in process, in the writings of non-violent activists and theorists of non-violence, at least five central conceptions tend to recur.

First, and most notably, the relationship between self and other is radically revised. In opposition both to Hegelian and Sartrian conceptions of an essential competitive relationship between self and other, and to psychological conceptions of a mature self as independent and separate from others, non-violent relationships presuppose selves defined by interdependent, mutually enhancing relationships to others. More controversially, in non-violent battle, an 'enemy' becomes an opponent who can change. The Christian injunction to "love" one's enemies is variously interpreted, but it precludes humiliating, mutilating, or killing an opponent.

A second conception, equally central to articulations of non-violence, is a critique of the distinction between means and ends. Ends are variously described in terms, for example, of Truth (Gandhi), reconciliation in a "beloved community" (King), or "maintaining connection" (Gilligan). Invariably, the daily processes of relationship and the means of struggle are taken to express and to define, incrementally, the end. The way one fights—or lives—not only represents the goal but instantiates its current realization.

Third, while insisting that evil be named and acknowledged, many non-violent activists urge FORGIVENESS and reconciliation. In King's words, "Forgiveness does not mean ignoring what has been done or putting a false label on an evil act. It means rather that the evil act is no longer a barrier to the relationship." Forgiveness is necessary to the (re)constitution of a beloved and just community. It is also an expression—and therefore contributes to the definition—of "love" for an enemy.

Fourth, many theorists of non-violence agree with PLATO (c. 430–347 B.C.E.) that it is better to suffer than to commit an injustice. For Gandhi and King, "self-suffering" (Hindi: *tapasya*) becomes a principle of non-violence. A self-sufferer assumes, insofar as possible, all the pain of battle. Willingness to suffer is considered a prerequisite of endurance and a testament to seriousness and COURAGE. It is also a weapon that induces shame and guilt in a conscientious opponent and SYMPATHY in bystanders. There is much ambivalence among non-violent thinkers about self-destructive acts—for example, "fasting to the death"—and about manipulation by shame and guilt. Gilligan, in contrast to the emphasis on *self*-suffering, speaks of including oneself in the circle of CARE. For her, the injunction that "*no-one* should be hurt" is the "premise of nonviolence."

Finally, many writers from various traditions take as essential to non-violence responsive, uncoerced speech that maintains connectedness without denying difference or preventing nonviolent dispute. "Conversation," "dialogue," or "voice" are opposed to "exit"—breaking connection—and to both force and silence. In non-violent struggle, responsive communication involves a commitment to truthfulness and openness except in urgent situations where dissemblance is necessary (falsifying documents, for example). Non-violent activists are almost always ready to talk with enemies or strangers, avoiding only those meetings which will be used by clearly violent leaders to serve their ends.

Theorists of non-violence contest the view that violence is "naturally" human while non-violence is an extraordinary moral feat. They cite ethological and anthropological evidence that, among humans and many other animals, cooperative caring activities are more prevalent than hitherto believed. Even violent societies contain non-violent practices and individuals; some societies, despite instances of violence, are pervasively non-violent. Most theorists of non-violence believe that both violence and non-violence are "natural" to men and women, and that both emerge from and vary with identifiable social conditions. It is therefore possible to identify and create political, economic, educational, and sexual arrangements that promote non-violent relationships and societies.

See also: ABORTION; ANIMALS, TREATMENT OF; ARENDT; BLACKMAIL; CAPITAL PUNISHMENT; CARE; CIVIL DISOBEDIENCE; COERCION; COMPETITION; CONSENT; CORRECTIONAL ETHICS; DETERRENCE, THREATS, AND RETALIATION; EUTHANASIA; EVIL; EXPLOITATION; FORGIVENESS; GANDHI; GUILT AND SHAME; HARM AND OFFENSE; HOLOCAUST; HOMICIDE; INFANTICIDE; KILLING/LETTING DIE; KING; NATURE AND ETHICS; OPPRESSION; PACIFISM; PAIN AND SUFFERING; POLICE ETHICS; PUNISHMENT; RACISM AND RELATED ISSUES; RAPE; REVENGE; REVOLUTION; SELF-DEFENSE; SEXUAL ABUSE AND HARASSMENT; SUICIDE; TERRORISM; THOREAU; TORTURE; WAR AND PEACE.

Bibliography

Arendt, Hannah. *On Violence.* New York: Harcourt Brace, 1969.

Bok, Sissela. *Toward a Strategy for Peace.* New York: Pantheon, 1989.

Bondurant, Joan. *Conquest of Violence: The Gandhian Philosophy of Conflict.* Berkeley: University of California Press, 1971.

Camus, Albert. *Neither Victims Nor Executioners.* New York: Continuum, 1980 [1946].

Cotta, Sergio. *Why Violence: A Philosophical Interpretation.* Gainesville: University of Florida Press, 1985.

Deming, Barbara. *We Are All Part of One Another.* Philadelphia: New Society, 1984. For a clear, secular statement of the principles of nonviolence, see especially "Revolution and Equilibrium."

Gandhi, Mohandas. *Non-Violent Resistance.* New York: Schocken, 1961. Collection of articles.

———. *Satyagraha in South Africa.* Ahmedabad: Navajivan, 1928.

Gilligan, Carol. *In a Different Voice.* Cambridge, MA: Harvard University Press, 1982.

Gilligan, Carol, Jill McClean Taylor, and Janie Victoria Ward. *Mapping the Moral Domain.* Cambridge, MA: Harvard University Press, 1989.

Habermas, Jürgen. *Communication and the Evolution of Society.* Boston: Beacon Press, 1979.

———. *Theory of Communicative Action.* 2 vols. Boston: Beacon Press, 1986–1988.

Harris, Adrienne, and Ynestra King, eds. *Rocking the Ship of State: Toward a Feminist Peace Politics.* Boulder, CO: Westview Press, 1989.

Holmes, Robert L. *On War and Morality.* Princeton, NJ: Princeton University Press, 1989. Excellent review of attempts to define violence; bibliography.

Kaunda, Kenneth. *The Riddle of Violence.* New York: Harper and Row, 1980.

King, Martin Luther, Jr. *A Testament of Hope: The Essential Writings of Martin Luther King Jr.* Edited by James Melvin Washington. New York: Harper and Row, 1986. The quotation from King is from "Loving Your Enemies," a sermon delivered Christmas, 1957, in Montgomery, Alabama.

Lorenz, Konrad. *On Aggression.* New York: Harcourt Brace, 1966 [1963].

Morgan, Robin. *Demon Lover.* New York: Norton, 1989.

Ruddick, Sara. Maternal Thinking: Toward a Politics of Peace. Boston: Beacon Press, 1989.

Scarry, Elaine. *The Body in Pain.* Oxford: Oxford University Press, 1975. See chapter 2, "The Structure of War."

Shaffer, Jerome, ed. *Violence.* New York: David McKay, 1971.

Tanner, Nancy MakePeace. *On Becoming Human.* Cambridge: Cambridge University Press, 1981.

Tiger, Lionel. *Men in Groups.* New York: Random House, 1969.

Waal, Frans de. *Peacemaking Among Primates.* Cambridge, MA: Harvard University Press, 1989.

Walker, Alice. *Meridian.* New York: Washington Square Press, 1976.

Weil, Simone. *Iliad, or The Poem of Force.* Wallingford, PA: Pendle Hill, 1956.

Sara Ruddick

virtue ethics

The recent use of 'virtue ethics' to distinguish one standpoint within ethics from others would have been unintelligible in Greek philosophy, for which, since a virtue was an EXCELLENCE (*arete*) and ethics concerned excellences of CHARACTER, all ethics was virtue ethics. Contemporary virtue ethics is in part a revival of some Greek preoccupations, transformed by the need to address the problems of modern moral philosophy.

SOCRATES (c. 470–399 B.C.E.), in the course of exposing Athenian incoherences about such virtues as COURAGE and piety, posed the four core questions of Greek virtue ethics: What makes a particular human quality a virtue? How is the knowledge of what the VIRTUES are related to the possession of the virtues? Are the several virtues aspects of a single virtue or are they otherwise connected? And how are the virtues exercised in achieving the specifically human good or goods? PLATO (c. 430–347 B.C.E.) and ARISTOTLE (384–322 B.C.E.), in extending Socrates' enquiries, established the necessary psychological, political, and metaphysical dimensions of any adequate theory of the virtues. So in the *Republic,* in pursuing answers to these Socratic questions, Plato identified temperateness as the specific excellence of the appetitive part of the *psyche,* courage and WISDOM as the excellences of the spirited and rational parts, and justice as the excellence of a right ordering of the parts within a *psyche* in which reason rules. Each virtue is also the excellence of a function discharged in a well-ordered *polis* by the appropriate group of citizens. The knowledge both of what each virtue is and of how each exemplifies the single form of virtue, that knowledge which constitutes possession of the virtues by those in whom reason rules, is a knowledge of timeless forms in the light afforded by the Form of the Good, that supreme good toward which every human life informed by the virtues moves in a rational progress.

That the virtues are both partly constitutive of the supreme human good and to be possessed, not only for their own sake as genuine excellences, but also for the sake of that good, is a thesis inherited by Aristotle. But his different conception of forms and his constructive critique of Plato's psychology and politics entailed a correspondingly different account of that good and of the virtues, one which both provided distinctive answers to the Socratic questions and, unlike Plato's, defended an emended and rationally justifiable version of contemporary educated Athenian beliefs about the virtues. Aristotle's thesis has four central features.

First, virtues are dispositions not only to act, but also to judge and to feel in accordance with the dictates of right reason, and the practice of the virtues is required for the life of EUDAIMONIA, the achievement of which is the human *telos.* To have the virtues is to function well as a human being.

Secondly, the virtues fall into two classes: the intellectual virtues, those excellences informing the activities specific to reason, to be acquired only through education, and the moral virtues, the excellences of the nonrational parts of the soul when these are obedient to reason, to be acquired only through habituation and training. But right action arising from moral virtue also requires the virtue of intelligent judgment, and intelligent judgment in turn requires moral virtue. Thus, PHRONESIS, or practical intelligence, is a key virtue that unifies the intellectual and the moral. Examples of intellectual virtues include not only *phronesis,* but also deliberative excellence and contemplative wisdom. Examples of moral virtues include courage, temperateness, liberality, magnanimity, and justice. To act from a moral virtue is to act in accordance with a mean between some excess and some defect, so that to fail in virtue is always to exhibit a vice of either excess or defect. Thus, for example, the vices of cowardice, which involves too much fear and too little confidence, and of rashness, which involves too little fear and overconfidence, are both failures to observe that mean which is courage.

Thirdly, since *phronesis* issues in right action of every kind, to possess it one must also possess all the moral virtues, for these direct us to the right ends, while *phronesis* selects the right means. So in their relations to *phronesis,* the virtues are a unity. *Phronesis* aims at the supreme human good, and dialectical arguments inform us what that good is and how the virtues relate to it. These are what the sciences of politics and of ethics supply, and we study ethics and politics in order to become good. But no such knowledge is able to instruct us as to what action is right to perform in the circumstances of particular situations; only *phronesis* so instructs us, and *phronesis* has no standard external to itself. So the *phronimos* is the standard of right action. To act rightly is to do what a good person would do in these particular circumstances.

The legislator who makes the laws for a particular *polis* must therefore possess *phronesis*. And so must the judge who applies and extends such laws in new and unforeseen types of situation. But in possessing the moral virtues, he will recognize that, just as it is always wrong to act contrary to the virtues, so certain types of action (for example, murder, theft, and adultery) are always bad, independently of circumstance. Aristotle said nothing about how precisely the knowledge of the universal wrongness of these types of action is related to the possession of *phronesis*. This silence concerns what was to become a central problem area for later virtue ethics.

Fourthly, it is only within the *polis* that the life of *eudaimonia* can be lived out, and thus it is in and through the life of the *polis* that the virtues are exercised. Moreover, apart from the education afforded by the *polis,* especially by the better kind of *polis,* human beings are incapable of the rationality required for virtue. Thus, some human beings are incapable by nature, among them both barbarians and women. Here again Aristotle has to be put in question.

Stoic thinkers, inheriting the Socratic questions through the CYNICS and rejecting Aristotelian teleology, developed rival theses in both these areas. The virtuous person came to be reconceived as a citizen of the cosmos, not of the *polis;* and the rules, conformity to which constitutes the life of virtue, are universal standards, prescribed by nature and by reason. To be wise is to understand oneself rightly as part of nature and to have a consistent character, guided only by reason, not by irrational PASSION. Virtue is single. The names of the virtues distinguish different types of situation in which one and the same virtue is required. Virtue is to be pursued only for its own sake, and each person is either wholly or not at all virtuous. Different Stoic thinkers formulated these positions in different ways, agreeing in a conception of the life of virtue which made it independent of social forms and INSTITUTIONS and making it possible for CICERO (106–43 B.C.E.), pupil of the Stoic Posidonius (135?–51 B.C.E.), to use STOICISM in framing an eclectic account of the virtues,

one which claimed both universality and the sanction of traditional Roman attitudes.

The Latin *'virtus'* had originally named the quality of a *vir,* 'manliness.' This etymological difference from *'arete'* developed into a catalogue of the virtues unlike Greek philosophical catalogues in, for example, the importance attached to *fides* as well as to courage and in its lack of respect for moral theorizing. Yet Cicero in *De officiis* amended a Stoic framework within which he retold traditional Roman moral anecdotes to exemplify virtues and duties characterized in Stoic and sometimes in Platonic terms. When, from the Renaissance onward, Cicero's moral teachings again became influential, his Stoic discussion of the nature and limits of *beneficiis* provided classical authority for treating generalized BENEVOLENCE as a central virtue, albeit one unknown to older Roman or to Aristotelian or Platonic ethics. But by then the question of how to judge between the apparently competing claims of very different catalogues of the virtues had been even more sharply raised by Judaism, Christianity, and ISLAM.

The virtues enjoined by the God of the Hebrew scriptures, and by all three theisms, included HUMILITY, patience, peacemaking, and CHARITY, virtues either unknown in or less important to the classical world. The problems of whether or how to integrate theistic doctrines of the virtues with Platonic, Aristotelian, or Stoic accounts were accompanied by that of how to reconcile an ethics of virtues with one of divine law, one binding human beings universally. Rival types of medieval attempt to solve these problems ranged between two extremes: at one, the rejection of the philosophical accounts in order to preserve theological doctrine from distortion or contamination; at the other, the construction of large, synthetic, generally Aristotelian frameworks in and through which a comprehensive classification of the virtues and a systematic statement of the relationship between obedience to the precepts of divine law and possession of the virtues were attempted. In the greatest of these Aristotelian syntheses, that of THOMAS AQUINAS (1225?–1274), even some of the rejections were incorporated; and conclusions about the virtues were presented as definitive insofar as they were supported by those constructive arguments which had hitherto withstood the strongest objections available from any source.

The political dimension of Aquinas's standpoint

is his insistence both that, within every human society and for every human being, a real possibility of acquiring the virtues exists and that, within every society, positive law requires our obedience just insofar as it accords with God's law as apprehended by reason, the NATURAL LAW. His psychology adds to an Aristotelian account of reason, passions, and appetites a version of AUGUSTINE's (354–430) conception of the will. Augustine had contended that only a will informed by charity, a gift of grace, can issue in genuinely virtuous action. Without charity, apparently just, courageous, or temperate acts are not virtuous, but give expression to the sinful PRIDE of the will. The apparent virtues of the pagan Romans were thus not real. For 'charity' names what is virtuous in every virtue. So the unity of the virtues was once more asserted, although in a new way. Aquinas combined Augustinian, Platonic, and Aristotelian theses in characterizing the virtues. A psychology of reason, will, passions, and appetites provided a revised understanding of Plato's four central virtues, temperateness being the virtue of the concupiscible part of the soul, courage of the irascible, and justice of the will, when each is rationally conformed to the mean. The virtue specific to reason is Aristotle's 'phronesis,' translated by 'prudentia.' Revealed divine law provides independent authority on how to act. But the primary, universal, unvarying precepts of the natural law are discoverable by every rational person, brought to bear upon detailed questions of practice through the exercise of prudentia and the other cardinal virtues. The whole range of virtues recognized by Aristotle is also recognized by Aquinas, but his account of them sometimes differs, and the other Aristotelian moral virtues are characterized as aspects or parts of temperateness, courage, and justice. Each of these latter for its adequate exercise requires the others and also prudentia. Thus, no one can have any of the cardinal virtues adequately without having all of them. This Aristotelian conception of the unity of the virtues is reinforced by Augustine's, since the four virtues are held by themselves to be insufficient for the perfect obedience required by divine law. They need to be informed and supplemented by the grace-given theological virtues of charity, faith, and HOPE. So informed, the virtues are those dispositions by the exercise of which humans attain their ultimate end, not the imperfect HAPPINESS of this life, but perfected happiness in eternal friendship with God.

Aquinas drew heavily upon Ibn Sina (AVICENNA, 980–1037), IBN RUSHD (Averroës, 1126–1198), and other contributors to the Islamic debates about the relationship of sharia, Islamic law, to Platonic and Aristotelian theses. He also drew upon the discussion by MAIMONIDES (1135–1204) of how the understanding of Torah similarly relates, as well as on various disparate strands of earlier Christian thinking. But it is important to emphasize that Aquinas is atypical in both the scale and method of his synthetic project. Generally, the medieval debates present a series of shifting, often eclectic attitudes both to the original Socratic questions and to the problems which developed out of attempts to answer them. Before Aquinas, ABELARD (1079–1142) conjoined elements of Cicero's revised Stoicism with an Augustinian view of charity and a partially Aristotelian conception of a virtue to devise a view of virtuous action of which right INTENTION is the crucial constituent. After Aquinas, Buridan (1300–1358) offered another rival mode of partial synthesis when he combined Aristotelian, Stoic, and Augustinian elements. The failure even in the Middle Ages to accept Aquinas's systematic view left all the major questions concerning the virtues open to further debate, debate increasingly informed by the Renaissance rejection of Aristotle's teleology. And secular discussion separated itself from the theology.

At the eighteenth-century beginnings of modern moral philosophy, therefore, the questions of virtue ethics seemed ready to be reopened, in a new intellectual context. MACHIAVELLI (1469–1527) had suggested, contrary to Cicero's moral teaching, that the successful aspirant to princely power needs to learn when *not* to be virtuous, that is, to be prepared to use violence and DECEIT, exemplifying in so doing that courageous, assertive energy which constitutes virtú. MANDEVILLE (1670–1733) had argued that such vices of individuals as ENVY and vanity promote profitable trade and that deceitfulness is of great commercial utility, while virtue confers no similar public benefit. HOBBES (1588–1679) and LOCKE (1632–1704) had argued that self-interest requires adherence to morality, not its flouting. Thus, the problem of the place of self-interest in the moral life had been posed in a new way. Any compelling account of the virtues had to supply an answer to the questions of why any reasonable human being should obey those rules which prescribe impartial or generous treatment to others and treat as virtues those qualities which issue in just or generous actions. Moreover, the eighteenth-century Enlightenment view demanded that MORAL RULES and virtues must be grounded in invariant human nature rather than in the particularities of local custom or tradition; thus, rules and virtues must be the same for all human beings. In establishing what these rules and virtues are and why they are owed allegiance, the relationship of rules prescribing duties and obligations to virtues is a central question.

In the eighteenth and nineteenth centuries, four rival answers were given to this question. HUME (1711–1776) treated a primary set of virtues, the natural virtues, as both prior to and the basis of rules enjoining just and obligatory actions. KANT (1724–1804) treated virtues as secondary, as dispositions supportive of those precepts enjoining upon the will unconditional duties which rational persons prescribe to themselves as the dictates of PRACTICAL REASON. SIDGWICK (1838–1900), in an unsuccessful eclectic attempt at synthesis, understood the virtues as personal qualities which are manifested both in the performance of acts required by duty and of good acts beyond what duty requires. And NIETZSCHE (1844–1900) asserted that both virtues and rules, as understood from Socrates and Plato to Kant and JOHN STUART MILL (1806–1873), were devices of a slavish herd morality, now to be rejected and transcended.

Hume's is the only modern account of the virtues comparable in scope and philosophical development to those of Aristotle and Aquinas. HUTCHESON (1694–1746) had treated the virtues as natural affections. Adding benevolence as a central virtue to his catalogue of virtues drawn partly from ancient authors, he meant by 'prudentia' not 'phronesis,' but the habit of considering in advance what is and is not advantageous, a habit which helps to guide the other affections. Hume followed Hutcheson in making reason the servant of the passions, a deviser of means to the ends proposed by the passions, and in defining the virtues in terms of the passions. In his account of the natural virtues, Hume equated "with regard to our mental qualities, *virtue* and the power of producing love or pride, *vice* and the power of producing humility or hatred" (*Treatise III,* iii, 1 [1737]).

The natural virtues include benevolence, courage, INTEGRITY, greatness of mind, various "natural abilities" (*e.g.,* PRUDENCE, patience, and TEMPERANCE),

eloquence, good humor, and cleanliness. These virtues are qualities which elicit from us, by reason of the constitution of our human nature, immediate approval on each occasion on which we encounter them. This is not the case with the virtue of justice, a virtue which not only often requires acts contrary to the interest of particular individuals, who nonetheless recognize them as just, but also acts contrary to the public interest. The benefits conferred by justice derive from the systematic operation of rules contrived by artifice. The sentiment which is annexed to the approbation of that system, a sentiment in whose formation sympathy plays a key part, constitutes justice as an artificial virtue. Promising, from which all contractual obligations arise, is another artifice, and so is government, contrived to uphold justice as well as to protect from external threats. The LOYALTY which is due to government is similarly artificial. Underlying Hume's account is a PSYCHOLOGY, ascribed to all normal human beings, in which both an initial sympathy for others and the reinforcement of that sympathy by the PLEASURE which each of us takes in our reciprocated affections, make LOVE and pride function as they do. There is thus a universal agreement of human beings in fundamental judgments about the virtues, one reinforced by the use of rules to correct the partiality of the passions, although often disguised by variations in social custom and circumstance.

Kant, by contrast, took the passions to provide no basis for moral agreement, but recognized that there are antecedent dispositions to morality among the feelings. These can serve morality only insofar as they are organized in the service of a rationally directed will. Perfection in virtue, in the singular, is the end of every such rational will. "To think of a number of virtues (as we inevitably do) is only to think of the different moral objects to which the one principle of virtue directs the will" (XIII, Introduction to Part II, *Metaphysic of Morals* [1785]). Virtue requires control over the passions and self-mastery; no measure of passion issues in a genuinely virtuous action. Kant thereby rejected the Aristotelian doctrines of the mean and of *eudaimonia* as well as Hume's account. The conflicts between Kantian, Humean, and Aristotelian (including Thomistic) accounts of virtue define the central debates of contemporary virtue ethics, but only when the conflict between Nietzsche's and all three earlier positions is added to them.

In *Also sprach Zarathustra* (1883–1885), Nietzsche denounced all attempts to connect virtue with happiness or with reward and PUNISHMENT. Such attempts have produced those "small virtues" which diminish human beings. The only virtue to be prized is that of those who will greatly, whose self is asserted in their actions, and whose virtue expresses that self in its overcoming, so rejecting that diminishing and corrupting unselfishness and lack of SELF-KNOWLEDGE expressed in the virtues as understood by all those who have followed Socrates.

Recent work in virtue ethics has mostly been either by Thomistic writers, indebted to Jacques Maritain (1882–1973) or Yves Simon, or from within the analytic school, although designed to overcome the limitations of previous analytic ethics. Philippa FOOT has drawn upon Aristotle and Aquinas in defining the central problems of any adequate contemporary virtue ethics, more especially those concerning both the relationship of virtues to benefits, harms, and happiness and the unity of the virtues. G. H. von Wright and Myles Burnyeat have shown that what it is to possess some particular virtue cannot be understood solely in terms of any antecedent characterization of types of virtuous act by means of rules or maxims, thus raising the question of the relationship of rules to virtues within morality. Philosophers have taken very different views on this, whether they are concerned with the virtues in general or with the detailed study of particular virtues.

James D. Wallace has integrated rules and virtues, using a partially Aristotelian conception of human function and excellence to argue that the different virtues function, each in its own specific way, to sustain the convention-informed, rule-following modes of social life from which human activity derives its central features. Annette Baier has developed a contemporary version of Hume's doctrine of the virtues, emphasizing how Hume uses empirically informed accounts of human passions, virtues, and institutions to relate nature to artifice, so that rules find a subordinate place within a virtue ethics.

Thus, Aristotle, Aquinas, and Hume all reappear in contemporary guise; and so do Kant and Nietzsche. Kurt BAIER has followed Kant in concluding that what morality requires is a good will, expressed in obedience to rules which specify what types of action it is rational to require of everyone. Virtues have at best a secondary place in morality, amplifying and supporting moral rules. Harold Alderman, by contrast, has developed Nietzschean themes in arguing that how one ought to act should be decided neither by applying some universal rule nor by identifying some final good, but by imagining what some ideal individual would do and acting accordingly, thus making those virtues one's own.

Contemporary theological writers have also disagreed about the virtues in ways which revive and transform doctrines from the past history of virtue ethics. Thus, Stanley Hauerwas has reformulated Thomistic theses within a Protestant theological framework. Both he and Gilbert Meilaender have enquired what a specifically Christian view of the virtues requires—what, on a Christian view, the place of the nontheological virtues in public life ought to be and what the relationship between these is. But if recent theological writing has contributed to philosophical virtue ethics, it has also shared in its two major limitations.

The first of these arises from an acceptance of the compartmentalizations of contemporary academic philosophy, whereby theses about the virtues are debated within moral philosophy in a way which detaches them from the theoretical contexts in which they were originally at home. So Aristotelian and Thomistic theses about the virtues are integral parts of complex, unified bodies of political, psychological, and metaphysical theory. They stand or fall, for the most part, as parts of those wholes. And Hume's naturalistic epistemology and psychology provided a similar theoretical context, detached from which his account of the virtues becomes something quite different and much inferior.

A second limitation is the lack of recognition accorded to conceptions of the virtues in other than Western cultures. A. S. Cua and David Wong have recently noted differences and similarities between ancient Greek and ancient Chinese virtue ethics, but adequate importance still has to be accorded to the study not only of what the philosophy and practice of CHINA have contributed to virtue ethics, but also to the philosophy and practice of JAPAN, INDIA, AFRICA, and elsewhere.

See also: ANSCOMBE; ARISTOTELIAN ETHICS; AVICENNA; BENEFICENCE; BENEVOLENCE; BUDDHIST ETHICS; CHARACTER; CHARITY; CHRISTIAN ETHICS; CIVIC GOOD AND VIRTUE; CONFUCIAN ETHICS; COURAGE; DEONTOLOGY; DUTY AND OBLIGATION; *EUDAIMONIA*, -ISM; EXCELLENCE; FAIRNESS; FIDELITY; FINAL GOOD;

FOOT; FRANKENA; FRIENDSHIP; GENEROSITY; GOOD, THEORIES OF THE; HAPPINESS; HOPE; HUMILITY; IBN RUSHD; ISLAMIC ETHICS; JEWISH ETHICS; JUSTICE (various entries); LOVE; LOYALTY; MACINTYRE; MORAL REASONING; MORAL SAINTS; NATURAL LAW; PAUL; PHRONESIS; PRACTICAL REASON[ING]; PRIDE; PRUDENCE; SELF-CONTROL; SELF-KNOWLEDGE; STOICISM; SYMPATHY; TAOIST ETHICS; TEMPERANCE; THEOLOGICAL ETHICS; VIRTUES; WISDOM.

Bibliography

Abelard, Peter. *Peter Abelard's "Ethics."* Translated by D. E. Luscombe. Oxford: Oxford University Press, 1971.

Alderman, Harold. *Nietzsche's Gift.* Athens: Ohio University Press, 1977.

Aristotle. See especially *Nicomachean Ethics; Eudemian Ethics; Politics.*

Augustine, Saint. See *De doctrina christiana; De trinitate; De civitate Dei* (413–426)—especially Book 5.

Averroës (Ibn Rushd). *On Plato's Republic.* Translated by R. Lerner. Ithaca, N.Y.: Cornell University Press, 1974 [1st pub. ed. 1474].

Baier, Annette. *Postures of the Mind.* Minneapolis: University of Minnesota Press, 1985.

Burnyeat, Myles. "Virtues in Action." In *The Philosophy of Socrates,* edited by Gregory B. Vlastos. Garden City, N.Y.: Doubleday, 1971.

Cicero. See *De finibus bonorum et malorum; Tusculan Disputations; De officiis; De re publica; De legibus.*

Confucius. *The Analects (Lun Yü).* Translated by D.C. Lau. New York: Viking Penguin, 1979.

Cua, Antonio S. "Reflections on Moral Theory and Understanding Moral Traditions." In *Interpreting Across Boundaries,* edited by G. J. Larson and E. Deutsch. Princeton, N.J.: Princeton University Press, 1988.

Foot, Philippa. *Virtues and Vices.* Berkeley: University of California Press, 1978.

French, Peter A., T. E. Uehling, and H. K. Wettstein, eds. *Ethical Theory: Character and Virtue.* Midwest Studies in Philosophy, vol. 13. Notre Dame, Ind.: University of Notre Dame Press, 1988. Articles by twenty-nine philosophers; with the Kruschwitz anthology, a good introduction to contemporary discussions; excellent bibliography. See especially "Radical Virtue Ethics" by Kurt Baier.

Geach, Peter T. *The Virtues.* Cambridge: Cambridge University Press, 1977.

Hauerwas, Stanley. *A Community of Character.* Notre Dame, Ind.: University of Notre Dame Press, 1981.

Hoff Sommers, Christina, ed. *Vice and Virtue in Everyday Life: Introductory Readings in Ethics.* New York: Harcourt Brace Jovanovich, 1985.

Hume, David. *A Treatise of Human Nature.* 1739–1740. Especially books 2 and 3.

———. *An Enquiry Concerning the Principles of Morals.* 1751.

Hutcheson, Francis. *An Inquiry into the Original of Our Ideas of Beauty and Virtue.* 1725.

———. *Philosophiae moralis institutio compendaria.* 1742.

Kant, Immanuel. *Foundations of the Metaphysic of Morals.* 1785.

———. *Metaphysic of Morals.* 1797.

Kruschwitz, Robert B., and Robert C. Roberts, eds. *The Virtues: Contemporary Essays in Moral Character.* Belmont, Cal.: Wadsworth, 1987. 17 essays by philosophers. See especially "By Virtue of a Virtue" by Harold Alderman.

Leaman, Oliver. *Medieval Islamic Philosophy.* Cambridge: Cambridge University Press, 1985. Useful bibliography.

Long, A. A., and D. N. Sedley, eds. *The Hellenistic Philosophers.* 2 vols. Cambridge: Cambridge University Press, 1987. Texts, translations of, commentary on principal sources for Epicurean and Stoic writings. See especially chapters 20–25, 56–67.

Machiavelli, Niccolò. *The Prince.* 1513.

———. *The Discourses on the First Ten Books of Titus Livius.* 1519.

MacIntyre, Alasdair. *After Virtue.* 2d ed. Notre Dame, Ind.: University of Notre Dame Press, 1984.

———. *Whose Justice? Which Rationality?* Notre Dame, Ind.: University of Notre Dame Press, 1988.

Maimonides, Moses. *Ethical Writings.* Edited by R. L. Weiss, with C. Butterworth. New York: Dover, 1974.

———. *The Guide for the Perplexed.* [1200?]

Mandeville, Bernard. *The Fable of the Bees or Private Vices Made Public Benefits.* 6th ed. 1729 [1705].

Maritain, Jacques. *Neufs leçons sur les notions premières de la philosophie morale.* Paris: P. Tequi, 1951.

———. *La philosophie morale: Examen historique et critique des grandes systèmes.* Paris: Gallimard, 1960.

Markus, R. A. "Augustine—Human Action: Will and Virtue." Chapter 25 in *The Cambridge History of Later Greek and Early Medieval Philosophy.* Cambridge: Cambridge University Press, 1967.

Meilaender, Gilbert. *The Theory and Practice of Virtue.* Notre Dame, Ind.: University of Notre Dame Press, 1984.

Nietzsche, Friedrich. See *The Gay Science* (1882); *Thus Spake Zarathustra* (1883–1885); *Beyond Good and Evil* (1886); *On the Genealogy of Morals* (1887); *Twilight of the Idols* (1888).

Pincoffs, Edmund L. *Quandaries and Virtues.* Lawrence: University of Kansas Press, 1986.

Plato. See his *Charmides, Euthyphro, Laches, Protagoras, Phaedrus, Gorgias, Meno, Republic, Laws.*

Simon, Yves. *The Definition of Moral Virtue.* Edited by Vukan Kuic. New York: Fordham University Press, 1986.

Slote, Michael. *Goods and Virtues.* Oxford: Oxford University Press, 1990.

Thomas Aquinas. See *Summa theologiae* (1266–1273), especially Ia–Iae q. 55–89 and IIa–IIae, especially q. 1–170; *Quaestiones disputatae de virtutibus* (1256–1259); *Commentaries on the Ethics, the Politics* (1266–1272).

Trianosky, Gregory. "What Is Virtue Ethics All About? Recent Work on the Virtues." *American Philosophical Quarterly* 27, 4 (1990): 335–44.

Wallace, James. *Virtues and Vices.* Ithaca, N.Y.: Cornell University Press, 1978.

Walsh, James J. "Buridan on the Connection of the Virtues." *Journal of the History of Philosophy* 24, no. 4 (1986): 453–82.

Walton, Douglas. *Courage: A Philosophical Investigation.* Berkeley: University of California Press, 1986.

Wong, David. *Moral Relativity.* Berkeley: University of California Press, 1986.

———. "Universalism Versus Love with Distinctions: An Ancient Debate Revived." *Journal of Chinese Philosophy* 16, 4 (1989): 252–72.

Wright, G. H. von. *The Varieties of Goodness.* London: Routledge and Kegan Paul, 1964.

Yearley, Lee. *Mencius and Aquinas: Theories of Virtue and Conceptions of Courage.* Albany: State University of New York Press, 1990.

———. "Recent Work on Virtue." *Religious Studies Review* 16, no. 1 (1990): 1–9. Includes bibliography, especially of recent theological writing.

Alasdair MacIntyre

virtues

What kind of thing is to be counted as a virtue? While much of the discussion of the virtues applies by parity of reasoning to the vices, we will not here directly take up the problem what is to count as a vice.

Writers who attempt to define virtue and vice tiptoe through a minefield of philosophical difficulties. While it is noncontroversial that WISDOM, justice, TEMPERANCE, and COURAGE—and the many other generally recognized virtues—are desirable qualities of persons, and it is generally accepted that they are dispositions of some kind, agreement thereafter must be hard-earned. In what follows, we will recognize some of the more prominent moves that have been made in the definitional enterprise.

Dispositions

In philosophical discussion, typical examples of dispositions are of glass to shatter when struck, or of sugar cubes to dissolve when immersed in water. To attribute a disposition to something is to say that, normally, in certain exigencies (being struck or tossed into water), it will respond in a certain way (shatter or dissolve). Roughly, individuals have a given disposition if they tend to act or react in certain ways in certain sorts of circumstances. The virtues and vices, if they are dispositions, seem to belong among personality traits. But such traits—for example, the tendency to be abrupt, anecdotal, assertive, or artistic—need not be virtues or vices. What sets off the virtues from other personality traits? But, first, *are* the virtues dispositions, and, if so, what kind of dispositions are they?

Why should not one act constitute sufficient ground for the claim that a person is courageous, say, or cowardly—a very courageous or cowardly act? Rosetti, unbidden and fully aware of the risk, creeps forward for hours under murderously heavy fire to rescue her wounded friend; or Swinburne runs away and hides in terror, leaving his fiancée to be raped by a gang of street thugs. But what is the one dramatically courageous or cowardly act supposed to show? Is it not that, no matter how well courage might have been camouflaged by Rosetti's modesty, or cowardice successfully dissimulated by Swinburne, the deeds reveal a covert disposition? Whatever the outcome of the discussion of examples of this kind, the defender of the dispositional analysis can argue that there are few deeds so grotesquely abhorrent or so supremely good that we could safely rest a claim concerning the CHARACTER of a person solely on that deed. The argument from the single deed seems to show, at best, that there may be extreme cases in which the description of the deed alone is sufficient ground for the attribution of a virtue or vice.

Habits, Skills, or Innate Faculties

What kind of dispositions are the virtues, then? Are they habits? This may seem an appealing notion, since both virtues and habits seem to have a certain explanatory force; pointing to patterns of behavior, they tell us why people behave as they do. ARISTOTLE's (384–322 B.C.E.) term *hexis* is sometimes translated as "habit," but it is clear that he regarded the habits formed early in life as conducive to, rather than constitutive of, virtue and vice. There are at least three related reasons for preferring the more comprehensive notion of disposition to that of habit. The first is that "habit" is a term whose scope is too narrow to accommodate the virtues. We must stretch the term unmercifully if we are to speak of the habit of wisdom, of HUMILITY, or of courage. Second, habits tend to be evidence for the presence of a virtue, as the habit of falling behind in battle may be evidence of cowardice. Finally, and most importantly, habits tend to be determinate, whereas virtues tend to be determinable traits.

When we say of Millay that she has a habit of falling behind, twitching her foot, or mispronouncing "miscellaneous," we refer to one particular aspect of her behavior. We could teach a child what "falling behind" or "twitching a foot" means by drawing its attention to those aspects. This is not true of virtues and vices, since there is no single observable way in which they are evinced. We cannot teach a child what courage means by pointing to Jonson who is ahead of the troops rather than behind them. The child must learn to use the term against a variety of backgrounds, to apply not only to going ahead in battle, but also to speaking up when to do so is dangerous, to risking one's fortune for a principle, to defending another person from attack, and so on, indefinitely. Should the child identify courage with the habit of walking in front of the troops rather than behind them, it would not yet have learned the meaning of courage. The same seems to be true of all of the virtues and vices. There is no way of defining justice, temperance, wisdom, GENEROSITY, kindness, BENEVOLENCE, sensitivity, or the corresponding vices "by ostentation," that is, by pointing out a particular instance of behavior.

The determinable quality of the virtues also partially distinguishes them from skills. Although virtues may be learned, and are in this respect like skills, yet they are not exhibited in the way that typical skills are. We cannot point to a sequence of learned actions as a way of defining a virtue. But, on the other hand, since learning does seem to have something to do with having at least some of the virtues, we cannot suppose that the virtues are innate. This is of course to leave open the possibility that some persons have more innate aptitude for the acquisition of a virtue than do others.

The Stability and Evaluative Nature of Virtues and Vices

To say that a person is just is to characterize that person. The implication is that the virtue of justice, and other virtues, are not fleeting or ephemeral dispositions, but are relatively stable, long-lasting ones. We may use terms like just and generous in answering the question "What kind of person is Jones?" where what is wanted is a general appraisal, a kind of evaluative description. It will not do, in mentioning a person's virtues and vices, to say that he is angry unless we mean that he is typically an "angry man," or that she is happy, unless we mean that she is typically so when others are not happy.

To attribute a virtue to a person is to describe him or her in a vocabulary suitable to our purpose of determining what we think of him or her, what good or bad dispositions we should take into account. For this reason, goodness, evilness, despicableness, or praiseworthiness are not virtues and vices so much as descriptively empty summary judgments. We must know what the speaker would count as evidence for them if we are to understand how the judgment was reached.

Rational Dispositions

Supposing it be granted that virtues and vices are dispositions, but not the kind of dispositions that habits are. Then how broadly are we to understand "disposition?" Should we include tendencies to have certain kinds of beliefs, desires, feelings, or emotions, or to reason or be motivated in certain ways—as well as to act in certain ways? Most, if not all, contemporary philosophers prefer a conception of virtue that is not purely behavioral, but differences crop up over what nonbehavioral elements should predominate in our understanding of virtue and vice.

One view is that it is the disposition to act for a particular sort of reason or practical principle that distinguishes the virtues from other dispositions and from each other. Vice may, on this view, consist either in tending to act on wrong principles or in failing to act on one's right principle (the failing the Greeks called *akrasia*). This emphasis on the place of reason in the virtues is consistent with the Socratic thesis that to be virtuous is to have knowledge, and with the Aristotelian conception of the virtuous person as one who seeks the mean between extremes. It is an advantage of this view that it helps, in another way, to set off the virtues as dispositions from habits. Suppose that Jonson throws himself on a live grenade, thereby saving the lives of several of his comrades. This could have been an act engendered by habit if Jonson had been conditioned to do it by repeated simulated emergencies and appropriate training. To say that he did it by habit, however, is, *prima facie*, to remove it from the sphere of virtuous action. We could imagine a (miraculously surviving) Jonson disclaiming praise by saying, however implausibly, that he covered the grenade from habit. Mere habitual action seems insufficient ground for the attribution of a virtue or a vice. Something more seems required, and, on the present account, it is the reason Jonson had for his deed. His disposition is informed by his belief concerning his duty to his fellow soldiers. That belief will result in different actions according to the circumstances, and might even require that he not act as he had been trained, that he violate the ingrained pattern of habits. For example, if he were carrying a crucial message between commanders in the field, he might reason (in an instant) that his duty to save the lives immediately surrounding him is outweighed by his duty to deliver the message, thereby perhaps saving a great many more lives.

A second advantage of such a definition is that it accounts for the determinable character of the virtues by providing an account of why the exercise of the virtue might require different sorts of action in different circumstances. The principle on which one acts is not a blind rule, but a guide to, or a hint about, how one should conduct oneself in the exigencies that arise in life. It is because the child cannot grasp such a principle that it is unable easily to learn what justice, courage, or temperance are.

There are at least two difficulties with such an account of virtues, however. The first is that it seems to rule out many qualities that intuitively seem to be virtues; for example, wisdom, cheerfulness, imaginativeness, CIVILITY, gracefulness, and resourcefulness. For these qualities and a great many others, it is difficult to see that any special belief need be held in order for the quality to be present. This difficulty might possibly be avoided if the definition is not one of the virtues in general but only of some important subset of the virtues, for example, of the moral virtues.

But then the second difficulty is that, even for those qualities that do seem typically to be accompanied by a belief held as a principle, it does not follow that holding that belief is a necessary or sufficient condition of having the quality. For example, while we might say of courage that the principle is that one should never give in to fear, still it is difficult to show that only those persons who hold such a principle are entitled to be called courageous. Why cannot a person be courageous who does not know or who never appeals to any such principle, or who appeals to some other principle? If it be granted that such a person can be courageous, then the defender of the belief-held-as-principle definition might argue that one can unconsciously hold a belief as a principle, and that it is for this reason that a courageous person may be unable to cite the principle on which he or she acts. But the notion of a principle unconsciously held is a difficult one to grasp, and it incurs the danger of begging the question whether the definition in question is an acceptable one, since persons pointed to as virtuous but not holding a principle may too easily be classed as unconsciously holding a principle.

Motivational Dispositions

Still, the conception of virtue as resting on something interior, something that cannot be reduced to a behavioral pattern, is a powerful one. Mere behavior, most philosophers would agree, is not enough, since such a pattern is consistent with very different sorts of motivation. If, from fear of his commanding officer, a soldier does what a courageous person would do in battle, he is not therefore courageous. We need to know, if not what principle or principles he holds, at least what motivates him to act in the way that he does. Are virtues and vices, then, best understood as patterns of motivation? If the motivations of a person are, in turn, patterns of wants and aversions, then to say that a person is courageous, just, temperate, or wise is to say what kind of thing that person tends to want or want to avoid. It is to substitute an analysis based on inner dispositions for one that starts from outer, or behavioral, dispositions.

Several points can be made in favor of such an understanding of the virtues and vices. The first is that the motivational account has more potential explanatory power than the merely behavioral one. It says something about why Rosetti acts courageously or wisely, and does not merely refer us to the pattern of her actions in the past. Even if we must still ask why she has the particular pattern of wants and aversions that she now exhibits, nevertheless we seem to be moving closer to the source of her virtues and vices in probing her motivations. Wants and aversions are sometimes analyzed as symptoms of NEEDS, so that further analysis along this line might lead to an account of the virtues and vices in purely naturalistic, law-governed terms. The second, related, point is that the motivational account is more illuminating for purposes of moral assessment than is the behavioral one. If Jonson's throwing himself on a live grenade is motivated by the desire to save his comrades, then we have strong evidence for his being a courageous man—evidence that we would not have had if his motivation had been fear of his commanding officer.

We should notice that a motivational analysis of the virtues and vices requires a companion inquiry into the beliefs of the agent. Jonson's motivation could not have been loyalty to his comrades if he had believed that the grenade was a dummy; his motivation might instead have been a craving for recognition or adulation, evidence for a vice rather than for a virtue. The present account of the virtues and vices, then, might be called a motivation/belief one. It provides an analysis of Jonson's INTENTION in acting as he did; and we seem to need to know a person's intention in acting if we are to judge that he is or is not virtuous or vicious. So the third advantage of the present account is that it reserves a meaningful place for inquiries into the intention with which an action was done. A fourth advantage may at first glance seem to be a disadvantage. It is that some virtues and vices seemingly resistant to a motivation/belief analysis turn out to be amenable to such an account once it is recognized that the absence as well as the presence of a motivation or belief may be relevant. For example, justice might be understood as the tendency not to allow considerations of PARTIALITY to govern one's decisions; or courage might be analyzed as the absence of overweening concern to protect one's own well-being.

Unfortunately, there are disadvantages too. The first is that it is difficult to say, without circularity, just what pattern of motivations/beliefs grounds the claim that a person has a particular virtue or vice. How can we say, in general terms, what that pattern is for INTEGRITY or temperance? The second is that

there are a great many intuitively virtuous or vicious dispositions that arguably do not rest on motivation/belief at all—for example, wisdom, belligerence, sensibleness, and vindictiveness. The third difficulty is that we are still left with no way of distinguishing virtues and vices from other personality traits, since at least some of them, too, might be understood as consisting in given patterns of motivation and belief.

The Commendatory Force of Virtue Terms

To attribute a virtue to a person is often understood as praising or commending the individual in some way, not merely saying that that person has a desirable trait. On a broad definition, we might count wittiness or warmth as virtues, but these qualities might be gifts of inheritance or early childhood experience; they may provide no reason for the commendation of a person as their fortunate bearer. If the commendatory aspect of virtue is to be preserved, then the list of desirable traits that are virtues must be restricted to those that are to some degree self-inculcated. There must be some indication that the trait was acquired by the efforts of its bearer, that there was work, sacrifice, self-restraint, or conscious self-development in its acquisition.

This conception of virtue is consistent with the Aristotelian notion that the virtues are *aretai*, excellences, since EXCELLENCE is the result of self-cultivation. The belief that a virtue must be at least a partially self-engendered, and therefore commendable, excellence, has led some writers to specify the overcoming of some human frailty or natural recalcitrance as the defining characteristic of the virtues. Persistence is thus a virtue because of our natural tendency to give up difficult tasks rather easily; justice is a virtue because we are normally partial to kith and kin; or temperance is a virtue because it is a trait that is acquired at the expense of resisting temptations to extravagant habits of diet or self-expression. A difficulty with the restriction of virtues to the traits for which we are to some degree responsible is that the status of the trait as a virtue turns on the degree of RESPONSIBILITY for its self-inculcation. But to say to what degree a person is responsible even for a salient trait is often, if not always, difficult or impossible. Early childhood influences, the sociological conditions in which the person was raised, the contingencies of life are "responsible" too. But if virtue terms are not necessarily, or are only indefinitely, commendatory, perhaps it would be better simply to rest with the broader notion that virtues are generally desirable personality traits.

Teleological vs. Functional Accounts of Virtue

A pervasive notion in the discussion of the virtues, from Aristotle forward, has been that to be a virtue a trait must in some way be instrumental to the achievement of some good. It may be so by counteracting the emotions that obscure our judgment of what is beneficial or harmful, by correcting harmful tendencies in human nature, by enabling us to achieve the goods that are internal to practices, or by enhancing the possibilities of human flourishing. Such conceptions of the virtues are easily made consistent with the insistence that reason or motivation are essential constituents of virtue, and with the commendatory nature of most ascriptions of virtue. A particular attraction of these teleological accounts is that they can tie our judgment of what is and is not a virtue into a more general, teleological, ethical theory. Not only dispositions, but acts, policies, and practices are thus judged against the same standard as conducive to or at least partially constitutive of some good. The difficulty they share is that, unless the notion of the good is to be left descriptively empty, they must specify what is to count as good before they are in position to distinguish the virtues from other personality traits; and that specification has been a subject of continuing philosophical controversy.

Alternative to teleological accounts of the virtues are functional theories, which emphasize the mutually irreducible ways in which particular personality traits may be generally desirable, given the vicissitudes of human life. Such accounts need posit no theory of the good, but must answer the charge that they provide no unified criterion by means of which virtues may be distinguished from other traits of personality.

Pseudo-Virtues and the Relativity of Virtue

A common aim of the definition of the virtues has been to provide a standard against which pseudo-virtues, traits that merely seem at the time or in the circumstances to be desirable, can be distinguished from traits that are desirable in larger perspective,

or from an impartial point of view. Thus, Thucydides (c. 460–c. 399 B.C.E.) speaks of a time of internal and external strife in Greece when "inconsiderate boldness was counted true-hearted manliness . . . ; modesty, the cloak of cowardice; to be wise in everything, to be lazy in everything." The possibility of recognizing that what had been considered virtues were pseudo-virtues may seem to imply that there is a pantheon of virtues that is immune to the vicissitudes of history or culture. It is forcefully argued by some writers, however, that what has counted as a virtue is entirely relative to context, and that the meaning of virtue terms tends to shift through the history of their usage. Other writers insist that there are some dispositions that are nearly universally desirable.

See also: ALTRUISM; BENEFICENCE; BENEVOLENCE; CHARACTER; CHARITY; CIVILITY; COURAGE; DIGNITY; FAIRNESS; FIDELITY; GENEROSITY; GRATITUDE; HUMILITY; INTEGRITY; LOYALTY; PRUDENCE; SELF-CONTROL; SYMPATHY; TEMPERANCE; TOLERATION; WISDOM. *AND SEE:* ARISTOTLE; EXCELLENCE; INTENTION; MacINTYRE; MORAL DEVELOPMENT; MORAL PURITY; MORAL SAINTS; MOTIVES; PLATO; REASONS FOR ACTION; TELEOLOGICAL ETHICS; VIRTUE ETHICS; WEAKNESS OF WILL.

Bibliography

Abba, Giuseppe. "Virtu e dovere: Valuatzione di un recente debattito." *Salesianum* 49 (1987): 421–84. Contains comprehensive bibliography of recent philosophical and theological writings on the virtues.

Allport, Gordon, and Henry Odbert. "Trait-names: A Psycho-lexical Study." *Psychological Monographs* 47, no. 1 (1936). Extensive lists of trait names.

Anscombe, G. E. M. "Modern Moral Philosophy." *Philosophy* 33 (1958): 1–19. A ground-breaking early article.

Becker, Lawrence C. "Unity, Coincidence, and Conflict in the Virtues." *Philosophia* 20/1–2 (1990): 127–43.

Brandt, Richard. "Traits of Character: A Conceptual Analysis." *American Philosophical Quarterly* 7 (1970): 32–37. Motivational theory.

Brickhouse, Thomas C., and Nicholas D. Smith. "Socrates and the Unity of the Virtues." *Journal of Ethics* 1/4 (1997): 311–24.

Churchland, Paul M. "Toward a Cognitive Neurobiology of the Moral Virtues." *Topoi* 17/2 (1998): 83–96.

Foot, Philippa. *Virtues and Vices and Other Essays in Moral Philosophy.* Berkeley: University of California Press, 1978. Argues that the virtues are correctives to human nature.

Geach, Peter T. *The Virtues.* Cambridge: Cambridge University Press, 1977. Defense of the Catholic canon of the virtues.

Hunt, Lester. "Character and Thought." *American Philosophical Quarterly* 15 (1978): 177–86. An "intellectual" conception of the virtues.

Kruschwitz, Robert B., and Robert C. Roberts, eds. *The Virtues: Contemporary Essays on Moral Character.* Belmont, CA: Wadsworth, 1987. Contains a usefully arranged bibliography.

MacIntyre, Alasdair. *After Virtue: A Study in Moral Theory.* 2d ed. Notre Dame, IN: University of Notre Dame Press, 1984 [1981]. Perhaps the most widely discussed recent work.

———. *Dependent Rational Animals: Why Human Beings Need the Virtues.* Chicago: Open Court, 1999.

Pence, Gregory E. "Recent Work on the Virtues." *American Philosophical Quarterly* 21 (1984): 281–97. A critical survey.

Pincoffs, Edmund L. *Quandaries and Virtues: Against Reductivism in Ethics.* Lawrence: University Press of Kansas, 1986. A broad, functionalist approach.

Thucydides. *The Peloponnesian War.* For an outcry against the reign of the pseudo-virtues, see vol. I, book 3.

Wallace, James D. *Virtues and Vices.* Ithaca, NY: Cornell University Press, 1978. A biologically oriented functional approach.

Wright, G. H. von. *The Varieties of Goodness.* London: Routledge and Kegan Paul, 1963. For an excellent short introductory analysis, see chapter 7, "Virtue."

Edmund L. Pincoffs

Vitoria, Francisco de (1486?–1546)

A Spanish Late Scholastic theologian and moral and political philosopher, Vitoria entered the Dominican Order and was trained in his native Burgos and, after 1507, in Paris, where he came into contact with the new humanist movement. It appears that, during this time, he defended Desiderius Erasmus (1466–1536) at some disputes, though he would later harshly criticize his theological views. Vitoria taught theology with the Dominicans in Paris and later occupied chairs at Valladolid and Salamanca. He is recognized as one of the main reformers and revitalizers of Scholastic thought in the sixteenth century, and was instrumental in bringing about the substitution of the *Sentences* of Peter Lombard (1095?–1160) by the *Summa theologiae* of THOMAS AQUINAS (1225?–1274) as the basic theological textbook in Scholastic classrooms. His main contributions are in political philosophy and the philosophy of law. He left very few publications, and all his manuscripts were lost after his death. What is known of his work comes mainly from carefully taken transcripts of his lessons at Salamanca. These include his lectures or commentaries on Aquinas's *Summa* (1526–1542), and his *relectiones* or annual lectures on, amongst other topics, civil power (1528), HOMICIDE (1530), marriage (1531), the power of the Church, of the Councils, and of the Pope (1532, 1533, and 1534), the justice of the Spanish conquest of the Americas (1539), and just war (1539).

Like his Late Scholastic successors Domingo de Soto (1495–1560) and Francisco SUÁREZ (1548–1617), Vitoria was an Aristotelian naturalist. The origins of political POWER are found in God, who created human beings naturally driven to social life. The purpose of civil power is human flourishing, which is impossible outside a self-sufficient, structured group. Political power belongs originally to such commonwealth, which must, however, convene on some sort of government in order to exercise it. Thus, Vitoria distinguished between political power (*potestas*) as potency (*potentia*) and as AUTHORITY (*auctoritas*). The first is a Divine or natural institution; the second is contingent upon human convention. Not surprisingly, later liberal contractarians such as Thomas HOBBES (1588–1679) dismissed this distinction as it supposes that political power arises not out of a free self-interested agreement between individuals, but out of a "utility and necessity so urgent that only gods could resist it."

Vitoria distinguished eternal, natural, and civil or positive law. Eternal law ultimately refers to those Divine Ideas which in the Christian tradition were conceived to be principles guiding all creation. Natural law is derived from the former as the application of divine law to rational creatures. Civil or positive law is a human product which, while abiding by NATURAL LAW, supplements it by ruling about matters which are decidable through mere convention. Between natural and positive law, Vitoria made room for a certain international law (*ius gentium*) which is enacted by the "whole world, which is in a sense a commonwealth," and which "does not only have the force of pacts . . . between men but truly has the force of law." On account of this doctrine, he is commonly described as the founder of modern international law. Though there is perhaps some anachronism in the title, it is not altogether undeserved. His view that the *ius gentium* is not reducible to the law which holds within particular commonwealths, nor to conventional treaties between nations, appears to adumbrate the peculiar place, distinct from universal morality and from mere matters of choice, which concerns about cultural identity and plurality have within a common, global order.

Vitoria's talents found their most notable expression in his discussions of practical matters, and in particular of the European conquest of native American societies. In his first lecture *On the Indians,* he examined whether such wars were justified. Vitoria first established that pre-Columbian Americans "had as true dominion, both private and public, as any Christian," and that they lived in sovereign commonwealths ruled by legitimate rulers. He then dismissed several unjust titles actually used to usurp their rightful dues. He argued that neither the Pope nor the Emperor were masters of the whole world, and that even if they were, they could not depose legitimate rulers nor take over justly owned land. Claims based on the right of discovery were as invalid in this case as they would have been "if they had discovered us." Refusal of the Christian faith could not justify a war of conquest since it is wrong to induce someone to pretend—out of fear—that she believes. The conquest could not be justified either by claiming that the Indians were mortal sinners or that God had delivered them to their conquerors. Nor did the Indians themselves legitimately choose to be ruled by the Spaniards upon meeting them, since people cannot change rulers at a whim, nor can rulers themselves change them without the CONSENT of the people.

The just titles by which the Indians could come under Spanish rule include that such conquest be absolutely necessary and inevitable in order to defend the RIGHTS and safety of Spaniards, or to protect Christian missionaries or Christian converts, or to defend the innocent from a tyrant. A legitimate and truly free choice of the Indian commonwealth would also constitute a just title, as would the aiding of lawful allies. Finally, incapacity for self-rule, as in the case of children or the mentally retarded, might provide just grounds for taking them over. Vitoria suggested that none of these just titles actually did apply. In his lectures, he used academic language and was careful to give due consideration to all arguments and sides of the dispute. All the same, his considered view was that war had monstrous effects

and could be justified only as the unavoidable response to commensurable harm, something which was clearly not applicable in the case of, for example, the terrible massacre of the Incas at Cajamarca in 1532. The Spanish conquest of the Americas, and particularly of Perú, was in the end morally abhorrent: "there was no other cause for this war than sheer robbery" he wrote with indignation to one of his superiors.

Vitoria's *On the Indians* provided some of the theoretical backing to the denunciation—by Bartolomé de Las Casas (1474–1566) and several others—of the devastation of the indigenous societies of the New World and the exploitation of native Americans.

See also: APPLIED ETHICS; ARISTOTLIAN ETHICS; AUTHORITY; CHRISTIAN ETHICS; COMMON GOOD; CONSENT; INTERNATIONAL JUSTICE: CONFLICT; INTERNATIONAL JUSTICE: DISTRIBUTION; LEGAL PHILOSOPHY; NATURAL LAW; POWER; PROPERTY; RIGHT HOLDERS; RIGHTS; SOCIAL AND POLITICAL PHILOSOPHY; SOCIAL CONTRACT; SUÁREZ; THOMAS AQUINAS; THEOLOGICAL ETHICS; WAR AND PEACE.

Bibliography

Works by Francisco de Vitoria

De Indis et de iure belli relectiones. Edited by Ernest Nys and translated by John Pawley Bate. Washington, D.C.: Carnegie Institution, 1917. Latin text with English translation. With an introduction and a photographic reproduction of a 1696 edition.

Comentarios a la Secunda secundae de Santo Tomás. Edited by Vicente Beltrán de Heredia. 6 vols. Salamanca: Universidad de Salamanca, 1932–1935 and 1952. Complete text of the lessons on Aquinas's *Summa theologiae* IIa-IIae.

Obras. Relecciones teológicas. Edited by Teófilo Urdanoz. Madrid: Biblioteca de Autores Cristianos, 1960. Latin text of all thirteen *relectiones* with a Spanish translation; not truly a critical edition, even though advertized as such. See especially pp. 158, 191, 665, and 685.

Relectio de iure belli, o, Paz dinámica. Edited by L. Pereña, *et al.* Madrid: Consejo Superior de Investigaciones Científicas, 1981. Critical edition and Spanish translation of the *relectio* on just war. Includes selections from other works by Vitoria and related writings in Latin by Cano, de Soto, and Covarrubias.

Political Writings. Edited by Anthony Pagden and Jeremy Lawrance. Cambridge: Cambridge University Press, 1991. English translations of the *relectiones* on civil and ecclesiastical power, on temperance (selections), on the Indians, and on just war; the lectures on Aquinas's treatise on law in the *Summa theologiae* Ia-IIae; and other texts. With introduction, biographical notes, glossary, and bibliography. See especially pp. 10, 40, 250, 265, and 332.

Reflection on Homicide and Commentary on Summa theologiae IIa–IIae Q. 64 (Thomas Aquinas). Edited by John P. Doyle. Milwaukee: Marquette University Press, 1997. Latin text and English translation with an introduction and bibliography.

Works about Vitoria

Beltrán de Heredia, Vicente. *Francisco de Vitoria.* Barcelona: Editorial Labor, 1939. Increasingly dated work by one of the pioneers of Vitorian studies.

Castilla Urbano, Francisco. *El pensamiento de Francisco de Vitoria: Filosofía política e indio americano.* Barcelona: Anthropos, 1992. A general account with a useful bibliography.

Fernández Buey, Francisco. *La gran perturbación: Discurso del indio metropolitano.* Barcelona: Ediciones Destino, 1995. On the "clash between cultures" with an extensive section on Vitoria's *De Indis.*

Hernández Martín, Ramón. *Francisco de Vitoria: Vida y pensamiento internacionalista.* Madrid: Biblioteca de Autores Cristianos, 1995. Useful for biographical information.

Pagden, Anthony. *The Fall of Natural Man. The American Indian and the Origins of Comparative Ethnology.* Cambridge: Cambridge University Press, 1986.

———. "Dispossessing the Barbarian: The Language of Spanish Thomism and the Debate over the Property Rights of the American Indians." In *The Languages of Political Theory in Early-Modern Europe,* edited by Anthony Pagden, pp. 79–98. Cambridge: Cambridge University Press, 1987.

Skinner, Quentin. *The Foundations of Modern Political Thought.* 2 vols. Cambridge: Cambridge University Press, 1978. Classic study; deals with Vitoria in vol. 2.

Truyol Serra, Antonio, *et al. Actualité de la pensée juridique de Francisco de Vitoria.* Brussels: Bruylant, 1988. Papers on Vitoria's conception of international law and just war and on his life and intellectual development.

Jorge Secada

Voltaire [Francois-Marie Arouet de] (1694–1778)

French poet, playwright, novelist, historian, popularizer of science, social reformer, and philosopher, Voltaire was born in Paris into a prosperous middle-class family. He was sent to the Jesuit school of Louis le Grand, where he received an excellent classical education. Against the wishes of his family, he embarked on a literary career in which he was spectacularly successful almost from the start. He achieved great fame with his epic poem *La Henriade* (1723), which celebrated Henry IV (1553–1610), the last liberal French king. After two periods of imprisonment in the Bastille, Voltaire went to England in 1726, where he met all the most distinguished figures of the world of letters. His views both on philosophical and social issues were largely shaped by his experiences in England. Samuel CLARKE (1675–1729) helped him to see the importance of Newton (1642–1727), whom Voltaire revered as the greatest man who ever lived. He also became an ardent disciple of LOCKE (1632–1704), and was greatly impressed by the writings of the deists, especially Collins (1676–1729) and Toland (1670–1722).

On returning to France in 1729, Voltaire wrote the *Lettres philosophiques,* which appeared first in London in 1733 in English translation as *Letters Concerning the English Nation,* and a year later in Paris. This slim volume was aptly described by Voltaire's biographer, Gustave Lanson (1857–1934), as the first bomb hurled against the *ancien régime* and became the inspiration of liberal reformers throughout the European continent for the rest of the century. In the *Lettres,* Voltaire praised English INSTITUTIONS and, by implication, condemned conditions in France—the wealth, intolerance, and immense power of the church, the despotism of the king, and the privileges of the aristocracy. He recommended equal status for merchants and nobles, a fair distribution of taxes, and TOLERATION for all religions. The *Lettres* also contain an exposition and defense of the empiricism of Locke and the methods and achievements of Newton, accompanied by satires of the theories of ARISTOTLE (384–322 B.C.E.) and DESCARTES (1596–1650). From then until his death over forty years later, Voltaire championed these causes in a seemingly endless stream of plays, poems, historical works, volumes of popular science, and such celebrated books as *Candide* (1759) and the *Philosophical Dictionary* (1764). In 1759, Voltaire purchased a magnificent estate at Ferney, a small town near Geneva and a few miles inside French territory, where he lived unmolested by French, German, or Swiss authorities until shortly before his death.

The last sixteen years of Voltaire's life were devoted to two campaigns that shook Europe like nothing since LUTHER's (1483–1546) break with the Church of Rome. One was a campaign against judicial barbarism in the course of which he came to the assistance of numerous victims of persecution and brutal laws that were administered in an unbelievably arbitrary fashion. The other was a campaign not just against the Roman Catholic Church, but Christianity itself, which Voltaire regarded as "the most ridiculous, the most absurd, and bloody religion that has ever infected the world." When he returned to Paris in the year of his death, there were huge celebrations in his honor. The government and the royal family, however, ignored his presence, and when he died, the newspapers were not allowed to report the event. He had to be buried surreptitiously outside the city.

Voltaire was not primarily a philosopher, but he took philosophical questions very seriously. On several issues he held views which, though largely derivative, are of considerable interest. His fullest treatments of the foundations of ethics are found in the *Traité de métaphysiques,* which was written between 1734 and 1737 but not published until after his death, and in *Le philosophe ignorant* of 1766. The views are substantially identical in these two works, but the opposition to any form of ethical skepticism is more emphatic in the latter of the two. Voltaire rejects the derivation of moral principles from theological premises and he equally rejects the kind of rationalism advocated by Samuel Clarke. There are no moral qualities or relations existing independently of the NEEDS and emotions of human beings or, more generally, of organisms capable of experiencing PLEASURE and pain. Locke had shown to Voltaire's satisfaction that the so-called secondary qualities like hot and cold, colors and smells, lack objective existence. Exactly the same is true of moral qualities. At the same time, Voltaire was very much opposed to moral skepticism, especially in the form given to it by HOBBES (1588–1679). Hobbes taught that "there are no laws in the world but the laws of convention" and that "there is no justice and injustice but what has been agreed upon as such in a country." Suppose Hobbes had been alone with Cromwell on an island and suppose Cromwell attempted to kill Hobbes because of Hobbes's royalism. Would such an attempt not be as unjust on that island as in England?

Voltaire would probably maintain that his imaginary example not only shows that Hobbes's theory is wrong but also that some form of UTILITARIANISM must be correct. The word "utilitarianism" was not coined until the nineteenth century, but there can be no doubt that, like several of the other Encyclopedists, Voltaire was in fact a utilitarian. Moral laws, such as that HOMICIDE is wrong, are "natural laws" having the same status as any true empirical proposition. They are, "one and all," statements about the useful or harmful effects on society. "The well-being of society" is the "sole standard for measuring moral good and evil."

An important element in Voltaire's position that is logically distinct from his utilitarianism is his belief in a natural sentiment of BENEVOLENCE. In the 1730s, Voltaire read MANDEVILLE's (1670–1733) *Fable of the Bees* (1723) with great interest. He accepted some of its teachings, but rejected its psychological EGOISM. "If one should see an infant being destroyed," Mandeville had written, "he would endeavor to save it." This would not, however, be due to genuine SYMPATHY but "to prevent his own *amour-propre* from being revolted." Voltaire maintained exactly the opposite. We would try to save the child because we are so constructed as to feel pity for it. This pity is part of the *"bienveillance naturelle,"* the natural benevolence that is just as much part of our innate constitution as our self-interest. "If . . . the most savage man saw a sweet child being devoured by some animal," Voltaire writes in reply to Mandeville, he would feel "an anxiety born of pity, and a desire to run to his aid." It is true that this feeling of pity is often overwhelmed by purely selfish impulses, and it is not deplorable that this should be so. Otherwise we might fail to take steps to protect our own lives. However, the benevolence is very real; it is one of the basic ties in any society and it helps the preservation of our species.

Not only do human beings possess a natural sentiment of benevolence, but they also have an innate sense of justice. This topic is discussed in many places, perhaps most interestingly in one of the earliest (October 1737) of the letters to Frederick the Great (1712–1786). Suppose there were only four men on earth and suppose that one of them eats his companion's supper. The others will surely revolt because their sense of justice would be outraged. Both in this letter and in other places Voltaire is uncomfortable about his assertion of a natural sense of justice because it seems to be in conflict with his rejection of innate ideas. In the letter to Frederick, he insists that nobody "carries with him at birth" the idea that we must be just, but God has so constructed us that at a certain age everybody comes to acknowledge this truth. He compares the situation with our ability to walk. When we are born we cannot walk, but we are born with feet and legs and when we are strong enough we learn to walk. The subject is discussed at some length in *The Ignorant Philosopher*, where Voltaire raises the question at what age human beings "become acquainted with what is just and unjust" and he answers "at the age when we realize that two and two make four." Both here and elsewhere Voltaire comes perilously close to endorsing the position of Clarke which he had rejected in no uncertain terms in many of his other discussions. He thought that he could reconcile his views about justice with his Lockean empiricism, but it is doubtful that he was successful in this attempt.

See also: BENEVOLENCE; CLARKE; DESCARTES; EGO-ISM; ELITE, CONCEPT OF; EMOTION; EQUALITY; HOBBES; LOCKE; MANDEVILLE; MORAL DEVELOP-MENT; NATURAL LAW; RELIGION; RUSSELL; SHAFTES-BURY; SKEPTICISM IN ETHICS; THEOLOGICAL ETHICS; UTILITARIANISM.

Bibliography

Works by Voltaire

Oeuvres completes. Edited by Pierre de Beaumarchais the Marquis de Condorcet and Jacques Decroix. 70 vols. Kehl: De L'Imprimerie de la Société Littéraire-Typographique 1784–1789. First major edition of the complete works; called the Kehl edition.
Oeuvres de Voltaire. Edited by A. J. Q. Beuchot. 72 vols. Paris: Lefevre, 1829–1834. Also highly regarded.
Oeuvres completes. Edited by Louis Moland. 52 vols. Paris: Garnier, 1877–1885. Based on Beuchot.
Complete Works. Edited by W. H. Barber. 135 vols. Oxford: Voltaire Foundation, Taylor Institution, 1968–. Definitive ed. in progress. Vols. 85–135 are the 2d ed. of Theodore Besterman's collection of the correspondence, originally published in 107 vols., Geneva, 1953–1965.
Selections. Edited by Paul Edwards. New York: Macmillan, 1989. Contains the first English translation of the *Traité de métaphysiques* as well as all of the discussions of ethical topics in *Le philosophe ignorant.*

Works about Voltaire

Ayer, A. J. *Voltaire.* London: Weidenfield, 1986. Last chapter contains critical discussion.

Cassirer, Ernst. *Philosophy of the Enlightenment.* Princeton: Princeton University Press, 1955 [1932]. English translation of discussion of the conflict between Voltaire's empiricism and his inclination to regard moral principles as logically necessary.
Lanson, Gustave. *Voltaire.* 2d ed. Paris: Hachette, 1960 [1910]. Biography; English translation.
Mason, Haydn. *Voltaire: A Biography.* Baltimore: Johns Hopkins University Press, 1981.

Paul Edwards

voltarism

A thesis about some phenomenon is voluntaristic if the thesis claims that the will is the source of the phenomenon. Quite often, voluntaristic theses contrast with rationalistic theses. The latter maintain that, with respect to the same phenomenon, reason either is the source or is prior to the will.

Kinds of Voluntarism

Psychological voluntarism maintains that the will always determines both the ends at which one's actions aim and the means one chooses to bring about those ends. David HUME (1711–1776) argued that "reason is and ought only to be the slave of the passions," in opposition to rationalistic doctrines like PLATO's (c. 430–347 B.C.E.) claim that "knowledge is a noble thing and fit to command," which will not allow a person "to do anything which is contrary to what his knowledge bids him do."

Ethical voluntarism is a thesis about what is good or bad and what is right or wrong. Goodness is identified with what is approved, badness with what is disapproved. The identification can be claimed to be a metaethical thesis, so that 'is good,' for instance, is alleged to *mean* 'is the object of any man's Appetite or Desire' (Thomas HOBBES [1588–1679]), or it can be put forward as a metaphysical thesis. In the latter case, voluntarists deny that goodness and badness are intrinsic properties of things, asserting instead that they are relational properties founded in the positive and negative attitudes of conscious beings. If the world had no beings with desires or aversions, it would contain no goodness or badness. The will as center of DESIRE and aversion does not *respond* to the goodness and badness antecedently lodged in things; it *confers* goodness and badness on things by its activity. This sort of position diverges from Plato's philosophy, then, not only in assigning priority to the will over reason, but also in denying the independent ontological status of goodness. Ethical voluntarism is subjectivistic insofar as it locates the source of ethical value in a willing subject. It need not be relativistic: an ethical voluntarist can consistently claim that there are features that necessarily characterize the will such that certain kinds of thing are universally good or universally bad.

Ethical voluntarists regard the notions of rightness and wrongness either as derivative or as fundamental. The former kind of voluntarist characterizes rightness and wrongness teleologically, in terms of the tendency to satisfy positive and negative desires respectively. The latter kind of voluntarist characterizes rightness and wrongness formally, as conformity with or contrariness to commands or other expressions of the will, as long as it is understood that the will is not merely carrying out the dictates of reason.

The scope of ethical voluntarism can be indicated by considering different answers to the question of *whose* will is the source of value.

(a) *The individual.* As he is sometimes portrayed by Plato, Protagoras of Abdera (c. 490–421 B.C.E.) held an account according to which each person is the sole AUTHORITY of what is good-for-that-person and bad-for-that-person. Although the account is put in cognitive terminology, it is easy to imagine it rephrased in volitional language: theft is bad-for-Jones because Jones disapproves of it; good-for-Smith because Smith approves. This type of voluntarism is relativistic. There is no answering the question whether theft is *simply* good or bad; the closest approximation to that would be everyone's approving or everyone's disapproving theft.

(b) *The experts.* Plato nevertheless also attributes to Protagoras the thesis that some conditions (including, presumably, some desires) are better than others, and that it is the function of experts like Protagoras to replace in people worse desires with better ones. It is hard to see how the appeal to the preferences of experts can be made in a way that identifies the experts without abandoning voluntarism.

(c) *Society.* One version of this answer is majoritarian, maintaining that a thing is good in a society if and only if a majority of the society's members desire or approve of it. Another, more holistic, version allows for the possibility that there is a societal will or that there are societal desires that cannot be specified by the aggregation of the individual desires of its members.

(d) *God.* Theological voluntarism maintains that nothing is good or bad, right or wrong, unless God's will determines it so. Some theological voluntarists have maintained nevertheless that God is essentially good, suggesting that his essential goodness precludes him from willing certain types of things as good or right. It is not clear that this maneuver is consistent with voluntarism.

See also: DELIBERATION AND CHOICE; FREE WILL; FREEDOM AND DETERMINISM; MORAL RELATIVISM; PHILOSOPHY OF RELIGION; RATIONAL CHOICE; RATIONALITY VS. REASONABLENESS; SUBJECTIVISM; THEOLOGICAL ETHICS; VOLUNTARY ACTS.

Bibliography

Hobbes, Thomas. *Leviathan.* 1651. See part I, chapter 6.

Hume, David. *A Treatise of Human Nature.* 1737. Book II, part 3, section 3.

Idziak, Janine Marie, ed. *Divine Command Morality: Historical and Contemporary Readings.* New York: Edwin Mellen Press, 1979. Convenient source for material on theological voluntarism.

Plato. *Protagoras. Theaetetus.*

Rousseau, Jean-Jacques. *The Social Contract.* 1762. Defends a distinction between the will of all individual people and the general will.

William E. Mann

voluntary acts

Whether an event occurs voluntarily is commonly and plausibly thought to be of ethical significance, for reasons that will emerge and be discussed shortly. In light of this, it would be useful to have at hand an acceptable account of what sorts of events may occur voluntarily and under what conditions they may do so.

One such account that some philosophers have advocated is simply this: all and only acts occur voluntarily. While perhaps initially plausible, each half of this account has its difficulties.

The claim that all acts occur voluntarily is usually based on the observation that it is the very voluntariness of an episode of behavior that renders that episode an instance of genuine ACTION as opposed to something that an individual merely undergoes.

While one can do things involuntarily, in some broad sense of "do" (one typically sneezes involuntarily, salivates involuntarily, and so on), it is frequently claimed that only if one's behavior proceeds from one's will or volition does it constitute genuine action. (This, it is alleged, constitutes the difference between sneezing and blowing one's nose, between salivating and spitting.) There are three chief difficulties with this view.

First, the view appears to presuppose either a faculty of volition or the existence of volitions, both of which have seemed objectionable to many philosophers, either because (it is alleged) they are unduly mysterious or because there is no empirical evidence that they exist or occur. The accuracy of this allegation of course depends on what willing is taken to be. If—as is often the case—it is identified with such phenomena as desiring, intending, deciding, or choosing, then skepticism concerning its existence or occurrence is hard to support.

The second difficulty with the claim that all acts occur voluntarily is that, if this is taken to imply that all acts proceed from desires, intentions, or such, there appear to be acts that do not meet this condition. Consider someone who is nervously tapping his foot. He (or she) may be quite unaware that he is doing this; when it is brought to his attention and he is asked whether he wanted or intended to do it, he may claim that he had no such DESIRE or INTENTION. He might of course be mistaken about this, but why think so? Yet it seems that his foot-tapping is properly said to be a genuine action, rather than something that he merely undergoes.

The third difficulty with the claim that all acts occur voluntarily is that some acts are performed in ignorance or unintentionally, as when one runs into a lamppost when swerving to avoid a child. Even if this act proceeds from a volition (e.g., a desire or intention to avoid the child), one may well hesitate to call it a voluntary act, since the volition did not itself concern running into the lamppost.

The claim that only acts occur voluntarily may initially seem plausible in light of the fact that voluntariness is surely closely connected with the will, and the will is traditionally viewed as expressing itself in action. Nonetheless, there are some who talk of not only acts being voluntary but also beliefs, thoughts, attitudes, and omissions being voluntary. Perhaps this difficulty is fairly easily accommodated. It can be argued that only acts (or, perhaps, some essential part of acts, such as volitions) are directly voluntary; beliefs, thoughts, attitudes, and omissions (if they are not acts) can occur voluntarily also, but only indirectly, that is, only as consequences of events that are directly voluntary.

The various difficulties just discussed may suggest this more restrictive account of voluntariness: all and only intentional acts occur directly voluntarily. But each half of this account also faces difficulties.

The claim that all intentional acts occur (directly) voluntarily is problematic, in that some intentional acts are such that one is in some sense bound to do them, and this feature renders the claim that they occur voluntarily suspect. There are various ways in which one may be bound to do an act. One may find it impossible to act differently, in that one's desire to do the act is literally overwhelming, and this (except perhaps in certain special cases of the sort discussed by Harry Frankfurt) would appear to render one's performance of the act wholly beyond one's control; this may apply, for example, to certain kinds of addicts. Or one may find it not impossible but still very difficult or costly to act differently, so that, even if one has a desire to act differently and is strictly in control of whether or not one does so, nonetheless one is or feels compelled to act as one does; this can apply to a wide variety of cases—for example, to those who succumb to WEAKNESS OF WILL, to those who are forced (e.g., at gunpoint) to act in certain ways, and to those who reluctantly abide by the requirements of morality, custom, or convention. Or, finally, one may find it neither impossible nor difficult to act differently but nonetheless be in some sense bound to act as one does because one's desires have been manipulated in such a way that one's autonomy has been compromised, as when, for example, one has been bombarded by subliminal messages to purchase a certain product. In all of these cases, the agent in question would appear to act intentionally, and yet one may well hesitate to say that the act was a voluntary one.

The claim that only intentional acts occur (directly) voluntarily faces two difficulties. First, it seems that one can do something voluntarily but not intentionally when one does something that is an essential part of an intentional action. For example, a concert pianist may, during the course of playing a complicated passage, depress a certain key automatically, paying no attention to that aspect of what is being done. It has seemed to some incorrect to say that in this case the pianist depresses the key intentionally, but correct to say that the pianist does so voluntarily. Secondly, it seems that one can do something voluntarily but not intentionally when one produces a foreseen effect that forms no part of one's objective. For example, it may be no part of my plan to get my hands dirty when I work on my car; but, if I do get them dirty, I do so voluntarily. (One should note, however, that intention still plays a role in this case, in that I intend not to avoid getting my hands dirty if need be.)

In response to these difficulties, one might seek further for some such single account of voluntariness, but at this point the suspicion may well arise that the term "voluntary" is ambiguous and that any proposed single account of this sort would therefore prove problematic. Perhaps, then, a more promising tack is to distinguish various senses of "voluntary."

If one took this tack, the following, still rather rough account of voluntariness might recommend itself. With respect to direct voluntariness, we might say this: all acts (except perhaps for those such as nervously tapping one's foot) and only acts occur in what may be called a minimally voluntary way. Second, all and only those acts that are either intentional, or essential parts of something intentional, or foreseen side-effects of something intentional occur in what may be called a moderately voluntary way. Third, all and only those acts that are both moderately voluntary and such that one is not bound to do them occur in what may be called a fully voluntary way. These various senses of "voluntary," it should be noted, are related, in that each concerns the root notion of acting in accordance with one's will. Acts that are fully voluntary perhaps give fullest expression to this idea, but those which are merely moderately voluntary clearly also capture the idea to some extent. And even those which are merely minimally voluntary give some expression to it, since, it can be argued, even if not all acts can be said to be intentional without qualification, nonetheless all (except perhaps for acts like that of nervously tapping one's foot) are intentional under some description. (Thus, it may be said, one's running into a lamppost just is the same act, under a different description, as one's swerving to avoid the child.) One complication here is that an act that is performed due to some overwhelming or manipulated desire is,

in a sense, an act that is performed in accordance with one's will, and yet it has been said that such an act is not fully voluntary. This is because the notion of full voluntariness involves not just acting in accordance with one's will, but acting in accordance with a will that is operating freely.

This threefold account of direct voluntariness could be supplemented by an account of indirect voluntariness. Presumably this account must also be threefold, since (except possibly in the case of minimal voluntariness) not all consequences of voluntary acts should be said to occur voluntarily. However, the details of this account will not be explored here.

Not only may one act voluntarily, one may, of course, fail to act voluntarily. There are various ways in which this may occur. If to act voluntarily is to act in accordance with one's (free) will, then one way to fail to act voluntarily is to act in accordance with a will that is not operating freely (as when one does something due to an overwhelming or manipulated desire). Another way is to act against one's will (as when one reluctantly obeys a gunman, or reluctantly toes the conventional line). Another way is to do something in some sense independently of one's will (as when one acts unintentionally—nervously tapping one's foot, or running into a lamppost). Another way, of course, is not to act at all. When one acts, but not voluntarily, philosophers usually say that one acts nonvoluntarily; when one does something but does not perform a genuine action (such as when one sneezes or salivates), they usually say that one acts involuntarily (in a broad or loose sense of "act" that does not connote genuine action). According to this usage, then, so-called nonvoluntary acts are nonetheless (except perhaps in cases like that of nervously tapping one's foot) minimally voluntary; it is involuntary "acts" that are not even minimally voluntary.

Finally, what of the ethical significance of voluntary acts? This, of course, depends on the sort of voluntariness at issue. Even acts that are minimally voluntary have some such significance, since such voluntariness indicates genuine agency and thus furnishes an essential condition for the moral evaluation of agents and their acts. An act's being moderately voluntary is significant in that it indicates the presence of a certain intention (if not the intention to do something, at least the intention not to avoid doing it), and this is typically taken to be a key factor in the moral evaluation of agents and their acts, in terms of both moral RESPONSIBILITY and morally right and wrong action. An act's being fully voluntary carries with it the significance of an act's being moderately voluntary; in addition, it is an act that the agent is free or not bound to do, and this is frequently taken to be a further key factor in the moral evaluation of agents and their acts, again in terms of both moral responsibility and morally right and wrong action. It is for these reasons that moral philosophers, from the time of ARISTOTLE (384–322 B.C.E.) onward, have paid so much attention to the notion of a voluntary act.

See also: ACTION; ACTS AND OMISSIONS; AGENT-CENTERED MORALITY; ANSCOMBE; AUTONOMY OF MORAL AGENTS; CASUISTRY; CAUSATION AND RESPONSIBILITY; COERCION; CONSEQUENTIALISM; DELIBERATION AND CHOICE; DESIRE; FREE WILL; FREEDOM AND DETERMINISM; INTENTION; INTRANSITIVITY; MERIT AND DESERT; MOTIVES; PRICHARD; REASONS FOR ACTION; RESPONSIBILITY; THEOLOGICAL ETHICS; VOLUNTARISM; WEAKNESS OF WILL.

Bibliography

Anscombe, G. E. M. *Intention.* Oxford: Blackwell, 1957.

Aristotle. *Nicomachean Ethics.* Book II.

Aune, Bruce. *Reason and Action.* Dordrecht: Reidel, 1977. See especially chapter 2.

Austin, J. L. "A Plea for Excuses." *Proceedings of the Aristotelian Society* 57 (1956–1957): 1–30. Reprinted in White (19–42).

Davidson, Donald. "Actions, Reasons, and Causes." *Journal of Philosophy* 60 (1963): 685–700. Reprinted in White (79–94).

Fitzgerald, P. J. "Voluntary and Involuntary Acts." In *Oxford Essays in Jurisprudence,* ed. by A. G. Guest, pp. 1–28. Reprinted in White (pp. 120–43).

Frankfurt, Harry G. "Alternate Possibilities and Moral Responsibility." *Journal of Philosophy* 66 (1969): 829–39.

Prichard, H. A. *Moral Obligation.* Oxford: Clarendon Press, 1949. See especially pp. 187–98, reprinted under the title "Acting, Willing, Desiring" in White (pp. 59–69).

White, Alan R. "Introduction." In his (as ed.) *The Philosophy of Action,* pp. 1–18. Oxford: Oxford University Press, 1968.

Michael J. Zimmerman

Walzer, Michael (1935–)

Michael Walzer was educated at Brandeis and Harvard universities. He taught at Princeton and Harvard before moving to the Institute for Advanced Study at Princeton, where he is Professor of Social Studies. His books include *The Revolution of the Saints* (1965), *Just and Unjust Wars* (1977), *Spheres of Justice* (1983) and *Thick and Thin* (1994). In addition, he is an editor of both *Dissent* and *The New Republic*.

Walzer describes his moral philosophy as a historical and contextual one, contrasting it to moral philosophies that take a proceduralist form. Proceduralist theories that rely on an original position (such as John RAWLS's theory of justice), on an ideal of practical discourse (such as Jürgen HABERMAS's discourse ethics), or on an appropriately constrained conversation (such as Bruce Ackerman's account of social justice) are all meant to correct for prejudice, convention, and PARTIALITY. Hence, they are meant to issue in NORMS and principles with universal moral authority.

In Walzer's view, however, proceduralist moral philosophies ignore two crucial features of moral reflection. First, they ignore the moral world that communities already possess. Members of the communities for whom moral philosophy hopes to design principles already act and interact in certain ways, take certain norms and values seriously, understand their goods to have certain meanings, and orient themselves in certain ways toward each other and themselves. Hence, proceduralist moral philosophies must be able to show a community why it should abandon its way of life to live according to the principles proceduralist theories justify. Moreover, they must show the community this necessity in ways that make sense to that community and hence link up to the way of life it already has.

Second, proceduralist moral philosophies ignore their own historical and cultural conditions. Those who specify the conditions of an original position, define an ideal of practical discourse, or choose appropriate constraints for conversation already themselves inhabit a moral world. They already take seriously such ideals as freedom and EQUALITY and hence structure their design procedures so as to mirror the principles they take to be fundamental. Walzer's moral theory begins with the historical and cultural roots of these procedures. The principles that are meant to issue from proceduralist theories develop out of the struggles, issues, and histories of particular communities. They can be thinned out sufficiently to claim universal applicability. Nonetheless, Walzer insists, the ideals at their core are grounded not in procedure but in history and practice and in the reiterated ways specific communities understand themselves.

If moral principles are grounded in the understandings members of a community share, then moral philosophy, for Walzer, involves a consideration of those shared understandings. Moral philosophy is interpretive insofar as it tries to grasp the meaning and significance of the goods a community holds, the practices it pursues, and the values and norms it possesses. This sort of interpretive approach is not a mere apology for the *status quo,* in Walzer's view. Rather, moral reflection can be critical of practices, norms, or the distribution a particular community has of its social goods to the extent that it can show that those practices, norms, and distributive ideas violate the shared understandings of the particular society to which they belong. Walzer's ideal moral critic is thus the internal or connected one who holds the practices of his or her society up to its own ideals and checks its ideals against one another. The point of a connected form of social criticism is not to justify everything that a particular society does, but to show the way in which it may be violating its own self-understandings of how its members should act and interact and of what the society takes itself to be.

Walzer's theory of complex equality is taken from an analysis of the meaning of social goods and serves to illustrate his account of social criticism in general. His claim is that different cultural and historical communities conceive and create what they take as their social goods in different ways. Whether and how education, PROPERTY, political office, and physical health are social goods are questions different communities have decided differently both from one another and at different points in their own history. How these communities may justly distribute these goods also differs, for the distributive principles appropriate to different goods depends on what those goods are, or, in other words, their meaning for the culture or society for which they are a good. If medical care is conceived and created as a need for a particular community because of the way in which it understands the good of physical health, then, according to Walzer, medical care should be distributed according to principles governing the distribution of needs: namely, to all those who need it and to the degree that they need it. In contrast, if yachts and luxury goods are conceived and created as commodities, then they can be justly distributed according to principles appropriate to commodities—namely, the ability to pay.

This account of distributive principles based on the shared understanding particular communities have of their particular social goods remains both contextual and pluralistic. If education does not have the meaning in ancient Athens that it currently has in the United States, then it is illegitimate to require ancient Athens to have provided for it through communal funds in the way that the United States does. Similarly, if the shared understanding Americans have of medical care differs from their shared understanding of yachts, then to demand that they be distributed in the same way violates their autonomous meanings.

Distribution of goods according to their social meanings results in equality of a particular kind, Walzer thinks. Members of a society are equal not when they all have the same amount of every good the society creates and conceives. Rather, they are equal when different kinds of goods are distributed autonomously, according to their own internal social meanings, and when no distribution of any one sort of good is affected by the distribution of another. Violations of equality occur not when one individual has more money or more things than another, but when money buys more than things: when it buys education and political office, or when it provides the sole access to social goods whose shared meanings entail different principles of distribution. If only commodities are distributed to those who can afford them, then the threat that differences in wealth can mount subsides. If money also buys security, influence, education, and health (goods denied to those without money), then equality disappears.

Walzer has appealed to his interpretive and contextual moral theory not only to examine principles of distributive justice, but also to provide important insights into the character and possibility of a moral universalism, into just war theory, and into contemporary issues surrounding TOLERATION. Important criticisms of his work range from questions about his particular interpretations of shared understandings to questions about whether a contextual approach can successfully avoid relativism. To the former criticism, Walzer answers that it is precisely the task of social critics to show the validity of their interpretations of shared meanings and to make their interpretations compelling. To the latter criticism, Walzer replies by emphasizing a distinction between "thick" and "thin" moral principles. The principles that a moral universalism seeks to apply to all societies are not the thick principles grounded in particular histories and traditions, with their particular nuances and contextual connections. Rather, they are such principles appropriately thinned out for special occasions to allow for a connection to the vulnerabilities of all human beings. Thin principles allow for a universal condemnation and even a struggle against TORTURE, DECEIT, tyranny, OPPRESSION, and the like. At the level of particular societies engaged in constructing and maintaining a common life, morality is thicker and more complicated.

See also: CIVIL DISOBEDIENCE; CIVIL RIGHTS AND CIVIC DUTIES; COMMUNITARIANISM; EQUALITY; INTERESTS; INTERNATIONAL JUSTICE [entries]; JUSTICE, DISTRIBUTIVE; MILITARY ETHICS; MORAL COMMUNITY, BOUNDARIES OF; MORAL PLURALISM; MORAL RELATIVISM; MULTICULTURALISM; NEEDS; NORMS; POLITICAL SYSTEMS; PUBLIC GOOD; SOCIAL AND POLITICAL PHILOSOPHY; TOLERATION; WAR AND PEACE.

Bibliography

Works by Walzer

The Revolution of the Saints: A Study in the Origins of Radical Politics. Cambridge: Harvard University Press, 1965.

Obligations: Essays on Disobedience, War and Citizenship. Cambridge: Harvard University Press, 1970.

Just and Unjust Wars: A Moral Argument with Historical Illustrations. 2d ed. New York: Basic Books, 1992 (1977).

Radical Principles: Reflections of an Unreconstructed Democrat. New York: Basic Books, 1980.

Spheres of Justice: A Defense of Pluralism and Equality. New York: Basic Books, 1983.

Exodus and Revolution. New York: Basic Books, 1985.

Interpretation and Social Criticism. Cambridge: Harvard University Press, 1987.

The Company of Critics: Political Commitment and Social Criticism in the Twentieth Century. New York: Basic Books, 1988.

Thick and Thin: Moral Argument at Home and Abroad. Notre Dame: University of Notre Dame Press, 1994.

On Toleration. New Haven: Yale University Press, 1997.

Works about Walzer

Barry, Brian. "Social Criticism and Political Philosophy." *Philosophy and Public Affairs* (Fall 1990).

Dworkin, Ronald. "To Each His Own." *New York Review of Books* (April 14, 1983).

Ethics and International Affairs (no. 11, 1997). Special Issue on *Just and Unjust Wars.*

Galston, William A. "Democracy, Philosophy: The Political Thought of Michael Walzer." *Political Theory* 17 (Fall 1989).

Raz, Joseph. "Morality as Interpretation." *Ethics* 101/2 (January 1991).

Shapiro, Ian. *Political Criticism.* Berkeley: University of California Press, 1991.

Warnke, Georgia. *Justice and Interpretation.* Cambridge: MIT Press, 1993.

Georgia Warnke

Wang Yang-ming (1472–1529)

Also known by his private name Wang Shou-jen and posthumous title Wen-ch'eng (Completion of Culture), Wang was an original and dynamic thinker distinguished by his radical interpretation of Confucian thought in opposition to that of Ch'eng I (1033–1107) and CHU HSI (1130–1200). Aside from being a devoted teacher, Wang had a remarkable political and military career. He was Governor of Kiangsi and held various positions in the departments of public works, justice, military affairs, and others, and successfully suppressed rebellions in Fukien and Kwangsi. His fundamental ideas and doctrines are contained in the *Instructions of Practical Living (Ch'uan-hsi lu),* which is a collection of conversations and letters compiled by his disciples Nan Ta-chi (1487–1541) and Ch'ien Te-hung (1496–1574). The essay entitled "Inquiry on the *Great Learning,*" written a little over a year before his death, is a valuable statement of his mature philosophy.

Because of the unsystematic character of Wang's thought and his recurrent stress on personal realization, different interpretations are quite possible. Many scholars today see in Wang's philosophy an unusual synthesis of the ethical, metaphysical, and cosmological ideas that prevailed in Sung Confucianism. From the point of view of ethical theory, it is perhaps instructive to present his principal doctrines in the light of his focus on personal realization as the key to understanding the spirit of Confucian ethics. As is widely acknowledged by scholars, Wang's main teachings—such as the unity of moral knowledge and ACTION, the vision of the sage as a great person of *jen* (humanity), who "forms one body with Heaven and Earth and the myriad things," and the innate capacity of all humans to attain sagehood—were not intended as theoretical doctrines, but as compendious statements of the culmination of his own quest for understanding the spirit of Confucian learning.

Wang's quest for the spirit of Confucian learning

may be seen as a search for an answer to the question, "How can one become a Confucian sage?" In some ways, this is reminiscent of KIERKEGAARD's (1813–1855) "How can one become a Christian?" Such a question is intelligible in the light of understanding and commitment to the Confucian vision of *jen* as having an actuating or transformative significance in one's own life. Understanding the vision involves an appreciation of the unity and harmony of all existent things. According to Wang, "The great man regards Heaven, Earth, and myriad things as one body. He regards the world as one family and the country as one person. . . . Forming one body with Heaven, Earth, and the myriad things is not only true of the great man. Even the mind of the small person is no different. Only he makes it small." Wang went on to point out that the *jen* person also forms one body with plants, stones, tiles, mountains, and rivers.

What he envisaged is an ideal of the universe as a harmonious moral community. A commitment to the vision of *jen* (humanity) is more a commitment to the task of clarifying the concrete significance of the vision as an ideal theme rather than as an ideal norm that has preceptive import. An ideal theme is more a unifying perspective, or point of orientation, than a fixed principle of conduct. Wang sometimes used the term *tao* (way) instead of *jen* for expressing his vision, but these terms are not semantically equivalent. *Jen* stresses the significance of Wang's moral vision as residing in affectionate human relationships, a habitat which is capable of indefinite expansion and ultimately embraces the whole universe. *Tao* stresses the ongoing course of changing circumstances that calls for an exercise of the agent's sense of rightness (*yi*) in coping with them. Wang reminded his students that the concrete significance of *tao* cannot be exhausted with any claim to finality (*tao wu chung-ch'iung*). In order to focus on the inherent moral character of human *hsin* (mind and heart), Wang often used the term *t'ien-li* (heavenly principle) to express his notion of the highest good. In his view, if the mind is free from selfish desires and is completely invested with *t'ien-li,* and "if it is the mind that is sincere in its filial piety to parents, then in the winter it will naturally think of the cold of parents and seek a way to provide warmth for them, and in the summer it will naturally think of the heat of parents and see a way to provide coolness for them. These are all the offshoots of the mind that

is sincere in its filial piety." While Wang did not always deprecate the pursuit of factual knowledge, he mainly directed his attention to its governing ethical significance. Unlike Chu Hsi, he showed little interest in discovering the *li* or rationales of all existent things. For him, the investigation of things emphasized in the *Great Learning* does not consist literally in factual inquiry, but in the rectification of the mind that deviates from his moral vision. For him, "things" are the objectives of the moral will. To investigate is to rectify, to get rid of evil thoughts and to do good. Rectification of the mind involves, in particular, an acknowledgment of the unity of moral knowledge and action (*chih-hsing ho-i*), an enlargement of the scope of moral concern in the light of the vision of *jen,* rather than extensive acquisition of factual knowledge.

For contemporary moral philosophy, Wang's varying remarks on the unity of knowledge and action provide an interesting case study for the problem of moral commitment and achievement. Underlying Wang's doctrine is the question of understanding the moving POWER, actuating force, or import of moral knowledge as a form of practical as distinct from theoretical knowledge. This question, of course, presupposes that moral knowledge has a cognitive content, which for Wang consists of various Confucian notions of virtue such as filiality, sincerity, righteousness, and INTEGRITY. For this reason, Wang sometimes expressed his doctrine as one of the unity of moral learning and conduct, or of the simultaneous pursuit of moral learning and practice. The term "knowledge" (*chih*) carries both a prospective and retrospective emphasis, embodying a distinction between knowledge *anterior* to action and knowledge *posterior* to action. Prospective moral knowledge, for the most part, is a product of learning, an acknowledgment of the *projective* significance of the standards embedded in the various notions of virtue. It is this notion that is implicit in Wang's compendious remark that "knowledge is the direction of action and action is the effort of knowledge." As prospective knowledge, and by virtue of its cognitive content, it provides a direction or a leading idea (*chu-yi*) for actual conduct. Another compendious remark appears to make use of both prospective and retrospective senses of moral knowledge: "knowledge is the beginning of action and action is the completion of knowledge." Alternatively put, prospective knowledge is a task, and retrospective knowledge is an accomplishment, or the experience of actual practice. Wang's stress on personal realization of his moral vision is a stress on retrospective moral knowledge. For Wang, the transition from prospective to retrospective knowledge involves a variety of intellectual acts (inquiry, understanding, sifting, or discrimination) and volitional acts (involving resolution, INTENTION, moral DESIRE, and the purity of moral motives in the endeavor to achieve the ideal of *jen*). More especially, in his mature thought, Wang constantly focused on extending *liang-chih,* commonly rendered as "innate or intuitive knowledge of the good."

Again, like Wang's other doctrines, understanding his conception of *liang-chih* requires personal realization. He was reported to have said:

My doctrine of *liang-chih* was arrived at through a hundred deaths and a thousand sufferings. I cannot but concisely express it by a single utterance. Only I fear that when a student receives this teaching, it is all too easy for him to regard the teaching as something to play with occasionally without any real understanding, as it involves concrete and substantial effort.

For coherent explication, it is difficult to state his view without reconstruction. While we have no evidence that Wang would encourage such an attempt, he did admit that *liang-chih* has a diversity of compatible interpretations. From his varying remarks, it is possible to offer a plausible interpretation. *Liang-chih,* a notion indebted to MENCIUS (fourth century B.C.E.), is viewed as inherent in every person's mind, inborn rather than acquired, that is, its presence does not depend on learning or deliberation. It is said to be indestructible and omnipresent, though subject to obscuration by the insistence of selfish desires.

Fundamentally, it is an ability to distinguish the right from the wrong, as well as the good from the bad. The knowledge (*chih*) involved is not propositional knowledge, but acknowledgment, particularly of the actuating import of Wang's vision of *jen.* In this sense, *liang-chih* is the ability of moral DISCRIMINATION; it is akin to HUTCHESON's (1694–1746) notion of moral sense or BUTLER's (1692–1752) principle of reflection or CONSCIENCE. As informed by the vision of *jen, liang-chih* is moral consciousness, the seat of self-reliance in the pursuit of the vision. More especially, it is *liang-chih* that renders perspicuous the possibility of realizing the ideal of "forming one body" with all things in the universe. As invested with the ideal, the mind of *liang-chih* is not a repository of fixed rules or principles of conduct. Thus, it has a crucial role to play in guiding deliberation in coping with changing and exigent circumstances of human life.

Wang believed that *liang-chih* can provide unerring guidance, but it is unclear how he could account for failure in extending *liang-chih* and the relation between moral and factual knowledge. In some ways, Wang's doctrine of *liang-chih,* to adopt SIDGWICK's (1838–1900) distinction, is reminiscent of "perceptual" rather than "dogmatic" or "philosophical" INTUITIONISM. On the whole, his conceptions of moral mind, knowledge, and action, and the vision of *jen* repay close study, particularly, as a contribution to MORAL PSYCHOLOGY and to the history of ideas, in view of Wang's extensive influence in JAPAN and among major modern Chinese thinkers, *e.g.,* Liang Ch'i-chao (1873–1929) and Hsiung Shih-li (1885–1968). In recent Chinese thought responsive to Western philosophy, Wang's influence is evident in the works of T'ang Chun-i, Thomé H. Fang, and Mou Tsung-san.

See also: ACTION; CHINA; CHU HSI; COMPARATIVE ETHICS; CONFUCIAN ETHICS; CONFUCIUS; HSÜN TZU; MENCIUS; MORAL COMMUNITY, BOUNDARIES OF; MORAL PURITY; PRACTICAL WISDOM; SELF-KNOWLEDGE; WISDOM.

Bibliography

Works by Wang Yang-ming

Instructions for Practical Living and Other Neo-Confucian Writings. Translated by Wing-Tsit Chan. New York: Columbia University Press, 1963.

The Philosophical Letters of Wang Yang-ming. Translated by Julia Ching. Columbia: University of South Carolina Press, 1972.

Works about Wang Yang-ming

Chang, Carsun. *The Development of Neo-Confucian Thought.* Vol. 2. New York: Bookman Associates, 1962.

———. "Proceedings of East-West Philosophers' Conference on Wang Yang-ming: A Comparative Study." *Philosophy East and West* 23, nos. 1, 2 (1973).

Ching, Julia. *To Acquire Wisdom: The Way of Wang Yang-ming.* New York: Columbia University Press, 1976.

Cua, A. S. *The Unity of Knowledge and Action: A Study in Wang Yang-ming's Moral Psychology.* Honolulu: University Press of Hawaii, 1982.

———. "Between Commitment and Realization: Wang Yang-ming's Vision of the Universe as a Moral Community." *Philosophy East and West* 43, no. 4 (1993).

Tu Wei-ming. *Neo-Confucian Thought in Action: Wang Yang-ming's Youth (1472–1509).* Berkeley: University of California Press, 1976.

A. S. Cua

war and peace

When, if ever, is it morally permissible or obligatory for a state or collective to prepare for or engage in the deliberate organized violence known as "war"? Once a state or collective has resorted to war, are there any moral constraints upon the strategies and weapons which it employs? These questions have been addressed over several centuries, in many cultures, by "just war" theorists. The fundamental presumption of just war theory is that war is a moral activity; that is, whatever EVIL it brings, war can be conducted and judged according to recognizable moral standards. The two dominant alternatives to just war theory, realism and PACIFISM, reject even the attempt to assess war morally. "Realists" claim that organized violence is not intrinsically immoral and that moral judgments are at best irrelevant, and often inimical, to the "interests" of state which should guide decisions about war. Pacifists and nonviolent activists argue that wars cannot be judged morally because war or any other organized injuring and killing is always wrong; the attempt to censure selectively certain particular causes or practices of war indirectly legitimates the institution of war as a whole. In recent decades, the theory of "nuclear deterrence," which justifies the development and deployment of nuclear weapons, both challenges and contributes to just war theory, realism, and pacifism.

Just War Theory

Just war theorists presume that war is at least lamentable and usually horrifying. Nonetheless, these theorists argue, a state or collective is sometimes justified and occasionally obliged to resort to war.

There are two exemplary causes for war; self-preservative defense and rescue.

A state or politically organized group justly resorts to violence in response to violent attacks which seriously threaten its territory, cultural or ethnic integrity, HUMAN RIGHTS, or economic viability. The classic just defense is directed against actual attackers and is intended to disarm or repel them. However, most just war theorists define "just defense" more broadly to include, for example, preemptive attacks against armies massed to attack, strikes against the munitions and barracks of potential attackers, or invasions intended to weaken or control potential enemies. "Defense" then comes to designate a violent response to a real or perceived *threat* to the state or political entity. Similarly, although defense strictly construed is no longer justified when attackers are repelled or disarmed, many just war theorists allow for punitive or invasive attacks against a repelled and retreating attacker, sometimes, but not always, with the stated aim of deterring future attack.

Second, a state or collective may resort to violence on behalf of people who are suffering from unjust violence. If, for example, a state is murderously assaulting a group of its citizens or another state, a collective within or outside the state may justly intervene. Like "unjust attack," "murderous assault" can be expanded to include a threatened assault that calls for preemptive intervention. When intervention on behalf of the assaulted involves violating the assaulting state's borders, it can conflict with international law. Moreover, since, according to most just war theorists, even a murderous state has the right to defend itself against attack, both the rescuers of assaulted citizens and the defenders of the attacked state seem to be justly resorting to war. However, the question whether both (or all) sides in a war can in fact resort to war justly is much debated in just war theory.

In addition to legitimating military defense and rescue, just war theory is invoked to legitimate other kinds of war. Most notably, people invoke the language and concepts of just war theory to defend resorting to violence in order to spread—or at least prevent the erosion of—religious beliefs or political values such as DEMOCRACY. Moreover, wars which are described and defended in terms of POWER relations—for example, interventions intended to "restore the balance of power"—are also often defended in moral terms—as, for example, an intervention necessary to repel an unjustly aggressive invader. The justice of various causes of resorting to war is a matter of dispute within just war theory. What is indisputable within the theory is that a war is justifiable only if there are morally adequate grounds for undertaking it, or, in the terms of the theory, only if there is *jus ad bellum.*

In most versions of just war theory, the LEGITIMACY of a cause is necessary but not sufficient to justify resorting to violence. No matter how legitimate its cause, violence must be a 'last resort,' following upon the failure of nonviolent efforts to achieve just aims. The good to be achieved by going to war should at best significantly outweigh, and must at least be proportionate to, the costs of war and the suffering which war brings. A corollary of this requirement is that those going to war must anticipate success—or at least anticipate that violence will *predictably* increase the chances of achieving collective aims. The theory rules out self-sacrificial, heroic displays of violence which cannot predictably serve some collective end.

The decision to resort to violence must be made by the right people, and the 'just cause' that they adduce must reflect the actual reasons for fighting—for example, the claim that one is rescuing assaulted people cannot be used to describe or conceal territorial conquest or imperialist gain. Traditionally, just war theory had a conservative commitment to existing states and their governments. Only state leaders could legitimately declare war. Less conservatively, the decision to resort to violence must be taken by recognized political leaders acting with the support of substantial numbers of people. According to just war theory, small group or vanguard violence is unjustified no matter how legitimate its cause. On the other hand, many militarized cadres ("terrorists") describe their commitments in the language of just war theory.

The discussion of *jus ad bellum* is initially framed in terms of a state's, or at least a political collective's, decision to resort to violence. An individual is, then, morally permitted to participate in a just war. In most versions of the theory, individuals also have the right to abstain from a war if they are conscientiously opposed to war itself or, according to some theorists, if they are seriously and conscientiously opposed to a particular war. Because just war theorists believe that going to war is a *morally* serious

act, it would seem that soldiers should not be conscripted, terrorized, bribed, or deceived into fighting wars to which they do not conscientiously subscribe. However, most just war theorists support conscripting and coercively enlisting men—and very occasionally women—in a just cause. Similarly, smaller revolutionary or "guerilla" groups who cannot resort to conscription cite the justice of their cause in excuse of intimidating and sometimes violent tactics of procurement.

At the heart of just war theory is a paradox. It is impermissible to resort to war except where there is an urgent cause whose justice overrides considerations of the multiple suffering and evil that accompany war. Yet even a just cause does not legitimate all military strategies deemed instrumental or even necessary to achieve it. A war is just only if it is conducted justly. Whatever the justice of their cause, strategists, rulers, commanders, and individual soldiers should be constrained by the moral strictures of *jus in bello* as well as by military considerations. Similarly, even the most illegitimate aggressor should conduct its wars morally.

Moral constraints limit the targets, perpetrators, and weapons of attack. Ideally, only combatants are the object of attack—that is, only those people who are themselves attacking (or are clearly prepared and poised for attack). Once combatants surrender or are disarmed, they are no longer legitimate targets. Ideally, the weapons of a just war are discriminatory. It is possible to aim them only at combatants, and their effect is limited to the damage required to disarm, disable, or repel attackers. Weapons which will almost certainly maim noncombatants (*e.g.*, explosives dropped on cities) or which are gratuitously cruel (*e.g.*, dumdum bullets) or which cause damage to victims and bystanders even after surrender (*e.g.*, chemical defoliants) violate constraints of war.

As just war theorists recognize, some war practices violate the ideal constraints of *jus in bello*. Many standard, allegedly effective military strategies and weapons predictably afflict civilians or continue to have deleterious effects after a war. Even in declared wars waged by uniformed armies, it is difficult to distinguish combatants from noncombatants—for example, from munitions makers, intelligence gatherers, or farmers producing food for soldiers. Efforts to distinguish a class of "innocents" whose blood cannot be shed are no more successful. For example, the conscripted soldier may be no less "innocent" than an entrepreneur who sought war or a preacher who fomented the loyalties or HATE necessary to fight.

Faced with the disparity between ideals of war and its practice, just war theorists sometimes invoke the doctrine of DOUBLE EFFECT. The nub of this complexly elaborated doctrine is a distinction between effects which are intended and those that are merely foreseen but undesired. It is the intentional act rather than the foreseen consequence which is morally decisive. War makers should intend to kill only combatants; they can permissibly act on this INTENTION knowing that their weapons and strategies can afflict bystanders and are irreparably harmful.

Just war theorists (see especially Michael WALZER) may also appeal to the idea of "supreme emergency." In "supreme emergencies," a morally outrageous act—for example, the bombing of civilian populations—may, at a particular time, be the only feasible tactic in a just and urgent cause. Walzer's example is Britain's bombing of German cities *before* precision bombing or any other more acceptable measures were developed for resisting the great evil of Nazism. Recognizing that the appeal to "supreme emergencies" strains the very idea of *jus in bello,* Walzer underlines the irresolvable moral cost: "rights violated for the sake of victory are genuine rights, deeply founded and in principle inviolable."

Both the principle of "double effect" and the concept of "supreme emergency" reflect the determination of just war theorists to maintain the distinction between war and massacre, legitimate violence and murder, in the face of actual weaponry, strategies, and military realities that put these distinctions at risk.

Realism

States and other collectives often resort to violence to achieve political aims. According to realists, their decisions may be misguided in several ways: military force may be ineffective or inappropriate for achieving a particular aim; leaders or citizens may be prey to masculinist fantasies or patriotic romance; strategists may be uninformed about their opponent's strength or imprudent in assessing risks. War-making is subject to many kinds of censure; it is not, according to realists, subject to moral assessment. States make war. States act in state INTERESTS. In state relations, power is the only medium of ex-change; the strong exact what they can from the weak.

There are many kinds of realist positions. Some argue that "might makes right," that superior force not only does but should prevail. Other realists lament a reign of force they deem inevitable. Some believe that people as well as states are fundamentally governed by self-interest, others that individual morality is simply inapplicable to state relations. Still others believe that, while distinctive moral considerations may govern state actions, the preservation of the state is a moral imperative that overrides any other moral claims and that furtherance of state interests is a statesman's primary obligation. A realist may justify the existence of a particular state or a system of competitive self-interested states on the grounds that they promote *moral* life and the international stability on which morality depends. But a state's actions, including the violence it prepares for and undertakes, are then judged in terms of benefit to the state.

Realists write as though states were the agents of war, but smaller collectives can adapt realist arguments to their purposes. Nor do states war only against states; a militarized state can, in its self-interest, turn upon its own "dissident" or "minority" citizens. Realists should have no moral scruples about conscripting, hiring, or coercively enlisting soldiers. Like the wars it makes possible, effective procurement of soldiers can be justified in terms of state (or collective, or cadre) interests.

Many realists argue that, once war is undertaken, it should be conducted "realistically," that is, strategies and weapons should be assessed solely in terms of their military effectiveness. These realists would, for example, release or quarter prisoners when this was conducive to war aims or had no military import, but kill prisoners when quartering or releasing them was strategically costly. Although realists assess strategies in terms of their military effectiveness, they tend to recognize two checks on the appeal to "military necessity." When strategies conflict with international law, some realists are unwilling to declare the laws ineffectual and therefore invalid. Second, in choosing between strategies, realists may chose a less effective strategy on the ground that it spares more lives—principally the lives on one's own side but also lives of conquered people, especially if their labor can be put to use. Although not morally required to save lives if a more deadly strategy is markedly superior on military grounds, nothing prevents realists from acting humanely whenever military necessity allows.

It is possible for realists to reject moral constraints on going to war yet condemn those who conduct themselves "immorally" in battle. It is also possible to adhere to the strictures of *jus ad bellum,* but reject moral constraints on strategy. This realism *in bello* can be defended on moral grounds. Given the horrors of war, it is wrong to refrain from militarily effective acts that would hasten victory. Moreover, if organized violence cannot be controlled, it is fraudulent (unrealistic) to pretend otherwise.

Clearly, realist arguments can be used in support of war and in excuse of massacre. But realism is not necessarily more conducive to militarism or violence than just war theory. According to some realists, moralistic attitudes prevent people from going to war when they should and constrain them from fighting as effectively as they are able. But moral sentiments also inspire battle and excuse excesses of violence against an evil enemy. In refusing to distinguish the good from the evil cause, the legitimate from the illegitimate strategy, realists undermine the passion as well as the logic that fuels "just" and patriotic war.

Pacifism and Nonviolent Action

Even if soldiers and strategists are constrained by the principles of *jus in bello,* in waging war they commit themselves to war's business: out-injuring, and out-killing massed and anonymous others. Pacifists agree with just war theorists that many causes are worth fighting for, some worth dying for. But they argue that no cause justifies the deliberate, organized violence intrinsic to waging war.

"Absolute pacifists" reject any violence against humans and sometimes even against animals or the PROPERTY of humans. "Contextual pacifists" train for nonviolent resistance and look critically at every call to violence; but they refuse to rule out in advance an exceptional circumstance—more often an individual, but sometimes a collective assault—in which they would use violence to disarm and dislodge attackers or oppressors even if that meant killing them. These contextual pacifists are distinguished from the most anti-violent just war theorists only by the centrality and force, within their moral or religious lives, of their repudiation of violence and

their commitment to discover or invent strategies of nonviolent struggle.

Pacifists give various reasons for renouncing violence. Many secular as well as religious pacifists believe in the inviolability of human souls and the preciousness of human bodily lives. Whatever their metaphysical assumptions, most pacifists believe that war and other violence harms individuals who engage in it, morally, psychologically, and physically. They also believe that violence endangers the state or collective that relies on it and damages the natural habitat on which all warring parties depend. Most pacifists also believe that war fosters CORRUPTION, poverty, secrecy, tyrannical government, and violent OPPRESSION of "dissident" or "minority" citizens. Many pacifists also believe that military violence fuels and is fueled by racial, sexual, and domestic violence. In training soldiers, militarists use the rhetoric, and often tacitly condone the practice, of violence against women and the enemy "race." Even among civilians, war legitimates racist hate for "the enemy" and reasserts a cultural and conceptual connection between "masculinity" and the right to violence. Finally, pacifists fear that moderation and violence are intrinsically opposed; armies are rarely able to prevent the irrational and immoral escalation of enmity and destruction (see Clausewitz). What AUGUSTINE (354–430) (cited in J. Teichman) called war's "real evils"—"love of violence, revengeful cruelty, fierce and implacable enmity, wild resistance, and the lust for power, and such like"—may be intrinsic to organized violence.

The principal moral objection to pacifists is that, by washing their own hands of violence, they let violence be done to others. Although there is a quietist, private strain within pacifism, expressed in merely personal commitment to withdraw from violence, most pacifists are committed to resisting evil and redressing injustice. The pacifists' counterpart to military violence is nonviolent action. In more or less coherent campaigns, nonviolent activists engage in propaganda, demonstrations, strikes, sit-ins, boycotts, CIVIL DISOBEDIENCE, and other tactics of nonviolent struggle to achieve their aims. For pacifists and their critics, the relative *effectiveness* of this kind of nonviolent action, compared to military action, is a central *moral* issue.

Critics charge that nonviolent campaigns are at the mercy of armed forces that can quickly turn upon them. Moreover, pacifists are committed to negotiation and COMPROMISE on all but the most serious moral issues. Therefore, out of principle as well as weakness, pacifists will appease violent aggressors.

Pacifists reply that because militarists have to fund, procure, and arm an effective military force before they can effectively engage an attacker, they are at least as likely as nonviolent activists to placate an armed aggressor. While it takes time to plan and prepare for an effective nonviolent campaign, nonviolent activists claim that they are more able to engage in some action quickly. And because they work without massive armies, highly destructive weapons, and complex, computerized command and control systems, nonviolent fighters are more able than their military counterparts to revise or postpone their campaigns in the light of unpredicted damage.

Pacifists admit that activists and bystanders are massacred in nonviolent campaigns, but point out that those engaged in armed struggle, as well as the greater number of civilians routinely affected and often targeted by chemical and explosive weapons, are similarly vulnerable to slaughter. On the pacifist view, when lengthy military and nonviolent campaigns are considered and compared as a whole, there is considerably less mutilation, killing, and psychological destruction in the latter than the former. In general, pacifists claim that the effectiveness of violence is routinely overestimated. If a war has a clear winner, it also has a clear loser for whom violence has failed. The advantages gained by even a clear winner may be lost within decades. Most wars exhaust all participants; no one achieves the war aims which justified war in the first instance; winners and losers are depleted and demoralized. At best, the effects of violence are unpredictable and loosely related to the respective moral claims and virtues of belligerents.

By contrast, pacifists point to several instances of nonviolent actions whose successes, they believe, are underreported and minimized. While the successes of nonviolent action are only partial, pacifists claim that they are no more compromised than typical military victories. Nonetheless, most pacifists recognize a moral obligation to increase and to reveal the effectiveness of nonviolent action. However damaging and destructive violence may be, so long as nonviolent action is or is perceived to be at the mercy of violence, and military action is or is perceived to be the only means to resist evil and redress injustice, good people will continue to resort to war.

Whatever its effectiveness, nonviolent action is coercive, often hurtful, and frequently provokes violent response. Like just war theorists, nonviolent activists assess their means of struggle, trying to eliminate those that are violent, threaten to become violent, or are especially likely to provoke violent response. There is, for example, lively debate among pacifists about destruction of property and self-destructive activities like hunger strikes. Like the most just of wars, nonviolent action, however restrained, is morally risky. Like just war theorists, most pacifists believe that only actual or imminent serious injustice or assault justifies full-scale COERCION. However, pacifists also point out that nonviolent coercion admits of degrees and, on their view, is more controllable and less harmful than violence. Therefore, nonviolent activists need not be as morally certain of the rightness of their cause as their just war counterparts.

Deterrence

The detonation of nuclear weapons would kill millions of bystanders both within warring states and around the globe, perhaps destroying the human species and the habitat necessary for human life. They would almost certainly destroy the political culture and might well destroy the physical existence of any peoples who suffered their effects, almost certainly including peoples of the state who first detonated the weapons. Hence, the use of these weapons would be immoral according to just war theory and irrational according to realists. Moreover, because of the danger of accident, misperception, computer and communication breakdown, and unintended escalation of nonnuclear wars, the mere deployment of nuclear weapons threatens those who possess them as well as external parties. Hence the need for a distinctive theory which, unlike the three considered so far, addresses the rationality and morality of deploying the weapons that it would be immoral and irrational to detonate.

According to their advocates, nuclear weapons are meant to deter first-strike attacks on the possessing state by other nuclear states ("basic deterrence") as well as conventional or nuclear attacks on any state the nuclear state has promised to protect ("extended deterrence"). Both basic and extended deterrence appear to depend upon a potential attacker's belief that the possessing state intends to detonate the weapons they have deployed. Since this detonation appears to be suicidal, the intention is suspect.

Over the last few decades, some realists have defended the "rationality" of nuclear deployment by claiming that nuclear weapons can be usefully detonated and that therefore the intention to use them is credible. Some argue that the human species and perhaps the state in question can survive even major nuclear "exchanges." Most of these realists promulgate the concept of limited nuclear war and advocate developing strategies and weapons for waging these wars. Critics of any nuclear war underline the certain or probable massive destruction of even limited nuclear exchange. They also claim that the well-known difficulty of containing any military violence is exacerbated for weapons whose system for command, communication, and control is technologically complex, vulnerable to attack, and has proved barely reliable in peacetime circumstances.

Some realists argue that the mere deployment of weapons, and therefore the mere possibility of their use, is sufficient to deter attack ("existential deterrence"), and that therefore the effectiveness of the weapons does not depend upon an intention to use them. These realists adduce in support of their claim the fact that no nuclear weapons have been detonated (except in tests) since 1945 and even more that there have been no large-scale wars between states that possess or are protected by nuclear weapons. Moreover, they argue, any reasonable government would be extremely reluctant to risk provoking a nuclear armed state even if the chance of actual retaliation were slight.

Critics place less confidence in the associative, *post facto* connection of deterrence and (comparative) peace and underline the dangers of accidental detonation and the irrationality of trusting in the rationality of leaders. Noting the present social and economic harms to a state of nuclear deployment and the radical and undeniable destruction these weapons portend, they urge, on realist grounds alone, that states should develop and depend upon less lethal and costly forms of deterrence.

Just war theorists confront not only the possible irrationality but also the possible immorality of deploying nuclear weapons. Some just war theorists argue that a minimal, discriminatory ("counterforce") and contained use of nuclear weapons is consonant with the requirements of *jus in bello*. Most

just war theorists, citing the intrinsic destructiveness and "collateral damage" to populations of even small nuclear weapons and the great risk of escalation, argue that the *use* of nuclear weapons is unconscionable. They then confront the question whether it is moral to intend, or even to appear to intend, to perform an act that is immoral. And to this some respond that such an intention is permissible only if the intention itself is both necessary and sufficient to deter evil, thus raising again the question of the "rationality" of deterrence.

Nuclear deployment raises many other moral issues concerning, for example, the effect on children and others of their government's commitment to terror (or "balance of terror"), the effect on a society of the secrecy and hierarchy on which nuclear deployment depends, the covert use of nuclear weapons to intimidate and exploit other states, and the social injustices that are exacerbated by funneling scarce resources into weaponry. Despite the cumulative force of such moral challenges, many just war theorists, at least in the context of the Cold War (roughly, 1945–1989) between the United States and the then Soviet Union, remained sufficiently convinced of the efficacy and necessity of deterrence to support continuing deployment, especially when combined with determined though gradual and stable arms reduction.

But even when the Cold War was intense, some just war theorists were sufficiently troubled by the cumulative moral charges against deterrence to declare themselves "nuclear pacifists." Others became nuclear pacifists out of a "realistic" appreciation of the consummate danger of nuclear weapons and the inherent irrationality of nuclear strategies. At the least, nuclear pacifists publicly renounce the intention to use nuclear weapons and actively support unilateral disarmament initiatives. Usually, they argue that, in a nuclear age, with nuclear weapons proliferating, the entire system of war is too dangerous and costly to maintain. Moreover, they see no strategic or conceptual abyss—no "firebreak"—between nuclear and increasingly destructive "conventional" weapons. Hence, reflecting upon the irrationality and immorality of nuclear deployment leads them to reexamine the efficacy and legitimacy of any organized violence.

Theories of deterrence and nuclear pacifism developed in response to particular weapons within the context of a particular "cold war." It now seems likely that nuclear weapons will be substantially reduced and that the danger of war among the "Super" and "Western" powers will recede. If this hope is borne out, discussions of war and morality will center once again upon just war, realist, and pacifist responses to traditional forms of struggle, such as resistance to tyranny, state conflicts, civil strife, and imperialist conquest. But nuclear weapons will not disappear from those states that currently deploy them. Moreover, states that are just developing nuclear capacity will likely develop their own distinctive forms of deterrence theory or nuclear pacifism as they decide about the rationality and morality of the deployment and detonation of nuclear weapons. Hence, the insights developed by people who have been or will be forced to think in the nuclear shadow should continue to shape new understandings of the morality of war and nonviolent action.

See also: BARGAINING; COERCION; COLLECTIVE RESPONSIBILITY; COMPROMISE; COOPERATION, CONFLICT, AND COORDINATION; COST-BENEFIT ANALYSIS; DETERRENCE, THREATS, AND RETALIATION; DOUBLE EFFECT; GANDHI; GOVERNMENT, ETHICS IN; HOLOCAUST; HUMAN RIGHTS; INTERNATIONAL JUSTICE: CONFLICT; KING; LOYALTY; MACHIAVELLI; MILITARY ETHICS; NUCLEAR ETHICS; OPPRESSION; PACIFISM; POWER; RACISM AND RELATED ISSUES; REVENGE; REVOLUTION; RISK; RISK ANALYSIS; SELF-DEFENSE; TERRORISM; TORTURE; VIOLENCE AND NON-VIOLENCE; WALZER.

Bibliography

Bok, Sissela. *Toward a Strategy for Peace.* New York: Pantheon, 1989.

Bondurant, Joan. *Conquest of Violence: The Gandhian Philosophy of Conflict.* Berkeley: University of California Press, 1971.

Cady, Duane. *From Warism to Pacifism: A Moral Continuum.* Philadelphia: Temple University Press, 1989.

Catholic Church. National Conference of Catholic Bishops. "The Challenge of Peace: God's Promise and Our Response." In *Catholics and Nuclear War: A Commentary on "The Challenge of Peace," The U.S. Catholic Bishops' Pastoral Letter on War and Peace,* edited by Philip J. Murnion. New York: Crossroad Publishing, 1983. A reluctant defense of deterrence and thorough statement of just war theory. Volume also contains many interesting commentaries.

Clausewitz, Karl von. *On War.* Princeton: Princeton University Press, 1976 [1833]. Realism.

Deming, Barbara. *We Are All Part of One Another.* Philadelphia: New Society, 1984. For a clear, secular statement of the principles of nonviolence, see especially "Revolution and Equilibrium."

Dyson, Freeman. *Weapons and Hope.* New York: Harper and Row, 1984. Historical account of the development of concepts of deterrence and nuclear war fighting.

Gallie, W. G. *Philosophers of Peace and War: Kant, Clausewitz, Marx, Engels, and Tolstoy.* Oxford: Oxford University Press, 1978. Issues not framed in terms of just war theory.

Gandhi, Mohandas K. *Nonviolent Resistance.* New York: Schocken, 1961. Collection of articles.

———. *Satyagraha in South Africa.* Ahmedabad: Navajivan, 1928.

Holmes, Robert L. *On War and Morality.* Princeton: Princeton University Press, 1989. A very useful and thorough overview of the just war theories, deterrence, realism, and pacifism from a pacifist perspective. Useful bibliography.

Horsburgh, H. J. N. *Nonviolence and Aggression.* Oxford: Oxford University Press, 1978. Pacifism.

Johnson, James T. *Can Modern War Be Just*? New Haven: Yale University Press, 1984. On just war theory.

Kahn, Herman. *On Thermonuclear War.* Princeton: Princeton University Press, 1961. A classic discussion of deterrence.

Kant, Immanuel. "Perpetual Peace: A Philosophical Sketch." In *Kant's Political Writings,* edited by Hans Reiss. Cambridge: Cambridge University Press, 1970 [1795]. A useful discussion which does not frame issues in terms of just war theory.

Kennan, George. *American Diplomacy, 1900–1950.* Chicago: University of Chicago Press, 1951. Realism.

———. "Morality and Foreign Policy." *Foreign Affairs* 64, no. 3 (Winter 1985/86): 205–18. Realism.

Kenny, Anthony. *The Logic of Deterrence.* Chicago: University of Chicago Press, 1985.

King, Martin Luther, Jr. *A Testament of Hope: The Essential Writings of Martin Luther King Jr.* Edited by James Melvin Washington. New York: Harper and Row, 1986.

Lackey, Douglas P. *Moral Principles and Nuclear Weapons.* Totowa, NJ: Roman and Allanheld, 1984.

Machiavelli, Niccolo. *The Prince and the Discourses.* New York: Random House, 1950 [1513; 1519]. Realism.

Morgenthau, Hans. *Politics Among Nations: The Struggle for Power and Peace.* Rev. ed. New York: Knopf, 1973 [1948]. Realism.

Scarry, Elaine. *The Body in Pain.* Oxford: Oxford University Press, 1985.

Schell, Jonathan. *The Fate of the Earth.* New York: Knopf, 1982. Deterrence.

———. *The Abolition.* New York: Knopf, 1984. Deterrence.

Sharp, Gene. *Making Europe Unconquerable: The Poten-

tial of Civilian Based Deterrence and Defense. New York: Ballinger, 1985. Pacifism.

Teichman, Jenny. *Pacifism and the Just War.* Oxford: Basil Blackwell, 1986.

Walzer, Michael. *Just and Unjust Wars.* 2d ed. New York: Basic Books, 1992 (1977). A thorough examination and defense of just war theory with ancillary discussions of realism, nonviolence, and deterrence.

Sara Ruddick

weakness of will

This topic is discussed by philosophers mainly in connection with disputes between adherents of internalism and their opponents, the externalists. Substantially the same dispute divides advocates of PRESCRIPTIVISM from descriptivists. According to prescriptivists and internalists, in the sense in which the term is here used, one cannot hold a moral or other evaluative opinion without prescribing or desiring that it be acted on, or being motivated to act on it oneself if one is the subject of it. To descriptivists and externalists this has seemed obviously false (Ewing). The existence of cases in which people (the weak-willed or acratic) think that they ought to be doing something but are not disposed to do it seems an obvious objection to prescriptivism and internalism.

On the other hand, there is a problem for externalists and descriptivists too. For if there were no connection between the thought that one ought to do something and the disposition to do it, there would be no puzzle about weakness of will; but there clearly is a puzzle. If we do not do what we say we think we ought to be doing, an explanation is called for. Those who say "Yes I ought. So what?" are thought to have something wrong, not merely with their morals, but with their understanding of morality (of the word "ought"). The only way to sort out these problems which afflict the two sides is by a careful analysis of the different contexts and the different senses in which we can say "I ought" but not do what we say we ought, in order to determine whether there are any cases which impugn one or other of the two positions. Such an analysis might leave each side in possession of part of the field, and resolve one of the central problems in ethical theory. But it has not yet been achieved.

The problem first arose when SOCRATES (c. 470–399 B.C.E.), as reported by PLATO (c. 430–347

B.C.E.) (*e.g., Protagoras* 352ff.) and ARISTOTLE (384–322 B.C.E.; 1145b 25), denied the possibility of *akrasia* or weakness of will. All these philosophers were in part prescriptivists, though their prescriptivism was overlaid with a belief in the objectivity of prescriptions (for the notion of 'objective prescriptions' see Mackie and Hare). This is easiest to see in Aristotle; he normally speaks as if moral judgments were descriptive, but the prime source of them, *phronēsis* or PRACTICAL WISDOM, is said to be a prescriptive faculty (*epitaktikē,* 1143a 8). And the fact that the conclusions of his practical syllogisms are actions, or prescriptions treated as surrogates for actions (*De motu animalium* 701a 20) shows that the first, evaluative or normative, premise of the syllogism also must be prescriptive; otherwise (since the second premise is normally descriptive) the syllogism would be invalid.

Akrasia is therefore a problem for Aristotle; but he tackles it in a far more sophisticated and subtle way than Socrates. Instead of denying the existence of *akrasia* as Socrates does, and instead of roundly rejecting Socrates' view, as some expositors have misinterpreted him as doing, Aristotle says that this view "is clearly at variance with what appears to the case" (1145b 28). But at the end of the first and main part of his discussion he says "It does seem as if what Socrates was after actually happens" (1147b 14).

His own solution is "very Socratic" (Robinson). It consists (after several tentative approximations) in an application of the same doctrine of the practical syllogism which, for him, generated the problem. All deliberate, though not (according to Aristotle) all intentional, actions are the result of such syllogisms. It must be remembered that the practical syllogism is not merely an account of how we act on a moral principle, but, much more generally, an account of how deliberate ACTION of any sort is produced. It is Aristotle's less crude version of the drive-stimulus-response account of the genesis of all action, beloved of many modern psychologists. The acratic act (the act counter to our best judgment, as Davidson calls it) is also the result of such a syllogism, but one which is at odds with another, better, syllogism. This "good" syllogism has a universal premise which prohibits our eating; he does not say what it is; it might be "Nothing sticky should be eaten" (*cf.* Sorabji) or "No portion not allotted to one by one's hosts should be eaten" (*cf.* Austin). But there is also present a "bad" universal premise, that any sweet thing is nice, which has its own "minor" premise (This is sweet), and is allied with, or indeed tantamount to, a desire. This combination is as effective in moving us to action as the premise he has mentioned just before (1147a 25ff.) that any sweet thing should be eaten—which, he says, when combined with a factual premise to the effect that this is sweet, leads necessarily to the person's eating it, if he can and is not prevented.

So what has happened to the "good" syllogism and its universal premise? The latter is there (1147a 32, b 16) but has been rendered ineffective, so that the abstention it calls for is inhibited. The affect which inhibits it is not an affect *of* the good premise that is present, but of a particular perceptual "minor" premise which is needed to bring it to bear on the present case (1147b 9ff.). On this factual premise (a belief about an object of perception) depends what we do; it is the last link in the chain leading to action. But this, Aristotle says, "either, affected as he is, he does not have, or he has it not as knowledge, but merely says it, as a drunkard might say the verses of Empedocles" (*cf.* 1147a 20). So, not paying real attention to the fact that the food is sticky, or not his portion, he eats it.

It is no objection to this solution that we *blame* the acratic (1145b 10, 1148a 3, b 6); for blame goes with INTENTION, and the acratic's act is not merely intentional, but deliberate. There is, in a sense, ignorance of the good particular premise; but not (at the time, though there is afterward, 1150b 30), the *pain* which has to accompany actions done in excusable ignorance (1110a 19). And Aristotle is careful to say that *akrasia* is not WICKEDNESS, but is perhaps so in a manner of speaking (1151a 5).

He later says that there are two kinds of *akrasia.* One of them he calls 'impetuousness': someone acts against a good principle because he does not deliberate and is led on by the bad desire. The other he calls simply 'weakness': someone has deliberated in the (sc. immediate) past, but does not abide by the results of his deliberation. Both these types are consistent with the earlier explanation, and with prescriptivism. In the second case, the factual premise of the good syllogism is not present *now,* although that syllogism was complete earlier.

But difficulties can be raised for this solution. Externalists and descriptivists are apt to insist that there are cases in which someone has *all* the ingredients of the good syllogism fully present to his mind, and yet does not act on its conclusion. This would be a problem for Aristotle, as for any prescriptivist. It can only be resolved by further analysis. We have to distinguish between a large number of *different* possible cases, expanding Aristotle's list. All of them could be called 'acting counter to one's best judgment.' It may be that no one of these cases provides a counterexample to the prescriptivist position, but that, by lumping together features of different cases, descriptivists create the illusion of a counterexample.

Let us start with the easier cases, calling the subject of them S.

(1) S thinks in general, or dispositionally, that one ought, but does not apply this prescription to the particular present case. This is somewhat like Aristotle's tentative suggestion in 1146b 31.

(2) S says he ought, but does not really think it (the case of the hypocrite). Obviously, this creates no problem.

(3) S says he ought, but does not really understand what he is saying (*cf.* Aristotle's case of the drunkard, 1147a 20).

(4) S thinks he ought, but cannot. If the impossibility is due to physical inability, this creates no problem either, unless we misinterpret the dictum that 'ought' implies 'can' (Hare 1963). It is true that if S cannot, then the question of whether he ought does not arise as a question asking for a prescription for action. But I can certainly say that someone (myself, for example) ought but cannot, meaning, often, that if I could, it *would* be the case that I ought, though actually it is not.

(5) S thinks that he ought, but in a nonprescriptive sense of 'ought.' For example, he thinks that it is required by the current morality, though he does not himself accept this as a prescription for action.

(6) S thinks that he ought, but in a weak sense of 'thinks.' He has a *feeling* of obligation to do it (a feeling of compunction at not doing it). Such feelings are, in one perfectly good sense, cases of 'thinking that one ought'; but they do not amount to the full acceptance of prescriptions. Or (6a) S *thinks* that he ought in the sense

that thinking is not being certain enough to act on one's thought.

However, human moral psychology is too complex and subtle to be captured in this simple list. We must therefore add at least

(4a) S thinks that he ought, but cannot, not through physical inability, but because he cannot resist the temptation not to. Here the matter becomes very difficult, because it is hard to say what counts as being able to resist temptations. Try holding an arm out horizontally and keeping it there as long as possible. The time will come when one lowers it; but *could* one have gone on a bit longer? All serious temptations are like this. There is no determinate point at which S stops being able to resist—only a point at which we stop blaming him for not resisting. We blame him, if we do, for not being strongminded enough (*cf.* Aristotle 1145a 9). All inability is not compulsion in the pathological sense.

(7) S thinks with part of himself that he ought, in as prescriptive a sense of 'ought' as one wishes, but another part of him resists this and 'prevents' him doing it. This seems to have been Plato's solution (*Republic* 439e*ff.*, and *cf.* Aristotle 1102b 14). It was the reason for his division of the soul or mind into parts, which reminds us of Freud's (1856–1939) division, though it is not identical. It is also implied by Euripides (480 or 484–406 B.C.E.; *Medea* 1078, *Hippolytus* 380), Ovid (43 B.C.E.–C.E. 7; *Metamorphoses* 7, 20) and St. PAUL (C.E. 5?–67?; *Rom.* 7). The difficulty is to interpret it. For we do not really believe that "it is no longer I who am the agent, but sin that has its lodging in me." Otherwise *I* would not be to blame.

None of these cases presents a counterexample to prescriptivism and internalism. But to understand the matter fully we have to remember that moral thinking takes place at different levels. At the intuitive level (the only level considered by some anti-

prescriptivists), we do treat moral principles as *given*. We have learnt them, and not forgotten. We question them only with great reluctance. We say, even, that we *know* that it is wrong to tell lies, for example. This lends color to cognitivism and descriptivism. At this level, it is indeed possible for someone who knows, and *a fortiori* believes, that it is wrong to lie, nevertheless to tell a lie. When he does so, he will no doubt suffer compunction, and will describe himself as thinking or knowing that he ought not to tell it (*cf.* (6) above). If the intuitive level were all that there is to moral thinking, there would be, as externalists and descriptivists maintain, no problem about weakness of will.

Even at the intuitive level, moral principles are prescriptive; but at that level their prescriptivity is so heavily overlaid by the conviction of their truth that sometimes the believer in them can affirm their truth although he is not absolutely set on obeying them, and does not. This is what gives rise to the problem. It is in some ways analogous to the problem of conflicts of duties. There too we have the impossibility of obeying two principles, both of which are in some sense 'in' us (*cf.* Aristotle 1147a 32). In either case we shall act on one of the principles, and which we act on reveals what we finally prescribe to ourselves. But that does not stop the principle that is *not* acted on remaining in our consciousness and nagging us, so that we can go on saying that we *know* we ought to be observing it. Anyone who has succumbed to a temptation will understand this.

The literature on this subject is vast. For a short selection of more elaborate, subtle, and sophisticated, but not necessarily more correct, treatments, with diverse interpretations of Aristotle's account (some of them quite unbelievable), and voluminous references, see the works in the following bibliography.

See also: AGENCY AND DISABILITY; ARISTOTLE; CAUSATION AND RESPONSIBILITY; DELIBERATION AND CHOICE; DESIRE; EXTERNALISM AND INTERNALISM; FREEDOM AND DETERMINISM; INTENTION; MORAL PERCEPTION; MORAL PSYCHOLOGY; MOTIVES; OUGHT IMPLIES CAN; PRACTICAL WISDOM; PRESCRIPTIVISM; WICKEDNESS.

Bibliography

Aristotle. *On the Movement of Animals. Nicomachean Ethics.* Refs. to NE unless otherwise indicated; Bekker pagination.

Austin, J. L. "A Plea for Excuses." *Proceedings of the Aristotelian Society* 57 (1956/7). See p. 24n. Reprinted in his *Philosophical Papers* (Oxford: Oxford University Press, 1961), p. 123n.

Charles, D. *Aristotle's Philosophy of Action.* London: Duckworth, 1984. See chapters 3, 4.

Charlton, W. *Weakness of Will.* Oxford: Basil Blackwell, 1988.

Davidson, D. "How Is Weakness of the Will Possible?" In *Moral Concepts,* edited by Joel Feinberg. Oxford: Oxford University Press, 1970. See p. 93 for the acratic act. Reprinted in his *Essays on Actions and Events* (Oxford: Oxford University Press, 1980).

Euripides. *Hippolytus. Medea.*

Ewing, A. C. *Second Thoughts in Moral Philosophy.* London: Routledge and Kegan Paul, 1959. See chapter 1.

Hardie, W. F. R. *Aristotle's Ethical Theory.* Oxford: Oxford University Press, 1968. Chapter 13. (2d, enlarged ed., 1980.)

Hare, R. M. *Freedom and Reason.* Oxford: Oxford University Press, 1963. See chapter 5. For passage noted in article, p. 51.

———. *Moral Thinking.* Oxford: Oxford University Press, 1981. Especially pp. 57–60.

———. *Plato.* Oxford: Oxford University Press, 1982. For "objective prescriptions," see p. 57.

Kenny, Anthony. *Aristotle's Theory of the Will.* London: Duckworth, 1979. Especially chapter 14.

Mackie, J. L. *Ethics: Inventing Right and Wrong.* Harmondsworth: Penguin, 1977. For "objective prescriptions," see chapter 1.

Mele, Alfred R. *Irrationality.* Oxford: Oxford University Press, 1987. Large bibliography.

Mortimore, G., ed. *Weakness of Will.* London: Macmillan, 1971.

Ovid. *Metamorphoses.*

Paul, the Apostle. *Epistle to the Romans. New English Bible* translation.

Pears, David. *Motivated Irrationality.* Oxford: Oxford University Press, 1984.

Plato. *Protagoras.* Stephanus pagination.

Robinson, R. "L'Acrasie, selon Aristote." *Revue Philosophique* (July–September 1955). For passage noted, see p. 265. English translation, "Aristotle on Akrasia," in his *Essays on Greek Philosophy* (Oxford: Oxford University Press, 1969), and in *Articles on Aristotle: Vol. 2, Ethics and Politics,* ed. by J. Barnes, *et al.* (New York: St. Martin's Press, 1977).

Sorabji, Richard. *Necessity, Cause and Blame.* Ithaca, N.Y.: Cornell University Press, 1980. For passage noted here, see p. 473.

Urmson, J. O. *Aristotle's Ethics.* Oxford: Basil Blackwell, 1988. See especially chapter 7.

Walsh, J. J. *Aristotle's Conception of Moral Weakness.* New York: Columbia University Press, 1963.

R. M. Hare

Weber, Max (1864–1920)

Born in the German city of Erfurt, Weber grew up in Berlin. At the gymnasium there, he read widely in history and philosophy, studied the classics, and received an excellent training in languages. Weber began his university studies as a student of law at Heidelberg in 1882, transferring later to Berlin and Göttingen. In addition to law, he studied history, economics, and philosophy. Weber completed his doctoral dissertation in 1889, and two years later presented his *Habilitationsschrift* which formally qualified him for a university appointment. After holding several university positions, he accepted a chair in political economy at Freiburg in 1894 when he was only thirty. In 1896, he moved back to Heidelberg as a full professor. This meteoric rise in the stodgy German university system was halted by a nervous collapse that cut short his university career just as it was beginning. His illness incapacitated him for nearly five years and prevented further teaching for almost two decades.

Weber resumed his scholarly activities in 1903 as co-editor and the guiding spirit of the *Archiv für Sozialwissenschaft und Sozialpolitik,* which became the leading social science journal in Germany. From this time on, he lived as a private scholar, except for a brief period at the end of his life. Long periods of intense scholarly activity were followed by relapses into depression and inability to work. He eventually accepted a chair at Munich in 1919, where he fell ill with pneumonia and died the following year.

Weber published the first of his famous methodological essays, "'Objectivity' in Social Science and Social Policy," in 1904. As with his other methodological writings, he was primarily concerned with the nature of the social sciences and the special epistemological presuppositions that underlie all social scientific inquiry. In this influential treatise, Weber insisted on the rigorous distinction between empirical knowledge and value-judgments. While scientific truths are demonstrable, he said, value-judgments are not. To judge the validity of values, Weber held, was a matter of faith. Consequently, value-judgments must be excluded from all social scientific work.

The following year, he published his controversial study, *The Protestant Ethic and the Spirit of Capitalism,* in which he attempted to demonstrate a link between ascetic religious belief and economic development. In brief, he argued that the Calvinist believer's conception of his relationship to God and other men served to direct his activity into capitalist endeavors.

Weber pursued the general relationship of RELIGION and society further in his large-scale comparative SOCIOLOGY of world religions, where he examined the consequences of different theological doctrines for men's economic activities. He also planned a comprehensive treatise on economy, politics, and society. Although he never completed either of these ambitious projects, by the time of his death he had written volumes on the religion of CHINA, INDIA, and ancient Judaism. Weber's multivolume work, *Economy and Society,* and the great bulk of his many publications, did not appear until after his death in 1920.

Weber's concern with religious and other values is also seen in his writings on the legitimacy of institutional arrangements. He argued that the concept of LEGITIMACY has both an "empirical" and a "normative" meaning, and cautioned the social scientist to use only the former. While he is never explicit about the normative meaning, the empirical meaning of legitimacy concerns its binding influence on people's actions. Every institutional arrangement, he says, attempts to establish and cultivate a belief in its legitimacy. An economic or political system is legitimate, in Weber's view, to the extent that people believe that it is appropriate for their society. For Weber, then, legitimacy is completely a matter of belief or opinion.

Those acting subject to an institutional arrangement may, argues Weber, ascribe legitimacy to it in several ways: (1) on rational or legal grounds, based on a belief in the "legality" of normative rules and the right of those elevated to AUTHORITY under such rules to issue commands; (2) on traditional grounds, *i.e.,* a belief in the legitimacy of what has always existed; (3) on charismatic grounds, that is, by virtue of devotion to the specific and exceptional sanctity, heroism, or exemplary CHARACTER of an individual; and (4) by virtue of a rational belief in some absolute value, such as NATURAL LAW.

Although Weber speaks of four ways that claims to legitimacy may be grounded, in subsequent analyses he excluded (4) above and developed his three well-known "pure" types of legitimacy: rational, traditional, and charismatic. Even had he continued to consider all four types, however, he would have been subject to the criticism that his concept of legitimacy is, in one sense, incomprehensible. This is because it makes it impossible (or meaningless) to pose the important normative question: Is this government (economic system, or whatever) really legitimate? Weber has already assimilated this question into the, for him, primary question: Is this government (economic system, etc.) believed to be legitimate?

For Weber, and for those who follow him, questions about the legitimacy of a particular economic, political, or other institution are purely "empirical": answers require only that we observe whether people "believe" in them or obey their dictates. A government that engenders and maintains this belief through the use of secret police and propaganda is thus still legitimate. Political decisions accepted by the citizenry are legitimate, no matter how arbitrary or unrelated to specifiable rules. Since legitimacy is defined in terms of belief or acquiescence, no "normative" considerations need be involved. For those scholars accepting Weber's views, there are no criteria (other than belief) by which to make judgments about the legitimacy or illegitimacy of the institutional arrangements that concern them.

Weber emphasized the centrality of values—the ideas over which people struggle—at the individual as well as the societal level. He spoke of the scholar's soul being at stake in the practice of his or her vocation, and stressed the need for INTEGRITY and individual RESPONSIBILITY in one's life and work. At the same time, he disclaimed the possibility of any objective way of ranking values or justifying science or any other institution within the totality of human life.

Whatever his arguments about the validity of values, Weber's own values reveal themselves in his contributions to numerous areas of scholarly interest: the university, bureaucracy, POWER, social stratification, legal history, urbanism, and music, to name only a few. There was hardly a human concern left unexamined by this great universal scholar.

See also: AUTHORITY; CONVENTIONS; ECONOMIC SYSTEMS; GOVERNMENT, ETHICS IN; INSTITUTIONS; INTEGRITY; LEGITIMACY; METAPHYSICS AND EPISTEMOLOGY; POLITICAL SYSTEMS; POWER; PRECEDENT;

Weber, Max

RELIGION; RESPONSIBILITY; SOCIOLOGY; VALUE, CONCEPT OF.

Bibliography

Works by Max Weber

Ancient Judaism. Das antike Judentum, translated and edited by Hans H. Gerth and Don Martindale. Glencoe, IL: Free Press, 1952 [1917–1919].

Critique of Stammler. Translated and edited by Guy Oakes. New York: Free Press, 1977 [1907].

Economy and Society: An Outline of Interpretive Sociology. 2 vols. Edited, revised, and partially translated by Guenther Roth and Claus Wittich. Berkeley: University of California Press, 1978 [1922].

From Max Weber: Essays in Sociology, 1906–1924. Translated and edited by Hans H. Gerth and C. Wright Mills. New York: Oxford University Press, 1946.

General Economic History. Translated by Frank Knight. New York: Collier, 1961 [1923].

"'Objectivity' in Social Science and Social Policy." In *The Methodology of the Social Sciences.* Translated and edited by Edward A. Shils and Henry A. Finch. Glencoe, IL: Free Press, 1949 [1904].

Roscher and Knies: The Logical Problems of Historical Economics. Translated and edited by Guy Oakes. New York: Free Press, 1975 [1903–1906].

The Agrarian Sociology of Ancient Civilizations. Translated by R. I. Frank. London: New Left Books, 1976 [1909].

The City. Translated by Don Martindale and Gertrud Neuwirth. Glencoe, IL: Free Press, 1958 [1921].

The Protestant Ethic and the Spirit of Capitalism. Translation by Talcott Parsons of *Die protestantische Ethik und der Geist des Kapitalismus.* New York: Scribner's 1958 [1904–1905].

The Rational and Social Foundations of Music. Translated by Don Martindale, Johannes Riedel, and Gertrud Neuwirth. Carbondale: Southern Illinois University Press, 1968 [1921].

The Religion of China: Confucianism and Taoism. Translated and edited by Hans H. Gerth. Glencoe, IL: Free Press, 1952 [1916].

The Religion of India: The Sociology of Hinduism and Buddhism. Translated and edited by Hans H. Gerth and Don Martindale. Glencoe, IL: Free Press, 1958 [1917].

The Sociology of Religion. Translated by Ephraim Fischoff. Boston: Beacon Press, 1963 [1922].

Works about Max Weber

Bendix, Reinhard. *Max Weber: An Intellectual Portrait.* Garden City, NY: Doubleday, 1960. An invaluable guide to Weber's life and his work.

Bendix, Reinhard, and Guenther Roth. *Scholarship and Partisanship: Essays on Max Weber.* Berkeley: University of California Press, 1979. Helps to locate Weber's position in the intellectual topography of the twentieth century.

Green, Martin. *The von Richtofen Sisters: The Triumphant and the Tragic Modes of Love.* New York: Basic Books, 1974. Illuminates certain aspects of Weber's private life neglected in his wife's biography.

Marshall, Gordon. *Presbyteries and Profits.* Oxford: Clarendon Press, 1980. A good defense of the Protestant ethic thesis.

Mommsen, Wolfgang. *The Age of Bureaucracy: Perspectives on the Political Sociology of Max Weber.* Cambridge: Cambridge University Press, 1971. An excellent discussion of the relationship between Weber's methodology and his political theory.

Mommsen, Wolfgang, and Jürgen Osterhammel, eds. *Max Weber and His Contemporaries.* London: Allen & Unwin, 1987. An exploration of European intellectual life in the late nineteenth and early twentieth centuries.

Runciman, W. G. *A Critique of Max Weber's Philosophy of Social Science.* Cambridge: Cambridge University Press, 1972. A useful critique of Weber's methodological views.

Swedberg, Richard. *Max Weber and the Idea of Economic Sociology.* Princeton: Princeton University Press, 1998. Makes accessible Weber's ideas about economic sociology.

Weber, Marianne. *Max Weber: A Biography.* Translated by H. Zohn. New York: Wiley, 1975.

Derek L. Phillips

Weil, Simone (1909–1943)

Weil was a French philosopher, political activist, factory worker, and critic of the politics and culture of her time; later in life her thought turned in an increasingly religious and Christian direction.

Weil's early writings, especially her major essay "Reflections on the Causes of Liberty and Social Oppression" (1934), develop a powerful and original critique of the orthodox MARXISM of ENGELS (1820–1895), Lenin (1870–1924), and the European Communist parties.

Weil argues that a critique of capitalism, and political action grounded in that critique, must rest on a firmly moral basis. That basis is this: capitalist work organization (which Weil regarded as having been adopted also in the Soviet Union) undermines the DIGNITY of the workers and treats them as things. Drawing partly on her own factory experience, Weil powerfully describes this process of degradation and later broadens the description in her analysis of war in *"The Iliad,* or Poem of Force" (1940).

Weil regards her moral critique as drawing on KANT's (1724–1804) notion of treating others as ends, and she credits MARX (1818–1883) with applying this notion to the process of production. But she faults Marx for abandoning this focus in his social and political analysis, where he (wrongly, in Weil's view) views PROPERTY relations as the ultimate determinant of a society's CHARACTER. Weil also rejects the orthodox Marxist contention that the course of history itself condemns capitalism; more generally, she rejects all historically grounded notions of progress.

Weil's early essays discuss dignity primarily in individualistic and intellectualistic terms—as guiding one's actions by the use of one's reason and judgment. To be unable to exercise this capacity (especially in a work setting) is what it is to be oppressed. Weil's later writing conceptualizes the negation of dignity not so much as OPPRESSION but as "affliction"; she no longer sees its fundamental source in changeable social INSTITUTIONS. Affliction is not simple suffering but a deeply internalized sense of worthlessness akin to a spiritual death.

For Weil, the fundamental ethical stance toward the world is one of "attention" or attentive LOVE. Attention toward other human beings involves stripping away those elements of one's individual psychology which prevent fully taking in the reality of the specific other person. Thus, attention goes beyond pity, SYMPATHY, or BENEVOLENCE. In its purest and most complete state, this form of attention (especially toward the afflicted) is extraordinarily difficult to accomplish. It seems to be a law of PSYCHOLOGY that we turn away from the afflicted; to turn toward them with loving attention, we must counteract this natural force (which Weil calls "gravity"). Ultimately, only God's grace allows us to love the afflicted.

Weil criticizes the idea of "RIGHTS," regarding it as entirely inadequate to express the much more profound concept of "justice," understood in what she takes to be a Platonic sense. For her, the notion of "rights" is too legalistic; its connotation is too commercial, distributive, and comparative; it is grounded in the false value of individual personality; and the demand for rights tends to block out the recognition of hurt and degradation. In place of rights, Weil sets 'obligations to sustain needs' as the standard by which to construct and assess a social order. She articulates a rich (if sometimes idiosyncratic and arbitrary) theory of human NEEDS, listing many of them in seemingly contrary pairs—LIBERTY and order, EQUALITY and hierarchy, private and collective property.

In most of her writing, Weil is suspicious of "collectivities" as a force that constrains and even crushes individuals. But in her late work, *The Need for Roots* (1949), she articulates a moral and political foundation for COMMUNITARIANISM by seeing (some) human collectivities, and especially nations, as (potentially) "vital mediums," giving identity, sustenance, and meaning to individual lives.

See also: AUTONOMY OF MORAL AGENTS; BENEVOLENCE; CARE; DIGNITY; EXPLOITATION; INTERESTS; KANT; MARX; MARXISM; NEEDS; POWER; PROPERTY; WORK.

Bibliography

Works by Simone Weil

The Simone Weil Reader. Edited by G. Panichas. Nyack, N.Y.: Moyer Bell, 1977. The major essays on moral topics: *"The Iliad,* Poem of Might" (1940); "Human Personality" (1943); "The Love of God and Affliction" (1942).

Waiting for God. New York: Harper and Row, 1973 (1950). See "Forms of the Implicit Love of God," a major moral and religious essay.

The Need for Roots. New York: Routledge, 1988 (1949). The primary statement of Weil's later political (but also moral and religious) thought. Her only book length work.

"Reflections on the Causes of Liberty and Social Oppression." In *Oppression and Liberty.* Amherst: University of Massachusetts Press, 1973. The major work of her early political philosophy and her assessment of Marxism.

Works about Weil

Blum, Lawrence A., and Victor Seidler. *A Truer Liberty: Simone Weil and Marxism.* New York: Routledge, 1989. Exploration of her political philosophy, especially her relation to Marxism.

Dietz, Mary. *Between the Human and the Divine: The Political Thought of Simone Weil.* Totowa, N.J.: Rowman and Littlefield, 1988. Major overview of all of Weil's political thought; very good bibliography.

Little, J. P. *Simone Weil: Waiting on Truth.* Oxford: Berg, 1988.

McLellan, David. *Utopian Pessimist: The Life and Thought of Simone Weil.* New York: Poseidon, 1990.

Springsted, Eric. *Simone Weil and the Suffering of Love.* Cambridge, Mass.: Cowley Press, 1986. Brief account of her religious and moral thought.

Winch, Peter. *Simone Weil: "The Just Balance."* Cambridge: Cambridge University Press, 1989. Exploration of some major philosophical concerns in Weil's work.

Lawrence Blum

welfare rights and social policy

Welfare rights are legal protections for the fulfillment of the basic needs of those who cannot, unaided, fulfill those needs for themselves. An example is public assistance for the unemployed so that they can continue to pay for food and shelter even though they have not found paid work. Such protections against economic deprivation, when in force, are together called the welfare state. The welfare state is a set of public interventions in a market economy. Intended to place limits upon the worst economic outcomes that can befall individuals, it guarantees the legal right to some minimal levels or types of welfare. The central contemporary debates about social policy toward welfare rights, then, take the form of discussions about the welfare state, specifically about the interrelated issues of its scope and form, its mesh with the market economy it presupposes, and its justification. Those who believe that many but not all economic outcomes should be left to the play of market forces develop specific social policies to protect welfare rights.

The relation between legal rights and moral rights to welfare is neither as straightforward nor as essential to current debates as one might initially suspect. The great Western theorists of RIGHTS, such as John LOCKE (1632–1704), have assumed moral—indeed, natural—rights to various types of welfare provision. *The Second Treatise of Government* (1690) assumed a set of natural rights to subsistence: "Men, being once born, have a right to their Preservation, and consequently to Meat and Drink, and such other things, as Nature affords for their Subsistence." However, the recognition of a moral right to such subsistence supplies is neither sufficient for, nor necessary to, the creation of a legal right to them. Even if a moral right to subsistence is granted, provisions for the enjoyment of that right might still be made by voluntary associations of individuals not working through the state. Additional considerations are needed to establish that the kind of legal provisions that constitute a welfare state is the appropriate implementation of moral rights to welfare. Some of those additional considerations might even seem reason enough in themselves to justify a welfare state of some extent, in which case the acknowledgment of moral rights to welfare would not even be necessary to the argument for the legal rights.

The scope and form of welfare rights are central issues of current social policy. Simple decency, not to mention the prevention of social disorder, obviously requires that the homeless and the hungry not simply be left to freeze or starve in the streets. The interesting ethical questions concern how far to rise above utter heartlessness and specifically what public arrangements to make. What should be left to private CHARITY or to bureaucratic discretion, and what should be a matter of compulsory (tax-supported) and primarily nondiscretionary public provision? Should there be unemployment compensation, as mentioned above, or economic policies designed to produce full employment, or a right to a job with the government as employer of last resort, or some combination of two or more of these options? Should the eligibility for whatever is guaranteed be universal across the society, or should it be 'means-tested,' that is, should potential recipients be required to prove their need for the service or commodity in question? The answers to questions like these depend in part upon how alternative arrangements would mesh with the underlying market economy and in part upon which of several alternative justifications are the basis for creating the legal right.

The mesh with market mechanisms is discussed most often in terms of incentive and disincentive effects of alternative arrangements. For example, an issue central to debates about reform of the welfare system in the United States has been the relative economic positions of the 'working poor,' people with full-time jobs who nevertheless earn too little to fulfill their basic material NEEDS, and the chronically unemployed who claim whichever welfare rights they are entitled to by law. It is often asserted that, unless the working poor are economically better off than the unemployed receiving welfare benefits, the unemployed will not have sufficient incentive to seek employment. One proposed solution to this alleged problem is to make looking for work or accepting available jobs a condition for receiving welfare benefits. Another proposal is to insist that something less than the economic level of the working poor should in effect constitute a ceiling upon the maximum economic level to be guaranteed to the unemployed. However, these putative solutions make controversial empirical and ethical assumptions.

Such proposals tend to assume that those who make use of welfare rights are mostly healthy, adult white males with a good education and no competing claims upon their attention. The degree of the "feminization" of poverty in the United States means, however, that a large proportion of those who must call upon their welfare rights are single mothers whose young, dependent children make demanding competing claims upon their time. Moreover, among the unemployed men is a disproportionately high percentage of inadequately educated nonwhites. These proposals also presuppose that most people will be motivated to work only by the prospect of otherwise unacceptable economic conditions. To assume that the actual economic level of the working poor is an acceptable ceiling on the economic level of those exercising their welfare rights is to assume as well that this level is otherwise just and ethically acceptable.

The justifications for social policies creating welfare rights will naturally have strong implications for the appropriate level of guarantees. If that level is higher than the current actual level of the worst-off working poor, and if it is indeed necessary to maintain an incentive-providing INEQUALITY between the worst-off working and the best-off unemployed, then it may be ethically necessary to raise the economic level of the worst-off working poor by means of some other social policy, such as tax policy. For example, strong contemporary arguments for welfare rights base those rights not upon universal moral rights, but upon the requirements of citizenship or democratic participation in the specific society whose laws guarantee the rights. Meaningful citizenship or participation in democratic self-government may in fact require certain levels of guarantees of, for example, public education and public health. And other plausible justifying considerations, such as the democratic ideal of equal minimum SELF-RESPECT, would appear to set other requirements for both the scope and form of welfare rights. For example, 'means-testing,' which may initially seem an obvious requirement for efficiency, may be so stigmatizing as to be incompatible with self-respect. Still other possible justifications, such as the promotion of community,

the requirements of justice, or the protection of the vulnerable against EXPLOITATION, would carry their own implications for scope and form.

See also: ALTRUISM; BENEVOLENCE; CHARITY; CIVIL RIGHTS AND CIVIC DUTIES; COLLECTIVE RESPONSIBILITY; COMMUNITARIANISM; COOPERATIVE SURPLUS; DIGNITY; ECONOMIC ANALYSIS; ECONOMIC SYSTEMS; ENTITLEMENTS; EQUALITY; GENEROSITY; HUMAN RIGHTS; INEQUALITY; JUSTICE, DISTRIBUTIVE; LIBERTY, ECONOMIC; MERIT AND DESERT; NEEDS; PROPERTY; PUBLIC AND PRIVATE MORALITY; PUBLIC HEALTH POLICY; PUBLIC POLICY; PUBLIC POLICY ANALYSIS; RIGHTS; SELF-RESPECT; SOCIAL AND POLITICAL PHILOSOPHY; SOCIAL CONTRACT; SYMPATHY; TOLERATION; WORK.

Bibliography

Brown, Peter G., Conrad Johnson, and Paul Vernier, eds. *Income Support: Conceptual and Policy Issues.* Maryland Studies in Public Philosophy. Savage, MD: Rowman and Littlefield, 1981. Ethical issues in the implementation of welfare systems and the formulation of welfare reforms. For benefit adequacy *vs.* work incentives, see especially "Conflicting Objectives and the Priorities Problem" by Norman Daniels, 147–64.

Ehrenreich, Barbara, and Francis Fox Piven. "The Feminization of Poverty." *Dissent* 31 (1984): 162–70.

Goodin, Robert E. *Reasons for Welfare: The Political Theory of the Welfare State.* Studies in Moral, Political, and Legal Philosophy. Princeton: Princeton University Press, 1988. Comprehensive discussion and extensive bibliography.

Goodin, Robert E., Bruce Headey, *et al. The Real Worlds of Welfare Capitalism.* New York: Cambridge University Press, 1999.

Gutmann, Amy, ed. *Democracy and the Welfare State.* Studies from the Project on the Federal Social Role. Princeton: Princeton University Press, 1988. Thorough integration of both empirical and ethical considerations. See especially "Race, Class, Power, and the American Welfare State" by Jennifer L. Hochschild, 157–84.

Locke, John. *Second Treatise of Government.* 1690. See chapter 5, paragraph 25.

Marshall, T. H. "Citizenship and Social Class." In his *Class, Citizenship, and Social Development,* 65–122. Westport, CT: Greenwood Press, 1973. Classic lecture on welfare rights, originally presented in 1949.

Moon, J. Donald, ed. *Responsibility, Rights & Welfare: The Theory of the Welfare State.* Boulder, CO: Westview Press, 1988. Includes valuable historical perspectives.

Wellman, Carl. *Welfare Rights.* Savage, MD: Rowman and

Littlefield, 1982. A philosopher's detailed attention to social policy.

Henry Shue

Westermarck, Edward [Alexander] (1862–1939)

A Swedish-speaking Finn who wrote his major works in English, Westermarck was for a half century an internationally known researcher and writer on sociological, philosophical, and anthropological topics. His published works fall into three categories: the history of human marriage, the origin and development of the moral ideas, and the civilizations of Morocco. In each area, Westermarck's once dominant position has been severely challenged, leading to neglect or misinterpretation of his views, although in recent years scholars in a variety of disciplines have utilized and defended his writings.

The education Westermarck received at the University of Helsinki was Germanic in inspiration, and he likened it to a shallow stream that gave the impression of depth only because it was so muddy. Instead he turned to British writers—David HUME (1711–1776), Adam SMITH (1723–1790), Charles DARWIN (1809–1882), and James George Frazer (1854–1941)—as models. Intrigued by some questions about the origin of sexual modesty, Westermarck conducted armchair research in the British Museum, resulting in his first book, *The History of Human Marriage* (1891). Arguing against the prevailing opinion that early humans were sexually promiscuous, he cited recorded facts about human social customs and similarities among higher primates to demonstrate the universality of marriage. Émile DURKHEIM (1858–1917) took him to task for "resting sociology on Darwinism," but Westermarck's appeal to evolutionary theory was far from uncritical.

A more general subject had also captured Westermarck's imagination: the nature of moral disagreement. Are different ethical viewpoints due to defects in knowledge or are they simply a matter of contrary feelings? His investigation of moral behavior culminated in a mammoth two-volume work, *The Origin and Development of the Moral Ideas* (1906–1908).

While he agreed that reason has a large role to play in forming our moral judgments, Westermarck argued that morality is basically derived from sentiment and is socially conditioned: "Society is the school in which men learn to distinguish between right and wrong." He supported this conclusion with a mass of sociological and historical examples, organized by such categories as human sacrifice, SLAVERY, the right of PROPERTY, and SUICIDE. He appealed to descriptive data in tracing the origins of moral concepts ("good," "ought," "right," "duty," etc.) to their ultimate source in retributive emotions of indignation or approval, but he did not simply equate moral judgments with reports or expressions of emotions. Instead, pointing to basic similarities in human moral consciousness, he stressed that moral judgments are generalizations from emotions and represent a move toward IMPARTIALITY and disinterestedness; they make a claim, albeit falsely, to objectivity. In speaking of "the error we commit by attributing objectivity to moral estimates," Westermarck echoes Hume and anticipates the error theory of John Mackie (1917–1981).

What consequences follow from this denial of ethical objectivity? Normative pronouncements would lose their validity but would not therefore be wholly arbitrary, because they are part of a scientifically explainable moral consciousness. At the metaethical level, moral judgments, minus the claim to objectivity, would function along emotivist or prescriptivist lines. Insofar as theory influences practice, people would become more discriminating and tolerant in their moral opinions.

Never one to draw artificial boundaries between disciplines, Westermarck was already hard at work on his next major project: the study of Moroccan civilization. His linguistically sensitive field research, much admired by his pupil Bronislaw Malinowski (1884–1942), occupied him for four decades and generated several monographs, particularly the two-volume *Ritual and Belief in Morocco* (1926). Toward the end of his life, he defended his research methods against functionalist critics, arguing that there is no incompatibility between studying cultural phenomena within a single culture and across several cultures. In fact, his entire moral philosophy, which eschewed the normative in favor of the descriptive and the metaethical, rested on the possibility of comparison for its empirical base.

Westermarck's last major philosophical work was *Ethical Relativity* (1932). Although it incorporated major chunks of his earlier writings, this slimmer volume also contained a critique of the theories of

JOHN STUART MILL (1806–1873), Herbert SPENCER (1820–1903), F. H. BRADLEY (1846–1924), Leonard Hobhouse (1864–1929), and others; an attempt to trace the "emotional background" of normative ethical theories, especially utilitarian and Kantian; and a defense against attacks by his philosophical opponents. Most notable among Westermarck's critics was G. E. MOORE (1873–1958), who argued in his *Philosophical Studies* (1922) that Westermarck's SUBJECTIVISM could not account for ethical disagreement. In reply, Westermarck again distanced himself from the view that Moore mistakenly attributed to him, namely that moral judgments are reports of individual moral feelings.

Other controversies surrounded Westermarck during his lifetime. In *Three Essays on Sex and Marriage* (1934), he took issue with Sigmund Freud's (1856–1939) theory of the Oedipus complex, and in *Christianity and Morals* (1939), he argued that the moral influence of Christianity has been on balance negative. Even these more minor pieces are part of the puzzle that human behavior presented to Westermarck, and his moral philosophy cannot be understood except as an effort to provide a synthesis of diverse insights gleaned from several humanistic and social scientific disciplines.

See also: COMPARATIVE ETHICS; CONVENTIONS; CULTURAL STUDIES; DARWIN; DURKHEIM; EMOTION; EMOTIVISM; EVOLUTION; MOORE; MORAL REALISM; MORAL RELATIVISM; MULTICULTURALISM; PHILOSOPHICAL ANTHROPOLOGY; PRESCRIPTIVISM; SOCIAL PSYCHOLOGY; SOCIOLOGY; SUBJECTIVISM; THEORY AND PRACTICE.

Bibliography

Works by Westermarck

The History of Human Marriage. London: Macmillan, 1891. An expanded 5th edition was published in 3 volumes in 1921.

The Origin and Development of the Moral Ideas. 2 vols. London: Macmillan, 1906–1908.

Ritual and Belief in Morocco. 2 vols. London: Macmillan, 1926.

Memories of My Life. Translated by Anna Barwell. London: George Allen and Unwin, 1929.

Ethical Relativity. London: Kegan Paul, Trench, Trubner, 1932.

Three Essays on Sex and Marriage. London: Macmillan, 1934.

Christianity and Morals. London: Kegan Paul, Trench, Trubner, 1939.

Works about Westermarck

Ihanus, Juhani. *Multiple Origins: Edward Westermarck in Search of Mankind.* Translated by Maarika Toivonen. European Studies in the History of Science and Ideas, 6. Frankfurt am Main: Peter Lang, 1999. A useful study of Westermarck's writings, emphasizing anthropology and psychology.

Lagerborg, Rolf. *Om Edvard Westermarck och verkan från hans verkstad under hans tolv sista år 1927–1939.* Helsinki: Svenska Litteratursällskapets, 1951. Biographical pastiche emphasizing Westermarck's Finnish activities.

Mackie, J. L. "Edward Alexander Westermarck." In vol. 8 of *The Encyclopedia of Philosophy,* edited by Paul Edwards, 284–86. New York: Macmillan, 1968.

Moore, G. E. "The Nature of Moral Philosophy." In his *Philosophical Studies,* 310–39. London: Kegan Paul, Trench, Trubner, 1922.

Stocking, George W. *After Tylor: British Social Anthropology, 1888–1951.* Madison: University of Wisconsin Press, 1995. See pp. 151–63. A leading historian of anthropology assesses Westermarck's writings on marriage and Morocco.

Stroup, Timothy. *Westermarck's Ethics.* Åbo: Åbo akademi, 1982. The only full-scale treatment of his moral philosophy.

———, ed. *Edward Westermarck: Essays on His Life and Works.* Helsinki: Acta Philosophica Fennica, 1982. Articles by philosophers, sociologists, and anthropologists; the most complete bibliography of Westermarck's writings.

Wolf, Arthur P. *Sexual Attraction and Childhood Association: A Chinese Brief for Westermarck.* Stanford: Stanford University Press, 1995. Discusses the Westermarck-Freud disputes over the Oedipus complex and the incest taboo in light of empirical data from China.

Timothy Stroup

Whewell, William (1794–1866)

British philosopher, intellectual historian and scientist. The son of a Lancashire carpenter, Whewell went to Trinity College, Cambridge, on an exhibition from his grammar school. After graduating in 1816, he remained at Trinity, first as Fellow and, after 1841, as Master. He wrote on mathematics, physics, and mineralogy; on the history and philosophy of science; on moral philosophy; and on natural and moral theology. In 1826 he was ordained priest.

Against the British empiricist tradition, both in

science and ethics, he upheld the Kantian doctrine that, while concepts without percepts are empty, percepts without concepts are blind. Science develops by bringing accepted facts under more and more advanced concepts (which he called 'ideas'), testing results at each stage by whether their implications are themselves facts. Fact and theory are thus relative to one another: facts are expressible only in terms of concepts; and a phenomenon "is a Fact or a Theory, according as it is considered as standing on one side or the other of the Inductive Bracket." Science is not simply cumulative: accepted facts may be revised by new theories.

Unlike facts in the natural sciences, the facts of morality are 'preceptive.' That murder is wrong is the fact that the inner nature of human beings as practically rational is such that, if they think clearly and pertinently, they will conclude that, no matter what practical problem may confront them, committing murder is an irrational solution of it. The sets of rules of conduct imposed by law and public opinion in a society are the preceptive form of what the society accepts as moral facts; and the task of moral philosophy is to develop a set of 'ideas' that will explain and, where necessary, correct them. Moral facts are largely, but not wholly, what a Christian society accepts them as being. Beyond philosophy, Christian revelation for the most part confirms what is thus accepted, but sometimes corrects it.

Whewell explained accepted moral facts as deriving from five 'superior rules,' which are in turn derived from the Supreme Rule of Morality, that "We ought to do what is conformable to the Rules to which Reason directs us." They enjoin humanity, justice, truth, purity, and order (*i.e.,* the observance of positive laws). Since the first four superior rules are consistent (none requires what another forbids), they cannot be in conflict; but they can be in conflict with the rule of order, because positive laws, such as the United States Fugitive Slave Act (enacted 1850; repealed 1864), sometimes require what they forbid. In such cases, Whewell held that, although positive law is immoral and it is a duty to strive to change it, it should nevertheless be observed.

Whewell's moral epistemology, without his recognition of divine revelation, largely survives in Henry Sidgwick's (1838–1900) *Methods of Ethics* (1874), but Sidgwick claimed that reason leads us to the principles of egoism and utilitarianism, and not to Whewell's five superior rules, which are too

imprecise either for strict philosophy or for casuistry. This charge dissolves when Whewell's treatment of casuistical problems is studied.

See also: COMMON SENSE MORALISTS; JOHN STUART MILL; MORAL PERCEPTION; MORAL REASONING; SIDGWICK.

Bibliography

Works by Whewell

The Elements of Morality, Including Polity. 1st ed. 2 vols. Cambridge, 1845. Publishing history: 2d ed. (2 vols.), 1848; 3d ed. (2 vols. plus important supplement containing replies to criticisms), 1854; 4th ed. (1 vol.), 1864. U.S. editions have been pirated reprints of the first.

Selected Writings on the History of Science. Edited by Yehuda Elkana. Chicago: University of Chicago Press, 1984. The best readily available selection of Whewell's epistemological writing, with a useful editorial introduction.

Works about Whewell

Schneewind, Jerome B. *Sidgwick's Ethics and Victorian Moral Philosophy.* Oxford: Clarendon Press, 1977. Chapter 3. An authoritative account of Whewell's moral philosophy and its intellectual setting; useful bibliographies.

Todhunter, Isaac. *William Whewell D.D.: An Account of His Writings with Selections from His Literary and Scientific Correspondence.* 2 vols. London: Macmillan, 1876. Depreciates Whewell's moral philosophy, but a mine of bibliographical and biographical information.

Alan Donagan

wickedness

Wickedness may be defined as intentional wrongdoing. The central puzzle about it is: "in what sense can people intend to do wrong?" Wrongdoing is seldom if ever anyone's explicit INTENTION—yet, if people do not intend to be wicked, how can they be held responsible and blamed for what they do? Though SOCRATES (c. 470–399 B.C.E.) raised this difficulty, philosophers, especially modern philosophers, have paid it little attention. In recent times, two sets of doubts have obscured the concept still further. The old, humane doubts about whether wrongdoers know what they are doing have been compounded by quite different, more modern (subjectivist or relativist) doubts about whether any acts are really wrong at all. The whole practice of blame has fallen under suspicion. Yet if we are to discriminate as we need to between better and worse among the wildly varying actions and agents that surround us, we all need to use blame as well as praise. Nor can we sensibly attribute RESPONSIBILITY for good actions without attributing it for bad ones as well. These problems greatly increase current difficulties about PUNISHMENT, about moral differences between cultures, about MORAL EDUCATION, and about the standing of "moral judgment" generally.

The Older Dispute about Responsibility

Socrates put forward the paradoxical view that "nobody does wrong willingly" because "virtue is knowledge" (see PLATO's [c. 430–347 B.C.] *Protagoras* 352–358). Wrongdoing springs, he said, from a specially profound and sinister kind of ignorance, a "lie in the soul" which does not constitute an excuse (as modern thinkers might hope) because it is itself in some way voluntary. This is a strongly intellectualist account of vice and virtue, identifying virtue with true knowledge of the good. ARISTOTLE (384–322 B.C.E.) shrewdly criticized this view, pointing out that the kind of "ignorance" Socrates described is highly peculiar. For one thing, it is often intermittent, since we often know perfectly well that a certain action is wrong, but we lose sight of this when we ourselves are tempted to commit it. "Incontinence"—vacillating WEAKNESS OF WILL—is, he said, at least as common a cause of wrongdoing as confident self-justification.

Many philosophers have followed Aristotle's lead in noting the crucial part played by nonintellectual, noncognitive factors such as feeling in shaping motivation. Unfortunately, however, some have often treated the issue as a sharp, simple competition between reason (or knowledge) and feeling for the position of sole determinant of conduct, as if these were quite separate forces and were the only two possible causes of action. Socrates' rationalist insistence on knowledge as the sole determinant was balanced by the reply of HUME (1711–1776) that feeling is the only possible cause of action—"reason is, and ought only to be, the slave of the passions." Until recently, few prominent philosophers followed Aristotle and Bishop Joseph BUTLER (1692–1752) in trying to work out a richer, more subtle, and less

polemical vocabulary for describing the complexities of motivation, which could do justice to both elements. Today, however, this less conflict-ridden approach is probably becoming more popular.

Public versus Private

Besides this war declared between feeling and reason, there has also been a misleading division between the inner, personal or spiritual perspective on wrongdoing and the outer, social one. In the Middle Ages, religious thought stressed chiefly the inner angle, concentrating on personal responsibility for sin. Some modern political theorists—especially utilitarians—have often treated wrongdoing more as a public nuisance, comparable to disease, and concentrated on finding the right kind of social engineering to control it. This attitude, though often useful for public action, easily leads to a mechanistic or deterministic approach in which personal responsibility vanishes completely. Libertarian thinkers have revolted strongly against the obvious inadequacies of this approach. Friedrich NIETZSCHE (1844–1900) and Jean-Paul SARTRE (1905–1980) have stressed the reality of free choice, and have moreover expanded the notion of it remarkably. They have suggested that freedom is not just a matter of choosing between existing values, but of actually "creating" or "inventing" new values of one's own.

What Is Immoralism?

On this view, does the idea of wrongdoing still have any meaning? These writers are not altogether easy to understand on this point. Three quite different interpretations seem available:

(1) that it is indeed wrong to sin against one's own standards,
(2) that the only thing really wrong is the moral cowardice or BAD FAITH that prevents people from inventing these individual standards at all, or
(3) that the whole notion of wrongness has simply vanished.

View (3) seems to underlie the current notion that the whole practice of "making moral judgments" ought to be abandoned—a proposal which seems itself clearly to be a moral judgment. People often understand the title of Nietzsche's *Beyond Good and Evil* (1887) in this way, and take this program to be the one he described by his term "immoralism."

Nietzsche does indeed sometimes talk like this. But then it was his declared practice to spray acute remarks with very varying tendencies all round his topics, leaving his readers to work out how to relate them. Elsewhere—and especially in *Beyond Good and Evil* itself—he firmly and explicitly aims his attacks against particular current moral attitudes and standards, confidently making new and different moral judgments about what should replace them. He was a serious moralist who wanted to change the world, and he absolutely needed to make these new moral judgments in order to do so. He could not possibly afford to make the quite different move of outlawing moral judgment as such. IMMORALISM for him meant primarily the attack on current standards. Accordingly, neither he nor Sartre—also a committed real-world moralist—actually worked out a way of making this strange move intelligible. Anyone genuinely anxious to make it today needs to show how it is to be understood.

Conclusion

Current difficulties about using the concept of wickedness arise largely because certain admirable projects—for curtailing punishment, for honoring cultural differences, and for respecting individual freedom—have been too clumsily and paradoxically expressed. These projects really call for different moral judgments, emphasizing different values and stigmatizing different kinds of wrongdoing. They cannot intelligibly demand the abolition of all moral judgments and the loss of the concept.

See also: BAD FAITH; CRUELTY; DECEIT; DESIRE; EMOTION; EVIL; GUILT AND SHAME; IMMORALISM; INTENTION; MORAL PSYCHOLOGY; MORAL REASONING; MORAL RELATIVISM; MULTICULTURALISM; PASSION; PUBLIC AND PRIVATE MORALITY; PUNISHMENT; RESPONSIBILITY; SUBJECTIVISM; TOLERATION; VIRTUES; VOLUNTARY ACTS; WEAKNESS OF WILL.

Bibliography

Aristotle. *Nicomachean Ethics.* Book VII, chapters 1–10. A most useful general discussion. For Socrates, see chapters 2–3.

Butler, Joseph. *Fifteen Sermons.* 1722. See Sermon VII, *Upon the Character of Balaam;* and Sermon X, *Upon Self-Deceit.* For his very helpful general views on moral psychology, see the Preface to the sermons.

Hume, David. *A Treatise of Human Nature.* 1737. See Book III, part 1, section 1.

Midgley, Mary. *Wickedness: A Philosophical Essay.* London; New York: Routledge and Kegan Paul, 1984.

———. *Can't We Make Moral Judgments?* 1991. New York: St. Martin's Press.

Nietzsche, Friedrich. Beyond Good and Evil. The Genealogy of Morals. Thus Spake Zarathustra. 1883–1887.

Plato. *Protagoras.* See pp. 352–358 for Socrates' paradoxes. See also *Republic* p. 381 (Book II, chapter 9) for the Lie in the Soul.

Sartre, Jean-Paul. *Existentialism Is a Humanism.* Translated by Philip Mairet. London: Eyre and Methuen, 1948. Translation of *L'Existentialisme est un humanisme,* 1946.

Mary Midgley

William of Ockham (c. 1285–1347)

Born in England and educated at Oxford, Ockham was the preeminent Franciscan thinker of the mid-fourteenth century. Because of his role in the bitter dispute between the Franciscans and Pope John XXII (1316–1334) over evangelical poverty, he was excommunicated in 1328. After that he abandoned philosophy and theology proper, producing instead a series of political tracts on the ecclesiastical and secular power of the papacy.

Ockham's moral doctrine has often been summarily dismissed as voluntaristic, authoritarian, fideistic, and even skeptical. Though the first two charges are at least defensible, recent work suggests that Ockham's ethical writings are more subtle and, in short, more Aristotelian than is commonly recognized. Because the relevant texts are dispersed throughout Ockham's nonpolitical works, the recent publication of a complete critical edition of those works should spur more definitive research into his ethics.

Right Reason and Divine Commands

According to Ockham, moral theory is divided into (a) *positive moral science,* which "contains human and divine laws that obligate one to pursue or to avoid what is neither good nor evil except because it is prohibited or commanded by a superior whose role it is to establish the laws," and (b) *nonpositive moral science,* which "directs human acts apart from any precept of a superior, in the way that principles known either *per se* or through experience direct them . . . [principles] that Aristotle talks about in moral philosophy" (*OT* IX, 177). The latter is a demonstrative science that is "more certain than many others, because all can have greater experience of their own acts than of other things."

A perennial theoretical challenge for Christian Aristotelians has been to integrate the positive moral doctrine found in divine revelation with a nonpositive moral doctrine of the sort found in ARISTOTLE (384–322 B.C.E.). The former enjoins us to conform our wills to God's will by fulfilling the moral obligations imposed upon us by divine commands. The latter enjoins us to pursue the good proper to human nature by living according to 'right reason,' that is, in accord with those dictates of PRACTICAL REASON that lead us toward genuine human flourishing.

THOMAS AQUINAS (1225?–1274) held that, in creating human beings, God *necessarily* legislates in a way that harmonizes with right reason. The law God promulgates for human beings is thus *necessarily* a *natural* law, a law that morally obligates us to pursue genuine human flourishing according to the dictates of right reason. So although moral obligation derives, strictly speaking, from divine commands, it is metaphysically impossible that God should command us to steal, murder, commit adultery, or do anything else directly opposed to what is good by nature for human beings.

Ockham retorts that such a view unjustifiably restricts God's freedom and detracts from God's GENEROSITY. While agreeing with Aquinas in general about the content of the laws God has *actually* ordained, he maintains that God was (and is) free to both command and reward acts such as theft, murder, and adultery, which, as things now stand, are morally evil and supernaturally demeritorious, and to prohibit and punish other acts—even the very act of loving God—which under the present dispensation are morally good and supernaturally meritorious (*OT* V, 352–3).

Some conclude that, on Ockham's reckoning, human nature itself and thus the dictates of right reason are infinitely malleable according to divine whim. But this conclusion seems to stem from the mistaken idea that Ockham's nominalism regarding universals rules out a thoroughgoing Aristotelian essentialism.

A second interpretation is that, according to Ockham, it is true but only *contingently* true that the law God has promulgated for human beings is a *natural* law: "*Given the ordination that is now in force,* no act is perfectly virtuous unless it is elicited in conformity with right reason" (*OT* VIII, 394). To be sure, right reason dictates that we obey the commands (if any) of our Creator. But even if God commanded us to be thieves or murderers or adulterers, right reason would still dictate in addition that we avoid theft, murder, and adultery—and so we would find ourselves in the desperate position of being morally obligated to perform acts which are contrary to right reason and which thwart genuine human flourishing. We are spared this plight only by God's freely bestowed generosity.

On yet a third interpretation, Ockham, like DUNS SCOTUS (c. 1266–1308), holds that God's law is indeed necessarily a NATURAL LAW—so that there are some general dictates of right reason that God cannot countermand; but he denies, against Thomas Aquinas, that human flourishing *necessarily* rules out specific acts like theft, murder, and adultery.

Moral Goodness and Virtue

According to Ockham, 'morally good' as predicated of a human act "connotes that the agent is obligated to that act" (*OT* V, 353). This term applies (a) *directly* to interior acts of willing or willing-against that are intrinsically good (given standing divine precepts) and (b) only *indirectly* or by 'extrinsic denomination' to other interior or exterior acts insofar as they conform to intrinsically good interior acts. Further, an interior act is intrinsically good only if it has as part of its intentional object the motive of conforming one's will to the dictates of right reason or to the will of God.

A virtue is a habit of the will inclining one toward good acts. The highest degree of a given virtue attainable by an unbeliever is to be habitually disposed to will the good acts associated with that virtue "precisely and solely because they are dictated by right reason" (*OT* VIII, 335). Perfect virtue, which requires the special assistance of supernatural grace, is a fixed disposition to will what is dictated by right reason "precisely out of love for God."

Ockham also discussed topics such as the theological VIRTUES of faith, HOPE, and CHARITY, the connectedness of the moral virtues among themselves and with the theological virtues, and the relation of the virtues to habits of the sentient appetite. These discussions are all rich and insightful, and they provide fertile ground for further study.

See also: ARISTOTLE; CHARITY; CHRISTIAN ETHICS; DUNS SCOTUS; DUTY AND OBLIGATION; HOPE; NATURAL LAW; PHILOSOPHY OF RELIGION; PRACTICAL REASON; RELIGION; THEOLOGICAL ETHICS; THOMAS AQUINAS; VIRTUE ETHICS; VIRTUES; VOLUNTARISM.

Bibliography

Works by William of Ockham

Opera philosophica. 7 vols. St. Bonaventure, N.Y.: Franciscan Institute Press, 1974–1988. Critical edition of Ockham's philosophical works.

Opera theologica (OT). 10 vols. St. Bonaventure, N.Y.: Franciscan Institute Press, 1967–1986. Critical edition of Ockham's theological works. The following are central texts for his ethical theory: *OT* I, 276–507. *OT* II, 321. *OT* III, 440–568. *OT* IV, 597–610; 680–91. *OT* V, 338–58. *OT* VI, 149–61; 192–219; 351–428. *OT* VII, 39–61; 192–238; 340–61. *OT* VIII, 243–450. *OT* IX, 99–106; 167–92; 238–46; 253–91; 585–92; 596–99.

Opera politica. 3 vols. Manchester: Manchester University Press, 1940–1963. Critical edition of certain of Ockham's political writings, including the *Opus nonaginta dierum.*

Works about Ockham

Adams, Marilyn McCord. *William Ockham.* 2 vols. Notre Dame, Ind.: University of Notre Dame Press, 1987. The definitive contemporary work on Ockham's metaphysics, epistemology, and theology. See especially chapters 30–31.

———. "The Structure of Ockham's Moral Theory." *Franciscan Studies* 46 (1986): 1–35. A sustained defense of the second interpretation noted above.

Clark, David W. "Voluntarism and Rationalism in the Ethics of Ockham." *Franciscan Studies* 31 (1971): 72–87. Argues that Ockham's ethics falls between pure voluntarism and pure rationalism.

———. "William of Ockham on Right Reason." *Speculum* 48 (1973): 13–36. A useful introduction to its topic.

Freppert, Lucan. *The Basis of Morality According to William Ockham.* Chicago: Franciscan Herald Press, 1988. A 1961 dissertation; the best comprehensive study of Ockham's ethics.

Kent, Bonnie D. "Aristotle and the Franciscans: Gerald Odonis's Commentary on the *Nicomachean Ethics.*"

Dissertation. New York: Columbia University, 1984. An excellent study of the distinctively Franciscan appropriation of Aristotle's ethical theory in the late thirteenth and early fourteenth centuries.

McDonnell, Kevin. "Does Ockham Have a Natural Law Theory?" *Franciscan Studies* 34 (1974): 383–92. Contains references to Ockham's use of the term 'natural law,' which occurs only in his political works.

Obermann, Heiko. *The Harvest of Medieval Theology: Gabriel Biel and Late Medieval Nominalism.* 2d ed. Grand Rapids, Mich.: William Eerdmans, 1967. See especially chapter 4.

Suk, Othmar. "The Connection of the Virtues According to Ockham." *Franciscan Studies* 10 (1950): 9–32; 91–113. A close commentary on *OT* VIII, 323–407.

Urban, Linwood. "William of Ockham's Theological Ethics." *Franciscan Studies* 33 (1973): 310–50. A sustained defense of the third interpretation noted above.

Alfred J. Freddoso

Williams, Bernard (Arthur Owen) (1929–)

Bernard Williams has been professor of philosophy in Oxford, Cambridge, London, and the University of California at Berkeley. He has written on many areas, including an important book on DESCARTES (1596–1650). In ethics his central work is *Ethics and the Limits of Philosophy* (1985; cited here as *Ethics*). But he also wrote an introductory work, *Morality* (1976), as well as many important articles which have been collected into three books. His *Shame and Necessity* (1993) is a study of early Greek ethical thought.

In ethics Williams first became widely known for his criticism of UTILITARIANISM. His chief contribution here is the second half of *Utilitarianism, For and Against* (1973), which was coauthored by J. J. C. Smart who is in favour of utilitarianism. His particular objections include the problem of whether utilitarians can consistently think of themselves as being such. Williams also critices what he calls "government house utilitarianism": a ruling group, for utilitarian reasons, proposes a code of rules which the others are meant to follow for non-utilitarian reasons. Here, the rule utilitarianism problem of keeping the two sets of reasons distinct is partially expressed as the social problem of keeping the motivation of the two groups distinct.

The most influential criticism in this examination of utilitarianism concerns what Williams calls IN-

TEGRITY. In one example, a bandit chief tells you that if you kill one of his captives he will allow the others to go free, but if you don't he will kill the lot. On utilitarian grounds, the right thing to do should be straightforward: do what causes the fewest deaths—that is, kill the one captive. But, according to Williams, the answer is not that straightforward. He wants to show that it matters to us not just what happens (the consequences), but also who does it: can we properly set ourselves, as agents persisting through time, to do such dreadful acts without damaging our psychological identity or our integrity?

Williams relies here on developing a richer PSY-CHOLOGY and understanding of motivation than is found in utilitarianism and other leading moral theories, such as Kantianism. His most important paper on motivation, justification, and value is called "Internal and External Reasons" (in *Moral Luck*). For Williams, an 'internal' reason is one which is connected to an already existing motivational state, such as a desire; an external reason is one which is not so connected. (Williams's use of these terms is not the same as others' and so requires caution.) His claim is that all reasons are internal. This means that I do not have a (proper) reason for ACTION arising from the mere fact that, or from my perception that, for example, something is unjust. I have a reason only if there is something contingently about me such that I am motivated to be just (or to achieve things toward which justice is a means). Therefore, there are no REASONS FOR ACTION which apply to all rational agents as such. Whether something is a reason for a person's action depends upon that person's antecedent idiosyncratic psychological states.

This idea (which can also be found in chapter four of *Ethics*) works against any theory which supposes independent, universal, moral truths, which are taken automatically to provide reasons for action. It works against utilitarianism, where the greatest HAPPINESS is supposed to provide reason for anyone. It works against Kantianism, where pure reason, uncontaminated by DESIRE, is supposed to provide reasons for anyone. These Williams takes to fall to his fuller psychology, in particular the use of emotions rather than reason in ethical discovery.

Although Williams used the word 'morality' in an early lecture (and as the title of an early book), his preferred term is not 'morality' but 'ethics'. In this, as in other respects, he takes us back from the Kantian (or Christian) world to Greek thought. Instead of the Kantian idea of individual voluntary action as the centre of moral obligation leading to guilt at moral failure and blame by others, Williams proposes shame rather than blame as the central notion. Using early Greek thought, he claims that the voluntary is too weak a notion to found obligations.

For Williams, ethical requirements are more tangled, plural, and conflicting than they are on a Kantian model. In two earlier papers (collected in *Problems of the Self*, 1973), he developed this idea to show that ethical judgments are much more analogous to desires than to beliefs. Again, he uses emotions in his analysis, particularly the emotion of regret; and again his examples are drawn from classical Greek tragedy. His central example is Agamemnon under incompatible obligations to his daughter and to his fleet. If there is a single right answer in ethics, he should fulfil either one or the other of these obligations (otherwise, it should not matter which he does). But, Williams shows, whatever happens, Agamemnon will regret something. Taking this emotion of regret as an index of moral discovery, it follows that whatever Agamemnon does, he has done something wrong. Hence, values are plural and potentially conflicting.

Williams takes this to mean that such judgments are much more analogous to desires than they are to beliefs. If two beliefs conflict, then at least one of them must be wrong. But the Agamemnon example demonstrates that this is not the case for evaluative beliefs. Here we keep both incompatible beliefs, without thinking that we should withdraw either. To use the desire analogy: I may be caught between incompatible desires, but that doesn't mean that I should suppress or withdraw one or the other of them.

From this Williams claims that we should not ascribe a realistic status to their objects: evaluative beliefs are not beliefs about how—independently of our desires—things give us good reasons for action. Again, this runs counter to 'external' reasons and to central portions of the Kantian project. For Williams, evaluations differ from scientific beliefs which tend to converge on an independent truth (*Ethics*, chapter 8).

These points can be put in another way by considering the importance of MORAL LUCK (see the title essay in *Moral Luck*, 1981). For Kant, luck cannot enter into moral evaluation: I can be blamed only for what I did voluntarily (for my intentions). By contrast, Williams suggests that our evaluations do depend upon luck. For example, if I drive carefully, and through no fault of my own strike and kill a child, I may still feel 'agent-centred regret', that is, not just regret that the accident happened, but regret that I did it. Even though it was plainly bad luck, I may still feel that I should make some recompense.

Williams's central example to show the importance of moral luck is the case of the artist, Paul Gauguin (1848–1903). Gauguin left his wife and family to go to the South Seas to paint. If he produces great paintings, he is justified. If he doesn't, he is reprehensible for having left his family. But whether he succeeds is partially beyond his control. It is not simply a matter of having the right intentions. For Kant, OUGHT IMPLIES CAN: we may be properly evaluated only for those things we are able to do. But for Williams, such evaluation sometimes hinges ultimately on a matter of luck.

See also: EXTERNALISM AND INTERNALISM; GUILT AND SHAME; INTEGRITY; INTENTION; KANTIAN ETHICS; MORAL LUCK; MOTIVES; OUGHT IMPLIES CAN; REASONS FOR ACTION; UTILITARIANISM; VOLUNTARISM.

Bibliography

Works by Bernard Williams

Problems of the Self. Cambridge: Cambridge University Press, 1973. A selection of early papers.

Morality. Cambridge: Cambridge University Press, 1976. Simple, introductory account, with useful treatments of subjectivism and amoralism.

Moral Luck. Cambridge: Cambridge University Press, 1981. Essays from 1973–1980; a collection of the most important of Williams's papers on ethics.

Ethics and the Limits of Philosophy. London: Fontana, 1985. His most important book in ethics.

Shame and Necessity. Berkeley: University of California Press, 1993. A study of early Greek ethical thought.

Making Sense of Humanity and Other Philosophical Papers. Cambridge: Cambridge University Press, 1995. Papers collected from 1982–1993.

Smart, J. J. C., and Bernard Williams. *Utilitarianism: For and Against.* Cambridge: Cambridge University Press, 1973.

About Williams

Altham, J. E. J., and Ross Harrison, eds. *World, Mind, and Ethics: Essays on the Ethical Philosophy of Bernard Williams.* Cambridge: Cambridge University Press, 1995. Critical essays.

Ross Harrison

wisdom

The love of wisdom is supposed to be the defining characteristic of philosophers, but, with the notable exception of NIETZSCHE (1844–1900), philosophers have become noticeably less ardent in post-medieval times. This indicates a significant difference between modern sensibility and its classical and medieval predecessors. Premodern thinkers had been as fractious as modern ones, most of them nevertheless shared belief in a moral order in reality, in wisdom consisting in knowing and living according to this order, and in a life being good to the extent to which it is guided by wisdom. Modern sensibility has grown—is growing—increasingly doubtful of this belief because it is accustoming itself to the death of God, as Nietzsche put it. If there is an order in reality, it is assumed to be morally neutral, and good lives are thought to take a plurality of forms, depending on the plurality of moral ideals that humanity has constructed, rather than found inherent in the scheme of things. The modern neglect of wisdom is but a symptom of the doubt concerning the existence of the object about which wisdom has been supposed to provide knowledge. This neglect is a failing, however, because knowing how to live a good life is as important now as it has always been. The need for wisdom, therefore, has not been diminished by modern doubts about an indigenous moral order.

Wisdom may be understood in a moral and a nonmoral sense. In both senses, it involves deep knowledge, but in the moral sense the knowledge aims primarily at living a good life, whereas in the nonmoral sense its primary aim is established by some specific theoretical or practical endeavor. It is wisdom in the moral sense that will be discussed here. In that sense, moral wisdom, hereafter wisdom, is a virtue essential to living a good life. Its possession is a matter of degree; more of it makes a life better, less makes it worse.

The VIRTUES required for a good life control natural human tendencies by directing them toward seeking appropriate objects in appropriate ways. For instance, COURAGE controls the fear of danger, moderation controls the desire for PLEASURE, and justice controls the inclination toward PARTIALITY. Most virtues thus have specific outwardly directed, readily observable actions associated with them. If these actions are habitually and appropriately performed, then the relevant virtue can be justifiably ascribed to the agent. Wisdom is unlike these virtues because the specific action associated with it is directed inward and it is normally observable only by the agent. Wisdom is a virtue of reflection: the knowledge involved in it is not of how to act in some particular area of life, but of how to reflect on complex situations that may arise in any area of life. Wisdom is thus a second-order virtue that controls reflection rather than outward action. That is why there is no specific outward, observable action that normally merits being called wise. The performance or non-performance of any such action may, on occasion, be wise—or foolish—depending on the quality of the reflection that prompts it. Of the identical outward actions of two people, one may be wise, the other not.

Wisdom is thus characterized by directing the reflection associated with it inward, toward the agent, rather than outward, toward the world. The reflection is prompted by a complex situation the agent encounters in the world, and it aims to respond appropriately to it. But the quiddity of the reflection is inward because it has to do with what happens between encountering the situation and responding to it. And what happens there is that the agent endeavors to form a good judgment about what to do by evaluating the available possibilities in the light of his or her knowledge of the good. The reflection involved in wisdom is thus analyzable into a certain kind of judgment, evaluation, and knowledge, each of which reflects the agent's conception of what is involved in living a good life. That conception is the agent's standard of evaluation, the criterion of what makes the judgment good, and the embodiment of the knowledge that bears on the agent's life and conduct. Each may succeed or fail for various reasons, one of the most important of which is whether the conception of a good life they reflect is reasonable, in that the conception is suitable to the agent's CHARACTER and circumstances.

PLATO (c. 430–347 B.C.E.), the first major philosopher who wrote systematically about wisdom, stressed the central role of knowledge of the good in all the virtues. He saw the different virtues as applications of that knowledge to different areas of life. Because one of the great benefits wisdom provides is knowledge of the good, Plato thought that wisdom is not merely one virtue among others, but the most important of all the virtues. The assumption underlying this view is that knowledge of the good necessarily motivates one to act in conformity to it. Plato expressed this in the Socratic paradox: no one does EVIL knowingly. The thought behind it is that only ignorance can lead to ACTION contrary to the good, for everyone naturally seeks to have as good a life as possible.

If all moral situations were simple, Plato would have been right. In simple situations, the agents have a conception of a good life, they encounter some situation in which they have to reflect on what to do, and their moral task is to bring the knowledge, evaluation, and judgment that follow from their conception of a good life to bear on the situation at hand. If they had made no mistake in forming their conception of a good life or in applying it, then they will do what is good. If they end up doing evil, it is only because they made a mistake. The wiser they are, the less likely it is that they will be mistaken.

As ARISTOTLE (384–322 B.C.E.) saw, however, many moral situations are complex, not simple. The fundamental reason for this is that the contingency of life, the conflict of values, and the prevalence of evil often interfere with the formation of a reasonable conception of a good life, with the knowledge, evaluation, and judgment that follow from it, and with their application to moral situations. What rightly conducted reflection reveals in such cases is not how to do what the agent recognizes as the good, but the existence of insuperable obstacles in the way of forming and applying the agent's conception of a good life. These obstacles are not the products of poor reflection; they are conditions that exist independently of human efforts, and they may doom them. Aristotle expressed this by saying that the goods internal to a good life depend on goods external to them, and external goods are often beyond the control of the agents who seek them.

The contingency of life unavoidably places agents at the mercy of conditions they have neither created nor can decisively influence. Their genetic inheritance, circumstances of upbringing, level of energy, native intelligence, the conditions of their society, their good or bad luck, whether they fall afoul of injustice, whether their efforts are disparaged, all have an inevitable influence on their conception of a good life and on how well they can reflect. The frequent conflicts between the perfectly reasonable values to which agents have committed themselves also present obstacles that may have a formative influence on how well they can live and reflect. The moral and nonmoral components of their conception of a good life, their political convictions, religious beliefs, aesthetic preferences, and personal projects, their loyalties to INSTITUTIONS and persons, their fears and ambitions, the long-, medium-, and short-term satisfactions they seek often totally or proportionally exclude each other. These conflicts are produced by the very nature of values, not by the shortcomings of reflection on them. The prevalence of evil presents a further obstacle inherent in the human condition. Plato saw that the good has a naturally motivating force. But he did not see that greed, aggression, hatred, selfishness, CRUELTY, ENVY, and malevolence motivate moral monsters routinely and many others occasionally to act in ways contrary to the good.

In Stoic and Christian thought, these obstacles were acknowledged, but they were ascribed to human failings, and not counted as evidence against the existence of a moral order. The Stoics attributed them to uncontrolled desires and Christians to original sin. Modern sensibility does not countenance the cosmic optimism this view encourages. It demands evidence for the existence of a moral order, but the available evidence tells against it because all evidence comes from the world in which contingency, conflict, and evil are rampant.

These obstacles to living according to one's conception of a good life have it in common that they decrease the agent's control. They are obstacles inherent in the scheme of things, not in the agent's reflection. Improved reflection, therefore, cannot remove them. This is what makes many moral situations complex, and this is what vitiates Plato's view that better reflection will lead to better lives. It may do so, of course, but only if the contingency of life, the conflict of values, and the prevalence of evil do not prevent it.

This makes it apparent that wisdom is needed in both simple and complex situations, but it is needed in them for different reasons. In both situations, wisdom copes with obstacles. In simple situations, the obstacles are created by defects in the agent's reflection. Coping with them requires making one's con-

ception of a good life more reasonable and improving the knowledge, evaluation, and judgment that guide one's response. In simple situations, coping with obstacles means overcoming them. In complex situations, the obstacles cannot be overcome because they are inherent in the scheme of things. They will persist even if the agent's conception of a good life is thoroughly reasonable and the knowledge, evaluation, and judgment that it prompts are faultless. Coping with such obstacles requires understanding that commitment to reason and the good may not be sufficient to make one's life good, and it requires one to respond to this lamentable fact by strengthening rather than weakening the commitment. In complex situations, coping with the obstacles means learning to live with them as well as it is possible. Learning this is a matter of growing in depth.

The beginning of depth is the willingness to reflect on the facts of complex moral situations. These facts are that the contingency of life, the conflict of values, and the prevalence of evil permanently endanger human efforts to live a good life and that they do so regardless of how reasonable and well-directed the efforts are. Willingness to reflect on these facts is rare because there is a powerful motive for ignoring them: the expectation that commitment to reason and the good will make lives good. If this expectation is false, then an abyss opens up, for the questions of why be reasonable and why be motivated by the good, indeed why be motivated by anything, if success is independent of effort, will seem to have no convincing answers. If reflection destroys this expectation, it leads to hopelessness, and then it may be reasonable not to reflect, for thereby one may avoid the hopelessness to which it leads.

There is, however, a better alternative available: realizing that the expectation that leads to hopelessness is false. If the expectation is abandoned, then hopelessness will not result from its disappointment. But if it is abandoned, then the daunting significance of the facts will have to be faced. Reflection will lead people to realize then that their own chances of a good life are endangered. If reflection does not help to change this fact, what good does it do? Why strive for greater depth, if all it brings is the realization that all that one values is at risk?

To these questions, there are two answers. The first is that greater depth will lead to understanding that one is at risk, not that one is doomed. The outcome of facing the risk at which the contingency of life, the conflict of values, and the prevalence of evil put the efforts to live a good life can be success, not just failure. The good of greater depth is that of freeing oneself from false expectations, accepting the uncertain outcome of one's efforts, and not allowing the uncertainty to weaken one's efforts. To do otherwise is to increase the odds against oneself, but this time by the avoidable failure to cultivate the depth of understanding that would enable one to make the necessary efforts despite the risk of failure.

The second answer is that greater depth will lead to controlling one's natural tendency to respond inappropriately to the uncertainties of human existence in general and to those of one's own efforts in particular. The variety of inappropriate responses is great, and it is pointless to try to catalog all of them. Some common ones, however, are worth noticing. One is the cultivation of an ironic detachment that endeavors to view one's own efforts, as well as those of humanity, as having no more significance than the events in an ant heap. Another is to endeavor to deceive oneself by refusing to acknowledge the uncertainties. A further one is to adopt the heroic posture of celebrating one's efforts as a doomed Promethean struggle in which the struggle, not its outcome, is what is seen as mattering. Blind faith, resignation, cynicism, indulgence in the pleasures of the moment, and RESENTMENT against the scheme of things are some other inappropriate responses. All of them involve the sentimental falsification of the facts; they differ only in the feelings that are allowed to go astray. For they are all efforts to make too much or too little of the facts and thereby make them suitable objects of the overflowing feelings they provoke. The greater one's depth is, the more it will make one's feelings fit the facts and the less it will permit the falsification of the facts to fit one's feelings. The reason for cultivating this depth is to avoid the inappropriate responses that will worsen one's already uncertain prospects of living a good life.

The upshot of this account is that wisdom is a virtue that is needed when the smooth flow of life is interrupted by obstacles. The obstacles may be the result of the shortcomings of one's conception of a good life, or of the knowledge, evaluation, and judgment that follow from it. Wisdom leads to identifying these shortcomings and to trying to correct them. The situations in which this could be done are simple because they have a simple cause and a simple remedy: the cause is insufficient wisdom and the remedy is the cultivation of greater wisdom. The interruption, however, may be the result of obstacles that no amount of wisdom can remove because they are created by the contingency of life, the conflict of values, and the prevalence of evil, each of which lies beyond the agent's control. Wisdom helps then to understand that this is so, strengthen the motivation to do what is possible to make one's life better, and avoid inappropriate responses. These situations are complex because they reveal the uncertainties of human existence. They can only be endured, not changed. And enduring them depends on the reflectiveness and depth that wisdom provides to those who have it.

See also: AUTONOMY OF MORAL AGENTS; CHARACTER; *EUDAIMONIA,* -ISM; EVIL; EXTERNALISM AND INTERNALISM; GOOD, THEORIES OF THE; MORAL DEVELOPMENT; MORAL LUCK; MORAL REALISM; NIETZSCHE; PRACTICAL REASON[ING]; PRACTICAL WISDOM; PRUDENCE; RATIONALITY VS. REASONABLENESS; SITUATION ETHICS; TEMPERANCE; VALUE, CONCEPT OF; VALUE, THEORY OF; VIRTUE ETHICS; VIRTUES.

Bibliography

Annas, Julia. *The Morality of Happiness.* Oxford: Oxford University Press, 1993. A history of ancient theories of a good life and the place of wisdom in them.

Aristotle. *Nicomachean Ethics.* Translated by W. D. Ross, revised by J. O. Urmson. In *The Complete Works of Aristotle,* edited by Jonathan Barnes. Princeton: Princeton University Press, 1984. The fullest classical view of the place of wisdom in a good life.

Collins, J. D. *The Lure of Wisdom.* Milwaukee: Marquette University Press, 1962. Wisdom in the context of Christian thought.

Den Uyl, Douglas. *The Virtue of Prudence.* New York: Lang, 1991. History and analysis of the practical wisdom in Aristotle, Aquinas, Hobbes, Adam Smith, and Kant.

Gilson, Etienne. *Wisdom and Love in Saint Thomas Aquinas.* Milwaukee: Marquette University Press, 1951. Wisdom in Thomist thought.

Hampshire, Stuart. *Thought and Action.* London: Chatto & Windus, 1960. An account of the nature of the reflection associated with wisdom.

Kekes, John. *Moral Wisdom and Good Lives.* Ithaca, NY: Cornell University Press, 1995. A contemporary account of wisdom; bibliography.

Nietzsche, Friedrich. *The Birth of Tragedy.* In *Basic Writings of Nietzsche,* edited, translated, and with commentaries by Walter Kaufmann. New York: Random

House, 1968. Tr. of *Die Geburt der Tragödie* [1872]. The first modern attempt to free wisdom from classical and medieval assumptions.

————. *Thus Spoke Zarathustra.* In *The Portable Nietzsche,* translated and edited by Walter Kaufmann. Harmondsworth: Penguin, 1954. Translation of *Also sprach Zarathustra* [1883–1885]. Nietzsche's mature but scattered thoughts about wisdom.

Nussbaum, Martha C. *The Therapy of Desire.* Princeton: Princeton University Press, 1994. History of Hellenistic accounts of wisdom.

Plato. *Euthydemus.* Translated by W. H. D. Rowse. In *Plato: The Collected Dialogues,* edited by Edith Hamilton and Huntington Cairns. Princeton: Princeton University Press, 1961. Dialogue on wisdom.

————. *The Republic.* Translated by Robin Waterfield. Oxford: Oxford University Press, 1993. Wisdom in the context of a good society and a good life.

Rice, E. F. *The Renaissance Idea of Wisdom.* Cambridge: Harvard University Press, 1958. Traces the changes in the understanding of wisdom from ancient theories up to and including the Renaissance.

John Kekes

Wittgenstein, Ludwig [Josef Johann] (1889–1951)

A member of a distinguished Austrian family, Ludwig Wittgenstein was educated as an engineer; an interest in mathematics led him to philosophical questions. He went to Cambridge to study with Bertrand RUSSELL (1872–1970), under whose encouragement he began the logical writings that developed into the *Tractatus Logico-Philosophicus.* Written while he was a soldier in the World War I, it was published shortly thereafter. Wittgenstein then left philosophy. He returned to philosophical studies in 1929, and lectured at Cambridge during the 1930s and again for a brief period as professor of philosophy after World War II, publishing nothing after 1929. His teaching and his posthumously published writings, especially *Philosophical Investigations,* have been enormously influential.

Wittgenstein wrote a lecture on ethics around 1930; besides that there are remarks of his, explicitly ethical in character or content, in several places. The final pages of the *Tractatus* contain a sequence of such remarks; and there are thoughts about ethics in his *Notebooks 1914–1916.* Although there is not in his later work any philosophical investigation of specifically ethical concepts, a great many of the re-marks, drawn largely from the years after 1929 and published in English as *Culture and Value,* bear on ethics. His published writings contain little else that is explicitly ethical. He did, however, say that the point of the *Tractatus—i.e.,* of the whole book, not just what is explicitly about ethics—is ethical. And so any discussion of Wittgenstein's thought about ethics in that early period must make clear how what appears to be a book on logic in relation to language has an ethical point. Further, although he made no comparable remark about the point of his later writings, it has been said (see, *e.g.,* J. C. Edwards) that they too have an ethical intention.

So one difficulty in thinking about 'Wittgenstein's ethics' is becoming clear how or whether one can responsibly see as bearing on ethics what is explicitly concerned with something else. A related difficulty can be put so: unless you understand the ethical as it was to him (as expressed, for example, in remarks in *Culture and Value,* pp. 35–40, on COURAGE and on the conditions in which what one says can have truth in it), you will find it hard to grasp what he tries to accomplish in philosophy, because you will not see what mastery of the will enters philosophical thought as he engages in it. You may not see what it is to cheat in philosophy, and you may not catch yourself at it. But unless you understand the difficulty of philosophy as he thought of it, through yourself having worked through the philosophy, worked through it without cheating, you cannot see the force of the remarks with explicitly ethical content.

And there is one other difficulty. We have an idea that ethics is a branch of thought and discourse, and that philosophical ethics is a branch of philosophy containing both normative judgments and reflection on the objectivity of ethical thought, its epistemology, and perhaps its metaphysical basis or implications. To speak of 'Wittgenstein's ethics' is to suggest that some thoughts and remarks of his belong either in ethics (the branch of thought) or in philosophical ethics (the branch of philosophy). At the time of his early writings, he took the idea of ethics as branch of thought to be an illusion, and the idea of philosophical ethics to be a related one. It was no part of his intention to contribute anything to either except a *quietus.* How far his later view about ethics as a possible subject of thought diverges from current philosophical conceptions it is impossible to say with comparable definiteness; but it should not simply be assumed, if we speak of 'Wittgenstein's ethics,' that what is in question fits readily with our ideas of what the subject is.

Much of Wittgenstein's ethical thinking concerns the character of our times, from which he felt himself distant. His ethical remarks in the *Tractatus* come after and depend for their significance on a sequence (6.362–6.3751) containing a criticism of the modern *Weltanschauung* as resting entirely on an illusion. In his remarks about ethics, the idea of illusion and of false consolation in thought (supported by laziness, lack of courage, weakness) are important, and these ideas are, during the whole of his life, connected with his view of what is involved in philosophy and with his critical elucidations of what he found alien in the spirit of the times.

Ethics in the *Tractatus*

The *Tractatus* is a difficult book, not only because it is extremely compressed but also because it ends by stating that the propositions it contains are nonsense. Some readers ascribe to Wittgenstein the view that, although the propositions in the text count as nonsense, in accordance with the view of language which the book takes, they are nevertheless intended to convey to its readers truths that cannot be put into words, truths concerning the relation between language and what it depends on, the nature of the self, and ethics. Thus, for example, when Wittgenstein says (*Tr.* 6.423) that it is impossible to speak about the will so far as it is the bearer of the ethical (in contrast to the will, of no relevance to ethics, that is the subject of empirical PSYCHOLOGY), this may be read as meant to convey the truth that beyond the will that words reach, there is something else that they cannot refer to. But it is instead possible to take Wittgenstein's final description of his propositions as nonsense to mean not only that they do not express thoughts as ordinary propositions do, but also that they do not convey or in any other way enable us to grasp ineffable truths. To call proposition 6.423 nonsense, on this reading, does not mean that, although it cannot be spoken of, *there is* the will as bearer of the ethical. On this reading, an aim of the book is to enable us to give up the following analogy: just as the line between true and false propositions marks the division between what is the case and what is not, the line between what it makes sense to say and what it does not make sense to say marks the division between what may be thought and what

is beyond that and not thinkable. If we do not give up the analogy, we shall read Wittgenstein as claiming that ineffable truths that cannot be put into words are given in language in some other way. If we do give up the analogy, we shall read him as saying that we inevitably treat what is internal to language's being language as if it were a peculiar state of affairs. The sentences of the *Tractatus* engage in this masquerade in order to enable us to live without engaging in it. They fake the appearance of the expression of thoughts, but not to convey the ineffable; they are self-conscious fakes, intended to free us from what is less conscious fakery, what is illusion.

The relation of all this to ethics can best be seen if Wittgenstein's remarks on ethics in the *Tractatus* are taken with his remarks about solipsism (5.6–5.641). He says that what the solipsist is getting at is right; only it cannot be said. The solipsist says such things as "I am unique: there is no other subject of experience." When Wittgenstein says that what the solipsist is getting at is right, this is read by some (*e.g.,* Norman Malcolm) as an acceptance of the truth, though beyond words, of some sort of solipsism, as if what the solipsist were getting at were given us by his words. Alternatively, what the solipsist is getting at may be taken to be nothing but what belongs to language as language, which he tries to put using words like "I" or "self." And Wittgenstein may then be read as self-consciously borrowing apparently solipsistic language in his discussion of these issues. On this reading of the *Tractatus*, the borrowing *ends;* solipsism is not an unspeakable truth; the aim of the borrowing is that we are as it were at peace with the absence of the Subject in any proposition and do not try to think of the intelligibility of propositions in terms of a *relation* to something. And Wittgenstein makes clear the connection between this treatment of the self and a denial of synthetic *a priori* truths, explicable in terms of a relation between experience and a thinking subject. Solipsism, thought through strictly, coincides, he says, with pure realism; *i.e.,* he criticizes as a kind of intellectual cheating the *im*pure realism that will insist on some idea of a transcendental self *in relation to* the world. 'Pure realism' means: do not imagine that you imagine that there is, or that you can be in, a relation to the world. The discussion of solipsism is already ethical; and the explicitly ethical remarks are closely related. The ethical impulse is something Wittgenstein does not criticize; it issues, though, in talk purporting to be about the sense of the world, or about what is good and EVIL.

The question is how we are to read Wittgenstein's criticism of ethical talk. On one sort of reading we shall be left with an account of value in relation to the will, an account with a strong Schopenhauerian flavor, which cannot be put into senseful discourse but which we read Wittgenstein as intending to convey. On the other sort of reading, the ethical impulse that leads us to talk of value, if it is followed through strictly, leads to a silence *not* taken as the silence of someone who recognizes some conveyed though unspeakable truth. "Followed through strictly": here we have to see the difference between Wittgenstein's thought and the characteristic approach of philosophical ethics, which looks for the right philosophical account of sentences taken to *express value-judgments.* Wittgenstein's aim undercuts ethics (though not as the logical positivists aimed to): he attempts not to find an account of such sentences but to change our view of them as expressive, to show that the sentences we start off thinking of as expressive of value-judgments do not express value-judgments or anything else. They cannot be picked out by what they mean; *e.g.,* by their meaning something necessary, or beyond the conditions of senseful discourse. The totality of ordinary meaningful propositions does not include any 'ethical propositions.' If one made plain everything that can be said, then two things together—(a) that everything that could be said *was* included (*nothing* was left out); and (b) that none of what was included was ethical—would show clearly the essential feature of ethics, which is that it is not a sphere of thought or expression at all. So making clear everything that can be said leaves the space for ethics clear, precisely in leaving for ethics nothing but silence: a silence not of recognition that what one wants to say cannot be said, but that there is nothing that one *wants to say.* This does not mean that there are not then in life tasks to be performed, but there are not ethical problems whose solutions are thoughts.

Two final points: First, Professor ANSCOMBE (1919–2001) picks out as what is 'most obviously wrong' in the *Tractatus* the view that what happens in the world does not have ethical value, a view that pushes the ethical will out of the world, and that thus requires an unacceptable account of what it is to *do* something. Thus Wittgenstein's later and very different discussions of will and intention (*e.g., Phil-*

osophical Investigations, sections 611–93) involve issues that underlay the *Tractatus* conception of ethics. Second, Wittgenstein's only sustained later discussion of ethics is in the "Lecture on Ethics," written during a period in which he was subjecting to criticism the fundamental ideas about logic in the *Tractatus.* Wittgenstein's ethical views were not, though, significantly changed from those in the *Tractatus;* and this has been taken (by, *e.g.,* P. M. S. Hacker) to support the view that they never really were integrated with the logical views of that book. The issues here go to the heart of one's understanding of Wittgenstein, and are explored in James Conant's "Must We Show What We Cannot Say?"

See also: ANALYTICAL PHILOSOPHY AND ETHICS; ANSCOMBE; FORMALISM; LOGIC AND ETHICS; METAETHICS; METAPHYSICS AND EPISTEMOLOGY; MORAL TERMS; RUSSELL; VALUE, CONCEPT OF; VALUE, THEORY OF; WITTGENSTEINIAN ETHICS.

Bibliography

Works by Ludwig Wittgenstein

Philosophical Investigations. Oxford: Blackwell, 1953.

Tractatus logico-philosophicus. Translated by D. F. Pears and B. F. McGuiness. London: Routledge and Kegan Paul, 1961 [1921]. Translation of *Logisch-philosophische Abhandlung.*

"Lecture on Ethics." *Philosophical Review* 74 (1965 [1930?]): 3–12.

"Letters to Ludwig von Ficker." Translated by Bruce Gillette. In *Wittgenstein: Sources and Perspectives,* edited by C. G. Luckhardt. Ithaca, N.Y.: Cornell University Press, 1979. Taken from his *Briefe an Ludwig von Ficker.*

Notebooks 1914–1916. Translated by G. E. M. Anscombe. Edited by G. H. von Wright and G. E. M. Anscombe. Oxford: Blackwell, 1979.

Culture and Value. Translated by Peter Winch. Edited by G. H. von Wright. Chicago: University of Chicago Press, 1998, 2d ed. [1994]. Translation of *Vermischte Bemerkungen.*

Works about Wittgenstein

Anscombe, G. E. M. *An Introduction to Wittgenstein's Tractatus.* London: Hutchinson, 1963. See pp. 171–72.

Canfield, John V., ed. *My World and Its Value.* Vol. 3 of *The Philosophy of Wittgenstein.* New York: Garland, 1986. See especially essays by Peter Geach, Peter Winch, A. Phillips Griffiths, Hidé Ishiguro, Friedrich

Waismann, Rush Rhees, Paul Engelmann, and B. F. McGuinness.

Cavell, Stanley. "Declining Decline: Wittgenstein as a Philosopher of Culture." In his This New Yet Unapproachable America, pp. 29–75. Albuquerque, N.M.: Living Batch Press, 1989.

Conant, James. "Must We Show What We Cannot Say?" In The Senses of Stanley Cavell, edited by Richard Fleming and Michael Payne, pp. 242–83. Lewisburg, Penn.: Bucknell University Press, 1989. See esp. p. 274.

Diamond, Cora. "Ethics, Imagination and the Method of Wittgenstein's Tractatus." In Bilder der Philosophie, edited by R. Heinrich and H. Vetter. Wiener Reihe 5 (1991). Reprinted in The New Wittgenstein, edited by Alice Crary and Rupert Read, 149–73. London: Routledge, 2000.

Edwards, James C. Ethics Without Philosophy: Wittgenstein and the Moral Life. Tampa: University Presses of Florida, 1982. See p. 4.

Griffiths, A. Phillips. "Wittgenstein, Schopenhauer, and Ethics." In Understanding Wittgenstein, 96–116. Royal Institute of Philosophy Lectures 7. London: Macmillan, 1974.

Hacker, P. M. S. Insight and Illusion. Oxford: Clarendon Press, 1986. See p. 106.

Johnston, Paul. Wittgenstein and Moral Philosophy. London and New York: Routledge, 1989.

Malcolm, Norman. "Wittgenstein and Idealism." In Idealism—Past and Present, edited by Godfrey Vesey, 249–67. Royal Institute of Philosophy Lectures 13. Cambridge: Cambridge University Press, 1982. See p. 249.

Redpath, Theodore. "Wittgenstein and Ethics." In Ludwig Wittgenstein: Philosophy and Language, edited by Alice Ambrose and Morris Lazerowitz, 95–119. London: George Allen and Unwin, 1972.

Rhees, Rush. "Critical Notice of Maurice Cornforth, Science Versus Idealism." Mind 56 (1947): 374–92. Reprinted as "Philosophy and Science" in his Without Answers, London: Routledge and Kegan Paul, 1969, pp. 23–49. See also in this volume "The Study of Philosophy," pp. 169–172.

Tilghman, B. R. "The Moral Dimension of the Philosophical Investigations." Philosophical Investigations 10 (1987): 99–117.

Winch, Peter. Ethics and Action. London: Routledge and Kegan Paul, 1972. See "Wittgenstein's Treatment of the Will" and "Can a Good Man Be Harmed?"

Cora Diamond

Wittgensteinian ethics

Ludwig WITTGENSTEIN's (1889–1951) influence on ethics has been to some degree through his discussion of ethical topics but also through the ideas and methods that he applied in treating quite different topics, and the style or spirit of his approach to philosophical problems.

The most important example of the first kind of influence is that of Wittgenstein's specifying of the *ethical* by the contrast between absolute and relative value, in his "Lecture on Ethics" (1929 or 1930). Relative value is exemplified by the goodness of a chair: its goodness is entirely a matter of how well it satisfies some determinate purposes; but absolute value (*e.g.,* the despicableness of some ACTION) would remain unchanged even as we imagine purposes and desires altering in all possible ways. The significance of the contrast is made clear by Roy Holland in "Is Goodness a Mystery?" and is connected by Holland to a criticism of any ethics taking notions like purpose, function, or DESIRE to be central. Holland extends the criticism to what he calls life-form arguments, arguments which, influenced by other elements in Wittgenstein's philosophy, explain ethical thought by reference to its social setting. Such accounts can, Holland argues, account for *most* features of ethical thought, but not for judgments of absolute value. Holland's argument shows that, if a philosopher, influenced by Wittgenstein, aims to show something of the *motley* of ethical thought, to present the variety of ethical thought in a perspicuous way, the presentation can include both absolute and relative judgments of value and can accord them quite different significance. The effect of his argument is to suggest a radical and damaging inadequacy in naturalistic approaches to ethics, which focus on the intelligibility of ordinary and conventional judgments of value and which exclude or explain away absolute value.

Among the notions used by Wittgenstein in his later work, and given application by others in ethics, are those of *practice, agreement in judgment,* and *form of life.* The most important application of this group of notions by Wittgenstein himself was in his discussions of *following a rule* (see, *e.g., Philosophical Investigations,* sections 143–252), and it is there we see their force. Given a certain training in following rules (*e.g.,* mathematical rules), we do not disagree about what constitutes going by the rule; we do not see it as an issue about which we have to make up our minds. Rather, if we need to, we simply apply the rule. Those who play chess do not dispute whether a move breaks the rules or not; and such agreement is part of the background of the thought of any player about what particular move to make. What is not clear is how these ideas about the role of agreement may be brought to our thought about right and wrong. D. Z. Phillips and H. O. Mounce have used Wittgenstein's discussion of agreement in judgment in arguing that, unless we agree in taking the wrongness of lying (for example) as a matter of course, we could not on particular occasions criticize or condemn someone for lying, and that the necessary agreement precludes discussion of why or whether honesty or chastity (say) has the moral character which in some contexts may be assigned to it without question. That this view involves misunderstanding of Wittgenstein's thought and distortion of the character of morality has, however, been argued by Rodger Beehler, and is implied by Stanley Cavell's discussion of the supposed analogy between defined practices like games and moral life (*The Claim of Reason*).

A quite different application of Wittgenstein's discussion of following rules is central in John McDowell's arguments for a kind of moral realism. McDowell takes Wittgenstein's discussion of rules to undercut the idea that, if what is in accordance with a rule is not a subjective matter, the accord must be graspable from a position outside, as it were, of our immersion in our practices of following rules. The discussion can then be turned against non-cognitivism in ethics, if it can be shown, as McDowell attempts to do, that the non-cognitivist is taken in by analogous spurious ideas of what ethical objectivity requires. The relevance of Wittgenstein's ideas to the issue of objectivity in ethics has also been argued by David Wiggins and by Sabina Lovibond.

One feature of Wittgenstein's approach to philosophical problems is the insistence that we not think what *must* be the case, but look and see what *is*. This comes out, for example, in his contrast between our philosophical conception of logical inference and the ways we actually make and criticize inferences (see his *Remarks on the Foundation of Mathematics*, Part I). Peter Winch's writings on ethics and, in particular, his discussions of ethical rationality are influenced by this feature of Wittgenstein's technique. In "The Universalizability of Moral Judgments" (1972) and "Particularity and Morals" (1987), Winch has called into question the philosophical ideas we have about the role universality *must* play in ethical reasoning. Philosophical pre-

conceptions about rationality in ethics are also questioned by Stanley Cavell (*The Claim of Reason* Part III); anyone wishing to learn how Wittgenstein's approach to philosophy may fruitfully be applied in ethics would do well to start by reading Winch and Cavell (Cavell, 1979 should be read with Cavell, 1962).

See also: GOOD, THEORIES OF THE; MORAL ABSOLUTES; MORAL REALISM; MORAL RELATIVISM; MORAL RULES; NATURALISM; PRACTICAL REASON[ING]; RATIONALITY VS. REASONABLENESS; UNIVERSALIZABILITY; VALUE, CONCEPT OF; VALUE, THEORY OF; WITTGENSTEIN.

Bibliography

Beehler, Rodger. *Moral Life.* Oxford: Blackwell, 1978.

Cavell, Stanley. "The Availability of Wittgenstein's Later Philosophy." *Philosophical Review* 71 (1962): 67–93. Reprinted in his *Must We Mean What We Say?* New York: Scribner's, 1969, pp. 44–72.

———. *The Claim of Reason.* Oxford: Clarendon Press, 1979. See chapters 11 and 12, esp. p. 324.

Diamond, Cora. *The Realistic Spirit: Wittgenstein, Philosophy, and the Mind.* Cambridge: MIT Press, 1991.

Holland, Roy. "Is Goodness a Mystery?" *The University of Leeds Review* 13 (1970): 57–72. Reprinted in his *Against Empiricism,* Oxford: Blackwell, 1980, pp. 92–109.

Lovibond, Sabina. *Realism and Imagination in Ethics.* Minneapolis: University of Minnesota Press, 1983.

McDowell, John. "Non-Cognitivism and Rule-Following." In his *Mind, Value, and Reality,* 198–218. Cambridge: Harvard University Press, 1998. Originally published in *Wittgenstein: To Follow a Rule,* edited by Steven H. Holtzman and Christopher M. Leich, 141–62. London: Routledge and Kegan Paul, 1981.

Norman, Richard. "On Seeing Things Differently." *Radical Philosophy* 1 (1972): 6–13. Reprinted in *The Philosophy of Society,* ed. by R. Beehler and Alan R. Drengson, London: Methuen, 1978, pp. 316–344.

O'Neill, Onora. "The Power of Example." *Philosophy* 61 (1986): 5–29.

Phillips, D. Z., and H. O. Mounce. *Moral Practices.* New York: Schocken Books, 1970.

Rhees, Rush. *Without Answers.* London: Routledge and Kegan Paul, 1969.

Wiggins, David. "Truth, Invention, and the Meaning of Life." *Proceedings of the British Academy* 62 (1976): 331–78. See pp. 368–72. Reprinted in his *Needs, Values, Truth: Essays in the Philosophy of Value,* Oxford: Basil Blackwell, 1987, pp. 87–137.

Winch, Peter. *Ethics and Action.* London: Routledge and Kegan Paul, 1972.

———. *Trying to Make Sense.* Oxford: Basil Blackwell, 1987.

Wittgenstein, Ludwig. *Philosophical Investigations.* Oxford: Basil Blackwell, 1953.

———. "Lecture on Ethics." *Philosophical Review* 74 (1965 [1930?]): 3–12. Reprinted in his *Philosophical Occasions,* ed. by James C. Klagge and Alfred Nordmann, Indianapolis: Hackett, 1993, pp. 37–44.

———. *Remarks on the Foundations of Mathematics.* Oxford: Basil Blackwell, 1978.

Cora Diamond

Wolff, Christian (1679–1754)

German professor of mathematics and philosophy at Halle (1707–1723 and 1740–1754) and Marburg (1723–1740). Wolff's publications covered all of philosophy and many of the natural sciences. Although he has been ridiculed for his lack of originality and sophistication, Wolff's unwavering rationalism and secularism, his lifelong concern for the practical application of philosophy, and his unflinching defense of intellectual freedom made him a prominent figure for the Enlightenment in Germany.

Wolff's 1703 habilitation thesis, *Philosophia practica universalis, mathematica methodo conscripta,* demonstrated the centrality of ethics in his philosophical thought. He argued that it is our duty to strive for the perfection of our mind, comprising both intellect and will, and body; that the primary instrument for such perfection is increased knowledge; but that since no one can achieve this end alone, we must each work with others in order to achieve our own perfection. Wolff's first work in moral philosophy thus already displayed his characteristic tendencies: perfectionism, COGNITIVISM, and a cooperative INDIVIDUALISM—individuals act for the perfection of themselves and other individuals, not for that of the human species in the abstract, maximizing these individual aims by acting cooperatively and collectively.

Wolff was appointed to teach mathematics at Pietist Halle in 1707, but soon began lecturing on philosophy as well. His argument that the means to human perfection could be discovered by pure reason independently of any religious revelation earned him the enmity of the Halle theological faculty. After his 1721 address, *Oratio de Sinarum philosophia practica* (*The Practical Philosophy of the Chinese*), in which Wolff argued that CONFUCIUS (551–479 B.C.E.) had been able to discover the natural laws of morality without any natural or revealed theology, the theologians had him expelled from Halle. This expulsion, and Wolff's subsequent defense of intellectual freedom, in which he argued that it was impossible for increased knowledge and the aims of good government to conflict, made him a hero to educated Europeans.

Wolff's most influential book in ethics, the *Vernünfftige Gedancken von der Menschen Thun und Lassen* or "German Ethics," was first published in 1720. The organization of this work necessitated the division of Wolff's subsequent Latin volumes, and influenced the structure of German moral philosophy from KANT (1724–1804) to HEGEL (1770–1831). Wolff divided moral philosophy into "universal practical philosophy" (the general theory of the nature of goodness, virtue, MORAL REASONING, and moral evaluation), ethics, economics, and politics (the latter two expounded in his *Vernünfftige Gedancken von dem gesellschaftlichen Leben der Menschen* or "German Politics" of 1721). Ethics concerned the duties we have independently of our membership in any social organization; these duties are, in this order, duties toward oneself, duties toward God, and duties toward others. Economics and politics concerned duties generated by membership in social organizations: economics by organizations smaller than the state, such as the household; and politics by the state. Although motivated by different considerations, Kant's division between the metaphysical foundations of morality and the metaphysics of morals and his division of the latter into doctrines of justice and virtue reflected Wolff's scheme. In addition, much of the detailed content of Kant's doctrine of virtue was also Wolffian. Wolff's moral philosophy in this work can be characterized under the four headings of perfectionism, NATURALISM, CONSEQUENTIALISM, and cognitivism.

According to Wolff, the fundamental law of practical philosophy is "Do what makes yourself and the condition of yourself and others more perfect, and omit what makes them more imperfect." In Wolff's metaphysics, perfection received a purely formal definition as maximal unity amidst variety. This carried over into his ethics, where perfection is sometimes characterized simply as maximal consistency among actions. But Wolff also defined perfection as maximal consistency with the essence and nature of human beings. The latter was defined in turn as the combination of a mind (consisting of intellect and will) and body in causal interaction with other objects. Thus, the abstract end of perfection became the more concrete end of preserving and improving the human mind, the human body, and the external conditions of human existence. Like DESCARTES (1596–1650), Wolff argued that PLEASURE results from the clear but indistinct perception of perfection. Continuing pleasure thus became a sign of perfection. Sometimes it seems as though pleasure is not just the sign of perfection but the substance of it, and Wolff's perfectionism threatens to degenerate into a refined UTILITARIANISM.

Wolff argued that the nature of human perfection can be known by unaided reason. He also argued that, according to the laws of nature, humans inevitably strive for their own perfection, and that only defective knowledge defeats this natural tendency. Thus, knowledge of the existence of God is not a prerequisite for virtue; even atheists could recognize the natural laws of morality. Wolff also opposed VOLUNTARISM, holding that our duties are not determined simply by commands of God's will, but are objectively determined by perfection of the essences perceived by God's intellect. He did concede, however, that God had created human (and all other) nature, and thus to act in accord with natural laws is to act in accord with divine law. Moreover, one can act according to the moral laws, recognizing their origin in the attributes of God, in order to glorify him. Wolff's *The Practical Philosophy of the Chinese* actually recognized three levels of virtue, levels that depend on whether the agent is motivated by natural law, natural theology, or revealed RELIGION. It was thus more conciliatory than the "German Ethics," even though it was the last straw for the Pietists. Insisting as he did that the laws of morality are also the laws of nature, Wolff did not recognize the possibility of a radical and inexplicable propensity toward EVIL, as Kant was later to do.

Wolff explicitly endorsed consequentialism, arguing that the virtuousness of actions was to be judged by whether they tended toward human perfection, and by the benevolent intentions of their agents. In *The Practical Philosophy of the Chinese*, Wolff argues that virtue requires agreement between our "inner" and "outer" actions, thus suggesting that motivation as well as outcome is morally relevant. However, his chapter on "Conscience" in the "German Ethics" is primarily concerned with the impor-

tance of acting out of clear and distinct knowledge of the outcomes of actions rather than out of the fear of punishments externally attached to actions by an earthly or divine ruler. Wolff's rigorous insistence on consequentialism was clearly part of his opposition to what he saw in religious ethics as an excessive emphasis on CONSCIENCE.

Wolff's theory of the will was strictly cognitivist. The will is simply the inclination of the mind toward an object which is perceived as good, and we therefore automatically will that which we hold to be good. Freedom, in turn, is simply the capacity of the soul to choose, among logically possible alternatives, that which appears best to it. Like LEIBNIZ (1646–1716), Wolff was content with the position that such choices were both certain and hypothetically necessary as long as they were not absolutely necessary. Not surprisingly, the charge of determinism was also leveled in his expulsion from Prussia.

Wolff's general theory of perfectionism was applied in an exhaustive catalogue of duties. Duties to the self are considered first, because we are each primarily responsible for our own welfare and are each in the best position to maximize our own perfection. This primacy of duties to the self, another influence on Kant, thus follows from Wolff's consequentialism. From his theory of human nature, Wolff concludes that our first duty to ourselves is in the improvement of our intellectual capacities and knowledge; given his theory of the will, the fundamental avenue to the improvement of the will is likewise the improvement of the intellect. Duties to our body include the duties to preserve and improve our health and to maximize our physical talents and capacities so that we may attain our other objectives. We also have duties to preserve and improve our external circumstances, which are necessary for the perfection of our body and mind.

Our duties to God, the second main class of duty that Wolff recognizes, are based on the duty to perform our other duties out of a recognition of their origin in the attributes of God as well as for their natural consequences for our own perfection.

Wolff's position on duties to others is complex. He does acknowledge some duty to advance perfection and HAPPINESS in general and not just in ourselves. But he also advances a self-referential argument: we will not always be able to maximize our own end of self-perfection with our own resources and will have to ask others for help, but we can reasonably expect such help only if we are also willing to extend it to others when we can. Wolff thus offers a rudimentary universalization argument. His discussion of duties to others also illustrates his consequentialism: in deciding whether to aid another, he argues, we must carefully calculate the total contribution to the perfection of all who will be affected and determine whether the RISK to the other or to ourself makes the greater difference to that end.

The details of Wolff's ethics sometimes appear silly, as when he instructs us on the valuable consequences of wearing reasonably but not excessively fashionable clothes and keeping them in good condition. But it must not be forgotten that Wolff was a devoted advocate of the rational pursuit of human happiness in a deeply dogmatic society, and that more sophisticated models of rationality (such as Kant's) could hardly have reached their audience without the preliminary labors of Wolff.

See also: APPLIED ETHICS; COLLECTIVE RESPONSIBILITY; CONFUCIUS; CONSCIENCE; CONSEQUENTIALISM; DUTY AND OBLIGATION; FREE WILL; FREEDOM AND DETERMINISM; HEGEL; INDIVIDUALISM; INTENTION; KANT; METAPHYSICS AND EPISTEMOLOGY; MORAL PERCEPTION; MORAL REASONING; MOTIVES; PERFECTIONISM; PRACTICAL REASON[ING]; RATIONAL CHOICE; SELF-KNOWLEDGE; SOCIAL AND POLITICAL PHILOSOPHY; VIRTUE ETHICS.

Bibliography

Works by Christian Wolff

"Philosophia practica universalis mathematica methodo conscripta." pp. 189–223. Hildesheim: Georg Olm, 1974 [1703]. Facsimile reprint of 1754 edition.

Vernünfftige Gedancken von Gott, der Welt, und der Seele des Menschen, auch allen Dingen überhaupt. Hildesheim: Georg Olm, 1983 [1720]. "German Metaphysics." Introduction by Charles A. Corr. Facsimile reprint of 1751 edition.

Vernünfftige Gedancken von der Menschen Thun und Lassen, zur Beförderung ihrer Glückseligkeit. Hildesheim: Georg Olm, 1976 [1720]. "German Ethics." Introduction by Hans Werner Arndt. Facsimile reprint of 4th ed., published 1733.

Vernünfftige Gedancken von dem Gesellschaftlichen Leben der Menschen und insonderheit dem Gemeinen Wesen. Hildesheim: Georg Olm, 1975 [1721]. "German Politics." Introduction by H. W. Arndt. Facsimile reprint of 4th ed., published 1736.

Ausführliche Nachricht von seinen eigenen Schriften die er in deutscher Sprache heraus gegeben. Hildesheim: Georg Olm, 1973 [1726]. Introduction by H. W. Arndt. See chapter 9, pp. 388–443. Facsimile reprint of 2d ed., published 1733.

Rede über die praktische Philosophie der Chinesen. Translated by Michael Albrecht. Latin-German ed. Hamburg: Felix Meiner, 1985 [1726].

Philosophia practica universalis, methodo scientifica pertractata. 2 vols. Hildesheim: Georg Olm, 1971; 1978 [1738–1739]. Afterword by Winfried Lenders. Facsimile reprint of 1st ed.

Philosophia moralis, sive ethica, methodo scientifica pertractata. 5 vols. Hildesheim: Georg Olm, 1970–1973 [1750–1753]. Afterword by W. Lenders. Facsimile reprint of 1st edition.

Preliminary Discourse on Philosophy in General. Translated by Richard J. Blackwell, New York: Bobbs-Merrill, 1963 [1728]. Translation of "Discursis preliminaris de philosophia in genere" from 3d ed. of *Philosophia rationalis sive logica, methodo scientifica pertractata,* pub. 1740.

Works about Wolff

Böckerstette, Heinrich. *Aporien der Freiheit und ihre Aufklärung durch Kant.* Stuttgart-Bad Cannstatt: Frommann-Holzboog, 1982. See pp. 64–160.

Campo, Mariano. *Christiano Wolff e il razionalismo precritico.* 2 vols. Hildesheim: Georg Olm, 1980 [1939].

Gelfert, Johannes. *Der Pflichtbegriff bei Christian Wolff und einigen anderen Philosophen der deutschen Aufklärung mit Rücksicht auf Kant.* Borna-Leipzig: Robert Noske, 1907.

Joesten, Klara. *Christian Wolff und die Grundlegung der praktischen Philosophie.* Leipzig: Weidmann, 1931.

Poser, Hans. "Die Bedeutung der Ethik Christian Wolffs für die Deutsche Aufklärung." In *Theoria Cum Praxi,* edited by Kurt Müller et al., vol. 1, pp. 206–17. Wiesbaden: Franz Steiner, 1980.

Riedel, Manfred. "'Emendation' der praktischen Philosophie: Metaphysik als Theorie der Praxis bei Leibniz und Wolff." In his *Metaphysik und Metapolitik,* 218–36. Frankfurt: Suhrkamp, 1975.

Schmucker, Josef. *Die Ursprünge der Ethik Kants,* 26–51. Meisenheim am Glan: Anton Hain, 1961.

Schneiders, Werner, ed. *Christian Wolff 1679–1754: Interpretation zu seiner Philosophie und deren Wirkung.* Hamburg: Felix Meiner, 1983. Includes articles on ethics by Anton Bissinger, Hans-Martin Bachmann, Christoph Link, and Marcel Thomann; extensive bibliography covers 1800–1982.

Stipperger, Emanuel. *Freiheit und Institution bei Christian Wolff.* Frankfurt; New York: Peter Lang, 1984.

Paul Guyer

Wollaston, William (1660–1724)

English moral philosopher and deist, William Wollaston defended a bold rationalist ethics along the lines of Samuel CLARKE (1675–1729). Wollaston described his proposed criterion of moral good and EVIL as novel, "something never met with anywhere." His only ethical work, *The Religion of Nature Delineated* (1722, 1724), was enormously popular, going through eight editions by 1750. Wollaston was highly esteemed and influential during his lifetime, but his views were sharply criticized, and in some cases even ridiculed, by HUTCHESON (1694–1746), HUME (1711–1776), PRICE (1723–1791), and BENTHAM (1748–1832). Unlike most writing of the period, Wollaston's is non-polemical, but his insistence throughout that morality is natural is in line with the standard rationalist criticism of HOBBES's (1588–1679) claim that there is no right or wrong in the state of nature and that morality is the result of a compact. This implied, critics thought, that morality is a human artifact with the result that standards of right and wrong were arbitrary and so not real.

Wollaston's aim was to find some rule or criterion to distinguish right from wrong actions. Immoral actions, he claims, have one feature in common. They offend against truth in that they treat things as if they were other than they in fact are. The criterion of morality is thus conformity to truth. Wollaston starts by defining truth as follows: "propositions are true which express things as they are." Whatever can be understood has meaning. Actions can be understood, so actions have meaning or significance: We say things with actions. Both actions and words thus express propositions. The meaning of words is always conventional, but many actions possess a natural, unalterable and nonvarying significance and, when they do, they express propositions more strongly than do words. Thus,

> whoever acts as if things were so, or not so, doth by his acts declare, that they are so, or not so; as plainly as he could by words, or with more reality. And if the things are otherwise, his acts contradict those propositions, which assert them to be as they are.

Immoral actions, then, express or imply a falsehood; they do not correspond to the way things are, denying things to be what they are. Suppose you are my benefactor and bestow favors on me, but I am ungrateful. According to Wollaston, my ingratitude implies that I never received any favors from you and in this sense it denies things to be what they are and so expresses a falsehood. The problem everybody finds with Wollaston's criterion of morality as conformity to truth is illustrated by this example. My action denies things to be what they are only if there is an antecedent duty of GRATITUDE. Wollaston's criterion is empty: particular duties can be derived from it only if there are antecedently and independently established moral duties.

Wollaston is aware of, but does not deal altogether satisfactorily with, three additional problems: since truth does not come in degrees, all wrong actions are equally wrong; since truths are consistent with one another, there cannot be conflicts of duty; and finally, since an action can be described in more than one way and so can express more than one proposition, criteria are needed for establishing the relevant description.

Wollaston goes on to argue that the pursuit of HAPPINESS and acting according to right reason coincide with the criterion of fidelity to truth. Thus, for Wollaston, morality is grounded upon a triple alliance of truth, happiness, and reason. He holds that a person is happy when the sum total of pleasures exceeds pains, and anticipating Bentham, introduces a calculus for comparing pleasures and pains which includes their intensity and duration. We all naturally aim at happiness and try to avoid unhappiness and have a duty to make ourselves and others happy. If we act in such a way as to make a creature who is susceptible of happiness unhappy, then we fail to treat that being according to its nature. Wollaston appeals to God's BENEVOLENCE to support the claim that happiness and truth coincide; God ensures that in the long run acting morally is in our interest. Reason is the faculty that discovers truths laid down by God, and so to act according to right reason and truth are the same thing. In the remainder of the book, Wollaston provides demonstrations of how particular duties may be derived from truth, happiness, and right reason. These include duties to God, society, ourselves, and our families.

See also: CLARKE; CUDWORTH; HISTORY OF WESTERN ETHICS: 8. SEVENTEENTH AND EIGHTEENTH CEN-

TURIES; MORAL SENSE THEORISTS; MORAL REALISM; NATURALISM; RATIONALITY VS. REASONABLENESS.

Bibliography

Work by William Wollaston

The Religion of Nature Delineated. Privately printed, 1722; first commercial ed., London, 1724. The *Life of Wollaston* is prefixed to the 6th ed., London, 1738.

Works about Wollaston

Bott, Thomas. *The Principal and Peculiar Notion Advanced in a Late Book, Intitled 'The Religion of Nature Delineated', Considered and Refuted.* London, 1724.

Clarke, John. *An Examination of the Notions of Moral Good and Evil, Advanced in a Late Book, Entitled 'The Religion of Nature Delineated.'* London, 1735.

Feinberg, Joel. "Wollaston and His Critics." *Journal of the History of Ideas* 38 (1977): 345–52.

Joynton, Olin. "The Problem of Circularity in Wollaston's Moral Philosophy." *Journal of the History of Philosophy* 22 (1984): 435–44.

Kydd, R. M. *Reason and Conduct in Hume's Treatise,* 31–35. New York: Russell and Russell, 1964.

Stedman, R. E. "The Ethics of Wollaston." *The Nineteenth Century and After* 118 (1935): 217–25.

Thompson, C. G. *The Ethics of William Wollaston.* Boston: Gorham Press, 1922.

Tweyman, Stanley. "Truth, Happiness and Obligation: The Moral Philosophy of William Wollaston." *Philosophy* 51 (1976): 35–46.

A sustained line of criticism of Wollaston's ethical theory was developed by the following British moralists:

Bentham, Jeremy. *An Introduction to the Principles of Morals and Legislation.* New York: Hafner Press, 1948 [1789]. See chapter 2, paragraph 14, footnote, example 8.

Hume, David. *A Treatise of Human Nature.* Oxford: Clarendon Press, 1987 [1737]. See book 3, part 1, section 1, pp. 461–63, and footnote.

Hutcheson, Francis. "Mr. Wollaston's Significancy of Truth, as the Idea of Virtue Considered." Section 3 of his *Illustrations Upon the Moral Sense,* edited by Bernard Peach, 146–58. Cambridge: Belknap Press of Harvard University Press, 1971 [1728].

Price, Richard. *A Review of the Principal Questions in Morals.* Edited by D. D. Raphael, 125–26. Oxford: Oxford University Press, 1948 [1758, 1787].

Charlotte Brown

Wollstonecraft [Godwin], Mary (1759–1797)

From the publication of her most significant philosophical work, *A Vindication of the Rights of Woman* (1792), until her death from complications following the birth of her second child (Mary Wollstonecraft Godwin, later Mary Shelley [1797–1851]), Mary Wollstonecraft was a major figure in the vigorous circle of English intellectuals committed to a "new philosophy of reason"—a philosophy aimed at radical reformation of social and political INSTITUTIONS. In *Mary, A Fiction* (1788), a thinly novelized set of reflections prompted by her experience as a governess in Ireland, and in *A Vindication of the Rights of Men* (1790), the first published response to Edmund BURKE's (1729–1797) *Reflections on the Revolution in France* (1790), she deploys the same unblinking commitment to the power of reason found in the *Rights of Woman.* The same is true of her reportage from Paris, where she lived from late 1793 to mid-1795, during a critical time in the French Revolution. Like most in her circle, she was filled with awe and enthusiasm for the early stages of the revolution, finding in it the hope that radical political EQUALITY could be achieved then and there, and that a social order founded on reason could be realized. Her *Letters Written During a Short Residence in Sweden, Norway and Denmark* (1795) concludes with the candid acknowledgment that her earlier enthusiasm had been misplaced. But her philosophical commitment to reason and equality never faltered, as is evident in the posthumously published fragment of *The Wrongs of Woman* (1798), a novel meant to parallel her essay on women's RIGHTS.

The philosophical project embodied in all her writing on women is the logical extension of the Enlightenment doctrine that reason is the source of the DIGNITY and moral worth of human beings and the ground of all claims to individual autonomy and HUMAN RIGHTS. In *A Vindication of the Rights of Woman,* she vigorously and clearly argued: Equality of reason means equal moral worth and equal claims to autonomy, LIBERTY, social and political rights. Women are the equals of men in reason; thus it is a denial of their dignity as human beings to deny them social and political equality. With a persistence and invective that troubles present-day feminists, Wollstonecraft grants that women in her day are typically inferior to men in almost every respect, including the exercise of their rational capacities. But she argues that their deficiencies with respect to reason are wholly created by oppressive social institutions and the debilitating sort of education they receive—that is, that their deficiencies are wholly artificial rather than natural and are the product of correctable human institutions. In a scathing, witty, and protracted attack on the views of Jean-Jacques ROUSSEAU (1712–1778), Dr. James Fordyce (1720–1796), and others, together with her reflections on the lives possible for women in England in her day, she argues for educational reform. If education were corrected, the moral equality of women and men would be plain. Men of good CONSCIENCE could then no longer deny them social and political equality. And all men should be able to acknowledge, she argues, the great social good that would result if women and men were equally able to realize their rational powers. Some of these points were echoed by JOHN STUART MILL (1806–1873) in *The Subjection of Women* (1869).

For more than a century and a half after her death, Wollstonecraft's work was in eclipse. In part this was due to its subject matter. Feminist writing has regularly been ridiculed and marginalized, and hers was no exception. In part, too, her star was eclipsed by the contempt heaped upon her whole circle after the excesses of the French Revolution. And perhaps some of the cause may be traced to people's scandalized reaction to her life (*e.g.,* to her love affairs, out-of-wedlock pregnancies, abandonment by the father of her first child, subsequent SUICIDE attempts, forced marriage to William GODWIN [1756–1836], and her tragic death). All of this was sensationalized by Godwin's apparently innocently motivated publication (after her death) of her intimate letters, and of course was repeatedly brought to public attention by the lives her children led. Whatever the reason for the earlier eclipse of her work, her place in the canon of political philosophy now seems secure.

See also: BURKE; DIGNITY; ENTITLEMENTS; EQUALITY; FEMINIST ETHICS; GODWIN; HUMAN RIGHTS; INSTITUTIONS; LIBERTY; JOHN STUART MILL; MORAL REASONING; OPPRESSION; PATERNALISM; REVOLUTION; RIGHTS; ROUSSEAU; SOCIAL AND POLITICAL PHILOSOPHY; WOMEN MORAL PHILOSOPHERS.

Bibliography

Works by Mary Wollstonecraft

Mary, A Fiction. Edited by Cary Kelly. Oxford: Oxford University Press, 1975 [1788].

A Vindication of the Rights of Men, in a Letter to the Right Honorable Edmund Burke. Edited by Eleanor Louise Nicholes. Facsimile ed. Delmar: Scholars Facsimiles and Reprints, 1980 [1790].

A Vindication of the Rights of Woman, With Strictures on Political and Moral Subjects. Edited by Carol H. Poston. 2d, Norton critical ed. New York: Norton, 1988 [1792]. Contains an authoritative text, with illuminating critical apparatus, historical and biographical material, valuable bibliography.

An Historical and Moral View of the Origin and Progress of the French Revolution and the Effect It Has Produced in Europe. Edited by Janet M. Todd. Facsimile ed. Delmar: Scholars Facsimiles and Reprints, 1980 [1794].

Letters from Sweden [Letters Written During a Short Residence in Sweden, Norway and Denmark]. Edited by Carol H. Poston. Lincoln: University of Nebraska Press, 1976 [1795].

Posthumous Works of the Author of a Vindication of the Rights of Woman. Edited by William Godwin. New York: Garland, 1974 [1798]. Includes the fragments of *The Wrongs of Woman* and letters to Imlay.

Lawrence C. Becker

women moral philosophers

The record of women engaging in moral philosophy dates at least to the fifth century B.C.E. This article presents women moral philosophers in chronological order, omitting those for whom separate entries appear, and omitting twentieth-century philosophers. Dates are sometimes speculative. Chronological ordering rather than a few generic groupings is necessary because no single characteristic describes moral philosophy as women generally engaged in it. Women wrote and taught in all major and many minor schools of moral philosophy. Their writings sometimes transcend and sometimes synthesize ideas from different schools. Most women moral philosophers were part of male-stream philosophic circles, and their writings generally reflect the prevailing philosophical views of their day.

Phintys of Sparta (c. 420 B.C.E.)

The author of two fragments from a book *On the Moderation of Women* disputes the view that it is unfitting for a woman to philosophize. She claims that COURAGE, justice, and WISDOM are common to both men and women. Phintys offers a duty-based contractual analysis of the moral discord created by adultery. The author recommends moderation in all things for a woman. She argues that the moderate woman (and the well-regulated city) disdains displays of arrogance and class differences.

Arete of Cyrene (c. 350 B.C.E.)

Arete is reputed to have taught philosophy for thirty-five years and to have written forty books, now lost. Daughter of Aristippus of Cyrene, Arete is her father's alleged successor to head the Cyrenaic school. Her son, Aristippus the Younger, had the nickname *"metrodidactus"* (mother-taught). Her views are assumed to be consistent with the CYRENAICS.

Perictione I (c. 350? B.C.E.)

Her fragment *On the Harmony of Women* recommends that particular VIRTUES be exercised in order to develop higher virtues which in turn bring HAPPINESS to a woman and her FAMILY. Beauty develops through the exercise of wisdom, not through physical adornment, which characterizes morally weak women. TEMPERANCE fosters the development of all other virtues. Intemperance is the first step toward "the sin of every vice." The author also addresses issues of filial piety and respect, and of POWER, class, and OPPRESSION.

Aesara of Lucania (c. 300 B.C.E.)

In a surviving fragment from her *Book on Human Nature,* the author presents a NATURAL LAW theory. Introspection about the nature of the human soul permits the discovery of the philosophic foundation for all human laws: those of individual, family and social morality, as well as those of medicine. The parts of the soul are mind, spiritedness, and DESIRE. Virtue (*harmonia*) is having the appropriate part of the soul influence particular actions.

Theano II (c. 300 B.C.E.)

Theano is known largely through the fragments of her correspondence that have survived. The letter to Euboule describes a woman's moral RESPONSIBILITY to raise children to become virtuous, harmonious adults. Failure to do so contributes to the personal disorder of the child's soul, and ultimately to social disorder. In children, virtue develops by cultivating the mind to moderate impulse and desire. Young children cannot understand how to apply the principle of *harmonia*. They require discipline and guidance in developing that understanding and internalizing virtuous habits.

Theano's letter to Nikostrate addresses a woman's responsibility to act justly toward her adulterous husband. Marriage is a contractual relationship between friends based on judgments about the benefits of sharing a life. That one party violates duties thus incurred does not relieve the other of the duty to provide an example of moral virtue for the adulterous spouse to emulate.

The letter to Kallisto addresses duties owed by the "mistress of the house" to servants and slaves. Considerateness and good will between mistress and slave must involve mutual recognition of slaves' moral worth. Law and custom subordinate slave and servant to the mistress, yet the maintenance of a harmonious social order requires that the mistress be attentive to slaves' psychological and moral welfare as well as their physical needs.

The (spurious) letter to Euridike urges her not to be jealous of her husband's relationship with a courtesan. A (spurious) letter to Tim(ai)onides admonishes that the gods know the untruthfulness of his slander.

Makrina of Neocaesaria (c. C.E. 300)

Makrina's moral philosophy was recorded by her brother, Gregory (c. 331–395), Bishop of Nyssa, in his dialogue *De anima et resurrectione;* details of her life are recorded in his *Vita Macrinae.* She addresses the unity and immortality of the soul, the role of the passions, knowledge of the good, and reincarnation of humans as nonhumans. Her views clearly show familiarity with those of PLATO (c. 430–347 B.C.E.), PLOTINUS (205–270), Porphyry (234–305), Philo of Alexandria (c. 20 B.C.E.–c. C.E. 40), Origen (180–

254), and others. Makrina held that women were made in God's image and therefore had rational souls which were capable of the kind of moral virtue that is important for salvation.

Asclepigenia of Athens (c. C.E. 430)

Daughter of Plutarch the Younger (d. 430). Together with Syrianus and her brother Hierius, Asclepigenia continued the neo-Platonic academy of Plotinus, upon the death of her father in 430. Proclus (c. 410–485) was her student; it is from a study of Plotinus and Proclus that we assume Asclepignia's views tended toward MYSTICISM, magic, and theurgy as ways of understanding the nature of virtue and the mysteries of metaphysics. Metaphysics was related not only to RELIGION but to ethics insofar as the practice of virtue was understood as the way to the contemplation of the Absolute.

Murasaki Shikibu (978–c. 1031)

Widely known as the greatest work of Japanese literature, her novel *Genji monogatari (The Tale of Genji)* includes a fully developed feminist existentialist moral philosophy. The heroine, Ukifune (whose name means "loose boat"), is adrift in an existentialist void which symbolizes her moral role as a woman in Japanese society, as well as her self-image. She faces and resolves the existentialist dilemmas of existence, moral worth, freedom, moral responsibility, dread, and death in the context of Māhāyāna Buddhism. Her life is thus a quest for *nirvana* and for entrance to the Western Paradise, which is closed to women.

Hildegard of Bingen (1098–1179)

All of Hildegard's works contain elements of her ethics and describe the cosmic consequences of human action. Hildegard's moral anthropology considers the woman to be a human being who may be different from man in temperament, but not in wisdom, moral worth, or moral capacity. The *Scivias* describes the moral and cosmological harmony of the universe as disrupted by Eve's seduction of Adam. Harmony must be restored through salvation. Humans, although provided by God with FREE WILL, have abdicated the moral responsibility of governance over the earth and have violated moral

law. The *Liber vitae meritorum* portrays the struggle between virtues and vices. Vice must be overcome in the human soul through repeated exemplification of opposing virtues. Many "vices" Hildegard describes, including depression, would today be described as psychological disorders. *Liber divinorum operum (De operatione Dei)* revises the visions of *Scivias* and explains her changed views. There is physical as well as moral correspondence between humans and the cosmos. Humans have a natural, rudimentary understanding of the moral law and a duty to be continuously sensitive to the correspondence between humans and the cosmos, particularly by studying the Books of Creation and Revelation.

Heloise (1101–1164)

A student of CICERO's (106–43 B.C.E.) philosophy, Heloise, in her *Epistolae,* recorded her arguments against marriage to ABELARD (1079–1142) on the grounds that the social constraints of marriage would kill their highly intellectualized, sensual relationship. Love for Abelard convinced her that marriage to him would be morally wrong. As a married cleric, his authority as a philosopher and a theologian would diminish. In her view (*Problemata Heloissae*), Heloise married in obedience to and out of love for Abelard and was therefore materially, but not morally, responsible for his castration by her uncle. Her action was morally right because it was a product of caring. To her, rectitude of action depends not on its consequences but on the INTENTION with which it is done.

Herrad, Abbess of Hohenbourg [Herrad of Landsberg] (d. 1191)

Her *Hortus deliciarum,* which contains nearly 1,200 textual extracts and more than 340 illustrations, offers an account of salvation through the study of ethics, cosmology, and biblical and church history. Philosophy nourishes all forms of knowledge through the seven liberal arts, and is itself divided into logic, ethics, and physics. Within the trivium, dialectic distinguishes true from false; ethics repels vice and induces virtue. Virtue is defined (Socratically) as including PRUDENCE, justice, temperance, and fortitude. Ethics is both practical (active, applied) and speculative (contemplative).

Beatrice of Nazareth [Beatrijs van Tienen] (1200 or 1205–1268)

Her *Seven Manieren van Minne* (*Seven Modes of Sacred Love*) offers epistemological and metaphysical accounts of the connection between intellectual and sensory knowledge, the relationship between cognitive and physical experience of God, and the roles which virtues and the passions play in acquiring that experience. Knowing God is characterized by exemplifying CARE, concern, and service to others.

Mechtild of Magdeberg (c. 1207–c. 1282)

Das fliessende Licht der Gottheit (*The Flowing Light of the Godhead*) contains Mechtild's views on metaphysics and cosmology, her moral anthropology, her religious and moral epistemology, and an ethics focusing on the experience of love. Mechtild emphasizes the development of those virtues which enhance the ability to experience God. She regards secular power as an obstacle to moral life. Virtue must be accompanied by good works in the service of love. Social relations are properly governed by virtues which facilitate living in close proximity with others in the development of a relationship with God. A Beguine, Mechtild emphasized service to the afflicted, HUMILITY, compassion, and the alleviation of psychological suffering.

Hadewych of Antwerp [Adelwip] (fl. c. 1240)

Hadewych's Augustinian-influenced *Visions, Letters and Strophic Poems* introduced Dutch translations of neo-Platonic epistemological and ethical terms used by the Church Fathers. God illuminates Reason which guides the soul to *Minne* (love) herself. Having fulfilled its function, Reason becomes useless. *Minne* assumes control of the soul which becomes godlike, conforming itself to God's will, but without losing its independence. Whoever assumes the duties of *Minne* must withdraw from the mystical experience of God's love and become dedicated to acts of loving service to others. Thus, Hadewych's moral epistemology implies her ethics.

Birgitta of Sweden [Birgitta Suecica] (1302–1373)

Birgitta's ethical views (*Revelationes; Sermo Angelicus*) are formed by her mariology, her concept of a trinitarian God, her concept of human nature, and her view of political authority. She depicts Mary as a woman of great ethical, spiritual, and intellectual qualities who actively taught Christ's doctrines. Humans must live according to God's will, although some are predestined for salvation and others for damnation. God gives secular authority to kings who must govern justly and who must be models of ethical behavior.

Catherine of Siena [Catherine Benincasa] (c. 1347–1380)

Catherine's moral philosophy is found in *Il Dialogo* and in her *Orazione* and *Lettere*. The highest moral good was love of God which required love of neighbor. Free will is a faculty of the soul unaffected by original sin. God respects this faculty and through baptism frees us to accept or refuse his grace when we reach the age of discernment. God's grace enables us to reason well and to conform ourselves to his will by binding ourselves through love to him. Love of God requires love of neighbor and therefore duties of love, patience, understanding, CHARITY, BENEVOLENCE, FORGIVENESS, as well as public works, and the morality of institutions of church and state. Poverty was an essential moral virtue. Attachment to material goods, not possession or mere enjoyment of those goods, constitutes the opposite vice.

Christine de Pizan [Christine Pisan] (1365–1431)

Pisan argued against female inferiority and subordination. Her *Cité des dames* constructs a walled city for the protection of women from physical as well as moral harm. The female moral virtues, Ladies Reason, Justice, and Duty, guide women. Through the voices of these rational moral virtues, Pisan argued that the oppression of women was contrary to the goal of improving society itself. Women are limited by specific social roles, therefore, they should work hard to avoid activities that dull their intellect and sap their strength to the detriment of the common social good.

Teresa of Avila, Saint [Teresa de Jesus] (1515–1582)

Four major works and 400 letters, poems, and treatises survive. *Life, Way of Perfection* and *Interior*

Castle are works of moral epistemology. Influenced by AUGUSTINE's (354–430) *Confessions,* Teresa offers an epistemological account of the roles of sensation and reason which implies a standard Christian account of virtue. Existence in unity with God requires knowledge of God which can be achieved only through a progressive program involving a life of humility, meditation, and exemplary conduct. Successive steps include the domination and exclusion of sensory data followed by quiet prayer and meditation, the transcendence of reason itself, cessation of perception, and then a state of total passivity and receptiveness in which the soul attains beatific vision and an uncomprehending certainty of unification with God. Although the soul cannot understand intellectually what has happened in its union with God, the experience of union is so intense that the soul is certain of its experience. Juan de Yepes y Alvarez (St. John of the Cross [1542–1591]) was among her students.

[Luisa] Oliva Sabuco de Nantes Barerra (b. 1562)

Her *Nueva filosofía de la naturaleza del hombre* (1588), explains moral action and moral emotion in relationship to psychology and physiology. MORAL DEVELOPMENT, as well as acting or failing to act virtuously, are explained in physiological and psychological terms. Sabuco cites the moral theories of the Greek and Roman philosophers as well as those of the Church Fathers. She claims that her view reveals a common bond among those theories. Sabuco illustrates applications of her theory with hundreds of examples of correlations between psychological function and dysfunction, physiological development, disease and health, and moral virtue and vice.

Marie le Jars de Gournay (1565–1645)

Michel de MONTAIGNE's (1533–1592) student and editor of his *Essais* (1580–1595), de Gournay, in her own work, disputed claims of women's natural inferiority. *Egalité des hommes et des femmes* argues that women are equal in the capacity for MORAL REASONING and action. Sexual differentiation was not part of the essence of human nature, but was necessary only for reproduction. Men and women are intellectual and moral equals. In *Grief des dames* (1626), she argued for social EQUALITY of the sexes.

Damaris Cudworth Masham (1659–1708)

Occasional Thoughts (1705) supported John LOCKE (1632–1704) against Edward Stillingfleet (1635–1699) on the question of the relative merits of revelation and reason. Masham, the daughter of Ralph CUDWORTH (1617–1688), argued that preferring revelation alone to revelation which stood up to scrutiny by reason would lead people to view Christianity as unreasonable. Principles of Christian morality are derivable from reason as well as from common sense although it is natural to be motivated by passion and hence to be inclined against virtue. Christianity articulates a rational basis of fear of God's PUNISHMENT for vice, thereby motivating virtuous action. *Discourse on the Love of God* (1696) argued against John Norris (1657–1711) that love of creatures was a necessary prerequisite for loving God. Objecting to Calvinist rejection of worldliness, she argued that only inordinate love of the world conflicts with love of God. There is virtue in social intercourse and in public life, not just in the contemplative life. Masham objected to the denial of educational opportunities to most women and to the double standard of morality imposed on women, particularly those regarding chastity.

Mary Astell (1666–1731)

Writing primarily on moral and religious epistemology (*Letters concerning the Love of God . . . ,* 1695) and on the morality of social institutions (*A Serious Proposal . . . ,* 1694), Astell agreed with Locke that intuition was the best source of knowledge, yet she argued for the existence of innate ideas and for Cartesian skepticism as an appropriate methodology with which to seek knowledge of those innate ideas. She urged women to require reason to govern passion and to suspend judgment in the absence of clear and distinct ideas. She intended her critiques and synthesis of Lockean and Cartesian epistemology to work to women's advantage by recognizing the role of passion, the potential for reason to dominate it, and the need for universal education to develop women's intellects.

Catherine Trotter Cockburn (1679–1749)

Trotter was an early defender of Locke's against claims that Locke's *Essay* (1690) did not provide a firm basis for morality. One argument of Trotter's comprehensive *Defence . . .* showed that Thomas Burnet (c. 1635–1715) of the Charterhouse wrongly claimed that the perception of good and evil was analogous to sensory perception and, like sensory perception, occurred independently of reason. Trotter argued that the ideas of good and evil merely coincided with descriptions of events or actions considered to be good or evil. Moral good and evil is defined exclusively in reference to human nature as defined by God through human creation. Consequently, knowledge of moral good and evil is possible through reflection on human nature. Her later pamphlets and letters continued to defend Lockean epistemology as providing a foundation for moral knowledge.

Harriet Martineau (1802–1876)

Sister of James (1805–1900) and an associate of William Johnson Fox (1786–1864), Thomas Carlyle (1795–1881), Harriet Taylor (see next listing), and JOHN STUART MILL (1806–1873), Martineau authored more than forty books totaling 600 editions and translations in many fields including philosophy. *Miscellanies* (1836) describes the development of religious epistemology in the context of personal religious experience. The type and degree of religious knowledge achieved by a person enables her to incorporate moral philosophy as a personal source of knowledge of ideal human behavior. Improvements in individual moral sensitivity to others' needs, in self-consciousness, reflection, and in analyticity accompany a greater knowledge of one's relationship to God and an increased internalization of principles of moral philosophy. *Illustrations of Political Economy* (1834) applies her moral and religious philosophy to issues including religious intolerance, labor disputes, the slave trade, and involuntary commitment of the mentally ill.

Harriet Hardy Taylor Mill (1807–1858)

Taylor is known for her views on equal social rights for women and egalitarian marriages, consistent with a utilitarian view of personal freedom as expressed in Mill's *On Liberty* (1859). Her collaboration with Mill notwithstanding, Taylor's views on women's rights to employment were strongly opposed to Mill's views. Taylor held that, in a society which denied women educational, civil, and political rights equal to those of men, a woman's decision to marry and have children is not a freely made commitment to forego employment, remain married, and raise children. While Taylor advocated no-fault divorce, Mill maintained that women renounced all rights to independent employment by selecting the career of wife, mother, and husband's counterpart. Taylor's untitled essays and her correspondence are preserved with Mill's. Her contributions to *On Liberty* and to *Principles of Political Economy* (1848) appear under Mill's authorship.

Clarisse Gauthier Coignet (b. 1823)

Editor of the weekly *La Morale indépendante*, Coignet argued for the teaching of secular ethics in secondary education. *La Morale independante dans son principe et son object*, and *De Kant à Bergson; reconciliation de la réligion et de la science dans un spiritualisme nouveau* (1911) analyze the relationship between moral philosophy and religion. She also wrote histories of ethics, moral analyses of social institutions, works of jurisprudence, and social philosophy, particularly concerning women's rights. She held that freedom was an irreducible first principle of human existence and therefore of moral science.

Clemence Royer (1830–1892)

Royer is known for her translation of Charles DARWIN's (1809–1882) *Origin of Species through Natural Selection* (1859) and for her analysis of the implications of EVOLUTION for moral theory. Royer's *Le Bien et la loi morale; Ethique et téleologie* (1881) was considered to surpass Herbert SPENCER's (1820–1903) *The Data of Ethics*. Human evolution depends upon continued human moral development which seeks to improve the happiness of entire societies. The good consists in utilitous action consistent with laws of human nature. There is a moral duty to increase happiness by protecting the development of happiness-producing characteristics of the species. This requires sacrificing egoistic pleasures in favor of promoting the common social welfare and happiness. In a just society, institutions which foster the development of humanistic concern have priority.

Antoinette Brown Blackwell (1825–1921)

The first ordained American woman, Blackwell published six books of philosophy as well as works of as poetry, theology, and fiction. *The Philosophy of Individuality* portrays mind and matter as dual aspects of human moral nature. *The Sexes Throughout Nature* analyzes the sexism inherent in evolutionary theory. Blackwell synthesized aspects of evolution and natural philosophy informed by Newtonian physics and Christian accounts of virtue. According to her synthesis, women and men make moral judgments differently; women bring compassion to justice and caring to rights. Blackwell argued that women reason inductively and men deductively, but that both forms of reasoning were of equal importance. Men and women are equally capable of moral action and moral decision making, although women excel in nurturing others.

Julie Velten Favre (1834–1896)

Favre supported early childhood education in the history of moral philosophy. Her works include *La Morale des Stoïciens* (1888), *La Morale de Socrate* (1888), *La Morale d'Aristote* (1889), *La Morale de Ciçeron* (1891), *La Morale de Plutarque* (1909), and *Montaigne, Moraliste et Pedagogue* (1887). These works contain her views on moral philosophy and analyze the application of moral theories to social institutions affecting women. Social roles assigned to women can help women develop special abilities to enhance the COMMON GOOD through nurturance; however, there is no reason to believe that women excel men at nurturance. All persons are, first, citizens of the world and, second, members of their family and state. Positive social justice is inseparable from love of others.

Hortense Allart de Meritens (fl. 1850)

Novum organum, ou Sainteté philosophique (1857) analyzes failures of earlier philosophies to adequately demonstrate God's existence and the moral imperative to be pious. She criticizes the failure of science to supplant religious ethics with a sci-entifically based natural rights theory, and sketches a system of natural religion and morality conceived as an object of science.

Mary Whiton Calkins (1863–1930)

First woman president of the American Psychological Association (1905) and of the American Philosophical Association (1918). Calkins authored seven books, of which *The Good Man and the Good* (1918) is on ethics. Ethics is a division of PSYCHOLOGY which must concern itself with moral facts. A good man is one who wills the good for its own sake and identifies himself as a member of a universal community of selves. Philosophical ethics should be studied in order to know the good, so as to become good. A mean between extremes, virtue is defined as a habit of will through which instinct is controlled in the interest of the good. God is the Greater Self which includes, yet transcends, the universe of selves. Linking ethics to her view of human nature, her metaphysics, and PHILOSOPHY OF RELIGION, she infers that the universal moral community of selves is the family of God.

L. Susan Stebbing (1885–1943)

Stebbing, in *Philosophy and the Physicists* (1937), comments on attempts by John Wisdom, Bertrand RUSSELL (1872–1970), and C. D. Broad (1887–1971) to wrestle with the question of moral responsibility in the context of physical indeterminacy. She claims that the acceptance of moral responsibility does not require a denial of causation. Theological doctrines of predestination and scientific doctrines of determinism permeate the language of moral philosophy, making discussions of moral freedom, responsibility, and culpability dependent upon metaphysics and subject to the same errors and inadequacies of theories of physics.

See also: ANSCOMBE; ARENDT; DE BEAUVOIR; FOOT; MURDOCH; RAND; STAEL; THOMSON; WEIL; WOLLSTONECRAFT.

Bibliography

Collected sources and works about women moral philosophers

Allen, Prudence. *The Concept of Woman: The Aristotelian Revolution, 750 BC–AD 1250.* Montreal: Eden Press,

1985. Reprinted, Grand Rapids, MI: W. B. Eerdmans, 1997. Contains important analyses and bibliographic references for sources who lived prior to the modern period. The forthcoming sequel to this volume will focus on the modern period.

Diogenes Laertius. *Lives of the Eminent Philosophers.* Arete of Cyrene's writings do not survive. Information about her can be found here, under the headings: Aristippus; Strabo, *Geography,* XVII 3, 22; Clement of Alexandria, *Stromates,* IV, XIX, 122, 1; and Eusebius of Caesarea, *Preparatio evangelica,* XIV, 18.32.764a.

Gregory of Nyssa. *De anima et resurrectione.* Translated by W. K. Lowther. London: Clark, 1916. For the views of his sister, Makrina of Neocaesaria.

Minge, J. P., ed. *Patrologiae cursus completus: Patrologia Graeca; Patrologia Latina.* Paris, 1844–1864. These volumes contain Greek or Latin texts of works from the late ancient through the late medieval period.

Thesleff, Holger. "Pythagorean Texts of the Hellenistic Period." *Acta Academiae Aboensis, Humanoira, Ser. A.* 30, no. 1 (1965). Includes fragments and letters by Aesara of Lucania, Phintys of Sparta, Perictione I, Theano II, and other women philosophers writing in the Pythagorean tradition whose writings were preserved by Stobaeus and Theodoret.

Waithe, Mary Ellen, ed. *A History of Women Philosophers.* 4 vols. Dordrecht; Boston: Martinus Nijhoff, 1987 (vol. 1); Kluwer Academic, 1989–1995 (vols. 2–4). Contains full bibliographies for (and some translations of) women philosophers mentioned in this article. Volume titles: Vol. 1: *Ancient Women Philosophers, 600 B.C.–500 A.D.* Vol. 2: *Medieval, Renaissance, and Enlightenment Women Philosophers, A.D. 500–1600.* Vol. 3: *Modern Women Philosophers, 1600–1900.* Vol. 4: *Contemporary Women Philosophers: 1900–Today.*

The following is a list of selected works, available in English, by women philosophers. For exhaustive bibliographies of all the philosophers mentioned in this article, refer to Allen and Waithe, listed above.

Astell, Mary. *A Serious Proposal to the Ladies . . .* London: R. Wilkins, 1694. Remainder of title: *. . . for the Advancement of Their True and Greatest Interest, by a Lover of her Sex.*

———. *Letters Concerning the Love of God . . .* London: J. Norris, 1695. Remainder of title: *. . . Between the Author of the Proposal to the Ladies and Mr. John Norris, Wherein his Discourse Shewing That it Ought to be Entire and Exclusive of all Other Loves, is Further Cleared and Justified.*

Calkins, Mary Whiton. *The Good Man and the Good.* New York: Macmillan, 1918.

Christine de Pisan. *The Book of the City of Ladies.* Translated by E. J. Richards. New York: Persea, 1982 [1405].

Cockburn, Catharine Trotter. *The Works of Mrs. Catharine Cockburn, Theological, Moral, Dramatic and Poetical.* Edited by Thomas Birch. 2 vols. London, 1751. "With an account of the author's life."

Heloise, and Peter Abelard. *The Letters of Abelard and Heloise.* Translated by C. K. Scott Moncrieff. New York: Knopf, 1926. Also see the translation by B. Radice (Harmondsworth: Penguin, 1974).

Herrad of Hohenbourg. *Hortus deliciarum.* 2 vols. Studies of the Warburg Institute, vol. 36. London: University of London, 1979. Vol. 1, Commentary; vol. 2, Reconstruction.

Hildegard of Bingen. *The Latin Scivias.* Translated by Bruce Hozeski. Santa Fe, NM: Bear, 1986.

Martineau, Harriet. *Miscellanies.* 2 vols. Boston: Hilliard, Gray, 1836.

———. *Illustrations of Political Economy.* 9 vols. London: C. Fox, 1834.

Masham, Damaris Cudworth. *A Discourse Concerning the Love of God.* London: A. & J. Churchil, 1696.

———. *Occasional Thoughts in Reference to a Virtuous or Christian Life.* London: A. & J. Churchil, 1705.

Mechthild von Magdeburg. *Revelations, or The Flowing Light of the Godhead.* Translated by L. Menzies. New York: Longmans, Green, 1953.

Murasaki Shikibu. *The Tale of Genji.* Edited by R. Bowring. Cambridge: Cambridge University Press, 1988 [c. 1001–1015].

Stebbing, L. Susan. *Philosophy and the Physicists.* London: Methuen, 1937.

Taylor (Mill), Harriet. Untitled essays on equality. In *Essays on Sex Equality: John Stuart Mill and Harriet Taylor Mill,* edited by Alice Rossi. Chicago: University of Chicago Press, 1970.

Teresa of Avila. *The Complete Works of St. Teresa of Jesus.* Translated by E. A. Peers. London: Sheed & Ward, 1946.

Mary Ellen Waithe

work

'Work,' any activity that produces services and products of value to others, is not synonymous with 'occupation,' a particular work activity and social role that one assumes on a regular basis. Nor is all work paid, as, for example, home child care. Yet 'work' as status and 'work' as activity are frequently confused, and the terms 'work,' 'occupation,' and 'employment' are almost interchangeable.

Despite the obvious importance of work, it is leisure that has been traditionally valorized. The ancient Greeks, for example, believed that labor brutalized the mind, making it unfit for contemplation. In Genesis, God's work is *intellectual,* not manual; and a lifetime of work is Adam's punishment. Later developments in the Christian Church led to THOMAS AQUINAS's (1225?–1274) theorizing a hierarchy of occupations based on their value to society (at that time, with the priesthood the highest and merchants the lowest). In the modern period, as ardent a defender of capitalism as Adam SMITH (1723–1790) commented that the worker, over a lifetime of labor, "becomes as stupid and ignorant as it is possible for a human creature to become." And Sigmund Freud (1856–1939) believed that, despite work's being a good source of sublimation, "the great majority of people only work under the stress of necessity, and this natural human aversion to work raises most difficult social problems."

Sociologist Max WEBER (1864–1920) coined the term "Protestant ethic" to describe the world view of the emerging middle class that spearheaded and underpinned developing capitalist ideology. In linking work and salvation, the Protestant emphasis on self-reliance, frugality, and deferred gratification, obedience, and rationality is ideally suited to the world of the capitalist entrepreneur whose profits would not be spent frivolously but rather reinvested in the business. By the late 1800s, the Protestant ethic was secularized into a "work ethic" or "success ethic" which offered a justification for the zeal of the early capitalists and resulting social inequities: wealth became a reward for hard work, poverty a result of laziness and lack of talent, and "work-centeredness" central to one's sense of personal worth.

Critics of the "work ethic" maintain that it is not an ethic at all but rather an ideological rationale propagated by the upper and middle classes to justify INEQUALITY and make work palatable by endowing it with moral value. The spirit of the work ethic, detractors argue, cannot apply if one is forced to work to survive, if one's options for work are severely limited, and if one's labor is not enriching. This criticism does not necessarily question the connection between hard work and CHARACTER but insists on attention to the quality of one's work life. In addition, critics note that a genealogy of "the" work ethic reveals its historicity; indeed, they note that the alleged universality of the ethic is an illusion. In Japan, for example, where work is itself prized, the influence of Confucianism (with its concomitant view of the essential goodness of human nature) leads to the view that *kigyo wa unmet kyodotai de aru* (enterprise and employees share a common des-

tiny). Finally, many critics maintain that capitalist ideology itself conceals mixed, if not contradictory impulses; advertising's emphasis on HEDONISM, for example, seems to undermine the impulse toward delayed gratification.

Philosophical analyses (by RAWLS and NOZICK, among others) of justice and resource allocation feature discussions of work and access to jobs as issues for distribution theories. Ethical analyses of work explore competing views of human nature implied in competing theories of management like theory *x* and theory *y*, where the former claims that workers would rather not work, are prone to laziness, and need almost constant supervision (an authoritarian model); and the latter that workers are motivated and productive if work is fulfilling (a communitarian model). The first model presupposes that work is inherently undesirable, the second that work's desirability depends on circumstances.

The Right to Work

The classical view (with roots in Smith and John LOCKE [1632–1704]) defends a free market where rational, self-interested, autonomous individuals with different abilities, INTERESTS, and preferences meet and make mutually beneficial exchanges. Despite the potential for conflict, particularly in a context of scarcity, this view maintains that the system minimizes conflict. The right to PROPERTY is the fundamental basis for the free market, and government exists to protect that right and to ensure that exchanges occur voluntarily. Employee rights then are special rights which derive from binding contractual agreements with employers.

The classical view has recently faced serious challenges, in particular that it depends on a flawed assumption that all participants in the market have similar BARGAINING power. Though the classical view rightly maintains that one is free to reject some particular job, the worker is *not* free to reject *all* jobs. Further, critics see work not as a necessary evil, but rather as constitutive of our nature as human beings. More radical critics argue for the rejection of capitalism itself; moderates defend reforms like, for example, employee bills of rights and affirmative action.

To have a right to *X* is to have a *prima facie* claim to *X* which generally overrides considerations of expediency. Analyses of RIGHTS also distinguish negative rights to noninterference from positive rights to certain social goods and services (strictly speaking, 'positive' and 'negative' refer to the obligations imposed on others). If one has a right to live and must work to live, does one have the right to work? The Universal Declaration of Human Rights (1981) states: "Everyone has the right to work, to free choice of employment, to just and favourable conditions of work and to protection against unemployment." Virtually everyone agrees that individuals should have the *opportunity* to pursue their desired employment without interference. Disagreement arises over whether this right is positive, since this notion conflicts with the competitive basis of the free market. Capitalists like Milton Friedman and classical libertarians like Robert Nozick reject the notion of such a right for three reasons: (1) it cannot be universal, particularly given limited resources; (2) it violates the fundamental right to property, requiring state intervention; and (3) it destroys initiative and motivation in guaranteeing work. Defenders of a positive right to work maintain that this right is too inextricably connected to self-esteem and human DIGNITY to make it dependent on the caprices of the market.

The Rights of Workers

No one questions whether workers have the right to life by virtue of being citizens. But do workers *qua* workers possess rights? For some analysts, workers are virtually "rightless" when they arrive at work. Others have argued (often using a Kantian/Rawlsian framework) that workers *qua* workers have certain ENTITLEMENTS. These may include:

The right to due process. The U.S. Supreme Court has ruled that the due process clause of the Fourteenth Amendment does not extend to the private sector of the economy. Employers (in the absence of a specific contract) may hire, fire, or demote "employees at will" without notice and without reason. The notion of "employment at will" has been challenged in recent literature (Werhane) as violating the right to equal consideration, since employment at will would allow for deserving and undeserving employees alike to be fired.

The right to privacy. Do employers have the right to use polygraphs to screen prospective employees or use surveillance to prevent employee theft? Some have argued that the right to PRIVACY—the right to control how much and what sort of information others can know about one—requires that there be limits to what employers may do.

The right to blow the whistle. Some maintain that whistle blowers—those who make public the immoral or illegal behavior of an employer or supervisor—are disloyal and deserve no protection; others that the right to free speech includes the right to blow the whistle and overrides LOYALTY when harm may come to innocent third parties; and still others that employees have no obligations of loyalty to employers because of the for-profit nature of their relationship.

The right to workplace safety. Do employers have an obligation to inform employees of potential hazards on the job? To compensate employees for work-related injury? To what extent are employers responsible for unforeseeable damages? If one accepts the notion of an implied contract, what are its conditions? Consider, for example, "informed refusal": can an employee refuse, without fear of reprisal, to work with certain dangerous substances?

Gender and race discrepancies in wages still exist, even after controlling for qualifications and types of occupations. Further, women and people of color tend to be segregated in lower paying, less prestigious occupations. Should we take active steps to try to remedy this inequality? If so, what steps? The classical view maintains that inequality *per se* is not unjust if it results from voluntary market transactions and that rational employers seek the most qualified and therefore do not discriminate. Critics maintain that institutional racism and sexism coupled with socialization explain present inequities and that voluntary measures are inadequate. Instead, affirmative action is essential to redress the inequity. At times this policy is defended on grounds of compensatory justice. Others, however, maintain that past injustices are morally irrelevant and that preferential hiring policies are justified by society's goal of eliminating racial and sexual inequality.

Meaningful Work

Some claim that the right to work is not enough if work is not meaningful. They defend a variety of strategies for workplace restructuring geared toward greater worker participation in workplace decisions and the "democratization" of work (Schwartz). Surveys repeatedly reveal that most people would continue to work, even with financial independence; yet, most people also report that they would change jobs if they could. This suggests that the interest, challenge, and autonomy thought to be essential to meaningful work are absent in most occupations. Braverman and others emphasize the fragmentation and dehumanization of work in modern "post-capitalism," the technological complexity that has made work demeaning and routine. An alternative view maintains that new technologies have made possible an improved standard of living, greater flexibility, increased decentralization, and freedom for real creativity.

Regardless, changes in contemporary culture require new ways of thinking about work. Predictions of incredible leisure have turned out not to be the case. In addition, traditional hierarchical arrangements "no longer seem practical or relevant" (Marshall). The transnational nature of large corporations ("corporations are particularly responsible for the diminished significance of national borders" [Byrne]), the increasing use of contract employees, the shift from manufacturing to service occupations, technological developments making work at home possible—such changes seem to force a revisioning of our notions of work and particularly of meaningful work.

Karl MARX (1818–1883) argued that capitalism's demand for ever greater profit leads to the degradation of work and the ALIENATION (a term originating in Roman law to refer to transference or divestiture of property) of the worker. Increasingly, detail work leads to greater efficiency and also ease in replacing individual workers. For Marx, alienation results from the capitalist mode of production because the worker has no control over the production process, does not own the products of her labor, and is separated from other workers who are not allies but competitors. The worker "does not fulfill himself in his work," resulting in a "self-estrangement," a "renunciation of life and of human needs."

For at least the early Marx, HEGEL's (1770–1831) concept of self-activity included a notion of creative work, a possibility undermined by capitalist development. Dealienation for Marx is based on a socialized mode of production and is not therefore simply a matter of making work more "interesting" or less bureaucratic. Would this entail that *all* wage labor, as a means to an end, is alienating?

The 1970s and 1980s in the United States were an important period of experimentation with new work systems (not so unlike the humane relations movement of the 1930s and the social relations movement of the 1950s), and the Quality of Working Life movement gained high visibility. A number of recent theories (in philosophy as well as organizational behavior) examine the possibility of "meaningful work" where "meaningfully redesigned jobs" might give workers a voice and reduce alienation (U.S. Department of Health, Education, and Welfare). Frequent references to companies like Volvo and Saab which use team-based approaches to production appear in the literature as examples of a new form of organization which reestablishes "the social basis of community" (Schleuning). Some argue that such efforts can appeal even to employers, for they "have resulted in increases in productivity" (U.S. Department of Health, Education, and Welfare). Critics, however, point to this fact as evidence of the vulnerability of the meaningful work movement, however well intentioned, to co-optation by owners.

For philosophers, the possibility of meaningful work is frequently tied to normative values like autonomy and self-fulfillment; yet this vision seems more resonant with an earlier era of individual crafts and guilds and might be anachronistic and sentimentalizing. And, clearly, if greater productivity is the necessary if not sufficient condition for acceptance of work redesign and increased democratization of the workplace, then such an agenda has nothing to do with workers' "rights" or with issues like autonomy and satisfaction.

The changing nature of TECHNOLOGY—including information systems, global communication, and automation—is obviously linked to the question of work and its meanings; but there is no consensus on how to interpret technology's potential. Where utopian perspectives may once have envisioned an endless world of leisure made possible by technological advances (indeed, radical feminist Shulamith Firestone even argued that advances in technology might free women of the burden of childbearing, and thus end women's biological disadvantage), even the most ardent defenders of technology would see such a perspective as naive. Technological determinists might maintain that alienation is an inevitable outcome of dominant technology. Dependent capitalism—the term used to describe the phenomenon of underdevelopment and poverty in the third world—seems to force an expanded understanding of alienation.

If self-fulfilling work is "agent-dependent" (Byrne), can *any* work be fulfilling? Even the presumption that high-skill jobs are high satisfaction jobs (and *vice versa*) has been shown not to be the case. And clearly job satisfaction is neither necessary nor sufficient to keeping a job. Indeed, "job satisfaction" must not be confused with nonalienation (at least from a Marxian point of view), given that such satisfaction may be the result of false consciousness, passivity, and the appeal of high wages. Some feminists have pointed to housework—its routinized nature, its endless cycles of repetition, and its absence of value as defined by the market—as paradigmatic of alienated labor; more recently, however, other feminists have suggested that housework's flexibility, its creative potential, and its dependence on individual initiative may suggest possibilities for rethinking work more generally. Communitarians might focus on the social embeddedness of human Being and the need for analyses of work to be framed in terms of that nature; in such a framework, satisfying work becomes a social responsibility shared communally because of what work contributes rather than seen as an individual right which one "brings" to the marketplace.

A deeper philosophical problem may underlie discussions of meaningful work and alienation: Do such perspectives posit a universal, essentialized human nature which is inevitably degraded by certain kinds of work? Is this subjective or objective? Clearly, subjective indicia like "misery" or its absence cannot be necessary or sufficient to a critique of work. Definitions of "good work" (*e.g.*, it "stimulates mind and body, sense of commitment, activities that generate purposeful actions, and close attention to the synergy of means and ends" [Schleuning]) are notoriously ambiguous and admit of enormous personal interpretation. Is there work that by definition is "meaningless"? It would seem that every evolved society has an ideology of work, a set of values (not necessarily internally coherent) associated with work and the division of labor. What work is, what work is valued, how work is accomplished and rewarded, and what is the relationship between work and lived experience—these sorts of questions reflect deeply felt and often conflictual assumptions about human nature and lived experience.

See also: BARGAINING; BUSINESS ETHICS; CHARACTER; CHRISTIAN ETHICS; COMPUTERS; CONTRACTS; DIGNITY; DISCRIMINATION; ELITE, CONCEPT OF; ENTITLEMENTS; EQUALITY; FEMINIST ETHICS; HUMANISM; INEQUALITY; INTERESTS; JUSTICE, DISTRIBUTIVE; LIBRARY AND INFORMATION PROFESSIONS; LOYALTY; MARX; MARXISM; MATERIALISM; NEEDS; OPPRESSION; POWER; PRIVACY; PROFESSIONAL ETHICS; PROPERTY; RACISM AND RELATED ISSUES; RIGHTS; SELF-RESPECT; SEXUAL ABUSE AND HARASSMENT; TECHNOLOGY.

Bibliography

Appelbaum, Eileen, and Rosemary Batt. *The New American Workplace*. Ithaca, NY: ILR Press, 1994.

Braverman, Harry. *Labor and Monopoly Capital*. New York: Monthly Review Press, 1974.

Byrne, Edmund F. *Work, Inc.: A Philosophical Inquiry*. Philadelphia: Temple University Press, 1990. Quotations are from p. 16.

Ewing, David. *Freedom Inside the Corporation*. New York: McGraw-Hill, 1977.

Firestone, Shulamith. *The Dialectic of Sex: The Case for Feminist Revolution*. New York: Bantam, 1972.

Fox, Mary Frank, and Sharlene Hesse-Biber. *Women at Work*. Palto Alto, CA: Mayfield Publishing, 1984.

Freud, Sigmund. *Civilization and Its Discontents*. Translation by James Strachey of *Das Unbehagen in der Kultur*. New York: W. W. Norton, 1961 [1930]. Passage quoted, p. 29.

Friedman, Milton. *Capitalism and Freedom*. Chicago: University of Chicago Press, 1962.

Gini, A. R., and T. J. Sullivan, eds. *It Comes with the Territory: An Inquiry Concerning Work and the Person*. New York: Random House, 1989.

Jackall, Robert. *Moral Mazes: The World of Corporate Managers*. New York: Oxford University Press, 1988.

Marshall, Edward M. *Transforming the Way We Work*. New York: American Management Association, 1995. Quoted from p. 1.

Marx, Karl. *The Economic and Philosophic Manuscripts of 1844*. Translated by Martin Milligan. New York: International Publishers, 1964. Quoted from pp. 110, 150.

Nozick, Robert. *Anarchy, State and Utopia*. New York: Basic Books, 1974.

Oldenquist, Andrew, and Menachem Rosner, eds. *Alienation, Community, and Work*. New York: Greenwood Press, 1991.

Rawls, John. *A Theory of Justice*. Cambridge: Harvard University Press, 1971.

Rose, Michael. *Re-Working the Work Ethic: Economic Values and Socio-Cultural Politics*. New York: Schocken Books, 1985.

Schacht, Richard. *Alienation*. Garden City, NY: Anchor Books, 1971.

Schleuning, Neala. *Idle Hands and Empty Nests: Work and Freedom in the U.S.* New York: Bergin and Garvey, 1990. Quoted from pp. 106, 128.

Schwartz, Adina. "Meaningful Work." *Ethics* 92 (1982): 634–46.

Smith, Adam. *The Wealth of Nations.* New York: 1904 [1776]. Quoted from p. 734.

United States. Department of Health, Education, and Welfare. *Work in America.* Cambridge: MIT Press, 1973. Quoted from pp. *xviii,* 112.

Weber, Max. *The Protestant Ethic and the Spirit of Capitalism.* Translation by Talcott Parsons of *Die protestantische Ethik und der Geist des Kapitalismus.* New York: Scribner's, 1958 [1904–1905].

Werhane, Patricia. *Persons, Rights and Corporations.* Englewood Cliffs, NJ: Prentice-Hall, 1985.

Westin, Alan F. *Whistle Blowing.* New York: McGraw-Hill, 1981.

Westin, Alan F., and Stephan Salisbury, eds. *Individual Rights in the Corporation.* New York: Pantheon, 1980.

Diane C. Raymond

Subject Index

This index lists subjects and names found in the text of the encyclopedia articles. The **bold-face** entries indicate main discussion of the subject. Alphabetization is word by word.

Volume key: Volume 1, pages 1–642; volume 2, pages 643–1266; volume 3, pages 1267–1977.

1833

act consequentialism: consequentialism, 304–307; moral absolutes, 1112; teleological ethics, 1692; torture, 1720–1721

act token, action, 13–14

act type: action, 13; duty and obligation, 424–425; moral absolutes, 1111, 1112; Ross, 1521; Suárez, 1663–1664; supererogation, 1673, 1674; teleological ethics, 1692; voluntary acts, 1773–1776

act utilitarianism: Bentham, 139; consequentialism, 305; Godwin, 613; idealized agents, 836; life and death, 997; Mill (John Stuart), 1102; moral absolutes, 1111, 1113, 1114; motives, 1187; norms, 1243; proportionality, 1393–1394; situation ethics, 1587; teleological ethics, 1692; torture, 1719–1720; twentieth-century Anglo-American ethics, 769; utilitarianism, 1739, 1740, 1742

act-consequentialism. See act consequentialism

action, 13–15; acts and omissions, 14, 15–18; altruism, 50, 51; American moral philosophy, 55; anger, 67; Anscombe, 74, 75, 76; Anselm, 77, 78; Arendt, 84; Aristotelian ethics, 87, 88; Aristotle, 92, 93, 94–95, 96; Augustine, 102, 103; authenticity, 106; authority, 109; autonomy of moral agents, 111–114; Balguy, 122; Buddhist ethics, 164; business ethics, 170; Butler, 175–176; casuistry, 187–189; categorical and hypothetical imperativess, 190–193; causation and responsibility, 194–197; character, 200–201; cheating, 206–207; China, 219; Christian ethics, 227; classical Greek ethics, 693, 694; cognitive science, 249, 251; coherentism, 253–254; collective responsibility, 255–257; commensurability, 258, 259, 260; common good, 264; common sense moralists, 267, 268; communitarianism, 270; Confucian ethics, 288; consequentialism, 304, 305, 306; conservatism, 314; constructivism, 318; conventions, 329, 330; courage, 352–355; Crusius, 363; deliberation and choice, 382, 383; Democritus, 390; deontology, 391–392, 394; desire, 398–399; deterrence, 400, 401; dignity, 405–406; Donegan, 417; double effect, 418–419; duty and obligation, 423–428; early Medieval ethics, 710, 713; economic analysis, 433; economic systems, 440; Edwards, 445; egoism, 446–448; environmental ethics, 467, 468; Epictetus, 473; excellence, 504; excuses, 506–508; externalism and internalism, 517, 518; feminist ethics, 532; final good, 549–551; fittingness, 551–553; Foot, 555; Frankena, 570; free will, 571–574; freedom and determinism, 77; Fuller, 585; Gandhi, 594; Gert, 609; Gewirth, 610–611; good, 620, 621; Hare, 651; Hellenistic ethics, 701; Holbach, 779;

Hutcheson, 818; hypocrisy, 820, 821; ideal observer, 827–828; idealized agents, 835–837; impartiality, 841–843; India, 846; individualism, 849; integrity, 863–864; intention, 866–868; James, 900; Jewish ethics, 909–910, 914; Kant, 930–931, 932, 933; Kantian ethics, 939, 942; karma, 943–945; later Medieval ethics, 717, 718–719; Lewis, 971; liberty, 979–980; Mandeville, 1040; mercy, 1074; merit and desert, 1075, 1076; metaphysics and epistemology, 1089; moral absolutes, 1111; moral attention, 1115–1116; moral development, 1118; moral reasoning, 1162; motives, 1185–1187; naturalism, 1213; Nietzsche, 1236; oppression, 1261–1262; ought implies can, 1265–1266; passion, 1279; Perry, 1293; person, 1295; personal relationships, 1300; philosophy of religion, 1311–1312; possibilism, 1349–1350; postmodernism, 1351; power, 1353–1354; practical reason[ing], 1355–1357; practical wisdom, 1358–1360; pragmatism, 1361; praxis, 1365; presocratic Greek ethics, 687; principlism, 1379; promises, 1386–1387, 1389; proportionality, 1393, 1394, 1395; prudence, 1398, 1399; psychology, 1406; rational choice, 1446–1451; rationality vs. reasonableness, 1453; Rawls, 1457; reasons for, 1461–1464; reflective equilibrium, 1467, 1468–1469; Reid, 1470–1472; religion, 1475; responsibility, 1486–1491; revenge, 1493; Ricoeur, 1499; right, 1499, 1500, 1501; right holders, 1502; rights, 1509–1510; Roman ethics, 705; Sartre, 1532; Schopenhauer, 1539; self-control, 1549; self-deception, 1552; seventeenth- and eighteenth-century ethics, 736; Singer, 1584, 1585; situation ethics, 1586–1587; skepticism, 1588, 1590; slippery slope argument, 1594; social psychology, 1615–1618; sociology, 1621; Socrates, 1624–1625, 1627; Stoicism, 1653, 1654, 1656; strategic interaction, 1657–1662; Thomas Aquinas, 1709; Thomson, 1712–1714; twentieth-century Anglo-American ethics, 765, 766–767, 768; twentieth-century Continental ethics, 759, 761–762; virtues, 1763–1766, 1767; voluntary acts, 1773–1776; Wang, 1779; weakness of will, 1789–1791; wickedness, 1800–1802; Wittgensteinian ethics, 1813; Wollaston, 1818. See also agent-centered morality; behavior; circumstances of action; collective action; conduct; right action

action theory: game theory, 593; strategic interaction, 1659

active enabling, altruism, 52

activity: Aristotle, 94; emotion, 456; perfectionism, 1291; Renaissance ethics, 723

acts. See act token; act type; act utilitarianism; action; acts and omissions; voluntary acts

acts and omissions, 15–18; Abelard, 2; action, 14; altruism, 52; consent, 301; deceit, 379; Donegan, 417; double effect, 418–419; evil, 498; Foot, 555; human rights, 799; killing and letting die, 947–950; negligence, 1224–1225; oppression, 1262; promises, 1386–1389; voluntary acts, 1774, 1775

Acts of the Apostles, common good, 263

actualism: possibilism, 1349–1350; social contract, 1608

act-utilitarianism. See act utilitarianism

Adam: Anselm, 77, 78; Augustine, 102; early Medieval ethics, 713; evil, 499; political systems, 1341; puritanism, 1428–1429; Schelling, 1536; seventeenth- and eighteenth-century ethics, 731, 735; women moral philosophers, 1822; work, 1827

Adams, E. M.: autonomy of ethics, 110, 111; naturalism, 1213

Adams, Robert Merrihew: philosophy of religion, 1311, 1312; responsibility, 1488; theological ethics, 1702

adaptive function: Darwin, 373; nineteenth-century British ethics, 7453

Addams, Jane, pacifism, 1267

addiction: autonomy of moral agents, 113; free will, 573

additivity problems, 19–21; intransitivity, 877–879; rational choice, 1449

Adeimantus, good, 621

adequacy, emotion, 456–457

adequacy of consideration, contracts, 326

adharma, Hindu ethics, 681

adjectives, moral terms, 1181

adjudication, Fuller, 585

Adler, Felix, 21–24

admiration, moral sense theorists, 1174

adolescence, sexual abuse, 1568–1569

adoption: economic liberty, 984; family, 522; reproductive technologies, 1478

Adorno, Theodor W.: critical theory, 357–358, 359; Habermas, 643

adultery: Augustine, 104; cheating, 205; Duns Scotus, 421; fidelity, 544, 545; later Medieval ethics, 719; moral absolutes, 1111, 1112; sexuality, 1571, 1573; women moral philosophers, 1821

adulthood, children, 207–210

Advaita Vedānta, India, 844, 847

advantage: bargaining, 123; exploitation, 515; Spinoza, 1640; virtue ethics, 1760

adversary system: legal ethics, 956; legal philosophy, 959

adversity. See harm

advertent negligence. See recklessness

advertising: censorship, 198; mass media, 1055, 1056

Aelred of Rievaulx: friendship, 582; love, 1020; mysticism, 1197

Aeneas, Roman ethics, 704, 707

Aenesidemus, skepticism, 1588–1589

Volume key: Volume 1, pages 1–642; volume 2, pages 643–1266; volume 3, pages 1267–1977.

1834

Aesara of Lucania, women moral philosophers, 1821
Aeschylus: literature, 1004; mortality, 1183; revenge, 1492; tragedy, 1721, 1722
Aesop, hypocrisy, 820
Aesopian moral, Africa, 34
aesthetic transcendence: American moral philosophy, 55; conservation ethics, 308
aestheticism, aesthetics, 24, 26
aesthetics, **24–33**; Africa, 34; Aristotelian ethics, 86, 89; autonomy of ethics, 110; conservation ethics, 308; emotion, 457; environmental ethics, 468; etiquette, 487; fittingness, 552, 553; forgery, 559–561; Gadamer, 590; happiness, 645, 648; hedonism, 666; idealist ethics, 830; Japan, 903; Marx, 1047; Nietzsche, 1235, 1237; nineteenth-century Continental ethics, 755, 756; Peirce, 1287; perfectionism, 1288; Schiller, 1537–1538; Shaftesbury, 1577–1578; sport, 1643; value concept, 1746; value theory, 1750
affect, cognitive science, 250
affections: Mencius, 1072; nature, 1218; personal relationships, 1301; Shaftesbury, 1577–1578
affective response, emotivism, 459
affirmative action: applied ethics, 83; business ethics, 171; civil rights, 240–241; correctional ethics, 342; discrimination, 414–415; Dworkin, 429; political correctness, 1337, 1339; public policy, 1418; public policy analysis, 1421; racism, 1435, 1438; self-respect, 1564; social and political philosophy, 1600; work, 1828, 1829
affliction, Weil, 1795
Africa, **33–36**; comparative ethics, 273; conservation ethics, 309; Schweitzer, 1541; virtue ethics, 1761
African American studies: multiculturalism, 1188; political correctness, 1338
African Americans: civil rights, 240–241; discrimination, 413, 414–415; equality, 481; groups, 636; Islam, 887; King, 950–951; medical ethics, 1069; multiculturalism, 1190–1191; Niebuhr, 1235; public policy, 1418; racism, 1433–1435, 1436, 1439; twentieth-century Anglo-American ethics, 769
After Virtue, MacIntyre, 1035
afterlife. *See* immortality; reincarnation
Agamemnon: moral dilemmas, 1125; Williams, 1805
agape: Augustine, 104–105; charity, 203; Christian ethics, 226; love, 1020–1023, 1024; religion, 1475; seventeenth- and eighteenth-century ethics, 733; theological ethics, 1704. *See also* Christian love
Age of Reasons, The, Paine, 1272
agency and disability, **36–40**; abortion, 3; acts and omissions, 16, 17; altruism, 52, 53; anger, 69; animals, 73; anthropology, 80; bargaining, 123;

Bentham, 139; bioethics, 141–145; consent, 302–303; death, 377; deceit, 380; discrimination, 413–416; equality, 481–482; euthanasia, 492; fairness, 520; family, 522, 523; feminist ethics, 528–537; fiduciary relationships, 547, 548; human rights, 798; idealized agents, 837; inequality, 852–853; infanticide, 855; lesbian ethics, 967; life and death, 994, 997, 998; medical ethics, 1063–1064; moral community, 1117; narrative, 1202, 1204; needs, 1221–1223; partiality, 1277; paternalism, 1282, 1283; political correctness, 1337; public health, 1416–1417; racism, 1433–1435; rape, 1443–1446; Rawls, 1455; reproductive technologies, 1477–1478, 1479, 1480; responsibility, 1491; right holders, 1502–1506; rights, 1509, 1511; self-defense, 1555; slippery slope argument, 1594–1595; suicide, 1670, 1671; theory and practice, 1708; Vitoria, 1769; Weil, 1795. *See also* autonomy of moral agents; disability
agency theory: action, 14; Aristotelian ethics, 87; Donegan, 417–418; free will, 571–574; happiness, 649–650
agent-centered morality, **40–43**; Abelard, 1–2; action, 14; agency and disability, 36; altruism, 50–53; anger, 67–69; animals, 71; Anselm, 77–78; applied ethics, 81–83; Arendt, 84; Aristotelian ethics, 86, 87, 89; Aristotle, 93; authority, 107–108; benevolence, 135; Bradley, 154; causation and responsibility, 194, 195; character, 201, 202; communitarianism, 269–270; Dewey, 403; Donegan, 417; double effect, 418–419; Duns Scotus, 420; early Medieval ethics, 712; emotion, 455; Epicurus, 476; ethics and morality, 486; evil, 500, 501; excuses, 506–508; exploitation, 515–516; feminist ethics, 530, 532, 534–535; fiduciary relationships, 548; final good, 549–551; fittingness, 551–554; free will, 572–574; Fuller, 585; Gert, 608–610; Gewirth, 610–611; Green, 631; Grotius, 633–634; groups, 635; guilt and shame, 639–640; Hegel, 672–673; Hellenistic ethics, 698; Holocaust, 780–784; ideal observer, 827–828; idealist ethics, 831, 834; idealized agents, 835–837; impartiality, 842; integrity, 863–866; intention, 866; James, 899–900; Jewish ethics, 910–911, 914; Kantian ethics, 939–942, 940; karma, 943–945; later Medieval ethics, 716, 718; Leibniz, 963–964; lesbian ethics, 967; liberalism, 973; Locke, 1009, 1010; loyalty, 1028; Luther, 1031; metaphysics and epistemology, 1089; moral absolutes, 1113; moral pluralism, 1139; moral sense theorists, 1178; motives, 1185–1187; narrative, 1202–1203; natural law, 1206; nineteenth-century Continental

ethics, 752; norms, 1243; ought implies can, 1266; paternalism, 1283; philosophy of religion, 1312; plagiarism, 1317; pleasure, 1327–1329; postmodernism, 1351–1352; practical wisdom, 1358–1360; pragmatism, 1361–1362, 1363–1364; reasons for action, 1462, 1463; responsibility, 1486–1491; right holders, 1502–1506; rights, 1511; Roman ethics, 705; Schiller, 1537–1538; self and social self, 1545; self-ownership, 1561–1563; seventeenth- and eighteenth-century ethics, 738; Shaftesbury, 1577–1578; social contract, 1607, 1609; sociology, 1621; Socrates, 1624–1627; Sophists, 1630; stakeholder, 1648; subjectivism, 1665–1666; sympathy, 1677, 1678; twentieth-century Anglo-American ethics, 766–767, 771; twentieth-century Continental ethics, 759; utilitarianism, 1743; voluntary acts, 1776; Williams, 1805, 1806; wisdom, 1807–1809; Wolff, 1816. *See also* autonomy of moral agents; idealized agents
agent-relative morality, 40–42
agents. *See* agent-centered morality; autonomy of moral agents; idealized agents
aggadah, Jewish ethics, 912
aggregate behavior patterns: individualism, 849; rational choice, 1447–1448, 1449
aggregate benefit, utilitarianism, 1740
aggregation, additivity, 19
aggression: hate, 660; international conflict, 872, 873; life and death, 995, 998; property, 1392; self-defense, 1554, 1555; sport, 1642; war and peace, 1783, 1786
Āghā Khān, Shī'ism, 1579
agnosticism, **43–45**; nineteenth-century British ethics, 744; Protagoras, 1394
Agrarian Justice, Paine, 1272
agreeableness, Hume, 808, 812
agreement: Balguy, 122; bargaining, 123; Barry, 126; compromise, 281; contracts, 326–328; conventions, 329; economic liberty, 981; fairness, 521; moral rules, 1168; Murphy, 1195; personal relationships, 1299; social contract, 1607, 1608, 1609
agribusiness, 45–47
agricultural ethics, **45–48**; cosmopolitan ethics, 346; environmental ethics, 468; genetic engineering, 603
ahimsā: competition, 278; Gandhi, 593, 594; Hindu ethics, 682, 683; India, 846; Jainism, 897, 898
Ahriman, competition, 277
AI (artificial intelligence), practical reason[ing], 1356
AIDS (acquired immune deficiency syndrome): bioethics, 144; medical ethics, 1070; public health, 1417
Aiken, Henry: autonomy of moral agents, 112, 113; moral point of view, 1141
Aiken, William, agricultural ethics, 46
Ailred of Rievaulx. *See* Aelred of Rievaulx

Volume key: Volume 1, pages 1–642; volume 2, pages 643–1266; volume 3, pages 1267–1977.

1835

Subject Index

Volume key: Volume 1, pages 1–642; volume 2, pages 643–1266; volume 3, pages 1267–1977.

1836

Volume key: Volume 1, pages 1–642; volume 2, pages 643–1266; volume 3, pages 1267–1977.

1837

Volume key: Volume 1, pages 1–642; volume 2, pages 643–1266; volume 3, pages 1267–1977.

1838

Volume key: Volume 1, pages 1–642; volume 2, pages 643–1266; volume 3, pages 1267–1977.

1839

Subject Index

Volume key: Volume 1, pages 1–642; volume 2, pages 643–1266; volume 3, pages 1267–1977.

Ayn Rand Institute, Rand, 1442
Ayn Rand Society, Rand, 1442
Ayurvedic medicine, medical ethics, 1066
Azor, Juan, casuistry, 188

Baader, Franz von, Schelling, 1536
babies: cradle arguments, 355–357; right holders, 1503, 1504, 1505. *See also* children and ethical theory; infants
Babylonian myth, competition, 277
baby-selling, reproductive technologies, 1478
Bacharach, Michael, economic analysis, 433
backward-looking nature, justice, rectificatory, 927
Bacon, Francis: legal ethics, 955; revenge, 1494; seventeenth- and eighteenth-century ethics, 730; Spinoza, 1638–1639
bad: analytic philosophy, 64, 65, 66; Brentano, 158; classical Greek ethics, 693–695; comparative ethics, 275; competition, 277; death, 377, 378; envy, 472; forms of consciousness, 564; Hellenistic ethics, 701; karma, 944; naturalistic fallacy, 1215–1217; Nietzsche, 1238; passion, 1281; proportionality, 1394–1395; resentment, 1482; Russell, 1527; Santayana, 1529; Suárez, 1663; technology and nature, 1690, 1691; value concept, 1745; virtue ethics, 1758; voluntarism, 1772–1773. *See also* double effect; harm; immoralism; vice; wrong, concepts of
bad actions: Anscombe, 75; social psychology, 1616–1617
bad consequences, 159
bad faith, **118–120**; authenticity, 106; existential ethics, 512; hypocrisy, 819–820, 822; phenomenology, 1306; Sartre, 1531; self-deception, 1552; wickedness, 1801
bad intention: Abelard, 2; Arendt, 84
bad judgment, Arendt, 84
Baden school, neo-Kantianism, 1226
Bahya ibn Pakuda, Jewish ethics, 913
Baier, Annette: agency and disability, 38; egoism, 449; emotion, 456; right holders, 1504, 1505; sympathy, 1678, 1679; virtue ethics, 1761
Baier, Kurt E. M., **120–121**; analytic philosophy, 64, 66; ethics and morality, 485; Frankena, 570; impartiality, 841; moral education, 1129; moral point of view, 1141, 1142, 1143, 1144; moral rules, 1168–1169, 1170; naturalism, 1213; revolution, 1497; twentieth-century Anglo-American ethics, 767; virtue ethics, 1761
Bain, Alexander, Mill (John Stuart), 1100
Bakke case, discrimination, 414
balance: American moral philosophy, 55; Democritus, 390; gratitude, 629–630; library, 986; principlism, 1379; technology and nature, 1691; utilitarianism, 1738–1739
balance of burdens, justice, rectificatory, 927

balance of power: Niebuhr, 1235; war and peace, 1782–1783
balancing metaphor, additivity, 20
Balguy, John, **121–122**
banality of evil, Arendt, 84
Bandura, A., moral development, 1121
Bangladesh famine, public policy, 1418
baptism: Christian ethics, 225; puritanism, 1428
Barabbas, amnesty and pardon, 57
barbarians, virtue ethics, 1758
barbarity, genocide, 607
Barber, Benjamin R., political systems, 1345
Barber, Bernard, trust, 1728, 1730
Barbeyrac, Jean, Pufendorf, 1424
bargaining, **123–125**; blackmail, 151, 153; compromise, 282; consent, 301; contracts, 326, 327, 328; deterrence, 400; economic analysis, 438; economic liberty, 982; exploitation, 516; fairness, 521; Marxism, 1049; rational choice, 1450; strategic interaction, 1658; work, 1828
Barker, Ernest: liberalism, 972; social contract, 1609
Barnes, W.H.F., good, 620
Barnevelt, Jan van Olden, Grotius, 633
Baron, Hans, humanism, 802
Baron, Marcia: partiality, 1276; supererogation, 1674
Baron, Robert S., social psychology, 1614
Barratt, Alfred, nineteenth-century British ethics, 747
Barry, Brian (M.), **125–127**; cooperation, conflict, and coordination, 335; economic analysis, 438; equality, 480; Hobbes, 775; political systems, 1345; reciprocity, 1465
Barry, William, agnosticism, 44
BART case, engineering ethics, 463
Barth, John, commensurability, 261
Barth, Karl, Christian ethics, 226–227
Bartok, Bela, moral realism, 1155
base emotions, hate, 60
basic acts, action, 14
basic good. *See* good, theories of the
basic needs, needs, 1221, 1222
basic rights. *See* human rights
basic strategies, metaethics, 1079
basis for rational consistency, Barry, 125
Batson, C. Daniel, social psychology, 1616
Baudelaire, Charles-Pierre, nihilism, 1240
Bauer, Bruno: Engels, 460; humanism, 801; Marx, 1043
Bauer, Yehuda, genocide, 607
Bauman, Zygmunt, postmodernism, 1351
Bayles, Michael D., library, 986
Beagle voyage, Darwin, 373, 374
Beardsley, Monroe, aesthetics, 30–32
beastiality, sexuality, 1572
beastly methods, Machiavelli, 1033–1034
beata vita, Cicero, 232
beatitude: later Medieval ethics, 716–717, 718; Renaissance ethics, 723–724, 728, 729; Suárez, 1663
Beatitudes, moral absolutes, 1112
Beatrice of Nazareth [Beatrijs van Tienen], women moral philosophers, 1822

beatus, Cicero, 232
Beauchamp, Tom L.: beneficence, 132; consent, 302; principlism, 1378, 1379
beauty: aesthetics, 24–32; Africa, 34; Bradley, 155; Edwards, 446; Japan, 903; Kant, 935; love, 1018; moral education, 1128; organic unity, 1264; Renaissance ethics, 724; Ross, 1521; Schiller, 1537, 1538; Shaftesbury, 1578; twentieth-century Anglo-American ethics, 766; twentieth-century Continental ethics, 764; value concept, 1745; women moral philosophers, 1821
Beauvoir, Simone de. *See* de Beauvior, Simone
Beccaria, Cesare, Marchesi di, **127–128**; Bentham, 137, 138; capital punishment, 183
Beck, Lewis White, twentieth-century Anglo-American ethics, 771
Becker, Ernest, life and death, 995–996
Becker, Lawrence C.: property, 1390, 1391–1392; reciprocity, 1465; self and social self, 1545; social psychology, 1618; trust, 1729
Beckett, Samuel, the absurd, 7
becoming. *See* being and becoming
Bedau, Hugo, correctional ethics, 341
Beecher, Henry K., pain, 1270
Beehler, Rodger: Murphy, 1193; Wittgensteinian ethics, 1814
Beetham, David, legitimacy, 961
Beethoven, Ludwig van: aesthetics, 25; Nietzsche, 1238; Schiller, 1537
Beguines, women moral philosophers, 1823
behavior: agent-centered morality, 40–43; analytic philosophy, 66; Aristotle, 93; autonomy of moral agents, 113; Bentham, 140; biological ethics, 148; Buddhist ethics, 166; conventions, 329; Darwin, 374; deliberation and choice, 383–384; Dewey, 402–404; dignity, 405; egoism, 446–447; envy, 471; etiquette, 487, 488; fittingness, 552; Foucault, 568; guilt and shame, 639; Hsün Tzu, 794; hypocrisy, 823; immoralism, 838–840; individualism, 849; James, 899; Locke, 1009, 1011; love, 1026; metaphysics and epistemology, 1091; moral development, 1118–1124; moral relativism, 1166; natural law, 1209; norms, 1242–1243; privacy, 1381, 1382, 1383; prudence, 1397, 1399; public and private morality, 1410–1413; public health, 1415; racism, 1437, 1438; rational choice, 1447–1448, 1448, 1449, 1451; reasons for action, 1461–1464; religion, 1475; risk aversion, 1519; self and social self, 1545; self-control, 1549; social psychology, 1613–1618; twentieth-century Continental ethics, 762–763; utilitarianism, 1737; value theory, 1752; virtues, 1763–1764; voluntary acts, 1773–1776. *See also* action; reasons for action; voluntary acts
being: Edwards, 446; existential ethics, 509, 510–514; Heidegger, 675–676;

Volume key: Volume 1, pages 1–642; volume 2, pages 643–1266; volume 3, pages 1267–1977.

1841

Volume key: Volume 1, pages 1–642; volume 2, pages 643–1266; volume 3, pages 1267–1977.

1842

Volume key: Volume 1, pages 1–642; volume 2, pages 643–1266; volume 3, pages 1267–1977.

1843

Volume key: Volume 1, pages 1–642; volume 2, pages 643–1266; volume 3, pages 1267–1977.

1844

Volume key: Volume 1, pages 1–642; volume 2, pages 643–1266; volume 3, pages 1267–1977.

1845

Volume key: Volume 1, pages 1–642; volume 2, pages 643–1266; volume 3, pages 1267–1977.

1846

Volume key: Volume 1, pages 1–642; volume 2, pages 643–1266; volume 3, pages 1267–1977.

1847

Volume key: Volume 1, pages 1–642; volume 2, pages 643–1266; volume 3, pages 1267–1977.

1848

Volume key: Volume 1, pages 1–642; volume 2, pages 643–1266; volume 3, pages 1267–1977.

1849

Volume key: Volume 1, pages 1–642; volume 2, pages 643–1266; volume 3, pages 1267–1977.

1850

mass media, 1054–1056; moral realism, 1158; moral terms, 1180–1182; non-violence, 1756; praxis, 1365; promises, 1386–1387; right holders, 1504; twentieth-century Continental ethics, 764, 765. *See also* language; mass media; meaning; semantics

communion: Christian ethics, 223; hope, 791

communism: China, 221; competition, 278; Engels, 460, 462; Feuerbach, 541; humanism, 801; Marx, 1042; Marxism, 1051, 1054; neo-Kantianism, 1227, 1228; phenomenology, 1306; property, 1392; Rand, 1441; Soviet ethical theory, 1633–1634; Suárez, 1664; Weil, 1794. *See also* socialism

Communist League, Marx, 1042

Communist Manifesto: forms of consciousness, 566; Marx, 1042; Marxism, 1053

Communist Party: political correctness, 1337, 1338; Soviet ethical theory, 1633; Weil, 1794

communitarianism, **269–272**; Africa, 33, 34; agency and disability, 38; Aristotelian ethics, 86; autonomy of moral agents, 113; Bradley, 155; business ethics, 174; civic good, 236; comparative ethics, 273–274; cosmopolitan ethics, 348; duty and obligation, 428; family, 523; feminist ethics, 530, 531, 535; Feuerbach, 541; Gandhi, 594; good, 623; Hegel, 674; humanism, 802; individualism, 850; international distributive justice, 875; liberalism, 973; nineteenth-century British ethics, 745; nineteenth-century Continental ethics, 753; obedience to law, 1254–1255; perfectionism, 1291; pride, 1376; Royce, 1525–1526; self and social self, 1545–1546; social and political philosophy, 1602; sociology, 1621; Staël, 1644; Suárez, 1664; Taylor, 1685; Tufts, 1732; twentieth-century Anglo-American ethics, 765, 771; Weil, 1795; work, 1831

community: abortion, 3, 4; agency and disability, 38; American moral philosophy, 54, 55; Aristotelian ethics, 86; Aristotle, 91, 96, 97; civility, 243; common good, 263; communitarianism, 269, 270–271; comparative ethics, 273–274; duty and obligation, 427; egoism, 448; environmental ethics, 469–470; equality, 483; etiquette, 487; feminist ethics, 530, 535; honor, 789, 790; Hume, 808–809; idealist ethics, 832, 833, 834; individualism, 848, 849; international distributive justice, 875; Islamic business ethics, 888; Islamic ethics, 889; Kantian ethics, 941; Leopold, 966; lesbian ethics, 967; library, 987; MacIntyre, 1035; moral purity, 151–152; multiculturalism, 1189; Murphy, 1195; mysticism, 1197; obedience to law, 1254–1255,

1256; police ethics, 1332, 1334, 1335–1336; Protagoras, 1396–1397; public and private morality, 1410; public goods, 1413–1415; punishment, 1427; Rawls, 1457; Reid, 1471; rights, 1511; risk, 1513–1514; self-deception, 1552; social and political philosophy, 1602; sociology, 1621; Sophists, 1630; twentieth-century Anglo-American ethics, 771; twentieth-century Continental ethics, 764. *See also* communitarianism; moral community, boundaries of

comparative economic systems. *See* economic systems

comparative ethics, **273–277**; business ethics, 173–174; Gassendi, 595–597; golden rule, 617; moral relativism, 1164–1165; Taoist ethics, 1680–1684; virtue ethics, 1761

comparison: additivity, 19; analogical argument, 60–61; commensurability, 258, 259; economic systems, 440, 441; passion, 1280; rational choice, 1448; resentment, 1483; value theory, 1750

compassion: altruism, 51; autonomy of moral agents, 113, 114; beneficence, 132; benevolence, 134; Buddhist ethics, 166, 168; care, 186; egoism, 448; emotion, 454; euthanasia, 492; evil, 499; feminist ethics, 529; forgiveness, 561; idealist ethics, 833, 834; India, 847; Jainism, 897, 898; Japan, 902; Jesus, 907; literature, 1006; medical ethics, 1063; mercy, 1075; moral sense theorists, 1174; nāgārjuna, 1200; postmodernism, 1352; Schopenhauer, 1539; sympathy, 1676, 1678, 1679

compatibilism: free will, 572–573; freedom and determinism, 575, 576–577; Leibniz, 964

compensation: Anselm, 77; correctional ethics, 340; discrimination, 415–416; international distributive justice, 876; justice, rectificatory, 926; land ethics, 953; rights, 1511; risk, 1513; suicide, 1668

competency: consent, 302–303; euthanasia, 492; library, 986; medical ethics, 1068; psychology, 1406; trust, 1729, 1731

competition, **277–280**; business ethics, 171, 173; economic systems, 439, 441; Epicureanism, 475; Epicurus, 477; evolution, 501; Hobbes, 773; land ethics, 953; library, 991; Marx, 1045; Marxism, 1051; mass media, 1055; materialism, 1057; moral sense theorists, 1173; perfectionism, 1291; plagiarism, 1317; racism, 1435; reproductive technologies, 1479; Roman ethics, 704, 706; sport, 1642–1643; sympathy, 1678; work, 1829

complacency, hypocrisy, 822

complementary fallacy, comparative ethics, 276

complexity, wisdom, 1807, 1808

compliance: authority, 108; contractarianism, 323; legitimacy,

962; metaethics, 1086; skepticism, 1591–1592

composites, journalism, 915, 916

comprehensive theory, metaethics, 1084

comprehensiveness: coherentism, 252; final good, 549–550

compromise, **280–282**; consent, 303; contractarianism, 321; corruption, 345; fairness, 520, 521; nursing ethics, 1251; self and social self, 1547; war and peace, 1786

compulsion: excuses, 507; freedom and determinism, 575; psychology, 1406; voluntary acts, 1774

compulsoriness, public goods, 1413, 1415

compulsory heterosexuality, sexuality, 1575

computers, **283–287**; library, 986, 988–989, 990, 991; police ethics, 1334

Comte, Auguste, Mill (John Stuart), 1100, 1103

con artist, hypocrisy, 820

Conant, James, Wittgenstein, 1812

concentration, India, 846

concentration camps: collective responsibility, 257; Holocaust, 784; medical ethics, 1069

Concept of Law, The, Hart, 655–656, 657

conception (biological): abortion, 2–6. *See also* reproduction (biological)

conception of good, Barry, 126

concepts: analytic philosophy, 64–66; deontology, 396; Whewell, 1800

conceptual hedonism, pleasure, 1327

conceptual paradox, blackmail, 151–152

conceptual slope arguments, slippery slope, 1594

conceptual unity, Confucian ethics, 289–290

concern: sympathy, 1676; theory and practice, 1707. *See also* altruism; compassion; empathy; other-regarding; personal relationships

concession, bargaining, 123

conclusion, analogical argument, 61

concrete happiness, Bentham, 138

concrete narratives. *See* narrative ethics

Condition of the Working Class in England, The, Engels, 460

conditional predication, Jainism, 898

conditions for justice. *See* justice, circumstances of

conditions for morality, biological theory, 149

Condorcet, Marquis de: equality, 483; rational choice, 1447, 1448–1449

conduct: applied ethics, 80–83; casuistry, 188; Christian ethics, 224; communitarianism, 270; Confucian ethics, 288; deontology, 391–393; etiquette, 487, 488; existential ethics, 513; forms of consciousness, 564; golden rule, 615–617; government ethics, 627–628; harm and offense, 654; Hart, 657; idealized agents, 836, 837; India, 846; Jainism, 897; Locke, 1009; military ethics, 1094; moral education, 1128, 1129; moral luck, 1135–1136; moral perception, 1137, 1138; moral realism, 1158;

Volume key: Volume 1, pages 1–642; volume 2, pages 643–1266; volume 3, pages 1267–1977.

1851

Volume key: Volume 1, pages 1–642; volume 2, pages 643–1266; volume 3, pages 1267–1977.

1852

consequences: American moral philosophy, 55; Anscombe, 75; Augustine, 103; authenticity, 106; Ayer, 116; collective responsibility, 257; democracy, 386; deontology, 392–393; double effect, 419; Foot, 555; free will, 574; Godwin, 613; good, 623; homicide, 785; hypocrisy, 821; inequality, 851; infanticide, 855; karma, 944; killing and letting die, 949; legitimacy, 961; moral education, 1129; moral luck, 1136; moral reasoning, 1161; negligence, 1224–1225; philosophy of religion, 1311; pragmatism, 1363; Reid, 1471; rights, 1511; risk analysis, 1515–1517; Singer, 1584–1585; situation ethics, 1587; slavery, 1593; slippery slope argument, 1596; strategic interaction, 1660; technology, 1687; teleological ethics, 1692; theory and practice, 1707; torture, 1720; twentieth-century Anglo-American ethics, 766, 768, 769; utilitarianism, 1741–1742, 1743; voluntary acts, 1774

consequentialism, **304–307**; acts and omissions, 17; additivity, 19–20; Adler, 23; agent-centered morality, 41; American moral philosophy, 54; anger, 69; Anscombe, 75; blackmail, 153; causation and responsibility, 196–197; Christian ethics, 227; collective responsibility, 256, 257; cooperation, conflict, and coordination, 334, 335; deontology, 391, 392, 393, 394, 396; discrimination, 414–415; Donegan, 417; double effect, 419; duty and obligation, 424–425; economic analysis, 434; economic systems, 440, 442; Foot, 555; formalism, 563; future generations, 586–588; government ethics, 628; Hindu ethics, 680, 683; international distributive justice, 875; Kantian ethics, 939, 940; legal ethics, 956; logic, 1016; moral absolutes, 1112, 1113; moral luck, 1135, 1136; moral reasoning, 1163; motives, 1185; partiality, 1275, 1276–1277; paternalism, 1283; perfectionism, 1288; pleasure, 1327; pragmatism, 1362; pride, 1377; principlism, 1378; public and private morality, 1412; racism, 1437; revenge, 1493; secrecy and confidentiality, 1542–1543; sexuality, 1571; Soviet ethical theory, 1634; strategic interaction, 1659–1660; suicide, 1670; teleological ethics, 1692, 1693; theism, 1700; torture, 1719–1720; twentieth-century Anglo-American ethics, 771; utilitarianism, 1740; Wolff, 1815, 1816, 1817

conservation ethics, **307–310**; environmental ethics, 468–470; Leopold, 965–966; technology and nature, 1691

conservatism, **311–317**; Bradley, 154; Burke, 169; Crusius, 363; Descartes, 397, 398; euthanasia, 494–496; Hegel, 669–670, 674; liberalism,

973; naturalism, 1213; Objectivism, 1259; person, 1297; political correctness, 1337; precedent, 1367; racism, 1438; Rand, 1441; Roman ethics, 706; sexuality, 1570; slippery slope argument, 1594–1596; twentieth-century Anglo-American ethics, 767, 769, 771. *See also* reactionary thought

consideration, contracts, 326

consistency: authenticity, 106; autonomy of moral agents, 112; coherentism, 252; compromise, 282; Lewis, 971; moral pluralism, 1139; rationality vs. reasonableness, 1452, 1453

constancy: fidelity, 544; Hume, 807

Constant, Benjamin: liberalism, 973, 975; Staël, 1644

constant-sum game, game theory, 592

constituencies: business ethics, 171; stakeholder, 1645–1646

constituents: government ethics, 626–627; public policy analysis, 1420

Constitution (U.S.). *See* United States Constitution

constitutionalism: economic systems, 443; government ethics, 625; Hegel, 669, 670; Hobbes, 773–774; human rights, 796, 797; Kant, 935, 937; liberalism, 973; libertarianism, 976, 977

constraints: liberty, 979; moral development, 1121

constructivism, **317–320**; international distributive justice, 876; psychology, 1407–1408; Rawls, 1457; social contract, 1612

consumer culture: cultural studies, 365; mass media, 1055; materialism, 1058

consumer surplus, cost-benefit analysis, 350

consummatory experiences: American moral philosophy, 55; pragmatism, 1362

consumption: cost-benefit analysis, 350; cultural studies, 365; economic systems, 439; exploitation, 516; libertarianism, 977; mass media, 1055; public goods, 1413, 1414; public health, 1415

contemplation: Aristotle, 97; conservation ethics, 308; Maimonides, 1036; mysticism, 1197; Renaissance ethics, 723, 724; virtue ethics, 1757

contemporary ethics: Aristotelian ethics, 85–90; bioethics, 141–145; communitarianism, 270; conservation ethics, 310; double effect, 418, 419; duty and obligation, 425, 428; Dworkin, 430; equality, 482–483; eudaimonism, 491; existential ethics, 510–514; fairness, 520–521; feminist ethics, 528, 533–538; Foot, 555–556; friendship, 582–589; future generations, 586–588; genetic engineering, 602–606; good, 621–622; honor, 789–790; human rights, 796–799; hypocrisy, 822–823; infanticide, 854–856; Islamic ethics, 893; Jainism, 898; justice, distributive, 924; liberalism, 973–

974; MacIntyre, 1035; moral absolutes, 1112–1113; moral education, 1129–1130; natural law, 1209–1210; neo-Kantianism, 1227–1228; paternalism, 1282; person, 1298; personal relationships, 1299, 1300–1302; public policy, 1418–1419; reproductive technologies, 1475–1480; self and social self, 1545–1546; social and political philosophy, 1601–1602, 1605–1606; social contract, 1610–1612; suicide, 1670; sympathy, 1676; theory and practice, 1708; twentieth-century Angol-American ethics, 765–773; twentieth-century Continental ethics, 758–765; virtue ethics, 1757, 1760, 1761

contempt: anger, 68; pride, 1374, 1377; racism, 1435, 1436, 1437

contentment: Democritus, 390; happiness, 645; meaning of life, 1002

context: analytic philosophy, 66; principlism, 1380; self-defense, 1554; situation ethics, 1586–1587; slippery slope argument, 1595–1596; social psychology, 1614–1618; weakness of will, 1789. *See also* circumstances of action; situation ethics

contextual pacifists, war and peace, 1785

contextualism: communitarianism, 270; comparative ethics, 276; formalism, 563; Murphy, 1193; Walzer, 1778

continence: puritanism, 1430; temperance, 1694

contingency: authenticity, 106; conservatism, 315, 316; economic analysis, 433

continuing education, bioethics, 142

contraception: abortion, 3; Anscombe, 76; family, 522; future generations, 586; Islamic medical ethics, 895; privacy, 1381; sexuality, 1571; technology and nature, 1690. *See also* birth control

contractarianism, **320–325**; censorship, 199; common good, 262, 263, 265; cooperative surplus, 337–338; deontology, 391, 392, 395; economic systems, 443, 444; egoism, 449; future generations, 588; good, 622; Hobbes, 773, 774; human rights, 797; Hume, 811; idealized agents, 837; killing and letting die, 949; liberalism, 973, 974; libertarianism, 977; medical ethics, 1063; Prichard, 1373; property, 1391; Rawls, 1454–1459; revenge, 1493; skepticism, 1591; social and political philosophy, 1601–1603; stakeholder, 1647; theory and practice, 1707–1708; twentieth-century Anglo-American ethics, 770–771, 772; Vitoria, 1768. *See also* social contract

contracts, **326–328**; agency and disability, 36; Aristotelian ethics, 87; bargaining, 123, 124; bribery, 159; coercion, 245–248; Confucian ethics, 292; conservatism, 311; contractarianism, 323; conventions, 329; economic liberty, 982;

Volume key: Volume 1, pages 1–642; volume 2, pages 643–1266; volume 3, pages 1267–1977.

1853

Volume key: Volume 1, pages 1–642; volume 2, pages 643–1266; volume 3, pages 1267–1977.

1854

Volume key: Volume 1, pages 1–642; volume 2, pages 643–1266; volume 3, pages 1267–1977.

Volume key: Volume 1, pages 1–642; volume 2, pages 643–1266; volume 3, pages 1267–1977.

1856

Volume key: Volume 1, pages 1–642; volume 2, pages 643–1266; volume 3, pages 1267–1977.

1857

Volume key: Volume 1, pages 1–642; volume 2, pages 643–1266; volume 3, pages 1267–1977.

1858

Devlin, Patrick: Hart, 657; sexuality, 1573

Dewey, John, **402–405**; Adler, 21; aesthetics, 31; American moral philosophy, 54, 55, 56; applied ethics, 81; Aristotelian ethics, 89; cognitive science, 249, 251; Emerson, 452–450; Fuller, 584; humanism, 802; Mead, 1060; moral development, 1120, 1123; moral education, 1130; moral reasoning, 1163; Murphy, 1193; naturalism, 121; nature, 1219; Nietzsche, 1236; pragmatism, 1361, 1362, 1363; public and private morality, 1410; public policy, 1418; self and social self, 1544; Soviet ethical theory, 1635; Stevenson, 1649; Tufts, 1732; twentieth-century Anglo-American ethics, 767, 768; value theory, 1750

dharma: Buddha, 161; forms of consciousness, 564; Hindu ethics, 677–681, 682, 683; India, 845–846, 847

Dharma ʾāstras: Hindu ethics, 680; India, 845, 846, 847

Diagnostic and Statistical Manual of Mental Disorders: DSM-III-R and DSM-IV: Gert, 609; psychoanalysis, 1405

dialectic: Aristotle, 91; classical Greek ethics, 694; conservatism, 311; deliberation and choice, 382; existential ethics, 509; Gewirth, 610–611; historiography, 684; Japan, 903; Nietzsche, 1239; nineteenth-century British ethics, 739, 743; phenomenology, 1306; Rand, 1440; Ricoeur, 1499; Sartre, 1532; self and social self, 1544; Sidgwick, 1581; Soviet ethical theory, 1631; Sunnīsm, 1673; twentieth-century Anglo-American ethics, 771

dialogue: non-violence, 1756; Socrates, 1624

Diamond, Cora: Murdoch, 1192; Murphy, 1193

Dickens, Charles: hypocrisy, 821; integrity, 865; literature, 1005, 1006

Dickinson, Emily: Emerson, 451; transcendentalism, 1724

"dictatorship of proletariat," Marxism, 1050

Diderot, Denis: hypocrisy, 822; Montesquieu, 1108; nature, 1218; Shaftesbury, 1577

Dido, Roman ethics, 704

die, right to: analogical argument, 59, 60, 61, 63; applied ethics, 82; dignity, 406; euthanasia, 492–494, 495; suicide, 1668, 1671

dietary restrictions, moral purity, 1152

difference: equality, 484; feminist ethics, 529, 530, 531, 532, 533, 534, 536, 537; formalism, 563; moral relativism, 1164–1165; multiculturalism, 1189–1190; racism, 1435; self and social self, 1546

difference principle: cooperation, conflict, and coordination, 335; justice, distributive, 922, 923; Rawls, 1456; risk aversion, 1519, 1520;

twentieth-century Anglo-American ethics, 770, 772

Digambara, Jainism, 898

Diggs, B. J., practical reason[ing], 1357

dignity, **405–406**; Adler, 22; agency and disability, 39; anger, 69; Aristotelian ethics, 87, 88, 89; cosmopolitan ethics, 347; cruelty, 361; deontology, 393, 395; Dworkin, 430; Epictetus, 474; equality, 482; etiquette, 487; euthanasia, 492, 493, 494; Gandhi, 594; government ethics, 627; Hegel, 672; Hume, 807; Jewish ethics, 911; Kant, 936; Kantian ethics, 939, 940; legal ethics, 956; liberalism, 974; Mill (James), 1098; moral psychology, 1159; multiculturalism, 1188, 1189; nineteenth-century Continental ethics, 753, 754; oppression, 1261; privacy, 1382, 1383; Pufendorf, 1424; rights, 1509; Schiller, 1537, 1538; secrecy and confidentiality, 1542; torture, 1719; twentieth-century Continental ethics, 764; Weil, 1794–1795; Wollstonecraft, 1819; work, 1829

dikaiosyne, integrity, 865

dike, presocratic Greek ethics, 688, 690

dilemmas. *See* moral dilemmas

dimensions, justice, rectificatory, 926

diminishing marginal utility: Bentham, 139; economic analysis, 434, 435, 436; equality, 483; interests, 870; justice, distributive, 922; risk aversion, 1518, 1519; utilitarianism, 1741

dimished responsibility, psychology, 1406

Dimmesdale (fictional), hypocrisy, 821

Dio Chrysostom, Cynics, 370

Diogenes of Sinope, Cynics, 368–370

Diogenes Laertius: cradle arguments, 356; Cyrenaics, 371; Epicurus, 476; Gassendi, 595, 596; golden rule, 614; hedonism, 664, 665; Hellenistic ethics, 697; Renaissance ethics, 724, 727; Stoicism, 1652

Dionysian value: Nietzsche, 1237–1238, 1239; nihilism, 1241; puritanism, 1431; tragedy, 1723

Dionysius, Cicero, 232

diplomacy: etiquette, 487; government ethics, 625; international conflict, 872–873; legitimacy, 961

direct intention, intention, 868

direct utilitarian. *See* act utilitarianism

direct vs. indirect duties, animals, 70–71, 72

direction of development, Mencius, 1071, 1072, 1073

directives, authority, 107–108

directness, Nietzsche, 1236

dirty hands, **407–410**; compromise, 282; existential ethics, 513; feminist ethics, 532; government ethics, 626, 628; moral luck, 1136; public and private morality, 1411

disability: abortion, 3; agency and disability, 36–40; American moral philosophy, 55–56; animals, 73; fairness, 520; family, 522; genetic engineering, 604; Gert, 609; idealized agents, 837; inequality, 852;

infanticide, 854, 855; life and death, 994, 997; moral community, 1117; political correctness, 1337; public health, 1416–1417, 1417; right holders, 1502, 1504, 1505, 1506; suicide, 1669; theory and practice, 1708. *See also* agency and disability; mental disability

disability adjusted life years (DALYs), medical ethics, 1063

disagreement: Balguy, 122; moral realism, 1156–1158, 1159; Stevenson, 1650; theological ethics, 1705; Westermarck, 1798

disalienation: phenomenology, 1306; Sartre, 1532

disappointment, value concept, 1747–1748

disapproval: guilt and shame, 640; homosexuality, 786–787; ideal observer, 827, 828; moral sense theorists, 1173, 1174, 1176, 1177; toleration, 1717; voluntarism, 1772

disarmament, nuclear ethics, 1247, 1248

disasters: applied ethics, 82; engineering ethics, 463; nuclear ethics, 1249; public policy, 1418

discipleship, Christian ethics, 227

discipline, Locke, 1010, 1011

disclosure, bargaining, 123

discounting the future, **410–413**; future generations, 586; risk, 1513

discourse. *See* moral discourse; language

discourse ethics: critical theory, 360; Habermas, 643–644; Mead, 1060; social contract, 1612. *See also* moral discourse; moral terms

Discourse on Method, Descartes, 397

Discourse on the Origin of Inequality: competition, 278; Rousseau, 1521–1522, 1523

Discourse on the Sciences and Arts, Rousseau, 1521, 1522

Discourses, Machiavelli, 1034

discretion: correctional ethics, 341, 342; fidelity, 544; Hume, 807; police ethics, 1335

discrimination, **413–416**; applied ethics, 83; civil rights, 240–241; conservatism, 312; Dworkin, 429; equality, 478–479, 483; feminist ethics, 528–538; fittingness, 553; groups, 636, 637; human rights, 796; library, 989; multiculturalism, 1188, 1189; oppression, 1261; partiality, 1277; police ethics, 1332, 1335–1336; political correctness, 1338, 1339; public policy, 1418; public policy analysis, 1421; racism, 1436, 1437, 1439; sexual abuse, 1567; twentieth-century Anglo-American ethics, 769, 770; work, 1829

disdain, guilt and shame, 640

disease: competition, 279; medical ethics, 1064; moral community, 1117; public health, 1416, 1417

disgust, harm and offense, 654

disharmony: harm and offense, 653; seventeenth- and eighteenth-century ethics, 736

dishonor, Locke, 1008

disintegrative dualisms, Chuang Tzu, 231

Volume key: Volume 1, pages 1–642; volume 2, pages 643–1266; volume 3, pages 1267–1977.

1859

Volume key: Volume 1, pages 1–642; volume 2, pages 643–1266; volume 3, pages 1267–1977.

1860

Domitian, Emperor of Rome, Epictetus, 473

Donagan, Alan, **416–418**; Kantian ethics, 941, 942; love, 1024, 1025–1026; moral absolutes, 1113; moral pluralism, 1139; nineteenth-century British ethics, 742; twentieth-century Anglo-American ethics, 771, 772

Donatism: Augustine, 102–103; suicide, 1669

Donne, John, suicide, 1669

Doris, John M., social psychology, 1618

Dostoyevsky, Fyodor: duty and obligation, 423; immoralism, 838; literature, 1005; Rand, 1440; Soviet ethical theory, 1634

double effect, **418–420**; acts and omissions, 17; Anscombe, 76; Foot, 555; intention, 867–868; moral absolutes, 1113–1114; nuclear ethics, 1249; proportionality, 1394–1395; psychology, 1406; self-defense, 1555–1556; war and peace, 1784

Double Helix, The, analogical argument, 59

double standard: family, 523; women moral philosophers, 1824

"doublethink," self-deception, 1551

doubt: agnosticism, 44; skepticism, 1590

Douglas, Mary, moral purity, 1151

Douglass, Frederick: cruelty, 361, 362; King, 950; multiculturalism, 1190

Dougle Arguments (Dissoi Logi), Sophists, 1628

Downie, R. S.: love, 1024, 1025–1026; person, 1296

dowry, Africa, 33

draft (conscription): amnesty and pardon, 58; war and peace, 1783–1784

drama: the absurd, 7; fittingness, 552; literature, 1004–1005; natural law, 1206; neo-Stoicism, 1229; presocratic Greek ethics, 686; self-deception, 1552; tragedy, 1721–1723

dread: existential ethics, 509; risk analysis, 1516

dreams: Augustine, 104; bad faith, 119

Dretske, Fred, action, 14

Dreyfus affair: economic systems, 422; James, 900

drinking: hedonism, 666; Renaissance ethics, 727; seventeenth- and eighteenth-century ethics, 735

drives: moral development, 1120–1121; self and social self, 1545

drive-stimulus-response, weakness of will, 1789

Drobnitsky, O. G., Soviet ethical theory, 1634

drug dealing: correctional ethics, 341; economic liberty, 982, 985; libertarianism, 977

drug taking: Kant, 935; sport, 1643

drug testing, business ethics, 173

drunkenness, self-respect, 1564

D'Souza, Dinesh Anthony, racism, 1436, 1437

Du Bois, W.E.B.: civil rights, 241; King, 950; multiculturalism, 1190; racism, 1436

Du Vair, Guillaume: neo-Stoicism, 1229, 1230; Renaissance ethics, 726

dual dynamics, Japan, 904

dualism: bad faith, 118; Durkheim, 422–423; evil, 499; Kant, 933; lesbian ethics, 967; person, 1294; Plato, 1325; Pufendorf, 1423; seventeenth- and eighteenth-century ethics, 737–738; social and political philosophy, 1604; Taoist ethics, 1680–1684

Dualism of the Practical Reason: nineteenth-century British ethics, 745; Sidgwick, 1582

due process: agricultural ethics, 45, 46, 47; business ethics, 173; human rights, 796, 799; privacy, 1381; technology, 1688; work, 1829

dueling, honor, 789

Dufrenne, Mikel, Ricoeur, 1499

Dummett, Michael, political systems, 1344

Duncan-Jones, Austin, Butler, 176

Duns Scotus, John, **420–422**; Donegan, 417; later Medieval ethics, 718, 719; natural law, 1207; philosophy of religion, 1311; seventeenth- and eighteenth-century ethics, 732; theological ethics, 1702; William of Ockham, 1803

duplicity: deceit, 378; Rousseau, 1522

Dupuit, Jules, cost-benefit analysis, 350

duration: hedonism, 666; intransitivity, 878

duress, excuses, 507

Durkheim, Émile, **422–423**; individualism, 849; institutions, 859; moral development, 1120, 1121; moral education, 1129, 1130; punishment, 1426; sociology, 1619–1620; Staël, 1644; strategic interaction, 1658; suicide, 1669; Westermarck, 1798

Dürrenmatt, Friedrich, moral absolutes, 1113

Dussel, Enrique, praxis, 1365

Dutch Reform Church, Grotius, 633

duties: beneficence, 129; Bradley, 155; children, 210; Jesus, 908; Jewish ethics, 913; medical ethics, 1068. *See also* duty and obligation; duty, moral

Duties of the Clergy, early Medieval ethics, 710

duty, civic. *See* civic duties

duty, legal: acts and omissions, 16–17; amnesty and pardon, 58; bargaining, 124

duty, moral: acts and omissions, 16–17; agency and disability, 39; agent-centered morality, 41; amnesty and pardon, 58; analytic philosophy, 64; animals, 71–72, 73; Anscombe, 75; anthropology, 80; Aristotelian ethics, 87, 89; autonomy of moral agents, 112; bargaining, 124; beneficence, 128–132; benevolence, 134, 136; Bentham, 140; Bradley, 154, 155; Butler, 177; Calvin, 178; casuistry, 188; children, 210; China, 211; constructivism, 317–318; contractarianism, 324; cosmopolitan ethics, 346; courage, 353, 354;

deontology, 391, 392, 394–395; duty and obligation, 423; Edwards, 445, 446; egoism, 447; emotion, 457; Gert, 609; Godwin, 613; good, 623; gratitude, 630; happiness, 648; Hart, 656; Hegel, 672–673; Hobbes, 775; Holbach, 778–779; idealist ethics, 831–832, 833; immoralism, 839; Jesus, 908; Jewish ethics, 913; Kant, 930, 933, 934, 935; Kantian ethics, 939, 941; killing and letting die, 947–948; land ethics, 953; love, 1024, 1025; Malebranche, 1038; Mo Tzu, 1105; moral absolutes, 1113; moral development, 1120; moral rules, 1168, 1169; moral saints, 1170, 1171–1172; moral sense theorists, 1174, 1175; motives, 1185, 1187; natural law, 1206; nineteenth-century British ethics, 743; nineteenth-century Continental ethics, 752; obedience to law, 1254; Paley, 1274; partiality, 1275, 1276, 1277; person, 1295; Prichard, 1373; Pufendorf, 1423; rationality vs. reasonableness, 1453; Reid, 1470–1472; religion, 1474; responsibility, 1487; right, 1500, 1501; rights, 1507; Ross, 1521; Schweitzer, 1541; self-respect, 1564; seventeenth- and eighteenth-century ethics, 738; theological ethics, 1702, 1703, 1704, 1705; twentieth-century Anglo-American ethics, 767; Wolff, 1815–1817; Wollaston, 1818; women moral philosophers, 1821. *See also* categorical and hypothetical imperatives

duty and obligation, **423–428**; abortion, 6; agency and disability, 38; agent-centered morality, 41; American moral philosophy, 55; animals, 71, 72, 73; Anscombe, 75; Anselm, 77; anthropology, 80; Aristotelian ethics, 87, 89; Aristotle, 93; Augustine, 102; authority, 108; autonomy of moral agents, 112, 113; bargaining, 124; beneficence, 129–130, 131; Bentham, 140; Calvin, 178; care, 185–187; children, 208–210; civic duties, 241; Clarke, 245; consent, 300; constructivism, 317–318; deontology, 391–396; Dworkin, 429; equality, 482; ethics and morality, 485, 486; fairness, 521; family, 522; Fénelon, 540; fidelity, 544, 545; fiduciary relationships, 546–548; fittingness, 553; future generations, 588; Gert, 609; Godwin, 613; golden rule, 616; Hegel, 670; Hobbes, 774–775, 775; Holbach, 778–779; idealist ethics, 831; immoralism, 839–840; Jesus, 908; Jewish ethics, 911, 913, 914; Kant, 930–931, 934; liberalism, 975; love, 1024; moral community, 1117; moral development, 1120, 1122; moral saints, 1170–1172; moral sense theorists, 1174, 1175, 1176, 1178; nineteenth-century Continental ethics, 752; obedience to law, 1255–1256; person, 1293; personal relationships, 1301–1302; philosophy of religion, 1312; police ethics, 1333;

Volume key: Volume 1, pages 1–642; volume 2, pages 643–1266; volume 3, pages 1267–1977.

1861

duty and obligation, *continued*
pragmatism, 1363; Prichard, 1373;
public health, 1416; Pufendorf, 1423;
Reid, 1470–1472; religion, 1474;
responsibility, 1486, 1487; revenge,
1493; right, 1500, 1501; right
holders, 1503; rights, 1507–1508,
1510; risk, 1513–1514; Schweitzer,
1541; self and social self, 1546; self-
deception, 1551; self-ownership,
1563; self-respect, 1564; social
contract, 1607, 1608, 1609; Soviet
ethical theory, 1631; stakeholder,
1648; supererogation, 1673–1675;
theological ethics, 1702, 1703, 1704,
1705; theory and practice, 1707–
1708; Thomson, 1712–1713; virtue
ethics, 1760; weakness of will, 1791;
Wolff, 1815–1817; Wollaston, 1818;
women moral philosophers, 1821.
See also duty, moral; obligation
duty for duty's sake: Bradley, 154, 155;
nineteenth-century British ethics, 743
duty-and-interest-junction principle,
Bentham, 140
Dworkin, Andrea, lesbian ethics, 967
Dworkin, Ronald, **428–431**; autonomy
of ethics, 110, 111, 113; deontology,
393; euthanasia, 493, 495; Hart, 657;
human rights, 798; inequality, 852;
justice, rectificatory, 927; land ethics,
953; legal philosophy, 958; liberalism,
975; neutral principles, 1232; police
ethics, 1335; political systems, 1341;
right, 1501; social and political
philosophy, 1604; social contract,
1610
dyadic deontic logics, logic, 1015
dying. *See* death; die, right to; killing and
letting die; life and death

Eadmer, Anselm, 78
Eagly, Alice H., social psychology, 1614
earth ethic, Leopold, 966
earthquakes, evil, 498
Eastern moral thought. *See* non-Western
thought
Eastern Orthodoxy, Christian ethics, 223
Ebreo, Leone, Renaissance ethics, 724
Eckhart, Meister: Buber, 160; mysticism,
1197, 1198
ecocentrism, environmental ethics, 469–
470
ecofeminism: environmental ethics, 470;
feminist ethics, 534
ecojustice, environmental ethics, 470
ecology: agricultural ethics, 45, 46;
conservation ethics, 309, 310;
environmental ethics, 468, 469; land
ethics, 953, 954; Leopold, 965; right
holders, 1504; technology and nature,
1691
economic analysis, **432–439**; agricultural
ethics, 45, 46, 47; altruism, 50;
bargaining, 123–124; Barry, 126;
Bentham, 139; blackmail, 152; civil
rights, 239, 240–241; competition,
277–279; conservation ethics, 308;
cooperative surplus, 337; cost-benefit
analysis, 349–352; deliberation and
choice, 384; democracy, 387;
discounting the future, 410–411;

economic systems, 441–444; Engels,
460; entitlements, 465–467; forms of
consciousness, 565, 566; game
theory, 592; human rights, 799;
inequality, 852; interests, 868;
international distributive justice,
874–877; land ethics, 954; legal
philosophy, 959; liberalism, 973, 974;
libertarianism, 976–977; Marx,
1042–1047; Marxism, 1048–1054;
mass media, 1055; materialism, 1057;
Mill (John Stuart), 1100–1103; neo-
Kantianism, 1227–1228; nineteenth-
century Continental ethics, 754–755;
nuclear ethics, 1249; Objectivism,
1259; political systems, 1345;
prudence, 1400; public goods, 1414;
public health, 1417; public policy
analysis, 1421–1422; racism, 1435,
1438; rational choice, 1446, 1447,
1448, 1450–1451; reciprocity, 1464,
1466; risk aversion, 1518–1520; self
and social self, 1544, 1545; sexuality,
1573; Smith, 1596, 1598–1599;
social contract, 1611; stakeholder,
1645–1648; strategic interaction,
1658; sympathy, 1676; technology,
1688, 1689; value theory, 1750,
1751; Weber, 1793; welfare, 1796–
1797; work, 1828–1831
Economic and Philosophical Manscripts,
humanism, 801–802
economic deprivation. *See* poverty;
welfare rights and social policy
economic development: corruption, 345;
cost-benefit analysis, 350;
international distributive justice,
874–877
economic efficiency, bargaining, 123
economic growth, materialism, 1057
economic liberty. *See* liberty, economic
economic sanctions, blackmail, 152
economic systems, **439–445**;
competition, 277; cooperative
surplus, 337; cosmopolitan ethics,
346–349; Dworkin, 430; economic
liberty, 981–985; Engels, 460–462;
equality, 482, 483; exploitation, 516;
fairness, 520; family, 523; feminist
ethics, 533–534, 537; Hegel, 670–
671; inequality, 852; institutions,
858, 859–863; international
distributive justice, 877; Islamic
business ethics, 888; liberalism, 973;
materialism, 1057, 1058; merit and
desert, 1076; nineteenth-century
Continental ethics, 754–755;
Objectivism, 1259; public and private
morality, 1410; Rawls, 1456, 1459;
twentieth-century Anglo-American
ethics, 769; twentieth-century
Continental ethics, 763; welfare,
1796–1797; work, 1828–1831. *See
also* market system
economics. *See* economic analysis;
economic systems
economists: bargaining, 123; Barry, 125,
126
Economy and Society, Weber, 1793
ecosystems. *See* ecology
ecstasy, mysticism, 1198
ecstatic nihilism, nihilism, 1241

Edelstein, Ludwig, medical ethics, 1067
Edgeworth, Francis Ysidro: economic
analysis, 434; nineteenth-century
British ethics, 747; rational choice,
1448
Edinburgh Review, nineteenth-century
British ethics, 740–741
Edo period, Japan, 902
education: academic ethics, 8–10;
academic freedom, 10–12; Adler, 21–
23; aesthetics, 30; autonomy of moral
agents, 113; bioethics, 141, 142;
China, 214; civil rights, 238, 240;
competition, 279; computers, 283–
284; conservatism, 315; correctional
ethics, 339; Dewey, 404;
discrimination, 413; equality, 478;
family, 522; Green, 632; human
rights, 797, 799; humanism, 800–
801, 802; idealist ethics, 831;
institutions, 858; library, 987;
medical ethics, 1068; moral
development, 1118, 1122, 1123;
moral education, 1127, 1129, 1130;
multiculturalism, 1188–1190;
personal relationships, 1299; political
correctness, 1337–1340; racism,
1433; Rousseau, 1522, 1523;
Schiller, 1538; Soviet ethical theory,
1631; Stewart, 1652; tragedy, 1722;
Tufts, 1732; twentieth-century
Continental ethics, 762; value theory,
1752; virtue ethics, 1757, 1758;
welfare, 1797; Wollstonecraft, 1820;
women moral philosophers, 1824,
1825, 1826. *See also* colleges and
universities; moral education
Educational Amendments of 1972 (U.S.),
political correctness, 1338
educational software, computers, 286
Edwards, J. C., Wittgenstein, 1810
Edwards, Jonathan, **445–446**; Christian
ethics, 227
Edwards, Paul, emotivism, 459
Edwards, Rem B., nineteenth-century
British ethics, 741
efficiency: conservation ethics, 308;
deontology, 393; economic systems,
440, 441, 442, 443; rationality, 1451;
work, 1830
egalitarianism. *See* equality
egg donation. *See* ova donation
ego psychology: moral development,
1121; psychoanalysis, 1402–1404
egocentrism: partiality, 1275; Seneca,
1566
egoism, **446–450**; altruism, 53; Baier,
120, 121; Bentham, 139–140; Butler,
175, 177; consequentialism, 305;
Durkheim, 422; duty and obligation,
423; egoism, 446–450; existential
ethics, 513; Feuerbach, 541; Gert,
608; good, 622; government ethics,
625; happiness, 648–649; Hobbes,
777; Holbach, 779; human rights,
797; individualism, 850; Kantian
ethics, 939, 943; love, 1023;
Mandeville, 1040; Marxism, 1054;
metaethics, 1086; Mill (James), 1098;
moral attention, 1116; moral
development, 1120, 1124; moral
psychology, 1146, 1147, 1148, 1149;

Volume key: Volume 1, pages 1–642; volume 2, pages 643–1266; volume 3, pages 1267–1977.

1862

Murdoch, 1192; natural law, 1209; Nietzsche, 1236; nineteenth-century British ethics, 739–740, 743, 745; obedience to law, 1257; perfectionism, 1288; pleasure, 1326–1327; Rand, 1440, 1441; revolution, 1498; rights, 1511; Schopenhauer, 1539; self and social self, 1546; seventeenth- and eighteenth-century ethics, 731, 732, 735, 736–737; Sidgwick, 1581, 1582; social and political philosophy, 1601; Socrates, 1625–1626; Soviet ethical theory, 1633; Spinoza, 1640; utilitarianism, 1737; value concept, 1746; Voltaire, 1770

Ehrenfels, Christian von, value theory, 1750

Eichmann, Adolf, Arendt, 84

Eichmann in Jerusalem, Arendt, 84

Eidos, forms of consciousness, 564

eigentlich, authenticity, 105

Eigentlichkeit, bad faith, 119

Eightfold Path: Buddha, 162; Buddhist ethics, 164, 165

Eighth Ammendment (U.S.), cruelty, 361

Eisenstadt v. Baird, privacy, 1381

Either/Or: authenticity, 106; existential ethics, 509; nineteenth-century Continental ethics, 755

elder care, feminist ethics, 536

Eleans: Hellenistic ethics, 696, 697, 698; Levinas, 969

Eleazar, hypocrisy, 820

elected officials, cosmopolitan ethics, 348

elections: democracy, 386, 388; public and private morality, 1411; rational choice, 1448–1449, 1450; Rousseau, 1524. *See also* voting; voting rights

electricity, nuclear ethics, 1249

electronic mail, computers, 283, 284

electronic media: computers, 283–284; freedom of the press, 580; library, 990

electronic surveillance, police ethics, 1334

elegance, aesthetics, 24

elenchus, classical Greek ethics, 692

Elfstrom, Gerard, military ethics, 1094

eligibility, economic systems, 440, 443

Eliot, George: integrity, 864; literature, 1005, 1006

Eliot, T. S.: Bradley, 155; elite, 450

elite, concept of, **450–451**; anthropology, 79; autonomy of moral agents, 113; classical Greek ethics, 692; democracy, 387; discrimination, 415; equality, 481, 482, 483, 484; Hegel, 672; Jewish ethics, 913, 914; Locke, 1008, 1009; moral realism, 1156; Nietzsche, 1236, 1238; nineteenth-century Continental ethics, 756, 757; perfectionism, 1291; political correctness, 1339; political systems, 1342; racism, 1434; Roman ethics, 704; social and political philosophy, 1604; work, 1827

elitism. *See* elite, concept of

Elizabeth I, Queen of England, neo-Stoicism, 1230

Elizabeth, Princess of Bohemia, neo-Stoicism, 1231

Elizabeth, Princess of the Palatine, Descartes, 397

Elkins, S. M., slavery, 1593

Ellis, Havelock, gay ethics, 598

Elliston, Frederick, police ethics, 1334–1335

Ellsworth, Phoebe C., social psychology, 1614

eloquence: Hume, 807; virtue ethics, 1760

Elshtain, Jean Bethke, public and private morality, 1412

Elster, Jon: individualism, 849; institutions, 859; revolution, 1495

emanation, philosophy of religion, 1312

emancipation: agency and disability, 36; critical theory, 360; cultural studies, 366; feminist ethics, 528, 537; revolution, 1498; Soviet ethical theory, 1633. *See also* liberation

emancipatory morality, critical theory, 358

embarrassment, Africa, 35

embezzlement, correctional ethics, 341

embryo: analogical argument, 60; applied ethics, 82, 83; genetic engineering, 604, 605; reproductive technologies, 1475, 1476, 1478, 1479; slippery slope argument, 1594, 1595; Thomson, 1714

Emerson, Ralph Waldo, **451–454**; American moral philosophy, 54; autonomy of ethics, 110; conservation ethics, 307; liberalism, 975; Royce, 1525; Thoreau, 1714, 1715; transcendentalism, 1724, 1725, 1726, 1727

emigration, cosmopolitan ethics, 346

Émile: moral development, 1119; Rousseau, 1521, 1522–1523

eminent domain, rights, 1511

emotion, **454–458**; Anscombe, 74; beneficence, 129, 131; benevolence, 134; Brentano, 157–158; Buddha, 162; Buddhist ethics, 164; care, 185; character, 200, 201; China, 216, 217–218; cognitive science, 250; collective responsibility, 257; common sense moralists, 268; communitarianism, 270–271; comparative ethics, 274; Confucian ethics, 294; emotivism, 458, 459; feminist ethics, 530; government ethics, 625; hope, 791–793; Jainism, 898; life and death, 995; literature, 1006; moral education, 1130; Objectivism, 1257; partiality, 1275; personal relationships, 1299; persuasive definition, 1304; Plato, 1322; principlism, 1380; Seneca, 1566; Stoicism, 1654; suffering, 1270; sympathy, 1676; Westermarck, 1798, 1799. *See also* emotions; emotivism; feelings; passion

emotional numbness, sympathy, 1677

emotions: aesthetics, 27; American moral philosophy, 54; analytic philosophy, 66; anger, 67–69; Aristotle, 93, 94; classical Greek ethics, 694, 695; Gert, 608; gratitude, 630; guilt and shame, 639–640; happiness, 644–

650; hate, 659–662; Hellenistic ethics, 701; Husserl, 817; immoralism, 839; James, 899; literature, 1005, 1006; Mencius, 1071; Mo Tzu, 1105; moral development, 1124; moral psychology, 1145–1150; naturalism, 1212–1213; nature, 1217; neo-Stoicism, 1229, 1231; ought implies can, 1266; Plato, 1320; practical wisdom, 1358; Price, 1372; Renaissance ethics, 725–726; resentment, 1483; Scheler, 1533, 1534; self-control, 1559, 1594; self-esteem, 1557; self-knowledge, 1560; Seneca, 1565, 1566; sexuality, 1570; Stoicism, 1655; sympathy, 1676–1679; tragedy, 1722–1723; twentieth-century Continental ethics, 759–760; Westermarck, 1798; wickedness, 1801; Williams, 1805. *See also* feelings

emotive-good-reasons theory, naturalism, 1213, 1214

emotivism, **458–460**; analytic philosophy, 65–66; Ayer, 116–117; Brentano, 157; common sense moralists, 269; emotion, 457; Foot, 554; Frankena, 570; good, 620; happiness, 648–649; intuitionism, 880; Kierkegaard, 945; metaethics, 1080, 1084; Murphy, 1194; naturalism, 1212–1213, 1214; naturalistic fallacy, 1216–1217; nature, 1219; nineteenth-century British ethics, 740; prescriptivism, 1369, 1370; Stevenson, 1649–1650; subjectivism, 1666; twentieth-century Anglo-American ethics, 768; value theory, 1751

empathy: Arendt, 84; cognitive science, 250–251; coherentism, 254; feminist ethics, 536; groups, 637; Habermas, 643; ideal observer, 828; lesbian ethics, 968; moral development, 1123–1124; Smith, 1598; sympathy, 1675

Empedocles: literature, 1005; presocratic Greek ethics, 687

empiricism: American moral philosophy, 54; Ayer, 116; beneficence, 129; Bentham, 139; Bradley, 154; Darwin, 374–375; Gassendi, 595; Holbach, 778–789; idealist ethics, 832; individualism, 850; Lewis, 971; Mead, 1060; metaphysics and epistemology, 1091; Mill (John Stuart), 1100; moral realism, 1154, 1155, 1156; nineteenth-century British ethics, 742; public policy analysis, 1422; seventeenth- and eighteenth-century ethics, 733; social psychology, 1613–1618; sociology, 1620, 1621; Staël, 1644; Stewart, 1651; theism, 1701

employee-employer issues. *See* employment

employment: business ethics, 173, 174; computers, 284; discrimination, 413, 414–415; duty and obligation, 425; human rights, 797; public health, 1416, 1417; sexual abuse, 1567;

Volume key: Volume 1, pages 1–642; volume 2, pages 643–1266; volume 3, pages 1267–1977.

1863

Volume key: Volume 1, pages 1–642; volume 2, pages 643–1266; volume 3, pages 1267–1977.

1864

Volume key: Volume 1, pages 1–642; volume 2, pages 643–1266; volume 3, pages 1267–1977.

1865

Subject Index

Volume key: Volume 1, pages 1–642; volume 2, pages 643–1266; volume 3, pages 1267–1977.

1866

Volume key: Volume 1, pages 1–642; volume 2, pages 643–1266; volume 3, pages 1267–1977.

Subject Index

Volume key: Volume 1, pages 1–642; volume 2, pages 643–1266; volume 3, pages 1267–1977.

1868

Volume key: Volume 1, pages 1–642; volume 2, pages 643–1266; volume 3, pages 1267–1977.

1869

Volume key: Volume 1, pages 1–642; volume 2, pages 643–1266; volume 3, pages 1267–1977.

1870

Volume key: Volume 1, pages 1–642; volume 2, pages 643–1266; volume 3, pages 1267–1977.

1871

freedom of expression. *See* censorship; free speech; freedom of the press

freedom of religion: Calvin, 179; censorship, 198; human rights, 797; Jefferson, 905; liberalism, 974; multiculturalism, 1190; privacy, 1381; Rawls, 1459; toleration, 1717–1718

freedom of speech. *See* free speech

freedom of the press, **578–581**; blackmail, 153; censorship, 197, 198; harm and offense, 654; Jefferson, 905; privacy, 1381; secrecy and confidentiality, 1542

freedom of the will. *See* free will

Freedom to Read Policy Statement, library, 986

Freeman, R. Edward, stakeholder, 1646

free-market capitalism. *See* market system

Freemen, Samuel, agent-centered morality, 41

free-rider problem: contractarianism, 322; conventions, 332

freethinkers, agnosticism, 44

French, Peter, collective responsibility, 255, 256

French Academy, Montesquieu, 1108

French Enlightenment. *See* Enlightenment

French Revolution: amnesty and pardon, 57; applied ethics, 81; Burke, 169; duty and obligation, 425; equality, 479; Godwin, 613; individualism, 848; Kant, 929, 936, 937; Paine, 1272; praxis, 1366; Price, 1371, 1372; Schiller, 1538; Staël, 1644; Wollstonecraft, 1819, 1820

Freud, Anna, altruism, 50, 51

Freud, Sigmund: anger, 68; bad faith, 118; feminist ethics, 530; guilt and shame, 639, 640; hate, 660–661; life and death, 995; moral development, 1120, 1123; moral psychology, 1149; mortality, 1184; Nietzsche, 1237; passion, 1281; psychoanlaysis, 1402–1404, 1405; psychology, 1407; religion, 174; self and social self, 1544; self-deception, 1551, 1552; self-knowledge, 1560; sexual abuse, 1568; sexuality, 1571; Smith, 1597; suicide, 1670; value theory, 1751; weakness of will, 1791; Westermarck, 1799; work, 1828

Freudianism, narrative, 1201

Frey, R. G., agricultural ethics, 46

Fried, Charles: moral absolutes, 1113; privacy, 1381

Friedlander, Benedict, gay ethics, 598

Friedlander, Henry, euthanasia, 496

Friedman, Marilyn, partiality, 1276

Friedman, Milton, work, 1829

Friedrich, Carl, corruption, 345

friendliness: character, 202; Hume, 807

friends: altruism, 50; Aristotelian ethics, 86, 89; Aristotle, 96; benevolence, 135; death, 377; deceit, 378; fidelity, 544; Hume, 810; moral psychology, 1148, 1149; partiality, 1275, 1277; personal relationships, 1299, 1300, 1302; Reid, 1471; Roman ethics, 707; self-knowledge, 1559; Stoicism, 1653;

suicide, 1670; theory and practice, 1707

friendship, **581–584**; academic ethics, 9; altruism, 52, 53; Aristotelian ethics, 86; Aristotle, 96–97; character, 202; children, 210; civic good, 234; common good, 263, 264; communitarianism, 270, 271; cradle arguments, 356; Cyrenaics, 371; deliberation and choice, 382; deontology, 393; duty and obligation, 427; egoism, 448; Emerson, 452; Epicurus, 477; eudaimonia, 490, 491; excellence, 505; externalism and internalism, 518; fidelity, 544, 545; gay ethics, 597; Godwin, 613; good, 623; gratitude, 629; hypocrisy, 819, 820, 821; Kant, 935; lesbian ethics, 968; love, 1018–1019, 1020, 1021, 1022, 1024; loyalty, 1027; materialism, 1059; Mill (James), 1098; moral psychology, 1148, 1149; moral sense theorists, 1175; Objectivism, 1258; passion, 1279; perfectionism, 1288; personal relationships, 1299, 1300–1302; practical wisdom, 1358; Protagoras, 1396; public and private morality, 1412; Rawls, 1457; reciprocity, 1464, 1466; self-deception, 1552; Seneca, 1566; Sophists, 1630; sympathy, 1678; theological ethics, 1704; trust, 1728; utilitarianism, 1740

Fries, Jakob, Frierich, Hegel, 673

Froehlich, Thomas J., library, 986, 987

Frogs, tragedy, 1721

Frolov, Ivan T., Soviet ethical theory, 1633

Fromm, Erich: cruelty, 361; psychoanalysis, 1403

Fronto, Marcus Cornelius, Seneca, 1565

frozen embryos, reproductive technologies, 1476, 1478

frugality: Hume, 807; work, 1828

frui-uti distinction, Augustine, 104

frustration: classical Greek ethics, 691; happiness, 645, 646; Marx, 1046; revenge, 1493

Fry, Sara T., nursing ethics, 1251

Frye, Marilyn, lesbian ethics, 067

Fukuyama, Francis, trust, 1730

fulfillment: American moral philosophy, 55; Jewish ethics, 912; metaphysics and epistemology, 1089; self-deception, 1542; subjectivism, 1665; value concept, 1745

full self-ownership, self-ownership, 1562–1563

full virtue, Aristotle, 95

Fuller, Buckminster, technology and nature, 1690

Fuller, Lon Luvois, **584–586**

Fuller, Margaret, transcendentalism, 1724, 1726–1727

function, homosexuality, 787

functional theory: institutions, 859–860, 862; sociology, 1621; virtues, 1767

functional-kind, psychology, 1408

fundamental attribution error, social psychology, 1615

fundamental criteria, MacIntyre, 1035

fundamental equality, equality, 478, 479–483

fundamental good: classical Greek ethics, 691; utilitarianism, 1738. *See also* intrinsic value

fundamental moral values, twentieth-century Continental ethics, 760

fundamental property, value theory, 1750

fundamentalism: Africa, 35; strategic interaction, 1659

funerals: etiquette, 487; Mencius, 1071, 1072; mortality, 1183

Fung Yu-lan: China, 221; Confucian ethics, 287

fuqaha, Islamic ethics, 891

Furies, presocratic Greek ethics, 687

Furnish, V. P., love, 1020

future benefits, institutions, 862

future distribution, Marx, 1045

future generations, **586–589**; agricultural ethics, 46; American moral philosophy, 54; conservation ethics, 307, 308; cost-benefit analysis, 351; critical theory, 358; Darwin, 373; deontology, 393; discounting the future, 411–412; discrimination, 414; economic systems, 440; environmental ethics, 468; evil, 500; evolution, 502; fiduciary relationships, 547; genetic engineering, 603, 604; integrity, 865; libertarianism, 978; Marx, 1045, 1047; moral community, 1170; nuclear ethics, 1249; reciprocity, 1464; reproductive technologies, 1478; right holders, 1505; risk, 1514; Royce, 1526; self-ownership, 1563; sexuality, 1572; twentieth-century Anglo-American ethics, 772; twentieth-century Continental ethics, 765

future goods. *See* discounting the future

Fyodorov, N., Soviet ethical theory, 1634

Gabriel, Archangel, Islam, 887

Gadamer, Hans-Georg, **590–591**; psychology, 1407, 1408, 1409

Gaia hypothesis, Leopold, 966

Gains-Preservation Principle, needs, 1223

Gaita, Raimond, integrity, 864

Galápagos islands, Darwin, 373, 374

Galatians, Paul, 1284, 1285

Galileo, academic freedom, 10

Galtung, Johan, pacifism, 1268

Gamaliel, Paul, 1284

gambling: economic liberty, 982, 985; risk aversion, 1518, 1519

game theory, **591–593**; applied ethics, 82; competition, 278; cooperation, conflict, and coordination, 333–336; cooperative surplus, 337; economic analysis, 437–438; Hume, 810; nineteenth-century British ethics, 747; Pascal, 1278; public goods, 1414; rational choice, 1447, 1448, 1450, 1451; strategic interaction, 1658, 1660–1661, 1662

games: game theory, 592; impartiality, 842; sport, 1641–1643; stakeholder, 1646; strategic interaction, 1660

Volume key: Volume 1, pages 1–642; volume 2, pages 643–1266; volume 3, pages 1267–1977.

1872

Volume key: Volume 1, pages 1–642; volume 2, pages 643–1266; volume 3, pages 1267–1977.

1873

Subject Index

German Idealism: Buber, 160; Marx, 1043; Schelling, 1535–1536; Taylor, 1686

German Ideology, The: Marx, 1042, 1043; Marxism, 1052, 1054

German Romanticism: Fichte, 543; moral imagination, 1131; Taylor, 1686

German Social Democratic Party, neo-Kantianism, 1227

Germany: academic freedom, 10; Brentano, 157–158; collective responsibility, 257; democracy, 387; evolution, 502; existential ethics, 509; Feuerbach, 541; Fichte, 542, 543; Hegel, 669–675; Heidegger, 675–676; Holocaust, 779–784; Husserl, 816–817; idealist ethics, 831; individualism, 848, 849; Jewish ethics, 914; Kant, 929–930; Kantian ethics, 939–943; liberalism, 972; Luther, 1031; moral imagination, 1131; mysticism, 1198; natural law, 1207; neo-Kantianism, 1226–1228; Nietzsche, 1235–1239; nineteenth-century Continental ethics, 752–758; praxis, 1364–1365; reproductive technologies, 1480; Scheler, 1535–1536; Schelling, 1535–1536; Schiller, 1537–1538; Schopenhauer, 1539; self and social self, 1544; social psychology, 1617; tragedy, 1723; twentieth-century Continental ethics, 758–761; Weber, 1792–1793; Wolff, 1815–1817. *See also* Nazism

Gerondi, Jonah, Jewish ethics, 913

Gerson, Jean, natural law, 1208

Gert, Bernard, **608–610**; beneficence, 132; principlism, 1378, 1379

gestalt psychology: additivity, 20; value theory, 1751

Gewirth, Alan, **610–612**; agricultural ethics, 45; Baier, 120; golden rule, 616; human rights, 797; Kantian ethics, 941–942; moral pluralism, 1140; moral point of view, 1141; moral reasoning, 1161; naturalism, 1214; partiality, 1276; right holders, 1505–1506; technology, 1687; twentieth-century Anglo-American ethics, 771

Ghazālī, al-: Ibn Rushd, 825; Ibn Ṭufayl, 827

Giannotti, Donato, prudence, 1400

Gibbard, Allan: metaethics, 1084; reciprocity, 1465; social psychology, 1613, 1618

Gibbon, Edward: Epicureanism, 475; Hume, 812

Gibson, Mary, Marxism, 1052

Gierke, Otto, individualism, 849

GIFT (gamete intrafallopian transfer), reproductive technologies, 1476

gift promises, contracts, 326, 328

gifts: amnesty and pardon, 58; Emerson, 452; generosity, 601; gratitude, 630; mercy, 1075; reciprocity, 1465; self-ownership, 1562, 1563

Gilbert, Daniel T., social psychology, 1615

Gilbert, Margaret, collective responsibility, 257

Gilgamesh, King, mortality, 1183

Gilligan, Carol: autonomy of moral agents, 114; beneficence, 132; care, 186; charity, 204; cognitive science, 249; feminist ethics, 529, 532, 533; lesbian ethics, 967, 968; moral development, 1123; moral pluralism, 1140; non-violence, 1755; nursing ethics, 1251; principlism, 1380; self and social self, 1546; sympathy, 1679

Gillon, Ranaan, principlism, 1378

Ginet, Carl: free will, 572; freedom and determinism, 576

Gītā. Hindu ethics, 681

Glanville, Joseph, Locke, 1008

glasnost, Soviet ethical theory, 1633, 1635

Glass, Stephen, journalism, 915

Glaubert, Gustav, literature, 1005

Glaucon: good, 621; presocratic Greek ethics, 689; Sophists, 1629

Gleig, George, nineteenth-century British ethics, 746

global climate change, conservation ethics, 310

global communication, computers, 283

global justice. *See* international justice: conflict; international justice: distribution

global nature, bioethics, 143–144

global point of view, practical wisdom, 1358

globalism: business ethics, 173–174; competition, 279; cosmopolitan ethics, 346–349; feminist ethics, 537–538; international distributive justice, 874–877

glory: civic good, 234; Hobbes, 777; Machiavelli, 1034; Roman ethics, 703, 704, 707

Glover, Jonathan: death, 378; moral absolutes, 1113

gnome, prudence, 1399

goals: competition, 279; Descartes, 397–398; Marx, 1045; moral pluralism, 1139; perfectionism, 1288, 1289–1290; political systems, 1342–1343; practical reason[ing], 1355, 1356; public policy analysis, 1421, 1422; Santayana, 1530; teleological ethics, 1691–1693

God: Abelard, 2; the absurd, 7, 8; Africa, 34; agency and disability, 37; agnosticism, 43–44; alienation, 49; amnesty and pardon, 57, 58; Anselm, 77, 78; atheism, 98–101; Augustine, 102, 103, 104–105; autonomy of moral agents, 111; biological theory, 149; Butler, 176–177; Calvin, 178–179; Cambridge Platonists, 179–180; Christian ethics, 222, 224, 225, 226, 227; common good, 264; common sense moralists, 267; comparative ethics, 274; conservation ethics, 307, 308–309; Crusius, 363; Cudworth, 364; Cumberland, 367, 368; deceit, 380; Descartes, 397; dirty hands, 408; Duns Scotus, 420, 421, 422; duty and obligation, 423; early Medieval ethics, 710, 711, 712; Edwards, 446; equality, 480; eudaimonism, 491; euthanasia, 494;

evil, 498–499, 500–501; existential ethics, 509; family, 523; Fénelon, 539–540; Fichte, 542; fiduciary relationships, 547; fittingness, 552, 553; free will, 572; freedom and determinism, 575; friendship, 582; Grotius, 633, 634, 735; historiography, 684; Hobbes, 774; homicide, 785; honor, 788; hope, 791; humanism, 801, 802; humilty, 815; hypocrisy, 820, 821, 822; idealist ethics, 833; India, 844; Islam, 882, 883, 884, 885, 886; Islamic business ethics, 887; Islamic ethics, 889–890, 892; Jefferson, 906; Jesus, 906, 907, 908; Jewish ethics, 909, 910, 911–912, 913, 914; Kant, 933; Kierkegaard, 946–947; King, 951; later Medieval ethics, 716, 717, 719; Leibniz, 963–964; liberalism, 974; life and death, 994, 998; Locke, 1007, 1008, 1009, 1010; love, 1020, 1022; Luther, 1031; Maimonides, 1036; Malebranche, 1037–1038; Montaigne, 1107; Montesquieu, 1105; moral attention, 1115–1116; moral education, 1128; moral sense theorists, 1175, 1176, 1177, 1178; mysticism, 1197, 1198; natural law, 1209; nineteenth-century Continental ethics, 756; Pascal, 1278; Paul, 1285; person, 1294; philosophy of religion, 1310–1313; Plotinus, 1330; pride, 1376; prudence, 1398; puritanism, 1429; Reid, 1471; religion, 1473, 1474–1475; Renaissance ethics, 722, 723–724, 728, 729; Schelling, 1535, 1536; seventeenth- and eighteenth-century ethics, 730–731, 732, 733, 734, 738; Shaftesbury, 1578; Spinoza, 1638–1640; Suárez, 1663, 1664; suicide, 1669, 1670; Sunnīsm, 1673; supererogation, 1673; theism, 1699–1701; theological ethics, 1702–1706; tragedy, 1723; virtue ethics, 1758, 1759; voluntarism, 1773; Wolff, 1816; Wollaston, 1818; women moral philosophers, 1823, 1824, 1826; work, 1827. *See also* death of God; God's will; *headings beginning with divine*

Goddess, Hindu ethics, 681

gods: agnosticism, 43; Aristotelian ethics, 87, 88; Aristotle, 97; Ayer, 116; classical Greek ethics, 693, 694, 695; competition, 278; deceit, 380; Epictetus, 473; Epicureanism, 474; evil, 499; Hellenistic ethics, 700, 701; Hindu ethics, 681; India, 845; Jewish ethics, 911; Lucretius, 1029–1030; mysticism, 1197; natural law, 1206; presocratic Greek ethics, 687, 689; Protagoras, 1397; Renaissance ethics, 723; Stoicism, 1653; tragedy, tragedy, 1723

God's goodness: Balguy, 122; Jewish ethics, 909; religion, 1474, 1475

God's image: conservation ethics, 307, 308–309; person, 1294; women moral philosophers, 1822

God's law. *See* divine law

God's love. *See* divine love

Volume key: Volume 1, pages 1–642; volume 2, pages 643–1266; volume 3, pages 1267–1977.

1874

Volume key: Volume 1, pages 1–642; volume 2, pages 643–1266; volume 3, pages 1267–1977.

1875

good will, *continued*
idealized agents, 836; integrity, 865; Kant, 930–931, 932; Kantian ethics, 939; Luther, 1031; person, 1295; stakeholder, 1647; sympathy, 1676; value concept, 1745; virtue ethics, 1761

good works: Christian ethics, 224; early medieval ethic, 712; women moral philosophers, 1823

Goodin, Robert, partiality, 1277

Goodman, Nelson: aesthetics, 30; forgery, 560, 561; moral realism, 1154; reflective equilibrium, 1467

goodness: analytic philosophy, 65; Anscombe, 75; Anselm, 78; atheism, 99, 100; Balguy, 122; civility, 242; classical Greek ethics, 691, 694, 695; commensurability, 258, 259, 260; Confucius, 295; consequentialism, 304; early Medieval ethics, 711; economic analysis, 437; euthanasia, 496; friendship, 581, 582; good, 620, 622; Hartmann, 658; Hellenistic ethics, 700, 701; Hsün Tzu, 795; Hutcheson, 818; idealist ethics, 834; later Medieval ethics, 716, 718; Luther, 1031; metaethics, 1083; Moore, 1109–1110; moral development, 123; moral sense theorists, 1176, 1177; motives, 1185; philosophy of religion, 1311, 1312; Plato, 1319; rationality vs. reasonableness, 1453; Rawls, 1457; religion, 1474, 1475; Roman ethics, 704; Rousseau, 1522; Scheler, 1534; theism, 1699–1700; theological ethics, 1705; twentieth-century Anglo-American ethics, 766; twentieth-century Continental ethics, 760; utilitarianism, 1739–1740; voluntarism, 1772–1773; William of Ockham, 1803–1804; Wittgensteinian ethics, 1813. *See also* good, theories of the

Goodpaster, Kenneth E., environmental ethics, 468

Goodrich case (A7D), engineering ethics, 463

goods: bargaining, 123; cooperative surplus, 336–338; naturalistic fallacy, 1216; value concept, 1746. *See also* external goods; instrinsic goods; primary goods; public goods

goodwill: love, 1019, 1022; moral absolutes, 1114; reciprocity, 1464

Gorbachev, Mihail, Soviet ethical theory, 1633

Gordon, Lewis, racism, 1437, 1439

Gordon, Robert, emotion, 456

Gorgias: presocratic Greek ethics, 689–690; Sophists, 1628, 1630

Gorovitz, Samuel, slippery slope argument, 1596

Gospels: casuistry, 188, 189; Christian ethics, 225, 227; Jesus, 906–908, 909; neo-Stoicism, 1230; Paul, 1285, 1286; Renaissance ethics, 728, 729; theological ethics, 1703–1704

Gough, J. W., social contract, 1609

Gould, Carol, self and social self, 1545, 1546

Gournay, Marie le Jars de, women moral philosophers, 1824

government: academic freedom, 10–13; Africa, 35; agricultural ethics, 45; amnesty and pardon, 56–58; Anscombe, 76; anthropology, 79; censorship, 198–199; civic duties, 241; civic good, 234, 235; conservation ethics, 308; conservatism, 314–315; conventions, 329; cooperative surplus, 337; democracy, 385–388; Dworkin, 430; economic analysis, 432; economic systems, 443–444; equality, 480; etiquette, 487; fiduciary relationships, 547–548; Godwin, 613; Grotius, 633–634; Hsün Tzu, 794; human rights, 797–798; individualism, 850; institutions, 862; interests, 868, 870; international conflict, 871–873, 872; international distributive justice, 874–877; Kant, 935–936; land ethics, 953; legal philosophy, 960; legitimacy, 960–962; liberalism, 973, 975; libertarianism, 976, 977; life and death, 995; Machiavelli, 1034; neo-Stoicism, 1232–1234; norms, 1244; Nozick, 1246; obedience to law, 1255, 1256; Objectivism, 1259; oppression, 1261; paternalism, 1282; perfectionism, 1290–1291; Plato, 1320, 1321; police ethics, 1332; political systems, 1340–1346; public and private morality, 1410–1413; public health, 1416–1417; public policy, 1418; public policy analysis, 1420; Rawls, 1458–1459; reproductive technologies, 1480; revolution, 1495–1498; right to life, 1033; risk analysis, 1515–1517; Roman ethics, 706; Rousseau, 1524; social and political philosophy, 1600–1606; social contract, 1607–1612; strategic interaction, 1658, 1659; Suárez, 1663–1664; suicide, 1671; terrorism, 1696; virtue ethics, 1760; Vitoria, 1768; Weber, 1793

government, ethics in, **624–629**; Christian ethics, 225; civility, 243; computers, 284; corruption, 344, 345; deceit, 378, 380; discrimination, 414–415; freedom of the press, 578–579; Hsün Tzu, 794; human rights, 797; hypocrisy, 819, 821, 823; interests, 866, 868; loyalty, 1027–1028; nineteenth-century British ethics, 740–741; presocratic Greek ethics, 687; public and private morality, 1410–1413; racism, 1433–1435; Rawls, 1458–1459; reflective equilibrium, 1468; secrecy and confidentiality, 1542, 1543; transcendentalism, 1726; trust, 1730; welfare, 1796–1797. See also *political ethics*

government ownership, conservation ethics, 308

government regulation. See public policy; regulation

Govier, Trudy, trust, 1730

grace. See divine grace

gracefulness, virtues, 1765

gradualism: neo-Kantianism, 1227; slippery slope argument, 1594–1596

Grail legend, moral attention, 1115

grammar laundering, journalism, 916

Gramsci, Antonio: cultural studies, 365, 366; oppression, 1263; praxis, 1365; twentieth-century Continental ethics, 763

grandparenthood: family, 522; reproductive technologies, 1478

Gratian of Bologna: early Medieval ethics, 713–714; natural law, 1207

gratitude, **629–631**; acts and omissions, 16; Balguy, 122; Buddhist ethics, 168; children, 208, 210; Cyrenaics, 371; deontology, 392; fairness, 521; fittingness, 553; free will, 572; Godwin, 613; Hume, 807; ideal observer, 828; Jesus, 908; Kant, 935; medical ethics, 1067; moral development, 1122; moral sense theorists, 1177, 1178; obedience to law, 1256; reciprocity, 1464, 1466; Reid, 1471; religion, 1475; Shaftesbury, 1578

gratuities, police ethics, 1333

grave desecration, death, 377

gravity, early Medieval ethics, 711

Gray, Robert, sexuality, 1574

Great Britain: academic freedom, 12; amnesty and pardon, 58; Anscombe, 75; Balguy, 121–122; Bentham, 137–140; Bradley, 154–155; Burke, 169; Butler, 175–177; Cambridg Platonists, 179–180; Clarke, 244–245; cultural studies, 365–366; Darwin, 375; Epicureanism, 475; fiduciary relationships, 546; freedom of the press, 579–580; Godwin, 612–613; Green, 631–632; Hart, 655–657; Hutcheson, 817–819; idealist ethics, 832; individualism, 848, 849; intuitionism, 879–882; liberalism, 972, 973; literature, 1006; Locke, 1007–1011; medical ethics, 1068; Mill (James), 1097–1098; Mill (John Stuart), 1098–1103; Moore, 1109–1110; moral sense theorists, 1173–1178; needs, 1222; neo-Stoicism, 1230; nineteenth-century ethics, 739–751; pacifism, 1268; Paine, 1272, 1721; Paley, 1273–1274; police ethics, 1332, 1335–1336; political systems, 1345–1346; Price, 1371–1372; Prichard, 1373; puritanism, 1430, 1431; reproductive technologies, 1477, 1480; Russell, 1526–1528; self and social self, 1544; Shaftesbury, 1577–1578; Sidgwick, 1580–1581; Spencer, 1637–1638; suicide, 1671; twentieth-century Anglo-American ethics, 765–772, 765–773; Whewell, 1799–1800; William of Ockham, 1802–1804; Williams, 1804–1806; Wollaston, 1818–1819; Wollstonecraft, 1819–1820. *See also* Scottish Enlightenment

Great Learning (Ta Hsüeh): Chu Hsi, 228, 229; Confucian ethics, 287

"Great Speech," Sophists, 1629

Great Ultimate, China, 214, 218–219

Volume key: Volume 1, pages 1–642; volume 2, pages 643–1266; volume 3, pages 1267–1977.

1876

Volume key: Volume 1, pages 1–642; volume 2, pages 643–1266; volume 3, pages 1267–1977.

1877

Subject Index

Habermas, Jürgen, **643–644**; the absurd, 7; Gadamer, 591; government ethics, 628; legitimacy, 961, 962; Mead, 1060; neo-Kantianism, 1228; praxis, 1365; self and social self, 1545; social contract, 1612; sociology, 1621–1622; twentieth-century Continental ethics, 758, 763–764; Walzer, 1777

habit: American moral philosophy, 55; Christian ethics, 224; Dewey, 404; Duns Scotus, 421; institutions, 860–861; James, 900; later Medieval ethics, 718; Locke, 1009; moral education, 1128, 1130; passion, 1279; pragmatism, 1363; prudence, 1397–1398, 1399; virtues, 1763–1764, 1765; William of Ockham, 1803, 1804

habituation, character, 202

Hacker, P.M.S., Wittgenstein, 1812

hïth: Islam, 883, 884, 885; Islamic ethics, 891; Islamic medical ethics, 895

Hadwych of Antwerp [Adelwip], women moral philosophers, 1823

Haeckel, Ernst, evolution, 502

Hague Convention, genocide, 607

Haight, Mary, self-deception, 1552

haiku, Japan, 903

Haji, Ishtiyaque, responsibility, 1490

hajj, Islam, 884

Haksar, Vinit, equality, 481, 482

Halbfass, Wilhelm, India, 845, 846, 847

Hall, Everett W.: moral point of view, 1141; value theory, 1751

Hall, Stuart, cultural studies, 365

Halldén, Sören, persuasive definition, 1304

Halperin, David, gay ethics, 599

Hamilton, Alexander, amnesty and pardon, 57

Hamilton, Charles V., racism, 1436

Hamilton, V. Lee, social psychology, 1617

Hamilton, William: biological theory, 148; Mill (John Stuart), 1100

Hamlet, guilt and shame, 639

Hampshire, Stuart: aesthetics, 26–27; Gandhi, 594; Hart, 655; liberalism, 975; moral point of view, 1141; naturalism, 1213

Hampton, Jean, Hobbes, 774, 775, 776, 777

Han dynasty: China, 210–217; Chu Hsi, 228; Hsün Tzu, 794, 795; Taoist ethics, 1683–1684

Han Fei Tzu, China, 211, 213, 214

Han Learning school, China, 220

Han Yü: China, 217; Confucius, 297; Mencius, 1072

Hand, Learned, Dworkin, 428

handicaps. *See* disability

Haney, Craig, social psychology, 1615, 1617

happiness, 156–157, **644–650**; the absurd, 7; Anselm, 77; Aristotelian ethics, 87; Aristotle, 91–97; Avicenna, 115; Ayer, 116, 117; Baier, 120; beneficence, 130, 131; Bentham, 137–140; biological theory, 146; Brandt, 156–157; Buddha, 161;

Buddhist ethics, 164; business ethics, 174; Butler, 175, 176; charity, 204; Cicero, 232; civic good, 233, 234; Clarke, 245; classical Greek ethics, 691, 695; common good, 264, 265; consequentialism, 304, 306; conservatism, 315; cradle arguments, 357; Crusius, 363; Cynics, 369; Cyrenaics', 371; deontology, 393; Dewey, 402; discounting the future, 411; early Medieval ethics, 710, 712, 713; Edwards, 445, 446; egoism, 449; elite, 450, 451; Epictetus, 473; Epicureanism, 474; Epicurus, 476, 477; equality, 479; ethics and morality, 486; eudaimonia, 489, 491; eudaimonism, 491; excellence, 505; existential ethics, 513; fairness, 521; Fénelon, 540; Feuerbach, 541; final good, 549; Foot, 554, 555, 556; Gassendi, 596; gay ethics, 599; Godwin, 613; good, 620, 621, 622, 623; government ethics, 626; hedonism, 668; Hellenistic ethics, 697–701; Holbach, 778, 779; Hutcheson, 818; ideal observer, 827; idealist ethics, 833; India, 844, 847; inequality, 851; Islamic ethics, 891; Jainism, 898; James, 900; Jefferson, 905, 906; Jewish ethics, 912; justice, distributive, 921, 922; Kant, 933, 935; Kantian ethics, 9450; later Medieval ethics, 717; Leibniz, 964; liberalism, 974; life and death, 997; Locke, 1008–1009; love, 1022; Lucretius, 1029–1030; Marxism, 1048, 1051; materialism, 1057, 1058, 1059; Mill (James), 1098; Mill (John Stuart), 1100, 1101, 1102; moral education, 1128; moral luck, 1135; moral psychology, 1146, 1147; moral reasoning, 1163; moral rules, 1168; moral sense theorists, 1175, 1176; mortality, 1183; motives, 1186; natural law, 1206; nature, 1218; nineteenth-century British ethics, 740; nineteenth-century Continental ethics, 753; Objectivism, 1258; pain and suffering, 1269, 1271; Paley, 1275; paternalism, 1282; person, 1294; philosophy of religion, 1310; phronesis, 1314; Plato, 1319–1320, 1322, 1324–1325; Plotinus, 1329, 1330–1331; practical wisdom, 1358; Price, 1372; prudence, 1399; psychology, 1406; Rawls, 1457; Renaissance ethics, 720, 722–723, 725, 727, 729; Roman ethics, 704; Seneca, 1566; seventeenth- and eighteenth-century ethics, 732; Singer, 1585; skepticism, 1588; social and political philosophy, 1603; social contract, 1611; Socrates, 1624, 1625–1627; Spencer, 1637; Stewart, 1651; Stoicism, 1652, 1653, 1655, 1656; Suárez, 1663; sympathy, 1677; teleological ethics, 1692–1693; Thomas Aquinas, 1710; tragedy, 1722; utilitarianism, 1738, 1739; value concept, 1745; virtue ethics, 1759, 1761; Williams, 1805; Wolff, 1816, 1817; Wollaston, 1818; women

moral philosophers, 1821, 1825. *See also* greatest happiness

hara-kiri, suicide, 1670

hard determinism, free will, 572, 573–574

hard paternalism, paternalism, 1283, 1284

hard realism, life and death, 995

Hardin, Russell: Barry, 126; game theory, 593; institutions, 851; political systems, 1345; social contract, 1612; strategic interaction, 1661; trust, 1730; twentieth-century Anglo-American ethics, 771–772

Hare, J. H., military ethics, 1094

Hare, R[ichard] M[ervyn], **650–652**; agent-centered morality, 41; analytic philosophy, 65, 66; Anscombe, 75; autonomy of moral agents, 112, 113; emotivism, 459; ethics and morality, 485; Frankena, 570; impartiality, 841; Kantian ethics, 940; logic, 1012; love, 1023, 1024; metaethics, 1080, 1082, 1084; moral education, 1129; moral point of view, 1141; moral rules, 1168; moral terms, 1180, 1181, 1182; Murphy, 1195; naturalism, 1213; ought implies can, 1265; prescriptivism, 1369, 1370; responsibility, 1490; skepticism, 1591; theory and practice, 1707; twentieth-century Anglo-American ethics, 768, 769, 771; universalizability, 1734, 1735, 1736, 1737; weakness of will, 1789, 1790

Hargrove, Eugene C., environmental ethics, 468

harm: amnesty and pardon, 58; analogical argument, 63; applied ethics, 81; atheism, 98–99; blackmail, 153; classical Greek ethics, 693; collective responsibility, 256–257; cruelty, 360–362; death, 377, 378; deceit, 381; Descartes, 397; deterrence, 400, 401; discounting the future, 413; envy, 471; Epicurus, 477; euthanasia, 495–496; future generations, 587–588; genetic engineering, 604; Gewirth, 611; group, 636–637, 638; homicide, 785; hypocrisy, 821; infanticide, 855; intention, 867; Jainism, 898; killing and letting die, 949; land ethics, 953; legal philosophy, 958, 959; life and death, 997, 998; moral luck, 1136; moral rules, 1167, 1169, 1170; negligence, 1224–1225; neutral principles, 1232; non-violence, 1755; nuclear ethics, 1247; paternalism, 1283; Plato, 1322; principlism, 1379; property, 1392; prudence, 1399; public health, 1416; rape, 1444, 1445; resentment, 1482; revenge, 1493, 1494; right holders, 1504; rights, 1508, 1511; risk, 1513–1514; risk analysis, 1515, 1516, 1517; self-deception, 1551, 1552; self-defense, 1554, 1555, 1556; sexuality, 1570, 1571, 1572, 1573; social and political philosophy, 1604; social psychology, 1616–1617; suicide, 1668; technology, 1688; terrorism, 1696–

Volume key: Volume 1, pages 1–642; volume 2, pages 643–1266; volume 3, pages 1267–1977.

1878

1698; theory and practcie, 1707; Thomson, 1712–1714; torture, 1719–1720; violence, 1753–1754; virtue ethics, 1761; war and peace, 1785; work, 1829. *See also* injury; non-maleficence

harm and offense, **652–655**; anger, 67; coercion, 246; deterrence, 400–401; Hart, 657; pornography, 1347–1348; punishment, 1425–1427; revenge, 1493; social and political philosophy, 1604; social psychology, 1616–1617

harm prevention: paternalism, 1282; social psychology, 1616–1617

Harman, Gilbert: contractarianism, 322; intention, 867, 868; metaethics, 1085; moral realism, 1156; moral reasoning, 1162

harmony: Africa, 34; alienation, 49; classical Greek ethics, 694; compromise, 281; etiquette, 487; Hegel, 673; Hellenistic ethics, 701; Hsün Tzu, 795; Hume, 813; integrity, 865; Rousseau, 1522; seventeenth- and eighteenth-century ethics, 736; Shaftesbury, 1578; temperance, 1693

Harré, Rom, psychology, 1408

Harrington, James: civic good, 235; humanism, 802

Harris, George W., Aristotelian ethics, 88–89

Harrison, Ross, Bentham, 138, 140

Harsanyi, John: contractarianism, 321–322, 324; economic analysis, 435–436, 438; social contract, 1611; technology, 1688

Hart, H.L.A. (Herbert Lionel Adolphus), **655–657**; Baier, 120; contracts, 584; Dworkin, 428–429; fairness, 521; legal ethics, 957; negligence, 1224; norms, 1243; revolution, 1497; right, 1500, 1501; sexuality, 1573

Hartland, E. Sidney, collective responsibility, 256

Hartley, David: Bentham, 139; Mill (James), 1097

Hartmann, Heinz, psychoanalysis, 1403

Hartmann, Nicolai, **658–659**; Gadamer, 590; phenomenology, 1305, 1306; twentieth-century Continental ethics, 758, 760; value theory, 1751

Hartsock, Nancy, sexuality, 1575

Hastings, Warren, Burke, 169

Hastings Center: applied ethics, 83; bioethics, 141; medical ethics, 1069

hate, **659–662**; Brentano, 158; Holocaust, 784; homosexuality, 786; racism, 1436, 1437; rape, 1445, 1446; resentment, 1482, 1483, 1484; revenge, 1493; twentieth-century Continental ethics, 759; war and peace, 1785

hate crimes, political correctness, 1339

hate speech, political correctness, 1337, 1339

Hauerwas, Stanley: prudence, 1400; theological ethics, 1702; virtue ethics, 1761

Hauptman, Robert, library, 986, 987, 988, 989

Hawthorne, Nathaniel: hypocrisy, 821; transcendentalism, 1724

Hayek, Friedrich A. von: economic systems, 442; individualism, 849, 850; justice, distributive, 921, 923; liberalism, 973, 975; naturalism, 1213; Objectivism, 1259; strategic interaction, 1660; twentieth-century Anglo-American ethics, 770

Ḥayy Ibn Yaqẓān, Ibn Ṭufayl, 826, 827

hazardous technology: engineering ethics, 462–464; technology, 1687–1689. *See also* health hazards

Hazlitt, William: Godwin, 612; hypocrisy, 820–821

Heal, G. M., discounting the future, 411

Healing, Avicenna, 115

healing: Christian ethics, 222; medical ethics, 1062–1064, 1066–1070

health: abortion, 3; bioethics, 144; business ethics, 173; *eudaimonia,* 490, 491; excellence, 505; Gandhi, 594; genetic engineering, 603, 604; good, 620; human rights, 796; Mencius, 1071; narrative, 1204; psychoanalysis, 1404; Renaissance ethics, 720, 725; Socrates, 1626–1627; Sophists, 1630; Wolff, 1816

health care: American moral philosophy, 56; bioethics, 142, 143, 144, 145; civil rights, 238; collective responsibility, 256; entitlements, 466; Islamic medical ethics, 894–895; life and death, 996; medical ethics, 1062, 1063–1064; moral community, 1117; nursing ethics, 1250–1252; paternalism, 1282, 1283; professional ethics, 1384; public health, 1416–1417; Schweitzer, 1541; suicide, 1671; welfare, 1797. *See also* medicine

health hazards: deceit, 379; engineering ethics, 462–464; genetic engineering, 603; nuclear ethics, 1249; risk analysis, 1515, 1516; technology, 1688–1689; work, 1829

heart: Jesus, 907; Mencius, 1072

Heartbreak House, pacifism, 1267

heaven: China, 211, 212, 213; early Medieval ethics, 712; Hsün Tzu, 795; India, 843, 846; Locke, 1008, 1009, 1010; Mencius, 1071, 1072; philosophy of religion, 1313. *See also* immortality

Hebdige, Dick, cultural studies, 365

Hebrew Bible: beneficence, 129; Christian ethics, 225, 226, 227; existential ethics, 509; Jesus, 907, 908; Jewish ethics, 911, 911–912, 913, 914; theological ethics;, 1703, 1705; virtue ethics, 1758, 1759. *See also* Bible; specific books

Hebrew-Christian ethics. *See* Judeo-Christian ethics

Hecataeus of Miletus, presocratic Greek ethics, 688

Hedge, Frederick, transcendentalism, 1724

hedone, Cicero, 231

hedonic calculus, hedonism, 666

hedonic tone theory, hedonism, 663

hedonism, **662–669**; Aristotle, 92; Bentham, 139, 140; Bradley, 154, 155; Buddha, 162; Buddhist ethics,

165; Butler, 176, 177; China, 215; classical Greek ethics, 693; cost-benefit analysis, 351; cradle arguments, 356; Cyrenaics, 370–372; Epicureanism, 475; Epicurus, 477; good, 620; Hellenistic ethics, 697, 698; idealist ethics, 830, 832, 834; Jefferson, 906; Jewish ethics, 913; Kierkegaard, 945; Leibniz, 964; life and death, 997; Locke, 1007–1008, 1010; Mill (James), 1098; moral luck, 1135; naturalistic fallacy, 1216; nineteenth-century British ethics, 740, 741, 742–743, 745, 747; organic unity, 1264; Peirce, 1287; Plato, 1319, 1324; pleasure, 1326–1329; psychology, 1406; puritanism, 1429; Renaissance ethics, 727; Russell, 1527–1528; Sidgwick, 1581; Socrates, 1625, 1626, 1627; suicide, 1670; temperance, 1695; utilitarianism, 1738, 1740, 1743; value concept, 1746, 1747–1748; value theory, 1751; work, 1828

Heep, Uriah (fictional), hypocrisy, 821, 823

Hegel, Georg Wilhelm Friedrich, **669–675**; additivity, 20; Adler, 22; alienation, 48–49; Aristotelian ethics, 86; Bradley, 154, 155; Camus, 181; capital punishment, 183; common sense moralists, 268; communitarianism, 269; competition, 278; conservatism, 311; critical theory, 359; duty and obligation, 423, 427; elite, 450–451; Engels, 460, 461, 462; existential ethics, 509, 511; feminist ethics, 530; Feuerbach, 541; Fichte, 543; formalism, 563; Frankena, 569; Hellenistic ethics, 696; historiography, 683–684; *humanism, 802;* hypocrisy, 822; idealist ethics, 830, 831–832, 833; Kant, 931; Kierkegaard, 946; King, 950; liberalism, 972, 973; Marx, 1043; Mead, 1060; multiculturalism, 1188; neo-Kantianism, 1227; Nietzsche, 1237; nihilism, 1240; nineteenth-century British ethics, 739, 742, 743; nineteenth-century Continental ethics, 752, 753–754, 756; obedience to law, 1254–1255; Objectivism, 1258; organic unity, 1265; perfectionism, 1288; personal relationships, 1299, 1302; praxis, 1364–1365; property, 1390, 1392; proportionality, 1394; psychology, 1409; punishment, 1427; Ricoeur, 1499; Royce, 1525; Schelling, 1535; self and social self, 1544; self-deception, 1552; social and political philosophy, 1599–1600; Taylor, 1685, 1686; tragedy, 1723; twentieth-century Anglo-American ethics, 765, 771; twentieth-century Continental ethics, 758, 762, 764; violence and non-violence, 1755; Wolff, 1815; work, 1830

hegemony: cultural studies, 366; oppression, 1263

Hegesias, Cyrenaics, 370–371, 372

Heian period, Japan, 902

Volume key: Volume 1, pages 1–642; volume 2, pages 643–1266; volume 3, pages 1267–1977.

1879

Subject Index

Heidegger, Martin, **675–676**; authenticity, 105, 106; bad faith, 119; charity, 204; existential ethics, 509, 510, 511; Gadamer, 590, 591; Hartmann, 658; humanism, 802; Levinas, 969; moral purity, 1153; mortality, 1183–1184, 1185; Nietzsche, 1236; nihilism, 1240, 1241; philosophical anthropology, 1309; postmodernism, 1350, 1351; psychology, 1407; Schelling, 1536; self and social self, 1545; Soviet ethical theory, 1635; Taylor, 1685; technology and nature, 1690; twentieth-century Continental ethics, 758

hekousia, Aristotle, 94

Held, Virginia: cognitive science, 249; collective responsibility, 256; egoism, 449; moral pluralism, 1139, 1140; self and social self, 1546

Helen of Troy, presocratic Greek ethics, 689–690

hell: early Medieval ethics, 713; Locke, 1008, 1009, 1010; nature, 1219; philosophy of religion, 1313; puritanism, 1431

Hellenistic ethics: character, 201; children, 208; cradle arguments, 355–357; Cynics, 368–370; emotion, 455; excellence, 505; gay ethics, 598; good, 621; history of Western ethics, 690, 696–703; Islam, 885; Islamic ethics, 892; Jesus, 907–909; medical ethics, 1067; moral development, 1119; natural law, 1206; Paul, 1285, 1286; person, 1294; practical wisdom, 1358; Renaissance ethics, 724–726; Roman ethics, 703–704, 706; skepticism, 1588; Stoicism, 1653, 1655; Sunnīsm, 1672; women moral philosophers, 1821, 1822. *See also* Epicurianism; Stoicism

Hellenized Judaism, Jesus, 907

Heloise: Abelard, 1; women moral philosophers, 1822

helpfulness: beneficence, 132; duty and obligation, 426; moral rules, 1169, 1170; reciprocity, 1464; social psychology, 1615–1616; sympathy, 1675. *See also* altruism

Helvetius, Claude: Beccaria, 127; Bentham, 137, 138; Montesquieu, 1108; pleasure, 1329; seventeenth- and eighteenth-century ethics, 735

Hemings, Sally, Jefferson, 906

hemophilia, genetic engineering, 604

Hempel, Carl, moral realism, 1154

Henefin, Mary Sue, reproductive technologies, 1476

Henkin, Louis, human rights, 797

Henry, IV, King of France, Voltaire, 1770

Henry VIII, King of England, medical ethics, 1068

Henson, Richard G., life and death, 997

Heraclitus: classical Greek ethics, 690; competition, 278; King, 950; literature, 1004; presocratic Greek ethics, 686, 687–688

Herbert, Edward, Baron of Cherbury, religion, 1473

herd morality: existential ethics, 509, 510; hate, 659; Nietzsche, 1236, 1238; nineteenth-century Continental ethics, 756, 757–758

Herder, Johann Gottfried: Hegel, 674; humanism, 801

hereditary titles. *See* nobility

heresy: Abelard, 1, 2; Augustine, 102–103

Herman, Barbara: Aristotelian ethics, 89; moral perception, 1138; partiality, 1276

Hermarchus of Mytilene, Epicureanism, 474

hermeneutics: additivity, 20; Christian ethics, 223; Confucian ethics, 287; Gadamer, 590–591; Japan, 903; Ricoeur, 1499; Taylor, 1685

Hermeren, Goran, autonomy of ethics, 109

Herodotus: Mill (John Stuart), 1099; presocratic Greek ethics, 688

heroes: competition, 277; elite, 451; engineering ethics, 464; existential ethics, 510; honor, 789; literature, 1005; moral saints, 1170–1172; Nietzsche, 1239; presocratic Greek ethics, 686; Roman ethics, 704; supererogation, 1673, 1674, 1675; theory and practice, 1707; tragedy, 1722, 1723; twentieth-century Continental ethics, 764, 765

heroism: Emerson, 452; religion, 1475

Herrad, Abbess of Honehbourg [Herrad of Landsberg], women moral philosophers, 1822

Herskovits, Melville, anthropology, 79, 80

Hesiod: presocratic Greek ethics, 686, 687; tragedy, 1721

heterogeneity, applied ethics, 81

heterogeneity of the good, Pufendorf, 1424

heteronomous activity, person, 1295

heterosexism: family, 523; feminist ethics, 528, 530, 534; gay ethics, 598, 599, 600; political correctness, 1339

heterosexual desire, twentieth-century Continental ethics, 761

heterosexuality, sexual abuse, 1567

heuristic elite, elite, 450

hexis: Aristotle, 92; character, 200; virtues, 1763–1764

Heyd, David, supererogation, 1675

Hick, John, evil, 499

Hicks, John, economic analysis, 433

hierarchies: Brentano, 157–158; early Medieval ethics, 711; elite, 450, 451; feminist ethics, 530; final good, 549; happiness, 645, 647; Hartmann, 658; Hindu ethics, 678–680, 681, 682, 683; Holocaust, 783; Husserl, 816; Ibn Rushd, 825; intuitionism, 880; Kantian ethics, 9450; lesbian ethics, 967; loyalty, 1028; Malebranche, 1038; moral realism, 1156; narrative, 1202; natural law, 1207; Nietzsche, 1237; nursing ethics, 1250–1251; pacifism, 1267; perfectionism, 1289–1290; phenomenology, 1306; Plotinus, 1329, 1330; postmodernism, 1351; principlism,

1379, 1380; resentment, 1483; rights, 1510; Scheler, 1533–1534; Stoicism, 1653; strategic interaction, 1659; temperance, 1695; twentieth-century Continental ethics, 759–760; work, 1827. *See also* ordinality

Hierius, women moral philosophers, 1822

Hierocles: cradle arguments, 356; Epicureanism, 475

higher law. *See* natural law

higher morality, nineteenth-century Continental ethics, 757, 758

higher persons: immoralism, 839; twentieth-century Continental ethics, 760

higher pleasures: Godwin, 613; Mill (John Stuart), 1101; pleasure, 1328; puritanism, 1429, 1430

higher values: resentment, 1484–1485; twentieth-century Continental ethics, 759, 760

higher-order motives, motives, 1182

highest good (*summum bonum*): Cicero, 231; classical Greek ethics, 693; Democritus, 389–390; early Medieval ethics, 713, 720; Gassendi, 59, 596; good, 620, 621, 622–623; Hellenistic ethics, 702; Hobbes, 775, 777; hope, 791; Husserl, 817; idealist ethics, 833; Kant, 932, 936; karma, 944; Kierkegaard, 946; life and death, 998; nineteenth-century Continental ethics, 752; Peirce, 1287; perfectionism, 1289; philosophy of religion, 1310; Renaissance ethics, 720, 721, 723, 724–725, 727, 728; Roman ethics, 704; virtue ethics, 1757, 1759; Wang, 1780

highest use, conservation ethics, 308

highly evolved, naturalistic fallacy, 1215

Hildebrand, Dietrich von, phenomenology, 1305, 1306–1307

Hildegard of Bingen, women moral philosophers, 1822

Hill, Thomas E., Jr.: partiality, 1276; self-respect, 1565

Himmelfarb, Gertrude, Moore, 1110

Himmler, Heinrich, Holocaust, 781, 783

Hindu ethics, **676–683**; Buddhist ethics, 163; comparative ethics, 274, 275; Jainism, 898; medical ethics, 1066

Hinduism: competition, 277; forms of consciousness, 564; Gandhi, 593; Hindu ethics, 676–683; India, 843–844, 845, 846–847; Jainism, 897, 898; karma, 944; life and death, 998; love, 1026; suicide, 1670

Hintikka, Jaakko, logic, 1014

Hippias, Sophists, 1628, 1629, 1630

Hippocratic Oath, medical ethics, 1063, 1067

Hippolytus, weakness of will, 1791

Hirshleifer, Jack, cooperative surplus, 337

Hirst, E. W., golden rule, 615

historical materialism: critical theory, 359; Marx, 1042, 1043–1045, 1046

historiography, **683–685**; Aristotelian ethics, 85–90; Donegan, 417, 418; Durkheim, 422; Gassendi, 595, 596; Hegel, 674; Hume, 805, 809, 811–

Volume key: Volume 1, pages 1–642; volume 2, pages 643–1266; volume 3, pages 1267–1977.

1880

Volume key: Volume 1, pages 1–642; volume 2, pages 643–1266; volume 3, pages 1267–1977.

1881

honor, *continued*
good, 620; gratitude, 630; guilt and shame, 639; Hsün Tzu, 795; integrity, 864; Japan, 901, 902; Locke, 1008, 1009; Machiavelli, 1033; Price, 1372; pride, 1375; rape, 1444; revenge, 1494; Roman ethics, 704, 706; twentieth-century Continental ethics, 764

Honoré, A. M.: Hart, 655; property, 1390

honors: fairness, 521; Sophists, 1630

Hook, Sidney, humanism, 802

Hooker, Richard: Christian ethics, 224, 226; seventeenth- and eighteenth-century ethics, 731

Hooker, Worthington, medical ethics, 1069

Hoover, Herbert, individualism, 848–849

hope, **791–793**; the absurd, 7; Augustine, 104; Buddha, 162; Buddhist ethics, 168; Camus, 181, 182; Christian ethics, 224; eudaimonism, 491; euthanasia, 493; Fénelon, 540; later Medieval ethics, 718; virtue ethics, 1759; William of Ockham, 1804

hopefulness, Jesus, 907

hopelessness, wisdom, 1808

Hopkins, E. Washburn, India, 843, 845

Horace, Roman ethics, 707

Horgan, Terence, moral realism, 1157

Horkheimer, Max, critical theory, 358, 359

Horney, Karen, psychoanalysis, 1403

Horton, B., land ethics, 952

Horton, John, obedience to law, 1255

Hospers, John, Russell, 1527

hospitality, character, 202

hospitals: bioethics, 145; collective responsibility, 256; medical ethics, 1063, 1064

hostility: correctional ethics, 341; moral development, 1120

House of Representatives, U.S. *See* United States Congress

House Un-American Activities Committee (U.S.), Rand, 1441

housework, work, 1831

housing, racism, 1433

Hovot ha-Levavot, Jewish ethics, 913

Howison, G. H., idealist ethics, 830, 833

Hsi K'ang, China, 215

Hsiang Hsiu, China, 215

hsin: Confucius, 296; Mencius, 1072; Wang, 1780

hsing: China, 212, 214, 217; Chu Hsi, 229; Mencius, 1071

Hsiung Shih-li: China, 221; Wang, 1781

hsüeh, Confucius, 296

Hsün Tzu, **793–796**; China, 211, 213, 214, 215; comparative ethics, 275; Confucian ethics, 287, 288, 290, 291, 292, 293; Confucius, 296; Mencius, 1072

Hsün Yüeh, China, 214, 215, 217

Hu Shih, China, 221

Huai-nan Tzu: China, 215; Taoist ethics, 1680, 1684

Huang Tsung-hsi, China, 220

hubris, presocratic Greek ethics, 686

hudor, moral realism, 1157

Hudson, W. D., moral reasoning, 1161

Hudson v. McMillian, correctional ethics, 341

Hughes, Martin, terrorism, 1697

Hugo, Victor, Rand, 1440

Huig de Groot. *See* Grotius, Hugo

Hui-neng, China, 216, 217

Hull, John, agency and disability, 37

human acts, Thomas Aquinas, 1709

human agency, communitarianism, 270

human beings: abortion, 4; animals, 70–72, 73; Anselm, 77–78; Aristotelian ethics, 87–88; Aristotle, 91–97; atheism, 101; bad faith, 119; character, 200–202; classical Greek ethics, 693–695; conservation ethics, 309; cosmopolitan ethics, 346–349; Darwin, 374, 375; deceit, 379; deliberation and choice, 382–384; dignity, 405–406; Duns Scotus, 421–422; egoism, 449; Engels, 416, 460; environmental ethics, 469, 470; Epictetus, 473; equality, 479, 480, 480–481, 482; *eudaimonia,* 489; evolution, 502–503; excellence, 504; existential ethics, 510–514; Feuerbach, 541; fiduciary relationships, 547; free will, 571–574; future generations, 588; genetic engineering, 603–606; Green, 631–632; Hellenistic ethics, 700–701; Hobbes, 773, 774; Hsün Tzu, 795; humanism, 801, 802; immoralism, 839; Islamic ethics, 889–890; life and death, 993, 997; love, 1021, 1023, 1024; moral development, 1119, 1120; mortality, 1184–1185; nihilism, 1240–1241; nineteenth-century Continental ethics, 753, 755, 756, 757; person, 1293–1294, 1296; philosophical anthropology, 1308–1309; Plotinus, 1330, 1331; psychoanalysis, 1404–1405; psychology, 1407–1409; right holders, 1502, 1504, 1505; self and social self, 1544; self-control, 1549; social and political philosophy, 1601; Spinoza, 1639; Stoicism, 1653; technology and nature, 1690; transcendentalism, 1726, 1727; twentieth-century Anglo-American ethics, 772; twentieth-century Continental ethics, 761–763, 764; value concept, 1745, 1746; virtue ethics, 1757–1761. *See also* human nature; humanity; person, concept of

human cloning: analogical argument, 59–60, 61, 62, 63; reproductive technologies, 1478, 1480

human condition: authenticity, 106; bad faith, 119; Camus, 181–182; de Beauvoir, 375–376; meaning of life, 1000–1002; presocratic Greek ethics, 687; Sartre, 1531

human depravity: Augustine, 102; Seneca, 1565

human development, Green, 631

human dignity. *See* dignity

human emancipation. *See* emancipation

human existence. *See* human beings; human condition

human flourishing. *See* flourishing

Human Genome Organization, reproductive technologies, 1479

Human Genome Project: computers, 283; genetic engineering, 606; Gert, 609; reproductive technologies, 1476, 1479

human good. *See* good, theories of the

human growth hormone, genetic engineering, 603

human nature: American moral philosophy, 54, 55; anger, 67–69; Anselm, 77; Aristotle, 96; authenticity, 106; benevolence, 134; Bentham, 137–138, 139–140; Butler, 175–176; China, 214; Chu Hsi, 228–229; cognitive science, 251; Confucian ethics, 288; conservatism, 313, 315, 316; correctional ethics, 340, 343; Cynics, 369; deontology, 394–395; Dewey, 402–403; Duns Scotus, 420–422; Durkheim, 422–423; duty and obligation, 425; egoism, 446–447; Emerson, 453; envy, 472; golden rule, 616–617; government ethics, 625; Hegel, 670, 674; Hellenistic ethics, 701; Holbach, 779; honor, 788; Hsün Tzu, 784; Hume, 804–805, 808, 813; ideal observer, 827; India, 846; Japan, 901, 904; Jefferson, 905, 906; Kant, 934; Kantian ethics, 942; life and death, 995; love, 1026; MacIntyre, 1035; Maimonides, 1036; Mill (John Stuart), 1102; Mo Tzu, 1105; moral absolutes, 1112; moral psychology, 1145–1150; moral sense theorists, 1173–1178; motives, 1186; natural law, 1205, 1206, 1207; nature, 1217, 1218; nineteenth-century British ethics, 740; nineteenth-century Continental ethics, 753; partiality, 1276; perfectionism, 1289, 1920; presocratic Greek ethics, 688–689; psychology, 1406, 1408–1409; racism, 1435; religion, 1474; Renaissance ethics, 725; Roman ethics, 705, 706; Sartre, 1531; seventeenth- and eighteenth-century ethics, 733, 735, 737; social and political philosophy, 1600, 1604–1605; sociology, 1621; twentieth-century Continental ethics, 763; violence and non-violence, 1756; virtue ethics, 1759, 1760; William of Ockham, 1803; Wolff, 1816; work, 1828

human perfectibility: Augustine, 102; conservatism, 315; Mandeville, 1040

human reality, bad faith, 118–119

human reproduction. *See* reproduction (biological); reproductive rights; reproductive technologies

human rights, **796–800**; animals, 72–73; Barry, 126; bioethics, 143–144; Calvin, 179; Camus, 182; capital punishment, 183, 184; censorship, 199; civil disobedience, 236, 237; civil rights, 239; correctional ethics, 341; cosmopolitan ethics, 346–349; deontology, 393; dignity, 406; duty and obligation, 424, 425, 426; equality, 478, 479–480; feminist

Volume key: Volume 1, pages 1–642; volume 2, pages 643–1266; volume 3, pages 1267–1977.

1882

ethics, 536–537; formalism, 563; government ethics, 626; Hegel, 671; international distributive justice, 875–876; land ethics, 953; legal philosophy, 958; libertarianism, 977–978; Marxism, 1050–1051; person, 1297; public policy, 1418; Pufendorf, 1423; rationality vs. reasonableness, 1453; Rawls, 1459; reproductive technologies, 1476; rights, 1509–1510, 1511; self-defense, 1554, 1555; slavery, 1593; social contract, 1611; suicide, 1669; torture, 1719–1720; twentieth-century Anglo-American ethics, 769, 771; war and peace, 1782; Wollstonecraft, 1819; work, 1829

human sacrifice: Hindu ethics, 682; infanticide, 855–856; Westermarck, 1798. *See also* sacrificial offerings

human subject research: bioethics, 142; medical ethics, 1069; principlism, 1378; social psychology, 1613–1618

human welfare: academic freedom, 10, 11; American moral philosophy, 55–56; Breen, 631–632; human rights, 796–799; inequality, 851–853; land ethics, 953; moral absolutes, 1113; paternalism, 1282; public policy analysis, 1421–1422; rights, 1511; Socrates, 1626; theory and practice, 1707; utilitarianism, 1737–1744. *See also* flourishing; well-being

humaneness: benevolence, 134; Japan, 901

humanism, **800–803**; civic good, 234; Descartes, 398; early Medieval ethics, 798; elite, 450; feminist ethics, 531, 537; Grotius, 633; Heidegger, 675; Islam, 886; Locke, 1008; nineteenth-century Continental ethics, 753; Objectivism, 1258; phenomenology, 1306; psychology, 1407; Rand, 1441; Renaissance ethics, 720–729; resentment, 1482; Sartre, 1531; Soviet ethical theory, 1633, 1635; twentieth-century Continental ethics, 763; Vitoria, 1768–1769

humanism-secularism, Adler, 21

humanitarianism, resentment, 1484–1485

humanitas, humanism, 801, 802

humanities: political correctness, 1338; practical reason[ing], 1355–1356

humanity: Aristotelian ethics, 88; China, 211, 214, 216, 218, 221; Chu Hsi, 228–229; Confucian ethics, 287–294; Confucius, 295–296; cosmopolitan ethics, 346–349; deontology, 393; dignity, 405; Hsün Tzu, 795; humanism, 801; Hume, 807; Kant, 931, 934, 935, 937; Kantian ethics, 941; liberalism, 972, 974; love, 1024–1026; Montaigne, 1107; mortality, 1183; natural law, 1205–1209; Nietzsche, 1239; nihilism, 1240; nineteenth-century Continental ethics, 753; partiality, 1276; resentment, 1483, 1484–1485; Rousseau, 1522; Seneca, 1566; Taoist ethics, 1682; technology and nature,

1690–1691; twentieth-century Continental ethics, 762–763, 764; Wang, 1780

Humboldt, Wilhelm von: individualism, 850; liberalism, 972, 973; perfectionism, 1291

Hume, David, **803–815**; action, 15; agnosticism, 43, 44; anger, 69; Anscombe, 74; applied ethics, 81; Aristotle, 93; autonomy of ethics, 110; benevolence, 134; Bentham, 138, 139; biological theory, 146, 147; Butler, 177; Cambridge Platonists, 180; care, 186; causation and responsibility, 194, 196, 197; cognitive science, 249; common sense moralists, 268; comparative ethics, 275; Confucian ethics, 289; contractarianism, 321, 322, 323, 324; cooperation, conflict, and coordination, 335; Cudworth, 364; Darwin, 375; deliberation and choice, 383; desire, 399; Emerson, 452; emotion, 457; emotivism, 458; entitlements, 465; environmental ethics, 469; ethics and morality, 486; evolution, 502; excuses, 507; existential ethics, 510; forms of consciousness, 565; Frankena, 470; free will, 572, 573; freedom and determinism, 57; game theory, 593; good, 620; gratitude, 630; happiness, 648–649; Hart, 657; hate, 660, 661; hope, 791; Husserl, 816; Hutcheson, 818; ideal observer, 828; idealist ethics, 832; internalism, 517, 518; Jefferson, 905; justice, circumstances of, 918, 919, 920; libertarianism, 977; literature, 1004; logic, 1011; Mandeville, 1040; medical ethics, 1068; metaethics, 1081; metaphysics and epistemology, 1090; Mill (James), 1097; moral imagination, 1131; moral psychology, 1145; moral purity, 1152; moral realism, 1154; moral reasoning, 1161, 1162, 1163; moral sense theorists, 1173, 1174, 1175, 1176–1178; motives, 1186; naturalism, 1214; nature, 1218; nineteenth-century British ethics, 746; norms, 1242–1243; obedience to law, 1254, 1255; Paley, 1273; passion, 1279, 1280, 1281; personal relationships, 1299; pleasure, 1328; Price, 1363; pride, 1375, 1376–1377; property, 1390; public and private morality, 1412; racism, 1434; rational choice, 1446, 1449; rationality vs. reasonableness, 1452, 1453, 1454; Reid, 1470; seventeenth- and eighteenth-century ethics, 737; Shaftesbury, 1577, 1578; skepticism, 1588, 1591; Smith, 598, 1597; social and political philosophy, 1602; social contract, 1608; Stewart, 1651; strategic interaction, 1657, 1658–1659, 1661–1662; suicide, 1669; sympathy, 1676, 1677, 1678, 1679; theism, 1699–1700; twentieth-century Anglo-American ethics, 769, 772; virtue ethics, 1760, 1761; voluntarism, 1772; Westermarck,

1798; wickedness, 1801; Wollaston, 1818

humiliation: euthanasia, 496–497; rape, 1446; revenge, 1493; sexuality, 1571, 1574; violence, 1750

humility, **815–816**; Buddhist ethics, 168; Descartes, 398; early Medieval ethics, 711, 712; genetic engineering, 604; honor, 788; hope, 791; Islamic ethics, 890; Jesus, 907; Jewish ethics, 913, 914; mysticism, 1197; Nietzsche, 1236; Pascal, 1278; postmodernism, 1352; pride, 1375, 1376, 1377; resentment, 1482, 1483, 1484; self-esteem, 1557; theological ethics, 1702; twentieth-century Continental ethics, 759, 760; virtue ethics, 1758; virtues, 1764; women moral philosophers, 1823, 1824

humor: character, 201; persuasive definition, 1304

hunger: agricultural ethics, 45; classical Greek ethics, 694; Epicurus, 477; equality, 482; feminist ethics, 531, 533; international distributive justice, 874, 876; killing and letting die, 947, 948, 950; life and death, 996, 997; moral community, 1117; needs, 1222; public policy, 1418; welfare, 1796. *See also* famine

hunger strikes: Gandhi, 594; violence and non-violence, 1754, 1755. *See also* fasting

Hung-jen, China, 216

hunting: animals, 72; Leopold, 966

Hurka, Thomas, Aristotelian ethics, 90

Hurley, Patrick: analogical argument, 61, 62, 63; persuasive definition, 1303

Hurley, Susan L., economic analysis, 433

Hurych, Jitka M., library, 986

Husak, Douglas, human rights, 799

Husserl, Edmund [Gustav Albrecht], **816–817**; bad faith, 118; existential ethics, 510, 511; Hartmann, 658; Levinas, 969; phenomenology, 1305, 1306, 1307; philosophical anthropology, 1309; Ricoeur, 1499; Scheler, 1534; twentieth-century Continental ethics, 759

Hutcheson, Francis, **817–819**; Balguy, 121–122; Bentham, 138; Cambridge Platonists, 180; common sense moralists, 267; Cudworth, 364; Edwards, 446; Emerson, 452; fittingness, 553; Frankena, 570; Hume, 805; ideal observer, 827–828; intuitionism, 879; Jefferson, 905; Kant, 929; Mandeville, 1040; Mill (James), 1098; moral sense theorists, 1173, 1174–1176, 1177, 1178; natural law, 1209; nineteenth-century British ethics, 740, 746; Paley, 1273; Price, 1371; seventeenth- and eighteenth-century ethics, 736, 737; Shaftesbury, 1577, 1578; Smith, 1596–1597; virtue ethics, 1760; Wang, 1781; Wollaston, 1818

Hutterites, Christian ethics, 225

Huxley, Aldous: genetic engineering, 605; perfectionism, 1290

Huxley, Julian, evolution, 502

Volume key: Volume 1, pages 1–642; volume 2, pages 643–1266; volume 3, pages 1267–1977.

1883

Volume key: Volume 1, pages 1–642; volume 2, pages 643–1266; volume 3, pages 1267–1977.

1884

Volume key: Volume 1, pages 1–642; volume 2, pages 643–1266; volume 3, pages 1267–1977.

1885

Volume key: Volume 1, pages 1–642; volume 2, pages 643–1266; volume 3, pages 1267–1977.

1886

Volume key: Volume 1, pages 1–642; volume 2, pages 643–1266; volume 3, pages 1267–1977.

1887

Volume key: Volume 1, pages 1–642; volume 2, pages 643–1266; volume 3, pages 1267–1977.

1888

Volume key: Volume 1, pages 1–642; volume 2, pages 643–1266; volume 3, pages 1267–1977.

1889

Subject Index

Jainism, **897–899**; Hindu ethics, 677, 682; India, 843, 844, 845, 846, 847; theory and practice, 1707

James I, King of England, Suárez, 1663

James, Henry: integrity, 865; literature, 1005, 1006

James, William, **899–901**; Adler, 21; agnosticism, 44; American moral philosophy, 54–55, 56; Emerson, 452; emotion, 455; existential ethics, 511; Fuller, 584; hate, 659; humanism, 802; Japan, 903; mysticism, 1198; Nietzsche, 1236; nineteenth-century British ethics, 747; Perry, 1293; pragmatism, 1361, 1362, 1363; Santayana, 1530

Jansen, Cornelius, Pascal, 1278

Jansenism: casuistry, 189; Fénelon, 539, 540; Pascal, 1278

Japan, **901–905**; business ethics, 174; collective responsibility, 257; comparative ethics, 273; Nāgārjuna, 1200; suicide, 1670; virtue ethics, 1761; Wang, 1781; women moral philosophers, 1822; work, 1828

Jaspers, Karl: authenticity, 106; collective responsibility, 256; existential ethics, 510; twentieth-century Continental ethics, 758

jealousy: Democritus, 390; emotion, 454, 455, 456, 457; envy, 471; happiness, 645; moral development, 1120; sexuality, 1570

Jefferson, Thomas, **905–906**; agricultural ethics, 46; government ethics, 627; Jesus, 907; social contract, 1611; Stewart, 1652

Jefferson, Tony, cultural studies, 365

Jehovah's Witnesses, Holocaust, 779–780

jen: China, 211, 214, 216, 218, 221; Chu Hsi, 228–229; Confucian ethics, 287–294; Confucius, 295–296; Wang, 1780, 1781

Jerome, Saint: Lucretius, 1029; suicide, 1669

Jerusalem, genocide, 607

Jesuits: casuistry, 188, 189; Hume, 804; hypocrisy, 822; moral absolutes, 1112; natural law, 1207; neo-Stoicism, 1229–1230; Pascal, 1278; religion, 1474; Renaissance ethics, 720; seventeenth- and eighteenth-century ethics, 731; Suárez, 1663–1664

Jesus of Nazareth, **906–909**; Abelard, 2; the absurd, 8; amnesty and pardon, 57; Anselm, 77; atheism, 99; Augustine, 103, 104; beneficence, 129, 130; Calvin, 178; Christian ethics, 222, 224, 225, 226–227; Emerson, 452; happiness, 645; humanism, 801; hypocrisy, 820; Islam, 883; love, 1020, 1023; Luther, 1031; medical ethics, 1067; mysticism, 1197; narrative, 1203; neo-Stoicism, 1230, 1231; Niebuhr, 1235; Nietzsche, 1238; Paul, 1284, 1285, 1286; Renaissance ethics, 729; Scheler, 1534; seventeenth- and eighteenth-century ethics, 730–731, 734; Spinoza, 1638, 1639; suicide,

1670; theological ethics, 1703–1704; women moral philosophers, 1823

Jevons, William Stanley, economic analysis, 433

Jewish ethics, **909–915**; beneficence, 129; bioethics, 142; Buber, 160–161; casuistry, 188; charity, 203; comparative ethics, 275; Donegan, 417; early Medieval ethics, 713; golden rule, 614; hypocrisy, 820; Jesus, 907–908, 909; Maimonides, 1036–1037; medical ethics, 1066; moral absolutes, 1111; virtue ethics, 1758, 1759. *See also* Judeo-Christian ethics

Jewish ritual, Christian ethics, 222

Jewish tradition, Jesus, 907

Jews: discrimination, 415; genocide, 607; Holocaust, 779–784; racism, 1433; Spinoza, 1638. *See also* Jewish ethics; Judaism

Jina, Jainism, 897

Job: hypocrisy, 820; neo-Stoicism, 1230

jobs. *See* work

Jocasta, sexual abuse, 1568

John XXII, Pope, William of Ockham, 1802

John: Jesus, 907; theological ethics, 1704

John Cassian. *See* Cassian, John, Saint

John Chrysostom. *See* Chrysostom, John, Saint

John of the Cross, Saint: mysticism, 1198; women moral philosophers, 1824

John Paul II, Pope (Karol Wojtyla), sexuality, 1572

John the Baptist, Saint, Jesus, 906

Johnsen, D. Bruce, cooperative surplus, 337

Johnson, James Turner, military ethics, 1094

Johnson, Mark, cognitive science, 250

Johnson, Samuel, civility, 242

joint action. *See* collective action

joint ownership, self-ownership, 1562

joint supply, public goods, 1413, 1414

Jonsen, Albert R.: casuistry, 188; medical ethics, 1069, 1070; persuasive definition, 1304; principlism, 1379

Jorgensen's Paradox, logic, 1006

Josephus, suicide, 1669

journalism, **915–918**; applied ethics, 81; censorship, 197–199; cultural studies, 365; deceit, 380; freedom of the press, 578–580; nihilism, 1240; secrecy and confidentiality, 1542. *See also* mass media

Journalist and the Murderer, The, journalism, 916

journalist-source relationships, journalism, 916

journals: applied ethics, 83; nineteenth-century British ethics, 745–746

joy: Descartes, 397; feminist ethics, 530; happiness, 645; hate, 659; literature, 1005; puritanism, 1431; Renaissance ethics, 725

Joyful Silence, The, Nietzsche, 1238–1239

Joynt, Carey B., military ethics, 1094

Juan Chi, China, 215

Judah the Pious, Jewish ethics, 914

Judaism: beneficence, 129; Buber, 160–161; Camus, 182; Christian ethics, 222, 223; competition, 277; Hegel, 670; hypocrisy, 820; Jesus, 906, 907; Jewish ethics, 909–915; Levinas, 970; love, 1020, 1026; Maimonides, 1036–1037; moral purity, 1151; Nietzsche, 1237; Paul, 1284, 1285–1286; person, 1294; philosophy of religion, 1310; Renaissance ethics, 724; Spinoza, 1638–1639; suicide, 1669, 1670; technology and nature, 1690; theism, 1699; theological ethics, 1702, 1703; virtue ethics, 1758, 1759; Weber, 1793

Judas, suicide, 1669

Judeo-Christian ethics: competition, 277; conservation ethics, 309; generosity, 601; happiness, 645; love, 1020–1024, 1026; twentieth-century Anglo-American ethics, 769

judges: Bentham, 139, 140; Dworkin, 429–430; philosophy of religion, 1313; precedent, 1367; professional ethics, 1385

judgments: action, 13–15; aesthetics, 28–29; analytic philosophy, 64–65, 66; anger, 67–68; Anselm, 77; Arendt, 84, 85; atheism, 98–99; Augustine, 103; authority, 107–109; autonomy of ethics, 110; Ayer, 117; bad faith, 119; Barry, 125; beneficence, 130; Bentham, 138, 140; business ethics, 173; Cambridge Platonists, 179; coherentism, 252–253; common sense moralists, 267–268; courage, 354, 355; deceit, 380; deliberation and choice, 382, 383, 384; duty and obligation, 427; economic analysis, 435; emotivism, 458; environmental ethics, 470; euthanasia, 493; excellence, 505; fidelity, 544; fiduciary relationships, 548; Foot, 554–555; formalism, 563; forms of consciousness, 565, 566; Frankena, 574; future generations, 588; golden rule, 616; government ethics, 627; happiness, 647; Hare, 651; Hellenistic ethics, 697, 698; Holbach, 779; Holocaust, 780–781; intuitionism, 880–881; Islam, 885; Islamic business ethics, 888; Kant, 930; later Medieval ethics, 719; liberty, 980; loyalty, 1028; metaethics, 1079, 1083, 1084, 1085; moral development, 1120, 1121, 1122; moral dilemmas, 1126; moral education, 1130; moral realism, 1154–1160; moral reasoning, 1160–1163; moral relativism, 1166, 1166–1167; moral sense theorists, 1174, 1176, 1177, 1178; moral terms, 1180, 1181, 1182; mysticism, 1198; negligence, 1224–1225; nineteenth-century Continental ethics, 754; ought implies can, 1266; philosophy of religion, 1313; precedent, 1366–1368; prescriptivism, 1369–1371; prudence, 1399, 1400; reflective equilibrium, 1467–1469; Reid, 1470; Russell, 1527; self-control, 1549, 1550; self-deception, 1551;

Volume key: Volume 1, pages 1–642; volume 2, pages 643–1266; volume 3, pages 1267–1977.

1890

Volume key: Volume 1, pages 1–642; volume 2, pages 643–1266; volume 3, pages 1267–1977.

1891

Volume key: Volume 1, pages 1–642; volume 2, pages 643–1266; volume 3, pages 1267–1977.

1892

Volume key: Volume 1, pages 1–642; volume 2, pages 643–1266; volume 3, pages 1267–1977.

1893

Subject Index

Kohl, Marvin, life and death, 997
Kohlberg, Lawrence: cognitive science, 249; moral development, 1122–1123; moral education, 1129, 1130; psychoanalysis, 1402; Smith, 1597
Köhler, Wolfgang, value theory, 1751
Kohut, Heinz, psychoanalysis, 1403–1404
Kokutai, Japan, 902
Kolenda, Konstantin, Murphy, 1194, 1195
Kolnai, Aurel, twentieth-century Continental ethics, 758
Koran. *See* Qur'an
Korea, Nāgārjuna, 1200
Körner, Christian Gottfried, Schiller, 1537
Korotich, Vitaly, Soviet ethical theory, 1635
Korsgaard, Christine: immoralism, 839; Kantian ethics, 942–943
kosmos, presocratic Greek ethics, 687
Kreutzer Sonata, The, puritanism, *1430*
Kripke, Saul: logic, 1014; moral realism, 1157
Kristeva, Julia, self and social self, 1546
Kropotkin, Pyotr, nature, 1218
Kṣatriya, Hindu ethics, 678, 679
Ku Yen-wu, China, 220
Kuflick, Arthur, autonomy of moral agents, 113
Kuhn, Thomas: commensurability, 258; historiography, 683; intransitivity, 879; moral realism, 1155
Kuhse, Helga, nursing ethics, 1252
Kuki Shūzō, Japan, 903
K'ung Ch'iu, Confucius, 295
K'ung Chung-ni, Confucius, 295
K'ung Fu Tzu (Master K'ung), Confucius, 295
K'ung Tzu, Confucius, 295
kung-ming, Confucian ethics, 290
Kuo Hsiang, China, 215, 216
Kymlicka, Will, multiculturalism, 1191
kyosei, business ethics, 174

La Bruyère, Jean de, passion, 1280
La Mettrie, Julien, nature, 1218
labor: alienation, 48–49; bargaining, 124; blackmail, 152, 153; Engels, 460, 461, 462; exploitation, 516; Marx, 1043, 1046; Marxism, 1049–1054; Nozick, 1246; oppression, 1262; property, 1391–1392; risk analysis, 1516; self-ownership, 1562; threats, 400; value theory, 1750; welfare, 1796–1797; work, 1828. *See also* division of labor; employment; work; working class
Lachs, John, euthanasia, 493, 496
Laclos, Pierre, hypocrisy, 821
Ladd, John: public and private morality, 1412; stakeholder, 1647
Laelius, Roman ethics, 705
laissez faire: evolution, 501, 502; individualism, 848; Marxism, 1048–1049, 1051; Objectivism, 1259; Rand, 1440
Lakoff, George, cognitive science, 250
Lakoff, Sanford, equality, 480
Lamarck, Jean Baptiste de, Darwin, 373

Lamb, James W., freedom and determinism, 576
land ethics, **952–954**; agricultural ethics, 45, 46; conservation ethics, 309, 310; environmental ethics, 469–470; Leopold, 965–966
land mines ban, cosmopolitan ethics, 348
land reform, land ethics, 952
land use: agricultural ethics, 45, 46; land ethics, 952–954
land-community ethics, land ethics, 953
Landesman, Bruce, secrecy and confidentiality, 1542
Landino, Epicureanism, 475
Lane, Rose Wilder, Rand, 1441
Lanfranc, early Medieval ethics, 712
Lang, Berel, Holocaust, 782–783
Lange, Carl G.: emotion, 455; James, 899
Langford, C. H., Frankena, 569
language: analytic philosophy, 64–66; animals, 70; autonomy of ethics, 110; Ayer, 116, 117; Bentham, 137, 138; common sense moralists, 269; conventions, 328–329; deceit, 379–380; emotivism, 458; feminist ethics, 534; Gadamer, 590, 591; journalism, 916; Kantian ethics, 942–943; moral development, 1124; moral realism, 1156–1158; moral reasoning, 1161; moral terms, 1179–1182; Murphy, 1194–1195; oppression, 1263; ought implies can, 1265, 1266; persuasive definition, 1303–1305; plagiarism, 1316–1317; political correctness, 1337, 1338–1339; postmodernism, 1350–1351; prescriptivism, 1369–1371; Prichard, 1373; puritanism, 1430; sexual abuse, 1568; sexuality, 1575; Soviet ethical theory, 1631; Stevenson, 1649, 1650; Taylor, 1686; twentieth-century Anglo-American ethics, 768; value theory, 1751; Westermarck, 1798; Wittgenstein, 1811, 1812. *See also* linguistics; meaning; semantics
Language, Truth and Logic, analytic philosophy, 65
Lanson, Gustave, Voltaire, 1770
Lao Tzu, **955**; China, 211, 212, 213, 214, 215, 216; Chuang Tzu, 230; comparative ethics, 275; competition, 278; military ethics, 1093; Taoist ethics, 1680
Lao Tzu. See Lao Tzu
Lao-Chuang philosophy. *See* Taoism
Laplace, Pierre Simon de, freedom and determinism, 575
Las Casas, Bartolomé de, Vitoria, 1769
Latané, Bibb, social psychology, 1615
Latin America, amnesty and pardon, 58
Latin Church Fathers. *See* Church Fathers
Latin literature, humanism, 801
Lau, D. C., land ethics, 955
Lauwers, Luc, discounting the future, 412
law: analogical argument, 59, 60; Bentham, 137, 139, 140; bioethics, 145; casuistry, 188; censorship, 198; cheating, 205; China, 215; classical Greek ethics, 694; competition, 278; computers, 283; Confucian ethics,

294; consent, 302; conventions, 329; correctional ethics, 343; democracy, 385, 387, 388; Democritus, 389, 390; deontology, 394; dignity, 406; discrimination, 413–414; Donegan, 417; duty and obligation, 424, 425, 428; Dworkin, 429–430; early Medieval ethics, 712, 713–714; etiquette, 487, 488; excuses, 508; feminist ethics, 533–534; fiduciary relationships, 546; freedom of the press, 580; Fuller, 584–585; government ethics, 626; Grotius, 633–634; guilt and shame, 639; harm and offense, 652–655; Hart, 655–657; Hobbes, 774; homicide, 785; human rights, 796, 797; innocence, 856–857; Islam, 883, 884–885; Islamic business ethics, 887–888; Islamic ethics, 889; Islamic medical ethics, 894, 895; Jewish ethics, 909–915; Kant, 930–931, 935; legal ethics, 955–957; legal philosophy, 957–960; legitimacy, 960–961; Leibniz, 963–964; liberalism, 975; libertarianism, 977; Locke, 1007–1009; moral education, 1128; natural law, 1205; negligence, 1224–1225; nineteenth-century British ethics, 741, 742; paternalism, 1282; police ethics, 1333, 1334; political correctness, 1338, 1339, 1340; pornography, 1348; pragmatism, 1363–1364; precedent, 1366–1367; presocratic Greek ethics, 688, 689; privacy, 1381–1382; property, 1390–1393; proportionality, 1394; prudence, 1400; public and private morality, 1410; Pufendorf, 1423; rape, 1444; rational choice, 1447, 1450; Rawls, 1458–1459; right, 1500, 1501; right holders, 1505, 1506; rights, 1506, 1507, 1509; Roman ethics, 706; seventeenth- and eighteenth-century ethics, 731–732, 737–738; social and political philosophy, 1601, 1603; social contract, 1608, 1609–1610; Sophists, 1629–1630; Soviet ethical theory, 1631; suicide, 1669, 1671; technology, 1688; twentieth-century Continental ethics, 764; virtue ethics, 1758; welfare, 1796–1797; William of Ockham, 1802–1803. *See also* civil law; criminal justice; jurisprudence; legal ethics; legal philosophy; moral law; natural law; obedience to law
law enforcement: common good, 265; computers, 283; punishment, 1425–1427. *See also* correctional ethics; criminal justice; police ethics
Law, Liberty, and Morality, Hart, 657
law of equal freedom, nineteenth-century British ethics, 744
Law of Peoples, The, Rawls, 1459
Lawrence, D. H.: persuasive definition, 1304; puritanism, 1429, 1431
laws of nature: causation and responsibility, 194; competition, 278; cradle arguments, 355; Cudworth, 364; Cumberland, 367; Hobbes, 773–777; moral sense theorists, 1173,

Volume key: Volume 1, pages 1–642; volume 2, pages 643–1266; volume 3, pages 1267–1977.

1894

Volume key: Volume 1, pages 1–642; volume 2, pages 643–1266; volume 3, pages 1267–1977.

1895

Volume key: Volume 1, pages 1–642; volume 2, pages 643–1266; volume 3, pages 1267–1977.

1896

linguistic analysis: Christian ethics, 223; metaethics, 1080

linguistics: nineteenth-century British ethics, 740; ought implies can, 1265; postmodernism, 1350–1351; social and political philosophy, 1599, 1600; Soviet ethical theory, 1632; twentieth-century Anglo-American ethics, 768; value theory, 1751

linguistic solipsism, Kantian ethics, 942–943

Lipsius, Justus: neo-Stoicism, 1229, 1230; Renaissance ethics, 726

Lisbon earthquake, evil, 498

literacy, Africa, 35

literary criticism, Baier, 120

literature: historiography, 684; humanism, 801

literature and ethics, **1004–1007**; authenticity, 106; cruelty, 361; deceit, 379, 380; Emerson, 452; emotion, 457; envy, 471; etiquette, 488; feminist ethics, 529; fittingness, 552; guilt and shame, 639; humanism, 801; hypocrisy, 821, 822–823; integrity, 864, 865; Jewish ethics, 912–914; Lucretius, 1029–1030; medical ethics, 1064; moral absolutes, 1113; moral development, 1118; moral dilemmas, 1125; mortality, 1183; narrative, 1201, 1202–1203; nihilism, 1240; pacifism, 1267; plagiarism, 1316–1317; political correctness, 1337, 1338; presocratic Greek, 686, 687; puritanism, 1430, 1431; Rand, 1440, 1441; revenge, 1492; self-deception, 1552; Soviet ethical theory, 1634; Staël, 1644; Thoreau, 1714–1716; tragedy, 1721–1723; transcendentalism, 1724–1727; twentieth-century Anglo-American ethics, 772; Voltaire, 1770; Williams, 1805; women moral philosophers, 1822

litigiousness, legal ethics, 957

Littleton, Christine A., feminist ethics, 534

liturgy, Hindu ethics, 678

Liu Hsiang, Hsün Tzu, 794

Lively, Jack: nineteenth-century British ethics, 741; political systems, 1343

Lives of the Philosophers, Renaissance ethics, 727

living well. *See* eudaimonia

loathing, hate, 660

lobbyists: corruption, 344; government ethics, 627

local-miracle compatibilists, freedom and determinism, 577

Lockard, Joan S., self-deception, 1552

Locke, John, **1007–1011**; applied ethics, 81; atheism, 98; Beccaria, 127; Bentham, 137; children, 208; consent, 299, 300; contractarianism, 321, 323; conventions, 329; correctional ethics, 341; duty and obligation, 425; Edwards, 445; entitlements, 466; equality, 482; fiduciary relationship, 547–548; Foucault, 568; freedom and determinism, 575; Gassendi, 595;

government ethics, 626; Hobbes, 773; homicide, 785; human rights, 796; Hutcheson, 818; individualism, 849, 850; Jefferson, 905, 906; justice, distributive, 920, 923; legitimacy, 961, 962; Leibniz, 964; liberalism, 972, 973, 974; libertarianism, 976; Malebranche, 1037; moral development, 1119; moral education, 1128–1129; moral sense theorists, 1175; mysticism, 1198; natural law, 1209; Nozick, 1246; obedience to law, 1255, 1256; oppression, 1261; Paine, 1272; person, 1294–1295, 1298; police ethics, 1332; political systems, 1341; property, 1391–1392; Pufendorf, 1424; Rawls, 1454; Reid, 1470; religion, 1473; right to life, 1002, 1003; self and social self, 1544; self-defense, 1554; self-ownership, 1561, 1562–1563; seventeenth- and eighteenth-century ethics, 732; social and political philosophy, 1600, 1601, 1602; social contract, 1608, 1610–1611; twentieth-century Anglo-American ethics, 770; virtue ethics, 1759; Voltaire, 1770, 1772; welfare, 1796; women moral philosophers, 1824, 1825; work, 1828

Lockean proviso: Nozick, 1246; property, 1392

Loewer, Barry, logic, 1015

logic: analogical argument, 61–64; coherentism, 252; moral realism, 1154–1155; universalizability, 1734, 1736

logic and ethics, **1011–1017**; Avicenna, 115; Ayer, 116; deliberation and choice, 383; duty and obligation, 424; early Medieval ethics, 712; Gassendi, 596; Jainism, 898; Peirce, 1287; persuasive definition, 1303; public policy, 1418; Russell, 1526; Scheler, 1533; slippery slope argument, 1595–1596; twentieth-century Anglo-American ethics, 769; twentieth-century Continental ethics, 759; universalizability, 1734, 1736; Wittgenstein, 1812, 1814

logic of place, Japan, 903

logic of species, Japan, 903

logical ethical naturalist, naturalism, 1214

logical fallacy, slippery slope argument, 1595–1596

logical positivism: autonomy of ethics, 110; Ayer, 116; common sense moralists, 268; emotivism, 458; moral realism, 1154; nature, 1219; nineteenth-century British ethics, 740; twentieth-century Anglo-American ethics, 768; Wittgenstein, 1812

logos: Hellenistic ethics, 701; natural law, 1206; presocratic Greek ethics, 687; Sophists, 1631; Stoicism, 1653

Lomasky, Loren: human rights, 797, 799; person, 1298

London Metropolitan Police, police ethics, 1332

longing, love, 1017

losers, competition, 278

loss: innocence, 858; life and death, 994, 995; risk, 1513; risk analysis, 1515; risk aversion, 1518–1520

loss of face, guilt and shame, 639

loss of freedom, Gert, 609

loss of honor, honor, 789

loss of pleasure, Gert, 609

Lossky, N. O., Rand, 1440

Lotze, R. H., value theory, 1750

Louis XII, King of France, Machiavelli, 1033

Louis XIV, King of France: Fénelon, 539; Pascal, 1278

Louis, Duc de Bourgogne, Fénelon, 539, 540

love, **1017–1027**; altruism, 52; anger, 68; Aristotelian ethics, 86, 89; Augustine, 104–105; autonomy of moral agents, 113; beneficence, 129, 131; benevolence, 134, 135; biological theory, 147; Brentano, 158; Buddhist ethics, 165; Camus, 182; character, 202; charity, 203, 204; children, 209; China, 211, 213; Christian ethics, 222, 224, 225; common good, 264; Confucian ethics, 290; Cudworth, 364; deontology, 393; Duns Scotus, 421; early Medieval ethics, 710; economic liberty, 983, 984; Edwards, 446; Emerson, 452; emotion, 454, 455, 456, 457; feminist ethics, 529, 535; Fénelon, 539, 540; Feuerbach, 541; fidelity, 544, 545; forgiveness, 561; friendship, 581, 583; Gandhi, 594; gay ethics, 597, 598, 599; golden rule, 614–617; gratitude, 629; happiness, 648, 649, 650; hate, 659, 660–661; hedonism, 666; Hindu ethics, 682; Hume, 804, 809; innocence, 858; interests, 870; Islam, 886; Jesus, 907, 908; Kant, 935; King, 950; later Medieval ethics, 717; life and death, 999; literature, 1005, 1006; Lucretius, 1030; Luther, 1031; Malebranche, 1038; materialism, 1058, 1059; Mencius, 1071, 1072; Mo Tzu, 1104–1105; moral attention, 1115; moral psychology, 1147–1150; moral sense theorists, 1175, 1176, 1178; mysticism, 1197; Niebuhr, 1235; nineteenth-century Continental ethics, 753; non-violence, 1755; Objectivism, 1258; pacifism, 1268; partiality, 1276; passion, 1279–1280; Paul, 1286; personal relationships, 1301; persuasive definition, 1304; Plato, 1319, 1323–1324; Rawls, 1457; reciprocity, 1466; religion, 1474, 1475; Renaissance ethics, 724, 727; resentment, 1483, 1485; Scheler, 1533, 1534; Schelling, 1536; self-deception, 1551, 1552; seventeenth- and eighteenth-century ethics, 730–731, 733, 734, 735, 736, 738; sexuality, 1570, 1571, 1572, 1575; situation ethics, 1586; Sophists, 1629; Soviet ethical theory, 1634, 1635; Spinoza, 1639, 1640; Suárez, 1664; sympathy, 1676, 1678; theological ethics, 1703–1704, 1705; theory and practice, 1707;

Volume key: Volume 1, pages 1–642; volume 2, pages 643–1266; volume 3, pages 1267–1977.

love, *continued*
Thomasius, 1711; twentieth-century Continental ethics, 759, 760, 762, 764; virtue ethics, 1760; Weil, 1795; women moral philosophers, 1822, 1823, 1824. *See also* Christian love; divine love

love of the remote, twentieth-century Continental ethics, 760

Lovibond, Sabina: narrative, 1203; Wittgensteinian ethics, 1814

Loving v. Virginia, privacy, 1381

loving-kindness, euthanasia, 496

Lowenberg, J., Royce, 1525

loyalty, **1027–1029**; American moral philosophy, 54–55; Aristotelian ethics, 86; autonomy of moral agents, 113; business ethics, 172; Christian ethics, 222; classical Greek ethics, 692; conventions, 332; externalism and internalism, 518; fidelity, 543; idealist ethics, 833; integrity, 864; Japan, 901, 902; Jesus, 907; legitimacy, 960, 961, 962; moral development, 1122; moral purity, 1153; partiality, 1275, 1276; personal relationships, 1301; police ethics, 1332; professional ethics, 1385; reciprocity, 1466; self-esteem, 1558; trust, 1730; virtue ethics, 1760; work, 1829

Loyola. *See* Ignatius of Loyola, Saint

Lu Hsiang-shan: China, 219; Chu Hsi, 228; Confucian ethics, 287

Luce, R. W., economic analysis, 437

lucidity, Camus, 182

Lucifer, envy, 472

Lucilius, Seneca, 1565

luck. *See* moral luck

Lucretia, suicide, 1669

Lucretius (Titus Lucretius Carus), **1029–1031**; Epicureanism, 475; Epicurus, 476; free will, 572; Hellenistic ethics, 696–697; literature, 1004, 1005; nature, 1217; Renaissance ethics, 727; Roman ethics, 703, 706–707

Lugoñes, Maria: lesbian ethics, 967; moral purity, 1153

Luhmann, Niklas: power, 1354; trust, 1730

Lukács, Georg: praxis, 1365; self and social self, 1545; twentieth-century Continental ethics, 763

Lukasiewicz, Jan, fate and fatalism, 526

Luke: beneficence, 129, 130; golden rule, 614; hypocrisy, 820; Jesus, 906, 907; love, 1020–1021; theological ethics, 1704

Lukes, Steven, Soviet ethical theory, 1633

lump sum redistribution, economic systems, 441

lun, Confucian ethics, 288, 292

Lun Yü (Analects): China, 211, 214, 219; Confucian ethics, 288–290, 293, 295; Mencius, 1071

lust, puritanism, 1431

Luther, Martin, **1031–1032**; Christian ethics, 225–226; government ethics, 625; liberalism, 972; natural law, 1208; seventeenth- and eighteenth-

century ethics, 731, 732; supererogation, 1673; theological ethics, 1702; Voltaire, 1770

Lutheranism: Christian ethics, 225–226; natural law, 1209; Renaissance ethics, 729

Lu-Wang School: China, 219; Chu Hsi, 228, 229

Luxembourg, Rosa, self and social self, 1545

luxury: civic good, 235; Cynics, 369; seventeenth- and eighteenth-century ethics, 735

Luzzatto, Moses Haim, Jewish ethics, 914

Lyceum, Hellenistic ethics, 699–700

Lycophron, Sophists, 1628, 1629

lying. *See* deceit; lies

Lynch, William, hope, 791

lynching: James, 900; revenge, 1492

Lyons, David: fairness, 521; human rights, 797; twentieth-century Anglo-American ethics, 769

Lyotard, Jean-François, postmodernism, 1351, 1352

Macabees, hypocrisy, 820

Macaulay, Thomas Babington: legal ethics, 955; nineteenth-century British ethics, 740–741

MacCormick, Neil, right holders, 1503, 1505, 1506

Macdonald, G. F., institutions, 859

MacDonald, Margaret, emotivism, 459

Machan, Tibor, Rand, 1442

Machiavelli, Niccolò [di Bernardo dei], **1033–1035**; civic good, 234–235; dirty hands, 407, 409; government ethics, 624, 628; humanism, 802; institutions, 859; Soviet ethical theory, 1633; stakeholder, 1646–1647, 1648; virtue ethics, 1759

MacIntyre, Alasdair C., **1035–1036**; Anscombe, 74; Aristotelian ethics, 86; communitarianism, 270, 271–272; Gandhi, 574; integrity, 864–865; international distributive justice, 875; literature, 1006; loyalty, 1028; narrative, 1203; natural law, 1210; naturalism, 1213; partiality, 1275, 1276; prudence, 1400; psychology, 1408, 1409; self and social self, 1545–1546; theological ethics, 1702; twentieth-century Anglo-American ethics, 772

Mack, Eric: human rights, 799; Rand, 1442

Mackie, J. L.: metaethics, 1083, 1085; metaphysics and epistemology, 1088; moral point of view, 1141, 1142; Russell, 1527; skepticism, 1591; universalizability, 1735; value concept, 1747; weakness of will, 1789; Westermarck, 1798

MacKinnon, Catharine, sexual abuse, 1567

Mackintosh, James: Mill (James), 1098; nineteenth-century British ethics, 741, 744, 745, 746

Maclagan, W. G., love, 1024, 1025–1026

Macpherson, C. B., self and social self, 1545

Macrobius, later Medieval ethics, 715

macroeconomics, public policy analysis, 1421

Mad Ch'anist School, China, 220

Mādhyamika Buddhism, Nāgārjuna, 1200–1201

Madison, James: civic good, 235; elite, 451; liberalism, 973

Madonna (entertainer), materialism, 1059

Magna Carta (England): police ethics, 1332; social contract, 1609

magnanimity: Aristotelian ethics, 87; Aristotle, 96; Hume, 807; theological ethics, 1702; virtue ethics, 1758

Mahābhārata: competition, 278; Hindu ethics, 679, 680; India, 680

Mahāvīra, Jainism, 897

Mahāyāna Buddhism: Buddha, 162; Buddhist ethics, 165–167; China, 216; competition, 277; India, 84717718; Nāgārjuna, 1200–1201; women moral philosophers, 1822

Mahdī, Muḥammad al-, Shī'ism, 1579

Maimonides, Moses, **1036–1037**; Jewish ethics, 912–913; virtue ethics, 1759

Maine, Henry: nineteenth-century British ethics, 746; social contract, 1607

mainstream beliefs, moral relativism, 1165

majority decision: democracy, 386, 388; rational choice, 1448–1449; voluntarism, 1773

Makrina of Neocaesaria, women moral philosophers, 1821–1822

malady definition, Gert, 609

Malcolm, Janet, journalism, 916

Malcolm, Norman, Wittgenstein, 1811

male bias: feminist ethics, 528, 531, 533–537; gay ethics, 598; multiculturalism, 1188, 1190; personal relationships, 1302; political correctness, 1338; principlism, 1380; self and social self, 1546

male comradship, gay ethics, 598

Malebranche, Nicolas, **1037–1039**; Fénelon, 539, 540; seventeenth- and eighteenth-century ethics, 733, 734

malice: Balguy, 122; Bentham, 139; blackmail, 153; freedom of the press, 579; hate, 660, 661; hedonism, 667, 668; resentment, 1483; revenge, 1493, 1494

Malice Objection, hedonism, 667, 668

malicious joy, hate, 659, 660

Malinowski, Bronislaw: institutions, 859; Westermarck, 1798

Mallock, W. H., agnosticism, 44

Mally, Ernst, logic, 1003

Malone, Patrick S., social psychology, 1615

Malthus, Thomas Robert, Darwin, 373

management: business ethics, 173, 174; conservatism, 315; stakeholder, 1645, 1647, 1648. *See also* employment

Mandela, Nelson, civility, 243

Mandeville, Bernard, **1039–1041**; individualism, 850; moral sense theorists, 1174; nineteenth-century British ethics, 746; seventeenth- and

Volume key: Volume 1, pages 1–642; volume 2, pages 643–1266; volume 3, pages 1267–1977.

1898

Volume key: Volume 1, pages 1–642; volume 2, pages 643–1266; volume 3, pages 1267–1977.

master-slave relationship: Hegel, 672;
Objectivism, 1258; self and social
self, 1544; twentieth-century
Continental ethics, 758
masturbation: puritanism, 1430;
sexuality, 1572, 1574
material comforts: emotion, 455;
happiness, 645, 646; Hellenistic
ethics, 701; seventeenth- and
eighteenth-century ethics, 735
material good, life, 993
material goods: justice, distributive, 921,
922; materialism, 1058
material needs, Marx, 1043
material principles of justice, justice,
distributive, 920
material theories, metaethics, 1081
material values, phenomenology, 1306
materialism, **1057–1060**; conservation
ethics, 308; critical theory, 358;
Cudworth, 364; Hobbes, 775, 776;
Holbach, 778–779; mass media,
1055; nature, 1217; puritanism,
1431; transcendentalism, 1725
materialist conception of history: critical
theory, 359; Marx, 1042, 1043–1045,
1046
materials, library, 987–988
maternal virtues, family, 522
maternity leave, feminist ethics, 534
mathematics: Ayer, 116; classical Greek
ethics, 694, 695; economic analysis,
438; engineering ethics, 463, 464; al-
Fārābī, 525; game theory, 591–592;
historiography, 684; Hobbes, 773;
nineteenth-century British ethics, 747;
Pascal, 1278; Peirce, 1287; rational
choice, 1448; Russell, 1526;
seventeenth- and eighteenth-century
ethics, 734; Stewart, 1651
Matheron, Alexander, Spinoza, 1640
Matters of Need, needs, 1221, 1222
Matthew: beneficence, 129, 130;
forgiveness, 562; golden rule, 614;
hypocrisy, 820; Jesus, 907, 908; love,
1020; mysticism, 1197; seventeenth-
and eighteenth-century ethics, 730–
731; theological ethics, 1704
maturation, psychology, 1406
Māturīdī, Sunnīsm, 1673
maturity: children, 210; responsibility,
1487; twentieth-century Continental
ethics, 763
Maurice, Frederick Denison, nineteenth-
century British ethics, 747
maximal hedonism, pleasure, 1326
maximization: game theory, 592; justice,
distributive, 921; moral absolutes,
1113, 1114; stakeholder, 1647;
theory and practice, 1707;
utilitarianism, 1741
maxims: casuistry, 187; Descartes, 397,
398
maximum good: deontology, 391–393,
394, 395; economic systems, 442;
egoism, 448; twentieth-century
Anglo-American ethics, 770, 771
maximum pleasure, economic analysis,
433
May, Larry, collective responsibility, 255,
256, 257
Maya, suicide, 1670

Mayeroff, Milton, altruism, 52
McCarthy, Bernard, correctional ethics,
341
McCarthyism, political correctness, 1338
McCloskey, Henry J., right holders, 1502
McConnell, Terrance, moral pluralism,
1139
McDermott, John, American moral
philosophy, 56
McDowell, John: integrity, 865; moral
realism, 1158; social psychology,
1618; Wittgensteinian ethics, 1814
McGinniss, Joe, journalism, 916
McGuigan, Jim, cultural studies, 366
McLean, Iain, institutions, 862
McTaggart, John McTaggart, idealist
ethics, 830, 833
Mead, George Herbert, **1060–1062**;
pragmatism, 1361; psychology, 1407–
1408; self and social self, 1544–
1545; Tufts, 1732
Mead, Margaret, twentieth-century
Anglo-American ethics, 769
mean: Aristotelian ethics, 87; Aristotle,
92, 93; character, 200–201;
generosity, 601; Jewish ethics, 913;
moral perception, 1137; *phronesis*,
1314; Renaissance ethics, 721–722,
725, 726; temperance, 1694; virtue
ethics, 1758, 1760; virtues, 1764–
1765; women moral philosophers,
1826. *See also* moderation
meaning: analytic philosophy, 64–65;
Ayer, 116–117; emotivism, 458–459;
life, 1000–1002; moral realism,
1154, 1156–1158; moral reasoning,
1161; moral terms, 1180, 1181;
persuasive definition, 1305;
phenomenology, 1307;
postmodernism, 1351; prescriptivism,
1370; Santayana, 1529; Stevenson,
1650; trust, 1731; twentieth-century
Continental ethics, 764; work, 1829–
1831
meaning of life. *See* life, meaning of
meaningful vs. meaningless life:
euthanasia, 493–494; work, 1829–
1831
means and ends: American moral
philosophy, 55; anthropology, 80;
Aristotelian ethics, 87, 88; autonomy
of moral agents, 112; courage, 352;
de Beauvoir, 376; deliberation and
choice, 382; democracy, 387;
deontology, 391, 393, 394; Donegan,
418; double effect, 418–419;
economic analysis, 432; existential
ethics, 512–513; exploitation, 515;
Foot, 555; good, 620; government
ethics, 627; Green, 632; Hume, 811;
intention, 867–868; Kant, 930, 931–
932, 935; Kantian ethics, 940, 942;
liberalism, 974–975; libertarianism,
976; moral reasoning, 1162–1163;
moral sense theorists, 1175; natural
law, 1209; non-violence, 1755;
phronesis, 1314, 1315, 1316; police
ethics, 1333; practical reason[ing],
1356; practical wisdom, 1358–1359,
1360; pragmatism, 1362, 1363;
prudence, 1398; public and private
morality, 1411; public policy analysis,

1420, 1421; punishment, 1425;
rational choice, 1448; rationality,
1451, 1453; rationality vs.
reasonableness, 1452, 1453;
revolution, 1495; sexuality, 1572;
situation ethics, 1587; Soviet ethical
theory, 1633; Stevenson, 1649;
strategic interaction, 1660;
teleological ethics, 1692–1693;
twentieth-century Continental ethics,
762; value concept, 1745, 1746;
virtue ethics, 1757–1758, 1760;
virtues, 1767; voluntarism, 1772; war
and peace, 1786; work, 1831. *See
also* end in itself
means of production: Engels, 460, 461,
462; exploitation, 516; Marx, 1046;
Marxism, 1049; revolution, 1496
means-ends dichotomy. *See* means and
ends
measurement, commensurability, 258,
260
Mecca. *See* Mekka
Mechtild of Magdeberg, women moral
philosophers, 1823
Medea: emotion, 455; weakness of will,
1791
meden agan, presocratic Greek ethics,
686
media. *See* journalism; mass media
mediation, Fuller, 585
medical education, medical ethics, 1068
medical ethics, **1062–1066**; analogical
argument, 59, 60, 61, 62, 63; applied
ethics, 81, 82, 83; autonomy of moral
agents, 113, 114; bargaining, 124;
bioethics, 141–142, 143, 144, 145;
charity, 204; collective responsibility,
256; computers, 284; consent, 302;
conservatism, 315; cruelty, 362;
deceit, 379; dignity, 406; double
effect, 419; euthanasia, 492; fiduciary
relationships, 546; genetic
engineering, 603, 604; Gert, 609;
Hare, 651; honor, 790; Islamic, 894–
895; Jewish, 910; killing and letting
die, 948; library, 989; life and death,
995, 996, 997; narrative, 1204;
nature, 1218; nursing, 1250–1252;
principlism, 1378, 1379; professional
ethics, 1384; public health, 1416–
1417; public policy analysis, 1421;
reproductive technologies, 1476,
1476–1477, 1480; risk, 1513; risk
analysis, 1516; secrecy and
confidentiality, 1542, 1543; sexual
abuse, 1568; slippery slope argument,
1594; suicide, 1669, 1671
medical ethics, historical, **1066–1071**;
Avicenna, 115; Ibn Rushd, 825; Ibn
Tufayl, 826; Islam, 885; Islamic,
894–895; nursing, 1250–1252;
Schweitzer, 1541
medical etiquette, medical ethics, 1069
medical guilds, medical ethics, 1068
medically assisted suicide. *See* physician-
assisted suicide
Medici, Lorenzo de,' Renaissance ethics,
724
medicine. *See* health; health care;
medical ethics; nursing ethics; public
health policy

Volume key: Volume 1, pages 1–642; volume 2, pages 643–1266; volume 3, pages 1267–1977.

1900

Medicus Politicus, medical ethics, 1068
medieval period. *See* Middle Ages
Medina, Islam, 882–883
Medina, Bartolomé de, casuistry, 188
meditation: Buddhist ethics, 164; China, 217; India, 847; Japan, 902; literature, 1004; Roman ethics, 708; women moral philosophers, 1824
Meditations: Marcus Aurelius, 1041; neo-Stoicism, 1230; person, 1294; Roman ethics, 708
meekness: Jesus, 907; resentment, 1483, 1484. *See also* humility
Mehring, Franz, neo-Kantianism, 1227
mei, Confucian ethics, 292
Meiji period, Japan, 901, 902
Meiklejohn, Alexander, freedom of the press, 578
Meilaender, Gilbert: prudence, 1400–1401; virtue ethics, 1761
Meinong, Alexius, value theory, 1750
Meister Eckhart. *See* Eckhart, Meister
mei-te, Confucian ethics, 289, 292
Mekka: Islam, 882, 883, 884; Islamic business ethics, 887
Melanchthon, Philipp: Christian ethics, 223; natural law, 1208; Renaissance ethics, 729
Melanesia, homosexuality, 788
Melden, A. I., right holders, 1504, 1505
Mele, Alfred R.: intention, 867; self-control, 1549; temperance, 1694
Melian Dialogue: international conflict, 872; presocratic Greek ethics, 689
Mellema, Gregory, collective responsibility, 256
Melville, Herman: envy, 471; transcendentalism, 1724
membership, contractarianism, 324
Memmius, Gaius, Lucretius, 1029
memory: animals, 70; mortality, 1184; person, 1295, 1298; prudence, 1399; Stewart, 1651
men: autonomy of moral agents, 114; civic good, 234; Darwin, 374, 375; discrimination, 414–415; family, 522–524; feminist ethics, 528, 531, 533–537; gay ethics, 597–600; homosexuality, 786–788; honor, 789; lesbian ethics, 968; liberalism, 974; library, 989; moral development, 1123; moral education, 1129; personal relationships, 1302; rape, 1443, 1444–1446; sexual abuse, 1567, 1568; sexuality, 1570–1575; violence and non-violence, 1754, 1756; war and peace, 1785
Mencius, **1071–1073**; China, 211, 212, 213, 214–221; Chu Hsi, 228; Confucian ethics, 287, 288, 290, 293; Confucius, 296, 297; Hsün Tzu, 794, 795; Mo Tzu, 1104, 1105; moral absolutes, 1111; Wang, 1781
Mencius, Book of, Chu Hsi, 228, 229
Mencken, H. L., Rand, 1441
Mendelssohn, Moses: Jewish ethics, 914; Schiller, 1538
Meng K'o. *See* Mencius
Meng Tzu. *See* Mencius
Meng Tzu: China, 219; Mencius, 1071
mental calmness: good, 621; Roman ethics, 708

mental capacity, children, 208
mental cruelty: cruelty, 361–362; torture, 1719
mental disability: agency and disability, 36–39; consent, 302; deceit, 380; evil, 498; excuses, 507; free will, 573; Gert, 609; Holocaust, 781–782; moral community, 1117; political correctness, 1337; psychology, 1406; responsibility, 1491; right holders, 1502, 1504, 1505, 1506; rights, 1509; suicide, 1670; theory and practice, 1708
mental health: idealist ethics, 830–834; psychoanalysis, 1404; rationality vs. reasonableness, 1452, 1453; self-esteem, 1557
mental illness: psychoanalysis, 1405; psychology, 1406; suicide, 1668, 1670, 1671. *See also* psychopathology
mental pleasure, Hellenistic ethics, 700
mental reservations, deceit, 379
mental states: Brentano, 157; idealist ethics, 829–834; intention, 866, 867; Kant, 933; meaning of life, 1001, 1002; Murdoch, 1192; Objectivism, 1257; psychoanalysis, 1404–1406; violence, 1753. *See also* mind
mental suffering: cruelty, 361–362; rape, 1445; torture, 1719; violence, 1753
mercy, **1073–1075**; amnesty and pardon, 57, 58; anger, 69; Anselm, 78; Buddhist ethics, 168; Christian ethics, 225; early Medieval ethics, 712; euthanasia, 493–494, 495, 946; forgiveness, 561; Hume, 807; infanticide, 855; life and death, 997–998; Machiavelli, 1033; supererogation, 1673
merit and desert, **1075–1079**; academic freedom, 11–13; Africa, 35; beneficence, 129; discrimination, 414, 415; entitlements, 466; intention, 867; karma, 944–945; legal philosophy, 958; mercy, 1075; moral sense theorists, 117; perfectionism, 1291; plagiarism, 1316–1317; Price, 1372; responsibility, 1487, 1491; self-respect, 1564; Shaftesbury, 1577, 1578; supererogation, 1673–1674, 1675
Meritens, Hortense Allart de, women moral philosophers, 1826
meritocracy, discrimination, 415
Merleau-Ponty, Maurice: Ricoeur, 1499; Sartre, 1531; Taylor, 1685
Merrill, Ronald E., Objectivism, 1258
Merteuil, Marquis de (fictional), hypocrisy, 821
meson, character, 200–201
mestiza, gay ethics, 600
metaethical reasoning, moral reasoning, 1160–1161
metaethical relativism, moral relativism, 1165–1166
metaethics, **1079–1087**; analytic philosophy, 66; applied ethics, 80–81; atheism, 98; Ayer, 117; emotivism, 458; euthanasia, 496; Frankena, 570; Hare, 651; Jewish ethics, 910, 911–912, 913; later

Medieval ethics, 719; libertarianism, 977–978; medical ethics, 1064; moral point of view; moral realism, 1155; moral relativism, 1165–1166; Murphy, 1193; Nietzsche, 1235–1239; philosophy of religion, 1311; skepticism, 1592; Stevenson, 1649, 1650; technology, 1687; twentieth-century Anglo-American ethics, 765; utilitarianism, 1743; Westermarck, 1798
Metamorphoses, weakness of will, 1791
metanarratives, critical theory, 359
metanormative theory, Nietzsche, 1235–1236
metaphor: additivity, 20; Japan, 901; Jesus, 907
metaphysics: the absurd, 7; action, 13; Adler, 22; aesthetics, 31; Anscombe, 74; Anselm, 78; autonomy of moral agents, 112, 113; Avicenna, 115; Ayer, 116; Cambridge Platonists, 180; classical Greek ethics, 695; conservatism, 311, 312; Cudworth, 363–364; Descartes, 396; Edwards, 445; emotivism, 458; Fénelon, 539; Gassendi, 596; Hegel, 674; Heidegger, 676; Hellenistic ethics, 699; historiography, 684; Hobbes, 775, 776, 777; humilty, 815; Husserl, 817; idealist ethics, 829–834; Japan, 903; Kant, 930, 933, 934–936; later Medieval ethics, 716, 718; Leibniz, 963, 964; Malebranche, 1038; materialism, 1059; mysticism, 1197, 1198; naturalism, 1212, 1214; naturalistic fallacy, 1216; nature, 1217; Nietzsche, 1236, 1237; nihilism, 1240–1241; nineteenth-century Continental ethics, 752; Peirce, 1287; perfectionism, 1289; Perry, 1293; person, 1298; Plotinus, 1329; Reid, 1470; religion, 1474; Royce, 1525–1526; Schopenhauer, 1539; seventeenth- and eighteenth-century ethics, 733, 734; sport, 1643; Stoicism, 1656; teleological ethics, 1692, 1693; theism, 1699, 1700–1701; theological ethics, 1705; women moral philosophers, 1826. *See also* metaphysics and epistemology
metaphysics and epistemology, **1087–1093**; autonomy of ethics, 110, 111; bad faith, 118, 119; Cudworth, 363–364; Descartes, 396–398; historiography, 684; Hobbes, 773; Jainism, 898; James, 899; Mill (John Stuart), 1100; Nozick, 1246; Objectivism, 1257; Peirce, 1287; Plato, 1322; Reid, 1470; seventeenth-and eighteenth-century ethics, 733
metaphysics of desert, merit and desert, 1078
metaphysics of experience, Japan, 903
method, beneficence, 131
methodological notions: individualism, 849; moral realism, 1154; Sidgwick, 1581
Mexican War, Thoreau, 1715
Meyer, Philip, journalism, 917
Meyers, Diana, moral purity, 1153

Volume key: Volume 1, pages 1–642; volume 2, pages 643–1266; volume 3, pages 1267–1977.

1901

Miami Herald v. Tornillo, freedom of the press, 580
microeconomics: public policy analysis, 1421, 1422; rational choice, 1447. *See also* cost-benefit analysis
Midas, King (legendary), Nietzsche, 1238, 1239
Middle Ages: casuistry, 188; Christian ethics, 223; conscience, 298, 299; Gewirth, 610; history of Western Ethics, 709–720; honor, 789; humanism, 8091; Jewish ethics, 912–914; liberalism, 974; Maimonides, 1036–1037; medical ethics, 1067; military ethics, 1094; mysticism, 1197–1198; natural law, 1205, 1207–1208; neo-Stoicism, 1229; person, 1294; pleasure, 1329; Renaissance ethics, 728; social contract, 1609–1610; suicide, 1669, 1670; theological ethics, 1702, 1703; virtue ethics, 1758–1759; William of Ockham, 1802–1804; women moral philosophers, 1822–1823. *See also* Scholasticism
middle class: individualism, 848; work, 1828. *See also* bourgeoisie
middle ground. *See* mean
middle way: Buddha, 162; Buddhist ethics, 164, 165, 167; Nāgārjuna, 1200
Midgley, Mary, altruism, 51
Mies, Ludwig von, Rand, 1441
mildness: Aristotle, 96; character, 202
Miles, Robert, racism, 1436
Milesians, presocratic Greek ethics, 687
Milgram, Stanley: Holocaust, 783; social psychology, 1616–1617
militarism. *See* war; war and peace
military draft: amnesty and pardon, 58; war and peace, 1783–1784
military ethics, **1093–1097**; civic good, 234; collective responsibility, 256; competition, 279; computers, 286; conscience, 298; cruelty, 362; etiquette, 487; Holocaust, 783; homicide, 786; honor, 789, 790; moral community, 1117; nuclear ethics, 1247–1249; Roman ethics, 707; terrorism, 1697–1698; torture, 1720; war and peace, 1783–1784, 1785
military life, conservatism, 313
military virtue, courage, 353
Mill, Harriet Hardy Taylor. *See* Taylor, Harriet Hardy
Mill, James, **1097–1098**; democracy, 386; good, 620; government ethics, 626; Mill (John Stuart), 1099, 1100; nineteenth-century British ethics, 740–741, 745, 746; political systems, 1343, 1344; Stewart, 1652
Mill, John Stuart, **1098–1104**; analytic philosophy, 64; animals, 71, 73; applied ethics, 81; Beccaria, 127; beneficence, 130–131; Bentham, 138, 140; casuistry, 189; censorship, 197; children, 208, 209; China, 221; commensurability, 261; common sense moralists, 267, 268; consequentialism, 306; conservation ethics, 308; deceit, 380; democracy,

386; deontology, 392; Emerson, 453; engineering ethics, 464; Epicureanism, 475; Epicurus, 477; equality, 483; evil, 499; existential ethics, 509, 512; externalism and internalism, 518; feminist ethics, 528, 533; final good, 550; freedom of the press, 578; gay ethics, 599; Godwin, 613; good, 620, 622–623; Green, 631, 632; happiness, 644–645, 648–649; harm and offense, 652, 653; Hart, 657; hedonism, 663, 665, 666–667; human rights, 797; Hume, 812; Hutcheson, 818, 819; idealist ethics, 832; individualism, 849; justice, distributive, 921; legal philosophy, 959; liberalism, 972, 973, 974, 975; life and death, 999; logic, 1012; love, 1023; Mill (James), 1097; moral rules, 1168, 1169, 1170; moral sense theorists, 1178; motives, 1186–1187; naturalism, 122; nature, 1218; neutral principles, 1232, 1233; nineteenth-century British ethics, 739, 740, 741–742, 743, 745, 747; pain and suffering, 1269, 1271; Paley, 1273; paternalism, 1282, 1283; perfectionism, 1291; personal relationships, 1300; pleasure, 1328; political correctness, 1339; political systems, 1344; psychology, 1406; public and private morality, 1410; puritanism, 1428, 1429, 1430; rational choice, 1446, 1448; reciprocity, 1465; reflective equilibrium, 1469; right, 1500; right holders, 1505; sexuality, 1573; Sidgwick, 1580; Singer, 1585; social and political philosophy, 1604; Staël, 1644; strategic interaction, 1660; sympathy, 1676, 1677; twentieth-century Anglo-American ethics, 766, 768–769; utilitarianism, 1737–1738, 1739; virtue ethics, 1760; Westermarck, 1799; Wollstonecraft, 1820; women moral philosophers, 1825
Millar, Alan, Butler, 176
Miller, Arthur G., social psychology, 1617
Miller, David, equality, 483
Miller, Norman, social psychology, 1614
Miller, Richard: Engels, 461; Marxism, 1052, 1053; moral realism, 1155, 1158; revolution, 1495, 1496, 1497–1498
Millgram, Elijah, commensurability, 259, 260, 261
Mills, Claudia, racism, 1438
Mill's test, Hutcheson, 819
Mil'ner-Irinin, Ia. A., Soviet ethical theory, 1634–1635
Milton, John: censorship, 197; envy, 471; immoralism, 838; liberalism, 972
Mīmāsā, Hindu ethics, 680
mimesis, critical theory, 359
mind: American moral philosophy, 54; animals, 71, 72, 73; autonomy of ethics, 110; Baier, 121; Cambridge Platonists, 180; Chu Hsi, 229–230; classical Greek ethics, 694;

Cudworth, 364; Emerson, 452–453; existential ethics, 511; externalism and internalism, 518; Hsün Tzu, 794–795; hypocrisy, 823; idealist ethics, 829–834; India, 844; intention, 866, 867; Locke, 1008, 1010; Malebranche, 1038; Mencius, 1072; Nāgārjuna, 1200; Reid, 1470; self-deception, 1551; Spinoza, 1639–1640; suicide, 1670; Wang, 1780, 1781; weakness of will, 1791; Wolff, 1816
Mind (journal), nineteenth-century British ethics, 745–746
mind-body dichotomy: Malebranche, 1037; Objectivism, 1257; person, 1294; Plato, 1325; Plotinus, 1330, 1331; puritanism, 1431
Ming Confucianism: China, 220–221; Confucian ethics, 291
minimal ethics, critical theory, 359
minimal inconveniences, bargaining, 124
minimum standards of provision, needs, 1221–1222
minorities: business ethics, 173; conservatism, 312; democracy, 387–388; discrimination, 413, 414–415; gay ethics, 598, 599; government ethics, 627; groups, 637; human rights, 798; Marxism, 1050; multiculturalism, 1188–1190; oppression, 1262–1263; police ethics, 1335–1336; political correctness, 1337, 1338, 1339, 1340; right holders, 1503; self-respect, 1564; technology, 1688; twentieth-century Anglo-American ethics, 769; war and peace, 1785
minors: abortion, 3; agency and disability, 36; children, 207–210; fiduciary relationships, 547; pornography, 1347, 1348; right holders, 1502, 1503, 1504, 1505, 1506; sexual abuse, 1568–1569
Minow, Martha, self and social self, 1546
Mintz, Anne P., library, 991
miracles: Locke, 1010; Paley, 1273
Mirlees, J. A., economic analysis, 434
mirrors of nature, cradle arguments, 355–356
misanthropy, hate, 661
miscegenation, racism, 1435
Mischel, W. and H., moral development, 1121
misconduct, corruption, 344
misdirection, revenge, 1493
miserliness, Renaissance ethics, 721, 722
misery: hate, 661; Locke, 1008–1009; oppression, 1261
misfortune: death, 377; Democritus, 390
Mishneh Torah, Jewish ethics, 913
misogyny: hate, 661; lesbian ethics, 967; moral purity, 1152; rape, 1445
mission of proletariat, Marx, 1045
missionizing: Epicureanism, 474; Paul, 1284–1285; Vitoria, 1769
mistakes, excuses, 507
mitigating circumstances, excuses, 506, 507
Mittleid, sympathy, 1675
Mitty, Walter (fictional), bad faith, 119

Volume key: Volume 1, pages 1–642; volume 2, pages 643–1266; volume 3, pages 1267–1977.

1902

Volume key: Volume 1, pages 1–642; volume 2, pages 643–1266; volume 3, pages 1267–1977.

1903

Volume key: Volume 1, pages 1–642; volume 2, pages 643–1266; volume 3, pages 1267–1977.

1904

Volume key: Volume 1, pages 1–642; volume 2, pages 643–1266; volume 3, pages 1267–1977.

1905

Subject Index

Volume key: Volume 1, pages 1–642; volume 2, pages 643–1266; volume 3, pages 1267–1977.

1906

Scheler, 1533–1534; skepticism, 1588; sociology, 1619; sport, 1642; strategic interaction, 1662; Suárez, 1663–1664; suicide, 1669; Taylor, 1685–1686; temperance, 1695; theism, 1700–1701; toleration, 1717–1718; twentieth-century Continental ethics, 758, 759–760, 761, 764; value concept, 1747, 1748–1749; value theory, 1751, 1752; Williams, 1805; work, 1828

moral view: constructivism, 318; metaphysics and epistemology, 1090

moral virtues. *See* virtues

moral way of life, Mencius, 1072–1073

moral worth. *See* worth

Moralia in Job, early Medieval ethics, 711

moralism: aesthetics, 24; conservatism, 314, 316; economic liberty, 884–885; legal philosophy, 959; neutral principles, 1233; nineteenth-century Continental ethics, 757; oppression, 1263; resentment, 1484; social and political philosophy, 1604; Soviet ethical theory, 1631–1633; Stevenson, 1649, 1650

Moralität: formalism, 563; Hegel, 670, 671, 672, 673; hypocrisy, 822; psychology, 1409; twentieth-century Anglo-American ethics, 771

morality. *See* ethics and morality; moral point of view; moralism

morality in nature, Balguy, 121, 122

Morality of Law, The, Fuller, 584

morally engaged life, Maimonides, 1036

morally justifiable, justice, rectificatory, 927

morally meritorious person, merit and desert, 1076

morally optimal act, ideal observer, 828

More, Henry, Cambridge Platonists, 179, 180

More, Thomas: Renaissance ethics, 728; suicide, 1669

mores, homosexuality, 786

Morgan, Robin, sexuality, 1573

Morgenstern, Oskar: economic analysis, 433, 435; game theory, 591, 592

Morgenthau, Hans: government ethics, 624, 625; Niebuhr, 1235

Morillo, Carolyn R., egoism, 447

Morris, Charles, pragmatism, 1361

Morris, Herbert, collective responsibility, 256

Morrison v. Olson, government ethics, 628

mortal sin, hypocrisy, 822

mortality, **1182–1185**; death, 377–378; Epicurus, 477; life and death, 993–999; Lucretius, 1030; public health, 1416; Renaissance ethics, 727

Mosaic law: casuistry, 188; Paul, 1284, 1285; Spinoza, 1639

Moses: Calvin, 179; Islam, 883; Jesus, 907; philosophy of religion, 1310, 1311; Renaissance ethics, 729; Spinoza, 1638, 1639

Moses ben Maimon. *See* Maimonides, Moses

motherhood: abortion, 3, 4; de Beauvoir, 376; family, 522–523; feminist ethics,

528, 531, 533, 534, 536; lesbian ethics, 968; love, 1019; moral development, 1123; self and social self, 1546; welfare, 1797. *See also* family; parenthood; pregnancy

motion pictures. *See* film

motivation: altruism, 50, 51; American moral philosophy, 55; anger, 69; Anselm, 77; Aristotle, 92; Augustine, 103; benevolence, 134; classical Greek ethics, 694, 695; common good, 264; competition, 279; desire, 399; economic analysis, 433; economic systems, 440, 442; egoism, 446, 447, 448–449; emotion, 454, 457; envy, 471, 472; excuses, 507; externalism and internalism, 517–518; fidelity, 544; freedom, 575, 576; game theory, 593; gratitude, 630; Hobbes, 775, 777; Holbach, 779; Hsün Tzu, 794; ideal observer, 828; idealist ethics, 833; Kant, 932; Locke, 1009; Luther, 1031; Marxism, 1053–1054; metaphysics and epistemology, 1089–1090; moral development, 1120; moral education, 1129–1130; moral psychology, 1145–1150; moral sense theorists, 1174, 1175; Murphy, 1194; Paley, 1274; partiality, 1276; passion, 1279; psychology, 1406; Pufendorf, 1424; rape, 1445; rational choice, 1450, 1451; rationality vs. reasonableness, 1453–1454; Rawls, 1455; reasons for action, 1462, 1463–1464; religion, 1475; Renaissance ethics, 725; revenge, 1492, 1493, 1494; revolution, 1495–1497; Ricoeur, 1498; self-control, 1549–1550; seventeenth- and eighteenth-century ethics, 733, 734, 735, 737; social contract, 1612; sociology, 1621; Stoicism, 1654; subjectivism, 1665, 1666, 1667; sympathy, 1676, 1678; twentieth-century Anglo-American ethics, 765; utilitarianism, 1738, 1739; virtues, 1765–1766; welfare, 1797; wickedness, 1801; Williams, 1805; wisdom, 1809; Wolff, 1816; work, 1829

motives, **1185–1188**; action, 15; Anscombe, 74, 75; benevolence, 135; Bentham, 140; Butler, 176; Cambridge Platonists, 180; categorical and hypothetical imperatives, 190; character, 200; Clarke, 245; common good, 262; consequentialism, 304, 305; cooperation, conflict, and coordination, 334; cruelty, 361; Crusius, 363; Edwards, 445; excuses, 507, 508; externalism and internalism, 517; Frankena, 570; friendship, 583; guilt and shame, 639; Hegel, 671, 673; Hobbes, 773; Holocaust, 781, 783–784; homicide, 785; Hutcheson, 818; hypocrisy, 823; idealized agents, 836; Jefferson, 905; Jesus, 907; Jewish ethics, 914; journalism, 916; Locke, 1008–1009; medical ethics, 1063; metaethics, 1085; Mill (James), 1098; moral

absolutes, 1114; moral development, 1120; moral sense theorists, 1175, 1176, 1177, 1178; negligence, 1224–1225; nineteenth-century British ethics, 745; partiality, 1276; passion, 1279; personal relationships, 1300; Price, 1372; rationality vs. reasonableness, 1453–1454; Rawls, 1455; Reid, 1470, 1472; religion, 1472, 1473, 1474, 1475; resentment, 1484; revenge, 1493; Rousseau, 1522–1523; Royce, 1525; Schopenhauer, 1539; self and social self, 1545; self-knowledge, 1559; seventeenth- and eighteenth-century ethics, 734, 735, 736, 737; Shaftesbury, 1577, 1578; Smith, 1598; social contract, 1612; subjectivism, 1665, 1666, 1667; supererogation, 1675; sympathy, 1676; Taylor, 1685; trust, 1731

Mou Tsung-san: China, 221; Confucian ethics, 287; Wang, 1781

Mounce, H. O., Wittgensteinian ethics, 1814

mourning, mortality, 1184–1185

movies. *See* film

MPV. *See* moral point of view

Muḥammad, Prophet: Avicenna, 115; Islam, 882–883, 884, 885, 886; Islamic business ethics, 887, 888; Islamic ethics, 889–893; Shīʻism, 1579; Sunnīsm, 1672

Muʻāwiya, Shīʻism, 1579

Muir, John: conservation ethics, 307–309; elite, 450

multiculturalism, **1188–1191**; Hegel, 674; medical ethics, 1070; moral imagination, 1131–1132; moral relativism, 1164–1167; narrative, 1203–1204; political correctness, 1337, 1339; postmodernism, 1352; presocratic Greek ethics, 688; self and social self, 1546; social psychology, 1614; Taylor, 1685; value theory, 1752

Multiculturalism and "The Politics of Recognition," Taylor, 1685

multidimensional ethical forces, Japan, 901

multinational peace keeping, military ethics, 1096

multiple use, conservation ethics, 308

multiple-past compatibilists, freedom and determinism, 576–577

multiplicity: Levinas, 969; postmodernism, 1351

Multiplicity (film), analogical argument, 60

Münsterberg, H., value theory, 1750

Munzer, Thomas, Christian ethics, 225

Murasaki Shikibu, women moral philosophers, 1822

murder. *See* homicide

Murdoch, Iris, **1191–1192**; altruism, 52; emotion, 457; literature, 1004, 1005, 1006; moral attention, 1115, 1116; moral perception, 1137–1138

Murphy, Arthur Edward, **1193–1196**; moral point of view, 1141

Murphy, Jeffrie: consent, 301; hate, 660, 662; right holders, 1505

Volume key: Volume 1, pages 1–642; volume 2, pages 643–1266; volume 3, pages 1267–1977.

1907

Volume key: Volume 1, pages 1–642; volume 2, pages 643–1266; volume 3, pages 1267–1977.

1908

natural obligation: Balguy, 122; Hume, 809. *See also* obligation

natural order, presocratic Greek ethics, 687

natural properties: naturalistic fallacy, 1215, 1216; twentieth-century Anglo-American ethics, 767

natural reason, moral education, 1128

natural resources: conservation ethics, 308–310; cosmopolitan ethics, 346; economic systems, 439; entitlements, 466; environmental ethics, 467–470; future generations, 587, 588; land ethics, 952–953; Leopold, 965–966; libertarianism, 977–998; moral community, 1117; right holders, 1503, 1504, 1505, 1506; self-ownership, 1562. *See also* resource allocation

natural rights: Bradley, 155; children, 208–209; civil rights, 239; correctional ethics, 341; duty and obligation, 425; entitlements, 466–467; fiduciary relationships, 547–548; Gewirth, 611; human rights, 796; Jefferson, 905–906; libertarianism, 976, 977–978; Locke, 1009–1010; oppression, 1261; Price, 1372; psychology, 1407, 1409; right to life, 1002–1003; self-defense, 1554; seventeenth- and eighteenth-century ethics, 732, 733; social and political philosophy, 1601, 1602; social contract, 1609, 1610, 1611; welfare, 1796; women moral philosophers, 1826. *See also* civil rights; human rights; individual rights

natural selection: altruism, 51; biological theory, 146, 147, 149; Darwin, 373–374; egoism, 447; evolution, 501, 502–503; life and death, 995; nineteenth-century British ethics, 739, 740, 744; twentieth-century Anglo-American ethics, 765

natural sin, early Medieval ethics, 713

natural value, Hutcheson, 818

natural virtues: Aristotle, 95; benevolence, 134; virtue ethics, 1760

naturalism, **1212–1215**; Africa, 34; American moral philosophy, 55; analytic philosophy, 65; atheism, 98; autonomy of ethics, 110; China, 215; Cynics, 369; Darwin, 375; emotion, 457; Frankena, 569–570; Hobbes, 775, 776, 778; Hume, 804–805; idealist ethics, 832, 833, 834; logic, 1012; metaethics, 1080, 1081, 1082, 1083, 1085; metaphysics and epistemology, 1087–1091, 1093; Murphy, 1194; nature, 1217–1219; nineteenth-century British ethics, 740; nineteenth-century Continental ethics, 755; psychology, 1406, 1408, 1409; revenge, 1493; Schweitzer, 1540–1541; Soviet ethical theory, 1634; theism, 1700, 1701; twentieth-century Anglo-American ethics, 767–768; value concept, 1747, 1748; value theory, 1750; Vitoria, 1768–1769; Wolff, 1815; Wollaston, 1818

naturalistic fallacy, **1215–1217**; Ayer, 116; biological theory, 146–147, 148; critical theory, 358; evolution, 502; Frankena, 569; logic, 1012; metaethics, 1082; metaphysics and epistemology, 1088; Moore, 1109; naturalism, 1212; reproductive technologies, 1476; social psychology, 1613; twentieth-century Anglo-American ethics, 766

naturalization of morality, nineteenth-century Continental ethics, 757

natural-kind: psychoanalysis, 1404, 1405; psychology, 1408, 1409

nature: aesthetics, 29; alienation, 49; American moral philosophy, 54; animals, 73; Balguy, 121–122; competition, 278; conservation, 307–310; Cudworth, 364; Cynics, 369; equality, 480; evil, 499; Fichte, 543; Hobbes, 773, 774; Japan, 901, 902; natural law, 1205; Schelling, 1536; skepticism, 1587, 1588; Sophists, 1629; Spinoza, 1638–1639; Stewart, 161; Stoicism, 1653; technology, 1690–1691; value theory, 1750; violence, 1753; Wollaston, 1818. *See also* laws of nature; nature and ethics

Nature and Destiny of Man, The, Niebuhr, 1235

nature and ethics, **1217–1220**; agricultural ethics, 45–48; autonomy of ethics, 110; competition, 278; conservation ethics, 307–310; environmental ethics, 467, 468, 469, 470; evolution, 501–503; feminist ethics, 530; fittingness, 552; Grotius, 634; Hellenistic ethics, 698, 701; Leopold, 965–966; moral development, 1119; moral education, 1128; moral sense theorists, 1173, 1174; presocratic Greek ethics, 687, 688, 689; Renaissance ethics, 725; right holders, 1503, 1504, 1505, 1506; Rousseau, 1522, 1523; Schweitzer, 1540; seventeenth- and eighteenth-century ethics, 732; Taoist ethics, 1681–1684. *See also* natural law

nature preservationists, conservation ethics, 308, 309–310

naturopathy, medical ethics, 1069

Nausiphanes, Epicurus, 476

Navarrus, Martin, casuistry, 188

"Nazi personality," Holocaust, 781–782

Nazism: Arendt, 84; Buber, 160; censorship, 198; elite, 451; equality, 482; euthanasia, 492, 496; evolution, 502; genocide, 607; Holocaust, 779–784; homosexuality, 786; infanticide, 855–856; Levinas, 969; loyalty, 1027–1028; medical ethics, 1069; moral purity, 1153; oppression, 1262; racism, 1433; reproductive technologies, 1479; responsibility, 1488; social psychology, 1617; strategic interaction, 1660; terrorism, 1698; value theory, 1752

necessity: excuses, 507; logic, 1013, 1014; self-defense, 1555

needs, **1220–1224**; Africa, 34; altruism, 50; American moral philosophy, 54; Anscombe, 74; atheism, 101; Brandt,

157; care, 185; charity, 203; Christian ethics, 225; collective responsibility, 255; common good, 263, 264; Confucian ethics, 292; conservation ethics, 307–308; conservatism, 313; corruption, 345; critical theory, 358–359, 360; Darwin, 374; economic analysis, 437; economic systems, 443–444; entitlements, 466; equality, 481; family, 523; feminist ethics, 536; fiduciary relationships, 547; generosity, 602; good, 623; Green, 63; happiness, 646–647, 649; interests, 868, 869, 870; international distributive justice, 874, 876; Jesus, 908; Marx, 1043; Marxism, 1049, 1051; mass media, 1055; materialism, 1057, 1058; merit and desert, 1076; moral development, 1123, 1124; Murphy, 1194; nature, 1218; Objectivism, 1259; Plato, 1319; pleasure, 1327, 1328; Plotinus, 1330; postmodernism, 1352; psychology, 1406; reasonableness, 1452; rights, 1511; secrecy and confidentiality, 1542; self-deception, 1552; social contract, 1611; sociology, 1621; Soviet ethical theory, 1634; sympathy, 1677; theory and practice, 1707; tragedy, 1723; transcendentalism, 1726; twentieth-century Continental ethics, 764; value theory, 1752; Voltaire, 1770; Weil, 1795; welfare, 1796–1797

negation of values. *See* nihilism

negative duties: duty and obligation, 425; moral absolutes, 1113; moral rules, 1169; Thomson, 1712–1713

negative emotions: moral development, 1124; resentment, 1482, 1483

negative freedom, Green, 632

negative liberty: liberty, 979–980; Staël, 1644

negative polarity. *See* positive-negative polarity

negative rights: children, 208; Gewirth, 611; human rights, 799; moral absolutes, 1113; right to life, 1002–1003; rights, 1510, 1511; social contract, 1611; work, 1829

negative theology, the absurd, 7–8

negative values: Scheler, 1534; value concept, 1745, 1747, 1748

negativity, resentment, 1482, 1483

negligence, **1224–1226**; children, 209; evil, 498; family, 522; future generations, 587–588; legal philosophy, 958; moral luck, 1135–1136; responsibility, 1490; violence, 1754

negotiation: bargaining, 123–124; compromise, 282; war and peace, 1785–1786

neighbor: Aristotelian ethics, 89; Butler, 175; Christian ethics, 225; cosmopolitan ethics, 348; early Medieval ethics, 710; environmental ethics, 469; envy, 471; Godwin, 513; golden rule, 614–617; Jesus, 908; Kant, 935; Kierkegaard, 947; love, 1020–1021, 1022–1023, 1024, 1025; Luther, 1031; moral attention, 1115;

Volume key: Volume 1, pages 1–642; volume 2, pages 643–1266; volume 3, pages 1267–1977.

1909

Volume key: Volume 1, pages 1–642; volume 2, pages 643–1266; volume 3, pages 1267–1977.

1910

nondeductive arguments, analogical argument, 61, 62, 63
nondescriptivism, prescriptivism, 1369, 1370
non-dictatorship, rational choice, 1449
nonegoistic hedonism, pleasure, 1326–1327
nonexcludability, public goods, 1413
nonexistence, death, 378
nonhuman animals. *See* animals; animals, treatment of
nonimmanent critique, critical theory, 359
noninferential justification, intuitionism, 880–881
noninferential knowledge, metaphysics and epistemology, 1090–1091, 1092
noninterference, Marxism, 1051
nonintervention: international distributive justice, 875; libertarianism, 976; moral relativism, 1166–1167
nonjudgmentalism, moral relativism, 1166–1167
non-maleficence: animals, 71; autonomy of moral agents, 113; deceit, 380; deontology, 392; medical ethics, 1063, 1064; moral absolutes, 1113; moral rules, 1167, 1169, 1170; principlism, 1378, 1379
nonmoral merit, merit and desert, 1076
nonnaturalism: analytic philosophy, 65; intuitionism, 880; metaethics, 1083, 1085; metaphysics and epistemology, 1087
nonpersuasive evidence, bad faith, 118
nonpositive moral laws, later Medieval ethics, 719
nonprofit organizations, public policy analysis, 1420, 1421
nonrational desires, Plato, 1320–1321
nonrational impulses, Aristotle, 93, 94, 95–96
nonrationality, virtue ethics, 1757
nonrenewable resources, economic systems, 439
non-revolutionary militancy, Marxism, 1049
non-self: authenticity, 106; Japan, 904
nonsense, Ayer, 116
non-sentience, land ethics, 953
nonutilitarianism: additivity, 19–20; agent-centered morality, 41; justice, distributive, 921–922; Mill (John Stuart), 1100, 1101; Rawls, 1454–1458; risk aversion, 1519; utilitarianism, 1738, 1740
nonverbal communication: deceit, 379, 380; etiquette, 487; sexuality, 1573
nonviolence: Gandhi, 593, 594; Hindu ethics, 682, 683; India, 846, 847; King, 950, 951; lesbian ethics, 968; life and death, 998; moral development, 1123; pacifism, 1267; public policy, 1418; violence, 1754, 1755–1756; war and peace, 1782, 1785–1786. *See also* violence and non-violence
non-Western thought: bioethics, 142; Buddha, 161–162; Buddhist ethics, 163–168; business ethics, 173–174; China, 210–220; Chu Hsi, 228–229;

Chuang Tzu, 230–231; comparative ethics, 273–276; Confucian ethics, 287–294; Confucius, 295–297; Hindu ethics, 676–683; Hsün Tzu, 793–796; India, 843–848; Jainism, 897–898; Japan, 901–904; karma, 943–945; Lao Tzu, 955; Mencius, 1071–1073; Mo Tzu, 1104–1105; nāgārjuna, 1200–1201; Taoist ethics, 1680–1684; Wang, 1779–1781
normative criticism, critical theory, 358
normative egoism, egoism, 446, 447, 448, 449
normative ethics: applied ethics, 80–83; Christian ethics, 227; evolution, 501; feminist ethics, 529, 531, 532, 534, 536; forms of consciousness, 564–566; Hart, 656; Jewish ethics, 909, 910; Kantian ethics, 942–943; logic, 1016; metaethics, 1079, 1080; naturalism, 1212; Nietzsche, 1235–1239; nineteenth-century Continental ethics, 752; public policy analysis, 1421, 1422; rationality vs. reasonableness, 1452–1453; social contract, 1611; Stevenson, 1649; twentieth-century Anglo-American ethics, 765–766; Westermarck, 1798–1799
normative interest, business ethics, 172, 173
normative issues, metaethics, 1080
normative Judaism, Jewish ethics, 909
normative judgments: Barry, 125; moral terms, 1180
normative jurisprudence, legal philosophy, 957–958
normative moral theories, metaethics, 1081–1083
normative morality: homosexuality, 786; neutral principles, 1233
normative reasons, motives, 1186
normative relativism. *See* moral relativism
normative sciences, Peirce, 1287
normative theory: aesthetics, 24–26; critical theory, 358–360; Hare, 651; harm and offense, 652; motives, 1186; practical ethics, 81, 82; Singer, 1584–1585
normative-evaluative force, alienation, 49
norms, **1242–1245**; agency and disability, 38; alienation, 49; applied ethics, 81, 82; Aristotelian ethics, 89; biological theory, 149; casuistry, 187; China, 211, 216, 218; classical Greek ethics, 692; computers, 283; Confucius, 295, 296; contractarianism, 321; conventions, 331–332; critical theory, 358–359, 360; cultural studies, 366; desire, 399; Dewey, 402, 403, 404; duty and obligation, 425; Dworkin, 430; early Medieval ethics, 711; evolution, 503; existential ethics, 509, 510; feminist ethics, 529, 531–532, 534, 536, 537; forms of consciousness, 564–566; Fuller, 585; gay ethics, 597, 600; golden rule, 616, 617; government ethics, 627; Habermas, 643; Hegel, 673–675; Hindu ethics, 677–678; homosexuality, 786; honor, 789;

human rights, 797, 798–799; Husserl, 817; immoralism, 838, 839; India, 845, 846; institutions, 862, 863; Jewish ethics, 910; journalism, 917–918; Kantian ethics, 942; Lewis, 971; libertarianism, 976; Marxism, 1052; mass media, 1054; Mencius, 1071; metaethics, 1081, 1083; metaphysics and epistemology, 1090; Moore, 1110; moral absolutes, 1112; moral development, 1118, 1120; moral education, 1130; moral pluralism, 1139–1140; motives, 1186; multiculturalism, 1190; natural law, 1205; nineteenth-century Continental ethics, 753, 754–755, 755–756; personal relationships, 1301; phenomenology, 1306; political correctness, 1337, 1338; postmodernism, 1351; presocratic Greek ethics, 688; principlism, 1378; privacy, 1382–1383; professional ethics, 1834–1885; prudence, 1399; psychology, 1407; public and private morality, 1412; rationality vs. reasonableness, 1452; reciprocity, 1464, 1465, 1466; Ricoeur, 1499; Roman ethics, 704, 705; self and social self, 1545; skepticism, 1591; sociology, 1621, 1622; strategic interaction, 1659; Suárez, 1663; technology, 1687; technology and nature, 1691; trust, 1730; twentieth-century Continental ethics, 763, 764; Walzer, 1777, 1778
Norris, John, women moral philosophers, 1824
Norse myth, competition, 277
Norton, Bryan G., environmental ethics, 468
nothing, nihilism, 1240
not-I, Fichte, 542
Novak, William, cooperative surplus, 337
Novalis, Fichte, 543
novels: hypocrisy, 821; integrity, 865; literature, 1005–1006
Nowell-Smith, P. H.: Anscombe, 75; Frankena, 570; Murphy, 1195
Nozick, Robert, **1245–1247**; agent-centered morality, 41; coercion, 247; communitarianism, 270; deontology, 391, 393; entitlements, 465–466; envy, 471; equality, 482; euthanasia, 493; fairness, 521; human rights, 799; justice, distributive, 921, 923–924; justice, rectificatory, 927; land ethics, 952; life and death, 994; moral absolutes, 1113; property, 1391, 1392; Rand, 1442; right, 1501; social contract, 1610; twentieth-century Anglo-American ethics, 770; work, 1828, 1829
nuclear ethics, **1247–1250**; academic freedom, 11; discounting the future, 411; future generations, 586, 588; genetic engineering, 606; genocide, 607; life and death, 997; pacifism, 1267; public policy, 1418; risk analysis, 1515, 1516; social and political philosophy, 1600; technology, 1687, 1688, 1689; war and peace, 1786–1788

Volume key: Volume 1, pages 1–642; volume 2, pages 643–1266; volume 3, pages 1267–1977.

Subject Index

nuclear family, family, 522
nuclear power plants: nuclear ethics, 1249; risk analysis, 1515, 1516; technology, 1688
nuclear war. *See* nuclear ethics
nuclear waste disposal: discounting the future, 411; nuclear ethics, 1249
nuclear weapons. *See* nuclear ethics
numerical goals, discrimination, 414, 415
Nuremberg Code, medical ethics, 1069
Nuremberg war crimes trials: collective responsibility, 256; Holocaust, 781
nursing ethics, **1250–1253**; bioethics, 142, 145
nurturing. *See* care
Nussbaum, Martha: Aristotelian ethics, 87, 88, 89; commensurability, 260, 261; emotion, 455, 457; Gandhi, 594; justice, distributive, 920–921; moral luck, 1134, 1135; moral perception, 1138; Murdoch, 1192; narrative, 1201; Seneca, 1565, 1566
nutrition: agricultural ethics, 45, 47. *See also* famine; food; hunger
nutrition withdrawal, analogical argument, 59, 60, 63

Oakeshott, Michael: government ethics, 626; idealist ethics, 830
obedience: authority, 108; Cambridge Platonists, 179; children, 208; civic good, 233; classical Greek ethics, 692; conventions, 329; Crusius, 363; early Medieval ethics, 711; feminist ethics, 530; Holocaust, 783; Islamic ethics, 893; Jesus, 907; loyalty, 1028; Mo Tzu, 1105; moral purity, 1151, 1152; moral rules, 1169; mysticism, 1197; nursing ethics, 1250; religion, 1474–1475; resentment, 1482; social psychology, 1616–1617; theological ethics, 1703; work, 1828
obedience to law, **1254–1257**; amnesty and pardon, 58; cheating, 205–207; civic duties, 241; civil disobedience, 236–237; Democritus, 389–390; Gert, 611; Godwin, 613; good, 623; guilt and shame, 639; Hobbes, 775; Hume, 807; Jewish ethics, 910, 914; Kant, 931–932; Kantian ethics, 940; legitimacy, 960; Locke, 1008; moral education, 1128; moral sense theorists, 1178; prudence, 1400; public policy, 1418; Rawls, 1459; reciprocity, 1464, 1466; seventeenth- and eighteenth-century ethics, 731–732; social contract, 1608, 1609–1610; Sophists, 1629, 1630; Soviet ethical theory, 1631–1631; Suárez, 1663; Thomasius, 1711–1712; virtue ethics, 1758, 1759, 1761
objectification, sexuality, 1571, 1574
objective correlate, Husserl, 816
objective idealism, Scheler, 1535
objective oppression, oppression, 1261
objective prescriptions, weakness of will, 1789
objective spirit, Hegel, 671
objective values, James, 899, 900
objective wrongness, negligence, 1225
objectively bad transactions, bargaining, 124

objectives: practical reason[ing], 1356; rights, 1507, 1510; risk analysis, 1516
Objectivism, **1257–1260**; Hartmann, 658; Hegel, 673; Hobbes, 774, 775, 777; Islamic ethics, 892; moral realism, 1156, 1157, 1158; Objectivism, 1257; Rand, 1440, 1441–1442; Russell, 1527; theism, 1700
objectivity: alienation, 48; autonomy of ethics, 110, 113; constructivism, 319, 320; emotion, 456; happiness, 648–650; metaphysics and epistemology, 1087; negligence, 1224, 1225; perfectionism, 1288, 1289; political correctness, 1338; psychology, 1409; reasons for action, 1463–1464; religion, 1473; Russell, 1527; Stewart, 1651; twentieth-century Anglo-American ethics, 767; value concept, 1747; Wittgensteinian ethics, 1814; work, 1831
obligation: Balguy, 122; beneficence, 129–130, 131; benevolence, 136; Bentham, 137; consent, 300, 302; conventions, 330, 332; cosmopolitan ethics, 346, 348; courage, 354; Crusius, 362–363; duty and obligation, 424–425; fidelity, 544; Godwin, 612; good, 623; government ethics, 626, 627, 628; Hare, 651; Hobbes, 774, 775; Holbach, 778–779; homicide, 785, 786; honor, 788; hope, 793; Hume, 809; Hutcheson, 818; ideal observer, 827–828; idealized agents, 836; immoralism, 839, 840; India, 848; integrity, 865; international distributive justice, 876; Islam, 884; James, 900; Jesus, 908; Jewish ethics, 911, 914; Kant, 929–931, 934; Kantian ethics, 939, 941; Kierkegaard, 946; legal ethics, 956, 957; Locke, 1009, 1010; logic, 1012–1013, 1014, 1015, 1016; Marcus Aurelius, 1041; metaethics, 1085, 1086; Mill (John Stuart), 1103; moral dilemmas, 1126; moral pluralism, 1138, 1139; moral sense theorists, 1174, 1175, 1176; motives, 1186; natural law, 1205, 1207, 1208, 1209, 1210; nature, 1219; nineteenth-century Continental ethics, 752, 756; norms, 1243–1244; obedience to law, 1254–1256, 1255; oppression, 1262; personal relationships, 1301–1302; philosophy of religion, 1312; postmodernism, 1352; Prichard, 1373; principlism, 1379; promises, 1387–1389; public and private morality, 1412; public goods, 1415; Pufendorf, 1423; reciprocity, 1464, 1465, 1466; religion, 1474; Ricoeur, 1499; right, 1500, 1501; right holders, 1504, 1505; secrecy and confidentiality, 1542; self and social self, 1546, 1547; seventeenth- and eighteenth-century ethics, 732, 735; Shaftesbury, 1578; social contract, 1607, 1608; Sophists, 1630; Soviet ethical theory, 1631; stakeholder, 1648; subjectivism, 1666; theological

ethics, 1702, 1703, 1704, 1705; theory and practice, 1708; Thomasius, 1711–1712; Thomson, 1712–1713; trust, 1729–1730; twentieth-century Continental ethics, 764; utilitarianism, 1738, 1739–1740, 1742–1743; value concept, 1748; value theory, 1751; Weil, 1795; William of Ockham, 1803; work, 1829. *See also* duty and obligation
oblique intention, intention, 868
O'Brian, William V., military ethics, 1094
obscenity, pornography, 1348
observation, moral realism, 1155
observation by others: American moral philosophy, 55; ideal observer, 827–829; Mead, 1061; moral sense theorists, 1176, 1177, 1178; Smith, 1598; social psycholgy, 1613–1618; sociology, 1621
observational learning, moral development, 1121
obstacles, wisdom, 1808–1809
obstruction, liberty, 978–979
occasionalism, Malebranche, 1037
occupational risk: business ethics, 173; risk analysis, 1516–1517; technology, 1689; work, 1829
occupational segregation, discrimination, 413, 414–415
occupations: work, 1826, 1827. *See also* employment; professional ethics
Ockham, William of. *See* William of Ockham
O'Connor, Frank, Rand, 1441
O'Connor, Timothy, free will, 572
Octavian, Roman ethics, 703
odium, hate, 660
Odysseus, presocratic Greek ethics, 686
Odyssey, The, historiography, 684
Oedipus: guilt and shame, 639; Hegel, 672; moral luck, 1136; sexual abuse, 1568
Oedipus complex, Westermarck, 1799
Oedipus Rex, guilt and shame, 639
offense. *See* harm and offense
offenses: harm and offense, 654–655; punishment, 1425–1427; revenge, 1493; social and political philosophy, 1604
offer: bargaining, 123; blackmail, 151
officium, Roman ethics, 705
Ogden, C. K.: analytic philosophy, 65; emotivism, 458; Stevenson, 1650
oikeiosis: children, 208; Stoicism, 1653
Okin, Susan Moller, egoism, 449
Old Academy, Cicero, 232
Old Testament. *See* Bible; Hebrew Bible
Oldenquist, Andrew, partiality, 1275, 1276
oligarchy, political systems, 1342
Oliner, Samuel and Pearl, altruism, 51
Olson, Mancur, Jr.: cooperation, conflict, and coordination, 335; Marxism, 1053; rational choice, 1447, 1450
Olympus, presocratic Greek ethics, 687
omissions: deceit, 379; oppression, 1262; voluntary acts, 1774, 1775. *See also* acts and omissions
omnipotence: biological theory, 149; Cudworth, 364; Duns Scotus, 421;

Volume key: Volume 1, pages 1–642; volume 2, pages 643–1266; volume 3, pages 1267–1977.

1912

evil, 498, 499, 500–501; fittingness, 552; Islam, 885; philosophy of religion, 1311, 1312; Spinoza, 1639; Sunnīsm, 1673; theism, 1699; theological ethics, 1705

omniscience: early Medieval ethics, 712; freedom and determinism, 575; ideal observer, 829; philosophy of religion, 1310, 1312; Spinoza, 1639; theism, 1699

On Anger, Seneca, 1565–1566

On Good Spirits, classical Greek ethics, 691

On Liberty: beneficence, 131; harm and offense, 652; individualism, 849; legal philosophy, 959; Mill, 1099, 1100; paternalism, 1282; public and private morality, 1410; women moral philosophers, 1825

On Nature or on Not-being, presocratic Greek ethics, 689

On Right and Wrong, nineteenth-century British ethics, 747

On the Indians, Vitoria, 1769

On the Morals of the Catholic Church, early Medieval ethics, 710

On the Nature of Things: Lucretius, 1029; nature, 1217; Renaissance ethics, 727; Roman ethics, 703, 706–707

On the Origin of Species. See Origin of Species

On the Social Contract. See Social Contract, The

On Tranquility of Mind, Roman ethics, 707

On Truth, Sophists, 1628

onanism, sexuality, 1572

One (Good): mysticism, 1197; Plotinus, 1329, 1330

one person, one vote: equality, 484; Mill (John Stuart), 1100

O'Neill, Eugene, self-deception, 1552

O'Neill, Onora: civility, 243; twentieth-century Anglo-American ethics, 771

Onesimus, Paul, 1286

on-line databases, library, 988, 990–991

ontology: bad faith, 118, 119; existential ethics, 510, 511–514; Hobbes, 773; Malebranche, 1038; metaethics, 1083–1084; mortality, 1183, 1185; Pufendorf, 1423; Royce, 1525; Sartre, 1531, 1532; value theory, 1751

ontotheology, Schelling, 1536

open marriages, fidelity, 545

open question argument: metaethics, 1082; metaphysics and epistemology, 1088–1089; Moore, 1109

openness: democracy, 385; non-violence, 1756

operationalism, metaphysics and epistemology, 1091

opiate abuse, Kant, 935

opinion: honor, 789, 790. *See also* public opinion

opportunity. *See* equal opportunity

opposites, Taoist ethics, 1682

opposition, competition, 277

oppression, **1261–1264**; beneficence, 129; Burke, 169; Christian ethics, 227; competition, 279; cosmopolitan ethics, 346; critical theory, 358;

cultural studies, 366; elite, 451; environmental ethics, 470; fairness, 521; Gandhi, 594; Godwin, 612; Hindu ethics, 682; human rights, 798; King, 950; Locke, 1007; multiculturalism, 1189, 1190; narrative, 1202; neutral principles, 1233; political correctness, 1339; praxis, 1365; racism, 1436, 1437; reciprocity, 1466; revolution, 1495, 1497; Rousseau, 1522; self and social self, 1546; social and political philosophy, 1604; social contract, 1611; twentieth-century Continental ethics, 762; war and peace, 1785; Weil, 1795; Wollstonecraft, 1820; women moral philosophers, 1823

optimism: Descartes, 397; hope, 792; King, 950; nineteenth-century Continental ethics, 753; trust, 1729

optimization thesis, deontology, 393

oral tradition: etiquette, 488; Jesus, 906

order: conservatism, 315; cooperation, conflict, and coordination, 335; cooperative surplus, 337; Malebranche, 1038

order of the universe, Marcus Aurelius, 1042

orderliness, Plato, 1320, 1321

orders of creation, Christian ethics, 225

ordinality: economic analysis, 433, 434–437; economic systems, 441; game theory, 592, 593; rational choice, 1448–1449, 1450; risk analysis, 1516, 1517; strategic interaction, 1662. *See also* hierarchies

ordinary blackmail, blackmail, 152, 153

ordinary language: common sense moralists, 269; Prichard, 1373; Sidgwick, 1580

ordinary morality, common sense moralists, 266–269

ordinary vices, hypocrisy, 823

ordine, civic good, 234

orexis: deliberation and choice, 382; desire, 398

organ transplantation: economic liberty, 982–983, 984; Islamic medical ethics, 895; medical ethics, 1062, 1063, 1069

organic groups, communitarianism, 270–271

organic unity, **1264–1265**; additivity, 20; Brentano, 158; twentieth-century Anglo-American ethics, 766. *See also* unity

organization: business ethics, 170–174; groups, 637; Holocaust, 783; military ethics, 1093; paternalism, 1282; Perry, 1293; public and private morality, 1412; public policy analysis, 1420, 1421; right holders, 1502, 1503–1504; social contract, 1607; stakeholder, 1645–1649; suicide, 1669; twentieth-century Continental ethics, 759; work, 1830

organization values, business ethics, 172, 173

"oriental morality," Japan, 901

Origen: moral purity, 1152; women moral philosophers, 1821–1822

Origin of Species: agnosticism, 43; biological theory, 147; Darwin, 373, 374; evolution, 501; nineteenth-century British ethics, 743, 744; women moral philosophers, 1825

Origin of the Family, Private Property and the State, The, feminist ethics, 528

original acquisition, property, 1391

original position: idealized agents, 836; Rousseau, 1522

original sin: Augustine, 102; character, 201; common sense moralists, 267; Descartes, 397; evil, 499; MacIntyre, 1035; Nietzsche, 1236; puritanism, 1429; Renaissance ethics, 729; seventeenth- and eighteenth-century ethics, 731; wisdom, 1808

originality: Godwin, 614; individualism, 848; plagiarism, 1316–1317

Orphic cult, moral purity, 1152

Ortega y Gasset, José, authenticity, 106

Orwell, George: hate, 660; self-deception, 1551

ostinazione, civic good, 234

Othello, hypocrisy, 821

Other, concept of the: de Beauvoir, 376; feminist ethics, 537; Levinas, 969–970; moral purity, 1152; mortality, 1184; political correctness, 1339; twentieth-century Continental ethics, 761

other, ethical relationship with. *See* other-regarding

otherness: alienation, 49; bad faith, 118, 119

other-regarding: altruism, 50–53; Aristotle, 96–97; beneficence, 128–132; benevolence, 134–136; Bentham, 139–140; children, 210; cosmopolitan ethics, 346–349; deceit, 381; ethics and morality, 485, 486; existential ethics, 512; golden rule, 614–617; good, 621–622; Green, 631–632; harm and offense, 652–653; ideal observer, 827–829; Jainism, 898; Jesus, 907–908; Jewish ethics, 914; Lewis, 971; love, 1018; Mencius, 1073; Mo Tzu, 1104–1105; moral attention, 1115–1116; moral development, 1120, 1124; moral education, 1129; moral imagination, 1133; moral psychology, 1146–1147, 1148–1150; moral saints, 1172; moral sense theorists, 1174–1178; needs, 1221–1223; Plato, 1322, 1323–1324, 1325; postmodernism, 1352; Protagoras, 1396; reasonableness, 1452; Reid, 1471; resentment, 1484; Russell, 1528; self-control, 1549; self-respect, 1564; Shaftesbury, 1577; social psychology, 1613–1618; Stoicism, 1653; suicide, 1668; supererogation, 1674; sympathy, 1676, 1677; theory and practice, 1707; twentieth-century Continental ethics, 761; utilitarianism, 1737; violence and non-violence, 1755; Wolff, 1816–1817. *See also* neighbor; personal relationships; self and social self

Volume key: Volume 1, pages 1–642; volume 2, pages 643–1266; volume 3, pages 1267–1977.

1913

others, observation by. *See* observation by others; spectator point of view

Otto, Rudolf, religion, 1473

ought: analytic philosophy, 64, 65, 66; Anscombe, 74, 75; duty and obligation, 423–428; Hart, 656; logic, 1013; moral reasoning, 1161; moral relativism, 1166; moral terms, 1180, 1181; naturalism, 1212; naturalistic fallacy, 1216; practical reason[ing], 1355, 1356; reasons for action, 1462; Royce, 1525; value theory, 1751; weakness of will, 1789. *See also* is/ought problem

ought implies can, **1265–1266**; Augustine, 102, 104; categorical and hypothetical imperatives, 190; ethics and morality, 485; Hobbes, 774; Kant, 930; moral dilemmas, 1126; moral luck, 1135; nineteenth-century British ethics, 744; rationality vs. reasonableness, 1453; Williams, 1806

Our Mutual Friend, hypocrisy, 821

outcomes: economic analysis, 433, 437; fairness, 420; Foot, 555; game theory, 591, 592; hope, 791–792; inequality, 852; institutions, 862; Marxism, 1048–1049; negligence, 1224; political systems, 1343–1345; power, 1353; risk, 1513–1515; risk analysis, 1515–1518; risk aversion, 1518–1520; self-ownership, 1563; situation ethics, 1587; social contract, 1612; strategic interaction, 1659, 1660, 1662; subjectivism, 1667; suicide, 1670; Wolff, 1816. *See also* ends; means and ends

Outlines of the History of Ethics for English Readers, nineteenth-century British ethics, 746

outsiders, international distributive justice, 875

Ou-yang Ching-wu, China, 221

ova donation: analogical argument, 61, 63; family, 522; reproductive technologies, 1475–1480

overman: existential ethics, 510; Nietzsche, 1238, 1239

Oversoul, conservation ethics, 307

Ovid, weakness of will, 1791

ownership: property, 1390–1393; self-ownership, 1561–1563

Oxford Intuitionists, Prichard, 1373

Oxford Realists, Prichard, 1373

Oxford University: Green, 631, 632; Taylor, 1684, 1685; twentieth-century Anglo-American ethics, 766, 770, 772

Oyster Objection, hedonism, 666

ozone shield, conservation ethics, 310

pacifism, **1267–1269**; Anscombe, 76; civility, 243; conscience, 298; Gandhi, 593, 594; Jesus, 908; life and death, 995, 998, 999; moral absolutes, 1111; public policy, 1418; right to life, 1003; self-defense, 1552; twentieth-century Anglo-American ethics, 770; war and peace, 1782, 1785–1786, 1788. *See also* nonviolence

Padgug, Robert, sexuality, 1575

paganism: Abelard, 2; Avicenna, 115, 116; Fénelon, 540; Islam, 882; Jewish ethics, 911; later Medieval ethics, 715; Renaissance ethics, 728, 729

Pai-chang, Buddhist ethics, 167

pain: abortion, 5; additivity, 20; agricultural ethics, 47; Anselm, 77; Bentham, 137, 138; classical Greek ethics, 691; cruelty, 361; deontology, 393; egoism, 446; emotion, 455, 456; Epictetus, 473; Epicureanism, 474; Epicurus, 477; Gert, 609; good, 620, 621, 623; happiness, 647; hate, 659; hedonism, 662–668; Hellenistic ethics, 700, 701; human rights, 798; ideal observer, 828; idealist ethics, 830, 831, 834; India, 844; Kant, 933; Locke, 1008–1009, 1010; Mill (John Stuart), 1101; moral community, 1117; moral education, 1129; moral reasoning, 1163; moral rules, 1169; naturalistic fallacy, 1215; nature, 1218; person, 1296; Plato, 1320; psychology, 1406; puritanism, 1429; Renaissance ethics, 727; Roman ethics, 706; self-control, 1548; seventeenth- and eighteenth-century ethics, 735; sexuality, 1571; Socrates, 1626; utilitarianism, 1738–1739; violence and non-violence, 1754; Voltaire, 1770; Wollaston, 1818

pain and suffering, **1269–1271**; animals, 71; atheism, 101; China, 217; Cicero, 232; cradle arguments, 356; cruelty, 361; Cyrenaics, 371, 372; death, 377; early Medieval ethics, 712; emotion, 456; environmental ethics, 468; *eudaimonia,* 489; euthanasia, 492–497; evil, 498, 499–500; fittingness, 552, 553; Gert, 609; harm and offense, 654; hate, 661–662; hedonism, 667; Hindu ethics, 678; impartiality, 842; killing and letting die, 949; Malebranche, 1038; nineteenth-century Continental ethics, 753; suicide, 1661; sympathy, 1675, 1678; theism, 1700; torture, 1719–1720; violence, 1754

Paine, Thomas [Tom], **1271–1273**; Godwin, 612

Pakistan, Islamic medical ethics, 895

Paley, Grace, pacifism, 1267

Paley [variant: Payley], William, **1273–1275**; Darwin, 374; nineteenth-century British ethics, 739, 741; philosophy of religion, 1311; religion, 1474; seventeenth- and eighteenth-century ethics, 735; theism, 1700; theological ethics, 1702

Pamphilus, Epicurus, 476

Panaetius: Cicero, 232; natural law, 1206; Roman ethics, 705–706; Stoicism, 1652, 1656

Pandora's jar, evil, 498, 499

Pangloss, Dr. (fictional), fittingness, 553

pantheism, Schelling, 1536

papal encyclicals, Christian ethics, 224

parables, Jesus, 907

paradigm cases: casuistry, 187, 188; conventions, 330; moral rules, 1168

paradigms: Jesus, 907; tragedy, 1721

paradox: the absurd, 7, 8; aesthetics, 29; blackmail, 151–152; classical Greek ethics, 693; deterrence, 401; existential ethics, 510; logic, 1013–1014; moral absolutes, 1113; nineteenth-century British ethics, 739; oppression, 1263; Socrates, 1623–1624; stakeholder, 1647–1648; twentieth-century Anglo-American ethics, 769; twentieth-century Continental ethics, 762; war and peace, 1783; wickedness, 1801; wisdom, 1807

"Paradoxes of Derived Obligation, The," logic, 1013–1014

parallel examples, killing and letting die, 948

pardon. *See* amnesty and pardon

parens patriae doctrine, fiduciary relationships, 547

Parent, William, privacy, 1382

parenthood: analogical argument, 63; anthropology, 80; Aristotelian ethics, 89; children, 208–210; Christian ethics, 225; Confucian ethics, 289, 290; Confucius, 295; cosmopolitan ethics, 348; duty and obligation, 426; early Medieval ethics, 712; entitlements, 466; family, 522–524; feminist ethics, 528, 531, 533, 534, 536, 537; fiduciary relationships, 547; fittingness, 553; happiness, 648; homosexuality, 787; Japan, 901–902; love, 102, 1019, 1024; Mencius, 1072, 1073; Mo Tzu, 1104, 1105; moral development, 1120, 1121, 1122, 1124; moral education, 1129; moral psychology, 1148, 1149; partiality, 1277; personal relationships, 1299, 1301; privacy, 1381; reciprocity, 1464, 1466; reproductive technologies, 1475–1480; right holders, 1503, 1505; rights, 1509; sympathy, 1677. *See also* motherhood; reproduction (biological); reproductive rights

Pareto, Vilfredo: economic analysis, 435; economic systems, 440; game theory, 592; libertarianism, 977; rational choice, 1448, 1449

Pareto criterion (optimal): economic analysis, 435, 436, 437; economic systems, 440, 441, 442; rational choice, 1448, 1449; Rawls, 1456

Parfit, Derek: additivity, 19; Arendt, 85; Baier, 120; discounting the future, 411; egoism, 448; inequality, 851, 853; institutions, 861; person, 1298; twentieth-century Anglo-American ethics, 772

Paris Commune: Marxism, 1050, 1052; revolution, 1495

parity of reasons, killing and letting die, 9458

Parker, DeWitt H.: Frankena, 569, 570; value theory, 1751

Parker, Robert, moral purity, 1151

parliamentary democracies, Marxism, 1049, 1050, 1053

Parmenides: classical Greek ethics, 690; literature, 1004; presocratic Greek ethics, 688

Volume key: Volume 1, pages 1–642; volume 2, pages 643–1266; volume 3, pages 1267–1977.

parole, correctional ethics, 340, 341–342

Parsons, Talcott: power, 1354; sociology, 1621

partiality, **1275–1277**; academic ethics, 9; corruption, 344; family, 523; feminist ethics, 531, 536; Hume, 813; impartiality, 841–843; Marxism, 1050; Mencius, 1073; Mo Tzu, 1105; stakeholder, 1647–1648; strategic interaction, 1659; twentieth-century Anglo-American ethics, 770; wisdom, 1807

participatory democracy: civic good, 234; liberalism, 973

particular volitions, Malebranche, 1038

particular-interest principle, infanticide, 854

particularism: Adler, 22; Christian ethics, 224; intuitionism, 880; personal relationships, 1302

partisanship, legal ethics, 956, 957

Pascal, Blaise, **1278–1279**; casuistry, 189; Descartes, 398; existential ethics, 509; hypocrisy, 822; Locke, 1008, 1009, 1010; moral absolutes, 1112; religion, 1474; Scheler, 1533; slavery, 1593

Pascal's wager: Locke, 1010; Pascal, 1278

Paskins, Barrie A., terrorism, 1697

passion, **1279–1281**; anger, 68, 69; Buddha, 161; emotion, 456; Gandhi, 594; Hellenistic ethics, 699; Hobbes, 773, 777; Holbach, 779; hope, 791; Hume, 805, 809, 812–813; ideal observer, 827; lesbian ethics, 968; liberty, 979; moral reasoning, 1162; moral sense theorists, 1174, 1175, 1178; neo-Stoicism, 1230–1231; Nietzsche, 1239; partiality, 1275; *phronesis*, 1314, 1315; presocratic Greek ethics, 686; pride, 1375, 1377; puritanism, 1430; resentment, 1482; Ricoeur, 1499; Rousseau, 1522, 1523; self-control, 1549; Seneca, 1565; Shaftesbury, 1577; Stoicism, 1655; sympathy, 1675; virtue ethics, 1758, 1760, 1761; wickedness, 1801; women moral philosophers, 1824

Passion of the Soul, Descartes, 397

passive citizens, Kant, 936

passive nihilism, nihilism, 1241

passive threat, self-defense, 1554

passivity: emotion, 456, 457; love, 1022

Passmore, John: environmental ethics, 467–468; land ethics, 953

Passover, amnesty and pardon, 57

past, fixity of, fatalism, 527

Pateman, Carole: obedience to law, 1256; political systems, 1344; self and social self, 1545

patents: computers, 285; property, 1392; reproductive technologies, 1479

Pater, Walter: aesthetics, 24; gay ethics, 598

paternalism, **1282–1284**; agency and disability, 36, 39; anthropology, 80; autonomy of moral agents, 113, 114; bargaining, 123, 124; consent, 303; dignity, 406; economic liberty, 984–985; family, 522, 523; feminist ethics, 537; Gert, 609; Hart, 657; humilty,

816; interests, 869; Kant, 931; liberalism, 973; Locke, 1011; medical ethics, 1063; nursing ethics, 1250–1251, 1252; oppression, 1261; public health, 1417; public policy analysis, 1421; racism, 1437; reciprocity, 1466; reproductive technologies, 1480; risk, 1613; sexual abuse, 1569; sexuality, 1572; social contract, 1611; utilitarianism, 1742. *See also* autonomy of moral agents

Paterson, Isabel, Rand, 1441

pathos of distance, Nietzsche, 1237

patience: early Medieval ethics, 712; Emerson, 453; family, 522; hope, 791; Hume, 807; virtue ethics, 1758, 1760; women moral philosophers, 1823

patients: Islamic medical ethics, 894; sexual abuse, 1568

patient's rights: applied ethics, 82; medical ethics, 1063, 1069; nursing ethics, 1250, 1251, 1252; principlism, 1378, 1379

Paton, H. J.: moral point of view, 1142; twentieth-century Anglo-American ethics, 771

patria, civic good, 233, 234

patriarchy: animals, 73; environmental ethics, 470; feminist ethics, 537; Hume, 811; lesbian ethics, 968; persuasive definition, 1304; public and private morality, 1412; reproductive technologies, 1480

patriotism: civic good, 235; Holocaust, 784; international distributive justice, 875; loyalty, 1028

Patristic thought. *See* Church Fathers

Patrizi, Francesco, Renaissance ethics, 724

Patterson, Orlando, slavery, 1593

Paul, the Apostle, Saint, **1284–1286**; Abelard, 2; Augustine, 104; charity, 203; Christian ethics, 222–223; cosmopolitan ethics, 347; natural law, 1207; neo-Stoicism, 1230; Paley, 1273; puritanism, 1429; Renaissance ethics, 723; seventeenth- and eighteenth-century ethics, 731; weakness of will, 1791

Paulhus, Delroy L., self-deception, 1552

Pauline principle, double effect, 419

payback retaliation, revenge, 1492–1493

Payley, William. *See* Paley, William

payoffs: cooperation, conflict, and coordination, 333; game theory, 592; moral reasoning, 1163. *See also* ends; outcomes

PC. *See* political correctness

peace: civic good, 233; common good, 265; conservatism, 315; cosmopolitan ethics, 347; government ethics, 625; Hobbes, 766; Hume, 807, 811, 813; Kant, 936, 937; life and death, 995, 999; pacifism, 1267–1269; war and peace, 1782, 1785–1786

Peace Corps, American moral philosophy, 54

peace of mind. *See* ataraxia; serenity; tranquility

Peace Pledge Union, pacifism, 1268

peacefulness, early Medieval ethics, 712

peacemaking, virtue ethics, 1758

pedagogy. *See* educatation

pederasty: gay ethics, 598; sexual abuse, 1568–1569

peer review, academic ethics, 9

Peirce, C[harles] S[anders], **1287–1288**; American moral philosophy, 54; analogical argument, 61–62; Aristotelian ethics, 89; James, 899; pragmatism, 1361–1362; Royce, 1525

Peirce, J., engineering ethics, 464

Pelagianism: Augustine, 102, 104; Christian ethics, 224

Pelagius, religion, 1474

Peloponnesian War: government ethics, 624, 625; Socrates, 1622

penal system: amnesty and pardon, 58; Avicenna, 115; Bentham, 137; capital punishment, 183; correctional ethics, 338–342; Locke, 1008; moral education, 1130; police ethics, 1335; punishment, 1426, 1427; rape, 1443. *See also* criminal justice

penalties. *See* punishment; sanctions

penalty: liberty, 979; sport, 1643

penance: Christian ethics, 224; early Medieval ethics, 710

Pence, Gregory E., reproductive technologies, 1480

Penelhum, Terence, Butler, 176, 177

penitence: casuistry, 188; Christian ethics, 224; punishment, 1427; Spinoza, 1639

Pennock, J. Roland, political systems, 1342

penology. *See* correctional ethics; penal system

Pentateuch, Jewish ethics, 911

Pepper, Stephen C., value theory, 1751

perception. *See* moral perception

perceptual intuitionism: Sidgwick, 1581, 1582; Wang, 1781

Percival, Thomas, medical ethics, 1068

perfect agent. *See* idealized agents

perfect duties: Aristotelian ethics, 87, 89; duty and obligation, 425, 426; moral rules, 1169; Pufendorf, 1423; supererogation, 1674

perfect goodness: Balguy, 122; theological ethics, 1705

perfect universal duties, duty and obligation, 426

perfect universe, Duns Scotus, 421

perfectibility: Augustine, 102; conservatism, 315; Mandeville, 1040

perfection: Christian ethics, 226; Crusius, 363; early Medieval ethics, 711; excellence, 504; idealist ethics, 833; idealized agents, 836–837; Islam, 883; Islamic ethics, 893; James, 899; later Medieval ethics, 718; Leibniz, 964; Malebranche, 1038; moral saints, 1171, 1172; Murdoch, 1192; mysticism, 1197; philosophy of religion, 1312; religion, 1474; seventeenth- and eighteenth-century ethics, 733, 734; Stoicism, 1653, 1655; twentieth-century Continental ethics, 764; virtue ethics, 1760

Volume key: Volume 1, pages 1–642; volume 2, pages 643–1266; volume 3, pages 1267–1977.

1915

perfectionism, **1288–1292**; Adler, 23; Aristotelian ethics, 90; atheism, 98; Christian ethics, 226; Crusius, 363; duty and obligation, 424; early Medieval ethics, 710; Emerson, 452; equality, 483; gay ethics, 599; Kantian ethics, 939; libertarianism, 976; social and political philosophy, 1602; teleological ethics, 1692; Wolff, 1815–1817

performance: forgery, 560–561; promises, 1388–1389; sport, 1643

Periander, presocratic Greek ethics, 687

Pericles: Arendt, 84; liberalism, 972; Protagoras, 1396

Perictione I, women moral philosophers, 1821

Peripatetics: final good, 549; Renaissance ethics, 721, 722, 723, 725

Perkins, Rollin M., consent, 302

Perlman, S. J., forgiveness, 562

permanence, love, 1022

permanent minority. *See* minorities

permission: consent, 300; logic, 1012, 1013

perpetrators, Holocaust, 780–784

perplexities, Confucian ethics, 293

Perry, Gaylord, sport, 1642

Perry, R[alph] B[arton], **1292–1293**; American moral philosophy, 55; Frankena, 569, 570; good, 620; life and death, 998; naturalism, 1212; twentieth-century Anglo-American ethics, 767; value theory, 1750, 1751

persecution: conservatism, 311; cosmopolitan ethics, 346; genocide, 607–608; Holocaust, 779–784; Levinas, 970. *See also* oppression

perseverance, Hume, 807

Persian Letters, The, Montesquieu, 1108

Persians, tragedy, 1721

persistence: civic good, 234; virtues, 1766

Persius, neo-Stoicism, 1230

person, concept of, **1293–1299**; abortion, 3–6; analogical argument, 60, 63; applied ethics, 83; deontology, 393; fate and fatalism, 526; homicide, 786; infanticide, 854–855; life and death, 997, 998; philosophy of religion, 1312; privacy, 1382; psychoanalysis, 1404; psychology, 1407–1409; rape, 1444, 1446; Rawls, 1455; reproductive technologies, 1476, 1480; right holders, 1504, 1505; right to life, 1003; Scheler, 1534; self and social self, 1544; slippery slope argument, 1594; Thomson, 1714; value concept, 1746; violence, 1754

person-affecting consequentialism, future generations, 587, 588

personal being, psychology, 1408

personal cruelty, cruelty, 361, 362

personal entitlements, rights, 1508, 1510

personal God: the absurd, 8; Kant, 933; philosophy of religion, 1312

personal good. *See* individual good; well-being

personal happiness, good, 623

personal idealism, idealist ethics, 833, 834

personal identity. *See* identity

personal information: privacy, 1382; secrecy and confidentiality, 1542

personal integration: Aristotelian ethics, 88, 89, 90; Foucault, 568; moral purity, 1153

"personal is political," gay ethics, 598

personal liberties. *See* individual rights

personal life, Aristotelian ethics, 88, 89

personal love, twentieth-century Continental ethics, 760

personal merits: Confucian ethics, 289; Hume, 808

personal models: mass media, 1054; moral development, 1121; moral education, 1128, 1129; twentieth-century Continental ethics, 759

personal moral anger, anger, 68

personal morality, Nietzsche, 1236

personal pacifism, pacifism, 1267–1268

personal relationships, **1299–1303**; academic ethics, 9; agency and disability, 39; agent-centered morality, 41; alienation, 49; altruism, 52; anger, 67–69; Aristotelian ethics, 86, 87, 89; Aristotle, 96–97; atheism, 101; autonomy of moral agents, 114; care, 185–187; cheating, 205; children, 207; computers, 283, 284; cosmopolitan ethics, 348; duty and obligation, 427–428; entitlements, 466; environmental ethics, 469, 470; envy, 471–472; etiquette, 487; exploitation, 515; family, 523; feminist ethics, 529, 532–533, 535, 537; fidelity, 543, 544, 545; forgiveness, 561–562; formalism, 563; free will, 574; friendship, 581–583; gay ethics, 597–600; guilt and shame, 640; happiness, 645; Hume, 810; hypocrisy, 819, 820, 821; innocence, 858; interests, 870; Islamic business ethics, 887; Jewish ethics, 909; Kant, 935; lesbian ethics, 967–968; love, 1018–1026; loyalty, 1027; Mo Tzu, 1104–1105; moral absolutes, 1114; moral development, 1122–1123; moral pluralism, 1140; moral psychology, 1148–1150; moral sense theorists, 1175, 1177; nineteenth-century Continental ethics, 753, 754, 755; Objectivism, 1258; oppression, 1261; partiality, 1275–1277; person, 1293; pride, 1377; principlism, 1380; privacy, 1381, 1382; rationality vs. reasonableness, 1451–1454; reciprocity, 1465, 1466; right holders, 1504; self and social self, 1546; self-control, 1549; self-esteem, 1557–1558; self-ownership, 1563; Seneca, 1566; sexuality, 1571, 1573, 1575; suicide, 1670; sympathy, 1677, 1678; trust, 1729, 1730–1731; twentieth-century Anglo-American ethics, 772; twentieth-century Continental ethics, 758, 760–761, 763

personal responsibility: collective responsibility, 255; responsibility, 1486

personal sacrifice: common good, 263, 264–265; consequentialism, 305; courage, 354

personal sin, early Medieval ethics, 713

personal transformation: Taoist ethics, 1682; twentieth-century Continental ethics, 758, 761–763, 764–765

personal values: feminist ethics, 535; idealist ethics, 834; rational choice, 1447–1448; value concept, 1747

personal worth: Aristotelian ethics, 88; economic liberty, 985; environmental ethics, 468; equality, 481; guilt and shame, 650; love, 1025; pride, 1375

personalism: humanism, 801; situation ethics, 1586

personality: character, 201–202; guilt and shame, 640; Holocaust, 781–782; Hume, 806–807; moral development, 1121; moral perception, 1138; nineteenth-century British ethics, 742; property, 1392; sexuality, 1570; twentieth-century Continental ethics, 760

personality disintegration, Aristotelian ethics, 89

personhood. *See* person, concept of

perspective, happiness, 649

perspective of others. *See* spectator point of view

perspectivism: Murdoch, 1192; social and political philosophy, 1602, 1603

persuasion: corruption, 344; power, 1354; presocratic Greek ethics, 690

persuasive definition, **1303–1305**; Moore, 1109; twentieth-century Anglo-American ethics, 768

perversion, sexuality, 1572, 1573, 1574, 1575

pessimism: conservatism, 315, 316; Descartes, 397; hope, 792; Hume, 812; nihilism, 1240, 1241; nineteenth-century Continental ethics, 753; Pascal, 1278

pesticides, agricultural ethics, 45, 46, 47

Peter Cantor of Paris, casuistry, 188

Peter Lombard: Duns Scotus, 420; later Medieval ethics, 716; Vitoria, 1768

Peter of Ailly, natural law, 1208

Peter of Celle, mysticism, 1197

Peters, R. S., revolution, 1497

Peters, Richard, moral education, 1129

Petrarch, Renaissance ethics, 720, 725

petrochemical industry, agricultural ethics, 45

Petrovic, Gajo: self and social self, 1545; twentieth-century Continental ethics, 763

Pettit, Philip, institutions, 859, 862

Pfänder, Alexander, phenomenology, 1307

Phaedo, Hellenistic ethics, 697

Pharisees: hypocrisy, 820; Paul, 1284

Phelan, Shane, gay ethics, 600

phenomenology, **1305–1308**; agnosticism, 44; Christian ethics, 223, 224; Confucian ethics, 287; existential ethics, 509, 510, 511, 512; Hartmann, 658; Hegel, 669, 670, 672; Heidegger, 675–676; Husserl, 816–817; idealist ethics, 831; James, 900; Japan, 903; Levinas, 969–970; Lewis, 971; nineteenth-century Continental ethics, 752, 753; Peirce, 1287; philosophical anthropology,

Volume key: Volume 1, pages 1–642; volume 2, pages 643–1266; volume 3, pages 1267–1977.

1916

Volume key: Volume 1, pages 1–642; volume 2, pages 643–1266; volume 3, pages 1267–1977.

1917

Volume key: Volume 1, pages 1–642; volume 2, pages 643–1266; volume 3, pages 1267–1977.

1918

Volume key: Volume 1, pages 1–642; volume 2, pages 643–1266; volume 3, pages 1267–1977.

1919

Volume key: Volume 1, pages 1–642; volume 2, pages 643–1266; volume 3, pages 1267–1977.

1920

Volume key: Volume 1, pages 1–642; volume 2, pages 643–1266; volume 3, pages 1267–1977.

1921

Volume key: Volume 1, pages 1–642; volume 2, pages 643–1266; volume 3, pages 1267–1977.

1922

Volume key: Volume 1, pages 1–642; volume 2, pages 643–1266; volume 3, pages 1267–1977.

1923

Volume key: Volume 1, pages 1–642; volume 2, pages 643–1266; volume 3, pages 1267–1977.

1924

Volume key: Volume 1, pages 1–642; volume 2, pages 643–1266; volume 3, pages 1267–1977.

1925

rationality, *continued*
communitarianism, 269; comparative ethics, 274, 275; competition, 278; compromise, 281; constructivism, 318; conventions, 330; critical theory, 359; Cynics, 369; deontology, 391; desire, 399; Donegan, 417; economic analysis, 437; egoism, 447, 448–449; Epictetus, 473; Epicurus, 476–477; feminist ethics, 534–535; final good, 549; Foot, 555; Gert, 608–610; golden rule, 616; government ethics, 625; Hellenistic ethics, 698; Kantian ethics, 941, 942; later Medieval ethics, 717; Lewis, 971; love, 1024–1025; metaethics, 1085; moral point of view, 1143; moral sense theorists, 1175; natural law, 1209; nineteenth-century Continental ethics, 753, 754; Objectivism, 1258; pain and suffering, 1270; perfectionism, 1290; person, 1294; Price, 1372; psychology, 1409; public goods, 1415; rationality vs. reasonableness, 1451–1454; Rawls, 1457, 1458, 1459; reasons for action, 1461–1464; Renaissance ethics, 725; revolution, 1498; right holders, 1504; Roman ethics, 706; self and social self, 1544; self-control, 1550; self-deception, 1551; seventeenth- and eighteenth-century ethics, 737–738; skepticism, 1592; social and political philosophy, 1600, 1602; social contract, 1611, 1612; Stoicism, 1653, 1654; Taylor, 1685, 1686; Thomas Aquinas, 1709; twentieth-century Anglo-American ethics, 772; virtue ethics, 1758; war and peace, 1787; Wittgensteinian ethics, 1814; Wolff, 1817; work, 1828

rationality vs. reasonableness, **1451–1454**; categorical and hypothetical imperatives, 189–193; hope, 792–793; motives, 1186–1187; Pascal, 1278; Rawls, 1458; reflective equilibrium, 1468–1469

rationalization: moral relativism, 1165; racism, 1437; self-deception, 1551

ratios, classical Greek ethics, 694

Ravizza, Mark, free will, 573

Rawls, John, **1454–1461**; agency and disability, 36; agent-centered morality, 41; American moral philosophy, 55–56; animals, 70; applied ethics, 82; Aristotelian ethics, 86; autonomy of ethics, 111; autonomy of moral agents, 112, 113; Baier, 120; Barry, 126; beneficence, 132; censorship, 197; cheating, 207; children, 208; civil disobedience, 237; civility, 242, 243; common sense moralists, 269; communitarianism, 270, 271, 272; consequentialism, 306; constructivism, 317–320; contractarianism, 321–324; cooperation, conflict, and coordination, 334, 335; cooperative surplus, 336, 337–338; deontology, 391, 393, 394, 395; discounting the future, 411; duty and obligation, 424, 428; economic analysis, 432, 436,

437; envy, 471, 472; equality, 482, 484; euthanasia, 493; fairness, 521; fidelity, 544; good, 623; Green, 632; Habermas, 643; human rights, 797; idealized agents, 836, 837; impartiality, 84; inequality, 851, 852; institutions, 858; international distributive justice, 876; intuitionism, 880; justice, circumstances of, 919; justice, distributive, 921–924; justice, rectificatory, 927; Kantian ethics, 941; King, 951; legitimacy, 961; liberalism, 972, 974, 975; Marxism, 1052; merit and desert, 1076; metaethics, 1082–1083; moral absolutes, 1112; moral point of view, 1141, 1142; moral reasoning, 1161; moral rules, 1168–1169; motives, 1185, 1187; multiculturalism, 1190; naturalism, 1213; Nozick, 1245; obedience to law, 1256; political systems, 1345; psychology, 1408, 1409; racism, 1438; rational choice, 1447, 1451; rationality vs. reasonableness, 1452–1453; reciprocity, 1465; reflective equilibrium, 1467–1469; right holders, 1505; risk aversion, 1519, 1520; self and social self, 1545; self-respect, 1564; slavery, 1593; social and political philosophy, 1600, 1601–1602, 1603, 1604; social contract, 1612; stakeholder, 1647; technology, 1688; twentieth-century Anglo-American ethics, 770–771, 772; utilitarianism, 1741; Walzer, 1777; work, 1828

Raymond, Janice, lesbian ethics, 967

Raz, Joseph: authority, 107; commensurability, 258, 259; consent, 303; right, 1501

Rāzī, al-, Islamic medical ethics, 894

reactionary thought: Hegel, 669–670; individualism, 848; nineteenth-century British ethics, 743

reactive attitudes: anger, 67; free will, 572–573; ideal observer, 827–829; resentment, 1482

real goods, Hobbes, 776, 777

realism: cosmopolitan ethics, 348; international conflict, 872; life and death, 995; metaethics, 1084, 1085; Niebuhr, 1235; Objectivism, 1257; Prichard, 1373; war and peace, 1782, 1784–1785, 1786, 1788. *See also* legal realism; moral realism

realistic pessimism, conservatism, 315, 316

reality: comparative ethics, 274; conservatism, 311, 312; idealist ethics, 830, 831, 832, 833; Janism, 898; moral attention, 1116; nineteenth-century Continental ethics, 752; Plotinus, 1329; political correctness, 1338; postmodernism, 1351

realization, personal, Mead, 1061

realization, transcendentalism, 1726

Realms of Being, Santayana, 1529

reason: American moral philosophy, 55; anger, 68–69; animals, 70, 71; Anselm, 77; Aristotle, 92, 95; Baier,

120; Balguy, 122; beneficence, 130; benevolence, 134, 135; classical Greek ethics, 691, 694; competition, 278; conservatism, 311; Duns Scotus, 420–421; duty and obligation, 425; emotion, 454, 455–456; Epictetus, 473; *eudaimonia*, 490; Fichte, 542; fittingness, 553; Godwin, 612; government ethics, 627; Hellenistic ethics, 697, 701; Hobbes, 777; homicide, 785; idealist ethics, 830; Kant, 930, 931–933; later Medieval ethics, 716; Montesquieu, 1106; moral education, 1128; moral psychology, 1145–1146, 1147, 1148; motives, 1185; narrative, 1203; natural law, 1206, 1207; Objectivism, 1257, 1258; Pascal, 1278; passion, 1279; person, 1294, 1295; *phronesis*, 1314–1316; Plato, 1319; postmodernism, 1351; rationality vs. reasonableness, 1452; Rawls, 1459; Roman ethics, 706; self-control, 1549; Seneca, 1566; seventeenth- and eighteenth-century ethics, 731, 734–735; skepticism, 1588; social and political philosophy, 1600; Socrates, 1624–1625; twentieth-century Anglo-American ethics, 700; virtue ethics, 1757, 1758, 1760; voluntarism, 1773; wickedness, 1801; Wolff, 1815; Wollstonecraft, 1819–1820; women moral philosophers, 1824

reasonableness: anger, 68–69; happiness, 648; moral sense theorists, 1175; rationality vs., 1452–1453; Rawls, 1458. *See also* rationality vs. reasonableness

reasoned discussion, bargaining, 123

reasoning: analogical, 59–63; animals, 70, 71; classical Greek ethics, 690–691, 692; formalism, 563; later Medieval ethics, 718; Locke, 1009; moral education, 1128–1129; moral sense theorists, 1175; Nāgārjuna, 1200; naturalism, 1213–1214; partiality, 1276; rationality, 1452. *See also* moral reasoning; practical reason[ing]; reasons for action

reasonless choices, naturalism, 1214

reasons for action, **1461–1464**; abortion, 3; action, 15; additivity, 20; agent-centered morality, 40–42; altruism, 51–53; authority, 108, 109; Balguy, 121–122; categorical and hypothetical imperatives, 189–193; classical Greek ethics, 693; coercion, 246–248; consent, 303; contractarianism, 322; deontology, 393–396; desire, 398–399; dirty hands, 407–410; Duns Scotus, 420–421; duty and obligation, 425; egoism, 446–449; externalism and internalism, 518; free will, 573; Hart, 656; immoralism, 838–839; intention, 866–868; Jesus, 907; Kantian ethics, 942; Kierkegaard, 956; killing and letting die, 948–949; metaethics, 1085; metaphysics and epistemology, 1089; moral point of view, 1141–1144; moral realism, 1158; moral reasoning, 1162; moral

Volume key: Volume 1, pages 1–642; volume 2, pages 643–1266; volume 3, pages 1267–1977.

1926

Volume key: Volume 1, pages 1–642; volume 2, pages 643–1266; volume 3, pages 1267–1977.

1927

religion, *continued*
moral education, 1128; moral purity, 1152, 1153; multiculturalism, 1190; mysticism, 1196–1198; nature, 1218, 1219; Niebuhr, 1234–1235; nineteenth-century British ethics, 739, 740, 745; nineteenth-century Continental ethics, 755, 756; pacifism, 1267; Pascal, 1278; Peirce, 1287; person, 1294; pragmatism, 1361; praxis, 1365; privacy, 1381; psychoanalysis, 1403; Pufendorf, 1424; puritanism, 1428–1431; Rawls, 1458, 1459; Renaissance ethics, 726; revenge, 1493; seventeenth- and eighteenth-century ethics, 730, 735, 738; sexuality, 1570, 1572; social and political philosophy, 1604; Soviet ethical theory, 1631, 1635; Spinoza, 1638–1640; suicide, 1669, 1670, 1671; Sunnism, 1672–1673; supererogation, 1673; Taoist ethics, 1680–1684; technology and nature, 1690, 1691; theism, 1699–1701; theological ethics, 1702–1706; Thomas Aquinas, 1708–1710; Thoreau, 1715; toleration, 1717–1718; tragedy, 1721; Tufts, 1732; Voltaire, 1770; Wang, 1779–1781; war and peace, 1782; Weber, 1793; Wolff, 1816; women moral philosophers, 1822–1825, 1826. *See also* God; philosophy of religion; theology
religion, philosophy of. *See* philosophy of religion
remarriage, family, 522
remedy of specific performance, contracts, 327
remorse, collective responsibility, 257
remoteness, hedonism, 666
Renaissance: civic good, 234–235; early Medieval ethics, 712; history of Western ethics, 720–729; humanism, 801, 802; individualism, 849; liberalism, 974; Machiavelli, 1033–1034; natural law, 1208–1209; neo-Stoicism, 1229; prudence, 1400; Roman ethics, 706; social contract, 1609–1610; virtue ethics, 1759
Renan, Joseph-Ernest, nihilism, 1240
renewal, Islamic ethics, 893
renunciation, Hindu ethics, 680, 682
reparation: correctional ethics, 340; deontology, 392
repentance: Christian ethics, 225, 226; forgiveness, 562; twentieth-century Continental ethics, 759
representation: civic good, 235–236; cosmopolitan ethics, 348; cultural studies, 366; economic analysis, 433; government ethics, 626–627, 628; Hegel, 669, 670; individualism, 850; Kant, 936; liberalism, 973; political correctness, 1339; political systems, 1343, 1344; Rawls, 1459; Staël, 1644; transcendentalism, 1726
representative democracy: Bentham, 137, 139; democracy, 387; government ethics, 626–627; Mill (John Stuart), 1100
repression (emotional), resentment, 1483

repression (political): conservatism, 312, 313; Holocaust, 784; Marxism, 1050; oppression, 1262
reproach, guilt and shame, 640
reproduction (biological): abortion, 2–5; competition, 279; Darwin, 374; economic liberty, 984; feminist ethics, 528, 530, 534, 535; future generations, 587; homosexuality, 787; Hume, 811; lesbian ethics, 968; rape, 1444; reproductive technologies, 1475–1480; sexuality, 1570, 1571, 1572, 1574. *See also* birth control; pregnancy
reproductive rights: abortion, 3–6; applied ethics, 82–83; family, 522; feminist ethics, 528, 530; privacy, 1381; public and private morality, 1410; public policy, 1418; reproductive technologies, 1477
reproductive technologies, **1475–1482**; analogical argument, 60, 61, 62, 63; economic liberty, 982, 984; family, 522; feminist ethics, 528, 530; genetic engineering, 605; Islamic medical ethics, 895; slippery slope argument, 1594
republicanism: civic good, 234, 235, 236; government ethics, 625; Grotius, 633; humanism, 802; Kant, 936, 937; Machiavelli, 1034; Roman ethics, 706
repulsion, pornography, 1348
reputation: Africa, 34; blackmail, 153; freedom of the press, 579; interests, 869–870; journalism, 917; Locke, 1008; revenge, 1494; Sophists, 1630; trust, 1729
requirements: bargaining, 123; metaphysics and epistemology, 1090; moral dilemmas, 1126; reasons for action, 1462–1463; skepticism, 1591–1592; subjectivism, 1665; value theory, 1751
res publica, civic good, 233–234
res publica est res populi, civic good, 234
rescue: acts and omissions, 15–18; bargaining, 124; Holocaust, 780; moral absolutes, 1111, 1112, 1113, 1114; moral dilemma, 1126; moral rules, 1170; motives, 1187; war and peace, 1782, 1783
research: academic ethics, 9; academic freedom, 12–13; anthropology, 79; bioethics, 141, 142; genetic engineering, 606; Gert, 609; library, 991; medical ethics, 1069; pain and suffering, 1270; plagiarism, 1317; principlism, 1378; public health, 1415; public policy analysis, 1420–1421; reproductive technologies, 1475, 1476; social psychology, 1613–1618; sociology, 1620–1622
research centers, applied ethics, 83
research ethics, Gert, 609
resentment, **1482–1486**; altruism, 51; anger, 67, 68, 69; Aristotle, 93; elite, 451; envy, 471–472; evil, 500; forgiveness, 561–562; free will, 572; happiness, 645; harm and offense, 654; hate, 659, 661; Hume, 811; ideal observer, 828; moral

development, 1120; moral psychology, 1150; moral sense theorists, 1177; Nietzsche, 1236, 1237; passion, 1281; racism, 1434; revenge, 1493; self-knowledge, 1560; twentieth-century Continental ethics, 759, 760
resignation: Islam, 885; Japan, 904; neo-Stoicism, 1229, 1230
resistance, Hindu ethics, 682
resoluteness: Heidegger, 675, 676; revolution, 1498
resolution: compromise, 281; Wang, 1781
Resolutiones morales, casuistry, 188
resolve, American moral philosophy, 54
resource allocation: bargaining, 123; beneficence, 130; Bentham, 138–139; bioethics, 141; cosmopolitan ethics, 346; economic liberty, 982; economic systems, 439–444; inequality, 852; institutions, 861–862; interests, 869; international distributive justice, 874–877; justice, distributive, 921; libertarianism, 977–978; Marx, 1046; Marxism, 1048–1049, 1051; materialism, 1058, 1059; needs, 1221–1223; racism, 1435, 1438; rational choice, 1450; reproductive technologies, 1479; theory and practice, 1707; Walzer, 1778; work, 1828. *See also* distribution; justice, distributive; natural resources
Resource Conservation Ethic, conservation ethics, 308, 309–310
resourcefulness, virtues, 1765
respect: anger, 68; Aristotelian ethics, 89; atheism, 101; Camus, 182; civility, 242–243; compromise, 281; Confucian ethics, 289, 290; deontology, 395; Donegan, 417; equality, 481; feminist ethics, 535; happiness, 645; honor, 789–790; human rights, 798; Kant, 935; Kantian ethics, 941; love, 1024–1026; moral development, 1121; oppression, 1261; principlism, 1378; Santayana, 1530; sexuality, 1571, 1572; toleration, 1717, 1718; twentieth-century Continental ethics, 764; value concept, 1746. *See also* self-respect
respectability, Smith, 1597
responsibility, **1486–1492**; abortion, 3, 6; academic ethics, 8–10; acts and omissions, 15–18; Adler, 23; Africa, 35; agency and disability, 36–39; agricultural ethics, 45; anger, 68; Aristotle, 94–95; authenticity, 105, 106; bad faith, 118, 119; beneficence, 132; bioethics, 143; Bradley, 154; Buber, 160–161; business ethics, 171; care, 185–187; causation and responsibility, 194–197; children, 207–210; China, 217; Christian ethics, 226; coercion, 246; cognitive science, 249; collective responsibility, 255–257; common sense moralists, 267; computers, 283, 286; consent, 301; conservation ethics, 307; contracts, 328; cooperation, conflict, and coordination, 335; cosmopolitan

Volume key: Volume 1, pages 1–642; volume 2, pages 643–1266; volume 3, pages 1267–1977.

1928

Volume key: Volume 1, pages 1–642; volume 2, pages 643–1266; volume 3, pages 1267–1977.

1929

Volume key: Volume 1, pages 1–642; volume 2, pages 643–1266; volume 3, pages 1267–1977.

1930

Volume key: Volume 1, pages 1–642; volume 2, pages 643–1266; volume 3, pages 1267–1977.

1931

Volume key: Volume 1, pages 1–642; volume 2, pages 643–1266; volume 3, pages 1267–1977.

1932

Volume key: Volume 1, pages 1–642; volume 2, pages 643–1266; volume 3, pages 1267–1977.

1933

Subject Index

self-actualization: alienation, 48, 49; economic liberty, 984; Marx, 1047

self-advancement, Marxism, 1048, 1051, 1053

self-alienation: alienation, 48–49; Hegel, 673

self-assertion: individualism, 849; Marxism, 1054; nineteenth-century Continental ethics, 757–758; passion, 1279

self-awareness: existential ethics, 512; Foucault, 567–568; right holders, 1504; Roman ethics, 705, 707–708

self-censorship: Emerson, 453; emotion, 456

self-concept: communitarianism, 270, 272; constructivism, 319; free will, 574; Hegel, 672; homicide, 786; pride, 1374; psychoanalysis, 1404; psychology, 1407–1408

self-concern: benevolence, 135; Plato, 1323–1324

self-condemnation, moral purity, 1150

self-confidence, self-respect, 1564

self-consciousness: abortion, 4; cradle arguments, 356–357; economic liberty, 982; elite, 451; Epicureanism, 474; equality, 481; Foucault, 567–568; gay ethics, 600; idealist ethics, 833; India, 844; Japan, 903; Kantian ethics, 941; nineteenth-century British ethics, 742; philosophical anthropology, 1309; pride, 1375; Rousseau, 1522; self and social self, 1544, 1545

self-contemplation, Roman ethics, 708

self-control, **1548–1551**; anger, 68–69; autonomy of moral agents, 112, 113; character, 201; classical Greek ethics, 694; Cynics, 369; Cyrenaics, 371; Descartes, 397; emotion, 456; Engels, 462; Epictetus, 473–474; Epicurus, 476; *eudaimonia,* 490; euthanasia, 493; evil, 499; Foucault, 568; Gandhi, 594; Hellenistic ethics, 697; idealized agents, 836; India, 846; international conflict, 872; moral education, 1128, 1129; moral purity, 1151, 1152, 1153; resentment, 1482; Roman ethics, 705; self-ownership, 1563; self-respect, 1565; seventeenth- and eighteenth-century ethics, 730; Smith, 1597, 1599; Sophists, 1630; temperance, 1694, 1695; twentieth-century Continental ethics, 760, 763; virtue ethics, 1760

self-creation, Nietzsche, 1238–1239

self-cultivation: China, 212, 218, 219, 220; Emerson, 452; Foucault, 567–568; virtues, 1766

self-deception, **1551–1553**; authenticity, 105–106; bad faith, 118, 119; deceit, 380, 381; existential ethics, 513; happiness, 649; Holocaust, 782–783; hypocrisy, 819–820, 822, 823; Kant, 935; meaning of life, 1001; moral imagination, 1132–1133; moral sense theorists, 1178; prescriptivism, 1370; resentment, 1482; self-control, 1549; self-esteem, 1557; self-knowledge, 1560; self-respect, 1564; Taylor,

1685; twentieth-century Continental ethics, 761

self-defense, **1553–1556**; abortion, 3; anger, 69; deceit, 379; deterrence, 401; double effect, 419; harm and offense, 653; homicide, 785, 786; human rights, 799; innocence, 857; military ethics, 1094; Mill (John Stuart), 1103; moral pluralism, 1139; moral rules, 1169; nuclear ethics, 1247, 1248; passion, 1279; police ethics, 1334; Rawls, 1459; right, 1500; right holders, 1503; war and peace, 1782

self-defilement, Augustine, 103

self-definition: Emerson, 453; philosophical anthropology, 1309; Roman ethics, 705

self-delusion, hypocrisy, 820

self-denial: Christian ethics, 225, 226; good, 622; Jesus, 907; moral purity, 1152; Nietzsche, 1236; Soviet ethical theory, 1634; Suárez, 1664; sympathy, 1677

self-dependence, transcendentalism, 1725, 1726

self-destruction: non-violence, 1755; suicide, 1668–1672; theory and practice, 1707

self-destructiveness: revenge, 1493; theory and practice, 1707; war and peace, 1786

self-determination: abortion, 3; agency and disability, 38–39; autonomy of moral agents, 111–114; Cambridge Platonists, 180; children, 209–210; Christian ethics, 223; Edwards, 445; euthanasia, 492, 493, 494, 495, 496; Hindu ethics, 682; Kant, 931; karma, 944; later Medieval ethics, 718; person, 1295; Price, 1372; right holders, 1503; sexuality, 1571; Shaftesbury, 1578; suicide, 1671

self-development: lesbian ethics, 967; psychoanalysis, 1402; self and social self, 1545; Wolff, 1816

self-devotion, Green, 632

self-direction, seventeenth- and eighteenth-century ethics, 730, 735–738

self-discipline: classical Greek ethics, 692; ethics and morality, 486

self-disclosure, Chuang Tzu, 230

self-discovery, narrative, 1204

self-esteem, **1556–1558**; altruism, 51; beneficence, 130; envy, 471, 472; honor, 789; materialism, 1058; Objectivism, 1258; oppression, 1261; pride, 1374, 1375, 1377; racism, 1434; resentment, 1483, 1485; revenge, 1494; self-deception, 1552; self-respect, 1564; sympathy, 1677; work, 1829

self-estrangement, work, 1830

self-evaluation: self-esteem, 1556–1558; self-respect, 1564

self-evident beliefs: intuitionism, 880; Ross, 1521

self-evident judgments, twentieth-century Continental ethics, 759

self-examination: Foucault, 568; Hsün Tzu, 795

self-exploitation, economic liberty, 984

self-expression: Emerson, 452, 453; etiquette, 487; freedom of the press, 579; oppression, 1261

self-fragmentation, Aristotelian ethics, 90

self-fulfillment: self-deception, 1552; work, 1830–1831

self-governance: seventeenth- and eighteenth-century ethics, 738; social and political philosophy, 1604

self-government: autonomy of moral agents, 112, 113; Price, 1372; welfare, 1797

self-growth: Emerson, 452, 453; Foucault, 567–568

self-harm: rights, 1508; risk, 1513; self-respect, 1564; social psychology, 1616–1617

self-hatred, resentment, 1482, 1485

selfhood, Heidegger, 675, 676

self-identification, groups, 635

self-identity: bad faith, 119; moral psychology, 1147; sympathy, 1677–1678

self-image: authenticity, 106; Hegel, 672; racism, 1439; self-deception, 1551

self-immolation, Hindu ethics, 682

self-importance, forgiveness, 561

self-improvement: deontology, 392; Descartes, 397; duty and obligation, 428; Emerson, 453; Foucault, 567–568; Roman ethics, 707

self-incrimination, privacy, 1381

self-indulgence: Epicureanism, 475; Jewish ethics, 913; temperance, 1694, 1695

self-integration, moral purity, 1150

self-interest: agent-centered morality, 42; altruism, 50, 51, 53; Baier, 120; beneficence, 131; Bentham, 139, 140; business ethics, 174; cooperative surplus, 337; cosmopolitan ethics, 348; Democritus, 389–390; economic systems, 440; egoism, 446, 447–449; euthanasia, 494; final good, 549; Foot, 555; good, 622; harm and offense, 653; Hegel, 673; Hobbes, 775, 777; Hsün Tzu, 784; Hume, 809, 811, 813; hypocrisy, 819; interests, 870–871; Marxism, 1053–1054; Mo Tzu, 1105; moral point of view, 1143, 1144; moral psychology, 1146, 1147; moral relativism, 1165; moral sense theorists, 1173, 1174; motives, 1187; norms, 1243, 1244; Objectivism, 1258; prudence, 1399, 1400; public goods, 1414; rational choice, 1447, 1450, 1451; rationality vs. reasonableness, 1452; Renaissance ethics, 724; revolution, 1495, 1496, 1497; self and social self, 1544; seventeenth- and eighteenth-century ethics, 731, 735–736; sexuality, 1570; Shaftesbury, 1578; Smith, 1598; sociology, 1621; Sophists, 1629, 1630; Soviet ethical theory, 1633, 1634; strategic interaction, 1662; subjectivism, 1665, 1666; suicide, 1670; sympathy, 1676, 1678; teleological ethics, 1692; theory and practice, 1707; twentieth-century

Volume key: Volume 1, pages 1–642; volume 2, pages 643–1266; volume 3, pages 1267–1977.

1934

Volume key: Volume 1, pages 1–642; volume 2, pages 643–1266; volume 3, pages 1267–1977.

1935

Subject Index

sentences (language), moral terms, 1180

sentencing reform, correctional ethics, 342

sentience: agency and disability, 39; animals, 71–72, 73; Bentham, 139; cruelty, 36–362; environmental ethics, 468; euthanasia, 494; Frankena, 570; impartiality, 842; land ethics, 953; Leibniz, 964; life and death, 993–999; love, 1023; moral community, 1117; moral sense theorists, 1177–1178; person, 1296, 1298; right holders, 1502

sentiment: emotion, 457; Hume, 805; Schiller, 1537; seventeenth- and eighteenth-century ethics, 737; Shaftesbury, 1577, 1578; sympathy, 1677, 1678–1679; Voltaire, 1771; Westermarck, 1798

sentimentalism: Adler, 22; Balguy, 121; Kant, 929; moral sense theorists, 1173–1178; Paley, 1273; seventeenth- and eighteenth-century ethics, 737; Shaftesbury, 1578; sympathy, 1679

separate intelligences, biological theory, 149

separation, alienation, 48, 49

separation of powers, liberalism, 975

separatism: lesbian ethics, 968; racism, 1435

Septuagint, hypocrisy, 820

Serebnick, Judith, library, 987

serenity: Cicero, 231–232; Hume, 807; Marcus Aurelius, 1042; Seneca, 1565; Stoicism, 1655

service: academic ethics, 9–10; library, 986; Schweitzer, 1542

servility: forgiveness, 562; Kant, 935; pride, 1376; self-respect, 1564; sympathy, 1679

settled state, character, 200

seven capital sins, early Medieval ethics, 711

seven deadly sins, Christian ethics, 224

Seven Sages, presocratic Greek ethics, 686–687

sex offenders, correctional ethics, 340

sex selection: infanticide, 854; reproductive technologies, 1476, 1478

sex vs. gender, de Beauvoir, 376

sexism: anger, 68; animals, 71; autonomy of moral agents, 113; critical theory, 360; cultural studies, 366; discrimination, 413, 414–415; equality, 481; family, 523; feminist ethics, 528, 531, 533–536; fittingness, 553; gay ethics, 598; hate, 661; humanism, 803; multiculturalism, 1188, 1189; partiality, 1277; political correctness, 1337, 1339; violence, 1754; women moral philosophers, 1826; work, 1829. *See also* heterosexism

Sextus Empiricus, skepticism, 1588, 1589

sexual abuse and harassment, **1567–1570**; abortion, 3; academic ethics, 9; consent, 302; correctional ethics, 342; cruelty, 361; family, 523; feminist ethics, 528, 534, 537;

political correctness, 1337, 1338, 1339; pornography, 1347, 1348; public policy analysis, 1421; rape, 1443–1446; sexuality, 1571, 1572, 1573, 1574; war and peace, 1785

sexual equality: applied ethics, 81; family, 523; feminist ethics, 533–534; sexual abuse, 1567–1568; Wollstonecraft, 1819–1820; women moral philosophers, 1824, 1825

sexual explicitness, pornography, 1348

sexual exploitation: academic ethics, 9; consent, 302; feminist ethics, 528, 534, 537; sexual abuse and harassment, 1567–1569

sexual identity, gay ethics, 599

Sexual Inversion, gay ethics, 598

sexual liberation, Bentham, 137

sexual orientation. *See* gay ethics; homosexuality; lesbian ethics

sexual selection, Darwin, 373, 374

sexuality and sexual ethics, **1570–1577**; anthropology, 79; bargaining, 123; Bentham, 137; cruelty, 361; early Medieval ethics, 710; economic liberty, 982, 984, 985; family, 523; feminist ethics, 528, 532–533, 534, 535, 537; fidelity, 544; freedom of the press, 579; gay ethics, 597–600; hedonism, 665; Hellenistic ethics, 697; Hindu ethics, 680; homosexuality, 786–788; Hume, 807, 811; Islam, 884; Jewish ethics, 911; Kant, 935; lesbian ethics, 967; love, 1018; Maimonides, 1036; moral development, 1120; moral purity, 1152; pornography, 1346–1348; privacy, 1381; psychoanalysis, 1402–1403, 1404–1405; psychology, 1406, 1409; puritanism, 1428–1429, 1430–1431; racism, 1436, 1437; rape, 1443–1446; Renaissance ethics, 727; self-respect, 1564; seventeenth- and eighteenth-century ethics, 735; sexual abuse, 1567–1569; social and political philosophy, 1604; twentieth-century Anglo-American ethics, 770; twentieth-century Continental ethics, 761; Westermarck, 1798, 1799; women moral philosophers, 1822, 1824

shadow-price, conservation ethics, 308

Shaffer, Peter, puritanism, 1431

Shaftesbury, [Anthony Ashley Cooper] 3rd Earl of, **1577–1579**; Balguy, 121; Cambridge Platonists, 180; Cudworth, 364; Hutcheson, 817, 818; intuitionism, 879; Jefferson, 905; Mandeville, 1040; moral sense theorists, 1173; passion, 1280; seventeenth- and eighteenth-century ethics, 736, 737, 738

Shakespeare, William: aesthetics, 25; envy, 471; hypocrisy, 821; literature, 1005; tragedy, 1723

shame: Africa, 35; anger, 67; Aristotle, 93; Cicero, 232; collective responsibility, 255, 257; emotion, 456; groups, 635; guilt and shame, 639–640; harm and offense, 654; honor, 789, 790; Locke, 1008; moral psychology, 1149–1150; nihilism,

1240; non-violence, 1755; passion, 1280; privacy, 1383; resentment, 1484; revenge, 1494; self-esteem, 1557; sexuality, 1571, 1574; suicide, 1669; twentieth-century Continental ethics, 759; Williams, 1805. *See also* guilt and shame

shamelessness, Cynics, 369

Shannon, Thomas A., reproductive technologies, 1477, 1480

Shan-tao, Buddhist ethics, 168

Shao Yung, China, 218

shared moral emotions, Mencius, 1073

shared responsibility, collective responsibility, 255–257

shared values: strategic interaction, 1658; Walzer, 1777–1778

Shari'a: Islam, 883, 884–885; Islamic business ethics, 887–888; Islamic ethics, 889; Islamic medical ethics, 894, 895; Shi'ism, 1580; virtue ethics, 1759

sharing: feminist ethics, 530; friendship, 582

Sharp, Frank C.: Cumberland, 367; ideal observer, 828

Shaver, Donna A., library, 988

Shaw, George Bernard, pacifism, 1267

Shelley, Mary Wollstonecraft Godwin: Godwin, 613; Wollstonecraft, 1819

sheng, Chu Hsi, 228

Shen-hsui, China, 216

Sherman, Lawrence, police ethics, 1333

Shestov, Lev, Soviet ethical theory, 1634

shield, contracts, 328

Shi'ism, **1579–1580**; Islam, 883, 884; Sunnism, 1673

Shinran: Buddhist ethics, 168; Japan, 903

Shinto: competition, 277; Japan, 901, 902; suicide, 1670

Shklar, Judith, hypocrisy, 821, 822, 823

shock: harm and offense, 654; journalism, 917

Shockley, William, racism, 1434

shortcomings, guilt and shame, 640

Shrader-Frechette, Kristin, agricultural ethics, 45

shu: Confucian ethics, 291; Confucius, 296

Shue, Henry, human rights, 797, 799

shyness, hate, 661

Sibley, Mulford, life and death, 998

sickle cell anemia, genetic engineering, 604

side constraints: moral absolutes, 1113; rights, 1510

Sidgwick, Henry, **1580–1584**; Adler, 21; altruism, 52; analytic philosophy, 64; Anscombe, 75; atheism, 98; beneficence, 130, 131; casuistry, 189; commensurability, 261; common sense moralists, 268, 269; consequentialism, 305, 306; deceit, 380; discounting the future, 411; egoism, 447; Epicurus, 477; ethics and morality, 486; fidelity, 544; golden rule, 615; happiness, 644–645; hedonism, 663; humilty, 815; international conflict, 873; intuitionism, 879; love, 1017, 1024; moral reasoning, 1161, 1162; Murphy, 1193; natural law, 1210;

Volume key: Volume 1, pages 1–642; volume 2, pages 643–1266; volume 3, pages 1267–1977.

1936

Volume key: Volume 1, pages 1–642; volume 2, pages 643–1266; volume 3, pages 1267–1977.

1937

Subject Index

Volume key: Volume 1, pages 1–642; volume 2, pages 643–1266; volume 3, pages 1267–1977.

1938

Volume key: Volume 1, pages 1–642; volume 2, pages 643–1266; volume 3, pages 1267–1977.

Volume key: Volume 1, pages 1–642; volume 2, pages 643–1266; volume 3, pages 1267–1977.

1940

Volume key: Volume 1, pages 1–642; volume 2, pages 643–1266; volume 3, pages 1267–1977.

1941

Volume key: Volume 1, pages 1–642; volume 2, pages 643–1266; volume 3, pages 1267–1977.

1942

police ethics, 1334; risk analysis, 1515

technology, **1687–1690**; agricultural ethics, 45; analogical argument, 59–60, 61, 62, 63; computers, 283–286; conservatism, 315; cosmopolitan ethics, 349; Cynics, 369; engineering ethics, 462–464; freedom of the press, 580; genetic engineering, 605–606; international distributive justice, 876; library, 989–991; Marxism, 1049; medical ethics, 1069; nuclear ethics, 1247–1249; postmodernism, 1351; praxis, 1366; reproductive technologies, 1475–1480; slippery slope argument, 1594; technology and nature, 1690–1691; work, 1830

technology and nature, **1690–1691**; reproductive technologies, 1475–1480

Teichman, Jenny: pacifism, 1267, 1268; war and peace, 1785

teleion, Aristotle, 91

teleological ethics, **1289–1291**; moral absolutes, 1112; perfectionism, 1289–1291

teleologism: action, 14; agent-centered morality, 41; autonomy of ethics, 110; Butler, 177; Christian ethics, 224, 227; duty and obligation, 424; economic systems, 440, 442; environmental ethics, 468; hope, 792; Husserl, 817; Kierkegaard, 946; liberalism, 974–975; libertarianism, 976; Mill (John Stuart), 1100–1101; moral reasoning, 1161; nineteenth-century Continental ethics, 756, 757; theism, 1700; twentieth-century Anglo-American ethics, 771; virtues, 1767; voluntarism, 1773. *See also* end in itself; good, theories of

television: cultural studies, 365; freedom of the press, 580; mass media, 1054–1056

Telfer, Elizabeth: love, 1024, 1025–1256; person, 1296; self-respect, 1565

telos: cradle arguments, 355–357; deliberation and choice, 382; final good, 549; Foucault, 568; Jesus, 908; liberalism, 974; MacIntyre, 1035; natural law, 1206; teleological ethics, 1691–1693; virtue ethics, 1757

Temkin, Larry, inequality, 853

temperance, **1693–1696**; Aristotle, 96; Augustine, 105; benevolence, 134; civic good, 234; classical Greek ethics, 692, 694; emotion, 454; *eudaimonia*, 490; excellence, 504; Hellenistic ethics, 697; Hume, 807; later Medieval ethics, 718; Plato, 1320; practical wisdom, 1358; presocratic Greek ethics, 688, 689; Protagoras, 1396; prudence, 1398; puritanism, 1430; Roman ethics, 705; self-control, 1549; social psychology, 1618; Sophists, 1630; Stoicism, 1653; Thomas Aquinas, 1709; virtue ethics, 1758, 1759, 1760; virtues, 1763, 1764, 1766; women moral philosophers, 1821, 1822. *See also* moderation

temporality: authenticity, 105; discounting the future, 410–412; freedom and determinism, 575; Royce, 1525

Temps modernes, Les, Sartre, 1531

temptation: early Medieval ethics, 711; pride, 1376; self-control, 1548–1549

Ten Commandments (Decalogue): Abelard, 1; Buber, 161; Buddhist ethics, 163; Calvin, 178; Christian ethics, 226; later Medieval ethics, 719; love, 1020, 1021, 1022–1024, 1025; medical ethics, 1066; moral absolutes, 1111; moral rules, 1169; philosophy of religion, 1310, 1311; Renaissance ethics, 729; seventeenth- and eighteenth-century ethics, 730–731; suicide, 1669; theological ethics, 1703

Ten Modes, skepticism, 1589

tenacity, self-respect, 1565

tenderness, Hume, 807

tenure: academic ethics, 10; academic freedom, 11–12, 13

Teraspulsky, Laurie, social psychology, 1615

Teresa, Mother, theological ethics, 1705

Teresa of Avila, Saint [Teresa de Jesus]: mysticism, 1198; women moral philosophers, 1823–1824

term limits, government ethics, 626

terminal illness: analogical argument, 59; dignity dignity, 406; euthanasia, 492–497; killing and letting die, 948; life and death, 997; moral community, 1117; suicide, 1671; violence, 1754

terminology. *See* moral terms

terms of bargains, bargaining, 124

territoriality: international conflict, 872–873; property, 1392; war and peace, 1782, 1783

territories: legitimacy, 961; Rawls, 1459

terrorism, **1696–1699**; deliberation and choice, 384; duty and obligation, 425; Hare, 651; life and death, 996, 997; military ethics, 1096; nuclear ethics, 1249; rape, 1445, 1446; war and peace, 1783

Tertullian, the absurd, 8

tests: competition, 277; impartiality, 841–843; public health, 1417

tetrapharmakos, Epicureanism, 474

TGI (transaction generated information), computers, 284–285

Thalberg, Irving, action, 14

Thales: golden rule, 614; presocratic Greek ethics, 687

thankfulness, gratitude, 630

Thatcher, Margaret, materialism, 1057

Theano II, women moral philosophers, 1821

Theater of the Absurd, the absurd, 7

theft: conventions, 332; correctional ethics, 341; Duns Scotus, 421; evil, 498; forgery, 558; plagiarism, 1316–1317

theism, **1699–1702**; agnosticism, 43, 44; atheism, 100, 101; Butler, 177–178; Camus, 182; Duns Scotus, 420, 421, 422; evil, 498–501; Hindu ethics, 677, 681–682, 683; historiography, 684; humanism, 802; Hume, 808; Kant, 933; Locke, 1010; mysticism, 1198; nineteenth-century British ethics, 740, 745; Pascal, 1278; philosophy of religion, 1310, 1311–1313; religion, 1473; seventeenth- and eighteenth-century ethics, 733, 738; skepticism, 1591; theological ethics, 1702–1706; virtue ethics, 1758; Wolff, 1816; women moral philosophers, 1826. *See also* God; monotheism

theocrats, individualism, 848

theodicy: evil, 498–500; Malebranche, 1038

Theodorus, Cyrenaics, 370–371, 372

theological ethics, **1702–1706**; Ayer, 116, 117; Balguy, 121; Bentham, 138; Butler, 176–177; Cambridge Platonists, 180; charity, 203, 204; Clarke, 245; double effect, 418–419; early Medieval ethics, 709–714; Edward, 445–446; eudaimonism, 491; Fénelon, 539–540; golden rule, 615, 616; later Medieval ethics, 718; medical ethics, 1069–1070; moral absolutes, 1113; moral sense theorists, 1174, 1176; Niebuhr, 1234–1235; nineteenth-century British ethics, 739; Paley, 1273–1274; Thomas Aquinas, 1708–1710; virtue ethics, 1761

theological rationalism, philosophy of religion, 1311–1312

theological voluntarism, philosophy of religion, 1311–1312

theology: Abelard, 1–2; the absurd, 7–8; agnosticism, 44; alienation, 48; Anselm, 77–78; Augustine, 102–105; Buddhist ethics, 163–168; Cambridge Platonists, 179–180; casuistry, 188–189; Christian ethics, 222, 224, 226, 227; conscience, 298; Crusius, 362–363; Cyrenaics, 371; evil, 499–500; Grotius, 633; Hindu ethics, 676–683; humanism, 801; Hume, 808; Ibn Rushd, 825; Ibn Ţufayl, 826; Islam, 883–884, 885; Islamic ethics, 889–893; Jewish ethics, 910–915; Kant, 933; later Medieval ethics, 716; Leibniz, 963; liberalism, 974; Malebranche, 1037–1038; mysticism, 1197; natural law, 1207–1208; nature, 1219; philosophy of religion, 1310–1313; pride, 1376; Renaissance ethics, 729; right to life, 1003; Schelling, 1536; seventeenth- and eighteenth-century ethics, 731, 734, 735; Shi'ism, 1580; Sunnism, 1673; Taoist ethics, 1680–1684; Thomas Aquinas, 1709–1711; Voltaire, 1770; voluntarism, 1773; Weber, 1793; William of Ockham, 1803–1804; women moral philosophers, 1826. *See also* theism; theological ethics

Theophrastus, Hellenistic ethics, 696, 699

theoretical hypotheses, moral realism, 1155

theoretical knowledge, *phronesis*, 1314

theoretical perfectionism, perfectionism, 1289, 1290

Volume key: Volume 1, pages 1–642; volume 2, pages 643–1266; volume 3, pages 1267–1977.

1943

theoretical philosophical scrutiny, bioethics, 143

theoretical reason[ing]: Kant, 932–933; moral realism, 1155; practical reason[ing], 1357

theoretical wisdom. *See sophia*

theôria, Aristotle, 97

theory and practice, **1706–1708**; applied ethics, 81–82; bioethics, 142; duty and obligation, 427–428; engineering ethics, 463–464; al-Fārābī, 525; Fichte, 542; Kant, 932–933; Maimonides, 1036; Montaigne, 1107; moral attention, 1115–1116; nature, 1220; *phronesis*, 1314–1316; practical reason[ing], 1357; pragmatism, 1361–1362; praxis, 1364–1366; reflective equilibrium, 1468–1469; Schweitzer, 1541; situation ethics, 1586–1587; skepticism, 1591; twentieth-century Anglo-American ethics, 769; twentieth-century Continental ethics, 764; Whewell, 1800

Theory of Forms. *See* Form of the Good

theory of intrinsic value, Brentano, 157

Theory of Justice, A: communitarianism, 271; economic analysis, 432, 437; Green, 632; institutions, 858; justice, distributive, 921–924; moral rules, 1168; multiculturalism, 1190; psychology, 1409; Rawls, 1454, 1455, 1456, 1457–1458; reflective equilibrium, 1467, 1468; self and social self, 1545; social and political philosophy, 1603, 1605; social contract, 1612; twentieth-century Anglo-American ethics, 770

theory of justification, metaethics, 1081

Theory of Moral Sentiments, The: moral sense theorists, 1174; nineteenth-century British ethics, 746; prudence, 1400; Smith, 1597

theory of the good. *See* good, theories of the

theory of the right. *See* right, concepts of

theory of values. *See* value, theory of

theosis, Christian ethics, 223

therapeutic deception, medical ethics, 1062

therapist, sexual abuse, 1568

Theravada Buddhism, China, 216

Thérèse, Saint: elite, 450; happiness, 648

Thermodontine, lesbian ethics, 968

Thessalonians, Paul, 1284

thinking. *See* thought

Third World: anthropology, 80; feminist ethics, 528, 537; gay ethics, 600; international distributive justice, 874–877; library, 991, 992; multiculturalism, 1188; Niebuhr, 1235; work, 1830

third-party beneficiaries: rights, 1508; utilitarianism, 1742

third-party harm: self-defense, 1556; sexuality, 1573; violence and non-violence, 1754, 1755; war and peace, 1786; work, 1829

Thiroux, Jacques P., engineering ethics, 463

thirst, classical Greek ethics, 694

Thirty Years War: Grotius, 633; military ethics, 1094

Thomas, Laurence, egoism, 448

Thomas à Kempis, humility, 815

Thomas Aquinas, Saint, **1708–1711**; animals, 70; autonomy of ethics, 110; beneficence, 129; casuistry, 187; charity, 203; children, 208; Christian ethics, 223, 224, 227; Chu Hsi, 228; civil disobedience, 237; common good, 262, 263, 264; common sense moralists, 267; conscience, 298; courage, 353, 354; Donegan, 417, 418; double effect, 418; Duns Scotus, 420; early Medieval ethics, 711; eudaimonism, 491; Foot, 555; free will, 573; friendship, 582; generosity, 601; gratitude, 629–630; happiness, 648; honor, 788; hope, 791; Hume, 807; humilty, 815; hypocrisy, 821–822; King, 950; later Medieval ethics, 716, 717, 719; love, 1020; MacIntyre, 1035; Maimonides, 1036; military ethics, 1094; moral absolutes, 1111–1112; moral development, 1119; multiculturalism, 1190; mysticism, 1197; natural law, 1205, 1207, 1208, 1209, 1210; nature, 1218; neo-Stoicism, 1231; perfectionism, 1288, 1289, 1290; philosophy of religion, 1312; practical wisdom, 1358; prudence, 1398–1399, 1400; Renaissance ethics, 721; right to life, 1003; self-defense, 1555–1556; seventeenth- and eighteenth-century ethics, 731; sexuality, 1572; Suárez, 1663; suicide, 1669; supererogation, 1673; theism, 1700; theological ethics, 1702, 1703, 1705; twentieth-century Anglo-American ethics, 772; virtue ethics, 1758–1759, 1760, 1761; Vitoria, 1768; William of Ockham, 1803; work, 1827

Thomasius, Christian, **1711–1712**; Pufendorf, 1423, 1424; seventeenth- and eighteenth-century ethics, 733

Thomism. *See* Thomas Aquinas, Saint

Thompson, Kenneth, Niebuhr, 1235

Thomson, Judith Jarvis, **1712–1714**; abortion, 5; action, 14; euthanasia, 493; life and death, 994; self-defense, 1554; technology, 1688

Thoreau, Henry David, **1714–1717**; civil disobedience, 236, 237; conservation ethics, 307, 309; elite, 451; King, 950; public and private morality, 1411; transcendentalism, 1724, 1725, 1726, 1727

Thornton, James, moral point of view, 1141, 1143

"Thou shalt" expressions, Buber, 161

thought: analogical, 59–63; Anscombe, 75; Arendt, 84; Aristotle, 92, 96; Ayer, 117; classical Greek ethics, 694; excellence, 504; feminist ethics, 536; Fichte, 542; forms of consciousness, 464, 564; Foucault, 568; immoralism, 838; James, 899; moral attention, 1115–1116; moral reasoning, 1160–1163; Murdoch, 1192; political correctness, 1338; sexuality, 1573; voluntary acts, 1774;

weakness of will, 1789, 1791; Wittgenstein, 1811

thought homogenization, Japan, 902

thought-experiments, moral realism, 1157–1158

thoughtlessness, responsibility, 1488, 1490

Thrasymachus: good, 621; government ethics, 624; presocratic Greek ethics, 90, 689; Sophists, 1628, 1629; strategic interaction, 1658

threats: bargaining, 123; blackmail, 151–152; conventions, 330; courage, 3352; economic liberty, 982; promises, 1386; punishment, 1425; rape, 1443; self-defense, 1554, 1555, 1556; social and political philosophy, 1601. *See also* deterrence, threats, and retaliation

Three Mile Island, nuclear ethics, 1249

Three People's Principle, China, 221

threefold body, Buddha, 162

Thucydides: government ethics, 624, 625; international conflict, 871–872; presocratic Greek ethics, 686, 688, 689; Sophists, 1628; virtues, 1767

thumos, anger, 68

Thurber, James, bad faith, 119

Thus Spoke Zarathustra: elite, 450; existential ethics, 510; generosity, 601; Nietzsche, 1236, 1237, 1238, 1239; tragedy, 1723; virtue ethics, 1761

ti, China, 211

Tieck, Ludwig, Fichte, 543

t'ien, China, 211, 212, 213

t'ien ming, China, 215

Tilak, G. B., Hindu ethics, 682

Tillich, Paul: Christian ethics, 227–228; King, 950

Tim(ai)onides, women moral philosophers, 1821

time: beneficence, 130; Plotinus, 1331

timidity, courage, 353

Timmons, Mark, moral realism, 1157

Timon of Phlius, Hellenistic ethics, 698

tipping, bribery, 159

Tīrthankaras, Jainism, 897

title, property, 1392

Title IV (Civil Rights Act of 1964), political correctness, 1338

Title IX (Educational Amendments of 1972), political correctness, 1338

Title VII (Civil Rights Act of 1964), civil rights, 240–241

Titus, genocide, 607

TMI case, engineering ethics, 463

Tocqueville, Alexis de: democracy, 387; individualism, 849; liberalism, 972, 973

token state, causation and responsibility, 195

tokens, action, 13–14

Toland, John: Locke, 1010; Voltaire, 1770

toleration, **1717–1719**; applied ethics, 81; Calvin, 179; Cambridge Platonists, 179; censorship, 198; civility, 242, 243; Emerson, 453; James, 900; liberalism, 974; Locke, 1010, 1011; moral relativism, 1166, 1167; multiculturalism, 1189;

Volume key: Volume 1, pages 1–642; volume 2, pages 643–1266; volume 3, pages 1267–1977.

1944

Volume key: Volume 1, pages 1–642; volume 2, pages 643–1266; volume 3, pages 1267–1977.

1945

Volume key: Volume 1, pages 1–642; volume 2, pages 643–1266; volume 3, pages 1267–1977.

1946

Volume key: Volume 1, pages 1–642; volume 2, pages 643–1266; volume 3, pages 1267–1977.

1947

Volume key: Volume 1, pages 1–642; volume 2, pages 643–1266; volume 3, pages 1267–1977.

1948

Volume key: Volume 1, pages 1–642; volume 2, pages 643–1266; volume 3, pages 1267–1977.

1949

Volume key: Volume 1, pages 1–642; volume 2, pages 643–1266; volume 3, pages 1267–1977.

Volume key: Volume 1, pages 1–642; volume 2, pages 643–1266; volume 3, pages 1267–1977.

1951

Volume key: Volume 1, pages 1–642; volume 2, pages 643–1266; volume 3, pages 1267–1977.

1952

Volume key: Volume 1, pages 1–642; volume 2, pages 643–1266; volume 3, pages 1267–1977.

1953

Volume key: Volume 1, pages 1–642; volume 2, pages 643–1266; volume 3, pages 1267–1977.

1954

Citation Index

The following index lists the 3700 authors (or editors) of the books and articles cited in the bibliographies in this encyclopedia. Corporate authors, legal cases, and journals cited separately are listed at the beginning of the index. Works mentioned in five or more bibliographies are listed by title under the author's or editor's name. Works that are co-authored or co-edited are represented under the names of each co-author or co-editor. Anthologies are represented, under the name(s) of the editor(s), only when they have a separate bibliographic entry. Authors of articles mentioned in the annotations of such anthologies are also listed. Translators and editors of compilations of works by one author are not listed. **Boldface** indicates the first page of the bibliography in biographical entries.

The reader should note that a name may appear more than once on any of the pages given, and that the form of the name that appears in the bibliography may vary slightly from the form of the name in this list. Such variation is the inevitable result of different citation styles used by the authors of the *Encyclopedia* entries. The editors have made every effort to insure that two people with the same, or similar, names have not been combined into one listing (see, for examples, John Marshall, Susan Wolf, and Michael Zimmerman), and that no one is listed twice when once would have sufficed. The editors tender apologies to anyone who has been inadvertently merged with an unsuspecting colleague in the one case, or twinned in the other case.

Journals cited separately

Bioethics, 1066
Cahiers staëliens, 1645
Cambridge Quarterly of Health Care Ethics: CQ: The International Journal for Health Care Ethics Committees, 1066
Criminal Justice Ethics, 1336
Economics and Philosophy, 438
Ethics: An International Journal of Social, Political, and Legal Philosophy, 1066
Gossip: A Journal of Lesbian Feminist Ethics, 968
Hastings Center Report, 1066
Holocaust and Genocide Studies, 608
Human Life Review, 1004
Hypatia: A Journal of Feminist Philosophy, 187
IRB: A Review of Human Subjects Research, 1066
JAMA: The Journal of the American Medical Association, 1066
The Journal of Ayn Rand Studies, 1260
Journal of Chinese Philosophy, 222, 276

Journal of Clinical Ethics, 1066
Journal of Indian Philosophy, 276
Journal of Law, Medicine and Ethics, 1066
Journal of Medical Ethics, 1066
Journal of Medicine and Philosophy, 1066
Journal of the Armenian Assembly of America, 608
Journal of the Philosophy of Sport, 1643
Kennedy Institute of Ethics Journal, 1066
Law and Philosophy, 586
Law, Medicine and Health Care, 1066
Lesbian Ethics, 545, 968
The Locke Newsletter, 1011
Milbank Quarterly, 1066
New England Journal of Medicine, 1066
Philosophy and Public Affairs, 1066
Philosophy East and West, 222, 277
Risk Analysis: An International Journal, 1514
Social Philosophy and Policy, 137, 871
Social Theory and Practice, 431
The Thoreau Quarterly, 1717
Utilitas, 141

Corporate authors

ACI Writing Assistance Center, 1318
American Association of University Professors, 10
American Fertility Society. Ethics Committee, 1481
American Library Association, 992
American Psychiatric Association, 1405
Amnesty International, 184, 1721
Armistice International, 1721
Canada. Royal Commission on New Reproductive Technologies, 1481
Carnegie Commission, 1056
Catholic Church. Congregation for the Doctrine of the Faith, 1481
Catholic Church. National Conference of Catholic Bishops, 1788
Council for International Organizations of Medical Sciences: CIOMS, 145
Group of Lisbon, 175
International Organisation of Islamic Medicine, 896
National Academy of Sciences (U.S.). Committee on Risk and Decision-Making, 1517

Volume key: Volume 1, pages 1–642; volume 2, pages 643–1266; volume 3, pages 1267–1977.

Citation Index

National Council for Research on Women (U.S.), 1340

New York State Task Force on Life and the Law, 146

United Nations Educational, Scientific, and Cultural Organization: UNESCO, 581

United States. Congress, 629, 1481

United States. Department of Commerce, 40

United States. Department of Health, Education, and Welfare, 1832

United States. Employment Standards Administration, 416

United States. National Commission for the Protection of Human Subjects of Biomedical and Behavioral Research, 1381

United States. President's Commission for the Study of Ethical Problems in Medicine and Biomedical and Behavioral Research, 146, 1065, 1417

United States. Presidential Clemency Board, 59

University of Birmingham (Great Britain). Centre for Contemporary Cultural Studies, 367

Legal cases

Biddle v. Perovich, 59
Bowers v. Hardwick, 1384
Boyd v. United States, 1384
Brown v. Board of Education of Topeka, 416
Carey v. Population Services International, 1384
Eisenstadt v. Baird, 1384
Griswald v. Connecticut, 1384
Hudson v. McMillian, 343
Katz v. United States, 1384
Loving v. Virginia, 1384
Morrison v. Olson, 629
Olmstead v. United States, 1384
Rieser v. District of Columbia, 343
Roe v. Wade, 1384
Sidis v. F-R Publishing Company, 1384
Skinner v. Oklahoma, 1384
Stanley v. Georgia, 1384
United States v. Wilson, 59
Whitley v. Albers, 343
Whren et al. v. United States, 1337

Authors

Abba, Giuseppe, 1767
Abbey, Edward, 954
Abbott, Thomas Kingsmill, 617
Abel, G., 1232
Abelard, Peter, **2**, 1313, 1762, 1827
Aboulafia, Mitchell, 1062, 1547
Abrams, M. H., 748
Abu al-Hasan al-Ash'ari, 1673
Acker, James R., 184
Ackerman, Bruce A., 975, 1234, 1393, 1606
Ackerman, Felicia, 489

Ackrill, J. L., 98, 527
Acton, H. B., 279
Adam, A., 540
Adams, E. M., 111, 1214, 1220
Adams, Marilyn McCord, 577, 1701, 1804
Adams, Robert Merrihew, 508, 1173, 1188, 1313, 1491, 1701
Adamson, Robert, 835
Addelson, Kathryn Pyne, 538
Adkins, A. W. H., 690, 1397
Adler, Felix, **23**, 617
Adler, Jacob, 1427
Adler, Renata, 580
Adorno, Theodor W., 107, 360, 367, 1056
Aelred, of Rievaulx, 583, 1026
Aesara, of Lucania, 1827
Aeschylus, 1494
Agger, Ben, 366
Ahmad, Khursheed, 889
Aiken, H. D., 114, 1144
Aiken, Linda H., 1252
Aiken, William, 47, 524
Ainslie, George, 412
Aitken, Robert, 1198
Al-Ash ari Ali ibn Ismäil, 894
al-Farabi. *See* Farabi, al-
Al-Hibri, Azizah, 1016
Alan, of Lille, 714
Albee, Ernest, 738
Albee, Ernest, *A History of English Utilitarianism*, 368, 748, 1179, 1274, 1583
Albertus Magnus, 720
Alderman, Harold, 1239, 1762
Alexander, Jeffrey C., 1622
Alexander, Larry, 1368
Alexander, Richard D., 150
Alexander, Samuel, 748
Alexy, Robert, 617
Algra, K., 702
Allen, Gay Wilson, 900
Allen, Jeffner, 968
Allen, Prudence, 1826
Allen, R. G. D., 439
Allen, Wayne F., 451
Allinson, Robert, 294
Allison, David B., 1241
Allison, Henry, 938, 1641
Allison, Lincoln, 316
Allport, Gordon W., 1618, 1767
Almeder, Robert F., 1514
Alpern, Kenneth, 160
Alston, William P., 111
Altham, J. E. J., 1806
Althusser, Louis, 803, 1109
Alvarez, A., 1671
Ambrose, of Milan, 714
Ames, Bruce, 1517
Ames, Roger T., 231, 295, 297, 1073, 1552, 1684
Anderberg, Thomas, 1671
Anderson, Charles R., 1716
Anderson, Elizabeth, 262, 396, 438, 1140, 1514
Anderson, Quentin, 1727
Anderson, Thomas C., 1532
Anderson, W. French, 1481
Andolsen, Barbara Hilkert, 1026

Andre, Judith, 985
André, Y., 1039
Andreopoulos, George J., 608
Andrew, of Neufchateau, 1706
Andrews, Kenneth R., 174
Andrews, Lori B., 1481
Andrews, Richard, 954
Anechiarico, Frank, 345
Anees, A. A., 895
Anesaki, M., 169
Ang, Ien, 366
Angehrn, Emil, 1048
Angus, Ian, 1056
Annas, Julia, 478, 696, 1326, 1590. *The Morality of Happiness*, 90, 136, 357, 372, 486, 491, 505, 551, 650, 702, 1360, 1693, 1809
Ansbro, John J., 951
Anscombe, G. E. M., 20, **76**, 527, 858, 1210, 1812. *Intention*, 15, 76, 384, 868, 1357, 1776. "Modern Moral Philosophy," 20, 307, 420, 868, 1114, 1475, 1693, 1767
Anselm, **78**, 1075
Antonaccio, Maria, 1192
Appelbaum, Eileen, 1831
Appiah, K. Anthony, 1191, 1439
Apressyan, R. G., 1636
Aquinas, Thomas. *See* Thomas Aquinas
Åqvist, Lennart, 1016, 1350, 1373
Arblaster, Anthony, 975
Archard, David, 210, 303, 524
Ardal, Páll S., 814
Arendt, Hannah, **85**, 109, 257, 362, 381, 451, 608, 1354, 1756
Arendt, Hannah, *The Human Condition*, 85, 451, 1366, 1383, 1413, 1547
Aries, Philippe, 210, 714
Aristotle, 64, **97**, 262, 505, 641, 685, 790, 1007, 1026, 1281, 1357, 1724, 1791. *Eudemian Ethics*, 98, 202, 505, 551, 583, 1762. *Nicomachean Ethics*, 69, 97, 98, 136, 202, 236, 266, 355, 384, 399, 484, 491, 505, 508, 522, 551, 574, 577, 602, 623, 631, 638, 650, 668, 837, 925, 928, 1026, 1086, 1124, 1130, 1150, 1163, 1185, 1292, 1298, 1309, 1316, 1360, 1377, 1401, 1413, 1427, 1466, 1491, 1550, 1561. *Politics*, 202, 236, 388, 1130, 1263, 1298, 1309, 1346, 1762
Arius Didymus, 551
Armour, Leslie, 1279
Armstrong, A. H., 714, 1331
Armstrong, David, 197
Arneson, Richard J., 522, 853, 1284, 1461
Arnim, I. von, 1657
Arnold, E. Vernon, 709, 1567
Arnold, Peter J., 1643
Arnold, Robert M., 1066
Aron, Raymond, 873
Aroskar, Mila A., 1252
Arras, John D., 1065, 1380
Arrow, Kenneth J., 438, 444, 1346, 1451, 1461, 1520
Arthur, John, 133, 960, 1191
Arvin, Newton, 454
Asch, Adrienne, 524
Asch, Solomon E., 1618

Volume key: Volume 1, pages 1–642; volume 2, pages 643–1266; volume 3, pages 1267–1977.

1956

Volume key: Volume 1, pages 1–642; volume 2, pages 643–1266; volume 3, pages 1267–1977.

1957

Citation Index

Volume key: Volume 1, pages 1–642; volume 2, pages 643–1266; volume 3, pages 1267–1977.

1958

Volume key: Volume 1, pages 1–642; volume 2, pages 643–1266; volume 3, pages 1267–1977.

Volume key: Volume 1, pages 1–642; volume 2, pages 643–1266; volume 3, pages 1267–1977.

1960

Volume key: Volume 1, pages 1–642; volume 2, pages 643–1266; volume 3, pages 1267–1977.

1961

Citation Index

Volume key: Volume 1, pages 1–642; volume 2, pages 643–1266; volume 3, pages 1267–1977.

Volume key: Volume 1, pages 1–642; volume 2, pages 643–1266; volume 3, pages 1267–1977.

1963

Citation Index

Hampshire, Stuart, 32, 629, 975, 1134, 1144, 1215, 1360, 1809
Hampton, Jean, 388, 778, 1415, 1606, 1613. *Forgiveness and Mercy*, 70, 562, 662, 1075, 1428, 1494
Haney, Craig, 1619
Hanmer, T. J., 1125
Hannaford, Robert V., 618
Hannay, Alastair, 295, 947
Hansson, Bengt, 1016
Hardie, W. F. R., 98, 491, 790, 1792
Hardimon, Michel, 675
Hardin, Garrett, 133
Hardin, Russell, 127, 336, 593, 863, 1244, 1250, 1346, 1451, 1584, 1613, 1731
Harding, Walter, 1717
Hare, John E., 629, 1096, 1474
Hare, Peter H., 501, 685
Hare, R. M., 618, **651**, 652, 1127, 1144, 1164, 1182, 1371, 1594, 1636, 1721, 1737, 1792. *Freedom and Reason*, 114, 151, 428, 618, 1026, 1170, 1266, 1371, 1737, 1792. *The Language of Morals*, 67, 428, 651, 1016, 1087, 1130, 1170, 1215, 1217, 1371, 1492, 1592, 1749. *Moral Thinking*, 42, 618, 652, 843, 1016, 1026, 1087, 1170, 1182, 1215, 1371, 1708, 1737, 1792
Hargrove, Eugene C., 470
Harman, Gilbert, 829, 868, 1167, 1188, 1599, 1619, 1714. *The Nature of Morality*, 325, 1087, 1160, 1164, 1592
Harré, Rom, 197, 1410
Harris, Adrienne, 1756
Harris, C. R. S., 422
Harris, Errol E., 1641
Harris, George W., 90, 406, 1137, 1558, 1561
Harris, John, 42, 73
Harris, Leonard, 1440
Harris, Paul, 238
Harrison, Jonathan, 814, 829
Harrison, Ross, 141, 1583, 1806
Harsanyi, John, 325, 438, 444, 1461, 1520, 1613, 1689
Hart, H. L. A., 420, 522, **657**, 928, 975, 1004, 1245, 1416, 1428, 1461, 1498, 1512. *Essays on Bentham*, 128, 141, 657, 1502, 1512. *Punishment and Responsibility*. 508, 657, 858, 1225, 1428, 1492
Hartland, E. Sidney, 257
Hartley, L. P., 472
Hartman, Edwin M., 174
Hartmann, Heinz, 1405
Hartmann, Nicolai, **659**, 1308, 1753
Hartsock, Nancy, 1576
Hartung, Gerald, 1211, 1425
Hasegawa Nyozekan, 904
Haslett, D. W., 444
Hathout, H., 896
Hauerwas, Stanley, 101, 1401, 1706, 1762
Hauptman, Robert, 992
Hausman, Daniel M., 438, 445
Havard, William C., 1583
Hawkins, Gordon, 1428

Hawley, John Stratton, 683
Haworth, Lawrence, 114
Hayek, F. A. von, 445, 851, 925, 975, 1041, 1215, 1245, 1662
Hays, Richard B., 1286
Hays, Samuel P., 310
Hayward, F. H., 1583
Hazard, Geoffrey C., 957
Hazelton, Roger, 659
Hazlitt, William, 824
Head, John G., 266
Headley, Bruce, 1797
Heal, G. M., 412
Hearn, Jeff, 1263
Hebdige, Dick, 367
Heffernan, J., 954
Heffernan, William C., 1336
Hegel, G. W. F., 20, 50, 276, 280, 543, **675**, 702, 835, 1547, 1553, 1724. *Philosophie des Rechts*, 20, 316, 675, 824, 835, 1393, 1395, 1428
Hegeman, Elizabeth, 1651
Heidegger, Martin, **676**, 803, 1241, 1353, 1537, 1691. *Being and Time*, 50, 107, 514, 676, 1153, 1185, 1309, 1547
Heidsieck, François, 790
Heimsoeth, Heinz, 659
Heinekamp, Albert, 965
Heiss, Robert, 659
Held, David, 360, 644
Held, Virginia, 251, 257, 449, 538, 1056, 1140, 1419, 1454, 1547
Helm, Paul, 1313, 1475, 1701
Heloise, 1827
Hempel, Carl G., 1160
Hendel, Charles W., 814, 1525
Henefin, Mary Sue, 1481
Henkin, Louis, 800
Hennessey, Patricia, 6
Henrich, Dieter, 1538
Henry, P., 1331
Hense, O., 370
Henson, Richard G., 999
Herford, R., Travers, 915
Herman, Barbara, 685, 939, 1576. *The Practice of Moral Judgment*, 90, 396, 428, 564, 866, 939, 943, 1138, 1164, 1277
Herman, Edward S., 567
Herman, Judith Lewis, 1569
Hermeren, Goran, 111
Hernández Martín, Ramón, 1770
Herrad, of Hohenbourg, 1827
Hertzler, J. O., 618
Heslep, R., 416
Hesse-Biber, Sharlene, 1831
Hestevold, H. Scott, 1075, 1395
Hetcher, Steven, 1245
Hewison, Nancy S., 992
Heyd, David, 355, 589, 1676, 1718
Heyer, George S., Jr., 78
Heywood, Paul, 345
Hick, John, 501
Hicks, John, 439
Hiers, Richard H., 909
Higgins, Ann, 1125, 1131
Higgins, Kathleen M., 1239
Hildebrand, Dietrich von, 1308
Hildegard, of Bingen, 1827

Hill, John, 1111
Hill, Sharon Bishop, 114
Hill, Thomas E., Jr., 320. *Autonomy and Self-Respect*, 114, 406, 939, 1558, 1565. *Dignity and Practical Reason in Kant's Moral Theory*, 193, 320, 406, 939, 943, 1558, 1676
Hillman, Robert A., 328
Hilpinen, Risto, 1016
Hinchman, Lewis P., 85
Hinchman, Sandra K., 85
Hindrey, Rodrick, 683
Hinsley, F. H., 874
Hintikka, Jaakko, 527, 1016
Hiriyanna, Mysore, 945
Hirsch, Emil R., 618
Hirschmann, Albert, 204
Hirshleifer, Jack, 338
Hirshman, Lisa, 1569
Hirst, E. W., 618
Hittinger, R., 1211
Hoagland, Sarah Lucia, 538, 545, 968
Hobart, R. E., 578
Hobbes, Thomas, 238, 578, 624, **778**, 1329. *Leviathan*, 207, 257, 280, 325, 332, 449, 484, 618, 624, 778, 790, 800, 874, 975, 1150, 1215, 1281, 1413, 1454, 1502, 1613, 1662, 1773
Hobhouse, Leonard, 484, 851, 975
Hoche, Hans-Ulrich, 618, 1737
Hochschild, Jennifer L., 1797
Hochstrasser, T. J., 1211
Hodges, D. C., 618
Hodgson, D. H., 401
Hodgson, Marshall G. S., 887, 894
Hodgson, Shadworth, 749
Hoebel, E. Adamson, 786
Hoekema, David A., 401
Hoffman, Joshua, 578
Hoffman, Martin, 1125
Hoffman, Michael, 251
Hoffman, Stacey, 257, 638
Hoffman, Stanley, 877, 1096
Hofmann, E., 1645
Hoggart, Richard, 367
Hohfeld, Wesley Newcomb, 1502, 1512
Hohler, T. P., 543
Hoistad, R., 370
Holbach, Paul Henri Thiry, **779**
Holland, A. J. 685
Holland, Roy, 1814
Holland, Thomas E., 1502
Hollingdale, R. J., 1239
Hollis, Martin, 439
Holloran, Thomas E., 1649
Holmes, Helen Bequaert, 1481
Holmes, Robert L., 1096, 1756, 1788
Holmes, Stephen, 871, 976
Holmstrom, Nancy, 416, 1054, 1498
Holzhey, Helmut, 1228
Honderich, Ted, 574, 1395, 1428
Honoré, A. M., 657, 928, 1393
Hont, Istvan, 1211
Hood, Roger, 185
Hook, Sidney, 13, 659, 999
Hooker, Brad, 1668
Hooker, Michael, 160
hooks, bell, 367
Hoose, Bernard, 1114, 1395

Volume key: Volume 1, pages 1–642; volume 2, pages 643–1266; volume 3, pages 1267–1977.

1964

Volume key: Volume 1, pages 1–642; volume 2, pages 643–1266; volume 3, pages 1267–1977.

1965

Volume key: Volume 1, pages 1–642; volume 2, pages 643–1266; volume 3, pages 1267–1977.

Volume key: Volume 1, pages 1–642; volume 2, pages 643–1266; volume 3, pages 1267–1977.

Volume key: Volume 1, pages 1–642; volume 2, pages 643–1266; volume 3, pages 1267–1977.

1968

Volume key: Volume 1, pages 1–642; volume 2, pages 643–1266; volume 3, pages 1267–1977.

1969

Citation Index

Nietzsche, Friedrich, 107, 362, 497, 514, 602, 824, 841, **1239**, 1241, 1292, 1553, 1724, 1762, 1809, 1810. *Beyond Good and Evil*, 32, 280, 841, 1292, 1377, 1762, 1802. *On the Genealogy of Morals*, 362, 641, 841, 1281, 1353, 1428, 1486, 1762
Nill, Michael, 391, 1397, 1631
Nisbett, Richard E., 1619
Nishida Kitaro, 904, 905
Nishitani Keiji, 905
Nissenbaum, Helen, 287, 1383
Nitecki, Doris V., 150
Nitecki, Matthew H., 150
Nivison, David S., 222, 295, 297, 1073
Noddings, Nel, *Caring*, 187, 539, 969, 1130, 1252, 1303, 1679
Noonan, John T., 160, 228, 1004, 1576
Norcross, Alastair, 879, 950
Norman, Ralph V., 272
Norman, Richard, 1814
North, Helen, 1696
Norton, Bryan G., 470
Norton, David, 819
Norton, David Fate, 814
Novak, David, 1672
Novak, Michael, 175
Novak, William, 338
Novitz, David, 1134
Nowell-Smith, P. H., 1215, 1374
Noxon, J., 814
Nozick, Robert, 21, 125, 248, 396, 497, 999, **1246**, 1247, 1292, 1561. *Anarchy, State, and Utopia*, 42, 272, 445, 467, 472, 484, 517, 522, 800, 925, 928, 954, 978, 1115, 1246, 1263, 1393, 1416, 1461, 1502, 1512, 1563, 1606, 1613, 1831
Nussbaum, Martha, 90, 439, 505, 539, 702, 877, 925, 1036, 1205, 1292, 1461, 1576, 1724. *The Fragility of Goodness*, 90, 202, 262, 491, 506, 624, 1137, 1138, 1225, 1360, 1724. *Love's Knowledge*, 202, 1007, 1130, 1134, 1138, 1205, 1360. *The Therapy of Desire*, 70, 90, 458, 506, 624, 650, 702, 709, 1030, 1360, 1567, 1810
Nygren, Anders, 204, 228, 1027
Nyiri, J. C., 317

O'Brien, Conor C., 170
O'Brien, D., 1331
O'Brien, David, 1383
O'Brien, William V., 1096
O'Connell, Laurence J., 1380
O'Connell, Sean, 1553
O'Connor, Alan, 367
O'Connor, D. J., 1211
O'Connor, Timothy, 197, 574
O'Donovan, Oliver, 1027
O'Driscoll, Lyla, 1075
O'Flaherty, Wendy Doniger, 683, 945
O'Gorman, Frank, 170
O'Hear, Anthony, 317
O'Meara, John Joseph, 715
O'Neill, J., 851
O'Neill, Onora, 280, 320, 524, 548, 877, 939, 1636, 1814. *Constructions of Reason*, 194, 244, 320, 939, 1188.

Towards Justice and Virtue, 90, 205, 320, 428, 564
O'Neill, William, 1260
Oakes, Guy, 1228
Oakeshott, Michael, 317, 629
Oates, W. J., 624
Obermann, Heiko, 1804
Odbert, Henry, 1767
Oddie, Graham, 950
Odin, Steve, 905
Oestrich, G., 1232
Ogden, C. K., 459, 1651
Okin, Susan Moller, 449, 524, 539
Olafson, Frederick A., 1309
Oldenquist, Andrew, 1029, 1277, 1831
Oliner, Pearl M., 53
Oliner, Samuel P., 53
Olivecrona, Karl, 739
Oliver, F. S., 345
Ollig, Hans-Ludwig, 1228
Olson, Mancur, Jr., 336, 1054, 1416, 1451
Ong, Walter, 280
Oppenheim, Charles, 992
Oppenheim, Felix E., 981
Oppenheimer, Helen, 1377
Oppermann, H., 709
Ortega y Gasset, José, 107, 514
Osborn, Eric, 228
Osler, M. J., 597, 1232
Osler, William, 999
Osterhammel, Jürgen, 1794
Osterhoudt, Robert G., 1643
Otto, Rudolph, 1199
Outka, Gene, 101, 137, 228, 947, 1027, 1115, 1475
Ovid, 1792
Owens, David, 569
Ozment, Steven E., 1199

p'Bitek, Okot, 36
Packe, Michael St. John, 1104
Packer, Barbara L., 454, 1728
Padgug, Robert, 1576
Paetzold, Ramona, 1569
Pagden, Anthony, 1770
Page, Alfred N., 439
Paine, Thomas, **1272**, 1273
Paley, William, 750, 790, **1274**, 1313
Palladini, Fiammetta, 1425
Palmer, Julie Gage, 606
Palmer, R., 591
Panichas, George A., 1116
Panizza, Letizia, 730
Panzer, Elisha A., 445
Parekh, Bhikhu, 141
Parens, Erik, 524
Parent, William, 1383
Parenti, Michael, 1056
Pareto, Vilfredo, 439, 451
Parfit, Derek, 396, 589, 853, 879, 1668. *Reasons and Persons*, 21, 42, 378, 413, 449, 551, 589, 624, 863, 879, 1079, 1118, 1299, 1464, 1667
Pargetter, R., 1350, 1550
Park, Dorothy G., 659
Parker, DeWitt H., 1753
Parker, Robert, 1153
Parkin, Charles W., 170
Parkin, John, 368

Parsons, Charles, 1419
Parsons, Kathryn Pyne, 33
Parsons, Talcott, 1245, 1622
Partridge, Ernest, 471, 548
Pascal, Blaise, 189, 1115, **1279**
Paskins, Barrie A., 1096, 1699
Passerin d'Entrèves, Alessandro, 428, 739, 1211
Passmore, John, 181, 364, 471, 814, 954
Pastin, Mark, 160
Pateman, Carole, 389, 1257, 1346, 1548, 1613
Pater, Walter, 33
Paterson, David, 74
Paton, H. J., 939, 1144, 1651
Patrides, C. A., 181
Patten, Steven, 462, 1048, 1104
Patterson, O., 1594
Paul, Ellen Frankel, 205, 1250
Paul, Gregor, 295
Paul, J., 1638
Paul, Jeffrey, 925, 1247
Paul, Sherman, 454, 1717
Paul, the Apostle, 205, 1792
Pauley, W. C. De. *See* De Pauley, W. C.
Paulhus, Delroy L., 1553
Paulsen, Monrad G., 1225
Paxton, Michael, 1443
Payne, Robert, 1377
Payner, Richard J., 1199
Pears, David, 1553, 1792
Peffer, R. G., 1048
Peikoff, Leonard, 1260
Peirce, Charles Sanders, 64, **1288**, 1364
Peirce, J., 464
Pelczynski, Z. B., 675
Pelczynski, Zbigniew, 981
Pelligrino, Edmund D., 548
Pembroke, S. G., 357
Pence, Gregory E., 1065, 1481, 1768
Pence, Terry, 1253
Penelhum, Terence, 177, 669, 814, 1271
Penner, T., 1326, 1628
Pennock, J., Roland, 248, 282, 976, 1346, 1393
Peperzak, Adriaan, 971
Pepper, Stephen C., 1753
Perelman, C., 484
Perictione I., 1827
Peristiany, J. G., 641
Perkins, Rollin M., 304
Perlin, Seymour, 1672
Perrin, Norman, 909
Perry, David L., 1329
Perry, John, 1299
Perry, Michael J., 800
Perry, Ralph B., 901, 999, **1293**. *General Theory of Value*, 56, 1215, 1293, 1749, 1753
Petchesky, Rosalind Pollack, 6
Peterken, G. F., 310
Peters, Edward, 362, 1721
Peters, Julie, 539
Peters, R. S., 109, 925, 1131, 1454, 1498, 1606
Peterson, Merrill D., 906
Peterson, Richard A., 1691
Peterson, Susan Rae, 1446
Petrovic, Gajo, 50, 1548
Pettit, Philip, 385, 444, 863

Volume key: Volume 1, pages 1–642; volume 2, pages 643–1266; volume 3, pages 1267–1977.

1970

Volume key: Volume 1, pages 1–642; volume 2, pages 643–1266; volume 3, pages 1267–1977.

1971

Citation Index

Ricoeur, Paul, 793, 1308, **1499**
Ridolfi, R., 1034
Riedel, Manfred, 675, 1817
Rieff, Philip, 1406
Riegel, Jeffrey, 1073
Riker, William, 389
Riley, Patrick, 1211
Rintelen, Fritz-Joachim von, 817
Rispler-Chaim, V., 896
Risser, James, 591
Rist, John M., 105, 702, 709, 1331
Ritchie, David G., 750, 1512
Robbins, John W., 1260
Robbins, Lionel, 439
Roberts, H. R. T., 59
Roberts, Kevin W. S., 445
Roberts, Robert C., 506, 784, 1561, 1762, 1768
Roberts, Tom Aerwyn, 137, 1179
Robertson, John, 519
Robertson, John A., 1481
Robin, Richard, 1288
Robinet, A., 1039
Robins, Michael H., 1358, 1389
Robinson, Fiona, 539
Robinson, George M., 10, 13, 1318
Robinson, Nehemiah, 608
Robinson, R., 1792
Robinson, Richard, 459, 1305, 1651
Robinson, Richard H., 163, 1201
Rochot, Bernard, 597
Rockefeller, Stephen, 40
Rodis-Lewis, Geneviève, 398, 1039
Roe, Emery, 1205
Roebuck, Julian B., 1336
Roemer, John, 388, 925, 517, 1048
Roemig, R. F., 182
Roetz, Heiner, 297
Rogerson, S., 286
Rohatyn, Denis, 1111
Rollin, Bernard, 74, 606
Rolston, Holmes, 150
Rolston, Holmes III, 471
Romilly, Jacqueline de, 1631
Rommen, H. A., 739
Rommetveit, Ragnar, 1245
Roquebert, Michel, 1269
Rorty, Amélie, 458, 506, 631, 999, 1299, 1360, 1377, 1550, 1551, 1553, 1558. *Essays on Aristotle's Ethics*, 98, 202, 492, 506, 696, 1360
Rorty, Richard, 685, 976, 1353, 1364
Rose, Michael, 1831
Rose-Ackerman, Susan, 345
Rosen, Bernard, 790
Rosen, Fred, 141
Rosen, Jay, 918
Rosenbaum, Alan S., 800
Rosenbaum, Stuart E., 184
Rosenkrantz, Gary, 578
Rosenthal, David M., 84
Rosenthal, Sandra B., 1062
Rosner, Brian S., 1286
Rosner, Menachem, 1831
Ross, Alf, 332
Ross, Jacob Joshua, 524
Ross, Lee, 1619
Ross, W. D., 882, 1127, 1374. **1521**. *The Right and the Good*, 21, 207, 381, 396, 545, 882, 928, 1017, 1079,

1115, 1170, 1217, 1292, 1374, 1389, 1521, 1749
Rossi, Alice, 538
Rossiter, Clinton, 317
Rost, H. T. D., 618
Roth, Alois, 817
Roth, Guenther, 1794
Rothbard, Murray N., 978, 1563
Rothstein, Mark A., 1481
Rotter, Julian B., 1731
Rougemont, Denis de. *See* de Rougemont, Denis
Rousseau, Jean-Jacques, 236, 332, 389, 1263, **1524**, 1612, 1613. *Émile*, 858, 1125, 1131, 1151, 1524. *The Social Contract*, 236, 266, 325, 332, 389, 1263, 1346, 1454, 1524, 1613, 1773
Routley, Richard, 471, 1250
Routley, Val, 1250
Rowland, Robyn, 1481
Rowley, Harold Henry, 618
Royce, Josiah, 56, 758, 835, 1029, **1526**
Rubin, Richard, 992
Ruby, Jay, 918
Rucker, Darnell, 1733
Ruddick, Sara, 969, 1303. *Maternal Thinking*, 524, 539, 969, 1548, 1756
Ruddick, William, 524, 548, 1419
Ruder, David S., 1649
Rudmin, Floyd, 1059
Ruggerio, Guido de, 976
Ruja, Harry, 1528
Runciman, W.G., 1794
Ruse, Michael, 150, 375, 503
Rush, Florence, 1569
Russell, Bertrand, 238, 332, 685, 1269, 1354, 1419, **1528**, 1576
Russell, Diana E. H., 1349, 1569
Russell, H. J., 619
Russell, Paul, 814
Russett, Cynthia Eagle, 503
Rutherford, R. B., 709
Ruthven, Malise, 1721
Ryan, Alan, 485, 633, 981, 999, 1104, 1393
Ryan, Cheney C., 1097
Ryan, Richard, 1131
Rybalks, M., 514
Ryder, Richard, 74
Ryle, Gilbert, 669, 824, 1271

Saadia ben Joseph (Saadya Gaon), 915
Sabel, Charles F., 1422
Sabini, John, 473
Sachdev, Paul, 6
Sachedina, Abdulaziz A., 1580
Sachs, A., 619
Sachs, David, 1558, 1565
Saddhatisa, Hammalawa, 169
Sade, D. A. F., 362
Sadr, Ayatullah Baqir al-, 889
Sadurski, Wojciech, 1079, 1428
Sagoff, Mark, 352, 471, 954, 1419, 1515
Sahlins, Marshall, 1467
St. Clair, William, 614
Salisbury, Stephan, 1832
Salmon, Merrilee H., 64
Salmond, John William, 1502
Salt, Henry, 74
Samuel, Herbert Louis, 619

Samuel, Otto, 659
Samuelson, N., 915
Samuelson, Paul A., 445, 1451
Sanborn, Frank B., 1717
Sandbach, F. H., 702
Sandel, Michael J., 236, 272, 497, 1413. *Liberalism and the Limits of Justice*, 272, 564, 877, 1461, 1548
Sandkühler, Hans Jörg, 1228
Sandurski, M. J., 928
Santas, G., 1628
Santayana, George 56, 317, 454, 999, 1030, 1134, 1220, 1432, **1530**
Santoni, Ron, 120
Santos, C., 1665
Santurri, Edmund N., 1027
Sapontzis, Steve F., 1118
Sappho, 969
Sarasohn, Lisa, 597
Sartori, Giovanni, 389
Sartorius, Rolf, 926, 1284
Sartre, Jean-Paul, 8, 107, 120, 410, 458, 514, 803, 1007, 1215, 1308, 1366, 1440, **1532**, 1802. *Being and Nothingness*, 8, 120, 641, 824, 999, 1241, 1308, 1532, 1548, 1553
Satris, Stephen, 1651
Saunders, J. L., 1232
Saunders, John Turk, 578
Savage, L. J., 1520
Sayce, R. A., 1108
Sayre, F., 370
Sayre, Kenneth, 1689
Sayre-McCord, Geoffrey, 255, 1087, 1093, 1215
Scanlan, James P., 1636
Scanlon, Thomas M., 114, 125, 199, 325, 396, 416, 497, 522, 1048, 1065, 1461, 1467, 1613
Scarman, Leslie George, 1337
Scarre, Geoffrey, 524
Scarry, Elaine, 1756, 1788
Schabas, William A., 185
Schacht, Richard, 50, 758, 765, 1831
Schaffner, Kenneth F., 64
Schaper, Eva, 33
Schapiro, Renie, 1066
Scharfstein, Ben-Ami, 1199
Schatzberg, Michael G., 1263
Schauer, Frederick F., 199, 581, 1349, 1596
Scheffler, Israel, 1364
Scheffler, Samuel, 42, 43, 194, 307, 410, 1115, 1277, 1461. *Consequentialism and its Critics*, 43, 307, 396, 1115, 1744
Scheick, William J., 1273
Scheler, Max, 53, 1486, **1534**, 1553, 1679
Schell, Jonathan, 1788
Schelling, Friedrich, **1536**
Schelling, Thomas C., 401, 863, 1422, 1515, 1517
Scherer, Donald, 1118
Schiffer, Stephen, 400
Schiller, F. C. S., 1553
Schiller, Friedrich von, 33, **1538**
Schiller, Herbert, 1056
Schilpp, Paul, 161, 515, 1530
Schinzinger, Roland, 464

Volume key: Volume 1, pages 1–642; volume 2, pages 643–1266; volume 3, pages 1267–1977.

1972

Volume key: Volume 1, pages 1–642; volume 2, pages 643–1266; volume 3, pages 1267–1977.

1973

Volume key: Volume 1, pages 1–642; volume 2, pages 643–1266; volume 3, pages 1267–1977.

1974

Volume key: Volume 1, pages 1–642; volume 2, pages 643–1266; volume 3, pages 1267–1977.

Citation Index

Wallace, Gerry, 1494
Wallace, James D., *Virtues and Vices*, 299, 355, 602, 1696, 1763, 1768
Wallace, R. Jay, 574, 578
Wallace, Ronald S., 179
Walliman, Isidor, 608
Wallwork, Ernest, 423, 1027
Walsh, James, 763, 1792
Walsh, W. H., 258, 675, 835
Walter Burley, 720
Walters, LeRoy, 606, 1065, 1071
Walton, Clarence, 175
Walton, Craig, 1039
Walton, Douglas N., 355, 384, 1305, 1358, 1596, 1763
Walton, Richard E., 498
Walz, Kenneth, 629
Walzer, Michael, 40, 410, 874, 1000, 1137, 1346, 1419, 1548, **1779**. *Just and Unjust Wars*, 349, 410, 874, 1000, 1097, 1396, 1419, 1699, 1779, 1789. *Spheres of Justice*, 272, 791, 800, 877, 926, 985, 1141, 1548, 1779
Wang Yang-ming, **1781**
Waquet, Jean-Claude, 346
Ward, Janie Victoria, 1125, 1756
Ward, Mrs. Pauline, 633
Wardell, Mark L., 1622
Wardlaw, Grant, 1699
Wardle, John, 816
Ware, Robert, 462
Warnke, Georgia, 591, 1779
Warnock, G. J., 134, 487, 1182, 1389, 1651
Warnock, Mary, 1217, 1482
Warren, Karen, 471
Warren, Mark E., 1731
Warren, Mary Anne, 6, 1004, 1506
Warrender, Howard, 778
Warriner, D., 954
Wartenberg, Thomas, 1354
Wartofsky, Marx W., 1548
Washington, George, 244
Wasserman, David, 40, 146, 1556
Wasserstrom, Richard A., 185, 258, 416, 858, 957, 1097, 1368, 1420, 1436
Waterlow, Sarah, 527
Watkins, J. W. N., 778
Watson, Burton, 222
Watson, Gary, 114, 578, 1212, 1551, 1696
Watson, Stephen, 1517
Watsuji Tetsuro, 905
Watt, W. M., 887
Wattles, Jeffrey, 619
Watts, Tim J., 992
Weale, Albert, 304, 485
Weber, David R., 238
Weber, Marianne, 1794
Weber, Max, 410, 963, 1354, 1622, **1794**, 1832
Weeks, Jeffrey, 601
Weil, Simone, 428, 791, 1116, 1269, 1757, **1795**
Weil, Vivian, 464
Weimar, David, 1422
Weiner, Paul B., 993
Weinsheimer, Joel C., 591
Weinstein, D. (David), 1638

Weir, Robert F., 1672
Weisenberg, Matisyohu, 1271
Weiss, Paul, 619, 1643
Weiss, R., 631
Weiss, Raymond L., 1037
Weisstub, David N., 1066
Weithman, Paul J., 1461
Weldon, Fay, 1494
Wellbank, J. H., 1461
Wellman, Carl, 800, 1502, 1506, 1512, 1797
Wells, Donald A., 1097
Wendel, François, 179
Wendell, Susan, 40, 539, 1349
Wensinck, A. J., 887
Wenz, Peter S., 471
Werhane, Patricia, 160, 174, 800, 1832
Werkmeister, W. H., 659
Werpehowski, William, 1027
Werth, James L., 1672
Wertheimer, Alan, 125, 248, 517, 1577
Wertheimer, Roger, 1004
Wertz, S. K., 64
Wessell, Leonard P., 1538
Wesson, Robert, 151
West, Celeste, 993
West, Henry R., 1104
Westerman, Pauline C., 1212
Westermann, William Lynn, 1594
Westermarck, Edward, 277, 619, 791, 829, **1799**
Westin, Alan F., 1384, 1832
Wettstein, Howard K., 505, 1762
Wetzel, James, 105
Whately, Richard, 619, 751
Wheelwright, Philip, 619
Whelan, Frederick, 814
Whewell, William, 751, **1800**
Whichcote, Benjamin, 181
Whicher, Stephen, 454
Whitbeck, Caroline, 464, 1548
White, Alan R., 1776
White, James Boyd, 1007
White, Louise G., 1422
White, Morton, 906, 1266, 1364
White, N.P., 326
White, Nicholas, 1584
White, Robert W., 1151
White, Stephen A. 506
White, Stephen K. 170, 644
Whitehead, Alfred North, 501
Whiting, Jennifer, 90, 98, 428, 939
Whitmarsh, Anne, 376
Whittaker, Charles E. 238
Widerker, David, 528
Wiesel, Elie, 1000
Wiggins, David, 90, 98, 194, 262, 1002, 1224, 1316, 1361, 1410, 1668, 1749, 1814
Wiggins, G., 1125
Wigmore, John Henry, 1543
Wijesekara, O. H., de A., 169
Wildavsky, Aaron, 1514, 1517
Wilde, Oscar, 33
Wilder, Amos, 909
Wildt, Andreas, 675
Wilenius, R., 1665
Wilensky, Robert, 1358
Wiles, Peter J. D., 445
Wilkins, Barry, 877

Wilkins, Burleigh Taylor, 170
Wilkinson, Paul, 1699
Willey, Thomas E., 1228
William, of Auxerre, 720
William, of Ockham, 1313, 1502, **1804**
Williams, Bernard, 18, 21, 43, 54, 262, 378, 396, 410, 439, 485, 487, 519, 551, 773, 837, 841, 874, 943, 1127, 1167, 1464, 1596, 1668, 1750, **1806**. *Ethics and the Limits of Philosophy*, 43, 91, 194, 428, 458, 487, 551, 841, 943, 976, 1087, 1141, 1361, 1593, 1619, 1806. *Moral Luck*, 43, 91, 1137, 1188, 1225, 1277, 1492, 1806. *Shame and Necessity*, 506, 641, 791, 841, 1806. *Utilitarianism: For and Against*, 519, 866, 926, 1744, 1806
Williams, Glanville, 508, 786, 856
Williams, Howard, 939
Williams, Linda, 1349
Williams, Patricia A., 151
Williams, Paul, 2
Williams, Raymond, 33, 367, 1056
Williams, William, 74, 1691
Williams, William H., 1104
Williigenburg, Theodoor van, 1469
Willis, Richard H., 1467
Wills, Garry, 105
Wilm, Carl Emil, 1539
Wilson, Allan, 993
Wilson, Catherine, 43
Wilson, David Sloan, 449
Wilson, Edward O., 150, 151, 1000
Wilson, John, 751
Winch, Peter, 77, 765, 866, 1796, 1812, 1813, 1814, 1815
Windelband, Wilhelm, 1228
Wing, Adrien Katherine, 539
Wingren, Gustaf, 1032
Winiger, Kathleen J., 1576
Winkler, John J., 1724
Winkler, Kenneth P., 819
Winkler, R., 1517
Winner, Langdon, 1691
Winslow, Gerald R., 1253
Winston, Kenneth, 586
Winter, Eggert, 1228
Wise, Sue, 1569
Witteveen, Willem, 586
Wittgenstein, Ludwig, 1182, **1812**, 1815
Wittmann, Michael, 817
Wojtyla, Karol [Pope John Paul II], 1535, 1577
Wokler, Robert, 1525
Wolf, Arthur P., 1799
Wolf, Susan M., 1066
Wolf, Susan [R.], 40, 410, 574, 784, 838, 1151, 1173
Wolfe, Susan J., 969
Wolff, Christian, **1817**
Wolff, Hans M., 1712
Wolff, Jonathan, 1247
Wolff, Robert Paul, 939, 963, 1029, 1257, 1264, 1719
Wolfson, Harry A., 1037
Wolgast, Elizabeth H., 1512
Wollacott, J., 1056
Wollaston, William, 1179, **1819**
Wollheim, Richard, 156, 378, 641, 751, 1007

Volume key: Volume 1, pages 1–642; volume 2, pages 643–1266; volume 3, pages 1267–1977.

Wollstonecraft, Mary, 614, **1820**
Wolper, Andrea, 539
Wolter, Allan B., 422
Wong, David B., 277, 282, 1073, 1106, 1167, 1763
Wood, Allen W., 462, 517, 675, 939, 1048
Wood, Gordon, 236
Wood, Robert E., 161
Woodard, J. David, 316
Woods, Michael, 1316
Woodward, Diana, 993
Woodward, James, 589
Woodward, Kathleen, 70
Woolf, Virginia, 1269
Wootton, Barbara, 1428
Woozley, A. D., 866, 1257, 1467
Wright, Crispin, 156, 1668
Wright, G. H., von, 385, 1016, 1017, 1358, 1389, 1753. *The Varieties of Goodness*, 355, 619, 1164, 1358, 1696, 1750, 1763, 1768
Wright, Jack C., 1619

Wright, John P., 815
Wright, Richard A., 36
Wriglesworth, J. L., 439
Wrong, Denis H., 1354
Wundt, Max, 1712
Wyatt-Brown, Bertram, 791, 1594
Wykoff, Leslie W., 992
Wyschogrod, Edith, 1353

Yearley, Lee H., 1073, 1763
Yeazell, Stephen, 258
Yoder, John Howard, 185, 909
Young, H. Peyton, 1245
Young, Iris Marion, 538, 539, 1191, 1548, 1607
Young, Katherine, 683
Young, Oran R., 125
Young, Robert, 115, 1079, 1699
Young-Bruehl, Elisabeth, 85, 1440
Youngner, Stuart J., 1066
Yourgrau, Palle, 378
Yovel, Yirmiahu, 939
Yuan Dao, 1684

Zaehner, R. C., 1199
Zahir, F. I., 896
Zahn, Gordon, 1269
Zaitchik, Alan, 1079
Zanta, L., 1232
Zashin, Elliot M., 238
Zeckhauser, Richard, 1422
Zeller, Eduard, 703, 709
Zemach, Eddy, 33
Zillmer, Eric A., 784
Zimbardo, Philip, 1619
Zimmer, Heinrich, 899
Zimmerman, David, 248, 1086, 1164, 1592
Zimmerman, Michael E., 107
Zimmerman, Michael J., 508, 1266, 1492
Zimring, Franklin E., 1428
Zink, S., 1329
Zinn, Howard, 238
Zolo, Danilo, 349
Zucker, Marjorie B., 1672
Zwarg, Christina, 1728
Zwiebach, Burton, 238

Volume key: Volume 1, pages 1–642; volume 2, pages 643–1266; volume 3, pages 1267–1977.